The Lights *of* Revelation

& the Secrets *of* Interpretation

The Lights *of* Revelation

& *the* Secrets *of* Interpretation

Ḥizb I

of the Commentary on the Qur'ān by

al-Bayḍāwī

Arabic Edition & English Translation

With introduction & notes by

Gibril Fouad Haddad

Foreword by

Osman Bakar

BEACON BOOKS

ubd Press

First published in the UK by Beacon Books and Media Ltd
Innospace, Chester Street, Manchester M1 5GD, UK
and in Brunei Darussalam by UBD Press, Universiti Brunei Darussalam, Jalan Tungku Link, Gadong BE 1410.

Indexing, cover design and typesetting by author. Fonts: Lotus Linotype (Arabic) and Minion Tra (English). Cover illustration: Title page of Berlin Staatsbibliothek Hs. or. 8180, the oldest manuscript of al-Bayḍāwī's *Anwār al-Tanzīl* known, reproduced courtesy of the Department of Conservation and Digitization at the Staatsbibliothek zu Berlin—Preußischer Kulturbesitz.

Printed in the UK

www.beaconbooks.net

Cataloging-in-Publication Data
Perpustakaan Dewan Bahasa dan Pustaka Brunei
A catalogue record for this book is available from the British Library

al-Bayḍāwī, ʿAbd Allāh ibn ʿUmar, -1286?

The Lights of Revelation and the Secrets of Interpretation: *Ḥizb* One of the Commentary on the Qur'ān by al-Bayḍāwī. Arabic edition and English translation and notes by Gibril Fouad Haddad.
xlv+854 p. 23 cm. Indices.
1. Qur'an—Commentaries—Early works to 1800. I. Haddad, Gibril Fouad, 1960- . II. Title. III. Title: *Anwār al-tanzīl wa-asrār al-taʾwīl*. English and Arabic.

ISBN Paperback 978-0-9926335-7-8
ISBN Hardback 978-0-9926335-8-5

To His Majesty

Sultan Haji Hassanal Bolkiah
Muʿizzaddin Waddaulah
Sultan and Yang Di-Pertuan
of Brunei Darussalam

بسم الله الرحمن الرحيم

اللهم صل على محمد وآل محمد

﴿ الٓرۚ كِتَٰبٌ أَنزَلۡنَٰهُ إِلَيۡكَ لِتُخۡرِجَ ٱلنَّاسَ مِنَ ٱلظُّلُمَٰتِ إِلَى ٱلنُّورِ بِإِذۡنِ رَبِّهِمۡ إِلَىٰ صِرَٰطِ ٱلۡعَزِيزِ ٱلۡحَمِيدِ ١ ﴾ إبراهيم عليه السلام

﴿ وَتِلۡكَ ٱلۡأَمۡثَٰلُ نَضۡرِبُهَا لِلنَّاسِۖ وَمَا يَعۡقِلُهَآ إِلَّا ٱلۡعَٰلِمُونَ ٤٣ ﴾

العنكبوت

﴿ بَلۡ هُوَ ءَايَٰتُۢ بَيِّنَٰتٞ فِي صُدُورِ ٱلَّذِينَ أُوتُواْ ٱلۡعِلۡمَۚ وَمَا يَجۡحَدُ بِـَٔايَٰتِنَآ إِلَّا ٱلظَّٰلِمُونَ ٤٩ ﴾ العنكبوت

أَهْلُ الْقُرآنِ هُمْ  **أَهْلُ اللَّهِ وَخَاصَّتُهُ**

اللَّهُمَّ اجْعَلْنَا مِنَ الْوَاصِلِينَ لِلْعَيْنِ، دُونَ السَّامِعِينَ لِلأَثَرِ.

Figure 1: Title page of Berlin Staatsbibliothek Hs. or. 8180, the oldest ms. of *Anwār al-Tanzīl* known, copied in 758/1357 in 414 folios 18.5x27 cm. in size. The illuminator wrote:

كتابُ انوَار التنزيل في اسرار التَاويل
تَصنيف الإمام العَلّامة خَاتم العُلما
وَالمحققين حجّة الإسلَام وَالمسلمينَ
القَاضِي نَاصِر الدّين عُمر ابن مُحمد البيضاوي رحمه الله

"The book of *The Lights of Revelation Concerning the Secrets of Interpretation* / authored by the Imam, the Savant, the Seal of Scholars / and Verifying Authorities, the Proof of Religion and Muslims / the Qadi Nāṣir al-Dīn ʿUmar b. Muḥammad al-Bayḍāwī—may Allah have mercy on him!" The above text contains mistakes: the title alters the original's conjunction *wāw* ⁽and⁾ in *wa-Asrār* ⁽and the Secrets⁾ to the preposition *fī* ⁽concerning⁾ and the author is misidentified as ʿUmar b. Muḥammad, the father of the actual author Nāṣir al-Dīn ʿAbd Allāh b. ʿUmar b. Muḥammad al-Bayḍāwī (as correctly added at the bottom, outside the decorative margin, by the copyist by way of rectification). The middle text is a wakf document. It begins with laud of the Creator and an invocation of blessings "on him who was addressed with the words *Were it not for you* [i.e. the Prophet Muḥammad]—and were it not for him the universes would not have been created" then describes the endowment status of the manuscript as a work of mercy on the owner's part, al-Sayyid al-Ḥājjī Aḥmad b. al-Ḥājjī ʿUmar, for the benefit of "Ḥājjī Maḥmūd *madrasa* teachers in this locality" as well as the owner himself, his children and his great-grandchildren, "never to be bought or sold… or altered… or leave this locality," followed by the names of seven witnesses. The mid-page seal bears the inscription

توكلي على خالقي / يا حنان / يا منان / عبده سليمان

My reliance is on my Creator /
O Cherisher! / O Bestower! / His servant Sulaymān.

In the left margin is a partial ownership notice, [م]لكه [ا]لفقي[ر] الشريف "owned by the pauper, the sherif...."

كتاب أنوار التنزيل وأسرار التأويل
تصنيف الإمام العلامة خاتم العلماء

حمد لمن هو خالق البرايا وشكر لمن هو أظهر علينا الآلاء وصلوة على من هو مخاطب بخطاب لولاك
ولولاه لما خلق الأفلاك وبعد فيقول السيد الحاج أحمد بن الحاج عمر غفر الله لهما لما كان دار الدنيا
دار غرور ودار عبور ودار المحن ودار الوهن والآخرة خير وأبقى لمن هو اختار الباقيات
الصالحات وعمل بالأعمال الصالحات أردت أن أوقف أنوار التنزيل وأسرار التأويل
ليكون ذريعة في الآخرة وسببا لنجاتي عنه وستر أمن النار يا رب تقبل منا بقبول حسن
وارض عني برضاء الحسن ووقفت وحبست لهذا التفسير الشريف
والكتاب اللطيف لمن هو مدرس في مدرسة الحاجي محمود
بحيث لا يباع ولا يشترى ولا يرهن ولا يسترهن ولا يودع ولا يستودع ولا يبدل ولا يمنع
لمن هو أهل بالنظر في هذه البلدة ولا يخرج من هذه البلدة وجعلت توليته لي ما دمت حيا ثم لأولادي
ثم أولاد أولادي فمن بدله بعد ما سمعه فإنما إثمه على الذين يبدلونه

ثم غنيمة زاده السيد علي چلبي — مصطفى — قوقو زاده الحاج — السيد ابراهيم خليل افندي — ابراهيم افندي — السيد مصطفى افندي — الحاجي ولي الدين

والمحققين محيي الإسلام والمسلمين
القاضي ناصر الدين عبد الله بن عمر البيضاوي رحمه الله

ناصر الدين عبد الله بن عمر ... البيضاوي

Contents

Dedication to HM The Sultan of Brunei Darussalam v
Epigraphs and Prayer vii
Title page of oldest known manuscript of *Anwār al-Tanzīl* viii
Illustrations and Tables xxi
Foreword by Prof. Datuk Dr. Osman bin Bakar xxv
Acknowledgments xliii
Abbreviations xlv

Introduction: al-Bayḍāwī and his *Anwār al-Tanzīl wa-Asrār al-Ta'wīl* in hermeneutical tradition 1

I. BIOBIBLIOGRAPHY *& RAISON D'ETRE* OF THE PRESENT WORK

Bayḍāwī's teachers and chain of transmission in Shāfiʿī *fiqh* 5
Bayḍāwī's students 8
Bayḍāwī's peers 10
Bayḍāwī's *Tafsīr* and other works in law, legal theory, grammar and parsing, history, logic, sufis, poetry and astronomy 13
Purpose of the present work, the first full-length study in English and first bilingual edition of Bayḍāwī's *Tafsir* 17

II. BACKGROUND, METHODOLOGY, SOURCES, SALIENT FEATURES

Transmission, analysis and polysemy in Quranic exegesis 19
Passive anonymizers *qīla/ruwiya/quri'a* for weak transmission 21
The connection of *aḥruf* ⁽dialects/idioms⁾ with polysemy 22
Semantic and stylistic invariables (*kulliyyāt al-Qur'ān*) 26
Bayḍāwī's synthesis of Perso-Khurasanian hermeneutics 29
Comparison of the Basran and Kufan schools of grammar 31
Three examples of Bayḍāwī's succinct treatment of complex linguistic and theological questions 33-41

a. Is *Allāh* an underived proper name or is it etymologically derived from *ilāh* ⁽deity⁾? 33

b. Does Allah task one beyond one's capacity, such as tasking Abū Lahab and Abū Jahl to believe? 35
c. *Naskh*: The pre-Islamic viability and post-Islamic inviability of Judaism, Christianity and other superseded faiths 37
Expert scholarly exertion (*ijtihād*) and other qualifications 41
The 22 disciplines of exegesis, including scientific training 42
Scientific and philosophical discourse in the *Anwār*: physiology, meteorology, geophysics, mineralogy, embryology, psychology, psycholinguistics, empiricism versus materialism 43
More on the exegete's musts: piety, orthodoxy and parsing 47
Bayḍāwī's main sources 48-60
1. Purging Zamakhsharī's *Kashshāf* 48—Rebuttal of Muʿtazila and other sects 51—Controverted slips into Muʿtazilism 53
2. al-Rāghib's *Mufradāt Alfāẓ al-Qur'ān* and his *Tafsīr* 57
3. al-Rāzī's *Mafātīḥ al-Ghayb* 58
Sufism in *Anwār al-Tanzīl*: the vision of Allah; self-extinction; the pleasures of Paradise reflect levels of knowledge of Allah in *dunyā*; "slaughter the cow of your ego" 60

III: Reception of the *Tafsīr* in the *Umma* and the West

The *Anwār* as a textbook and its scholastic marginalia 62
Epigones and epitomes 64
Gradual disuse of the *Anwār* in the last 75 years 65
Recourse to *Anwār al-Tanzīl* in middle Orientalism (17-18th c.): France, Germany, England, Holland, and Rome 66
Western confusion over al-Bayḍāwī's *Tafsīr* 69

IV: Translation issues and backdrop to the present work

Post-Kemal Azhari-Salafi fatwas against Qur'ān translation 72
Our rendering of the Magnificent Qur'ān 75
Anwār al-Tanzīl in partial translation: Urdu, French, English 76
The present edition and translation of the *Anwār* 79

V: SOURCES USED AND OUR *ISNĀD* (CHAIN OF TRANSMISSION)

Manuscripts, editions & commentaries used in this work 82-92
Manuscripts: Berlin-Riyadh (x3)-Cambridge (x3)-Baltimore-Damascus-Nablus-Irbil-Mecca-Alukah
Editions: Istanbul (x2)-Leipzig-Bulaq (x2)-Teheran-Cairo (x4) Deoband-Beirut (x2)-Damascus-Mecca-Karachi
Commentaries: Zakariyyā Anṣārī-Suyūṭī-Ibn Kamāl Bāshā-'Iṣām al-Isfarāyīnī-al-Munāwī-Sa'dī Çelebi-Shaykh Zādah-Sayālkūtī-Khafājī-Kāzarūnī-Qūnawī-Kawrā'ī
Illustrative samples from the sources used 93-118
Our chain of transmission to Bayḍāwī's *Anwār al-Tanzīl* 119

The First *Ḥizb* of the Qur'ān (1:1-2:74): A Baydawian Rendering in English 123-139

The First *Ḥizb* of al-Bayḍāwī's *Anwār al-Tanzīl*: Critical Edition of the Text and English Translation 143-680

Bayḍāwī's Preamble 143-147
Tafsīr is the chief science and foundation of all disciplines 145

SŪRAT AL-FĀTIḤA 147-213

Fourteen names of the Fatiha 147
The *basmala* is part of the Fatiha 151
Basmala implies a verb standing for whatever act follows 153
Monotheism magnified in the positioning of the *basmala* 154
Morphology and desinence of the *bā'* in the *basmala* 156
Etymology and morphology of *ism* (name) 157
The name is primarily other than the named 159
The divine name *Allāh*: etymology and morphology 161
No word can designate the reality of the divine Self 166
Raḥmān and *raḥīm* are synonyms 168
Longer cognates point to additional meanings 169
Raḥmān cannot be pluralized or feminized 172

Al-rabb originally means "nurturing" 177
The Ghazalian microcosm of human beings 179
Definitions of *mālik*, *malik* and *dīn* 181
Dīn as "sacred law" and as "obedience" 184
Addressing Allah as if seeing Him 186
Who is the speaker in *naʿbudu* and *nastaʿīn*? 191
Why *iyyāka* was put first before the verbs 192
The quest for self-extinction in the object of worship 192
Putting the means (*wasīla*) first ensures fulfillment 194
Varieties of divine guidance 195
Prayer for guidance, self-extinction, and vision of Allah 197
Meaning and variants of *sirāṭ/ṣirāṭ* 198
Typology of the divine favors 201
Divine favor is safety from wrath and misguidance 203
Emotional and physical divine attributes are metaphorical 205
Who are *those who incur anger and those who are astray*? 207
Meaning and recitation of *Āmīn* 209
Reports on the immense merits of the Fātiḥa 212

SŪRAT AL-BAQARA 214-679
Definition of the Disjointed Letters 214
Interpretation of the Disjointed Letters 216
Phonemes and their attributes 218
Syllabic combinations of the *Fawātiḥ* and their significance 225
Interpretation of the Opening Letters continued 227
Seven other interpretations and their rebuttals 229
The preferred interpretation 237
More interpretations yet 238
Sufi phonology of *alif lām mīm* 239
Declension of the Opening Letters 240
Do the Opening Letters constitute integral verses? 242
Why *That is the Book* instead of *This is the Book*? 243
The Qur'ān's rational invalidation of doubt 245

The specific beneficiaries of Quranic *hudā* ‹guidance› 247
Levels of *taqwā* ‹guarding oneself› 248
Parsing of verses 2:1-2 250
Belief in the unseen is part and parcel of *taqwā* 255
Various doctrines on what the integrals of belief are 259
Ashʿarī definition of belief as confirmation in the heart 260
Meanings and types of *ghayb* ‹unseen› 263
Meanings of "establishing the prayer" 265
The Muʿtazili claim that *rizq* can only be *ḥalāl* 268
The meaning of *infāq* ‹spending› 271
Highlighting of the Jews and Christians who accept Islam 273
Meaning of *mā unzila* ‹what was sent down› 275
The renouncing of Jewish and Christian eschatologies 277
Meaning of *yūqinūn* ‹they are certain› 278
Highlighting of the recipients of divine guidance 280
Divine guidance is unfathomable, invaluable and direct 282
The intense Quranic valorization of the *muttaqīn* ‹wary› 284
A non-Sunni view that Muslim sinners are in hell forever 285
Parsing of *inna* ‹verily› and its function 286
Definition of *kufr* and its vestimentary symbols 289
The Muʿtazili (and Shiʿi) view that the Qurʾān is created 290
Repeatedly warning them is the same as not warning at all 292
The doctrine that Allah can task one beyond capacity 295
Gradual sealing up and blinding of the heart and psyche 298
Non-Sunni views of the divine "sealing" and "misguiding" 300
More on how Allah seals the senses of the unbelievers 303
Parsing of mass-transmitted and irregular readings 306
Semantics of *ʿadhāb* ‹punishment› 308
The hypocrites exposed 310
The delusions of the Israelites 313
The unbelievers' duplicity defines their identity 315
"They deceive Allah" is not literal 317

The unbelievers' literal and figurative heart disease 323
The prohibition of lying 327
The spread of corruption in the land 329
The corrupters protest they are in fact civilizers 330
"Human beings" as types of belief or groups of converts 332
Zendiks' view that mere verbal profession is belief 334
The difference between "knowing" and "realizing" 336
The human devils 340
Rhetorical difference between verbal and nominal clauses 341
The scoffing of the hypocrites 341
The divine scoffing 343
Non-Sunni figurations of divine reinforcing of *ṭughyān* 345
The purchase of ruin at the price of guidance 348
Parables, similes and proverbs 353
"The one" stands for a collective: analysis of *al-ladhī* 354
How Allah takes away light 359
Parables of error: hypocrites, atheists and false Sufis 362
Loss of hearing, speech and sight as a simile of unbelief 364
A cloubdburst filled with darkness, thunder and lightning 369
The meteorological cause of thunder 372
Analysis of *kāda* ⁽it was almost fact⁾ 377
Linguistic precedents and the diachronic status of poets 380
Effects are from causes yet befall only through divine will 382
For Ashʿarīs the term *shay'* applies only to existing entities 384
Human enablement and divine omnipotence 386
Multi-tiered allegories in the Qur'ān and Arabic poetry 387
Allegorical interpretation of the storm and its elements 391
Stylistic alarm through *iltifāt* ⁽apostrophic redirection⁾ 393
The frequent Quranic summons *yā ayyuhā* 395
Belief, worship are universal duties, as Allah created all 396
A worshipper's *taqwā* is wariness between fear and hope 402
Knowledge of Allah and of His rights over His creatures 404

Earth's levelness and rotundity at one and the same time 406
The divine paradigms of fecundation and growth 408
Rain formation 409
The plural of paucity standing for collectivity or abundance 410
Worship entails faith in the omnipotence of the worshipped 413
Why human beings are under obligation to worship Allah 416
Quranic polysemy and the allegories of human creation 417
Why the Qur'ān was sectioned into suras 421
Interpretations of the divine challenge 422
Meanings of *shahīd* in Arabic usage 424
Meanings of *dūn* in Arabic usage 425
Truthfulness is to report accurately what one knows 429
The meaning of the stones of hell (*ḥijāra*) 433
Proofs of Prophethood in the divine challenge 437
Meanings of the word *janna* and the names of paradise 443
The rivers of paradise 447
The fruits of paradise 449
Allegorical interpretation of "similar fruits" of paradise 454
The actual states of paradise are beyond comparison 456
Sunni understanding of *khulūd* as literally "a long time" 457
Perfection of resurrected bodies & rebuttal of materialists 459
Method, power of similes/proverbs even in divine speech 461
Definition of shame; meaning of its attribution to Allah 464
"Additive" particles in the Qur'ān play a stylistic role 468
Sizes great and small are all relative in the divine sight 471
Definition of *ḥaqq* 474
Definitions of the divine will 476
The three types of *fāsiq* 480
The Muʿtazilis' intermediary damnation for sinful Muslims 481
Types of divine covenants 484
Types of breaches condemned by Allah 486
The three different possible addressees in *kayfa takfurūn?* 489

The definition of life in creatures 493
The description of Allah as possessing *ḥayāt* (life) 494
Istiwā' literally means symmetry 498
Timing of the respective creations of heaven and earth 499
The number of the heavenly spheres 501
Divine creatorship, wisdom and resuscitatorship 501
The superiority of human beings to angels 504
Grammar and usage of *idh* and *idhā* 505
The angels: name, nature and functions 507
The hierarchic intermediacy of prophets and angels 511
The divine disclosure and the angels' verbal engagement 513
Angels wonder at divine wisdom eradicating human sins 514
The angels inquired without objecting nor boasting 516
Complex humans and simple angels: mission of vicegerency 517
The affirmation of divine transcendence 519
The modality of the divine teaching of Adam 520
The meaning of *Ādam* 521
The meaning of the teaching of the names 523
The divine silencing of the angels' misassumption 526
The divine foreknowledge of Iblīs's planned disobedience 531
Nine fundamental lessons in the *khilāfa* and *asmā'* verses 532
The angels' prostration to Adam 535
Adam as archetype of everything in existence 537
Iblīs's refusal to use Adam as a means to Allah 540
Iblīs was originally an angel per the vast majority 542
Certain angels are not infallible; *jinn* meaning "invisible" 545
Ash'arīs define "the believer" as one who dies as a Muslim 549
Husbands are liable primarily, ahead of wives 550
Paradise already exists and is beyond this world 550
Wisdom of pre-emptive prohibition for the heart's haleness 552
The Forbidden Tree 553
How Satan duped Adam and Eve 554

The fall from paradise to earth 556
The divine gift of human repentance 558
Women follow behind men with regard to legal status 561
Adam represents all repentants and followers of guidance 562
Meaning, etymology and interpretation of *āya* 566
Adam's mistake in light of the infallibility of prophets 567
Other paradigms and teachings in Adam's story 573
The divine address to all learned people and the Israelites 574
Levels of the respective divine and human covenants, 577
Self-extinction in Allah is the last level of *tawḥīd* 578
The divine reminder to the people of the Covenant 580
Time-contextual suitability of variant heavenly rulings 582
Jews and Christians are expected to become Muslims 583
The rabbinate & clergy feared losing their worldly status 586
The first step of wariness (*taqwā*) is dread (*rahba*) 587
The Jews and Christians' deliberate muddling of the truth 588
Non-Muslim worship is as zero prayer and zero charity 589
The pillars of Islam are universally binding 590
They enjoined virtue and even Islam but practiced neither 591
The benefits of prayer 595
The divine preferentiation of the Israelites at one time 599
The non-Sunni claim that once in hellfire always in hellfire 604
Ordeals and blessings are both divine tests 608
Āl means *ahl* ⁽family, people⁾ including the chief figure 610
Meaning of the Israelites' "looking on" at the Red Sea 611
The qualitative differences between Israelites and Muslims 612
The Book and the *Furqān* given to Mūsā 615
Autogenocide atoned for the enormity of the golden calf 618
Significance of the divine name *al-Bāri'* ⁽Producer of all⁾ 621
Prophet's vision of Allah in *dunyā*; believers' vision in *ākhira* 623
Allah's successive gifts; the Israelites' successive treasons 625
The harm of ingratitude to Allah is only reflexive 626

The effortless avenue of divine forgiveness 627
The divine honoring of well-doers no matter what 630
The parody of *Ḥiṭṭa* and the mockery of forgiveness 630
The miracle of Mūsā's water-rock in the desert 632
Deniers of miracles wrought for Mūsā and the Israelites 637
They longed for the rustic food they were used to 638
The stamping of odious states on the Israelites 641
Islam abrogates previous faiths 648
Refutation of Sībawayh regarding the *fā'* of apodosis 649
The Damoclean mountain to extract Israelite obedience 650
The expression *law* ⁽if it were⁾ 652
The simianization of the Sabbath-breakers 653
The story of the divinatory yellow cow 656
Abrogation, other scenarios of the cow's particularization 660
"Yellow" is the established gloss; al-Ḥasan said "black" 662
Surūr ⁽gladness⁾ among the types of mirth 663
All is by His will but His order may differ from His will 666
Divine teachings in the story of the yellow cow 673
Slaying one's ego to know one's enemy & revive one's soul 675
Hearts are harder than rocks that feel and surrender 676

Arabic-English glossary of technical terms 681
Glossary of persons and sects cited by al-Bayḍāwī 691
Bibliography 775
Index of Sura References 789
Index of Hadiths & Early Reports 791
Index of Poetic Verses 811
General Index 815
Other Works by Gibril Fouad Haddad 851
Other Publications by Beacon Books and UBD Press 854

Illustrations and Tables

Figure 1	Title page of Berlin Hs. or. 8180, the earliest extant ms. of *Anwār al-Tanzīl* known, copied 758/1357 in Shiraz and Damascus. Staatsbibliothek zu Berlin - Preußischer Kulturbesitz.
Figure 2	Incipit page of Berlin Hs. or. 8180.
Figure 3	Berlin Hs. or. 8180 folio 30v: end of *Ḥizb I*.
Figure 4	Riyadh, King Saʿūd University, ms. Tafsīr 1036 folio 2a: Bayḍāwī, *Anwār al-Tanzīl*, Surat al-Fātiḥa. Ms. copied 850/1446.
Figure 5	Cambridge Ms. Add. 3586. *Anwār al-Tanzīl*, folio 2b: preamble and Fatiha. Copied 874/1470.
Figure 6	Title page (folio 1a) of 908/1503 Cambridge ms. Gg 3.20 of *Anwār al-Tanzīl*.
Figure 7	End of the first *ḥizb* (f. 25a), Cambridge Gg 3.20.
Figure 8	Walters Art Museum, Baltimore, ms. W.584 p. 152: Shaykh al-Islam Ibn Kamāl Bāshā's (Kemalpaşazade d. 940/1534) commentary on al-Bayḍāwī, Surat al-Fātiḥa. Copied 966/1559.
Figure 9	Zakariyyā al-Anṣārī (823-926/1420-1520), *Ḥāshiya* entitled *Fatḥ al-Jalīl bi-Bayān Khafī Anwār al-Tanzīl*. Ẓāhiriyya ms. *ʿUlūm al-Qur'ān* 266, f° 1. Copied 990/1582.
Figure 10	*Tafsīr al-Bayḍāwī*. Alukah website unidentified complete ms. (www.alukah.net/library/0/52999). F° 4a: End of Sūrat al-Fātiḥā and beginning of Sūrat al-Baqara. Copied 1067/1657.
Figure 11	*Tafsīr al-Bayḍāwī*. Jāmiʿat Ṣalāḥ al-Dīn (Irbil, Iraq) ms. 51, f° 1: Incipit (preamble and Fatiha). Copied 1150/1737.

Figure 12 *Tafsīr al-Bayḍāwī*, f° 1b of ms 298 Najah National University of Nablus (West Bank, State of Palestine) from the library of the Mufti of Jaffa. Undated.

Figure 13 Folio 1b (Incipit) of undated Cambridge ms. Add. 3179 of *Tafsīr al-Bayḍāwī* in *nastaʿliq* Indian script.

Figure 14 Incipit of pre-1242/1827 ms. 1729 of *Anwār al-Tanzīl*, Jāmiʿat Umm al-Qurā, Mecca.

Figure 15 Title page of Sacy's 1829 *Anthologie Grammaticale Arabe* which begins with a translation of Bayḍāwī's commentary on Sūrat al-Baqara (2:1-7).

Figure 16 First page of Sacy's translation of Bayḍāwī.

Figure 17 Title page of earliest known edition of *Anwār al-Tanzīl*, printed at Dār al-Ṭibāʿat al-ʿĀmira, Istanbul 1257/1841.

Figure 18 Incipit of Istanbul 1257/1841 edition with *Tafsīr al-Jalālayn* in the margins.

Figure 19 Title page of the 1848 Leipzig edition of *Tafsīr al-Bayḍāwī* by Heinrich Fleischer, one of the first Qur'ān commentaries published in Europe.

Figure 20 Page 3 of Fleischer's 1848 edition: Fatiha.

Figure 21 Page 1 (Incipit) of Teheran 1272/1856 lithograph edition of a marginalia by the Shiʿi Safavid Bahā' al-Dīn al-ʿĀmilī (953-1030/1546-1621), *Taʿlīqāt Anwār al-Tanzīl*, surrounding Bayḍāwī's text.

Figure 22 Title page of the 1330/1912 Egyptian edition of al-Bayḍāwī's *Tafsīr* with al-Kāzarūnī's (d. after 1102/1691) 1100-page, four-volume *Ḥāshiya*.

Figure 23 Incipit of the 1912 Bayḍāwī/Kāzarūnī edition.

Figure 24 Last page of the 1912 edition bearing a eulogy by its chief editor, the Moroccan-born Azharī Shāfiʿī jurist Muḥammad al-Zuhrī al-Ghamrāwī.

Figure 25 Ibn Ḥabīb al-Dimashqī (d. 779/1377), *Durrat al-Aslāk fī Dawlat al-Atrāk* ("Year 685"), ms. Leipzig Vollers 0661, folios 85b-86a and details showing Bayḍāwī's obitus. Copied in Aleppo, in 1071/1660.

Table 1 Appeal to *tafsīrs* in early European renderings of Qur'ān—including Bayḍāwī—from du Ryer (1647) to George Sale (1734).

Table 2 Teacher-student lineages of Western Arabist scholars who worked on al-Bayḍāwī, 1800-2000.

Foreword

by

Prof. Datuk Dr. Osman bin Bakar*

In the Name of God, the Most Gracious, the Most Merciful

Exegeses of sacred texts occupy a special place in the intellectual and literary traditions of the world. Not least, this particular genre of literary works owes its importance to the central role it plays in explaining and articulating the spiritual and moral teachings of the religions with which the texts are respectively associated. For religions with a sacred language such as Islam, exegesis of sacred texts is seen to assume an even greater role and function, particularly in the advancement of spiritual knowledge. Since in Islam the Quran, which is its most fundamental sacred text, is the verbatim revelation of the Word of God, revealed in the Arabic language, exegesis (*tafsīr*) is known to embrace broader dimensions of knowledge than what are normally found, for example, in the Christian tradition, which is known not to have a sacred language. Language, which in this particular instance is Arabic, plays a more central and also a more specific role in exegesis. Indeed, knowledge of classical Arabic with all its unique characteristics and features is universally acknowledged in the Islamic tradition as a fundamental prerequisite for the well-established traditional science of Quranic exegesis (*ʿilm tafsīr al-Qurʾān*).

* Distinguished Professor and Director, Sultan Omar Ali Saifuddien Centre for Islamic Studies, Universiti Brunei Darussalam; Emeritus Professor of Philosophy of Science, Department of Science and Technology Studies, University of Malaya in Kuala Lumpur, Malaysia.

The special place and role of Quranic exegesis in Islamic tradition deserves emphasis, especially in our modern times when much of the traditional knowledge about the science of exegesis has either been lost or forgotten. There is increasing confusion in the contemporary Muslim *umma* with regard to the understanding of the Quran because, in the name of individual rights, more and more people are venturing into the interpretation of its verses without having the necessary prior knowledge and expertise in the science of exegesis. It is as if in the name of individual human rights a person is free to build a house on his own land as he pleases, even though he lacks the necessary knowledge of the art of architecture and construction. He may, of course, proceed with its construction but only to face its consequences later on. Some of the consequences could even be immediate such as, for example, having to face actions by authorities in the public department concerned. Analogously, the Muslim *umma* is now facing the consequences of malpractices in interpretations of the Quran that clearly violate some of the most fundamental principles of the traditional science of exegesis, a good example of which is the principle of coherence and inner consistency of the Quran as a whole. A rampant malpractice in this regard is indulgence in interpretations of Quranic verses that seek to justify and to serve sectarian purposes and interests.

The consequences of exegetical malpractices, which are now very much visible in Muslim societies, include confusion in many Muslim minds and fortification of various forms of sectarianism and extremism. These negative consequences are more than sufficient reasons to impress upon the Muslim *umma* the kind of harm that could come to them from deviationist practices in Quranic interpretations. A good lesson to be learnt from these consequences is that there is a real need for Muslim scholars as intellectual guardians of the *umma* to reaffirm the good epistemological understanding of the traditional science of Quranic exegesis[1] while addressing the issues raised against it by its critics, some of which are indeed legitimate. The science of Quranic exegesis as traditionally understood and as affirmed in this foreword as well as in the work which it prefaces is not a static or an outdated science or body of knowledge that has outlived its usefulness as its modernist critics imagine it to be. On the contrary, this science is at once perennial and contemporary. It is perennial in the sense that the principles on which it is based are true and useful at all times as seen from the perspective of tawhidic epistemology.[2] And it is contemporary in the sense that the same principles are dynamic enough to allow themselves to be freshly applied to new human problems and new knowledge claims.

The traditionality of the traditional science of exegesis is essentially not an issue of temporality but rather of primacy that concerns the issue of ultimate origin. From the traditional perspective, the origin of the science is divine, meaning the Quran itself. Thus, traditional Muslim scholars of exegesis (*al-mufassirūn*) insisted that the best interpreter of the Quran is none other than the Quran itself, an idea which they turned into a fundamental methodological principle of the science. By this idea they mean that God clarifies and details each verse with knowledge contained in other verses. They appealed to the Quran itself in support of their view. This principle of what may be described as "the self-explanatory nature" of the Quran, which they had formulated, is contained in the following verse:

> For We have certainly brought them a Book, which We have detailed with knowledge (*faṣṣalnāhu ʿala ʿilm*), a guidance and a mercy for a people who believe.[3]

They also understood the meaning of human origin to be quite different from its secular understanding. While in the secular understanding the idea of human origin takes the meaning of being completely cut off from the divine source, the traditional perspective insists on the preservation of a metaphysical link between human ideas and their divine roots. From the point of view of human experience, this metaphysical link may be said to admit of various degrees of divine inspiration. The Quran presents the Prophet Muhammad—upon him blessings and peace!—as the best human recipient of divine inspiration, since the inspiration he received is the most intense of all. He is thus viewed as the best human interpreter of the Quran, and the Prophetic Hadiths are traditionally seen as the first and foremost commentary on the Quran. Indeed, tradition maintains that the Prophet's *Sunna* is his total personification of the Quran. These equivalent teachings concerning the inner relationship between the Prophet and the Quran, which emphasize the idea of the former as the best exegetical authority next to the latter, were made the second methodological principle of the traditional science of exegesis.

All authentic exegetical works are spiritually inspired. The greater the intensity of its inspiration, the better the quality of an exegetical work will be. For all exegetes (sing: *mufassir*), in the wake of the Prophet, also have a working mind that seeks to preserve its metaphysical link with the Divine Source of the Quran, although in their case the intensity of the link is much less than the one experienced by the Prophet. However, to the extent that this metaphysical link exists in the mind of the exegete and is manifested in his exegetical work, the work in question deserves to be considered traditional in character. The quality of exegesis is determined by many factors, the two most important of which are the intensity of spiritual inspiration received by the exegete in question and the quality of his creative thinking (*ijtihad*). It is this combined spiritual-intellectual quality found in the exegete as reflected in his work that in turn determines the quality of his exegesis. On the basis of this consideration, Islamic exegetical tradition established a guiding principle according to which the first generation of exegetes that emerged from within the ranks of the Prophet's companions—such as ʿAlī b. Abī Ṭālib, Ibn ʿAbbās, Abū'l-Dardā' and Ibn Masʿūd—are viewed as the most authoritative in exegesis after the Prophet (upon him blessings and peace).[4] However, this guiding principle does not exclude the possibility of distinguished exegetes of very high rank emerging in the *umma* from time to time in Islamic history. We have in mind the appearance of such eminent spiritual and intellectual authorities as al-Ṭabarī (839-923), al-Ghazzālī (1058-1111), al- Zamakhsharī (c. 1074-c. 1144), Fakhr al-Dīn al-Rāzī (1149-1209), Muḥyiddīn Ibn ʿArabī (1164-1240) and Ibn Kathīr (c. 1300-1373), who produced exegeses of either part or the whole of the Quran. Also deserving inclusion in this list of famous and influential exegetes is Ibn Kathir's contemporary, al-Bayḍāwī,[5] whose commentary on the Quran is partially translated and studied in this work by Dr Gibril Fouad Haddad, undertaken during his Visiting Fellowship at the Sultan Omar ʿAli Saifuddien Centre for Islamic Studies (SOASCIS), Universiti Brunei Darussalam.[6]

The first generation of exegetes of the *umma* occupy a special place in the history of Islam, because they were among the best companions of the Prophet—the first and greatest human interpreter of the Quran—and therefore lived the closest to the source of the Revelation; they were generally regarded by the *umma* as men of distinction in spiritual matters; and they were the *umma*'s first intellectuals, noted for their depth of learning and well-versed in the inner mysteries of the knowledge content of the Quran. As such their views on Quranic exegesis became an eminent source of inspiration for all later exegetes until our own times.

The Quran is a book of divine guidance in all aspects of human life and thought. The key to its authentic understanding is exegesis, which is traditionally understood to embrace both *tafsīr* and *taʾwīl*.[7] It is thus not surprising that right from the beginning of Islam the science of exegesis (*ʿilm al-tafsīr*) became the most important branch of the Quranic sciences (*ʿulum al-Qurʾān*). Al-Bayḍāwī referred to this science as "the queen of the religious sciences (*raʾīs al-ʿulūm al-dīniyya*)" and the foundation of all disciplines.[8] The foundation of the science of exegesis was laid down by the Prophet himself, with those of his companions gifted with an exegetical mind—such as those mentioned earlier—contributing to the science as its virtual co-founders. For this reason, apart from the Prophet (upon him blessings and peace), the names of these co-founders almost always appear in the exegetical works of later Muslim scholars. Many good and creative (*ijtihādī*) minds during the past fourteen centuries and more of Islamic history contributed to the advancement of this science, which has remained traditional in its character without being conservative (as this term is pejoratively understood by its critics). In the light of the foregoing discussion on the principles and inherent dynamism of the traditional science of exegesis, we maintain that this science, which is itself still capable of growing and developing within the bounds of Islamic tradition and orthodoxy, would be necessary and sufficient to help the *umma* deepen their understanding of the Quran.

The various traditional exegetical works produced over the centuries all provide a good illustration of particular principles of the science of exegesis being applied in actual exegetical works. Epistemologically speaking, one methodological principle of exegesis, which no exegetist could really avoid applying due to its very nature, is the principle of scientific[9] exposition (*tafṣīl ʿalā ʿilm*), which is mentioned in the Quran.[10] This Quranic idea provides a scriptural support for the exegesis-related intellectual activity traditionally known as *tafsīr bil-raʾy* ("exegesis by personal opinion"). Al-Ghazzālī, for example, has soundly established this type of *tafsīr* as lawful.[11] As he argued it, the practice of explaining the Quran by personal opinion is traceable to the well-known exegetists among the Companions of the Prophet—upon him blessings and peace—such as Ibn ʿAbbās and Ibn Masʿūd, but their kind of personal opinions is not to be equated with the *tafsīr bil-raʾy* that the Prophet prohibited.[12] Al-Ghazzālī distinguished between personal opinion that is valid and personal opinion that is corrupt due to it being affected by lower passion (*hawā*). Quite clearly, if *tafsīr bil-raʾy* is to be accepted as a valid methodological approach to Quranic explanation then it has to be in conformity with the Quranic doctrine of *tafṣīl ʿalā ʿilm*. Since the elucidation and exposition of the Quran is to be in accordance with true knowledge, for that is what *ʿalā ʿilm* really means, only true and valid personal opinions can have any place and role in the exposition (*tafṣīl*) of the Quran. What this means is that it is only scholars knowledgeable in many academic disciplines who would be able to produce high quality exegetical works. Furthermore, following al-Ghazzālī, we are observing the close connection that exists between the quality of personal opinions and the state of the soul. In this perspective, *tafsīr bil-raʾy* is seen not only as an intellectual-rational pursuit but also as one having a spiritual-moral dimension. In other words, while every exegetist may be applying the method of *tafsīr ʿalā ʿilm* in the explanation of the

Quran, only those with a broad command of both *naqlīy* (transmitted) and *'aqlīy* (acquired through intellect-reason) knowledge[13] and a praiseworthy moral character have a clear advantage to produce excellent works of exegesis.

Insofar as we are positing the Quran and the Hadiths as the two best interpreters of the Quran we may speak of the divine and Prophetic exegetical models. Since it is desirable for Muslims to emulate the Prophetic exegetical model, which is itself an emulation of the divine model, they should undertake the task of further developing the traditional science of exegesis with its various branches, particularly the branch now popularly known as scientific[14] exegesis (*tafsīr 'ilmīy*) that interprets and explains verses pertaining to natural and cosmic phenomena, that is strongly supported by the epistemological project of *tafṣīl 'alā 'ilm* in accordance with the state of knowledge in their time. The nature of this project is such that contemporary Muslim academics and Muslims need to have good knowledge of past Quranic exegetical works as well as modern knowledge in all disciplines.

Sad to say, due to a host of reasons, not least language barriers, the contemporary Muslim knowledge of the classical works of *tafsīr* is rather limited and their general appreciation of this particular category of religious writings has suffered a decline. Since many Western and secular-educated Muslims do not have knowledge of Arabic they are unable to access the great works in Islam on exegesis of the Quran, practically all of which are written in this language, even if they are aware of their existence. In the light of the issues that we have raised in the foregoing pages and for many more reasons, Dr. Haddad's present work is most welcome. Dr. Haddad is to be praised for undertaking the admirable task of critically editing and rendering into

English the first tenth of one of the most influential works of *tafsīr* in the history of Islam. The work in question, al-Bayḍāwī's *Anwār al-Tanzīl* ("The Lights of Revelation"), which has also been referred to as *Tafsīr al-Bayḍāwī*, is noteworthy, first because of its literary and scholarly merits, and second because of the eminence of its author. Al-Bayḍāwī was a prolific scholar of 13th-14th century Islam,[15] authoring works in the sciences of the Sharia like jurisprudence (*fiqh*) and principles of jurisprudence (*uṣūl al-fiqh*), dialectical theology (*kalām*), Sufism and ethics (*taṣawwuf*), grammar, and epistemology.[16]

Anwār al-Tanzīl is important and significant, because of its fame and influence. In Dr. Haddad's own estimation, this work "became and remained for seven centuries the most studied of all *Tafsīrs*,"[17] and it is to be regarded as "the most important commentary on the Quran in the history of Islam."[18] The work won praise during the author's own life-time and invited "glowing testimonies" from later scholars until modern times. Perhaps significantly as well was its use as a textbook, especially in the madrasas of Mamluk Egypt and Ottoman Turkey.[19] To show its worldwide popularity Dr. Haddad refers to the textual evidences in the form of abundant printed editions and commentaries and super-commentaries written on it, samples of which he included in his book. In modern terms and equivalents, *Tafsīr al-Bayḍāwī* deserves to be treated as a best-seller of all times ever since its publication seven centuries ago, one of the most cited books in the field of exegesis (*tafsīr*), and as a book that enjoys many excellent reviews. The book was among the very first commentaries of the Quran to be published in Europe in the nineteenth century.

Given the important role that the book can play in contributing to the revival of the traditional science of exegesis in the contemporary world we consider it fortunate indeed that it is now made available in the English language, even if only partially. It is the fate of the Muslim *umma* that, for a large segment of its modern intelligentsia, English has emerged as the main language of Islamic discourse and literary output. No amount of resistance from Boko Haram-like movements in the Islamic world is going to change this fact. When it comes to academic and intellectual matters, many contemporary Muslims find themselves more fluent and more at ease in English rather than in any other language, including their own mother tongue. It is through works on Islam and its civilization made available in the English language that most of them have the opportunity to learn about their own spiritual and intellectual traditions. It is in the light of this changing reality in our scholarly and intellectual life in modern times that the importance and significance of Dr. Haddad's present work needs to be understood and appreciated.

We have referred earlier to the epistemological project which we termed *tafṣīl ʿalā ʿilm* in the context of our current effort to revive and advance the traditional science of exegesis (*ʿilm al-tafsīr*), an effort equivalent to what is presently referred to by some scholars as *al-tajdīd fīl-tafsīr* (Renewal in Quranic Commentary). Through Dr. Haddad's present book we are able to see the relevance of both al-Bayḍāwī the scholar and his literary output, particularly *Anwār al-Tanzīl,* to the project. Dr. Haddad provides data and information that show how al-Bayḍāwī understood and actually applied the methodological principle of *tafṣīl ʿalā ʿilm* to his exegesis of the Quran. Hopefully, some others will further pursue a study of this aspect of al-Bayḍāwī's religious thought. The *Tafsīr Bayḍāwī* partially translated by Dr. Haddad is limited to the exegesis of the first *ḥizb* of the Quran, which comprises its first chapter (*Surat al-Fātiḥa*) and the first seventy-four verses of its second chapter (*Surat al-Baqara*). Concerning the value of *Tafsīr Bayḍāwī* to contemporary scholars of the science of Quranic exegesis that can be derived from Dr. Haddad's present work someone may argue that his study would not bring out the real worth of the *tafsīr*, since it is limited to a small portion of the Quran. But going through Dr. Haddad's Introduction and the rich footnotes to his translation of the Quranic text it seems clear that not only is he aware of the issue at hand but he also provides an interesting response to it. His work seems to inform us that even on the basis of an exegesis of the first *ḥizb* alone, we can already see the traditional character of al-Bayḍāwī's exegesis with all its major dimensions and characteristics of which we have spoken earlier.

The argument presented here is that it is not necessary to wait until the later chapters, let alone until the end of the Quran, in order to see the major features of al-Bayḍāwī's *tafsīr* that qualify it to be treated as a meritorious exegetical work. In his interpretation of the selected verses of the Quran it is possible to see al-Bayḍāwī applying the foundational and methodological principles of the traditional science of exegesis. Thanks to Dr. Haddad's Introduction and notes to the translation we are able to see al-Bayḍāwī's application of the exegetical principles all the clearer. Of special interest to us is al-Bayḍāwī's practice of the methodological principles of *tafsīr al-Qur'ān bil-Qur'ān*, which Dr. Haddad translated as "self-exegesis"[20] and *tafṣīl 'alā 'ilm* of which *al-tafsīr al-'ilmīy* is an important dimension. Dr. Haddad refers to al-Bayḍāwī's appreciation of the role of science in exegesis when he insisted on conversance with "the givens of modern science."[21] We know that among the first seventy-four verses in *Surat al-Baqara* there are several that pertain to natural phenomena, which are the objects of natural science. We are now in a position to examine first-hand how al-Bayḍāwī interpreted these science-related verses in the light of 13th-14th century Islamic science to which the prominent scientist, Quṭb al-Dīn al-Shīrāzī (1236-1311), a fellow native of Shiraz, was a significant contributor.

In his Introduction Dr. Haddad also discusses al-Bayḍāwī's commitment to the idea of multi-disciplinary expertise as a crucial asset to the production of an enlightened and a high-quality work of exegesis. Al-Bayḍāwī insisted that none should practice or undertake to speak about exegesis (*tafsīr*) unless he "excels in the religious sciences in their totality—roots and branches—and has proved superior in the crafts of the Arabic language and the literary arts in all their varieties."[22] He himself possessed the kind of multi-disciplinary expertise that he wanted all aspiring scholars of the discipline to have. In our view, the idea of knowledge-based explanation or exposition (*tafṣīl ʿalā ʿilm*) of Quranic verses that we have repeatedly mentioned is equivalent in meaning to the idea of multi-disciplinary expertise emphasized by al-Bayḍāwī. Although as just quoted, al-Bayḍāwī's emphasis was on the totality of the religious sciences, he did not exclude the role of "modern" or contemporaneous sciences in exegesis. This means that, for al-Bayḍāwī, the idea of *ʿilm* in the doctrine of *tafṣīl ʿalā ʿilm* would embrace both the *naqlīy* (transmitted) and *ʿaqlīy* (intellectual-rational) sciences. Such an understanding would have a significant impact on the development of a contemporary science of Quranic exegesis.

The rich data and information that Dr. Haddad has provided in his present work have a significance that extends beyond the domain of exegesis. We would like to briefly address issues pertaining to two discipline, namely epistemology and Islamic history. The epistemological issue raised by Dr. Haddad's book pertains to al-Bayḍāwī's choice of the term religious sciences (*al-ʿulūm al-dīniyya*). Bayḍāwī mentioned *al-ʿulūm al-dīniyya* in the introduction to his *tafsīr*.[23] We are interested in the coinage of this term. We first encountered this term more than three decades ago when we undertook a study of Quṭb al-Dīn al-Shīrāzī's classification of knowledge in which the term appears. His classification was treated in a Persian work titled *Durrat al-Tāj*.[24] *Al-ʿulūm al-dīniyya* played an important role in this classification as a category of knowledge. We are interested in finding out who coined the term and when. It is interesting to know that al-Bayḍāwī also used the term, since both hailed from Shiraz. But this piece of information does not help much towards finding the answer to our question, since Quṭb al-Dīn al-Shīrāzī was an older contemporary of al-Bayḍāwī. In the usage of the term al-Bayḍāwī could not have preceded Quṭb al-Dīn. What we can do is to research on the issue of the currency of the term in 13th and 14th-century Persian Islam, which could also prove to be its source. A comparative study of the understanding of the term by Quṭb al-Dīn al-Shīrāzī and al-Bayḍāwī could, however, throw some light on the issue.

The contents of Dr. Haddad's book also raise historical issues that pertain to Islamic intellectual history. If it is indeed our objective to have a broader and clearer picture of the Islamic intellectual history then it is worth taking up the issue of the various possible historical connections between the various scholars located in different parts of the Islamic world and the issue of the ideas that linked them to each other as mentioned in Dr. Haddad's book. The significance of his book in this particular respect is that it could help fill certain gaps in our current picture of the Islamic intellectual tradition. Past Muslim scholars are known to play a much more important role than other groups in maintaining and promoting intra-ummatic links. As such, there is a need for more research on the kind of intellectual world in which al-Bayḍāwī lived and thought and his connections to that world.

In conclusion, we would like to once again congratulate Dr. Haddad for this important work, which we believe will benefit not only teachers and students in the discipline of Quranic exegesis (*'ilm al-tafsīr*) but also those in the other disciplines, both religious and intellectual-rational. We are proud to say that this work, which the author successfully completed within the eighteen months period of his Visiting Research Fellowship at SOASCIS—a commendable scholarly feat—represents a good example of a scholarly work based on research done at the Centre. This book is the sixth to be published within the last one year. The first four books were published by UBD Press at the same in November 2014 and the fifth volume, a Springer publication, is to be released before the end of 2015. We hope, in his new appointment as a Senior Assistant Professor at SOASCIS, that Dr Haddad will continue to publish well-researched, scholarly works in line with the Centre's objective to position itself as a world leading research centre in Islamic studies. *Wa-mā tawfīqī illā bi'Llāh.*

Brunei Darussalam
10 Muharram 1437
23 October 2015

NOTES

[1] For a more recent work in English on the history of the science of Quranic exegesis, see Mahmoud M. Ayoub, *The Qur'an and Its Interpreters*, vol. 1, Introduction, pp. 1- 40.

[2] *Tawhidic* epistemology expounds the idea of the hierarchy and unity of truths, the highest of which is the Absolute Truth (*al-Ḥaqq*), which in Islam is one of the Names of God, and the lowest of which is the empirical truths. For a detailed exposition of tawhidic epistemology, see Osman Bakar, "The Qur'anic Identity of the Muslim *Ummah*: Tawhidic Epistemology as its Foundation and Sustainer" in *Islam and Civilisational Renewal*, vol. 3, no. 3 (2012), pp. 438-454 and in *Islamic Civilisation and the Modern World: Thematic Essays* (Brunei Darussalam: UBD Press, 2014), chapter 2.

[3] The Quran, al-Aʿrāf 7:52. According to this verse, the Quran explains itself in detail "with knowledge." The key phrase, *faṣṣalnāhu ʿalā ʿilm* ("We have detailed it, i.e. the Quran, with knowledge") appears general and comprehensive enough in its meaning to admit all forms and kinds of knowledge, including scientific knowledge as detailed explanations of each verse of the Quran. The principle of *tafṣīl ʿalā ʿilm* (elucidation or exposition with knowledge) is thus of fundamental importance to Quranic exegesis (*ʿilm al-tafsīr*).

[4] Al-Ghazzālī, for example, considers these early Muslim figures as scholars of Quranic exegesis. For al-Ghazzālī's discussion of their views on exegesis, see Muhammad Abul Quasem, *The Recitation and Interpretation of the Qur'an: Al-Ghazali's Theory* (London: Routledge & Kegan Paul, 1982), Chapter Four, pp. 86-104; for references to their own interpretations of verses in the first three chapters of the Quran, see Mahmoud M. Ayoub, *The Qur'an and Its Interpreters*, vols. I and II. The late Muhammad Abdul-Rauf, a modern Muslim scholar who served as professor at al-Azhar University in Cairo and as the first rector of International Islamic University, Malaysia, described ʿAlī b. Abī Ṭālib as the first Muslim intellectual. See his *Imam Ali Ibn Abi Talib: The First Intellectual Muslim Thinker* (Cairo: Al-Saadawi Publications, 1996).

[5] His full name is Qāḍī Nāṣir al-Dīn ʿAbd Allāh b. ʿUmar al-Bayḍāwī. The exact dates of his birth and death are not known. It appears that he flourished during the period between the last decade of the thirteenth century

and the second decade of the fourteenth century. See Gibril F. Haddad's discussion of this issue in the Introduction of his present work.

[6] SOASCIS is one of the few graduate centres of Islamic studies in the world exclusively devoted to producing Masters and PhDs by research in Islamic civilization and contemporary issues as well as undertaking research on various aspects of the field. Having completed his Visiting Fellowship at SOASCIS with an admirable scholarly output in the form of this lengthy book Dr Haddad was appointed in 2015 as a Senior Assistant Professor at the Centre.

[7] The terms *tafsīr* and *ta'wīl*, which are variously understood by exegetists, are found in the Quran itself. Some exegetists use the word *tafsīr* to mean interpretation in a broad sense such that *ta'wīl* is included and treated as a special kind of it. Some others use the word *tafsīr*, which occurs only once in the Quran (25:33), with the more specific meaning of "external explanation of the Book" or exoteric exegesis (*ẓāhir al-tafsīr*) to contrast it with *ta'wīl*, which is understood to mean "symbolic or hermeneutic interpretation" or esoteric exegesis of the Book. In the eighth book of his *Iḥyā' 'Ulūm al-Dīn* (The Revival of the Religious Sciences), entitled *The Book of Recitation and Interpretation of the Quran*, al-Ghazzālī used the term *ẓāhir al-tafsīr* to distinguish it from *ta'wīl*. Many leading exegetical authorities, especially among the Sufis, including Ibn 'Arabī, understand *tafsīr* and *ta'wīl* as two qualitatively different but interdependent interpretive modes or processes of understanding the meanings of the Quran.

[8] Al-Bayḍāwī wrote: "...truly the greatest of the sciences in scope and the highest in rank and radiance (*sharafan wa-manāran*) is the science of exegesis [of the Quran] (*'ilm al-tafsīr*), the chief and head of all the religious sciences (*al-'ulūm al-dīniyya*), the edifice of the bases of the sacred law and their foundation." See Gibril Fouad Haddad, *The Lights of Revelation and the Secrets of Interpretation: Ḥizb I of the Commentary on the Qur'ān by al-Bayḍāwī* (London: UBD Press and Beacon Books, 2015), p. 145.

[9] The word "scientific" is used here in the comprehensive sense of the Arabic term *'ilmīy* as understood and practiced in traditional Islamic scholarship that extends in its methodological application to all branches of knowledge, including the religious sciences.

[10] *The Quran*, 7:52. See note 3.

[11] Muhammad Abul Quasem, *The Recitation and Interpretation of the Quran*, pp. 86-94.

[12] Al-Ghazzālī quoted the following Prophetic hadith: "The man who explains the Quran according to his personal opinion (*bi-ra'yihi*) shall take his place in Hell" (al-Tirmidhi, *Sunan*, Tafsīr, 1). See M. Abul Quasem, *The Recitation and Interpretation of the Qur'an*, p. 86.

[13] For a detailed study of these two categories of knowledge in the Islamic tradition see Osman Bakar, *Classification of Knowledge in Islam* (Kuala Lumpur: Institute for Policy Studies, 1992; reprint, Cambridge: Islamic Texts Society, 1997).

[14] This time the word "scientific" is used in a more specific sense to refer to the methodological characteristics of the study of the natural world.

[15] For detailed information on al-Bayḍāwī's writings see Gibril F. Haddad, *The Lights of Revelation*, pp. 13-16.

[16] Dr. Haddad informs us that al-Bayḍāwī wrote a work entitled *Mawḍū'āt al-'Ulūm* which therefore, as the title suggests, pertains to epistemology (theory of knowledge). Dr. Haddad says it deals with the classification of the sciences. See G. F. Haddad, *The Lights of Revelation*, p. 16. Our comment is that even if the work does not deal explicitly with the classification of the sciences it is still correct to refer to it as a treatise on epistemology, since the topic of subject-matter or object of study (*mawḍū'*) of a science comes under the purview of the philosophical discipline of epistemology.

[17] G. F. Haddad, *The Lights of Revelation*, p. 18.

[18] G. F. Haddad, *The Lights of Revelation*, p. 1.

[19] G. F. Haddad, *The Lights of Revelation*, p. 91.

[20] G. F. Haddad, *The Lights of Revelation*, p. 49. In the practice of self-exegesis al-Bayḍāwī claimed the superiority of his *Anwār al-Tanzīl* to many other *tafsīrs*, including al-Zamakhsharī's *Kashshāf*.

[21] G. F. Haddad, *The Lights of Revelation*, p. 43.

[22] G. F. Haddad, *The Lights of Revelation*, pp. 14, 145.

[23] G. F. Haddad, *The Lights of Revelation*, p. 145.

[24] See Osman Bakar, *Classification of Knowledge in Islam*, Chapter 11.

Acknowledgments

This work is the fruit of an 18-month fellowship at Universiti Brunei Darussalam. My thanks go to the Chair Professor and Director of the Sultan Omar Ali Saifuddien Centre for Islamic Studies (SOASCIS) at UBD Prof. Datuk Dr. Osman Bakar; the Privy Councillor to the State of Perak, Malaysia, and Fellow at the Oxford Centre for Islamic Studies Dr. Muhammad Afifi al-Akiti; Dr. Sayyid Hamid al-Mahdali of the Usul al-Din faculty, Universiti Islam Sultan Sharif Ali (UNISSA) in Brunei; and the Qur'ān canonist of Damascus Dr. Muhammad Samer al-Nass (I read the first *rub'* of this *tafsīr* with the latter two), for their support and encouragement. Thanks also to Dr. Ibrahim Zayn at the International Islamic University of Malaysia who first suggested for me to translate al-Bayḍāwī and to Dr. Muhammad Munir al-Hayek of Abu al-Nur Institute in Damascus for proofreading the Fatiha part of my edition. Thanks to my *sharīf* mentors in the service of Qur'ān and Hadith, especially my beloved *murshid*s the late Mawlana Shaykh Muhammad Nazim Adil Naqshbandi and Mawlana Shaykh Muhammad Hisham Kabbani; and the erudite senior Hadith master and head of the Departments of the Qur'ān and Sunna in the Universities of Damascus and Aleppo, Dr. Nur al-Din 'Itr. The debt I owe them can never be repaid but I hope to be granted, because of them, a *nisba* to the Qur'ān and the Family of the Prophet ﷺ that benefits here and hereafter. Lastly, thanks to the head of the Near and Middle Eastern Department at the University of Cambridge, Mrs. Yasmin Faghihi; the Department of Conservation and Digitization at the Staatsbibliothek zu Berlin—Preußischer Kulturbesitz; and my family.

This work was prepared amid daily reminders of the trials of the Syrian people. They remain in our prayers and it is also dedicated to them.

Abbreviations

α	Cambridge 874/1470 ms. of *Anwār al-Tanzīl*
A	Ẓāhiriyya 990/1582 ms. of Zakariyyā al-Anṣārī, *Ḥāshiya*
Afandī	Muḥibb al-Dīn Afandī, *Sharḥ Shawāhid al-Kashshāf*
Ahkām	Maḥmūd Khalīl al-Ḥuṣarī, *Aḥkām Qirā'at al-Qur'ān*
Ak	Alukah 1067/1657 manuscript of *Anwār al-Tanzīl*
AQ	'Abd al-Qādir Ḥassūna's 1996 ed., *Anwār* with Kāzarūnī
B	Berlin 758/1357 ms., *Anwār al-Tanzīl*
β	Undated Cambridge ms., *Anwār al-Tanzīl*
C	Cairo 1375/1955 ed. of *Anwār al-Tanzīl*
ÇZ	Çelebi and Zādah *Ḥāshiyas* (Riyadh 1170/1757 ms.)
D	Deobandi ed. *al-Taqrīr al-Ḥāwī fī Ḥall Tafsīr al-Bayḍāwī*
ε	Cambridge 908/1502 manuscript of *Anwār al-Tanzīl*
F	Fleischer's 1848 edition of the *Anwār* (Leipzig)
G	Gujarātī's *Ḥāshiyat al-ʿAlawī* on the *Anwār* (2012 ed.)
H	Ḥallāq-Aṭrash 2000 edition of *Anwār al-Tanzīl*
I	Irbil 1150/1737 ms. of the *Anwār* at Jāmiʿat Ṣalāḥ al-Dīn
Iṣ	'Iṣām al-Dīn al-Isfarāyīnī, *Ḥāshiya* on al-Bayḍāwī ms.
J	Jār Allāh al-Zamakhsharī and his *Tafsīr al-Kashshāf*
K	al-Kāzarūnī, *Ḥāshiya* on al-Bayḍāwī (1912 ed.)
Kh	Khafājī, *Ḥāshiyat ʿInāyat al-Qāḍī* on Bayḍāwī (1867 ed.)
L	Istanbul 1257/1841 edition of *Anwār al-Tanzīl*
Lisān	Ibn Manẓūr, *Lisān al-ʿArab*
M	Mecca pre-1242/1827 ms. of *Anwār al-Tanzīl*
MM	Muḥammad Marʿashlī 1998 ed. of *Anwār al-Tanzīl*
MQ	'Abd al-Laṭīf al-Khaṭīb, *Muʿjam al-Qirā'āt*
N	Nablus undated ms. of *Tafsīr al-Bayḍāwī*, Jāmiʿat al-Najāḥ
P	Pakistan 2010 ed. of the *Anwār* with al-Kawrā'ī's *Taʿlīqāt*
Q	al-Qūnawī, 2001 ed. of the *Ḥāshiya* on al-Bayḍāwī
R	Riyadh 850/1446 ms. of *Anwār al-Tanzīl*
S	al-Suyūṭī, *Ḥāshiyat Nawāhid al-Abkār* on Bayḍāwī (2003)
Sk	al-Sayālkūtī, *Ḥāshiya* on al-Bayḍāwī (1270/1854)
T	Teheran 1272/1856 lithographic edition of the *Anwār*
U	'Uthmāniyya 1317/1899 ed. of *Anwār al-Tanzīl*
Ul	'Uthmāniyya 1305/1888 lithograph ed. of *Anwār al-Tanzīl*
W	Walters 966/1559 ms. of Ibn Kamāl Bāsha's *Ḥāshiya*
Z	Shaykh Zādah, 1306/1889 ed. of *Ḥāshiya* on al-Bayḍāwī

Introduction: al-Bayḍāwī and his *Anwār al-Tanzīl wa-Asrār al-Ta'wīl* in hermeneutical tradition

Among the major exegeses of the Qur'ān none has received more attention on the part of Muslim teachers and scholars than the *tafsīr* by the elusive Turco-Perso-Arab Shāfi'ī-Ash'arī-Sufi master of Shīrāz and Tabriz, *Qāḍī al-quḍāt* Nāṣir al-Dīn Abū Sa'īd (also Abū al-Khayr and Abū Muḥammad) 'Abd Allāh b. 'Umar b. Muḥammad b. 'Alī al-Bayḍāwī, *Anwār al-Tanzīl wa-Asrār al-Ta'wīl* (The Lights of Revelation and the Secrets of Interpretation). Who was Qadi al-Bayḍāwī and why did his medium-sized work become the most important commentary on Qur'ān in the history of Islam? The details of his life are scanty. The meticulous Syrian historian Shams al-Dīn al-Dhahabī (673-748/1275-1347) shows no knowledge of him and does not mention him in all of *Tārīkh al-Islām al-Kabīr*, *Siyar A'lām al-Nubalā'* and *al-'Ibar fī Tārīkh man 'Abar*. Nor does Kamāl al-Dīn Abū al-Faḍl Ibn al-Fuwaṭī al-Ḥanbalī (642-723/1244-1323) document him in his *Majma' al-Ādāb fī Mu'jam al-Alqāb*.[1]

Bayḍāwī was born in al-Bayḍā' (Beyza), "the White"—thus named because of its white tower that could be seen from afar[2]—between Iṣṭakhr and Shīrāz, Fars Province, before or during the reign of the Ilkhānī Atābak Abū Bakr b. Sa'd-i-Zangī (628-658/1231-1260). A few years after his father's death he was appointed *qāḍī al-mamālik* of Fars then, briefly, *qāḍī al-quḍāt* in Shīrāz. He moved to Tabriz, Azerbaijan Province where he died and was buried in the Jarāndāb cemetery. His birthdate is unknown and his obitus variously claimed as:

[1] Ed. Muḥammad al-Kāẓim, 6 vols. (Teheran: Wizārat al-Thaqāfa wal-Irshād al-Islāmī, 1416/1995).

[2] Abū al-'Abbās Aḥmad al-Qalqashandī, *Ṣubḥ al-A'shā fī Kitābat al-Inshā*, 14 vols. (Cairo: Maṭba'at Dār al-Kutub al-Miṣriyya, 1340/1922) 4:346.

(i) "682/1283 or later;"
(ii) 685/1286 (most famously);
(iii) 691/1292;
(iv) 692/1293;
(v) 708/1308 (likely);
(vi) 716/1316 (likely);
(vii) and 719/1319.[3]

[3] Respectively in **(i)** Muḥammad Muḥsin Aghā Buzurg al-Ṭihrānī, (1293-1389/1876-1969) *al-Dharī'a ilā Taṣānīf al-Shī'a*, ed. Sayyid Aḥmad al-Ḥusaynī, 26 vols. (Beirut: Dār al-Aḍwā', 1983) 6:41; **(ii)** Ḥamdullāh Mustawfī al-Qazwīnī (682-750/1283-1349), *The Ta'rīkh-i Guzida or "Select History,"* ed. and trans. Edward G. Browne, 2 vols. (Leyden: E.J. Brill and London: Luzac & Co., 1913) 1:811, 2:222 §95 [ed. based on an 857/1453 Persian ms.; but Charles Rieu (1820-1902), *Supplement to the Catalogue of the Arabic Manuscripts in the British Museum* (London: Longmans & co., 1894) p. 68 §116 says "Ḥamdullah Mustaufi… states that he died after 710" in Rieu's reading of a London ms. of *Ta'rīkh-i Guzida* while a later ed. by 'Abd al-Ḥusayn Navā'ī (Teheran: Amīr Kabīr, 1339 [Persian]/1960) p. 706, 7f. claims "716/1316," cf. Josef van Ess, "Biobibliographische Notizen zur islamischen Theologie." *Die Welt des Orients*, Bd. 9, H. 2 (1978) p. 264 and Edwin E. Calverley and James W. Pollock in *Nature, Man and God in Medieval Islam: 'Abd Allah Baydawi's text* Ṭawāli' al-Anwār min Maṭāli' al-Anẓār *Along with Mahmud Isfahani's Commentary* Maṭāli' al-Anẓār, Sharḥ Ṭawāli' al-Anwār, 3 vols. (Leiden: Brill, 2001) 1:xxix, xxxvii]; Ṣalāḥ al-Dīn Khalīl b. Aybak al-Ṣafadī (691-764/1292-1363), *al-Wāfī bil-Wafayāt*, ed. Aḥmad al-Arnā'ūṭ and Turkī Muṣṭafā, 29 vols. (Beirut: Dār Iḥyā' al-Turāth al-'Arabī, 1420/2000) 17:206 as he heard it directly from the expert biographer Abū al-Khayr Najm al-Dīn Sa'īd b. 'Abd Allāh al-Dihlī al-Baghdādī al-Ḥanbalī (712-749/1312-1348); 'Imād al-Dīn Ismā'īl b. 'Umar b. Kathīr (700-774/1301-1373), *al-Bidāya wal-Nihāya*, ed. 'Abd Allāh al-Turkī, 21 vols. (Cairo: Dār Hajar, 1417/1997) 17:606; Ibn Ḥabīb al-Ḥalabī al-Dimashqī (d. 779/1377), *Durrat al-Aslāk fī Dawlat al-Atrāk*, ms. Leipzig Vollers 0661, folio 86a; Ibn Shākir al-Kutbī (686-784/1287-1382) [in *'Uyūn al-Tārīkh*?] according to Shihāb al-Dīn Ibn al-'Imād al-Dimashqī, *Shadharāt al-Dhahab fī Akhbār man Dhahab*, ed. 'Abd al-Qādir and Maḥmūd al-Arnā'ūṭ, 10 vols. (Damascus and Beirut: Dār Ibn Kathīr, 1406/1986) 7:685, Year 685; al-Suyūṭī (849-911/1445-1505), *Bughyat al-Wu'āt fī Ṭabaqāt al-Lughawiyyīn wal-Nuḥāt*, ed. Muḥammad Abū al-Faḍl Ibrāhīm, 2nd ed., 2 vols. (Beirut: Dār al-Fikr, 1399/1979) 2:50-51; Shams al-Dīn Muḥammad b. 'Alī al-Dāwūdī (d. 945/1538), *Ṭabaqāt al-Mufassirīn*, ed. 'Alī Muḥammad 'Umar, 2nd ed., 2 vols. (Cairo: Maktabat Wahba, 1415/1994) 1:242-243; Aḥmad b. Muḥammad al-Adnahwī (11th/17th c.), *Ṭabaqāt al-Mufassirīn*, ed. Sulaymān b. Ṣāliḥ al-Khizzī (Medina: Maktabat al-'Ulūm wal-Ḥikam, 1417/1997) pp. 254-255; Abū al-Ṭayyib Mawlūd al-Sarīrī

The fifth and sixth datings are circumstancially supported by the chronology relative to the obituaries of at least seven contemporaries that fall either too far (four students) or too close

al-Sūsī, *Muʿjam al-Uṣūliyyīn* (Beirut: Dār al-Kutub al-ʿIlmiyya, 1423/2002) pp. 305-306; ʿĀdil Nuwayhiḍ, *Muʿjam al-Mufassirīn*, 2nd ed., 2 vols. ([Beirut]: Mu'assasat Nuwayhiḍ al-Thaqāfiyya, 1409/1988) 1:318 among many others. This is also the dating held by Ziriklī and Kaḥḥāla in *al-Aʿlām* and *Muʿjam al-Mu'allifīn* respectively but this date implies the Qadi died early in life. **(iii)** Ibn al-Subkī (727-771/1327-1370) in *Ṭabaqāt al-Shāfiʿiyya al-Wusṭā* as cited in the footnotes to *Ṭabaqāt al-Shāfiʿiyya al-Kubrā*, ed. Maḥmūd al-Ṭannāḥī and ʿAbd al-Fattāḥ al-Ḥilw, 2nd. ed., 10 vols. (Jīza: Dār Hijr, 1992) 8:16-17; Jamāl al-Dīn al-Isnawī (d. 772/1371), *Ṭabaqāt al-Shāfiʿiyya*, ed. Kamāl Yūsuf al-Ḥūt, 2 vols. (Beirut: Dār al-Kutub al-ʿIlmiyya, 1407/1987) 1:136; Ibn al-Maṭarī al-ʿUbādī, *Dhayl Ṭabaqāt al-Shāfiʿiyyīn*, 3rd vol. of Ibn Kathīr's *Ṭabaqāt al-Fuqahā' al-Shāfiʿiyyīn*, ed. Muḥammad Zaynuhum ʿAzb and Aḥmad Hāshim, 3 vols. (Cairo: Maktabat al-Thaqāfat al-Dīniyya, 1413/1993) 3:96; Ismāʿīl Bāshā Baghdādī (d.1339/1921), *Hadiyyat al-ʿĀrifīn: Asmā' al-Mu'allifīn wa-Āthār al-Muṣannifīn*, 2 vols. (Istanbul: Milli egitim basimevi, 1951-1955, rept. Beirut: Dār Iḥyā' al-Turāth al-ʿArabī, n.d.) 1:462-463. **(iv)** ʿAbd Allāh b. Asʿad al-Yāfiʿī (698-768/1299-1367), *Mir'āt al-Jinān wa-ʿIbrat al-Yaqẓān fī Maʿrifat Mā Yuʿtabar min Ḥawādith al-Zamān*, ed. Khalīl al-Manṣūr, 4 vols. (Beirut: Dār al-Kutub al-ʿIlmiyya, 1417/1997) 4:165; al-ʿUbādī, *Dhayl* (3:96); Muḥammad Bāqir Khvānṣārī (1226-1313/1811-1895), *Rawḍāt al-Jannāt fī Aḥwāl al-ʿUlamā' wal-Sādāt*, 8 vols. (Beirut: al-Dār al-Islāmiyya, 1411/1991) 5:127-130 §464. **(v)** Abū al-ʿAbbās Aḥmad b. Abī al-Khayr Zarkūb Shīrāzī (681-789/1282-1387) in *Shīrāznāmah*, ed. Bahman Karimi (Teheran: Maṭbaʿa-i Rawshanā'ī, 1310[Persian]/1931) p. 136, cf. Lutpi Ibrahim, *Theological Questions at Issue between az-Zamakhsharī and al-Bayḍāwī with special reference to* al-Kashshāf *and* Anwār at-Tanzīl, unpub. Ph.D. thesis (Edinburgh: University of Edinburgh, 1977) p. 38 and van Ess, "Notizen" (p. 263 n. 60). Also see notes 25, 163. **(vi)** *Anon. British Museum ms. 3328* (fol. 201a) in Lutpi Ibrahim, *Questions* pp. 37-38; Rieu, *Supplement* p. 68 §116; Rudolf Sellheim, *Materialien zur arabischen Literaturgeschichte*, 2 vols. (Wiesbaden: Steiner, 1976) pp. 289-91; cf. Carl Brockelmann, art. "Baiḍāwī" in *EI*[1] (2:590-591), James Robson, art. "BAYḌĀWĪ" in *EI*[2] (1:1129) and van Ess p. 264: "Sehon Rieu hat eine Bemerkung auf dem Vorsatzblatt einer Handschrift von Baiḍāwīs *Tafsīr* im Britischen Museum bekanntgemacht, wo es ganz präzise heißt, daß der Verfasser am Ende seines Lebens allem weltlichenStreben entsagt habe und i. J. 716/1316 gestorben sei." This is also the gist of a note found by Rieu in another London ms. which van Ess cites as "*K. al-Aqālim*, einer Umarbeitung von Qazwīnīs *Āṯār al-bilād*," and the "post-710" dating cited. **(vii)** Khafājī (977-1069/1569-1659), *ʿInāyat al-Qāḍī wa-Kifāyat al-Rāḍī ʿalā Tafsīr al-Bayḍāwī*, ed. Muḥammad Ṣabbāgh, 8 vols. (Bulāq: Dār al-Ṭibāʿa al-ʿĀmira, 1283/1867, rept. Beirut: Dār Ṣādir, 1975) 1:3, "based on the Persian sources."

(the Qadi's father, his teacher Būshanjānī, al-Būṣīrī) to the date 685 for it to be correct. (As for the Ilkhān vizier Rashīd al-Dīn Faḍl Allāh's letter mentioning Bayḍāwī among fifty scholarly recipients of gifts[4] it is spurious.) Furthermore, the fact that Nasafī (d. 710/1310) and Ibn al-Ṣā'igh (d. 714/1314) were already epitomizing him shows the *Anwār* was finished early and achieved fame quickly. This matches the reason given for his appointment as qadi of Bayḍā' under the Ilkhan Arghun (683-690/1284-1291) "due to the prestige of his *Tafsīr*"[5]—all well before the move to Tabriz, which most likely was after 685. Lastly, the autograph master of the *Anwār* was being recopied in (and probably also before) 720/1320 not in Tabriz but in Shīrāz.[6]

The editor of Bayḍāwī's *al-Ghāyat al-Quṣwā* quotes Ibn al-Ḥabīb al-Ḥalabī al-Dimashqī (d. 779/1377) as saying "his demise was in the town of Tabriz, aged 100" and sources it to "the Muḥammad III ms. of *Durrat al-Aslāk* (1:57)"[7]; but no such words are found in the entry on Bayḍāwī in the Leipzig ms. of the *Durra* (see illustrations section below at the very end).[8]

[4] "Possibly in the years 710-712" Van Ess, "Notizen" (pp. 265-268). The letter is a bombastic and anachronistic Indian forgery mixing top names with obscure Indian ones cf. Ruben Levy, "Letters of Rashīd al-Dīn," *JRAS* 78 (1946) pp. 74-78.

[5] Khwāndamīr (d. 942/1536), *Ḥabīb al-Siyar* and Khvānṣārī per van Ess p. 264.

[6] Cf. Rosemarie Quiring-Zoche, "An early manuscript [758/1357] of al-Bayḍāwī's *Anwār al-tanzīl* and the model it has been copied from," in *From Codicology to Technology: Islamic Manuscripts and Their Place in Scholarship*, ed. Stephanie Brinkmann and Beate Wiesmüller (Berlin: Frank & Timme, 2009) pp. 39-41. Compare the data to the bizarre claim that "the *Anwār al-tanzīl* seems to have been slow gaining widespread recognition" in *Encyclopædia Iranica*, art. "BAYŻĀWĪ." See pp. 16, 63 above also.

[7] Bayḍāwī, *al-Ghāyat al-Quṣwā fī Dirāyat al-Fatwā*, ed. 'Alī Muḥyī al-Dīn 'Alī Qarah Dāghī, 2 vols. (Shubrā Miṣr: Dār al-Naṣr lil-Ṭibā'at al-Islāmiyya, 1402/1982) 1:54. This claim is reduplicated in the 1988 *Turkish Encyclopedia* (cf. Quiring-Zoche p. 35), by 'Abd al-Raḥmān al-Shihrī in his lessons on al-Bayḍāwī (see note 119 below) and by Sa'īd Fawda in the introduction to his edition of Bayḍāwī's *Miṣbāḥ al-Arwāḥ*.

[8] Ibn Ḥabīb, *Durrat al-Aslāk fī Dawlat al-Atrāk* (year 685), ms. Leipzig Vollers 0661, folios 85b-86a. http://refaiya.uni-leipzig.de/receive/RefaiyaBook_islamhs_00002925

His teachers

Bayḍāwī was raised in a scholarly family that counted no less than three provincial head judges: his father "*qāḍī al-quḍāt*, Imām al-Ḥaqq wal-Dīn, Abū al-Qāsim 'Umar," his paternal grandfather "*qāḍī al-quḍāt* Fakhr al-Dīn Abī 'Abd Allāh Muḥammad b. Ṣadr al-Dīn Abī al-Ḥasan 'Alī" and his paternal great-uncle "*Aqḍā al-quḍāt* Shams al-Dīn Abū Naṣr Aḥmad b. 'Alī" as he names them in his preamble to *Tuḥfat al-Abrār*, which no doubt motivated him to perpetuate the titular tradition. He took sacred law (*fiqh*) from his father through a prestigious chain of transmission:[9]

Qadi 'Abd Allāh b. 'Umar al-Bayḍāwī

↓

His father 'Umar b. Muḥammad b. 'Alī (d. 673 or 675?/1275 or 1277?)

↓

His father Fakhr al-Dīn Muḥammad b. Ṣadr al-Dīn 'Alī

↓

Mujīr al-Dīn Maḥmūd b. Abī al-Mubārak al-Baghdādī (d. 592/1196)

↓

Abū Manṣūr Sa'īd b. Muḥammad al-Razzāz (462-539/1070-1145)

↓

Abū Ḥāmid Muḥammad al-Ghazālī (450-505/1058-1111)

↓

'Abd al-Malik al-Juwaynī (Imām al-Ḥaramayn) (419-478/1028-1085)

↓

His father Abū Muḥammad 'Abd Allāh b. Yūsuf (d. 438/1047)

↓

Abū Bakr 'Abd Allāh b. Aḥmad al-Qaffāl [al-Ṣaghīr] (d. 417/1026)

↓

Abū Zayd Muḥammad b. Aḥmad al-Fāshānī (301-371/914-982)

↓

Qadi Abū al-'Abbās Aḥmad b. 'Umar b. Surayj (249-306/863-918)

↓

[9] Bayḍāwī, *Ghāya* (1:184f.); 'Ubādī, *Dhayl Ṭabaqāt al-Fuqahā' al-Shāfi'iyyīn* (3:97).

Abū al-Qāsim ʿUthmān b. Saʿīd b. Bashshār al-Anmāṭī (d. 228/843)

Ismāʿīl b. Yaḥyā al-Muzanī (175-264/791-878) | al-Rabīʿ b. Sulaymān al-Murādī (174-270/790-825)

Imam Abū ʿAbd Allāh Muḥammad b. Idrīs al-Shāfiʿī
(150-204/767-819)

Imām al-Ḥaram Muslim b. Khālid al-Zanjī (d. 179 or 180/795 or 796) | Mālik b. Anas al-Aṣbaḥī (93-179/712-795)

Ibn Jurayj (d. 150/767) | Nāfiʿ Mawlā Ibn ʿUmar (d. 117/735)

ʿAṭāʾ b. Abī Rabāḥ (d. 114/732) | Ibn ʿUmar (10BH-73 or 74/612-692 or 693)

Ibn ʿAbbās (2 or 3BH-68/619-688)

THE PROPHET MUḤAMMAD ﷺ

Also among al-Bayḍāwī's teachers:

• Muḥammad b. Muḥammad al-Kathḥitāʾī (or Kathḥitānī), a Sufi scholar who was teacher to the Sultan Aḥmad Āghā b. Hūlāgū (d. 682/1283). He relatedly petitioned the latter to grant Bayḍāwī the post of chief judge of Fars in *dunyā*-deprecatory tones:

> This is an excellent learned man who requests a share with Your lordship in hell; I mean he bids you grant him the length of a prayer-rug in the Fire, namely the chair of judgeship.

"When al-Bayḍāwī heard the way his teacher had submitted his request he divested himself from his ambition and retired from the world"[10] Something like retirement would account for the obscurity that shrouds the latter part of the Qadi's life.

[10] Thus in Subkī, *Ṭabaqāt* (5:59) but paraphrased in Khvānṣārī, *Rawḍāt* (5:128-129).

- The erudite and saintly Sharaf al-Dīn ʿUmar b. al-Zakī b. Bahrām al-Būshakānī or Būshanjānī (d. 677/1279 or 680/1282) who also taught Quṭb al-Dīn al-Shīrāzī. It is said all the works of the Qadi al-Bayḍāwī—his star pupil—were first drafts of his which the Qadi reworked and finalized. The latter wrote him a long elegy that was engraved at his gravesite then effaced.[11]

- *Qāḍī al-quḍāt* Taqī al-Dīn Abū al-Ḥasan ʿAlī b. al-Ḥasan b. Aḥmad al-Shīrāzī. This and the following entries are uncertain.

- *Qāḍī al-quḍāt* Sirāj al-Dīn Abū al-ʿIzz Mukarram b. al-ʿAlāʾ b. Naṣr al-Qālī (d. 621/1224!) with his chain to Tāj al-Qurrāʾ Ibn Ḥamza al-Kirmānī and Imām al-Wāḥidī; both he and the previous in *fiqh* and canonical readings according to al-ʿUbādī.

- "Najm al-Dīn ʿAbd al-Wāḥid, from Shaykh Muwaffaq al-Dīn al-Kāzarānī, from Abū al-Faraj Masʿūd b. al-Ḥasan al-Thaqafī;"

- (more likely through intermediaries:) Abū Aḥmad ʿAbd al-Wahhab b. ʿAlī b. Sakīna al-Ṣūfī al-Baghdādī (d. 606/1210);

- (more likely through intermediaries:) Mukhliṣ al-Dīn Abū Aḥmad Maʿmar b. ʿAbd al-Wāḥid b. al-Fākhir al-Qurashī al-ʿAbshamī al-Aṣbahānī (d. 564/1169), both of them in hadith.[12]

Al-Bayḍāwī's connection with the philosopher Naṣīr al-Dīn Muḥammad b. Muḥammad b. al-Ḥasan al-Ṭūsī (d. 672/1274) and likewise his tutelage under the Sufi shaykh Abū Ḥafṣ ʿUmar b. Muḥammad b. ʿAbd Allāh al-Suhrawardī (539-632/1145-1235) are unsupported beyond their mention in a late Shiʿi source, the philosopher Abū al-Qāsim b. Abī Ḥāmid b. Naṣr al-Bayān al-Kāzarūnī's (d. after 1014/1605) *Sullam al-Samāwāt*, who also

[11] Muʿīn al-Dīn Abū al-Qāsim al-Junayd b. Maḥmūd al-ʿUmarī al-Shīrāzī (d. after 740/1340), *Shadd al-Izār fī Ḥaṭṭ al-Awzār ʿan Zuwwār al-Mazār* (Teheran: Maṭbaʿat al-Majlis, 1368/1949) pp. 297-299 §214 and al-ʿUbādī, *Dhayl* (3:95).
[12] The last five as documented by al-ʿUbādī, *Dhayl* (3:94-95).

alone attributed to the Qadi a commentary on al-Ṭūsī's *Fuṣūl.*[13]

His students

Among al-Bayḍāwī's students as mentioned by the sources:

- the hadith scholar Abū al-Qāsim Kamāl al-Dīn ʿUmar b. Ilyās b. Yūnus al-Marāghī al-Adharbayjānī al-Ṣūfī al-Dimashqī (643-732/1245-1332) the teacher of Badr al-Dīn al-Nābulusī, he studied *uṣūl*, *fiqh* and *kalām* under al-Bayḍāwī and read with him the *Minhāj*, the *Ghāya* and the *Ṭawāliʿ* in those three disciplines respectively as well as *Anwār al-Tanzīl.*[14]

- ʿAbd al-Raḥmān b. Aḥmad al-Aṣfahānī: he read the *Ghāya* and other works with al-Bayḍāwī. His son Maḥmūd (674-749/1275-1348) wrote commentaries on al-Bayḍāwī's *Minhāj* and his *Ṭawāliʿ.*[15]

- Rūḥ al-Dīn b. Jalāl al-Dīn al-Ṭayyār, a Tabriz disciple who produced a commentrary on al-Bayḍāwī's *Miṣbāḥ al-Arwāḥ.*[16]

- Qadi Zayn al-Dīn ʿAlī b. Rūzbahān b. Muḥammad al-Khānjī (d. 707/1308!): a Tabriz disciple who authored *al-Nihāya fi Sharḥ*

[13] As cited by Khvānṣārī in *Rawḍāt al-Jannāt* (5:129). Cf. al-Baghdādī, *Hadiyyat al-ʿĀrifīn* (1:463a) and Qarah Dāghī, introduction to *al-Ghāyat al-Quṣwā* (1:63-65).

[14] Ibn Ḥajar al-ʿAsqalānī, *al-Durar al-Kāmina fī Aʿyān al-Miʾat al-Thāmina*, 4 vols. (Hyderabad Deccan: Maṭbaʿat Dāʾirat al-Maʿārif al-ʿUthmāniyya, 1350/1931) 3:156-157 and Aḥmad Sardār al-Ḥalabī, *Iʿlām al-Ṭalabat al-Nājiḥīn* (see note at the very end of this introduction). Ibn Ḥajar said al-Dhahabī included him in his *Muʿjam* and described him as his teacher, and this is reproduced uncritically by contemporaries such as Qarah Dāghī, *Ghāya* (1:65-66) and Yūsuf Aḥmad ʿAlī, *al-Bayḍāwī wa-Manhajuh fil-Tafsīr*, unpub. doctoral diss. (Mecca: Jāmiʿat Umm al-Qurā, n.d.) p. 23; however, al-Marāghī is not mentioned in the two editions of al-Dhahabī's *Muʿjam al-Shuyūkh* and we have seen that the latter shows no knowledge of al-Bayḍāwī at all, which would be unlikely if he studied under so close a student of his. The correct Dhahabī is no doubt the son, Abū Hurayra Ibn al-Dhahabī, rather than the father.

[15] Cf. Qarah Dāghī (1:67).

[16] al-Shīrāzī, *Shadd al-Izār* (p. 211).

al-Ghāya, a commentary on al-Bayḍāwī's large work on Shāfiʿī sacred law; a commentary on the latter's *Minhāj* in legal theory; a work on grammar; a commentary on Ibn al-Ḥājib's *Kāfiya* entitled *al-Shukūk*; and a commentary on the latter's work on legal theory which al-Bayḍawī also commented, *Mukhtaṣar al-Muntahā*, entitled *al-Muʿtabar*.[17]

• Qadi Rūḥ al-Dīn Abū Ṭāhir b. Abī al-Maʿālī, a pious bilingual scholar of Tabriz who also authored a complete commentary on *Sharḥ al-Ghāya*. "He died on Laylat al-Raghā'ib [the night before the first Jumuʿa of Rajab] of 753 [17 August 1352]."[18]

• Tāj al-Dīn ʿAlī b. ʿAbd Allāh b. Abī al-Ḥasan b. Abī Bakr al-Tibrīzī al-Shāfiʿi (d. 746/1345) a student of al-Quṭb al-Shīrāzī:[19] although not a student of the Qadi since "he was able to reach al-Bayḍāwī but did not take anything from him," he deserves mention in view of the fact that that proximity took place before the year 716/1316—at which time he left Khurasan and entered Baghdad—which strengthens the probability that the Qadi was alive beyond the year 685.

• Fakhr al-Dīn Aḥmad b. al-Ḥasan b. Yūsuf al-Jārabardī al-Shāfiʿī (d. 746/1346): yet another famed Tabriz commentator of the *Minhāj* and the *Kāfiya*, part of the *Ḥāwī* (in Shāfiʿī law) and al-Zamakhsharī's *Kashshāf* who also "reportedly met al-Bayḍāwī."[20]

• Tāj al-Dīn al-Hankī: Ibn al-Subkī and others mentioned him among al-Bayḍāwī's students, which is unlikely.[21]

As for Jamāl al-Dīn Muḥammad b. Abī Bakr b. Muḥammad al-Kisā'ī al-Muqrī' who taught and died in Tabriz, he was not a

17 al-Shīrāzī, *Shadd al-Izār* (pp. 212-213).
18 al-Shīrāzī, *Shadd al-Izār* (pp. 391-392).
19 al-Dāwūdī, *Ṭabaqāt al-Mufassirīn* (1:406-407 §354).
20 Ibn al-Subkī, *Ṭabaqāt* (5:169) and others, cf. Qarah Dāghī (1:67-68).
21 In the entry on al-Ījī who studied under him: *Ṭabaqāt* (9:8), cf. Qarah Dāghī (1:68).

student of Nāṣir al-Dīn al-Bayḍāwī but of his father Imām al-Dīn as explicitly stated by the author of *Shadd al-Izār*.[22]

His peers

Among the many prominent scholars in al-Bayḍāwī's synchronic layer three stood out in Shiraz and Tabriz:

- Quṭb al-Dīn Abū al-Thanā' Maḥmūd b. Mas'ūd b. Muṣliḥ al-Fārisī al-Kāzarūnī al-Shīrāzī al-Shāfi'ī (634-710/1237-1311), the Qadi's jocular, wealthy and generous countryman and (probably slightly older) school colleague (under al-Būshakānī), a well-travelled, world-savvy familiar of kings, "the scholar of non-Arabs" (al-Dhahabī), "held in high esteem by the Mongols" (Ibn al-Wardī) yet humble savant, qadi of Malatya, physician (under his father's tutelage), astronomer, mathematician, opticist, chess-player, diplomat and prestidigitator (*yutqin al-sha'badha*).

He authored commentaries on Ibn Sīnā's *Kulliyyāt* (in which he cited the Sufi savant Shams al-Dīn Muḥammad b. Aḥmad al-Ḥakīm al-Kutbī among his teachers) and *Qānūn* (which he taught in Damascus with the *Shifā'*); al-Suhrawardī's *Ḥikmat al-Ishrāq*; al-Sakkākī's *Miftāḥ al-'Ulūm* on rhetoric; and his teacher Naṣīr al-Dīn al-Ṭūsī's *Tadhkira* on astronomy, in which he authored original works such as *Nihāyat al-Idrāk* and *Tuḥfat al-Sāmī*. He also authored *Ghurrat al-Tāj* in sapience (*ḥikma*). All of the above works are in Persian. The Mongolian Ilkhan sultan Abagha (1234-1282) reportedly told him: "You are the best of al-Naṣīr's students and he is quite old so be sure not to miss out any of his knowledge." to which he replied: "I have taken everything I need." Whenever he finished writing a book he would fast and keep vigil next to his finished copy.

[22] al-Shīrāzī, *Shadd al-Izār* (p. 117), contrary to Yūsuf Aḥmad 'Alī's assumption in *al-Bayḍāwī wa-Manhajuh fil-Tafsīr* (p. 21).

He reputedly took *taṣawwuf* in Konya from Ṣadr al-Dīn Qūnawī the stepson of Ibn ʿArabī.[23] According to one account he was assiduous in praying in congregation, "always dressing in the Sufi fashion" (al-Suyūṭī) and humbled himself before the ulema; another says he loved wine and clowning.[24] Toward the last part of his life in Tabriz he turned to hadith—in which he narrated Ibn al-Athīr's *Jāmiʿ al-Uṣūl* and al-Baghawī's *Sharḥ al-Sunna*—jurisprudence, *taṣawwuf* and *tafsīr*, authoring a slim commentary on al-Zamakhsharī's *Kashshāf*; and marginalia on Ibn al-Ḥājib's *Mukhtaṣar Muntahā al-Sūl wal-Amal fī ʿIlmay al-Uṣūl wal-Jadal* on legal principles and dialectic. He would say: "I wish I lived in the Prophet's—upon him blessings and peace—time, even blind and deaf, as long as he might look at me once."[25]

[23] Yūsuf Sarkīs, *Muʿjam al-Maṭbūʿāt al-ʿArabiyya wal-Muʿarraba*, 2 vols. (Cairo: Maṭbaʿat Sarkīs, 1346/1928) 2:1532.

[24] al-Isnawī, *Ṭabaqāt al-Shāfiʿiyya* (2:32 §718) and Ibn Qāḍī Shuhba, *Ṭabaqāt al-Shāfiʿiyya*, ed. ʿAbd al-ʿAlīm Khān, 5 vols. (Hyderabad Deccan: Dā'irat al-Maʿārif al-ʿUthmāniyya, 1398/1987) 2:311 §523.

[25] Cf. Ibn Ḥajar, *al-Durar al-Kāmina* (4:339-340 §924); al-Subkī, *Ṭabaqāt al-Shāfiʿiyya al-Kubrā* (10:385); al-Suyūṭī, *Bughyat al-Wuʿāt* (2:282 §1983); al-Shīrāzī, *Shadd al-Izār* (p. 110-111); Ibn Taghrī Bardī, *al-Nujūm al-Zāhira fī Mulūk Miṣr wal-Qāhira*, ed. Muḥammad Shams al-Dīn, 16 vols. (Beirut: Dār al-Kutub al-ʿIlmiyya, 1413/1992) 9:213; al-Shawkānī, *al-Badr al-Ṭāliʿ bi-Maḥāsin man baʿd al-Qarn al-Sābiʿ*, 2 vols. (Cairo: Maṭbaʿat al-Saʿāda, 1348/1929) 2:299-300 §542; Nuwayhiḍ, *Muʿjam* (2:667-668); Osman Bakar, *Classification of Knowledge in Islam* (Kuala Lumpur: ISTAC and IIUM, 2006) pp. 229-248. Except for al-Adnahwī in his *Ṭabaqāt al-Mufassirīn* (p. 198-199 §§239, 241), the sources confuse him with another Quṭb al-Shīrāzī, Maḥmūd b. Muḥammad (d. 581/1185), author of a large *tafsīr*, *Fatḥ al-Mannān fī Tafsīr al-Qur'ān*. Ibn Kathīr (d. 774/1373), *Bidāya* (17:606) said the Qadi requested to be buried next to Quṭb al-Dīn, cf. al-Sūsī, *Muʿjam al-Uṣūliyyīn* (p. 306)—which confirms his post-710 obitus—but it is the other way around (Quṭb al-Dīn requests) in Ibn Rāfiʿ's (d. 774) version in *Tārīkh ʿUlamā' Baghdād*, ed. ʿAbbās ʿAzzāwī, 2nd ed. (Beirut: Dār al-ʿArabiyya lil-Masmūʿāt, 2000) p. 183. Quṭb al-Dīn had built a tomb for his teacher Naṣīr al-Dīn Ṭūsī in the Tabriz cemetery, so it would have been expected for him to wish to be buried there. Khvānṣārī, *Rawḍāt* (6:45) merely states the Quṭb and the Qadi's graves were adjacent. The latter "was destroyed by the Safavids some time before 984/1576" per the *Encyclopædia Iranica* unsourced.

• The precocious *Qāḍī al-quḍat* of Fāris, Majd al-Dīn Ismāʿīl b. Yaḥyā b. Ismāʿīl al-Tamīmī al-Shīrāzī al-Bālī (662-756/1264-1355) who, like the Qadi, hailed from a prestigious scholarly family and was appointed head judge in Shīrāz at 15, then Bayḍāwī replaced him for only a period of six months in 673/1275,[26] after which Majd al-Dīn was reappointed as head judge, a post he retained for the next 75 years to his death. He became famous for his piety, knowledge and courage in the face of Shiʿism when the latter threatened to become the state religion. Among his works: *al-Qawāʿid al-Rukniyya* in law, a commentary on Ibn al-Ḥājib in *usūl*, an epitome on *kalām* and prolific poetry.[27]

• Jamāl al-Dīn Abū Manṣūr al-Ḥasan b. Yūsuf b. ʿAlī b. al-Muṭahhar al-Asadī al-Ḥillī (648-726/1250-1325) was another philosopher-theologian-astronomer and Avicennan graduate of Naṣīr al-Dīn al-Ṭūsī under whom he studied (like Quṭb al-Dīn) in the Maragheh observatory[28] in Azerbaijan and whose *Miṣbāḥ al-Mutahajjid* he abridged in ten chapters, after which he wrote his own *al-Bāb al-Ḥādi ʿAshar* (The Eleventh Chapter) on Imami doctrine. Like al-Bayḍāwī and al-Bālī he hailed from a prestigious family of scholars in Hilla, Iraq—the center of Shiʿi Islam at the time—and like al-Shīrāzī also became known as *al-ʿAllāma*. In Baghdad he studied the Sunni and Muʿtazili doctrines, which he would later use in his debates and efforts to propagate Twelver Shiʿism. He was also a gifted writer who left many influential books: *Tabṣirat al-Mutaʿallimīn fī Aḥkām al-Dīn, Tahdhīb Ṭuruq al-Wuṣūl ilā ʿIlm al-Uṣūl, Qawāʿid al-Anām fī Maʿrifat al-Ḥalāl*

[26] Zarkūb Shīrāzī, *Shīrāznāmah* (p. 136) cf. Ibrahim, *Theological Questions* (p. 32)

[27] al-Subkī, *Ṭabaqāt al-Shāfiʿiyya al-Kubrā* (9:400-403) cf. Qarah Dāghī, introduction to al-Bayḍāwī's *al-Ghāyat al-Quswā* (1:69) and Calverley-Pollock, *Nature, Man and God* (1:xxx-xxxii).

[28] "The NASA of its day," cf. Osman Bakar, *Islamic Civilisation and the Modern World: Thematic Essays* (Brunei Darussalam: UBD Press, 2014) pp. 87, 104.

wal-Ḥarām, Kanz al-ʿIrfān fī Fiqh al-Qurʾān, Mukhtalaf al-Shīʿa fī Aḥkām al-Sharīʿa and others. He is credited for integrating the Sunni theory of *ijtihād* into Shiʿi jurisprudence.[29] He moved to Tabriz in 704/1305 and influenced the Ilkhan ruler Uljaytu (679-717/1280-1317) who reportedly converted to Shiʿism in 710/1310 "when al-Hilli issued a fatwa in his favor that abolished a troublesome divorce"[30] then back again to Sunnism before his death from poisoning.[31] Aḥmad b. Taymiyya predictably hated him with a passion[32] and wrote his four-volume *Minhāj al-Sunna al-Nabawiyya* in refutation of him.

Bayḍāwī's *Tafsīr* and his other works

As a revised and improved version of al-Zamakhsharī's landmark *Tafsīr al-Kashshaf, Anwār al-Tanzīl* contains the most concise analysis of the Quranic use of Arabic grammar and style to date and was viewed early on as a foremost demonstration of the Qurʾān's essential and structural inimitability (*iʿjāz maʿnawī wa-lughawī*) in Sunni literature: contemporaries were already citing

[29] "As to [*ijtihād*] not being a Shi'a term formerly, there is no doubt; if there is any uncertainty, it is about the date of its acceptance by the Shi'ah. It is not improbable that this term like several groups of people in the seventh century was converted to Shi'ism at the hands of the absolute Ayatullah, al-'Allamah al-Hilli" Ayatullah Murtadha Mutahhari, "The role of *ijtihād* in legislation," *al-Tawḥīd* (Tehran: Islamic Propagation Organization) vol. 4 no. 2. See http://www.al-islam.org/al-tawhid/vol4-n2/role-ijtihad-legislation-ayatullah-murtadha-mutahhari. All URLs are are of October 2014.

[30] Jalāl al-Dīn ʿAbd al-Raḥmān, *al-Qāḍī al-Bayḍāwī wa-Atharuhu fī Uṣūl al-Fiqh* (Cairo: Dār al-Kitāb al-Jāmiʿī, 1981) p. 183 cf. Calverley, *Nature* (1:xxxvi).

[31] Qarah Dāghī, introduction to al-Bayḍāwī's *Ghāya* (1:69-70), cf. Calverley-Pollock, *Nature, Man and God* (1:xxxv-xxxvi). Their claim that debates took place between al-Ḥillī and the Qadi, appears based on Khvānṣārī's assertion in his *Rawḍāt al-Jannāt* (5:130) of a cordial correspondence between them on the issue of *istiṣḥāb* ʿpresumption of continuity of a *status quo ante*ʾ.

[32] He was heard by al-Ṣafadī calling him "Ibn al-Munajjas" (son of the defiled) instead of Ibn al-Muṭahhar (son of the purified), cf. Ibn Taghrī Bardī, *al-Nujūm al-Zāhira* (9:192) and al-Ṣafadī's own chapter on Ibn Taymiyya in *al-Wāfī bil-Wafayāt*.

it as already mentioned, and it was being copied in Damascus no later than 758/1356.[33] Its success crowns Bayḍāwī's intent to pour into his magnum opus—not only as a doctor of the creed, legal theorist and jurisprudent of the first rank but also as a litterateur and historian in Arabic and Persian—the quintessence of his skills and scholarly experience.[34] This comes as no surprise since *tafsīr*, the most encompassing of the Islamic disciplines, demands the widest array of knowledge from its expert: "The Book of Allah cannot be explained unless all of the disciplines are mobilized for it."[35] Such a rule held especially true for the arts of language, as al-Bayḍāwī points out:

> Truly the greatest of the sciences in scope and highest in rank and radiance is the science of exegesis of the Qur'ān—the chief and head of all the religious sciences, the edifice of the bases of the sacred law and their foundation. *None* is suited to practice it or undertake to speak about it but he who excels in the religious sciences in their totality—roots and branches! —and has proved superior in the crafts of the Arabic language and the literary arts in all their varieties.[36]

Thus al-Bayḍāwī aimed to set the standard in the genre just as

[33] See p. 4, notes 156 and 163 and Quiring-Zoche, "An early manuscript" (p. 38).
[34] See Yūsuf Aḥmad 'Alī, *al-Bayḍāwī wa-Manhajuh*; Muḥammad al-Zuḥaylī, *al-Qāḍī al-Bayḍāwī* 2nd ed. (Damascus: Dār al-Qalam, 1420/1999) pp. 121-145; Muḥammad Ḥusayn al-Dhahabī, *al-Tafsīr wal-Mufassirūn*, 7th ed., 3 vols. (Cairo: Maktabat Wahba, 2000) 1:211-216; al-Suyūṭī, *Nawāhid al-Abkār wa-Shawārid al-Afkār*, ed. Aḥmad Ḥājj Muḥammad 'Uthmān, unpublished Ph.D. dissertation, 3 vols. (Mecca: Jāmi'at Umm al-Qurā, 1423-24/2002-2003) 1:13; Ḥājjī Khalīfa, *Kashf al-Ẓunūn 'an Asāmī al-Kutub wal-Funūn*, ed. Muḥammad Sharaf al-Dīn Yāltaqāyā and Rif'at Bīlkah al-Kilīsī. 2 vols. (Istanbul : Maṭābi' Wikālat al-Ma'ārif al-Jalīla, 1941-1943, rept. Beirut: Dār Iḥyā' al-Turāth al-'Arabī, n.d.) 1:186-194. Most tend to consider the *Anwār* his last work.
[35] Ibn 'Aṭiyya (d. 546/1151), *al-Muḥarrar al-Wajīz fī Tafsīr al-Kitāb al-'Azīz*, ed. 'Abd al-Salām Muḥammad, 6 vols. (Beirut: Dār al-Kutub al-'Ilmiyya, 1422/2001), preamble.
[36] al-Bayḍāwī, *Anwār al-Tanzīl wa-Asrār al-Ta'wīl al-Musammā Tafsīr al-Bayḍāwī*, ed. Muḥammad Ṣubḥī b. Ḥasan Ḥallāq and Maḥmūd Aḥmad al-Aṭrash (Damascus: Dār al-Rashīd; Beirut: Mu'assasat al-Īmān, 1421/2000) 1:5 (Preamble).

he had aimed to in other fields with his works in legal theory (*uṣūl al-fiqh*), grammar (*naḥw*), credal doctrine (*kalām*), sacred law (*fiqh*), history and poetry, all of them well-recopied works:

• his survey of *uṣūl al-fiqh* (legal theory), *Minhāj al-Wuṣūl ilā ʿIlm al-Uṣūl*, which crowns his three previous commentaries in that discipline: on al-Rāzī's *Maḥṣūl* and *Muntakhab* and Ibn al-Ḥājib al-Mālikī's (570-646/1175-1248) *Mukhtaṣar al-Muntahā*;

• his works of *naḥw* (grammar) and *iʿrāb* (parsing): a commentary on Ibn al-Ḥājib's *Kāfiya fīl-Naḥw* and an abridgment of the latter entitled *Lubb al-Albāb fī ʿIlm al-Iʿrāb*;

• his works of *kalām* (dialectic theology): *Maṭāliʿ al-Anẓār*; its commentary *Tawāliʿ al-Anwār*; *Miṣbāḥ al-Arwāḥ*; *al-Īḍāḥ*; *Sharḥ al-Muntakhab*, an epitome of a work by al-Rāzī; and *Muntahā al-Munā Sharḥ Asmāʾ Allāh al-Ḥusnā*, published in 2006.

• his two large reference-works of Shāfiʿī *fiqh* (law), *al-Ghāyat al-Quṣwā fī Dirāyat al-Fatwā* (The Ultimate in Knowledge of Legal Responses)[37] and his four-volume commentary on Abū Isḥāq al-Shīrāzī's (393-476/1003-1083) *al-Tanbīh*;

• *Tuḥfat al-Abrār*, his three-volume hadith commentary on al-Baghawī's *Maṣābīḥ al-Sunna*.

• his concise "history of the world" entitled *Niẓām al-Tawārīkh* in Persian, described as "a history textbook which he wrote impartially, in a moderate literary format and the same style he had used for law and jurisprudence."[38] It went on to receive Arabic and Turkish translations—with an abundance of manuscripts in

[37] And not "The Most Extreme Transgression" [!!] as Peter G. Riddell translated it in his article "al-Baydawi" in *The Qurʾān: an Encyclopedia*, ed. Oliver Leaman (London and New York: Routledge, 2006) p. 116.

[38] ʿAbbās al-ʿAzzāwī, *al-Taʿrīf bil-Muʾarrikhīn fī ʿAhd al-Maghūl wal-Turkmān* (Baghdad: Sharikat al-Tijāra wal-Ṭibāʿat al-Maḥdūda, 1376/1957) p. 116.

the libraries of Europe and Turkey—as well as a commentary in Hindustani published in Hyderabad in 1930. An oft-published history of China in Persian is also attributed to him.[39]

Al-Bayḍāwī also authored a work on sufism, *Tahdhīb al-Akhlāq*, heretofore unpublished; *Mawḍūʿāt al-ʿUlūm* on the classification of the sciences; a brief on *hay'a* ⟨astronomy⟩; and, in poetry, *Tafrīj al-Shidda*, an exquisite *tasbīʿ* ⟨sevening⟩ or addition of five hemistichs to each verse of Būṣīrī's (608-696/1211-1297) masterpiece *al-Burda* anaphorically repeating *Allāh*.[40] Tāj al-Dīn al-Subkī's teacher, the Shāfiʿī biographer and hadith master of the Two Sanctuaries Ibn al-Maṭarī (ʿAfīf al-Dīn Abū al-Siyāda/Abū Jaʿfar ʿAbd Allāh b. Muḥammad b. Aḥmad al-Anṣārī al-ʿUbādī 698-765/1299-1364) expressed his admiration for these paradigmatic writings as "works that travelled the lands east and west producing imams" only a brief time after their author's death.[41]

[39] See [Ṣādiq] Rizāzādah Shafaq (d.1892), *Tārīkh al-Adab al-Fārisī*, trans. Muḥammad Mūsā Hindāwī (Cairo: Dār al-Fikr al-ʿArabī, 1948) p. 198; Zuḥaylī, *al-Qāḍī al-Bayḍāwī* (pp. 32 and 165-166); Lutpi Ibrahim, *Theological Questions* (pp. 42-43) and "Bayḍāwī's Life and Works," *Islamic Studies* 18 no. 4 (Winter 1979) 311-321. Edward G. Browne (1862-1926) was unaware of the success of the *Niẓām*; in his *Literary History of Persia*, 4 vols. (London: Unwin, 1908-1928) 3:63, 100-101 he dismissed it as a "dull and jejune little book [in which Bayḍāwī] practically ignores all history except that which is connected with Islám and the Muhammadan peoples, the ancient Kings of Persia, and the Hebrew Prophets and Patriarchs" and shows no knowledge of his history of China. The latter is a spurious attribution acc. to Antoine-Isaac Silvestre de Sacy, "Extrait du Commentaire de BÉÏDHAWI sur l'Alcoran" in his *Anthologie Grammaticale Arabe* (Paris: Imprimerie Royale, 1829) p. 37 n. 1 and ʿAlī, *al-Bayḍāwī wa-Manhajuh* (p. 29). See also David S. Margoliouth, *Chrestomathia Baidawiana: The Commentary of El-Baiḍāwī on Sura III* (London: Luzac & Co., 1894) p. xv.

[40] ʿAlī, *al-Bayḍāwī wa-Manhajuh* (pp. 24-29); al-Zuḥaylī, *al-Qāḍī al-Bayḍāwī* (p. 176); and see note 13 above. On the *Mawḍūʿāt* see ʿAbbās Sulaymān, *Taṣnīf al-ʿUlūm bayna al-Ṭūsī wal-Bayḍāwī*. Būṣīrī's obitus further buttresses a post-685 obitus for Bayḍāwī.

[41] Ibn al-Maṭarī al-ʿUbādī, *Dhayl Ṭabaqāt al-Fuqahā' al-Shāfiʿiyyīn*, third vol. of Ibn Kathīr's *Ṭabaqāt al-Fuqahā' al-Shāfiʿiyyīn* (3:97). Due to the incomplete identification of that author as only العبادي on the part of the two editors, library catalogues have invariably confused him with an earlier one who also authored a *Ṭabaqāt al-Shāfiʿiyya*,

Raison d'être of the present work

The aim of *tafsīr* works was nothing less than to renew and boost the relationship of the community of Islam with its most fundamental text. That was certainly al-Bayḍāwī's intent, and it appears to have received the greatest share of acceptance in the *Umma* as can be inferred from the more than 1,400 documented extant manuscripts of *Anwār al-Tanzīl* and the more than 300 supercommentaries of it in the libraries of the world (with countless thousands of manuscripts still waiting to be catalogued); no other *tafsīr* has received as much attention.[42] It is also the *tafsīr* that has received the most editions and reprints since the 1950s—albeit none meeting modern critical standards.[43]

The success of Bayḍāwī's intention can also be gleaned from the glowing testimonies of later scholars and the fact that the

Abū ʿĀṣim Muḥammad b. Aḥmad al-ʿAbbādī, who predates Ibn Kathīr and Bayḍāwī.

[42] See *al-Fahras al-Shāmil lil-Turāth al-ʿArabī al-Islāmī al-Makhṭūṭ: ʿUlūm al-Qur'ān, Makhṭūṭāt al-Tafsīr wa-ʿUlūmih*, 2 vols. (Amman: al-Majmaʿ al-Malakī li-Buḥūth al-Ḥaḍārat al-Islāmiyya, 1989) 1:280-344. Nuwayhiḍ, *Muʿjam* (2:855-860) documents 135 authors of marginalia on the *Anwār*. The Syrian national library alone (Maktabat al-Asad) boasts no less than 81 partial or complete manuscripts and rare editions of the *Anwār* : *Fahras al-Makhṭūṭāt al-ʿArabiyya al-Maḥfūẓa fī Maktabat al-Asad al-Waṭaniyya*, 5 vols. (Damascus: Manshūrāt Maktabat al-Asad, 1996) 4:46-93; and 147 partial or full marginalia (4:123-124, 301, 307-403, 473-490, 519-525, 691-693).

[43] Cf. *al-Qur'ān al-Karīm wa-bi-Hāmishihi al-Tafsīr al-Musammā Anwār al-Tanzīl* etc., 2 vols. (Cairo : Maṭbaʿat Muṣṭafā al-Bābī al-Ḥalabī, 1951, 1955); *Anwār al-Tanzīl wa-Asrār al-Ta'wīl* (Beirut: Dār al-Jīl, n.d.); ditto, 2 vols. (Beirut: Mu'assasat Shaʿbān, n.d.); ditto, 2 vols. (Beirut: Dār Ṣādir, 2001), based on the earliest Istanbul edition of 1257/1841; *Tafsīr al-Bayḍāwī al-Musammā Anwār al-Tanzīl* etc., 5 vols., ed. Ḥamza al-Naṣartī et al. (Cairo: Maktabat al-Ahrām and Maktabat al-Jumhūriyya, 1418/1997); ditto, 2 vols. (Beirut: Dār al-Kutub al-ʿIlmiyya, 1988, 1999, 2006, 2008 and 2011); ditto, with al-Kāzarūnī's *Ḥāshiya*, ed. ʿAbd al-Qādir ʿIrfān al-ʿAshshā Ḥassūna, 5 vols. (Beirut: Dār al-Fikr, 1996, 2005, 2009), hereafter AQ; *Anwār al-Tanzīl* etc., 2 vols. (Cairo: al-Hay'at al-ʿĀmma li-Quṣūr al-Thaqāfa, 2011); *Anwār al-Tanzīl wa-Asrār al-Ta'wīl al-Maʿrūf bi-Tafsīr al-Bayḍāwī*, ed. Muḥammad ʿAbd al-Raḥmān al-Marʿashlī (Beirut: Dār Iḥyā' al-Turāth al-ʿArabī and Mu'assasat al-Tārīkh al-ʿArabī, 1418/1998), hereafter MM; and the 2000 ed. already mentioned (see note 36), hereafter H.

Anwār became and remained for seven centuries the most studied of all *Tafsīrs*:

> The scholars have placed it, ever since it first emerged and became famous in the second half of the seventh [Hijri] century, on a pedestal of reliance and acceptance and they devoted themselves to it as the principal reference-work in *tafsīr*... and the main requirement of teaching from the deep reaches of India to the farthermost Maghreb.[44]

Yet there has been, to date, no full-length work in English on this most taught, most copied, and most commented-upon exegesis of the Qur'ān in Islam and the first *tafsīr* to be published in Europe (Leipzig, 1846). Brimming as it does with allusive subtexts and run-on sentences, the style of the *Anwār* is so compact as to make its language seem arcane. Its technicality—born of the author's interlocked references to the "mediate disciplines" (*'ulūm al-āla*: grammar, style, logic, rhetoric, legal principles, history and hadith science) and the five "end disciplines" (*'ulūm al-maqāṣid*, namely *'aqīda*, *tafsīr*, hadith, *fiqh* and *sīra*)—is daunting and makes rendering into another language an arduous labor. Compounding the problem is the fact that modern Arabic editions are chock-full of textual corruptions.[45] Yet, more than a trusted edition and inspired translation, readers need a vademecum that demonstrates the refined methodology of the au-

[44] Muḥammad al-Fāḍil b. al-Ṭāhir b. 'Āshūr, *al-Tafsīr wa-Rijāluh*, Silsilat al-Buḥūth al-Islāmiyya no. 2, year 28 (Cairo: Majma' al-Buḥūth al-Islāmiyya fil-Azhar, 1970; rept. 1417/ 1997) pp. 112, 118.

[45] See notes 287, 292, 348, 350, 412, 462, 512, 514, 598, 604, 615, 638, 663, 800, 864-865, 938, 946, 960-961, 964, 995, 1025, 1028, 1037, 1086, 1090, 1094, 1154, 1244, 1256, 1259, 1280, 1293, 1300, 1302, 1309, 1365, 1369 for seemingly endless examples of corruption in the modern editions in the first *Ḥizb* alone, particularly the three Arab editions of 1996, 1998 and 2000 (AQ, MM and H respectively). The above do not include equally frequent misvowelizations in the same editions. Older editions often had ulema for editors and therefore tended to be free of such errors.

thor and shows what made his work the mainstream analytical commentary (*al-tafsīr al-taḥlīlī*) par excellence. The present work aims to demonstrate those aspects of al-Bayḍāwī's work through a critical edition, translation and study of the first *ḥizb* of *Anwār al-Tanzīl*—the first tenth of the entire book in size—toward the re-discovery of a proven success story in the defense and illustration of the Book of Allah.

The tradition of transmission (*athar*), analysis (*taḥlīl*) and polysemy (*al-wujūh wal-naẓā'ir*) in Quranic exegesis

Works of "transmissive exegesis" or *tafsīr bil-athar*—a genre made famous by Ibn Jarīr al-Ṭabarī (224-310/839-ca.922) with his celebrated *Jāmiʿ al-Bayān ʿan Taʾwīl Āy al-Qurʾān* (Encyclopedia of Elucidations for Interpreting the Verses of the Qur'ān)—hinged on the compilation of exegetical hadiths and reports.[46] The method of *Anwār al-Tanzīl*, however, hinges on linguistic and stylistic analysis and critique. Historians of *tafsīr* put it in the ineptly-named category of "speculative exegesis" (*tafsīr bil-ra'y*) when it would be more correct and precise to label it a linguistic-analytical exegesis or *tafsīr lughawī taḥlīlī*.[47]

Jāmiʿ al-Bayān itself, the greatest transmissive *tafsīr*, was an

[46] The famous transmissive *tafsīrs* are, in chronological order: Ṭabarī's *Jāmiʿ al-Bayān*; Ibn Abī Ḥātim's *Tafsīr*; Māwardī's *al-Nukat wal-ʿUyūn*; Baghawī's *Maʿālim al-Tanzīl*; Ibn ʿAṭiyya's *al-Muḥarrar al-Wajīz*; al-Khāzin's *Lubāb al-Ta'wīl*; Ibn Kathīr's *Tafsīr*; al-Thaʿālibī's *al-Jawāhir al-Ḥisān* and Suyūṭī's *al-Durr al-Manthūr*. For a chronological review of the lost and extant works most representative of that genre see the introduction to Ḥikmat Bashīr Yāsīn, *al-Tafsīr al-Ṣaḥīḥ: Mawsūʿat al-Ṣaḥīḥ al-Masbūr min al-Tafsīr bil-Ma'thūr*, 4 vols. (Medina: Dār al-Ma'āthir, 1420/ 1999) 1:17-25.

[47] The mostly-linguistic *tafsīrs* are: Zamakhsharī's *Kashshāf*; Rāzī's *Mafātīḥ al-Ghayb*; Bayḍāwī's *Anwār al-Tanzīl*; Nasafī's *Madārik al-Tanzīl*; Abū Ḥayyān's *al-Baḥr al-Muḥīṭ*; al-Samīn al-Ḥalabī's *al-Durr al-Maṣūn*; Niẓām al-Dīn Naysābūrī's *Gharā'ib al-Qur'ān*; *Tafsīr al-Jalālayn*; Shirbīnī's *al-Sirāj al-Munīr*; Abū al-Suʿūd's *Irshād al-ʿAql al-Salīm*; and Ālūsī's *Rūḥ al-Maʿānī* cf. Muḥammad Ḥusayn al-Dhahabī, *ʿIlm al-Tafsīr* (Cairo: Dār al-Maʿārif, [1977]) p. 66-67; also: Musāʿid al-Ṭayyār, *al-Tafsīr al-Lughawī*.

analytical commentary as well, since it devotes many pages to the discussion of language and its intricacies among other issues[48]—as do also Ibn al-Jawzī in *Zād al-Masīr*, Ibn Kathīr in his *Tafsīr* and al-Shinqīṭī in *Aḍwā' al-Bayān fī Īḍāḥ al-Qur'ān bil-Qur'ān*.[49] Even more so does al-Bayḍāwī's *tafsīr* constantly exert "proof-based preference of one of several scenarios for interpreting any given term" (*tarjīḥ aḥad iḥtimālāt al-lafẓ bil-dalīl*).[50]

Such choices constitute *ijtihād*—expert scholarly exertion[51]—informed by a prestigious Iraqi-Khurasanian lexicological tradition. Quranic polysemy was studied within the sub-genre of *al-wujūh wal-naẓā'ir*, where *wujūh* or "aspects" refers to variant meanings while *naẓā'ir* or "analogues" are the multiple instances of homonyms that convey them.[52] After initial forays by the Successors 'Ikrima Mawlā Ibn 'Abbās (d. 105/723) and the Syrian Khārijī post-Successor 'Alī b. Abī Ṭalḥa (d. 143/760) the first full-length work on the subject, *al-Wujūh wal-Naẓā'ir fil-Qur'ān*, was penned by the exegete Muqātil b. Sulaymān al-Balkhī (d. 150/767)—the author of the first extant comprehensive *tafsīr*.[53]

[48] E.g., al-Ṭabarī's long introduction and his complex analysis of the *alif lām* of *al-ḥamdu* in the second verse of the Fātiḥa in which he discusses grammar and cites poetry in support of his arguments: *Tafsīr al-Ṭabarī: Jāmi' al-Bayān 'an Ta'wīl Āy al-Qur'ān*, ed. 'Abd Allāh b. 'Abd al-Muḥsin al-Turkī et al., 26 vols. (Cairo: Dār Hajar, 1422/2001) 1:138-141. On this *tafsīr* as a work of linguistic analysis of the Qur'ān see Musā'id al-Ṭayyār, *al-Tafsīr al-Lughawī lil-Qur'ān* (Dammam: Dār Ibn al-Jawzī, 1422/2001) pp. 185-205 and 'Itr, *'Ulūm al-Qur'ān* (pp.77-81).

[49] The only pure complete *tafsīr bil-ma'thūr* being al-Suyūṭī's *al-Durr al-Manthūr*, cf. Maḥmūd al-Naqrāshī al-Sayyid 'Alī, *Manāhij al-Mufassirīn min al-'Aṣr al-Awwal ilā al-'Aṣr al-Ḥadīth* (al-Quṣaym [Saudi Arabia]: Maktabat al-Nahḍa, 1986) pp. 88-200.

[50] Abd al-Salām Muḥammad, introduction to his edition of Ibn 'Aṭiyya's *al-Muḥarrar al-Wajīz* (1:5).

[51] See section on "*ijtihād* and other qualifications" further down.

[52] The similarly-termed *al-ashbāh wal-naẓā'ir* also flourished in law and grammar as shown by the works of Ibn Nujaym, Ibn al-Wakīl and al-Suyūṭī with that title.

[53] Muqātil b. Sulaymān, *al-Wujūh wal-Naẓā'ir*, ed. Ḥātim Ṣāliḥ al-Ḍāmin (Dubai:

Many built on his pioneering work, notably Yaḥyā b. Sallām al-Taymī al-Baṣrī (124-200/743-815)[54] and the Khārijī linguist and exegete Abū ʿUbayda Maʿmar b. al-Muthannā al-Taymī (110-210 /728-825)—who adduced poetry for the first time—with a *tafsīr* entitled *Majāz al-Qur'ān*, among over two dozen other studies in that genre.[55] Examples of *wujūh* and *naẓā'ir* they gave include *hudā* (17 different meanings), *kufr* (4), *shirk* (3), *maraḍ* (4), *sū'* (11), *fasād* (6), *mashy* (4), *libās* (4), *raḥma* (14), *fitna* (14), *dhikr* (19), *umma* (9), *ṣalāt* (6), *khayr* (8), *rūḥ* (9), *qaḍā'* (15), *duʿā'* (6), etc. These works formed the basis of al-Rāghib al-Aṣfahānī's (d. 502/1108) lexicon *Mufradāt Alfāẓ al-Qur'ān* and Zamakhsharī's *tafsīr* and lexicons such as *Asrār al-Balāgha*, *al-Mustaqṣā min Amthāl al-ʿArab*, *al-Fā'iq fī Gharīb al-Ḥadīth*, etc., both of which authors are among al-Bayḍāwī's main sources.

Passive anonymizers *qīla/ruwiya/quri'a* to cite weaker views

When presenting a variety of interpretations of the same term or passage (ranging from imperceptible nuance to diametrical opposites) al-Bayḍāwī, in keeping with al-Zamakhsharī's text and scholarly tradition, usually begins with what he considers the main view then lists other views. He almost always presents the first view as fact which he himself asserts while he introduces subsequent ones with *wa-qīla* ʿit is also said'. The rhetorical tenor in the use of such a passive anonymizer is that the gloss,

Markaz Jumʿat al-Mājid lil-Thaqāfa wal-Turāth, 1427/2006).

54 See Yaḥyā b. Sallām, *al-Taṣārīf: Tafsīr al-Qur'ān mimmā Ishtabahat Asmā'uhu wa-Taṣarrafat Maʿānīh*, ed. Hind Shalabī (Amman: Mu'assasat Āl al-Bayt, 2007).

55 Also published were al-Ḥīrī's *Wujūh al-Qur'ān*; al-Dāmighānī's *al-Wujūh wal-Naẓā'ir*; Ibn al-Jawzī's *Nuzhat al-Aʿyun al-Nawāẓir fī ʿIlm al-Wujūh wal-Naẓā'ir*; Ibn ʿImād al-Balbīsī's *Kashf al-Sarā'ir fī Maʿnā al-Wujūh wal-Ashbāh wal-Naẓā'ir*; Suyūṭī's *Itqān* (Type 39); and his monograph *Muʿtarak al-Aqrān fī Mushtarak al-Qur'ān*. See Muḥammad Yūsuf al-Sharbajī, "*ʿIlm al-wujūh wal-naẓā'ir fil-Qur'ān al-karīm*," *Majallat Jāmiʿat Dimashq*, vol. 19 no. 2 (2003) pp. 455-491.

report or reading it introduces is weaker than what precedes:

> Whatever he cites of variant glosses (*wujūh al-tafsīr*) in second, third, or fourth place by introducing it with the term *qīla* ‹it was said›: this is weak either in the sense of *marjūḥ* ‹prevailed over› or in that of *mardūd* ‹rejected›.[56]

For example, in his explanation of the Name *Allāh* in al-Fātiḥa (1:1), the Qadi first states positively that

> *ilāh* ‹deity›, originally, is for every object of worship; then overwhelming usage confined it to the One Who is rightfully worshipped. It is derived from *alaha* ‹he worshipped›.

He then proceeds to mention five other views, each of which he introduces with *wa-qīla* since he deems them all less probable than the first. Similarly he defines the Sabians (al-Baqara 2:62) as

> a nation between Christians and Jews. It is also said that the origin of their religion is the religion of Nūḥ—upon him peace. It is also said they are angelolaters. It is also said they are astrolaters.[57]

The connection of *aḥruf* ‹dialects/idioms› with polysemy

Since the Qur'ān describes the "words of Allah" as infinite (al-Kahf 18:109, Luqmān 31:27) and commands reflection, thought, analysis, contemplation, study, deliberation, understanding etc. through hearts, hearing, sights and minds (e.g., Āl 'Imrān 3:79, Yūsuf 12:2, al-Ḥijr 15:75, al-Naḥl 16:44, Saba' 34:44), it is in the context of the inexhaustible quality of its meanings that scholars interpreted the mass-transmitted (*mutawātir*) but ambiguous

[56] Ḥājjī Khalīfa, *Kashf al-Ẓunūn* (1:187a); but al-Bayḍāwī does follow J's lead in this: for example see note 1341.

[57] Hadith scholars routinely use passive anonymizers when introducing a narration not with the active identifier *rawā Fulān* ‹X narrates› but with *ruwya*, *yurwā* (it is narrated›. This *tamrīḍ* ‹verbal form of dubiosity› insinuates that, in their eyes, the report is weak. This is not an absolute rule: see notes 360, 648 and Shihrī, class 9 after 21'.

(*mutashābih*) Prophetic hadith of the "seven *aḥruf*":

> Jibrīl made me read according to one *ḥarf* so I asked him again; and I kept asking him for more and he went on giving me more, until he ended up at seven *aḥruf*.[58]

Seven explanations are transmitted on the seven *aḥrūf*:

- they are "seven from among the Arabic dialects/idioms"—the most established position;[59]
- or "seven" denotes open-ended multitude to allow any number of meanings, spellings, or pronunciations for the same words or passages, "because seven indicates multitude among units just as 70 does among two-digit numbers and 700 among three-digit numbers, without a specific number being intended;"[60]
- or—in Abū al-Faḍl al-Rāzī's *istiqrā'* (comprehensive induction) —the combination of reading variants with grammatical, morphological, inflectional, and/or syntactical variants, all of which can be subsumed under seven broad types of differences.[61]

[58] Narrated from Ibn 'Abbās by al-Bukhārī and Muslim.

[59] Ibn Manẓūr, *Lisān al-'Arab* (*s.v. ḥarf*).

[60] al-Suyūṭī, *al-Itqān fī 'Ulūm al-Qur'ān* (Type 16).

[61] These types are (i) noun number and gender differences, e.g. *hum li-amānātihim/amānatihim* in al-Mu'minūn (23:8); (ii) tense differences, e.g. *qāla/qul rabbī ya'lamu* in al-Anbiyā' (21:4) and *Rabbanā bā'id/Rabbunā bā'ada* in Saba' (34:19); (iii) inflectional differences, e.g. *wa-lā tas'al/tus'alu* and *wa-lā yuḍārru/yuḍārra* in al-Baqara (2:119 and 2:282) and *dhūl-'arshi al-majīdū/al-majīdī* in al-Burūj (85:15); (iv) word addition or omission, e.g. *sāri'ū/wa-sāri'ū* in Āl 'Imrān (3:133) and *wal-nahāri idhā tajallā wa-mā khalaqa al-dhakara wal-unthā/wal-nahāri idhā tajallā wal-dhakari wal-unthā* in al-Layl (92:3); (v) word order, e.g. *wa-qatalū wa-qutilū/wa-qutilū wa-qatalū* in Āl 'Imrān (Q 3:195) and *wa-jā'at sakratu al-mawti bil-ḥaqq/wa-jā'at sakratu al-ḥaqqi bil-mawt* in Qāf (50:19); (vi) letter change, e.g. *wa-nẓur ilā al-'iẓāmi kayfa nunshizuhā/nunshiruhā* in al-Baqara (2:259), *tablū/tatlū* in Yūnus (10:30) and *wa-ṭalḥin manḍūd/wa-ṭāl'in manḍūd* in al-Wāqi'a (56:29); and (vii) dialectical differences, e.g. different tribal pronunciations entailing *fatḥ* vs. *imāla* such as *hal atāka ḥadīthu Mūsā/hal atéka ḥadīthu Mūsé* in al-Nāzi'āt (79:15); *idghām* vs. *iẓhār* e.g. *la-qad jā'akum/la-qaj-jā'akum* in al-Tawba (9:127) and *qad sami'a/qas-sami'a* in al-

• or they are ambiguous and unfathomable (*mutashābihāt*), "because the term *ḥarf* lexically can denote an alphabetical letter, or a word, or a meaning, or an orientation;"[62]

• or they represent various types, modalities or statuses of legal and other rulings;[63]

• or the sciences of the articles of the creed;[64]

• or the canonical and non-canonical readings—an anachronism according to Abū al-Qāsim al-Hudhalī (403-465/1012-1074).[65]

Another remarkable and oft-quoted Prophetic hadith mentions, in addition to the seven dialects of the Qur'ān on the whole, "the outward and inward aspects (*ẓahr wa-baṭn*) of each and every verse," the "boundary" (*ḥadd*) of every *ḥarf*," and the "way up" and "vantage-point" of every boundary:

> ʿAbd Allāh b. Masʿūd said that the Messenger of Allah—upon him blessings and peace—said: "The Qur'ān was sent down according to seven wordings; every verse in

Mujādila (58:1); *tas-hīl* vs. *taḥqīq*, e.g. *a'andhartahum/āndhartahum/āandhartahum* in al-Baqara 2:6 and *a'innā/ayinnā/āyinnā la-mardūdūna* in al-Nāziʿāt (79:10); or *tafkhīm* vs. *tarqīq*, e.g. the alif in *salāt* pronounced two ways. Abū al-Faḍl ʿAbd al-Raḥmān b. Aḥmad al-Rāzī, *Maʿānī al-Aḥruf al-Sabʿa*, ed. Ḥasan Ḍiyā' al-Dīn ʿItr (Beirut: Dār al-Nawādir, 1433/2012) and Muḥammad ʿAbd al-ʿAẓīm al-Zarqānī, *Manāhil al-ʿIrfān fī ʿUlūm al-Qur'ān*, ed. Fawwāz Aḥmad Zamarlī, 2 vols. (Beirut: Dār al-Kitāb al-ʿArabī, 1415/1995) 1:132-134.

62 al-Suyūṭī, *Itqān* (Type 16).

63 Such as (i) abrogating vs. abrogated (*al-nāsikh wal-mansūkh*); (ii) general vs. particular (*al-khāṣṣ wal-ʿāmm*); (iii) absolute vs. restricted (*al-muṭlaq wal-muqayyad*); (iv) textual vs. interpretive (*al-naṣṣ wal-mu'awwal*); (v) indeterminate and explicited (*al-mujmal wal-mufassar*); (vi) exception (*istithna'*); and (vii) types of exception. See al-Zarkashī, *al-Burhān fī ʿUlūm al-Qur'ān* (type 11) and Ḥasan ʿItr, *al-Aḥruf al-Sabʿa wa-Manzilat al-Qirā'āt minhā* (Beirut: Dār al-Bashā'ir al-Islāmiyya, 1409/1988) p. 122.

64 al-Suyūṭī, *Itqān* (Type 16) and al-Zarkashī, *Burhān* (type 11).

65 In his *Kāmil fil-Qirā'āt al-ʿAshr wal-Arbaʿa al-Zā'ida ʿalayhā*, ed. Jamāl al-Shāyib ([Cairo?]: Mu'assasat Samā lil-Tawzīʿ wal-Nashra, 1428/2007) p. 91.

each of them has a surface and an inward.[66] [Another wording has:] every wording has a surface and an inward, each wording has a boundary and each boundary has a way up/vantage-point [to more meanings].[67]

عَنْ عَبْدِ الله بْنِ مَسْعُودٍ رضي الله عنه، قَالَ: قَالَ رَسُولُ الله ﷺ: أُنْزِلَ الْقُرْآنُ عَلَى سَبْعَةِ أَحْرُفٍ، لِكُلِّ آيَةٍ مِنْهَا ظَهْرٌ وَبَطْنٌ. رواه ابن حبان في صحيحه. وجاء بلفظ: أُنْزِلَ الْقُرْآنُ عَلَى سَبْعَةِ أَحْرُفٍ، لِكُلِّ حَرْفٍ مِنْهَا ظَهْرٌ وَبَطْنٌ، وَلِكُلِّ حَرْفٍ حَدٌّ، وَلِكُلِّ حَدٍّ مُطَّلَعٌ. ويجوز: مَطْلَعٌ (مَعًا). رواه الفريابي والطبري والبغوي في تفاسيرهم والطبراني في الكبير والطحاوي في مشكل الآثار ورواه البزار وأبو يعلى في المسند.

In another hadith the Prophet—upon him blessings and peace—said: "Qur'ān is tractable and bears many aspects (*al-Qur'ān dhalūlun dhū wujūh*); therefore construe it according to its most beautiful aspects."[68] Al-Māwardī (364-450/974-1058) explained "tractable" here to mean both easy to memorize and "the repository of its meanings, so that those who strive to understand not fall short." He explains the "many aspects" as polysemy in line with the Qur'ān's miraculous nature, and also in reference to the multiple aspects of Quranic discourse. The "beautiful aspects" are either the extraction of the best interpretive meanings or the encouragement to practice its most beautiful aspects, for example strictness versus dispensations, forgiveness versus revenge.[69]

66 Ibn Ḥibbān, *Ṣaḥīḥ Ibn Ḥibbān bi-Tartīb Ibn Balbān*, ed Shu'ayb al-Arnā'ūṭ, 2nd ed., 18 vols. (Beirut: Mu'assasat al-Risāla, 1414/1993) 1:276 §75.

67 Al-Ṭabarī, *Tafsīr* (1:22) and others.

68 Narrated by al-Dāraquṭnī, *Sunan* (*Kitāb al-Nawādir*).

69 al-Māwardī, *al-Nukat wal-'Uyūn: Tafsīr al-Māwardī*, ed. Sayyid b. 'Abd al-Maqṣūd

Another famous typology of the interpretive facets of Qur'ān was given by Ibn 'Abbās (3BH-68/620-688):

> *Tafsīr* has four different perspectives (*awjuh*): one is familiar to Arabs because its is their own language, one is a type no one has any excuse not to know, one is a perspective known only to the people of learning and one is known only to Allah.[70]

The third of Ibn 'Abbas's four categories—the type of *tafsīr* "known only to the people of learning"—was most probably the type taught by the Prophet (upon him blessings and peace) more than any other type. As if to comment on that type for the benefit of scholars and students of knowledge specifically, the Companion Abū al-Dardā'—one of the main teachers of Qur'ān in Damascus in his time—said his students: "You will never understand deeply until you see that the Qur'ān has many different aspects/perspectives/meanings (*wujūhan kathīra*)."[71]

Semantic and stylistic invariables (*kulliyyāt al-Qur'ān*)

In contradistinction to the polysemy/*wujūh* genre all of the above exegetes also contributed to what became known as the invariables/*kulliyyāt* genre. The most basic units of meaning in the Qur'ān are words.[72] Such words are either monosemic (conveying a single meaning) or polysemic (conveying two or more meanings). Ibn 'Abbās and his students divided monosemes into two types:

b.'Abd al-Raḥīm, 6 vols. (Beirut: Dār al-Kutub al-'Ilmiyya, 1992), introduction.

70 Narrated by al-Ṭabarī, *Tafsīr* (1:70).

71 Narrated by Abū Dāwūd in *Kitāb al-Zuhd Riwāyat Ibn al-A'rābī 'anh*, ed. Abū Tamīm Yāsir b. Ibrāhīm and Abū Bilāl Ghunaym b. 'Abbās (Cairo: Dār al-Mishkāt lil-Nashr wal-Tawzī', 1414/1993) p. 212 §242.

72 The Disjointed Letters (*al-ḥurūf al-muqaṭṭa'a*) are also carriers of meaning but those meanings are not determined and therefore remain ambiguities (*mutashābihāt*).

(i) "semantic invariables that know no exception" (*kulliyyāt maʿnawiyya muṭṭarida*), such as *ifk*, a Quraysh idiom which invariably means *kadhib* or "lying;"[73] or *al-sāʿa*, which invariably means the Day of Resurrection;[74] or *sulṭān*, which invariably means "authoritative proof" (*ḥujja*)[75] among many others;[76] and

(ii) "semantic invariables with exceptions" (*kulliyyāt maʿnawiyya aghlabiyya/ ghayr muṭṭarida*) such as the following:

• *bukm* (lit. mute) always means "incapable of uttering the declaration of faith" except in two places where it means literally mute and incapable of speaking:[77]

> *and We shall assemble them on the Day of Resurrection on their faces, blind, dumb and deaf* (*ʿumyan wa-bukman wa-ṣumman*) al-Isrāʾ (17:97)

and

> *Two men, one of them dumb, having control of nothing, and he is a burden on his owner…* (al-Naḥl 16:76)

• *al-ẓulumāt wal-nūr* (lit. darkness and light) always means "unbelief and faith" except in a single verse where it literally means "darkness and light":[78]

73 Ibn Ḥasnūn, *al-Lughāt fīl-Qurʾān*, ed. Ṣalāḥ al-Dīn al-Munajjid (Cairo: Maṭbaʿat al-Risāla, 1365/1946) p. 44.

74 al-Samīn al-Ḥalabī, *ʿUmdat al-Ḥuffāẓ fī Tafsīr Ashraf al-Alfāẓ*, ed. Muḥammad Bāsil ʿUyūn al-Sūd, 4 vols. (Beirut: Dār al-Kutub al-ʿIlmiyya, 1417/1998) 1:255.

75 al-Bukhārī, *Ṣaḥīḥ* (*Tafsīr*, Sūrat al-Isrāʾ).

76 See Burayk b. Saʿīd al-Qarnī, *Kulliyyāt al-Alfāẓ fīl-Tafsīr*, 2 vols. (Ryadh: pub. by author, 1426/2006) and Ayyūb b. Mūsā al-Kafawī, *al-Kulliyyāt: Muʿjam fīl-Muṣṭalaḥāt wal-Furūq al-Lughawiyya*. ed. ʿAdnān Darwīsh and Muḥammad al-Maṣrī, 2nd ed. (Beirut: Muʾassasat al-Risāla, 1413/1993).

77 al-Zarkashī, *al-Burhān fī ʿUlūm al-Qurʾān*, ed. Muḥammad Abū al-Faḍl Ibrāhīm, 3rd ed., 4 vols. (Cairo: Dār al-Turāth, 1404/1984) 1:137, cf. al-Qarnī, *Kulliyyāt* (2:616).

78 al-Rāzī, *Tafsīr al-Fakhr al-Rāzī al-Mushtahar bil-Tafsīr al-Kabīr wa-Mafātīḥ al-Ghayb*, 32 vols. (Beirut: Dār al-Fikr, 1401/1981) 7:16, cf. al-Qarnī, *Kulliyyāt* (2:717).

Praise be to Allah, Who has created the heavens and the earth and has appointed darkness and light. (al-Anʿām 6:1)

• *nikāḥ* (lit. copulation) always means "marriage" except in one verse, where it means "puberty" (*al-ḥulum*):[79]

Test well the orphans until they reach puberty (al-Nisā' 4:6).

The Qur'ān also contains stylistic invariables (*kulliyyāt al-asālīb*). Among them:

• the regular pairing of deterrence with encouragement; or of the divine Names/Attributes of punishment with the Names/Attributes of mercy,[80] as in the verse:

Know that Allah is severe in punishment and that Allah is all-Forgiving, Most Merciful (al-Mā'ida 5:98)

• "When Allah precludes something from creation and asserts it for Himself, it invariably means that such assertion precludes any partner for Him in absolute terms,"[81] as in the verses:

None in the heavens and the earth knows the Unseen except Allah (al-Naml 27:65)

and

None will manifest it at its proper time but He (al-Aʿrāf 7:187)

and

Everything shall perish except His Face (al-Qaṣaṣ 28:88).

[79] al-Zarkashī, *Burhān* (1:140), cf. al-Qarnī, *Kulliyyāt* (2:779).

[80] al-Shāṭibī, *al-Muwāfaqāt*, ed. Mashhūr Ḥasan Salmān, 6 vols. (al-Khubar: Dār Ibn ʿAffān, 1417/1997) 4:167 and Ibn al-Qayyim, *Jalā' al-Afhām*, ed. Zā'id b. Aḥmad al-Nushayrī (Mecca: Dār ʿIlm al-Fawā'id, 1425/2004) p. 188. Cf. al-Qarnī, *Kulliyyāt* (1:119-120).

[81] Muḥammad al-Amīn al-Shinqīṭī, *Aḍwā' al-Bayān fī Īḍāḥ al-Qur'ān bil-Qur'ān*, 9 vols. (Mecca: Dār ʿIlm al-Fawā'id, 1426/2005) 1:211, cf. al-Qarnī, *Kulliyyāt* (1:121).

The contemporary exegete Muhammad Amīn al-Shinqīṭī (1325-1393/1905-1974) adduced the above rule, on the basis of those three examples, as the proof that the *wāw* affixed to *al-rāsikhūn* in the verse *wa-mā yaʿlamu taʾwīlahu illā Allāh wal-rāsikhūna fīl-ʿilmi* (Āl ʿImrān 3:7) is not a conjunction of coordination (*wāw al-ʿaṭf*) but rather a resumptive (*wāw istiʾnāfiyya*) that initiates an independent clause after a fullstop. Allah thus precluded knowledge of the "actual/ultimate reference"—the literal Quranic meaning of *taʾwīl*, otherwise conventionally defined as "the exposition of the referent of the Quranic meaning per the dictates of [linguistic and other] rules and minute investigation"[82]—of the *mutashābihāt* from other than Himself.[83] This is the position of those who consider that the recitational pause after *illā Allāh* here is not merely optional but binding.[84]

Bayḍāwī's synthesis of Perso-Khurasanian hermeneutics

At the same time as he produced, with *Anwār al-Tanzīl*, a reference-work on polysemy, stylistic registers and linguistic invariables, al-Bayḍāwī integrated in it his expertise on parsing

[82] Nūr al-Dīn ʿItr, *ʿUlūm al-Qurʾān al-Karīm*, 6th ed. (Damascus: published by author, 1416/1996) p. 73. *Taʾwīl* has also been claimed to be of the *kulliyyāt al-muṭṭarida* in the Qurʾān in the sense of the reality of something referred to, while lexically it means its actual or ultimate referent (*al-ḥaqīqa wal-ʿāqiba al-latī taʾūl ilayhā al-umūr*) cf. al-Qarnī, *Kulliyyāt* (1:246-262). In this sense, as a Quranic vocable, *taʾwīl* means "meaning" even more literally than *tafsīr*. On the difference between the two terms see also al-Zarkashī, *Burhān* (2:172); al-Dhahabī, *al-Tafsīr wal-Mufassirūn* (1:22); Ibrāhīm ʿAbd al-Raḥmān Khalīfa, *Dirāsāt fī Manāhij al-Mufassirīn* (Cairo: Maktabat al-Azhar, 1979) pp. 10-25; Fāṭima Muḥammad Mardīnī, *al-Tafsīr wal-Mufassirūn* (Damascus: Dār Ghār Ḥirāʾ and Bayt al-Ḥikma, 1430/2009) pp. 12-19 and Ḥāmid b. ʿAlī al-ʿImādī (d. 1171/1758), *al-Tafṣīl fīl-Farq bayn al-Tafsīr wal-Taʾwīl*, ed. Ḥāzim Saʿīd al-Bayyātī, in *al-Aḥmadiyya* 15 (Ramaḍān 1424/October 2003) 15-60.

[83] al-Shinqīṭī, *Aḍwāʾ al-Bayān* (1:211) cf. al-Qarnī, *Kulliyyāt* (1:121).

[84] The majority stopped; Ibn ʿAbbās, Mujāhid, al-Rabīʿ b. Sulaymān, the Shāfiʿīs, Ibn Fūrak, Aḥmad al-Qurṭubī, Ibn ʿAṭiyya, al-Bayḍāwī and Ibn ʿĀshūr in *al-Taḥrīr wal-Tanwīr*, 30 vols. (Tunis: al-Dār al-Tūnisiyya lil-Nashr, 1984) 1:116, 3:164-165, did not.

or desintential syntax (*iʿrāb*), a branch of learning in which he authored, as mentioned, *Lubb al-Albāb fī ʿIlm al-Iʿrāb*, which received several commentaries.[85] He also digested the literature on miraculous inimitability (*iʿjāz*) to which he was heir through two pioneering models of *tafsīr*, each of which had broken the mould of the genre in its time. He integrated the sura-by-sura linguistic method the Ḥanafī Muʿtazili Jār Allāh Maḥmūd al-Zamakhsharī (467-538/1074-1143) of Khwarizm (near Samarqand) used in his *Kashshāf ʿan Ḥaqāʾiq Ghawāmiḍ al-Tanzīl wa-ʿUyūn al-Aqāwīl fī Wujūh al-Taʾwīl* (Laying Bare the Realities of the Enigmas of Revelation and Choicest Statements on the Various Aspects of Interpretation) with the multidisciplinarian tradition inaugurated by Fakhr al-Dīn al-Rāzī (543-606/1148-1210) of Ray—near present-day Teheran—in his large *Mafātīḥ al-Ghayb* (Keys to the Unseen), but without the prolixity of either. As just mentioned, he also relied on the works of al-Rāghib al-Aṣfahānī:

> This *tafsīr* is a magnificent book that needs no introduction. He summarized in it the material of the *Kashshāf* related to parsing, semantics and rhetorics; from the *Tafsīr al-Kabīr* [of Rāzī] whatever is related to sapience and dialectics, and from al-Rāghib's *tafsīr* whatever is related to etymologies, arcane truths and subtle allusions, adding to that whatever his mind reined in of rational perspectives and plausible variants....[86]

These three sources are discussed further down. In addition, al-Bayḍāwī also benefited from the works of many prominent predecessors in Perso-Khurasanian linguistic exegesis such as:

Muqātil b. Sulaymān (d. 150/767) in Balkh and Basra,
Sahl al-Tustarī (203-283/819-896) in Tustar,

[85] See ʿAlī, *al-Bayḍāwī wa-Manhajuh* pp. 26-27.
[86] Muṣṭafā b. ʿAbd Allāh , known as Ḥājjī Khalīfa and Kâtip Çelebi, *Kashf al-Ẓunūn* (1:187). For examples of those main three influences on al-Bayḍāwī see Yūsuf Aḥmad ʿAlī, *al-Bayḍāwī* (pp. 65-74).

Ibn Jarīr al-Ṭabarī (224-310/839-ca.922) in Amol,
Ibn Abī Ḥātim al-Rāzī (240-327/854-939) in Ray,
Ghulām Tha'lab al-Zāhid (261-345/875-956) in Baghdad,
al-Qaffāl al-Shāshī al-Kabīr (291-365/904-976) in Tashkent,
Abū al-Ḥasan al-Jurjānī (d. 392/1002) in Ray and Nishapur,
Ibn Fūrak (d. 406/1015) in Ray and Nishapur,
al-Sulamī (325-412/937-1021) in Nishapur,
al-Tha'labī (d. 427/1036) in Nishapur,
Abū al-Faḍl al-Rāzī (370-454/981-1062) in Nishapur,
al-Qushayrī (376-465/986-1073) in Nishapur,
al-Wāḥidī (398?-468/1008?-1076) in Nishapur,
ʿAbd al-Qāhir al-Jurjānī (d. 471/1078) in Jurjān,
al-Samʿānī (426-489/1035-1096) in Merv and Nishapur,
al-Ghazālī (450-505/1058-1111) in Ṭūs (near Mashhad),
al-Baghawī (433-516/1042-1122) in Merv,
al-Taymī al-Aṣfahānī (457-535/1065-1141) in Ispahan,
al-Shahrastānī (479-548/1086-1153) in Khwarizm-Nishapur,
Bayān al-Ḥaqq al-Ghaznawī (d. after 553/1158) in Nishapur,
Rūzbahān Baqlī (522-606/1128-1210) in Shiraz,
and al-Khuwayy (583-637/1187-ca.1239) in Khurasan.[87]

Comparison of the Basran and Kufan schools of grammar

Al-Bayḍāwī also wove into the *Anwār* a comparative critique of the Basran and Kufan schools of grammar and philology; a grammar-oriented review of the different narrations of mass-transmitted (*mutawātir*) canonical readings of the Qur'ān and anomalous (*shādhdh*), non-canonical ones;[88] references to the

[87] Qāḍī al-quḍāt Abū al-ʿAbbās Aḥmad b. Khalīl b. Saʿāda al-Khuwayy al-Barmakī al-Khurāsānī *thumma* al-Dimashqī was a jurist, jurisprudent, and prosodist of the first rank from Azerbaijan whose great contribution was the completion of his teacher al-Fakhr al-Rāzī's *Tafsīr*, cf. Nuwayhiḍ, *Muʿjam al-Mufassirīn* (1:35) and Ibn al-Subkī, *Ṭabaqāt al-Shāfiʿiyya al-Kubrā* (8:16-17). See p. 59.

[88] See Muḥammad Ghiyāth al-Janbāz, *al-Qirā'āt al-Shādhdha wa-Tawjīhuhā fī Tafsīr*

Sunni schools of law on legal issues—chiefly the Shāfiʿī—and the Sunni schools of doctrine, in particular the Ashʿarī; and sufism.

In the linguistic minutiae that are the province of grammatical polemics and school differences al-Bayḍāwī sides with the Basrians and mostly promotes their positions. When discussing the etymology of the word *ism* ⟨noun⟩, for example, he names them, affiliates himself with them, states their view and evidence from usage and poetry, then proceeds to reject that of the Kufans, first without naming them, then explicitly:

> Our Basrian colleagues hold that *ism* is of the nouns whose endings are elided (*ḥudhifat aʿjāzuhā*) due to frequent use and whose initials have an indeclinable mute case (*bināʾ ʿala al-sukūn*), after which a conjunctive compression (*hamzat al-waṣl*) was affixed to them as an initial—since [Arabs] have it that one begins with a vowelized consonant (*mutaḥarrik*) and stops at a quiescent one (*sākin*). ...
>
> Transposition is unlikely and irregular (*al-qalbu ghayru muṭṭarid*); [rather,] its derivation (*ishtiqāq*) is from *sumūw* ⟨highness⟩, as [a name] constitutes eminence and a mark of distinction for the referent (*musammā*). The Kufans derive it from *sima*, with *wism* as its root, from which the *wāw* was [presumably] elided and then a glottal stop (*hamza*) compensated for it to minimize [vowel] weakness (*iʿlāl*). This [derivation] was rejected because the *hamza* is not a familiar replacement for initial elisions (*mā ḥudhifa ṣadruh*) in their language [Arabs].

By "transposition" al-Bayḍāwī means the presumed transposition of the initial *wāw* of *wasm* ⟨mark⟩ into the initial *hamza* of *ism*—the etymology preferred by the Kufans—as opposed to the Basrian view that *ism* comes from *s-m-w* rather than *w-s-m*.

al-Bayḍāwī (Mecca: Dār Ṭaybat al-Khaḍrāʾ lil-Nashr wal-Tawzīʿ, 2011).

Three examples of Bayḍāwī's succinct treatment of complex linguistic and theological questions

Al-Bayḍāwī's concentration of information into a very concise amount of words lent his work intertextual and hypertextual qualities as illustrated by the following three doctrinal passages. The first one bears on the derivation or underived nature of the name *Allāh*; the second on the Ashʿarī and Māturīdī doctrine that Allah may task one beyond one's strength; the third on Islam's abrogation of previous faiths:

a. Is *Allāh* an underived proper name or etymologically derived?

When al-Bayḍāwī states in his commentary on the first verse of the Fātiḥa, "It was also said *Allāh* is a proper name for His own essence" (*ʿalamun li-dhātihi al-makhṣūṣa*) he is citing al-Rāzī's terminology and definition in *Mafātīḥ al-Ghayb*, as confirmed by his citation of al-Rāzī's subsequent argument that

> if it were a descriptive, the statement "There is no god but Allah" would not constitute pure monotheism—as in, for example, "There is no god but the all-Merciful," which does not preclude partnership.[89]

That al-Bayḍāwī agrees with this argument can be gleaned from his autograph marginal comments on al-Zamakhsharī as cited by the Shāfiʿī-Ashʿarī author of the largest extant supercommentary on the *Kashshāf*, Sharaf al-Dīn al-Ḥusayn b. ʿAbd Allāh al-Ṭībī (d. 743/1343):

> *al-Raḥmān*, even though it is reserved for the Creator—exalted is He!, it remains that such has transpired with a separate proof; linguistically, it [only] means someone who shows utmost mercy.[90]

[89] Bayḍāwī, *Anwār* (al-Fātiḥa 1:1) cf. al-Rāzī, *Mafātīḥ al-Ghayb*, *sub* al-Baqara 2:163.
[90] al-Ṭībī, *Futūḥ al-Ghayb fīl-Kashfi ʿan Qināʿ al-Rayb*, ed. Ḥikmat Bashīr Yāsīn, unpublished Ph.D. diss., 7 vols. (Medina: al-Jāmiʿa al-Islāmiyya, 1413-1416/1992-1996)

Yet, far from agreeing with al-Rāzī's conclusion, he goes on to say, "The prevalent view (*al-aẓhar*), however, is that it is originally a descriptive." Al-Suyūṭī (849-911/1445-1505) takes strong exception in his supercommentary—"the correct view, based on transmission and evidence, is that it is a proper name from the start!"—while al-Qūnawī points out that "[al-Bayḍāwī's] intent was to disprove the claim [made by al-Zamakhsharī] that [*Allāh*] is underived—whether a proper name or a descriptive."[91] Al-Shawkānī in the introduction to *Nayl al-Awṭār* labels the view that *Allāh* is a proper name as the position of the majority then proceeds to describe it as "originating from *al-ilāh*," i.e., derived.[92]

Al-Bayḍāwī goes on to explain:

> but when overwhelming usage made [the name *Allāh*] His [and His alone], wherein it applied to no other and became like a distinguishing mark for Him—as also took place, for example, with al-Thurayyā and al-Ṣaʿiq—it was treated as a proper name.

The abstruse examples of al-Thurayyā and al-Ṣaʿiq are elucidated by al-Qūnawī who states in his *Ḥāshiya* that *thurayyā* is originally the diminutive of *tharwā* (multitudinous)—which metonymically became the name of the Pleiades cluster of stars *al-thurayyā*—while the adjective *ṣaʿiq* (thunderstruck) became

1:88, citing al-Bayḍāwī's words in the margins of the *Kashshāf*.

91 al-Suyūṭī, *Nawāhid* (1:142) and *al-Ashbāh wal-Naẓā'ir fil Naḥw*, 4 vols. (Hyderabad Deccan: Dā'irat al-Maʿārif al-ʿUthmāniyya, 1359-1361/1940-1942) 4:5; al-Qūnawī, *Ḥāshiyat al-Qūnawī ʿalā Tafsīr al-Imām al-Bayḍāwī*, ed. ʿAbd Allāh Maḥmūd ʿUmar, 20 vols. (Beirut: Dār al-Kutub al-ʿIlmiyya, 1422/2001) 1:131. Al-Suyūṭī goes on in the *Nawāhid* (1:127) to quote al-Taftāzānī's (722-792/1322-1390) saying: "Just as imagination is bewildered regarding His Essence and Attributes, so are they confounded whether the word that signifies Him is a noun or an adjective, derived or underived, a proper name or not, etc."

92 Muḥammad b. ʿAlī al-Shawkānī, *Nayl al-Awṭār min Asrār Muntaqā al-Akhbār*, ed. Muḥammad Ṣubḥī Ḥallāq, 16 vols. (Dammam: Dār Ibn al-Jawzī, 1427/2006) 1:113.

the surname of Khuwaylid b. Nufayl.[93] The two names patently illustrate how descriptives can become proper names through overwhelming usage. Thus Bayḍāwī tempers the minority view without wholly capitulating to the majority one.

b. Does Allah task one beyond one's capacity, for example tasking Abū Lahab and Abū Jahl to believe when He knows and announces they will not?

Al-Bayḍāwī brings up the familiar doctrinal issue of "tasking beyond capacity" (*al-taklīf bi-mā lā yuṭāq*) in his commentary on the verse *Verily those who rejected belief, it is the same for them whether you warn them or you do not warn them* (al-Baqara 2:6) saying:

> This verse was adduced as a proof by those who say that it is possible that one be tasked beyond capacity, since Allah Most High said about them that they will not believe and [yet] has commanded them to believe; therefore, should they believe, His report would turn into a lie, and [furthermore] their belief would comprise belief in the fact that they will not believe, which is a contradiction.

Al-Qūnawī further explains the above hypothesis: "For example, if Abū Lahab were to believe, he would have to believe in everything the Prophet—upon him blessings and peace—brought, including the announcement that he would never believe."[94] Since the above is a logical impossibility, it follows that Abū Lahab is inherently unable to believe, yet he is tasked to, and therefore Allah *may* task one beyond one's capacity. Al-Bayḍāwī rejects this reasoning as unsubstantiated:

> The truth is that tasking one with what is inherently impossible, even if it is rationally conceivable—in light of the fact that [legal] rulings do not call for an ulterior benefit, least of

[93] Al-Qūnawī, *Ḥāshiya* (1:131-132).
[94] Al-Qūnawī, *Ḥāshiya* (2:37).

> all obedience (*min ḥaythu inna al-aḥkām lā tastadʿī gharaḍan siyyamā al-imtithāl*)—nevertheless a review of the evidence yields no such occurrence.

"Meaning," al-Qūnawī comments, "the legal responsibilities (*takālīf*) have all been reviewed and followed up, but no inherent impossibility could be found among them. As for what appears to be a tasking with something impossible, it is subject to contextualization and interpretation (*muwajjah mu'awwal*)."[95]

Ashʿarīs and Māturīdīs had posited two scenarios wherein one can be commanded to do something one is unable to do: (i) physical inability, in which case legal responsibility (*taklīf*) is cancelled; here, the legally responsible person (*mukallaf*) is psychologically aware of his physical inability and thus cannot conceive of fulfilling the command, and so the inability is not wilful; (ii) wilful avoidance and opposition, as with those like Abū Jahl and Abū Lahab who were commanded to believe although Allah knew they would not, and who *will be plunged in a flaming fire* (al-Masad 111:3); here, the *mukallaf* is psychologically aware of his ability and thus can conceive of fulfilling the command, so that his inability is wilful. The latter category of inability, moreover, is the general status of all unbelievers. It also shows that ability for unbelief differs from ability for belief, and that the inner reality of this matter remains hidden lest volition (*ikhtiyār*) turn to coercion (*jabr*)—the doctrine of the Jabriyya ʿDeterministsʾ—even if, ontologically, both scenarios derive directly from divine will and power.[96]

[95] Al-Qūnawī, *Ḥāshiya* (2:38).

[96] See Ibn Fūrak, *Maqālāt al-Ashʿarī*, ed. Aḥmad al-Sāyiḥ (Cairo: Maktabat al-Thaqāfat al-Dīniyya, 1425/2005) pp. 110-113; al-Ashʿarī, *al-Lumaʿ fīl-Radd ʿalā Ahl al-Zaygh wal-Bidaʿ*, ed. Muḥammad Ḥusayn al-Ḍāwī (Beirut: Dār al-Kutub al-ʿIlmiyya, 1421/2000) p. 62-63 and *al-Ibāna ʿan Uṣūl al-Diyāna*, ed. Bashīr Muḥammad ʿUyūn, 3rd ed. (Damascus: Maktabat Dār al-Bayān, 1416/1996) p. 134-135; Maymūn al-Nasafī,

Furthermore, as al-Bayḍāwī states (end of commentary on al-Baqara 2:6), the ability to obey is very much present even in the case of the unbelievers, and the divine disclosure of the absence of obedience does not constitute a nullification of that ability:

> As for the [divine] report that something is taking place or not, it does not contradict the [human] ability to enact it; for example, when Allah Most High reports what He will do or what His slave will do by choice. The benefit of warning—even after knowing that it will have no successful outcome—is to bind one to admit the proof, and also for the Messenger to reap the merit of conveyance. That is why He said, *it is the same for them* (al-Baqara 2:6) and not "it is the same for you" the way He told the idol-worshippers, *it is the same to you all whether you call unto them or you are silent* (al-A'rāf 7:193).

c. *Naskh*: The pre-Islamic viability and post-Islamic inviability of Judaism, Christianity and other superseded faiths

Al-Bayḍāwī succinctly recapitulates both glosses of the four categories cited in the firt part of the verse *Verily those who believed and those who Judaized and the Nazarenes and the Sabians* ... (al-Baqara 2:62). The first gloss—and the more established one—is that of Ibn 'Abbās, and understands the first *those who believed* as referring to all followers of pre-Islamic dispensations, including Jews, Christians and Sabians: if they were sincere, orthodox within their creed and congruent in deeds, their

Tabṣirat al-Adilla fī Uṣūl al-Dīn, ed. Claude Salamé, 2 vols. (Damascus: Institut Français de Damas, 1993) 2:544-545; al-Taftāzānī, *Sharḥ al-'Aqā'id al-Nasafiyya*, ed. Muḥammad 'Adnān Darwīsh (Damascus: N.p., 1411/1990) p. 145-150; al-Bunānī, *Ḥāshiya* on al-Maḥallī's *Sharḥ* on Ibn al-Subkī's *Jam' al-Jawāmi'*, 2 vols. ([Cairo: s.n.], 1285/1868, rept. Beirut: Dār al-Fikr, 1402/1982) 1:206, *mas'ala: yajūz al-taklīf bil-muḥāl muṭlaqan*; al-Haytamī, *al-Fatḥ al-Mubīn bi-Sharḥ al-Arba'īn*, ed. Muḥammad Ḥasan Ismā'īl (Beirut: Dār al-Kutub al-'Ilmiyya, 2007) p. 180-181, discussion of *qaḍā'* in the commentary on the second of the Forty Hadiths and his *al-Minaḥ al-Makkiyya fī Sharḥ al-Hamziyya*, ed. Bassām Muḥammad Bārūd, 3 vols. (Abū Dhabī: al-Mujamma' al-Thaqāfī and Beirut: Dār al-Ḥāwī, 1418/1998) 2:822, "by consensus."

reward is assured. The second gloss is that of Sufyān al-Thawrī (97-161/716-778) and understands the entire four categories as archetypes of unbelievers in the time of the Prophet, beginning with the hypocrites who "*believed* in claim only;" all four categories, however, are promised paradise if their adherents decide to believe truly in the Prophet Muḥammad and act accordingly.

Al-Bayḍāwī then supplies the respective conclusions of both glosses in his commentary on the second part of the verse, *whoever believed in the One God and the Last Day and did good, undoubtedly for them is their reward with their Nurturer Himself and they have nothing to fear nor shall they grieve* (al-Baqara 2:62):

> [It means] "whoever among them had followed his religion *before it became abrogated*, confirming with all his heart original creation and the final return and acting upon the dictates of his religious law;" it was also said, "whoever believes out of those unbelievers with unalloyed belief and enters Islam truthfully." [emphasis mine]

By using the term *naskh* ⟨abrogation⟩ the Qadi makes clear that in either case it is indisputable that all previous faiths and dispensations are superseded by the Muḥammadan one and that Islam abrogates Judaism, Christianity, Sabianism and—a fortiori—all other previous faiths and creeds. This position is in conformity with Ashʿarism as well as other Sunni doctrinal schools without dissent from the Shiʿis, Muʿtazilis, Khawārij and the rest of Muslim groups and sects. This unbreached consensus is that each successive prophet in history is considered to have abrogated part or all of his predecessor's law—as illustrated by the Gospel's abrogation of some of the rulings of the Torah (cf. Āl ʿImrān 3:48-50)—until the final and all-encompassing abrogation of all previous dispensations by the mission of the Seal of

Prophets (al-Aḥzāb 33:40), who was prophesied in those two Books (al-Aʿrāf 7:156-158) and sent universally to all people (Sabaʾ 34:28) with the very last, greatest, and most complete of all heavenly Scriptures, with the best of all human nations as its recipient (al-Baqara 2:143, Āl ʿImrān 3:109), and so until the end of times.[97] Furthermore, the incorruptibility of the final Revelation and its supersession of previous dispensations are expressed in the Quranic term *muhayminan* ⁽trustee, trustworthy, custodian, watcher⁾ in the verse *And unto you have We revealed the Scripture with the truth, confirming whatever Scripture was before it, and a watcher over it* (al-Māʾida 5:48). Al-Rāzī said:

> First, (a) [It means] ward (*raqīb*), witness (*shāhid*), and guardian (*ḥāfiẓ*); (b) it means "trusted" (*amīn*) over the Books that preceded it. Second, this is the case only because the Qurʾān is the Book that never becomes abrogated, nor is It subject to substitution (*tabdīl*) and tampering (*taḥrīf*), as the Most High said: *We have without doubt sent down the Remembrance; and We will assuredly guard it* (al-Ḥijr 15:9). If this is the case then the testimony of the Qurʾān remains forever that the [pristine] Torah, Gospel and Psalms are the pure truth, and that whatever is true in these Books can be known forever. Third, the author of the *Kashshāf* said it is also read *muhaymanan*, meaning "witnessed over" on the part of Allah Most High in that He preserves it from tampering and substitution.[98]

Al-Ghazālī specified there is "consensus in the agreement of the entire Community that the sacred law of Muḥammad—upon him blessings and peace—abrogates the laws of his predecessors either *in toto* or in whatever contravenes it; this is agreed upon and whoever denies it violates consensus."[99] It is notewor-

[97] Cf. Ibn Kathīr, *Tafsīr* (5:244-250 under al-Māʾida 5:48).

[98] Al-Rāzī, *Mafātīḥ al-Ghayb* (12:12).

[99] Al-Ghazālī, *al-Mustaṣfā min ʿIlm al-Uṣūl*, 2 vols. (Bulaq: al-Maṭbaʿat al-Amīriyya,

thy that this stipulation encompasses laws and rulings but not (i) historical reports, nor (ii) credal foundations such as pure monotheism, resurrection, prophetology, angelology and the hereafter which all stand unchanged since the first revelation, as conveyed in the titles of al-Shawkānī's two monographs *Irshād al-Thiqāt ilā Ittifāq al-Sharā'i' 'alā al-Tawḥīd wal-Ma'ād wal-Nubuwwāt* (Guiding the Trusted to the Agreement of All Sacred Laws Over the Oneness of Resurrection and Prophecy) and *al-Maqālat al-Fākhira fī Ittifāq al-Sharā'i' 'alā Ithbāt al-Dār al-Ākhira* (The Splendid Statements on the Agreement of All Sacred Laws in Affirming the Abode of the Hereafter).[100]

Another eminent Khurasanian Shāfi'ī-Ash'ari exegete, al-Shahrastānī, offered a teleological reading of *naskh*, which he compared to organic growth in the introduction to his *tafsīr*:

> It was said that [abrogation] is a completion (*takmīl*) in that the objectives of legal rulings, once they reach their endpoint and farthest limit, are completed with other rulings that possess nobler and more perfect objectives. We say the same thing about organisms, as in the replacement (*intisākh*) of the zygote (*nuṭfa*) by the blastocyst (*'alaqa*) and the latter's replacement with a grooved embryo (*muḍgha*), to the seventh stage which is another creation. So the sacred laws began with Adam—upon him peace—and end up with Resurrection, which is the other birth; and every law is replacing the previous one, that is, completing it to the next stage of another perfection.... Do not think for a moment that any law cancels out another or that its rulings are lifted and others put in its place! For the zygote among organisms, if it were to be eradicated or taken out, would not reach to the

1322) 1:111, cf. 'Alā' al-Dīn al-Bukhārī, *Kashf al-Asrār 'an Uṣūl Fakhr al-Islām al-Pazdawī*, ed. Muḥammad al-Mu'taṣim bil-Lāh al-Baghdādī, 2nd ed., 4 vols. (Beirut: Dār al-Kitāb al-'Arabī, 1414/1994) 3:345.

[100] *Al-Fatḥ al-Rabbānī min Fatāwā al-Imām al-Shawkānī*, ed. Muḥammad Ṣubḥī Ḥallāq, 12 vols. (Ṣan'ā': Maktabat al-Jīl al-Jadīd, 1423/2002) 1:473-585.

> second or third stage, but rather, its progress to completion has ended, and there is no further form of perfection coming in the wake of its own fulfillment. It is the same with the first law if it were to be eradicated.... Likewise, the last law—the noblest of them all—comprises rulings that have never been substituted—these are the foundations of the creed, and they are *the clear revelations which are the substance of the Book* (Āl ʿImrān 3:7)—together with substitutable rulings which are the branches of the creed—these are the ambiguous verses *whereof Allah effaces what He will, and confirms* (al-Raʿd 13:39). And He does not efface except for a perfection fulfilled, nor does He confirm but for a principle directed toward perfection."[101]

Expert scholarly exertion (*ijtihād*) and other qualifications

The above two examples show the multi-layered quality of the *Anwār* and al-Bayḍāwī's at times hermetic combination of what al-Fāḍil b. ʿĀshūr (1327-1390/1909-1970) called

> concision (*ikhtiṣār*), minute precision (*diqqat al-taʿbīr*), strict scholarly terminology (*iltizām al-muṣṭalaḥ al-ʿilmī*) and the economic use of implied mental inferences for meanings that branch out of the text and then serve as basis for the passage that follows.[102]

The result, history shows, appeared as both a very modern and a very classical hermeneutics for its time, and the ultimate didactic tool because of its brevity and orthodoxy. In light of the standing garnered by the *Anwār* it would therefore not be an exaggeration to say that al-Bayḍāwī's achievement was an example of expert scholarly exertion (*ijtihād*)[103] at work and of renew-

[101] *Tafsīr al-Shahrastānī al-musammā Mafātīḥ al-Asrār wa-Maṣābīḥ al-Abrār*, ed. Muḥammad ʿAlī Ādharshab, 2 vols. (Tehran: Markaz al-Buḥūth wal-Dirāsāt lil-Turāth al-Makhṭūṭ, 1429/2008) 1:52-53.

[102] Muḥammad al-Fāḍil b. ʿĀshūr, *al-Tafsīr wa-Rijāluh* (pp. 114-115).

[103] See the comprehensive definition of *ijtihād* and the *mujtahid* in Ibn al-Subkī, *Jamʿ*

al (*tajdīd*) in the sacred sense of the word, as told in the Prophetic hadith: "Verily Allah shall send to this Nation, at the onset of every hundred years, one/those who will renew their religion for them."[104] Al-Bayḍāwī himself, in describing exegesis as a sum total of the sciences for none but the most accomplished in each of them, is assimilating *tafsīr* to full-fledged *ijtihād*.

The 22 disciplines of exegesis, including scientific training

Ijtihād, furthermore, buttressed the edifice of exegesis and protected it from erosion through the dedicated sub-disciplines of Quranic studies applied by qualified experts as defined, for example, by al-Suyūṭī in his *Itqān* (Type 78, *shurūṭ al-mufassir*) and as summarized by Ibn Ḥajar al-Haytamī (909-973/1503-1565):

> The tools of exegesis are fifteen different disciplines:
> • philology (*al-lugha*),
> • grammar (*al-naḥw*),[105]
> • morphology (*al-taṣrīf*),
> • etymology (*al-ishtiqāq*),
> • style/diction (*al-ma'ānī*),
> • rhetoric (*al-bayān*),
> • tropes (*al-badī'*),[106]

al-Jawāmi' fī Uṣūl al-Fiqh, ed. 'Abd al-Mun'im Khalīl Ibrāhīm, 2nd ed. (Beirut: Dār al-Kutub al-'Ilmiyya, 1423/2002) pp. 118-119.

[104] Narrated from Abū Hurayra by Abū Dāwūd, *Sunan* (*Malāḥim, Bāb mā yudhkaru fī qarn al-mi'a*), al-Ḥākim, *al-Mustadrak 'alā al-Ṣaḥīḥayn*, with al-Dhahabī's *Talkhīṣ al-Mustadrak*, 5 vols. (Beirut: Dār al-Ma'rifa, 1986, rept. of 1334/1916 Hyderabad edition with indices by our teacher Yūsuf al-Mar'ashlī) 4:522, and others.

[105] Of which one of the greatest representatives was al-Wāḥidī, followed by Bayḍāwī, both of whose *tafsīrs* can be characterized as concise applied grammars of the Arabic language, without which true exegesis is impossible. Yet sadly we see nowadays many people embarking on both *tafsīr* and translation with neither specialized *Sharī'a* training nor even understanding of Arabic grammar—in the service of corruption.

[106] Al-Bayḍāwī took much of his discussion on those three types—*ma'ānī, bayān* and *badī'*—from al-Zamakhsharī and, to a certain extent, al-Rāghib. The first two are con-

- Quranic readings (*al-qirā'āt*),[107]
- principles of creed and principles of law (*al-aṣlayn*),
- circumstances of revelation (*asbāb al-nuzūl*),
- historical accounts (*al-qaṣaṣ*),
- abrogating evidence (*al-nāsikh*),
- abrogated evidence (*al-mansūkh*),
- sacred law (*al-fiqh*),
- hadiths that explicate the vague and the anonymous (*al-aḥādīth al-mubayyina li-tafsīr al-mujmal wal-mubham*),
- and a knowledge that stems from a spiritual gift (*'ilm al-mawhiba*), which is a knowledge Allah imparts to whoever puts into practice what they know.[108]

Scientific discourse in *Anwār al-Tanzīl*

Our teacher Dr. Nūr al-Dīn 'Itr added a sixteenth requirement, "to be conversant with the givens of modern science."[109] This aspect of exegesis is associated with modern times but already emerges in the hermeneutics of the *Anwār*—to Suyūṭī's chagrin in his supercommentary—as can be gleaned from the Qadi's discussion of the physiological causes of surdity under *deaf, dumb, blind* (al-Baqara 2:18); the meteorological cause of thunder under *a cloudburst from the sky* (2:19); Earth's levelness and rotundity at one and the same time and rain formation under *Who has made for you the earth a bed* (2:22); the proper-

sidered essential while the third is a *'ilm taḥsīnī* (embellishing discipline).

107 This discipline is studied under the genre of *tawjīh al-qirā'āt* (polysemic Quranic readings) and al-Bayḍāwī made profound use of it insofar as it sheds light on the layers of meaning in the Qur'ān.

108 Al-Haytamī as quoted by his student Mullā 'Alī al-Qārī in *Mirqāt al-Mafātīḥ Sharḥ Mishkāt al-Maṣābīḥ* (commentary on the hadith *Man qāla fil-Qur'āni bi-ra'yihi fa-aṣāba fa-qad akhṭa'*: "Whoever speaks about the Qur'ān based on his mere opinion and is correct, is incorrect").

109 'Itr, *'Ulūm al-Qur'ān al-Karīm* (p. 88) cf. Muḥammad Riḍā's preamble to *al-Manār*.

ties of minerals (2nd quotation below); the psychological and physiological definitions of mercy under the *Basmala* (1:1); of anger (1:7); of the "appetitive" and "wrathful" faculties in man in counterpoise with the "rational," which make him complex as opposed to the simplicity of angels (2:30); of the lifeless character of primitive fetal states as "elements and nutrients and humors and zygotes and morsels of flesh, formed and unformed" under *when you had been dead* (2:28); and of shyness, the middle between impudence and timidity (2:26). The above discussions, particularly the latter, connect empirical observation with language and Arabic etymology in a manner much closer to modern psycholinguistics than Isidore of Seville (560-636CE) had achieved with Latin and ancient science in his *Etymologies*:

> *Ḥayā'* ⟨shame⟩ is the psyche's aversion to reprehensible matters out of fear of blame. It is an intermediate between impudence—audacity to do reprehensible matters with utter disregard for consequences—and timidity, the cowing of the psyche into complete inaction. It stems from *ḥayāt* ⟨life⟩, for it is a dejection that takes over the vital impulse and deters it from doing this or that. Hence it is said *ḥayiya al-rajulu* ⟨the man felt shame⟩ just as they say *nasiya* and *ḥashiya* when one's *nasā* ⟨sciatic nerves⟩ and *ḥashā* ⟨bowels⟩ are ailing.

In his commentary on eternity under *wa-hum fīhā khālidūn* (2:25) Bayḍāwī argues against materialists that the incorruptibility of compound bodies in paradise can easily be conceived by observing the full internal cohesion of certain minerals, even though they are foolish to assume this world and the next are comparable. He rebuts them again in his discussion of the evidentiary probability of miracles on the strength of empirical observation of the wonders of the natural world at the conclusion of his commentary on *"Strike with your staff!" whereupon there burst forth from it twelve springs* (al-Baqara 2:60):

> Whoever denies the like of these stunning miracles, it is because of his utmost ignorance of Allah and his lack of pondering the wonders of His handiwork. For when it is conceivable that there might be stones that shave hair, shrink away from vinegar or attract metal, it is not inconceivable that Allah may create a rock and make it disposed to attract subterranean water, or attract winds from the globe and turn that into water through a process of cooling and the like.

A *naqlī atharī* hadithist at heart, al-Suyūṭī lashes out ("the reference-point of exegesis is transmission!") at what he somewhat unfairly characterizes as a text-dismissive philosophical bent in Bayḍāwī's approach, for example on the Qadi's view that *Allāh* is originally not an underived proper name (al-Fatiha 1:1); his position that the prevalent interpretation of the Disjointed Letters is that they symbolize the substance of the Qur'ān as speech composed of the same stuff of which its deniers compose their own speech (al-Baqara 2:1); his position that the divine *khatm* and *ghishāwa* are metaphorical (al-Baqara 2:7); his gloss on thunder as "caused by the disturbance of cloud formations and their mutual collision when driven by the wind" (al-Baqara 2:19) etc. Even when the Qadi turns literalist—as in his allowing the literalization of *maraḍ* ⁽sickness⁾ in the verse *in their hearts is a sickness* (al-Baqara 2:10), in the process supplying flawless medico-spiritual definitions of sickness—al-Suyūṭī chafes because that gloss, yet again, goes against the grain:

> [al-Bayḍāwī:] *al-maraḍ* ⁽sickness⁾ is literally what happens to the body and brings it out of its proper equilibrium, inevitably causing its erratic behavior. Figuratively, it denotes psychological states that impair the psyche's integrity such as ignorance, misbelief, envy, rancor and viciousness, because they block one from the acquisition of redeeming qualities or lead to the ruin of true eternal life. The noble verse can be interpreted both ways.

> [al-Suyūṭī:] I say: what the exegetes concluded was to interpret the verse figuratively, as that was what Ibn Jarīr [al-Ṭabarī] and Ibn Abī Ḥātim narrated from Ibn Masʿūd, Ibn ʿAbbās, Abū al-ʿĀliya, Mujāhid, ʿIkrima, al-Ḥasan, al-Rabīʿ and Qatāda. Neither of them reported anything other than that from anyone; and the reference-point of exegesis is transmission. One wonders at the author and at the writer of the *Kashshāf*, how in most Quranic and Hadithic passages they interpret what is apparently literal as transferred meaning and metaphor without justification, when the imams of hadith and eminent authorities explicitly state that what is meant is the literal meaning of the manifest [locution]! And the Sharīf [al-Jurjānī] colludes with them in that, as do the rest of those who tread that path: they all abandon the imams of hadith with their verdict that 'literalists claim' (*zaʿama ahl al-ẓāhir*)! But they have no ground to stand on other than their rule that transferred meaning is more expressive than the literal meaning. Yet here, its exegesis has emerged from the Companions and Successors as a transferred meaning and no other—but that was not enough for them and they added the literal meaning! Really none of those who commented the *Kashshāf* trod the path of the hadith scholars more than al-Ṭībī, for he was truly, in addition to his arch-mastery in the rational disciplines, a Sufi *muḥaddith*.[110]

In reality, far from ignoring or rejecting hadith-based exegesis, al-Bayḍāwī on the contrary always puts it in first place and supersedes it only with Qur'ān-based glosses as, for example, in his discussion of who is ultimately meant by *ghayr al-maghḍūbi ʿalayhim wa-lā al-ḍāllīn* (al-Fātiḥa 1:7). More to the point here, he combines such exegesis with scientific explanations which he often concludes with a fine sapiental and doctrinal observation. This method, inherited from al-Rāzī, surpasses what the latter

[110] Al-Suyūṭī, *Nawāhid* (1:381). See note 1134 for a hadithic error on his own part. For more on Bayḍāwī's scientific discourse see A.H. Johns, "Exegesis as an Expression of Islamic Humanism—Approaches, Concerns and Insights of al-Baydawi" in *Hamdard Islamicus* 22 no. 4 (1999), pp. 37-58.

had achieved in his own *tafsīr* because of the Qadi's economy in both style and content as very effectively illustrated by his take on plant biology in his commentary on *He sent down, out of the sky, water whereby He produced some fruits* (al-Baqara 2:22):

> The budding of fruits is by the power of Allah Most High and His will; however, (i) He made water that mixes with soil a means in their production and a material for them, just like the sperm-drop for animals; that is, He made it His custom to pour out their forms and modalities over the material of their admixture; (ii) or He devised in water an active force and in the earth a receptive force, out of the combination of which are generated the different kinds of fruit. ... [In] His originating them in a gradational manner from state to state, ... He renews [His] paradigms for those who can see and makes them more confident of His irrepressible might, which would not be the case if they were created in one go.

More on exegetes' musts: piety, orthodoxy—and parsing

Additional criteria mentioned by al-Suyūṭī include:

- to aim to explain the Qur'ān through itself in the first place;
- to aim to explain it through the Sunna after the Qur'ān;[111]
- to possess sound belief;
- to be impeccable in the practice of the religion;
- to purify one's intention through simple living;
- to be thoroughly accomplished in the art of parsing so that the variance in meanings will not confuse one.[112]

[111] This condition came as a reminder to exegetes—already in al-Suyūṭī's time—that the obligation to refer back to the Hadith in any type of exegesis of the Qur'ān is not negotiable but rather comparable (and only second) to the obligation to refer back to the Qur'ān itself.

[112] al-Suyūṭī, *al-Itqān fī 'Ulūm al-Qur'ān*, ed. Markaz al-Dirāsāt al-Qur'āniyya, 7 vols. (Medina: Mujamma' al-Malik Fahd li-Ṭibā'at al-Muṣḥaf al-Sharīf, 1426/2005) 6:2274-2276, Type 78, beginning.

al-Bayḍāwī's main sources:
1. His reworking and purging of al-Zamakhsharī's *Kashshāf*

The *Anwār* has been called "the leading abridgment" of Jār Allāh al-Zamakhsharī's *Kashshāf* (*sayyid al-mukhtaṣarāt minh*) or, more precisely, "an emendation, expurgation and abridgment" (*tahdhīb wa-tanqīḥ wa-ikhtiṣār*) and "thoroughgoing revision" of it[113]—in either case Jār Allāh proving to be al-Bayḍāwī's principal source as for so many others in the golden age of Persianate marginalia on the *Kashshāf* that was the long eighth century (680-816).[114] Jār Allāh and al-Bayḍāwī do cover the same aspects:

(i) morphology, establishing the form or forms of each word;

(ii) etymology, mentioning the various schools of grammar and the Quranic verses, hadiths and poetic examples adduced by each in support of their respective positions (al-Bayḍāwī never fails to clarify his own preference in the process);

[113] "Abridgment": Ibn al-Subkī in *Ṭabaqāt al-Shāfiʿiyya al-Kubrā*, al-Suyūṭī in *Ṭabaqāt al-Lughawiyyīn wal-Nuḥāt* and others; "master abridgment": al-Suyūṭī in the *Nawāhid* and Ḥājjī Khalīfa in *Kashf al-Ẓunūn*; "emendation, expurgation and abridgment": Khvānṣārī, *Rawḍāt al-Jannat* (5:128); "thoroughgoing revision": Calverley-Pollock, *Nature, Man and God* (1:xxxiii).

[114] By Būshakānī (d. 680/1282), Quṭb Shīrāzī (634-710/1237-1311), Nasafī (d. 710/1311), Ṭībī (d. 743/1343), Qazwīnī (d. 745/1345), Jārabardī (d. 746/1346), al-Fāḍil al-Yamanī (d. 750?/1349?), Quṭb Rāzī (d. 766/1365), Bābirtī (d. 786/1384), Taftāzānī (722-792/1322-1390), Bulqīnī (724-805/1324-1403), Sayyid Jurjānī (740-816/1340-1413)... Jār Allāh himself was influenced by the Shāfiʿī ʿAbd al-Qāhir Jurjānī's (d. 471/1079) landmark *Dalāʾil al-Iʿjāz* and *Asrār al-Balāgha* which codified what became 'composition theory' (*naẓariyyat al-naẓm*) in Quranic syntax. See Ḥātim Ṣāliḥ al-Ḍāmin, *Naẓariyyat al-Naẓm: Tārīkh wa-Taṭawwur* (Baghdad: Manshūrāt Wizārat al-Thaqāfa wal-Iʿlām, 1399/1979); Darwīsh al-Jundī, *Naẓariyyat ʿAbd al-Qāhir fil-Naẓm* (Cairo: Maktabat Nahḍat Miṣr, 1960) and *al-Naẓm al-Qurʾānī fil-Kashshāf* (Cairo: Maktabat Nahḍat Miṣr, 1969); Aḥmad Badawī, *ʿAbd al-Qāhir al-Jurjānī*, 2nd ed. (Cairo: Maktabat Miṣr, 1962); Jāḥiẓ, Rummānī, Khaṭṭābī and Jurjānī, *Rasāʾil fil-Iʿjāz* in *Iʿjāz al-Qurʾān al-Karīm ʿAbr al-Tārīkh*, ed. ʿĪsā Bullāṭā (Beirut: al-Muʾassasat al-ʿArabiyya, 2006) pp. 27-86; and Badri N. Zubir, *Balāghah as an Instrument of Qurʾān Interpretation: A Study of al-Kashshāf* (Kuala Lumpur: IIUM Press, 2008).

(iii) phonetics, establishing how words are pronounced in close conjunction with form, notably for *alif lām mīm* (verse 2:1);

(iv) syntax and grammar, establishing in what way or ways the verses' verbal units form clauses in order to supply meanings—frequently through lexical and syntactic polysemy or invariability;

(v) historical canonicity of the text as Quranic and variants of irregular (*shādhdh*) readings;

(vi) the merits of verses and suras mentioned in the hadiths.

Yet everything is in the Qadi's reworking and, of course, he parts ways with his source in both content and form. From the viewpoints of doctrinal authority and multi-discipline coverage, furthermore, the *Anwār* claimed superiority to the *Kashshāf* on the following fronts:

- al-Bayḍāwī showed greater mastery of the Qur'ān's intra-textuality and "self-exegesis" (*tafsīr al-Qur'ān bil-Qur'ān*) as well as inter-textual illustrative proofs from the Hadith—the two primary authoritative sources for exegesis—and the sayings of the leading Companions and Successors.[115]

- al-Bayḍāwī connected Quranic proof-texts to their legal applications and rulings better than Zamakhsharī, principally with reference to the two main schools of his region at the time, the Shāfi'ī then the Ḥanafī. Of particular note are his citations of the principal reference-works in the two schools, such as Abū Isḥāq al-Shīrāzī's *al-Tanbīh fīl-Fiqh*—which he commented in a separate work[116]—and his *Muhadhdhab*; Ghazālī's *al-Wajīz*; and al-Kāsānī's (d. 587/1191) *Badā'i' al-Ṣanā'i'*. He even quoted from Suḥnūn's (160-240/777-854) *Mudawwana* in Mālikī *fiqh*.

[115] Cf. 'Ali, *al-Bayḍāwī wa-Manhajuh* (pp. 32-45 and 46-64).
[116] Cf. 'Alī, *al-Bayḍāwī wa-Manhajuh* (pp. 28-29).

As a rule he did not source his citations, in keeping with the unencumbered practice of compendia.[117]

• He adduced points of legal principles taken from al-Ghazālī's *Mustaṣfā* and al-Rāzī's *Maḥṣūl*, which he also used in his own book on *uṣūl al-fiqh*, the *Minhāj*, while Zamakhsharī's approach lacks this aspect entirely. Furthermore, he was more adept than his predecessor at expounding the interpretive dichotomies of meaning-inference from proof-texts such as "unqualified versus qualified" (*al-muṭlaq wal-muqayyad*), "general versus specific" (*al-ʿāmm wal-khāṣṣ*) etc. as he had already codified these categories in his works on legal theory, especially the *Minhāj*. This, moreover, allowed him to reference *ʿulūm al-Qurʾān* (hermeneutics) and its role in textual exposition better than Zamakhsharī.[118]

• al-Bayḍāwī benefited greatly from al-Zamakhsharī in explaining the huge role of rhetoric in the unfolding of the miraculous linguistic inimitability of the Qurʾān, but he explained that role more successfully and with greater transparency.[119]

• al-Zamakhsharī's approach to syntax and etymology heavily relies on Sībawayh (148-180 /765-796), Abū ʿAlī al-Fārisī (288-377/901-987) and his student Ibn Jinnī (322-395/934-1005), which at times produces exegesis in isolation of established views, as if in a vacuum. Al-Bayḍāwī, however, casts a wider net of grammatical tradition and includes into his purview many

[117] Cf. ʿAlī, *al-Bayḍāwī wa-Manhajuh* (pp. 75-79).

[118] Cf. ʿAlī, *al-Bayḍāwī wa-Manhajuh* (pp. 80-83).

[119] See ʿAbd al-Raḥmān al-Shihrī's second audio lesson on *Anwār al-Tanzīl* posted at http://ar.islamway.net/lesson/132243, around 25'25" and 56'50". Al-Shihrī teaches Qurʾān and its sciences at King Saʿūd University in Riyadh and is the director of that city's Markaz Tafsīr lil-Dirāsāt al-Qurʾāniyya. As a result he tends to rail without compunction against al-Bayḍāwī and al-Rāzī's Ashʿarism, which he libels as "meaning-corruption" (*taḥrīf*), going so far as to accuse the latter of having "greatly damaged the science of grammar and the science of exegesis" (third audio lesson around 16')!

more authorities such as Khalīl al-Farāhīdī (100-178/719-794), Thaʿlab [Aḥmad b. Yaḥyā al-Shaybānī] (200-291/816-904), al-Zajjāj (241-311/855-923), Abū Manṣūr al-Azharī (282-370/895-980), al-Mubarrid (210-286/825-899) and others.[120] When, for example, the *Kashshāf* claims that *ṣalāt* is thus named "because the praying person moves his buttocks" (*ṣalā*, dual *ṣalawayn*), al-Bayḍāwī rejects that view and reasserts the derivation of *ṣalāt* as a transference or metaphorization (*naql*) of the literal meaning of *ṣallā* ʿhe supplicatesʾ to apply to *ṣalāt* and its forms from beginning to end, in line with past and future exegetes.[121]

Bayḍāwī's refutation of the non-Sunni sects in his *Tafsīr*

• He refuted al-Zamakhsharī's Muʿtazili doctrinal stances as well as others of the non-Sunni sects in a rapid-fire succession of points on many key issues, among them:

(i) the Muʿtazili concept of "the [third] station between the two stations [of heaven and hell];"[122]

(ii) the Muʿtazili denial of intercession;[123]

(iii) the Muʿtazili claims that it is obligatory for Allah to reward good-doers and that He has no choice but to always do "what is fittest and best" (*al-aṣlaḥ/al-aḥsan*);[124]

[120] Cf. ʿAlī, *al-Bayḍāwī wa-Manhajuh* (pp. 84-89). See our biographical glossary on these grammarians.

[121] Cf. al-Suyūṭī, *Nawāhid* (1:305).

[122] In his discussion of the definition of *īmān* under al-Baqara 2:3 and his discussion of *fāsiq* under 2:26. Cf. ʿAlī, *al-Bayḍāwī wa-Manhajuh* (pp. 317-318).

[123] In his discussion of *wa-lā hum yunṣarūn* under al-Baqara 2:48 and *khulūd* under 2:25. Cf. ʿAlī, *al-Bayḍāwī wa-Manhajuh* (pp. 319-321).

[124] In his commentary on *Māliki yawm al-dīn* under al-Fātiḥa 1:4, the reinforcement of the unbelievers' rebellion in 2:15 and on *mādhā arāda-l-Lāhu bi-hādhā mathalan* under al-Baqara 2:26. Also his statement in his commentary on *uʿbudū Rabbakum al-ladhī khalaqakum* (al-Baqara 2:21) that the obedient servant is not obligatorily entitled to divine reward and his commentary on *anna lahum jannāt* (al-Baqara 2:25).

(iv) the Mu'tazili and Qadari claim that Allah does not create the acts of evil-doers;[125]

(v) the Mu'tazili and Shi'i claim that Allah is not literally seen on the Day of Resurrection;[126]

(vi) the Mu'tazili and Shi'i claim that the Qur'ān is created;[127]

(vii) the Mu'tazili claim that God-given sustenance (*rizq*) necessarily excludes the illicit;[128]

(viii) the Mu'tazili and Karrāmī claim that Allah creates His own will;[129]

(ix) the Mu'tazili doctrine that paradise and hell have not yet been created;[130]

(x) the Mu'tazili claim that human reason is the arbiter of right and wrong rather than divine law;[131]

(xi) the Ḥashwiyya claim that prophets are not infallible;[132]

(xii) the Shi'i claim that 'Alī b. Abī Ṭālib was appointed by Quranic stipulation as successor to the Prophet—upon him and his house blessings and peace;[133]

Also in his commentary on *mā kānū li-yu'minū illā an yashā'a Allāh* under al-An'ām 6:111, cf. 'Alī, *al-Bayḍāwī wa-Manhajuh* (pp. 321-323).

[125] In his discussion of the divine "sealing" and "misguiding" under al-Baqara 2:7, the divine "scoffing" and reinforcement of the unbelievers' rebellion in 2:15 and *mādhā arāda-l-Lāhu bi-hādhā mathalan* under al-Baqara 2:26.

[126] In his commentary on *ilā Rabbihā nāẓiratun* under al-Qiyāma 75:23 cf. 'Alī, *al-Bayḍāwī wa-Manhajuh* (pp. 323-325).

[127] In his discussion of the Qur'ān citing past historical events under al-Baqara 2:6.

[128] In his commentary on *wa-mimmā razaqnāhum yunfiqūn* under al-Baqara 2:3.

[129] In his discussion of *in shā'a-l-Lāh* under al-Baqara 2:70.

[130] In his discussion on *u'iddat lil-kāfirīn* under al-Baqara 2:24.

[131] In his discussion on who defines what the *ṣāliḥāt* are under al-Baqara 2:25.

[132] Under *fa-azallahumā al-shayṭān* (al-Baqara 2:36) cf. 'Alī, *Bayḍāwī* (pp. 326-328).

[133] In his commentary on *waliyyukum Allāhu wa-Rasūluhu wal-ladhīna āmanū* under al-Mā'ida 5:55 cf. 'Alī, *al-Bayḍāwī wa-Manhajuh* (pp. 329-322).

(xiii) the Shiʿi claims that *Ahl al-Bayt* are Fāṭima, ʿAlī and their two children exclusively; that the relatives of the Prophet—upon him and his house blessings and peace—such as the above and the Twelve Imams are infallible; and that their consensus is an irrefutable proof;[134]

(xiv) the Muʿtazili claim that humans are all inferior to angels;[135]

(xv) and the Muʿtazili and Qadari claim that Allah does not know of things before they come into being.[136]

Controverted aspects in *Anwār al-Tanzīl*

Although Qadi al-Bayḍāwī aimed to expunge the *Kashshāf* of its "rank Muʿtazilism"[137] he did not completely succeed, as can be gleaned from what al-Suyūṭī calls "*Kashshāf* copyism" (see note 1174) in his erotically-entitled supercommentary *Nawāhid al-Abkār wa-Shawārid al-Afkār*, a finding supported by other Sunni readings of the first or both of the two works, such as

- *al-Intiṣāf min al-Kashshāf* by the Mālikī Nāṣir al-Dīn Aḥmad b. Muḥammad b. Manṣūr al-Jarawī al-Iskandarī, known as Ibn al-Munayyir (620-683/1223-1284);
- *Shaddākat al-Muʿtazila* by Ibn al-ʿAmīd Atqānī (d. 758/1357);
- *Tajrīd al-Kashshāf* by Ibn Abī al-Qāsim (769-837/1368-1434);
- *al-Itḥāf bi-Tamyīz mā Tabiʿa fīhi al-Bayḍāwī Ṣāḥib al-Kashshāf* by al-Suyūṭī's student the Mālikī *Sīra* historian Muḥammad b.

[134] In his commentary on *li-yudhhiba ʿankumu al-rijsa ahla al-bayt* under al-Aḥzāb 33:33 cf. ʿAlī, *al-Bayḍāwī wa-Manhajuh* (pp. 332-333).
[135] At the very end of his commentary on *qāla yā Ādamu anbiʾhum* (al-Baqara 2:33). See our article "The title *Best of Creation*" at http://www.livingislam.org/n/bc_e.html
[136] At the very end of his commentary on *qāla yā Ādamu anbiʾhum* (al-Baqara 2:33), cf. Imām al-Ḥaramayn, *al-Irshād ilā Qawāṭiʿ al-Adilla* (p. 256, *dhamm al-qadariyya*).
[137] Khvānṣārī, *Rawḍāt al-Jannat* (5:128).

ʿAlī al-Ṣāliḥī (d. 942/1536);

- *Kashf al-Aqwāl al-Mubtadhala fī Sabqi Qalam al-Bayḍāwī li-Madhhab al-Muʿtazila* by Aḥmad al-Nūbī (d. 1037?/1627?);
- *Rafʿ al-Ikhtilāf ʿan Kalāmay al-Qāḍī wal-Kashshāf* by Shaykh ʿAbd al-Ghanī al-Nābulusī (1050-1143/1640-ca.1730);
- *al-Inṣāf bil-Muḥākama bayna al-Tamyīz wal-Itḥāf* by Murtaḍā al-Zabīdī (1145-1205/1732-1790),
- and recent studies of uneven reliability.[138]

The first of the aspects mentioned in the previous section—al-Bayḍāwī's greater mastery of probative exegetical proof-texts from the two main sources of the Qur'ān and Sunna—shines in his Ashʿarī fine-tuning[139] of al-Zamakhsharī's over-interpretive stance on the Divine Attributes, his inappropriate take on Prophetic infallibility and his overall lack of mastery in Hadith. Yet, at times, the Qadi reduplicates those and other failings part and parcel, for example neglecting to inject—in his commentary on al-Baqara 2:10—a qualifier that would turn the Muʿtazili asser-

[138] See Ṣāliḥ al-Ghāmidī, *al-Masā'il al-Iʿtizāliyya fī Tafsīr al-Kashshāf lil-Zamakhsharī fī Ḍaw'i mā Warada fī Kitāb al-Intiṣāf li-bnil-Munayyir: ʿArḍ wa-Naqd*, 2 vols. (Ḥā'il (Saudi Arabia): Dār al-Andalus, 1418/1998)—with the caveat that as an anti-Ashʿarī Wahhabi, al-Ghāmidī is unreliable: he undermines Ibn al-Munayyir at every turn and leans to Qadarism on the one hand (e.g., denying *kasb*) and anthropomorphism on the other; Muḥammad Ḥusayn al-Dhahabī, *al-Tafsīr wal-Mufassirūn* (1:211); Yūsuf Aḥmad ʿAlī, *al-Bayḍāwī wa-Manhajuh* (pp. 65-68, 91-99, 246-255); Lutpi Ibrahim, *Theological Questions*; the Ḥashwī authors of *al-Mawsūʿat al-Muyassara fī Tarājim A'immat al-Tafsīr wal-Iqrā' wal-Naḥw wal-Lugha*, ed. Walīd al-Zubayrī et al. (Manchester and Medina: Majallat al-Ḥikma, 1424/2003) 2:1378-1383; the genuinely outraged Fāṭima Mardīnī, *al-Tafsīr wal-Mufassirūn* (pp. 84-85); and the morbidly prejudiced Sharīfa Aḥmad al-Mālikī, *al-Bayḍāwī wa-Ārā'uh al-Iʿtiqādiyya: ʿArḍ wa-Naqd min Khilāl Tafsīrih*, unpub. Master's diss. (Mecca: Jāmiʿat Umm al-Qurā, 1430/2009).

[139] See the description of Ashʿarī's "middle road" on many points of doctrine between the opposite extremes of Muʿtazilism and anthropomorphism in Ibn ʿAsākir, *Tabyīn Kadhib al-Muftarī*, ed. Aḥmad Ḥijāzī al-Saqqā (Beirut: Dār al-Jīl, 1995) pp. 150-151.

tion that "*kadhib* ⁽lying⁾ is categorically prohibited in its entirety" into the agreed-upon orthodox position, which is that some types of *kadhib* are indeed established as licit. This is promptly pointed out by Suyūṭī in his supercommentary. On *ḥadhara-l-mawt* ⁽for fear of death⁾ (al-Baqara 2:19) Bayḍāwī sides with the Mu'tazili definition of death as pure inexistence, interpreting away *khalaqa* ⁽created⁾ in the verse *Who created death and life* (al-Mulk 67:2) as "appointed" whereas the Ash'arī-Sunni position is that death is an accident (*'araḍ*) and that it is actually created, as pointed out again by al-Suyūṭī.[140] On *al-ḥajar* ⁽stones⁾ in the verse *beware the fire whose fuel is people and stones* (al-Baqara 2:24), Bayḍāwī begins by saying "they are the idols they carved and worshipped... It was also said they are the gold and silver they used to hoard." He then mentions, as a third possible gloss, "it was also said they are brimstone—a pinpointing that has no proof." In saying this he follows Zamakhsharī's position, which itself is the weak and baseless one since the gloss of the *ḥijāra* as brimstone is well-established in the earliest *tafsīr*s and the vast majority of subsequent ones as pointed out by al-Suyūṭī and al-Khafājī. Likewise he interprets away the *kursī* in al-Baqara 2:255 as imagery, not reality and again is called out by al-Suyūṭī.

Al-Bayḍāwī also followed the *Kashshāf* in (i) doubting the authenticity of an undeniably sound and famous hadith ("No newborn is born except the devil touches it at the time of its birth whereupon it begins to cry from that touch except Maryam and her son"[141]) and (ii) dismissing any notion of literal touch as mere *takhyīl wa-taṣwīr* ⁽imagery and visualization⁾ in the commentary

[140] This issue runs parallel to the Mu'tazili, Bahai and Christian claim that evil and death are "insubstantial" and "do not have an objective reality" but "are only the absence of good/life" cf. Augustine of Hippo's doctrine in *De civitate Dei*. See note 766.

[141] al-Bukhārī, *Ṣaḥīḥ* (*Anbiyā', Bāb qawlihi ta'ālā Wa-dhkur fīl-Kitābi Maryam*); Muslim, *Ṣaḥīḥ* (*Faḍā'il, Bāb faḍā'il 'Īsā 'alayhi al-Salām*).

on the supplication of Maryam's mother at the time of her birth (Āl 'Imrān 3:35-36). Al-Khafājī, Ibn Ḥajar and especially al-Suyūṭī[142] trounced this interpretation just as al-Rāzī, al-Taftāzānī and Ibn al-Munayyir had done before them. Ibn Ḥajar pointed out that the hadith does not problematize the doctrine of Prophetic infallibility as it does not preclude other than Maryam and her son being similarly protected (contrary to al-Ṭībī's musing that it may be exclusive to the two of them) in light of other verses such as *I verily shall adorn the path of error for them in the earth and I shall mislead them every one except such of them as are Your perfectly devoted slaves* (al-Ḥijr 15:39-40, cf. 15:42; al-Isrā' 17:65; Ṣād 38:82-83).[143]

Likewise Bayḍāwī was seen as imitating Zamakhsharī's rude attribution of a *zalla* (lapse) to the Prophet—upon him blessings and peace—in his sworn avoidance of his concubine Māriya the Copt implied in the verse, *O Prophet! Why do you make prohibited that which Allah made lawful for you,* etc. (al-Taḥrīm 66:1).[144] The Qadi did the same in his commentary on *lā a'budu mā ta'budūn* (al-Kāfirūn 109:2), in the claim that in pre-Islamic times the polytheists "were labeled (*kānū mawsūmīn*) as worshipping idols, just as he was not labeled as worshipping Allah" although he himself stated elsewhere "he had worshipped according to a revealed law before Islam" and weakened the view that he had not—in conformity with Sunni consensus.[145]

[142] al-Suyūṭī, *Nawāhid* (2:522-523).

[143] See Ibn Ḥajar, *Fatḥ al-Bārī bi-Sharḥ Ṣaḥīḥ al-Bukhārī*, ed. Muḥammad Fu'ād 'Abd al-Bāqī et al., 13 vols. (Beirut, Dār al-Ma'rifa, 1379/1959) 8:212 (*Tafsīr* Āl 'Imrān 3:36).

[144] Al-Khafājī took Bayḍāwī to task for this just as Ibn al-Munayyir had lashed at al-Zamakhsharī for it, cf. Yūsuf Aḥmad 'Alī, *al-Bayḍāwī wa-Manhajuh* (pp. 249-250), and this rudeness was the reason al-Taqī al-Subkī stopped teaching the *Kashshāf*.

[145] al-Bayḍāwī, *Minhāj al-Wuṣūl ilā 'Ilm al-Uṣūl*, ed. Muṣṭafā Shaykh Muṣṭafā (Beirut: Mu'assasat al-Risāla, 2006) p. 73 (*fil-Sunna, al-mas'ala al-khāmisa*). Cf. 'Alī, *al-Bayḍāwī wa-Manhajuh* (pp. 253-255). These are the type of lapses implied in the gibe

2. al-Rāghib's *Mufradāt* and his *Tafsīr*

Next in order of importance of inspiration in the *Anwār* among the books of *tafsīr* come the works of two major Khurasanian Ashʿarī authorities with a predilection for linguistics and rhetoric: al-Rāghib al-Aṣfahānī and al-Fakhr al-Rāzī.

Al-Ḥusayn b. Muḥammad b. al-Mufaḍḍal, known as Abū al-Qāsim al-Rāghib al-Aṣfahānī (d. 502/ca.1108) and cited by al-Rāzī "among our [Shāfiʿī-Ashʿarī] colleagues (*min aṣḥābinā*),"[146] produced several exegetical works, among them (i) a *tafsīr* (yet unpublished but for Sūrat Āl ʿImrān and two thirds of al-Nisā');[147] (ii) his magnum opus, the erudite *Mufradāt Alfāẓ al-Qur'ān*, framed as a glossary of *gharīb* or difficult terms of Qur'ān as shown by its alternate title of *al-Mufradāt fī Gharīb al-Qur'ān*—Abū Ḥayyān's student the Syro-Egyptian exegete al-Samīn al-Ḥalabī (d. 756/1355) critiqued it and expanded on it in *'Umdat al-Ḥuffāẓ fī Tafsīr Ashraf al-Alfāẓ*; and (iii) *Ḥall Mutashābihāt al-Qur'ān*, also known by the alternate titles of *Durrat al-Ta'wīl fī Mutashābih al-Tanzīl* and *Kashf Mushkilāt al-Qur'ān*, a work dedicated to the elucidation of obscure meanings and seemingly contradictory passages as its last title indicates, in the tradition of similarly-named works.[148]

that al-Zamakhsharī "misled many of those who do not normally hold false positions into promoting many false exegeses... when they themselves knew and believed otherwise." Aḥmad b. Taymiyya, *Muqaddima fī Uṣūl al-Tafsīr* (Beirut: Dār Maktabat al-Ḥayāt, 1980) p. 38. The latter (661-728/1263/1328) had no knowledge of Bayḍāwī.

146 al-Rāzī, *Asās al-Taqdīs*, ed. Aḥmad Ḥijāzī al-Saqqā (Cairo: Maktabat al-Kulliyyāt al-Azhariyya, 1406/1986) p. 17.

147 al-Rāghib al-Aṣfahānī, *Tafsīr al-Rāghib al-Aṣfahānī: min awwal sūrat Āl ʿImrān wa-ḥattā nihāyat al-āya 113 min sūrat al-Nisā'*, ed. ʿĀdil ʿAlī al-Shidī, 2 vols. (Riyadh: Madār al-Waṭan lil-Nashr, 1424/2003).

148 Such as Ibn Qutayba's (213-276/828-886) *Ta'wīl Mushkil al-Qur'ān*, Ibn Fūrak's (330-406/942-1015) *Mushkil al-Ḥadīth wa-Bayānuh*, Bayān al-Ḥaqq al-Naysābūrī's (d. 553/1158) *Bāhir al-Burhān fī Maʿānī Mushkilāt al-Qur'ān*, and Ibn ʿAbd al-Salām's

3. al-Rāzī's *Mafātīḥ al-Ghayb*

Another Shāfiʿī savant and doctrinaire (*mutakallim*), the *Shaykh al-Islām*, jurisprudent, philologist, genealogist, heresiographer, logician and physician Abū ʿAbd Allāh Muḥammad b. ʿUmar al-Qurashī al-Bakrī al-Taymī al-Ṭabaristānī, known as Ibn al-Khaṭīb and as Fakhr al-Dīn al-Rāzī (543-606/1148-1209), produced *Mafātīḥ al-Ghayb* (Keys to the Invisible), also known as *al-Tafsīr al-Kabīr*, generally hailed as a masterpiece of erudition and perhaps the greatest *tafsīr bil-ra'y* in the literature, in 12 to 30 volumes depending on the edition. The author spent the last fifteen years of his life writing it and died before finishing it.[149] He included in it his knowledge of the natural sciences of his time, Arabic grammar, rhetoric and philology, as well as the various positions of the scholars of *fiqh* (particularly the Shāfiʿī school), *kalām*, logic and philosophy, with frequent references to Hadith, *Sīra* and hermeneutical literature (notably Wāḥidī's *Tafsīrs*). He forwarded his doctrinal preferences in refutation of the Qur'anic commentaries of non-Sunnis (such as the Muʿtazilis al-Aṣamm, al-Jubbā'ī, Qāḍī ʿAbd al-Jabbār, al-Kaʿbī, Abū Muslim al-Aṣfahānī and al-Zamakhsharī) and non-Shāfiʿīs (particularly Ḥanafīs). The exegete Abū Ḥayyān al-Andalusī criticized its prolixity in acerbic terms[150] while the Ḥanafī Maḥmūd al-Ālūsī gave point-by-point replies in defense of his school in his own commentary entitled *Rūḥ al-Maʿānī*. A contemporary wrote:

(577-660/ca.1181-1262) luminous *Fawā'id fī Mushkil al-Qur'ān*. More recent efforts —by non-Ashʿarī scholars—include *Dafʿ Īhām al-Iḍṭirāb ʿan Āyāt al-Kitāb* by the late Muḥammad al-Amīn al-Shinqīṭī and Aḥmad al-Quṣayyir's 2007 doctoral thesis at Jāmiʿat Umm al-Qurā, *al-Aḥādīth al-Mushkila al-Wārida fī Tafsīr al-Qur'ān al-Karīm*.

149 Cf. Ibn Khallikān, *Wafayāt al-Aʿyān wa-Anbā' Abnā' al-Zamān*, ed. Iḥsān ʿAbbās, 8 vols. (Beirut: Dār al-Thaqāfa, rept. Dār Ṣādir, 1972) 1:249.

150 To the point he said: "One of the scholars said that his *Tafsīr* contains everything but *tafsīr*!" cf Ḥajjī Khalīfa, *Kashf al-Ẓunūn* (1:431).

> [al-Rāzī] gave the science of *tafsīr* its due in full.... I could cite a thousand proofs to this effect. Among its excellences is its near-complete exemption of Israelite reports: whenever he mentions one it is only in order to show its falsehood, as he did in the stories of Hārūt and Mārūt, Dāwūd and Sulaymān. He also addressed the narrations that cast aspersions on the Prophet's infallibility and demonstrated their falsehood, as in the story of the cranes.[151]

The *Mafātīḥ* was completed first by al-Rāzī's student *Qāḍī al-quḍāt* Shams al-Dīn Aḥmad b. Khalīl al-Khuwayy al-Dimashqī (d. 637/1240),[152] then by Najm al-Dīn Aḥmad b. Muḥammad al-Qamūlī (d. 727/1327).[153] It has been claimed (by al-Shihāb al-Khafājī in *Sharḥ al-Shifā* and Ḥājjī Khalīfa in *Kashf al-Ẓunūn*) that al-Rāzī stopped at Sūrat al-Anbiyā' but a study by ʿAbd al-Raḥmān al-Maʿallamī (1895-1966) asserts that al-Rāzī's hand shows for Sūras 1-28, 37-46, 57-59 and 67-114; furthermore, the continuator was most probably Shams al-Dīn al-Khuwayy alone since internal clues make al-Qamūlī implausible.[154]

[151] Muḥammad Abū Shahba, *al-Isrā'īliyyāt wal-Mawḍūʿāt fī Kutub al-Tafsīr*, 4th ed. (Cairo: Maktabat al-Sunna, 1408/1988) p. 134. See also ʿAbd al-ʿAzīz al-Majdūb, *al-Imām al-Ḥakīm Fakhr al-Dīn al-Rāzī min Khilāl Tafsīrih* (Tunis: Dār Suḥnūn; Beirut: Dār Ibn Ḥazm, 1429/2008) and Michel Lagarde, *Les secrets de l'invisible: Essai sur le Grand Commentaire de Faḫr al-Dîn al-Râzî* (Beirut: Albouraq, 2008). Contrary to Abū Shahba's assumption, al-Ṭabarī and other hadith-strong authorities authenticated the story of the cranes cf. Ibn Ḥajar, *Fatḥ* (8:439-440); al-Bayḍāwī rejects it under al-Najm but assumes its correctness under al-Ḥajj 22:52-55 and al-Kūrānī validates the latter as the correct position: "He—upon him peace—only uttered those words after their casting forth by the devil impersonating the angel by Allah's enablement as a test... not from his own caprice." *al-Lumʿat al-Saniyya fī Taḥqīq al-Ilqā' fīl-Umniyya*, ed. and transl. Alfred Guillaume, *Bulletin of the SOAS* 20 no. 1/3 (1957) pp. 291-303.

[152] In Ibn Abī Uṣaybiʿa (d. 668/1270), *ʿUyūn al-Anbā' fī Ṭabaqāt al-Aṭibbā'*, ed. Nizār Riḍā (Beirut: Dār Maktabat al-Ḥayāt, n.d.) p. 647. Ibn Abī Uṣaybiʿa was a student of both al-Rāzī and al-Khuwayy.

[153] In Ibn al-Subkī, *Ṭabaqāt al-Shāfiʿiyya al-Kubrā* (9:31).

[154] ʿAbd al-Raḥmān al-Maʿallamī, *Majmūʿ fīhi... Baḥth Ḥawla Tafsīr al-Rāzī*, ed. Mājid ʿAbd al-ʿAzīz al-Ziyādī (Mecca: al-Maktaba al-Makkiyya, 1417/1996) pp. 99-134.

In language al-Bayḍāwī also relies on other works according to need, such as Abū al-Baqā' al-'Ukbarī's (538-616/1144-1219) grammatical analyses of the Qur'ān *al-Tibyān fī I'rāb al-Qur'ān* and *I'rāb al-Qirā'āt al-Shawādhdh* among others.[155]

Sufism in *Anwār al-Tanzīl*

While *Anwār al-Tanzīl* is not considered a Sufi work, its spiritual overtones bear the same unmistakable stamp of classical *taṣawwuf* as do the intense devotionalism and treatment of the Prophet Muḥammad's perfected attributes and intercessory status in al-Bayḍāwī's *Tasbī' al-Burda* ("Sevening" of Būṣīrī's panegyric poem the *Burda*). These aspects often match it with earlier Khurasanian *tafsīr*s more eminently described as such—by al-Tustarī, al-Sulamī, al-Qushayrī and Ruzbihan Baqli. In the Fātiḥa for example, Bayḍāwī observes that *iyyāka na'budu wa-iyyāka nasta'īn* ⁽You do we worship and You do we ask for help⁾ (al-Fātiḥa 1:5) shows a grammatical shift in discourse from the third person in the first four verses to the second, the famous *iltifāt* ⁽apostrophic redirection⁾ of Arabic stylistics; but his point is to introduce the Sunni and Sufi doctrine of *mushāhada/ru'ya* ⁽vision of Allah⁾ and show "absence becoming vision":

> [This] forms a progression from demonstration to sight and a move from absence to witnessing. It is as if the object of knowledge is now being seen, the rationally conceivable is beheld, and absence turns to presence! ... He followed up with what constitutes the farthest reach of the knower's quest, which is to probe the depth of arrival and become one of the people of reciprocal vision, whereupon he sees Him with his very eyes and converses with Him directly.

He then pauses and makes the reader a partner in his supplication: "O Allah! Make us of those who reach the very source and not just hear the report!" The above passages respectively

[155] Cf. 'Alī, *al-Bayḍāwī wa-Manhajuh* (p. 86-87) and see note 120 above.

paraphrase two Sufi-foundational hadiths: *al-iḥsān an taʿbuda Allāh kaʾannaka tarāh* (Excellence is to worship Allah as if you see Him) and *laysa al-khabaru kal-muʿāyana* (News of something is not like seeing it directly). He then crowns his discourse with the Sufi theme of *fanāʾ* (self-extinction in Allah):

> truly the sage's arrival is realized only when he becomes immersed in awareness of the presence of the Holy One, oblivious to everything else, to the point he is not even aware of himself or any of his own states, except insofar as being is aware of Him and connected to Him.

In his recapitulation of the meanings of *ihdinā al-ṣirāṭa al-mustaqīm* (show us the straight path) (al-Fātiḥa 1:6), al-Bayḍāwī again utters, through a Sufi prosopopœia, an impassioned prayer for self-extinction and vision of Allah:

> What is asked, then, is (i) more of what they were conferred of guidance; (ii) or firmness with it; (iii) or the acquirement of the ranks that result from it. When spoken by the accomplished knower of Allah it means, "Direct us on the path of wayfaring in You so that You will eradicate from us the pitch-darkness of our states and take away the dense screens of our material bodies, so that we can be illuminated with the light of Your holiness and we can see You with Your light!"

The theme of *fanāʾ* as the culmination of spiritual wayfaring recurs in the commentary on *laʿallakum tattaqūn* (perhaps you will beware) (al-Baqara 2:21). The delicious "consimilar fruits" (2:25) enjoyed by the people of paradise are not just food but an allegory of the learning and acts of obedience they were provided in the world, and of how much the latter, also, differ proportionately in pleasure from believer to believer. Another Sufi passage is the comparison of the slaughtering of the Yellow Heifer to the mastering of one's soul made famous by al-Sulamī and al-Qushayrī earlier. Al-Bayḍāwī's own treatment of this comparison in his commentary on al-Baqara 2:73, however, is much more elaborate as he takes care to tie every aspect of the text and subtext of the Quranic and *atharī* accounts to the metaphor of the subdued ego, cementing together tenor and vehicle in the most pointed manner possible:

> whoever wants to know his worst enemy—which strives in every way to inflict death upon him—the way is to slaughter the cow in his own self, namely the appetitive faculty at the time the rapacity of adolescence is gone but the weakness of old age has not yet taken over, when it still excites [his] admiration and looks ravishing [to him], has not yet been brought low in the pursuit of this world and is still free of its stain, without any speck of its disgrace on it. Then the effect of that [slaying] will reach his soul and it will come alive....

The above lines inspired superb comments by Shaykh Zādah and al-Qūnawī which further helped clarify al-Bayḍāwī's design and which we have excerpted in the footnotes. Other passages include the Qadi's denounciation of pseudo-Sufis under the verse *and He left them in darknesses, sightless* (al-Baqara 2:17); his commentary on al-Mā'ida 5:115 ("One of the Sufis said...") and that on the *snorting coursers* in al-ʿĀdiyat (100) as representing the perfect souls *sparking off* gnoses, *slaying* lower desires, *raising up* longing *and entering* the gatherings on high.

The *Anwār* as a textbook and its scholastic marginalia

We have seen how al-Bayḍāwī can be described as possessing the criteria of *ijtihād* listed by Ibn al-Subkī and those of *tafsīr* listed by al-Suyūṭī and al-Haytamī; and, more importantly, how he was able to synthesize various analytical approaches into a seamlessly woven text for the benefit of subsequent generations. This is one of the reasons his *Tafsīr* enjoyed such success in the Muslim world from its earliest emergence—as illustrated by its inclusion in al-Nasafī's *Madārik al-Tanzīl* and its earliest extant supercommentary, *al-Ḥusām al-Māḍī fī Sharḥ Gharīb al-Qāḍī* by Abū Bakr b. Aḥmad b. al-Ṣā'igh al-Ḥanbalī (d. 714/1314)[156]—and became required study in the madrasa curricula of Mamlūk and Ottoman Egypt, Turkey (where *tafsīr*s were mostly supercommentaries on the *Anwār*),[157] Zaytūna in Tunisia and the rest of the Arab world, as well as South and Southeast Asia. It is an indication of its great demand in India that it was the first *tafsīr* printed at NKP, the historical Lucknow press founded in 1858 by Munshi Newal Kishore (1836-1885), a Hindu.[158] The 1912 Cairo edition—together with a 1,100-page *ḥāshiya* by Kāzarūnī (d. after 1102/1691)—was required reading for sixth-year Azhar students[159] and still is today for seventh-year *madrasa* students in parts of the Indian Subcontinent,[160] particularly the first *ḥizb* or first *juz'* which have been translated and commented on their own.[161] Ismāʿīl Bāshā al-Baghdādī (d. 1339/1921) identifies by title and author about 69 complete and partial supercommentaries (*ḥawāshī, taʿlīqāt*) on the *Anwār* in *Īḍāḥ al-Maknūn*; Brockelmann lists 83.[162] The most renowned are, in chronological order, those of Zakariyyā al-Anṣārī, al-Suyūṭī, Ibn Kamāl

[156] Nuwayhiḍ, *Muʿjam al-Mufassirīn* (1:107); *al-Fahras al-Shāmil* (*Tafsīr* 1:320 §2).

[157] Cf. Susan Gunasti, "Political patronage and the writing of Qur'ān commentaries among the Ottoman Turks," *Journal of Islamic Studies* 24/3 (2013) pp. 335-357.

[158] A 2nd ed. print dated 1282/1865 is kept at the library of the University of Oxford.

[159] ʿAfīf al-Dīn Abū al-Faḍl ʿAbd Allāh b. Ḥasan al-Ṣiddīqī al-Kāzarūnī, *Ḥāshiyat al-Kāzarūnī ʿalā Tafsīr al-Bayḍāwī*, ed. Muḥammad al-Zuhrī al-Ghamrāwī, 4 vols. (Cairo: Dār al-Kutub al-ʿArabiyya al-Kubrā, 1330/1912). See Figures 22-24.

[160] Cf. http://www.jamiabinoria.net/darulifta/pages/nisab.htm.

[161] Cf. the edition, Urdu translation and commentary on *Ḥizb* I by Sayyid Fakhrul Ḥasan, *al-Taqrīr al-Ḥāwī fī Ḥall al-Bayḍāwī*, 4 vols. in 1 (Deoband: Kutubkhanah-i Fakhriyah, 1970; rept. Karachi: Islami Kutubkhanah-i, 2004) and the Arabic edition and commentary on *Juz'* I by ʿAbd al-Karīm al-Kawrā'ī (Karachi: Maktabat al-Bushrā, 2010). An annotated ed. of the first *juz'* was penned by Muḥammad Abu al-Ḥasan, *Taysīr al-Bayḍāwī: Taʿlīqāt wa-Sharḥ ʿalā Anwār al-Tanzīl* (Cairo: Dār al-Anṣār, 1979).

[162] Ismāʿīl Bāshā al-Baghdādī, *Kitāb Īḍāḥ al-Maknūn fīl-Dhayl ʿalā Kashf al-Ẓunūn ʿan Asāmī al-Kutub wal-Funūn*, 2 vols. (Teheran: Maktabat al-Islāmiyya wal-Jaʿfarī Tibrīzī, 1967; rept. Beirut: Dār Iḥyā' al-Turāth al-ʿArabī, n.d.) 1:138-142.

Bāshā, ʿIṣām al-Dīn al-Isfarāyīnī, Saʿdī Çelebi, Shaykh Zādah, al-ʿĀmilī, al-Sayālkūtī, al-Khafājī, al-Kāzarūnī and al-Qūnawī, all of which we have used and whose supports we describe in the section on manuscripts and editions' sigla.

Epigones and epitomes

Several major commentaries built on Bayḍāwī's precedent in *tafsīr taḥlīlī* literature. Najm al-Dīn ʿAbd Allāh al-Nasafī's (d. 710/1310) *Madārik al-Tanzīl wa-Ḥaqā'iq al-Ta'wīl* echoed *Anwār al-Tanzīl*'s title and quoted entire passages from it.[163] Jalāl al-Dīn al-Maḥāllī (791-864/1389-1460) wrote a concise *tafsīr* from Surat al-Kahf to the end (with the Fātiḥa) after which Jalāl al-Dīn al-Suyūṭī (849-911/1445-1505) completed it. Then came the larger *al-Sirāj al-Munīr fīl-Iʿānati ʿalā Maʿrifati Baʿḍi Maʿānī Kalām Rabbinā al-Ḥakīm al-Khabīr* by the Cairene al-Shirbīnī (d. 977/1570), *Irshād al-ʿAql al-Salīm ilā Mazāyā al-Kitāb al-Karīm* by the Ottoman mufti Abū al-Suʿūd al-ʿImādī (900-982/1495-1574) and *Rūḥ al-Maʿānī* by al-Ālūsī (1217-1270/1802-1854).

The *Anwār* also received adaptations and anthologies: the qadi, hadith scholar, Prophetologist, heresy-hunter and poet of Beirut and Jerusalem Shaykh Yūsuf b. Ismāʿīl al-Nabhānī (1265-1350/1849-1932) penned the briefest *tafsīr* yet, entitled *Qurrat al-ʿAyn min al-Bayḍāwī wal-Jalālayn*, in which he epitomized the *Anwār* and the *Jalālayn*. This work received several editions. An 843-page epitome of the *Anwār* was also produced in 1984 by another Beirut qadi, Muḥammad b. Aḥmad Kanʿān (1944-2011)—*Mawāhib al-Jalīl min Tafsīr al-Bayḍāwī*—and published, like the *Qurrat al-ʿAyn*, in the margins of the Qur'ān. The same

[163] Cf. Dhahabī, *al-Tafsīr wal-Mufassirūn* (1:217); ʿAṭiyya al-Jubūrī, *Dirāsāt fīl-Tafsīr wa-Rijālih* (Cairo: al-Maṭbaʿa al-ʿArabiyya, 1971) p. 107; ʿAbd al-Ḥalīm Maḥmūd, *Manāhij al-Mufassirīn* (Cairo: Dār al-Kitāb al-Miṣrī and Beirut: Dār al-Kitāb al-Lubnānī, 1421/2000) pp. 217-220; and ʿAlī, *al-Bayḍāwī* (pp. 305-307). This shows the swift spread of the *Anwār* by the time of Bayḍāwī's death.

author published similarly substantial abridgments of the *Manār* and Ibn Kathīr's *Tafsīr*. More recently Zakī Muḥammad Abū Sarī' Faraghlī authored another two-volume epitome, *Irshād al-Sārī ilā Durar Tafsīr al-Bayḍāwī*, published in 1995 in Cairo.

Gradual disuse of the *Anwār*

The trend in the last 75 years, however, has been the shelving of this remarkable work and its replacement by prolix but purportedly more relevant works written in everyday language, paraphrasing or outlining the Qur'ān and aiming to address scientific discoveries or progressive doctrines such as *Tafsīr al-Manār* by the Egyptian reformist Muḥammad 'Abduh and his Lebanese student Muḥammad Rashīd Riḍā who scoffed at what they called

> the dry type of *tafsīr*, alienating one from Allah and His Book, namely that wherewith one aims to analyze vocables and parse sentences and clarify the purpose of those expressions and allusions among other artistic subtleties: such should not be called a *tafsīr* but is rather some kind of training in the artslike grammar, rhetoric and other than that.[164]

Other notable works include *Tafsīr al-Jawharī* by Ṭanṭāwī b. Jawharī; *Tafhīm al-Qur'ān* by Abū al-A'lā al-Mawdūdī, who relatedly influenced Ḥasan Bannā', Ruhollah Khomeini and Sayyid Quṭb; *Fī Ẓilāl al-Qur'ān* by Quṭb; and Marāghī's (d. 1371/1952) *Tafsīr*, which the latter said he wrote "without the proud concision of bygone times but self-explanatory, addressing the need of contemporaries in style and arrangement, easily accessible"[165] Comparable shorter works today include *Taysīr al-Karīm al-Raḥmān fī Tafsīr Kalām al-Mannān* by 'Abd al-Raḥmān al-Sa'dī

164 Muḥammad Rashīd Riḍā, *Tafsīr al-Qur'ān al-Ḥakīm al-Mushtahar bi-ismi Tafsīr al-Manār*, 2nd ed., 12 vols. (Cairo: Dār al-Manār, 1366-1368/1947-1949) 1:24.

165 Aḥmad b. Muṣṭafā al-Marāghī, *Tafsīr al-Marāghī*, 30 vols. (Cairo: Muṣṭafā Babī al-Ḥalabī, 1365/1946), preamble. On 20th-century *tafsīrs* see Faḍl Ḥasan 'Abbās, *al-Mufassirūn: Maḍarisuhum wa-Manāhijuhum* (Amman: Dār al-Nafā'is, 2007).

(1889-1956); the partial *Tafsīr* of Maḥmūd Shalṭūt (1310-1383/1893-1963); *Zahrat al-Tafāsīr* by Muḥammad Abū Zahra (1315-1394/1898-1974); *al-Wajīz fī Tafsīr al-Qur'ān* by the philologist Shawqī Ḍayf (1910-2005); *Zubdat al-Tafsīr*—an abridgment of Shawkānī's *Fatḥ al-Qadīr* by a student of al-Shinqīṭī, Muḥammad Sulaymān Ashqar (1930-2009); *al-Tafsīr al-Manhajī* by Ahmad Nawfal (b. 1946); *al-Tafsīr al-Muyassar* by 'Ā'iḍ al-Qaranī (b. 1959); the anonymized *al-Tafsīr al-Muyassar* at Mujamma' al-Malik Fahd;[166] and *Aysar al-Tafāsīr* by Abū Bakr Jābir al-Jazā'irī (b. 1921)—a Saudi-sponsored bowdlerizing of the *Jalālayn*. Among larger and medium-sized works came the multiple *tafsīrs* of our Syrian teachers Muḥammad 'Alī al-Ṣābūnī (b. 1930), Wahbat al-Zuḥaylī (b. 1932) and 'Abd al-Raḥmān Ḥabannaka (1345-1425/1927-2004); a *tafsīr* by Muḥammad Sayyid Ṭanṭāwī (1928-2010) in Egypt and the 10-volume collective *al-Tafsīr al-Mawḍū'ī* published in Sharjah in 2010. In comparison to the classical tradition some of the above-mentioned works, at times, seem doctrinaire or read like glossaries and paraphrases interspersed with historical notes, or revisionist critiques of past *tafsīrs*. Lastly, all took note of the late Muḥammad Mutawallī al-Sha'rāwī's (1911-1998) *tafsīr*—first televised to Arab audiences then published in print—and *Taḥrīr al-Ma'nā al-Sadīd wa-Tanwīr al-'Aql al-Jadīd fī Tafsīr al-Kitāb al-Majīd*, known as *al-Taḥrīr wal-Tanwīr*, by Muḥammad al-Ṭāhir b. 'Āshūr (1296-1394/1879-1973) rector of Zaytūna, the most accomplished modern *tafsīr*.

The recourse to *Anwār al-Tanzīl* and other *tafsīrs* in primitive and middle Orientalism

The first two (commissioned) translators of the Qur'ān in the medieval West, Robert of Ketton (*Lex Mahumet pseudoprophete*,

[166] By Ḥikmat Bashīr, Ḥāzim Ḥaydar, Muṣṭafā Muslim, 'Abd al-'Azīz Ismā'īl, Bakr Abū Zayd and others, cf. http://www.ahlalhdeeth.com/vb/showthread.php?t=145628

July 1143CE) and Mark of Toledo (*Liber Alchorani*, 1211CE), predated Bayḍāwī but were already making "careful use of Qur'ānic commentaries as they translated" according to a recent study—much more so Ketton, hence his aggressively paraphrastic, *ad sensum* rendering as opposed to Toledo's more cautious *ad verbum* literalism.[167] Ketton

> had altered the meaning of Qur'ānic terms as he translated them; he had often left out what was explicitly in the text but incorporated into his Latin version what was only implicit in the Arabic original.... a freewheeling paraphrase.... [which] nevertheless reflected what Muslims themselves thought to be the meaning of the Qur'ān. The most vivid signs of this are the numerous passages in all parts of his Latin Qur'ān where Robert has incorporated into his paraphrase glosses, explanations, and other exegetical material drawn from one or several Arabic Qur'ānic *tafsīr*s or commentaries.... [T]here is much more to [his] translation than mere paraphrasing.[168]

Later works (Table 1) beginning with the gentleman-litterateur André du Ryer's 1647 French *L'Alcoran*, followed by his Arabic-nescient adapters in English, Dutch and German, then the rabid Catholic Islamophobe Ludovico Marracci's *Alcorani textus* and

[167] See Thomas E. Burman, "*Tafsīr* and Translation: Traditional Arabic Qur'ān Exegesis and the Latin Qur'āns [*sic*] of Robert of Ketton and Mark of Toledo," *Speculum* 73 no. 3 (July 1998) 702-732, esp. 707-711, 726, 730-731, cf. Muhammad Sultan Shah, "The Earliest Translations of the Qur'ān: Latin, French and English," *The Islamic Quarterly* 57 no. 1 (2013) pp. 53-76.

[168] Burman, "*Tafsīr* and Translation" (pp. 705, 707, 710). He goes on to show that Ketton's rendering conforms to Ṭabarī's *Tafsīr*, Rāghib's *Mufradāt* (both of which were in circulation in Muslim Europe at the time) and Zamakhsharī's *Kashshāf*. It became the more popular and boasts 24 extant manuscripts as opposed to the half dozen of the punctilious Toledo, cf. Burman, *Reading the Qur'ān in Latin Christendom, 1140-1560* (Philadelphia: University of Pennsylvania Press, 2007) p. 122. Thus, although *Lex Mahumet* was published only four centuries later (by the German reformist Theodorus 'Bibliander,' a Greek form of the name Buchmann), its manuscript form never hampered its wide reduplication, contrary to the claim that it "remained hidden for nearly four centuries in manuscript form": Shah, "Earliest Translations" (p. 53).

Date, place	Author	Title	Explicit references to *tafsīrs*
1543 Basel	Theodorus Bibliander (ed.)	[Latin] *Lex Saracenorum, quam Alcoran vocant*	None—1st ed. of Ketton's Latin.
1547 [Venice]	Andrea Arrivabene	[Italian] *L'Alcorano di Macometto*	None—translation of the Latin ed.
1616 Nürnberg	H. Salomon Schweiggern	[German] *Alcoranus Mahometicus*	None—translation of the Italian ed.
1647 Paris	André du Ryer	[French] *L'ALCORAN DE MAHOMET*	*Gelaldin, le Bedaoi* [Bayḍāwī] & *Tenoir.*
1648 London	Alexander Ross	[English] *The Alcoran of Mahomet*	Same—translation of du Ryer.
1658 Amsterdam	Glazemaker	[Dutch] *Mahomet's Koran*	Same—translation of du Ryer.
1688 Hamburg	Johan Lange	[German] *Vollstaendiges türckisches Gesetz-Buch oder Alkoran*	Same—translation of Ross.
1698 Padua	Ludovico Marracci	[Latin] *Alcorani textus universus*	Yaḥyā, *Kashshāf*, Tha'labī, Bayḍāwī, *Jalālayn* and more.
1734 London	George Sale	[English] *The Koran* [first direct English translation]	All of the above *tafsīrs* and more.

Table 1: Appeal to *tafsīrs* in early European renderings of Qur'ān—including Bayḍāwī—from du Ryer (1647) to George Sale (1734).

culminating with the landmark 1734 *The Koran: commonly called the Alcoran of Mohammed, translated into English immediatly from the original Arabic: with explanatory notes, taken from the most approved commentators* by George Sale "the leading Arabist of the age,"[169] all explicitly cited these *tafsīrs* or their authors:

[169] Nabil Matar, "Alexander Ross and the first English translation of the Qur'ān," *The Muslim World* 88 no.1 (January 1998) p. 91. "One of Du Ryer's great achievements... is his pioneering use of well-known commentaries on the Qur'ān such as those of al-Bayḍāwī and the *Jalālayn*.... Marracci, Sale and Edward Lane (in *Selections from the Kuran*, 1843) were to follow his lead." Aḥmad Gunny, review of *André du Ryer and Oriental Studies in 17th-c. France, Journal of Islamic Studies* 16 no. 3 (2005) p. 411.

- Yaḥyā b. Sallām al-Taymī al-Baṣrī (124-200/743-815), *Taṣārīf*;
- Abū Isḥāq al-Thaʿlabī (d. 427/1036), *al-Kashf wal-Bayān*;
- al-Zamakhsharī (467-538/1074-1143), *al-Kashshāf*;
- al-Rāzī (543-606/1148-1210), *Mafātīḥ al-Ghayb*;
- al-Bayḍāwī (d. 685/1286), *Anwār al-Tanzīl*;
- al-Fayrūzābādī (729-817/1329-1415), *Tanwīr al-Miqbās*;
- al-Maḥallī (791-864/1389-1460) and al-Suyūṭī, *Jalālayn*.[170]

Western confusion over al-Bayḍāwī's *Tafsīr*

Modern Orientalism reduplicated the misconstruction of al-Bayḍāwī's *Anwār al-Tanzīl* by ʿAbduh, Riḍā and Marāghī as little more than the medieval scholastics of a bygone age; the blindness of its own three patriarchs to the significance of that work is equally staggering. Theodor Nöldeke (1836-1930) imparted—in *Geschichte des Qorâns*, written at age 22—a clueless assessment that was sadly destined to inform every entry on Bayḍāwī in successive editions of the *Encyclopædia of Islam* (characterized below as a "knot of misguided judgment") and other European and American blurbs. Ignaz Goldziher (1850-1921) in his *Richtungen der islamischen Koranauslegung* gave Bayḍāwī all of eight cursory references while discussing other issues. Lastly Snouck Hurgronje (1857-1936) was so unfamiliar with *Anwār al-Tanzīl* that he thought the first Malay *tafsīr*, *Tarjumān al-Mustafīd*, was a translation of it, misleading generations of later publishers and academes into thinking the same (see three sections down). In light of the above it is easy to imagine why the landmark set by Heinrich Fleischer (1801-1888, a graduate of Silvestre de Sacy

[170] See, e.g., André du Ryer, *LAlcoran de Mahomet* (Paris: Antoine de Sommaville, 1647) pp. 8, 29; Ludovico Marracci, *Alcorani textus universus* etc., 2 vols. in 1 (Padua: Ex Typographia Seminarii, 1698) 1:34-41 cf. Carlo A. Nallino, "Le fonti arabe manoscritte dell'opera di Ludovico Marracci sul Corano," *Raccolta di scritti*, 6 vols. (Roma: Istituto per l'Oriente, 1939-48) 2:109 and Sale, *Koran* (London: J. Wilcox, 1734): http://posner.library.cmu.edu/Posner/books/book.cgi?OCLC=1135206.

and teacher to Goldziher) with his 1848 edition of the *Anwār*, the first European edition of any *tafsīr*, never bore fruit—Nöldeke even deplored it as a waste of Fleischer's talent! This amateurism of fin-de-siècle Orientalism (on which modern "Islam studies" are based) is diagnosed well by a Lebanese-Canadian historian of *tafsīr* who, in the process, sums up al-Fāḍil b. ʿĀshūr's analysis of *Anwār al-Tanzīl* as the arch-*tafsīr* of Islamic civilization:

> If one reads the *Encyclopedia of Islam*'s article on al-Bayḍāwī, one can get a fair idea of the sort of judgment befuddling the field of *tafsīr*. Let me quote here a sample from the article: "His works are generally not original, but based on works by other authors. He is noted for the brevity of his treatment of his various subjects, but his works suffer on this account from a lack of completeness, and he has been blamed for inaccuracy. His most famous work is his commentary on the Qur'ān… which is largely a condensed and amended edition of al-Zamakhsharī's *al-Kashshāf*" (*EI*, 2nd edition, *sub* al-Bayḍāwī). The factual information is wrong. The work is based on more than one work; in addition to *al-Kashshāf*, it draws equally on al-Razī's Qur'ān commentary, and the dictionary of al-Rāghib al-Aṣbahānī. But the work is actually a distillation of the whole tradition of *tafsīr*. The author of this encyclopedia entry is, moreoever, unable to explain why this Qur'ān commentary[,] of all the Qur'ān commentaries in Islam, was edited in Europe in the 19th century. He mentions the edition done by H.O. Fleischer in two volumes (Leipzig, 1846-8), which incidentally was badly received. Is it possible that Europe of the mid 19th century was more aware of the significance of al-Bayḍāwī's work than later in its history; that soon the romantic prejudice would make such an interest on the part of Europe out of place? ...
>
> Al-Bayḍāwī's work is indeed a work based on a well-hewn tradition; it is a summary and a polishing of this tradition. The romantic modernist tradition damns such a work as derivative. I do believe that this knot of misguided judgment is impossible to refute simply because it is founded on so many

questionable but in our day axiomatic presuppositions vis-à-vis the medieval tradition. We as modern agents are incapable of not damning the medieval past—and nothing makes us more uncomfortable than the notion of an unoriginal gloss or an epitome, or a hundred-times-over copied summary of a work already summarized. It is simply suffocating. ...

Ibn ʿĀshūr considers al-Bayḍāwī's commentary to be a sifting and a bringing-to-perfection of the six centuries of the *tafsīr* tradition. It summed up the different insights, permitted the reader a clear vision of the scope of the discussions of the Qurʾān and allowed the reader the possibility of using the work as a gateway to the genre. All this was done with the most polished style, a perfection of diction that was the result of the maturation of the genre (Ibn ʿĀshūr 1970: 93). Its simplicity is precisely the source of its complexity, its very nature an invitation for a gloss and for researching anew the history of the tradition. The moment it appeared, it became clear that this was the text par excellence to use in teaching *tafsīr* in seminaries. Its publication also heralded a moment of unification for the genre; here was at last a book on a very complicated field that was unanimously used as the first reference tool by all scholars. After its appearance no one could escape this work. As the text for teaching *tafsīr* in the seminary, al-Bayḍāwī's commentary was glossed by each generation of professors. It was in fact the most glossed text in the history of *tafsīr*. ...

Ibn ʿĀshūr believes that the spread of the teaching of this commentary resulted in the standardization of the higher educational systems (or a unification) in all Muslim lands, with the result that all higher educational system[s] were now following the Persianate method (*al-ṭarīqa al-ʿajamiyya*). ...

Intellectual historians of the modern Middle East have never explained for us why the glosses on al-Zamakhsharī's and al-Bayḍāwī's commentaries were the eaerliest works to be published in the 19th century. But then such a question is impossible to raise as long as we continue to do Islamic religious history the way we have been doing it so far. Such a question has no place yet in our envisioning of the develop-

> ment of the modern Islamic world. Why were these rather voluminous works made consistently available? Part of the answer is that they were essential for the seminary system. As a matter of fact… [t]hey were always published with at least one gloss if not more, thus always embedded in a gloss, surrounded by the apparatus of the seminary system. It is an immense loss for the field that now with the penetration of the romantic ideal into all levels of Muslim society, including that of traditional scholars, the Islamic world has ceased to publish any of these glosses; what little we have available of the glosses were almost published in the 19th century before the dismantling of the Ottoman *madrasa* system.[171]

Qur'ān translation and Post-Kemal Azhari-Salafi fatwas

Al-Sarakhsī (d. 490/1097) in his *Mabsūṭ* attributes—without chain of transmission—a Farsi rendering of the Fātiḥa to Salmān al-Fārisī.[172] Other than the 1606 "Toledo Qur'ān" in Spanish and Shāh Waliyyullāh's (1114-1176/1702-1763) *Fatḥ al-Raḥmān* (a Persian translation he designed for the uneducated public in both literal and interpretive style and throughout which he uses the name *Khudā* for *Allāh*),[173] stand-alone integral Muslim translations of the Qur'ān before late colonial times are a rarity.[174]

[171] Walid A. Saleh, "Marginalia and Peripheries: A Tunisian Historian and the History of Qur'anic Exegesis," *Numen* 58 (2011) pp. 304-309. Cf. Theodor Nöldeke et al., *History of the Qur'ān*, trans. Wolfgang Behn (Leiden: Brill, 2013), p. 356.

[172] Shams al-Dīn al-Sarakhsī, *Kitāb al-Mabsūṭ*, 30 vols. (Cairo: Maṭba'at al-Sa'āda, 1331/1913, rept. Beirut: Dār al-Ma'rifa, n.d.) 1:37.

[173] See *World Bibliography of Translations of the Meanings of the Holy Qur'ān*, ed. Ekmeleddin Ihsanoglu et al. (Istanbul: IRCICA, 1406/1986) pp. 356-364 and study by Miṣbāḥ Allāh 'Abd al-Bāqī, *al-Imām Waliyyullāh al-Dihlawī wa-Tarjamatuhu lil-Qur'ān*, in *Majallat al-Buḥūth wal-Dirāsāt al-Qur'āniyya* vol. 6 (Year 3) pp. 153-260.

[174] See Consuelo López-Morillas, *El Corán de Toledo : edición y estudio del manuscrito 235 de la Biblioteca de Castilla-La Mancha* (Gijón: Trea, 2011). In the brief section entitled "Histoire de la traduction du Coran" in the introduction to his 1959 French translation Muḥammad Ḥamīdullah (1326-1423/1908-2002) cites six pre-seventh/13th century examples of what he calls Persian translations, all of which are *tafsīrs* rather than translations: *al-Qur'ān al-Majīd ma'a Ma'ānīh bil-Faransiyya*, 12th ed.

The translation of the text of the Qur'ān into a non-Arabic medium was—according to prominent latter-day Azhari authorities—a damnable sin. Through the efforts of its erudite "Salafi" Ḥusayni rector at the time, Muḥammad Shākir (1866-1939), al-Azhar University in Cairo recommended in 1925 that English translations of the Qur'ān be burnt; Shākir also published a fatwa in the Egyptian daily *al-Ahrām* and in his essay *al-Qawl al-Faṣl fī Tarjamat al-Qur'ān al-Karīm ilā al-Lughāt al-Aʿjamiyya* (The Final Word on Translating the Noble Qur'ān into non-Arab Languages) that "all who help any Qur'ān translation project will burn in Hell for evermore." The Lebanese "Salafi" hadith scholar Muḥammad Rashīd Riḍā (1282-1354/1865-1935) asserted the same in his 1926 essay *Tarjamat al-Qur'ān wamā fīhā min al-Mafāsid wa-Munāfāt al-Islām* (The Translation of Qur'ān and the Vices and Negation of Islam It Entails), as did another Azhari

(Paris: Dār al-Nūr, 1406/1986), introduction (pp. liii-liv). He states "Au temps du Samanide Mansour ibn Nouh, un comité de savants traduisit en 345H le Coran en Persan, et y ajouta la traduction résumée du commentaire de Tabari;" in reality it was only an oft-recopied abridged translation of Ṭabarī's *Tārīkh* rather than his commentary which Manṣūr's minister Abū ʿAlī Muḥammad al-Balʿamī (d. 386/ 996) had made, cf. Edward G. Browne, *Literary History of Persia* (1:11, 1:356, 1:368-369, 1:477); Charles Storey, *Persian Literature: A Bio-Bibliographical Survey*, 5 vols. in 12 (London: Luzac and Co., 1927) 1:1-2. He continues, "une autre traduction persane, anonyme... se trouve à Cambridge, que Browne a décrite;" again what Browne described was a commentary of Qur'ān rather than a translation: Browne, *Literary History* (1:477-478) and "Description of an Old Persian Commentary on the Kur'án," *Journal of the Royal Asiatic Society of Great Britain and Ireland* (July 1894) pp. 417-524; Storey, *Persian Literature* 1:2-3. "Sourâbâdi nous a laissé une autre traduction...": yet again this is a *tafsīr* by Abū Bakr ʿAtīq b. Muḥammad al-Sūrābādī (mid-fifth/11th c.) as explicitly listed by his own source: Storey, *Persian Literature* 1:3. Works by the arch-Ashʿarī Shāhfūr ʿImād al-Dīn Abū al-Muẓaffar Ṭāhir b. Muḥammad Isfarāyīnī (d. 471/1079), Abū Naṣr Aḥmad b. al-Ḥasan b. Aḥmad al-Sulaymānī al-Zāhidī (fl. 519/1125), and al-Harawī al-Anṣārī are all Persian *tafsīrs*. See also the British Library's Delhi 1868 and 1890 Waliyyullāh Persian and Hindustani interlinear editions entitled *Qur'ān Majīd* and Travis Zadeh, *The vernacular Qur'an: Translation and the Rise of Persian Exegesis* (Oxford : Oxford University Press, 2012).

rector, Muḥammad Ḥasanayn Makhlūf al-ʿAdawī (1861-1936), in his 1932 *Kalima ḥawla Tarjamat al-Qur'ān al-Karīm*. Understandably the above were largely reacting to the fall of the Ottoman caliphate and the anti-Arabic aspects of Kemalism.

In practical terms, however, colonialism had made translation a virtual legal exigency: it is not surprising that in the first 60 years of the 20th century virtually all English translations by Muslims came out of British India starting with Muḥammad ʿAbd al-Ḥakīm Khan's (1905) and including Pickthall's landmark *Meaning of the Glorious Koran* (1930).[175] A British convert and arguably the most English Muslim translator of all, Muḥammad Marmaduke Pickthall (1875-1936) helped turn the tide by travelling to Cairo and courageously addressing the ulema of Azhar ("Sheykh Rashid Rida was somewhere near me on the right") in 1930 to defend his forthcoming translation around the same time that *al-Ahrām* had published a diatribe against it. Yet another rector (1928-1930, 1935-1945), Muḥammad b. Muṣṭafā b. Muḥammad al-Marāghī (1881-1945)—brother of the *mufassir* Aḥmad al-Marāghī and a student of Muḥammad ʿAbduh (1849-1905)—supported him against the position of Shākir et al.: "Go on in God's name in the way that is clear to you, and pay no heed to what any of us say." As Pickthall wrote, "It was evident that there were two opinions in al-Azhar itself."[176] Today, less

[175] See Ḥamīdullah, introduction to his *al-Qur'ān al-Majīd* (pp. lxx-lxxiii).

[176] See Pickthall, "Arabs and non-Arabs, and the question of translating the Qur'ān," *Islamic Culture* (July 1931) pp. 422-433 and Ann Fremantle's biography *Loyal Enemy*, epitomized by Timothy J. Winter, "Marmaduke Pickthall: A Brief Biography," *Seasons: Semiannual Journal of the Zaytuna Institute* (Spring 2004) pp. 23-39. The rector spoke English, wrote on the topic of translations of the Qur'ān and addressed the 1936 World Congress of Religions in London on the subject of "Human Fellowship" (*al-zamālat al-insāniyya*). When he proposed the same year that al-Azhar itself produce an English translation he was rebuffed by the two top judges Muḥammad Sulaymān with *Ḥadath al-Aḥdāth fil-Islām: al-Iqdām ʿalā Tarjamat al-Qur'ān* and Muḥammad

than a century later, the discipline of *tafsīr* translation is counted among the requisites of scholarly production. In a 2013 Mecca colloquium entitled "Renewal in Quranic commentary" (*al-tajdīd fīl-tafsīr*), it was highlighted as part and parcel of the process of *ijtihād* and *tajdīd* in Islamic civilization.[177]

Our rendering of the Magnificent Qur'ān

The Qur'ān cannot be veraciously enough translated into any language; but Shāh Waliyyullāh famously advocated (at the end of *al-Fawz al-Kabīr fī Uṣūl al-Tafsīr*) that it be, on the one hand, rendered as word-for-word and literally as possible—*verbatim et literatim*; yet, at the same time, intelligibly and clearly, *ad sensum*, even if the word count rises. The present English rendering of its first 74 verses is ultimately my own[178] but in my quest for prudent literalism I have appreciated—archaisms aside and despite rare inaccuracies and slips into interpretation—the scrupulous choices of Muhammad Marmaduke Pickthall (1875-1936) and the Deobandi Baydawist Abdul Majid Daryabadi (1892–1977). Muhammad Taqi Usmani (b. 1943), Arthur John Arberry (1905-1969) and John Penrice (1818-1892) also deserve mention among top Qur'ān Arabists with an eye to precision, even if the latter only produced a glossary rather than a translation.[179]

Muṣṭafā al-Shāṭir with *al-Qawl al-Sadīd fī Ḥukm al-Qur'ān al-Majīd* among others, cf. ʿUmar Riḍā Kaḥḥāla, *Muʿjam al-Muʾallifīn*, 4 vols. (Beirut: Mu'assasat al-Risāla, 1414/1993), entry "Muḥammad al-Marāghī."

[177] See proceedings, 25th conference on *Tafsīr* at the Center for *Tafsīr* of Jāmiʿat Umm al-Qurā in Mecca on 5 February 2013, http://vb.tafsir.net/tafsir34944/ as of May2016.

[178] With devoted thanks to my parents and many language teachers at École Notre-Dame de Jamhour (Lebanon); King's School, Canterbury (UK); Columbia University (New York); City University of New York; and École Normale Supérieure (Paris).

[179] The rest of the 50-odd English renderings in circulation as of 2016 are marred by inaccuracy, (over)interpretation, translatese (ungrammaticalness, neologism, bathos, gibberish), archaism, untranslationese (transcribing instead of translating), bias and replication. Their marginalia vary from historico-glossarial to ideological and from

Anwār al-Tanzīl in partial translation: Urdu, French, English

Formal renderings of al-Bayḍāwī's *Tafsīr* in other languages have been rare and partial due to the inherent difficulty of the text. Many if not most of the *ḥawāshī* themselves are partial due to the added fact that since al-Bayḍāwī's method is encapsulated in the first quarter of his *tafsīr*, a sample was enough to give an idea of the whole. Al-Suyūṭī, for example, stopped his at Sūrat al-Tawba and al-Sayālkūtī at al-Baqara 2:229; similarly, modern Urdu translations and supercommentaries destined for school use content themselves with the first *juz'* or, as we have, the first *ḥizb*.[180] As a result, other than the didactic Urdu works just mentioned, only six texts stand out to date—five by European Arabists and the sixth by a Hartford missionary.

The very influential Baron Antoine-Isaac Silvestre de Sacy (1758-1838), "Fondateur de l'orientalisme moderne.... immense savant,"[181] inaugurated European Baydawian studies with his French translation of the commentary on the first seven verses of Sūrat al-Baqara (part of a grammar chrestomathy), which my former teacher at Columbia Pierre Cachia (b. 1921) used for a retranslation of that on *alif lām mīm*.[182] David Samuel Margoliouth (1858-1940) in 1894 brought out a translation of the commentary on Āl 'Imrān for students of Arabic at the Oxford Oriental School; *A translation of Baidawi's Commentary on the first Sura*

minimalist to oversized. Of late, the 2,000-page *Study Quran* (2015) is a skillful apology for Perennialism, a New Age, unislamic doctrine interpolated and redacted into an apparatus of ostensibly mainstream exegetical literature. See our review at academia.edu/24894666/The_Study_Quran_Review_Haddad_02Mar2016_MWBR

180 See note 161.

181 Sylvette Larzul, "Silvestre de Sacy, Antoine-Isaac," *Dictionnaire des orientalistes de langue française*, ed. François Pouillon (Paris: Editions Karthala, 2012) p. 953.

182 Sacy, *Anthologie Grammaticale Arabe* (pp. 1-62) and Pierre J.E. Cachia, "Bayḍāwī on the *Fawātiḥ*: A Translation of His Commentary on *alif-lām-mīm* in Sūrah 2, v. 1," *Journal of Semitic Studies* 13 (1968) 218-231.

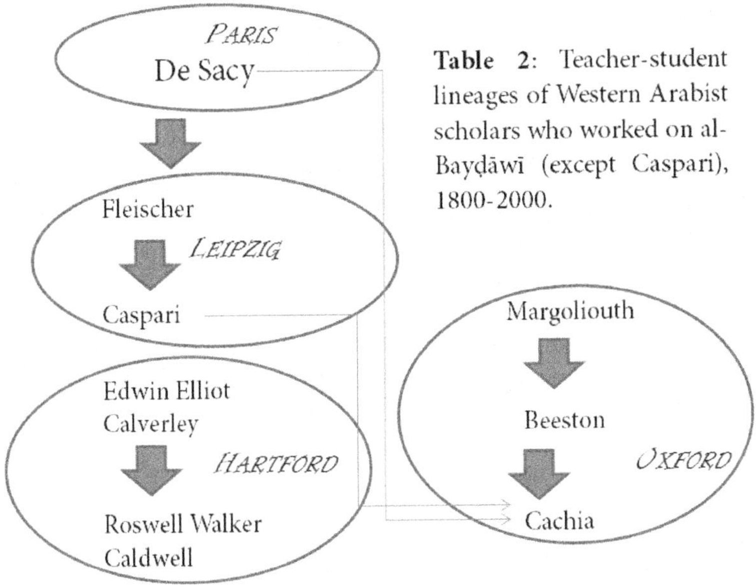

Table 2: Teacher-student lineages of Western Arabist scholars who worked on al-Bayḍāwī (except Caspari), 1800-2000.

of the Koran by Roswell Walker Caldwell (1885-1973)—his 1933 M.A. thesis—remains unpublished (I have not seen it); and in 1963 another Oxonian, Alfred Felix Landon Beeston (1911-1995) —Margoliouth's student and Cachia's teacher)—published his translation of the commentary on Sūrat Yūsuf, again for students of Arabic. The latter work was in fact a reworking of an earlier effort by two Glaswegian academes published in the Fifties.[183] The above were obviously interested in Bayḍāwī as applied grammar, not exegesis. Āl ʿImrān and Yūsuf were picked for their Biblical themes: Margoliouth was a priest in the Church of England, his father and uncle converts from Judaism to Anglicanism and Beeston a devout Catholic. Caldwell was a Presbyterian missionary in Egypt for two decades leading up to his

183 See David S. Margoliouth, *Chrestomathia Baidawiana*; A.F.L. Beeston, *Bayḍāwī's Commentary on Sūrah 12 of the Qur'ān* (Oxford: Clarendon Press, 1963, rept. 1974 and 1978); and Eric F.F. Bishop and Mohamed Kaddal, *The Light of Inspiration and Secret of Interpretation, being a translation of the Chapter of Joseph (Sūrat Yūsuf) with the commentary of Nasir id-Din al-Baidāwī* (Glasgow: Jackson, 1957).

thesis at Hatford Seminary—under another missionary and future Bayḍāwī specialist, the newly appointed Professor of Arabic and Islamic studies at the Kennedy School of Missions, Edwin Elliot Calverley (1882-1971). (See Table 2.) *Qur'ān and Its Exegesis*—an English version of Helmut Gätje's (1927-1986) 1971 German anthology from Zamakhsharī, Bayḍāwī and others—aspired to precision despite a trite introduction and mediocre notes.

The Acehnese Shaṭṭārī Sufi, *mufassir*, Shāfiʿī jurist and author of 30 books ʿAbd al-Ra'ūf b. ʿAlī al-Fanṣūrī Singkol or al-Singkīlī (1024-1104/1615-1693) penned the first Malay *tafsīr*, a volume in Jāwī script entitled *Tarjumān al-Mustafīd* (The Translator for the Seeker of Benefit) in which he based himself on *Tafsīr al-Jalālayn* but interspersed *ḥikāyāt* ʿstoriesʾ and *fawā'id* ʿbenefitsʾ from Shāfiʿī *tafsīrs* such as Bayḍāwī's and al-Khāzin's *Lubāb al-Ta'wīl*. An enduring misrepresentation of the *Tarjumān* began when its first printed edition (Istanbul 1302 /1884)—followed by subsequent editions to date—added to its title-page the subtitle "a Jawi translation of Bayḍāwī's *tafsīr*" and that is how it and its author came to be (mis)cited even in scholarly literature, when the briefest glimpse at its first page suffices to show that it is not a translation of al-Bayḍāwī at all.[184]

[184] Cf. ʿAbd al-Ra'ūf b. ʿAlī al-Fanṣūrī al-Jāwī, *al-Qur'ān al-Karīm wa-bi-hāmishih Tarjumān al-Mustafīd, wa-huwa al-tarjamat al-Jāwiyya lil-tafsīr al-musammā Anwār al-Tanzīl wa-Asrār al-Ta'wīl lil-Imām al-Qāḍī... al-Bayḍāwī*, ed. Muḥammad Idrīs ʿAbd al-Ra'ūf al-Marbawī al-Azharī, 4th ed., 2 vols. (Singapore: Pustaka National, 1370/1951). Peter Riddell, "The Sources of ʿAbd al-Ra'ūf's *Tarjumān al-Mustafīd*," *JMBRAS* 57 no. 2 (1984) pp. 113-118 has attributed responsibility for that misleading moniker to the Dutch Orientalist Snouck Hurgronje (1857-1936). See also Anthony H. Johns, "Quranic Exegesis in the Malay World" in *Approaches to the History of the Interpretation of the Qur'ān*, ed. Andrew Rippin (OUP, 1988) pp. 263-266 and Martin van Bruinessen, "*Kitab kuning*: Books in Arabic script used in the Pesantren milieu," *Bijdragen tot de Taal-, Land- en Volkenkunde* 146 no. 2/3 (1990) p. 253. Riddell yet states 20 years later that Bayḍāwī "served as an important source for ʿAbd al-Ra'uf al-Singkili's Malay commentary upon the whole Qur'ān, *Tarjumān al-mustafīd* (The

The present edition and translation of the *Anwār*

This edition, translation and study of *Ḥizb* I of *Anwār al-Tanzīl* is based on the manuscripts and editions described in the next section. I have added vowelization to the Arabic text and my own punctuation (according to modern usage in each language), paragraph structure and bulleting/numbering to help the reader make sense of Bayḍāwī's many run-on sentences. I have also added about two dozen superscript or marginal annotations (e.g. صح / معاً / بالمدّ / بالتشديد / بالضمّتين / بالفتح) to confirm a rare or unexpected word or spelling, or valid dual or triple vowelizations. I have used the *Muṣḥaf al-Madīnat al-Nabawiyya lil-Nashr al-Ḥāsūbī* software for the Quranic type with its added verse numbering and decorative brackets. Whenever poetry is quoted the meter of the verse(s) is identified between square brackets. The requisite invocations placed after names of prophets and angels (*ʿalayhi/m al-salām*), Companions (*raḍya Allāhu ʿanhu/ā/um*) and scholars (*raḥimahu Allāh*) are, in many cases, also added by scribes and should not automatically be assumed to be from the pen of the original author. The above are all standard editorial practices for classical Arabic texts, as is the use of parentheses in lieu of quotation marks for single words or brief phrases.

The English follows the *OED* standard (with U.S. spelling) for the most part and reflects the collected terminology of three major Arabic-English grammars and lexicons: Wright's *Grammar of the Arabic Language*, Howell's *Grammar of Classical Arabic* and Lane's *Lexicon*. I have benefited from Cachia's *Monitor*—an epitome and concatenation of Wright and Howell—and, somewhat, Penrice's *Dictionary*.[185] In his analysis of Arabic grammar

interpreter of that which gives benefit) [*sic*], written around 1085/1675." In *The Qur'ān: An Encyclopedia*, ed. Oliver Leaman (New York: Routledge, 2006) p. 118.

[185] William Wright, *A Grammar of the Arabic Language, Translated from the German of [Carl P.] Caspari*, 3rd ed., rev. W. Robertson Smith and M.J. de Goeje, ed. Pierre

and rhetoric, coinage of English equivalents and knowledge of probative sources E.W. Lane deserves special mention.

I have striven to be as consistent as possible in my translation of Bayḍāwī's Arabic while avoiding monolithism. When trying to meet the needs of context, I have not hesitated to use more than a single correct English rendering of the same term, as in:

ḥudūth:	contingency, temporal origin(ation), recency
lāzim:	inseparable, inevitable, concomitant
muqtaḍā:	corollary, exigency, dictate, presupposition
shubha:	skepticism, suspicion, misgivings
taḍammun:	a containing, entailing, implying
aṣl:	literal meaning/origin, etymon, root, original case
kunh:	totality, extent, ultimate reality

This studied disparity is validated by Quranic usage where, for example, *ishtarā* (an auto-antonym) at times means "purchase" (al-Baqara 2:16) and at times "trade off" (al-Baqara 2:41). It also boils down to selecting single terms for indissociably compound meanings, as when the Qadi's ubiquitous *fīl-aṣl* is rendered "originally" or—almost as often—"literally" (cf. "implied original wording" under *wa-mā ẓalamūnā* (al-Baqara 2:57).

I have appended a biographical glossary of persons, groups and sects mentioned by name in the *Anwār* and a bilingual Arabic-English glossary of Bayḍāwī's technical terms that covers

Cachia, 2 vols. (Cambridge: University Press, 1955; rept. Beirut: Librairie du Liban, 1996); Mortimer Howell, *Grammar of the Classical Arabic Language*, 4 vols. in 11 (Allahabad: NW Provinces Govt. Press, 1880-1911); Edward William Lane, *Arabic-English Lexicon*, 8 vols. (London and Edinburgh: Williams and Norgate, 1863-1893), rept. 2 vols. (Cambridge: Islamic Texts Society, 1984); Pierre Cachia, *The Monitor: A Dictionary of Arabic Grammatical Terms* (Beirut: Librairie du Liban and London: Longman, 1973); John Penrice, *Dictionary and Glossary of the Kor-ân* (1873, rept. Delhi: Adam Publishers, 1991). Cf. also Magdi Wahba, *A Dictionary of Literary Terms: English-French-Arabic* (Beirut: Librairie du Liban, 1974, rept. 1983); Abdul-Raof Hussein, *Arabic Rhetoric: A Pragmatic Analysis* (New York: Routledge, 2006); and Hasan Ghazala, *A Dictionary of Stylistics and Rhetoric* (Malta: Elga Publications, 2000).

principally grammar but also rhetoric, prosody, phonetics, credal doctrine and anything else that warrants inclusion as specialized terminology. These glossaries may serve as correctives and addenda to the manuals of the classical Arabists and provide help for specialists of al-Bayḍāwī as well as *tafsīr* students and translators in general. The index of Quranic verses and hadiths covers not only those cited by Bayḍāwī but also those mentioned in my own introduction and notes.

Our hope is that this work will be of benefit towards a better understanding of the endeavors of al-Bayḍāwī and his peers in illustrating the inexhaustible nature of Divine Speech and the glory of the Quranic medium. Its mistakes are my own and it only skims the surface of the author's idiom and the wealth of the Arabic and English languages. May it nevertheless serve as a helpful reference for linguistic exegesis as a genre and a science, Quranic grammar and style, Sunni classicism, Ashʿarī culture, and the authoritative exposition of the inimitable discourse that made *The Book* the enduring, unmatchable wonder of the ages.

Manuscripts and editions used in this work (listed in descending order of antiquity) and their sigla

Berlin 758/1357 manuscript (B): *Anwār al-Tanzīl* complete, very legibly written in a small *naskh* hand with copious vowelization and rubrication of the Quranic text by Qawwām b. al-Ḥusayn b. Muḥammad al-Shīrāzī who completed it on a Thursday morning in Ṣafar 758/February 1357 in the Khānqāh al-Khātūniyya in Damascus per its colophon on folio 414a. This well-preserved codex is the oldest known ms. of Bayḍāwī's *Tafsīr* and we have collated the final form of this work primarily against its text. Ms. Staatsbibliothek Preußischer Kulturbesitz, Berlin Hs. or. 8180 in 414 folios.[186]

Riyadh 850/1446 manuscript (C): *Anwār al-Tanzīl* from its preamble to the end of Sūrat al-Kahf, 257 folios in a very legible hand by Ibrāhīm b. Muḥammad, more reliably vowelized than any other we have seen. King Saʿūd University ms. Tafsīr 1036.[187]

Cambridge 874/1470 manuscript (α): Commentary on the first six suras from the *Anwār*, entitled *Tafsīr al-Qāḍī al-Bayḍāwī min Sūrat al-Baqara ilā Ākhir Sūrat al-Anʿām* in 115 folios with a colophon on the penultimate folio dating the conclusion of the copy "in the mid-morning of al-Arbiʿāʾ (Wednesday) in the first 10 days of the sacred month of Muḥarram 874 after the Hijra." Ms. Cambridge Add. 3586 written in elegant small *naskh* hand in black ink with red ("rubrication") lines highlighting the Quranic text and vowelized in places.[188]

[186] See its description in full in Rosemarie Quiring-Zoche, "An early manuscript."

[187] http://makhtota.ksu.edu.sa and www.al-mostafa.com

[188] See further description in E.G. Browne, *Hand-List of the Muḥammadan Manuscripts in the Library of the University of Cambridge* (Cambridge: University Press, 1900) p. 252. Browne misunderstands its copy as "dated the 10th of Muḥarram, A.H. 874" whereas the correct dating is actually either Wednesday 2 Muharram 874 (12

Cambridge 908/1503 manuscript (ε): *Anwār al-Tanzīl* copied in full by Muḥammad b. Muḥammad b. Ḥasan b. ʿAlī b. Aḥmad b. Muḥammad al-Khalīlī al-Makhzūmī al-Ḥanafī in an "small, ill-formed hand" (Browne) of 329 folios in black ink with rubrication of the Quranic text. This ms. has suffered some damage caused by fire but most of it is intact including the first *ḥizb*. The colophon dates the termination of its copy on "al-Ithnayn 7 Rabīʿ al-Awwal 908" although most probably Rabīʿ al-Thānī.[189]

Baltimore 966/1559 manuscript (W): Supercommentary by Shaykh al-Islam Ibn Kamāl Bāshā (Kemalpaşazade 873-940/1469-1534) on al-Bayḍāwī's *Tafsīr*, Surat al-Baqara from 2:21 to 2:95, with a fragment of Surat al-Fātiḥa at the end. Kept at the Walters Art Museum in Baltimore, USA (Walters ms. W.584).[190]

Damascus 990/1582 manuscript (A): *Fatḥ al-Jalīl bi-Bayān Khafī Anwār al-Tanzīl* (The Disclosure of the All-Majestic Clarifying the Obscurities of *The Lights of Revelation*), a supercommentary by Shaykh al-Islam Zakariyyā al-Anṣārī (823-926/1420-1520) the last surviving student of Ibn Ḥajar and a major Shāfiʿī jurist, hadith master, linguist, and specialist of canonical readings in his time. Ẓāhiriyya ms. *ʿUlūm al-Qur'ān* 266, Damascus. E.W. Lane quotes from it in his *Lexicon*.

Nablus undated manuscript (N): *Tafsīr al-Bayḍāwī*, ms. 298 Najah National University of Nablus (West Bank, State of Palestine), from the library of the Mufti of Jaffa. Undated. The imaged text reaches to Sūrat al-Baqara verse 4, after which it

July 1469) or Wednesday 9 Muḥarram 874 (19 July 1469).

189 Browne, *Hand-List* (p. 17) misreads the year as 708 (*thamānin wa-sabʿimi'atin*) but it is certain that it says 908 (*thamānin wa-tisʿimi'atin*). The pinpointing of the day, however, is problematic as given since 7 Rabīʿ al-Awwal 908 falls on a Saturday, not a Monday. As for 7 Rabīʿ al-Awwal 708 it falls on a Sunday. If, however, the month is Rabīʿ al-Thānī 908 then the 7th does fall on a Monday.

190 http://art.thewalters.org/viewwoa.aspx?id=2150

jumps to verse 181.[191]

Cambridge undated manuscript (β): *Tafsīr al-Bayḍāwī* in 498 folios written in legible *nastaʿlīq* hand but devoid of dating or colophon. Its first-folio notice indicates a non-Arab owner.[192]

Ryadh 1059/1649 manuscript (Iṣ): Ibrāhīm b. Muḥammad b. ʿArab Shāh, known as ʿIṣām al-Dīn al-Isfarāyīnī (873-945/1468-1538), who flourished in Isfarāyīn and Samarqand, authored a *Ḥāshiya* on al-Bayḍāwī which was copied far and wide. King Saʿūd University ms. 6096.[193]

Alukah 1067/1657 manuscript (Ak): *Tafsīr al-Bayḍāwī*, an elegantly copied and knowledgeably vowelized complete manuscript of unknown provenance. Its first page is stamped with a marker from the Saudi Ḥajj and Awqāf Ministry.[194]

Irbil (Iraq) 1150/1737 manuscript (I): complete and partly vowelized *Anwār al-Tanzīl*, Jāmiʿat Ṣalāḥ al-Dīn ms. 51.[195]

Riyadh 1170/1757 manuscript (ÇZ): Saʿdī Çelebi—known as Tacizade (d. 945/1538)—and Shaykh Zādah's respective *Ḥāshiyas* on the *Anwār*. King Saʿūd University ms. 6750.[196]

Mecca pre-1242/1827 manuscript (M): *Anwār al-Tanzīl* from the beginning to the end of Sūrat al-Fātiḥa. Jāmiʿat Umm al-Qurā University ms. 1729.[197]

Istanbul 1257/1841 edition (L): This two-volume printed edition of the *Anwār* with *Tafsīr al-Jalālayn* in the margins, pub-

[191] http://manuscripts.najah.edu/node/298
[192] See further description in E.G. Browne, *Hand-List* (p. 17).
[193] http://makhtota.ksu.edu.sa/makhtota/6518/1
[194] http://www.alukah.net/library/0/52999
[195] https://archive.org/details/Makh6o6atHamdiSalafi-2
[196] http://makhtota.ksu.edu.sa/makhtota/6750/10
[197] http://libback.uqu.edu.sa/hipres/SCRIPT/ind1729.pdf

lished at Dār al-Ṭibāʿat al-ʿĀmira, is the earliest to our knowledge. It was reprinted there in 1283/1867 and in Bulaq in 1285/1868 and 1303/1886.

Leipzig 1264/1848 edition (F): This complete edition of the *Anwār*—said to be the first *tafsīr* published in Europe—entitled *Beidhawii Commentarius in Coranum: ex codd. Parisiensibus, Dresdensibus et Lipsiensibus,*[198] was based on late manuscripts (10-11/16-17th centuries) which the editor did not describe, nor did he provide a critical apparatus.[199] To this nevertheless remarkable work Fleischer's student Winand Fell added several indices (1878). Its original publication coincides with that of the Būlāq edition of Shaykh Zādah's *Ḥāshiya* on the *Anwār* in 1263/1847 in three volumes.[200]

Bulaq 1270/1854 edition (Sk): This one-volume edition and supercommentary from the Fātiḥa to verse 229 of al-Baqara by ʿAbd al-Ḥakīm b. Shams al-Dīn al-Sayālkūtī (d. 1066/1656), an Indian specialist of logic who taught in Shāh Jahān Ābād and authored commentaries on logic, the *Nasafiyya*, *Mawāqif* and *ʿAḍudiyya*, was prized by teachers for its concision. Reprinted Quetta (Pakistan): Maktabat-i Islāmīyah, 1977.

[198] "Editit indicibusque instruxit H.O. Fleischer. Lipsiae: Sumptibus F.C.G. Vogelii, 1846-1848." See http://ar.wikisource.org/wiki/ملف:أنوار_التنزيل.pdf

[199] The half dozen Paris mss. described in Baron de Slane's *Catalogue des manuscrits arabes* (Paris: Imprimerie Nationale, 1883-1895) pp. 143-144 § 627-633 date from the 10th/16th century or later while those of Dresden and Leipzig date from "the 1070s/1660s and the 1080/1670s" respectively according to Fleischer, cf. Quiring-Zoche, "An early manuscript" (pp. 33-34). The oldest copy of the *Anwār* at the Bibliothèque Nationale de France is indeed ms. Arabe 628, copied in 969/1562. The German Orientalist Johann Fück (1894–1974) praised Fleischer's edition but also briefly mentioned its flaws in his *Die arabischen Studien in Europa* (Leipzig: Otto Harrassowitz, 1955) p. 171; transl. by ʿUmar Luṭfī al-ʿĀlim, *Tārīkh Ḥarakat al-Istishrāq* (Damascus: Dār Qutayba, 1996); 2nd ed. (Beirut: Dār al-Madār al-Islāmī, 2001) p. 171.

[200] Prints of it are kept at Bayerische StaatsBibliothek in Munich and in Oxford.

Teheran 1272/1856 lithograph (T): Bahā' al-Dīn Muḥammad b. Ḥusayn al-ʿĀmilī's (953-1030/1546-1621) *Taʿlīqāt Anwār al-Tanzīl* is an edition of the *Anwār* with marginalia by the Shaykh al-Islam of the Safavid state and chief Shiʿi authority in his time.[201] The author of *al-Dharīʿa* lists 23 *ḥawāshī* on the *Anwār* purported to be Shiʿi works and he includes Sayālkūtī's (see previous entry), to whom he attributes authorship of a book of Rafidi creed entitled *Ithbāt al-Imāma* on which basis he claims him to have been a crypto-Shiʿi (*mutasattir bil-taqiyya*).[202]

Istanbul 1282/1865 edition (Z): An edition and supercommentary by the recluse Turkish master Muḥyī al-Dīn Muḥammad b. Muṣliḥ al-Dīn Muṣṭafā b. Shams al-Dīn al-Qūjawī al-Rūmī al-Ḥanafī, known as Shaykh Zādah (d. 951/1544), in eight volumes for beginners which he then rewrote into four.[203] He said:

> When I hesitate regarding a verse of the Qur'ān I turn to Allah Most High, then my chest expands until it becomes as big as the world, and two moons rise—I know not what they are—followed by a great light which shows me the Preserved Tablet, then I extract the meaning of the verse out of it.[204]

Ḥājjī Khalīfa praised it over all other supercommentaries for its ease and clarity in its explanation of Bayḍāwī's language .[205]

[201] http://upload.wikimedia.org/wikisource/ar/e/e5/أنوار_التنزيل_وأسرار_التأويل.pdf IIUM libraries in Malaysia have two copies of this work dated 1019/1610, one at Gombak Central Library and one at ISTAC.

[202] Aghā Buzurg al-Ṭihrānī, *al-Dharīʿa* (1:83 and 6:41-44).

[203] Muḥyī al-Dīn Muḥammad b. Muṣṭafā Shaykh Zādah, *Ḥāshiyat Muḥyī al-Dīn Shaykh Zādah*, 3 vols. (Istanbul: Maktaba ʿUthmāniyya, 1282/1865; rept. Istanbul: Hakikat Kitabevi, 1990).

[204] In Najm al-Dīn al-Ghazzī, *al-Kawākib al-Sā'ira bi-Aʿyān al-Mi'at al-ʿĀshira*, ed. Khalīl al-Manṣūr, 3 vols. (Beirut: Dār al-Kutub al-ʿIlmiyya, 1418/1997) 2:58. Together with Sakhāwī's *al-Ḍaw' al-Lāmiʿ li-Ahl al-Qarn al-Tāsiʿ* this work illustrates that the 9th and 10th Hijri centuries were dominated by al-Bayḍāwī's *Tafsīr* among scholars.

[205] In Nuwayhiḍ, *Muʿjam al-Mufassirīn* (2:637-638). *Zādah* meant "son of" in Ottoman Turkish as did "Oghli," so that "ʿArab Zādah" means "Son of Arabs." cf. Ḥassān

Many other Ottoman scholars who wrote on the *Anwār* are also known as "Zādah."[206]

Bulaq 1283/1867 edition (Kh): The eight-volume *'Ināyat al-Qāḍī wa-Kifāyat al-Rāḍī* (The Diligence of the Judge and Sufficiency of the Appreciative) by Shihāb al-Dīn Aḥmad b. Muḥammad b. Aḥmad al-Khafājī (977-1069/1569-1659) is one of the most relied-upon supercommentaries of al-Bayḍāwī and is prized for its clarity and balanced documentation of disputed issues by an accomplished and well-travelled Egyptian qadi and foremost philologist who mastered both the Ḥanafī and Shāfi'ī schools of law and authored a glossary of Arabized words, *Shifā' al-Ghalīl fī-mā fī Kalām al-'Arab min al-Dakhīl.*

Cairo 1305/1888 lithograph (Ul): a hand-written edition facing the Ottoman calligraphy of the Qur'ān, published at Cairo's al-

Ḥallāq and 'Abbās Ṣabbāgh, *al-Mu'jam al-Jāmi' fil-Muṣṭalaḥāt al-'Uthmāniyya* (Beirut: Dār al-Nahḍat al-'Arabiyya, 1430/2009) p. 106. The French Orientalist Baron Antoine-Isaac Silvestre de Sacy named his son "Samuel-Ustazade Silvestre de Sacy."

[206] Among them: Muḥammad b. Muḥammad al-Anṭākī, known as 'Arab Zādah (919-969/1513-1562); Muḥammad b. 'Abd al-Wahhāb b. 'Abd al-Karīm, known as 'Abd al-Karīm Zādah (d. 975/1568), who owned a quill he reserved exclusively for writing the Divine Name; the exegete, judge, jurist and poet 'Alā' al-Dīn 'Alī b. Muḥammad, known as Ḥinnāwī Zādah (918-979/1512-1572) who also authored marginalia on the *Kashshāf*; Muḥammad b. 'Abd al-Laṭīf, known as Bukhārī Zādah (d. 986 /1578); the Constantinople-born jurist and qadi of Cairo and the Two Holy Sanctuaries Aḥmad b. Muhammad b. Ramaḍān al-Rūmī, known as Nashānjī Zādah (934-986/1528-1578) who also authored a work of parsing (*I'rāb al-Qur'ān*); Kamāl al-Dīn Muḥammad b. Aḥmad b. Muṣṭafā b. Khalīl (959-1030/1552-1621), a foremost linguist, judge, historian and the son of the encyclopedist Ṭāsh Kubrī Zādah (901-968/1495-1561): both are known by the name "Ṭāshköprüzāde" which is shared by others as well; his grandfather Muṣliḥ al-Dīn Muṣṭafā (901-968/1495-1561) was preceptor to Sultan Selīm I; 'Abd al-Raḥmān b. Muḥammad b. Sulaymān al-Rūmī al-Ḥanafī (d. 1078/1667), a jurist from Gallipoli who is also known as Dāmād Shaykh al-Islām; and Muṣṭafā b. Aḥmad al-Bursawī, known as Ghazzī Zādah (d. 1204/1790), a bilingual litterateur who authored a *Ḥāshiya* he named *Tazyīn al-Maqāmāt*. Cf. Nuwayhiḍ, *Mu'jam al-Mufassirīn* (2:625; 2:571; 1:385; 2:555; 1:73; 2:486; 1:277; 2:674).

Maṭbaʿat al-ʿUthmāniyya al-ʿĀmira.[207] This edition was reprinted in 1329 and then again recently by Dār al-Jīl in Beirut.

Cairo 1317-1324/1899-1906 edition (U): This is a frequently republished edition of no less than four parallel-text *Tafsīrs*: al-Bayḍāwī's *Anwār* on top, ʿAlāʾ al-Dīn al-Khāzin's (d. 725/1325) *Lubāb al-Taʾwīl fī Maʿānī al-Tanzīl*—in which he said he summarized al-Baghawī's (433-516/1042-1122) *Maʿālim al-Tanzīl*—on the bottom, al-Nasafī's (d. 701/1302) *Madārik al-Tanzīl wa-Ḥaqāʾiq al-Taʾwīl* on the top margin and *Tanwīr al-Miqbās min Tafsīr Ibn ʿAbbās* by al-Fayrūzābādī (d. 817/1414) on the bottom margin, at al-Maṭbaʿat al-ʿUthmāniyya al-ʿĀmira.

Cairo 1330/1912 edition (K): This 1100-page, 4-volume edition and *ḥāshiya* of al-Bayḍāwī's *Tafsīr* by the Hanafi scholar ʿAfīf al-Dīn Abū al-Faḍl ʿAbd Allāh b. Ḥasan al-Khaṭīb al-Qurashī al-Ṣiddīqī al-Ḥanafī al-Kāzarūnī (d. after 1102/1691) was taught to sixth-year students at al-Azhar. The author should not be confused with his namesake Muḥammad al-Khaṭīb al-Ṣiddīqī al-Kāzarūnī (d. 940/1534) the author of a *Risāla fī Iʿjāz al-Qurʾān*. Published at Dār al-Kutub al-ʿArabiyya al-Kubrā.[208] The latter should not be confused with his namesake Muḥammad al-Khaṭīb al-Ṣiddīqī al-Kāzarūnī (d. 940/1534) the author of a *Risāla fī Iʿjāz al-Qurʾān*.

Cairo 1375/1955 edition (C): This 622-page ["2nd"] edition of the *Anwār* in the margins of the *Muṣḥaf*—two volumes in a single oversize tome—was meticulously published by Muṣṭafā al-Bābī al-Ḥalabī. It is the last of the classical editions and the first to include some very light punctuation such as commas, colons, periods, quotation, interrogation and exclamation marks.

207 http://ar.wikisource.org/wiki/ملف:تفسير_البيضاوي.pdf

208 Cf. note 159.

Deoband 1970 edition (D): *al-Taqrīr al-Ḥāwī fī Ḥall al-Bayḍāwī* (The Comprehensive Resolution of al-Bayḍāwī's Difficulties) is a four-part edition (published as a single tome totalling 773 pp.) containing the Arabic text of *Anwār al-Tanzīl* (*Ḥizb* I) on top of each page with a word-for-word translation in the middle of the page and an Urdu commentary in the bottom half and following pages, all by Sayyid Fakhrulḥasan (d. after 1985). Reprinted in Karachi at Islamī Kutubkhānah in 2004.

Riyadh 1409/1989 edition: ʿAbd al-Raʾūf al-Munāwī's (d. 1031/1622) three-volume *al-Fatḥ al-Samāwī fī Takhrīj Aḥādīth al-Bayḍāwī* (The Heavenly Opening in the Documentation of the Hadiths of al-Bayḍāwī) was published at Dār al-ʿĀṣima. Al-Munāwī appears to have taken the entirety of his material verbatim from al-Suyūṭī's own documentation (in his *Nawāhid al-Abkār*) of the Prophetic, Companion, and Successor reports cited by al-Bayḍāwī which—since the latter so often takes its hadithic material from the *Kashshāf*—nicely complements Zaylaʿī's documentation of the hadiths found in the latter, entitled *Takhrīj al-Aḥādīth wal-Āthār al-Wāqiʿa fī Tafsīr al-Kashshāf*. The latter received two editions more detailed than Ibn Ḥajar's concise treatment of the same topic entitled *al-Kafī al-Shāf fī Takhrīj Aḥādīth al-Kashshāf*, published in one volume.[209]

Beirut 1996 edition (AQ): ʿAbd al-Qādir ʿIrfān Ḥassūna's all-too-lightly annotated five-volume edition of the *Anwār* together with al-Kāzarūnī's *Ḥāshiya* was reprinted several times at Dār al-Fikr. This edition is full of typographical blunders and misreadings of al-Bayḍāwī's text.

[209] Two other important hadith documentations of the *Anwār*, both of them still in manuscript form, remained inaccessible to this writer: *Tuḥfat al-Rāwī fī Takhrīj Aḥādīth Tafsīr al-Bayḍāwī* by Muḥammad b. Ḥasan b. Himmāt al-Dimashqī (d. 1175/1762) and *Fayḍ al-Bārī fī Takhrīj Aḥādīth Tafsīr al-Bayḍāwī* by ʿAbd Allāh b. Ṣibghat Allāh al-Madrāsī (d. 1288/1871).

Beirut 1418/1998 edition (MM): By Muḥammad ʿAbd al-Raḥmān al-Marʿashlī at Dār Iḥyāʾ al-Turāth al-ʿArabī and Muʾassasat al-Tārīkh al-ʿArabī in five volumes. This edition is full of the same type of errors as the previous one and, in its superficial introductory study of the *Anwār* and related literature, fails to identify the manuscript(s) on which it is based. The two editions are probably the worst available on the market today.

Damascus and Beirut 1421/2000 edition (H): Muḥammad Ṣubḥī b. Ḥasan Ḥallāq and Maḥmūd Aḥmad al-Aṭrash contributed to make this the most elaborate edition the *Anwār* has received so far, with paragraph divisions, a modicum of footnotes, sparse vowelization and rubrication in three oversize volumes. Like the preceding two editions, this one is also crammed with misspellings, misvowelizations and misinterpretations, in addition to lacking the required critical identification of its source and the manuscript(s) that it used—if any.

Beirut 1422/2001 edition (Q): *Ḥāshiyat al-Qūnawī*. Deemed by two successive sultans (Muṣṭafā Khān and ʿAbd al-Ḥamīd Khān) the foremost scholar of Constantinople in his time, Konya-born ʿIṣām al-Dīn Ismāʿīl b. Muḥammad b. Muṣṭafā al-Qūnawī (d. 1195/1781) authored a large supercommentary which received a 20-volume edition, together with Ibn al-Tamjīd's *Ḥāshiya*. His is among the most useful of all marginalia for a close reading of al-Bayḍāwī's text and has been relied upon in this work. He cites, endorses or takes issue with many of the prior marginalia such as Suyūṭī, Shaykh Zādah, Khafājī and Sayālkūtī as well as Abū al-Suʿūd, usually without naming them. If he cites "the two masters" (*al-shaykhān*) he means Zamakhsharī and Bayḍāwī (e.g. under *thumma ʿaraḍahum ʿalā al-malāʾika* in al-Baqara 2:31 cf. Q 3:138). The edition, however, suffers from the avalanche of typos, paginal reshuffling and other editorial blunders typically associated with its publisher, Dār al-Kutub al-ʿIlmiyya.

Mecca 1424/2003 edition (S): al-Suyūṭī (849-911/1445-1505) wrote a *ḥāshiya* entitled *Nawāhid al-Abkār wa-Shawārid al-Afkār* (The Budding Breasts of Virgins and Vagrant Thoughts), to about the 50th verse of Sūrat al-Tawba in which he focusses on issues of grammar and philology by epitomizing the prestigious *Kashshāf* Sunni supercommentaries of al-Ṭībī, Saʿd al-Dīn al-Taftāzānī (722-792/1322-1390, whom al-Suyūṭī calls *al-Saʿd*), al-Sharīf al-Jurjānī (740-816/1340-1413, whom al-Suyūṭī calls *al-Sayyid*), Quṭb al-Dīn al-Shīrāzī, Akmal al-Dīn al-Bābirtī (714?-786/1314?-1384) and Abū Ḥayyān (d. 745/1344) as well as al-Rāzī, with an abundant documentation of the hadiths of the *Anwār* and sparse discussions of creed and doctrinal issues. He takes issue with al-Bayḍāwī in several places. This is an unpublished Ph.D. dissertation that is useful for its sourcing of the hundreds of materials and personas cited by al-Suyūṭī but marred by the Wahhabi dissertator's detraction of his own material in his introduction and footnotes.

Pakistan 1431/2010 edition (P): *Anwār al-Tanzīl* (*Juzʾ* I) with *Taʿlīqāt* by the late ʿAbd al-Karīm al-Kawrāʾī. This meticulous work in Arabic by a scholar of the Indian Subcontinent includes interlinear lexical and grammatical glosses as well as generous marginalia that incorporate excerpts and paraphrases from all the classics. It has received several editions leading up to a mostly mistake-free and best typeset text to date (Karachi: Maktabat al-Bushrā, 1431/2010).

Barelwi 1433/2012 edition (G): *Ḥāshiyat al-ʿAlawī ʿalā Tafsīr al-Bayḍāwī* in three volumes, a marginalia by the major Gujarati scholar of Yemeni origin Wajīh al-Dīn Aḥmad b. Naṣr Allāh b.

ʿImād al-Dīn al-Aḥmad Ābādī al-Ḥusaynī (911-998/1505-1590). This edition is based on a manuscript that ends shortly after the beginning of Sūrat al-Ḥijr and shows the brilliance of the supercommentator in all the sciences—including philology and hadith—but is not served well by its textual reprint of the *Tafsīr* itself, as the editor relied on the faulty modern editions rather than original manuscripts.[210]

A partial ms. of the *Anwār* at Universiti Brunei Darussalam

UBD owns a partial, undated paper manuscript of *Anwār al-Tanzīl* consisting in a single unpaginated volume of 22x17cm. written in an ordinary, legible script hand in black ink with rubrications. Its pages are slightly damaged by lice. It was not assigned any shelf-mark. It starts with Sūrat al-Qaṣaṣ and ends with Sūrat al-ʿĀdiyāt.[211]

[210] Wajīh al-Dīn al-ʿAlawī, *Ḥashiyat al-ʿAlawī ʿalā Tafsīr al-Bayḍāwī*, ed. Muḥammad Ḥanīf Khān al-Riḍawī al-Barelwī, 3 vols. (Breilly, India: Imam Aḥmad Riḍā Academy, 1433/2012).

[211] Main library, University Brunei Darussalam. No. Perolehan: 1000297745. Diterim pada: 21.12.00.

Illustrative samples from the sources used for this edition and translation

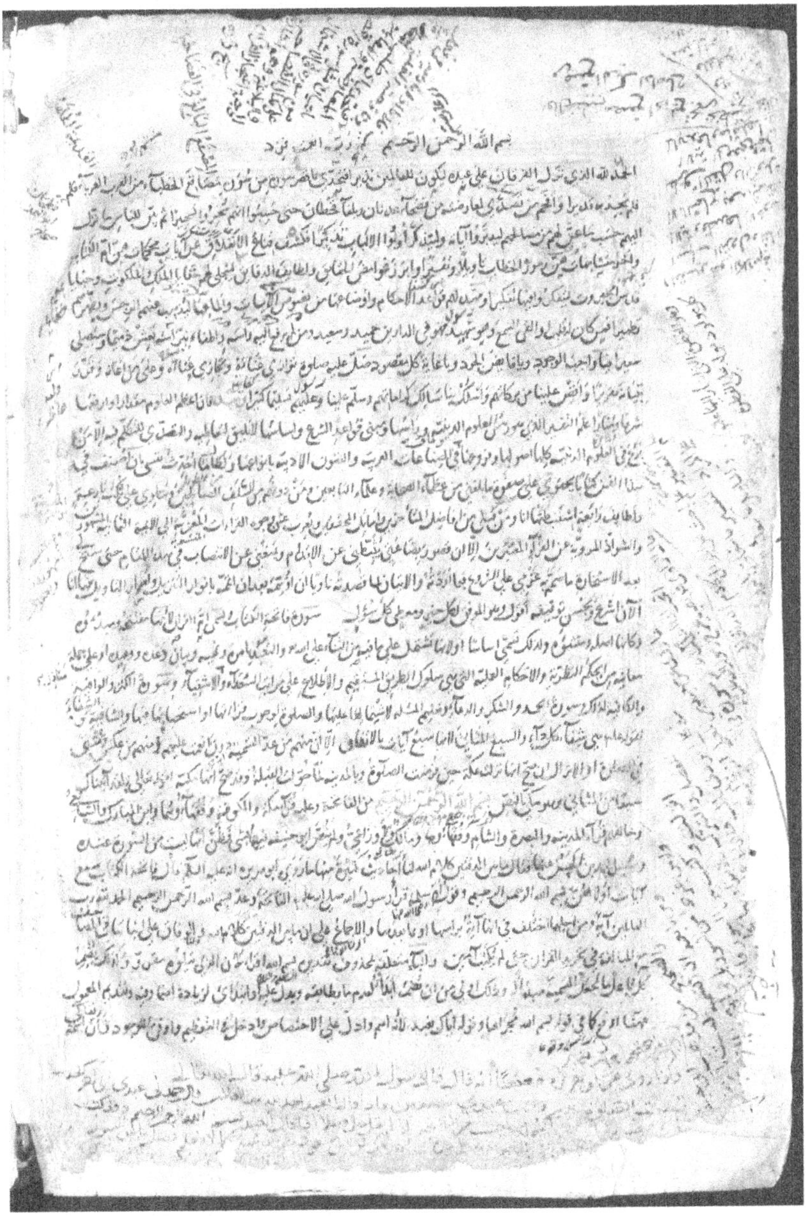

Figure 2: Incipit page of Berlin Hs. or. 8180 with Bayḍāwī's title clearly stated on line 15 as *Anwār al-Tanzīl wa-Asrār al-Ta'wīl.*

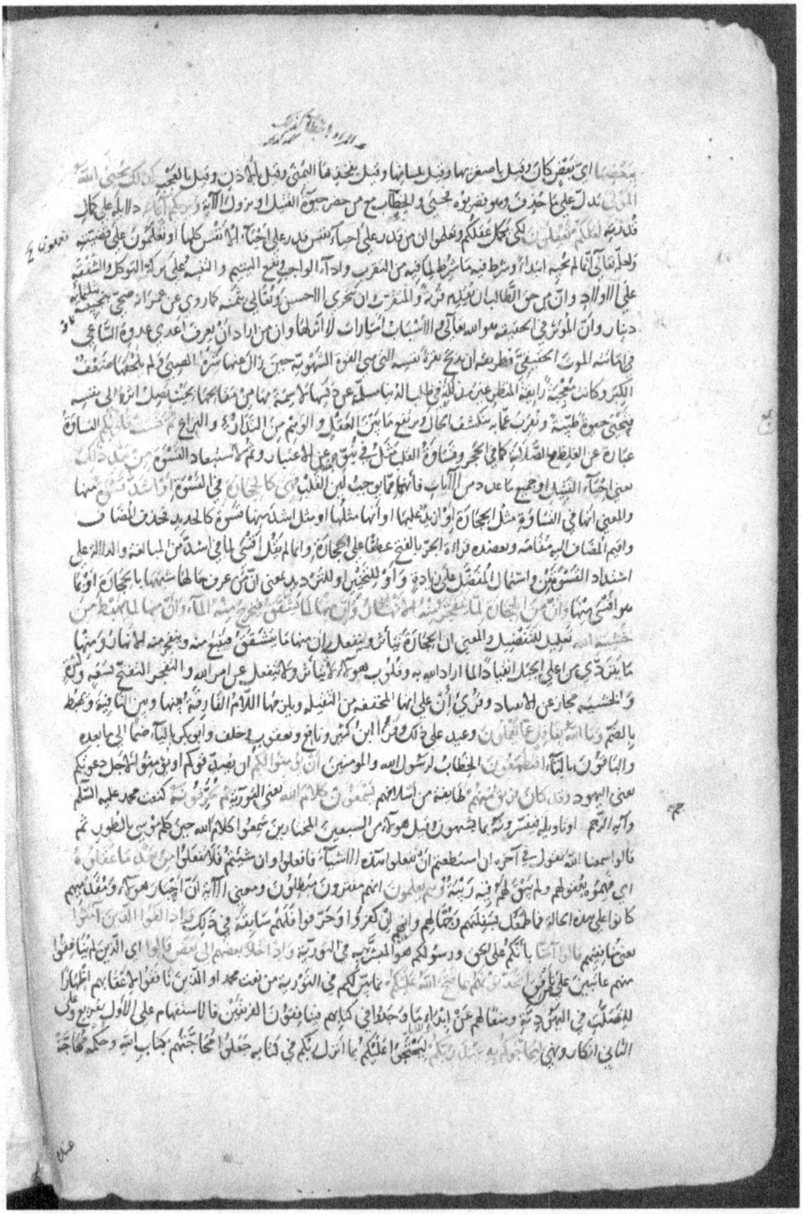

Figure 3: Berlin Hs. or. 8180 folio 30v: end of *Ḥizb I* (below mid-page): *Allah is not at all unaware of what you do.*

Figure 4: Riyadh, King Sa'ūd University, ms. Tafsīr 1036 folio 2a: Bayḍāwī, *Anwār al-Tanzīl*, Surat al-Fātiḥa. Ms. copied 850/1446. Top line: "***Allāh*** is originally *ilāh* 'deity, from which the *hamza* 'glottal stop' [*i*] was elided and compensated by *al-*; hence, one says *Yā Allāh* 'O Allah' disjunctively; but it is used specifically for the One Who is rightfully worshipped."

Figure 5: Cambridge Ms. Add. 3586. *Anwār al-Tanzīl*, folio 2b: Incipit (preamble and beginning of Fatiha) with the top fifth word misspelled as *Qur'ān* instead of *Furqān*. Copied 874 /1470.

كتاب أنوار التنزيل وأسرار التأويل
تصنيف الشيخ الإمام
العالم العلامة ناصر
الدين محمد البيضاوي
طاب ثراه وجعل الجنة
مثواه آمين

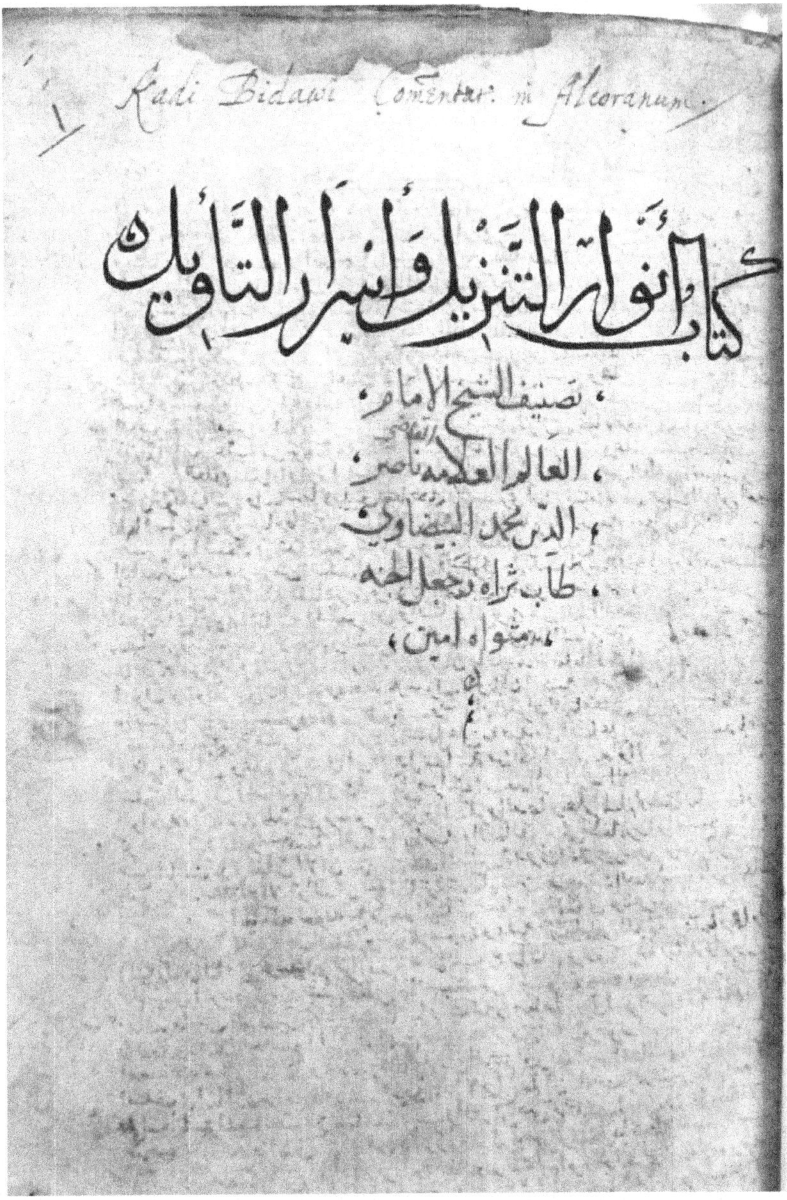

Figure 6: Title page (folio 1a) of 908/1503 Cambridge ms. Gg 3.20 of *Anwār al-Tanzīl*.

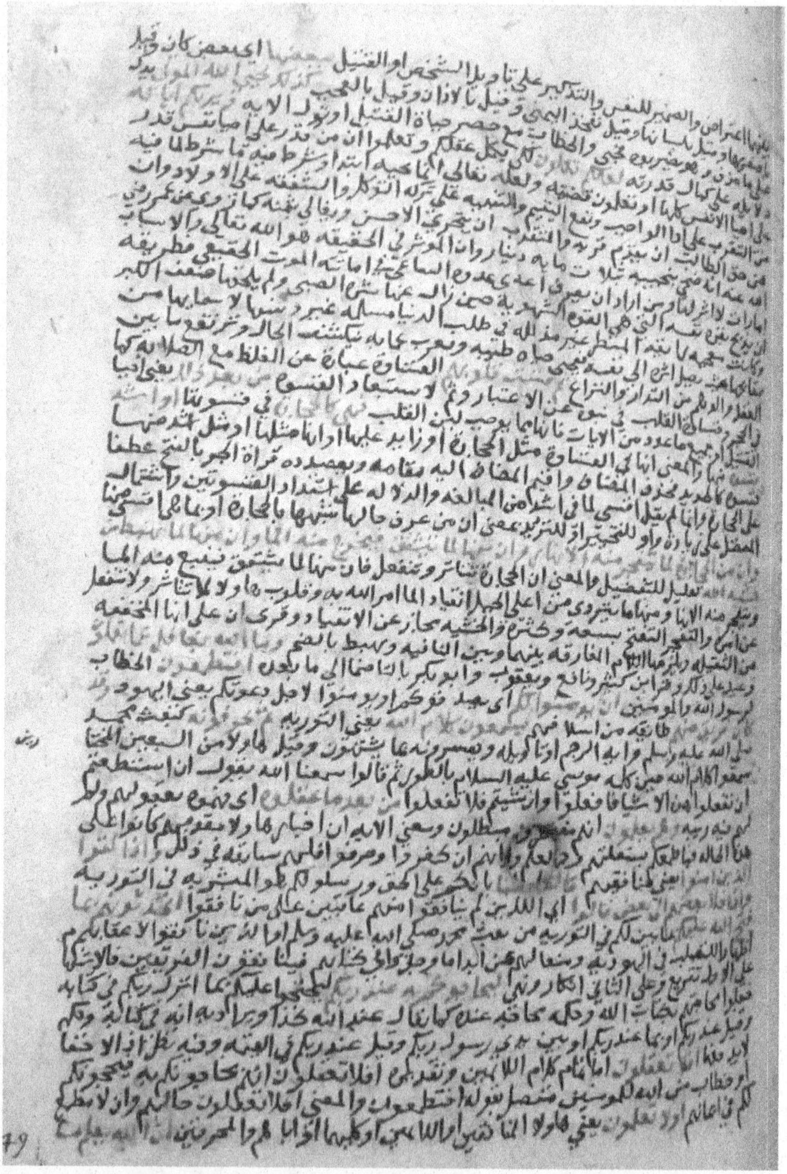

Figure 7: *Allah is not at all unaware of what you do* (mid-page): End of the first *ḥizb* (folio 25a), 908/1503 Cambridge ms. Gg 3.20 of *Anwār al-Tanzīl*. A burn mark can be seen.

Figure 8: Walters Art Museum, Baltimore, ms. W.584 p. 152: Shaykh al-Islam Ibn Kamāl Bāshā's (Kemalpaşazade d. 940/1534) commentary on al-Bayḍāwī, Surat al-Fātiḥa. Copied 966/1559.

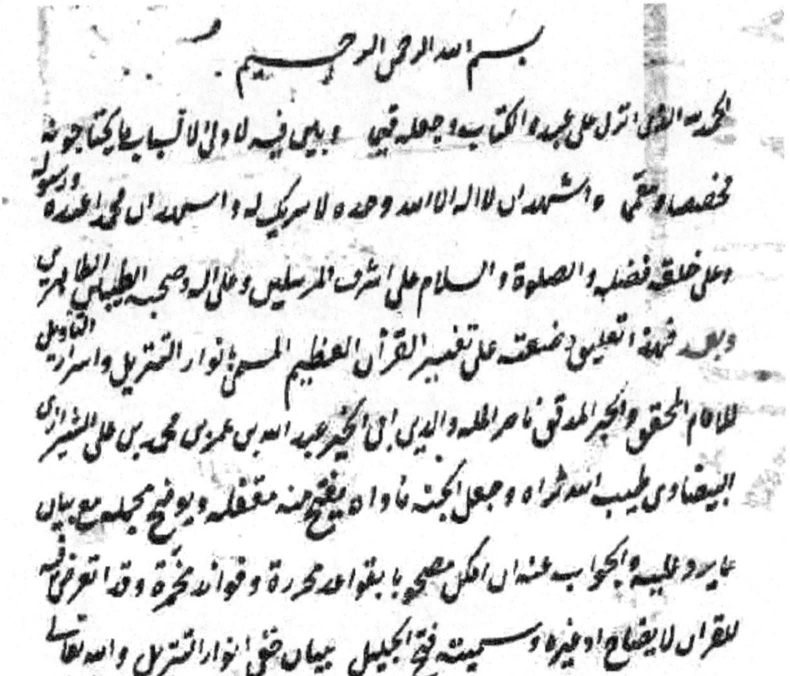

Figure 9: Zakariyyā al-Anṣārī's (823-926/1420-1520) *Ḥāshiya* entitled *Fatḥ al-Jalīl bi-Bayān Khafī Anwār al-Tanzīl*. Ẓāhiriyya ms. *'Ulūm al-Qur'ān* 266, f° 1. Copied 990/1582.

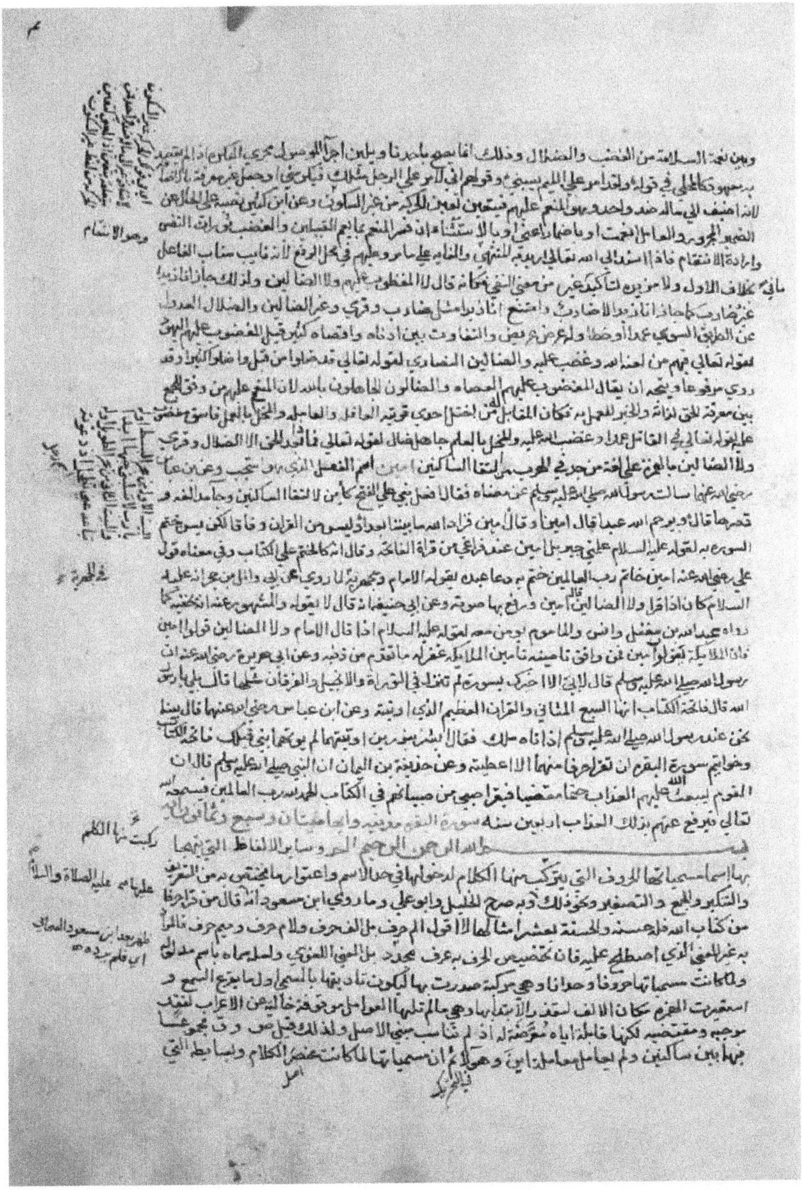

Figure 10: *Tafsīr al-Bayḍāwī*. Alukah website unidentified complete ms. (www.alukah.net/library/0/52999). Copied 1067/1657. F° 4a: End of Sūrat al-Fātiḥā and beginning of Sūrat al-Baqara.

Figure 11: *Tafsīr al-Bayḍāwī*. Jāmiʿat Ṣalāḥ al-Dīn (Irbil, Iraq) ms. 51, fº 1: Incipit (preamble and Fatiha). Copied 1150/1737.

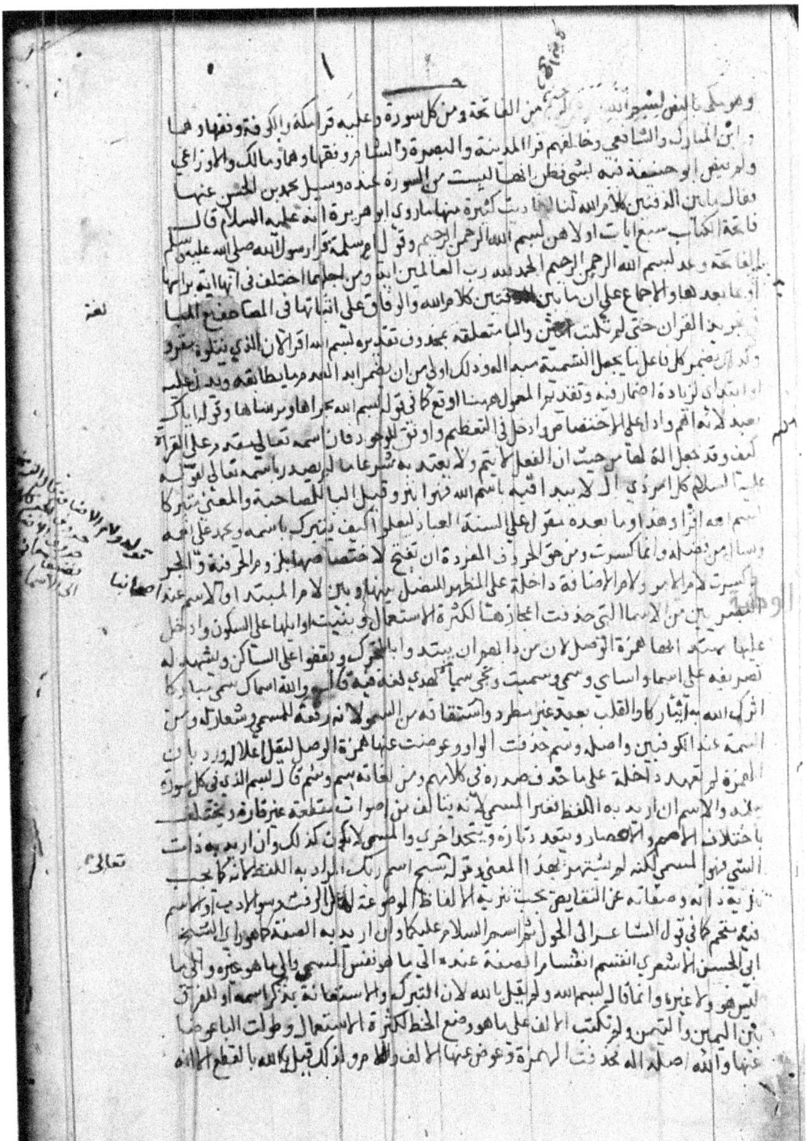

Figure 12: *Tafsīr al-Bayḍāwī*, f° 1b of ms 298 Najah National University of Nablus (West Bank, State of Palestine) from the library of the Mufti of Jaffa. Undated.

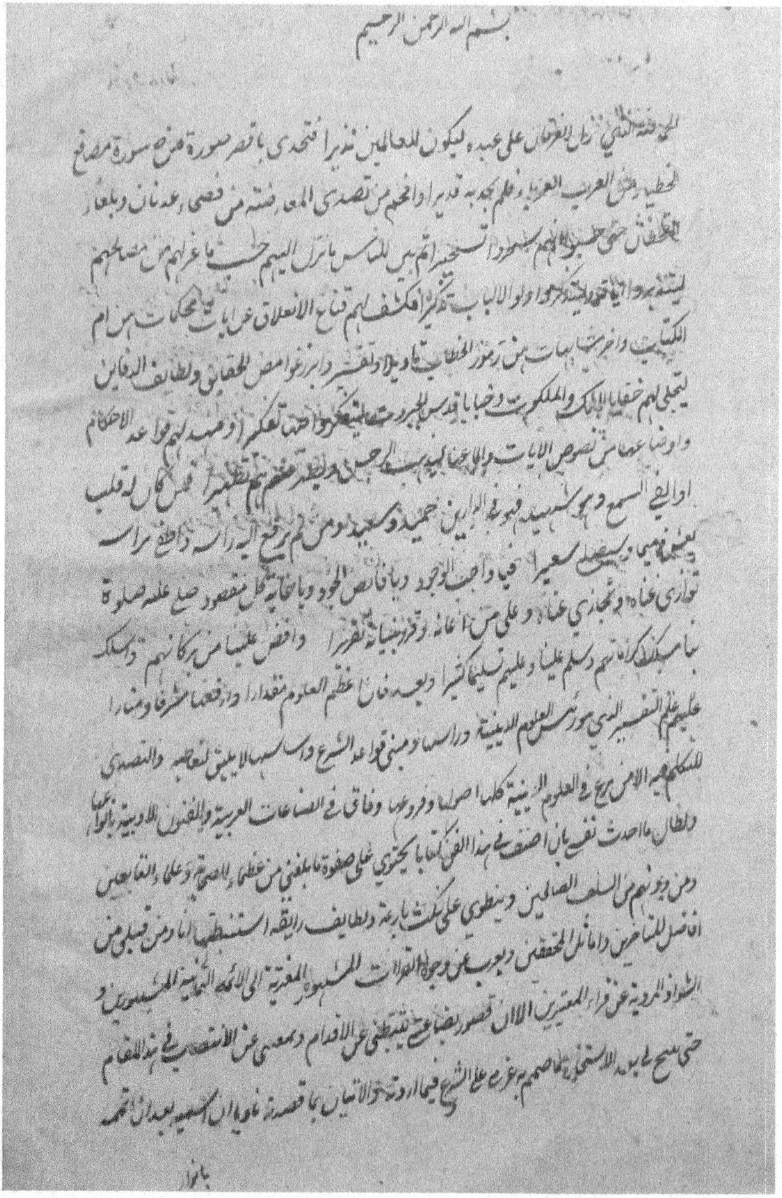
بسم الله الرحمن الرحيم

Figure 13: Folio 1b (Incipit) of undated Cambridge ms. Add. 3179 of *Tafsīr al-Bayḍāwī* in *nastaʿliq* Indian script.

Figure 14: Incipit of pre-1242/1827 ms. 1729 of *Anwār al-Tanzīl*, Jāmiʿat Umm al-Qurā, Mecca.

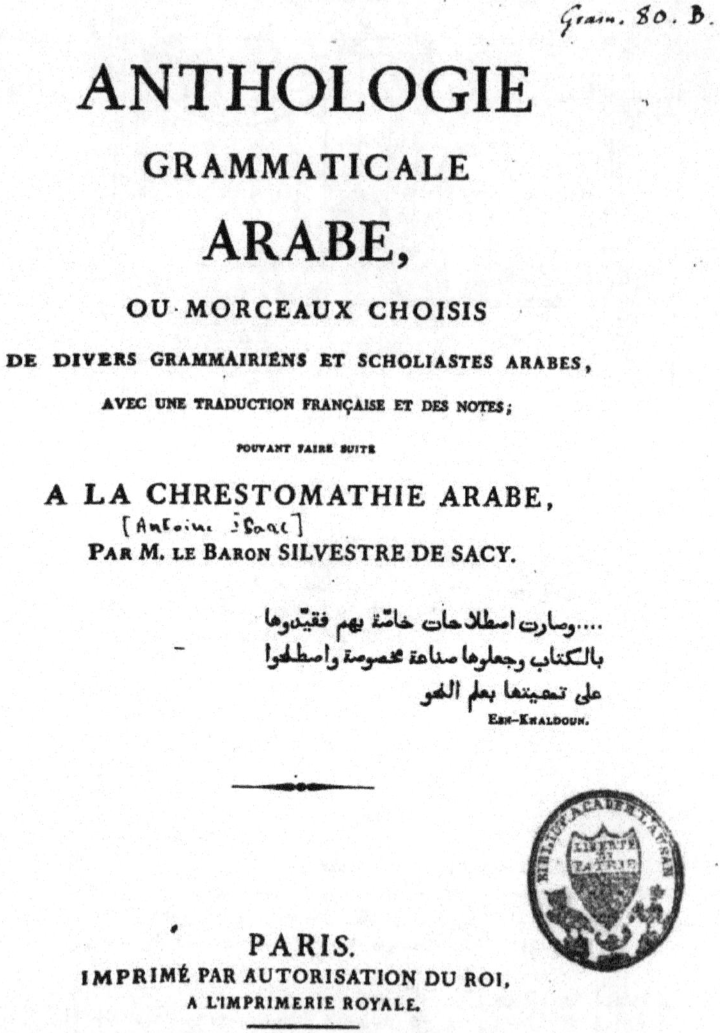

ANTHOLOGIE
GRAMMATICALE
ARABE,
OU MORCEAUX CHOISIS
DE DIVERS GRAMMAIRIENS ET SCHOLIASTES ARABES,
AVEC UNE TRADUCTION FRANÇAISE ET DES NOTES;
POUVANT FAIRE SUITE
A LA CHRESTOMATHIE ARABE,
[Antoine Isaac]
PAR M. LE BARON SILVESTRE DE SACY.

....وصارت اصطلاحات خاصّة بهم فقيّدوها
بالكتاب وجعلوها صناعة مخصوصة واصطلحوا
على تسميتها بعلم النحو
EBN-KHALDOUN.

PARIS.
IMPRIMÉ PAR AUTORISATION DU ROI,
A L'IMPRIMERIE ROYALE.
1829.

Figure 15: Title page of Sacy's 1829 *Anthologie Grammaticale Arabe* which begins with a translation of Bayḍāwī's commentary on Sūrat al-Baqara (2:1-7).

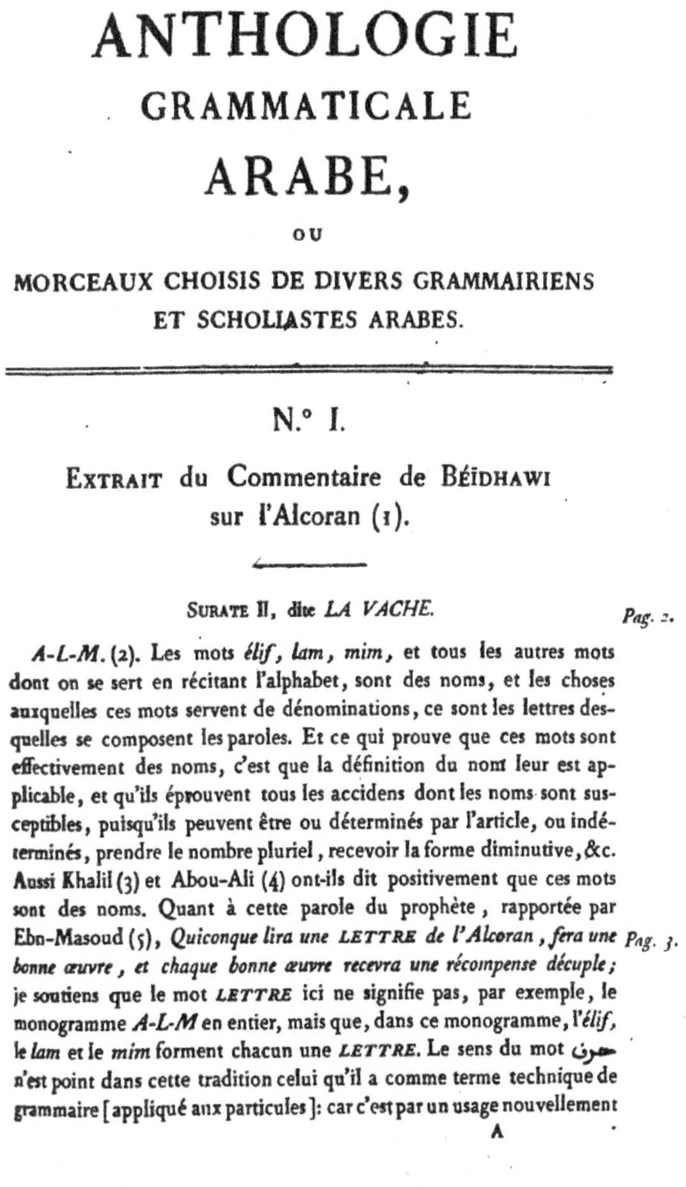

ANTHOLOGIE GRAMMATICALE ARABE,

OU

MORCEAUX CHOISIS DE DIVERS GRAMMAIRIENS ET SCHOLIASTES ARABES.

N.° I.

EXTRAIT du Commentaire de BÉÏDHAWI sur l'Alcoran (1).

SURATE II, dite *LA VACHE.* Pag. 2.

A-L-M. (2). Les mots *élif, lam, mim,* et tous les autres mots dont on se sert en récitant l'alphabet, sont des noms, et les choses auxquelles ces mots servent de dénominations, ce sont les lettres desquelles se composent les paroles. Et ce qui prouve que ces mots sont effectivement des noms, c'est que la définition du nom leur est applicable, et qu'ils éprouvent tous les accidens dont les noms sont susceptibles, puisqu'ils peuvent être ou déterminés par l'article, ou indéterminés, prendre le nombre pluriel, recevoir la forme diminutive, &c. Aussi Khalil (3) et Abou-Ali (4) ont-ils dit positivement que ces mots sont des noms. Quant à cette parole du prophète, rapportée par Ebn-Masoud (5), *Quiconque lira une* LETTRE *de l'Alcoran, fera une* Pag. 3.
bonne œuvre, et chaque bonne œuvre recevra une récompense décuple; je soutiens que le mot *LETTRE* ici ne signifie pas, par exemple, le monogramme *A-L-M* en entier, mais que, dans ce monogramme, l'*élif*, le *lam* et le *mim* forment chacun une *LETTRE*. Le sens du mot حرف n'est point dans cette tradition celui qu'il a comme terme technique de grammaire [appliqué aux particules]: car c'est par un usage nouvellement

A

Figure 16: First page of Sacy's translation of Bayḍāwī.

قاضی بیضاوی

هذا الجزء الاول من تفسیر انوار التنزیل واسرار التأویل تألیف امام
المحققین وقدوة اجل المدققین * القاضی ناصر الدین ابو الخیر عبد الله بن
عمر بن محمد الشیرازی البیضاوی والبیضاء قریة من اعمال
شیراز توفی بسنة احدی وتسعین وسبعمائه * وبهامشه تفسیر
الجلالین تألیف العلامة محمد بن احمد المحلی
رضی الله عنهم ونفعنا الله بهم آمین

شرکت صحافیهٔ عثمانیه

شرکتمزك بدایت تشکلندنبرو کتب ورسائل عربیه وترکیه غایت مصحح
واهون فیئاتله نشر اولندیغی کبی لله الحمد اشبو بیك اوجیوز ایکی سنه سی
دخی (انوار التنزیل) نام تفسیر شریفك تصحیحنه اهتمام ایله طبعنه موفق
اولنوب برنجی شعبه سی حکاکلرده (۳) نومرولو وایکنجی شعبه
سی صحافلر چارشوسنده (٦٨) دکانلرده اوچنجی شعبه سی
ازمیرده کاغدجیلر ایچنده بکارلی زاده حافظ احمد طلعت
افندینك (١٦) نومرولی دکانده کرك
ومصارفات نقلیه سی ضم ایله استانبول
فیئاتنه صاتلقده در

وسلانیکده استانبول چارشوسنده مصطفی
صدقی افندینك دکاننده دخی صاتلقده در

Figure 17: Title page of the earliest known edition of *Anwār al-Tanzīl*, printed at Dār al-Ṭibāʿat al-ʿĀmira, Istanbul 1257/1841.

قاضی بیضاوی

بسم الله الرحمن الرحيم

الحمد لله الذى نزل الفرقان على عبده ليكون للعالمين نذيرا * فتحدى
باقصر سورة من سوره مصاقع الخطباء من العرب العرباء فلم يجد به
قديرا * وافحم من تصدى لمعارضته من فصحاء عدنان وبلغاء قحطان
حتى حسبوا انهم سحروا تسحيرا * ثم بين للناس مانزل اليهم حسب
ماعن لهم من مصالحهم ليدبروا آياته وليتذكر اولوا الباب تذكيرا *
فكشف لهم قناع الانغلاق عن آيات محكمات هن ام الكتاب * واخر
متشابهات هن رموز الخطاب * تأويلا وتفسيرا * وابرز غوامض الحقائق
* ولطائف الدقائق * ليتجلى لهم خفايا الملك والملكوت وخبايا قدس الجبروت
* ليتفكروا فيها تفكيرا * ومهد لهم قواعد الاحكام واوضاعها * من نصوص
الآيات والماعها * ليذهب عنهم الرجس ويطهرهم تطهيرا * فمن كان له قلب
اوالقى السمع وهو شهيد * فهو فى الدارين حميد وسعيد * ومن لم يرفع اليه رأسه *
واطفأ نبراسه * يعش ذميما ويصلى سعيرا * فيا واجب الوجود * ويا فائض
الجود * ويا غاية كل مقصود * صل عليه صلوة توازى غناءه * وتجازى
عناءه * وعلى من اعانه وقرر تبيانه تقريرا * وافض علينا من بركاتهم *
واسلك بنا مسالك كراماتهم * وسلم عليهم وعلينا تسليما كثيرا * وبعد *
فان اعظم العلوم مقدارا * وارفعها شرفا ومنارا * علم التفسير الذى
هو رئيس العلوم الدينية ورأسها * ومبنى قواعد الشرع واساسها *

لايليق

تفسير الجلالين

بسم الله الرحمن الرحيم

الحمد لله حمدا موافيا لنعمه
مكافئا لمزيده * والصلاة
والسلام على سيدنا محمد وآله
وصحبه وجنوده * هذا ما
اشتدت اليه حاجة الراغبين *
فى تكملة تفسير القرآن الكريم
الذى ألفه الامام العلامة
المحقق جلال الدين * محمد بن
أحمد المحلى الشافعى رحمه
الله وتتميم مافاته وهو من أول
سورة البقرة الى آخر
الاسراء بتتمة على نمطه من
ذكر ما يفهم به كلام الله تعالى
والاعتماد على أرجح الاقوال
واعراب مايحتاج اليه وتنبيه
على القراآت المختلفة المشهورة
على وجه لطيف وتعبير
وجيز وترك التطويل بذكر
أقوال غير مرضية *
وأعاريب محلها كتب
العربية * والله أسأل النفع به
فى الدنيا واحسن الجزاء
عليه فى العقبى بمنه وكرمه

Figure 18: Incipit of the earliest known edition of *Anwār al-Tanzīl* (Istanbul 1257/1841) with *Tafsīr al-Jalālayn* in the margins, published at Dār al-Ṭibāʿat al-ʿĀmira.

BEIDHAWII

COMMENTARIUS IN CORANUM

EX CODD. PARISIENSIBUS DRESDENSIBUS ET LIPSIENSIBUS

EDIDIT

INDICIBUSQUE INSTRUXIT

H. O. FLEISCHER

DR. THEOL. ET PHILOS. ET LL. OO. P. O. LIPS.

VOLUMEN II.

LIPSIAE, MDCCCXLVIII

SUMTIBUS FRIDERICI CHRISTIANI GUILIELMI VOGELII.

TYPIS GUIL. VOGELII, FILII.

Figure 19: Title page of 1848 Leipzig edition of *Tafsīr al-Bayḍāwī*, among the very first Qurʾān commentaries published in Europe.

٣ سورة فاتحة الكتاب ١

سُورَةُ فَاتِحَةِ ٱلْكِتَابِ

مكّيّة وآيها سبع آيات

وتسمّى امّ القران لانّها مفتتحه ومبدأه فكانّها اصله ومنشأه ولذلك تسمّى اساسا او لانّها تشتمل على ما فيه من الثناء على اللّه والتعبّد بامره ونهيه وبيان وعده ووعيده او على جملة معانيه من الحِكَم النظريّة والأحكام العمليّة الّتى هى سلوك الطريق المستقيم والاطّلاع على مراتب السعداء ومنازل الاشقياء وسورةَ الكنزِ والوافيةَ والكافيةَ لذلك وسورةَ الحمد والشكرِ والدعاء وتعليمِ المسئلة لاشتمالها عليها والصلوةِ لوجوب قراءتها او استحبابها فيها والشافيةَ والشفاء لقوله صلعم هى شفاء كلّ داء والسبعَ المثانى لانّها سبع آيات بالاتّفاق الّا انّ منهم من عدّ التسمية دون انعمت عليهم ومنهم من عكس وتُثنّى فى الصلوة او الانزال ان صحّ انّها نزلت بمكّة حين فُرضت الصلوة وبالمدينة لمّا حُوّلت القبلة وقد صحّ انّها مكّيّة لقوله تعالى ولقد آتيناك سبعا من المثانى وهو مكّىّ بالنصّ

بِسْمِ ٱللّٰهِ ٱلرَّحْمٰنِ ٱلرَّحِيمِ

من الفاتحة وعليه قُرّاء مكّة والكوفة وفقهاؤهما وابن المبارك والشافعىّ وخالفهم قرّاء المدينة والبصرة والشأم وفقهاؤها ومالك والاوزاعىّ ولم ينصّ ابو حنيفة فيه بشىء فظُنّ انّها ليست من السورة عنده وسئل محمّد بن الحسن عنها فقال ما بين الدفّتين كلام اللّه لنا احاديث كثيرة منها ما روى ابو هريرة انّه عم قال فاتحة الكتاب سبع آيات أُولاهنّ بسم اللّه الرحمن الرحيم وقول امّ سلمة قرأ رسول اللّه الفاتحة وعدّ بسم اللّه الرحمن الرحيم الحمد للّه ربّ العالمين آية ومن اجلهما اختلف فى انّها آية برأسها او بما بعدها والإجماعُ على انّ ما بين الدفّتين كلام اللّه والوِفاقُ على اِثباتها فى المصاحف مع المبالغة فى تجريد القران حتّى لم يكتب آمين ، والباء متعلّقة بمحذوف تقديرُه بسم اللّه أَقْرأُ لانّ الّذى يتلوه مقروء وكذلك يضمر كلُّ فاعل ما يَجْعل التسميةَ مبدأً له وذلك أَوْلَى من ان يضمر أَبْدأُ لعدم ما يطابقه ويدلّ عليه او ابتدائىْ لزيادة اضمارٍ فيه وتقديمُ المعمول ههنا اوقعُ كما فى قوله بسم اللّه مجراها وقولِه ايّاك نعبد لانّه اهمُّ وادلُّ على الاختصاص وادخلُ فى التعظيم واوفقُ للوجود فانّ اسمه تعالى متقدّم على القراءة كيف لا وقد جُعِل آلةً لها من حيث انّ الفعل لا يتمّ ولا يعتدّ به شرعا ما لم يصدَّر باسمه لقوله عم كلّ امرٍ ذى بالٍ لم يُبْدأ فيه باسم اللّه فهو ابتر وقيل الباء للمصاحبة والمعنى متبرّكا باسم اللّه اقرأُ وهذا وما بعده مقول على أَلسنة العباد ليعلموا كيف يُتبرّك باسمه ويحمد على نعمه ويسأل من فضله وانّما كُسرت ومِنْ حقّ الحروف المفردة ان تُفْتَح لاختصاصها بلزوم الحرفيّة والجرّ كما كسرت لام الامر ولام الاضافة داخلةً على المُظْهَر للفصل بينهما وبين لام الابتداء ، والاسم عند اصحابنا البصريّين من الاسماء الّتى حُذفت أَعجازها لكثرة الاستعمال وبُنيت اوائلها على السكون وأُدخل عليها مبتدأً بها همزة الوصل لانّ مِنْ دأبهم ان يبتدؤا بالمتحرّك ويقفوا على الساكن

Figure 20: Page 3 of Fleischer's 1848 edition: Fatiha.

Figure 21: Page 1 (Incipit) of the Teheran 1272/1856 lithograph edition of the marginalia by the Shiʿi Safavid Shaykh al-Islam Bahāʾ al-Dīn al-ʿĀmilī (953-1030/1546-1621), *Taʿlīqāt Anwār al-Tanzīl*, surrounding al-Bayḍāwī's text.

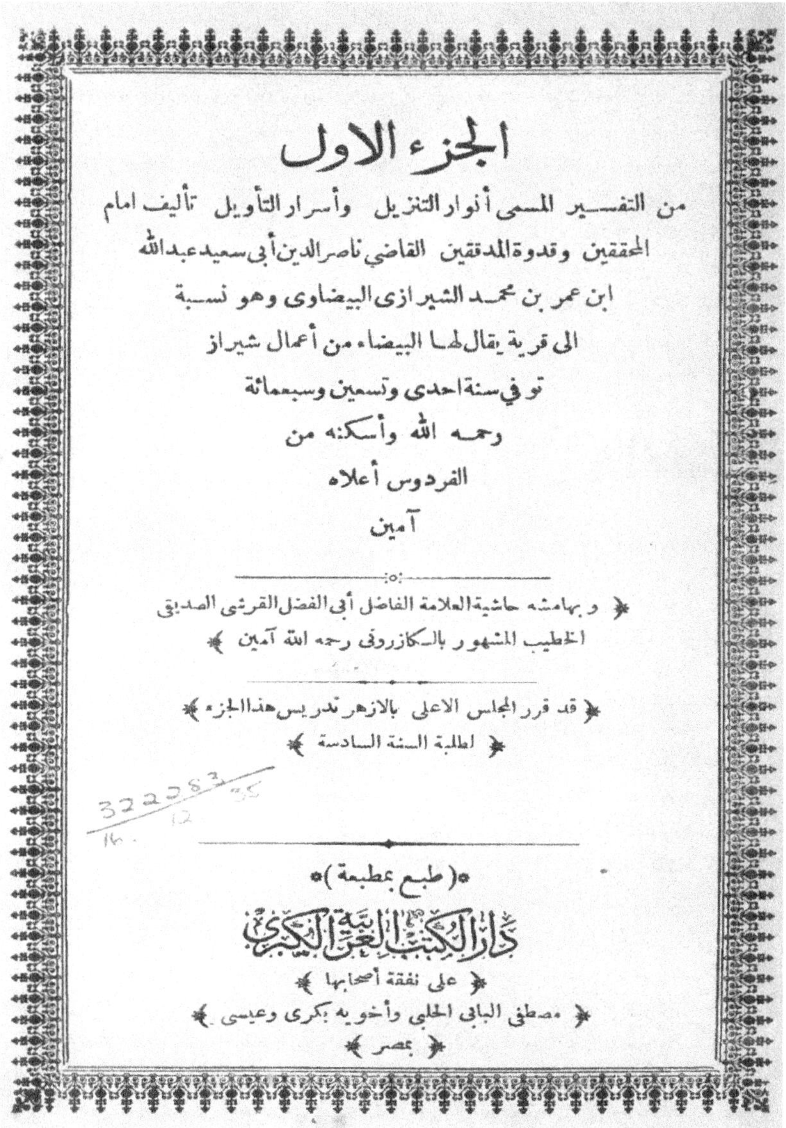

الجزء الاول

من التفسير المسمى أنوار التنزيل وأسرار التأويل تأليف امام
المحققين وقدوة المدققين القاضي ناصر الدين أبي سعيد عبد الله
ابن عمر بن محمد الشيرازي البيضاوي وهو نسبة
الى قرية يقال لها البيضاء من أعمال شيراز
توفي سنة احدى وتسعين وسبعمائة
رحمه الله وأسكنه من
الفردوس أعلاه
آمين

وبهامشه حاشية العلامة الفاضل أبي الفضل القرشي الصديقي
الخطيب المشهور بالكازروني رحمه الله آمين

قد قرر المجلس الاعلى بالازهر تدريس هذا الجزء
لطلبة السنة السادسة

(طبع بمطبعة)
دار الكتب العربية الكبرى
على نفقة أصحابها
مصطفى البابي الحلبي وأخويه بكرى وعيسى
بمصر

Figure 22: Title page of the 1330/1912 Egyptian edition of al-Bayḍāwī's *Tafsīr* with al-Kāzarūnī's (d. after 1102/1691) 1100-page, four-volume *Ḥāshiya*: "The higher council in al-Azhar has decreed this book be taught to 6th-year students."

بسم الله الرحمن الرحيم رب تمم بالخير

(قوله الحمد لله الذى نزل الفرقان على عبده ليكون للعالمين نذيرا) قال صاحب الكشاف فى خطبته الحمد لله الذى أنزل
القرآن كلاما مؤلفا منظما وقال الشريف فى الحاشية دل بلامى التعريف والملك على اختصاص الحمد به تعالى وقال فى حاشية شرح
المختصر دل الشارح فى قوله الحمد لله بلامى التعريف والاختصاص على اختصاص جنس الحمد به تعالى المستلزم لاختصاص المحامد
كلها تحقيقا على قاعدة أهل الحق وأورد بعض العلماء انه أطبق شراح الكشاف وغيرهم ممن تلاهم على ذلك ولى فيه بحث
لان الظاهر ان اللام انما يدل على الاختصاص بمعنى التعلق الخاص لا بمعنى الانحصار يدل على ذلك انهم ماعدوه من طرق
الحصر كما عدوا سائر الحروف المشهورة بالحصر منها وان قولك المال لزيد لو كان مفيدا لحصر المال على زيد كان قولك
ما المال الا لزيد مفيدا لحصر المال على صفة الانحصار على زيد لا على قصر المال فى زيد ولو كان لله الحمد مفيدا لقصر الحمد
على الاختصاص بالله تعالى لا على قصره على الله تعالى لان قولك الحمد لله لما كان دالا على اختصاص الحمد به يعنى كونه مقصورا
عليه تعالى لم يكن تقديم الظرف مفيدا للاختصاص الحاصل بدونه بل قصر ذلك على الاختصاص على المبتدأ واللازم منتف
كيف لا وصاحب الكشاف نفسه قد قال فى سورة التغابن قدم الظرفان فى قوله له الملك وله الحمد ليدل تقديمهما على اختصاص
الملك والحمد بالله عز وجل أقول الجواب عما ذكر أولا ان قوله انهم ماعدوه من طرق الحصر ان أراد به (٢) انهم ماعدوه
من الطرق المذكورة فى باب القصر من أبواب علم المعانى فعدم ذكره فيه لا يدل على عدم كونه من
طرقه فانهم ما حصروا الطرق فيما ذكر فى الباب المذكور يدل على ذلك ان صاحب التلخيص
وغيره ذكروا ان كون الخبر المحلى باللام يدل على القصر كزيد المنطلق مثلا فانه يدل على
قصر الانطلاق على زيد ولم يذكروا ذلك فى باب القصر وان أرادوا انهم لم يعدوه من طرق
القصر أصلا فممنوع فان قولهم اللام للاختصاص يدل ظاهرا على انه للقصر وعما ذكره ثانيا
انه يمكن ان يكون قولهم اللام للاختصاص انه فى الاصل للاختصاص والحصر ثم يستعمل
فى معان أخر كالتعلق الخاص أو يكون مستعملا فيهما بالاشتراك ومنه قولك ما المال
الا لزيد فتأمل نظير ذلك ما قالوا ان اللام فى الاصل للتعليل ثم يستعمل فى مجرد ترتب الشئ كما فى قوله تعالى فالتقطه آل فرعون
ليكون لهم عدوا وحزنا ثم اذا سلمنا ما ذكروه وانه يلزم قصر المال على صفة الاختصاص بزيد فلا نسلم أن هذا لا يدل على
انحصاره فى زيد بل يدل عليه بطريق المبالغة فانه يفيد انه ليس للمال الا صفة كونه مقصورا على الاختصاص لا يتجاوز الى صفة
الاشتراك بينه وبين غيره فلو كان غير زيد ذا مال لم يكن مقصورا على صفة الاختصاص بل له صفة الاشتراك فتدبر وعما ذكر ثالثا
ان قول صاحب الكشاف قدم الظرفان الخ يجوز ان يكون معناه انه لما كان اللام قد يجيء لغير القصر فلو قيل الحمد له لم يكن نصا فى
حصر الحمد عليه تعالى فقدم الظرفان ليكون نصا فاللام فى له الحمد لمجرد التعلق فيكون النص على القصر مستفادا من التقديم
ثم انه لو لم يكن اللام للقصر لم يكن الحمد لله مفيدا لقصر الحمد على الله تعالى وكان معناه مجرد تعلق الحمد بالله تعالى فلا يفهم منه ما هو
الغرض الاصلى من قصر الحمد عليه تعالى * واعلم ان بين العبارة المنقولة من أول خطبة الكشاف وبين الفقرة الاولى من خطبة
الكتاب فرقا من وجوه الاول ان المراد من الانزال الانزال الى السماء الدنيا فانه روى انه أنزل من اللوح المحفوظ الى السماء الدنيا
دفعة ثم نزل بحسب المصالح منجما ولهذا لم يقيد صاحب الكشاف أنزل بقوله على عبده ولم يتعرض المصنف للانزال المذكور دفعة
واحدة لان ظهور اعجازه وعموم فيضه وهدايته بالتنزيل على عبده ليكون للعالمين نذيرا ولا يخفى مناسبة الانزال للقرآن الذى
هو الجمع فى الاصل كما سيجيء وملاءمة التنزيل للفرقان الثانى ان عبارة المصنف مشتملة على فائدة التنزيل وهى الانذار
الثالث الاشارة الى كونه صلى الله عليه وسلم مبعوثا الى كافة الخلق بقوله ليكون للعالمين نذيرا على ما قرر ان اللام فى للعالمين

﴿ بسم الله الرحمن الرحيم ﴾

الحمد لله الذى نزل
الفرقان على عبده
ليكون للعالمين نذيرا

Figure 23: First page of the 1912 Bayḍāwī/Kāzarūnī edition with al-Bayḍāwī's text in the box.

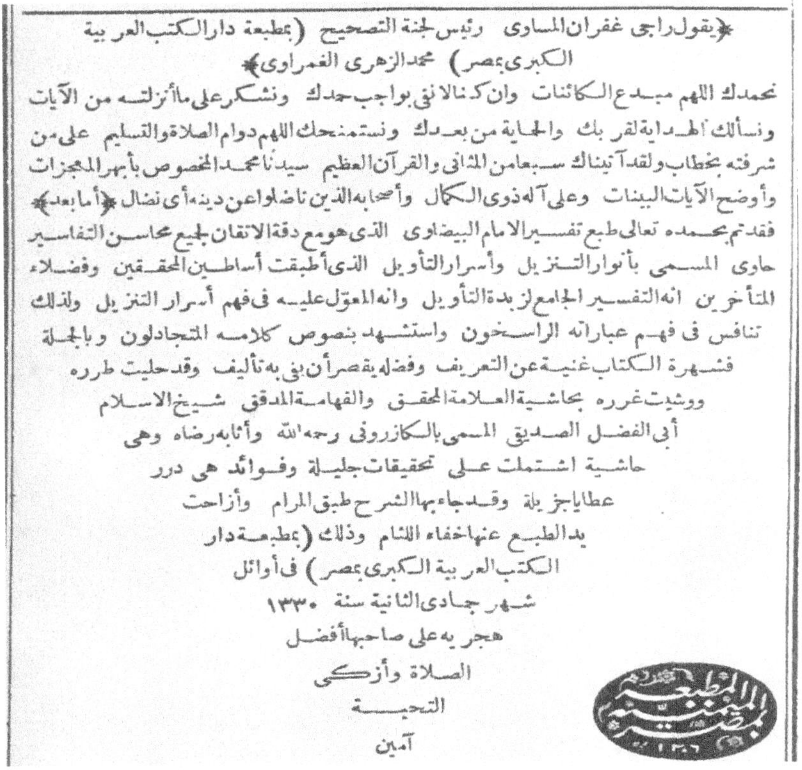

﴿يقول راجي غفران المساوي رئيس لجنة التصحيح (بمطبعة دار الكتب العربية
الكبرى بمصر) محمد الزهري الغمراوي﴾
نحمدك اللهم مبدع الكائنات وان كنا لا نفي بواجب حمدك ونشكر على ما أنزلته من الآيات
ونسألك الهداية لقربك والحماية من بعدك ونستمنحك اللهم دوام الصلاة والتسليم على من
شرفته بخطاب ولقد آتيناك سبعا من المثاني والقرآن العظيم سيدنا محمد المخصوص بأبهر المعجزات
وأوضح الآيات البينات وعلى آله ذوي الكمال وأصحابه الذين ناضلوا عن دينه أي نضال ﴿أما بعد﴾
فقد تم بحمده تعالى طبع تفسير الامام البيضاوي الذي هو مع دقة الاتقان لجميع محاسن التفاسير
حاوي المسمى بأنوار التنزيل وأسرار التأويل الذي أطبقت أساطين المحققين وفضلاء
المتأخرين انه التفسير الجامع لزبدة التأويل وانه المعول عليه في فهم أسرار التنزيل ولذلك
تنافس في فهم عباراته الراسخون واستشهد بنصوص كلامه المتجادلون وبالجملة
فشهرة الكتاب غنية عن التعريف وفضله يقصر أن يفي به تأليف وقد حليت طرره
ووشيت غرره بحاشية العلامة المحقق والفهامة المدقق شيخ الاسلام
أبي الفضل الصديقي المسمى بالكازروني رحمه الله وأثابه رضاه وهي
حاشية اشتملت على تحقيقات جليلة وفوائد هي درر
عطايا جزيلة وقد جاء بها الشرح طبق المرام وأزاحت
يد الطبع عنها خفاء اللثام وذلك (بمطبعة دار
الكتب العربية الكبرى بمصر) في أوائل
شهر جمادى الثانية سنة ١٣٣٠
هجريه على صاحبها أفضل
الصلاة وأزكى
التحية
آمين

Figure 24: Last page of the 1912 Bayḍāwī edition bearing a eulogy by its chief editor, the Moroccan-born Azharī Shāfiʿī jurist Muḥammad al-Zuhrī al-Ghamrāwī: "By the Grace of Allah the printing of Imam al-Bayḍāwī's Qur'ān commentary is done. In addition to its extreme meticulousness, it encompasses all the excellences of other commentaries. It is named *Anwār al-Tanzīl wa-Asrār al-Ta'wīl* and there is consensus among the foremost authoritative scholars past and present that this *tafsīr* gathers up the cream of exegesis and is the ultimate reference in understanding the secrets of revelation. Those who are firmly rooted in learning have competed in understanding its phrases and debaters quote it verbatim. In sum, the fame of this book needs no introduction and its merit cannot be overemphasized."

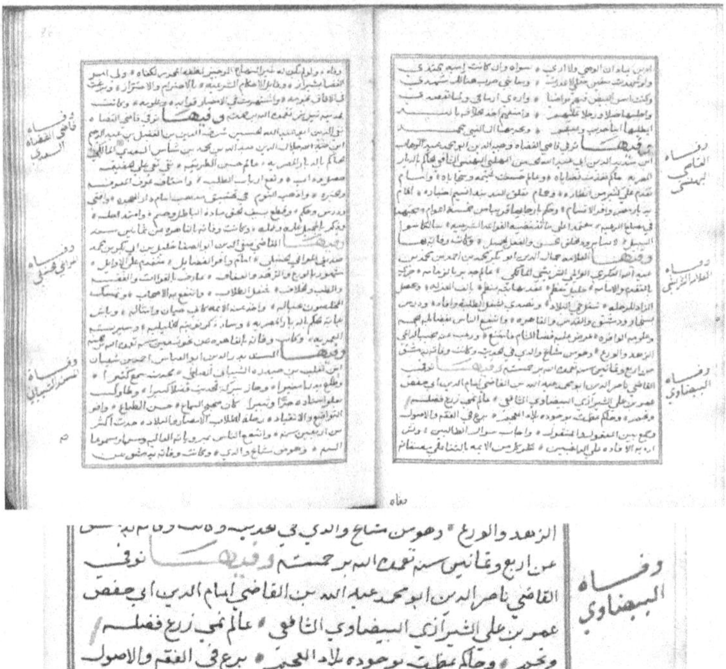

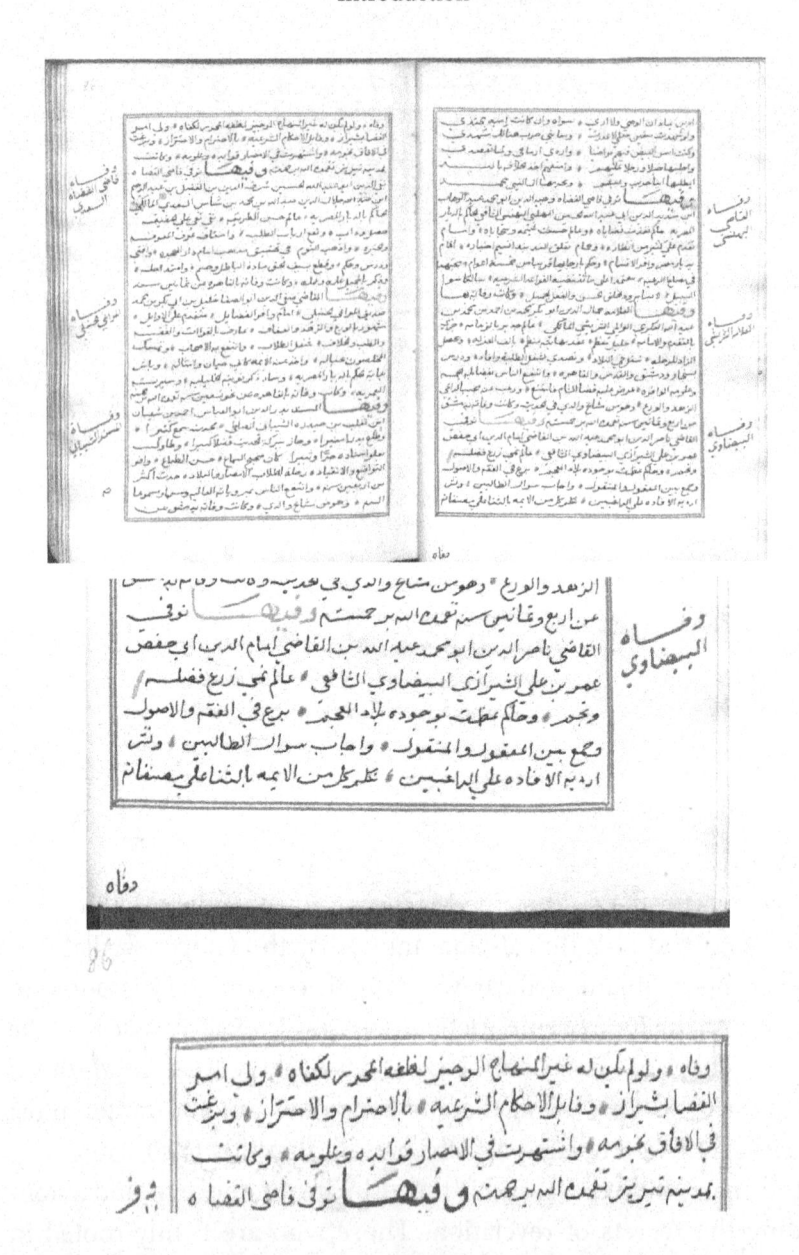

Figure 25: Ibn Ḥabīb al-Dimashqī (d. 779/1377), *Durrat al-Aslāk fī Dawlat al-Atrāk* ("Year 685"), ms. Leipzig Vollers 0661, folios 85b-86a and details showing Bayḍāwī's obitus. Copied in Aleppo in 1071/1660.

Our chain of transmission (*sanad al-riwāya*) to Bayḍāwī's *Anwār al-Tanzīl*

I, the needy pauper Abū Ḥammād Gibril b. Fouad Haddad al-Ṣāliḥī narrate al-Bayḍāwī's *Anwār al-Tanzīl wa-Asrār al-Ta'wīl*:

1a- from my teachers the Renewer of Sunni education, *Ḥāfiẓ*, chair of the Departments of Qur'ān and Sunna in the universities of Damascus and Aleppo and author of 50 books, Dr. Nūr al-Dīn ʿItr b. Muḥammad b. Ḥasan al-Ḥusaynī al-Azharī al-Ḥanafī (b. 1356/1937) and 1b- the *muqri'* and *muḥaddith* of Damascus, Muḥammad Sāmer b. Mamdūḥ b. Sharīf al-Naṣṣ al-Ḥanafī, MD,

2a- the former from his teacher, maternal uncle and father-in-law Shaykh Abū al-Najīb ʿAbd Allāh b. Muḥammad Najīb b. Muḥammad Sirāj al-Dīn al-Ḥusaynī al-Ḥalabī al-Ḥanafī al-Rifāʿī (1343-1422/1925-2001), the saintly *Ḥāfiẓ* and Shaykh al-Islām of Aleppo; 2b- the latter from our teacher the *faqīh* Shaykh Muḥammad Adīb b. Aḥmad b. al-Ḥājj Dīb Kallās (1921-2009),

3a- the former from his father the hadith scholar and exegete, Shaykh Muḥammad Najīb Sirāj al-Dīn al-Ḥusaynī al-Ḥalabī (1274-1373/1858-1954), 3b- the latter from the Mufti of Shām, Sayyid Muḥammad Abū al-Yusr ʿĀbidīn (1307-1401/1890-1981),

4- both Shaykh Najīb and Sayyid Abū al-Yusr from the great *Muḥaddith al-Akbar* of Damascus, the Sayyid and Shaykh Badr al-Dīn Muḥammad b. Yūsuf al-Ḥasanī al-Maghribī al-Dimashqī (1267-1354/1851-1935),

5- from his main teacher Burhān al-Dīn Ibrāhīm b. ʿAlī al-Saqqā al-Azharī al-Miṣrī al-Shāfiʿī (1212-1298/1797-1881),

6- from his teacher the saintly blind imam and hadith scholar Muḥammad b. Sālim b. Nāṣir al-Fishnī al-Miṣrī known as Shaykh Thuʿaylib (or Thuʿaylīb) (1151-1239/1738-1824),

7- from his two erudite teachers the hadith scholars Shihāb al-Dīn Aḥmad b. ʿAbd al-Fattāḥ al-Mullawī (d. 1181/1767) and Shihāb al-Dīn Aḥmad b. al-Ḥasan al-Jūharī (d. 1181/1767),

8- both from the *musnid* and hadith master ʿAbd Allāh b. Sālim b. Muḥammad al-Baṣrī al-Makkī (1049-1143/1639-1731),

9- from his teacher the blind *musnid* Shams al-Dīn Muḥammad b. al-ʿAlāʾ al-Bābilī al-Qāhirī al-Shāfiʿī (1000-1077/1592-1666),

10- from the erudite hadith scholars al-Shihāb Aḥmad b. ʿĪsā b. ʿAllāb b. Jamīl al-Kalbī al-Mālikī al-Miṣrī al-Ṣūfī al-Azharī (d. 1027/1618) and Abū al-Najā Sālim b. ʿIzz al-Dīn Muḥammad al-Sanhūrī al-Mālikī al-Miṣrī (d. 1025/1616 or 1015/1606),

11- both from their teacher the erudite *musnid, ḥāfiẓ* and jurist Najm al-Dīn Muḥammad b. Aḥmad b. ʿAlī b. Abī Bakr al-Ghayṭī al-Shāfiʿī al-Iskandarī (900-982/1495-1574), the second also from the erudite arch-jurist al-Shihāb Aḥmad b. Ḥajar al-Haytamī al-Makkī al-Shāfiʿī (909-973/1503-1566),

12- both from their teacher, the centenarian Shaykh al-Islam, jurisprudent, hadith scholar, canonist, Sufi and qadi Zayn al-Dīn Abū Yaḥyā Zakariyyāʾ b. Muḥammad al-Anṣārī al-Miṣrī al-Shāfiʿī (823-926/1420-1520),

13- from the erudite hadith scholar Abū al-Faḍl Muḥammad b. Muḥammad b. Abī Bakr al-Anṣārī al-Dhirwī al-Makkī al-Shāfiʿī, known as Ibn al-Marjānī (796-876/1394-1472) and the hadith arch-master Abū al-Faḍl Aḥmad b. ʿAlī b. Ḥajar al-ʿAsqalānī (773-852/1372-1448),

14- both from the erudite hadith scholar Abū Hurayra Zayn al-Dīn ʿAbd al-Raḥmān b. Shams al-Dīn Muḥammad b. Aḥmad al-Dhahabī al-Dimashqī (715-799/1315-1397),

15- from the Azeri-Damascene Sufi hadith scholar al-Kamāl Abū Ḥafṣ or Abū al-Qāsim ʿUmar b. Ilyās b. Yūnus al-Marāghī al-Adharbayjānī al-Dimashqī (643-732/1245-1332),[212]

from the Imam and Qadi Nāṣir al-Dīn

ʿAbd Allah b. ʿUmar al-Bayḍāwī,

may the mercy of Allah

be upon him and

all of the

above.

Āmīn.

[212] Cf. Aḥmad Sardār al-Ḥalabī, *Iʿlām al-Ṭalabat al-Nājiḥīn fīmā ʿAlā min Asānīd al-Shaykh ʿAbd Allāh Sirāj al-Dīn* (Aleppo: Dār al-Qalam al-ʿArabī, 1414/1994) p. 101; Muḥammad Amīn Ibn ʿĀbidīn, *Thabat Ibn ʿĀbidīn al-Musammā ʿUqūd al-Laʾālī fīl-Asānīd al-ʿAwālī*, ed. Muḥammad b. Ibrāhīm al-Ḥusayn (Beirut: Dār al-Bashāʾir al-Islāmiyya, 1431/2010) p. 392-393 §51; ʿĪsā b. Muḥammad al-Thaʿālibī al-Makkī, *Thabat Shams al-Dīn al-Bābilī* with Murtaḍā al-Zabīdī, *al-Murabbī al-Kābulī fīman Rawā ʿan al-Babilī*, ed. Muḥammad b. Nāṣir al-ʿAjamī (Beirut: Dār al-Bashāʾir al-Islāmiyya, 1425/2004) pp. 91 §55, pp. 189-190 §12, p. 194 §22; al-Muḥibbī, *Khulāṣat al-Athar fī Aʿyān al-Qarn al-Ḥādī ʿAshar*, 4 vols. (Cairo: al-Maṭbaʿat al-Wahbiyya, 1284/1867) 1:266; al-Sakhāwī, *al-Ḍawʾ al-Lāmiʿ li-Ahl al-Qarn al-Tāsiʿ*, 12 vols. in 6 (Cairo: Maktabat al-Qudsī, 1354/1935; rept. Beirut: Dār al-Jīl, 1992) 9:67 §172; *Thabat Shaykh al-Islām al-Qāḍī Zakariyyā al-Anṣārī*, ed. Muḥammad b. Ibrāhīm al-Ḥusayn (Beirut: Dār al-Bashāʾir al-Islāmiyya, 1431/2010) p. 331; Muḥammad al-Sinbāwī, *Thabat al-Amīr al-Kabīr*, ed. Muḥammad Ibrāhīm al-Ḥusayn (Beirut: Dār al-Bashāʾir al-Islāmiyya, 1430/2009; and ʿAbd al-Raḥmān b. Aḥmad al-Kuzbarī et al., *Majmūʿ al-Athbāt al-Ḥadīthiyya li-Āl al-Kuzbarī al-Dimashqiyyīn*, ed. ʿUmar al-Nushūqātī (Damascus: Dār al-Nawādir, 1428/2007) pp. 57, 61, 97-98, 233, 355.

The First *Ḥizb* of the Qur'an (1:1-2:74)

A Baydawian Rendering in English

with paginal index of corresponding commentary

1 The Sura of the Opening 147

1 *In the Name of the One God, the All-Beneficent,* 151
the Most Merciful!

2 *Praise be to the One God, the Nurturer of the* 173
worlds,

3 *the All-Beneficent, the Most Merciful,* 180

4 *the Owner of the Day of reckoning!* 180

5 *You do we worship and You do we ask for help!* 186

6 *Show us the straight path,* 195

7 *the path of those You have favored, other than* 200
those who incurred anger nor those who are
astray!

214 **2** **The Sura of the Cow**
(Medinan, numbering 287 verses)

214 1 *In the Name of the One God, the All-Beneficent,*
the Most Merciful! Alif; lām; mīm:

243 2 *that is the Book no doubt ∴ therein, ∴ a Guidance*
for those who beware—

255 3 *those who believe in the unseen and establish the*
prayer, spending out of what We provided them,

273 4 *and those who believe in what was sent down to*
you and what was sent down before you; and of
the hereafter they are certain:

280 5 *Those are upon guidance from their Nurturer*
and those—they are the successful!

285 6 *Verily those who rejected belief, it is the same for*
them whether you warn them or you do not
warn them.

[7]*The One God has sealed over their hearts and* 297
over their hearing; and over their sights there is a
pall; and theirs is an immense punishment.

[8]*And of people there are those who say: "We be-* 309
lieve in the One God and in the Last Day," when
they are not believers at all.

[9]*They deceive the One God and those who do* 317
believe; but they delude only themselves.

[10]*In their hearts is a sickness, so the One God in-* 323
creased their sickness; and theirs is a painful
punishment because they used to lie.

[11]*And when it is said to them: "Do not spread* 328
corruption in the land," they say: "Nay, but we
are civilizers!"

[12]*Behold! Truly it is they who are the workers of* 330
corruption; but they do not realize.

[13]*And when it is said to them, "Believe as human* 332
beings believe!" they say, "Us? Believe as the fools

believe?" Behold! Truly it is they who are the fools; but they do not know.

337 [14]*And when they light upon those who believe
they say: "We believe." And when they retire unto
their devils they say: "Truly we are with you, we
only make scoff."*

342 [15]*The One God scoffs at them and keeps reinforcing them in their rebellion all bewildered!*

348 [16]*Those are they who purchased error at the price
of guidance; so their trading profited nothing and
they were not guided at all.*

352 [17]*Their likeness is as the likeness of the one that
kindled a fire; as soon as it illuminated his surroundings, the One God took away their light and
He left them in darknesses, sightless:*

364 [18]*deaf, dumb, blind—so they will not return;*

369 [19]*or as a cloudburst from the sky filled with
darknesses, thunder and lightning: they put their*

fingers into their ears from the thunderstrokes for fear of death; and all the while the One God surrounds the unbelievers.

20*Lightning almost snatches away their sights:* 377
every time it shines for them they walk in that, and when it darkens over them they stand; and if the One God willed He would take away their hearing and sights. Truly the One God is over all things almighty!

21*O you people! Worship your Nurturer Who* 393
created you and those before you; perhaps you will beware;

22*Who has made for you the earth a bed and the* 404
sky a building, and sent down, out of the sky, water whereby He produced some fruits as sustenance for you. Therefore do not set up peers to the One God when you know full well!

23*And if you are in doubt of what We brought* 418
down on Our slave, then produce a sura of its

like, and call your witnesses as against the One God if you are truthful;

429 **24***but if you do not—and you will not—then beware the fire whose fuel is people and stones! It was readied for the unbelievers.*

439 **25***And give glad tidings to those who believe and do righteous deeds, that for them are gardens underneath which run the rivers. Whenever they are provided thereof with fruit as a provision they say: "This is what was provided to us in former times;" and they are supplied with it, all looking similar, and they have therein spouses immaculate, and they will be therein, perduring.*

461 **26***Verily the One God is not ashamed to strike some similitude—of a gnat or what is more than that. As for those who believe, they know it is the truth from their Nurturer; but as for those who disbelieve, they say: "What did the One God mean by [using] this as a simile?" He misleads many thereby and He guides many thereby; but*

*He misleads none thereby other than the de-
praved,*

27 *those who breach the covenant of the One God* 482
*after its thorough fastening, and cut what the One
God commanded to be joined, and spread corruption on earth: those—they are the losers!*

28 *How do you disbelieve in the One God when* 488
*you had been dead then He gave you life, then He
will make you die, then He will give you life, then
unto Him you shall be returned?*

29 *He it is Who created for you what is in the* 495
*earth—all of it; further, He proceeded to the sky
and He levelled them as seven skies, and He is
most knowing of all things.*

30 *And behold! Your Nurturer said to the angels,* 504
*"Verily I am setting on earth a successor." They
said: "Will you set in it those who will spread
corruption in it and shed blood, while we extol
with Your praise and we hallow for You?" He
said, "Verily I know what you do not know."*

520 **31** *And He taught Adam the names—all of them. Then He displayed them before the angels and He said, "Inform Me of the names of these, if you are truthful."*

527 **32** *They said, "Extolled are You! We know nothing except what You taught us. Truly You—and You alone—are the most Knowing, the most Wise."*

530 **33** *He said, "O Adam, inform them of their names!" When he informed them of their names He said, "Did I not tell you? Verily I know what is invisible in the heavens and the earth; and I know what you disclose and what you try to keep hidden."*

535 **34** *And behold! We said to the angels, "Prostrate to Adam!" So they prostrated, except Iblīs: he refused and was arrogant, and he was of the unbelievers.*

550 **35** *And We said: "O Adam! inhabit the Garden—you and your wife—and eat from it in plenty,*

wherever you both wish, but do not approach this Tree lest you be of the wrongdoers!"

[36]*Then Satan caused them to slip from it and he* 554
drove them out of what they were both in. And We said: "All go down, one another's enemy! and you can have in the earth a settlement and some benefit until a certain time."

[37]*Then Adam welcomed from his Nurturer cer-* 558
tain words, whereupon He relented towards him. Truly He—and He alone—is the Oft-Relenting, the Most Merciful.

[38]*We said: "Go down from it, all of you! And if* 563
ever comes to you—as it will—a guidance from Me: then whoever follows My guidance, there shall be no fear for them, nor shall they grieve."

[39]*As for those who disbelieve and belie Our signs:* 565
those are the dwellers of the fire; they will abide therein forever.

575 **40***O sons of Isrāʾīl! Remember My favor which I lavished on you and fulfill My covenant, I shall fulfill the covenant made to you; and Me do dread!*

581 **41***And believe in what I have sent down in confirmation of what is with you, and do not be the first disbeliever therein; and do not purchase with My signs some paltry gain. And of Me do beware!*

588 **42***And do not confound the truth with falsehood and conceal the truth when you know full well!*

589 **43***And establish the prayer and remit the charity tax, and bow with those who bow.*

591 **44***Do you order people to practice virtue and forget yourselves? Yet you rehearse the Book! Have you no understanding?*

594 **45***And seek help in endurance and prayer; and truly that is too much except for those who are humble!—*

46 *those who presume that they are going to meet* 598
their Nurturer and are returning back to Him.

47 *O sons of Isrāʾīl! Remember My favor which I* 599
lavished on you, and that I have preferred you
over the worlds;

48 *—and beware a day a soul cannot pay any-* 601
thing on behalf of another soul, and no interces-
sion will be accepted from it, and no redemption
taken, nor will they get any help!—

49 *and when We saved you from the house of* 605
Pharaoh as they persecuted you with evil tor-
ment, massacring your sons and sparing your
females: and in that you faced a trial, on the part
of your Nurturer, tremendous!

50 *And when We parted the sea with you, where-* 609
upon We saved you and drowned the house of
Pharaoh as you looked on.

613 **51** *And when We promised Mūsā forty nights, then you resorted to the Calf after him, transgressing!*

615 **52** *Then We pardoned you after that act: perhaps you will give thanks.*

615 **53** *And when We gave Mūsā the Book and discernment: perhaps you will be guided.*

617 **54** *And when Mūsā said to his nation: "My nation! truly you have wronged yourselves by resorting to the Calf, therefore repent to your Producer and kill yourselves! Such indeed is best for you in the sight of your Producer." Then He relented towards you. Truly He—and He alone—is the Oft-Relenting, the Most Merciful!*

622 **55** *And when you said: "O Mūsā, we will not believe merely for your sake; but only when we see the One God openly." So the thunderstroke seized you as you looked on!*

56*Then We raised you up after your death. Per-* 625
haps you will be thankful.

57*And We overshadowed you with clouds, and* 626
We brought down upon you manna and game:
"Eat of the agreeable things We provided you!"
And they did not wrong Us, but rather they were
wronging themselves.

58*And when We said, "Enter this town and eat* 627
from it wherever you wish in plenty; and enter
the gate submissively and say: A reprieve!"
whereby We shall forgive you your errors; and We
will increase the well-doers.

59*Then those who did wrong replaced what they* 630
had been told with some other words. So We sent
down on the wrong-doers a bane from the sky
because of their transgressions.

60*And when Mūsā sought water for his nation, so* 632
We said, "Strike with your staff the rock;" where-
upon there burst forth from it twelve springs.

Each people knew well their drinking-place. "Eat and drink of the provision of the One God, and do not wreak havoc in the land by spreading corruption!"

637 **61** *And when you all said: "O Mūsā, we will no longer put up with the same food; therefore call upon your Nurturer for us and He will bring out for us of what the earth grows—of its herbs and its cucumbers and its grains and its lentils and its onions." He said: "Will you take what is inferior in exchange for what is best? Go down into some city! Then you shall have what you ask." And humiliation and misery were pitched upon them, and they finally bore the anger of the One God. That is on account of their constant disbelief in the signs of the One God and their killing the prophets unrightly. That is on account of their disobedience and constant transgressions.*

645 **62** *Verily those who believed and those who Judaized and the Nazarenes and the Sabians: whoever believed in the One God and in the Last Day and*

did good, undoubtedly for them is their reward with their Nurturer Himself, and they have nothing to fear, nor shall they grieve.

63 *And when We took your binding promise, and* 650
We made the mountain hang above you: "Take what We gave you with strength and remember what is in it! Perhaps you will beware."

64 *Yet you turned away even after that. Indeed,* 651
were it not for the favor of the One God over you and His mercy, you would have been of the losers!

65 *And you know very well of those among you* 653
who transgressed in the Sabbath, whereupon We said to them: "Be apes, kept at bay!"

66 *Then We made it a deterrent punishment for* 655
all behind it and all ahead of it, and an admonishment for those who beware.

67 *And when Mūsā said to his nation: Verily the* 656
One God commands you to slaughter a cow. They said: "Are you making us your laughing-stock?"

He said: "I take refuge in the One God from ever being of the ignorant!"

658 **68** *They said: "Call upon your Nurturer for us to make clear to us what it is." He said: "Verily He says it is a cow neither cull nor yearling, middling between that, so do what you are commanded!"*

662 **69** *They said: "Call upon your Nurturer for us to make clear to us what her color is." He said: "Verily He says it is a yellow cow of intensely bright color that gladdens the beholders."*

664 **70** *They said: "Call upon your Nurturer for us to make clear to us what she is. Verily cows all look the same to us. Then we will be, if the One God wills, assuredly well-guided."*

668 **71** *He said: "Verily He says it is a cow unbroken to plowing the earth or watering tillage, flawless, without one spot on her." They said: "Now you have given the precise terms!" Finally they slaughtered it—after they almost did not.*

72 And when you killed a soul, then jostled one 671
another over it—but the One God was to be the
discloser of what you were concealing—

73 so We said: "Strike it with part of her." Thus 672
does the One God revive the dead and show you
His signs! Perhaps you will understand.

74 Yet your hearts hardened, even after that. In- 676
deed, they are like rocks, or more intense yet in
hardness; but truly there are certain rocks out of
which rivers burst forth; and truly there are some
that cleave asunder so that water issues from
them; and truly there are some that crash down
in fear of the One God! And the One God is not
at all unaware of what you do.

The Lights *of* Revelation

& the Secrets *of* Interpretation

Ḥizb I

of the Commentary on the Qur'ān by

al-Bayḍāwī

ARABIC EDITION & ENGLISH TRANSLATION

With notes by

Gibril Fouad Haddad

الحزب الأوّل من تفسير أنوار التنزيل وأسرار التأويل

لِلْإمام المُحقِّق القُدْوَة أبي الخَير نَاصِر الدِّين

البيضاوي

حقّقه وضبط نصّه وشَكَلَه وترجم معانيه إلى الإنجليزية وعلّق عليه
وخرّج أدلّته وشواهده على 30 أصلاً **د. جبريل فؤاد حداد**

بسم الله الرحمن الرحيم

الحَمْدُ لله ﴿ٱلَّذِى نَزَّلَ ٱلْفُرْقَانَ عَلَىٰ عَبْدِهِۦ لِيَكُونَ لِلْعَٰلَمِينَ نَذِيرًا﴾، فَتَحَدَّى بِأَقْصَرِ سُورَةٍ مِنْ سُوَرِهِ مَصَاقِعَ الخُطَبَاءِ مِنَ العَرَبِ العَرْبَاءِ، فَلَمْ يَجِدْ بِهِ قَدِيراً؛ وَأَفْحَمَ مَنْ تَصَدَّى لِمُعَارَضَتِهِ مِنْ فُصَحَاءِ عَدْنَانَ وَبُلَغَاءِ قَحْطَانَ حَتَّى حَسِبُوا أَنَّهُمْ سُحِّرُوا تَسْحِيراً؛ ثُمَّ بَيَّنَ ﴿لِلنَّاسِ مَا نُزِّلَ إِلَيْهِمْ﴾ حَسَبَما عَنَّ لَهُمْ مِنْ مَصَالِحِهِمْ ﴿لِّيَدَّبَّرُوٓا۟ ءَايَٰتِهِۦ وَلِيَتَذَكَّرَ أُو۟لُوا۟ ٱلْأَلْبَٰبِ﴾ تَذْكِيراً؛ فَكَشَفَ لَهُمْ قِنَاعَ الانْغِلَاقِ عَنْ آيَاتٍ مُحْكَمَاتٍ ﴿هُنَّ أُمُّ ٱلْكِتَٰبِ وَأُخَرُ مُتَشَٰبِهَٰتٌ﴾ هُنَّ رُمُوزُ الخِطَابِ تَأْوِيلاً وَتَفْسِيراً؛ ....

Glory to Allah *Who sent down the Discernment on His slave for him to be a warner to the worlds* (al-Furqān 25:1)! He challenged, with the shortest of its suras, the champions of eloquence among pure-blooded Arabs and found none capable [of response]. He confuted those who set out to oppose it—of the orators of ʿAdnān and declaimers of Qaḥṭān[213]—until they thought they had been completely bewitched. Then he expounded *for humankind what was revealed to them* (al-Naḥl 16:44) within their purview of their own welfare, *so that they may ponder its verses and people of intellect may heed* (Ṣād 38:29) carefully. He dispelled for them opacity from *clear verses which are the substance of the Book and others, allegorical* (Āl ʿImrān 3:7), which are the figures of speech through interpretation and exegesis....

[213] The ancestors of the Arabs. ʿAdnān ʿResidentʾ gave birth to Maʿadd ʿToughʾ, to whom Quraysh and the Prophet Muḥammad—upon him blessings and peace—are traced, while Qaḥṭān ʿHardʾ gave birth to the eponym Yaʿrub ʿSpeaks most clearlyʾ, to whom ʿĀd and Thamūd are traced, cf. Ibn Durayd, *al-Ishtiqāq*, ed. ʿAbd al-Salām Muḥammad Hārūn (Beirut: Dār al-Jīl, 1411/1991) pp. 5, 31, 217, 361.

وَأَبْرَزَ غَوَامِضَ الْحَقَائِقِ وَلَطَائِفَ الدَّقَائِقِ، لِيَتَجَلَّى لَهُمْ خَفَايَا الْمُلْكِ وَالْمَلَكُوتِ وَخَبَايَا قُدْسِ الْجَبَرُوتِ، لِيَتَفَكَّرُوا فِيهَا تَفْكِيراً؛ وَمَهَّدَ لَهُمْ قَوَاعِدَ الْأَحْكَامِ وَأَوْضَاعَهَا، مِنْ نُصُوصِ الْآيَاتِ وَأَلْمَاعِهَا، لِيُذْهِبَ عَنْهُمُ الرِّجْسَ وَيُطَهِّرَهُمْ تَطْهِيراً. فَمَنْ ﴿كَانَ لَهُۥ قَلْبٌ أَوْ أَلْقَى ٱلسَّمْعَ وَهُوَ شَهِيدٌ﴾، فَهُوَ فِي الدَّارَيْنِ حَمِيدٌ وَسَعِيدٌ؛ وَمَنْ لَمْ يَرْفَعْ إِلَيْهِ رَأْسَهُ، وَأَطْفَأَ نِبْرَاسَهُ، يَعِشْ ذَمِيماً وَيَصْلَ سَعِيراً.

فَيَا وَاجِبَ الْوُجُودِ، وَيَا فَائِضَ الْجُودِ، وَيَا غَايَةَ كُلِّ مَقْصُودٍ، صَلِّ عَلَيْهِ صَلَاةً تُوَازِي غَنَاءَهُ، وَتُجَازِي عَنَاءَهُ، وَعَلَى مَنْ أَعَانَهُ وَقَرَّرَ تِبْيَانَهُ تَقْرِيراً؛

He shed light on the complexities of great truths and the subtleties of nuances, so that the undisclosed matters of visible Sovereignty and preternal Dominion and the hidden ones in the world of Holiness and Might be made manifest[214] to them, and they would think on them and reflect. He laid down for them the foundations of laws and their applications out of the texts of verses and their hints, *to remove uncleanness far* from them and cleanse them *with a thorough cleansing* (al-Aḥzāb 33:33). Whoever, then, *has a heart or gives ear with full intelligence* (Qāf 50:37) shall be in both abodes praised and blessed! But whoever disdains him and puts out his beacon shall live in contempt and be thrown into a scorching fire (cf. al-Inshiqāq 84:12).

Therefore—O Necessary Being! O Outpourer of munificence! O Goal of every pursuit!—bless him with a blessing that matches his boon and repays his struggle, as well as those who aided him and inculcated his message/buttressed his edifice[215] most firmly;

[214] α, AQ, B, D, F, H, I, K, M, MM, R, Sk, T: ليتجلّى Ak, N, S: لتتجلى Kh: لتنجلي A, L, P, Q, U, Ul, Z: لينجلي β, ε: لِتجلى

[215] α, Ak, B, ε, K, Kh, M, N, Q, R: تِبيانَه β, I, L, Sk, T, U, Z: بنيانه See Q (1:37) on var.

وَأَفِضْ عَلَيْنَا مِنْ بَرَكَاتِهِمْ وَاسْلُكْ بِنَا مَسَالِكَ كَرَامَاتِهِمْ، وَسَلِّمْ عَلَيْهِمْ وَعَلَيْنَا تَسْلِيماً كَثِيراً.

وَبَعْدُ، فَإِنَّ أَعْظَمَ الْعُلُومِ مِقْدَاراً وَأَرْفَعَهَا شَرَفاً وَمَنَاراً: عِلْمُ التَّفْسِيرِ الَّذِي هُوَ رَئِيسُ الْعُلُومِ الدِّينِيَّةِ وَرَأْسُهَا، وَمَبْنَى قَوَاعِدِ الشَّرْعِ وَأَسَاسُهَا. لَا يَلِيقُ لِتَعَاطِيهِ وَالتَّصَدِّي لِلتَّكَلُّمِ فِيهِ إِلَّا مَنْ بَرَعَ فِي الْعُلُومِ الدِّينِيَّةِ كُلِّهَا - أُصُولِهَا وَفُرُوعِهَا - وَفَاقَ فِي الصِّنَاعَاتِ الْعَرَبِيَّةِ وَالْفُنُونِ الْأَدَبِيَّةِ بِأَنْوَاعِهَا.

وَلَطَالَمَا أُحَدِّثُ نَفْسِي بِأَنْ أُصَنِّفَ فِي هَذَا الْفَنِّ كِتَاباً يَحْتَوِي عَلَى

pour down on us from their vast blessings; cause us to tread the path of their miraculous gifts; and greet them[216] and us with an abundant greeting of Peace!

[*Tafsīr* is the chief science and foundation of all disciplines]

To proceed: truly the greatest of the sciences in scope and the highest in rank and radiance is the science of exegesis, which is the chief and head of all the religious sciences, the framework of the bases of the sacred law and their foundation. None is suited to practice it or venture to speak about it but he who excels in the religious sciences in their totality—roots and branches[217]—and has proved superior in the crafts of the Arabic language and the literary arts in all their varieties.

And I have—by Allah!—long contemplated authoring a book in this discipline that would contain ....

216 "Those who aided him etc." are respectively the Companions (*ṣaḥāba*) and Successors (*ṭābiʿīn*) according to Qūnawī, *Ḥāshiyat al-Qūnawī ʿalā Tafsīr al-Imām al-Bayḍāwī,* printed with Ibn al-Tamjīd, *Ḥāshiyat Ibn al-Tamjīd,* 20 vols. ed. ʿAbd Allāh Maḥmūd ʿUmar (Beirut: Dār al-Kutub al-ʿIlmiyya, 1422/2001) 1:37, hereafter Q.

217 Cf. Ibn ʿAṭiyya (d. 546/ca. 1151) and Abū Ḥayyān (d. 745/1344)—among others—in the introductions to their respective *tafsīrs*.

صَفْوَةِ مَا بَلَغَنِي مِنْ عُظَمَاءِ الصَّحَابَةِ وَعُلَمَاءِ التَّابِعِينَ وَمَنْ دُونَهُمْ مِنَ السَّلَفِ الصَّالِحِينَ؛ وَيَنْطَوِي عَلَى نُكَتٍ بَارِعَةٍ وَلَطَائِفَ رَائِعَةٍ، اِسْتَنْبَطْتُهَا أَنَا وَمَنْ قَبْلِي مِنْ أَفَاضِلِ الْمُتَأَخِّرِينَ وَأَمَاثِلِ الْمُحَقِّقِينَ؛ وَيُعْرِبُ عَنْ وُجُوهِ الْقِرَاءَاتِ الْمَشْهُورَةِ الْمَعْزِيَّةِ إِلَى الْأَئِمَّةِ الثَّمَانِيَةِ الْمَشْهُورِينَ، وَالشَّوَاذِّ الْمَرْوِيَّةِ عَنِ الْقُرَّاءِ الْمُعْتَبَرِينَ، ....

the essence of all that has reached me from the major Companions and ulema of the Successors and the rest of the pious early Muslims including brilliant allusions and marvelous subtleties[218] I and those before me have brought to light among the preeminent latter-day [scholars] and worthiest authorities. It would also clarify the variants of the famous [Quranic] readings that are sourced[219] to the famous eight Imams[220] and the irregular variants narrated from the notable Readers. ....

[218] Q (1:426) defined the *nukta* when commenting on the Qadi's statement, toward the very end of his commentary on 2:2, "Each of these sentences, moreover, holds an allusive point in the purest rhetorical style (*nukta dhāt jazāla*):" "The *nukta* is the subtle question that is brought out perspicuously and cogitatively. It derives from 'he scratched the ground with his spear,' leaving its trace there: the nuance was named *nukta* because thoughts leave their trace on it." Al-Nābulusī said in *al-Ajwiba 'alā Mi'atin wa-Wāḥidin wa-Sittīna Su'ālan*, ed. Imtithāl al-Ṣaghīr (Damascus: Dār al-Fārābī lil-Ma'ārif, 1422/2001), Question 126, p. 301: "Shaykh Khālid [al-Azharī] said in *Sharḥ al-Qawā'id* [=*Sharḥ Qawā'id al-I'rāb*]: 'The allusive point is the nuance (*al-nukta hiya al-daqīqa*).'" On Companions and Successors see biographical glossary.

[219] All mss. and eds.: المعزية AQ, MM, Q: المعزوّة

[220] The seven canonical Readers (*qurrā'*) are Nāfi', Ibn Kathīr, Abū 'Amr b. al-'Alā', Ibn 'Āmir, 'Āṣim, Ḥamza, and al-Kisā'ī. The "famous eight" includes Ya'qūb and the "famous ten" Abū Ja'far Ibn al-Qa'qā' and Khalaf al-Bazzār (see our biographical glossary). Cf. Ibn al-Bādhish, *Kitāb al-Iqnā' fīl-Qirā'āt al-Sab'*, ed. 'Abd al-Majīd Qaṭāmish, 2 vols. (Damascus: Dār al-Fikr, 1403/1983); Ibn Ghalbūn, *al-Tadhkira fīl-Qirā'āt al-Thamān*, ed. Ayman Rushdī Suwayd, 2 vols. (Jeddah: al-Jamā'a al-Khayriyya li-Taḥfīẓ al-Qur'ān, 1412/ 1991); and Ibn al-Jazarī, *Sharḥ Ṭayyibat al-Nashr fīl-Qirā'āt al-'Ashr*, ed. Anas Mahra, 2nd ed. (Beirut: Dār al-Kutub al-'Ilmiyya, 1420/2000).

إِلَّا أَنَّ قُصُورَ بِضَاعَتِي يُثَبِّطُنِي عَنِ الْإِقْدَامِ، وَيَمْنَعُنِي عَنِ الِانْتِصَابِ فِي هَذَا الْمَقَامِ؛ حَتَّى سَنَحَ لِي ـ بَعْدَ الِاسْتِخَارَةِ ـ مَا صَمَّمَ بِهِ عَزْمِي عَلَى الشُّرُوعِ فِيمَا أَرَدْتُهُ، وَالْإِتْيَانِ بِمَا قَصَدْتُهُ، نَاوِياً أَنْ أُسَمِّيَهُ بَعْدَ أَنْ أُتَمِّمَهُ بِـ

أَنْوَار التَّنْزِيلِ وَأَسْرَار التَّأْوِيلِ.

فَهَا أَنَا الْآنَ أَشْرَعُ، وَبِحُسْنِ تَوْفِيقِهِ أَقُولُ ـ وَهُوَ الْمُوَفِّقُ لِكُلِّ خَيْرٍ، وَمُعْطِي كُلِّ مَسْؤُولٍ ـ:

(١) سُورَةُ فَاتِحَةِ الْكِتَابِ

وَتُسَمَّى (٢) أُمَّ الْقُرْآنِ، (أ) لِأَنَّهَا مُفْتَتَحُهُ وَمَبْدَؤُهُ؛ فَكَأَنَّهَا أَصْلُهُ وَمَنْشَؤُهُ،

But I felt unqualified—and this unnerved me and blocked me from rising to the task. Then came to me, after the consultative prayer, that which sealed my resolve to embark upon my plan and realize my project, with the intention to name it, after I finish it, ***The Lights of Revelation and the Secrets of Interpretation***.

Now do I begin and, asking for the best of God-given success —it is He Who is the facilitator of every good and the granter of every request!—I say:

[Fourteen names of the Fatiha]

1. The Sura of the Opening of the Book[221]

It is also named

2. "the Mother of the Qur'ān," (i) because it is its inception and starting-point—as it were, its origin and birthplace;[222]

221 A, ε, I, Iṣ, L, N, R, T, U, Ul, W: سورة فاتحة الكتاب β: سورة الفاتحة α: missing ill. Ak: سورة فاتحة الكتاب مكية وايها سبع ايات F, K: سورة فاتحة الكتاب مكية وقيل مدنية وايها سبع ايات

وَلِذَلِكَ تُسَمَّى (٣) أَسَاساً؛ (ب) أَوْ لِأَنَّهَا تَشْتَمِلُ عَلَى مَا فِيهِ مِنَ الثَّنَاءِ عَلَى اللهِ سُبْحَانَهُ وَتَعَالَى، وَالتَّعَبُّدِ بِأَمْرِهِ وَنَهْيِهِ، وَبَيَانِ وَعْدِهِ وَوَعِيدِهِ؛ (ج) أَوْ عَلَى جُمْلَةِ مَعَانِيهِ مِنَ الْحِكَمِ النَّظَرِيَّةِ وَالْأَحْكَامِ الْعَمَلِيَّةِ، الَّتِي هِيَ سُلُوكُ الطَّرِيقِ الْمُسْتَقِيمِ وَالِاطِّلَاعُ عَلَى مَرَاتِبِ السُّعَدَاءِ وَمَنَازِلِ الْأَشْقِيَاءِ؛ (٤) وَسُورَةَ الْكَنْزِ، (٥) وَالْوَافِيَةَ، (٦) وَالْكَافِيَةَ لِذٰلِكَ؛ (٧) وَسُورَةَ الْحَمْدِ، (٨) وَالشُّكْرِ، (٩) وَالدُّعَاءِ،

whence it is also named

3. "a foundation;" (ii) or because it rounds up the Quranic contents of the praise of Allah Most High and Exalted, [the modalities of] worshipping through His commands and prohibitions, and the exposition of His promises and threats; (iii) or because it contains the aggregate of its meanings of intellective wisdoms and practical rulings, which is to walk in the straight way and behold the stations of the elect and the homes of the wretched.[223]

It is also named 4. "the Sura of the Treasure;" hence, likewise:

5. "the Abundant" and

6. "the Sufficient;"

7. "the Sura of Praise,"

8. "of Thanksgiving,"

9. "of Supplication" and of

[222] B, K: ومنشؤه α: ومنشاءه β, R, W: ومنشاؤه Ak, ε, N: ومنشاوه A: ومنشأوه F, I: ومنشأه T: ومنشاه

[223] "To elaborate [on al-Bayḍāwī's sentence], it encompasses four categories of sciences which are the pivot of the religion: the principles, the branches, sufism, and history." Al-Suyūṭī, *Nawāhid al-Abkār wa-Shawārid al-Afkār*, ed. Aḥmad Ḥājj Muḥammad ʿUthmān, unpublished Ph.D. dissertation, 3 vols. (Mecca: Jāmiʿat Umm al-Qurā, 1423-24/2002-2003) 1:39-40, hereafter S. He cites 20-odd names of the Fatiḥa in his *Itqān*.

(١٠) وَتَعْلِيمِ الْمَسْأَلَةِ لِاشْتِمَالِهَا عَلَيْهَا؛ (١١) وَالصَّلَاةِ، لِوُجُوبِ قِرَاءَتِهَا أَوِ اسْتِحْبَابِهَا فِيهَا؛ (١٢) وَالشَّافِيَةِ، (١٣) وَالشِّفَاءِ، لِقَوْلِهِ عَلَيْهِ الصَّلَاةُ وَالسَّلَامُ: هِيَ شِفَاءٌ مِنْ كُلِّ دَاءٍ؛

10. "Teaching how to Beseech," since it includes the above;

11. "of Prayer" as it is obligatory or desirable to recite it in it;[224]

12. "the Healer" and

13. "the Cure" due to his statement—upon him blessings and peace: "It is a panacea;"[225]

[224] I.e., obligatory according to the Shāfiʿīs and as related from some Companions such as Ibn ʿAbbās to that effect, cf. al-Khafājī, *ʿInāyat al-Qāḍī wa-Kifāyat al-Rāḍī*, ed. Muḥammad al-Ṣabbāgh, 8 vols. (Bulāq: Dār al-Ṭibāʿat al-ʿĀmira, 1283/1867) 1:24, hereafter Kh; "obligatory or desirable" according to the Shāfiʿīs and Ḥanafīs respectively (S, Q) and per Muḥyī al-Dīn Muḥammad b. Muṣṭafā Shaykh Zādah, *Ḥāshiyat Muḥyī al-Dīn Shaykh Zādah*, 3 vols. (Istanbul: Maktaba ʿUthmāniyya, 1306/1889) 1:12=*Ḥāshiyat Muḥyī al-Dīn Shaykh Zādah*, ed. Muḥammad ʿAbd al-Qādir Shāhīn, 8 vols. (Beirut: Dār al-Kutub al-ʿIlmiyya, 1419/1999) 1:26, hereafter Z.

[225] Narrated from ʿAbd Allāh b. Jābir by al-Bayhaqī in *Shuʿab al-Īmān* (Branch 19, *Taʿẓīm al-Qurʾān, Faṣl fī faḍāʾil al-Suwar wal-Āyāt*) and, in short form, Aḥmad b. Ḥanbal, *Musnad*, ed. Shuʿayb al-Arnāʾūṭ et al., 50 vols. (Beirut: Muʾassasat al-Risāla, 1419/1999) 29:139 §17597 (*"isnāduhu ḥasan fil-mutābaʿāt"*); also in *mursal* mode (i.e., directly from the Prophet without Companion-link) from the Successor ʿAbd al-Malik b. ʿUmayr, by al-Dārimī in his *Sunan* (*Faḍāʾil al-Qurʾān, Faḍl Fātiḥat al-Kitāb*) through trustworthy narrators—hence declared *ṣaḥīḥ mursal* in S (1:43-44) and "good-chained" in *al-Durr al-Manthūr fil-Tafsīr bil-Maʾthūr*, ed. ʿAbd Allāh b. ʿAbd al-Muḥsin al-Turkī, 17 vols. (Cairo: Markaz Hajar lil-Buḥūth, 1424/2003) 1:16—and al-Bayhaqī who said it bears witness to the previous report and that of the Prophet's calling the Fātiḥa a *ruqya* ⁽incantatory remedy⁾: narrated from Abū Saʿīd al-Khudrī in the two *Ṣaḥīḥs* and *Sunan*. Dīnawarī's narration of the panacea report as Ibn ʿUmayr's own saying in *al-Mujālasa wa-Jawāhir al-ʿIlm*, ed. Mashhūr Ḥasan Salmān, 9 vols. (Beirut: Dār Ibn Ḥazm, 1419/1998) 4:321-322 §1482 is a sub-narrator's inaccuracy. Cf. Aḥmad al-Ghumārī, *al-Mudāwī li-ʿIlal al-Jāmiʿ al-Ṣaghīr wa-Sharḥay al-Munāwī*, 6 vols. (Cairo: Dār al-Kutbī and al-Maktabat al-Makkiyya, 1996) 4:561 §2386/5827 and Abū ʿĀṣim Nabīl al-Ghamrī, *Fatḥ al-Mannān Sharḥ wa-Taḥqīq Kitāb al-Dārimī Abī Muḥammad ʿAbd Allāh b. ʿAbd al-Raḥmān*, 10 vols. (Mecca and Beirut: al-Maktaba

(١٤) وَالسَّبْعَ الْمَثَانِي، لِأَنَّهَا سَبْعُ آيَاتٍ بِالْاِتِّفَاقِ، إِلَّا أَنَّ مِنْهُمْ مَنْ عَدَّ التَّسْمِيَةَ دُونَ ﴿أَنعَمتَ عَلَيهِمْ﴾، وَمِنْهُمْ مَنْ عَكَسَ.

وَتُثَنَّى فِي الصَّلَاةِ، أَوِ الْإِنْزَالِ إِنْ صَحَّ أَنَّهَا نَزَلَتْ بِمَكَّةَ حِينَ فُرِضَتِ الصَّلَاةُ، وَبِالْمَدِينَةِ حِينَ حُوِّلَتِ الْقِبْلَةُ؛ وَقَدْ صَحَّ أَنَّهَا مَكِّيَّةٌ لِقَوْلِهِ تَعَالَى: ﴿وَلَقَدْ ءَاتَيْنَٰكَ سَبْعًا مِّنَ ٱلْمَثَانِي﴾ [الحجر ٨٧]، وَهُوَ مَكِّيٌّ بِالنَّصِّ.

14. "the Seven Oft-Repeated," as it is formed of seven verses by general agreement[226]—only some counted the theonymic invocation without [stopping after] *those You have favored* while others did the opposite.[227] It is repeated inside prayer, or was revealed repeatedly—provided it is true[228] that it was revealed both in Mecca when prayer was made obligatory and in Medina when the direction of prayer was changed. It is soundly established as Meccan[229] since Allah Most High said, *We have certainly given you seven of the oft-repeated* (al-Ḥijr 15:87), which is Meccan as established textually.[230]

al-Makkiyya and Dār al-Bashā'ir al-Islāmiyya, 1419/ 1999) 10:482-483 §3635.

226 By consensus (*ijmā'*) acc. to al-Ṭaḥāwī, *Sharḥ Ma'ānī al-Āthār*, ed. Muḥammad Zahrī al-Najjār et al. 5 vols. (Beirut: 'Ālam al-Kutub, 1414/1994) 1:201 §1194 and Ibn 'Abd al-Barr, *al-Istidhkār*, ed. 'Abd al-Mu'ṭī Amīn Qal'ajī, 30 vols. (Damascus and Beirut: Dār Qutayba; Aleppo and Cairo: Dār al-Waḥy, 1414/1993) 4:201 §4742. Ibn Ḥajar, *Fatḥ* (8:159) cites odd dissents by Ḥusayn b. 'Alī al-Ju'fī and 'Amr b. 'Ubayd.

227 See al-Dānī, *al-Bayān fī 'Add Āy al-Qur'ān*, ed. Ghānim al-Ḥamd (Kuwait: Markaz al-Makhṭūṭāt wal-Turāth wal-Wathā'iq, 1414/1994) and others.

228 The Qadi begins with the strong gloss and proceeds with the weaker one(s).

229 Narrated from 'Alī and Qatāda (S) "rebutting Mujāhid who said it is Medinan" (W) although the latter is also related from the Prophet—upon him blessings and peace—cf. *Tafsīr Muqātil b. Sulaymān*, ed. 'Abd Allah Shaḥḥāta, 5 vols. (Beirut: Mu'assasat al-Tārīkh al-'Arabī, 1423/2002) 1:35. Nasafī considered it both Meccan and Madinan.

230 "Because the verses that precede and follow deal with the unbelievers in Mecca" (Z); "By *textually* he means the Sunna, for that is authentically established from Ibn 'Abbās—Allah be well-pleased with him and his father—and a Companion's statement

﴿بِسۡمِ ٱللَّهِ ٱلرَّحۡمَٰنِ ٱلرَّحِيمِ ۝١﴾: مِنَ الْفَاتِحَةِ؛ وَعَلَيْهِ قُرَّاءُ مَكَّةَ، وَالْكُوفَةِ، وَفُقَهَاؤُهُمَا، وَابْنُ الْمُبَارَكِ، وَالشَّافِعِيُّ. وَخَالَفَهُمْ قُرَّاءُ الْمَدِينَةِ، وَالْبَصْرَةِ، وَالشَّامِ، وَفُقَهَاؤُهَا، وَمَالِكٌ، وَالْأَوْزَاعِيُّ. وَلَمْ يَنُصَّ أَبُو حَنِيفَةَ فِيهِ بِشَيْءٍ، فَظُنَّ أَنَّهَا لَيْسَتْ مِنَ السُّورَةِ عِنْدَهُ. وَسُئِلَ مُحَمَّدُ بْنُ الْحَسَنِ عَنْهَا، فَقَالَ: مَا بَيْنَ الدَّفَّتَيْنِ كَلَامُ اللهِ تَعَالَى.

وَلَنَا أَحَادِيثُ كَثِيرَةٌ؛ مِنْهَا: ....

[The *basmala* is part of the Fatiha]

[1:1] **bi-smi-l-Lāhi-r-raḥmāni-r-raḥīmi** ⁽*In the Name of the One God, the All-Beneficent, the Most Merciful*⁾ is part of the Fatiha.[231] This is the position of the Quranic readers and jurists of Mecca and al-Kūfa, Ibn al-Mubārak and al-Shāfiʿī. A contrary view was held by the readers and jurists of Medina, Basra, Greater Syria, Mālik and al-Awzāʿī. Abū Ḥanīfa did not stipulate anything on it so it is thought he did not deem it part of the sura. Muḥammad b. al-Ḥasan was asked about it and he said "Everything that is between the two covers is the word of Allah Most High."[232]

We [Shāfiʿīs] have many hadiths [as proofs]; among them:

concerning the Qur'ān, especially with regard to revelation, has the status of a raised report" (A); "which is supported by its being the position of ʿAlī, Ibn ʿAbbās, Qatāda, Ubay b. Kaʿb and the majority of the scholars after them" (Q); "It is the position of Ibn ʿAbbās and the majority of the Companions and commentators of Qur'ān" (Kh).

[231] β, ε, K, L, M, N, Q, U, Ul, Z: addition: ومن كل سورة missing in α, B, ÇZ, F, I, Kh, R, Sk, T, W. Kh comments: والمصنف سكت عن سائر السور Ak: وقيل من كل سورة. "Kufan, Basrian, Medinan and Syrian counters concurred the *basmala* is not an initial *āya* for every sura, differing only over the Fatiha." Al-Ṭāhir b. ʿĀshūr, *al-Taḥrīr wal-Tanwīr*, 30 vols. (Tunis: al-Dār al-Tūnisiyya lil-Nashr, 1984) 1:78 (eighth introduction).

[232] A reply that suggests he considered the *basmala* part of the Qur'ān. The expression *mā bayn al-daffatayn* refers to the ʿUthmānic Codex, in which they wrote the *basmala* at the beginning of every Sura, without Sura names, *Āmīn*, the numbering of the Suras or their verses or places of revelation, pause signs, dotting and vowelization.

مَا رَوَى أَبُو هُرَيْرَةَ رَضِيَ اللهُ تَعَالَى عَنْهُ، أَنَّهُ عَلَيْهِ الصَّلَاةُ وَالسَّلَامُ قَالَ: فَاتِحَةُ الْكِتَابِ سَبْعُ آيَاتٍ، أُوْلَاهُنَّ ﴿بِسْمِ ٱللَّهِ ٱلرَّحْمَٰنِ ٱلرَّحِيمِ﴾؛ وَقَوْلُ أُمِّ سَلَمَةَ رَضِيَ اللهُ عَنْهَا: قَرَأَ رَسُولُ اللهِ ﷺ الْفَاتِحَةَ، وَعَدَّ ﴿بِسْمِ ٱللَّهِ ٱلرَّحْمَٰنِ ٱلرَّحِيمِ ٱلْحَمْدُ لِلَّهِ رَبِّ ٱلْعَٰلَمِينَ﴾ آيَةً.

(i) Abū Hurayra, Allah be well-pleased with him, narrated that the Prophet, upon him blessings and peace, said:

> The Opening of the Book is seven verses, the first of which being *In the Name of Allah, the All-Beneficent, the Most Merciful.*[233]

(ii) There is also the saying of Umm Salama, Allah be well-pleased with her:

> The Messenger of Allah—upon him blessings and peace—recited the Fatiha and counted *In the Name of Allah, the Beneficent, the Merciful, Praise be to Allah, the Nurturer of the worlds* as one verse.[234]

[233] Narrated by Ibn Mardūyah in his *Tafsīr* with a very weak chain cited by Ibn Kathīr in his *Tafsīr al-Qur'ān al-'Aẓīm*, ed. Muṣṭafā al-Sayyid Muḥammad et al., 15 vols. (Jīza: Mu'assasat Qurṭuba, 1421/2000) 1:154-155; Ṭabarānī with a good corroborant chain in *al-Mu'jam al-Awsaṭ*, ed. Ṭāriq b. 'Awaḍ Allāh b. Muḥammad and 'Abd al-Muḥsin al-Ḥusaynī, 10 vols. (Cairo: Dār al-Ḥaramayn, 1415/1995) 5:208 §5102; al-Dāraquṭnī in his *Sunan* (*Ṣalāt, al-Jahr bi-bi-smi-l-Lāh al-Raḥmān al-Raḥīm*) and, through him, al-Bayhaqī both in the *Sunan al-Kubrā* and *Shu'ab al-Īmān* with a weak chain made fair by the report's corroborants while in his *'Ilal al-Wārida fil Aḥādīth al-Nabawiyya*, ed. Maḥfūẓ al-Raḥmān Zayn Allāh al-Salafī, 16 vols. (Riyadh: Dār Ṭayba, 1405/1985) 8:148 §1468, Dāraquṭnī avers it is Abū Hurayra's saying. Also narrated as a saying of the *Tābi'ī* Muḥammad b. Ka'b al-Quraẓī by al-Qāsim b. Sallām, *Faḍā'il al-Qur'ān*, ed. Marwān al-'Aṭiyya et al. (Damascus and Beirut: Dār Ibn Kathīr, 1415/1995) p. 217.

[234] The versions of this fair report all mention that the phrases *In the Name of Allah, the Beneficent, the Merciful; Praise be to Allah, Nurturer of the worlds* were counted as two verses cf. al-Munāwī, *al-Fatḥ al-Samāwī bi-Takhrīj Aḥādīth al-Qāḍī al-Bayḍāwī*, ed. Aḥmad Mujtabā al-Salafī, 3 vols. (Riyadh: Dār al-'Āṣima, 1409/1989) 1:94-96 §3.

وَمِنْ أَجْلِهِمَا اخْتُلِفَ فِي أَنَّهَا آيَةٌ بِرَأْسِهَا أَمْ بِمَا بَعْدَهَا. وَالْإِجْمَاعُ عَلَى أَنَّ مَا بَيْنَ الدَّفَّتَيْنِ كَلَامُ اللهِ سُبْحَانَهُ وَتَعَالَى، وَالْوِفَاقُ عَلَى إِثْبَاتِهَا فِي الْمَصَاحِفِ، مَعَ الْمُبَالَغَةِ فِي تَجْرِيدِ الْقُرْآنِ، حَتَّى لَمْ تُكْتَبْ (آمِين).

وَالْبَاءُ مُتَعَلِّقَةٌ بِمَحْذُوفٍ، تَقْدِيرُهُ: (بِسْمِ اللهِ أَقْرَأُ)، لِأَنَّ الَّذِي يَتْلُوهُ مَقْرُوءٌ؛ وَكَذَلِكَ يُضْمِرُ كُلُّ فَاعِلٍ مَا ....

Because of these two [reports] there was a difference of opinion whether it forms a verse on its own or together with what follows. There is consensus that everything that is between the two covers is the word of Allah Most High, and all concur on including it in the written volumes while going to every length to admit only what constitutes Qur'ān; hence *āmīn* was not written.[235]

[*Basmala* implies a verb standing for whatever act follows]

The ***bā'*** [in *bi-smi-l-Lāh*] pertains to an ellipsis; its subaudition is "By the Name of Allah I recite," since what follows is being recited; and thus does every agent pronominally imply whatever

Narrated from Umm Salama by al-Dāraquṭnī, *Sunan*; Ibn Khuzayma, *Ṣaḥīḥ*; al-Ḥākim in *al-Mustadrak*; al-Ṭaḥāwī, *Sharḥ Ma'ānī al-Āthār*; al-Bayhaqī, *Sunan* and *Ma'rifat al-Sunan wal-Āthār*; as documented by Ibn Ḥajar, *Talkhīṣ al-Ḥabīr*, ed. Abū 'Āṣim Ḥasan b. 'Abbās, 4 vols. (Cairo: Mu'assasat Qurṭuba, 1416/1995) 1:430-421 §347.

[235] This is the strongest proof according to al-Bayhaqī in his *Khilāfiyyāt* and *Ma'rifat al-Sunan*, ed. 'Abd al-Mu'ṭī Amīn Qal'ajī, 15 vols. (Aleppo and Cairo: Dār al-Wa'ī, 1411/1991) 2:364. For more on the Shāfi'ī position see the chapters and sections on the *basmala* in al-Baghawī's *Sharḥ al-Sunna*; al-Khāzin's *Lubāb al-Ta'wīl fī Ma'ānī al-Tanzīl* (Fātiḥa); al-Rūyānī's *Baḥr al-Madhhab*, ed. Aḥmad 'Izzū 'Ināyat al-Dimashqī, 14 vols. (Beirut: Dār Iḥyā' al-Turāth al-'Arabī, 1413/2002) 2:136-140; al-Rāfi'ī's *al-'Azīz Sharḥ al-Wajīz*, ed. 'Alī Muḥammad Mu'awwaḍ and 'Ādil Aḥmad 'Abd al-Mawjūd, 13 vols. (Beirut: Dār al-Kutub al-'Ilmiyya, 1417/1997) 1:493-496 etc. especially Abū Shāma's *Kitāb al-Basmala* (and its abridgment by al-Dhahabī) and Aḥmad al-'Ālim's *Ḥukm al-Basmala fīl-Ṣalāt* (Beirut: Dār al-Gharb al-Islāmī, 1993). Non-Shāfi'īs held that it was written in not as part of any sura but as an independent, out-of-count divider between each two suras.

يَجْعَلُ التَّسْمِيَةَ مَبْدَأً لَهُ. وَذَلِكَ أَوْلَى مِنْ أَنْ يُضْمَرَ (أَبْدَأُ)، لِعَدَمِ مَا يُطَابِقُهُ وَيَدُلُّ عَلَيْهِ؛ أَوْ (ابْتِدَائِي)، لِزِيَادَةِ إِضْمَارٍ فِيهِ.

وَتَقْدِيمُ المَعْمُولِ هٰهُنَا أَوْقَعُ، كَمَا فِي قَوْلِهِ: ﴿بِسْمِ ٱللَّهِ مَجْرٜىٰهَا﴾ [هود ٤١]، وَقَوْلِهِ: ﴿إِيَّاكَ نَعْبُدُ﴾ ، لِأَنَّهُ أَهَمُّ، وَأَدَلُّ عَلَى الِاخْتِصَاصِ، وَأَدْخَلُ فِي التَّعْظِيمِ، وَأَوْفَقُ لِلْوُجُودِ، فَإِنَّ اسْمَهُ سُبْحَانَهُ وَتَعَالَى مُقَدَّمٌ عَلَى الْقِرَاءَةِ. كَيْفَ؟ وَقَدْ جُعِلَ آلَةً لَهَا مِنْ حَيْثُ إِنَّ الْفِعْلَ لَا يَتِمُّ وَلَا يُعْتَدُّ بِهِ شَرْعاً مَا لَمْ يُصَدَّرْ بِاسْمِهِ تَعَالَى، لِقَوْلِهِ عَلَيْهِ الصَّلَاةُ وَالسَّلَامُ: ....

[act] he initiates with a theonymic invocation. That is more suitable than to make it imply "I begin," to which nothing corresponds or points; or "[By the Name of Allah] is my beginning," which entails even more ellipsis.[236]

[Magnification of monotheism in the positioning of *basmala*]

Putting the governed element first here carries more effect — just as in His saying *In the name of Allah be its course!* (Hūd 11:41) and *You do we worship* (Fātiḥa 1:5)—because it has more weight and is more indicative of exclusivity, prompter in magnifying Allah and more evocative [of the primacy] of [His] existence. For His Name—may He be glorified and exalted!—truly precedes recitation. How [could it not],[237] when It was made an instrument by means of which recitation is carried out? And an act remains incomplete and unimportant in the Sacred Law as long as the Name of Allah Most High is not mentioned ahead of it, since the Prophet —upon him blessings and peace—said: .....

[236] I.e. of a nominal sentence and an annexation construct.
[237] α, A, Ak, B, ε, I, N, R, Sk, T: كَيفَ β, F, K, Kh, L, U, Ul: كيف لا

كُلُّ أَمْرٍ ذِي بَالٍ لَا يُبْدَأُ فِيهِ بِبِسْمِ اللهِ فَهُوَ أَبْتَرُ.

وَقِيلَ الْبَاءُ لِلْمُصَاحَبَةِ، وَالْمَعْنَى: (مُتَبَرِّكًا بِاسْمِ اللهِ تَعَالَى أَقْرَأُ)؛ وَهٰذَا، وَمَا بَعْدَهُ، إِلَى آخِرِ السُّورَةِ: مَقُولٌ عَلَى أَلْسِنَةِ الْعِبَادِ ....

Every important matter that is not begun with *bi-smi-l-Lāh* remains barren.[238]

It was also said the *bā'* denotes accompaniment in the sense, "With the blessing of the Name of Allah Most High do I read."[239] For this phrase and what follows it to the end of the sura is all represented as spoken by the believers [themselves] ....

[238] Narrated by al-Khaṭīb al-Baghdādī in *al-Jāmiʿ li-Akhlāq al-Rāwī wa-Ādāb al-Sāmiʿ*, ed. Muḥammad ʿAjāj al-Khaṭīb, 2 vols. (Beirut: Mu'assasat al-Risāla, 1412/1991) 2:87 §1232 and through him, al-Ruhāwī in his *Arbaʿīn*, Ibn al-Subkī in *Ṭabaqāt al-Shāfiʿiyyat al-Kubrā* and al-Sakhāwī in *al-Ajwibat al-Marḍiyya*. Although it is a very famous narration, it is considered by general agreement an aberrant wording narrated through one of al-Awzāʿī's trustworthy students (Mubashshir b. Ismāʿīl) while a dozen others relate from the latter the wording "that is not begun with *al-ḥamdu lillāh*." Hence the *basmala* version was unanimously disauthenticated as "flimsy" (*wāhin*), cf. Ibn Ḥajar, *Fatḥ al-Bārī bi-Sharḥ Ṣaḥīḥ al-Bukhārī*, ed. Muḥammad Fu'ād ʿAbd al-Bāqī et al., 13 vols. (Beirut, Dār al-Maʿrifa, 1379/1959), *Tafsīr, Say, O People of the Scripture, come to a common word between us and you*; and the exhaustive, meticulous study of the literature on this wording by the hadith master Muḥammad b. Jaʿfar al-Kattānī in *al-Aqāwīl al-Mufaṣṣila li-Bayān Ḥadīth al-Ibtidā' bil-Basmala*, ed. Muḥammad ʿIṣām ʿArār and Muḥammad al-Fātiḥ al-Kattānī (Damascus: privately printed, 1419/1998), while Ibn Jaʿfar's student, Aḥmad al-Ghumārī, demonstrated its forgery in his irate monograph *al-Istiʿādha wal-Ḥasbala mimman Ṣaḥḥaḥa Ḥadīth al-Basmala*, 2nd ed. (Damascus: Dār al-Baṣā'ir, 1405/1985). Those who declared it fair, such as al-Nawawī in his *Adhkār*, did so by subsuming it under the wording of *ḥamd* and in consideration of the Quranic precedent of beginning every sura thus. Al-Suyūṭī's grading of *ḥasan* for al-Ruhāwī's chain—which he cites in full in the *Nawāhid* (1:91-92)—is a mistake since it contains Aḥmad b. ʿImrān al-Nahshalī who is suspected of forgery and Farrūja Muḥammad b. Ṣāliḥ al-Baṣrī who is unknown. Note: al-Khaṭīb's version has "maimed" (*aqṭaʿ*) instead of "barren" (*abtar*).

[239] "Which is facilitated by the hadith 'By the Name of Allah, with Whose Name nothing can harm in heaven or on earth...'" (S).

لِيَعْلَمُوا كَيْفَ يُتَبَرَّكُ بِاسْمِهِ، وَيُحْمَدُ عَلَى نِعَمِهِ، وَيُسْأَلُ مِنْ فَضْلِهِ.

وَإِنَّمَا كُسِرَتْ - وَمِنْ حَقِّ الْحُرُوفِ الْمُفْرَدَةِ أَنْ تُفْتَحَ - لِاخْتِصَاصِهَا بِلُزُومِ الْحَرْفِيَّةِ وَالْجَرِّ، كَمَا كُسِرَتْ لَامُ الْأَمْرِ، وَلَامُ الْإِضَافَةِ - دَاخِلَةً عَلَى الْمُظْهَرِ - لِلْفَصْلِ بَيْنَهُمَا وَبَيْنَ لَامِ الْابْتِدَاءِ.

so that they may know how one obtains blessing from His Name and how He is glorified for His favors and petitioned for His bounty.

[Morphology and desinence of the *bā'* in the *basmala*]

The *bā'* received a *kasra*—although it would be right for single-letter particles to receive a *fatḥa*[240]—because it alone[241] is [both] invariably a particle as well as entailing prepositional attraction,[242] just as the imperative *lām* and the *lām* of annexation—when affixed to other than pronouns—both receive a *kasra* to distinguish them from the inchoative/inceptive *lām*.[243]

[240] I.e., because *fatḥa* is the next choice as an indeclinable case (*binā'*) after *sukūn*, the latter being unpronounceable for word initials. (Z)

[241] I.e., among the four sorts of particles (*ḥurūf*)—prepositions, adverbs, conjunctions, and interjections, cf. Wright, *Grammar* (1:278 §354).

[242] Al-Ṭībī said: "The *wāw* of oath invalidates this claim." (S)

[243] E.g., imperative/jussive/requisitive *lām* with *kasra*: *li-yalīnī ulū al-aḥlāmi wal-nuhā*; prepositional *lām* of (genitive) annexation with *kasra*: *lil-muttaqīn*; inchoative/inceptive *lām* with *fatḥa*: *la-Zaydun munṭaliq*. The latter denotes emphasis. Cf. Wright (1:283, 291); Edward William Lane, *Arabic-English Lexicon*, 8 vols. (London and Edinburgh: Williams and Norgate, 1863-1893), rept. 2 vols. (Cambridge: Islamic Texts Society, 1984), supplement, *lām*; our teacher Pierre Cachia, *The Monitor: A Dictionary of Arabic Grammatical Terms* (Beirut: Librairie du Liban and London: Longman, 1973), pp. 90-91; our teacher ʿAbd al-Ghanī al-Daqr, *Muʿjam al-Qawāʿid al-ʿArabiyya fīl-Naḥw wal-Taṣrīf* (Damascus: Dār al-Qalam, 1406/1986), "*al-lām*" pp. 377b-382a; and George M. Abdul-Massih and Hani George Tabri, *al-Khalīl: A Dictionary of Arabic Grammar Terminology* (Beirut: Librairie du Liban, 1410/1990), pp. 336b-344a.

وَ(الْإِسْمُ) عِنْدَ أَصْحَابِنَا الْبَصْرِيِّينَ: مِنَ الْأَسْمَاءِ الَّتِي حُذِفَتْ أَعْجَازُهَا لِكَثْرَةِ الْاِسْتِعْمَالِ، وَبُنِيَتْ أَوَائِلُهَا عَلَى السُّكُونِ، وَأُدْخِلَ عَلَيْهَا ـ مُبْتَدَأً بِهَا ـ هَمْزَةُ الْوَصْلِ، لِأَنَّ مِنْ دَأْبِهِمْ أَنْ يَبْتَدِئُوا بِالْمُتَحَرِّكِ وَيَقِفُوا عَلَى السَّاكِنِ.

وَيَشْهَدُ لَهُ تَصْرِيفُهُ عَلَى (أَسْمَاءٍ)، وَ(أَسَامِيَ)، وَ(سُمَيٍّ) وَ(سَمَّيْتُ).

وَمَجِيءُ (سُمًى) كَ(هُدًى): لُغَةٌ فِيهِ. قَالَ: [رَجَز]

[Etymology and morphology of *ism*]

Our Basrian colleagues[244] hold that *ism* is of the nouns whose endings are elided due to frequent use and whose initials have an indeclinable mute case, after which a conjunctive compression was affixed to them as an initial[245]—since they [Arabs] have it that one begins with a vowelized consonant and stops at a quiescent one.

Witnessing to this [derivation] is the inflection of *ism* into *asmāʾ*,[246] *asāmī*,[247] *sumayy*[248] and *sammayt*.[249]

The inflection *suman* ‹name›—as in *hudan* ‹guidance›—is a dialectical form.[250]

One [poet] said: ["The Trembling"][251]

244 This expression indicates that al-Bayḍāwī followed the Basrian school in grammar.

245 These are *ibn(a), ism, ist, ithn(at)ān, umruʾ, imraʾa,* and *aym Allāh* according to most grammarians. (S) Cf. Wright, *Grammar* (1:20).

246 I.e. instead of *awsām*. (S, Q)

247 Plural of *asmāʾ*, so it is the plural's plural (*jamʿ al-jamʿ*). (Q)

248 As the diminutive *sumayyun*—originally *sumaywun*—instead of *wusaymun* (S, Q); or as *samiyyun* ‹namesake› instead of *wasīmun*. (S, Sk)

249 Instead of *wasamtu*. (S, Q)

250 Originally *sumawun* and *sumuwun* where the final *wāw* was turned into *alif*. (S)

251 The meters of Arabic prosody are described—with illustrative examples—by Wright, *Grammar* (2:358-368) and Karam al-Bustānī, *al-Bayān* (Beirut: Maktabat Ṣādir, n.d.) pp. 117-139.

وَاللهُ أَسْمَاكَ سُمىً مُبَارَكاً ❋ آثَرَكَ اللهُ بِهِ إِيثَارَكَا

وَالْقَلْبُ بَعِيدٌ، غَيْرُ مُطَّرِدٍ. وَاشْتِقَاقُهُ (أ) مِنَ (السُّمُوِّ)، لِأَنَّهُ رِفْعَةٌ لِلْمُسَمَّى، وَشِعَارٌ لَهُ.

(ب) وَمِنَ (السِّمَةِ) عِنْدَ الْكُوفِيِّينَ، وَأَصْلُهُ (وِسْمٌ)، حُذِفَتِ الْوَاوُ، وَعُوِّضَتْ عَنْهَا هَمْزَةُ الْوَصْلِ لِيَقِلَّ إِعْلَالُهُ. وَرُدَّ بِأَنَّ الْهَمْزَةَ لَمْ تُعْهَدْ دَاخِلَةً عَلَى مَا حُذِفَ صَدْرُهُ فِي كَلَامِهِمْ.

وَمِنْ لُغَاتِهِ: (سِمٌ)، وَ(سُمٌ). قَالَ: [رَجَز]

And Allah named you with a name (suman) blessed,
by which He favored you, just as He favored you in other ways.[252]

Transposition is unlikely and irregular;[253] [rather,] its derivation is from *sumūw* ⟨highness⟩,[254] as it [the name] constitutes eminence and an ensign for the referent.

The Kufans derive it from *sima* ⟨brand, trace⟩, with *wism* as its root, from which the *wāw* was elided and then a *hamzat al-waṣl* ⟨conjunctive compression⟩ made up for it to minimize vowel-weakness.[255] This [derivation] was rejected because the *hamza* is not a familiar replacement for initial elisions in their language.

Also among its dialectical forms are *sim*[un] and *sum*[un]. The poet said: ["The Trembling"]

252 Spoken by the Khārijī poet Abū Khālid al-Qanānī (S) cf. al-Mubarrid, *al-Kāmil*, ed. Muḥammad Aḥmad al-Dālī, 2nd ed., 4 vols. (Beirut: Mu'assasat al-Risāla, 1412/1992) 3:1081, corrupted to "al-Qashānī" in the 'Ilmiyya edition of al-Qūnawī.

253 I.e., of the initial *wāw* of *wasm* ⟨mark⟩ into the initial *hamza* of *ism*, the etymology preferred by the Kufans. (S, Z, Q)

254 I.e., among the Basrians (Z).

255 Cf. Wright, *Grammar* (1:71-72) and Abdul-Massih, *Khalīl* (pp. 91b-95a).

مَعًا
بِسْمِ الَّذِي فِي كُلِّ سُورَةٍ سِمُهُ * ....

وَ(الْإِسْمُ)، إِنْ أُرِيدَ بِهِ اللَّفْظُ: فَغَيْرُ الْمُسَمَّى؛ لِأَنَّهُ يَتَأَلَّفُ مِنْ أَصْوَاتٍ مُتَقَطِّعَةٍ غَيْرِ قَارَّةٍ، وَيَخْتَلِفُ بِاخْتِلَافِ الْأُمَمِ وَالْأَعْصَارِ، وَيَتَعَدَّدُ تَارَةً، وَيَتَّحِدُ أُخْرَى؛ وَالْمُسَمَّى لَا يَكُونُ كَذَلِكَ. وَإِنْ أُرِيدَ بِهِ ذَاتُ الشَّيْءِ: فَهُوَ الْمُسَمَّى؛ لَكِنَّهُ لَمْ يَشْتَهِرْ بِهَذَا الْمَعْنَى. وَقَوْلُهُ تَعَالَى ﴿تَبَارَكَ اسْمُ رَبِّكَ﴾ [الرحمن ٧٨] و﴿سَبِّحِ اسْمَ رَبِّكَ الْأَعْلَى﴾ [الأعلى ١]: الْمُرَادُ بِهِ اللَّفْظُ، لِأَنَّهُ كَمَا يَجِبُ تَنْزِيهُ ذَاتِهِ سُبْحَانَهُ وَتَعَالَى وَصِفَاتِهِ عَنِ النَّقَائِصِ، ....

In the name of Him Whose Name (si/umuh) is in every sura.[256]

[The name is primarily other than the named]

If, by "name" one means the vocable (*lafz̤*), then it is other than the referent (*musammā*), since it is composed of separate, unfixed sounds,[257] differs according to nations and eras, and is at times multiple and at times single, contrary to the referent.

If, however, the thing itself is meant, then it is the very same as the referent; but this acceptation is not widespread: in the verses of Allah Most High, *Blessed be the Name of your Nurturer* (al-Raḥmān 55:78) and *Glorify the Name of your Nurturer the Most High* (al-Aʿlā 87:1), what is meant is the vocable. For just as it is obligatory to shield His essence—may He be glorified and exalt-

[256] Narrated from a man from Kalb by Abū Zayd al-Anṣārī, *al-Nawādir fīl-Lugha*, ed. Muḥammad Aḥmad (Beirut: Dār al-Shurūq, 1981/1401) p. 462; or spoken by Ruʾba b. ʿAjjāj cf. Muḥibb al-Dīn Afandī, *Sharḥ Shawāhid al-Kashshāf* known as *Tanzīl al-Āyāt ʿalā al-Shawāhid min al-Abyāt*, published with Ibn Ḥajar's *al-Kāfī al-Shāf fī Takhrīj Aḥādīth al-Kashshāf* (Beirut: Dār Iḥyāʾ al-Turāth al-ʿArabī, 1418/1997) p. 337; or Abū ʿIkrima al-Ḍabbī, cf. Ibn al-Anbārī, *Īḍāḥ al-Waqf wal-Ibtidāʾ*, ed. Muḥyī al-Dīn Ramaḍān, 2 vols. (Damascus: Mujammaʿ al-Lughat al-ʿArabiyya, 1391/1971) 1:215.

[257] "Because they are fluid (*sayyāla*), as their parts do not gather up in actuality." (Q)

يَجِبُ تَنْزِيهُ الْأَلْفَاظِ الْمَوْضُوعَةِ لَهَا عَنِ الرَّفَثِ وَسُوءِ الْأَدَبِ.

أَوِ (الِاسْمُ) فِيهِ مُقْحَمٌ، كَمَا فِي قَوْلِ الشَّاعِرِ: [طَوِيل]

إِلَى الْحَوْلِ ثُمَّ اسْمُ السَّلَامِ عَلَيْكُمَا * ....

وَإِنْ أُرِيدَ بِهِ الصِّفَةُ - كَمَا هُوَ رَأْيُ الشَّيْخِ أَبِي الْحَسَنِ الْأَشْعَرِيِّ - انْقَسَمَ انْقِسَامَ الصِّفَةِ عِنْدَهُ: إِلَى مَا هُوَ نَفْسُ الْمُسَمَّى، وَإِلَى مَا هُوَ غَيْرُهُ، وَإِلَى مَا لَيْسَ هُوَ وَلَا غَيْرَهُ.

ed!—and Attributes from [any attribution of] defects, it is also obligatory to keep the vocables that apply to them safe from any filth or impropriety.

Alternately, "the name" is intercalated,[258] as in the poet's saying, ["The Long"]

Up to one year—then the Name of Peace on you both![259]

If, however, the attribute is meant—as is the view of Shaykh Abū al-Ḥasan al-Ashʿarī—it is divided into the same subdivisions he gave attributes: (i) what is the referent itself, (ii) what is other than the referent, and (iii) what is neither the referent nor other than it.[260]

[258] This is the position of the Khārijī linguist and exegete Abū ʿUbayda Maʿmar b. al-Muthannā al-Taymī (110-210/728-825) in his commentary entitled *Majāz al-Qur'ān*, ed. Muḥammad Fu'ād Sezgin, 2nd ed., 2 vols. (Beirut: Mu'assasat al-Risāla, 1401/1981) 1:16: "*Bi-smi-l-Lāh* is none other than *bi-l-Lāh* because the name of something is the thing itself. Labīd said…" which al-Ṭabarī severely rebuts in his *Tafsīr* (1:117-120).

[259] Spoken by the Companion-poet Labīd b. Rabīʿa al-ʿĀmirī—one of the seven *Muʿallaqāt* authors—after he reached 130 years of age and said: "My two daughters wished for their father to live on / but am I aught but of Rabīʿa or Muḍar? / Rise both, declare what you know well. Neither / claw faces nor shave heads, but say / 'He is the man who never failed a friend / nor betrayed his beloved nor cheated nor deceived.' / Up to one year—then the Name of the Transcendant on you both; and whoso weeps a whole year is excused." (S)

[260] Cf. Daniel Gimaret, *La doctrine d'al-Ashʿarī* (Paris: Cerf, 1990) pp. 352-356.

وَإِنَّمَا قَالَ: (بِسْمِ الله)، وَلَمْ يَقُلْ: (بِالله)، لِأَنَّ التَّبَرُّكَ وَالْاسْتِعَانَةَ بِذِكْرِ اسْمِهِ؛ أَوْ لِلْفَرْقِ بَيْنَ الْيَمِينِ وَالتَّيَمُّنِ.

وَلَمْ تُكْتَبِ الْأَلِفُ عَلَى مَا هُوَ وَضْعُ الْخَطِّ: لِكَثْرَةِ الْاسْتِعْمَالِ؛ وَطُوِّلَتِ الْبَاءُ عِوَضاً عَنْهَا.

وَ(**اللهُ**): أَصْلُهُ (إِلٰهٌ)، فَحُذِفَتِ الْهَمْزَةُ وَعُوِّضَ عَنْهَا الْأَلِفُ وَاللَّامُ، وَلِذَلِكَ قِيلَ: (يَا أَللهُ)، بِالْقَطْعِ؛ إِلَّا أَنَّهُ مُخْتَصٌّ بِالْمَعْبُودِ بِالْحَقِّ؛ ....

He said "by the Name of Allah" instead of "by Allah" because the obtainment of blessing and the recourse to help are by the mention of His Name; or to differentiate between oath (*yamīn*) and propitiation (*tayammun*).

The *alif* was not written according to calligraphic convention because it is so heavily used, so the *bā'* was elongated to compensate for it.[261]

[The divine name *Allāh*: etymology and morphology]

Allāh is originally *ilāh* (deity), from which the *hamza* (glottal stop) was elided and compensated by *al-*; hence, one says *Yā Allāh* (O Allah) disjunctively;[262] but it is used specifically for the One Who is rightfully worshipped. ....

[261] A second justification for the elongation of the written *bā'* according to al-Bulqīnī is magnification (*ta'ẓīm*), since it begins the Book of Allah. (S) See on this theme the erudite Sufi mathematician Aḥmad b. Muḥammad al-'Adadī, known as Ibn Bannā' al-Marrākishī (654-721/1256-1321), *'Unwān al-Dalīl fī Marsūm Khaṭṭ al-Tanzīl*, ed. Hind Shalabī (Beirut: Dār al-Gharb al-Islāmī, 1990).

[262] I.e. not *Yallāh* contractively. The latter is a colloquialism used to signify "hurry up!," further corrupted in the Maghreb into the feminine and plural verbal forms *yallāhī* and *yallāhū* respectively. It has also been claimed to be an unrelated, underived Persian colloquialism: http://www.ahlalhdeeth.com/vb/showthread.php?t=169211.

وَ(الْإِلٰهُ) فِي الْأَصْلِ لِكُلِّ مَعْبُودٍ، ثُمَّ غَلَبَ عَلَى المَعْبُودِ بِالْحَقِّ. وَاشْتِقَاقُهُ مِنْ (أَلَهَ إِلٰهَةً) وَ(أُلُوهَةً) وَ(أُلُوهِيَّةً) بِمَعْنَى (عَبَدَ)؛ وَمِنْهُ (تَأَلَّهَ) وَ(اسْتَأْلَهَ).

وَقِيلَ: مِنْ (أَلِهَ)، إِذَا تَحَيَّرَ؛ لِأَنَّ الْعُقُولَ تَتَحَيَّرُ فِي مَعْرِفَتِهِ.

أَوْ مِنْ (أَلِهْتُ) إِلَى فُلَانٍ، أَيْ سَكَنْتُ إِلَيْهِ؛ لِأَنَّ الْقُلُوبَ تَطْمَئِنُّ بِذِكْرِهِ، وَالْأَرْوَاحَ تَسْكُنُ إِلَى مَعْرِفَتِهِ؛

أَوْ مِنْ (أَلِهَ)، إِذَا فَزِعَ مِنْ أَمْرٍ نَزَلَ عَلَيْهِ؛ ....

Ilāh ⁽deity⁾, originally, is for any object of worship; then overwhelming usage [confined it] to the One Who is rightfully worshipped. It is derived

(i) from *alaha*[263] ⁽he worshipped⁾—[infinitive nouns] *ilāhatan, ulūhatan* and *ulūhiyya*[264]—whence [verbs] *ta'allaha* and *ista'laha* ⁽he devoted himself to worship⁾. It is also said [to derive]

(ii) from *aliha* ⁽he became perplexed⁾, because minds are bewildered when it comes to knowing Him;

(iii) or from *alahtu ilā fulān* ⁽I took refuge with X⁾, that is, I found peace with him; for hearts grow tranquil with His remembrance and souls find peace with knowledge of Him;

(iv) or from *aliha* when one becomes distressed at some emer-

[263] Thus vowelized in M and N, while I and T have *aliha* which some deem the correct reading cf. (أله) يأله من باب تعب الاهة بمعنى عبد عبادة in Aḥmad b. Muḥammad al-Fayyūmī, *al-Miṣbāḥ al-Munīr fī Gharīb al-Sharḥ al-Kabīr lil-Rāfiʿī*, 2 vols. (Cairo: Maṭbaʿat al-Taqaddum, 1322/1904) 1:12 but S, K and others confirm the former as the correct *ḍabt*: قوله (من أله) بفتح الهمزة واللام كعبد وزناً ومعنىً (Q). Ditto in al-Jawharī, *al-Ṣiḥāḥ: Tāj al-Lugha wa-Ṣiḥāḥ al-ʿArabiyya*, ed. Aḥmad ʿAbd al-Ghafūr ʿAṭṭār, 4th ed., 6 vols. (Beirut: Dār al-ʿIlm lil-Malāyīn, 1410/1990); al-Fayrūzābādī, *al-Qāmūs al-Muḥīṭ*, ed. Yūsuf al-Shaykh Muḥammad al-Biqāʿī (Beirut: Dār al-Fikr, 1995/1410); and al-Rāghib, *Mufradāt*, entries *a-l-h*. *Aliha* comes up next but in different senses.

[264] Ak, B, ε, F, I, K, N, R, T: الهة والوهة والوهية α, β: الهة والوهية

مَعًا

وَ(آلَهَهُ غَيْرُهُ): أَجَارَهُ، إِذِ الْعَائِذُ يَفْزَعُ إِلَيْهِ، وَهُوَ يُجِيرُهُ ـ حَقِيقَةً أَوْ بِزَعْمِهِ؛

أَوْ مِنْ (أَلِهَ الْفَصِيلُ)، إِذَا وَلِعَ بِأُمِّهِ؛ إِذِ الْعِبَادُ يُولَعُونَ بِالتَّضَرُّعِ إِلَيْهِ فِي الشَّدَائِدِ؛

أَوْ مِنْ (وَلِهَ)، إِذَا تَحَيَّرَ وَتَخَبَّطَ عَقْلُهُ؛ وَكَأَنَّ أَصْلَهُ (وِلَاهٌ)، فَقُلِبَتِ الْوَاوُ هَمْزَةً لِاسْتِثْقَالِ الْكَسْرَةِ عَلَيْهَا اسْتِثْقَالَ الضَّمَّةِ فِي (وُجُوه)، فَقِيلَ: (إِلَهٌ)، كَ(إِعَاءٍ) وَ(إِشَاحٍ)؛ وَيَرُدُّهُ الْجَمْعُ عَلَى (آلِهَةٍ) دُونَ (أَوْلِهَةٍ)؛

gency. *Ālahahu ghayruhu* means "someone gave him protection" when a refuge-seeker flees to someone who then gives him protection, whether real or claimed.[265] Another use of *aliha* is for the newborn calf craving its mother, as creatures strongly yearn for Him and earnestly call on Him in difficulties.

(v) Another derivation is *waliha*, "he became perplexed, bewildered;" it is as if[266] its root were *wilāh*[267] then the *wāw* was transposed into a *hamza* ⁽glottal stop⁾ because of the heaviness of its *kasra*—in the same way the initial *ḍamma* weighed too heavily in *wujūh* ⁽faces⁾[268]—yielding *ilāh* ⁽deity⁾, as in *iʿā'* and *ishāḥ*.[269] This is invalidated by its plural being *āliha* rather than *awliha*.

265 Respectively corresponding to true and false belief. (Q)

266 Q, Sk: انما قال بلفظ التشبيه لان اصله لم يثبت في الاستعمال فهو قياس محض
Kh: لم يجزم به لعدم سماع ولاه إن كانت العبارة كأنّ بفتح الكاف والهمزة وتشديد النون، ويجوز أن يكون مخففاً بالألف ماضي كان الناقصة وما قيل من أنه لا يصح لأنه يجب حينئذ نصب ولاه ورسمه بألف وليس كذلك هو في النسخ ليس بشيء لأنه يجوز حكاية لفظه كما في بعض الحواشي فيمنع صرفه.

267 α, B, I: وِلاه T: وَلاه

268 Which became *ujūh* with *hamza* replacing the initial *wāw* (Q) cf. *Lisān*, art. *w-q-t*.

269 Respectively from *wiʿā'* ⁽vessel⁾ and *wishāḥ*, a wide diagonal leather chest-strap worn by women (cf. *Nihāya*, art. *w-sh-ḥ*), which Reinhart Dozy both mistranslates and mistakes for a plural in his *Dictionnaire détaillé des noms des vêtements chez les Arabes* (Amsterdam: Jean Müller, 1845, rept. Beirut: Librairie du Liban, n.d.), art. *wishāḥ*, whereas the plural is *awshiḥa* cf. "Whosoever straps on a sword in the way of Allah, he shall have a *wishāḥ* from the *awshiḥa* of Paradise" in Ibn Ḥajar, *al-Iṣāba fī Tamyīz al-Ṣaḥāba*, entry on ʿAtīqa b. al-Ḥārith al-Anṣārī.

وَقِيلَ: أَصْلُهُ (لَاهٍ)، مَصْدَرُ (لَاهَ يَلِيهُ لَيْهاً) وَ(لَاهاً)، إِذَا احْتَجَبَ وَارْتَفَعَ؛ لِأَنَّهُ ـ سُبْحَانَهُ وَتَعَالَى ـ مَحْجُوبٌ عَنْ إِدْرَاكِ الأَبْصَارِ، وَمُرْتَفِعٌ عَلَى كُلِّ شَيْءٍ وَعَمَّا لَا يَلِيقُ بِهِ؛ وَيَشْهَدُ لَهُ قَوْلُ الشَّاعِرِ: [بَسِيط]

كَحَلْفَةٍ مِنْ أَبِي رَبَاحٍ ۞ يَشْهَدُهَا لَاهُهُ الكِبَارُ

وَقِيلَ: عَلَمٌ لِذَاتِهِ المَخْصُوصَةِ؛ لِأَنَّهُ يُوصَفُ وَلَا يُوصَفُ بِهِ؛ وَلِأَنَّهُ

(vi) It was also said its root is *lāh*, the infinitive noun of the verb *lāha*—[aorist] *yalīhu*, [infinitive nouns] *layhan* and *lāhan*—meaning "he veiled himself and was or became elevated," for Allah—may He be glorified and exalted!—is veiled from the perception of sights and elevated above all things and anything that does not befit Him. Witnessing to it is the poet's saying: ["The Outspread"]

> Like a solemn oath of Abū Rabāḥ
>   witnessed by his tremendous god (*lāhuhu*).[270]

It was also said [**Allāh** is] a proper name for His own Essence,[271] because it is described but never serves to describe, and

---

[270] From a poem beginning with the verse, "Have you all not seen Iram and ʿĀd? || The night and the day reduced them to nought" (*alam taraw Iraman wa-ʿĀdā || awdā bihā/afnāhumu al-laylu wal-nahāru*). Some versions have the variants *ḥalqatin* ʿcircleʾ instead of *ḥalfatin* ʿoathʾ and *yasmaʿuhā* ʿheardʾ for *yashhaduhā* ʿwitnessedʾ. (S, Q, Z) Cf. *Dīwān al-Aʿshā al-Kabīr*, ed. Muḥammad Ḥusayn (Cairo: Maktabat al-Ādāb, [1950]) pp. 280-283 §53. α, I, N, R: رباح Ak, β, ε, T: رياح

[271] This terminology is borrowed from al-Rāzī's *Mafātīḥ al-Ghayb* in many places, al-Bayḍāwī's principal source for doctrinal and philosophical issues while Zamakhsharī's *Kashshāf* (henceforward J) is his principal source for grammar and rhetoric. He also borrows moral and doctrinal points from al-Rāghib al-Asfahānī, cf. Muḥammad al-Fāḍil b. ʿĀshūr, *al-Tafsīr wa-Rijāluh* (pp. 107-120); Muḥammad al-Zuḥaylī, *al-Qāḍī al-Bayḍāwī*, 2nd ed. (Damascus: Dār al-Qalam, 1420/1999) p. 121-138; and Yūsuf Aḥmad ʿAlī, *al-Bayḍāwī wa-Manhajuhu fīl-Tafsīr*, unpublished Ph.D. diss. (Mecca: Umm al-Qurā University, n.d.) p. 65-74.

لَا بُدَّ لَهُ مِنْ اِسْمٍ تَجْرِي عَلَيْهِ صِفَاتُهُ، وَلَا يَصْلُحُ لَهُ ـ مِمَّا يُطْلَقُ عَلَيْهِ ـ سِوَاهُ؛ وَلِأَنَّهُ لَوْ كَانَ وَصْفاً، لَمْ يَكُنْ قَوْلُ (لَا إِلٰهَ إِلَّا اللهُ) تَوْحِيداً، مِثْلَ: (لَا إِلٰهَ إِلَّا الرَّحْمٰنُ)، فَإِنَّهُ لَا يَمْنَعُ الشَّرِكَةَ.

وَالْأَظْهَرُ أَنَّهُ وَصْفٌ فِي أَصْلِهِ؛ لٰكِنَّهُ لَمَّا غَلَبَ عَلَيْهِ، بِحَيْثُ لَا يُسْتَعْمَلُ فِي غَيْرِهِ، وَصَارَ لَهُ كَالْعَلَمِ، ....

because He must have a name to which His Attributes apply; and there is none suitable for Him, among those by which He might be named, but that.

Furthermore, if it were a descriptive, the statement "There is no god but Allah" would not constitute pure monotheism—as in, for example, "There is no god but the all-Merciful," which does not preclude partnership.[272]

The predominant view, however, is that it is originally a descriptive;[273] but when overwhelming usage made it His, wherein it applies to no other and became like a proper name for Him ......

[272] A reasoning taken from al-Rāzī, *Tafsīr al-Fakhr al-Rāzī al-Mushtahar bil-Tafsīr al-Kabīr wa-Mafātīḥ al-Ghayb*, 32 vols. (Beirut: Dār al-Fikr, 1401/1981), *sub* 2:163. "Al-Ṭībī said [in *Futūḥ al-Ghayb* (1:88)]: 'The Qadi wrote in the margin: "*al-Raḥmān*, even though it is reserved for the Creator—exalted is He!, it remains that such has transpired with a separate proof; linguistically, it [only] means someone who shows utmost mercy."'" (S) This elucidation cited by al-Suyūṭī in his *Nawāhid* (1:240) suggests autograph marginalia penned by al-Bayḍāwī on J, which were in al-Ṭībī's possession as he worked on the latter.

[273] "The author's intent is to disprove the claim that it is underived, whether a proper name or a descriptive." (Q) "The correct view, based on transmission and evidence, is that it is a proper name" (S) cf. Suyūṭī's *Ashbāh wal-Naẓā'ir fil Naḥw* (4:5). Shawkānī in the introduction of *Nayl al-Awṭār* labels the view that *Allāh* is an underived proper name as the position of the majority (*al-jumhūr*). Al-Rāzī (who also prefers the latter position) in his *Kitāb Lawāmiʿ al-Bayyināt Sharḥ Asmā' Allāh Taʿālā wal-Ṣifāt*, ed. Muḥammad al-Naʿsānī (Cairo: al-Khānjī, 1323/1905) pp. 80, 83 says that it is derived according to the majority of the Muʿtazilis, many of the lexicographers and others.

مِثْلَ (الثُّرَيَّا)، وَ(الصَّعِقِ): أُجْرِيَ مُجْرَاهُ فِي إِجْرَاءِ الْأَوْصَافِ عَلَيْهِ، وَامْتِنَاعِ الْوَصْفِ بِهِ، وَعَدَمِ تَطَرُّقِ احْتِمَالِ الشَّرِكَةِ إِلَيْهِ؛ لِأَنَّ ذَاتَهُ مِنْ حَيْثُ هُوَ، بِلَا اعْتِبَارِ أَمْرٍ آخَرَ ـ حَقِيقِيٍّ أَوْ غَيْرِهِ ـ غَيْرُ مَعْقُولٍ لِلْبَشَرِ، فَلَا يُمْكِنُ أَنْ يُدَلَّ عَلَيْهِ بِلَفْظٍ؛ وَلِأَنَّهُ لَوْ دَلَّ عَلَى مُجَرَّدِ ذَاتِهِ الْمَخْصُوصَةِ، لَمَا أَفَادَ ظَاهِرُ قَوْلِهِ سُبْحَانَهُ وَتَعَالَى: ﴿وَهُوَ ٱللَّهُ فِي ٱلسَّمَٰوَٰتِ وَفِي ٱلْأَرْضِ﴾ [الأنعام ٣] مَعْنًى صَحِيحاً؛ ....

—as also took place, for example, with "al-Thurayyā" and "al-Ṣaʿiq"[274]—it was deemed as such in that (i) descriptives qualify it, (ii) it never serves as a descriptive, and (iii) any hint of possible partnership is precluded from it.

[No word can designate the reality of the divine Self]

For His essence, viewed as He Himself, without regard to any other aspect—intrinsic or otherwise[275]—is inconceivable to human beings and therefore cannot be designated with a word. Also, if it designated nothing but His own essence, then the letter of His statement—exalted is He!—*He is Allah in the heavens and on earth* (al-Anʿām 6:3) would not have made sense.[276] Further-

---

[274] Originally the diminutive of *tharwa*, "multitudinous"—which metonymically became the name of the Pleiades cluster of stars (*al-thurayyā*)—and the adjective "thunderstruck" (*ṣaʿiq*) which became the surname of Khuwaylid b. Nufayl. (Q)

[275] "Whether intrinsic (*ḥaqīqī*)—such as the positive, affirmative attributes (*al-ṣifāt al-ījābiyya al-thubūtiyya*)—or unintrinsic—such as the preclusive attributes (*al-ṣifāt al-salbiyya*).ʾ ʿAbd al-Nabī b. ʿAbd al-Rasūl Aḥmadnagrī, *Mawsūʿat Muṣṭalaḥāt Jāmiʿ al-ʿUlūm: al-Mulaqqab bi-Dustūr al-ʿUlamāʾ*, ed. Rafīq al-ʿAjam (Beirut: Maktabat Lubnān, 1997) art. *Allāh*.

[276] "Al-Ṭībī said: ʿI.e., with regard to temporal-local adverbiality (*al-ẓarfiyya*) which is impossible for His essence, hence it must have a meaning specific to descriptiveness (*al-waṣfiyya*), namely, "the One worshipped in the heavens and the earth."ʾ And what he said needs reconsideration." (S)

وَلِأَنَّ مَعْنَى الِاشْتِقَاقِ هُوَ كَوْنُ أَحَدِ اللَّفْظَيْنِ مُشَارِكاً لِلْآخَرِ فِي الْمَعْنَى وَالتَّرْكِيبِ، وَهُوَ حَاصِلٌ بَيْنَهُ وَبَيْنَ الْأُصُولِ الْمَذْكُورَةِ.

وَقِيلَ: أَصْلُهُ (لَاهَا) بِالسُّرْيَانِيَّةِ، فَعُرِّبَ بِحَذْفِ الْأَلِفِ الْأَخِيرَةِ، وَإِدْخَالِ اللَّامِ عَلَيْهِ.

وَتَفْخِيمُ لَامِهِ - إِذَا انْفَتَحَ مَا قَبْلَهُ أَوِ انْضَمَّ - سُنَّةٌ، وَقِيلَ: مُطْلَقاً.

وَحَذْفُ أَلِفِهِ لَحْنٌ، تَفْسُدُ بِهِ الصَّلَاةُ، وَلَا يَنْعَقِدُ بِهِ صَرِيحُ الْيَمِينِ؛ وَقَدْ جَاءَ لِضَرُورَةِ الشِّعْرِ: [وَافِر]

أَلَا لَا بَارَكَ اللَّـهُ [بالقصر] فِي سُهَيْلٍ ❋ إِذَا مَا اللهُ بَارَكَ فِي الرِّجَالِ

more, derivation means that one of two terms has meaning and form in common with the other, and this is precisely the case between it and the etymons mentioned.

It was also said its root is the Syriac *lāhā*, Arabized with the elision of the final *alif* and the insertion of an additional *lām*.[277]

The glottal accentuation of its *lām* when preceded by a *fatḥa* or *ḍamma* is a [linguistic] tradition; it was also said [it is thus accented] in all cases.[278]

The suppression of its *alif* is a solecism by which prayer becomes invalid and an oath falls short of being explicitly sworn; yet it has come up for the requirements of meter: ["The Exuberant"]

> *Lo! May Allah* [without *alif*] *never bless Suhayl*
> *every time that Allāh shall bless men.*[279]

[277] Al-Bulqīnī considered this derivation baseless. (S)
[278] I.e. even if preceded by *kasra*: a weak position. (S)
[279] *Alā lā bāraka <u>Allahu</u> fī Suhaylin || idhā mā-l-Lāhu bāraka fīl-rijāli.* The *alif* was dropped out of *Allāh* in the first hemistich so that it can read ˘--- | ˘-˘˘- | ˘-- to match

وَ﴿ٱلرَّحْمَٰنِ ٱلرَّحِيمِ﴾ : اِسْمَانِ بُنِيَا لِلْمُبَالَغَةِ مِنْ (رَحِمَ)، كَ(الْغَضْبَانِ) مِنْ (غَضِبَ)، وَ(الْعَلِيمِ) مِنْ (عَلِمَ).

وَ(الرَّحْمَةُ) فِي اللُّغَةِ: رِقَّةُ الْقَلْبِ وَانْعِطَافٌ يَقْتَضِي التَّفَضُّلَ وَالإِحْسَانَ؛ وَمِنْهُ: (الرَّحِمُ)، لِانْعِطَافِهَا عَلَى مَا فِيهَا. وَأَسْمَاءُ اللهِ تَعَالَى إِنَّمَا تُؤْخَذُ بِاعْتِبَارِ الْغَايَاتِ الَّتِي هِيَ أَفْعَالٌ، دُونَ الْمَبَادِي الَّتِي تَكُونُ انْفِعَالَاتٍ.

[*Raḥmān* and *raḥīm* are synonyms]

Al-raḥmān al-raḥīm are two intensive-form nouns derived from *raḥima* ⁽he showed compassion⁾, like *ghaḍbān* ⁽angry⁾ from *ghaḍiba* and *'alīm* ⁽knowing⁾ from *'alima*. *Raḥma* ⁽mercy⁾, lexically, is tenderness of the heart and a leaning that dictates the showing of favor and good treatment, whence *raḥim* ⁽womb⁾ since the latter curves around its content.[280] But the Names of Allah are taken only in consideration of outcomes, which are acts, and not of inceptions, which are affects.[281]

the same-footed second hemistich, and meet the requirement of the meter. Spoken by Quṭrub, cf. Ibn Jinnī, *Sirr Ṣinā'at al-I'rāb*, ed. Ḥasan Handāwī, 2nd ed., 2 vols. (Damascus: Dār al-Qalam, 1413/1993) 2:720-721 and his *al-Muḥtasab fī Tabyīn wujūh Shawādhdh al-Qirā'āt*, ed. 'Alī al-Najdī Nāṣif et al., 2nd ed., 2 vols. (Dār Sezgin, 1407/1987) 1:181.

280 "Either by way of metonymy (*al-majāz al-mursal*) by naming the cause and intending the result, or by way of a proverbial metaphor (*isti'āra tamthīliyya*)." (Q) The latter is "produced by retaining in one's mind all the elements of a comparison except the tenor" cf. Pierre Cachia, *The Arch Rhetorician or The Schemer's Skimmer: A Handbook of Late Arabic* badī' *drawn from 'Abd al-Ghanī an-Nābulusī's* Nafaḥāt al-azhār 'alā nasamāt al-asḥār (Wiesbaden: Harrasowitz Verlag, 1998) p. 88.

281 "Its upshot is that it is impossible to attribute literal compassion (*ḥaqīqat al-raḥma*) to Allah, therefore it is explained as that which compassion necessitates (*tufassaru bi-lāzimihā*)." (S) This method and its examples are demonstrated by Ibn 'Ādil, "Exposition of Attributes that Are Inattributable [literally] to Allah" in *al-Lubāb fī 'Ulūm al-Kitāb*, ed. 'Ādil Aḥmad 'Abd al-Mawjūd et al., 20 vols. (Beirut: Dār al-Kutub al-'Ilmiyya, 1419/1998) 1:154-155; Ibn 'Abd al-Salām, *al-Ishāra ilā al-Ījāz fī Ba'ḍ Anwā'*

وَ﴿ٱلرَّحۡمَٰنِ﴾ أَبْلَغُ مِنَ ﴿ٱلرَّحِيمِ﴾، لِأَنَّ زِيَادَةَ الْبِنَاءِ تَدُلُّ عَلَى زِيَادَةِ الْمَعْنَى، كَمَا فِي (قَطَعَ) وَ(قَطَّعَ)، وَ(كُبَارٌ) وَ(كُبَّارٌ). وَذٰلِكَ إِنَّمَا يُؤْخَذُ تَارَةً بِاعْتِبَارِ الْكَمِّيَّةِ، وَأُخْرَى بِاعْتِبَارِ الْكَيْفِيَّةِ؛ فَعَلَى الأَوَّلِ، قِيلَ: يَا رَحْمٰنَ الدُّنْيَا ـ لِأَنَّهُ يَعُمُّ الْمُؤْمِنَ وَالْكَافِرَ ـ وَرَحِيمَ الآخِرَةِ ـ لِأَنَّهُ يَخُصُّ الْمُؤْمِنَ؛ وَعَلَى الثَّانِي، قِيلَ: يَا رَحْمٰنَ الدُّنْيَا وَالآخِرَةِ، وَرَحِيمَ الدُّنْيَا؛ لِأَنَّ النِّعَمَ الأُخْرَوِيَّةَ كُلَّهَا

[Longer cognates point to additional meanings]

Al-raḥmān is more intensive than *al-raḥīm*—since addition in morphology spells addition in meaning,[282] as in *qaṭaʿa*, ⁽he cut⁾ and *qaṭṭaʿa* ⁽he cut to pieces⁾, or *kubār* ⁽big⁾ and *kubbār* ⁽huge⁾ —which must be understood in regard to quantity at times and modality at others. In the first case, it was said "O *raḥmān* of this world"—for the latter includes the believer and the unbeliever—"and *raḥīm* of the next!"—for it is exclusive to the believer. In the second case it was said "O *raḥmān* of this world and the next, and *raḥīm* of this world!" because next-worldly favors are all ....

al-Majāz, ed. ʿUthmān Ḥilmī ([Cairo:] al-Maṭbaʿat al-ʿĀmira, 1313/1895) pp. 104-112 in which he states: 'According to the Shaykh [al-Ashʿarī], *raḥma* means Allah's will *(irāda)*, for His slave, of whatever one showing compassion wills for the one who is shown it" and so for all states or acts connoting affect (*infiʿāl*), need, spatiality or corporeality such as friendship (*maḥabba*), love (*wudd*), good pleasure (*riḍā*), gratitude (*shukr*), laughter (*ḍaḥik*), happiness (*faraḥ*), patience (*ṣabr*), jealousy (*ghīra*), shame (*ḥayāʾ*), testing (*ibtilāʾ*), sarcasm (*sukhriyya*), mockery (*istihzāʾ*), scheming (*makr*), ruse (*khidʿ*), astonishment (*ʿajab*), distance (e.g. when qualified by *dhālika*, *dhālikum*), leisure (*farāgh*), hesitancy (*taraddud*), establishment [over the Throne] (*istiwāʾ*), baring of the shin (*kashf al-sāq*), wrath (*ghaḍab*), resentment (*sukhṭ* or *sakhaṭ*), grief (*asaf*), hatred and spite (*qilā*, *maqt*, *bughḍ*), enmity (*ʿadāwa*), and malediction (*laʿn*); and our translations of al-Bayhaqī's *al-Asmāʾ wal-Ṣifāt* and Ibn ʿAbd al-Salām's *al-Mulḥa fī Iʿtiqād Ahl al-Ḥaqq* published at al-Sunna Foundation of America (Islamic Doctrines & Beliefs series).

282 Usually, but not always; in some cases the reverse is true, e.g. *ḥadhir*/*ḥādhir* (S).

جِسَامٌ، وَأَمَّا النِّعَمُ الدُّنْيَوِيَّةُ: فَجَلِيلَةٌ وَحَقِيرَةٌ.

وَإِنَّمَا قُدِّمَ ـ وَالْقِيَاسُ يَقْتَضِي التَّرَقِّي مِنَ الْأَدْنَى إِلَى الْأَعْلَى ـ: (١) لِتَقَدُّمِ رَحْمَةِ الدُّنْيَا؛ (٢) وَلِأَنَّهُ صَارَ كَالْعَلَمِ مِنْ حَيْثُ إِنَّهُ لَا يُوصَفُ بِهِ غَيْرُهُ؛ لِأَنَّ مَعْنَاهُ: ....

momentous, while this-worldly favors are both weighty and trifling.[283] It was pointedly put first—although the rule dictates a progression from lower to higher:

1. because the mercy of this world takes place first;

2. and because it has become like a proper name since none other than Allah is described by it.[284] For its meaning is ....

[283] "He has followed the *Kashshāf* here." (S) "Neither of these two supplications has been transmitted. The one report to that effect is 'O *raḥmān* of this world and the next and their *raḥīm*!'" Al-Kāzarūnī, *Ḥāshiya* on al-Bayḍāwī, ed. Muḥammad al-Zuhrī al-Ghamrāwī, 4 vols. (Cairo: Dār al-Kutub al-ʿArabiyya al-Kubrā, 1330/1912), hereafter K. Cf. Ibn Kathīr, *Tafsīr* (1:198). The oft-quoted *duʿāʾ* K cites is part of a weak hadith narrated through Yūnus b. Yazīd al-Aylī who alternately reports it (i) from al-Zuhrī, from Anas cf. al-Ṭabarānī in *al-Muʿjam al-Ṣaghīr*, ed. ʿAbd al-Raḥmān Muḥammad ʿUthmān, 2 vols. (Medina: al-Maktaba al-Salafiyya, 1388/1968) 1:202, cf. al-Ḍiyāʾ al-Maqdisī, *al-Aḥādīth al-Mukhtāra*, ed. ʿAbd al-Malik Duhaysh, 4th ed., 13 vols. (Mecca: Maktabat al-Nahḍa, 1421/2001) 7:196-197 §2633; (ii) from al-Zuhrī, from Saʿīd b. al-Musayyab, from Muʿādh b. Jabal, cf. al-Ṭabarānī, *al-Muʿjam al-Kabīr*, ed. Ḥamdī ʿAbd al-Majīd al-Salafī, 2nd ed. 25 vols. (Baghdad: Wizārat al-Awqāf, 1984-1990, rept. Cairo: Maktabat Ibn Taymiyya, n.d.) 20:154 §323, 20:159 §332; and (iii) from al-Ḥakam b. ʿAbd Allāh al-Aylī (discarded and suspected of lying or forgery per al-Mundhirī in *al-Targhīb*), from al-Qāsim b. Muḥammad, from ʿĀʾisha, from her father by al-Ṭabarānī in *al-Duʿāʾ* (p. 327), al-Bazzār in his *Musnad*, al-Taymī in *al-Targhīb*, al-Ḥākim in *al-Mustadrak*, al-Bayhaqī in *al-Dalāʾil* and others. It is also related from Ibn Masʿūd with a forged chain and wording cf. Ibn al-Jawzī, *Mawḍūʿāt* (Salafiyya ed. 2:130-131), al-Suyūṭī in the *Laʾāliʾ* and others; also through ʿAbd al-ʿAzīz b. Ziyād—an unknown—from Anas in the wording, "O ʿAlī, shall I not teach you…" by al-Taymī al-Aṣfahānī in *al-Targhīb wal-Tarhīb*, ed. Ayman Shaʿbān, 3 vols. (Cairo: Dār al-Ḥadīth, 1993) 2:137-138 §1305; also *mursal* from the *Tābiʿī* ʿAbd al-Raḥmān b. Sābiṭ by Ibn Abī Shayba and others, and *mursal* from ʿAṭāʾ al-Khurāsānī, from Muʿādh by Ibn ʿAsākir.

الْمُنْعِمُ الْحَقِيقِيُّ الْبَالِغُ فِي الرَّحْمَةِ غَايَتَهَا، وَذٰلِكَ لَا يَصْدُقُ عَلَى غَيْرِهِ، لِأَنَّ مَنْ عَدَاهُ فَهُوَ مُسْتَعِيضٌ بِلُطْفِهِ وَإِنْعَامِهِ، يُرِيدُ بِهِ جَزِيلَ ثَوَابٍ، أَوْ جَمِيلَ ثَنَاءٍ؛ أَوْ يُزِيحُ رِقَّةَ الْجِنْسِيَّةِ أَوْ حُبَّ الْمَالِ عَنِ الْقَلْبِ. ثُمَّ إِنَّهُ كَالْوَاسِطَةِ فِي ذٰلِكَ لِأَنَّ ذَاتَ النِّعَمِ، وَوُجُودَهَا، وَالْقُدْرَةَ عَلَى إِيصَالِهَا، وَالدَّاعِيَةَ الْبَاعِثَةَ عَلَيْهِ، وَالتَّمَكُّنَ مِنَ الْاِنْتِفَاعِ بِهَا، وَالْقِوَى الَّتِي بِهَا يَحْصُلُ الِانْتِفَاعُ، إِلَى غَيْرِ ذٰلِكَ: مِنْ خَلْقِهِ، لَا يَقْدِرُ عَلَيْهَا أَحَدٌ غَيْرُهُ؛

"the true grantor of bounty who reaches the utmost in mercy." Such is untrue of any other than Him, since all others aim to obtain repayment in exchange for giving kindness and favor. One either wants lavish compensation, or fine praise or to allay[285] the sensitivity of human sympathy[286] and love of money from the heart. Moreover, one is like a mere intermediary in that, since the favors themselves, their existence, the power to deliver them, the motivation and stimulus to [obtain] them, the ability to benefit from them, the powers by which such benefit takes place, and so forth, all of this is His creation and none but He has power over it.

[284] By consensus per al-Kirmānī. (S) "As for their naming Musaylima the Arch-Liar 'the *raḥmān* of al-Yamāma,' it was prompted by their fanaticism in apostasy." (Q)

[285] α, L, Kh, Q, Sk, U, Ul, Z: يزيح ε: أو حميد ما يزيح A: او يزيح اي او مزيح كما في نسخة D, H, K, M, N, P: مزيح β, B, T: مزيل I: مزيح with superscript gloss: اي مزيل F: مُريح R: يُزيح أَنَفَة α, Ak: يزيل AQ, MM: مزيح

[286] *Riqqat al-jinsiyya* is the wording in the printed editions of *Anwār al-Tanzīl*, K, F, T and the *Kashshāf*—the latter making it the correct reading since it is the Qadi's source—while A has *riqq*, Ak *ribqat*, α *anafat*, B, Kh, Q and R *anafat al-khissa*, "the shame of meanness," and Z *ribqat al-khissa*, "the noose of meanness." The passage was skipped in S, who did not do a word by word commentary, while A explains: "That is, a human being is inherently a miser and loves money, so when he does someone a favor he only wants to curb the slavish grip of his human character by doing something that contradicts his basic nature—which is inherently miserly as is the common lot of those of his species—in order to be praised for doing so."

(٣) أَوْ لِأَنَّ الرَّحْمٰنَ، لَـمَّا دَلَّ عَلَى جَلَائِلِ النِّعَمِ وَأُصُولِهَا، ذَكَرَ الرَّحِيمَ لِيَتَنَاوَلَ مَا خَرَجَ مِنْهَا، فَيَكُونُ كَالتَّتِمَّةِ وَالرَّدِيفِ لَهُ؛

(٤) أَوْ لِلْمُحَافَظَةِ عَلَى رُؤُوسِ الْآيِ.

وَالْأَظْهَرُ أَنَّهُ غَيْرُ مَصْرُوفٍ ـ وَإِنْ حَظَرَ اخْتِصَاصُهُ بِاللهِ تَعَالَى أَنْ يَكُونَ لَهُ مُؤَنَّثٌ عَلَى (فَعْلَى) أَوْ (فَعْلَانَة) ـ إِلْحَاقاً لَهُ بِمَا هُوَ الْغَالِبُ فِي بَابِهِ.

وَإِنَّمَا خَصَّ التَّسْمِيَةَ بِهٰذِهِ الْأَسْمَاءِ لِيَعْلَمَ الْعَارِفُ أَنَّ الْمُسْتَحِقَّ لِأَنْ يُسْتَعَانَ

3. Or, after *al-raḥmān* pointed to the sublime and fundamental favors,[287] He mentioned *al-raḥīm* to address everything outside the first purview, like a complement and in tandem with it.

4. Another reason would be to harmonize verse endings.[288]

[*Raḥmān* cannot be pluralized or feminized]

The predominant view is that [*al-raḥmān*] is indeclinable[289] —regardless of the fact that its being used exclusively for Allah precludes its having a feminine with the forms *faʿlā* or *faʿlāna*[290] —if we sort it with the most frequent occurrences for its word type. He chose to be named by these Names so that the knower would realize that the one truly deserving to be sought for help

[287] "Sublime such as intellect, understanding, and all that serves as a means for the greatest felicity, and fundamental such as existence, life and the like." (Q) All mss. and eds.: وأصولها H: وأوصلها typo.

[288] The original term is "verse headings" (*ru'ūs*) but it means their endings (*awākhir*); by their keep is meant their mutual congruence in specific fashion (*tanāsub fī hay'atin makhṣūṣa*), namely that the penultimate letter be a mute *yā'* preceded by a *kasra*. (Q) The consonantal *fawāṣil* ⟨verse-endings⟩ of Qur'ān are what is called *sajʿ* ⟨rhyming prose⟩ in prose and *qāfiya* ⟨rhymes⟩ in poetry, with the categorical caveat that the Qur'ān is neither prose nor poetry. Cf. al-Suyūṭī, *Itqān* (Type 59).

[289] I.e., gender and number-wise, not case-wise since it accepts the nominative, accusative and genitive cases of a triptote, but without nunation.

[290] I.e., *raḥmā* or *raḥmāna*, the putative feminine forms of *rahīm* and *raḥmān*.

بِهِ فِي مَجَامِعِ الْأُمُورِ: هُوَ الْمَعْبُودُ الْحَقِيقِيُّ، الَّذِي هُوَ مُولِي النِّعَمِ كُلِّهَا، عَاجِلِهَا وَآجِلِهَا، جَلِيلِهَا وَحَقِيرِهَا؛ فَيَتَوَجَّهُ بِشَرَاشِرِهِ إِلَى جَنَابِ الْقُدْسِ، وَيَتَمَسَّكُ بِحَبْلِ التَّوْفِيقِ، وَيَشْغَلُ سِرَّهُ بِذِكْرِهِ وَالِاسْتِعْدَادِ بِهِ عَنْ غَيْرِهِ.

﴿ٱلْحَمْدُ لِلَّهِ﴾ (الْحَمْدُ): هُوَ الثَّنَاءُ عَلَى الْجَمِيلِ الِاخْتِيَارِيِّ، مِنْ نِعْمَةٍ أَوْ غَيْرِهَا؛ وَ(الْمَدْحُ): هُوَ الثَّنَاءُ عَلَى الْجَمِيلِ مُطْلَقاً. تَقُولُ: حَمِدْتُ زَيْداً عَلَى عِلْمِهِ وَكَرَمِهِ، وَلَا تَقُولُ: حَمِدْتُهُ عَلَى حُسْنِهِ؛ بَلْ مَدَحْتُهُ. وَقِيلَ هُمَا أَخَوَانِ.

وَ(الشُّكْرُ): مُقَابَلَةُ النِّعْمَةِ قَوْلاً وَعَمَلاً وَاعْتِقَاداً. قَالَ: [الطويل]

in all matters[291] is He Who is truly worshipped, Who is the grantor of all favors—both the immediate and the deferred, the sublime and the petty—turning therefore with every last shred of his being[292] to the Divine presence and firmly grasping the rope of God-given success, engrossing his inward being with His remembrance and taking Him as his sufficiency without any other.

[1:2] **al-ḥamdu li-l-Lāhi** ⁽*Praise be to the One God*⁾. *Ḥamd* is homage paid for a voluntary grace—whether a favor or something else—while *madḥ* ⁽compliment⁾ is homage paid for grace in unrestricted terms. You say, "I praised Zayd for his learning and generosity," but not "I praised him for his handsomeness," rather, "I complimented him." It is also said they are near- synonymous cognates.[293] As for *shukr* ⁽gratitude⁾, it is the matching of favor in speech, deed and conviction. [The poet] said: ["The Long"]

[291] *Majāmiʿ al-umūr* primarily means "all important matters" but can also mean all matters in absolute terms, which here is more obvious. (Q)

[292] *Bi-sharāshirihi*, "plural of *sharshara* which is used to mean the soul and the body, and it originally means the tips of the wings and the tail so it was used to mean the whole" (Q), an expression often used by the Qadi but invariably garbled to *bi-sharri asharrihi* in the 2000 edition of the *Anwār*.

[293] Lit. "brothers," a lexicographical term for words sharing two of their three root letters. Linguists refer to such cases as "the greater etymology" (*al-ishtiqāq al-akbar*)—

أَفَادَتْكُمُ النَّعْمَاءُ مِنِّي ثَلَاثَةً ❋ يَدِي وَلِسَانِي وَالضَّمِيرَ الْمُحَجَّبَا

فَهُوَ أَعَمُّ مِنْهُمَا مِنْ وَجْهٍ، وَأَخَصُّ مِنْ آخَرَ. وَلَمَّا كَانَ الْحَمْدُ مِنْ شُعَبِ الشُّكْرِ أَشْيَعَ لِلنِّعْمَةِ، وَأَدَلَّ عَلَى مَكَانِهَا ـ لِخَفَاءِ الِاعْتِقَادِ، وَمَا فِي إِدْآبِ الْجَوَارِحِ مِنَ الِاحْتِمَالِ ـ جُعِلَ رَأْسَ الشُّكْرِ وَالْعُمْدَةَ فِيهِ، فَقَالَ ـ عَلَيْهِ الصَّلَاةُ وَالسَّلَامُ: الْحَمْدُ رَأْسُ الشُّكْرِ، وَمَا شَكَرَ اللهَ مَنْ لَمْ يَحْمَدْهُ.

Graciousness earned you three things from me:
my hand, my tongue and conscience within.[294]

So the latter is more general than the first two from one perspective and more specific from another. Since praise, as an offshoot of gratitude, publicizes favors more and is more indicative of their existence—conviction remains hidden and the taxing[295] of the limbs is a burden—it was made the heading of gratitude and its mainstay. Hence he said, upon him blessings and peace:

> Praise is the head of thanks: he does not thank Allah, who does not praise Him [first].[296]

which the Qadi will mention shortly—and view it as indicative of shared meaning(s).

[294] The author of this oft-quoted verse remained unidentified in the commentaries.

[295] B: إِذْءَاب A: ادءآب Ak: إِدْآب I: إِدْابِ N: إِدْأَبِ Kh: إدآب كالاتعاب وزنا ومعنى S: إِدْآبِ K, Z: اداب α, β, T: اداب F: اذْءَاب D, H, L, MM, P, U: آداب Ul: آدآب ε: ادا omission.

[296] Narrated **(i)** *mursal*-chained from Qatāda (61-117/681-735), from ʿAbd Allāh b. ʿAmr by ʿAbd al-Razzāq in his *Muṣannaf* (*Bāb shukr al-ṭaʿām*) and, through him, al-Ḥakīm al-Tirmidhī in *Nawādir al-Uṣūl fī Maʿrifat Aḥādīth al-Rasūl*, ed. Tawfīq Maḥmūd Takla, 2nd ed., 7 vols. (Damascus: Dār al-Nawādir, 1432/2011) 4:88 §865 *Aṣl* 154; al-Baghawī in his *Tafsīr* at the end of Sūrat al-Isrā' and *Sharḥ al-Sunna*, ed. Shuʿayb al-Arnā'ūṭ, 2nd ed., 15 vols. (Beirut: al-Maktab al-Islāmī, 1403/1983) 5:50 §1271; al-Khaṭṭābī in *Gharīb al-Ḥadīth* (*s.v. shukr*); al-Bayhaqī in *Shuʿab al-Īmān* (Branch 33) and *al-Ādāb* (Beirut: Mu'assasat al-Kutub al-Thaqāfiyya, 1408/1988) p. 293 §888, and al-Thaʿlabī in his *Tafsīr* (*sub* 1:2); **(ii)** from Ibn ʿAbbās as his own statement by Ibn Abī Ḥātim, al-Ṭabarī and al-Baghawī in wordings merely equating *ḥamd* with *shukr* in their respective *Tafsīrs*—in this sense Ibn Abī al-Dunyā's monograph *al-Shukru lil-Lāh ʿazza wa-jall* is replete with reports that mention only *ḥamd*; and **(iii)**

وَ(الذَّمُّ): نَقِيضُ الحَمْدِ؛ وَ(الْكُفْرَانُ): نَقِيضُ الشُّكْرِ.

وَرَفْعُهُ بِالِابْتِدَاءِ، وَخَبَرُهُ: ﴿لِلَّهِ﴾. وَأَصْلُهُ النَّصْبُ ـ وَقَدْ قُرِئَ بِهِ ـ وَإِنَّمَا عُدِلَ عَنْهُ إِلَى الرَّفْعِ لِيَدُلَّ عَلَى عُمُومِ الحَمْدِ وَثَبَاتِهِ لَهُ دُونَ تَجَدُّدِهِ وَحُدُوثِهِ.

Blame, on the other hand, is the contrary of praise, and unthankfulness (*kufrān*) the contrary of gratitude.

It [*ḥamd*] is in the nominative case as an inchoative whose enunciative is *lillāh*, but its original [case] is accusative and thus did some recite it.[297] It was pointedly put in the nominative instead, to signify the universality and stability of praise for Allah without notion of renewal or temporal origination.[298] ....

from al-Nawwās b. Samʿān with a weak chain in al-Ṭabarānī's *Awsaṭ* (2:14 §1071), cf. al-Haythamī, *Majmaʿ al-Baḥrayn fī Zawā'id al-Muʿjamayn*, ed. ʿAbd al-Quddūs b. Muḥammad Nadhīr, 9 vols. (Riyadh: Maktabat al-Rushd, 1413/1992) 4:80-81 §2129, that the Prophet, upon him blessings and peace, fulfilled his oath to thank Allah if He returned to him his stolen camel al-Jadʿā' by saying *al-ḥamdu lillāh*. Cf. al-Zaylaʿī in *Takhrīj al-Aḥādīth wal-Āthār al-Wārida fī Tafsīr al-Kashshāf* (from al-Fātiḥa to al-Mā'ida), 3 vols., ed. ʿAlī ʿUmar Aḥmad Bādaḥdaḥ, unpublished Ph.D. dissertation (Mecca: Jāmiʿat Umm al-Qurā, 1416-1417/1995-1996) 1:495, al-Munāwī in *al-Fatḥ al-Samāwī* (1:99-102), and al-Suyūṭī in *al-Durr al-Manthūr* (1:54-55). The latter declared the first version fair in his *Jāmiʿ al-Ṣaghīr* (§3835) since its narrators are trustworthy as he stated in the introduction of *Tadrīb al-Rāwī*—although Qatāda is known for concealment of his authorities (*tadlīs*). Ibn Taymiyya declared it sound in his *Majmūʿ al-Fatāwā* (14:310, 14:315-317 but tracing it back to Abū Saʿīd al-Khudrī). It is overall authentic despite the grade of "weak" claimed by the usual contemporaries.

297 *Al-ḥamda lillāh* is the reading of Hārūn al-ʿAtakī, Ru'ba, Ibn ʿUyayna, Zayd b. ʿAlī, al-Ḥasan, and Ibn al-Sumayfiʿ with an inferred (*muqaddar*) verbal regent, while al-Ṭūsī mentioned that the accusative case here was a dialectical form. Cf. ʿAbd al-Laṭīf al-Khaṭīb, *Muʿjam al-Qirā'āt*, 11 vols. (Damascus, Dār Saʿd al-Dīn, 1422/2002), hereafter *MQ*. "When put in the accusative its meaning is, 'I praise Allah with much praise.' The accusative presumes an infinitive noun governed by a suppressed verb postulated as 'we praise' in the plural, as it is made to be spoken by Allah's slaves and matches His statements *we worship and we ask for help*." (Kh)

298 Nominative makes the phrase nominal, consisting of a *mubtada'* and *khabar*, while the accusative, as shown in the previous note, makes it verbal; the characteristics of

وَهُوَ مِنَ الْمَصَادِرِ الَّتِي تُنْصَبُ بِأَفْعَالٍ مُضْمَرَةٍ لَا تَكَادُ تُسْتَعْمَلُ مَعَهَا.

وَالتَّعْرِيفُ فِيهِ: (١) لِلْجِنْسِ؛ وَمَعْنَاهُ: الْإِشَارَةُ إِلَى مَا يَعْرِفُ كُلُّ أَحَدٍ أَنَّ الْحَمْدَ مَا هُوَ؛ (٢) أَوْ لِلْاِسْتِغْرَاقِ، إِذِ الْحَمْدُ فِي الْحَقِيقَةِ كُلُّهُ لَهُ؛ إِذْ مَا مِنْ خَيْرٍ إِلَّا وَهُوَ مُوْلِيهِ بِوَسَطٍ أَوْ بِغَيْرِ وَسَطٍ كَمَا قَالَ تَعَالَى ﴿وَمَا بِكُم مِّن نِّعۡمَةٍ فَمِنَ ٱللَّهِ﴾ [النحل ٥٣].

وَفِيهِ إِشْعَارٌ بِأَنَّهُ تَعَالَى حَيٌّ، قَادِرٌ، مُرِيدٌ، عَالِمٌ؛ إِذِ الْحَمْدُ لَا يَسْتَحِقُّهُ إِلَّا مَنْ كَانَ هٰذَا شَأْنُهُ.

It is of the infinitive nouns that are usually put in the accusative because of implied verbs that are almost never used with them.[299]

Its definite article is (i) for the species—meaning the designation of that which everyone knows praise to be; (ii) or for totality since praise, in reality, all belongs to Him: there is no goodness except He is its giver whether with an intermediary or without one,[300] as He said—may He be exalted: *And whatever blessing is with you, it is from Allah* (al-Naḥl 16:53).

There is also in it a proclamation that He is all-living, all-mighty, all-willing and all-knowing, since praise is not truly deserved but by the One of such exalted status.

nominal clauses are universality and fixity (*'umūm, thubūt*) e.g. *Zaydun munṭaliqun* while those of verbal sentences are renewal and novelty (*tajaddud, ḥudūth*) e.g. *Zaydun yanṭaliqu.* Also see notes 557, 673, 681 and Aḥmad al-Ḥāzimī, *Fatḥ Rabb al-Bariyya fī Sharḥ Naẓm al-Ājurrūmiyya* (Mecca: Maktabat al-Asadī, 1431/2010) pp. 13-14.

[299] E.g., *Ḥamdan lillāh* which opens one of the top three or four founding classics of Arabic philology, Ibn Qutayba's *Adab al-Kātib*. Another very common use of this construction is the expression *shukran* ("Thanks"). Al-Ṣan'ānī's *Thamarāt al-Naẓar fī 'Ilm al-Athar* begins with "*Ḥamdan laka yā Wāhiba kulli kamāl, wa-shukran laka yā Māniḥa al-jazīli min al-nawāl...*"

[300] Respectively what may involve the slave's will such as knowledge and all the types of learning that are part of what he acquires or what his will has no part in whatsoever such as beauty, courage, perception, motive abilities and so forth. (Q)

وَقُرِئَ (الْحَمْدِ لله) بِإِتْبَاعِ الدَّالِ اللَّامَ، وَبِالْعَكْسِ، تَنْزِيلاً لَهُمَا، مِنْ حَيْثُ إِنَّهُمَا يُسْتَعْمَلَانِ مَعاً، مَنْزِلَةَ كَلِمَةٍ وَاحِدَةٍ.

﴿رَبِّ ٱلْعَٰلَمِينَ﴾ (الرَّبُّ) فِي الْأَصْلِ مَصْدَرٌ بِمَعْنَى التَّرْبِيَةِ؛ وَهِيَ تَبْلِيغُ الشَّيْءِ إِلَى كَمَالِهِ شَيْئاً فَشَيْئاً. ثُمَّ وُصِفَ بِهِ لِلْمُبَالَغَةِ، كَالصَّوْمِ وَالْعَدْلِ.

وَقِيلَ: هُوَ نَعْتٌ من (رَبَّهُ يَرُبُّهُ) فَهُوَ (رَبٌّ)، كَقَوْلِكَ (نَمَّ يَنُمُّ) فَهُوَ (نَمٌّ)؛ ثُمَّ سُمِّيَ بِهِ الْمَالِكُ، لِأَنَّهُ يَحْفَظُ مَا يَمْلِكُهُ، وَيُرَبِّيهِ.

وَلَا يُطْلَقُ عَلَى غَيْرِهِ تَعَالَى ....

It was also read *al-ḥamdi lillāh* with the *d* following the case of the *l*, and also vice-versa [*al-ḥamdu lullāh*][301] virtually—since they are used together—as a single word.

[*Rabb* originally means "nurturing"]

rabbi-l-ʿālamīna ⁽*the Nurturer of the worlds*⁾: ***rabb*** is literally an infinitive noun that means nurturing, which is to make something reach its completeness little by little. Then it was used as a descriptive intensive like *ṣawm* and *ʿadl.*[302]

It is also said that *rabb* is a descriptive epithet from *rabbahu* ⁽he nurtured him⁾, [aorist] *yarubbuhu*, so one is a *rabb* ⁽nurturer⁾, as one would say *namma* ⁽he gossiped⁾, [aorist] *yanummu*, so one is a *namm* ⁽gossiper⁾. Then it was used to name the owner, because he preserves and nurtures what he owns.

It is not used in unqualified terms for anyone beside Allah

[301] Respectively by al-Ḥasan al-Baṣrī and Ibrāhīm b. Abī ʿAbla, each mode also constituting a dialectical form. (*MQ*) For a beautiful elucidation see the opening of al-Farrā''s (d. 207/822) *Maʿānī al-Qur'ān*, ed. Muḥammad ʿAlī al-Najjār and Aḥmad Yūsuf Najātī, 3rd ed., 3 vols. (Beirut: ʿĀlam al-Kutub, 1403/1983).

[302] The infinitive noun for "fasting," *ṣawm*, was used intensively to denote the person who fasts, *q.v.* in Ibn Sīdah's *Muḥkam* and al-Fayrūzābādī's *Qāmūs*, while the noun for "justice," *ʿadl*, was used to mean the upright person, notably in hadith and law.

إِلَّا مُقَيَّداً، كَقَوْلِهِ: ﴿ٱرْجِعْ إِلَىٰ رَبِّكَ﴾ [يوسف ٥٠].

وَ(الْعَالَمُ): اِسْمٌ لِمَا يُعْلَمُ بِهِ، كَالْخَاتَمِ وَالْقَالَبِ، غَلَبَ فِيمَا يُعْلَمُ بِهِ الصَّانِعُ تَعَالَى؛ وَهُوَ: كُلُّ مَا سِوَاهُ مِنَ الْجَوَاهِرِ وَالْأَعْرَاضِ؛ فَإِنَّهَا ـ لِإِمْكَانِهَا، وَافْتِقَارِهَا إِلَى مُؤَثِّرٍ وَاجِبٍ لِذَاتِهِ ـ تَدُلُّ عَلَى وُجُودِهِ.

وَإِنَّمَا جَمَعَهُ لِيَشْمُلَ مَا تَحْتَهُ مِنَ الْأَجْنَاسِ الْمُخْتَلِفَةِ؛ وَغَلَّبَ الْعُقَلَاءَ مِنْهُمْ، فَجَمَعَهُ بِالْيَاءِ وَالنُّونِ، كَسَائِرِ أَوْصَافِهِمْ.

وَقِيلَ: اِسْمٌ وُضِعَ لِذَوِي الْعِلْمِ مِنَ الْمَلَائِكَةِ وَالثَّقَلَيْنِ؛ وَتَنَاوُلُهُ لِغَيْرِهِمْ: عَلَى سَبِيلِ الِاسْتِتْبَاعِ.

Most High[303] except in a restricted sense, as in His saying, *Return unto your master* (Yūsuf 12:50).

ʿĀlam is a name for "that by which something is known" (*yuʿlam*), like *khātam* ⟨seal⟩ and *qālab* ⟨cast⟩. Its predominant usage became "that by which the exalted Maker is known"—namely, everything other than Him of substances and accidents which, because of their contingency and dependency on a self-necessary Mover, point to the latter's existence.

He made it plural so that it encompasses all the multifarious species it covers, predominantly their rational beings, giving its plural a *yā'* and a *nūn*, as for everything else that qualifies them.

It was also said that it is a name coined for those who possess *ʿilm* ⟨knowledge⟩—angels and the Two Weighty Ones,[304] applying to other things a posteriori.

303 I.e. in most cases according to al-Jurjānī and others. (S)

304 *Al-thaqalān*, i.e., humankind and jinn, thus named (i) "because they are the earth's burden (*thiql al-arḍ*) as it carries them alive and dead" per Ibn Qutayba, *Tafsīr Gharīb al-Qur'ān*, ed. al-Sayyid Aḥmad Ṣaqr ([Cairo]: Dār Iḥyā' al-Kutub al-ʿArabiyya, 1958;

وَقِيلَ: عَنَى بِهِ النَّاسَ هٰهُنَا؛ فَإِنَّ كُلَّ وَاحِدٍ مِنْهُمْ عَالَمٌ، مِنْ حَيْثُ إِنَّهُ يَشْتَمِلُ عَلَى نَظَائِرِ مَا فِي الْعَالَمِ الْكَبِيرِ مِنَ الْجَوَاهِرِ وَالْأَعْرَاضِ يُعْلَمُ بِهَا الصَّانِعُ، كَمَا يُعْلَمُ بِمَا أَبْدَعَهُ فِي الْعَالَمِ الْكَبِيرِ؛ وَلِذٰلِكَ سَوَّى بَيْنَ النَّظَرِ فِيهِمَا، وَقَالَ تَعَالَى: ﴿وَفِىٓ أَنفُسِكُمْ ۚ أَفَلَا تُبْصِرُونَ ﴿٢١﴾﴾ [الذاريات].

وَقُرِئَ (رَبَّ الْعَالَمِينَ) بِالنَّصْبِ (أ) عَلَى الْمَدْحِ؛ (ب) أَوِ النِّدَاءِ؛ (ج) أَوْ بِالْفِعْلِ الَّذِي دَلَّ عَلَيْهِ الْحَمْدُ.

[The Ghazalian *ʿālam al-ṣaghīr* ⟨microcosm⟩ of human beings]

It was also said that people are meant right here, for each one of them is a world—in the sense of comprising the equivalents of the substances and accidents the macrocosm contains—by which the Maker can be known,[305] just as He can be known through what He fashioned in the macrocosm. Hence He made studying each the same as studying the other and said, *And in yourselves. Can you then not see?* (al-Dhāriyāt 51:21).

It was also read *rabba al-ʿālamīn* in the accusative[306] (i) in the sense of a compliment;[307]

(ii) or as a vocative;

(iii) or governed by the verb which praise indicates.

repr. Beirut: al-Maktabat al-ʿIlmiyya, 1428/2007) p. 22; and (ii) honorifically—since Allah preferred them over other creatures by giving them reason—the Arabs naming important matters *thaqal*, cf. *Tahdhīb al-Lugha*, *Lisān al-ʿArab* and *Anwār* (*sub* 55:31).

[305] A concept dear to the Qadi who reiterates it under al-Baqara 2:34 and al-Dhāriyāt 51:21: "There is nothing in the world except its equivalent is found in human beings," and which al-Ghazālī expounded before him in his defense of his own *Iḥyāʾ ʿUlūm al-Dīn* entitled *al-Intiṣār li-mā fīl-Iḥyāʾ min al-Asrār*, from which al-Suyūṭī quotes at length (S 1:182-185) much to the ire of the Wahhabi editor of the *Nawāhid*—as it is a concept inherited from Greco-Christian tradition in full, cf. George Perrigo Conger, *Theories of Macrocosms and Microcosms in the History of Philosophy* (1922).

[306] By Zayd b. ʿAlī, Abū Zayd, Kisāʾī, Abū al-ʿĀliya, ʿĪsā b. ʿUmar, Ibn al-Sumayfiʿ. (*MQ*)

[307] "With an appropriate inferred verb governing it… and it is the weakest sense." (Z)

وَفِيهِ دَلِيلٌ عَلَى أَنَّ الْمُمْكِنَاتِ، كَمَا هِيَ مُفْتَقِرَةٌ إِلَى الْمُحْدِثِ حَالَ حُدُوثِهَا، فَهِيَ مُفْتَقِرَةٌ إِلَى الْمُبْقِي حَالَ بَقَائِهَا.

﴿ٱلرَّحْمَٰنِ ٱلرَّحِيمِ﴾: كَرَّرَهُ لِلتَّعْلِيلِ عَلَى مَا سَنَذْكُرُهُ.

﴿مَٰلِكِ يَوْمِ ٱلدِّينِ﴾: قِرَاءَةُ عَاصِمٍ، وَالْكِسَائِيِّ، وَيَعْقُوبَ؛ وَيَعْضُدُهُ قَوْلُهُ تَعَالَى: ﴿يَوْمَ لَا تَمْلِكُ نَفْسٌ لِّنَفْسٍ شَيْـًٔا وَٱلْأَمْرُ يَوْمَئِذٍ لِّلَّهِ ﴿١٩﴾﴾ [الانفطار].

وَقَرَأَ الْبَاقُونَ: ﴿مَلِكِ﴾؛ وَهُوَ الْمُخْتَارُ، لِأَنَّهُ قِرَاءَةُ أَهْلِ ....

It offers evidence that contingencies, just as they are utterly dependent on the Originator (*al-muḥdith*) upon their origination, so are they utterly dependent on the Perpetuator (*al-mubqī*) upon their endurance.

[1:3] **al-raḥmāni-r-raḥīmi** ⁽*the all-Beneficent, the most Merciful*⁾: He repeated it for justification in the sense we mention below.

[1:4] **māliki yawmi-d-dīni** ⁽*Owner of the Day of reckoning*⁾: *Māliki* is the reading of ʿĀṣim, al-Kisāʾī and Yaʿqūb. It is reinforced by the saying of Allah, *A day when no soul shall possess (tamliku) anything to help another; that day the Command belongs to Allah* (al-Infiṭār 82:19). The rest read *maliki* ⁽owner⁾.[308] The latter is our preference, since it is the reading of the residents ....

[308] *Māliki*: ʿĀṣim, al-Kisāʾī, Khalaf, Yaʿqūb, the Rightly-Guided Caliphs, Ibn Masʿūd, Ṭalḥa, al-Zubayr, ʿAbd al-Raḥmān b. ʿAwf, Ubay b. Kaʿb, Muʿādh b. Jabal, ʿUmar b. ʿAbd al-ʿAzīz, ʿAlqama, Qatāda, al-Aʿmash, al-Ḥasan, al-Zuhrī, al-Aswad, Abū Rajāʾ, Ibn Jubayr, al-Nakhaʿī, Ibn Sīrīn, al-Sulamī, Yaḥyā b. Yaʿmur. It is a Prophetic narration from Abū Hurayra, Umm Ḥuṣayn and Umm Salama and the choice of Abū Ḥātim and Abū Ṭāhir. *Maliki*: Ibn Kathīr, Nāfiʿ, Ibn ʿĀmir, Ḥamza, Abū ʿAmr, al-Kisāʾī also, Zayd, Abū al-Dardāʾ, Ibn ʿUmar, al-Miswar, Ibn ʿAbbās, Mujāhid, Marwān b. al-Ḥakam, Yaḥyā b. Waththāb, al-Aʿraj, Abū Jaʿfar, Shayba, Ibn Jurayj, al-Ḥajdarī, Ibn Jundab and Ibn Muḥayṣin and it is the choice of Abū ʿUbayd and the reading of many *Ṣaḥāba* and *Tābiʿīn*, also Prophet-related, which al-Ṭabarī deems the soundest. (*MQ*)

الْحَرَمَيْنِ، وَلِقَوْلِهِ تَعَالَى: ﴿لِمَنِ ٱلْمُلْكُ ٱلْيَوْمَ﴾ [غافر ١٦]؛ وَلِمَا فِيهِ مِنَ التَّعْظِيمِ.

وَ(الْمَالِكُ): هُوَ الْمُتَصَرِّفُ فِي الْأَعْيَانِ الْمَمْلُوكَةِ كَيْفَ يَشَاءُ، مِنَ (الْمِلْكِ).

وَ(الْمَلِكُ): هُوَ الْمُتَصَرِّفُ بِالْأَمْرِ وَالنَّهْيِ فِي الْمَأْمُورِينَ، مِنَ (الْمُلْكِ).

وَقُرِئَ (مَلْكِ) بِالتَّخْفِيفِ؛ وَ(مَلَكَ) بِلَفْظِ الْفِعْلِ؛ وَ(مَالِكاً) بِالنَّصْبِ عَلَى الْمَدْحِ، أَوِ الْحَالِ؛ وَ(مَالِكٌ) بِالرَّفْعِ مُنَوَّناً وَمُضَافاً عَلَى أَنَّهُ خَبَرُ مُبْتَدَءٍ مَحْذُوفٍ؛ وَ(مَلِكُ) مُضَافاً بِالرَّفْعِ وَالنَّصْبِ.

of the Two Sanctuaries and since He said: *Whose is the sovereignty (mulk) today?* (Ghāfir 40:16); and also because it entails more magnification.

[Definitions of *mālik*, *malik* and *dīn*]

Al-mālik ʿthe ownerʾ is the possessor of discretion over the concrete specifics owned in whatsoever way he wishes; it stems from *milk* ʿownershipʾ. *Al-malik* ʿthe sovereignʾ is the possessor of discretion of command and prohibition of those under his authority; it stems from *mulk* ʿsovereigntyʾ.

It was also read *malki* ʿkingʾ with alleviation; *malaka* ʿHe ownsʾ as a verb; *mālikan* ʿowningʾ in the accusative as a compliment[309] or as a participial state and *mālikun* in the nominative, [both] nunated; [*māliku*] as a governing annex, namely the enunciative of a suppressed inchoative; and *maliku* or *malika* ʿkingʾ as a governing annex in the nominative or the accusative.[310]

---

[309] See note 307.
[310] *Malki*: Related from Abū Hurayra, ʿĀṣim al-Ḥajdarī, Abū ʿAmr, Ibn ʿĀmir, and ʿUmar b. ʿAbd al-ʿAzīz; a dialectical form of the Bakr b. Wāʾil, originally *maliki* with a mid-consonant made quiescent. *Malaka yawma*: Anas b. Mālik, ʿAlī b. Abī Ṭālib, Abū Ḥaywa, Abū Ḥanīfa, Jubayr b. Muṭʿim, Yaḥyā b. Yaʿmur, Abū ʿĀṣim ʿUbayd b. ʿUmayr

وَ﴿يَوۡمِ ٱلدِّينِ﴾: يَوْمِ الْجَزَاءِ. وَمِنْهُ: كَمَا تَدِينُ تُدَانُ، ....

Yawmi-d-dīn is "the Day of Retribution;"[311] whence "As you judge, so shall you be judged"[312] ....

al-Laythī, Abū al-Maḥshar ʿĀṣim b. Maymūn al-Ḥajdarī, al-Ḥasan, and it is related from Ḥamza. *Mālika(n)*: al-Aʿmash, Ibn al-Sumayfiʿ, ʿUthmān b. Abī Sulaymān, ʿAbd al-Malik Qāḍī al-Hind, Abū Hurayra, ʿUmar b. ʿAbd al-ʿAzīz, Abū Ṣāliḥ al-Sammān, Abū ʿAbd al-Malik al-Shāmī, and Ibn Abī ʿAbla. *Mālikun yawma*: ʿĀṣim al-Ḥajdarī, ʿAwn al-ʿUqaylī, Khalaf b. Hishām, Abū ʿUbayd, and Abū Ḥātim. *Māliku yawmi*: Abū Hurayra, Abū Ḥaywa, ʿUmar b. ʿAbd al-ʿAzīz, Abū Rawḥ ʿAwn b. Abī Shaddād al-ʿUqaylī. *Maliku*: Saʿd b. Abī Waqqāṣ, ʿĀʾisha, Mawraq al-ʿIjlī, and Abū Ḥaywa, i.e. "He is the *malik*." *Malika*: Anas b. Mālik, al-Shaʿbī, Abū Nawfal, ʿUmar b. Muslim b. Abī ʿAdī, Abū Ḥaywa, Shurayḥ b. Yazīd, and Abū ʿUthmān al-Nahdī, as a vocative or compliment. There is also *milki, malīki, mallāk* among other readings. (*MQ*)

311 *Yawm al-jazāʾ*. "Al-Khuwayy said in his *Tafsīr*: 'There is a subtle difference between *dīn* and *jazāʾ*. *Dīn* is a name for (i) a computed *jazāʾ*, estimated to the amount dictated by the computation (ii) when it comes from the one directly concerned by the matter being requited. So *dīn* is not used for someone who requites on behalf of someone else, or gives much in return for little, but rather *jazāʾ*.'" (S) On al-Khuwayy see n. 87.

312 *Kamā tadīnu tudān*. Part of a longer hadith narrated **(i)** through trustworthy narrators but in *mursal* mode (see n. 225) from Abū Qilāba (d. 104/722), from the Prophet—upon him blessings and peace—by ʿAbd al-Razzāq, *Muṣannaf* and, through him, al-Bayhaqī, *al-Zuhd al-Kabīr* and *al-Asmāʾ wal-Ṣifāt*, ed. ʿAbd Allāh al-Ḥāshidī, 2 vols. (Jeddah: Maktabat al-Sawādī, 1413/1993) 1:197 §132 = ed. Muḥammad Zāhid al-Kawtharī (Beirut: Dār Iḥyāʾ al-Turāth al-ʿArabī, n.d., repr. of the 1358/1939 Cairo edition) p. 79; **(ii)** with a continuous *musnad* but very weak chain from Ibn ʿUmar by Ibn ʿAdī in *al-Kāmil fil-Ḍuʿafāʾ*, ed. ʿĀdil Aḥmad ʿAbd al-Mawjūd et al., 9 vols. (Beirut: Dār al-Kutub al-ʿIlmiyya, 1997) 7:348; and **(iii)** as a saying of Abū al-Dardāʾ and Mālik b. Dīnār, quoting the Torah, by Aḥmad, *al-Zuhd*. Its meaning is confirmed by several narrations in *Ṣaḥīḥ al-Bukhārī*: *lā tūkī fa-yūkā ʿalayki; lā tuḥṣī fa-yuḥṣiya ʿalayki; lā tūʿī fa-yūʿiya Allāh ʿalayki* all in *Kitāb al-Zakāt, al-taḥrīḍ ʿalā al-ṣadaqa* and the next chapter, also *Kitāb al-Hiba, hibat al-marʾa li-ghayr zawjihā*. A forged variant is narrated from Anas by Ibn Abī ʿĀṣim in *al-Sunna*. It is a leitmotiv of Judeo-Christian Scripture (cf. Judges 1:7, Psalms 137:8, Obadiah 1:15, Mark 4:24, Luke 6:38) and a famous Arabic proverb cf. Abū Hilāl al-ʿAskarī, (310-ca. 400/922-1010) *Jamharat al-Amthāl* (§1460), Abū al-Faḍl al-Maydānī, (d. 518) *Majmaʿ al-Amthāl*, s.v. *kamā*, and al-Zamakhsharī, *al-Mustaqṣā min Amthāl al-ʿArab*, s.v. *k-m-y*.

وَبَيْتُ الْحَمَاسَةِ: [هَزَجٌ]

وَلَمْ يَبْقَ سِوَى الْعُدْوَا * نِ دِنَّاهُمْ كَمَا دَانُوا

أَضَافَ اسْمَ الْفَاعِلِ إِلَى الظَّرْفِ، إِجْرَاءً لَهُ مُجْرَى الْمَفْعُولِ بِهِ عَلَى الْاِتِّسَاعِ، كَقَوْلِهِمْ: (يَا سَارِقَ اللَّيْلَةِ أَهْلَ الدَّارِ). وَمَعْنَاهُ: مَلَكَ الْأُمُورَ يَوْمَ الدِّينِ، عَلَى طَرِيقَةِ ﴿وَنَادَىٰٓ أَصْحَٰبُ ٱلْجَنَّةِ﴾ [الأعراف ٤٤]؛ ....

and the line from *al-Ḥamāsa:* ["The Trilling"]

And nothing's left but enmity:
we requited them (*dinnāhum*) *as they requited* (*dānū*).[313]

He annexed the agential noun to the [temporal-local] vessel,[314] treating the latter as a direct object by poetic licence as in their expression: "O robber of—tonight—the household!"[315] The meaning is (i) that He has complete control of all events on the Day of Judgment in the same style as in *And the dwellers of the Garden called out* (al-Aʿrāf 7:44),[316] ....

[313] Spoken by the knight Shahl b. Shaybān al-Zimmānī—nicknamed al-Find—about the Basūs war (S) cf. al-Tabrīzī, *Sharḥ Dīwān al-Ḥamāsa li-Abī Tammām*, ed. Ghurayd al-Shaykh, 2 vols. (Beirut: Dār al-Kutub al-ʿIlmiyya, 1421/2000) 1:23-25. The *Ḥamāsa* was a book of poetry famous for its brilliant and difficult style by Ḥabīb b. Aws Abū Tammām al-Ṭāʾī (d. 231). "He compiled poetry from the Arabs beginning with war matters then genealogy, encomia, lampoon and literature, but the title gave predominance to the opening material, *ḥamāsa* meaning brute strength and courage." (S)

[314] *Al-ẓarf*, the Basrian appellation for the *mafʿūl fīh*, defined as "an adverbial noun of place or of time implying the preposition *fī*" (Lane, *Lexicon*), "an accusative noun indicating the time or place of the verb and invariably implying the meaning of *fī*," Abdul-Massih, *Khalīl* (p. 264), both s.v. *al-ẓarf*.

[315] Al-Ṭībī said: "I.e, he made the temporal-local complement (*mafʿūl fīhi*) a virtual direct object (*mafʿūl bihi*)." (S) Namely, *al-layla* in the example and *yawm* in the Quranic verse.

[316] *And the dwellers of the Garden called out to the dwellers of the Fire: We have found that which our Nurturer promised us to be the Truth. Have you too found that which your Nurturer promised the Truth? They said: Yea, verily. And a crier in between them*

أَوْ: لَهُ المُلْكُ فِي هٰذَا الْيَوْمِ عَلَى وَجْهِ الِاسْتِمْرَارِ، لِتَكُونَ الْإِضَافَةُ حَقِيقِيَّةً، مُعَدَّةً لِوُقُوعِهِ صِفَةً لِلْمَعْرِفَةِ.

وَقِيلَ: (الدِّينُ): الشَّرِيعَةُ؛ وَقِيلَ: الطَّاعَةُ. وَالْمَعْنَى: يَوْمُ جَزَاءِ الدِّينِ.

وَتَخْصِيصُ الْيَوْمِ بِالْإِضَافَةِ: إِمَّا لِتَعْظِيمِهِ، أَوْ لِتَفَرُّدِهِ تَعَالَى بِنُفُوذِ الْأَمْرِ فِيهِ.

or (ii) that ownership is His on this day from a viewpoint of permanency, for the annexation to be literal and fit for its status of adjective for the definites.[317]

[*Dīn* as "sacred law" and as "obedience"]

It was also said that ***dīn*** means the sacred law and, also, obedience, in which case the sense is "the day of the requital for *dīn*."[318]

The reason for specifying the day with its annexation is either to magnify it, or because Allah Most High alone will have [His] order implemented on that day.[319]

cried: The curse of Allah is on evil-doers! I.e., describing in the past tense events that are to take place in the future. "The control has not yet been implemented, rather, it shall be so in the future; but because it is ascertained to befall, it is assimilated to the past and so was expressed in the past tense metaphorically (*isti'āratan*), as in *And the dwellers of the Garden called out*." (Q)

317 I.e. everything that precedes is equally literally qualified by the clause "Owner of the Day of Judgment." (K) So al-Bayḍāwī's sentence reads thus: that ownership is His on this day ontologically, from a viewpoint of timeless continuity without reference to past, present or future, so that the annexation of "Owner" to "Day" can be taken literally in both cases (i, ii) and be appropriate as an adjective for all the preceding definites—*Allāh*, *rabb al-'ālamīn*, *al-raḥmān* and *al-raḥīm*.

318 I.e. the day of recompense for obeying Allah and the rulings of sacred law. (Q)

319 I.e. directly, openly before all creation, literally, and indisputably, as opposed to the state of affairs in this world where liberty is given for naysayers to deny what they like. See on this figure of style Ibn 'Abd al-Salām on the hadith "I am the master of the children of Adam on the Day of Resurrection" in his *Bidāyat al-Sūl fī Tafḍīl al-Rasūl*.

وَإِجْرَاءُ هٰذِهِ الْأَوْصَافِ عَلَى اللهِ تَعَالَى ـ مِنْ كَوْنِهِ مُوجِداً لِلْعَالَمِينَ، رَبّاً لَهُمْ، مُنْعِماً عَلَيْهِمْ بِالنِّعَمِ كُلِّهَا، ظَاهِرِهَا وَبَاطِنِهَا، عَاجِلِهَا وَآجِلِهَا، مَالِكاً لِأُمُورِهِمْ يَوْمَ الثَّوَابِ وَالْعِقَابِ ـ: (أ) لِلدَّلَالَةِ عَلَى أَنَّهُ الْحَقِيقُ بِالْحَمْدِ، لَا أَحَدَ أَحَقُّ بِهِ مِنْهُ؛ بَلْ لَا يَسْتَحِقُّهُ عَلَى الْحَقِيقَةِ سِوَاهُ؛ فَإِنَّ تَرَتُّبَ الْحُكْمِ عَلَى الْوَصْفِ يُشْعِرُ بِعِلِّيَّتِهِ لَهُ؛ (ب) وَلِلْإِشْعَارِ، مِنْ طَرِيقِ الْمَفْهُومِ، عَلَى أَنَّ مَنْ لَمْ يَتَّصِفْ بِتِلْكَ الصِّفَاتِ: لَا يَسْتَأْهِلُ لِأَنْ يُحْمَدَ، فَضْلاً عَنْ أَنْ يُعْبَدَ؛ فَيَكُونَ دَلِيلاً عَلَى مَا بَعْدَهُ:

* فَالْوَصْفُ الْأَوَّلُ: لِبَيَانِ مَا هُوَ الْمُوجِبُ لِلْحَمْدِ؛ وَهُوَ الْإِيجَادُ وَالتَّرْبِيَةُ.

Allah is thus described—Originator of the worlds out of nothingness and their Nurturer, lavishing on them all His favors, outward and inward, immediate and deferred,[320] and in full possession of their affairs on the Day of reward and retribution:

(i) to show that He alone truly deserves praise and no one else deserves it more than He; nay, no one literally deserves it other than He—for making the description subsequent to the status proclaims that the latter causes the former[321]—

(ii) and to intimate, in substance, that whoever is not thus described is undeserving of praise, let alone worship.

Thus it all stands as a proof for what follows it—[namely]:

I. the first description [*Nurturer of the worlds*] serves to expose what compels praise, namely, origination and nurture;

[320] Outward favors are the creation of bodies and their strengths; inward ones, ensoulment, the gift of minds and noble characters; immediate ones are this-worldly while deferred ones are next-worldly. (Q)

[321] By "the status" (*al-ḥukm*) is meant the establishment of praise for Him. (Q)

❊ وَالثَّانِي وَالثَّالِثُ: لِلدَّلَالَةِ عَلَى أَنَّهُ مُتَفَضِّلٌ بِذٰلِكَ، مُخْتَارٌ فِيهِ، لَيْسَ يَصْدُرُ مِنْهُ لِإِيجَابٍ بِالذَّاتِ أَوْ وُجُوبٍ عَلَيْهِ قَضِيَّةً لِسَوَابِقِ الْأَعْمَالِ حَتَّى يَسْتَحِقَّ بِهِ الْحَمْدَ.

❊ وَالرَّابِعُ: لِتَحْقِيقِ الِاخْتِصَاصِ - فَإِنَّهُ مِمَّا لَا يَقْبَلُ الشَّرِكَةَ فِيهِ بِوَجْهٍ مَا - وَتَضْمِينِ الْوَعْدِ لِلْحَامِدِينَ، وَالْوَعِيدِ لِلْمُعْرِضِينَ.

﴿إِيَّاكَ نَعْبُدُ وَإِيَّاكَ نَسْتَعِينُ ۝٥﴾: ثُمَّ إِنَّهُ لَمَّا ذُكِرَ الْحَقِيقُ بِالْحَمْدِ، وَوُصِفَ بِصِفَاتٍ عِظَامٍ تَمَيَّزَ بِهَا عَنْ سَائِرِ الذَّوَاتِ، وَتَعَلَّقَ الْعِلْمُ بِمَعْلُومٍ مُعَيَّنٍ: ....

II-III. the second and third [*All-Beneficent, Most Merciful*] serve to show that He does it all as a favor and does so by choice, not that it issues from Him because of ontic necessity or any obligation of repayment for past deeds by discharging which He would purportedly deserve praise;[322]

IV. the fourth [*Owner of the Day of Judgment*] serves as a verification of exclusivity—as it consists in something which precludes partnership in any way whatsoever—and the comprisal of glad tidings for extollers with dire penalties for dissenters.

[Addressing Allah as if seeing Him]

[1:5] **iyyāka naʿbudu wa-iyyāka nastaʿīnu** (*You do we worship and You do we ask for help*): Then, after He Who deserves praise was mentioned and described with magnificent attributes by which He demarked Himself from all other entities, and after [our] knowledge now pertained to a specific object of knowledge,

[322] This clause contains a rebuttal of the philosophers and the Muʿtazila. (Q) See entry on the latter in our biographical glossary (par. iii).

خُوطِبَ بِذٰلِكَ ـ أَيْ: (يَا مَنْ هٰذَا شَأْنُهُ، نَخُصُّكَ بِالْعِبَادَةِ وَالْاِسْتِعَانَةِ) ـ لِيَكُونَ أَدَلَّ عَلَى الْاِخْتِصَاصِ، وَلِلتَّرَقِّي مِنَ الْبُرْهَانِ إِلَى الْعِيَانِ، وَالْاِنْتِقَالِ مِنَ الْغَيْبَةِ إِلَى الشُّهُودِ؛ فَكَأَنَّ الْمَعْلُومَ صَارَ عِيَاناً، وَالْمَعْقُولَ مُشَاهَداً، وَالْغَيْبَةَ حُضُوراً.

بَنَى أَوَّلَ الْكَلَامِ عَلَى مَا هُوَ مَبَادِئُ حَالِ الْعَارِفِ ـ مِنَ الذِّكْرِ، وَالْفِكْرِ، وَالتَّأَمُّلِ فِي أَسْمَائِهِ، وَالنَّظَرِ فِي آلَائِهِ، وَالْاِسْتِدْلَالِ بِصَنَائِعِهِ عَلَى عَظِيمِ شَأْنِهِ وَبَاهِرِ سُلْطَانِهِ ـ ثُمَّ قَفَّى بِمَا هُوَ مُنْتَهَى أَمْرِهِ، وَهُوَ: أَنْ يَخُوضَ لُجَّةَ الْوُصُولِ، وَيَصِيرَ مِنْ أَهْلِ الْمُشَاهَدَةِ، فَيَرَاهُ عِيَاناً، وَيُنَاجِيهِ شِفَاهاً.

He was addressed[323] accordingly, thus: "O You Whose status is such, we worship You and seek Your help exclusively!" This is more indicative of exclusivity and forms a progression from demonstration to sight and a move from absence to witnessing. It is as if the object of knowledge is now being seen, the rational concept is beheld, and absence turns to presence!

He built the first part of the discourse on the primary stages of the state of the knower—consisting in remembrance, reflection, contemplation of His Names, study of His bounties and the inference, from His handiwork, of His immense loftiness and astonishing power; then He followed up with what constitutes the farthest reach of his quest, which is to probe the depth of arrival and become one of the people of reciprocal vision, whereupon he sees Him with his very eyes and converses with Him directly.

[323] A variant yields "… entities, knowledge now pertained to a specific object; and so He was addressed" (Q, Sk). α, Ak, AQ, β, B, ÇZ, D, ε, F, H, MM, N, I, Iṣ, K, Kh, M, P, Q, T: خوطب تعلق العلم بمعلوم معين وتعلق العلم بمعلوم معين L, Q, Ul, U, Z: فخوطب تعلق العلم بمعلوم معين

اللّٰهُمَّ اجْعَلْنَا مِنَ الْوَاصِلِينَ لِلْعَيْنِ، دُونَ السَّامِعِينَ لِلْأَثَرِ!

وَمِنْ عَادَةِ الْعَرَبِ: التَّفَنُّنُ فِي الْكَلَامِ، وَالْعُدُولُ مِنْ أُسْلُوبٍ إِلَى آخَرَ، تَطْرِيَةً لَهُ وَتَنْشِيطاً لِلسَّامِعِ؛ فَيُعْدَلُ مِنَ الْخِطَابِ إِلَى الْغَيْبَةِ، وَمِنَ الْغَيْبَةِ إِلَى التَّكَلُّمِ وَبِالْعَكْسِ، كَقَوْلِهِ تَعَالَى: ﴿حَتَّىٰٓ إِذَا كُنتُمْ فِى ٱلْفُلْكِ وَجَرَيْنَ بِهِم﴾ [يونس ١٢] وَقَوْلِهِ: ﴿وَٱللَّهُ ٱلَّذِىٓ أَرْسَلَ ٱلرِّيَٰحَ فَتُثِيرُ سَحَابًا فَسُقْنَٰهُ﴾ [فاطر ٩] وَقَوْلِ امْرُئِ الْقَيْسِ: [مُتَقَارِبٌ]

تَطَاوَلَ لَيْلُكَ بِالْأَثْمُدِ * وَنَامَ الْخَلِيُّ وَلَمْ تَرْقُدِ

وَبَاتَتْ وَبَاتَتْ لَهُ لَيْلَةٌ * كَلَيْلَةِ ذِي الْعَائِرِ الْأَرْمَدِ

O Allah! Make us of those who reach the very source and not just hear the report!

The Arabs habitually practice refinement in their speech, switching from one style to another in order to refresh it and stimulate the listener. For example, one will switch from the second person to the third and from the third person to the first and back again,[324] as in the saying of Allah Most High *until, when you are in the ships and they sail with them* (Yūnus 10:22), and His saying, *And Allah it is Who sends the winds and they raise a cloud; then We lead it* (Fāṭir 35:9) and Umru' al-Qays's saying: ["The Tripping"]

Long is your night with antimonied [eyes],
while he sleeps who is care-free—but not you.
He spends the night; but for him, a night passes
such as the night of one eye-specked, inflamed.

[324] This is the rhetorical trope called *iltifāt* 'redirection' (S 1:212-219). Al-Bayḍāwī mentions it explicitly later on (verses 2:21, 2:28, 2:54, 2:83, 3:180, etc). See note 803.

وَذٰلِكَ مِنْ نَبَإٍ جَاءَنِي ❋ وَخُبِّرْتُهُ عَنْ أَبِي الْأَسْوَدِ

وَ(إِيَّا): ضَمِيرٌ مَنْصُوبٌ مُنْفَصِلٌ، وَمَا يَلْحَقُهُ مِنَ الْيَاءِ وَالْكَافِ وَالْهَاءِ: حُرُوفٌ زِيدَتْ لِبَيَانِ التَّكَلُّمِ وَالْخِطَابِ وَالْغَيْبَةِ، لَا مَحَلَّ لَهَا مِنَ الْإِعْرَابِ، كَالتَّاءِ فِي (أَنْتَ) وَالْكَافِ فِي (أَرَأَيْتَكَ). وَقَالَ الْخَلِيلُ: (إِيَّا): مُضَافٌ إِلَيْهَا؛ وَاحْتَجَّ بِمَا حَكَاهُ عَنْ بَعْضِ الْعَرَبِ: (إِذَا بَلَغَ الرَّجُلُ السِّتِّينَ، فَإِيَّاهُ وَإِيَّا الشَّوَابِّ)؛ وَهُوَ شَاذٌّ، لَا يُعْتَمَدُ عَلَيْهِ. وَقِيلَ: هِيَ الضَّمَائِرُ، وَ(إِيَّا): عُمْدَةٌ، فَإِنَّهَا لَمَّا فُصِلَتْ عَنِ الْعَوَامِلِ، تَعَذَّرَ النُّطْقُ بِهَا مُفْرَدَةً، فَضُمَّ إِلَيْهَا (إِيَّا) ....

And that is due to the unsettling news
I heard, which Abū al-Aswad told me.[325]

Iyyā is a disconnected pronoun in the accusative, and whatever *yā'* ⁽to me⁾, *kāf* ⁽to you⁾ or *hā'* ⁽to him⁾ are affixed to it, are letters added to determine the first, second and third persons respectively, all without desinential place, just like the *tā'* in *anta* ⁽you⁾ and the *kāf* in *ara'aytaka* ⁽imagine yourself⁾. Al-Khalīl, however, said that *iyyā* was a governed annex, adducing as proof what he reported from an Arab, "When a man reaches sixty years of age, let him beware young women!" (*fa'iyyāhu wa-iyyā al-shawābb*) but it is aberrant and unreliable. It was also said that they [*yā', kāf*, and *hā'*] were the pronouns, while *iyyā* is a prop: for when they became disconnected from the regents, it became unfeasible to pronounce them by themselves, so *iyyā* was joined to them ....

[325] Beginning of a poem of Umru' al-Qays narrated by al-Aṣma'ī, Abū 'Ubayda, Abū 'Amr al-Shaybānī and Ibn al-A'rābī. (S) Abū al-Aswad is the name of Umru' al-Qays's paternal cousin so the three lines start with the second person direct address, switch to the narrative third person, then to the first whereby we learn that the subject is the poet himself. *Dīwān Umru' al-Qays*, ed. Anwar Abū Sulaym et al. (Amman: Dār 'Ammār, 1412/1991) p. 238.

لِتَسْتَقِلَّ بِهِ. وَقِيلَ: الضَّمِيرُ هُوَ الْمَجْمُوعُ.

وَقُرِئَ (أَيَّاكَ) بِفَتْحِ الْهَمْزَةِ؛ وَ(هَيَّاكَ) بِقَلْبِهَا هَاءً.

وَ(الْعِبَادَةُ): أَقْصَى غَايَةِ الْخُضُوعِ وَالتَّذَلُّلِ - وَمِنْهُ: (طَرِيقٌ مُعَبَّدٌ) أَيْ مُذَلَّلٌ، وَ(ثَوْبٌ ذُو عَبَدَةٍ) إِذَا كَانَ فِي غَايَةِ الصَّفَاقَةِ - وَلِذٰلِكَ لَا يُسْتَعْمَلُ إِلَّا فِي الْخُضُوعِ لِلهِ تَعَالَى.

وَ(الِاسْتِعَانَةُ): طَلَبُ الْمَعُونَةِ؛ وَهِيَ: إِمَّا ضَرُورِيَّةٌ، أَوْ غَيْرُ ضَرُورِيَّةٍ. وَالضَّرُورِيَّةُ: مَا لَا يَتَأَتَّى الْفِعْلُ دُونَهُ: كَاقْتِدَارِ الْفَاعِلِ، وَتَصَوُّرِهِ، ....

and they can be used independently thanks to it. It was also said that the pronoun was the whole.

A variant reading has *ayyāka* with a *fatḥa* on the glottal stop, another *hayyāka* with its transposition into a *hā'*.[326]

'Ibāda ⟨worship⟩ is the farthermost point of submission and humility—whence *ṭarīq mu'abbad* ⟨a leveled path⟩ that is a well-trodden one, and *thawbun dhū 'abada* ⟨a sturdy garment⟩ when it is quite thick—hence, it is not used in any other sense than for submission to Allah.[327]

Isti'āna is the quest for support. The latter is either absolutely indispensable or not. The first type is what an act cannot be performed without, such as the empowerment of the doer, his conception of the act, ...

[326] *Ayyāka*: al-Faḍl al-Riqāshī, Sufyān al-Thawrī, and 'Alī b. Abī Ṭālib. Ibn 'Aṭiyya said it is a famous dialectical form. *Hayyāka*: Abū al-Sawwār al-Ghanawī—also a dialectical form. Other readings include *iyāka*, *hiyāka*, and *iyyéka* with *imāla*. (*MQ*)

[327] I.e. in the sacred law. As for the sense of "sturdy," it is meant to imply strength in worship like a tough, well-sewn garment. (Q)

وَحُصُولِ آلَةٍ وَمَادَّةٍ يُفْعَلُ بِهَا فِيهَا. وَعِنْدَ اسْتِجْمَاعِهَا، يُوصَفُ الرَّجُلُ بِالْاِسْتِطَاعَةِ، وَيَصِحُّ أَنْ يُكَلَّفَ بِالْفِعْلِ.

وَغَيْرُ الضَّرُورِيَّةِ: تَحْصِيلُ مَا يَتَيَسَّرُ بِهِ الْفِعْلُ وَيَسْهُلُ - كَالرَّاحِلَةِ فِي السَّفَرِ لِلْقَادِرِ عَلَى الْمَشْيِ - أَوْ يُقَرِّبُ الْفَاعِلَ إِلَى الْفِعْلِ وَيَحُثُّهُ عَلَيْهِ؛ وَهٰذَا الْقِسْمُ: لَا يَتَوَقَّفُ عَلَيْهِ صِحَّةُ التَّكْلِيفِ.

وَالْمُرَادُ: طَلَبُ الْمَعُونَةِ فِي الْمُهِمَّاتِ كُلِّهَا؛ أَوْ: فِي أَدَاءِ الْعِبَادَاتِ.

وَالضَّمِيرُ الْمُسْتَكِنُّ فِي الْفِعْلَيْنِ: لِلْقَارِئِ، ....

the availability of an instrument by which to act and material to act upon. When these conditions are met, a person is described as possessing ability and it is correct that he be legally responsible to do the act.

The second type [of assistance]—the dispensable—is the obtainment of what facilitates the act and by which it is more easily implemented—such as a mount on a trip for someone who is able to walk—or brings the doer nearer to the act and hastens it for him. This type does not form a criterion for the validity of legal responsibility.[328]

The meaning is the request for help in every task, or in the execution of all the types of worship.

[Those who are understood as saying *naʿbudu* and *nastaʿīn*]

The covert pronoun in both verbs represents the reciter ....

[328] The Determinists (al-Jabriyya) said this verse shows the creature could not act independently while the Absolute Libertarians (al-Qadariyya) said it showed he can act with total independence then asks for assistance. By defining and describing the two types of assistance the Qadi invalidates both claims and shows the parameters within which the creature asks for help in what he can do or for facilitation (*yusr*). (Sk)

وَمَنْ مَعَهُ مِنَ الْحَفَظَةِ، وَحَاضِرِي صَلَاةِ الْجَمَاعَةِ؛ أَوْ لَهُ، وَلِسَائِرِ الْمُوَحِّدِينَ: أَدْرَجَ عِبَادَتَهُ فِي تَضَاعِيفِ عِبَادَتِهِمْ، وَخَلَطَ حَاجَتَهُ بِحَاجَتِهِمْ، لَعَلَّهَا تُقْبَلُ بِبَرَكَتِهَا، وَيُجَابُ إِلَيْهَا؛ وَلِهٰذَا شُرِعَتِ الْجَمَاعَةُ.

وَقُدِّمَ الْمَفْعُولُ لِلتَّعْظِيمِ، وَالِاهْتِمَامِ بِهِ، وَالدَّلَالَةِ عَلَى الْحَصْرِ - وَلِذٰلِكَ قَالَ ابْنُ عَبَّاسٍ رَضِيَ اللهُ عَنْهُمَا: (مَعْنَاهُ: نَعْبُدُكَ وَلَا نَعْبُدُ غَيْرَكَ) - وَتَقْدِيمِ مَا هُوَ مُقَدَّمٌ فِي الْوُجُودِ، وَالتَّنْبِيهِ عَلَى أَنَّ الْعَابِدَ يَنْبَغِي أَنْ يَكُونَ نَظَرُهُ .....

and those with him of the recording angels and attendees of congregational prayer; or the reciter and the rest of the pure monotheists: one inserted one's worship into the folds of their own and mixed one's need with theirs so that, perhaps, the former would be accepted through the latter's blessing and be answered. This is why congregation was made law.

[Why *iyyāka* was put first before the verbs]

The [direct] object was put first for magnification, focus and the indication of exclusivity;[329] hence Ibn 'Abbās—may Allah be well-pleased with him and his father—said, "Its meaning is, 'We worship You, and we do not worship anyone other than You.'"[330]

[The quest for self-extinction in the object of worship]

The order also gives precedence to what possesses precedence in existence, cautioning that the worshipper must keep his eyes

[329] See S (1:222-229) on the linguistic and Quranic proofs that exclusivity (*ḥaṣr*) here is not from the usage and position of *iyyāka* but rather from the context of the subject (*min khuṣūṣ al-mādda lā min mawḍū' al-lafẓ*).

[330] Something similar is narrated by al-Ṭabarī (1:160) and Ibn Abī Ḥātim, *Tafsīr al-Qur'ān al-'Aẓīm Musnadan 'an Rasūl Allāh ṣallā Allāhu 'alayhi wa-sallama wal-Ṣaḥābati wal-Tābi'īn*, ed. As'ad Muḥammad al-Ṭayyib, 14 vols. (Mecca and Riyadh: Maktabat Nizār Muṣṭafā al-Bāz, 1417/1997) 1:29 §27, §30, cf. al-Munāwī, *Fatḥ* (1:103-104 §7), but with a chain said to be missing a link between al-Ḍaḥḥāk (22-102 or 105/643-721 or 723) and Ibn 'Abbās (3BH-68/620-688).

إِلَى الْمَعْبُودِ أَوَّلاً وَبِالذَّاتِ؛ وَمِنْهُ إِلَى الْعِبَادَةِ، لَا مِنْ حَيْثُ إِنَّهَا عِبَادَةٌ صَدَرَتْ عَنْهُ، بَلْ مِنْ حَيْثُ إِنَّهَا نِسْبَةٌ شَرِيفَةٌ إِلَيْهِ، وَوُصْلَةٌ سَنِيَّةٌ بَيْنَهُ وَبَيْنَ الْحَقِّ. فَإِنَّ الْعَارِفَ إِنَّمَا يَحِقُّ وُصُولُهُ إِذَا اسْتَغْرَقَ فِي مُلَاحَظَةِ جَنَابِ الْقُدْسِ وَغَابَ عَمَّا عَدَاهُ، حَتَّى إِنَّهُ لَا يُلَاحِظُ نَفْسَهُ وَلَا حَالاً مِنْ أَحْوَالِهَا إِلَّا مِنْ حَيْثُ إِنَّهَا مُلَاحِظَةٌ لَهُ وَمُنْتَسِبَةٌ إِلَيْهِ؛ وَلِذٰلِكَ فُضِّلَ مَا حَكَى اللهُ عَنْ حَبِيبِهِ ﷺ حِينَ قَالَ: ﴿لَا تَحْزَنْ إِنَّ ٱللَّهَ مَعَنَا﴾ [التوبة ٤٠] عَلَى مَا حَكَاهُ عَنْ كَلِيمِهِ عليه السلام حِينَ قَالَ: ﴿إِنَّ مَعِيَ رَبِّي سَيَهْدِينِ﴾ [الشعراء ٦٢].

وَكَرَّرَ الضَّمِيرَ لِلتَّنْصِيصِ عَلَى أَنَّهُ الْمُسْتَعَانُ بِهِ لَا غَيْرَ.

وَقُدِّمَتِ الْعِبَادَةُ عَلَى الِاسْتِعَانَةِ لِيَتَوَافَقَ رُؤُوسُ الْآيِ.

on the object of his worship first—and for His own sake—and thence to worship, viewed not as worship that issued from him, but from the perspective of a lofty connection to Him and a sublime link between oneself and the Real. For truly the sage's arrival is realized only when he becomes immersed in awareness of the presence of the Holy One, oblivious to everything else, to the point he is not even aware of himself or any of his own states, except insofar as being aware of Him and connected to Him. Hence what Allah related from His Beloved—upon him blessings and peace—as saying *Grieve not! Truly Allah is with us* (al-Tawba 9:40) is deemed superior to what He related from His Interlocutor—upon him peace—as saying *Verily, with me is my Nurturer: He shall guide me* (al-Shuʿarāʾ 26:62).

He repeated the personal pronoun as an unequivocal text that it is He Whose help is sought and no other.

Worship was put before seeking help so that the verse endings would match.

وَيُعْلَمُ مِنْهُ أَنَّ تَقْدِيمَ الْوَسِيلَةِ عَلَى طَلَبِ الْحَاجَةِ أَدْعَى إِلَى الْإِجَابَةِ.

وَأَقُولُ: لَمَّا نَسَبَ الْمُتَكَلِّمُ الْعِبَادَةَ إِلَى نَفْسِهِ، أَوْهَمَ ذٰلِكَ تَبَجُّحاً وَاعْتِدَاداً مِنْهُ بِمَا يَصْدُرُ عَنْهُ، فَعَقَّبَهُ بِقَوْلِهِ: ﴿وَإِيَّاكَ نَسْتَعِينُ﴾، لِيَدُلَّ عَلَى أَنَّ الْعِبَادَةَ أَيْضاً مِمَّا لَا يَتِمُّ وَلَا يَسْتَتِبُّ لَهُ إِلَّا بِمَعُونَةٍ مِنْهُ وَتَوْفِيقٍ.

وَقِيلَ: الوَاوُ لِلْحَالِ؛ وَالْمَعْنَى: (نَعْبُدُكَ مُسْتَعِينِينَ بِكَ).

وَقُرِئَ بِكَسْرِ النُّونِ فِيهِمَا، وَهِيَ لُغَةُ بَنِي تَمِيمٍ، فَإِنَّهُمْ يَكْسِرُونَ حُرُوفَ الْمُضَارَعَةِ ـ سِوَى الْيَاءِ ـ إِذَا لَمْ يَنْضَمَّ مَا بَعْدَهَا.

[Putting the means (*wasīla*) first ensures fulfillment]

It can be gleaned from it that putting the means ahead of asking one's need is more conducive to fulfillment.

And I say: When the speaker attributed to himself [the act of] worship, he gave the impression that he was boasting and accorded importance to his own doing, so he followed it up by saying *and You do we ask for help*, to indicate that worship is also something that does not become complete or consummate except with the help and the success He [alone] grants.

It was said the *wāw* ⁽and⁾ denotes a participial state whereby the meaning would be, "We worship You seeking Your help."

It was also read with a *kasra* under the *nūn* in both words [*niʿbudu, nistaʿīn*],[331] in the dialect of Banū Tamīm: they put a *kasra* under all aorist initials except the *yāʾ*, provided the next letter does not have a *ḍamma*.

[331] By Zayd b. ʿAlī, Yaḥyā b. Waththāb, ʿUbayd b. ʿUmayr al-Laythī, Zirr b. Ḥubaysh, al-Nakhaʿī, al-Muṭawwiʿī, and al-Aʿmash. It is a dialectical form of Tamīm, Qays, Asad, Rabīʿa, Hudhayl, and some of Quraysh. (*MQ*)

﴿ ٱهۡدِنَا ٱلصِّرَٰطَ ٱلۡمُسۡتَقِيمَ ﴾: (١) بَيَانٌ لِلْمَعُونَةِ الْمَطْلُوبَةِ؛ فَكَأَنَّهُ
قَالَ: كَيْفَ أُعِينُكُمْ؟ فَقَالُوا: اِهْدِنَا. (٢) أَوْ: إِفْرَادٌ لِمَا هُوَ الْمَقْصُودُ الْأَعْظَمُ.
وَ(الْهِدَايَةُ): دِلَالَةٌ بِلُطْفٍ؛ وَلِذٰلِكَ تُسْتَعْمَلُ فِي الْخَيْرِ؛ وَقَوْلُهُ تَعَالَى:
﴿ فَٱهۡدُوهُمۡ إِلَىٰ صِرَٰطِ ٱلۡجَحِيمِ ﴾ [الصافات ٢٣] وَارِدٌ عَلَى التَّهَكُّمِ. وَمِنْهُ
(الْهَدِيَّةُ) وَ(هَوَادِي الْوَحْشِ) لِمُقَدِّمَاتِهَا. وَالْفِعْلُ مِنْهُ: (هَدَى). وَأَصْلُهُ أَنْ
يُعَدَّى بِاللَّامِ، أَوْ (إِلَى)، فَعُومِلَ مُعَامَلَةَ (اخْتَارَ) فِي قَوْلِهِ تَعَالَى: ﴿ وَٱخۡتَارَ
مُوسَىٰ قَوۡمَهُۥ [سَبۡعِينَ رَجُلٗا] ﴾ [الأعراف ١٥٥].
وَهِدَايَةُ اللهِ تَعَالَى تَتَنَوَّعُ أَنْوَاعًا لَا يُحْصِيهَا عَدٌّ، كَمَا قَالَ تَعَالَى: ....

[1:6] **ihdinā-ṣ-ṣirāṭa-l-mustaqīma** ʿ*Show us the straight path*ʾ is (i) an exposition of the help being requested, as if He asked: "How shall I help you?" and they replied, "Direct us!" (*ihdinā*); (ii) or it is a singling out of the most sublime goal of all.

Hidāya ʿdirectionʾ is indication with kindness, hence it is applied to good things; the saying of Allah Most High *and point them to the path of hell* (al-Ṣāffāt 37:23) came by way of derision. Related to it are *hadiyya* ʿgiftʾ and *hawādī al-waḥsh* ʿthe leaders of the wild herdʾ to refer to its front-runners.

The verb for it is *hadā* ʿto guide, directʾ. By default it is transitively used with the *lām* or with *ilā*,[332] but it was used here in the same way as *ikhtāra* ʿselectedʾ in the verse *and Mūsā selected his nation [seventy men]* (al-Aʿrāf 7:155).[333]

[Varieties of divine guidance]

The guidance of Allah Most High is manifold and its varieties are beyond count, as He—may He be exalted—said, *If you ...*

[332] "In reality intransitiveness is the default in the Hijaz dialect and transitiveness is not the rule but merely another dialect" according to al-Shihrī, lesson 8, after 12'30".
[333] *Ay min qawmihi* ʿi.e. Mūsā selected *out of* his nationʾ. (Z)

﴿وَإِن تَعُدُّواْ نِعْمَتَ ٱللَّهِ لَا تُحْصُوهَآ﴾ [إبراهيم ٣٤]، وَلٰكِنَّهَا تَنْحَصِرُ فِي أَجْنَاسٍ مُتَرَتِّبَةٍ:

* الْأَوَّلُ: إِفَاضَةُ الْقُوَى الَّتِي بِهَا يَتَمَكَّنُ الْمَرْءُ مِنَ الِاهْتِدَاءِ إِلَى مَصَالِحِهِ، كَالْقُوَّةِ الْعَقْلِيَّةِ، وَالْحَوَاسِّ الْبَاطِنَةِ، وَالْمَشَاعِرِ الظَّاهِرَةِ.

* وَالثَّانِي: نَصْبُ الدَّلَائِلِ الْفَارِقَةِ بَيْنَ الْحَقِّ وَالْبَاطِلِ، وَالصَّلَاحِ وَالْفَسَادِ؛ وَإِلَيْهِ أَشَارَ حَيْثُ قَالَ: ﴿وَهَدَيْنَٰهُ ٱلنَّجْدَيْنِ ۝١٠﴾ [البلد] وَقَالَ: ﴿وَأَمَّا ثَمُودُ فَهَدَيْنَٰهُمْ فَٱسْتَحَبُّواْ ٱلْعَمَىٰ عَلَى ٱلْهُدَىٰ﴾ [فصّلت ١٧].

* وَالثَّالِثُ: الْهِدَايَةُ بِإِرْسَالِ الرُّسُلِ وَإِنْزَالِ الْكُتُبِ؛ وَإِيَّاهَا عَنَى بِقَوْلِهِ: ﴿وَجَعَلْنَٰهُمْ أَئِمَّةً يَهْدُونَ بِأَمْرِنَا﴾ [الأنبياء ٧٣] ....

would count the bounty of Allah you cannot number it (Ibrāhīm 14:34). However, they can be subsumed under sequential types:

• First, the bestowal of powers by which one is able to pursue one's own welfare such as intellective power,[334] sentiments, and external senses;

• Second, producing the proofs that demarcate truth from falsehood and righteousness from corruption. He referred to this type when He said, *Have We not shown him (hadaynāhu) the two roads?* (al-Balad 90:10) and *As for Thamūd, We guided them, but they preferred blindness over guidance* (Fuṣṣilat 41:17).

• Third, guidance by sending Messengers and revealing Books. This is what He meant when He said, *and We made them leaders guiding by Our command* (al-Anbiyā' 21:73) ....

[334] "The Imām [= al-Rāzī] said the mind is the primeval messenger (*al-rasūl al-aṣlī*)" (Q 1:239) but the Ash'arī position is that the created mind cannot make any creed obligatory, cf. al-Qushayrī, *al-Fuṣūl fīl-Uṣūl* in *Thalāth Rasā'il*, ed. Maḥmūd al-Ṭabalāwī (Shubrā Miṣr: Maṭba'at al-Amāna, 1988) §57-58 and al-Mutawallī, *Mughnī*, ed. Marie Bernand (Cairo: Institut Français d'Archéologie Orientale, 1986) p. 44.

وَقَوْلِهِ: ﴿إِنَّ هَٰذَا ٱلْقُرْءَانَ يَهْدِى لِلَّتِى هِىَ أَقْوَمُ﴾ [الإسراء ٩].

* وَالرَّابِعُ: أَنْ يَكْشِفَ عَلَى قُلُوبِهِمُ السَّرَائِرَ وَيُرِيَهُمُ الْأَشْيَاءَ كَمَا هِيَ بِالْوَحْيِ، أَوِ الْإِلْهَامِ، وَالْمَنَامَاتِ الصَّادِقَةِ؛ وَهٰذَا قِسْمٌ يَخْتَصُّ بِنَيْلِهِ الْأَنْبِيَاءُ وَالْأَوْلِيَاءُ؛ وَإِيَّاهُ عَنَى بِقَوْلِهِ: ﴿أُوْلَٰٓئِكَ ٱلَّذِينَ هَدَى ٱللَّهُ فَبِهُدَىٰهُمُ ٱقْتَدِهْ﴾ [الأنعام ٩٠]، وَقَوْلِهِ ﴿وَٱلَّذِينَ جَٰهَدُواْ فِينَا لَنَهْدِيَنَّهُمْ سُبُلَنَا﴾ [العنكبوت ٦٩].

فَالْمَطْلُوبُ: إِمَّا زِيَادَةُ مَا مُنِحُوهُ مِنَ الْهُدَى؛ أَوِ الثَّبَاتُ عَلَيْهِ؛ أَوْ حُصُولُ الْمَرَاتِبِ الْمُرَتَّبَةِ عَلَيْهِ. فَإِذَا قَالَهُ الْعَارِفُ بِاللهِ الْوَاصِلُ، عَنَى بِهِ: (أَرْشِدْنَا طَرِيقَ السَّيْرِ فِيكَ، لِتَمْحُوَ عَنَّا ظُلُمَاتِ أَحْوَالِنَا، وَتُمِيطَ غَوَاشِيَ أَبْدَانِنَا، ....

and *Truly this Qur'ān guides to what is straightest* (al-Isrā' 17:9).

• Fourth, He discloses secrets to their hearts and shows them things as they are, whether through revelation or inspiration and truthful dreams. This is something only Prophets and friends [of Allah] obtain. That is [respectively] what He means by saying, *Those are the ones whom Allah guided, so follow their guidance* (al-An'ām 6:90) and *As for those who strive in Us, We will most surely guide them (to) Our paths* (al-'Ankabūt 29:69).

[Prayer for guidance, self-extinction and for vision of Allah]

What is asked, then, is (i) more of what they were conferred of guidance; (ii) or firmness with it; (iii) or the acquirement of the ranks that result from it. When spoken by the accomplished knower of Allah he means, "Direct us on the path of wayfaring in You, so that You will eradicate from us the pitch-darkness of our states and take away the dense screens of our material bodies,[335]

[335] B: نمحو بالنون والتاء الفوقية والياء التحتية وكذا نميط Kh: لتمحو... وتميط Passim: ليمحو... وتميط بالوجوه الثلاثة
Sk: وتحيط... قوله لتمحو عنا قرئ بصيغة الخطاب والتكلم والغيبة بأن يكون الضمير راجعا الى السير

لِنَسْتَضِيءَ بِنُورِ قُدْسِكَ، فَنَرَاكَ بِنُورِكَ).

وَالْأَمْرُ وَالدُّعَاءُ يَتَشَارَكَانِ لَفْظاً وَمَعْنًى، وَيَتَفَاوَتَانِ بِالْاسْتِعْلَاءِ وَالتَّسَفُّلِ، وَقِيلَ: بِالرُّتْبَةِ.

وَ﴿السِّرَاطُ﴾: مِنْ (سَرَطَ الطَّعَامَ) إِذَا ابْتَلَعَهُ، فَكَأَنَّهُ يَسْرَطُ السَّابِلَةَ، وَلِذٰلِكَ سُمِّيَ لَقَماً، لِأَنَّهُ يَلْتَقِمُهُمْ. وَ﴿الصِّرَاطُ﴾: مِنْ قَلْبِ السِّينِ صاداً،

so that we can be illuminated with the light of Your holiness and we can see You with Your light!"

Command and supplication share the same wording and meaning but differ in [the connotation of] superiority and inferiority.[336] It was also said that they differ as to rank.[337]

[Meaning and variants of *sirāṭ/ṣirāṭ*]

Sirāṭ is from *saraṭa al-ṭaʿām*, "to swallow food," so it is as if it [the path] is gulping down the wayfarers. Hence it was also called[338] *laqam* ⁽mouthful⁾ because it devours them.[339]

Ṣirāṭ is from the transposition of the *sīn* into a *ṣād* ....

[336] I.e. respectively—superiority in command and inferiority in supplication. (P)

[337] I.e. height and lowliness are intrinsic to the speaker—whence command presupposes superiority and supplication presupposes inferiority exclusively—and this is the position of the Muʿtazila. (Q) The Sunni position makes the height of command and the lowliness of entreaty a matter of elective usage, e.g. intent and context, rather than intrinsic rank. Thus *ihdinā* here is an imperative meant as entreaty, not command.

[338] All mss. and eds.: سمّي β, R: يسمّى

[339] B, F, M, P: لَقَماً A: لقما بفتح الميم والقاف In the *Ṣiḥāḥ*: *al-laqam* is "the middle of the road" while *al-laqm* is "to swallow." Al-Jawharī, *Ṣiḥāḥ* (5:2031a, *l-q-m*). Al-Rāghib defines *sirāṭ* as "the downslope/the road made easy" (*al-ṭarīq al-mustas-hal*), "likewise it was named the gulped or gulping road (*al-ṭarīq al-laqm wal-multaqim*) if we consider that its wayfarer swallows it up." *Mufradāt Alfāẓ al-Qur'ān*, ed. Ṣafwān Dāwūdī, 4th ed. (Damascus: Dār al-Qalam, 1430/2009) p. 407, entry *s-r-ṭ*. However, he defines *al-laqam* not as the middle but as "the far end of the road" (*ṭaraf al-ṭarīq*): *Mufradāt* (p. 745, entry *l-q-m*). "As if it [the road] swallows them [the wayfarers] or vice-versa" (A).

لِيُطَابِقَ الطَّاءَ فِي الْإِطْبَاقِ. وَقَدْ يُشَمُّ الصَّادُ صَوْتَ الزَّايِ لِيَكُونَ أَقْرَبَ إِلَى الْمُبْدَلِ مِنْهُ. وَقَرَأَ ابْنُ كَثِيرٍ - بِرِوَايَةِ قُنْبُلٍ عَنْهُ - وَرُوَيْسٌ عَنْ يَعْقُوبَ: بِالْأَصْلِ؛ وَحَمْزَةُ: بِالْإِشْمَامِ؛ وَالْبَاقُونَ بِالصَّادِ، وَهُوَ لُغَةُ قُرَيْشٍ وَالثَّابِتُ فِي الْإِمَامِ.

وَجَمْعُهُ: (سُرُطٌ)، كَ(كُتُبٍ)؛ وَهُوَ كَ(الطَّرِيقِ) فِي التَّذْكِيرِ وَالتَّأْنِيثِ.

so that it can match the *ṭā'* in the over-covering [of the tongue and palate]. The *ṣād* is sometimes given a smack of *z*-sound to bring it closer to its alternant [*s*-sound]. Ibn Kathīr, as narrated by Qunbul, and Ruways, narrating from Ya'qūb, both read it in its original form [*s*]. Ḥamza read it with the *z*-sound.[340] The rest read it with *ṣ*, which is the dialect of Quraysh and the form fixed in the Master.[341]

Its plural is *suruṭ* as in *kutub* ‹books›, and it is indifferently put in the masculine or feminine, like *ṭarīq* ‹way›.[342]

[340] *Ṣzirāṭ*, a dialect of the 'Udhra, Kalb and Banū al-Qayn (*MQ*). *Ishmām* comes up again in the permutation of phonemes (see note 399) and elsewhere (note 653).

[341] *Al-Imām*, also known as *al-muṣḥāf al-imām* or Master Volume, the proper denomination of the 'Uthmānic codex in canonical readings and codicology, cf. the chapter-title *al-Imām al-ladhī kataba minhu 'Uthmān raḍya Allāhu 'anhu al-maṣāḥifa, wa-huwa muṣḥafuh* (The Imam from which 'Uthmān wrote the Quranic codices, and which is his volume) in Ibn Abī Dāwūd, *Kitāb al-Māṣāḥif*, 2 vols., ed. Muḥibb al-Dīn 'Abd al-Sabḥān Wā'iẓ, 2nd ed. (Beirut: Dār al-Bashā'ir al-Islāmiyya, 1423/2002) 1:245.

[342] "Masculine is the way of Banū Tamīm while feminine is the way of the people of Ḥijāz" (Z). The fact that the Qadi begins by addressing the word *sirāṭ* with an *s* (the minority reading of Qunbul, Ruways, Ibn Kathīr, Abū Ḥamdūn, al-Kisā'ī in one narration, al-Qawwās, 'Ubayd b. 'Aqīl from Shibl and from Abū 'Amr) then proceeds to the majority reading of *ṣirāṭ* (as taught by Nāfi', Abū 'Amr, Ibn 'Āmir, 'Āṣim, al-Kisā'ī in another narration, Abū Ja'far, Shayba, Qatāda, and Ibn Kathīr per al-Bizzī's narration) (*MQ*), might imply that his region and time followed one of the minority readings; however, he appears to be merely following the order of the *Kashshāf*. See also http://www.alukah.net/Web/alshehry/10823/46711/ on Bayḍāwī's preferred *qirā'a*.

و﴿ٱلْمُسْتَقِيمَ﴾: الْمُسْتَوِي؛ وَالْمُرَادُ بِهِ: طَرِيقُ الْحَقِّ؛ وَقِيلَ: هُوَ مِلَّةُ الْإِسْلَامِ.

﴿صِرَاطَ ٱلَّذِينَ أَنْعَمْتَ عَلَيْهِمْ﴾: بَدَلٌ مِنَ الْأَوَّلِ بَدَلَ الْكُلِّ [مِنَ الْكُلِّ]؛ وَهُوَ فِي حُكْمِ تَكْرِيرِ الْعَامِلِ مِنْ حَيْثُ إِنَّهُ الْمَقْصُودُ بِالنِّسْبَةِ؛ وَفَائِدَتُهُ: التَّوْكِيدُ، وَالتَّنْصِيصُ عَلَى أَنَّ طَرِيقَ الْمُسْلِمِينَ هُوَ الْمَشْهُودُ عَلَيْهِ بِالِاسْتِقَامَةِ عَلَى آكَدِ وَجْهٍ وَأَبْلَغِهِ؛ لِأَنَّهُ جُعِلَ كَالتَّفْسِيرِ وَالْبَيَانِ لَهُ. فَكَأَنَّهُ مِنَ الْبَيِّنِ الَّذِي لَا خَفَاءَ فِيهِ: أَنَّ الطَّرِيقَ الْمُسْتَقِيمَ مَا يَكُونُ طَرِيقَ الْمُؤْمِنِينَ.

Al-mustaqīm means "the straight." What is meant by it is the way of truth. It was also said it means the Muslim denomination.[343]

[1:7] ṣirāṭa-l-ladhīna anʿamta ʿalayhim ⟨*The path of those You have favored*⟩: A substitute of the first "path" substituting the whole <for the whole>,[344] and it is a virtual repetition of the regent in that it is the one purported by the referent ["show us the straight path"]. Its import is emphasis and the stipulation that the path of the Muslims is indeed the one attested as the path of virtue most emphatically and intensively, since it [the former] was made its [the latter's] explication and exposition, as if making it patently clear that the straight path is what forms the path of the believers.[345]

---

[343] "Both glosses are related from Ibn ʿAbbās… and they are not contrasting with one another (*laysā mutaghāyirayn*) contrary to what the author's wording suggests" (S).
[344] α, Ak, β, F, Kh, N, Q, R: بدل الكل من الكل All other eds. and mss.: بدل الكل
[345] al-Bayḍāwī differentiates between submission (*islām*) and belief (*īmān*) in his commentary on *wa-man yabtaghi ghayra al-islāmi dīnan* (Āl ʿImrān 3:85) and that on the hadith of Jibrīl in his *Tuḥfat al-Abrār Sharḥ Maṣābīḥ al-Sunna*, ed. Muḥammad Isḥāq Ibrāhīm, 3 vols. (Riyadh: Pub. by editor, 1432/2011) 1:88-91 in line with the Ashʿarī School but here he paraphrases the *Kashshāf* whose position is that of the Māturīdīs and Muʿtazilīs in who consider them undifferentiated, *al-muʾmin* standing for *al-*

وَقِيلَ: ﴿ٱلَّذِينَ أَنعَمتَ عَلَيهِمْ﴾: الْأَنْبِيَاءُ؛ وَقِيلَ: أَصْحَابُ مُوسَى وَعِيسَى ـ عَلَيْهِمَا السَّلَامُ ـ قَبْلَ التَّحْرِيفِ وَالنَّسْخِ.

وَقُرِئَ: (صِرَاطَ مَنْ أَنْعَمْتَ عَلَيْهِمْ).

وَالْإِنْعَامُ: إِيصَالُ النِّعْمَةِ؛ وَهِيَ فِي الْأَصْلِ: الْحَالَةُ الَّتِي يَسْتَلِذُّهَا الْإِنْسَانُ، فَأُطْلِقَتْ لِمَا يَسْتَلِذُّهُ مِنَ النَّعْمَةِ، وَهِيَ اللِّينُ.

وَنِعَمُ اللهِ ـ وَإِنْ كَانَتْ لَا تُحْصَى، كَمَا قَالَ: ﴿وَإِن تَعُدُّواْ نِعْمَتَ ٱللَّهِ لَا تُحْصُوهَآ﴾ [إبراهيم ٣٤] ـ ....

It was also said that *those You have favored* are the Prophets; or[346] the companions of Mūsā ⁽Moses⁾ and ʿĪsā ⁽Jesus⁾ —upon both blessings and peace—before textual corruption and abrogation.

It was also read *ṣirāṭa man anʿamta ʿalayhim* ⁽the path of whoever You have favored⁾.[347]

Inʿām ⁽favoring⁾ is the conveyance of *niʿma* ⁽favor⁾. The latter's original meaning is "a human being's state of enjoyment;" then it was used for the *naʿma* ⁽ease⁾ one enjoys, namely comfort.

[Typology of the divine favors]

The favors of Allah, although uncountable—as He said, *if you would count the bounty of Allah you cannot number it* ....

muslim and vice-versa. (Z) More in al-Qūnawī (1:253-256).

346 α, β, B, D, ε, I, L, Kh, M, P, Q, R, T, U, UL, Z and J: الأنبياء وقيل أصحاب موسى وعيسى Ak, AQ, F, H, K, MM, N: الأنبياء وقيل النبي ﷺ وأصحابه وقيل أصحاب موسى وعيسى "The first gloss, the believers, is in view of the fact that belief is the most perfect favor lavished by Allah on His servants in absolute terms; the second gloss, the Prophets, is in view of the fact that prophethood is the greatest favor in specific terms, while the third gloss is because every individual in this *Umma* must follow as they did." (Z)

347 By Ibn Masʿūd, Ibn al-Zubayr, Zayd b. ʿAlī, ʿUmar b. al-Khaṭṭāb, ʿAlī, ʿAlqama, and al-Aswad. (*MQ*) See Ibn Abī Dāwūd, *Maṣāḥif* (1:284-285,

تَنْحَصِرُ فِي جِنْسَيْنِ: دُنْيَوِيٍّ، وَأُخْرَوِيٍّ.

وَالْأَوَّلُ قِسْمَانِ: مَوْهِبِيٌّ، وَكَسْبِيٌّ.

* وَالْمَوْهِبِيُّ قِسْمَانِ: (١) رُوحَانِيٌّ: كَنَفْخِ الرُّوحِ فِيهِ، وَإِشْرَاقِهِ بِالْعَقْلِ، وَمَا يَتْبَعُهُ مِنَ الْقُوَى: كَالْفَهْمِ، وَالْفِكْرِ، وَالنُّطْقِ؛ (٢) وَجُسْمَانِيٌّ: كَتَخْلِيقِ الْبَدَنِ، وَالْقُوَى الْحَالَّةِ فِيهِ، وَالْهَيْئَاتِ الْعَارِضَةِ لَهُ، مِنَ الصِّحَّةِ وَكَمَالِ الْأَعْضَاءِ؛

* وَالْكَسْبِيُّ: تَزْكِيَةُ النَّفْسِ عَنِ الرَّذَائِلِ، وَتَحْلِيَتُهَا بِالْأَخْلَاقِ السَّنِيَّةِ، وَالْمَلَكَاتِ الْفَاضِلَةِ؛ وَتَزْيِينُ الْبَدَنِ بِالْهَيْئَاتِ الْمَطْبُوعَةِ، وَالْحُلِيِّ ....

(Ibrāhīm 14:34)—can be subsumed under two sets: this-worldly and next-worldly. The first is in two parts: gifted[348] and acquired.

The gifted is itself in two parts: (1) spiritual, such as people's ensoulment and enlightenment through the intellect and all the faculties that depend on it such as comprehension, reflection and speech[349]; and (2) corporeal, such as the fashioning of the body, the powers immanent in it, and its accidental aspects such as good health and well-proportioned limbs.

The acquired include the purification of the self from vices and its adornment with refined traits and worthy skills; the embellishment of the body with elegant miens and prized ....

[348] M: مَوْهَبِيّ All mss. and eds.: موهبى H: وهبى typo.

[349] All mss. and eds.: والنطق H: والنظر blunder. On Bayḍāwī's recourse to the Aristotelian classifications of faculties and powers see also pp. 196, 209, 418 and note 954; cf. Chart II in Osman Bakar, "Islamic Medical and Public Health System," *Islamic Civilisation and the Modern World: Thematic Essays* (Bandar Seri Begawan: Universiti Brunei Darussalam, 2014) p. 165, as taken from Hakim Abdur Razzack and Ummul Fazal, *Report on Arab (Unani) Medicine and the State of Kuwait: A Brief Survey* (s.l.: s.n., 1977).

الْمُسْتَحْسَنَةِ؛ وَحُصُولُ الْجَاهِ وَالْمَالِ.

وَالثَّانِي: أَنْ يَغْفِرَ لَهُ مَا فَرَطَ مِنْهُ، وَيَرْضَى عَنْهُ، وَيُبَوِّئَهُ فِي أَعْلَى عِلِّيِّينَ مَعَ الْمَلَائِكَةِ الْمُقَرَّبِينَ أَبَدَ الْآبِدِينَ.

وَالْمُرَادُ: هُوَ الْقِسْمُ الْأَخِيرُ، وَمَا يَكُونُ وُصْلَةً إِلَى نَيْلِهِ مِنَ الْقِسْمِ الْآخَرِ؛ فَإِنَّ مَا عَدَا ذٰلِكَ: يَشْتَرِكُ فِيهِ الْمُؤْمِنُ وَالْكَافِرُ.

﴿غَيْرِ ٱلْمَغْضُوبِ عَلَيْهِمْ وَلَا ٱلضَّآلِّينَ﴾: بَدَلٌ مِنَ ﴿ٱلَّذِينَ﴾ عَلَى مَعْنَى أَنَّ الْمُنْعَمَ عَلَيْهِمْ: هُمُ الَّذِينَ سَلِمُوا مِنَ الْغَضَبِ وَالضَّلَالِ؛ ....

ornaments; and the acquisition of repute and wealth.

The second [type of divine favor] is for Him to forgive one what one did thoughtlessly; be well-pleased with one; and make one dwell in the Highest with the angels brought near, forever and ever.

[The favor that is] meant is the latter [next-worldly] type and everything from the former[350] that serves as a link to attain it. The rest is all, without exception, the lot shared by both believers and unbelievers.

[Divine favor is safety from wrath and misguidance]

ghayri-l-maghḍūbi ʿalayhim wa-lā-ḍ-ḍāllīna ⁽*other than those who incurred anger nor those who are astray*⁾ is a substitute for ***al-ladhīna*** ⁽those [You have favored]⁾ in the sense that those who have been favored are those who are safe from anger and misguidance; ....

[350] α, A, Ak, β, B, D, ε, I, L, M, N, P, Q, R, T, U, Ul, Z: من القسم الآخر
Sk: من التقسيم الآخر F, K: من الآخر AQ, H, MM: من الآخرة blunder!
Kh: من القسم الآخر بفتح الخاء ومن تبعيضية لا بيانية

أَوْ: صِفَةٌ لَهُ مُبَيِّنَةٌ أَوْ مُقَيِّدَةٌ، عَلَى مَعْنَى أَنَّهُمْ جَمَعُوا بَيْنَ النِّعْمَةِ الْمُطْلَقَةِ - وَهِيَ نِعْمَةُ الْإِيْمَانِ - وَبَيْنَ السَّلَامَةِ مِنَ الْغَضَبِ وَالضَّلَالِ.

وَذٰلِكَ إِنَّمَا يَصِحُّ بِأَحَدِ تَأْوِيلَيْنِ: (١) إِجْرَاءُ الْمَوْصُولِ مُجْرَى النَّكِرَةِ، إِذْ لَمْ يُقْصَدْ بِهِ مَعْهُودٌ، كَالْمُحَلَّى فِي قَوْلِهِ: [كامل]

وَلَقَدْ أَمُرُّ عَلَى اللَّئِيمِ يَسُبُّنِي * ....

وَقَوْلِهِمْ: إِنِّي لَأَمُرُّ عَلَى الرَّجُلِ مِثْلِكَ فَيُكْرِمُنِي. أَوْ: (٢) جَعْلِ ﴿غَيْرِ﴾ ...

or, either an expository or a restrictive adjective for it in the sense that they have garnered [for themselves] absolute favor—namely the favor of belief—as well as safety from anger and misguidance.

The latter [adjectival sense] can be correct only through one of two possible interpretations:

(1) if we treat the relative pronoun [***al-ladhīna*** ‹those whom›] as an indefinite, as when[351] no one in particular is meant, such as the one described in the saying ["The Perfect"]

And I may pass by the scoundrel hurling insults at me,[352]

and their saying, "In truth, I do pass by the man such as yourself and he will show me benevolence;"

(2) if we make ***ghayr*** ‹other› ....

[351] α, AQ, B, F, I, L, Kh, M, N, Q, R, U, Ul, Z: اذ Ak, β, D, ε, H, MM, P, Sk, T: اذا

[352] Spoken by a man of the Banū Salūl; its continuation is: *I look the other way and say: This does not concern me* (S). A locus classicus of Arabic grammar discussed in Sībawayh's *Kitāb*, ed. ʿAbd al-Salām Muḥammad Hārūn, 5 vols. (Cairo: Maktabat al-Khānjī, 1385/1966) 3:24 among others in illustration—like the one that follows it—of definite and qualified constructs ("the depraved man hurling," "the man who resembles you") meant as indefinites, to refer to archetypes rather than particulars.

مَعْرِفَةً بِالْإِضَافَةِ، لِأَنَّهُ أُضِيفَ إِلَى مَا لَهُ ضِدٌّ وَاحِدٌ - وَهُوَ الْمُنْعَمُ عَلَيْهِمْ - فَيَتَعَيَّنُ تَعَيُّنَ (الْحَرَكَةِ) مِنْ (غَيْرِ السُّكُونِ).

وَعَنِ ابْنِ كَثِيرٍ: نَصْبُهُ عَلَى الْحَالِ مِنَ الضَّمِيرِ الْمَجْرُورِ، وَالْعَامِلُ: ﴿أَنْعَمْتَ﴾؛ أَوْ: بِإِضْمَارِ (أَعْنِي)؛ أَوْ: بِالْاسْتِثْنَاءِ، إِنْ فُسِّرَ النِّعَمُ بِمَا يَعُمُّ الْقَبِيلَيْنِ.

وَ(الْغَضَبُ): ثَوَرَانُ النَّفْسِ إِرَادَةَ الْانْتِقَامِ؛ فَإِذَا أُسْنِدَ إِلَى اللهِ تَعَالَى، أُرِيدَ بِهِ الْمُنْتَهَى وَالْغَايَةُ عَلَى مَا مَرَّ.

a definite by annexation, since it was annexed to something which has a single antonym—which is "those who have been favored"—so the latter is designated in the same way "movement" is designated by "other than stillness."

Ibn Kathīr relatedly read it in the accusative case [*ghayra*][353] as a participial state for the genitive-case pronoun [in the first *ʿalayhim*]—the regent being ***anʿamta*** ⟨You have favored⟩; or by implying "I mean;" or as an exceptive if the favoring is explained to include both parties.[354]

[Emotional and physical divine attributes are metaphorical]

Ghaḍab ⟨anger⟩ is "the flaring of the psyche in the pursuit of revenge" When attributed to Allah Most High the purport is culmination and outcome, as already discussed.[355]

353 This is also the reading of ʿUmar, ʿAlī, Ibn Masʿūd, ʿAbd Allāh b. al-Zubayr, and Ubay b. Kaʿb, and it is related from Ibn Muḥayṣin and al-Aʿmash. Al-Zajjāj supported it for its grammatical validity but al-Ṭabarī deemed it anomalous (*shādhdh*). (*MQ*)

354 "I.e., both believers and unbelievers, as if saying 'the path of those whom you have granted this and next-worldly favors to the exclusion of those who earn anger'..." (Q)

355 In the discussion of *al-raḥmān al-raḥīm*, in his sentence, "the Names of Allah are taken only in consideration of outcomes..." See p. 168 above and p. 466 below.

وَ﴿عَلَيْهِمْ﴾ فِي مَحَلِّ الرَّفْعِ، لِأَنَّهُ نَائِبُ مَنَابَ الْفَاعِلِ، بِخِلَافِ الْأَوَّلِ.

وَ﴿لَا﴾ مَزِيدَةٌ، لِتَأْكِيدِ مَا فِي ﴿غَيْرِ﴾ مِنْ مَعْنَى النَّفْيِ؛ فَكَأَنَّهُ قَالَ: (لَا الْمَغْضُوبِ عَلَيْهِمْ وَلَا الضَّالِّينَ). وَلِذٰلِكَ جَازَ: (أَنَا زَيْداً غَيْرُ ضَارِبٍ)، كَمَا جَازَ: (أَنَا زَيْداً لَا ضَارِبٌ)، وَإِنِ امْتَنَعَ (أَنَا زَيْداً مِثْلُ ضَارِبٍ).

[The second] ***ʿalayhim*** is construed as a nominative because it stands for the agent, unlike the first.[356]

Lā is additive to emphasize the sense of negation in ***ghayr***,[357] so it is like saying *lā al-maghḍūbi ʿalayhim wa-lā al-ḍāllīn* ⁽not those who earn Your anger and not those who are astray⁾. In the same way one can say *anā Zaydan ghayru ḍāribin* ⁽Zayd I will do other than strike⁾, just as one can say *anā Zaydan lā ḍāribun* ⁽Zayd I am not striking⁾, but not *anā Zaydan mithlu ḍāribin* ⁽Zayd I am quasi-striking⁾.

[356] "He means the annexed pronoun in the second *ʿalayhim* plays the role of subject of *al-maghḍūb*, the latter being devoid of pronoun.... Of the subtleties of this wording is that the servant addresses Allah when mentioning favor and explicitly ascribes the latter to Him as a means of drawing near to Him by its mention; but when it comes to mentioning anger, one shifts to the third person and leaves the ascription of anger to Him unexplicit out of *adab*. It is as if one said: 'You are the Owner of all favor, which is outpouring from Your presence; and those others deserve to incur anger.'" (Z 1:51)

[357] I.e., *other than those who earn Your anger and are astray*. Redundancy typifies the position of the Basrians while the Kufans consider *lā* here to signify *ghayr*. The Qadi refers to this grammatical view very often with regard to other particles as well such as *min, mā, lām, fā'* and *bā'* while modernists tend to view the label of "redundancy" as an affront to the perfection of the Book, cf. Muḥammad ʿAbduh as quoted in his student Rashīd Riḍā's *Tafsīr al-Manār*, 2nd ed., 12 vols. (Cairo: Dār al-Manār, 1366/1947) 1:379 *sub* al-Baqara 2:88 and Muḥammad ʿAbd Allāh Drāz, *al-Naba' al-ʿAẓīm: Naẓarāt Jadīda fil-Qur'ān al-Karīm*, 2nd ed. (Kuwait: Dār al-Kitāb al-ʿArabī, 1390/1970) p. 133. It is clear however, that redundancy is meant as a grammatical category not a qualifier of style, and that it is far from incompatible with rhetorical eloquence as demonstrated by the Qadi's words "to emphasize the sense of negation" and by his own explicit disclaimers while discussing the additive *mā* in *mathalan mā baʿūḍatan* (al-Baqara 2:26) and in *fa-bi-mā raḥmatin mina-l-Lāh* (Āl ʿImrān 3:159).

وَقُرِئَ: (وَغَيْرِ الضَّالِّينَ).

وَالضَّلَالُ: الْعُدُولُ عَنِ الطَّرِيقِ السَّوِيِّ ـ عَمْداً أَوْ خَطَأً؛ وَلَهُ عَرْضٌ عَرِيضٌ، وَالتَّفَاوُتُ مَا بَيْنَ أَدْنَاهُ وَأَقْصَاهُ كَثِيرٌ.

قِيلَ: ﴿ٱلْمَغْضُوبِ عَلَيْهِمْ﴾: الْيَهُودُ، لِقَوْلِهِ تَعَالَى فِيهِمْ: ﴿مَن لَّعَنَهُ ٱللَّهُ وَغَضِبَ عَلَيْهِ﴾ [المائدة ٦٠]؛ وَ﴿ٱلضَّآلِّينَ﴾: النَّصَارَى، لِقَوْلِهِ تَعَالَى ﴿قَدْ ضَلُّواْ مِن قَبْلُ وَأَضَلُّواْ كَثِيرًا﴾ [المائدة ٧٧]. وَقَدْ رُوِيَ مَرْفُوعاً.

وَيَتَّجِهُ أَنْ يُقَالَ: ﴿ٱلْمَغْضُوبِ عَلَيْهِمْ﴾: الْعُصَاةُ، وَ﴿ٱلضَّآلِّينَ﴾: الْجَاهِلُونَ ....

It was also read *wa-ghayri-ḍ-ḍāllīn*.[358]

Misguidance is deviation from the straight path deliberately or by mistake; its range is huge, with much disparity between its nearest and farthest [extents].

[Identifying *those who incur anger and those who are astray*]

It was said that *those who incurred anger* are the Jews, since Allah said of them *those whom Allah has cursed and on whom His wrath has fallen* (al-Mā'ida 5:60), while *those who are astray* are the Christians, since Allah said *they went astray before, and led astray many* (al-Mā'ida 5:77), and such has certainly been narrated as a Prophetic saying.[359]

It is pertinent to say that *those who incurred anger* are the sinners while *those who are astray* are those who do not know

[358] By ʿUmar, ʿAlī, Ubay b. Kaʿb, ʿAbd Allāh b. al-Zubayr, ʿAlqama and al-Aswad (*MQ*).
[359] From ʿAdī b. Ḥātim by Aḥmad, al-Tirmidhī who declared it fair, Ibn Ḥibbān, and others, as well as from Abū Dharr, Ibn ʿAbbās, Ibn Masʿūd, al-Rabīʿ b. Anas, Zayd b. Aslam and others. "Ibn Abī Ḥātim said: 'I am not aware of any disagreement over this [interpretation] among the exegetes.' This is an affirmation of consensus on his part; how dare one leave it aside, then, and leave the explicit Prophetic stipulation to turn to one's own opinion?" (S) More in the next note.

بِاللهِ، لِأَنَّ الْمُنْعَمَ عَلَيْهِ: مَنْ وُفِّقَ لِلْجَمْعِ بَيْنَ مَعْرِفَةِ الْحَقِّ لِذَاتِهِ، وَالْخَيْرِ لِلْعَمَلِ بِهِ؛ وَكَانَ الْمُقَابِلُ لَهُ: مَنِ اخْتَلَّ ....

Allah,[360] since the one who is granted favor is he who is graced with joining knowledge of truth for its own sake with the boon of putting it into practice; his counterpart is the transgressor in

[360] "This is truly bizarre (*hādhā min al-ʿajab al-ʿujāb*)—his weakening of the exegesis related from the Prophet, upon him blessings and peace, and all the Companions and Successors, and his invention of a conjectural exegesis which he then made the pertinent one! (*wa-khtirāʿuhu tafsīran bi-ra'yihi, wa-jaʿluhu annahu al-muttajah*)" (S). Al-Suyūṭī's characterization of the Qadi's words as a "weakening" of the narrated exegeses rests on the Qadi's expressions "it was said" (*qīla*) and "it was narrated" (*ruwiya*) in the passive voice which—like "it is cited" (*nuqila*), "it is told" (*ḥukiya*), and other such terms—according to general hadithic convention, convey dubiosity (*tamrīḍ*) in the authenticity of transmission as opposed to active-voice positive assertions (*jazm*) that convey certitude, e.g. "he said" (*qāla*), "he mentioned" (*dhakara*), "he narrated" (*rawā*), "he related" (*akhbara*), etc. Al-Bukhārī wields this formulaic distinction with proverbial mastery in his *Ṣaḥīḥ* and is subsequently cited as its archetypal master. Cf. al-Nawawī who set forth the rule of permitted and unpermitted usage in this respect in the section devoted to weak hadiths of the introduction to his commentary published under the title *Mā Tamassu ilayhi Ḥājatu al-Qārī li-Ṣaḥīḥ al-Imām al-Bukhārī*, ed. ʿAlī Ḥasan ʿAbd al-Ḥamīd (Beirut: Dār al-Kutub al-ʿIlmiyya, n.d.) p. 89-90, which Ṭāhir al-Jazā'irī reproduced in full in his *Tawjīh al-Naẓar ilā Uṣūl al-Athar*, 2nd ed., 2 vols. in one (Beirut: Dār al-Bashā'ir al-Islāmiyya, 1430/ 2009) 2:668-669. Nevertheless this rule was not etched in stone for the early scholars, cf. Nūr al-Dīn ʿItr, *Manhaj al-Naqd fī ʿUlūm al-Ḥadīth*, 3rd ed. (Damascus: Dār al-Fikr: 1981) p. 297 (*riwāyat al-ḥadīth al-ḍaʿīf*) and p. 377 (*ḥukm al-muʿallaq fīl-ṣaḥīḥayn*), as shown by al-Tirmidhī's free usage of the dubitative wording indifferently—both for certain and uncertain reports—and Bukhārī himself using "it is mentioned" (*yudhkaru*) in the same way on occasion. Ibn al-Ṣalāḥ in the first category (*ʿilm al-ṣaḥīḥ*) of his *ʿUlūm al-Ḥadīth* conceded the passive is used for both weak and sound reports, as underlined by al-ʿIrāqī in his commentary *al-Taqyīd wal-Īḍāḥ li-mā Uṭliqa wa-Ughliqa min Muqaddimat Ibn al-Ṣalāḥ*, ed. Muḥammad Rāghib al-Ṭabbākh (Aleppo: Pub. by editor, 1350/1931) p. 23: "Ibn al-Ṣalāḥ never said that the formula of *tamrīḍ* is not used other than for weak hadiths; on the contrary, his words convey that it is sometimes used for sound ones as well." Similarly al-Bulqīnī said *tamrīḍ* might indicate either rank in his *Maḥāsin al-Iṣṭilāḥ*, ed. ʿĀ'isha ʿAbd al-Raḥmān Bint al-Shāṭi' (Cairo: Dār al-Maʿrifa, 1411/1990) p. 169. As for the exegesis the Qadi forwards it is, in fairness, and just like the first exegesis he cites, far from "invented conjecture" but an eminently Quranic gloss.

إِحْدَى قُوَّتَيْهِ ـ الْعَاقِلَةِ وَالْعَامِلَةِ. وَالْمُخِلُّ بِالْعَمَلِ: فَاسِقٌ مَغْضُوبٌ عَلَيْهِ، لِقَوْلِهِ تَعَالَى فِي الْقَاتِلِ عَمْداً: ﴿وَغَضِبَ ٱللَّهُ عَلَيْهِ﴾ [النساء ٩٣]. وَالْمُخِلُّ بِالْعَقْلِ: جَاهِلٌ ضَالٌّ، لِقَوْلِهِ: ﴿فَمَاذَا بَعْدَ ٱلْحَقِّ إِلَّا ٱلضَّلَٰلُ﴾ [يونس ٣٢].

وَقُرِئَ: (وَلَا الضَّأَلِّينَ) بِالْهَمْزَةِ، عَلَى لُغَةِ مَنْ جَدَّ فِي الْهَرَبِ مِنِ الْتِقَاءِ السَّاكِنَيْنِ.

(آمِينَ): اِسْمُ الْفِعْلِ الَّذِي هُوَ (اِسْتَجِبْ). وَعَنِ ابْنِ عَبَّاسٍ، قَالَ: سَأَلْتُ رَسُولَ اللهِ ﷺ عَنْ مَعْنَاهُ، فَقَالَ: (افْعَلْ). ....

either his intellective or his active powers. The transgressor in deed is depraved and earns anger per the statement of Allah Most High about the deliberate murderer, *Allah is angry with him* (al-Nisā' 4:93) while the transgressor against his intellect is a misguided ignoramus per His statement *What is there, after truth, but error?* (Yūnus 10:32).

It was also read ***wa-lā-ḍ-ḍa'allīn***[361] in keeping with the dialectical form of those who will not countenance any meeting of two quiescent consonants.

[Meaning and recitation of *Āmīn*]

āmīna ⁽*amen*⁾ is a noun for the verb *istajib* ⁽do answer!⁾. It is related that Ibn 'Abbās said:

> I asked the Messenger of Allah—upon him blessings and peace—about its meaning and he said, "Do!"[362]

[361] By Ayyūb al-Sakhtiyānī, substituting a *hamza* for the quiescent *alif* to avoid the latter's meeting with the quiescent first *l*. (*MQ*)

[362] Narrated by al-Tha'labī, *al-Kashf wal-Bayān al-Ma'rūf bi-Tafsīr al-Tha'labī*, ed. Ibn 'Āshūr and Naẓīr al-Sā'idī, 10 vols. (Beirut: Dār Iḥyā' al-Turāth al-'Arabī, 1422/2002) 1:125—and cited by Abū al-Layth al-Samarqandī, Bayān al-Ḥaqq al-Ghaznawī and al-Qurṭubī in theirs—with a flimsy chain (*isnād wāhin*) through al-Kalbī, from Abū Ṣāliḥ, from Ibn 'Abbās cf. Ibn Ḥajar, *Kāfī* (p. 8 §4) and Munāwī, *Fatḥ* (1:106 §9)

بُنِيَ عَلَى الْفَتْحِ كَ(أَيْنَ) لِالْتِقَاءِ السَّاكِنَيْنِ وَجَاءَ مَدُّ أَلِفِه وَقَصْرُهَا؛ قَالَ: [بسيط]

.... ❊ وَيَرْحَمُ اللهُ عَبْداً قَالَ آمِينَا

وَقَالَ: [طَوِيل]

.... ❊ أَمِينَ فَزَادَ اللهُ مَا بَيْنَنَا بُعْدَا

وَلَيْسَ مِنَ الْقُرْآنِ وِفَاقاً؛ لٰكِنْ يُسَنُّ خَتْمُ السُّورَةِ بِهِ، لِقَوْلِهِ عَلَيْهِ الصَّلَاةُ وَالسَّلَامُ: عَلَّمَنِي جِبْرَئِيلُ آمِينَ عِنْدَ فَرَاغِي مِنْ قِرَاءَةِ الْفَاتِحَةِ؛ وَقَالَ: إِنَّهُ كَالْخَتْمِ عَلَى الْكِتَابِ. ....

It has an indeclinable *fatḥa* case ending, like *ayna* ⟨where⟩, due to the meeting of two quiescent consonants.[363] Its initial *alif* can be either long or short. [The poet] said: ["The Outspread"]

and may Allah have mercy on a slave who says āmīn![364]

and ["The Long"]

amīn! then Allah increased our mutual estrangement.[365]

It is not part of the Qur'ān by general agreement; but it is a sunna act to conclude the sura with it per his statements—upon him blessings and peace:

"Jibra'īl ⟨Gabriel⟩ taught me *āmīn* whenever I finish reciting the Fatiha;"[366] and "It is like the seal over the book"[367]

while Ibn Kathīr, *Tafsīr* (1:232) adduces another very weak chain through Juwaybir, from al-Ḍaḥḥāk, from Ibn 'Abbās. The *Lisān* and *Tahdhīb al-Lugha* include this gloss.

363 Translated as "the concurrence of vowelless consonants" by Margoliouth, *Chrestomathia* (p. 1).

364 In *Dīwān Majnūn Laylā*, its first hemistich being *O my Lord! do not deprive me of her love—ever!* (S)

365 Spoken by Khabīr b. al-Aḍbaṭ who had asked Fuṭḥul for a mount and was denied his request, its first hemistich being *Fuṭḥul went far from me for my asking him.* (S)

366 Something similar is narrated in *mursal* mode (on the latter term see note 225) from the Successor Abū Maysara by Ibn Abī Shayba, *Muṣannaf*, ed. Muḥammad 'Awwāma, 26 vols. (Beirut: Dār Qurṭuba, 1428/2006) 5:311 §8044 book of *ṣalāt*.

367 Narrated as a saying of the Companion Abū Zuhayr al-Numayrī by Abū Dāwūd in

وَفِي مَعْنَاهُ قَوْلُ عَلِيٍّ رَضِيَ اللهُ عَنْهُ: (آمِينَ) خَاتَـمُ رَبِّ الْعَـالَمِينَ، خَـتَمَ بِـهِ دُعَاءَ عَبْدِهِ.

يَقُولُهُ الْإِمَامُ؛ وَيَجْهَرُ بِهِ فِي الْجَهْرِيَّةِ، لِمَا رُوِيَ عَنْ وَائِلِ بْنِ حُجْرٍ أَنَّهُ عَلَيْهِ الصَّلَاةُ وَالسَّلَامُ كَانَ، إِذَا قَرَأَ ﴿وَلَا ٱلضَّآلِّينَ﴾، قَالَ: (آمِينَ)، وَرَفَعَ بِهَا صَوْتَهُ. وَعَنْ أَبِي حَنِيفَةَ أَنَّهُ لَا يَقُولُهُ؛ وَالْمَشْهُورُ عَنْهُ أَنَّـهُ يُخْفِيـهِ ــ كَـمَا رَوَاهُ عَبْدُ اللهِ بْنُ مُغَفَّلٍ وَأَنَسٌ.

In the same vein ʿAlī—Allah be well-pleased with him—said, "*Āmīn* is the seal of the Nurturer of the worlds, He has sealed with it His slave's supplication"[368]

The imam says it, pronouncing it aloud in the loud prayer, per Wāʾil b. Ḥujr's narration that he—upon him blessings and peace—would say *āmīn* after reciting ***wa-lā-ḍ-ḍāllīn*** and raise his voice saying it;[369] from Abū Ḥanīfa, however, it is related he does not say it; but the famous position related from him is that he does say it silently, just as narrated from ʿAbd Allāh b. Mughaffal and Anas.[370]

his *Sunan* (*Ṣalāt, al-taʾmīn warāʾ al-imām*) and al-Ṭabarānī in *al-Muʿjam al-Kabīr* (22:296-297 §756) with a fair chain per al-Suyūṭī in *al-Durr al-Manthūr* (1:17).

368 Narrated by al-Ṭabarānī only from Abū Hurayra, from the Prophet in *al-Duʿāʾ*, ed. Muḥammad Saʿīd al-Bukhārī, 3 vols. (Beirut: Dār al-Bashāʾir al-Islāmiyya, 1407/1987) 2:889 §219 with a weak or very weak chain cf. Ibn ʿAdī, *Kāmil* (*s.v.* "Muʾammal b. ʿAbd al-Raḥmān b. al-ʿAbbās") and al-Munāwī, *Fatḥ* (1:109 §12).

369 Narrated through Sufyān al-Thawrī in the *Sunan* and *Musnad* with a fair chain, cf. Ibn Ḥajar, *Kāfī* (p. 8 §6). The same is also authentically related from Abū Hurayra cf. Ibn Faraḥ al-Lakhmī, *Mukhtaṣar Khilāfiyyāt al-Bayhaqī*, ed. Dhayāb ʿAbd al-Karīm ʿAql, 5 vols. (Ryadh: Maktabat al-Rushd, 1417/1997) 2:68; Ibn al-Jawzī, *al-Taḥqīq fī Masāʾil al-Khilāf*, with al-Dhahabī's *Tanqīḥ al-Taḥqīq*, ed. ʿAbd al-Muʿṭī Amīn Qalʿajī, 12 vols. (Aleppo: Dār al-Waʿy al-ʿArabī, 1419/1998) 2:245-248; and al-Munāwī, *Fatḥ* (1:111-112). Shuʿba narrates, also from Wāʾil, that the Prophet remained silent but al-Bayhaqī said: "I know of no dissent among the people of learning that when Sufyān and Shuʿba differ, the chosen position is Sufyān's." Al-Lakhmī, *Mukhtaṣar* (2:64).

370 These two ascriptions are reduplicated from the *Kashshāf* and are unsubstantiated

وَالْمَأْمُومُ يُؤَمِّنُ مَعَهُ، لِقَوْلِهِ عَلَيْهِ الصَّلَاةُ وَالسَّلَامُ: إِذَا قَالَ الْإِمَامُ ﴿وَلَا ٱلضَّآلِّينَ﴾، فَقُولُوا: (آمِينَ)؛ فَإِنَّ الْمَلَائِكَةَ تَقُولُ (آمِينَ)؛ فَمَنْ وَافَقَ تَأْمِينُهُ تَأْمِينَ الْمَلَائِكَةِ، غُفِرَ لَهُ مَا تَقَدَّمَ مِنْ ذَنْبِهِ.

وَعَنْ أَبِي هُرَيْرَةَ - رَضِيَ اللهُ عَنْهُ - أَنَّ رَسُولَ اللهِ ﷺ قَالَ لِأُبَيٍّ: أَلَا أُخْبِرُكَ بِسُورَةٍ لَمْ يُنَزَّلْ فِي التَّوْرَاةِ وَالْإِنْجِيلِ وَالْقُرْآنِ مِثْلُهَا؟ قَالَ: قُلْتُ بَلَى يَا رَسُولَ اللهِ. قَالَ: فَاتِحَةُ الْكِتَابِ؛ إِنَّهَا السَّبْعُ الْمَثَانِي وَالْقُرْآنُ الْعَظِيمُ الَّذِي أُوتِيتُهُ.

The follower says *āmīn* together with him per his saying—upon him blessings and peace: "When the imam says *wa-lā-ḍ-ḍāllīn*, let all of you say *āmīn*; for the angels do say *āmīn*—and if one's *āmīn* coincides with theirs, one's sins are all forgiven."[371]

[Reports on the immense merits of the Fātiḥa]

Related from Abū Hurayra—Allah be well-pleased with him:

> The Messenger of Allah—upon him blessings and peace—said to Ubay: "Shall I not tell you of a sura the like of which was never sent down in all the Torah, the Gospel and the Qur'ān?" Ubay said: "Do tell me, Messenger of Allah!" He said: "The Opening of the Book! Truly it is the Seven Oft-Repeated and the magnificent Qur'ān that I was brought."[372]

according to al-Zayla'ī, Ibn Ḥajar and Abū Zur'a al-'Irāqī; rather, the silent *āmīn* is related from others: 'Alī and Ibn Mas'ūd in al-Ṭabarānī's *Kabīr* (9:301-302 §9304); 'Umar and 'Alī in al-Ṭabarī's *Tahdhīb* according to Ibn al-Turkmānī in *al-Jawhar al-Naqī* printed in the margins of al-Bayhaqī's *al-Sunan al-Kubrā*, 10 vols. (Beirut: Dār al-Fikr, n.d., repr. of the ed. published in Hyderabad, 1344-57/1925-1938) 2:48, 2:58.

[371] Narrated from Abū Hurayra by al-Bukhārī and Muslim. "The wording in [Muḥammad b. Ibrāhīm b. Ja'far] al-Jurjānī's (d. 408/1017) *Amālī* bears the addition 'and his future ones,' and al-Ghazālī relied on the latter wording in *al-Wasīṭ*." (S) Ibn Ḥajar in *Fatḥ al-Bārī* (2:265) showed it to be an aberrant addition.

[372] Narrated by al-Tirmidhī, *Sunan* (*ḥasan ṣaḥīḥ*), al-Nasā'ī in his, and al-Ḥākim who

صح

وَعَنِ ابْنِ عَبَّاسٍ رَضِيَ اللهُ عَنْهُمَا، قَالَ: بَيْنَا رَسُولُ اللهِ ﷺ جَالِسٌ، إِذْ أَتَاهُ مَلَكٌ، فَقَالَ: أَبْشِرْ بِنُورَيْنِ أُوتِيتَهُمَا، لَمْ يُؤْتَهُمَا نَبِيٌّ قَبْلَكَ: فَاتِحَةُ الْكِتَابِ، وَخَوَاتِيمُ سُورَةِ الْبَقَرَةِ؛ لَنْ تَقْرَأَ حَرْفاً مِنْهُمَا إِلَّا أُعْطِيتَهُ.

وَعَنْ حُذَيْفَةَ بْنِ الْيَمَانِ أَنَّ رَسُولَ اللهِ ﷺ قَالَ: إِنَّ الْقَوْمَ لَيَبْعَثُ اللهُ عَلَيْهِمُ الْعَذَابَ حَتْماً مَقْضِيّاً، فَيَقْرَأُ صَبِيٌّ مِنْ صِبْيَانِهِمْ فِي الْكِتَابِ: ﴿ٱلْحَمْدُ لِلَّهِ رَبِّ ٱلْعَٰلَمِينَ﴾، فَيَسْمَعُهُ اللهُ تَعَالَى، فَيَرْفَعُ عَنْهُمْ بِذٰلِكَ الْعَذَابَ أَرْبَعِينَ سَنَةً.

It is also related from Ibn ʿAbbās—Allah be well-pleased with him and his father:

> As the Messenger of Allah was sitting, lo and behold! an angel came to him and said, "Receive the glad tidings of two lights you have been given which no Prophet before you was ever given: the Opening of the Book and the closing verses of Surat al-Baqara. Never will you read a single letter of either but you shall be granted it."[373]

It is also related from Ḥudhayfa b. al-Yamān that the Messenger of Allah—upon him blessings and peace—said:

> Truly, Allah might visit on a people inevitable, destined punishment, whereupon a boy among them shall recite from the Book *Praise be to Allah, the Nurturer of the worlds*; Allah shall hear him and thereby lift from them punishment for forty years.[374]

graded it sound by Muslim's criterion.

[373] Narrated by Muslim in his *Ṣaḥīḥ* (with *baynamā*) and al-Nasāʾī in his *Sunan al-Kubrā* (with *baynā*) among others.

[374] Narrated by al-Thaʿlabī in his *Tafsīr* and forged by one of two "arch-liars" contained in its chain, Aḥmad b. ʿAbd Allāh al-Juwaybārī and Maʾmūn b. Aḥmad al-Harawī according to Abū Zurʿa al-ʿIrāqī; however, it is also related—without mention

سُورَةُ الْبَقَرَةِ مَدَنِيَّةٌ وَآيُهَا مِائَتَانِ وَسَبْعٌ وَثَمَانُونَ

بِسْمِ اللَّهِ الرَّحْمَٰنِ الرَّحِيمِ ﴿الٓمٓ ①﴾ وَسَائِرُ الْأَلْفَاظِ الَّتِي يُتَهَجَّى بِهَا: أَسْمَاءٌ، مُسَمَّيَاتُهَا الْحُرُوفُ الَّتِي رُكِّبَتْ مِنْهَا الْكَلِمُ، لِدُخُولِهَا فِي حَدِّ الْاِسْمِ، وَاعْتِوَارِ مَا يُخَصُّ بِهِ: مِنَ التَّعْرِيفِ، وَالتَّنْكِيرِ، وَالْجَمْعِ، وَالتَّصْغِيرِ، وَنَحْوِ ذٰلِكَ عَلَيْهَا؛ وَبِهِ صَرَّحَ الْخَلِيلُ وَأَبُو عَلِيٍّ.

[2:] The Sura of the Cow

Medinan, numbering 287 verses[375]

bi-smi-l-lāhi-r-raḥmāni-r-raḥīm ⁽*In the Name of the One God, the All-Beneficent, the Most Merciful*⁾.

[Definition of the Disjointed Letters]

[2:1] **alif, lām, mīm** ⁽A-L-M⁾ and the rest of the vocables[376] used for spelling are nouns—their referents[377] being the letters out of which words are formed—because they fall within the definition of nouns and share in what is peculiar to them—definiteness, indefiniteness, plural forms, diminutive forms and the like—as stated explicitly by al-Khalīl and Abū ʿAlī.

of the 40-year span—as a saying of the Successors Thābit b. ʿAjlān (in al-Dārimī's *Sunan, Kitāb Faḍāʾil al-Qurʾān, Bāb Taʿāhud al-Qurʾān*) and Mālik b. Dīnār (in Aḥmad's *Zuhd*), and the status of the latter is that of a Prophetic saying since its content cannot be deduced rationally but can only be reported from a higher source. (S) When a contemporary of Mullā ʿAlī al-Qārī named Sayyid Ṣibghat Allāh b. Rawḥ Allāh b. Jamāl Allāh al-Barwajī al-Madanī al-Ḥusaynī al-Naqshbandī (d. 1015/1606) declared that this hadith was forged, al-Qārī defended al-Bayḍāwī in a brief treatise entitled *Ṣanʿat Allāh fī Ṣīghat Ṣibghat Allāh*.

375 N: سُورَةُ الْبَقَرَةِ مَدَنِيَّةٌ وَآيُهَا مايتَانِ وَسَبْعٌ وَثَمَانُونَ آيَةً B omits آيَةً Ak, ε, I, K, Kh, L, T, MM, U, Ul, Z: ditto, without vowelization. R: وَهِيَ Q: سورة البقرة مائتان وثمانون وسبع آيات مدنية α, β: blank (absentee illuminator). "There is disagreement as to the number of its verses. Some said 286, some 287 or 285." (Kh)

376 Cf. Cachia, *Fawātiḥ* (p. 219).

377 In Cachia, *Fawātiḥ*: "denominates."

وَمَا رَوَى ابْنُ مَسْعُودٍ أَنَّهُ ـ عَلَيْهِ الصَّلَاةُ وَالسَّلَامُ ـ قَالَ: مَنْ قَرَأَ حَرْفاً مِنْ كِتَابِ اللهِ، فَلَهُ حَسَنَةٌ؛ وَالحَسَنَةُ بِعَشْرِ أَمْثَالِهَا؛ لَا أَقُولُ: ﴿الٓمٓ﴾ حَرْفٌ؛ بَلْ: أَلِفٌ حَرْفٌ، وَلَامٌ حَرْفٌ، وَمِيمٌ حَرْفٌ؛ فَالْمُرَادُ بِهِ: غَيْرُ الْمَعْنَى الَّذِي اصْطُلِحَ عَلَيْهِ، فَإِنَّ تَخْصِيصَهُ بِهِ عُرْفٌ مُجَدَّدٌ؛ بَلِ: الْمَعْنَى اللُّغَوِيُّ؛ وَلَعَلَّهُ سَمَّاهُ بِاسْمِ مَدْلُولِهِ. وَلَمَّا كَانَتْ مُسَمَّيَاتُهَا حُرُوفاً وُحْدَاناً ـ وَهِيَ مُرَكَّبَةٌ ـ: صُدِّرَتْ بِهَا، لِتَكُونَ تَأْدِيَتُهَا بِالْمُسَمَّى أَوَّلَ مَا يَقْرَعُ السَّمْعَ.

وَاسْتُعِيرَتِ الْهَمْزَةُ مَكَانَ الْأَلِفِ، لِتَعَذُّرِ الْاِبْتِدَاءِ بِهَا.

As for Ibn Mas'ūd's report that the Prophet—upon him blessings and peace—said,

> Whoever reads one letter of the Book of Allah has one good deed, and the good deed is [repaid] tenfold; I do not say *alif lām mīm* is a letter, but rather, *alif* is a letter, *lām* is a letter, and *mīm* is a letter:[378]

the intent here is other than the technical sense [of noun]—for such specific use is a modern convention—but rather the lexical sense; and he was probably naming it by the name of its referent.[379] Since the referents are discrete letters while they themselves are compounds, the latter [nouns] were made to begin with those [letters] so that their own rendering of the referents be the first thing heard.

The *hamza* was borrowed to replace the *alif* due to the impracticability of beginning with the latter.

[378] Narrated by al-Tirmidhī (*ḥasan ṣaḥīḥ gharīb*), al-Dārimī and Sa'īd b. Manṣūr in their *Sunan* (*Faḍā'il al-Qur'ān*) among others, all of them with *wa-lākin* instead of *bal*.

[379] "He followed the Imām [= al-Rāzī] in this; and to date its meaning remains unclear to me." (Sk) "The wording of the Imām was: 'He named it *ḥarf* figuratively since it is the name of the *ḥarf*, and the naming of one member of an inseparable pair as the other is a well-known trope (*majāz mashhūr*).'" (S) Cf. al-Rāzī, *Tafsīr* (2:2). "That the vocable is a name literally and a letter figuratively is not far-fetched." (Q)

وَهِيَ ـ مَا لَمْ تَلِهَا الْعَوَامِلُ ـ مَوْقُوفَةٌ، خَالِيَةٌ عَنِ الإِعْرَابِ، لِفَقْدِ مُوْجِبِهِ وَمُقْتَضِيهِ؛ لٰكِنَّهَا قَابِلَةٌ إِيَّاهُ وَمُعَرَّضَةٌ لَهُ، إِذْ لَمْ تُنَاسِبْ مَبْنِيَّ الْأَصْلِ ـ وَلِذٰلِكَ قِيلَ: ﴿صٓ﴾، وَ﴿قٓ﴾، مَجْمُوعاً فِيهِمَا بَيْنَ السَّاكِنَيْنِ ـ وَلَمْ تُعَامَلْ مُعَامَلَةَ (أَيْنَ) وَ(هٰؤُلَاءِ).

ثُمَّ إِنَّ مُسَمَّيَاتِهَا، لَمَّا كَانَتْ عُنْصُرَ الْكَلَامِ وَبَسَائِطَهُ الَّتِي يَتَرَكَّبُ مِنْهَا: اِفْتُتِحَتِ السُّورَةُ بِطَائِفَةٍ مِنْهَا، إِيقَاظاً لِمَنْ تُحُدِّيَ بِالْقُرْآنِ، وَتَنْبِيهاً عَلَى أَنَّ

Those [nouns], as long as they are ungoverned, are at a full stop and devoid of inflection since they are free of what compels it or dictates it.[380] However, they accept it and stand ready for it as they have nothing in common with indeclinables—hence it was said that in *ṣād* (Ṣād 38:1) and *qāf* (Qāf 50:1) both there is a meeting of two quiescent consonants—and thus were not treated like *ayna* ⟨where⟩ and *hā'ulā'i* ⟨those⟩.[381]

[Interpretation of the Disjointed Letters][382]

As for the referents themselves, since they form the constituents of speech and its basic building-blocks, the sura was opened with a group of them in order to awaken those whom the Qur'ān defied and as an intimation that ....

[380] "al-Ṭībī said: 'Namely, jointure' (*al-tarkīb*)" (S). "I.e., what imposes desinential syntax (*i'rāb*), namely, the regent (*al-'āmil*)" (Iṣ). Hence we do not read, e.g., *alifun lāmun mīmun*, or *ṣādun* or *qāfun* in the nominative.
[381] "Their quiescence stems from pausing (*sukūnuhā sukūn waqf*), for they deemed it permissible to have a meeting of quiescent consonants in pauses, even if the pause is unmarked (*wa-law 'alā ghayri ḥida*)." (Q) "Contrary to [words] whose quiescence is mandatory, in which case that is impermissible and the case becomes either *fatḥ* as in *ayna*, or with prepositional attraction (*jarr*) as in *hā'ulā'i*, or with *ḍamm* as in *ḥaythu* ⟨whereby⟩." (Sk)
[382] Or "monogrammes," cf. Sacy, *Anthologie* (p. vi).

الْمَتْلُوَّ عَلَيْهِمْ: كَلَامٌ مَنْظُومٌ مِمَّا يُنَظِّمُونَ مِنْهُ كَلَامَهُمْ؛ فَلَوْ كَانَ مِنْ عِنْدِ غَيْرِ اللهِ، لَمَا عَجَزُوا عَنْ آخِرِهِمْ - مَعَ تَظَاهُرِهِمْ وَقُوَّةِ فَصَاحَتِهِمْ - عَنِ الْإِتْيَانِ بِمَا يُدَانِيهِ؛ وَلِيَكُونَ أَوَّلُ مَا يَقْرَعُ الْأَسْمَاعَ مُسْتَقِلًّا بِنَوْعٍ مِنَ الْإِعْجَازِ. فَإِنَّ النُّطْقَ بِأَسْمَاءِ الْحُرُوفِ مُخْتَصٌّ بِمَنْ خَطَّ وَدَرَسَ؛ فَأَمَّا مِنَ الْأُمِّيِّ الَّذِي لَمْ يُخَالِطِ الْكُتَّابَ: فَمُسْتَبْعَدٌ، مُسْتَغْرَبٌ، خَارِقٌ لِلْعَادَةِ - كَالْكِتَابَةِ وَالتِّلَاوَةِ - سِيَّمَا وَقَدْ رَاعَى فِي ذٰلِكَ مَا يَعْجِزُ عَنْهُ الْأَدِيبُ الْأَرِيبُ، الْفَائِقُ فِي فَنِّهِ! وَهُوَ أَنَّـــهُ أَوْرَدَ فِي هٰذِهِ الْفَوَاتِحِ أَرْبَعَـــةَ عَشَرَ اِسْماً هِيَ نِصْفُ أَسَامِي حُرُوفِ الْمُعْجَمِ ....

what is being recited to them[383] is speech composed of the same stuff of which they compose their own speech. Hence, if it were from other than Allah, they would not have remained, to the last one of them, incapable—with their mutual abetment and the power of their pure idiom—to produce something approaching it. The very first thing heard was thus meant to stand out on its own with a kind of incapacitation: uttering the nouns of letters is the province of one who has written and studied; but from an illiterate who never sat at the feet of preceptors it is completely unexpected, strange to behold, and against all norms—as are writing and recitation—particularly since he had complied, in so doing, with rules that leave helpless even the most accomplished littérateur who surpasses all others in his art! Namely, he brought up, in those openers, fourteen nouns[384] which are half of the alphabetical letters ....

[383] α, A, Ak, β, B, ÇZ, D, ε, F, I, Kh, N, P, Q, Sk, S, T, U: المتلو عليهم AQ, H, K, L, MM, Ul, Z: اصل المتلو عليهم gloss.

[384] *Alif, lām, mīm, ṣād, rā', kāf, hā', yā', 'ayn, ṭā', sīn, ḥā', qāf*, and *nūn*. (Q)

ـ إِنْ لَمْ يُعَدَّ فِيهَا الْأَلِفُ حَرْفاً بِرَأْسِهَا ـ فِي تِسْعٍ وَعِشْرِينَ سُورَةٍ بِعَدَدِهَا إِذَا عُدَّ فِيهَا الْأَلِفُ الْأَصْلِيَّةُ، مُشْتَمِلَةً عَلَى أَنْصَافِ أَنْوَاعِهَا.

(١) فَذَكَرَ مِنَ الْمَهْمُوسَةِ ـ وَهِيَ مَا يَضْعُفُ الِاعْتِمَادُ عَلَى مَخْرَجِهِ، وَيَجْمَعُهَا (سَتَشْحَثُكَ خَصَفَهْ) ـ نِصْفَهَا: الحَاءُ، وَالْهَاءُ، وَالصَّادُ، وَالسِّينُ، وَالْكَافُ؛

—if we do not count *alif* one of them as a letter on its own[385]—in twenty-nine suras, the same number as them—if we count among them the pristine *alif*[386]—and comprising their most famous variants.

[Phonemes and their attributes]

Thus, he mentioned:

I. Of the voiceless phonemes—those with a weak articulation-point, which are joined in the phrase *sa-tashḥathuka khaṣafah* ⁽Khaṣafa will implore you⁾—one half, namely *ḥā'*, *hā'*, *ṣād*, *sīn*, and *kāf*,[387]

[385] The number of letters in the Arabic alphabet varies between 28 and 29 depending on making the *hamza* the same as the *alif* or counting them as distinct letters. "Ibn al-Jinnī said in *Nashr al-Ṣinā'a*: 'Know that the symbols of the alphabetical letters according to the entirety of the scholars are twenty-nine letters, beginning with *alif* and ending with *yā'* if we follow the most widespread arrangement of the alphabet, except for Abū al-'Abbās al-Mubarrid who counted them as 28, beginning with *bā'* and leaving out the *alif* at the beginning, saying it is a *hamza* which is not fixed as a single symbol, and it does not have a stable symbol but is written as a *yā'*, a *wāw* or an *alif* depending on circumstance.'" (Q)

[386] I.e. the unvowelized *alif*. (Q)

[387] "Voicelessness (*al-hams*) means, lexically, concealment (*al-khafā'*) and in nomenclature the concealment of the phoneme's vocalization due to its weakness... with the venting of breath alongside its utterance. The voiceless phonemes are the 10 gathered in the phrase *sakata fa-ḥaththahu shakhṣun* ("he fell silent so some person encouraged him"): *sīn, kāf, tā', fā', ḥā', thā', hā', shīn, khā'*, and *ṣād*." Maḥmūd Khalīl al-Ḥuṣarī (Shaykh al-Maqārī' al-Miṣriyya), *Aḥkām Qirā'at al-Qur'ān al-Karīm*, ed. Muḥammad

(٢) وَمِنَ الْبَوَاقِي المَجْهُورَةِ: نِصْفُهَا، يَجْمَعُهُ (لَنْ يُقْطَعَ أَمْرٌ)؛

(٣) وَمِنَ الشَّدِيدَةِ - الثَّمَانِيَةِ المَجْمُوعَةِ فِي (أَجَدْتَ طَبَقَكَ) -: أَرْبَعَةٌ، يَجْمَعُهَا (أَقِطُكَ)؛

(٤) وَمِنَ الْبَوَاقِي - الرِّخْوَةِ -: عَشَرَةٌ، يَجْمَعُهَا (حَمُسَ عَلَى نَصْرِهِ)؛

II. and of the remaining, outspoken phonemes, one half which are gathered in the phrase *lan yuqṭaʿa amrun* (no matter shall be decided);[388]

III. of the eight hard phonemes gathered in *ajadta ṭabaqak* (You have made a very good dish),[389] the four that are in *aqiṭuk* (your cheese),[390]

IV. and of the remaining, [21] limp phonemes, ten which are gathered in the phrase *ḥamusa ʿala naṣrihi* (he defended him zealously);[391]

Ṭalḥa Bilāl Minyār, 4th ed. (Cairo: al-Maktabat al-Makkiyya; Beirut: Dār al-Bashāʾir al-Islāmiyya, 1999) p. 83, hereafter *Aḥkām*. Cachia has "'mumbled' or 'whispered.'"

[388] I.e., *lām, nūn, yāʾ, qāf, ṭāʾ, ʿayn,* the vowelized *hamza, mīm,* and *rāʾ*. "Voicedness (*al-jahr*) is, lexically, the loud, strong voice. In nomenclature, it is the entrapment of breath at the utterance of a phoneme due to its strength and the strength of pressure on it at its exit (*makhraj*). It has 19 phonemes—everything other than the voiceless." *Aḥkām* (p. 84).

[389] I.e., *hamza, jīm, dāl, qāf, ṭāʾ, bāʾ, kāf* and *tāʾ*, also grouped in the phrase *ajid qaṭṭin bakat,* "it bothers me that Qaṭṭ wept" in the *Jazariyya,* section on the attributes of phonemes cf. Ṣalāḥ Ṣāliḥ Sayf, *al-ʿIqd al-Mufīd fī ʿIlm al-Tajwīd*, ed. Muḥammad Faqīr al-Afghānī (Amman: al-Maktabat al-Islāmiyya, 1987) p. 73. "Hardness is 'strength' lexically, and in nomenclature it means the complete entrapment of the voice passage at the utterance of the phoneme due to the full strength of its pressure at the exit. The hard phonemes are the eight gathered in the phrase *ajid qaṭṭin bakat.*" *Aḥkām* (p. 85).

[390] I.e., *hamza, qāf, ṭāʾ,* and *kāf*.

[391] I.e., *ḥāʾ, mīm, sīn, ʿayn, lām, alif, nūn, ṣād, rāʾ* and *hāʾ*. "Limpness (*rikhāwa*) is lexically 'softness' (*al-līn*) and, in nomenclature, the softness of the letter and of the voice

(٥) وَمِنَ الْمُطْبَقَةِ ـ الَّتِي هِيَ الصَّادُ، وَالضَّادُ، وَالطَّاءُ، وَالظَّاءُ ـ: نِصْفَهَا؛

(٦) وَمِنَ الْبَوَاقِي ـ الْمُنْفَتِحَةِ ـ: نِصْفَهَا؛

(٧) وَمِنَ الْقَلْقَلَةِ ـ وَهِيَ حُرُوفٌ تَضْطَرِبُ عِنْدَ خُرُوجِهَا، وَيَجْمَعُهَا (قَدْ طَبِجَ) ـ نِصْفَهَا الْأَقَلَّ لِقِلَّتِهَا؛

(٨) وَمِنَ اللِّينَتَيْنِ: الْيَاءُ، لِأَنَّهَا أَقَلُّ ثِقَلاً؛

V. Half of the over-covered phonemes, which are *ṣād, ḍād, ṭā'*, and *ẓā'*,[392]

VI. and half of the remaining, opened-up phonemes;

VII. Of the plosive phonemes—namely, the letters that shake upon exit and which are gathered in the phrase *qad ṭabija* ‹he finished beating the drum›—the lesser half due to their scarcity;[393]

VIII. Of the two soft phonemes the *yā'* because it is less heavy;[394]

passage during utterance due to its weakness and the weakness of the pressure on it at the exit. Its phonemes are 16, namely, all of the letters other than the eight hard ones already mentioned and the five median ones [of the fifth attribute, mediacy between hardness and limpness]... gathered in the phrase *lin 'Umar* ‹be lenient, 'Umar!›—namely *lām, nūn, 'ayn, mīm,* and *rā'*." *Aḥkām* (p. 86). The Qadi lumps together the median and limp phonemes while al-Jazarī differentiates them.

392 "Over-covering (*al-iṭbāq*) is lexically 'fastening' (*al-ilṣāq*) and, in nomenclature, the fastening of part of the tongue to the area of the upper palate nearest it, entrapping the sound between the two. Its phonemes are *ṣād, ḍād, ṭā'* and *ẓā'*." *Aḥkām* (p. 93).

393 "Plosiveness (*al-qalqala*) is lexically movement and agitation (*al-taḥarruk wal-iḍṭirāb*) and, in nomenclature, the great agitation of the sound of the quiescent phoneme at its exit so that it is fully articulated. Its letters are the five gathered in the phrase *quṭbu jaddin* ‹"pivot of fortune"› or *jiddin* ‹"earnestness"›, namely *qāf, ṭā', bā', jīm,* and *dāl*." *Aḥkām* (p. 98). Cachia has "resonant or movent" phonemes.

394 "Softness (*al-līn*) is lexically ease (*al-suhūla*) and, in nomenclature, the facility of the phoneme's exit without effort for the tongue. It is the attribute of two phonemes, the quiescent *wāw* and *yā'* following *fatḥa*, e.g. *khawf* and *quraysh*." *Aḥkām* (p. 103).

(٩) وَمِنَ الْمُسْتَعْلِيَةِ ـ وَهِيَ الَّتِي يَتَصَعَّدُ الصَّوْتُ بِهَا فِي الْحَنَكِ الْأَعْلَى، وَهِيَ سَبْعَةٌ: الْقَافُ، وَالصَّادُ، وَالطَّاءُ، وَالْخَاءُ، وَالْغَيْنُ، وَالضَّادُ، وَالظَّاءُ ـ: نِصْفُهَا الْأَقَلَّ؛

(١٠) وَمِنَ الْبَوَاقِي ـ الْمُنْخَفِضَةِ ـ: نِصْفُهَا؛

(١١) وَمِنْ حُرُوفِ الْبَدَلِ ـ وَهِيَ أَحَدَ عَشَرَ عَلَى مَا ذَكَرَهُ سِيبَوَيْهِ، وَاخْتَارَهُ ابْنُ جِنِّيٍّ، وَيَجْمَعُهَا (أَجِدُ طَوَيْتَ مِنْهَا) ـ: السِّتَّةَ الشَّائِعَةَ الْمَشْهُورَةَ، الَّتِي يَجْمَعُهَا (أَهْطَمَيْنِ)؛ وَقَدْ زَادَ بَعْضُهُمْ سَبْعَةً أُخْرَى، ....

IX. Of the self-elevated phonemes—those whose sound rises up in the upper palate, which are seven: *qāf, ṣād, ṭā', khā', ghayn, ḍād*, and *ẓā'*—their lesser half,[395]

X. and half of the remaining [22] depressed phonemes;[396]

XI. Of the letters of permutation—which are eleven according to Sībawayh and as chosen by Ibn Jinnī, gathered in the phrase *ajidu ṭawayta minhā* ⟨it bothers me that you are avoiding her⟩—the famous prevailing six that are gathered in the word *ahṭamayn* ⟨Two Crushers⟩,[397] while others add seven more: ....

[395] I.e., *qāf, ṣād* and *ṭā'*. "Self-elevation (*isti'lā'*) is lexically 'height' (*'ulūw*) and 'altitude' (*irtifā'*) and, in nomenclature, the tongue's rising to the upper palate upon uttering. Its phonemes are the seven gathered in the phrase *khuṣṣa ḍaghṭin qiẓ* ⟨live in a narrow bamboo hut!⟩ [= be content with little], namely, *khā', ṣād, ḍād, ghayn, ṭā', qāf,* and *ẓā'*. Ibn al-Jazarī said in the *Nashr*: 'The correct view is that they are the letters of amplification (*ḥurūf al-tafkhīm*), and the highest of them is *ṭā'*.'" *Aḥkām* (p. 90).

[396] "Subsidence (*istifāl*) is lexically lowering (*al-inkhifāḍ*) and, in nomenclature, the lowering of the tongue to the bottom of the mouth upon the phoneme's exit from the palate. Its phonemes are 22: all the letters other than the seven elevated ones already cited." *Aḥkām* (p. 91). I.e., *alif, ḥā', rā', sīn, 'ayn, kāf, lām, mīm, nūn, hā'* and *yā'*.

[397] I.e., *hamza, hā', ṭā', mīm, yā'* and *nūn*. *Ahṭamayn* is a dual name for two moun-

وَهِيَ: اللَّامُ فِي (أُصَيْلَال)، وَالصَّادُ وَالزَّايُ فِي (صِرَاط) وَ(زِرَاط)، وَالْفَاءُ فِي (أَجْدَاف)، وَالْعَيْنُ فِي (أَعِنَّ)، وَالثَّاءُ فِي (ثُرُوغِ الدَّلْوِ)، وَالْبَاءُ فِي (بَا اسْمُكَ)، حَتَّى صَارَتْ ثَمَانِيَةَ عَشَرَ؛ وَقَدْ ذَكَرَ مِنْهَا تِسْعَةً: السِّتَّةُ الْمَذْكُورَةُ، وَاللَّامُ، وَالصَّادُ، وَالْعَيْنُ.

(١٢) وَمِمَّا يُدْغَمُ فِي مِثْلِهِ، وَلَا يُدْغَمُ فِي الْمُقَارِبِ ـ وَهِيَ ....

the *lām* [for the final nūn] in *uṣaylāl*,[398] the *ṣād* and *zāy* in *ṣirāṭ* and *zirāṭ*,[399] the *fā'* [for the *thā'*] in *ajdāf*,[400] the *'ayn* [for the initial hamza] in *a'an*,[401] the *thā'* [for the *fā'*] in *thurūgh al-dalwi* ⸢the emptying of the pail⸣, and the *bā'* [for the *mīm*] in *bā-smuk?*[402] adding up to eighteen, of which He has mentioned nine: the six already mentioned then *lām, ṣād,* and *'ayn*.

XII. Of the phonemes that are contracted when geminated, but not when paired with an approximate phoneme—which are......

tains (Z). Among the similes Arabs use: "More crushing than locusts" (*aḥṭam min jarād*). Ibn Ḥamdūn, *al-Tadhkirat al-Ḥamdūniyya*, 10 vols. (Beirut: Dār Ṣādir, 1417/1997) 7:29 §94. Cachia's rendering as "two with great powers of digestion" (*Fawātiḥ* p. 223), coined from the literal meaning of *haṭama*, "to digest fast" (cf. *Lisān al-'Arab*, s.v. *h-ṭ-m*), is unsupported by usage. Permutation (or "substitution") is because *hamza* replaces *wāw*, e.g. *awāṣil* instead of *wawāṣil* as the pl. of *wāṣila*; *jīm* replaces *yā'*, e.g. *Abī 'Alijj* instead of *Abī 'Alīy*; *dāl* replaces *tā'*, e.g. *fuzdu, ijdama'ū* instead of *fuztu, ijtama'ū*; *ṭā'* replaces *tā'*, e.g. *iṣṭabir* instead of *iṣtabir*; *wāw* replaces *yā'*, e.g. *mūqin* instead of *muyqin*; or vice-versa, e.g. *mīqāt* instead of *miwqāt*; *tā'* replaces *wāw*, e.g. *tukhma* instead of *wukhma*; *mīm* replaces *wāw*, e.g. *fam* [instead of *fū*], etc. (Z)

398 Diminutive form of *aṣlān*, pl. of *aṣīl* ⸢dusk⸣, *uṣaylān*, with *n-l* permutation (S, Z, Q).

399 See note 340.

400 A *fā'-thā'* permutation in *ajdāth*, the plural of *jadath*, "grave." (Z)

401 I.e., the permutation of the initial hamza of *inna, anna, in* and *an* into a *'ayn*. (Q) "This is known as *'an'anatu Tamīm* ⸢the *'an*-twang of Tamīm⸣—they say *ashhadu 'anna Muḥammadan rasūlu-l-Lāh*." (S, Kh)

402 A, B, β, F, Kh, N, P, R, S, Sk, Ul: بَا اسمُكَ α, Ak, AQ, ÇZ, D, ε, H, I, K, L, MM, Q, T, U, Z: باسمك Orig. *mā-smuk* ⸢what is your name?⸣, a Māzin dialect permutation (S).

خَمْسَةَ عَشَرَ: الْهَمْزَةُ، وَالْهَاءُ، وَالْعَيْنُ، وَالصَّادُ، وَالطَّاءُ، وَالْمِيمُ، وَالْيَاءُ، وَالْخَاءُ، وَالْغَيْنُ، وَالضَّادُ، وَالْفَاءُ، وَالظَّاءُ، وَالشِّينُ، وَالزَّايُ، وَالْوَاوُ ـ: نِصْفَهَا الأَقَلَّ.

(١٣) وَمِمَّا يُدْغَمُ فِيهِمَا ـ وَهِيَ الثَّلَاثَةَ عَشَرَ الْبَاقِيَةُ ـ: نِصْفَهَا الأَكْثَرَ: الْحَاءُ، وَالْقَافُ، وَالْكَافُ، وَالرَّاءُ، وَالسِّينُ، وَاللَّامُ، وَالنُّونُ، لِمَا فِي الإِدْغَامِ مِنَ الْخِفَّةِ وَالْفَصَاحَةِ؛

(١٤) وَمِنَ الأَرْبَعَةِ الَّتِي لَا تُدْغَمُ فِيمَا يُقَارِبُهَا وَيُدْغَمُ فِيهَا مُقَارِبُهَا ـ وَهِيَ: الْمِيمُ، وَالزَّايُ، وَالسِّينُ، وَالْفَاءُ ـ: نِصْفَهَا.

(١٥) وَلَمَّا كَانَتْ الْحُرُوفُ الذَّلْقِيَّةُ ـ الَّتِي يُعْتَمَدُ عَلَيْهَا بِذَلْقِ اللِّسَانِ، وَهِيَ

fifteen: *hamza, hāʾ, ʿayn, ṣād, ṭāʾ, mīm, yāʾ, khāʾ, ghayn, ḍād, fāʾ, ẓāʾ, shīn, zāy,* and *wāw*—the lesser half;[403]

XIII. of those that are contracted in either case—namely, the remaining thirteen letters—the greater half: *ḥāʾ, qāf, kāf, rāʾ, sīn, lām,* and *nūn*, for the nimbleness and chasteness of contraction;

XIV. and of the four that are not contracted into their similar phonemes but into which their similar phonemes are contracted—namely, *mīm, zāy, sīn,* and *fāʾ*—half;[404]

XV. Since the tipped[405] phonemes that are relied upon because of[406] the tongue-tip—namely ....

[403] I.e., the first seven mentioned, the *hamza* counting as an *alif*. Cachia renders *yudgham* as "[converted then] incorporated," Sacy simply as "s'insèrent."

[404] I.e., *mīm* and *sīn*.

[405] *Dhalaqa dhalqan wa-dhalāqatan; dhalqīy, mudhlaq, dhawlaqīy*: *Aḥkām* (p. 75, 95).

[406] *Al ḥurūf al-dhalqiyya al-latī yuʿtamadu ʿalayhā bi-dhalqi al-lisān*. The *bāʾ* in *bi-dhalqi* is illative (*sababiyya*), not instrumental (*āliyya*), as the edged phonemes do not

سِتَّةٌ، يَجْمَعُهَا (رَبٌّ مُنْفِلٌ) ـ،

(١٦) وَالْحَلْقِيَّةُ ـ الَّتِي هِيَ الْحَاءُ، وَالْخَاءُ، وَالْعَيْنُ، وَالْغَيْنُ، وَالْهَاءُ، وَالْهَمْزَةُ ـ كَثِيرَةَ الْوُقُوعِ فِي الْكَلَامِ: ذَكَرَ ثُلُثَيْهِمَا.

(١٧) وَلَمَّا كَانَتْ أَبْنِيَةُ الْمَزِيدِ لَا تَتَجَاوَزُ عَنِ السُّبَاعِيَّةِ، ذَكَرَ مِنَ الزَّوَائِدِ الْعَشَرَةِ ـ الَّتِي يَجْمَعُهَا (الْيَوْمَ تَنْسَاهُ) ـ ....

the six gathered in the phrase *rabbun munfil* ⁽a lord lavishing spoils⁾[407]—

XVI. and the laryngeal phonemes—namely *ḥā', khā', 'ayn, ghayn, hā'* and *hamza*—are used very frequently in speech, He mentioned two thirds of them.[408]

XVII. Finally, since the augmentative forms are at most septiliteral,[409] He mentioned seven of the ten augmentative letters gathered in the phrase *al-yawma tansāh* ⁽today you will forget him⁾

necessarily involve the tongue-tip but require its proximity. (Q) Cachia reads *dhalaqī* which he calls "liquid" and asserts they should not be confused with the *dhawlaqiyya*, faulting both Bayḍāwī and Wright [1:5] here, cf. *Fawātiḥ* (p. 223-224n., misunderstands the *bā'*) and *Monitor* (p. 4, 38); see in their defense al-Ḥuṣarī as cited in the previous footnote and Aḥmad al-Ḥalwānī, *al-Laṭā'if al-Bahiyya Sharḥ al-Minḥat al-Saniyya*, ed. Muḥammad Muṭī' al-Ḥāfiẓ (Damascus: Maktabat al-Imām al-Awzā'ī, 1426 /2006) p. 48: "*wa tusammā... dhalqiyya wa-dhawlaqiyya.*" Sacy has "lingual."

407 "Pointedness (*dhalāqa*) lexically means the tongue's sharpness, eloquence and facility, and is usually applied to the edge of a thing and its extremity. In nomenclature it means the reliance of a letter on the edge of the tongue or the edge of the lip—both their edges—upon utterance. Its letters are called *ḥurūf al-dhalāqa, al-ḥurūf al-dhulq* and *al-ḥurūf al-mudhlaqa*. They are the six gathered in the phrase *farra min lubb* ⁽"he fled from the wise⁾. Its letters are *fā', rā', mīm, nūn, lām* and *bā'*." *Aḥkām* (p. 95).

408 I.e., *alif, bā', ḥā', rā', 'ayn, mīm, nūn,* and *hā'*. Cachia has "gutturals" after Sacy.

409 I.e., in nouns, excluding the feminine *hā'* and both the dual and affiliative (*nisba*-related) suffixes (Q 1:343), cf. al-Mubarrad, *Kitāb al-Muqtaḍab*, ed. Muḥammad 'Abd al-Khāliq 'Uḍayma (Cairo: Lajnat Iḥyā' al-Turāth al-Islāmī, 1415/1994) 1:191-198.

سَبْعَةَ أَحْرُفٍ مِنْهَا، تَنْبِيهاً عَلَى ذٰلِكَ.

وَلَوِ اسْتَقْرَيْتَ الْكَلِمَ وَتَرَاكِيبَهَا، وَجَدْتَ الْحُرُوفَ الْمَتْرُوكَةَ مِنْ كُلِّ جِنْسٍ مَكْثُورَةً بِالْمَذْكُورَةِ.

ثُمَّ إِنَّهُ ذَكَرَهَا مُفْرَدَةً، وَثُنَائِيَّةً، وَثُلَاثِيَّةً، وَرُبَاعِيَّةً، وَخُمَاسِيَّةً: إِيذَاناً بِأَنَّ الْمُتَحَدَّى بِهِ مُرَكَّبٌ مِنْ كَلِمَاتِهِمْ، الَّتِي أُصُولُهَا كَلِمَاتٌ مُفْرَدَةٌ، وَمُرَكَّبَةٌ مِنْ حَرْفَيْنِ فَصَاعِداً، إِلَى الْخَمْسَةِ.

وَذَكَرَ: (١) ثَلَاثَ مُفْرَدَاتٍ فِي ثَلَاثِ سُوَرٍ؛ لِأَنَّهَا تُوجَدُ فِي الْأَقْسَامِ الثَّلَاثَةِ: الْاِسْمِ، وَالْفِعْلِ، وَالْحَرْفِ؛

to underscore that fact.[410]

[Syllabic combinations of the *Fawātiḥ* and their significance]

If you were to inductively survey the language and its combinations you would find that the letters that were left out, in each category, are less in number than those that were mentioned.[411]

Further, He mentioned them single, paired, in threes, in fours and in fives: as a proclamation that the object of the challenge was formed of their own words, whose bases are single-letter words and words formed of two or more letters up to five.

Thus He mentioned:

1. three monoliterals in three suras, because they are found in the three parts of speech: the noun, the verb, and the particle;

[410] I.e., *alif, lām, yā', mīm, nūn, sīn,* and *hā'*. Cachia has "augmented forms [of nouns or verbs]," Sacy "*crémens* ou *lettres accessoires*" by which he means incremented. On *istiqrā'* ‹inductive survey› see the meticulous definition in al-Khafājī (1:277).

[411] "The upshot is, the letters mentioned in the *fawātiḥ* are more frequently used in the speech of the pure Arabs and their language than what was left out." (Q)

(٢) وَأَرْبَعَ ثُنَائِيَّاتٍ ـ لِأَنَّهَا تَكُونُ فِي الْحَرْفِ بِلَا حَذْفٍ، كَ(بَلْ)؛ وَفِي الْفِعْلِ بِحَذْفٍ، كَ(قُلْ)؛ وَفِي الِاسْمِ بِغَيْرِ حَذْفٍ، كَ(مَنْ)؛ وَبِهِ، كَ(دَمْ) ــ فِي تِسْعِ سُوَرٍ، لِوُقُوعِهَا فِي كُلِّ وَاحِدٍ مِنَ الْأَقْسَامِ الثَّلَاثَةِ، عَلَى ثَلَاثَةِ أَوْجُهٍ:

(أ) فَفِي الْأَسْمَاءِ: (مَنْ)، وَ(إِذْ)، وَ(ذُو)؛

(ب) وَفِي الْأَفْعَالِ: (قُلْ)، وَ(بِعْ)، وَ(خَفْ).

(ت) وَفِي الْحُرُوفِ: (مِنْ)، وَ(إِنْ)، وَ(مُذْ) عَلَى لُغَةِ مَنْ جَرَّ بِهَا.

(٣) وَثَلَاثَ ثُلَاثِيَّاتٍ ـ لِمَجِيئِهَا فِي الْأَقْسَامِ الثَّلَاثَةِ ـ فِي ثَلَاث عَشْرَةَ سُورَةٍ، تَنْبِيهاً عَلَى أَنَّ أُصُولَ الْأَبْنِيَةِ الْمُسْتَعْمَلَةِ ثَلَاثَةَ عَشَرَ: عَشْرَةٌ مِنْهَا لِلْأَسْمَاءِ، وَثَلَاثَةٌ لِلْأَفْعَالِ؛

2. four biliterals, because they are found in particles, without suppression, such as *bal* ⟨rather⟩; in verbs, with suppression, such as *qul* ⟨say!⟩;[412] and in nouns, without suppression, such as *man* ⟨who⟩, and with, such as *dam* ⟨blood⟩, in nine suras, since they [biliterals] occur in each of the three parts of speech in three ways:

(i) in nouns: *man*, *idh* ⟨when⟩, and *dhū* ⟨endowed with⟩;
(ii) in verbs: *qul* ⟨say!⟩, *biʿ* ⟨sell!⟩, and *khaf* ⟨fear!⟩; and
(iii) in particles: *min* ⟨from⟩, *in* ⟨if⟩, and *mudh* ⟨since⟩; the latter in the dialect of those who make it a preposition;

3. three triliterals—since these are found in the three parts of speech—in thirteen suras, to draw attention to the fact that the root structures being used amount to thirteen—ten of them for nouns and three of them for verbs;

[412] All mss. and eds.: بحذف كقل AQ, H, MM: بحذف ثقل كقل dittography.

(٤-٥) وَرُبَاعِيَّتَيْنِ، وَخُمَاسِيَّتَيْنِ، تَنْبِيهاً عَلَى أَنَّ لِكُلٍّ مِنْهُمَا أَصْلاً: كَ(جَعْفَرْ) وَ(سَفَرْجَلْ)؛ وَمُلْحَقاً: كَ(قَرْدَدْ) وَ(جَحَنْفَلْ).

وَلَعَلَّهَا فُرِّقَتْ عَلَى السُّوَرِ وَلَمْ تُعَدَّ بِأَجْمَعِهَا فِي أَوَّلِ الْقُرْآنِ لِهَٰذِهِ الْفَائِدَةِ، مَعَ مَا فِيهِ مِنْ إِعَادَةِ التَّحَدِّي، وَتَكْرِيرِ التَّنْبِيهِ، وَالْمُبَالَغَةِ فِيهِ.

وَالْمَعْنَى: أَنَّ هٰذَا الْمُتَحَدَّى بِهِ مُؤَلَّفٌ مِنْ جِنْسِ هٰذِهِ الْحُرُوفِ؛ أَوِ الْمُؤَلَّفُ مِنْهَا: كَذَا.

وَقِيلَ: هِيَ أَسْمَاءٌ لِلسُّوَرِ، وَعَلَيْهِ إِطْبَاقُ الْأَكْثَرِ. سُمِّيَتْ بِهَا إِشْعَاراً بِأَنَّهَا

4-5. two quadriliterals and two quintiliterals, to draw attention to the fact that each of these two categories has a true radical such as, respectively, *ja'far* ⁽brook⁾ and *safarjal* ⁽quince⁾, as well as quasi-quadriliterals and quintiliterals such as *qardad* ⁽rugged hill⁾ and *jaḥanfal* ⁽thick-snouted⁾;

These [combinations] may have been distributed over the suras as opposed to being all enumerated at the beginning of the Qur'ān for the purpose detailed above,[413] together with what such distribution conveys in the reiteration, repeated notice and heightened intensiveness of the challenge.

[Interpretation of the Opening Letters continued]

The meaning is, "That whereof the challenge consists in, is composed of the species of these letters;" or, "that which is composed of them, is such-and-such"

It was also said they are names for the suras, the majority concurring on this,[414] by which they were named to proclaim that....

[413] Sacy adds here between square brackets: "and which demonstrates the divine wisdom that presided over the use of these monograms." *Anthologie* (p. 6, my translation).
[414] "The exact words of the Imām [i.e., al-Rāzī in *Mafātiḥ al-ghayb*] are: 'It is the posi-

كَلِمَاتٌ مَعْرُوفَةُ التَّرْكِيبِ: فَلَوْ لَمْ تَكُنْ وَحْياً مِنَ اللهِ تَعَالَى، لَمْ تَتَسَاقَطْ مَقْدِرَتُهُمْ دُونَ مُعَارَضَتِهَا.

وَاسْتُدِلَّ عَلَيْهِ بِأَنَّهَا لَوْ لَمْ تَكُنْ مُفْهِمَةً، كَانَ الْخِطَابُ بِهَا كَالْخِطَابِ بِالْمُهْمَلِ، وَالتَّكَلُّمِ بِالزِّنْجِيِّ مَعَ الْعَرَبِيِّ، وَلَمْ يَكُنِ الْقُرْآنُ بِأَسْرِهِ بَيَاناً وَهُدًى، وَلَمَا أَمْكَنَ التَّحَدِّي بِهِ.

وَإِنْ كَانَتْ مُفْهِمَةً: فَإِمَّا أَنْ يُرَادَ بِهَا السُّوَرُ الَّتِي هِيَ مُسْتَهَلُّهَا عَلَى أَنَّهَا أَلْقَابُهَا، أَوْ غَيْرُ ذٰلِكَ.

وَالثَّانِي بَاطِلٌ، لِأَنَّهُ إِمَّا أَنْ يَكُونَ الْمُرَادُ ....

they are familiar verbal constructs; hence, if they did not consist in divine revelation, they would not utterly fall short of opposing them.

In support of the latter view, it was said that if they were not intelligible/meaningful,[415] any discourse that uses them would be outlandish, like addressing an Arab in Bantu: the Qur'ān would not form, in its entirety, a clear exposition and guidance, and it would not be possible to issue a challenge with it.

If they are intelligible, then either what is meant by them is the suras which they initiate—in the sense of being their epithets—or other than that.

The latter is false,[416] since the meaning must either be ....

tion of most of the theologians (*akthar al-mutakallimīn*) and was adopted by al-Khalīl and Sībawayh.' And a wonderful statement that is! For 'the majority' (*al-akthar*) in absolute terms did not adopt it." (S) It is the preferred view of 'Itr, *'Ulūm al-Qur'ān*, pp. 156-157 ("the majority of the exegetes and linguists—and others—said [so]").

415 (مفهمة) اسم فاعل من الإفهام... أو بزنة المفعول من الأفعال (Q).

416 This statement requires reconsideration since his own words "by which they were

مَا وُضِعَتْ لَهُ فِي لُغَةِ الْعَرَبِ: فَظَاهِرٌ أَنَّهُ لَيْسَ كَذٰلِكَ؛ أَوْ غَيْرَهُ: وَهُوَ بَاطِلٌ، لِأَنَّ الْقُرْآنَ نَزَلَ عَلَى لُغَتِهِمْ، لِقَوْلِهِ تَعَالَى: ﴿بِلِسَانٍ عَرَبِيٍّ مُّبِينٍ ١٩٥﴾ [الشعراء]. فَلَا يُحْمَلُ عَلَى مَا لَيْسَ فِي لُغَتِهِمْ.

لَا يُقَالُ [أوّلاً]: لِمَ لَا يَجُوزُ أَنْ تَكُونَ (١) مَزِيدَةً لِلتَّنْبِيهِ، وَالدَّلَالَةِ عَلَى انْقِطَاعِ كَلَامٍ وَاسْتِئْنَافِ آخَرَ؟ كَمَا قَالَهُ قُطْرُبٌ؛ ....

what they originally apply to in the Arabic language[417]—which is evidently not the case—or something else, which is false because the Qur'ān descended in their language—as Allah Most High said, *in a most eloquent Arabic tongue* (al-Shuʿarāʾ 26:195), and is therefore not understood in other than their language.

[Seven other interpretations and their rebuttals]

It cannot be said: Why is it not possible that [the Opening Letters] might be:

1. added[418] for admonition and to indicate the termination of one discourse and the start of another, as Quṭrub said;[419] ....

named to convey that they are familiar verbal constructs" presupposes the possibility of their being names for the suras other than the ones they initiate. (Q)

417 I.e., as alphabetical letters. (Q)

418 Sacy: "ajoutés d'une manière explétive."

419 "A weak view." (Z) "He said that when the unbelievers said, *Heed not this Qur'ān, and drown the hearing of it* (Fuṣṣilat 41:26), Allah desired to bring up something to them which they did not know because such would be a means to silence them and make them listen to their rebuttal by the Qur'ān, so Allah Most High revealed these letters. When they heard them, they said, bemused, 'Listen to what Muḥammad is bringing!' When they listened, the Qur'ān pounced on them; and so it was a means to silence them and a way for them to benefit from it." (Q) The view that the Opening Letters are designed to catch listeners by surprise and force their attention was espoused by al-Rāzī, al-Khuwayy, al-Suyūṭī in the *Itqān* and especially Muḥammad Rashīd Riḍā in the *Manār* and recent scholars such as Ṣubḥī al-Ṣāliḥ, Muḥammad ʿIzzat Darrūza, and ʿAbd al-Wahhāb Ḥammūda although strenuously rejected by

(٢) أَوْ إِشَارَةً إِلَى كَلِمَاتٍ هِيَ مِنْهَا، اِقْتُصِرَتْ عَلَيْهَا اِقْتِصَارَ الشَّاعِرِ فِي قَوْلِهِ

[رَجَز] قُلْتُ لَهَا قِفِي فَقَالَتْ قَاف * ....

كَمَا رُوِيَ عَنِ ابْنِ عَبَّاسٍ رَضِيَ اللهُ تَعَالَى عَنْهُمَا، قَالَ: الْأَلِفُ: آلَاءُ اللهِ؛ وَاللَّامُ: لُطْفُهُ؛ وَالْمِيمُ: مُلْكُهُ.

2. or an allusion to words from which they were excerpted, limited[420] to those letters the same way the poet did when he said,

["The Trembling"] *I told her, "Stop!" (qifī) so she said, "Qāf!"*[421]

Likewise it was related from Ibn ʿAbbās—may Allah be well-pleased with him and and his father:

• "*Alif* stands for the bounties (*ālāʾ*) of Allah, *lām* is His kindness (*luṭfuh*), and *mīm* is His sovereignty (*mulkuh*);"[422]

Ramaḍān ʿAbd al-Tawwāb; also, as "inceptions without specific meaning" (*fawātiḥ lā maʿnā lahā*) and dividers (*fawāṣil*), the latter being related from the linguists such as Abū ʿUbayda in *Majāz al-Qurʾān* and Ibn Jinnī in *al-Muḥtasab* on the basis of a saying to that effect by Mujāhid, and strengthened by al-Rāzī, al-Kirmānī and al-Ālūsī although strenuously rejected by al-Ṭabarī and Ibn Kathīr, cf. Sihām Khiḍr, *al-Iʿjāz al-Lughawī fī Fawātiḥ al-Suwar* (Beirut: Dār al-Kutub al-ʿIlmiyya, 2008) p. 207-224. The latter work is the most thorough presentation of the interpretations of the Opening Letters and their counter-rebuttals to date, also covering Muʿtazili, Shiʿi and others *tafsīrs*. See also Muḥammad Aḥmad Abū Firākh, *al-Muʿjam fī Fawātiḥ al-Suwar*, 2nd ed. (Kuwait: Sharikat Maktabat al-Bukhārī, 1413/1992).

420 *Iqtuṣirat* in all mss., "apparently erroneously copied with the feminine *tāʾ* because it is in the passive" cf. Q, Z but this is defended by Kh as correct and legitimate usage.

421 Spoken by al-Walīd b. ʿUqba b. Abī Muʿayṭ the governor of Iraq after his arrest by ʿUthmān for wine-bibbing cf. Ibn Jinnī, *al-Khaṣāʾiṣ*, ed. Muḥammad al-Najjār, 3 vols. (Cairo: Dār al-Kutub al-Miṣriyya, 1371/1952) 1:30, 80, 246, 2:361, with the wording: *"We said to her, 'Stop for us,' she said, 'Qāf!'"* which Kh said was a meterless corruption. *Qāf* here may stand for *waqaftu* ʿI stopʾ. Zajjāj said in *Maʿānī al-Qurʾān*, ed. ʿAbd al-Jalīl Shalabī, 5 vols. (Beirut: ʿĀlam al-Kutub, 1408/1988) 1:62: "Arabs may mention a single letter from the word meant, like their saying: 'I told her stop!, etc.'" Hence the hadith "Whoever helps to kill a Muslim even by half a word," i.e. code, a wink or gesture etc. See Muḥammad Kashshāsh, *al-Ishāra ghayr al-Shafawiyya fīl-Aḥādīth al-Nabawiyya* in *al-Aḥmadiyya* 13 (Muḥarram 1423/March 2003) 17-52.

وَعَنْهُ: أَنَّ ﴿الَر﴾، وَ﴿حَم﴾، وَ﴿ن﴾، مَجْمُوعُهَا: (الرَّحْمٰنُ).

وَعَنْهُ: أَنَّ ﴿الٓمٓ﴾ مَعْنَاهُ: (أَنَا اللهُ أَعْلَمُ). وَنَحْوُ ذٰلِكَ فِي سَائِرِ الْفَوَاتِحِ.

وَعَنْهُ: أَنَّ الْأَلِفَ: مِنَ اللهِ؛ وَاللَّامَ: مِنْ جِبْرَئِيلَ؛ وَالْمِيمَ: مِنْ مُحَمَّدٍ. أَيْ: الْقُرْآنُ مُنَزَّلٌ مِنَ اللهِ بِلِسَانِ جِبْرَئِيلَ عَلَى مُحَمَّدٍ، عَلَيْهِمَا الصَّلَاةُ وَالسَّلَامُ؛

- "*alif lām rāʾ*, *ḥā mīm*, and *nūn* all together form *al-Raḥmān*;"[423]
- "the meaning of *alif lām mīm* is, 'I, Allah, know best'"[424] and something similar for the rest of the Opening Letters;
- "*alif* is of Allah, *lām* of Jibraʾīl (Gabriel), *mīm* of Muḥammad,"[425] in the sense that the Qurʾān was brought down from Allah in the language of Jibraʾīl unto Muḥammad—upon both of them blessings and peace;

---

[422] Narrated as the saying of Abū al-ʿĀliya and al-Rabīʿ b. Anas in Ibn Abī Ḥātim, *Tafsīr* (1:33 §49 and 2:584 §3118); al-Ṭabarī, *Tafsīr* (1:209-210); *ibid.*, ed. Maḥmūd and Aḥmad Muḥammad Shākir, 2nd ed., 16 vols. (Cairo: Maktabat Ibn Taymiyya, 1374/1954) 1:208 §243; and al-Thaʿlabī in his *Tafsīr*, cf. al-Suyūṭī, *Durr* (1:121, 127), al-Munāwī, *Fatḥ* (1:124 §20).

[423] Narrated by Ibn Abī Ḥātim (also from Sālim b. ʿAbd Allāh) *Tafsīr* (1:32 §46, 48) with a weak chain and, with a somewhat similar wording, al-Ṭabarī, *Tafsīr* (Shākir ed. 1:207 §241; Turkī ed. 1:208); cf. al-Munāwī, *Fatḥ* (1:124-125 §21); but there are many reports that the Opening Letters are Divine Names, cf. al-Suyūṭī, *Durr* (1:121-123).

[424] Narrated by Ibn Abī Ḥātim, *Tafsīr* (1:32 §43); al-Ṭabarī (also from Saʿīd b. Jubayr), *Tafsīr* (Shākir ed. 1:207 §238-239; Turkī ed. 1:207-208); also al-Naḥḥās in *Maʿānī al-Qurʾān*, al-Baghawī in *Maʿālim al-Tanzīl*, al-Thaʿlabī, ʿAbd b. Ḥumayd, Ibn al-Mundhir etc., cf. al-Suyūṭī, *Durr* (1:121) and al-Munāwī, *Fatḥ* (1:125 §22).

[425] Al-Suyūṭī (and al-Munāwī in his wake) said "this is not related from Ibn ʿAbbās nor from any of the *Salaf*" but Sahl al-Tustarī does attribute it to Ibn ʿAbbās in his *Tafsīr* as do Ibn al-Jawzī, al-Qurṭubī, Abū Ḥayyān and others in theirs, while al-Rāzī attributes it to al-Ḍaḥḥāk in his. Qadi ʿIyāḍ cites it from Sahl in his *Shifā* (I, 4, *fī qasamih taʿālā bi-ʿaẓīm qadrih*) and it is cited without attribution in several early *Tafsīrs* such as Abū al-Muẓaffar al-Samʿānī, Ibn Juzay and others.

(٣) أَوْ: إِلَى مُدَدِ أَقْوَامٍ وَآجَالٍ بِحِسَابِ الْجُمَّلِ، كَمَا قَالَ أَبُو الْعَالِيَةِ، مُتَمَسِّكاً بِمَا رُوِيَ: أَنَّهُ عَلَيْهِ الصَّلَاةُ وَالسَّلَامُ، لَمَّا أَتَاهُ الْيَهُودُ، تَلَا عَلَيْهِمْ: ﴿الٓمٓ﴾ الْبَقَرَةَ؛ فَحَسَبُوهُ، وَقَالُوا: كَيْفَ نَدْخُلُ فِي دِينٍ مُدَّتُهُ إِحْدَى وَسَبْعُونَ سَنَةً؟ فَتَبَسَّمَ رَسُولُ اللهِ ﷺ، فَقَالُوا: فَهَلْ غَيْرُهُ؟ فَقَالَ: ﴿الٓمٓصٓ﴾، وَ﴿الٓر﴾، وَ﴿الٓمٓر﴾؛ فَقَالُوا: خَلَّطْتَ عَلَيْنَا، فَلَا نَدْرِي بِأَيِّهَا نَأْخُذُ. .....

3. or an allusion to the durations of certain peoples and lifespans according to numerology[426]—as stated by Abū al-ʿĀliya on the basis of the report that

> when the Jews came to him (upon him blessings and peace) he recited to them, *Alif, lām, mīm*, al-Baqara. They calculated it and said, "How are we to enter a religion the duration of which is seventy-one years?" The Messenger of Allah smiled. They said: "Is there more?" He said: "*Alif, lām, mīm, ṣād*; *alif, lām, rā'*; *alif, lām, mīm, rā'*." They said: "You are confusing us! We do not know which one to go by"[427]—

[426] *Al-jummal.* Gematria—divination through the extraction of secrets in the numbers behind names and letters, especially in sacred Scripture—is a Jewish science, also attributed by the scholars to Ādam, Idrīs (Enoch),ʿĪsā (Jesus), Pythagoras, Aristotle, the Chaldeans and Persians, etc., practiced or supported not only by non-Sunni sects and communities within Islām such as the "letterists" (*ḥurūfiyyūn*) among Shiʿis, notably Ismāʿīlīs, but also by those Sufis who deem licit the use of magic and talismans in traditional medicine and astrology on the basis of such works as *Shams al-Maʿārif* by the Maghrebine Aḥmad b. ʿAlī al-Būnī (d. 622/1225). Hermeneutic letterism was notoriously revived in our time by Rashād Khalīfa (who calculated that the Day of Resurrection would take place in the Hijri year 1710 (2280) and promoted the number 19, sacred to the Bahai sect) and his epigones. See Ṭāriq al-Qaḥṭānī, *Asrār al-Ḥurūf wa-Ḥisāb al-Jummal*, unpublished M.A. diss. (Mecca: Jamiʿat Umm al-Qurā, 1430/2009); al-Ṣanʿānī, *Risāla Sharīfa fīmā Yataʿallaq bil-Aʿdād wal-Ḥurūf*, ed. Mujāhid b. Ḥasan (Ṣanʿā': Maktabat Dar al-Quds, 1412/1991); and Khiḍr, *Iʿjāz* (p. 255, 265-266).

[427] Narrated by al-Bukhārī in *al-Tārīkh al-Kabīr*, 4 vols. in 8 (Hyderabad: Maktabat Jamʿiyyat Dā'irat al-Maʿārif al-ʿUthmāniyya, 1360-1384/1941-1969, repr. Beirut: Dār al-Kutub al-ʿIlmiyya, 2001) 2:208 §2209 and al-Ṭabarī who wavers regarding its con-

فَإِنَّ تِلَاوَتَهُ إِيَّاهَا بِهٰذَا التَّرْتِيبِ عَلَيْهِمْ، وَتَقْرِيرَهُمْ عَلَى اسْتِنْبَاطِهِمْ: دَلِيلٌ عَلَى ذٰلِكَ؛ وَهٰذِهِ الدِّلَالَةُ، وَإِنْ لَمْ تَكُنْ عَرَبِيَّةً، لٰكِنَّهَا لِاشْتِهَارِهَا فِيمَا بَيْنَ النَّاسِ، حَتَّى الْعَرَبِ، تُلْحِقُهَا بِالْمُعَرَّبَاتِ: كَـ(الْمِشْكَاةِ)، وَ(السِّجِّيلِ)، وَ(الْقُسْطَاسِ). مَعًا

(٤) أَوْ دَالَّةً عَلَى الْحُرُوفِ الْمَبْسُوطَةِ، مُقْسَماً بِهَا لِشَرَفِهَا مِنْ حَيْثُ إِنَّهَا بَسَائِطُ أَسْمَاءِ اللهِ تَعَالَى وَمَادَّةُ خِطَابِهِ.

since his recitation of them in that order to the Jews and his determination of their inference is proof of this. Although this [numerological] denotation is not Arab, nevertheless, because it is so famous among people, including Arabs, it is virtually a subset of Arabized words such as *mishkāt* ⁽niche⁾, *sijjīl* ⁽adobe⁾ and *qi/usṭās* ⁽scale⁾;[428]

4. or an allusion[429] to the discrete letters which are being sworn by because of their nobility, since they are the foundations of the Names of Allah and the materials of His Discourse;[430]

tent, *Tafsīr* (Shākir ed. 1:216-220 §246), both through Ibn Isḥāq with weak chains by agreement, also Ibn al-Mundhir through Ibn Jurayj cf. al-Suyūṭī, *Durr* (1:124-127) and Ibn Abī Ḥātim, *Tafsīr* (1:33 §49) cf. al-Munāwī, *Fatḥ* (1:126 §24), while very few scholars accepted this numerology-code view as valid, among them al-Suhaylī, cf. al-Khiḍr, *I'jāz* (p. 246-256). Cachia provides helpful calculations: "*alif-lām-mīm* (*Sūras* 2, 3, 29-32) 1+30+ 40=71; *alif-lām-mīm-ṣād* (*Sūra* 7) 1+30+40+90=161; *alif-lām-rā'* (*Sūras* 10-12, 14-15) 1+30+200=231; *alif-lām-mīm-rā'* (*Sūra* 13) 1+30+40+200=271."

[428] On these words see Ibn Qutayba, *Adab al-Kātib*, ed. Muḥammad al-Dālī (Beirut: Mu'assasat al-Risāla, 1402/1981) p. 496. For a comprehensive Arabized lexicon see al-Khafājī's *Shifā' al-Ghalīl fi-mā fī Kalām al-'Arab min al-Dakhīl*, ed. Muḥammad Kashshāsh (Beirut: Dār al-Kutub al-'Ilmiyya, 1418/1998).

[429] B, β, D, Kh, L, P, U, Ul, Z: دالّة Ak: او تكون داله I: دلالة corrected with first *lām* erased so as to read دالة α, F, R: دلالةً A, AQ, ε, H, K, MM, N, Q, Sk, T: دلالة

[430] This is al-Akhfash's explanation as cited by al-Rāzī (Kh, Z). It is also related from

هٰذا؛ و[ثانياً]: (٥) إِنَّ الْقَولَ بِأَنَّهَا أَسْمَاءُ السُّوَرِ يُخْرِجُهَا إِلَى مَا لَيْسَ فِي لُغَةِ الْعَرَبِ، لِأَنَّ التَّسْمِيَةَ بِثَلَاثَةِ أَسْمَاءٍ فَصَاعِداً مُسْتَنْكَرَةٌ عِنْدَهُمْ؛

(٦) وَيُؤَدِّي إِلَى اتِّحَادِ الِاسْمِ وَالْمُسَمَّى؛

(٧) وَيَسْتَدْعِي تَأَخُّرَ الْجُزْءِ عَنِ الْكُلِّ مِنْ حَيْثُ إِنَّ الِاسْمَ مُتَأَخِّرٌ عَنِ الْمُسَمَّى بِالرُّتْبَةِ؛

لِأَنَّا نَقُولُ:

furthermore, [it also cannot be said] that:

5. the view that they are names for the suras[431] make them alien to the Arabic language, because they considered it abhorrent[432] for something to have a name made of three or more words;[433]

6. moreover, it leads to the name and the named being one and the same;

7. and finally, it calls for the part to come second to the whole in that the name comes second to the named in sequence;[434]

because we say:

Ibn ʿAbbās, ʿIkrima and al-Kalbī, and was strengthened by Ibn Qutayba, al-Ṭabarī, al-Zarkashī, and especially Ibn al-Qayyim in his *Tibyān fī Aqsām al-Qurʾān* but weakened by al-Rāzī, cf. Khiḍr, *Iʿjāz* (p. 225-230).

431 Related from al-Ḥasan al-Baṣrī, Zayd b. Aslam and his son ʿAbd al-Raḥmān among exegetes; al-Khalīl, Sībawayh, and Ibn Qutayba among linguists; "the majority of the scholars" according to J. It is Rāzī's preferred view: Khiḍr, *Iʿjāz* (p. 171f.).

432 I, N, P, R: مستنكرة B: مستنكر with a superscript final ة α, Ak, β, ε, Kh: مستنكر AQ, F, H, K, L, MM, Q, T, U, Ul, Z: مستكره

433 I.e. compound Arabic names, e.g. Sarra Man Raʾā ⟨gladdens whoever sees⟩, Shābat Qarnāhā ⟨her two temples grayed⟩ and Taʾabbaṭa Sharran ⟨he took an armful of wickedness⟩ to which are compared the three-worded, four-worded, and five-worded names *alif lām mīm*, *alif lām mīm rā* and *ḥā mīm ʿayn sīn qāf* respectively, according to the view that the Letters are the names of suras. (Z, Kh, Q) See also four notes down.

434 Here Cachia misunderstands *rutba* to denote rank and incorrectly faults Sacy.

(١) إِنَّ هٰـذِهِ الْأَلْفَـاظَ لَمْ تُعْهَـدْ مَزِيـدَةً لِلتَّنْبِيـهِ وَالدَّلَالَـةِ عَـلَى الْانْقِطَـاعِ؛ وَالْاِسْتِئْنَافُ يَلْزَمُهَا وَغَيْرَهَا مِنْ حَيْثُ إِنَّهَا فَوَاتِحُ السُّوَرِ. وَلَا يَقْتَضِي ذٰلِكَ أَنْ لَا يَكُونَ لَهَا مَعْنًى فِي حَيِّزِهَا.

(٢) وَلَمْ تُسْتَعْمَلْ لِلْاِخْتِصَارِ مِنْ كَلِمَاتٍ مُعَيَّنَةٍ فِي لُغَتِهِمْ. أَمَّا الشِّعْرُ: فَشَاذٌّ؛ وَأَمَّا قَوْلُ ابْنِ عَبَّاسٍ: فَتَنْبِيهٌ عَلَى أَنَّ هٰذِهِ الْحُرُوفَ مَنْبَعُ الْأَسْـمَاءِ، وَمَبَـادِئُ الْخِطَابِ، وَتَمْثِيلٌ بِأَمْثِلَةٍ حَسَنَةٍ ـ أَلَا تَرَى أَنَّهُ عَـدَّ كُـلَّ حَـرْفٍ مِـنْ كَلِـمَاتٍ مُتَبَايِنَةٍ؟ ـ لَا تَفْسِيرٌ وَتَخْصِيصٌ بِهٰذِهِ الْمَـعَانِي دُونَ غَيْرِهَـا؛ إِذْ لَا مُخَصِّـصَ لَفْظاً وَمَعْنًى.

(٣) وَلَا بِحِسَابِ الْجُمَّلِ فَتُلْحَقَ بِالْمُعَرَّبَاتِ؛ وَالْحَدِيثُ: لَا دَلِيلَ فِيهِ، ....

1. Such words are not known to have been used as "added for admonition and to indicate termination." They have to be resumptive—just as others do—as the openers of suras. It does not follow from that that they have no meaning in themselves.

2. Nor were they used as abridgments of specific words in their language. As for the poetry cited, it shows irregular usage; and as for Ibn ʿAbbās's saying, it serves notice that those letters are the wellspring of the Names and the rudiments of discourse, an allegorization through fine examples—do you not see that he counted each letter as part of different words?—not an explication, and not a specification of those meanings at the exclusion of others,[435] as there is no specifier, whether lexical or semantic.

3. Nor were they used in numerological calculations for them to be classified as Arabized items. The hadith forms no proof, as

[435] I.e., bounties, kindness and sovereignty. (Q)

لِجَوَازِ أَنَّهُ عَلَيْهِ الصَّلَاةُ وَالسَّلَامُ تَبَسَّمَ تَعَجُّباً مِنْ جَهْلِهِمْ.

(٤) وَجَعْلُهَا مُقْسَماً بِهَا، وَإِنْ كَانَ غَيْرَ مُمْتَنِعٍ، لٰكِنَّهُ يُحْوِجُ إِلَى إِضْمَارِ أَشْيَاءَ لَا دَلِيلَ عَلَيْهَا.

(٥) وَالتَّسْمِيَةُ بِثَلَاثَةِ أَسْمَاءٍ: إِنَّمَا تَمْتَنِعُ إِذَا رُكِّبَتْ وَجُعِلَتْ اِسْماً وَاحِداً عَلَى طَرِيقَةِ بَعْلَبَكَّ؛ فَأَمَّا إِذَا نُثِرَتْ نَثْرَ أَسْمَاءِ الْعَدَدِ فَلَا، وَنَاهِيكَ بِتَسْوِيَةِ سِيبَوَيْهِ بَيْنَ التَّسْمِيَةِ بِالْجُمْلَةِ وَالْبَيْتِ مِنَ الشِّعْرِ وَطَائِفَةٍ مِنْ أَسْمَاءِ حُرُوفِ الْمُعْجَمِ.

it is possible that he—upon him blessings and peace—smiled out of wonder at their ignorance.

4. To treat them as the terms of an oath, although not precluded, nevertheless forces us to [assume] several elliptical terms, for which there is no proof.[436]

5. Naming something with three names is precluded only if they are combined into a single one in the manner of "Baʿlabakk;"[437] but if they are enumerated as discrete nouns,[438] then no. It is enough [proof] for you that Sībawayh made no difference between naming [something or someone] by using a sentence, a verse of poetry, or a group of the names of alphabetical letters.

[436] Namely: the verb of taking oath, its subject, the particle of swearing the oath, and the apodosis of the oath, all suppressed. (Q)

[437] Name of a famous city in Lebanon's Bekaa valley (known as Heliopolis in Greco-Roman antiquity) from which hailed many famous scholars, the name of which is formed by the "mixed compound" (*tarkīb mazjī*) (cf. Kh, Sk) of Baal—the name of an idol—and *bak*, of indeterminate meaning; similar to *ʿAbshamī*—a *nisba* coined from ʿAbd+Shams (Nūr al-Dīn ʿItr, class communication)—or the place-name Ḥaḍramawt (Kh, Q), presumably coined from *ḥaḍara+ mawt*. Al-Zabīdī gives further examples in *Tāj al-ʿArūs* (art. "Maʿdīkarib"). Cf. four notes up and Wright, *Grammar* (1:160).

[438] E.g., "Abū ʿAbd Allāh." (Q)

(٦) وَالْمُسَمَّى هُوَ مَجْمُوعُ السُّورَةِ، وَالِاسْمُ جُزْؤُهَا: فَلَا اتِّحَادَ.

(٧) وَهُوَ مُقَدَّمٌ مِنْ حَيْثُ ذَاتِهِ، مُؤَخَّرٌ بِاعْتِبَارِ كَوْنِهِ اِسْماً؛ فَلَا دَوْرَ، لِاخْتِلَافِ الْجِهَتَيْنِ.

وَالْوَجْهُ الْأَوَّلُ أَقْرَبُ إِلَى التَّحْقِيقِ، وَأَوْفَقُ لِلَطَائِفِ التَّنْزِيلِ، وَأَسْلَمُ مِنْ لُزُومِ ....

6. The named is the entire sura while the name is only part of it, so they are not one and the same.

7. The latter [part] comes first in itself,[439] while it comes second from the perspective of being a name [for the whole]; so there is no circular argument since the two aspects differ.[440]

[The preferred interpretation]

The first explanation is the likeliest to be right,[441] most in line with the subtleties of the revealed text and freest of the necessity

[439] A rebuttal of the claim that "it calls for the part to come second to the whole" (Sk).

[440] I.e., it does not necessitate the sequential priority of a thing to itself (Sk, Q, Z).

[441] I.e., as the Qadi stated at the beginning of his long discussion, the Opening Letters form an intimation to those who defy the Qur'ān that "its substance is speech composed of the same stuff of which they compose their own speech." Suyūṭī objects: "His claim of the preponderance of this explanation is unacceptable; it is a view without proof (*mā dhakarahu min tarjīḥihi mamnuʿ li'annahu qawlun lā dalīla ʿalayh*) and none of the predecessors said it. Rather, it is purely an opinion concerning the Book of Allah, unbacked by any authoritative reference and, needless to say, artificial and far-fetched!" (S) In reality this is the view of the majority of the linguists and exegetes and not just J, including Quṭrub, al-Farrā', al-Mubarrid, Abu al-Layth al-Samarqandī, al-Nasafī and, among latter-day scholars, al-Mizzī, Ibn Kathīr, Aḥmad b. Taymiyya, Abū al-Suʿūd in *Irshād al-ʿAql al-Salīm*, Sayyid Quṭb in *Fī Ẓilāl al-Qur'ān*, al-Ṭāhir b. ʿĀshūr in *al-Taḥrīr wal-Tanwīr*, al-Ṣābūnī in *Ṣafwat al-Tafāsīr*, cf. Khiḍr, *Iʿjāz* (p. 230-236) and our teacher Dr. Saʿīd al-Būṭī in his *tafsīr* lectures in the late 90s. For wild Orientalist speculations on the issue see James A. Bellamy, "The Mysterious Letters of the Qur'ān," *Journal of the American Oriental Society* 93 no.2 (Jul.-Sep. 1973) 267-285.

النَّقْلِ، وَوُقُوعِ الِاشْتِرَاكِ فِي الْأَعْلَامِ مِنْ وَاضِعٍ وَاحِدٍ؛ فَإِنَّهُ يَعُودُ بِالنَّقْضِ عَلَى مَا هُوَ مَقْصُودٌ بِالْعَلَمِيَّةِ.

وَقِيلَ: إِنَّهَا أَسْمَاءُ الْقُرْآنِ؛ وَلِذَٰلِكَ أُخْبِرَ عَنْهَا بِـ(الْكِتَابِ) وَ(الْقُرْآنِ).

وَقِيلَ: إِنَّهَا أَسْمَاءٌ لله تَعَالَى؛ وَيَدُلُّ عَلَيْهِ أَنَّ عَلِيّاً ـ كَرَّمَ اللهُ وَجْهَهُ ـ كَانَ يَقُولُ: يَا ﴿كٓهيعٓصٓ﴾، وَيَا ﴿حمٓ عٓسٓقٓ﴾؛ وَلَعَلَّهُ أَرَادَ: (يَا مُنَزِّلَهُمَا).

of metaphorizing,[442] or the eventual sharing [by several objects] of [the same] personal names given by one namer, since that ultimately contradicts the very purpose of name-identification.

[More interpretations yet]

8. It was also said they are names for the Qur'ān, hence the Book and the Qur'ān were predicated to them.[443]

9. It was also said they are names for Allah Most High.[444] This is indicated by the fact that ʿAlī—may Allah ennoble his countenance!—would say, "O *kāf hā yā ʿayn ṣād*! O *ḥā mīm ʿayn sīn qāf*!"[445] and he probably meant "O Revealer of them."

442 I.e., departing from the meanings that they are alphabetical letters to other meanings, namely the names of suras, the names of the Qur'ān, or Divine Names. (Q)

443 E.g., *alif lām mīm: That is the Book* (al-Baqara 2:1-2); *alif lām rā: those are the signs of the all-wise Book* (Yūnus 10:1); *alif lām rā: those are the signs of the all-clarifying Book* (Yūsuf 12:1); *alif lām rā: those are the signs of the Book* (al-Raʿd 13:1); *alif lām rā: those are the signs of the Book and an all-clarifying Qur'ān* (al-Ḥijr 15:1); cf. also al-Shuʿarā' 26:1-2; al-Naml 27:1; al-Qaṣaṣ 28:1-2; Luqmān 31:1-2. ʿAbd al-Razzāq, al-Ṭabarī, al-Baghawī, Rāzī, Ibn ʿAṭiyya, and Ibn Kathīr relate this position from Qatāda, Mujāhid, Ibn Jurayj, al-Kalbī, al-Suddī and Zayd b. Aslam cf. Khiḍr, *Iʿjāz* (p. 181).

444 As narrated from Ibn ʿAbbās with a sound chain by Ibn al-Mundhir in his *Tafsīr*, al-Bayhaqī in *al-Asmā' wal-Ṣifāt*, and Ibn Mardawayh in his *Tafsīr*. (S) This view is also related from Saʿīd b. Jubayr, Ibn Masʿūd, al-Shaʿbī, ʿĀmir, al-Suddī and others, as well as ʿAlī b. Abī Ṭālib, and it is al-Suyūṭī choice in his *Itqān* (Type 43).

445 Narrated by al-Ṭabarī in his *Tafsīr* and ʿUthmān b. Saʿīd al-Dārimī in his *Naqḍ al-Marrīsī*. (S) Also narrated from ʿAlī by Ibn Mājah in his *Tafsīr* and from Anas by Ibn

وَقِيلَ: الْأَلِفُ مِنْ أَقْصَى الْحَلْقِ، وَهُوَ مَبْدَأُ الْمَخَارِجِ؛ وَاللَّامُ: مِنْ طَرَفِ اللِّسَانِ، وَهُوَ أَوْسَطُهَا؛ وَالْمِيمُ: مِنَ الشَّفَةِ، وَهُوَ آخِرُهَا: جَمَعَ بَيْنَهَا، إِيمَاءً إِلَى أَنَّ الْعَبْدَ يَنْبَغِي أَنْ يَكُونَ أَوَّلُ كَلَامِهِ، وَأَوْسَطُهُ، وَآخِرُهُ: ذِكْرَ اللهِ تَعَالَى.

وَقِيلَ: إِنَّهُ سِرٌّ اسْتَأْثَرَ اللهُ بِعِلْمِهِ؛ وَقَدْ رُوِيَ عَنِ الْخُلَفَاءِ الْأَرْبَعَةِ وَغَيْرِهِمْ مِنَ الصَّحَابَةِ مَا يَقْرُبُ مِنْهُ؛ وَلَعَلَّهُمْ أَرَادُوا أَنَّهَا أَسْرَارٌ ....

[Sufi phonology of *alif lām mīm*]

10. It was also said that the *alif* is from the farthest end of the larynx, which is where the [phonemic] outlets begin; the *lām* is from the edge of the tongue, which is their middle-point; and the *mīm* is from the lip, which is their endpoint.[446] He brought them together as a sign that the beginning, middle and end of a slave's discourse should be the remembrance of Allah Most High.

11. It was also said that it is a secret known only to Allah. Something to that effect was related from the Four Caliphs and other Companions.[447] Perhaps they meant that they are secrets ....

Abī Ḥātim in his, also from Abū al-ʿĀliya, Saʿīd b. Jubayr, Imām Mālik and others, while Ibn ʿAṭiyya mentioned the possibility that they may be acronyms for the Divine Names rather than Names themselves, which is yet another view held by many, while others specified either Names, Attributes, or the Divine Essence; yet others added: "or other than *Allāh*" cf. Khiḍr, *Iʿjāz* (p. 184-196). The verses are from Sūrat Maryam (17:1) and Sūrat al-Shūrā (42:1-2) respectively.

446 Cf. Khiḍr, *Iʿjāz* (pp. 277-285).

447 Such as Ibn Masʿūd and Ibn ʿAbbās. It is the preference of al-Rabīʿ b. Khuthaym (d. 65/ca.684), al-Shaʿbī, Sufyān al-Thawrī, Ibn al-Anbārī, al-Ḥusayn b. al-Faḍl (d. 282/895), Abū Ḥātim, al-Fakhr al-Rāzī, al-Qurṭubī, Abū Ḥayyān, *Tafsīr al-Manār*, the *Jalālayn*, al-Ālūsī, al-Shawkānī, Muḥammad Abū Zahra, and Muḥammad Mutawallī al-Shaʿrānī among others. See the thorough documentation in Khiḍr, *Iʿjāz* (p. 144-148) and S (1:268-270) who quotes from the Afghan linguist al-Sijāwandī (Abū ʿAbd Allāh Muḥammad b. ʿAbd al-Rashīd b. Ṭayfūr al-Ghaznawī d. 560/1165 the author of *ʿAyn al-Maʿānī fī Tafsīr al-Kitāb al-ʿAzīz wal-Sabʿ al-Mathānī*): "The alphabetical letters are a test for the believer's confirmation and the unbeliever's denial as well as

بَيْنَ اللهِ تَعَالَى وَرَسُولِهِ، وَرُمُوزٌ لَمْ يُقْصَدْ بِهَا إِفْهَامُ غَيْرِهِ؛ إِذْ يَبْعُدُ الْخِطَابُ بِمَا لَا يُفِيدُ.

فَإِنْ جَعَلْتَهَا أَسْمَاءَ اللهِ تَعَالَى - أَوِ الْقُرْآنِ، أَوِ السُّوَرِ - كَانَ لَهَا حَظٌّ مِنَ الْإِعْرَابِ: إِمَّا الرَّفْعُ عَلَى الْاِبْتِدَاءِ، أَوِ الْخَبَرِ؛ أَوْ: النَّصْبُ، بِتَقْدِيرِ فِعْلِ الْقَسَمِ، عَلَى طَرِيقَةِ (اللهَ لَأَفْعَلَنَّ) بِالنَّصْبِ، أَوْ غَيْرِهِ، كَمَا ذُكِرَ؛ أَوْ: الْجَرُّ، عَلَى إِضْمَارِ حَرْفِ الْقَسَمِ.

وَيَتَأَتَّى الْإِعْرَابُ لَفْظاً، وَالْحِكَايَةُ، ....

between Allah Most High and His Prophet—symbols that were not intended for other than him to grasp,[448] since a completely uninformative address is unlikely.

[Declension of the Opening Letters]

If you consider them names for Allah, the Qurʾān, or suras, they can be inflected with: (i) the nominative, as inchoatives or enunciatives; (ii) the accusative, by subaudition of a verb denoting oath—as in *Allāha laʾafʿalanna* ⁽[I swear by] Allah I will do!⁾ with [*Allāh* in] the accusative[449]—or any other [verb] as already discussed; (iii) or the genitive if we imply a jurative particle.

Verbal declension is feasible, as is verbatim citation[450] ....

markers that raise attention.... I have spent years researching all facets of their meanings; interpretations that bear mention reached almost sixty, and I did not find the coolness of certainty until I forced myself to rest at this stage of my investigation."

448 Cf. Rūzbahān al-Baqlī al-Shīrāzī, *Tafsīr ʿArāʾis al-Bayān fī Ḥaqāʾiq al-Qurʾān*, ed. Aḥmad Farīd al-Mazyadī, 3 vols. (Beirut: Dār al-Kutub al-ʿIlmiyya, 1429/2008) 1:28.

449 I.e., *uqsimu bi-l-Lāhi laʾafʿalanna* ⁽I swear by Allah that I will do⁾. The suppression of the particle of oath (*bi*) *does* not take place unless the verb of oath (e.g., *uqsimu* or *ḥalaftu*) is also suppressed, following which the accusative takes place with the verb subauded. The latter cannot remain outwardly without the particle, as it is not said "*ḥalaftu-l-Lāha*" in chaste Arabic. (Q)

450 I.e. both "verbally" (*lafẓan*) and "constructively" (*maḥallan*), the latter consisting

فِيمَا كَانَتْ مُفْرَدَةً، أَوْ مُوَازِنَةً لِمُفْرَدٍ كـ﴿حمٓ﴾ - فَإِنَّهَا كـ(هَابِيلَ)؛ وَالْحِكَايَةُ لَيْسَتْ إِلَّا فِيمَا عَدَا ذٰلِكَ. وَسَيَعُودُ إِلَيْكَ ذِكْرُهُ مُفَصَّلاً إِنْ شَاءَ اللهُ تَعَالَى.

وَإِنْ أَبْقَيْتَهَا عَلَى مَعَانِيهَا: فَإِنْ قَدَّرْتَ بِالْمُؤَلَّفِ مِنْ هٰذِهِ الْحُرُوفِ: كَانَ فِي حَيِّزِ الرَّفْعِ بِالْابْتِدَاءِ أَوِ الْخَبَرِ عَلَى مَا مَرَّ.

وَإِنْ جَعَلْتَهَا مُقْسَماً بِهَا: يَكُونُ كُلُّ كَلِمَةٍ مِنْهَا مَنْصُوباً أَوْ مَجْرُوراً، عَلَى اللُّغَتَيْنِ فِي (اللهَ لَأَفْعَلَنَّ)، وَتَكُونُ جُمْلَةً قَسَمِيَّةً بِالْفِعْلِ الْمُقَدَّرِ لَهُ.

وَإِنْ جَعَلْتَهَا أَبْعَاضَ كَلِمَاتٍ، أَوْ أَصْوَاتاً مُنَزَّلَةً مَنْزِلَةَ ....

for those [letters] that are single [nouns];[451] or commensurable with single names, such as *ḥā mīm*, which is like "Hābīl" (Abel); and as citation exclusively in anything other than that.[452] There will be a more detailed discussion on this later if Allah wills.[453]

If, however, you leave them to their original meanings, then, provided you consider them composites, they are annexed to the nominative as inchoatives or enunciatives as already mentioned.

If you consider them oaths being sworn, then each of their words will be either in the accusative or the genitive per the two possible verbal forms in *Allāha laʾafʿalanna* (by Allah I will!), the sentence being juratory through its subauded verb; and if you consider them parts of words, or sounds to be treated ....

in the names being cited with a quasi-inherent final *sukūn* because that is how they are always cited (Z).

451 Such as *ṣād*, *nūn* and *qāf*.

452 E.g., *alif lām rā* or *kāf hā yā ʿayn ṣād* being cited as is, since verbal declension is impossible for them. (Z) On their declension see more in Khiḍr, *Iʿjāz* (pp. 140-143).

453 Namely in the Qadi's commentary on Ṣād (38:1).

حُرُوفِ التَّنْبِيهِ: لَمْ يَكُنْ لَهَا مَحَلٌّ مِنَ الإِعْرَابِ، كَالْجُمَلِ الْمُبْتَدَأَةِ، وَالْمُفْرَدَاتِ الْمَعْدُودَةِ.

وَيُوقَفُ عَلَيْهَا وَقْفَ التَّمَامِ إِذَا قَدَّرْتَ بِحَيْثُ لَا تَحْتَاجُ إِلَى مَا بَعْدَهَا.

وَلَيْسَ شَيْءٌ مِنْهَا آيَةً عِنْدَ غَيْرِ الْكُوفِيِّينَ. وَأَمَّا عِنْدَهُمْ، فَـ﴿الٓمٓ﴾ فِي مَوَاقِعِهَا، وَ﴿الٓمٓصٓ﴾، وَ﴿كٓهيعٓصٓ﴾، وَ﴿طه﴾، وَ﴿طسٓمٓ﴾، وَ﴿طسٓ﴾، وَ﴿يسٓ﴾، وَ﴿حمٓ﴾: آيَةٌ؛ وَ﴿حمٓ عٓسٓقٓ﴾: آيَتَانِ؛ وَالْبَوَاقِي لَيْسَتْ بِآيَاتٍ.

as admonitory interjections, then they are indeclinable, just like inceptive sentences and word-lists.

They require a "pause of termination [of meaning]" whenever you presume the latter to be the case, namely, when they do not need what follows.[454]

[Do the Opening Letters constitute integral verses?]

None of them constitutes a verse for other than the Kufans. The latter consider that *alif lām mīm* wherever it occurs; *alif lām mīm ṣād*; *kāf hā yā ʿayn ṣād*; *ṭā hā*; *ṭā sīn mīm*; *ṭā sīn*; *yā sīn* and *ḥā mīm* each constitute a verse, while *ḥā mīm, ʿayn sīn qāf* constitute two and the remainder are not verses.[455]

[454] Which is invariably the case. "Whether they are left with their original meanings and mentioned as discrete letters, or presumed to be composites of those letters as inchoatives or enunciatives, or deemed names for the suras or the Qur'ān, or Divine Names, and are put in the nominative as predicates by themselves, or the accusative through an inferred 'Mention!' or 'Read!' or made oaths with suppressed apodoses: in all of these cases, the pause is complete with them." (Q)

[455] Cf. al-Dānī, *al-Muktafā fīl-Waqf wal-Ibtidā*, ed. Yūsuf ʿAbd al-Raḥmān Marʿashlī, 2nd ed. (Beirut: Mu'assasat al-Risāla, 1407/1987) p. 158.

وَهٰذَا تَوْقِيفٌ: لَا مَجَالَ لِلْقِيَاسِ فِيهِ.

﴿ذَٰلِكَ ٱلْكِتَٰبُ﴾: ﴿ذَٰلِكَ﴾ إِشَارَةٌ:

(أ) إِلَى ﴿الٓمٓ﴾ إِنْ أُوِّلَ بِالْمُؤَلَّفِ مِنْ هٰذِهِ الْحُرُوفِ؛ أَوْ فُسِّرَ بِالسُّورَةِ؛ أَوِ الْقُرْآنِ. فَإِنَّهُ لَمَّا تَكَلَّمَ بِهِ وَتَقَضَّى، أَوْ وَصَلَ مِنَ الْمُرْسِلِ إِلَى الْمُرْسَلِ إِلَيْهِ: صَارَ مُتَبَاعِداً، أُشِيرَ إِلَيْهِ بِمَا يُشَارُ بِهِ إِلَى الْبَعِيدِ.

وَتَذْكِيرُهُ ـ مَتَى أُرِيدَ بِـ﴿الٓمٓ﴾ السُّورَةُ ـ لِتَذْكِيرِ الْكِتَابِ، فَإِنَّهُ خَبَرُهُ، أَوْ صِفَتُهُ الَّذِي هُوَ هُوَ.

This is a divine edict[456] that leaves no leeway for [normative] analogy.

[Why *That is the Book* instead of *This is the Book*?]

[2:2] **dhālika-l-kitābu** ⁽*That is the Book*⁾: *dhālika* ⁽that⁾ is a demonstrative pointing to *alif lām mīm* if the latter is interpreted as "the composites of these letters" or explained as the sura, or as the Qur'ān. For when it was spoken and done, or[457] when it reached the recipient [after being sent] by the Sender, it became distant and was thus[458] referred to with a demonstrative of distance.[459]

It was put in the masculine—in case the sura is meant by *alif lām mīm*— because *kitāb* is masculine, as the latter is its [*alif lām mīm*'s] enunciative, or its attribute, whereby "A" is "B".

456 Sacy and Cachia both misunderstood *tawqīf* to mean "punctuation."

457 All mss. and eds.: او وصل A: ووصل

458 α, Ak, β, H, I, K, L, MM, N, Q, Sk, U, Ul, Z: صار متباعداً أشير T: صار متباعداً فأشير D, P: صار متباعداً وأشير ε, F, R: أشير B, ÇZ: صارَ متباعداً with last clause missing entirely.

459 "The Imam said: 'The Qur'ān contains tremendous teachings and many sciences, and to examine them all is beyond human strength. Thus even though it is present with regard to its form, nevertheless it is invisible with regard to its secrets and realities. Hence it is right that it be referred to in the way the distant unseen is referred to.'" (S)

(ب) أَوْ: إِلَى ﴿ٱلْكِتَٰبُ﴾، فَيَكُونُ صِفَتَهُ. وَالْمُرَادُ بِهِ: الْكِتَابُ الْمَوْعُودُ إِنْزَالُهُ بِنَحْوِ قَوْلِهِ تَعَالَى: ﴿إِنَّا سَنُلْقِي عَلَيْكَ قَوْلًا ثَقِيلًا ۝٥﴾ [المزّمّل]، أَوْ فِي الْكُتُبِ الْمُتَقَدِّمَةِ.

وَهُوَ مَصْدَرٌ، سُمِّيَ بِهِ الْمَفْعُولُ لِلْمُبَالَغَةِ.

وَقِيلَ: (فِعَالٌ) بِمَعْنَى الْمَفْعُولِ، كَ(اللِّبَاسِ)؛ ثُمَّ أُطْلِقَ عَلَى الْمَنْظُومِ عِبَارَةً قَبْلَ أَنْ يُكْتَبَ، لِأَنَّهُ مِمَّا يُكْتَبُ.

وَأَصْلُ الْكَتْبِ: الْجَمْعُ؛ وَمِنْهُ: الْكَتِيبَةُ.

Or it points to ***al-kitāb*** ⟨the Book⟩ itself, which would then be its descriptive epithet,[460] in the sense of the Book that was promised to be revealed, either (i) with the like of His saying *Behold, We shall cast upon you a word of weight* (al-Muzzammil 73:5) or (ii) in the ancient Books.

Kitāb ⟨scripture⟩ is an infinitive noun by which the object [itself] was named for intensiveness.[461]

It was also said it is a *fiʿāl* form in the sense of the object as in *al-libās* ⟨garment⟩, then it was used for a literary composition in the sense of its expressions before that of its writing as it is the stuff of writing.

Katb originally means a multitude, whence *katība* ⟨batallion⟩.

460 "As regards the demonstrative pronouns, which are looked upon by the Arabs as substantives, either they may be placed in apposition to the substantive, or the substantive to them…. In both cases the apposition is a qualificative one, whence the first word in each is called by the Arabs المَوْصوف *that which is described,* and the second الصِّفَة *the description or descriptive epithet.*" Wright, *Grammar* (2:277 §136(b)).

461 I.e., instead of the objective form *maktūb*, as in *ʿadl* instead of *ʿādil* in the expression *rajulun ʿadlun* ⟨a just man⟩, see note 302.

﴿لَا رَيْبَ فِيهِ﴾: مَعْنَاهُ أَنَّهُ لِوُضُوحِهِ وَسُطُوعِ بُرْهَانِهِ، بِحَيْثُ لَا يَرْتَابُ الْعَاقِلُ ـ بَعْدَ النَّظَرِ الصَّحِيحِ ـ فِي كَوْنِهِ وَحْياً بَالِغاً حَدَّ الْإِعْجَازِ؛ لَا أَنَّ أَحَداً لَا يَرْتَابُ فِيهِ؛ أَلَا تَرَى إِلَى قَوْلِهِ تَعَالَى: ﴿وَإِن كُنتُمْ فِي رَيْبٍ مِّمَّا نَزَّلْنَا عَلَىٰ عَبْدِنَا﴾ [البقرة ٢٣] الْآيَةَ. فَإِنَّهُ مَا أَبْعَدَ عَنْهُمُ الرَّيْبَ، بَلْ: عَرَّفَهُمُ الطَّرِيقَ الْمُزِيحَ لَهُ؛ وَهُوَ أَنْ يَجْتَهِدُوا فِي مُعَارَضَةِ نَجْمٍ مِنْ نُجُومِهِ، وَيَبْذِلُوا فِيهَا غَايَةَ جُهْدِهِمْ، حَتَّى ـ إِذَا عَجَزُوا عَنْهَا ـ تَحَقَّقَ لَهُمْ أَنْ لَيْسَ فِيهِ مَجَالٌ لِلشُّبْهَةِ، وَلَا مَدْخَلٌ لِلرِّيْبَةِ.

وَقِيلَ: مَعْنَاهُ: لَا رَيْبَ فِيهِ لِلْمُتَّقِينَ، وَ﴿هُدًى﴾: حَالٌ مِنَ الضَّمِيرِ ....

[The Qurʾān's rational invalidation of doubt]

lā rayba fīhi ⁽*no doubt therein*⁾ means that, due to its clarity and the radiance of its proof, it follows that no rational being, after a sound examination, doubts that it constitutes revelation that qualifies as supernaturally inimitable. This is not to say that no one ever has doubts about it: do you not see that He said *And if you are in doubt concerning that which We revealed unto Our slave* [to the rest of] the verse (al-Baqara 2:23)? So He did not keep doubt away from them; rather, He showed them the way that removes[462] it, which consists in their striving to oppose any of its installments they like, and doing so to their utmost until, when they utterly fail, they realize that there is no room for skepticism and no leeway for doubt.[463]

It was also said its meaning is there is no doubt in it for those who beware, *hudan* being a complement of state for the pronoun

462 All mss. and editions: المزيح except AQ, H, MM: المريح typo.

463 "Al-Ṭībī said: 'Meaning: A reasoning person's doubt in such a context must inevitably be dispelled, as its hypothesis is that of impossibilities; but you are rational and reflecting people, so ponder it and try your best to see if any doubt remains.'" (S)

الْمَجْرُورِ؛ وَالْعَامِلُ فِيهِ: الظَّرْفُ الْوَاقِعُ صِفَةً لِلْمَنْفِيِّ.

وَ(الرَّيْبُ) فِي الْأَصْلِ: مَصْدَرُ (رَابَنِي الشَّيْءُ) إِذَا حَصَلَ فِيكَ الرِّيبَةُ؛ وَهِيَ قَلَقُ النَّفْسِ وَاضْطِرَابُهَا؛ سُمِّيَ بِهِ الشَّكُّ لِأَنَّهُ يُقْلِقُ النَّفْسَ، وَيُزِيلُ الطُّمَأْنِينَةَ.

وَفِي الْحَدِيثِ: **دَعْ مَا يَرِيبُكَ إِلَى مَا لَا يَرِيبُكَ؛ فَإِنَّ الشَّكَّ رِيبَةٌ، وَالصِّدْقَ طُمَأْنِينَةٌ.**

وَمِنْهُ: (رَيْبُ الزَّمَانِ)، لِنَوَائِبِهِ.

﴿هُدًى لِّلْمُتَّقِينَ﴾: يَهْدِيهِمْ ....

of the genitive, its regent being the temporal-local vessel [*fī*] that comes as an attribute for what is being negated.

Rayb is originally the infinitive noun of *rābanī al-shay'u* ⁽it unsettles me⁾ when you experience misgivings, the psyche's anxiety and its disturbance. It was used to name doubt because it causes anxiety in the psyche and does away with tranquility. A hadith states:

> Leave what causes you misgivings for what does not cause you misgivings; for truly, doubt is misgivings (*al-shakku rība*) and truthfulness is peace of mind.[464]

From it comes *raybu al-zamān* ⁽the vicissitudes of time⁾ for its trials.

hudan li-l-muttaqīna ⁽*a guidance for those who beware*⁾: it guides

[464] A Prophetic report narrated from al-Ḥasan b. ʿAlī by al-Nasā'ī, al-Tirmidhī (*ḥasan ṣaḥīḥ*), Aḥmad and many others. Al-Bukhārī cites its first half as a saying of the Basrian *Tābiʿī* Ḥassān b. Abī Sinān. The wording of the second half is verbatim as cited by J who was critiqued for its incoherence—cf. al-Ṭībī, *Futūḥ* (1:182) and S (1:276)—since the sources have: "Verily truthfulness/goodness (*al-ṣidqu/al-khayru*) is peace of mind and mendacity (*al-kadhibu*) is misgivings."

إِلَى الْحَقِّ.

وَ(الْهُدَى) فِي الْأَصْلِ: مَصْدَرٌ، كَـ(السُّرَى) وَ(التُّقَى)؛ وَمَعْنَاهُ: الدَّلَالَةُ.

وَقِيلَ: الدَّلَالَةُ الْمُوصِلَةُ إِلَى الْبُغْيَةِ، لِأَنَّهُ جُعِلَ مُقَابِلَ الضَّلَالَةِ فِي قَوْلِهِ تَعَالَى ﴿لَعَلَىٰ هُدًى أَوْ فِي ضَلَٰلٍ مُّبِينٍ﴾ [سبأ ٢٤]، وَلِأَنَّهُ لَا يُقَالُ (مَهْدِيٌّ) إِلَّا لِمَنِ اهْتَدَى إِلَى الْمَطْلُوبِ.

وَاخْتِصَاصُهُ بِالْمُتَّقِينَ: لِأَنَّهُمُ الْمُهْتَدُونَ بِهِ وَالْمُنْتَفِعُونَ بِنَصِّهِ ـ وَإِنْ كَانَتْ دَلَالَتُهُ عَامَّةً لِكُلِّ نَاظِرٍ مِنْ مُسْلِمٍ أَوْ كَافِرٍ؛ وَبِهَذَا الِاعْتِبَارِ قَالَ تَعَالَى: ﴿هُدًى لِّلنَّاسِ﴾[البقرة ١٨٥ وآل عمران ٤]. أَوْ: لِأَنَّهُ لَا يَنْتَفِعُ بِالتَّأَمُّلِ...

them to the truth.

[The specific beneficiaries of Quranic *hudā* ⁽guidance⁾]

Hudā is originally an infinitive noun—like *surā* ⁽night travel⁾ and *tuqā* ⁽wariness⁾—which means direction. It was also said it means the [specific] direction by which one reaches one's goal since it is considered the counterpart of misguidance in the saying of the Most High, *Surely, either we or you are upon right guidance, or in manifest error* (Saba' 34:24) and because the term *mahdī* ⁽well-guided⁾ is not used for other than one who found the right way to the object of the quest.

It refers specifically to the wary (i) because they are the ones that use it for right guidance and benefit from its text—although its direction includes every peruser, believer or unbeliever, in consideration of which Allah Most High said *a guidance for all people* (al-Baqara 2:185, Āl 'Imrān 3:4); (ii) or because none benefits by scrutinizing ....

فِيهِ إِلَّا مَنْ صَقَلَ الْعَقْلَ، وَاسْتَعْمَلَهُ فِي تَدَبُّرِ الْآيَاتِ، وَالنَّظَرِ فِي الْمُعْجِزَاتِ، وَتَعَرُّفِ النُّبُوَّاتِ؛ لِأَنَّهُ كَالْغِذَاءِ الصَّالِحِ لِحِفْظِ الصِّحَّةِ: فَإِنَّهُ لَا يَجْلِبُ نَفْعاً مَا لَمْ تَكُنِ الصِّحَّةُ حَاصِلَةً. وَإِلَيْهِ أَشَارَ بِقَوْلِهِ تَعَالَى: ﴿وَنُنَزِّلُ مِنَ ٱلْقُرْءَانِ مَا هُوَ شِفَآءٌ وَرَحْمَةٌ لِّلْمُؤْمِنِينَ وَلَا يَزِيدُ ٱلظَّٰلِمِينَ إِلَّا خَسَارًا ﴿٨٢﴾﴾ [الإسراء].

وَلَا يَقْدَحُ مَا فِيهِ مِنَ الْمُجْمَلِ وَالْمُتَشَابِهِ فِي كَوْنِهِ هُدًى لِمَا لَمْ يَنْفَكَّ عَنْ بَيَانٍ يُعَيِّنُ الْمُرَادَ مِنْهُ.

وَ(الْمُتَّقِي): اِسْمُ فَاعِلٍ، مِنْ قَوْلِهِمْ: (وَقَاهُ، فَاتَّقَى). وَالْوِقَايَةُ: فَرْطُ الصِّيَانَةِ. وَهُوَ فِي عُرْفِ الشَّرْعِ: ....

it except those who have burnished the intellect and used it to ponder the signs, peruse the inimitable miracles and recognize the matters of Prophethood. It is like a nutritious food suitable for conserving good health: it does not procure benefit unless there is already health. The Most High alluded to this in His saying, *And We reveal of the Qur'ān that which is a healing and a mercy for believers though it increase the evil-doers in naught save loss* (al-Isrā' 17:82).

Its unexplained and ambiguous content[465] does not undermine the fact that it is a guidance, since an exposition by which its import is determined[466] invariably goes with it.

[Levels of *taqwā* ⟨guarding oneself⟩]

Muttaqī ⟨wary⟩ is an active participle from *waqāhu, fa-ttaqā* ⟨he guarded him, so he guarded himself⟩, *wiqāya* being utmost maintenance. In the terminology of sacred law it is ....

[465] Sacy: "des passages amphibologiques ou obscurs."

[466] AQ, B, F, H, K, MM: يُعَيِّن α, Ak, I, N, Q, R, Sk, Ul, Z: نعين β, D, ε, Kh, L, P, T, U: تعيين

اِسْمٌ لِمَنْ يَقِي نَفْسَهُ مِمَّا يَضُرُّهُ فِي الآخِرَةِ.

وَلَهُ ثَلَاثُ مَرَاتِبَ: * الأُولَى: التَّوَقِّي مِنَ الْعَذَابِ الْمُخَلَّدِ، بِالتَّبَرِّي مِنَ الشِّرْكِ؛ وَعَلَيْهِ قَوْلُهُ تَعَالَى: ﴿وَأَلْزَمَهُمْ كَلِمَةَ التَّقْوَىٰ﴾ [الفتح ٢٦].

* والثَّانِيَةُ: التَّجَنُّبُ عَنْ كُلِّ مَا يُؤْثِمُ - مِنْ فِعْلٍ أَوْ تَرْكٍ - حَتَّى الصَّغَائِرِ عِنْدَ قَوْمٍ. وَهُوَ الْمُتَعَارَفُ بِاسْمِ التَّقْوَى فِي الشَّرْعِ؛ وَهُوَ الْمَعْنِيُّ بِقَوْلِهِ تَعَالَى: ﴿وَلَوْ أَنَّ أَهْلَ الْقُرَىٰ آمَنُوا وَاتَّقَوْا﴾ [الأعراف ٩٦].

* وَالثَّالِثَةُ: أَنْ يَتَنَزَّهَ عَمَّا يَشْغَلُ سِرَّهُ عَنِ الْحَقِّ، وَيَتَبَتَّلَ إِلَيْهِ بِشَرَاشِرِهِ. وَهُوَ التَّقْوَى الْحَقِيقِيُّ، الْمَطْلُوبُ ....

a name for one who guards himself from what harms him in the hereafter. It has three levels:

• First, guarding oneself against everlasting punishment by disowning idolatry, as in His saying, *and He imposed on them the word of wariness* (al-Fatḥ 48:26).

• Second, avoiding everything that constitutes sin—whether by commission or omission—including small sins according to some.[467] This is what is commonly known by the name of *taqwā* ʿwarinessʾ in sacred law and what is meant in His saying, *And if the people of the townships had believed and guarded themselves (wa-t-taqaw)* (al-Aʿrāf 7:96).

• Third, to keep oneself free of what engrosses one's inward away from the Real and to devote oneself to Him heart and soul. This is the true wariness that was demanded ....

[467] Bayḍāwī and J agree *taqwā* does not necessitate the latter, cf. Qur'ān 3:103, 134-136; 53:33; 64:17; contrary reports mean perfection. (S) "If avoiding *shirk* were not enough as *taqwā*, the affirmation of *tawḥīd* would not be called *kalimat al-taqwā*." (Z)

بِقَوْلِهِ تَعَالَى: ﴿يَٰٓأَيُّهَا ٱلَّذِينَ ءَامَنُواْ ٱتَّقُواْ ٱللَّهَ حَقَّ تُقَاتِهِۦ﴾ [آل عمران ١٠٢].

وَقَدْ فُسِّرَ قَوْلُهُ: ﴿هُدًى لِّلْمُتَّقِينَ﴾ هٰهُنَا عَلَى الْأَوْجُهِ الثَّلَاثَةِ.

وَاعْلَمْ أَنَّ الْآيَةَ تَحْتَمِلُ أَوْجُهاً مِنَ الْإِعْرَابِ:

(١) أَنْ يَكُونَ ﴿الٓمٓ﴾ مُبْتَدَأً، عَلَى أَنَّهُ اِسْمٌ لِلْقُرْآنِ، أَوِ السُّورَةِ، أَوْ مُقَدَّرٌ بِالْمُؤَلَّفِ مِنْهَا؛ وَ﴿ذَٰلِكَ﴾ خَبَرُهُ ـ وَإِنْ كَانَ أَخَصَّ مِنَ الْمُؤَلَّفِ مُطْلَقاً، وَالْأَصْلُ أَنَّ الْأَخَصَّ لَا يُحْمَلُ عَلَى الْأَعَمِّ ـ لِأَنَّ الْمُرَادَ بِهِ: الْمُؤَلَّفُ الْكَامِلُ فِي تَأْلِيفِهِ، الْبَالِغُ أَقْصَى دَرَجَاتِ الْفَصَاحَةِ وَمَرَاتِبِ الْبَلَاغَةِ؛ وَ﴿ٱلْكِتَٰبُ﴾: صِفَةُ ﴿ذَٰلِكَ﴾.

with His statement, *O Believers, beware Allah with true wariness of Him!* (Āl ʿImrān 3:102).

His saying *a Guidance for those who beware* here has been explained in all three senses.

[Parsing of verses 2:1-2]

Know that the verse supports various aspects of desinential syntax:

1. ***Alif lām mīm*** can be understood as an inchoative constituting a name for the Qurʾān or the Sura, or it can be subauded as "whatever [discourse] is formed of these [letters];" and ***dhālika*** is its enunciative—even if it is more specific than the composed whole in absolute terms, and in principle the more specific is not understood in terms of the more general—because what is meant by it is the work that is perfect in its composition, reaching the apex of pure style and top levels of eloquence, while ***al-kitāb*** is a descriptive epithet for ***dhālika***.

(٢) وَأَنْ يَكُونَ ﴿الٓمٓ﴾ خَبَرَ مُبْتَدَءٍ مَحْذُوفٍ، وَ﴿ذَٰلِكَ﴾ خَبَراً ثَانِياً ـ أَوْ بَدَلاً ـ وَ﴿ٱلْكِتَٰبُ﴾ صِفَتُهُ.

وَ﴿لَا رَيْبَ﴾ فِي المَشْهُورَةِ مَبْنِيٌّ لِتَضَمُّنِهِ مَعْنَى (مِنْ)، مَنْصُوبُ المَحَلِّ، عَلَى أَنَّهُ اِسْمُ ﴿لَا﴾ النَّافِيَةِ لِلْجِنْسِ، الْعَامِلَةِ عَمَلَ (إِنَّ)، لِأَنَّهَا نَقِيضَتُهَا وَلَازِمَةٌ لِلْأَسْمَاءِ لُزُومَهَا. وَفِي قِرَاءَةِ أَبِي الشَّعْثَاءِ: مَرْفُوعٌ بِـ﴿لَا﴾ الَّتِي بِمَعْنَى (لَيْسَ)؛

(أ) وَ﴿فِيهِ﴾: خَبَرُهُ ـ وَلَمْ يُقَدَّمْ كَمَا قُدِّمَ فِي قَوْلِهِ تَعَالَى: ﴿لَا فِيهَا غَوْلٌ﴾ [الصافات ٤٦]، لِأَنَّهُ لَمْ يُقْصَدْ ....

2. ***Alif lām mīm*** can also be understood as the enunciative of a suppressed inchoative, ***dhālika*** as a second enunciative or a substitute, and ***al-kitābu*** as its descriptive epithet.

Lā rayba ⟨no doubt⟩ in the famous one [viz., canonical reading] has an indeclinable fixed case ending[468] because it contains the meaning of *min* ⟨of⟩.[469] It is in the accusative case as the noun of "the ***lā*** ⟨no⟩ that negates the whole species," governing in the same way as *inna* ⟨verily⟩ because it is its antithesis and is inseparable from nouns just as *inna* is.

In the reading of Abū al-Sha'thā', however, it is in the nominative [*lā raybun*] with ***lā*** in the sense of *laysa*;[470] while

(a) ***fīh*** ⟨in it⟩ is its [***lā***'s] enunciative—which was not put first the way it was in the saying of Allah Most High *lā fīhā ghawlun* ⟨*Wherein is no headache* (al-Ṣāffāt 36:46)⟩ as the purport was not

468 Viz., *fatḥa*.
469 "The *min* of *istighrāq* ⟨totality⟩, as in *lā min raybi fīh* ⟨no doubt at all in it⟩." (Z)
470 An anomalous reading also related from Zuhayr al-Farqabī and Zayd b. 'Alī (*MQ*).

تَخْصِيصُ نَفْيِ الرَّيْبِ بِهِ مِنْ بَيْنِ سَائِرِ الْكُتُبِ كَمَا قُصِدَ ثَمَّةَ ـ؛

(ب) أَوْ: صِفَتُهُ، وَ﴿لِلْمُتَّقِينَ﴾ خَبَرُهُ، وَ﴿هُدًى﴾ نُصِبَ عَلَى الْحَالِ.

(ج) أَوْ: الْخَبَرُ مَحْذُوفٌ، كَمَا فِي ﴿لَا ضَيْرَ﴾ [الشعراء ٥٠] ـ فَلِذٰلِكَ وُقِفَ عَلَى ﴿لَا رَيْبَ﴾ ـ عَلَى أَنَّ ﴿فِيهِ﴾ خَبَرُ ﴿هُدًى﴾، قُدِّمَ عَلَيْهِ لِتَنْكِيرِهِ. وَالتَّقْدِيرُ: (لَا رَيْبَ فِيهِ، فِيهِ هُدًى).

(٣) وَأَنْ يَكُونَ ﴿ذَٰلِكَ﴾ مُبْتَدَأً، وَ﴿ٱلْكِتَٰبُ﴾ (أ) خَبَرَهُ، عَلَى مَعْنَى أَنَّهُ الْكِتَابُ الْكَامِلُ، الَّذِي يَسْتَأْهِلُ أَنْ يُسَمَّى كِتَاباً؛ (ب) أَوْ صِفَتُهُ، وَمَا بَعْدَهُ خَبَرُهُ. وَالْجُمْلَةُ خَبَرُ ﴿الٓمٓ﴾.

to single it out for the negation of doubt among all the other Scriptures the way it was purported in the latter case;[471]

(b) or [*fīh* is] its attribute, while ***lil-muttaqīn*** is its enunciative and ***hudan*** is in the accusative as a participial state;

(c) or the enunciative is suppressed, as in the expression *lā ḍayra* ⟨no harm⟩ (al-Shuʿarāʾ 26:50). This is why recitation can stop after *lā rayb*, in which case ***fīh*** is the enunciative of ***hudan*** and was placed before it because the latter is indefinite, the subaudition being "there is no doubt in it; in it there is guidance."

3. [Finally,] ***dhālika*** can be an inchoative of which ***al-kitāb*** is (a) the enunciative, in the sense that it is the perfect book—one that truly deserves to be called a book; (b) or the attribute, whereas the enunciative is what follows; and the [whole] sentence is the enunciative of ***alif lām mīm***.

[471] I.e., the way the wine of the hereafter alone was singled out among all wines as not causing illness. (Q)

وَالْأَوْلَى أَنْ يُقَالَ: إِنَّهَا أَرْبَعُ جُمَلٍ مُتَنَاسِقَةٍ، (أ) تُقَرِّرُ اللَّاحِقَةُ مِنْهَا السَّابِقَةَ، وَلِذٰلِكَ لَمْ يُدْخِلِ الْعَاطِفَ بَيْنَهَا.

* فَـ﴿الٓمٓ﴾: جُمْلَةٌ، دَلَّتْ عَلَى أَنَّ الْمُتَحَدَّى بِهِ هُوَ الْمُؤَلَّفُ مِنْ جِنْسِ مَا يُرَكِّبُونَ مِنْهُ كَلَامَهُمْ؛

* وَ﴿ذَٰلِكَ ٱلْكِتَٰبُ﴾: جُمْلَةٌ ثَانِيَةٌ، مُقَرِّرَةٌ لِجِهَةِ التَّحَدِّي؛

* وَ﴿لَا رَيْبَ فِيهِ﴾: ثَالِثَةٌ، تَشْهَدُ عَلَى كَمَالِهِ بِأَنَّ الْكِتَابَ الْمَنْعُوتَ بِغَايَةِ الْكَمَالِ، إِذْ لَا كَمَالَ أَعْلَى مِمَّا لِلْحَقِّ وَالْيَقِينِ.

* وَ﴿هُدًى لِّلْمُتَّقِينَ﴾: ـ بِمَا يُقَدَّرُ لَهُ مُبْتَدَأً ـ: رَابِعَةٌ، تُؤَكِّدُ كَوْنَهُ.........

It is more fitting to say they are well-coordinated sentences, (a) each reaffirming the one that precedes it, hence He did not insert a conjunction of coordination between any of its pairs. So:

- *Alif lām mīm* is a sentence indicating that the content of the challenge is that which is composed of the same material out of which they construct their speech;
- *That is the Book* is a second sentence reaffirming the aspect of challenge;
- *There is no doubt in it* is a third[472] that witnesses to its perfection, in that it is the Book that is characterized as the summit of perfection, since nothing possesses greater perfection than truth and certitude; and
- *a guidance for those who beware*—together with its inferred inchoative—is a fourth sentence,[473] emphasizing the fact that it is

[472] α, Ak, β, D, ε, I, N, R: فيه ثالثة AQ, H, K, Kh, L, MM, P, Q, T, U, Ul, Z: فيه جملة ثالثة

[473] B, D, ε, F, N, P, R, T: مبتدأً رابعةٌ Ak: ditto, with insertor squiggle in between and جملة added in the margin with glyph صح AQ, β, H, I, K, Kh, L, MM, Q, Sk, U, Ul, Z: مبتدأ أي هو جملة رابعة :α جملة رابعة

حقاً، لَا يَحُومُ الشَّكُّ حَوْلَهُ بِأَنَّهُ ﴿هُدًى لِّلْمُتَّقِينَ﴾؛

(ب) أَوْ تَسْتَتْبِعُ السَّابِقَةُ مِنْهَا اللَّاحِقَةَ اسْتِتْبَاعَ الدَّلِيلِ لِلْمَدْلُولِ؛ وَبَيَانُهُ: أَنَّهُ، لَمَّا نَبَّهَ أَوَّلاً عَلَى إِعْجَازِ الْمُتَحَدَّى بِهِ - مِنْ حَيْثُ إِنَّهُ مِنْ جِنْسِ كَلَامِهِمْ، وَقَدْ عَجَزُوا عَنْ مُعَارَضَتِهِ - اسْتُنْتِجَ مِنْهُ أَنَّهُ الْكِتَابُ الْبَالِغُ حَدَّ الْكَمَالِ؛ وَاسْتَلْزَمَ ذَٰلِكَ أَنْ لَا يَتَشَبَّثَ الرَّيْبُ بِأَطْرَافِهِ، إِذْ لَا أَنْقَصَ مِمَّا يَعْتَرِيهِ الشَّكُّ وَالشُّبْهَةُ. وَمَا كَانَ كَذَٰلِكَ: كَانَ - لَا مَحَالَةَ - ﴿هُدًى لِّلْمُتَّقِينَ﴾.

وَفِي كُلِّ وَاحِدَةٍ مِنْهَا: نُكْتَةٌ ذَاتُ جَزَالَةٍ.

* فَفِي الْأُولَى: الْحَذْفُ؛ وَالرَّمْزُ إِلَى الْمَقْصُودِ، مَعَ التَّعْلِيلِ؛

true and right, free of even the shadow of a doubt over the fact that it is guidance for the wary;

(b) or, each [sentence] making the next one follow it the way the sign makes [its] signification follow. In other words, after He first warned about the inimitability of the content of the challenge—i.e., its being the same species as their speech and yet they were completely unable to oppose it—the outcome was that it is the Book that reaches the apex of perfection. That inescapably means that no inkling of doubt mars it, since nothing is more defective than what raises doubt and suspicion. Hence, anything thus described must inevitably be a guidance for the wary.

Each of these [sentences], moreover, holds an allusive point in the purest rhetorical style.[474] Thus:

• the first sentence contains ellipsis[475] and symbolism of the purport as well as its rationale;

[474] On the *nukta* see note 218. *Jazāla* is the opposite of *rakāka* ʿlamenessʾ. (S)

[475] *Ḥadhf/maḥdhūf* and *iḍmār/muḍmar* have both been at times translated "ellipsis"

* وَفِي الثَّانِيَةِ: فَخَامَةُ التَّعْرِيفِ؛

* وَفِي الثَّالِثَةِ: تَأْخِيرُ الظَّرْفِ، حَذَراً عَنْ إِيهَامِ الْبَاطِلِ؛

* وَفِي الرَّابِعَةِ: الْحَذْفُ؛ وَالتَّوْصِيفُ بِالْمَصْدَرِ لِلْمُبَالَغَةِ؛ وَإِيرَادُهُ مُنَكَّراً لِلتَّعْظِيمِ؛ وَتَخْصِيصُ الْهُدَى بِالْمُتَّقِينَ بِاعْتِبَارِ الْغَايَةِ؛ وَتَسْمِيَةُ الْمُشَارِفِ لِلتَّقْوَى (مُتَّقِياً) إِيجَازاً، وَتَفْخِيماً لِشَأْنِهِ.

﴿ٱلَّذِينَ يُؤْمِنُونَ بِٱلْغَيْبِ﴾: إِمَّا ....

• the second, grandeur of the definite;[476]

• the third delays the local preposition lest falsehood[477] be suggested;

• the fourth (i) contains ellipsis and (ii) turns the infinitive noun into an attribute for intensiveness,[478] (iii) producing it as an indefinite for magnification.

(iv) Guidance was made particular to the wary in consideration of [their becoming so in] the end; also, naming *muttaqī* those who are approaching *taqwā* is for concision and in order to amplify their status.

[Belief in the unseen is part and parcel of *taqwā*]

[2:3] **al-ladhīna yuʾminūna bil-ghaybi** ⁽*those who believe in the unseen*⁾ is either: ....

and the latter also as "implied meaning" but see, on the respective differences between these two sets of terms as well as *taqdīr/muqaddar* (inferred meaning), Muṣṭafā Shāhir Khallūf's thorough study *Uslūb al-Ḥadhf fil-Qurʾān al-Karīm wa-Atharuh fil-Maʿānī wal-Iʿjāz* (Amman: Dār al-Fikr, 1430/2009) p. 33-40.

[476] I.e. the predicate was made definite in a way that conveys exclusivity (*taʿrīf al-musnad al-mufīd lil-ḥaṣr*). (Q)

[477] I.e., the ascription of doubt to all the other Books of Allah Most High. (Q)

[478] The infinitive noun *hudā* was made a descriptive (*juʿila waṣfan*), which is normally done with the present participial *hād*. (Q)

(I) مَوْصُولٌ بِـ﴿الْمُتَّقِينَ﴾:

(أ) عَلَى أَنَّهُ صِفَةٌ مَجْرُورَةٌ،

(١) مُقَيِّدَةٌ لَهُ ـ إِنْ فُسِّرَ (التَّقْوَى) بِـ(تَرْكِ مَا لَا يَنْبَغِي) ـ، مُتَرَتِّبَةٌ عَلَيْهِ تَرَتُّبَ التَّحْلِيَةِ عَلَى التَّخْلِيَةِ، وَالتَّصْوِيرِ عَلَى التَّصْقِيلِ؛

(٢) أَوْ: مُوَضِّحَةٌ ـ إِنْ فُسِّرَ بِمَا يَعُمُّ فِعْلَ الْحَسَنَاتِ وَتَرْكَ السَّيِّئَاتِ ـ لِاشْتِمَالِهِ عَلَى مَا هُوَ أَصْلُ الْأَعْمَالِ وَأَسَاسُ الْحَسَنَاتِ مِنَ الْإِيمَانِ، وَالصَّلَاةِ، وَالصَّدَقَةِ: فَإِنَّهَا أُمَّهَاتُ الْأَعْمَالِ النَّفْسَانِيَّةِ وَالْعِبَادَاتِ الْبَدَنِيَّةِ وَالْمَالِيَّةِ، الْمُسْتَتْبِعَةُ لِسَائِرِ الطَّاعَاتِ وَالتَّجَنُّبِ عَنِ الْمَعَاصِي غَالِباً.

I. a relative pronoun [whose antecedent is] ***al-muttaqīn***

(a) in the sense of a genitive-case attribute that

1. either restricts its sense—if *taqwā* is defined as the avoidance of everything unworthy—and follows it sequentially, the way adornment follows renouncement or fashioning follows burnishing;[479]

2. or elucidates [it][480]—if it is explained as encompassing the performance of good deeds and the avoidance of evil deeds, as it comprises the root of actions and basis of good deeds including belief, prayer, and alsmgiving. For these are the mothers of all personal deeds, corporal and monetary acts of worship which make the rest of the acts of religious obedience and avoidance of sins follow in the majority of cases.

[479] Note *jinās*-type paronomasia and alliterations: *taḥliya/takhliya, taṣwīr/taṣqīl*. See Zakariyyā al-Anṣārī, *Risāla fī Anwāʿ al-Jinās*, ed. Muthannā ʿAbd al-Rasūl al-Shukrī, in *Majallat Kulliyyat al-Tarbiya al-Asāsiyya/Jāmiʿat Bābil* 8 (May 2012) 52-76; al-Ṣafadī, *Jinān al-Jinās fī ʿIlm al-Badīʿ* (Constantinople: Maṭbaʿat al-Jawāʾib, 1299/1882); and ʿAlī al-Jindī, *Fann al-Jinās* (Cairo: Dār al-Fikr al-ʿArabī, 1954).

[480] I.e. as a defining attribute (*ṣifa kāshifa*). (Q)

أَلَا تَـــرَى إِلَى قَوْلِـــهِ تَعَـــالَى: ﴿إِنَّ ٱلصَّلَوٰةَ تَنْهَىٰ عَنِ ٱلْفَحْشَآءِ وَٱلْمُنكَرِ﴾ [العنكبوت ٤٥]، وَقَوْلِهِ عَلَيْهِ الصَّلَاةُ وَالسَّلَامُ:

الصَّلَاةُ عِمَادُ الدِّينِ.

وَ: الزَّكَاةُ قَنْطَرَةُ الإِسْلَامِ؟

Do you not see the saying of Allah Most High *truly, prayer prohibits gross indecency and wrongdoing* (al-ʿAnkabūt 29:45) and the sayings of the Prophet—upon him blessings and peace:

"Prayer is the pillar of the Religion"[481]

and

"The charity tax is the archway of Islam?"[482]

481 *Al-ṣalāt ʿimād al-dīn*. Thus narrated by (i) al-Bayhaqī in *Shuʿab al-Īmān*, ed. Muḥammad al-Saʿīd Basyūnī Zaghlūl, 7 vols. (Beirut: Dār al-Kutub al-ʿIlmiyya, 1410/1980) 3:39 §2807, from ʿUmar, although "ʿIkrima [= b. Khālid b. Saʿīd b. al-ʿĀṣ, very trustworthy] did not hear from ʿUmar and he probably meant Ibn ʿUmar" and (ii) Abū al-Qāsim al-Aṣfahānī al-Taymī in *al-Targhīb wal-Tarhīb* (3:33 §2016) from ʿAlī as stated by al-Zaylaʿī, *Takhrīj* (Ph.D. 1:42 §19), also al-Daylamī, *al-Firdaws bi-Maʾthūr al-Khiṭāb*, ed. al-Saʿīd b. Basyūnī Zaghlūl, 6 vols. (Beirut: Dār al-Kutub al-ʿIlmiyya, 1406 /1986) 2:404 §3795, both with a very weak chain containing discarded narrators. Al-Qārī said in *al-Asrār al-Marfūʿa* (entry *al-ṣalātu ʿimād al-dīn*): "Ibn al-Ṣalāḥ said in *Mushkil al-Wasīṭ* it is unrecognized while al-Nawawī in *al-Tanqīḥ* said it is rejected and a falsehood. However, Daylamī narrated it from ʿAlī—Allah be well-pleased with him—as mentioned by Suyūṭī; and al-Bayhaqī in the *Shuʿab* from ʿUmar—Allah be well-pleased with him—with a weak chain" It is narrated from Muʿādh by Tirmidhī *(ḥasan ṣaḥīḥ)* with the word *ʿamūd* for "pillar" instead of its synonym *ʿimād*. Ibn Ḥajar in *al-Talkhīṣ al-Ḥabīr*, ed. Ḥasan b. ʿAbbās b. Quṭb, 4 vols. (Cairo: Muʾassasat Qurṭuba and Dār al-Mishkāt, 1416/1995) 1:308, said "the latter is also narrated in *mursal* form by al-Faḍl b. Dukayn in *al-Ṣalāt*," but it is missing from the printed edition of his *Kitāb al-Ṣalāt*, ed. Ṣalāḥ al-Shalāḥī (Medina: Maktabat al-Ghurabāʾ al-Athariyya, 1417/1996).

482 Narrated from Abū al-Dardāʾ by al-Ṭabarānī in *al-Awsaṭ* (8:380-381 §8937), al-Bayhaqī in the *Shuʿab* (3:195 §3310), al-Quḍāʿī in *Musnad al-Shihāb*, ed. Ḥamdī ʿAbd al-Majīd al-Salafī, 2 vols. (Beirut: Muʾassasat al-Risāla, 1405/1985) 1:183-184 §191, al-Aṣfahānī in *al-Targhīb* (2:218 §1467), and Ibn Shāhīn in his *Afrād*, all through a weak

(٣) أَوْ: مَسُوقَةٌ لِلْمَدْحِ بِمَا تَضَمَّنَهُ ﴿الْمُتَّقِينَ﴾؛ وَتَخْصِيصُ الْإِيمَانِ بِالْغَيْبِ، وَإِقَامَةِ الصَّلَاةِ، وَإِيتَاءِ الزَّكَاةِ بِالذِّكْرِ: إِظْهَارٌ لِفَضْلِهَا عَلَى سَائِرِ مَا يَدْخُلُ تَحْتَ اسْمِ التَّقْوَى.

(ب) أَوْ: عَلَى أَنَّهُ مَدْحٌ مَنْصُوبٌ، أَوْ مَرْفُوعٌ، بِتَقْدِيرِ (أَعْنِي) أَوْ (هُمُ الَّذِينَ).

(II) وَإِمَّا مَفْصُولٌ عَنْهُ، مَرْفُوعٌ بِالْابْتِدَاءِ، وَخَبَرُهُ: ﴿أُوْلَٰئِكَ عَلَىٰ هُدًى﴾؛ فَيَكُونُ الْوَقْفُ عَلَى ﴿الْمُتَّقِينَ﴾ تَامّاً.

3. Or it is propounded as a compliment for what *muttaqīn* entails, while the specific mention of belief in the unseen, establishing prayer and remitting the obligatory almsgiving highlights their superiority over the rest of what is described as *taqwā*.

(b) Or in the sense of a compliment in the accusative or the nominative, the subaudition being respectively "I mean" or "they are the ones who."

II. Or a distinct pronoun in the nominative, as an inchoative whose predicate is *those are upon guidance from their Nurturer* (al-Baqara 2:5), making the pause at *al-muttaqīn* a full stop.

chain because of al-Ḍaḥḥāk b. Ḥumra cf. Ibn Ḥajar, *al-Kāfī al-Shāf* (p. 11 §16) but considered fair (*ḥasan*) by Ibn ʿAdī in *al-Kāmil* (4:154, 157) and al-Mundhirī in *al-Targhīb wal-Tarhīb*, cf. al-Zaylaʿī, *Takhrīj al-Kashshāf* (Ph.D. 1:43), al-Haythamī, *Majmaʿ al-Baḥrayn* (3:8-9 §1337) and *Majmaʿ al-Zawāʾid wa-Manbaʿ al-Fawāʾid*, 10 vols. (Beirut: Dār al-Fikr, 1412/1992) 3:198 §4327, and Aḥmad al-Ghumārī, *Fatḥ al-Wahhāb bi-Takhrīj Aḥādīth al-Shihāb*, ed. Ḥamdī ʿAbd al-Majīd al-Salafī, 2 vols. (Beirut: ʿĀlam al-Kutub and Maktabat al-Nahḍat al-ʿArabiyya, 1408/ 1988) 1:238-239 §190. Ibn al-Jawzī alone suggests it is a forgery in his *ʿIlal al-Mutanāhiya fīl-Aḥādīth al-Wāhiya*, "ed. Khalīl al-Mays" [the real editor is a certain Irshād al-Ḥaqq al-Atharī], 2 vols. (Beirut: Dār al-Kutub al-ʿIlmiyya, 1403/1983) 2:2.

وَ(الْإِيمَانُ) فِي اللُّغَةِ: عِبَارَةٌ عَنِ التَّصْدِيقِ، مَأْخُوذٌ مِنَ الْأَمْنِ، كَأَنَّ
بالمدّ الْمُصَدِّقَ آمَنَ الْمُصَدَّقَ مِنَ التَّكْذِيبِ وَالْمُخَالَفَةِ. وَتَعْدِيَتُهُ بِالْبَاءِ: لِتَضَمُّنِهِ
مَعْنَى الِاعْتِرَافِ. وَقَدْ يُطْلَقُ بِمَعْنَى الْوُثُوقِ، مِنْ حَيْثُ إِنَّ الْوَاثِقَ بِالشَّيْءِ
صَارَ ذَا أَمْنٍ مِنْهُ؛ وَمِنْهُ: (مَا آمَنْتُ أَنْ أَجِدَ صَحَابَةً). وَكِلَا الْوَجْهَيْنِ حَسَنٌ
بالمدّ
فِي ﴿يُؤْمِنُونَ بِٱلْغَيْبِ﴾.

وَأَمَّا فِي الشَّرْعِ: فَالتَّصْدِيقُ بِمَا عُلِمَ بِالضَّرُورَةِ أَنَّهُ مِنْ دِينِ مُحَمَّدٍ ﷺ،
كَالتَّوْحِيدِ، وَالنُّبُوَّةِ، وَالْبَعْثِ، وَالْجَزَاءِ؛ وَمَجْمُوعُ ثَلَاثَةِ أُمُورٍ: اِعْتِقَادُ الْحَقِّ،
وَالْإِقْرَارُ بِهِ، وَالْعَمَلُ بِمُقْتَضَاهُ عِنْدَ جُمْهُورِ الْمُحَدِّثِينَ، ....

[Various doctrines on what the integrals of belief are]

Īmān, lexically, expresses confirmation and stems from *amn* ⁽safety⁾, as if the confirmer gave the thing confirmed safety from belying and perjury. It was made transitive with the *bā'* because it implies confession. It can be used to mean *wuthūq* ⁽tying⁾, as one who ties something down has become safe from it; whence the expression "I did not clinch my travel mate(s) yet."[483] Both senses would be fine for *those who believe in the unseen.*

In the legal sense, it is the confirmation of what is absolutely necessary to know as part of the religion of Muḥammad—upon him blessings and peace—such as pure monotheism, prophethood, resurrection and requital. It is the sum of three things:[484] firm belief in the truth, affirmation of it, and acting upon its exigencies according to the vast majority of hadith scholars, ...

[483] An idiom of the Arabs, spoken when one adjourns a trip for lack of fellow travellers, cited in Abu Zayd al-Anṣārī's (2nd/8th c.) *al-Nawādir fīl-Lugha*, ed. Muḥammad ʿAbd al-Qādir Aḥmad (Beirut: Dār al-Shurūq, 1401/1980) p. 510-511.

[484] From this point, the Qadi paraphrases al-Rāghib's *Tafsīr*. (S)

وَالْمُعْتَزِلَةِ، وَالْخَوَارِجِ. فَمَنْ أَخَلَّ بِالِاعْتِقَادِ وَحْدَهُ: فَهُوَ مُنَافِقٌ؛ وَمَنْ أَخَلَّ بِالْإِقْرَارِ: فَكَافِرٌ؛ وَمَنْ أَخَلَّ بِالْعَمَلِ: فَفَاسِقٌ وِفَاقاً، وَكَافِرٌ عِنْدَ الْخَوَارِجِ، وَخَارِجٌ عَنِ الْإِيمَانِ غَيْرُ دَاخِلٍ فِي الْكُفْرِ عِنْدَ الْمُعْتَزِلَةِ. وَالَّذِي يَدُلُّ عَلَى أَنَّهُ التَّصْدِيقُ وَحْدَهُ: أَنَّهُ ـ سُبْحَانَهُ وَتَعَالَى ـ أَضَافَ الْإِيمَانَ إِلَى الْقَلْبِ، فَقَالَ:

the Muʿtazila and the Khawārij.[485] Thus, whoever comes short of belief is a hypocrite; whoever comes short of affirmation, an unbeliever; and whoever comes short of deeds, a transgressor by agreement. The Khawārij consider the latter an unbeliever and the Muʿtazila consider him outside belief and unbelief both.

[The Ashʿarī definition of belief as confirmation in the heart]

What indicates that it is confirmation alone[486] is that Allah Most High has annexed *īmān* to the heart and said, ...

[485] "In [al-Rāzī's] *al-Tafsīr al-Kabīr* [2:26 *sub* al-Baqara 2:3]: '*Īmān* is a name for the acts of the heart and the limbs and the affirmation by the tongue according to the Muʿtazila, the Khawārij, the Zaydiyya, and *Ahl al-Ḥadīth*.'" (Q 3:50) See p. 481 further down for the Qadi's commentary on *thereby He leads none astray save the transgressors* (al-Baqara 2:26): "and the Muʿtazila, since they said '*īmān* stands for...'"

[486] "In this preference he has followed Imam Fakhr al-Dīn; and this contradicts the position of their Imam both, al-Shāfiʿī—Allah be well-pleased with him—and the entirety of the Predecessors." (S 1:294) But then S himself says on the next page: "I say: the Predecessors posited deeds as a precondition for the perfection of *īmān*; the Muʿtazila, its validity;" whereas the Qadi is evidently discussing the absolute, irreducible core of *īmān* which he dissociates again from deeds elsewhere (cf. al-Baqara 2:25), since he says "whoever comes short of deeds is a transgressor by agreement" in conformity with S's representation of deeds as integral to the perfection of *īmān* and not the precondition of *īmān* itself. Al-Bayḍāwī's definition of *īmān* is that of Imam al-Ashʿarī in the *Lumaʿ*, ed. Muḥammad al-Ḍannāwī (Beirut: Dār al-Kutub al-ʿIlmiyya, 1421/2000), followed by most 5th-c. Ashʿarīs, cf. Ibn Fūrak, *Maqālāt al-Ashʿarī* (pp. 152-153); al-Bāqillānī, *al-Inṣāf fi-mā Yajib Iʿtiqāduh wa-lā Yajūz al-Jahlu bih*, ed. Muḥammad Zāhid al-Kawtharī, 2nd ed. (Cairo: al-Maktabat al-Azhariyya, 1421/2000) p. 52; Abū Manṣūr al-Baghdādī, *Uṣūl al-Dīn* (Istanbul: Maṭbaʿat al-Dawla, 1346/1928, rept. Beirut: Dār al-Kutub al-ʿIlmiyya, 1401/1981) pp. 247-248; Abū Isḥāq al-Shīrāzī, *ʿAqīdat al-Salaf* in *al-Ishāra ilā Madhhab Ahl al-Ḥaqq*, ed. Muḥammad al-Zubaydī (Beirut: Dār

﴿أُوْلَٰٓئِكَ كَتَبَ فِي قُلُوبِهِمُ ٱلْإِيمَٰنَ﴾ [المجادلة ٢٢]، ﴿وَقَلْبُهُۥ مُطْمَئِنٌّۢ
بِٱلْإِيمَٰنِ﴾ [النحل ١٠٦]، ﴿وَلَمْ تُؤْمِن قُلُوبُهُمْ﴾ [المائدة ٤١]، ﴿وَلَمَّا يَدْخُلِ
ٱلْإِيمَٰنُ فِي قُلُوبِكُمْ﴾ [الحجرات ١٤]؛ وَعَطَفَ عَلَيْهِ الْعَمَلَ الصَّالِحَ فِي
مَوَاضِعَ لَا تُحْصَى؛ وَقَرَنَهُ بِالْمَعَاصِي، فَقَالَ تَعَالَى ﴿وَإِن طَآئِفَتَانِ مِنَ ٱلْمُؤْمِنِينَ
ٱقْتَتَلُواْ﴾ [الحجرات ٩]، ﴿يَٰٓأَيُّهَا ٱلَّذِينَ ءَامَنُواْ كُتِبَ عَلَيْكُمُ ٱلْقِصَاصُ فِي ٱلْقَتْلَى﴾
[البقرة ١٧٨]، ﴿ٱلَّذِينَ ءَامَنُواْ وَلَمْ يَلْبِسُوٓاْ إِيمَٰنَهُم بِظُلْمٍ﴾ [الأنعام ٨٢]؛ ....

As for such, He has written faith upon their hearts (al-Mujādila 58:22), *and whose heart is at rest with the faith* (al-Naḥl 16:106), *but their hearts believe not* (al-Mā'ida 5:41), *for faith has not yet entered into your hearts* (al-Ḥujurāt 49:14), adjoining to it good deeds in countless places; and He paired it with sins when He said *And if two factions of the believers fall to fighting* (al-Ḥujurāt 49:9), *O you who believe! Retaliation is prescribed for you in the matter of the murdered* (al-Baqara 2:178), and *Those who believe and confound not their belief with wrongdoing* (al-Anʿām 6:82).

al-Kitāb al-ʿArabī, 1419/1999) p. 301 §35; Imām al-Ḥaramayn, *al-Irshād ilā Qawāṭiʿ al-Adilla fī Uṣūl al-Iʿtiqād*, ed. Muḥammad Mūsā and ʿAlī ʿAbd al-Ḥamīd (Cairo: Maktabat al-Khānjī, 1369/1950) p. 397 *bāb fil-Asmā' wal-Aḥkām, faṣl fī maʿnā al-īmān* and *al-ʿAqīda al-Niẓāmiyya*, ed. Muḥammad al-Zubaydī (Beirut: Dār Sabīl al-Rashād and Dār al-Nafā'is, 1424/2003) pp. 257-258. Cf. Ibn al-Munayyir on this verse and, *contra*, al-Taymī al-Aṣfahānī, *al-Ḥujja fī Bayān al-Maḥajja*, ed. Muḥammad al-Madkhalī, 2 vols. (Riyadh: Dār al-Rāya, 1990) 1:403-406. Ashʿarīs who were also from *Ahl al-Ḥadīth* such as al-Bayhaqī and al-Qushayrī, followed the *contra* position. See also ʿAlī al-Qārī's discussion in *Minaḥ al-Rawḍ al-Azhar fī Sharḥ al-Fiqh al-Akbar*, ed. Wahbī Sulaymān Ghāwjī (Beirut: Dār al-Bashā'ir al-Islāmiyya, 1419/1998) p. 251, Mūsā Lāshīn's in *Fatḥ al-Munʿim Sharḥ Ṣaḥīḥ Muslim*, 10 vols. (Cairo: Dār al-Shurūq, 1423-2002) 1:28-30; Richard M. Frank, "Knowledge and *Taqlīd*: The Foundations of Religious Belief in Classical Ashʿarism," *Journal of the American Oriental Society* 109.1 (1989) 37-61; and Gimaret, "La conception Ashʿarienne de la foi" in his *Doctrine d'al-Ashʿarī* (pp. 472-479).

مَعَ مَا فِيهِ مِنْ قِلَّةِ التَّغْيِيرِ، فَإِنَّهُ أَقْرَبُ إِلَى الْأَصْلِ؛ وَهُوَ مُتَعَيِّنُ الْإِرَادَةِ فِي الْآيَةِ، إِذِ الْمُعَدَّى بِالْبَاءِ هُوَ التَّصْدِيقُ وِفَاقًا.

ثُمَّ اخْتُلِفَ فِي أَنَّ مُجَرَّدَ التَّصْدِيقِ بِالْقَلْبِ: هَلْ هُوَ كَافٍ ـ لِأَنَّهُ الْمَقْصُودُ ـ أَمْ لَا بُدَّ مِنِ انْضِمَامِ الْإِقْرَارِ بِهِ لِلْمُتَمَكِّنِ مِنْهُ؟ وَلَعَلَّ الْحَقَّ هُوَ الثَّانِي، لِأَنَّهُ ـ تَعَالَى ـ ذَمَّ الْمُعَانِدَ أَكْثَرَ مِنْ ذَمِّ الْجَاهِلِ الْمُقَصِّرِ. وَلِلْمَانِعِ أَنْ يَجْعَلَ الذَّمَّ لِلْإِنْكَارِ، لَا لِعَدَمِ الْإِقْرَارِ لِلْمُتَمَكِّنِ مِنْهُ.

Moreover, the difference is minimal; for that [definition] is closer to the original meaning[487] and the latter is definitely meant in the verse since the intransitive form—made transitive with *bāʾ*—means "confirmation" by general agreement.

Then comes the difference of opinion whether pure confirmation with the heart is enough—for that is the purpose—or is it indispensable to also have affirmation for those able to provide it?[488] The truth might be the latter;[489] for Allah Most High has blamed the obdurate more than He has blamed the negligent ignoramus. One who holds the opposite view may deem the blame directed at denial, not at lack of affirmation for someone able to provide it.

[487] I.e., the difference between the legal meaning of *īmān* as a detail-specific confirmation (namely, of what is necessarily known to be part of the Religion) and the lexical meaning as confirmation in absolute terms, which is the original meaning. (Z, Q)

[488] "Those who defined *īmān* as confirmation (*taṣdīq*) with the heart and the tongue together are Abū Ḥanīfa and the generality of the jurists." (S) "Pazdawī in the *Kashf* [*al-Asrār*] said that affirmation expresses the heart's content and signals confirmation. Hence it is a 'potentially dispensable pillar' (*rukn yaḥtamil al-suqūṭ*)." (Q)

[489] He did not categorically assert it, for three reasons: conflicting evidence; rebuttal of the most literal evidence with the objection he is about to mention; and the fact that the preponderant Ashʿarī position is that affirmation is not an integral of *īmān* (*ʿadam kawn al-iqrār ruknan huwa al-rājiḥ ʿinda al-Ashāʿira*). (Q)

وَ﴿الْغَيْبُ﴾: (أ) مَصْدَرٌ؛ وُصِفَ بِهِ لِلْمُبَالَغَةِ، كَ(الشَّهَادَةِ) فِي قَوْلِهِ تَعَالَى: ﴿عَٰلِمُ ٱلْغَيْبِ وَٱلشَّهَٰدَةِ﴾ [الأنعام ٧٣ وغيرها] - وَالْعَرَبُ تُسَمِّي الْمُطْمَئِنَّ مِنَ الْأَرْضِ، وَالْخَمْصَةَ الَّتِي تَلِي الْكُلْيَةَ: (غَيْباً) - (ب) أَوْ: (فَيْعَلٌ) خُفِّفَ، كَ(قَيْلٍ).

وَالْمُرَادُ بِهِ: الْخَفِيُّ، الَّذِي لَا يُدْرِكُهُ الْحِسُّ، وَلَا تَقْتَضِيهِ بَدِيهَةُ الْعَقْلِ. وَهُوَ قِسْمَانِ: قِسْمٌ لَا دَلِيلَ عَلَيْهِ؛ وَهُوَ الْمَعْنِيُّ بِقَوْلِهِ تَعَالَى: ﴿وَعِندَهُۥ مَفَاتِحُ ٱلْغَيْبِ لَا يَعْلَمُهَآ إِلَّا هُوَ﴾ [الأنعام ٥٩]؛ وَقِسْمٌ نُصِبَ عَلَيْهِ دَلِيلٌ: كَالصَّانِعِ وَصِفَاتِهِ، وَالْيَوْمِ الْآخِرِ وَأَحْوَالِهِ؛ وَهُوَ الْمُرَادُ بِهِ فِي هٰذِهِ الْآيَةِ - هٰذَا، إِذَا جَعَلْتَهُ صِلَةً لِلْإِيمَانِ، وَأَوْقَعْتَهُ مَوْقِعَ الْمَفْعُولِ بِهِ. ....

Al-ghayb ʿthe unseenʾ is an infinitive noun used as a descriptive for intensiveness as was *shahāda* ʿthe seenʾ in the saying of Allah Most High *Knower of the unseen and the seen* (al-Anʿām 6:73 and elsewhere). The Arabs call depressed ground and the renal hilum *ghayb*. It could also be a lightened form of *fayʿal* like *qayl* ʿkingletʾ.[490]

[Meanings and types of *ghayb* ʿunseenʾ]

What is meant is something hidden, imperceptible, and unintuited. It is of two types: (i) what has no proof—and this is what is meant in the saying of Allah Most High *And with Him are the keys of the invisible. None but He knows them* (al-Anʿām 6:59); and (ii) what was given a proof, such as the Maker, His Attributes, the Last Day and its events. The latter [type] is what is meant in the verse under discussion—if you deem it connected back to belief and treat it as its direct object.

[490] I.e., *ghayyab* like *qayyal* respectively becoming *ghayb* and *qayl*. (Q)

وَإِنْ جَعَلْتَهُ حَالاً، عَلَى تَقْدِيرِ (مُلْتَبِسِينَ بِالْغَيْبِ): كَانَ بِمَعْنَى الْغَيْبَةِ وَالْخَفَاءِ؛ وَالمَعْنَى: أَنَّهُمْ يُؤْمِنُونَ غَائِبِينَ (أ) عَنْكُمْ ـ لَا كَالْمُنَافِقِينَ، الَّذِينَ ﴿إِذَا لَقُوا۟ ٱلَّذِينَ ءَامَنُوا۟ قَالُوٓا۟ ءَامَنَّا وَإِذَا خَلَوْا۟ إِلَىٰ شَيَـٰطِينِهِمْ قَالُوٓا۟ إِنَّا مَعَكُمْ إِنَّمَا نَحْنُ مُسْتَهْزِءُونَ ١٤﴾ [البقرة، بلفظ الواو أوّله: وَإِذَا]. أَوْ (ب) عَنِ الْمُؤْمَنِ بِهِ، لِمَا رُوِيَ أَنَّ ابْنَ مَسْعُودٍ رَضِيَ اللهُ تَعَالَى عَنْهُ قَالَ: وَالَّذِي لَا إِلٰهَ غَيْرُهُ، مَا آمَنَ أَحَدٌ أَفْضَلَ مِنْ إِيمَانٍ بِغَيْبٍ، ثُمَّ قَرَأَ هٰذِهِ الْآيَةَ.

If you say it is a participial state—with the subaudition that they themselves are characterized as unseen—then it means absence and invisibility. That is, "they believe (i) even when away from you, unlike the hypocrites who, *when they meet those who believe, they say: We believe; and when they retire unto their devils, they say: Surely we are with you, we were only mocking* (al-Baqara 2:14);" (ii) or, when away from the one who is the object of belief[491] on the basis of the narration from Ibn Mas'ūd—Allah be well-pleased with him: "By Him besides Whom there is no god, none has better belief than belief without seeing," then he recited this verse.[492]

[491] I.e. the Prophet Muḥammad—upon him blessings and peace. (Q)

[492] Narrated by Sa'īd b. Manṣūr, *Sunan*, ed. Sa'd b. 'Abd Allāh Āl Ḥumayyid, 5 vols. (Riyadh: Dār al-Ṣumay'ī, 1414/1993) 2:544 §180; al-Baghawī's grandfather Ibn Manī' al-Marwarūdhī (160-244/777-858) in his *Musnad* as adduced by al-Būṣīrī in *Itḥāf al-Khiyara al-Mahara bi-Zawā'id al-Masānīd al-'Ashara*, ed. Yāsir b. Ibrāhīm, 9 vols. (Riyadh: Dār al-Waṭan lil-Nashr, 1420/1999) 1:107 §74 and Ibn Ḥajar in *al-Maṭālib al-'Āliya bi-Zawā'id al-Masānīd al-Thamāniya*, ed. 'Abd Allāh b. 'Abd al-Muḥsin al-Tuwayjirī 19 vols. (Riyadh: Dār al-'Āṣima and Dār al-Ghayth, 1419/1998) 12:398 §2923; Ibn Abī Ḥātim and al-Baghawī in their *Tafsīrs* (*sub* Q 2:3); al-Ḥākim in the *Mustadrak* (*Tafsīr*, 2:260=Mar'ashlī ed. 3:403), with a chain that meets the standards of al-Bukhārī and Muslim according to al-Būṣīrī and al-Ḥākim; Ibn Mandah in *al-Īmān*, ed. 'Alī al-Fuqayhī, 2nd ed., 2 vols. (Beirut: Mu'assasat al-Risāla, 1406/1985) 1:371 §209; and al-Taymī al-Aṣfahānī in *al-Ḥujja* (1:486).

وَقِيلَ: المُرَادُ بِالْغَيْبِ: الْقَلْبُ، لِأَنَّهُ مَسْتُورٌ؛ وَالمَعْنَى: يُؤْمِنُونَ بِقُلُوبِهِمْ، لَا كَمَنْ ﴿يَقُولُونَ بِأَفْوَٰهِهِم مَّا لَيْسَ فِي قُلُوبِهِمْ﴾ [آل عمران ١٦٧].

فَالْبَاءُ، عَلَى الْأَوَّلِ: لِلتَّعْدِيَةِ؛ وَعَلَى الثَّانِي: لِلْمُصَاحَبَةِ. وَعَلَى الثَّالِثِ لِلْآلَةِ.

﴿وَيُقِيمُونَ ٱلصَّلَوٰةَ﴾: أَيْ (أ) يُعَدِّلُونَ أَرْكَانَهَا وَيَحْفَظُونَهَا مِنْ أَنْ يَقَعَ زَيْغٌ فِي أَفْعَالِهَا، مِنْ (أَقَامَ الْعُودَ) إِذَا قَوَّمَهُ؛ (ب) أَوْ: يُوَاظِبُونَ عَلَيْهَا، مِنْ (قَامَتِ السُّوقُ) إِذَا نَفَقَتْ، وَ(أَقَمْتَهَا) إِذَا جَعَلْتَهَا نَافِقَةً. قَالَ: [مُتَقَارِب]

أَقَامَتْ غَزَالَةُ سُوقَ الضِّرَابِ ❋ لِأَهْلِ الْعِرَاقَيْنِ حَولاً قَمِيطاً

It was also said that what is meant by *ghayb* is the heart because it is concealed, so that the meaning is "they believe with their hearts, not like those *who speak with their mouths what is not in their hearts* (Āl ʿImrān 3:167)."

So the [preposition] *bāʾ* in the first case is for transitiveness; in the second, accompaniment; in the third, instrumentality.

[Meanings of "establishing the prayer"]

wa-yuqīmūna al-ṣalāta ⁽*and establish the prayer*⁾, that is:

1. they make its integrals equal and protect it against any corruption of its acts; from *aqāma al-ʿūd* ⁽to straighten the staff⁾;

2. or, they perform it assiduously, from *qāmat al-sūq* ⁽the market is up⁾ when it is booming, and *aqamtahā* ⁽you made it an up market⁾, "you caused roaring trade." [The poet] said: ["The Tripping"]

Ghazāla pulled up the market of sword fights
for the Kufans and Basrians a full year.[493]

[493] Part of a long poem spoken by the Companion Ayman b. Khuraym al-Asadī—Allah be well-pleased with him and his father—cf. S (1:299-300), Afandī (p. 484), Ibn Sīdah,

فَإِنَّهُ إِذَا حُوفِظَ عَلَيْهَا، كَانَتْ كَالنَّافِقِ، الَّذِي يُرْغَبُ فِيهِ؛ وَإِذَا ضُيِّعَتْ، كَانَتْ كَالْكَاسِدِ، الْمَرْغُوبِ عَنْهُ؛

(ج) أَوْ: يَتَشَمَّرُونَ لِأَدَائِهَا مِنْ غَيْرِ فُتُورٍ وَلَا تَوَانٍ، مِنْ قَوْلِهِمْ: (قَامَ بِالْأَمْرِ وَأَقَامَهُ)، إِذَا جَدَّ فِيهِ وَتَجَلَّدَ؛ وَضِدُّهُ: (قَعَدَ عَنِ الْأَمْرِ وَتَقَاعَدَ).

(د) أَوْ: يُؤَدُّونَهَا؛ عَبَّرَ عَنِ الْأَدَاءِ بِالْإِقَامَةِ، لِاشْتِمَالِهَا عَلَى الْقِيَامِ، كَمَا عَبَّرَ عَنْهَا بِالْقُنُوتِ، وَالرُّكُوعِ، وَالسُّجُودِ، وَالتَّسْبِيحِ.

For when [the prayer] is well-kept it is like something saleable that is in high demand; but when it is neglected it is like a slumping market that is shunned.

3. Or, they hasten to perform it without slackness or delay, as in *qāma bil-amr wa-aqāmah* ⁽he rose to the task and got it done⁾ when one puts effort into it and shows endurance, its antonym being *qa'ada 'an al-amr wa-taqā'ad* ⁽ he sat it out and desisted⁾.

4. Or, they perform it: He named the performance (*adā'*) a raising up (*iqāma*) because it involves standing (*qiyām*), just as He also referred to it by the names of devotion (*qunūt*), bowing (*rukū'*), prostration (*sujūd*), and glorification (*tasbīḥ*).

al-Muḥkam wal-Muḥīṭ al-A'ẓam fīl-Lugha, ed. Ḥusayn Naṣṣār et al., 7 vols. (Cairo: Ma'had al-Makhṭūṭāt bi-Jāmi'at al-Duwal al-'Arabiyya, 1377/1958) *sub gh-z-l* and Abū al-Faraj al-Aṣfahānī, *al-Aghānī*, ed. Iḥsān 'Abbās et al., 3rd ed., 25 vols. (Beirut: Dār Ṣādir, 1429/2008) 20:199. Ghazāla was the Mosul-born Qur'ān-memorizer and wife of Shabīb b. Yazīd b. Nu'aym al-Shaybānī who led a Khārijī sub-sect that became known as the Shabībiyya and the Ḥarūriyya—after Ḥarūrā', the Iraqi town where the disgruntled ex-followers of 'Alī b. Abī Ṭālib first gathered in the wake of Ṣiffīn to wage war against the Muslim state. Shabīb fought al-Ḥajjāj and 'Abd al-Malik b. Marwān for a year with "200 shedders of sacred Muslim blood and with them fifty female heretics" (Khuraym). After his death she fought on for a year and was killed in turn. "'The market' is a *mukanniya* ⁽implicit⁾ and *takhyīliyya* ⁽conceptual/associative⁾ or a *tamthīliyya* ⁽proverbial⁾ or a *taṣrīḥiyya* ⁽explicit⁾ metaphor." (Kh)

وَالْأَوَّلُ أَظْهَرُ، لِأَنَّهُ أَشْهَرُ، وَإِلَى الْحَقِيقَةِ أَقْرَبُ وَأَفْيَدُ، لِتَضَمُّنِهِ التَّنْبِيهَ عَلَى أَنَّ الْحَقِيقَ بِالْمَدْحِ: مَنْ رَاعَى حُدُودَهَا الظَّاهِرَةَ ـ مِنَ الْفَرَائِضِ وَالسُّنَنِ ـ وَحُقُوقَهَا الْبَاطِنَةَ ـ مِنَ الْخُشُوعِ وَالْإِقْبَالِ بِقَلْبِهِ عَلَى اللهِ تَعَالَى؛ لَا الْمُصَلُّونَ ﴿ٱلَّذِينَ هُمْ عَن صَلَاتِهِمْ سَاهُونَ ۝٥﴾ [الماعون]. وَلِذَلِكَ ذَكَرَ فِي سِيَاقِ الْمَدْحِ: ﴿وَٱلْمُقِيمِينَ ٱلصَّلَوٰةَ﴾ [النساء ١٦٢]، وَفِي مَعْرِضِ الذَّمِّ: ﴿فَوَيْلٌ لِّلْمُصَلِّينَ ۝٤﴾ [الماعون].

وَ﴿ٱلصَّلَوٰةُ﴾: فَعَلَةٌ مِنْ (صَلَّى) إِذَا دَعَا؛ كَـ﴿ٱلزَّكَوٰةِ﴾ مِنْ (زَكَّى) ـ كُتِبَتَا بِالْوَاوِ عَلَى لَفْظِ الْمُفَخَّمِ. وَإِنَّمَا سُمِّيَ الْفِعْلُ الْمَخْصُوصُ بِهَا لِاشْتِمَالِهِ عَلَى الدُّعَاءِ.

The first of those meanings is the predominant one[494] because it is the most widespread. It is also the nearest to and most evocative of the literal meaning, since it entails a notification that the one who truly deserves praise is he who observes its outward boundaries—among obligations and sunnas—as well as its inward duties—of humility and turning to Allah with one's whole heart—contrary to *those who are heedless in their prayers* (al-Māʿūn 107:5). Hence He mentioned in a praiseful way *the diligent (muqīmūn) in prayer* (al-Nisā' 4:162) and in a blameful way *woe to those that pray* (al-Māʿūn 107:4).

Ṣalāt is a *faʿala*-form [stemming] from *ṣallā* ⁽he supplicates⁾, like *zakāt* from *zakkā* ⁽he purifies/he causes to grow⁾—both are written with a *wāw*, according to the pronunciation with glottal accentuation. The verb that denotes it was thus named because it comprises supplication.

[494] As narrated from Ibn ʿAbbās by al-Ṭabarī and Ibn Abī Ḥātim. (S)

وَقِيلَ: أَصْلُ (صَلَّى): حَرَّكَ الصَّلَوَيْنِ؛ لِأَنَّ الْمُصَلِّيَ يَفْعَلُهُ فِي رُكُوعِهِ وَسُجُودِهِ. وَاشْتِهَارُ هٰذَا اللَّفْظِ فِي الْمَعْنَى الثَّانِي مَعَ عَدَمِ اشْتِهَارِهِ فِي الْأَوَّلِ، لَا يَقْدَحُ فِي نَقْلِهِ عَنْهُ. وَإِنَّمَا سُمِّيَ الدَّاعِي (مُصَلِّياً) تَشْبِيهاً لَهُ فِي تَخَشُّعِهِ بِالرَّاكِعِ السَّاجِدِ.

﴿وَمِمَّا رَزَقْنَٰهُمْ يُنفِقُونَ﴾: (الرِّزْقُ) فِي اللُّغَةِ: الْحَظُّ؛ قَالَ تَعَالَى: ﴿وَتَجْعَلُونَ رِزْقَكُمْ أَنَّكُمْ تُكَذِّبُونَ ﴿٨٢﴾﴾ [الواقعة]. وَالْعُرْفُ خَصَّصَهُ بِتَخْصِيصِ الشَّيْءِ بِالْحَيَوَانِ، لِلِانْتِفَاعِ بِهِ وَتَمْكِينِهِ مِنْهُ.

وَأَمَّا الْمُعْتَزِلَةُ، لَمَّا اسْتَحَالُوا ....

It was also said that the root [meaning] of *ṣallā* is *ḥarraka al-ṣalawayn* ⁽he moved his haunches⁾,[495] because that is what the person at prayer does in his bowing and prostration. The fact that this vocable became famous in the latter sense, together with the fact that it was never famous in the former one, does not preclude its being transferred from it. However, the *dāʿī* ⁽supplicant⁾ was named a *muṣallī* ⁽one who prays⁾ by assimilation to him, in his active humility, as one bowing and prostrating.

wa-mim-mā razaqnāhum yunfiqūna ⁽*spending out of what We provided them*⁾: *rizq* ⁽provision⁾ lexically is a portion. Allah Most High said, *and you make it your livelihood to deny truth* (al-Wāqiʿa 56:82). By convention it concerns living things specifically, whereby they benefit from it and avail themselves of it.[496]

[The Muʿtazili claim that *rizq* can only be *ḥalāl*]

The Muʿtazila, on the other hand, by deeming it impossible

[495] AQ, β, B, D, H, J, K, Kh, L, MM, P, Q, Sk, T, U, Ul, Z: الصلوين I: الصَّلايَن α, Ak, R: الصَّلَى ε, N, S: الصلا

[496] "The commentator of the *Mawāqif* said: '*rizq* is everything from which a living thing derives benefit , whether shared or otherwise, permissible or prohibited.'" (Q)

عَلَى اللهِ تَعَالَى أَنْ يُمَكِّنَ مِنَ الْحَرَامِ - لِأَنَّهُ مَنَعَ مِنَ الْاِنْتِفَاعِ بِهِ، وَأَمَرَ بِالزَّجْرِ عَنْهُ - قَالُوا: الْحَرَامُ لَيْسَ بِرِزْقٍ؛ أَلَا تَرَى أَنَّهُ تَعَالَى أَسْنَدَ الرِّزْقَ هٰهُنَا إِلَى نَفْسِهِ، إِيذَاناً بِأَنَّهُمْ يُنْفِقُونَ الْحَلَالَ الْمُطْلَقَ؟ فَإِنَّ إِنْفَاقَ الْحَرَامِ لَا يُوجِبُ الْمَدْحَ؛ وَذَمَّ الْمُشْرِكِينَ عَلَى تَحْرِيمِ بَعْضِ مَا رَزَقَهُمُ اللهُ تَعَالَى بِقَوْلِهِ: ﴿قُلْ أَرَءَيْتُم مَّآ أَنزَلَ ٱللَّهُ لَكُم مِّن رِّزْقٍ فَجَعَلْتُم مِّنْهُ حَرَامًا وَحَلَٰلًا﴾ [يونس ٥٩].

وَأَصْحَابُنَا جَعَلُوا الْإِسْنَادَ لِلتَّعْظِيمِ، وَالتَّحْرِيضِ عَلَى الْإِنْفَاقِ، وَالذَّمَّ

for Allah to make the illicit available [as sustenance]—because He disallowed benefiting from it and ordered [us] to chide [anyone who does]—said: "The illicit does not constitute provision; do you not see that He—the Most High—has made Himself the source of provision right here, as a proclamation that they are spending the absolutely licit? For spending the illicit does not compel praise; and He actually condemned idolaters for declaring part of what Allah had provided them to be illicit by saying: *Say: Have you considered what provision Allah has sent down for you, how you have made some of it unlawful and some lawful?* (Yūnus 10:59)."[497]

Our [Ashʿarī] colleagues, however, said that the predication [of provision to Allah] is for self-magnification and as a stimulus [for people] to spend, while the condemnation ....

[497] "And this is a Qadarī innovation, for they consider that Allah Most High does not provide other than the licit; as for the illicit, the slave provides it to himself!... For *Ahl al-Sunna* there is no creator nor provider in their conviction except Allah Most High, in confirmation of His saying *Is there any creator other than Allah who provides you from heaven and earth? There is no god but He, so how are your perverted?* (Fāṭir 35:3) O Qadarīs!" Ibn al-Munayyir, *al-Intiṣāf* in the margins of J, *Kashshāf* (1:155). See also al-Qārī, *Minaḥ al-Rawḍ al-Azhar* (pp. 363-364 *al-ḥarāmu rizqun*).

لِتَحْرِيمِ مَا لَمْ يُحْرَمْ؛ وَاخْتِصَاصُ ﴿مَا رَزَقْنَٰهُمْ﴾ بِالْحَلَالِ: لِلْقَرِينَةِ؛ وَتَمَسَّكُوا لِشُمُولِ الرِّزْقِ لَهُ بِقَوْلِهِ ﷺ فِي حَدِيثِ عَمْرِو بْنِ قُرَّةَ: **لَقَدْ رَزَقَكَ اللهُ طَيِّبًا، فَاخْتَرْتَ مَا حَرَّمَ اللهُ عَلَيْكَ مِنْ رِزْقِهِ مَكَانَ مَا أَحَلَّ اللهُ لَكَ مِنْ حَلَالِهِ.** وَبِأَنَّهُ لَوْ لَمْ يَكُنْ رِزْقًا، لَمْ يَكُنِ الْمُتَغَذِّي بِهِ طُولَ عُمُرِهِ مَرْزُوقًا، وَلَيْسَ كَذَٰلِكَ، لِقَوْلِهِ تَعَالَى: ﴿وَمَا مِن دَآبَّةٍ فِي ٱلْأَرْضِ إِلَّا عَلَى ٱللَّهِ رِزْقُهَا﴾ [هود ٦].

وَ(أَنْفَقَ الشَّيْءَ) وَ(أَنْفَدَهُ) أَخَوَانِ؛ وَلَوْ اِسْتَقْرَيْتَ الْأَلْفَاظَ، وَجَدْتَ كُلَّ مَا فَاؤُهُ نُونٌ، وَعَيْنُهُ فَاءٌ ....

targets the forbiddance of what was never made forbidden; and that *what We provided them* is specific to the licit contextually.[498] They also adduced as evidence of its inclusion [in the meaning] of provision the Prophet's statement in the hadith of ʿAmr b. Qurra: "Allah has most certainly granted you pure sustenance! But you chose what Allah has forbidden you of His provision instead of what He made permissible for you of His licit sustenance."[499] Furthermore, if it were not provision, then the one who uses it for food all life long is not provided for, which is not the case since Allah Most High said, *And there is not a creature that creeps on earth but its sustenance depends on Allah* (Hūd 11:6).

Anfaqa al-shay' (he spent something) and *anfadah* (he spent it) are near-cognate synonyms.[500] If you were to inductively survey all vocables with an initial *nūn* and middle *fā'* you would find

[498] I.e. in the context of praise. (K)

[499] Narrated from Ṣafwān b. Umayya by Ibn Mājah, *Sunan* (penultimate hadith of the book of *Ḥudūd, bāb al-mukhannathīn*) with an extremely weak chain because of Bishr (or Bashīr) b. Numayr al-Baṣrī, accused of forgery and labeled "one of the pillars of lying" as well as Yaḥyā b. al-ʿAlā' al-Bajalī, likewise suspected and discarded.

[500] See notes 293 and 572 on *al-ishtiqāq al-akbar*.

دَالاًّ عَلَى مَعْنَى الذَّهَابِ وَالْخُرُوجِ.

وَالظَّاهِرُ مِنْ هٰذَا الْإِنْفَاقِ: صَرْفُ الْمَالِ فِي سَبِيلِ الْخَيْرِ مِنَ الْفَرْضِ وَالنَّفْلِ. وَمَنْ فَسَّرَهُ بِالزَّكَاةِ ذَكَرَ أَفْضَلَ أَنْوَاعِهِ وَالْأَصْلَ فِيهِ؛ أَوْ خَصَّصَهُ بِهَا، لِاقْتِرَانِهِ بِمَا هُوَ شَقِيقُهَا.

وَتَقْدِيمُ الْمَفْعُولِ: لِلْاهْتِمَامِ بِهِ، وَلِلْمُحَافَظَةِ عَلَى رُؤُوسِ الْآيِ. وَإِدْخَالُ (مِنْ) التَّبْعِيضِيَّةِ عَلَيْهِ: لِلْكَفِّ عَنِ الْإِسْرَافِ الْمَنْهِيِّ عَنْهُ.

they all share the two senses of "going" and "exiting."[501]

[The meaning of *infāq* ⟨spending⟩]

The manifest/dominant meaning of this expenditure is the use of [one's] wealth for good works—both obligatory and voluntary. Whoever explains it to mean *zakāt* ⟨charity tax⟩[502] has [either] mentioned the best of its varieties and its fundamental [meaning], or restricted it to that [sense] since it is paired with what constitutes its twin.[503]

The reason the direct object was put first is to emphasize its importance as well as to keep verse endings [consonant].[504] The insertion of the partitive preposition *min* ⟨of⟩ before it is to prevent wastefulness,[505] which is proscribed.[506]

501 E.g., *nafara, nafaza, nafasa, nafaʿa, nafā, nafaḍa, nafatha*, and the like. (S)

502 This is the *tafsīr* of Ibn ʿAbbās as narrated by al-Ṭabarī, who also narrated from Ibn Masʿūd that it refers to a man's expenditure on his family. (S)

503 I.e., *ṣalāt*. (Q)

504 See note 288.

505 α, A, Ak, β, B, D, ε, F, I, Kh, N, P, R, Sk, T: للكف عن الاسراف Q: كالكف عن الاسراف AQ, H, K, L, MM, Ul, Z: لمنع المكلف عن الإسراف gloss U: للتكلف عن اسراف typo.

506 "He followed in this the author of the *Kashshāf*, and a commentator has mentioned that this forms *iʿtizāl*, as Muʿtazilis say that *min* ⟨of⟩ is used in the verse to suggest that one must not give away all of one's property in charity but must retain some,

وَيَحْتَمِلُ أَنْ يُرَادَ بِهِ: الْإِنْفَاقُ مِنْ جَمِيعِ المَعَاوِنِ الَّتِي أَتَاهُمُ اللهُ مِنَ النِّعَمِ الظَّاهِرَةِ وَالْبَاطِنَةِ؛ وَيُؤَيِّدُهُ قَوْلُهُ عَلَيْهِ الصَّلَاةُ وَالسَّلَامُ: إِنَّ عِلْماً لَا يُقَالُ بِهِ، كَكَنْزٍ لَا يُنْفَقُ مِنْهُ. وَإِلَيْهِ ذَهَبَ مَنْ قَالَ: (وَمِمَّا خَصَّصْنَاهُمْ بِهِ مِنْ أَنْوَارِ....

It is also possible that by expenditure are meant all the resources Allah gave them, comprising outward and inward blessings. This [meaning] is supported by the saying of the Prophet —upon him blessings and peace:

> Verily, learning that is left unspoken is like a treasure left unspent![507]

This is the position of those who said [it means] "and of what We lavished on them of the lights ....

lest unbearable hardship follow. We say: *Min* signifies that expenditure must be out of the provision that is licit to the exclusion of the illicit; as for the dislike of spending all one's property in charity, it is not forbidden in absolute terms. Abū Bakr —Allah be well-pleased with him—gave away all his property in charity and the Prophet—upon him blessings and peace—did not disapprove of him. It is disliked only for someone who is unable to bear with hardship." (S) The default is actually dislike of extremes, the paradigm being *And let not your hand be chained to your neck nor open it with a complete opening, lest you sit down rebuked, denuded* (al-Isrā' 17:29) and the Prophet's explicit recommendations, rather than Abū Bakr's lone abnegation; hence the mainstream position is that of al-Bayḍāwī as shown by Q (1:487) in his commentary on the same passage and as evidenced from the Qur'ān and Sunna by such books as Ibn Abī al-Dunyā's *Amwāl* and Khallāl's *Ḥathth 'alā al-Tijāra wal-Ṣinā'a wal-'Amal.*

[507] Narrated from Abū Hurayra by Ibn 'Asākir, *Tārīkh Madīnat Dimashq*, ed. Muḥibb al-Dīn 'Amrawī, 80 vols. (Beirut: Dār al-Fikr, 1421/2001) 9:22 and Ibn 'Abd al-Barr, *Jāmi' Bayān al-'Ilm wa-Faḍlih*, ed. Abū al-Ashbāl al-Zuhayrī, 2 vols. (Dammam: Dār Ibn al-Jawzī, 1414/1994) 1:489 §774 and 1:491 §777; from Ibn 'Umar by al-Khila'ī, *al-Fawā'id al-Muntaqāt al-Ḥisān min al-Ṣiḥāḥ wal-Gharā'ib al-Ma'rūfa bil-Khila'iyyāt*, ed. Ṣāliḥ al-Laḥḥām (Amman: al-Dār al-'Uthmāniyya; Beirut: Mu'assasat al-Rayyān, 1431/2010) p. 401 §1033 and Ibn 'Abd al-Barr, *Jāmi'* (1:491 §778); from Ibn Mas'ūd by al-Quḍā'ī in *Musnad al-Shihāb* (1:180 §263); as a saying of Salmān al-Fārisī by Dārimī, *Sunan* (*Bāb al-balāgh 'an Rasūl Allāh*), Ibn Abī Shayba, *Muṣannaf* (19:203 §35810 *Kitāb al-zuhd*) and Ibn 'Abd al-Barr, *Jāmi'* (1:492 §779); and as a saying of Ibn 'Abbās by Bayhaqī, *al-Madkhal ilā al-Sunan al-Kubrā*, ed. Muḥammad al-Madkhalī (Kuwait: Dār al-Khulafā' lil-Kitāb al-Islāmī, 1984) p. 348 §578 and *Jāmi'* (1:490 §775).

الْمَعْرِفَةِ يُفِيضُونَ).

﴿وَٱلَّذِينَ يُؤْمِنُونَ بِمَآ أُنزِلَ إِلَيْكَ وَمَآ أُنزِلَ مِن قَبْلِكَ﴾: هُمْ مُؤْمِنُو أَهْلِ الْكِتَابِ، كَعَبْدِ اللهِ بْنِ سَلَامٍ - رَضِيَ اللهُ تَعَالَى عَنْهُ - وَأَضْرَابِهِ، مَعْطُوفُونَ:

(١) عَلَى ﴿ٱلَّذِينَ يُؤْمِنُونَ بِٱلْغَيْبِ﴾، دَاخِلُونَ مَعَهُمْ فِي جُمْلَةِ الْمُتَّقِينَ دُخُولَ أَخَصَّيْنِ تَحْتَ أَعَمَّ؛ إِذِ الْمُرَادُ بِأُولَئِكَ: الَّذِينَ آمَنُوا عَنْ شِرْكٍ وَإِنْكَارٍ، وَبِهَؤُلَاءِ: مُقَابِلُوهُمْ؛ فَكَانَتِ الْآيَتَانِ تَفْصِيلاً ﴿لِّلْمُتَّقِينَ﴾، وَهُوَ قَوْلُ ابْنِ عَبَّاسٍ رَضِيَ اللهُ عَنْهُمَا.

(٢) أَوْ عَلَى ﴿الْمُتَّقِينَ﴾، وَكَأَنَّهُ قَالَ: (﴿هُدًى لِّلْمُتَّقِينَ﴾ عَنِ الشِّرْكِ، ...

of spiritual knowledge they pour out."

[Highlighting of the Jews and Christians who accept Islam]

[2:4] **wa-l-ladhīna yu'minūna bi-mā unzila ilayka wa-mā unzila min qablika** ⁽*and those who believe in what was sent down to you and what was sent down before you*⁾: They are the faithful of the People of Scripture, such as ʿAbd Allāh b. Salām—may Allah be well-pleased with him—and his kind. They are adjoined with

1. *those who believe in the unseen* and like them are part of the God-fearing as particular subsets of the whole. For what is meant by the latter is those who believed renouncing idolatry and denial, while the former are their counterparts.[508] So the two verses are an elaboration of *al-muttaqīn*. This is what Ibn ʿAbbās — Allah be well-pleased with him and his father—said.[509]

2. Or with *the God-fearing*, as if He had said "*a guidance for the God-fearing* renouncing idolatry ....

[508] The "counterparts" are the People of Scripture, who moved from one religion to another religion, not from polytheism. (Z)
[509] As narrated by al-Ṭabarī. (S)

وَالَّذِينَ آمَنُوا مِنْ أَهْلِ الْمِلَلِ). (٣) وَيَحْتَمِلُ أَنْ يُرَادَ بِهِمُ الأَوَّلُونَ بِأَعْيَانِهِمْ؛ وَوُسِّطَ الْعَاطِفُ كَمَا وُسِّطَ فِي قَوْلِهِ: [مُتَقَارِب]

إِلَى الْمَلِكِ الْقَرْمِ وَابْنِ الْهُمَامِ * وَلَيْثِ الْكَتِيبَةِ فِي الْمُزْدَحَمْ

وَقَوْلِهِ: [سَرِيع]

يَا لَهْفَ زَيَّابَةَ لِلْحَارِثِ الـ * ـصَّائِحِ فَالْغَانِمِ فَالْآيِبِ

عَلَى مَعْنَى أَنَّهُمُ الْجَامِعُونَ بَيْنَ الْإِيمَانِ بِمَا يُدْرِكُهُ الْعَقْلُ جُمْلَةً، وَالْإِتْيَانِ بِمَا يُصَدِّقُهُ مِنَ الْعِبَادَاتِ الْبَدَنِيَّةِ وَالْمَالِيَّةِ، ....

and those who believed among the religious communities."

3. It is also possible that those that are meant are the first group specifically;[510] the copulative conjunction was put in the middle in the same way as in the following poetic verses:

["The Tripping"] *To the bull camel, king of magnificent designs*
***and** lion of the squadron in the midst of the fray*[511]

and

["The Swift"] *Alas and woe to Zayyāba*[512] *because of al-Ḥārith*
*who raids early, **and then** despoils, **and then** heads home.*[513]

[*And* was put in the middle] in the sense that they are joining, on the one hand, belief in what reason intuits broadly and the performance, in confirmation thereof, of corporal and monetary types of worship, ...

[510] I.e., those who believe in the unseen, establish the prayer, and spend. (Z)

[511] Spoken by an unknown, cf. Ibn al-Anbārī, *al-Inṣāf fī Masā'il al-Khilāf bayn al-Kūfiyyīn wal-Baṣriyyīn*, ed. Jawdat Mabrūk (Cairo: Maktabat al-Khānjī, 2002) p. 376.

[512] All mss. and eds.: زيّابة K: ذئابة AQ, H, MM: ذؤابة blunder.

[513] Spoken by Salama b. Dhuhl the son of Zayyāba. (S) In Abū Tammām al-Ṭā'ī, *Dīwān al-Ḥamāsa*, ed. Aḥmad Ḥasan Basaj (Beirut: Dār al-Kutub al-'Ilmiyya, 1418/1998) p. 26 §25.

وَبَيْنَ الْإِيمَانِ بِمَا لَا طَرِيقَ إِلَيْهِ غَيْرَ السَّمْعِ. وَكَرَّرَ الْمَوْصُولَ تَنْبِيهاً عَلَى تَغَايُرِ الْقَبِيلَيْنِ وَتَبَايُنِ السَّبِيلَيْنِ.

(٤) أَوْ طَائِفَةٌ مِنْهُمْ، وَهُمْ مُؤْمِنُو أَهْلِ الْكِتَابِ؛ ذَكَرَهُمْ مُخَصَّصِينَ عَنِ الْجُمْلَةِ، كَذِكْرِ جِبْرَئِيلَ وَمِيكَائِيلَ بَعْدَ الْمَلَائِكَةِ، تَعْظِيماً لِشَأْنِهِمْ وَتَرْغِيباً لِأَمْثَالِهِمْ.

وَ(الْإِنْزَالُ): نَقْلُ الشَّيْءِ مِنَ الْأَعْلَى إِلَى الْأَسْفَلِ؛ وَهُوَ إِنَّمَا يَلْحَقُ الْمَعَانِي بِتَوَسُّطِ لُحُوقِهِ الذَّوَاتِ الْحَامِلَةِ لَهَا. وَلَعَلَّ نُزُولَ ....

and, on the other, belief in what cannot possibly be grasped except[514] by actually hearing about it.[515]

He reiterated the relative pronoun to highlight the distinction between the two sides[516] and differentiate the two paths.[517]

4. Or a subset [of the first group], namely, the believers of the People of Scripture: He mentioned them to specify them out of the broader lot—in the same way Jibra'īl and Mīkā'īl are mentioned after the angels are mentioned—in order to emphasize their status and motivate their peers.

[Meaning of *mā unzila* ⟨what was sent down⟩]

Inzāl ⟨sending down⟩ is the moving of something from top to bottom. It is annexed to meanings only after annexation to their carriers themselves.[518] It may be that the descent ....

[514] All mss. and eds.: غير AQ, H, MM: عبر !! *taṣḥīf*.
[515] *al-sam'*, lit. "hearing," denotes all revealed knowledge about Allah, His Names and Attributes, angels, the Hereafter, and so forth.
[516] I.e., between what can be grasped through reason and what cannot be grasped other than through revealed communication (*al-sam'*). (Q)
[517] I.e., reason and transmission (*al-'aql wal-naql*). (Q)
[518] "So the meaning of the sending down of the Book by Allah is its being set into

الْكُتُبِ الإِلٰهِيَّةِ عَلَى الرُّسُلِ بِأَنْ يَتَلَقَّفَهُ الْمَلَكُ مِنَ اللهِ تَعَالَى تَلَقُّفاً رُوحَانِيّاً، أَوْ يَحْفَظَهُ مِنَ اللَّوْحِ الْمَحْفُوظِ، فَيَنْزِلُ بِهِ فَيُبَلِّغُهُ إِلَى الرَّسُولِ.

وَالْمُرَادُ بِـ﴿مَآ أُنزِلَ إِلَيْكَ﴾: الْقُرْآنُ بِأَسْرِهِ وَالشَّرِيعَةُ عَنْ آخِرِهَا. وَإِنَّمَا عَبَّرَ عَنْهُ بِلَفْظِ الْمَاضِي - وَإِنْ كَانَ بَعْضُهُ مُتَرَقَّباً - تَغْلِيباً لِلْمَوْجُودِ عَلَى مَا لَمْ يُوجَدْ، أَوْ تَنْزِيلاً لِلْمُنْتَظَرِ مَنْزِلَةَ الْوَاقِعِ؛ وَنَظِيرُهُ قَوْلُهُ تَعَالَى: ....

of the divine Books on the Messengers consists in the angel seizing [the Book] from Allah Most High spiritually, or in his memorizing it from the Preserved Tablet, after which he descends with it and conveys it to the Messenger.[519]

What is meant by *in what was sent down to you* is the Qur'an in its entirety and the sacred law to the last of it.[520] He expressed it in the past tense—although part of it remained to be revealed—only to let what is there predominate what is not yet there; or to give the awaited part the same status as the part already actualized. Another example would be the saying of Allah Most High,

motion by setting into motion its locus, which is the angel that carries it." (Z)

519 "Taken from the words of the Imam: 'If it is asked: How does Jibrīl hear the speech of Allah when His speech does not consists in letters and sounds? We say: It is possible that Allah creates hearing for His speech, then empowers him to express through wordings that pre-eternal speech.It is also possible that Allah created in His Preserved Tablet His Book in this particular manner of composition, after which Jibrīl read it and memorized it. It is also possible that He creates discrete sounds in this particular manner of composition in a particular body which Jibrīl then seizes, and He creates for him a *'ilm ḍarūrī* ('irrefutable, innate, indispensable, self-evident, imperative, intuitive, necessary, immediate knowledge as opposed to *'ilm muktasab*, acquired knowledge or derived from discursive reasoning') that such is the expression that will convey that pre-eternal speech.'" (S) See also Suyūṭī, *Itqān* (Type 16: *fī kayfiyyat inzālih*) and Binyamin Abrahamov, "Necessary knowledge in Islamic theology," *British Journal of Middle Eastern Studies*, vol. 20 no. 1 (1993) pp. 20-32.

520 "For the sending-down (*al-inzāl*) includes visible and hidden revelation (*al-waḥy al-ẓāhir wal-khafī*) so it includes all the sacred law (*fa-ya'umm al-sharī'a kullahā*)." (Sk)

﴿إِنَّا سَمِعْنَا كِتَٰبًا أُنزِلَ مِنۢ بَعْدِ مُوسَىٰ﴾ [الأحقاف ٣٠]. فَإِنَّ الْجِنَّ لَمْ يَسْمَعُوا جَمِيعَهُ، وَلَمْ يَكُنِ الْكِتَابُ كُلُّهُ مُنَزَّلاً حِينَئِذٍ.

وبـ﴿مَآ أُنزِلَ مِن قَبْلِكَ﴾: التَّـوْرَاةُ وَالْإِنْجِيـلُ وَسَـائِرُ الْكُتُـبِ السَّـابِقَةِ. وَالْإِيمَانُ بِهَا جُمْلَةً فَرْضُ عَيْنٍ، وَبِالْأَوَّلِ ـ دُونَ الثَّانِي ـ تَفْصِيلاً، مِـنْ حَيْـثُ إِنَّا مُتَعَبَّدُونَ بِتَفَاصِيلِهِ، فَرْضٌ، وَلَكِنْ عَلَى الْكِفَايَةِ؛ لِأَنَّ وُجُوبَـهُ عَـلَى كُـلِّ أَحَدٍ يُوجِبُ الْحَرَجَ وَفَسَادَ الْمَعَاشِ.

﴿وَبِٱلْءَاخِرَةِ هُمْ يُوقِنُونَ﴾ أَيْ يُوقِنُونَ إِيقَاناً زَالَ مَعَهُ مَا كَانُوا عَلَيْهِ ....

We have heard a Scripture that was sent down after [the time of] Mūsā (al-Aḥqāf 46:30); for the jinn had not heard all of it, nor had the Book entirely been revealed yet at that time.

And what was sent down before you is the Torah, the Gospel and the remainder of the previous Scriptures. Belief in them as an undifferentiated whole is a personal categorical obligation. Belief in the former[521]—and not the latter[522]— in every detail, in the sense of our being responsible to worship through its details, is [also] a categorical obligation, but communal, since its being obligatory for every individual would impose undue pressure and untenable living conditions.[523]

[The renouncing of Jewish and Christian eschatologies]

wa-bi-l-ʾākhirati hum yūqinūna ⁽*and of the hereafter they are certain*⁾: That is, they are certain with a certitude that eradicates what they previously believed: ....

[521] I.e., the Qur'ān. (Q)

[522] I.e., the previous Scriptures. (Q)

[523] "This indicates that 'belief in the Qur'ān' not only means belief in its being true, but also, together with the latter, belief in all that it contains in detail to the end of acting upon it." (Q)

مِنْ أَنَّ الْجَنَّةَ لَا يَدْخُلُهَا ﴿إِلَّا مَن كَانَ هُودًا أَوْ نَصَـٰرَىٰ﴾ [البقرة ١١١]، وَأَنَّ النَّارَ لَنْ تَمَسَّهُمْ ﴿إِلَّآ أَيَّامًا مَّعْـدُودَةً﴾ [البقرة ٨٠]، وَاخْتِلَافُهُمْ فِي نَعِيمِ الْجَنَّةِ: أَهُوَ مِنْ جِنْسِ نَعِيمِ الدُّنْيَا أَوْ غَيْرِهِ؟ وَفِي دَوَامِهِ وَانْقِطَاعِهِ.

وَفِي تَقْدِيمِ الصِّلَةِ وَبِنَاءِ ﴿يُوقِنُونَ﴾ عَلَى ﴿هُمْ﴾ تَعْرِيضٌ لِمَنْ عَدَاهُمْ مِنْ أَهْلِ الْكِتَابِ، وَبِأَنَّ اعْتِقَادَهُمْ فِي أَمْرِ الْآخِرَةِ غَيْرُ مُطَابِقٍ وَلَا صَادِرٍ عَنْ إِيقَانٍ.

وَ(الْيَقِينُ): إِتْقَانُ الْعِلْمِ بِنَفْيِ الشَّكِّ وَالشُّبْهَةِ عَنْهُ نَظَراً وَاسْتِدْلَالاً، وَلِذٰلِكَ لَا يُوصَفُ بِهِ ....

- that none enters Paradise *except Jews or Christians* (al-Baqara 2:110)
- and that hellfire will not touch them *but for a fews days* (al-Baqara 2:80, Āl ʿImrān 3:24), as well as their differing over
- the bliss of Paradise—is it of the same nature as the bliss of this world or something else?—
- and its eternality or finiteness.[524]

Giving precedence to the relative clause and assigning [the active-voice verb] *yūqinūn* ⟨they are certain⟩ [the detached subject pronoun] *hum* ⟨they⟩ is a hint at the rest of the People of Scripture and at the fact that their convictions with regard to the hereafter are neither correct nor stemming from certainty.

[Meaning of *yūqinūn* ⟨they are certain⟩]

Yaqīn ⟨certitude⟩ is the perfecting of a knowledge cleared of all doubt and ambiguity through investigative reasoning and proof-based deduction. Hence the word is not used to refer to

524 Ibn al-Qayyim documents these two issues in *Kitāb al-Rūḥ* and *Ḥādī al-Arwāḥ*.

عِلْمُ الْبَارِئِ، وَلَا الْعُلُومُ الضَّرُورِيَّةُ.

وَ(الْآخِرَةُ) تَأْنِيثُ (الْآخِرِ): صِفَةُ (الدَّارِ)، بِدَلِيلِ قَوْلِهِ تَعَالَى ﴿تِلْكَ ٱلدَّارُ ٱلْآخِرَةُ﴾ [القصص ٨٣] فَغُلِّبَتْ ـ كَـ(الدُّنْيَا).

وَعَنْ نَافِعٍ أَنَّهُ خَفَّفَهَا بِحَذْفِ الْهَمْزَةِ وَإِلْقَاءِ حَرَكَتِهَا عَلَى اللَّامِ.

وَقُرِئَ (يُؤْقِنُونَ) بِقَلْبِ الْوَاوِ هَمْزَةً لِضَمِّ مَا قَبْلَهَا، إِجْرَاءً لَهَا مَجْرَى الْمَضْمُومَةِ فِي (وُجُوهٍ) وَ(وُقِّتَتْ)؛ وَنَظِيرُهُ: [وَافِر]

لَحُبَّ الْمُؤْقِدَانِ إِلَيَّ مُؤْسَى * وَجَعْدَةُ إِذْ أَضَاءَهُمَا الْوَقُودُ
مَعًا

the knowledge of the Creator or to intuitive types of knowledge.

Al-ākhira ⁽the hereafter⁾ is the feminine of *al-ākhir* ⁽the next⁾. It is a descriptive attribute for "the abode" (*al-dār*)—as evinced by the saying of the Most High, *That is the abode of the hereafter* (al-Qaṣaṣ 28:83)—that was given predominance [as a noun] like *al-dunyā* ⁽the near → the world⁾.

It is related from Nāfiʿ that he would soften it by suppressing the *hamza* and displace its vowel to the *lām*.[525]

Another reading has *yu'qinūn* by transposition of *wāw* into a *hamza* due to the *ḍamma* preceding it, by treating it the way of *ḍamma*-vowelized letters in *wujūh* ⁽faces⁾ and *wuqqitat* ⁽it was timed⁾,[526] as illustrated in [the verse]: ["The Exuberant"]

Lovely to me were made the two fire-workers (al-mu'qidān), Mu'sā
and Jaʿda, when their lighting up the fires illuminates them.[527]

[525] I.e. *wa-bi-lākhirati* as did Warsh instead of *wa-bi-l'ākhirati* like the majority. (*MQ*)

[526] Respectively the plural of *wajh*—where the *wāw* is a transposition of the original *hamza* of *ujūh*—and *wuqqitat* from *uqqitat*. (Q, Z)

[527] I.e. the poet's two sons who were in charge of lighting fires for the towns. Spoken by Jarīr (d. 110 or 114/728 or 732) as part of a poem in praise of the caliph Hishām b. ʿAbd al-Malik b. Marwān al-Umawī and cited in illustration of *wāw*-to-*hamza* trans-

﴿أُوْلَٰٓئِكَ عَلَىٰ هُدٗى مِّن رَّبِّهِمۡۖ﴾: الْجُمْلَةُ فِي مَحَلِّ الرَّفْعِ إِنْ جُعِلَ أَحَدُ الْمَوْصُولَيْنِ مَفْصُولاً عَنِ (الْمُتَّقِينَ)، خَبَرٌ لَهُ؛ فَكَأَنَّهُ لَمَّا قِيلَ ﴿هُدٗى لِّلۡمُتَّقِينَ﴾ قِيلَ: مَا بَالُهُمْ خُصُّوا بِذٰلِكَ؟ فَأُجِيبَ بِقَوْلِهِ: ﴿ٱلَّذِينَ يُؤۡمِنُونَ بِٱلۡغَيۡبِ﴾ إِلَى آخِرِ الْآيَاتِ.

وَإِلَّا: فَاسْتِئْنَافٌ لَا مَحَلَّ لَهَا؛ فَكَأَنَّهُ نَتِيجَةُ الْأَحْكَامِ وَالصِّفَاتِ الْمُتَقَدِّمَةِ.

[Highlighting of the recipients of divine guidance]

[2:5] **ulāʾika ʿalā hudan min rabbihim** ⁽*those are upon guidance from their Nurturer*⁾: the clause is construed as a nominative if we take one of the two relative pronouns[528] as independent from *al-muttaqīn*, and this clause is its enunciative. In the latter case it is as if, when it was said, *a guidance for the God-fearing*, the question was asked, "Why are they singled out thus?"[529] and the answer came with His saying *those who believe in the unseen*, to the end of the verses.[530]

Otherwise it is a resumptive clause without desinential place, as if it were the consequence of the preceding rulings and attributes; ....

position in *mūqidān* and *Mūsa.* (S) Cf. *Dīwān Jarīr*, ed. Nuʿmān Amīn Ṭaha, 3rd ed., 2 vols. (Cairo: Dār al-Maʿārif, 1969-1971) 1:288 and Ibn Jinnī, *Khaṣāʾiṣ* (3:146, 219).

[528] I.e. if we make either one of the two *those who believe* in the previous two verses an inchoative (*mubtadaʾ*), (Q) as opposed to only the first of the two as claimed by J. (S)

[529] I.e., why or how did they get to deserve such honor? (S)

[530] "Al-Ṭībī said: 'He made His saying *hudan lil-muttaqīn* until His saying *yunfiqūn* the structural counterweight (*wāzana*) of His saying *al-ḥamdu lillāhi rabbi al-ʿālamīn* until His saying *māliki yawmi al-dīn*; and He made His saying *iyyāka naʿbudu wa-iyyāka nastaʿīn* the structural counterweight of *ulāʾika ʿalā hudan min rabbihim wa-ulāʾika humu al-mufliḥūn*. And herein is a subtle secret: namely, that Allah Most High represented at the opening of His precious Book the slave's praise of His Creator because of the latter's excellence towards him, whereby he rose up; then, here, the Creator praised His slave because of His guiding him, whereby he rose up again, all in one and the same style.'" (S 1:322)

أَوْ: جَوَابُ سَائِلٍ قَالَ: مَا لِلْمَوْصُوفِينَ بِهٰذِهِ الصِّفَاتِ اخْتُصُّوا بِالْهُدَى؟ وَنَظِيرُهُ: (أَحْسَنْتَ إِلَى زَيْدٍ صَدِيقِكَ الْقَدِيمِ حَقِيقٌ بِالْإِحْسَانِ). فَإِنَّ اسْمَ الْإِشَارَةِ هٰهُنَا كَإِعَادَةِ الْمَوْصُوفِ بِصِفَاتِهِ الْمَذْكُورَةِ، وَهُوَ أَبْلَغُ مِنْ أَنْ يُسْتَأْنَفَ بِإِعَادَةِ الْاِسْمِ وَحْدَهُ لِمَا فِيهِ مِنْ بَيَانِ الْمُقْتَضَى وَتَلْخِيصِهِ؛ فَإِنَّ تَرَتُّبَ الْحُكْمِ عَلَى الْوَصْفِ إِيذَانٌ بِأَنَّهُ الْمُوجِبُ لَهُ.

وَمَعْنَى الْاِسْتِعْلَاءِ فِي ﴿عَلَىٰ هُدًى﴾: تَمْثِيلُ تَمَكُّنِهِمْ مِنَ الْهُدَى وَاسْتِقْرَارِهِمْ عَلَيْهِ بِحَالِ مَنِ اعْتَلَى الشَّيْءَ وَرَكِبَهُ؛ وَقَدْ صَرَّحُوا بِهِ فِي قَوْلِهِمْ (اِمْتَطَى الْجَهْلَ وَغَوَى) وَ(اِقْتَعَدَ غَارِبَ الْهَوَى).

or [it is] the answer to the hypothetical question, "How were those thus described specified as having guidance?" Its [stylistic] equivalent would be, "You have treated your old friend Zayd well—deserving of good treatment." For the demonstrative noun [*ulā'ika*] here is virtually the reiteration of whatever had just been described with the above-mentioned attributes. Such [construction] is more powerful[531] than to resume by repeating the name alone,[532] as it entails exposition of the corollary and its summary: when a certain status follows in sequence to a certain description, it is a proclamation that the latter brings about the former.

The meaning of *isti'lā'* ⟨upon-ness⟩ in **'alā hudan** ⟨upon guidance⟩ is the assimilation of their mastery of guidance and their settling upon it to the state of someone who climbed on top of something and rode it. They said it explicitly in the phrases "He took ignorance for his mount and erred" and "He seated himself upon the withers of lust."

[531] *Ablagh* in the sense of *balāgha* ⟨eloquence⟩ or that of *mubālagha* ⟨hyperbole⟩. (Q)

[532] I.e. separately from all its attributes that were mentioned before. (Q)

وَذٰلِكَ إِنَّمَا يَحْصُلُ بِاسْتِفْرَاغِ الْفِكْرِ، وَإِدَامَةِ النَّظَرِ فِيمَا نُصِبَ مِنَ الْحُجَجِ، وَالْمُوَاظَبَةِ عَلَى مُحَاسَبَةِ النَّفْسِ فِي الْعَمَلِ.

وَنُكِّرَ ﴿هُدًى﴾ لِلتَّعْظِيمِ؛ فَكَأَنَّهُ أُرِيدَ بِهِ ضَرْبٌ لَا يُبَالَغُ كُنْهُهُ وَلَا يُقَادَرُ قَدْرُهُ؛ وَنَظِيرُهُ قَوْلُ الْهُذَلِيِّ: [طَوِيل]

فَلَا وَأَبِي الطَّيْرِ الْمُرِبَّةِ بِالضُّحَى * عَلَى خَالِدٍ لَقَدْ وَقَعْتِ عَلَى لَحْمِ

وَأُكِّدَ تَعْظِيمُهُ بِأَنَّ اللهَ تَعَالَى مَانِحُهُ وَالْمُوَفِّقُ لَهُ.

وَقَدْ أُدْغِمَتِ النُّونُ فِي الرَّاءِ بِغُنَّةٍ وَبِغَيْرِ غُنَّةٍ.

Such [control of and settling upon guidance] can only result from the complete dedication of one's thought and long contemplation of all the proofs that have been produced, together with assiduous self-accounting in one's deeds.

[Divine guidance is unfathomable, invaluable and direct]

Hudan was left indefinite for amplification,[533] as if a path was meant thereby, the totality of which cannot be fathomed nor its value be truly estimated, as in the saying of al-Hudhalī: ["The Long"]

Lo! I swear by the sire of the carrion-birds squatting mid-morning
on Khālid: Some flesh (laḥm[i]) you have chanced upon![534]

Its magnification was emphasized again by the fact that it is Allah Himself Who bestows it and grants one success for it.

The *nūn* was contracted into the *rā'* [*min rabbihim* → *mir-rabbihim*] with a nasal twang and without.

[533] As if to say, "and what guidance!" or that it is unfathomable. (Q)

[534] Cf. *Dīwān al-Hudhaliyyīn*, ed. Aḥmad al-Zayn and Maḥmūd Abū al-Wafā, 3 vols. (Cairo: Dār al-Kutub al-Miṣriyya, 1385/1965) 2:154. "This Khālid was an important person, so he gave his flesh importance by leaving it in the indefinite, and by extension he gave the birds that fell onto it importance." (S) On al-Hudhalī see our biographical glossary. Sacy completely mistranslates it "En vérité je ne suis pas tombé sur de la chair."

﴿وَأُوْلَٰٓئِكَ هُمُ ٱلْمُفْلِحُونَ﴾: كَرَّرَ فِيهِ اسْمَ الْإِشَارَةِ تَنْبِيهاً عَلَى أَنَّ اتِّصَافَهُمْ بِتِلْكَ الصِّفَاتِ يَقْتَضِي كُلَّ وَاحِدَةٍ مِنَ الْأَثَرَتَيْنِ، وَأَنَّ كُلًّا مِنْهُمَا كَافٍ فِي تَمْيِيزِهِمْ بِهَا عَنْ غَيْرِهِمْ.

وَوُسِّطَ الْعَاطِفُ، لِاخْتِلَافِ مَفْهُومِ الْجُمْلَتَيْنِ هٰهُنَا، بِخِلَافِ قَوْلِهِ ﴿أُوْلَٰٓئِكَ كَٱلْأَنْعَٰمِ بَلْ هُمْ أَضَلُّ أُوْلَٰٓئِكَ هُمُ ٱلْغَٰفِلُونَ﴾ [الأعراف ١٧٩]؛ فَإِنَّ التَّسْجِيلَ بِالْغَفْلَةِ وَالتَّشْبِيهَ بِالْبَهَائِمِ شَيْءٌ وَاحِدٌ: فَكَانَتِ الْجُمْلَةُ الثَّانِيَةُ مُقَرِّرَةً لِلْأُولَى، فَلَا تُنَاسِبُ الْعَطْفَ.

وَ﴿هُمْ﴾: (أ) فَصْلٌ، يَفْصِلُ الْخَبَرَ عَنِ الصِّفَةِ، وَيُؤَكِّدُ النِّسْبَةَ، وَيُفِيدُ اخْتِصَاصَ الْمُسْنَدِ بِالْمُسْنَدِ إِلَيْهِ؛ ....

wa-ulāʾika humu-l-mufliḥūn ⁽*and those—they are the successful!*⁾: He repeated the demonstrative noun here to draw attention to the fact that their description by those attributes necessitates each of these two superiorities, although either one suffices in itself to distinguish them from others.[535] The copulative was put in the middle because of the difference in what is understood from each clause right here, in contradistinction to His saying *Those are as cattle—rather, they are further astray! Those—they are the heedless* (al-Aʿrāf 7:179). For marking [them] as heedless and comparing them to dumb beasts is one and the same thing, so the second sentence confirms the first and is not suitable for [the sense of] adjunction.

Hum ⁽they⁾ is (i) a distinctive pronoun that sets apart the enunciative from the attribute, emphasizes affiliation and intimates the exclusive relation of predicate with subject; ....

[535] "Al-Sharīf [al-Jurjānī] said: 'Guidance is in the world and success in the hereafter, the affirmation of each being a desirable end in itself.'" (S)

(ب) أَوْ مُبْتَدَأٌ، وَ﴿ٱلْمُفْلِحُونَ﴾ خَبَرُهُ، وَالْجُمْلَةُ خَبَرُ ﴿أُوْلَٰٓئِكَ﴾.

وَ(الْمُفْلِحُ) ـ بِالْحَاءِ وَالْجِيمِ ـ: الْفَائِزُ بِالْمَطْلُوبِ، كَأَنَّهُ الَّذِي انْفَتَحَتْ لَهُ وُجُوهُ الظَّفَرِ. وَهٰذَا التَّرْكِيبُ، وَمَا يُشَارِكُهُ فِي الْفَاءِ وَالْعَيْنِ، نَحْوَ (فَلَقَ) وَ(فَلَذَ) وَ(فَلِيَ): يَدُلُّ عَلَى الشَّقِّ وَالْفَتْحِ.

وَتَعْرِيفُ (الْمُفْلِحِينَ): لِلدِّلَالَةِ عَلَى أَنَّ الْمُتَّقِينَ هُمُ النَّاسُ الَّذِينَ بَلَغَكَ أَنَّهُمُ الْمُفْلِحُونَ فِي الْآخِرَةِ؛ أَوْ: الْإِشَارَةِ إِلَى مَا يَعْرِفُهُ كُلُّ أَحَدٍ مِنْ حَقِيقَةِ الْمُفْلِحِينَ وَخُصُوصِيَّاتِهِمْ.

تَنْبِيهٌ: تَأَمَّلْ كَيْفَ نَبَّهَ ـ سُبْحَانَهُ وَتَعَالَى ـ ....

(ii) or it is an inchoative with *the successful* as its enunciative, and the entire clause is the enunciative of *ulāʾika* ‹those›.

Al-mufliḥ ‹the successful› with a *ḥāʾ*—or a *jīm* [*muflij*][536]—means the one who wins the prize, as if multiple winnings became open to him. This construction—and all that shares its first and second letters with it such as *falaqa* ‹cleave›, *faladha* ‹cut off› and *faliya* ‹be severed›—indicates slashing and opening.[537]

The definite article in *al-mufliḥūn* is to indicate that "those who beware are the people who—as you have already heard—are the successful ones in the hereafter;" or to refer to what everyone already knows concerning the true nature of the successful and their characteristics.[538]

[The intense Quranic valorization of the *muttaqīn* ‹wary›]

Nota bene: Observe how the Most High drew attention ....

[536] Per the view of the early grammarians that the common sharing of most root letters is indicative of a common etymology. (Kh) Also see note 293.

[537] Hence the planter (*al-zāriʿ*) is named *fallāḥ* ‹tiller›. (Z)

[538] Al-Ṭībī said: "The first gloss makes it a definite indicating previous knowledge (*lil-ʿahd*), the second indicating species (*lil-jins*)." (S)

عَلَى اخْتِصَاصِ الْمُتَّقِينَ بِنَيْلِ مَا لَا يَنَالُهُ كُلُّ أَحَدٍ مِنْ وُجُوهٍ شَتَّى؛ وَبِنَاءَ الْكَلَامِ عَلَى اسْمِ الْإِشَارَةِ لِلتَّعْلِيلِ مَعَ الْإِيجَازِ؛ وَتَكْرِيرَهُ؛ وَتَعْرِيفَ الْخَبَرِ؛ وَتَوْسِيطَ الْفَصْلِ؛ لِإِظْهَارِ قَدْرِهِمْ، وَالتَّرْغِيبِ فِي اقْتِفَاءِ أَثَرِهِمْ.

وَقَدْ تَشَبَّثَ بِهِ الْوَعِيدِيَّةُ فِي خُلُودِ الْفُسَّاقِ مِنْ أَهْلِ الْقِبْلَةِ فِي الْعَذَابِ؛ وَرُدَّ بِأَنَّ الْمُرَادَ بِالْمُفْلِحِينَ: الْكَامِلُونَ فِي الْفَلَاحِ؛ وَيَلْزَمُهُ عَدَمُ كَمَالِ الْفَلَاحِ لِمَنْ لَيْسَ عَلَى صِفَتِهِمْ، لَا عَدَمُ الْفَلَاحِ لَهُ رَأْساً.

﴿إِنَّ الَّذِينَ كَفَرُوا﴾: لَمَّا ذَكَرَ خَاصَّةَ عِبَادِهِ، وَخُلَاصَةَ أَوْلِيَائِهِ بِصِفَاتِهِمُ الَّتِي أَهَّلَتْهُمْ ....

to the fact that the wary alone obtain what no-one else does in many ways; how the discourse was built upon the demonstrative noun for justification together with concision; its repetition; the use of the definite for the enunciative; and the middle insertion of the distinctive pronoun, to display their immense worth and motivate people to follow in their footsteps.

[The non-Sunni view that Muslim sinners are in hell forever]

The Waʿīdiyya ⁽Punishists⁾[539] cleaved to this [description] to assert the eternality of hellfire for transgressors among the People of the *Qibla*. This [doctrine] was rejected because what is meant by *the successful* is those whose success is complete—which, by definition, means incomplete success for those who do not meet their criteria; not the utter absence of all success.

[2:6] **inna-l-ladhīna kafarū** ⁽*Verily those who rejected belief*⁾: Once He mentioned the special ones among His slaves and the quintessence of His friends by their attributes—which qualified them

[539] "Both the Muʿtazila and the Khawārij are meant." (Q 1:539) This is more accurate than to define them as only the former. See Glossary, *s.v.*

لِلْهُدَى وَالْفَلَاحِ، عَقَّبَهُمْ بِأَضْدَادِهِمْ: الْعُتَاةِ الْمَرَدَةِ، الَّذِينَ لَا يَنْفَعُ فِيهِمُ الْهُدَى، وَلَا تُغْنِي عَنْهُمُ الْآيَاتُ وَالنُّذُرُ. وَلَمْ يَعْطِفْ قِصَّتَهُمْ عَلَى قِصَّةِ الْمُؤْمِنِينَ كَمَا عَطَفَ فِي قَوْلِهِ تَعَالَى ﴿إِنَّ ٱلْأَبْرَارَ لَفِي نَعِيمٍ ﴿١٣﴾ وَإِنَّ ٱلْفُجَّارَ لَفِي جَحِيمٍ ﴿١٤﴾﴾ [الانفطار] لِتَبَايُنِهِمَا فِي الْغَرَضِ: فَإِنَّ الْأُولَى سِيقَتْ لِذِكْرِ الْكِتَابِ وَبَيَانِ شَأْنِهِ، وَالْأُخْرَى مَسُوقَةٌ لِشَرْحِ تَمَرُّدِهِمْ وَانْهِمَاكِهِمْ فِي الضَّلَالِ.

وَ﴿إِنَّ﴾ مِنَ الْحُرُوفِ الَّتِي تُشَابِهُ الْفِعْلَ: (أ) فِي عَدَدِ الْحُرُوفِ (ب) وَالْبِنَاءِ عَلَى الْفَتْحِ (ج) وَلُزُومِ الْأَسْمَاءِ (د) وَإِعْطَاءِ مَعَانِيهِ؛ وَالْمُتَعَدِّي ....

for guidance and success, He followed them up with their diametrical opposites: the arrogant and rebellious ones whom guidance benefits nothing, nor are the great signs and warnings of any use to them. He did not adjoin their narrative to that of the believers the way He did when He said, *Truly the virtuous are most surely in bliss* **and** *truly the criminals are most surely in the abyss* (al-Infiṭār 82:13-14) because they are different from one another in their respective objectives. The first [narrative] was told in order to mention the Book and expose its tremendous status while the latter was told in order to expand on their rebelliousness and engrossment in misguidance.

[Parsing of *inna* ⁽verily⁾ and its function]

Inna ⁽verily⁾ is one of the particles that resemble verbs in (i) the number of their letters,[540] (ii) their having an indeclinable *fatḥa* case ending,[541] (iii) their sticking to nouns and (iv) their imparting the meanings [of verbs],[542] especially transitive ones,

540 Because they have three letters or more. (Q)

541 Like verbs in the past tense. (S)

542 Such as emphasis (*ta'kīd*), literalization (*taḥqīq*), assimilation (*tashbīh*), rectification (*istidrāk*), wish (*tamannī*) and petition (*tarajjī*) just as verbs give their meanings of helping, striking, exiting and entering to the nouns that follow them. (Q, Z)

خَاصَّةً، فِي دُخُولِهَا عَلَى اسْمَيْنِ. وَلِـذٰلِكَ أُعْمِلَـتْ عَمَلَـهُ الْفَرْعِـيَّ - وَهُـوَ نَصْبُ الْجُزْءِ الْأَوَّلِ وَرَفْعُ الثَّانِي - إِيذَاناً بِأَنَّهُ فَرْعٌ فِي الْعَمَلِ، دَخِيلٌ فِيهِ.

وَقَالَ الْكُوفِيُّونَ: الْخَبَرُ قَبْلَ دُخُولِهَا كَانَ مَرْفُوعاً بِالْخَبَرِيَّـةِ، وَهِـيَ بَعْـدُ بَاقِيَةٌ، مُقْتَضِيَةٌ لِلرَّفْعِ قَضِيَّةً لِلِاسْتِصْحَابِ، فَلَا يَرْفَعُهُ الْحَرْفُ. وَأُجِيبَ بِأَنَّ اقْتِضَاءَ الْخَبَرِيَّةِ الرَّفْعَ مَشْرُوطٌ بِالتَّجَرُّدِ، لِتَخَلُّفِهِ عَنْهَا فِي خَبَرِ (كَانَ)، وَقَـدْ زَالَ بِدُخُولِهَا؛ فَتَعَيَّنَ إِعْمَالُ الْحَرْفِ.

وَفَائِدَتُهَا تَأْكِيدُ النِّسْبَةِ وَتَحْقِيقُهَا؛ وَلِذٰلِكَ يُتَلَقَّى بِهَا الْقَسَمُ، وَيُصَدَّرُ بِهَـا الْأَجْوِبَةُ، وَتُذْكَرُ فِي مَعْرِضِ الشَّكِّ؛ مِثْلُ قَوْلِهِ تَعَالَى: ....

in being affixed to two nouns. Hence they were given their subsidiary regency, which puts the first segment in the accusative case and the second in the nominative, as a signal that [the particle] is a subordinate in regency[543] and a newcomer in that.[544]

The Kufans said that before its affixing, the enunciative was in the nominative just as enunciatives should be, and remained so afterwards, necessitating the nominative by presumption of continuity so that it is not the particle that gives it that case. It was replied that the necessitation of its being in the nominative because it is an enunciative is conditional upon its being unaugmented, since [the nominative case] does not accompany it in the enunciative of *kāna*[545] but rather disappears when it is affixed; so the particle has to be given regency.

Its function is to emphasize affiliation and make it literal, hence it is used to pronounce oaths, initiate replies and in the face of doubt, as when Allah Most High said: ....

[543] I.e., the regency of the verb. (Z)
[544] I.e., not a regent in its origin. (Q, Z)
[545] Which is accusative.

﴿وَيَسْـَٔلُونَكَ عَن ذِي ٱلْقَرْنَيْنِ قُلْ سَأَتْلُوا۟ عَلَيْكُم مِّنْهُ ذِكْرًا ﴿٨٣﴾ إِنَّا مَكَّنَّا لَهُۥ فِى ٱلْأَرْضِ﴾[الكهف]، ﴿وَقَالَ مُوسَىٰ يَٰفِرْعَوْنُ إِنِّى رَسُولٌ مِّن رَّبِّ ٱلْعَٰلَمِينَ ﴿١٠٤﴾﴾[الكهف]. قَالَ الْمُبَرِّدُ: قَوْلُكَ (عَبْدُ اللهِ قَائِمٌ): إِخْبَارٌ عَنْ قِيَامِهِ؛ وَ(إِنَّ عَبْدَ اللهِ قَائِمٌ): جَوَابُ سَائِلٍ عَنْ قِيَامِهِ؛ وَ(إِنَّ عَبْدَ اللهِ لَقَائِمٌ): جَوَابُ مُنْكِرٍ لِقِيَامِهِ).

وَتَعْرِيفُ الْمَوْصُولِ: (أ) إِمَّا لِلْعَهْدِ؛ وَالْمُرَادُ بِهِ: نَاسٌ بِأَعْيَانِهِمْ، كَأَبِي لَهَبٍ، وَأَبِي جَهْلٍ، وَالْوَلِيدِ بْنِ الْمُغِيرَةِ، وَأَحْبَارِ الْيَهُودِ.

They will ask you of Dhūl-Qarnayn. Say: I shall recite to you something about him. Verily We (innā) established him in the land (al-Kahf 18:83-84), *And Mūsā said, O Firʿawn, verily I (innī) am a Messenger from the Nurturer of the worlds* (al-Aʿrāf 7:104). Al-Mubarrid said:

> You say *ʿAbd Allāh qā'im* (ʿAbd Allāh is standing) to report that he is standing; *inna ʿAbd Allāh qā'im* (verily ʿAbd Allāh is standing) in reply to someone asking about his standing; and *inna ʿAbd Allāh la-qā'im* (verily ʿAbd Allah is standing—I swear it) in reply to someone denying that he is standing.[546]

The definite article of the conjunctive noun [*al-ladhīna*]

(i) either denotes previous knowledge, in the sense of particular individuals like Abū Lahab, Abū Jahl, al-Walīd b. al-Mughīra and the rabbis of the Jews;[547]

[546] Attributed to al-Mubarrid who said it in reply to al-Kindī *al-mutafalsif* (al-Kindī the would-be philosopher) who was claiming that Arabic was redundant because all three expressions meant the same thing, cf. ʿAbd al-Qāhir al-Jurjānī, *Kitāb Dalā'il al-Iʿjāz*, ed. Maḥmūd Shākir (Cairo: Maktabat al-Khānjī, 1984; rept. Maṭbaʿat al-Madanī, 1413/1992) p. 315, cf. al-Rāzī, *Tafsīr* (*sub* al-Baqara 2:6) and al-Murādī (d. 749/1348), *al-Janā al-Dānī min Ḥurūf al-Maʿānī*, ed. Fakhr al-Dīn Qabāwa and Muḥammad Nadīm Fāḍil (Beirut: Dār al-Kutub al-ʿIlmiyya, 1413/1992) p. 131.

[547] 'Al-Ṭabarī narrates from Ibn ʿAbbās that the unbelievers among the Jews are

(ب) أَوْ لِلْجِنْسِ، مُتَنَاوِلاً مَنْ صَمَّمَ عَلَى الْكُفْرِ، وَغَيْرَهُمْ، فَخَصَّ مِنْهُمْ غَيْرَ الْمُصِرِّينَ بِمَا أُسْنِدَ إِلَيْهِ.

وَ(الْكُفْرُ) لُغَةً: سَتْرُ النِّعْمَةِ؛ وَأَصْلُهُ (الْكَفْرُ) بِالْفَتْحِ وَهُوَ السَّتْرُ، وَمِنْهُ قِيلَ لِلزَّارِعِ وَلِلَّيْلِ: (كَافِرٌ)، وَلِكِمَامِ الثَّمَرَةِ: (كَافُورٌ). وَفِي الشَّرْعِ: إِنْكَارُ مَا عُلِمَ بِالضَّرُورَةِ مَجِيءُ الرَّسُولِ ﷺ بِهِ. وَإِنَّمَا عُدَّ لُبْسُ الْغِيَارِ وَشَدُّ الزُّنَّارِ

(ii) or it refers to an entire class that extends both to those who persist upon unbelief with deaf ears[548] and the rest; then [later] He singled out those who did not persist with what was being attributed to them.[549]

[Definition of *kufr* and its vestimentary symbols]

Al-kufr lexically is "the cover-up of favor" Its origin is *al-kafr* with a *fatḥa*, which is the act of covering,[550] hence one calls the planter *kāfir*—also night—and the husk of the fruit is called *kāfūr*.

In legal terminology it is the denial of what is self-evidently known of what the Messenger—upon him blessings and peace—brought.[551] Wearing the badge and belt [of non-Muslims] ......

meant specifically." (S)

548 "To their death." (Q)

549 "And the specifier (*al-mukhaṣṣiṣ*) is the text that indicates that whoever repents among them does benefit from warnings." (Q)

550 Cf. al-Fārābī, *Dīwān al-Adab*, ed. Aḥmad Mukhtār ʿUmar and Ibrāhīm Anīs, 3 vols. (Cairo: Majmaʿ al-Lughat al-ʿArabiyya, 1974) 2:112, 158. *Kafr* also refers to a forlorn place that is hard of access, a back country: Ibn Fāris, *Muʿjam Maqāyīs al-Lugha*, ed. ʿAbd al-Salām Hārūn, 6 vols. (Beirut: al-Dār al-Islāmiyya, 1410/1990) 5:191, whence its use in the composite name of many a locality in the Arab world such as Kafr al-Shaykh In Egypt, Kafr Sūsa and Kafr Baṭna in Syria, or Kafr Shīma and Kafrayyā in Lebanon.

551 As defined by al-Rāzī. (S) "What is established through consensus is irrefutably counted as self-evident knowledge (*min al-ḍarūriyyāt*), and the falsehood of the doc-

وَنَحْوُهُمَا كُفراً لِأَنَّهَا تَدُلُّ عَلَى التَّكْذِيبِ، فَإِنَّ مَنْ صَدَّقَ الرَّسُولَ ﷺ لَا يَجْتَرِئُ عَلَيْهَا ظَاهِراً؛ لَا لِأَنَّهَا كُفْرٌ فِي أَنْفُسِهَا.

وَاحْتَجَّتِ الْمُعْتَزِلَةُ بِمَا جَاءَ فِي الْقُرْآنِ بِلَفْظِ الْمَاضِي عَلَى حُدُوثِهِ، لِاسْتِدْعَائِهِ سَابِقَةَ الْمُخْبَرِ عَنْهُ؛ وَأُجِيبَ: بِأَنَّهُ مُقْتَضَى التَّعَلُّقِ، وَحُدُوثُهُ لَا يَسْتَلْزِمُ حُدُوثَ الْكَلَامِ، كَمَا فِي الْعِلْمِ.

and the like counts as unbelief only insofar as it is indicative of rejection [of Islam], as anyone that confirms the veracity of the Messenger—upon him blessings and peace—would not dare to wear them visibly; but not because they constitute unbelief in themselves.

[The Muʿtazili (and Shiʿi) view that the Qur'ān is created]

The Muʿtazila adduced what the Qur'ān mentions in the past tense as a proof for their position that it has a temporal origin, since it requires that what is reported must precede in time. The answer is that it is an exigency of appurtenance, and the temporal origin of the latter does not necessarily mean the temporal origin of Speech; just as with respect to [divine] knowledge.[552]

trine of anthropomorphists likewise." (S 1:335).

[552] "I.e., the precedence in time of what is being reported is an exigency of His pre-existent speech becoming related to what is being reported; so the inseparable conclusion (*al-lāzim*) is the precedence of what is being reported over the becoming related and its contingency, which does not necessitate the contingency of the Attribute of Speech, just as what appertains to His knowledge that events occur: the appurtenance (*taʿalluq*) of the latter is contingent while knowledge is not." (Sk) "What we call 'pre-existent without beginning' (*azalī*) is the inward speech (*al-kalām al-nafsī*) that subsists in the Divine Essence (*al-qā'im bi-dhātih subḥānah*); and it is never described as past, present or future because it is timeless." (Z) On *kalām nafsī* see al-Qārī, *Minaḥ al-Rawḍ al-Azhar* (pp. 72-76), Muḥammad ʿAmrāwī, *al-Ajwibat al-Muḥarrara ʿan al-As'ilat al-ʿAshara* (Amman: Dār al-Fatḥ, 1432/2011) pp. 149-167 *limādhā qassama al-Ashāʿiratu al-kalāma ilā qismayn* and Saʿīd Fūda, *Tahdhīb Sharḥ al-Sanūsiyya Umm al-Barāhīn* (Amman: Dār al-Bayāriq, 1419/1998) pp. 55-60.

﴿سَوَآءٌ عَلَيۡهِمۡ ءَأَنذَرۡتَهُمۡ أَمۡ لَمۡ تُنذِرۡهُمۡ﴾: خَبَرُ ﴿إِنَّ﴾.

وَ﴿سَوَآءٌ﴾ اِسْمٌ بِمَعْنَى الِاسْتِوَاءِ، نُعِتَ بِهِ كَمَا نُعِتَ بِالْمَصَادِرِ؛ قَالَ اللهُ تَعَالَى: ﴿تَعَالَوۡاْ إِلَىٰ كَلِمَةٖ سَوَآءِۭ بَيۡنَنَا وَبَيۡنَكُمۡ﴾ [آل عمران].

رُفِعَ (أ) بِأَنَّهُ خَبَرُ ﴿إِنَّ﴾، وَمَا بَعْدَهُ مُرْتَفِعٌ بِهِ عَلَى الْفَاعِلِيَّةِ، كَأَنَّهُ قِيلَ: إِنَّ الَّذِينَ كَفَرُوا مُسْتَوٍ عَلَيْهِمْ إِنْذَارُكَ وَعَدَمُهُ؛

(ب) أَوْ بِأَنَّهُ خَبَرٌ لِمَا بَعْدَهُ بِمَعْنَى: إِنْذَارُكَ وَعَدَمُهُ سِيَّانِ عَلَيْهِمْ؛ وَالْفِعْلُ: إِنَّمَا يَمْتَنِعُ الْإِخْبَارُ عَنْهُ إِذَا أُرِيدَ بِهِ تَمَامُ مَا وُضِعَ لَهُ؛ أَمَّا لَوْ أُطْلِقَ

sawāʾun ʿalayhim aʾandhartahum am lam tundhirhum ⁽*it is the same for them whether you warn them or you do not warn them*⁾ is the enunciative of *inna.*

Sawāʾun ⁽the same⁾ is a noun that denotes equality, used as a qualificative in the same way infinitive nouns are also used. Allah Most High said, *Come to a word equitable (kalimatin sawāʾin) between us and you* (Āl ʿImrān 3:64). It was put in the nominative (i) as the enunciative of *inna*—and what follows it is also nominative in the sense of agency, as if it were being said: "Verily, those who rejected belief, it is indifferent to them whether you warn them or not;"

(ii) or as an enunciative for what immediately follows it, in the sense that "your warning them or not is all the same to them." Verbs are precluded from governing an enunciative only when its full semantic usage is meant.[553] However, when it is used as a syntactical absolute ....

[553] "By the 'full semantic usage' of verbs three things are meant: (i) the sense of an infinitive noun (*maṣdar*), which is the implied indication of the vocable used as a verb; (ii) the specified affiliation (*al-nisbat al-makhṣūṣa*) that correlates the sense of an infinitive noun to the subject itself; and (iii) whatever of the three tenses is specified." (Z)

وَأُرِيدَ بِهِ اللَّفْظُ، أَوْ مُطْلَقُ الْحَدَثِ الْمَدْلُولِ عَلَيْهِ ضِمْناً عَلَى الْاِتِّسَاعِ: فَهُوَ كَالْاِسْمِ فِي الْإِضَافَةِ وَالْإِسْنَادِ إِلَيْهِ، كَقَوْلِهِ تَعَالَى: ﴿وَإِذَا قِيلَ لَهُمْ ءَامِنُوا﴾، [البقرة ١٣] وَقَوْلِهِ: ﴿يَوْمُ يَنفَعُ ٱلصَّٰدِقِينَ صِدْقُهُمْ﴾ [المائدة ١١٩]، وَقَوْلِهِمْ: (تَسْمَعُ بِالْمُعَيْدِيِّ خَيْرٌ مِنْ أَنْ تَرَاهُ!).

وَإِنَّمَا عَدَلَ هٰهُنَا عَنِ الْمَصْدَرِ إِلَى الْفِعْلِ لِمَا فِيهِ مِنْ إِيهَامِ التَّجَدُّدِ. وَحَسُنَ دُخُولُ الْهَمْزَةِ وَ﴿أَمْ﴾ عَلَيْهِ، لِتَقْرِيرِ مَعْنَى الْاِسْتِوَاءِ وَتَأْكِيدِهِ؛ فَإِنَّهُمَا جُرِّدَتَا عَنْ مَعْنَى الْاِسْتِفْهَامِ لِمُجَرَّدِ الْاِسْتِوَاءِ، كَمَا جُرِّدَتْ حُرُوفُ النِّدَاءِ عَنِ .....

to mean the vocable or the unqualified temporal event[554] that is being signified inclusively and in a wider sense: then it is like a noun in annexation and predication, as in the saying of the Most High, *and when they are told: Believe!* (al-Baqara 2:13), *a day their truthfulness will benefit the truthful* (al-Māʾida 5:119)[555] and their saying, "Hearing of the Maʿadd man's reputation is better than actually seeing him!"[556]

[Repeatedly warning them is the same as not warning at all]

The reason He shifted here from the infinitive noun to the verb is because there is in the latter a suggestion of renewal;[557] and affixing the *hamza* and *am* ⁽or⁾ to it beautifully affirms and emphasizes the sense of sameness. They [*hamza* and *am*] were both stripped of any interrogative tenor for unalloyed equality, just as the vocative letters were stripped of their ....

554 Ak, β, B, ε, I, Iṣ, R, T: الحدث α: الحدوث

555 "The first verse illustrates how the verb is a subject [or a correlative of attribute] (*musnad ilayh*) where what is meant is the vocable, i.e. when they are told this vocable, namely, 'Believe' while the second illustrates how the verb is a governed annex (*muḍāf ilayh*), where what is meant is the actual event, i.e. the day the truthful benefit." (Z)

556 'You hear' here is in the sense of hearing and is the inchoative of 'better.' (Z) "A proverb used to refer to one whose news is more impressive than his appearance." (S)

557 Whereas nouns suggest firmness and definiteness. See notes 298, 673, 681.

الطَّلَبِ لِمُجَرَّدِ التَّخْصِيصِ فِي قَوْلِهِمْ: (اللَّهُمَّ اغْفِرْ لَنَا ـ أَيَّتُهَا الْعِصَابَةُ).

وَ(الْإِنْذَارُ): التَّخْوِيفُ؛ أُرِيدَ بِهِ التَّخْوِيفُ مِنْ عَذَابِ اللهِ. وَإِنَّمَا اقْتَصَرَ عَلَيْهِ دُونَ الْبِشَارَةِ، لِأَنَّهُ أَوْقَعُ فِي الْقَلْبِ وَأَشَدُّ تَأْثِيراً فِي النَّفْسِ، مِنْ حَيْثُ إِنَّ دَفْعَ الضُّرِّ أَهَمُّ مِنْ جَلْبِ النَّفْعِ؛ فَإِذَا لَمْ يَنْفَعْ فِيهِمْ، كَانَتِ الْبِشَارَةُ بِعَدَمِ النَّفْعِ أَوْلَى.

وَقُرِئَ ﴿ءَأَنذَرْتَهُمْ﴾ (أ) بِتَحْقِيقِ الْهَمْزَتَيْنِ؛ (ب) وَتَخْفِيفِ الثَّانِيَةِ بَيْنَ بَيْنَ وَقَلْبِهَا أَلِفاً ـ وَهُوَ لَحْنٌ، لِأَنَّ الْمُتَحَرِّكَةَ لَا تُقْلَبُ، وَلِأَنَّهُ يُؤَدِّي إِلَى .....

questing tenor for pure pin-pointing in the expression "O Allah, forgive us, exclusively this group [lit. 'O the group']!"[558]

Al-indhār ⁽warning⁾ is the instilling of fear, by which is meant instilling fear of the punishment of Allah. The latter was mentioned by itself, without mention of glad tidings, only because it shakes hearts and affects people more, as repelling harm is more urgent than to procure benefit; and since it availed them nothing, then a fortiori glad tidings will be useless.

A'andhartahum was read:

(i) with the full affirmation of the two *hamzas*;[559]

(ii) with the lightening of the second *hamza* in between[560] and its transposition into an *alif*—a solecism, as the vowelized consonant is not transposed and also because it leads to ....

[558] "An inapplicable example. Pin-pointing does not stem from the stripping of vocative particles as they are not even present there in the first place, but rather the names used [for pinpointing] resemble vocative particles, and those names are what was stripped [of their original tenor]." (S)

[559] By ʿĀṣim, Ḥamza, al-Kisāʾī, Ibn ʿĀmir, Ibn Dhakwān, Hishām, Rawḥ, Khalaf, al-Ḥasan, Ibn ʿAbbās, al-Aʿmash and Ibn Abī Isḥāq. It is the dialect of Tamīm. (*MQ*)

[560] I.e., in between *alif* and *hamza*.

جَمْعِ السَّاكِنَيْنِ عَلَى غَيْرِ حَدِّهِ؛ (ج) وَبِتَوْسِيطِ أَلِفٍ بَيْنَهُمَا مُحَقَّقَتَيْنِ؛ (د) وَبِتَوْسِيطِهَا وَالثَّانِيَةُ بَيْنَ بَيْنَ؛ (هـ) وَبِحَذْفِ الْاِسْتِفْهَامِيَّةِ؛ (و) وَبِحَذْفِهَا وَإِلْقَاءِ حَرَكَتِهَا عَلَى السَّاكِنِ قَبْلَهَا.

﴿لَا يُؤْمِنُونَ﴾ (١) جُمْلَةٌ مُفَسِّرَةٌ لِإِجْمَالِ مَا قَبْلَهَا فِيمَا فِيهِ الْاِسْتِوَاءُ، فَلَا مَحَلَّ لَهَا؛

the inordinate joining of two quiescent consonants;[561]

(iii) with a middle *alif* inserted between the two of them with the full affirmation of the two *hamzas*;[562]

(iv) with a middle *alif* inserted and the second *hamza* lightened in between;[563]

(v) with the interrogative one suppressed;[564]

(vi) the same, but with its vowel thrown back upon the preceding quiescent consonant.[565]

lā yu'minūna ⁽*they will not believe*⁾ is

1. an explicative sentence in light of the unexplained one before it with regard to the purview of equality, so it has no desinential syntax;

561 *Āndhartahum*: Ibn Kathīr, Nāfiʿ, Yaʿqūb, Abū ʿAmr in one narration, al-Aṣbahānī, Warsh, Hishām, Ruways and al-Azraq in one narration. From Warsh is also narrated something similar to Qālūn's reading. "The claim of solecism is J's but Abū Ḥayyān rejected it, saying it showed disrespect." (*MQ*) "He followed J here and this is a mistake, since that reading is well-established among the canonical seven and it is the narration of Warsh." (S)

562 *A'andhartahum*: Ibn Abī Isḥāq. (*MQ*)

563 *Āandhartahum*: Abū ʿAmr, Qālūn, Ismāʿīl b. Jaʿfar from Nāfiʿ, Hishām, al-Aʿmash, Abū Jaʿfar, al-Yazīdī, Ibn ʿAbbās and Ibn Abī Isḥāq. It is the dialect of Quraysh, the Hijaz and Saʿd b. Bakr. This was among the choices of Sībawayh and al-Khalīl, who considered it more probative than the Tamīm one. (*MQ*)

564 *Andhartahum*: al-Zuhrī and Ibn Muḥayṣin:. (*MQ*)

565 *ʿAlayhima ndhartahum*: Ubay. (*MQ*)

(٢) أَوْ حَالٌ مُؤَكِّدَةٌ؛ (٣) أَوْ بَدَلٌ عَنْهُ؛ (٤) أَوْ خَبَرُ ﴿إِنَّ﴾، وَالْجُمْلَةُ قَبْلَهَا اِعْتِرَاضٌ بِمَا هُوَ عِلَّةُ الْحُكْمِ.

وَالْآيَةُ مِمَّا احْتَجَّ بِهِ مَنْ جَوَّزَ تَكْلِيفَ مَا لَا يُطَاقُ: فَإِنَّهُ ـ سُبْحَانَهُ وَتَعَالَى ـ أَخْبَرَ عَنْهُمْ بِأَنَّهُمْ لَا يُؤْمِنُونَ وَأَمَرَهُمْ بِالْإِيمَانِ؛ فَلَوْ آمَنُوا، اِنْقَلَبَ خَبَرُهُ كَذِباً، وَشَمِلَ إِيمَانُهُمُ الإِيمَانَ بِأَنَّهُمْ لَا يُؤْمِنُونَ فَيَجْتَمِعُ الضِّدَّانِ.

وَالْحَقُّ أَنَّ التَّكْلِيفَ بِالْمُمْتَنِعِ لِذَاتِهِ، وَإِنْ جَازَ عَقْلاً ـ مِنْ حَيْثُ إِنَّ ....

2. or a participial state providing emphasis;

3. or a substitute for it;[566]

4. or the enunciative of *inna*, and the clause before it is a parenthetical statement of the reason for their status.[567]

[The doctrine that Allah can task one beyond capacity]

This verse was adduced as a proof by those who say that it is possible that one be tasked beyond capacity,[568] since Allah Most High has said about them that *they will not believe* and [yet] has commanded them to believe; therefore, should they believe, His report would turn into a lie, furthermore their belief would comprise belief in the fact that they will not believe, which is a contradiction.[569]

The truth is that tasking one with what is inherently impossible, even if it is rationally possible—from the perspective that

[566] I.e., a *badal al-kull min al-kull.* (Q) On this type see above, the very first sentence under al-Fātiḥa 1:7.

[567] Their status being their lack of belief on a permanent basis. (Q)

[568] See our introduction, section entitled "Does Allah task one beyond one's capacity, for example tasking Abū Lahab and Abū Jahl to believe when He knows and announces they will not?"

[569] For example, if Abū Lahab were to believe, he would have to believe in everything the Prophet—upon him blessings and peace—brought, including the announcement that he would never believe. (Q)

الْأَحْكَامَ لَا تَسْتَدْعِي غَرَضاً سِيَّمَا الِامْتِثَالَ ـ لَكِنَّهُ غَيْرُ وَاقِعٍ لِلِاسْتِقْرَاءِ. وَالْإِخْبَارُ بِوُقُوعِ الشَّيْءِ أَوْ عَدَمِهِ لَا يَنْفِي الْقُدْرَةَ عَلَيْهِ، كَإِخْبَارِهِ تَعَالَى عَمَّا يَفْعَلُهُ هُوَ، أَوِ الْعَبْدُ بِاخْتِيَارِهِ. وَفَائِدَةُ الْإِنْذَارِ بَعْدَ الْعِلْمِ بِأَنَّهُ لَا يَنْجَعُ: إِلْزَامُ الْحُجَّةِ، وَحِيَازَةُ الرَّسُولِ فَضْلَ الْإِبْلَاغِ؛ وَلِذٰلِكَ قَالَ ﴿سَوَآءٌ عَلَيْهِمْ﴾ وَلَمْ يَقُلْ (سَوَاءٌ عَلَيْكَ)، كَمَا قَالَ لِعَبَدَةِ الْأَصْنَامِ: ﴿سَوَآءٌ عَلَيْكُمْ أَدَعَوْتُمُوهُمْ أَمْ أَنتُمْ صَٰمِتُونَ﴾ [الأعراف ١٩٣].

وَفِي الْآيَةِ إِخْبَارٌ بِالْغَيْبِ عَلَى مَا هُوَ بِهِ ....

rulings do not have an ulterior motive, not even compliance[570] —nevertheless a review of the evidence yields no such occurrence.[571] As for the [divine] report that something is taking place or not, it does not contradict [one's own] ability to enact it; for example when Allah Most High reports what He will do, or what His slave will do by choice. The benefit of warning [naysayers]—even after knowing that it will have no successful outcome—is to bind one to admit the proof, and also for the Messenger to reap the merit of conveyance. That is why He said, *it is the same for them* and He did not say "it is the same for you" the way He told the idol-worshippers, *it is the same to you whether you all call unto them or you are silent* (al-Aʿrāf 7:193).

The verse also contains a precise report of the unseen ....

[570] "Because many do not follow those rulings, so if compliance were the ulterior goal it would necessarily imply [rulings] fall short." (Q) "My God, Your good pleasure is too holy to have an ulterior motive on Your part; how could it have an ulterior motive on mine?" Ibn ʿAṭāʾ Allāh, *Munājāt* in *Ibn ʿAṭāʾ Allāh et la naissance de la confrérie šādilite:* Ḥikam, ed. and trans. Paul Nwiya (Beirut: Dar al-Machreq, 1990) p. 221.

[571] "I.e., the legal responsibilities (*takālīf*) have all been reviewed and followed up, but no inherent impossibility could be found among them. As for what apparently seems to be a tasking with something impossible, it is subject to contextualization and reinterpretation (*muwajjah muʾawwal*), as will be mentioned later." (Q)

- إِنْ أُرِيدَ بِالْمَوْصُولِ أَشْخَاصٌ بِأَعْيَانِهِمْ - فَهِيَ مِنَ الْمُعْجِزَاتِ.

﴿خَتَمَ ٱللَّهُ عَلَىٰ قُلُوبِهِمْ وَعَلَىٰ سَمْعِهِمْ وَعَلَىٰٓ أَبْصَٰرِهِمْ غِشَٰوَةٌ﴾ تَعْلِيلٌ لِلْحُكْمِ السَّابِقِ وَبَيَانٌ لِمَا يَقْتَضِيهِ.

وَ(الخَتْمُ): الْكَتْمُ، سُمِّيَ بِهِ (أ) الْاِسْتِيثَاقُ مِنَ الشَّيْءِ بِضَرْبِ الخَاتَمِ عَلَيْهِ لِأَنَّهُ كَتْمٌ لَهُ، (ب) وَالْبُلُوغُ آخِرَهُ نَظَرًا إِلَى أَنَّهُ آخِرُ فِعْلٍ يُفْعَلُ فِي إِحْرَازِهِ.

—if, by the conjunctive noun, specific individuals are meant—in which case it is among the staggering miracles.

[2:7] **khatama-l-Lāhu ʿalā qulūbihim wa-ʿalā samʿihim wa-ʿalā abṣārihim ghishāwatun** ⁽*the One God has sealed over their hearts and over their hearing; and over their sights there is a pall*⁾ shows the reason for the prior ruling and expounds all that it dictates.

Al-khatm ⁽sealing⁾ is *al-katm* ⁽concealing⁾[572] and is used to name (i) the complete fastening[573] of something by striking a seal over it—because it is a concealment of it—and (ii) reaching the end of something, in view of the fact that it is the last thing one does before replacing it in its repository.[574]

[572] Another example of the type of near-cognates called *isthiqāq akbar* following J: see notes 293 and 500. It is better to say—as in the *Kashshāf*—that they are near-cognates (*akhawān*) in that there is a suggestion of similarity in meaning parallel to the similarity in for, rather than to explain one by the other which is an exaggeration (Kh). "It is possible that *katm* is among the lexical meanings of *khatm* as mentioned by one of the commentators who cited the *Qāmūs* to that effect." (Q)

[573] "*Istīthāq* is the *istifʿāl* form of *wuthūq* ⁽tying down⁾ and its meaning is the blocking of the doors and fastening of the padlocks over their contents for safe-keeping and to prevent access." (Kh)

[574] Hence the expression "I sealed (*khatamtu*) the Qur'ān." al-Rāghib, *Mufradāt, s.v.* "*Iḥrāz* is to put something in its *ḥirz*, which is what preserves it; hence laypeople call what they hang on themselves for protection a *ḥirz*. It means that whoever completes something has reaped it (*ḥāzahu*) through whatever means is used to reap its kind, such as memorizing the Qur'ān to its end, so it is as if he tied it down." (Kh)

وَ(الْغِشَاوَةُ): فِعَالَةٌ مِنْ (غَشَّاهُ) إِذَا غَطَّاهُ؛ بُنِيَتْ لِمَا يَشْتَمِلُ عَلَى الشَّيْءِ، كَالْعِصَابَةِ وَالْعِمَامَةِ. وَلَا خَتْمَ وَلَا تَغْشِيَةَ عَلَى الْحَقِيقَةِ؛ وَإِنَّمَا الْمُرَادُ بِهِمَا: (أ) أَنْ يُحْدِثَ فِي نُفُوسِهِمْ هَيْئَةً تُمَرِّنُهُمْ عَلَى اسْتِحْبَابِ الْكُفْرِ وَالْمَعَاصِي، وَاسْتِقْبَاحِ الْإِيمَانِ وَالطَّاعَاتِ بِسَبَبِ غَيِّهِمْ، وَانْهِمَاكِهِمْ فِي التَّقْلِيدِ، وَإِعْرَاضِهِمْ عَنِ النَّظَرِ الصَّحِيحِ، فَتَجْعَلَ قُلُوبَهُمْ بِحَيْثُ لَا يَنْفُذُ فِيهَا الْحَقُّ، وَأَسْمَاعَهُمْ تَعَافُ اسْتِمَاعَهُ؛ فَتَصِيرَ كَأَنَّهَا مُسْتَوْثَقٌ مِنْهَا بِالْخَتْمِ، .....

Ghishāwa ⁽pall⁾ is a *fi'āla* form of *ghashshāh* meaning "it covered him up" [a morphological formation] properly used for what encompasses something, such as *'iṣāba* ⁽head-wrap⁾ and *'imāma* ⁽turban⁾.[575]

[The gradual sealing up and blinding of the heart and psyche]

There is no seal nor pall in literal terms.[576] Rather, what is meant by them is (i) that He creates in their psyches a condition that makes them accustomed to love unbelief and sins more and more, and actively disparage faith and acts of obedience, because of their seduction, engrossment in conformism and shunning of genuine investigation, so that it makes their hearts impenetrable to truth and it makes their hearing not want to listen to it; and they both become virtually secured with the seal. Additionally,

575 "'*Iṣāba* is what is tied (*yu'ṣab*) around the head a little; increased, it is a *'imāma*." (Q)

576 "As per the *Kashshāf* verbatim; and this is one of the [interpretive] methods of *Ahl al-Sunna*: they take the creation of the condition about to be mentioned as the literal act of Allah (*fi'l Allāh ḥaqīqatan*), and its naming *khatm* and *ghāshiya* is figurative (*majāz*)." (S) "He wanted to invalidate the position of Ẓāhirīs who take them literally and resign their modality to the Knowledge of Allah Most High." (Q) "The stronger method is to say that they are a literal seal and a literal cover, since the hadiths to that effect are explicit.... Those who are not imbued with knowledge of hadith read them as metaphorical and figurative." (S 1:349).

وَأَبْصَارَهُمْ لَا تَجْتَلِي الْآيَاتِ الْمَنْصُوبَةَ لَهُمْ فِي الْأَنْفُسِ وَالْآفَاقِ ـ كَمَا تَجْتَلِيهَا أَعْيُنُ الْمُسْتَبْصِرِينَ ـ فَتَصِيرَ كَأَنَّهَا غُطِّيَ عَلَيْهَا وَحِيلَ بَيْنَهَا وَبَيْنَ الْإِبْصَارِ؛ وَسَمَّاهُ عَلَى الْاِسْتِعَارَةِ خَتْماً وَتَغْشِيَةً. (ب) أَوْ مَثَّلَ قُلُوبَهُمْ وَمَشَاعِرَهُمُ الْمَؤُوفَةَ بِهَا بِأَشْيَاءَ ضُرِبَ حِجَابٌ بَيْنَهَا وَبَيْنَ الْاِسْتِنْفَاعِ بِهَا خَتْماً وَتَغْطِيَةً.

وَقَدْ عَبَّرَ عَنْ إِحْدَاثِ هٰذِهِ الْهَيْئَةِ بِـ(الطَّبْعِ) فِي قَوْلِهِ تَعَالَى ﴿أُولَٰٓئِكَ ٱلَّذِينَ طَبَعَ ٱللَّهُ عَلَىٰ قُلُوبِهِمْ وَسَمْعِهِمْ وَأَبْصَٰرِهِمْ﴾ [النحل ١٠٨]؛ وَبِـ(الْإِغْفَالِ) فِي قَوْلِهِ تَعَالَى: ﴿وَلَا تُطِعْ مَنْ أَغْفَلْنَا قَلْبَهُۥ عَن ذِكْرِنَا﴾ [الكهف ٢٨]؛ وَبِـ(الْإِقْسَاءِ) فِي قَوْلِهِ تَعَالَى: ﴿وَجَعَلْنَا قُلُوبَهُمْ قَٰسِيَةً﴾ [المائدة ١٣].

it makes their sights not contemplate the great signs produced for them—both in themselves and the world at large—the way the eyes of those who strive to see[577] contemplate them, so that they become virtually blindfolded, their vision blocked. He named this [condition] "a seal" and "a pall" metaphorically.

(ii) Alternately, He represented their hearts and senses, infected by that [condition], as things segregated from any semblance of benefit, sealed off and covered up.

He expressed the creation of this condition as

(i) a stamping, when He said—may He be exalted—*Those are they whose hearts, hearing and sights Allah has stamped* (al-Naḥl 16: 108);

(ii) a making heedless, when He said, *and do not obey those whose hearts We have made heedless of our remembrance* (al-Kahf 18:28);

(iii) and a hardening when He said, *and We hardened their hearts* (al-Māʾida 5:13).

[577] *Mustabṣir* could also be translated figuratively as "those who have insight."

وَهِيَ ـ مِنْ حَيْثُ إِنَّ الْمُمْكِنَاتِ بِأَسْرِهَا مُسْتَنِدَةٌ إِلَى اللهِ تَعَالَى، وَاقِعَةٌ بِقُدْرَتِهِ ـ أُسْنِدَتْ إِلَيْهِ؛ وَمِنْ حَيْثُ إِنَّهَا مُسَبَّبَةٌ مِمَّا اقْتَرَفُوهُ ـ بِدَلِيلِ قَوْلِهِ تَعَالَى ﴿بَلْ طَبَعَ ٱللَّهُ عَلَيْهَا بِكُفْرِهِمْ﴾ [النساء ١٥٥]، وَقَوْلِهِ تَعَالَى ﴿ذَٰلِكَ بِأَنَّهُمْ ءَامَنُوا۟ ثُمَّ كَفَرُوا۟ فَطُبِعَ عَلَىٰ قُلُوبِهِمْ﴾ [المنافقون ٣] ـ: وَرَدَتِ الْآيَةُ نَاعِيَةً عَلَيْهِمْ شَنَاعَةَ صِفَتِهِمْ وَوَخَامَةَ عَاقِبَتِهِمْ.

وَاضْطَرَبَتِ الْمُعْتَزِلَةُ فِيهِ، فَذَكَرُوا وُجُوهاً مِنَ التَّأْوِيلِ:

الْأَوَّلُ: أَنَّ الْقَوْمَ لَمَّا أَعْرَضُوا عَنِ الْحَقِّ وَتَمَكَّنَ ذَٰلِكَ فِي قُلُوبِهِمْ حَتَّى صَارَ كَالطَّبِيعَةِ لَهُمْ، شُبِّهَ بِالْوَصْفِ الْخَلْقِيِّ الْمَجْبُولِ عَلَيْهِ.

These [acts]—from the perspective that all contingencies are attributed to Allah Most High and take place by His power—were all attributed to Him; and from the perspective of their being caused by what they committed—as indicated by the Most High when He said, *nay, Allah has stamped them through their unbelief* (al-Nisā' 4:155) and *that is because they believed then they disbelieved, so it was stamped over their hearts* (al-Munāfiqūn 63:3)—the verse came, exposing their hateful characteristics and baleful[578] end.

[Non-Sunni views of the divine "sealing" and "misguiding"]

The Muʿtazila floundered with regard to this verse[579] and mentioned several interpretive possibilities:

1. When those people turned away from the truth and that [aversion] took hold in their hearts until it became second nature to them, it was assimilated with a native physical trait.

[578] *Wakhāma* is pestilence and corruption in the land. (Q)
[579] "Because of their view that the *qabīḥ* ʿuglyʾ cannot be ascribed to Allah." (A)

الثَّانِي: أَنَّ الْمُرَادَ بِهِ تَمْثِيلُ حَالِ قُلُوبِهِمْ بِقُلُوبِ الْبَهَائِمِ الَّتِي خَلَقَهَا اللهُ تَعَالَى خَالِيَةً عَنِ الْفِطَنِ، أَوْ قُلُوبٍ مُقَدَّرٍ خَتَمَ اللهُ عَلَيْهَا؛ وَنَظِيرُهُ: (سَالَ بِهِ الْوَادِي) إِذَا هَلَكَ وَ(طَارَتْ بِهِ الْعَنْقَاءُ) إِذَا طَالَتْ غَيْبَتُهُ.

الثَّالِثُ: أَنَّ ذٰلِكَ فِي الْحَقِيقَةِ فِعْلُ الشَّيْطَانِ أَوِ الْكَافِرِ، لٰكِنْ ـ لَمَّا كَانَ صُدُورُهُ عَنْهُ بِإِقْدَارِهِ تَعَالَى إِيَّاهُ ـ أُسْنِدَ إِلَيْهِ إِسْنَادَ الْفِعْلِ إِلَى الْمُسَبِّبِ.

الرَّابِعُ: أَنَّ أَعْرَاقَهُمْ ـ لَمَّا رَسَخَتْ فِي الْكُفْرِ وَاسْتَحْكَمَتْ بِحَيْثُ لَمْ يَبْقَ طَرِيقٌ إِلَى تَحْصِيلِ إِيمَانِهِمْ سِوَى الْإِلْجَاءِ وَالْقَسْرِ، ثُمَّ لَمْ يَقْسِرْهُمْ إِبْقَاءً عَلَى غَرَضِ التَّكْلِيفِ ـ عَبَّرَ عَنْ تَرْكِهِ بِالْخَتْمِ، فَإِنَّهُ سَدٌّ لِإِيمَانِهِمْ. ....

2. What is meant is a proverbializing of the state of their hearts as being like the hearts of dumb beasts which Allah created devoid of wits—or like hearts subauded to have been stamped by Allah—equivalent to the expressions "the flood took him down the vale" to mean that he perished, or "the griffon took him and flew away" to mean that he has been absent too long.[580]

3. That, in reality, is the act of the devil or the unbeliever; but since such an act issues from them through their empowerment by Allah Most High, it was attributed to Him in the same way an act is attributed to the Causator.

4. When their roots[581] strengthened in unbelief and dominated to the point there remained no means of obtaining belief from them other than force or coercion—but He did not coerce them, as the purpose of legal responsibility must remain—He expressed His abandonment as a sealing, for it is a barrier to their belief.

[580] "I.e. it is a proverbializing without its actual parts being [literally] involved." (Q)
[581] "In the sense of native essence (*bi-maʿnā al-aṣl*)." (Q)

وَفِيهِ إِشْعَارٌ عَلَى تَمَادِي أَمْرِهِمْ فِي الْغَيِّ وَتَنَاهِي انْهِمَاكِهِمْ فِي الضَّلَالِ وَالْبَغْيِ.

الْخَامِسُ: أَنْ يَكُونَ حِكَايَةً لِمَا كَانَتِ الْكَفَرَةُ يَقُولُونَ -مِثْلَ: ﴿قُلُوبُنَا فِىٓ أَكِنَّةٍ مِّمَّا تَدْعُونَآ إِلَيْهِ وَفِىٓ ءَاذَانِنَا وَقْرٌ وَمِنۢ بَيْنِنَا وَبَيْنِكَ حِجَابٌ﴾ [فصلت ٥]- تَهَكُّماً وَاسْتِهْزَاءً بِهِمْ، كَقَوْلِهِ تَعَالَى ﴿لَمْ يَكُنِ ٱلَّذِينَ كَفَرُوا۟ مِنْ أَهْلِ ٱلْكِتَٰبِ وَٱلْمُشْرِكِينَ﴾ [البينة ١]، الْآيَةَ.

السَّادِسُ: أَنَّ ذٰلِكَ فِي الْآخِرَةِ؛ وَإِنَّمَا أَخْبَرَ عَنْهُ بِالْمَاضِي لِتَحَقُّقِهِ وَتَيَقُّنِ وُقُوعِهِ، ....

There is also in that a notification of their protracted insistence on error and their complete absorption with misguidance and rebellion.

5. It is a direct quotation of what the unbelievers used to say, such as *our hearts are under covers far from what you are summoning us to; in our ears there is a deafness; and between us and you there is a blind* (Fuṣṣilat 41:5) to deride and mock them, as in the saying of the Most High, *Never will those who rejected belief —the People of Scripture and the idolaters* (al-Bayyina 98:1) to the end of the verse.[582]

6. That takes place in the hereafter, but He related it in the past tense because of its factuality and the certitude of its occurrence,

[582] Al-Ṭībī said: "Because the unbelievers used to say, before the mission of the Prophet—upon him blessings and peace: 'We will never desist from what we follow until the prophet who was promised to us in the Torah and the Gospel comes to us.' *Then, when what they knew did come, they disbelieved* (al-Baqara 2:90); so Allah cited their words and how they broke their promise, but He couched it as a threat of punishment." (S, Q) "So the derision and quotation [in the second verse] is in the meaning, not verbatim." (Q)

وَيَشْهَدُ لَهُ قَوْلُهُ تَعَالَى: ﴿وَنَحْشُرُهُمْ يَوْمَ ٱلْقِيَـٰمَةِ عَلَىٰ وُجُوهِهِمْ عُمْيًا وَبُكْمًا وَصُمًّا﴾ [الإسراء ٩٧].

السَّابِعُ: أَنَّ الْمُرَادَ بِالْخَتْمِ: وَسْمُ قُلُوبِهِمْ بِسِمَةٍ تَعْرِفُهَا الْمَلَائِكَةُ، فَيُبْغِضُونَهُمْ وَيَنْفُرُونَ عَنْهُمْ.

وَعَلَى هٰذَا الْمِنْهَاجِ كَلَامُنَا وَكَلَامُهُمْ فِيمَا يُضَافُ إِلَى اللهِ تَعَالَى مِنْ طَبْعٍ وَإِضْلَالٍ وَنَحْوِهِمَا.

﴿وَعَلَىٰ سَمْعِهِمْ﴾ مَعْطُوفٌ ....

in testimony whereof the Most High said, *and We shall assemble them on the Day of Resurrection on their faces, blind, dumb and deaf* (al-Isrā' 17:97).

7. What is meant by the seal is the marking of their hearts with a mark the angels can recognize, so that they will hate them and flee from them.

All of the above shows the difference in method between our discourse and theirs with regard to what is ascribed to Allah Most High of "stamping" "misguiding" and the like.[583]

[More on how Allah seals the senses of the unbelievers]

Wa-ʿalā samʿihim ⁽and over their hearing⁾ is adjoined ....

[583] "Thus we—all the people of the Sunna—say it is attributed to Allah literally, as previously mentioned that contingencies are attributed, etc. and our refraining from attribution of certain matters is out of good manners (*lil-ta'addub*), not because ascription to the Most High is incorrect, as already discussed in the description of unlawful income (*al-suḥt*) as [His] provision (*rizq*). Really, the Muʿtazila go to unnatural lengths in figurative interpretation and they make arbitrary choices and are long-winded in that! This evokes a brilliant and subtle allusive point (*nukta bāriʿa laṭifa*), which is that since the truth is one, the people of truth suffice themselves with a single beautiful interpretation; but since falsehood is baseless and unstable, the people of falsehood are mystified with figurative interpretation and they pertinaciously cling to every defective and feeble matter." (Q 2:65)

عَلَى قُلُوبِهِمْ لِقَوْلِهِ تَعَالَى: ﴿وَخَتَمَ عَلَىٰ سَمْعِهِۦ وَقَلْبِهِۦ﴾ [الجاثية ٢٣]، وَلِلْوِفَاقِ عَلَى الْوَقْفِ عَلَيْهِ، وَلِأَنَّهُمَا ـ لَمَّا اشْتَرَكَا فِي الْإِدْرَاكِ مِنْ جَمِيعِ الْجَوَانِبِ ـ جَعَلَ مَا يَمْنَعُهُمَا مِنْ خَاصِّ فِعْلِهِمَا: الْخَتْمَ الَّذِي يَمْنَعُ مِنْ جَمِيعِ الْجِهَاتِ؛ وَإِدْرَاكُ الْأَبْصَارِ ـ لَمَّا اخْتَصَّ بِجِهَةِ الْمُقَابَلَةِ ـ جَعَلَ الْمَانِعَ لَهَا عَنْ فِعْلِهَا: الْغِشَاوَةَ الْمُخْتَصَّةَ بِتِلْكَ الْجِهَةِ.

وَكَرَّرَ الْجَارَّ لِيَكُونَ أَدَلَّ عَلَى شِدَّةِ الْخَتْمِ فِي الْمَوْضِعَيْنِ، وَاسْتِقْلَالِ كُلٍّ مِنْهُمَا بِالْحُكْمِ.

وَوَحَّدَ السَّمْعَ لِلْأَمْنِ مِنَ اللَّبْسِ، وَاعْتِبَارِ الْأَصْلِ: ....

to ***qulūbihim*** ⁽their hearts⁾ in light of His saying—may He be exalted—*and sealed over his hearing and his heart* (al-Jāthiya 45:23) and because there is agreement in pausing after it:[584] since the two of them are partners in perception from every aspect,[585] He made what blocks them from their specific function a seal that blocks from every direction.[586] As for the perception of sights, since it is specific to the frontward direction, the blocker of its function was made to be a pall specific to that direction.

He repeated the preposition [***ʿalā***] so that it will be more indicative of the sealing in both places as well as the pertinence of the ruling to each independently of the other.

He put ***samʿ*** ⁽hearing⁾ in the singular (i) because it is free of ambiguity (ii) and also in consideration of its literal origin, ……

584 "The agreement of Quranic readers over this shows it is unrelated to what follows it, otherwise it would necessarily mean that they agreed over a graceless pause." (Q)

585 "This is somewhat self-indulgent: if by the heart is meant the coniferous piece of flesh then it cannot perceive, but rather is the seat of knowledge; and if it is a spirit then it is obviously perceptive; but he appears to be meaning the physical organ." (Q)

586 "A rational proof, whereas what preceded was a transmissive one." (Q)

فَإِنَّهُ مَصْدَرٌ فِي أَصْلِهِ، وَالْمَصَادِرُ لَا تُجْمَعُ؛ أَوْ عَلَى تَقْدِيرِ مُضَافٍ مِثْلِ: (وَعَلَى حَوَاسِّ سَمْعِهِمْ).

وَ(الْأَبْصَارُ) جَمْعُ بَصَرٍ، وَهُوَ إِدْرَاكُ الْعَيْنِ؛ وَقَدْ يُطْلَقُ مَجَازاً عَلَى الْقُوَّةِ الْبَاصِرَةِ، وَعَلَى الْعُضْوِ؛ وَكَذَا السَّمْعُ. وَلَعَلَّ الْمُرَادَ (أ) بِهِمَا فِي الْآيَةِ: الْعُضْوُ، لِأَنَّهُ أَشَدُّ مُنَاسَبَةً لِلْخَتْمِ وَالتَّغْطِيَةِ؛ (ب) وَبِالْقَلْبِ: مَا هُوَ مَحَلُّ الْعِلْمِ؛ وَقَدْ يُطْلَقُ، وَيُرَادُ بِهِ الْعَقْلُ وَالْمَعْرِفَةُ، كَمَا قَالَ تَعَالَى: ﴿إِنَّ فِي ذَٰلِكَ لَذِكْرَىٰ لِمَن كَانَ لَهُۥ قَلْبٌ﴾ [ق ٣٧].

وَإِنَّمَا جَازَ إِمَالَتُهَا مَعَ الصَّادِ لِأَنَّ الرَّاءَ الْمَكْسُورَةَ تَغْلِبُ ....

as it is originally an infinitive noun and they are not put in the plural; (iii) unless we infer a governing annex, for example "and over their senses of hearing."

Abṣār is the plural of *baṣar* which is the eye's perception,[587] and can be used metaphorically for the faculty of sight as well as the organ—likewise ***samʿ*** (hearing). What is meant by both in the verse may be the organ, because it has a stronger correspondence to sealing and covering up. As for ***qalb*** (heart) what is meant is the seat of knowledge but it can also be used to mean the mind[588] and greater knowledge, as Allah Most High said, *verily therein is a reminder for him who has a heart* (Qāf 50:37).

The reason why it is permissible to give it an *é*-shaded phonetic deflection[589] with *ṣād* is because *rā'* with a *kasra* beats the

[587] "I.e., the perception of the person through the medium of the eye." (Q)

[588] Narrated from ʿAlī b. Abī Ṭālib by Bukhārī in *al-Adab al-Mufrad*, ed. Muḥammad Fu'ād ʿAbd al-Bāqī (Cairo: al-Maṭbaʿat al-Salafiyya, 1375/1956) p. 143 §547 *bāb: al-ʿaqlu fīl-qalb*.

[589] The *imāla*: *abṣérihim* أَبْصارِهِمْ is the reading of Abū ʿAmr, al-Dājūnī, Ibn Dhakwān through al-Ṣūrī, al-Dūrī from al-Kisā'ī, and al-Yazīdī. (*MQ*)

الْمُسْتَعْلِيَةَ لِمَا فِيهَا مِنَ التَّكْرِيرِ.

وَ﴿غِشَـٰوَةٌ﴾ رُفِعَ بِالْابْتِدَاءِ عِنْدَ سِيبَوَيْهِ، وَبِالْجَارِّ وَالْمَجْرُورِ عِنْدَ الْأَخْفَشِ، وَيُؤَيِّدُهُ الْعَطْفُ عَلَى الْجُمْلَةِ الْفِعْلِيَّةِ.

وَقُرِئَ بِالنَّصْبِ (أ) عَلَى تَقْدِيرِ: (وَجَعَلَ عَلَى أَبْصَارِهِمْ غِشَاوَةً)، أَوْ (ب) عَلَى حَذْفِ الْجَارِّ وَإِيصَالِ الْخَتْمِ بِنَفْسِهِ إِلَيْهِ، وَالْمَعْنَى: وَخَتَمَ عَلَى أَبْصَارِهِمْ بِغِشَاوَةٍ. وقرئ ....

self-elevated phoneme due to its repetitiveness.[590]

[Parsing of mass-transmitted and irregular readings]

Ghishāwatun has a nominative case (i) because it is an inchoative according to Sībawayh or (ii) by immediately following a preposition and its complement according to al-Akhfash,[591] a view supported by the adjunction with the verbal clause.[592]

It was also read with the accusative case (i) by inferring [the transitive verb] *wa-jaʿala ʿalā abṣārihim ghishāwatan* ⁽and He placed over their sights a pall⁾[593] (ii) or by suppressing the preposition and linking the sealing with it in the sense *wa-khatama ʿalā abṣārihim bi-ghishāwatin* ⁽and He sealed over their sights with a pall⁾.[594] It was also read ....

[590] "In that the *rā'* is a repetitive letter (*ḥarf takrīr*) which counts virtually as two letters (*qā'im maqāma ḥarfayn*)." (Z)

[591] "And the Kufans also, as the latter do not allow an inchoative to come after the enunciative, but because of the weakness of this view the author did not bother to mention it." (Q)

[592] "In the sense that *wa-ʿalā abṣārihim ghishāwatun* is a local-temporal/circumstancial clause (*jumla ẓarfiyya*) with a verb inferring the vessel (*ẓarf*), so the inference would be *wa-staqarrat ʿalā abṣārihim ghishāwatun* ⁽a pall has settled over their sights⁾, whereby there is congruence between it and the verbal clause [*khatama* etc.]." (Z)

[593] By al-Mufaḍḍal al-Ḍabbī; Ibn Nabhān and Abū Bakr from ʿĀṣim; a reading rejected by al-Ṭabarī, al-Zajjāj and Abū Ḥayyān. (*MQ*)

[594] "In the first sense the covering expressed the creating of that condition (*hay'a*) in

بِالضَّمِّ وَالرَّفْعِ؛ وَبِالْفَتْحِ وَالنَّصْبِ ـ وَهُمَا لُغَتَانِ فِيهَا ـ؛ وَ(غِشْوَةٌ) بِالْكَسْرِ،
مَرْفُوعَةً؛ وَبِالْفَتْحِ، مَرْفُوعَةً، وَمَنْصُوبَةً؛ وَ(عُشَاوَةٌ) مَعًا بِالْعَيْنِ الْغَيْرِ
الْمُعْجَمَةِ.

﴿وَلَهُمْ عَذَابٌ عَظِيمٌ﴾ وَعِيدٌ وَبَيَانٌ لِمَا يَسْتَحِقُّونَهُ.

(i) with *ḍamma* and nominative case-ending [*ghushāwatun*];

(ii) with *fatḥa* and accusative [*ghashāwatan*]—these are two dialectical variants here;

(iii) also *ghishwatun* with a *kasra* and the nominative;

(iv) [*ghashwatun/tan*] with *fatḥa* and the nominative or accusative;

(v) and *ʿa/u/ishāwatun/tan* with an undotted *ʿayn*.[595]

wa-lahum ʿadhābun ʿaẓīmun ⁽*and theirs is an immense punishment*⁾: [This is] a threat and exposition of what they deserve.

the sights just as the sealing expressed its creating in the hearts and hearing; in this sense, however, the sealing expresses the creating of the condition in all three organs. The upshot is that it exhibits the instrument of that creating in the sights explicitly for intensiveness, while it remains implicit and deductive for its two fellow organs. It is as if it was said: Allah has sealed over their hearts with layered coverings (*akinna*), and over their hearing with deafness (*waqr*) for example, and over their sights with a pall. So He sufficed Himself with the mention of the instrument in the third case." (Q 2:75).

595 *Ghushāwatun*: al-Ḥasan in one narration and Zayd b. ʿAlī, in the ʿUkl dialect; *ghashāwatan*: unidentified; *ghashāwatun*: al-Ḥasan and Abū Ḥaywa in the dialect of Rabīʿa; *ghishwatun*: Abū ʿAmr, Abū Ḥaywa; *ghashwatun*: ʿUbayd b. ʿUmayr, Aʿmash, Abū Ḥaywa; *ghashwatan*: Abū Ḥaywa, Sufyān Abū Rajāʾ, al-Aʿmash, Ibn Masʿūd; *ʿashāwatun*: Ṭāwūs; *ʿushāwatun*: al-Ḥasan; *ʿishāwatun*: unidentified. Also *ghashyatun*: Ibn Masʿūd and his students. Furthermore, when al-Kisāʾī paused, it is agreed upon that he would read it with *imāla*: *ghishāwéh* غِشَاوه. (*MQ*) "عشاوة is the infinitive noun for *aʿshā* ⁽nyctalops⁾, one who cannot see at night but sees in daytime, i.e. they see matters through their external aspects or worldly uses only, and they cannot see them through their internal aspects or next-worldly benefits, meaning they see the signs (*āyāt*) themselves and they do not see what they describe: sights of heedlessness rather than insights of wisening." (Q)

وَ(الْعَذَابُ) كَـ(النَّكَالِ) بِنَاءً وَمَعْنًى؛ تَقُولُ (عَذَبَ عَنِ الشَّيْءِ) وَ(نَكَلَ عَنْهُ) إِذَا أَمْسَكَ ـ وَمِنْهُ (الْمَاءُ الْعَذْبُ) لِأَنَّهُ يَقْمَعُ الْعَطَشَ وَيَرْدَعُهُ، وَلِذٰلِكَ سُمِّيَ (نُقَاخاً) وَ(فُرَاتاً) ـ ثُمَّ اتَّسَعَ فَأُطْلِقَ عَلَى كُلِّ أَلَمٍ فَادِحٍ وَإِنْ لَمْ يَكُنْ نَكَالاً ـ أَيْ: عِقَاباً يَرْدَعُ الْجَانِي عَنِ الْمُعَاوَدَةِ ـ فَهُوَ أَعَمُّ مِنْهُمَا. وَقِيلَ: اِشْتِقَاقُهُ مِنَ (التَّعْذِيبِ) الَّذِي هُوَ إِزَالَةُ الْعَذَبِ، كَـ(التَّقْذِيَةِ) وَ(التَّمْرِيضِ).

وَ(الْعَظِيمُ) نَقِيضُ الْحَقِيرِ، وَ(الْكَبِيرُ) ....

[Semantics of *ʿadhāb* ⟨punishment⟩]

Al-ʿadhāb ⟨punishment⟩ is like *al-nakāl* ⟨exemplary penalty⟩ in form and meaning;[596] you say *ʿadhaba ʿan al-shay'* ⟨to quit/hinder something⟩ and *nakala ʿanh* ⟨to desist from it⟩ in the sense of abstention, whence water that is *ʿadhb* ⟨sweet⟩, because it subdues thirst and curbs it, and that is why it was called *nuqākh* ⟨smiter⟩ and *furāt* ⟨grinder⟩.[597] Then it was extended to apply to any sort of heavy[598] pain, even other than a *nakāl*—which is the *ʿiqāb* ⟨sanction⟩ that deters the criminal from recidivating—and so it is more general in meaning than both of the latter.

It is also said it is derived from *taʿdhīb*, which is the elimination of *ʿadhib* ⟨sweetness⟩, as in *taqdhiya* ⟨removal of *qadhā*, impurities⟩ and *tamrīḍ* ⟨removal of *maraḍ*, sickness⟩.[599]

ʿAẓīm ⟨immense⟩ is contrary to *ḥaqīr* ⟨insignificant⟩ and *kabīr*

596 "Each one entails prevention, desistance, deterrence, and abstention." (Z) Al-Sajāwandī said: "ʿ*adhāb* is the inflicting of pain (*alam*) upon a living thing together with humiliation/contempt (*hawān*)." (S)

597 *Naqakha* means "to smite" and *farata* is the transposed form of *rafata*, "to grind," whence the names *nuqākh* and *furāt* for sweet, cool water as it tempers the vehemence of thirst. (Kh, Q, Z, Lane, *s.v.*).

598 α, A, Ak, B, F, I, Kh, L, P, Q, R, S, Sk, T, U, Ul, Z: فادح AQ, D, ε, H, K, MM: قادح

599 I.e., as a privative, in the same way as we say "fleecing," "dusting" and "boning" to signify the removal of fleece, dust, and bones.

نَقِيضُ الصَّغِيرِ؛ فَكَمَا أَنَّ الحَقِيرَ دُونَ الصَّغِيرِ، فَالْعَظِيمُ فَوْقَ الْكَبِيرِ. وَمَعْنَى التَّوْصِيفِ بِهِ: أَنَّهُ إِذَا قِيسَ بِسَائِرِ مَا يُجَانِسُهُ، قَصُرَ عَنْهُ جَمِيعُهُ وَحَقُرَ بِالْإِضَافَةِ إِلَيْهِ. وَمَعْنَى التَّنْكِيرِ فِي الْآيَةِ: أَنَّ عَلَى أَبْصَارِهِمْ نَوْعُ غِشَاوَةٍ لَيْسَ مِمَّا يَتَعَارَفُهُ النَّاسُ، وَهُوَ التَّعَامِي عَنِ الْآيَاتِ؛ وَلَهُمْ مِنَ الْآلَامِ الْعِظَامِ نَوْعٌ عَظِيمٌ لَا يَعْلَمُ كُنْهَهُ إِلَّا اللهُ.

﴿وَمِنَ ٱلنَّاسِ مَن يَقُولُ ءَامَنَّا بِٱللَّهِ وَبِٱلْيَوْمِ ٱلْءَاخِرِ﴾: لَمَّا افْتَتَحَ ـ سُبْحَانَهُ وَتَعَالَى ـ بِشَرْحِ حَالِ الْكِتَابِ، وَسَاقَ لِبَيَانِهِ ذِكْرَ الْمُؤْمِنِينَ الَّذِينَ أَخْلَصُوا دِينَهُمْ لله تَعَالَى وَوَاطَأَتْ فِيهِ قُلُوبُهُمْ أَلْسِنَتَهُمْ، وَثَنَّى بِأَضْدَادِهِمْ الَّذِينَ

ʿbigʾ is contrary to *ṣaghīr* ʿsmallʾ; just as the insignificant is less than the small, similarly, the immense is above the big. The meaning of its being thus qualified is that when compared to the things of the same class, they all fall short and appear insignificant next to it.

The meaning of the indefinite in the verse is that over their sights is a type of pall other than what people are familiar with, namely, wilful blindness to the great signs; and theirs is an immense type of immense pains, the totality of which none knows but Allah.

[2:8] **wa-mina al-nāsi man yaqūlu āmannā bi-l-Lāhi wa-bi-l-yawmi-l-ākhiri** ʿ*and of people there are those who say: We believe in the One God and in the Last Day*ʾ:

After He began by explaining the status of the Book and, to that end, mentioned the believers who devoted their religion wholly to Allah—wherein their hearts matched their tongues; and after, secondly, He described their opposites as those who …

مَحَّضُوا الْكُفْرَ ظَاهِراً وَبَاطِناً وَلَمْ يَلْتَفِتُوا لَفْتَةً رَأْساً، ثَلَّثَ بِالْقِسْمِ الثَّالِثِ الْمُذَبْذَبِ بَيْنَ الْقِسْمَيْنِ؛ وَهُمُ الَّذِينَ آمَنُوا بِأَفْوَاهِهِمْ وَلَمْ تُؤْمِنْ قُلُوبُهُمْ، تَكْمِيلاً لِلتَّقْسِيمِ. وَهُمْ أَخْبَثُ الْكَفَرَةِ وَأَبْغَضُهُمْ إِلَى اللهِ، لِأَنَّهُمْ مَوَّهُوا الْكُفْرَ وَخَلَطُوا بِهِ خِدَاعاً وَاسْتِهْزَاءً؛ وَلِذٰلِكَ طَوَّلَ فِي بَيَانِ خُبْثِهِمْ وَجَهْلِهِمْ وَاسْتَهْزَأَ بِهِمْ، وَتَهَكَّمَ بِأَفْعَالِهِمْ، وَسَجَّلَ عَلَى عَمَهِهِمْ وَطُغْيَانِهِمْ، وَضَرَبَ لَهُمُ الْأَمْثَالَ وَأَنْزَلَ فِيهِمْ ﴿إِنَّ ٱلْمُنَٰفِقِينَ فِي ٱلدَّرْكِ ٱلْأَسْفَلِ مِنَ ٱلنَّارِ﴾ [النساء ١٤٥]. وَقِصَّتُهُمْ عَنْ آخِرِهَا مَعْطُوفَةٌ عَلَى قِصَّةِ الْمُصِرِّينَ.

unequivocally rejected belief, outwardly and inwardly, paying it no heed from the very start, He then mentioned the third lot—those who waver back and forth between the two groups. They are those who believed with their mouths while their hearts never believed; and this completes the subdivision.

[The hypocrites exposed]

The latter are the most wicked of the unbelievers and the most loathsome to Allah, because they have embellished infidelity and injected it with deceit and scoffing. Therefore He exposed their wickedness and ignorance at length; mocked them and ridiculed their actions; passed judgment against their blindness of heart[600] and their tyranny; made them the stuff of proverbs; and revealed, concerning them: *Truly the hypocrites are in the lowest deep of the fire* (al-Nisā' 4:145). Their account from beginning to end is adjoined[601] to that of the obdurate.

[600] Ak, AQ, B, ÇZ, ε, F, H, Iş, K, Kh, MM, R, Sk: عمههم I: عمهم corr. to عمههم β, T: عمهم α, Q: عميهم D, L, U, Ul, Z: غيهم P: عميهم وفي نسخة غيهم

[601] Al-Taftāzānī and al-Jurjānī said the *'atf* here is not grammatical but logical and semantic. (S, Z) See note 909.

وَ(النَّاسُ): أَصْلُهُ (أُنَاسٌ)، لِقَوْلِهِـمْ: (إِنْسَـانٌ) وَ(إِنْسٌ) وَ(أَنَاسِيُّ)؛ فَحُذِفَتِ الْهَمْزَةُ حَذْفَهَا فِي (لُوقَةٍ)، وَعُوِّضَ عَنْهَا حَرْفُ التَّعْرِيفِ؛ وَلِذٰلِكَ لَا يَكَادُ يُجْمَعُ بَيْنَهُمَا. وَقَوْلُهُ: [كامل]

إِنَّ الْمَنَايَا يَطَّلِعْــ   *   ــنَ عَلَى الْإِنَاسِ الْآمِنِينَا

شَاذٌّ.

وَهُوَ اسْمُ جَمْعٍ كَـ(رُخَالٍ) ـ إِذْ لَمْ يَثْبُتْ (فُعَالٌ) فِي أَبْنِيَةِ الْجَمْعِ ـ مَأْخُوذٌ مِنْ (أَنِسَ) لِأَنَّهُمْ يَسْتَأْنِسُونَ بِأَمْثَالِهِمْ، أَوْ (آنَسَ) لِأَنَّهُمْ ظَاهِرُونَ مُبْصَرُونَ،

Al-nās 'people' is originally *unās*—just as they say *insān* 'human being', *ins* 'humanity', *anāsīy* 'humans'—after which the *hamza* was suppressed in the same way as in *lūqa* '<*alūqa*, ghee', and the definite article made up for it. That is why they are almost never found together;[602] as for the [poet's] saying, ["The Perfect"]

Death surely keeps bursting   upon unsuspecting folk (al-ināsˍ),[603]

it is anomalous.

It is a collective name like *rukhāl* 'ewes'[604]—since *fuʿāl* is unestablished among the plural forms—taken from (i) *anisa* 'to socialize', because they socialize with their likes;

(ii) or *ānasa* 'to observe', because they are visible in full view—

---

[602] I.e. *al-lūqa* is a noun stemming from *a-l-q*, not *l-w-q*, and its original form is *alūqa*. Hence the *hamza* and the definite article *alif lām* are hardly found together. (Z)

[603] Ibn Yaʿīsh said its author is unknown. (S) However, Abū Ḥātim al-Sijistānī in *Kitāb al-Muʿammarīn min al-ʿArab* (Cairo: Maṭbaʿat al-Saʿāda, 1323/1905) p. 34 attributes it to the tercentenarian king Dhū Jadan al-Ḥimyarī. Ibn Sīdah in *al-Mukhaṣṣaṣ*, ed. Muḥammad Maḥmūd al-Tarkazī al-Shinqīṭī et al., 17 vols. (Cairo: al-Maṭbaʿat al-Amīriyya, 1321/1903) 17:140, 145 attributes it to "Abū ʿUthmān" in his discussion on the derivations of the name *Allāh*.

[604] All mss. and eds. كُرخَال AQ, β, H, K, MM: كَرِجال ع: كَرخَال ! D: كَرُفَال typos.

وَلِذٰلِكَ سُمُّوا بَشَراً، كَمَا سُمِّيَ الْجِنُّ جِنّاً لِاجْتِنَانِهِمْ.

وَاللَّامُ فِيهِ: (أ) لِلْجِنْسِ، وَ(مَنْ) مَوْصُوفَةٌ ـ إِذْ لَا عَهْدَ ـ فَكَأَنَّهُ قَالَ: (وَمِنَ النَّاسِ نَاسٌ يَقُولُونَ)؛ (ب) أَوْ لِلْعَهْدِ، وَالْمَعْهُودُ هُمُ الَّذِينَ كَفَرُوا، وَ(مَنْ) مَوْصُولَةٌ، مُرَادٌ بِهَا: اِبْنُ أُبَيٍّ وَأَصْحَابُهُ وَنُظَرَاؤُهُ. فَإِنَّهُمْ ـ مِنْ حَيْثُ إِنَّهُمْ صَمَّمُوا عَلَى النِّفَاقِ ـ دَخَلُوا فِي عِدَادِ الْكُفَّارِ الْمَخْتُومِ عَلَى قُلُوبِهِمْ؛ وَاخْتِصَاصُهُمْ بِزِيَادَاتٍ زَادُوهَا عَلَى الْكُفْرِ لَا يَأْبَى دُخُولَهُمْ ....

hence they were called *bashar* ⟨flesh and blood⟩,[605] just as the jinn were thus called because they are made invisible.

The definite article in it denotes (i) the species,[606] in which case [the demonstrative pronoun] ***man*** ⟨those⟩ is an indefinite conjunctive, with no previous knowledge involved, as if He said, "And of people there are people who say";

(ii) or previous knowledge—where those previously known are those who committed unbelief—in which case *man* is a relative by which are meant Ibn Ubay, his friends and those like him:[607] from the perspective that they were intent on hypocrisy, they joined the number of the unbelievers whose hearts were sealed upon. The few additional characteristics that are exclusive to them on top of unbelief do not preclude their being subsumed

605 "He means that their flesh is visible while that of other [species] is covered with wool or feathers or other than that." (S)

606 "I.e. totality (*al-istighrāq*), because the Two Shaykhs [Sībawayh and al-Khalīl] use them interchangeably," (Q) as opposed to "previous knowledge" (*al-ʿahd*).

607 These are ʿAbd Allāh b. Ubay b. Salūl, Jadd b. Qays, Muʿattab b. Qushayr and their friends among the hypocrites of Medina, totalling 300 men and 170 women, most of them Jews as narrated from Abū al-ʿĀliya, al-Ḥasan and Qatāda by Ibn Kathīr in his *Tafsīr* and Badr al-Dīn b. Jamāʿa in *Ghurar al-Tibyān fī man lam Yusamma fil-Qurʾān*, ed. ʿAbd al-Jawād Khalaf (Damascus: Dār Qutayba, 1410/1990), under verse 3:8.

تَحْتَ هٰذَا الْجِنْسِ، فَإِنَّ الْأَجْنَاسَ إِنَّمَا تَتَنَوَّعُ بِزِيَادَاتٍ يَخْتَلِفُ فِيهَا أَبْعَاضُهَا؛ فَعَلَى هٰذَا، تَكُونُ الْآيَةُ تَقْسِيماً لِلْقِسْمِ الثَّانِي.

وَاخْتِصَاصُ الْإِيمَانِ بِاللهِ وَبِالْيَوْمِ الْآخِرِ بِالذِّكْرِ: (I) تَخْصِيصُ لِمَا هُوَ الْمَقْصُودُ الْأَعْظَمُ مِنَ الْإِيمَانِ؛ (II) وَادِّعَاءٌ بِأَنَّهُمُ احْتَازُوا الْإِيمَانَ مِنْ جَانِبَيْهِ وَأَحَاطُوا بِقُطْرَيْهِ؛ (III) وَإِيذَانٌ بِأَنَّهُمْ مُنَافِقُونَ فِيمَا يَظُنُّونَ أَنَّهُمْ مُخْلِصُونَ فِيهِ - فَكَيْفَ بِمَا يَقْصِدُونَ بِهِ النِّفَاقَ! لِأَنَّ الْقَوْمَ كَانُوا يَهُوداً، وَكَانُوا يُؤْمِنُونَ بِاللهِ وَبِالْيَوْمِ الْآخِرِ إِيمَاناً كَلَا إِيمَانَ؛ لِاعْتِقَادِهِمْ:

under that species; for categories vary in additional aspects in which individual parts differ. According to this [scenario] the verse would be a subset of the second group.

[The delusions of the Israelites]

The particular mention that belief is *in Allah and in the Last Day* exclusively of any other is

I. to single out the greatest objective of belief;

II. to [quote their] claim that they possess faith from start to finish and now encompass its two provinces;

III. to announce that they are hypocrites in whatever they think they are sincere in,[608] let alone that in which they intend duplicity! For those folk were Jews[609] who believed in Allah and the Last Day in a manner akin to no belief at all, since they believed:

[608] "This is not part of the *nifāq* which is the third subset; for, as he explicitly said, the latter consists in outward belief and inward unbelief, which is not the case here. At the most they are mistaken in what they believe to be right in; but they are not hypocrites in what they think to be sincere in, as error does not necessitate hypocrisy, as pointed out by one of the verifying scholars." (Q)

[609] Such as Ibn Ubay and his party, who were followers of the Torah. (Q)

(أ) التَّشْبِيهَ، (ب) وَاتِّخَاذَ الْوَلَدِ، (ج) وَأَنَّ الْجَنَّةَ لَا يَدْخُلُهَا غَيْرُهُمْ، (د) وَأَنَّ النَّارَ لَا تَمَسُّهُمْ إِلَّا أَيَّاماً مَعْدُودَةً، (ه) وَغَيْرَهَا؛ وَيُرُونَ الْمُؤْمِنِينَ أَنَّهُمْ
صح
آمَنُوا مِثْلَ إِيمَانِهِمْ؛

(IV) وَبَيَانٌ لِتَضَاعُفِ خُبْثِهِمْ وَإِفْرَاطِهِمْ فِي كُفْرِهِمْ؛ لِأَنَّ مَا قَالُوهُ، لَوْ صَدَرَ عَنْهُمْ لَا عَلَى وَجْهِ الْخِدَاعِ وَالنِّفَاقِ، وَعَقِيدَتُهُمْ عَقِيدَتُهُمْ: لَمْ يَكُنْ إِيمَاناً؛ فَكَيْفَ وَقَدْ قَالُوهُ تَمْوِيهاً عَلَى الْمُسْلِمِينَ وَتَهَكُّماً بِهِمْ؟ وَفِي تَكْرَارِ الْبَاءِ: ادِّعَاءُ الْإِيمَانِ بِكُلِّ وَاحِدٍ عَلَى الْأَصَالَةِ وَالِاسْتِحْكَامِ.

(i) in anthropomorphism;

(ii) in [divine] paternity;

(iii) that they alone would enter Paradise;

(iv) that hellfire would touch them only for a few days;

(v) and other than that.[610] Yet they advertized themselves to the believers as believing just like them.

IV. to expose their chronic depravity and extreme infidelity, because even if what they said had not come from them by way of deceit and duplicity—their beliefs being [known for] what they are—it would still not amount to faith,[611] let alone if they said it to beguile the Muslims and mock them.

In the repetition of [the preposition] ***bi*** ⁽in⁾ lies the protestation of belief in each individual item as genuine and solid.

610 Anthropomorphism: al-Aʿrāf 7:138 and al-Nisāʾ 4:153; paternity: al-Tawba 9:30; Paradise: al-Baqara 2:111; hellfire: al-Baqara 2:79 and Āl ʿImrān 3:24. (Q)

611 I.e. their profession of faith being famously contradicted by their actual practice makes liars of them even in their unduplicitous assertion "We believe in Allah and in the Last Day." (Q)

وَ(الْقَوْلُ) هُوَ (أ) التَّلَفُّظُ بِمَا يُفِيدُ؛ وَيُقَـالُ (ب) بِمَعْنَـى الْمَـقُولِ؛ (ج) وَلِلْمَعْنَى الْمُتَصَوَّرِ فِي النَّفْسِ الْمُعَبَّرِ عَنْهُ بِاللَّفْظِ؛ (د) وَلِلرَّأْيِ وَالْمَذْهَبِ مَجَازاً.

وَالْمُـرَادُ بِـ(الْيَوْمِ الْآخِرِ): مِنْ وَقْتِ الْحَشْرِ-إِلَى مَـا لَا يَنْتَهِـي؛ أَوْ إِلَى أَنْ يَدْخُلَ أَهْلُ الْجَنَّةِ الْجَنَّةَ وَأَهْلُ النَّارِ النَّارَ؛ لِأَنَّهُ آخِرُ الْأَوْقَاتِ الْمَـحْدُودَةِ.

﴿وَمَا هُم بِمُؤْمِنِينَ﴾ إِنْكَارُ مَا ادَّعَوْهُ وَنَفْيُ مَا انْتَحَلُوا إِثْبَاتَهُ. وَكَانَ أَصْلُهُ (وَمَا آمَنُوا) لِيُطَابِقَ قَوْلَهُمْ فِي التَّصْرِيحِ بِشَـأْنِ الْفِعْـلِ دُونَ الْفَاعِـلِ، لٰكِنَّـهُ عُكِسَ تَأْكِيداً، أَوْ مُبَالَغَةً فِي التَّكْذِيبِ؛ لِأَنَّ إِخْرَاجَ ذَوَاتِهِمْ مِنْ عِدَادِ الْمُؤْمِنِينَ أَبْلَغُ مِنْ نَفْيِ الْإِيمَانِ عَنْهُمْ فِي مَاضِي الزَّمَانِ. وَلِذٰلِكَ أَكَّدَ ....

Al-qawl ⁽to say⁾ is (i) to utter what conveys sense. It is also used in the sense of (ii) the thing stated; (iii) the meaning that is conceived mentally and expressed verbally; (iv) and for one's opinion and one's position—figuratively.

What is meant by *the Last Day* is from the time of Resurrection to no end, or until the people of Paradise enter Paradise and the people of hellfire enter hellfire, as that is the last of finite times.

wa-mā hum bi-muʾminīna ⁽*when they are not believers at all*⁾ is a rejection of what they asserted and a denial of what they claimed as firmly established.

[The unbelievers' duplicity defines their identity]

It would have been, normally, *wa-mā āmanū* ⁽when they did not believe⁾ so as to match their statement—which is explicitly verb-centered rather than agentive—but this was reversed for emphasis or intensification of denial. For expelling their very persons from among the believers is more significant than to deny that they possessed belief in the past. Hence He emphasized

النَّفْيَ بِالْبَاءِ، وَأَطْلَقَ الْإِيمَانَ، عَلَى مَعْنَى أَنَّهُمْ لَيْسُوا مِنَ الْإِيمَانِ فِي شَيْءٍ. وَيَحْتَمِلُ أَنْ يُقَيَّدَ بِمَا قَيَّدُوا بِهِ، لِأَنَّهُ جَوَابُهُ.

وَالْآيَةُ تَدُلُّ عَلَى أَنَّ مَنِ ادَّعَى الْإِيمَانَ وَخَالَفَ قَلْبُهُ لِسَانَهُ بِالْاعْتِقَادِ: لَمْ يَكُنْ مُؤْمِناً؛ لِأَنَّ مَنْ تَفَوَّهَ بِالشَّهَادَتَيْنِ فَارِغَ الْقَلْبِ عَمَّا يُوَافِقُهُ أَوْ يُنَافِيهِ: لَمْ يَكُنْ مُؤْمِناً. وَالْخِلَافُ مَعَ الْكَرَّامِيَّةِ فِي الثَّانِي؛ فَلَا يَنْهَضُ حُجَّةً عَلَيْهِمْ.

the negation with the [preposition] *bā'* ⁽=at all⁾ and put belief in absolute terms,[612] in the sense that they have nothing at all to do with belief. It is also possible to limit [the object of belief in the clause] to the same [objects] they limited [their affirmation] to, because it is its answer.

The verse indicates that whoever claims to have faith when his heart contradicts his tongue in his convictions is not a believer, because whoever pronounces the two testimonies of faith with a heart devoid of what conforms to it or denies it, is not a believer. The divergence [of *Ahl al-Sunna*] with the Karrāmiyya is [only] in the latter,[613] so [the verse] does not clinch the argument against them.[614]

[612] I.e. suppressing the direct objects "Allah and the Last Day," as negation of belief in unqualified terms makes negation of belief in qualified terms all the more certain. (Z)

[613] "Namely, whoever speaks the two testimonies with a heart devoid of what was mentioned: such is not a believer in our understanding, contrary to them; as for one who claims to have faith when his heart contradicts his tongue: he is an unbeliever by general agreement." (Z)

[614] "He means to rebut al-Māturīdī who said in *Ta'wīlāt al-Qur'ān*: 'The verse and its like clinch the argument against the Karrāmiyya, as they say that faith is the tongue's speech without confirmation.'" (Q 2:108) "It is a rebuttal of the Imam [Zamakhsharī] .... [The verse] does not indicate that when one with a void heart speaks something indicative of true belief he is not a believer for it to be adduced as a proof against the falsehood of the Karrāmiyya's position, who claim that belief is affirmation by tongue alone and nothing else. The *kufr* of him whose inward [conviction] goes against what

مَعًا
﴿يُخَٰدِعُونَ ٱللَّهَ وَٱلَّذِينَ ءَامَنُوا۟﴾: (الْخَدْعُ) أَنْ تُوهِمَ غَيْرَكَ خِلَافَ مَا تُخْفِيهِ مِنَ الْمَكْرُوهِ لِتُنْزِلَهُ عَمَّا هُوَ فِيهِ وَعَمَّا هُوَ بِصَدَدِهِ، مِنْ قَوْلِهِمْ (خَدَعَ الضَّبُّ) إِذَا تَوَارَى فِي جُحْرِهِ، وَ(ضَبٌّ خَادِعٌ) وَ(خَدِعٌ) إِذَا أَوْهَمَ الْحَارِشَ إِقْبَالَهُ عَلَيْهِ، ثُمَّ خَرَجَ مِنْ بَابٍ آخَرَ. وَأَصْلُهُ الْإِخْفَاءُ؛ وَمِنْهُ (الْمَخْدَعُ) لِلْخِزَانَةِ،
مَعًا
وَ(الْأَخْدَعَانِ) لِعِرْقَيْنِ خَفِيَّيْنِ فِي الْعُنُقِ.

وَالْمُخَادَعَةُ تَكُونُ بَيْنَ اثْنَيْنِ. وَخِدَاعُهُمْ مَعَ اللهِ لَيْسَ عَلَى ظَاهِرِهِ، لِأَنَّهُ لَا تَخْفَى عَلَيْهِ خَافِيَةٌ، وَلِأَنَّهُمْ لَمْ يَقْصِدُوا خَدِيعَتَهُ. بَلِ الْمُرَادُ:

[2:9] **yukhādiʿuna-l-Lāha wa-l-ladhīna āmanū** ⁽*they deceive the One God and those who do believe*⁾:

Kha/u/idʿ ⁽ruse⁾ is to suggest to someone other than the evil you conceal, in order to lure them away from where they stand or hoodwink them; as when they say *khadaʿa al-ḍabb* ⁽the lizard slinked⁾ when it concealed itself, or *ḍabbun khādiʿ* ⁽a slinking lizard⁾ and *khadiʿ* ⁽stealthy⁾ when it lets the baiter[615] think it is coming its way then leaves from another exit. Its basic meaning is concealment,[616] hence *ma/u/ikhdaʿ* ⁽concealed closet⁾ for storage space and *al-akhdaʿān* ⁽the two jugulars⁾ for two concealed veins in the neck.

["They deceive Allah" is not literal]

Mukhādaʿa ⁽deceit⁾ takes place between two parties. Their deceit with Allah is not literal, as absolutely nothing is hidden to Him and also because they do not intend to deceive Him. Rather, what is meant is:

he lets show does not necessitate the *kufr* of him whose inward [conviction] is devoid of what he declares outwardly and of what negates it." (Z 1:130)

615 All mss. and eds.: الحارش H: الحارس typo.

616 "He took this from the Imam [=al-Rāzī]." (S) Cf. al-Rāzī, *Mafātīḥ* (2:62).

(I) إِمَّا مُخَادَعَةُ رَسُولِهِ (أ) عَلَى حَذْفِ الْمُضَافِ، (ب) أَوْ عَلَى أَنَّ مُعَامَلَةَ الرَّسُولِ مُعَامَلَةُ اللهِ مِنْ حَيْثُ إِنَّهُ خَلِيفَتُهُ؛ كَمَا قَالَ تَعَالَى: ﴿مَّن يُطِعِ ٱلرَّسُولَ فَقَدْ أَطَاعَ ٱللَّهَ﴾ [النساء ٨٠]؛ ﴿إِنَّ ٱلَّذِينَ يُبَايِعُونَكَ إِنَّمَا يُبَايِعُونَ ٱللَّهَ﴾ [الفتح ١٠]؛

(II) وَإِمَّا أَنَّ صُورَةَ (أ) صَنِيعِهِمْ مَعَ اللهِ تَعَالَى - مِنْ إِظْهَارِ الْإِيمَانِ وَاسْتِبْطَانِ الْكُفْرِ -، (ب) وَصُنْعِ اللهِ مَعَهُمْ بِإِجْرَاءِ أَحْكَامِ الْمُسْلِمِينَ عَلَيْهِمْ - وَهُمْ عِنْدَهُ أَخْبَثُ الْكُفَّارِ وَأَهْلُ ﴿ٱلدَّرْكِ ٱلْأَسْفَلِ مِنَ ٱلنَّارِ﴾ [النساء ١٤٥] - اِسْتِدْرَاجاً لَهُمْ، (ج) وَامْتِثَالِ الرَّسُولِ ﷺ وَالْمُؤْمِنِينَ أَمْرَ اللهِ فِي إِخْفَاءِ حَالِهِمْ وَإِجْرَاءِ حُكْمِ الْإِسْلَامِ عَلَيْهِمْ، مُجَازَاةً لَهُمْ بِمِثْلِ صَنِيعِهِمْ: ....

(I) either the deceit of His Messenger if we say (i) that the governing annex was suppressed; (ii) or that interaction with the Messenger is interaction with Allah, from the perspective that he is His vicegerent, as He—exalted is He!—said, *Whoever obeys the Messenger obeys Allah* (al-Nisā' 4:80), *Verily those who swear allegiance to you swear allegiance to Allah Himself* (al-Fatḥ 48:10);

(II) or that the appearance (i) of their handiwork with Allah—in showing faith outwardly but concealing unbelief; (ii) of His design with them in letting the rulings of Muslims apply to them when they are, to Him, the filthiest unbelievers and the dwellers of *the lowest deep of the fire* (al-Nisā' 4:145), in order to beguile them; (iii) and of the compliance of the Messenger—upon him blessings and peace—and the believers to the command of Allah in keeping their state concealed and granting them the status of Islam, in requital[617] of their own exact handiwork: ……………..

[617] All mss. and eds.: مجازاة K, MM: مجاراة *taṣḥīf*.

صُورَةُ صَنِيعِ الْمُتَخَادِعَيْنِ.

وَيَحْتَمِلُ أَنْ يُرَادَ بِـ﴿يُخَادِعُونَ﴾ (يَخْدَعُونَ)، لِأَنَّهُ بَيَانٌ لِـ﴿يَقُولُ﴾؛ أَوْ اِسْتِئْنَافٌ بِذِكْرِ مَا هُوَ الْغَرَضُ مِنْهُ، إِلَّا أَنَّهُ أُخْرِجَ فِي زِنَةِ (فَاعَلَ) لِلْمُبَالَغَةِ، فَإِنَّ الزِّنَةَ، لَمَّا كَانَتْ لِلْمُغَالَبَةِ، وَالْفِعْلَ مَتَى غُولِبَ فِيهِ: كَانَ أَبْلَغَ مِنْهُ إِذَا جَاءَ بِلَا مُقَابَلَةِ مُعَارِضٍ وَمُبَارٍ اِسْتَصْحَبَتْ ذٰلِكَ. وَيَعْضُدُهُ قِرَاءَةُ مَنْ قَرَأَ ﴿يَخْدَعُونَ﴾.

وَكَانَ غَرَضُهُمْ فِي ذٰلِكَ (أ) أَنْ يَدْفَعُوا عَنْ أَنْفُسِهِمْ مَا ....

[all this] looks like the doing of two mutual deceivers.[618]

It is also possible that what is meant by ***yukhādiʿūn*** ⁽they deceive⁾ is *yakhdaʿūn* ⁽they delude⁾, because it is an elaboration of *[those] who say* (2:8)—or a resumptive clause—mentioning its purport; unless it was put in the *fāʿala* form for intensiveness.[619] For when the derived verbal form expresses predominance[620] and the verb reflects a contest with a superior force,[621] it is more expressive than when it comes without the attending contraposition of a challenger vying with it—which is bolstered by the reading ***yakhdaʿūn [al-Lāha]*** ⁽they delude [the One God]⁾.[622]

Their aim in that was (i) to repel from themselves whatever

[618] An example of "proverbial subordinate metaphor" (*istiʿāra tabaʿiyya tamthīliyya*) according to al-Taftāzānī. (S, Z)

[619] Ak, AQ, B, D, F, H, I, K, L, T, Ul: للمبالغة Kh, Q, U: للمقابلة P, MM: للمغالبة inversions. "As when they say *ṭābaqtu al-naʿl* ⁽I ranged the sandals in layers⁾ and *ʿāqabtu al-liṣṣ* ⁽I punished the robber⁾ due to the intensiveness of the act. Likewise *yukhāshī Allāh* means *yakhshā* ⁽he fears⁾ Allah greatly." (Z)

[620] α, Ak, B, D, ε, F, K, Kh, L, MM, P, Q, U: للمغالبة β, I: للمبالغة corr. to للمغالبة AQ, H, R, T, Ul: للمبالغة inversion.

[621] I.e. it is contested and opposition takes place between it and its companion. (Q)

[622] Ibn Masʿūd and Abū Ḥaywa. (*MQ*)

يَطْرُقُ بِهِ مَنْ سِوَاهُمْ مِنَ الْكَفَرَةِ؛ (ب) وَأَنْ يُفْعَلَ بِهِمْ مَا يُفْعَلُ بِالْمُؤْمِنِينَ مِنَ الْإِكْرَامِ وَالْإِعْطَاءِ؛ (ج) وَأَنْ يَخْتَلِطُوا بِالْمُسْلِمِينَ فَيَطَّلِعُوا عَلَى أَسْرَارِهِمْ وَيُذِيعُوهَا إِلَى مُنَابِذِيهِمْ؛ إِلَى غَيْرِ ذٰلِكَ مِنَ الْأَغْرَاضِ وَالْمَقَاصِدِ.

﴿وَمَا يُخَادِعُونَ إِلَّآ أَنفُسَهُمْ﴾ قِرَاءَةُ نَافِعٍ وَابْنِ كَثِيرٍ وَأَبِي عَمْرٍو. وَالْمَعْنَى: أَنَّ دَائِرَةَ الْخِدَاعِ رَاجِعَةٌ إِلَيْهِمْ وَضَرَرَهَا يَحِيقُ بِهِمْ؛ أَوْ أَنَّهُمْ فِي ذٰلِكَ خَدَعُوا أَنْفُسَهُمْ لَمَّا غَرُّوهَا بِذٰلِكَ، وَخَدَعَتْهُمْ أَنْفُسُهُمْ حَيْثُ حَدَّثَتْهُمْ بِالْأَمَانِي الْفَارِغَةِ وَحَمَلَتْهُمْ عَلَى مُخَادَعَةِ مَنْ لَا تَخْفَى عَلَيْهِ خَافِيَةٌ.

وَقَرَأَ الْبَاقُونَ ﴿وَمَا يَخْدَعُونَ﴾، لِأَنَّ الْمُخَادَعَةَ لَا تُتَصَوَّرُ إِلَّا بَيْنَ اثْنَيْنِ.

impugns others among the unbelievers; (ii) to be treated in the same way as the believers in honors and donations; (iii) to mix with the Muslims so as to be apprised of their secrets and broadcast them to their foes, among other aims and objectives.

wa-mā yukhādiʿūna illā anfusahum ‹*but they deceive only themselves*› is the reading of Nāfiʿ, Ibn Kathīr and Abū ʿAmr.

It means that the maze of deceit returns back to them and its harm surrounds them; or that in all this they have deceived themselves by deluding themselves into that [state], and their own souls deceived them by promising them vain hopes and pushing them to try to deceive the One from Whom nothing is hidden.

The rest read **wa-mā yakhdaʿūna** ‹*but they delude not*›[623] as *mukhādaʿa* ‹deceit› is inconceivable other than between two parties.[624]

[623] Ibn ʿĀmir, ʿĀṣim, Ḥamza, al-Kisāʾī, Abū Ḥaywa, Abū Jaʿfar, Yaʿqūb, Khalaf. (*MQ*)
[624] In the sense that the deceiver intends harm for the deceived through deceit. (Z)

وَقُرِئَ (أ) (يُخَدِّعُونَ) مِنْ (خَدَّعَ)، (ب) وَ(يَخَدِّعُونَ) بِمَعْنَى (يَخْتَدِعُونَ)، (ج) وَ(يُخْدَعُونَ) (د) وَ(يُخَادَعُونَ) عَلَى الْبِنَاءِ لِلْمَفْعُولِ.

وَنُصِبَ ﴿أَنفُسَهُمْ﴾ بِنَزْعِ الْخَافِضِ.

وَ(النَّفْسُ): ذَاتُ الشَّيْءِ وَحَقِيقَتُهُ. ثُمَّ قِيلَ (أ) لِلرُّوحِ، لِأَنَّ نَفْسَ الْحَيِّ بِهِ؛ (ب) وَلِلْقَلْبِ، لِأَنَّهُ مَحَلُّ الرُّوحِ أَوْ مُتَعَلَّقُهُ؛ (ج) وَلِلدَّمِ، لِأَنَّ قِوَامَهَا بِهِ؛

There are also the readings

1. *yukhaddiʿūn*,[625] from *khaddaʿa*;

2. *yakhaddiʿūn*,[626] in the sense of *yakhtadiʿūn*;

3. *yukhdaʿūn*[627] and

4. *yukhādaʿūn*,[628] [both of which] as passive constructs.[629]

Anfusahum ⁽themselves⁾ is in the accusative through removal of the genitival operative.[630] The *nafs* of something is the thing itself and its quiddity; then it came to denote:

• the spirit, because a living being is [alive] by [means of] it;

• the heart, because it is the place of the spirit or its connection-point;

• blood, because its mainstay is by means of it;

"The mention of this rationale suggests his preference goes to the latter reading." (Q)

625 By Qatāda and Muwarriq al-ʿIjlī. (*MQ*)

626 By Muwarriq al-ʿIjlī. (*MQ*)

627 By al-Jārūd b. Abī Sabra and Abū Ṭālūt ʿAbd al-Salām b. Shaddād. (*MQ*)

628 By Abū Ṭālūt, from his father. (*MQ*)

629 Other anomalous readings are *yakhddiʿūn* [similar to 2]; *yakhaddaʿūn*; *yukhdiʿūn*; *wa-mā yukhādiʿuhum illā anfusuhum*. (*MQ*)

630 Namely, the preposition *ʿan* ⁽from⁾. "I.e. *wa-mā yukhādiʿūna illā ʿan anfusihim*, in which case it would appear that the *mufāʿala* [of *mukhādaʿa*] is in the sense of the triliteral [i.e. *khudʿa*]." (Q)

(د) وَلِلْماءِ، لِفَرْطِ حَاجَتِهَا إِلَيْهِ؛ (ه) وَلِلرَّأْيِ فِي قَوْلِهِمْ (فُلَانٌ يُؤَامِرُ نَفْسَهُ) لِأَنَّهُ يَنْبَعِثُ عَنْهَا، أَوْ يُشْبِهُ ذَاتاً تَأْمُرُهُ وَتُشِيرُ عَلَيْهِ. وَالْمُرَادُ بِالْأَنْفُسِ هٰهُنَا: ذَوَاتُهُمْ؛ وَيَحْتَمِلُ حَمْلُهَا عَلَى أَرْوَاحِهِمْ وَآرَائِهِمْ.

﴿وَمَا يَشْعُرُونَ﴾: لَا يُحِسُّونَ لِذٰلِكَ، لِتَمَادِي غَفْلَتِهِمْ: جَعَلَ لُحُوقَ وَبَالِ الْخِدَاعِ وَرُجُوعَ ضَرَرِهِ إِلَيْهِمْ فِي الظُّهُورِ كَالْمَحْسُوسِ الَّذِي لَا يَخْفَى إِلَّا عَلَى مَؤُوفِ الْحَوَاسِّ. وَ(الشُّعُورُ): الْإِحْسَاسُ؛ وَمَشَاعِرُ الْإِنْسَانِ حَوَاسُّهُ.

- water,[631] because of its utmost dependence on it;
- opinion, in their expression, "X is advising with himself,"[632] because it proceeds from it or because opinion resembles someone that give commands and advice.

What is meant by *anfus* ⟨selves⟩ right here is their persons, and it is also possible to take it to refer to their spirits and their opinions.

wa-mā yashʿurūna ⟨*without realizing*⟩: they do not perceive that [that is happening] because of their pervasive heedlessness. He represented the fact that the calamity of deceit befell them and its harm returned back to them as a palpable matter that escapes only the notice of a senseless person. *Shuʿūr* ⟨sense⟩ is [the faculty of] perception, and a human being's *mashāʿir* ⟨sensations⟩ are his senses. ....

[631] "Such usage is not linguistically recognized, said Ibn al-Ṣā'igh in his marginalia on the *Kashshāf*, and not found in the lexicographies; what is found is *nafas* ⟨breath⟩. But this does not invalidate the author nor the *Kashshāf* because they are both expounding linguistic transference (*majāz lughawī*). So it does not harm that it is unestablished in the lexicographies. That is why he said, 'because of its utmost dependence on it': had his intent been to show what is established in language he would not have needed that. This transference is also a type of 'intending cause by mentioning result.'" (Q)
[632] "A euphemism (*kināya*) for hesitation." (Q)

وَأَصْلُهُ (الشِّعْرُ)، وَمِنْهُ (الشِّعَارُ).

﴿فِي قُلُوبِهِم مَّرَضٌ فَزَادَهُمُ ٱللَّهُ مَرَضًا﴾: الْمَرَضُ (أ) حَقِيقَةٌ فِيمَا يَعْرِضُ لِلْبَدَنِ فَيُخْرِجُهُ عَنِ الِاعْتِدَالِ الْخَاصِّ بِهِ وَيُوجِبُ الْخَلَلَ فِي أَفْعَالِهِ؛ (ب) وَمَجَازٌ فِي الْأَعْرَاضِ النَّفْسَانِيَّةِ الَّتِي تُخِلُّ بِكَمَالِهَا - كَالْجَهْلِ، وَسُوءِ الْعَقِيدَةِ، وَالْحَسَدِ، وَالضَّغِينَةِ، وَحُبِّ الْمَعَاصِي - لِأَنَّهَا مَانِعَةٌ مِنْ نَيْلِ الْفَضَائِلِ، أَوْ مُؤَدِّيَةٌ إِلَى زَوَالِ الْحَيَاةِ الْحَقِيقِيَّةِ الْأَبَدِيَّةِ.

وَالْآيَةُ الْكَرِيمَةُ تَحْتَمِلُهُمَا؛ فَإِنَّ (I) قُلُوبَهُمْ كَانَتْ مُتَأَلِّمَةً ....

Its root is *al-shiʿr* ⁽awareness⁾,[633] whence *shiʿār* ⁽ensign⁾.[634]

[The unbelievers' literal and figurative heart disease]

[2:10] **fī qulūbihim maraḍun fa-zādahumu-l-Lāhu maraḍan** ⁽*in their hearts is a sickness, so the One God increased their sickness*⁾: ***maraḍ*** ⁽sickness⁾ is literally what happens to the body and brings it out of its proper equilibrium, compelling it to behave erratically. Figuratively, it denotes psychological states that impair the psyche's integrity such as ignorance, misbelief, envy, rancor and viciousness, because they block one from the acquisition of redeeming qualities or lead to the ruin of true eternal life.[635]

The noble verse can carry either sense:[636] their hearts ached,

633 "Namely, understanding (*al-fahm*) and knowledge. One says *shaʿartu bi-sh-shayʾ*, meaning I am aware of it (*faṭantu lahu*); and *layta shiʿrī*, i.e. would that I knew." (Z)

634 "Namely, the battle-standard by which combatants recognize one another, and *al-shiʿār* is also a cloth worn directly over the skin and which one feels." (Z)

635 For a modern paraphrase of the similar defining principles of physical and mental sickness in spiritual diagnostication see Robert Thomson, *Natural Medicine* (New York: McGraw-Hill, 1978), particularly the introduction and chapter 2 (pp. 21-31), "The Eleven Principles of Natural Medicine."

636 I.e. literally and figuratively. (Q) See Suyūṭī's impassioned critique of Bayḍāwī's inclusion of the literal meaning as a possible gloss for this verse along with the figura-

تَحَرُّقاً عَلَى مَا فَاتَ عَنْهُمْ مِنَ الرِّيَاسَةِ، وَحَسَداً عَلَى مَا يَرَوْنَ مِنْ ثَبَاتِ أَمْرِ الرَّسُولِ ﷺ وَاسْتِعْلَاءِ شَأْنِهِ يَوْماً فَيَوْماً، وَزَادَ اللهُ غَمَّهُمْ بِمَا زَادَ فِي إِعْلَاءِ أَمْرِهِ وَإِشَادَةِ ذِكْرِهِ؛ (II) وَنُفُوسُهُمْ كَانَتْ مَؤُوفَةً بِالْكُفْرِ، وَسُوءِ الِاعْتِقَادِ، وَمُعَادَاةِ النَّبِيِّ ﷺ وَنَحْوِهَا، فَزَادَ اللهُ سُبْحَانَهُ وَتَعَالَى ذٰلِكَ بِالطَّبْعِ، أَوْ بِازْدِيَادِ التَّكَالِيفِ وَتَكْرِيرِ الْوَحْيِ وَتَضَاعُفِ النَّصْرِ.

وَكَانَ إِسْنَادُ الزِّيَادَةِ إِلَى اللهِ تَعَالَى مِنْ حَيْثُ إِنَّهُ مُسَبَّبٌ مِنْ فِعْلِهِ؛ وَإِسْنَادُهَا

gnawing the file[637] of all that had eluded them of leadership, envious of the visibly growing empowerment and ascendancy of the Messenger—upon him blessings and peace—day by day. Allah increased their grief by increasing the promotion of his cause and the celebration of his fame. Their souls were already infected[638] with unbelief, blasphemy, enmity to the Prophet—upon him blessings and peace—and so forth; then Allah increased that with a stamping[639] or through added liabilities, successive revelations and redoubled victories.[640]

The attribution of the increase to Allah Most High is from the perspective that it is caused by His act, ...

tive one, quoted in full in our introduction ("Scientific discourse in *Anwār al-Tanzīl*").

637 Z: اي احتراقا وتحزنا

Q: التحرق التفعل من الحرق وهو قطع الحديد بمبرد الحديد... حتى يسمع لها صوت وكنى بها عن شدة الغيظ والغضب وهو المراد هنا ولا بأس في حمله على حرق النار

Iş: اي يستحقون بعض اضراسهم ببعض حتى يسمع منه صوت وهذا كناية عن شدة الغيظ وليس من التحرّق بمعنى الاحراق

Sk: من حرق الاسنان اي سحق بعضها ببعض حتى سمع لها صريف وهو كناية عن شدة الغيظ

638 All mss. and eds.: مؤوفة or مؤفةً or مآوفة or مئوفة or ماؤفةً AQ, H, MM: موصوفة blunder

639 I.e. a sealing (*khatm*) (Q) in the sense of a disposition (*hay'a*) that blocks them from accepting truth in their hearts and senses, increasing the sickness of unbelief that was already in themselves. (Z)

640 All mss. and eds.: وتضاعف P: وتضاعيف typo

إِلَى السُّورَةِ فِي قَوْلِهِ تَعَالَى ﴿فَزَادَتْهُمْ رِجْسًا﴾ [التوبة ١٢٥]: لِكَوْنِهَا سَبَباً.

وَيَحْتَمِلُ أَنْ يُرَادَ بِالْمَرَضِ: مَا تَدَاخَلَ قُلُوبَهُمْ مِنَ الْجُبْنِ وَالْخَوَرِ حِينَ شَاهَدُوا شَوْكَةَ الْمُسْلِمِينَ، وَإِمْدَادَ اللهِ تَعَالَى لَهُمْ بِالْمَلَائِكَةِ، وَقَذْفِ الرُّعْبِ فِي قُلُوبِهِمْ، وَبِزِيَادَتِهِ تَضْعِيفَهُ بِمَا زَادَ لِرَسُولِ اللهِ ﷺ نُصْرَةً عَلَى الْأَعْدَاءِ وَتَبَسُّطاً فِي الْبِلَادِ.

﴿وَلَهُمْ عَذَابٌ أَلِيمٌ﴾، أَيْ: مُؤْلِمٌ؛ يُقَالُ: أَلِمَ فَهُوَ أَلِيمٌ، كَوَجِعَ فَهُوَ وَجِيعٌ. وُصِفَ بِهِ الْعَذَابُ لِلْمُبَالَغَةِ، كَقَوْلِهِ: [الوافر]

.... ❊ تَحِيَّةُ بَيْنِهِمْ ضَرْبٌ وَجِيعُ

while it is ascribed to the sura in His saying *it will increase their filth* (al-Tawba 9:125).

It is also possible that what is meant by sickness is the cowardice and feebleness that pervaded their hearts when they witnessed the might of the Muslims, how Allah was assisting them with angels and the casting of terror in their hearts, and its increase twice or more the like of what He increased victories for the Messenger of Allah—upon him blessings and peace—over enemies and spread his rule over the land.

wa-lahum ʿadhābun alīmun ⁽*and theirs is a painful punishment*⁾, that is, causing pain. It is said *alima* ⁽he felt pain⁾ so he is *alīm* ⁽in pain⁾ and *wajiʿa* ⁽he ailed⁾ so he is *wajīʿ* ⁽ailing⁾. Punishment was thus described for intensiveness as in his saying: ["The Exuberant"]

Their mutual greetings are agonizing blows[641]

[641] Second hemistich of a verse that begins "and cavalry-men approaching one another" (*wa-khaylun qad dalafat lahā bi-khayl*), spoken by the gigantic centenarian and valiant Companion-knight Abū Thawr ʿAmr b. Maʿdīkarb b. ʿAbd Allāh al-Zubaydī

عَلَى طَرِيقَةِ قَوْلِهِـمْ: (جَدَّ جِدُّهُ).

﴿بِمَا كَانُواْ يَكۡذِبُونَ﴾ قَرَأَهَا عَاصِمٌ وَحَمْزَةُ وَالْكِسَائِيُّ؛ وَالْمَعْنَى: بِسَبَبِ كَذِبِهِمْ أَوْ بِبَدَلِهِ، جَزَاءً لَهُمْ، وَهُوَ قَوْلُهُمْ ﴿ءَامَنَّا﴾. وَقَرَأَ الْبَاقُونَ ﴿يُكَذِّبُونَ﴾، (أ) مِنْ (كَذَّبَهُ) لِأَنَّهُمْ كَانُوا يُكَذِّبُونَ الرَّسُولَ ـ عَلَيْهِ الصَّلَاةُ وَالسَّلَامُ ـ بِقُلُوبِهِمْ ﴿وَإِذَا خَلَوۡاْ إِلَىٰ شَيَٰطِينِهِمۡ﴾ [البقرة ١٤]؛ (ب) أَوْ مِنْ (كَذَّبَ) الَّـذِي هُوَ لِلْمُبَالَغَةِ أَوْ لِلتَّكْثِيرِ مِثْلَ (بَيَّنَ الشَّيْءُ) وَ(مَوَّتَتِ الْبَهَائِمُ)؛ (ج) أَوْ مِـنْ (كَذَّبَ الْوَحْشِيُّ) ....

in the same was as they say *jadda jidduh* ⟨his energy soared⟩.[642]

bi-mā kānū yakdhibūna ⟨*because they used to lie*⟩, thus read by ʿĀṣim, Ḥamza and al-Kisāʾi,[643] whereby the meaning is "by reason of their lying" or "in exchange for it" to requite them for saying *We believe.* The rest read **yukadhdhibūn** ⟨*to belie*⟩,[644]

(i) from *kadhdhabah* ⟨he belied him⟩, because they used to belie the Messenger—upon him blessings and peace—in their hearts and *whenever they retired unto their devils* (al-Baqara 2:14);

(ii) or from *kadhdhaba* used for intensiveness or multiplication, as in *bayyana al-shay'* ⟨it became crystal-clear⟩ and *mawwatat al-bahā'im* ⟨the animals died en masse⟩;[645]

(iii) or from *kadhdhaba al-waḥshīy* ⟨the wild beast distrusted⟩,

as part of a long poem, cf. *Shiʿr ʿAmr b. Maʿdīkarib al-Zabīdi*, ed. Muṭāʿ al-Ṭarābīshī, 2nd ed. (Damascus: Majmaʿ al-Lugha al-ʿArabiyya, 1405/1985) p. 149.

642 I.e. by way of hypallage or transferred epithet. "Al-Ṭībī said 'i.e. by way of allegorical attribution (*isnād majāzī*)' while Shaykh Saʿd al-Dīn [al-Taftāzānī] said 'outwardly the attribution is to the infinitive noun (*maṣdar*).'" (S)

643 Also Khalaf, al-Ḥasan and al-Aʿmash. (*MQ*)

644 Namely Nāfiʿ, Ibn Kathīr, Abū ʿAmr, Ibn ʿĀmir, Abū Jaʿfar and Yaʿqūb, and it is the reading of most of the Medinans, Hijazis and Basrians. (*MQ*)

645 Emphatic forms of *bāna* and *mātat* respectively. (Q, S)

إِذَا جَرَى شَوْطاً وَوَقَفَ لِيَنْظُرَ مَا وَرَاءَهُ: فَإِنَّ الْمُنَافِقَ مُتَحَيِّرٌ مُتَرَدِّدٌ.

وَ(الْكَذِبُ) هُوَ الْخَبَرُ عَنِ الشَّيْءِ عَلَى خِلَافِ مَا هُوَ بِهِ. وَهُوَ حَرَامٌ كُلُّهُ، لِأَنَّهُ عُلِّلَ بِهِ اسْتِحْقَاقُ الْعَذَابِ، حَيْثُ رُتِّبَ عَلَيْهِ. وَمَا رُوِيَ أَنَّ إِبْرَاهِيمَ — عَلَيْهِ الصَّلَاةُ وَالسَّلَامُ - كَذَبَ ....

when it speeds for a distance then stops to look what is behind, for the hypocrite is perplexed and indecisive.

[The prohibition of lying]

Al-kadhib ⁽lying⁾ is to relate something as other than what it actually is. It is categorically prohibited in its entirety[646] because it was made a cause for deserving punishment, since the latter follows in sequence.[647] As for what was related[648] to the effect that "Ibrāhīm ⁽Abraham⁾—upon him blessings and peace—lied

646 I.e. at the basis but not according to contextual need (Sk). The claim that it is prohibited needs to be revised (K) as what is mentioned directly after proves it wrong (Q), especially according to the Shāfiʿī school (Q, Z). "He followed the *Kashshāf* in this but it is other than what they both said: there is a kind of lying that is permitted, a kind that is recommended, and a kind that is obligatory as resolved in the books of jurisprudence." (S) Suyūṭī counted this passage among the unwitting Muʿtazilisms of the *Anwār* and proceeded to list at length the many proofs for permissible lying, *Nawāhid* (1:386-390). See also to that effect al-Nawawī's discussion in the chapters on the prohibition of lying and the exposition of the kind of lying that is permitted in *Riyāḍ al-Ṣāliḥin min Kalām Sayyid al-Mursalīn*, ed. Muṣṭafā Muḥammad ʿUmāra (Cairo: Dār Iḥyā' al-Kutub al-ʿArabiyya, 1375/1955) pp. 560-566 (*Kitāb al-umūr al-manhy ʿanhā, Bāb taḥrīm al-kadhib*). In passing, S draws attention to the errors of those who rejected several authentic hadiths because they could not reconcile them with prophetic infallibility or other axiomatic doctrines such as Bāqillānī, Juwaynī, Ibn Fūrak, Qāḍī ʿIyāḍ, Ghazālī, Rāzī "and other greats."

647 An allusion to the *bā'* in *bi-mā kānū yakdhibūn* as causative (*sababiyya*). (Q)

648 Since the hadiths of "the three lies" are not dubious but well-established in the two *Ṣaḥīḥ*s, this might be an example of Bayḍāwī's use of the unattributive passive voice in introducing a report *without* conveying dubiousness (*tamrīḍ*)—not as assumed by Munāwī in the *Fatḥ* (1:142) or per the convention of latter-day hadith scholars, but indifferently, as in al-Tirmidhī's practice in his *Sunan*. See notes 57 and 360.

ثَلَاثَ كَذِبَاتٍ، فَالْمُرَادُ: التَّعْرِيضُ. وَلٰكِنْ لَمَّا شَابَهَ الْكَذِبَ فِي صُورَتِهِ، سُمِّيَ بِهِ.

﴿وَإِذَا قِيلَ لَهُمْ لَا تُفْسِدُوا فِي ٱلْأَرْضِ﴾: عَطْفٌ عَلَى ﴿يَكْذِبُونَ﴾ أَوْ ﴿يَقُولُ﴾. وَمَا رُوِيَ عَنْ سَلْمَانَ - رَضِيَ اللهُ عَنْهُ - أَنَّ أَهْلَ هٰذِهِ الْآيَةِ لَمْ يَأْتُوا بَعْدُ: فَلَعَلَّهُ أَرَادَ بِهِ أَنَّ أَهْلَهَا لَيْسَ الَّذِينَ كَانُوا فَقَطْ، بَلْ وَسَيَكُونُ مِنْ بَعْدُ مَنْ حَالُهُ حَالُهُمْ؛ لِأَنَّ الْآيَةَ مُتَّصِلَةٌ بِمَا قَبْلَهَا بِالضَّمِيرِ الَّذِي فِيهَا.

on three occasions,"[649] what is meant is equivocation; but because it had the appearance of a lie it was named one.[650]

[2:11] **wa-idhā qīla lahum lā tufsidū fīl-arḍi** ⁽*and when it is said to them: Do not spread corruption in the land*⁾: adjoined with *yukadhdhibūn* ⁽they belie⁾ or *yaqūlu* ⁽who say⁾.

What was narrated from Salmān—Allah be well-pleased with him—saying that those that are meant by this verse have not yet appeared:[651] perhaps he meant that those that are meant are not only those who already existed, but there will be in the future others whose state is identical. For the verse is connected with what precedes it through the pronoun that is in it.

649 Narrated from Abū Hurayra by al-Bukhārī (*Anbiyā', Bāb qawl Allāh ta'āla wa-ttakhā Allāh Ibrāhīma Khalīlan*) and Muslim (*Faḍā'il, Bāb faḍā'il Ibrāhīm*) as well as in the *Sunan*—except Ibn Mājah—and Aḥmad in his *Musnad*. (S)

650 Cf. al-Rāzī, *'Iṣmat al-Anbiyā'*, ed. Muḥammad Ḥijāzī (Cairo: Maktabat al-Thaqāfa al-Dīniyya, 1406/1986) p. 71. On the issue of the "three lies" attributed to the Prophet Ibrāhīm—upon him peace—see also Ibn Ḥimyar al-Sabtī, *Tanzīh al-Anbiyā' 'ammā Nasaba ilayhim Ḥuthālat al-Aghbiyā'*, ed. Muḥammad Riḍwān al-Dāya (Beirut and Damascus: Dār al-Fikr, 1411/1990) pp. 92-95 and 'Abd al-Raḥmān al-Ma'allamī, *al-Tankīl bi-mā fī Ta'nīb al-Kawtharī min al-Abāṭīl*, 2nd ed., ed. Muḥammad al-Albānī, 2 vols. (Riyadh: Maktabat al-Ma'ārif, 1406/1986) 2:248-253.

651 Narrated by al-Ṭabarī and Ibn Abī Ḥātim in their *Tafsīrs* for that verse with weak chains. See S (1:393) and al-Munāwī, *Fatḥ* (1:143-144 §36).

وَ(**الْفَسَادُ**): خُرُوجُ الشَّيْءِ عَنِ الِاعْتِدَالِ، وَ(الصَّلَاحُ) ضِدُّهُ، وَكِلَاهُمَا يَعُمَّانِ كُلَّ ضَارٍّ وَنَافِعٍ. وَكَانَ مِنْ فَسَادِهِمْ فِي الْأَرْضِ (أ) هَيْجُ الْحُرُوبِ وَالْفِتَنِ بِمُخَادَعَةِ الْمُسْلِمِينَ، (ب) وَمُمَالَأَةُ الْكُفَّارِ عَلَيْهِمْ بِإِفْشَاءِ الْأَسْرَارِ إِلَيْهِمْ؛ فَإِنَّ ذٰلِكَ يُؤَدِّي إِلَى فَسَادِ مَا فِى الْأَرْضِ مِنَ النَّاسِ وَالدَّوَابِّ وَالْحَرْثِ. وَمِنْهُ: إِظْهَارُ الْمَعَاصِي، وَالْإِهَانَةُ بِالدِّينِ؛ فَإِنَّ الْإِخْلَالَ بِالشَّرَائِعِ، وَالْإِعْرَاضَ عَنْهَا: مِمَّا يُوجِبُ الْهَرْجَ وَالْمَرْجَ وَيُخِلُّ بِنِظَامِ الْعَالَمِ.

وَالْقَائِلُ هُوَ اللهُ تَعَالَى، أَوِ الرَّسُولُ ﷺ، أَوْ بَعْضُ الْمُؤْمِنِينَ.

وَقَرَأَ الْكِسَائِيُّ وَهِشَامٌ (قُيْلَ) بِإِشْمَامِ الضَّمِّ الْأَوَّلِ.

[The spread of corruption in the land]

Al-fasād ⁽corruption⁾ is for something to no longer be in a state of equilibrium.[652] Its antonym is *ṣalāḥ* ⁽integrity⁾. The two of them comprise all matters harmful and beneficial. Their corruption in the land included (i) fomenting wars and seditions through their deception of Muslims and (ii) collective assistance of the unbelievers against Muslims by revealing the latter's secrets to them. All of that unquestionably leads to corruption of the people, livestock and tilth that are in the land. Also part of it is the publicizing of sins and contemning of religion. For violation of sacred laws and disregard of them are inevitable causes for massacres and undermine the order of the world.

The speaker here is Allah Most High, or the Messenger—upon him blessings and peace—or one of the believers.

Al-Kisā'ī and Hishām read *qwīla* with a smack of the pristine *ḍamma*.[653]

[652] I.e. the usefulness that is expected from it. (Q)

[653] As its original form comprised *ḍamm*, cf. Abdul-Massih, *Khalīl* (p. 79). Also read

﴿قَالُوٓا۟ إِنَّمَا نَحْنُ مُصْلِحُونَ﴾ جَوابٌ لِـ﴿إِذَا﴾ وَرَدٌّ لِلنَّاصِحِ عَلَى سَبِيلِ الْمُبالَغَةِ. وَالْمَعْنَى: أَنَّهُ لَا يَصِحُّ مُخاطَبَتُنا بِذٰلِكَ؛ فَإِنَّ شَأْنَنا لَيْسَ إِلَّا الْإِصْلاحَ، وَإِنَّ حالَنا مُتَمَحِّضَةٌ عَنْ شَوائِبِ الْفَسادِ؛ لِأَنَّ (إِنَّما) تُفِيدُ قَصْرَ ما دَخَلَتْ عَلَيْهِ عَلَى ما بَعْدَهُ، مِثْلَ (إِنَّما زَيْدٌ مُنْطَلِقٌ)، وَ(إِنَّما يَنْطَلِقُ زَيْدٌ).

وَإِنَّما قالُوا ذٰلِكَ لِأَنَّهُمْ تَصَوَّرُوا الْفَسادَ بِصُورَةِ الصَّلاحِ لِما فِي قُلُوبِهِمْ مِنَ الْمَرَضِ، كَما قالَ اللهُ تَعالَى: ﴿أَفَمَن زُيِّنَ لَهُۥ سُوٓءُ عَمَلِهِۦ فَرَءَاهُ حَسَنًا﴾ [فاطر ٨].

﴿أَلَآ إِنَّهُمْ هُمُ ٱلْمُفْسِدُونَ وَلَٰكِن لَّا يَشْعُرُونَ ﴿١٢﴾﴾ رَدٌّ لِما ادَّعَوْهُ أَبْلَغَ رَدٍّ

[The corrupters protest they are in fact civilizers]

qālū innamā naḥnu muṣliḥūna ⟨*they say: Nay, but we are civilizers*⟩ is the apodosis to *idhā* ⟨when⟩ and a reply to the honest adviser meant as an intensive. The meaning is: "It is not right to address us in such a way when, in reality, we stand for nothing but betterment, and our state is devoid of the least trace of corruption!" For *innamā* ⟨nothing but⟩ conveys restriction of whatever it prefixes to whatever follows; as in, for example, *innamā Zaydun munṭaliqun* ⟨Zayd alone is going⟩ and *innamā yanṭaliqu Zaydun* ⟨alone to go is Zayd⟩.

They only said this because they imagined corruption to be integrity due to the sickness in their hearts. As Allah said, *Is he for whom his evil-doing was made lovely, so that he considers it good—?* (Fāṭir 35:8).[654]

[2:12] **alā innahum humu-l-mufsidūna wa-lākin lā yashʿurūna** ⟨*behold! truly it is they who are the workers of corruption; but they do not realize*⟩: a rebuttal to their claim made more intensive

thus by Ruways, al-Ḥasan, al-Shanbūdhī, Nāfiʿ, Abū Jaʿfar, Ibn Muḥayṣin and Ibn ʿĀmir. It is the dialect of many Qays, ʿAqīl and their neighbors, and Banū Asad. (*MQ*)

[654] Example of anapodoton—a figure in which a main clause is suggested, as by the introduction of a subordinate clause, but does not occur nor is completed.

(I) لِلْاسْتِئْنَافِ بِهِ؛ (II) وَتَصْدِيرِهِ بِحَرْفَي التَّأْكِيدِ:

(١) ﴿أَلَآ﴾ الْمُنَبِّهَةِ عَلَى تَحْقِيقِ مَا بَعْدَهَا: فَإِنَّ هَمْزَةَ الِاسْتِفْهَامِ الَّتِي لِلْإِنْكَارِ، إِذَا دَخَلَتْ عَلَى النَّفْيِ، أَفَادَتْ تَحْقِيقاً، وَنَظِيرُهُ: (أ) ﴿أَلَيْسَ ذَٰلِكَ بِقَٰدِرٍ﴾ [القيامة ٤٠] ـ وَلِذٰلِكَ لَا تَكَادُ تَقَعُ الْجُمْلَةُ بَعْدَهَا إِلَّا مُصَدَّرَةً بِمَا يُتَلَقَّى بِهِ الْقَسَمُ ـ (ب) وَأُخْتُهَا (أَمَا)، الَّتِي هِيَ مِنْ طَلَائِعِ الْقَسَمِ.

(٢) وَ﴿إِنَّ﴾ الْمُقَرِّرَةِ لِلنِّسْبَةِ.

(III) وَتَعْرِيفِ الْخَبَرِ؛ (IV) وَتَوْسِيطِ الْفَصْلِ لِرَدِّ مَا فِي قَوْلِهِمْ ﴿إِنَّمَا نَحْنُ مُصْلِحُونَ﴾ مِنَ التَّعْرِيضِ لِلْمُؤْمِنِينَ، (V) وَالِاسْتِدْرَاكِ بِـ﴿لَّا يَشْعُرُونَ﴾.

I. by being a resumptive;

II. by being initiated with the two particles of emphasis:

1. *a-lā* ⁽is it not that!⁾, which serves notice that what follows is unquestionably true, for when the interrogative *hamza* that denotes negation is prefixed to a negative, it conveys unquestionable affirmation. Exactly like it are (i) *is not (a-laysa) that One certainly able* (al-Qiyāma 75:40)—hence any clause subsequent to it almost invariably starts with a juratory term—and (ii) the closely related *a-mā* ⁽is it not!⁾, one of the preambles of oaths;

2. *inna* ⁽truly⁾ which corroborates the relation.

III. by the definiteness[655] of the enunciative;

IV. by the middle position of the separative pronoun that serves to rebut the innuendo against the believers in their statement *nay, but we are civilizers;*[656]

V. and by the *correctio* with *lā yashʿurūn* ⁽they do not realize⁾.[657]

[655] With the generic definite article (*lām al-jins*), not the definite article that denotes previous knowledge (*lām al-ʿahd*). (Q)

[656] I.e. their innuendo that the believers are the corrupters. (Q)

[657] "Because the evidence of their being corrupters is now palpable; but they have no

﴿وَإِذَا قِيلَ لَهُمْ ءَامِنُوا۟﴾ مِنْ تَمَامِ النُّصْحِ وَالْإِرْشَادِ؛ فَإِنَّ كَمَالَ الْإِيمَانِ بِمَجْمُوعِ الْأَمْرَيْنِ: الْإِعْرَاضُ عَمَّا لَا يَنْبَغِي -وَهُوَ الْمَقْصُودُ بِقَوْلِهِ: ﴿لَا تُفْسِدُوا۟﴾؛ وَالْإِتْيَانُ بِمَا يَنْبَغِي -وَهُوَ الْمَطْلُوبُ بِقَوْلِهِ: ﴿ءَامِنُوا۟﴾.

﴿كَمَآ ءَامَنَ ٱلنَّاسُ﴾ فِي حَيِّزِ النَّصْبِ عَلَى الْمَصْدَرِ؛ وَ(مَا) مَصْدَرِيَّةٌ، أَوْ كَافَّةٌ، مِثْلُهَا فِي ﴿رُّبَمَا﴾ [الحجر ٢].

وَاللَّامُ فِي ﴿ٱلنَّاسُ﴾ (أ) لِلْجِنْسِ؛ وَالْمُرَادُ بِهِ: الْكَامِلُونَ فِي الْإِنْسَانِيَّةِ،

[2:13] **wa-idhā qīla lahum āminū** ⁽*and when it is said to them, Believe*⁾ to offer complete faithful advice and direction. For the perfection of faith lies in the sum of two matters: turning away from every reprehensible matter—this is what is meant by His saying *do not spread corruption*—and implementing what is required; this is what is demanded with His saying *believe.*

ka-mā āmana-n-nāsu ⁽*as human beings believe*⁾ is an annexure to the accusative as an infinitive noun. *Mā* ⁽what⁾ introduces a clause equivalent to the infinitive noun; or it is a neutralizing *mā*,[658] identical to the one in *ruba-mā* ⁽time after time⁾ (al-Ḥijr 15:2).

['Human beings' as archetypes of belief or groups of converts]

The [definite article] *lām* in *al-nās* is

(i) for the species, meaning thereby those of perfect humanity,....

sense to perceive it." (P, Q) See Badawī Ṭabāna, *Muʿjam al-Balāghā al-ʿArabiyya*, 3rd ed. (Riyadh: Dār al-Rifāʿī; Jeddah: Dār al-Manāra, 1408/ 1988) p. 221 §281 (*al-istidrāk wal-rujūʿ*); Cachia, *Arch Rhetorician* (p. 48 §72 and Arabic counterpart); and Gideon O. Burton, *Silva Rhetoricae: The Forest of Rhetoric*, http://rhetoric.byu.edu/ (*correctio*).

658 "The neutralizing/restringent *mā* (*mā al-kāffa*) is prefixed to certain verbs, verb-like particles (*al-ḥurūf al-mushabbaha bil-fiʿl*) and particles of prepositional attraction (*ḥurūf al-jarr*) and neutralizes (*takuffu*) their action... It is also called the superadded *mā* (*al-zāʾida*)." Abdul-Massih, *Khalīl* (pp. 352-353).

الْعَامِلُونَ بِقَضِيَّةِ الْعَقْلِ؛ فَإِنَّ اِسْمَ الْجِنْسِ، كَمَا يُسْتَعْمَلُ لِمُسَمَّاهُ مُطْلَقاً، يُسْتَعْمَلُ لِمَا يَسْتَجْمِعُ الْمَعَانِيَ الْمَخْصُوصَةَ بِهِ وَالْمَقْصُودَةَ مِنْهُ، وَلِذٰلِكَ يُسْلَبُ عَنْ غَيْرِهِ، فَيُقَالُ: (زَيْدٌ لَيْسَ بِإِنْسَانٍ). وَمِنْ هٰذَا الْبَابِ قَوْلُهُ تَعَالَى: ﴿صُمٌّ بُكْمٌ عُمْيٌ﴾ [البقرة ١٨] وَنَحْوُهُ؛ وَقَدْ جَمَعَهُمَا الشَّاعِرُ فِي قَوْلِهِ: [طويل]

.... ❋ إِذِ النَّاسُ نَاسٌ وَالزَّمَانُ زَمَانُ

(ب) أَوْ لِلْعَهْدِ؛ وَالْمُرَادُ بِهِ: الرَّسُولُ ﷺ وَمَنْ مَعَهُ، أَوْ مَنْ آمَنَ مِنْ أَهْلِ جِلْدَتِهِمْ، كَابْنِ سَلَامٍ ....

who act in conformity with the exigencies of intellect. For the nomen speciei, just as it is used for its referent in unqualified terms, is also used for what collects the meanings that are particular to it and intended by it.[659] Hence it can be divested from other than that, which is why one can say, "Zayd is no human being." To the latter category belongs the saying of the Most High, *deaf, dumb and blind* (al-Baqara 2:18) and the like. The poet put both [uses] together in his saying: ["The Long"]

when people were people and times were times.[660]

(ii) Alternately, it indicates previous knowledge, meaning the Messenger—upon him blessings and peace—and those with him, or those who believed of their kith and kin, such as Ibn Salām

[659] "This usage is a popular transferred meaning (*majāz muta'ārif*), whence it is said that when something is mentioned in absolute terms it is understood as its archetype." (Q)

[660] Said to have been etched in stone by a man of 'Ād, its first hemistich stating *Countries where we lived and which we loved*. This entire passage is from al-Rāghib's *Tafsīr*. (S) On the verse see also Abū al-Faraj al-Aṣfahānī, *Aghānī* (21:71-72) and Ṣadr al-Dīn 'Alī b. Abī al-Faraj al-Baṣrī, *al-Ḥamāsa al-Baṣriyya*, ed. 'Ādil Sulaymān Jamāl, 4 vols. (Cairo: Maktabat al-Khānjī, 1420/1999) 3:1071 §940.

وَأَصْحَابِهِ؛ وَالْمَعْنَى: آمَنُوا إِيمَاناً مَقْرُوناً بِالْإِخْلَاصِ، مُتَمَحِّضاً عَنْ شَوَائِبِ النِّفَاقِ، مُمَاثِلاً لِإِيمَانِهِمْ.

وَاسْتُدِلَّ بِهِ عَلَى قَبُولِ تَوْبَةِ الزِّنْدِيقِ، وَأَنَّ الْإِقْرَارَ بِاللِّسَانِ: إِيمَانٌ، وَإِلَّا لَمْ يُفِدِ التَّقْيِيدَ.

and his companions; in which case the meaning is, "Believe with a faith coupled with sincerity, purified from all taint of hypocrisy and identical with their belief."

[Zendiks and the view that mere verbal profession is belief]

It was adduced as evidence for the acceptability of the Zendik's repentance[661] and that oral affirmation constitutes belief,[662] otherwise[663] the qualification would not make sense.[664]

[661] "The Zendik in the convention of jurists is one who conceals staunch unbelief while displaying belief to protect himself. It is also related from *Sharḥ al-Maqāṣid* that if an unbeliever (*kāfir*) acknowledges the prophethood of the Prophet—upon him blessings and peace—and displays the signs of Islam together with his concealing convictions that are agreed upon as unbelief: such a person is specifically called a Zendik. There is a difference of opinion about the acceptability of his repentance and the correct position in the Hanafi school is that it is acceptable both before catching him and after. It was also said no, he is killed like the magician and the propagandist of atheism.... The rationale of the evidentiary nature of the verse for accepting the repentance of the Zendik is that hypocrites are part of the Zendiks; and since they were commanded to believe it is necessary to accept their repentance.... Hence that of the Zendiks is also acceptable because they are part of them." (Z)

[662] "I.e. the word *īmān* can be applied to it." (Q) Also see note 614 above and entry "Karrāmiyya" in biographical glossary.

[663] All mss. and eds.: والا لم يفد P: والا لم يفده AQ, H, MM: وان لم يفد typo

[664] "The Imam mentioned the same thing then rebutted it but the author omitted the rebuttal. His exact words were: 'Someone might adduce this verse as evidence that affirmation (*al-iqrār*) by itself is belief; for if it were not belief the referent of *īmān* would not be realized unless sincerity takes place therein, in which case His saying *Believe* would be enough to implement the demand, and the additional statement *as human beings believe* would be pointless (*laghw*). The answer is: real *īmān* in the Divine presence is the one that is coupled with sincerity. Outwardly, however, it is inaccessible except by way of outward affirmation. Undoubtedly, then, there was a need to emphasize

﴿قَالُوٓاْ أَنُؤۡمِنُ كَمَآ ءَامَنَ ٱلسُّفَهَآءُ﴾: الْهَمْزَةُ فِيهِ لِلْإِنْكَارِ، وَاللَّامُ مُشَارٌ بِهَا إِلَى ﴿ٱلنَّاسُ﴾، أَوِ الْجِنْسِ بِأَسْرِهِ، وَهُمْ مُنْدَرِجُونَ فِيهِ عَلَى زَعْمِهِمْ.

وَإِنَّمَا سَفَّهُوهُمْ (أ) لِاعْتِقَادِهِمْ فَسَادَ رَأْيِهِمْ؛ ....

qālū anuʾminu ka-mā āmana-s-sufahāʾu ⁽*they say, Us? Believe as the fools believe?*⁾: the [interrogative] *hamza* in it stands for denial[665] while the [definite article] *lām* alludes to *the human beings*, or the entire species[666] under which they[667] are subsumed according to them.

They declared them fools

(i) because they were convinced they held corrupt doctrines;

it *as humans beings believe*." (S 1:400) "The rationale of its evidentiary nature for saying that *īmān* is affirmation by itself whether coupled with sincerity or not, is that Allah Most High qualified it by saying *as human beings believe* in the sense of 'Believe with a faith coupled with sincerity and far from hypocrisy.' So if lone affirmation of the two testimonies were not belief the referent of *īmān* would not take place without sincerity; and His lone saying *as humans beings believe* would be correcting (*mustadrikan*) the assumption that the belief [they were] ordered to profess with His saying *Believe* is—in such a scenario—confirmation together with affirmation. Therefore there would be no need for His qualifying it by saying *as human beings believe*. The answer is that the belief that is demanded of them by His saying *Believe* is real belief that is credited as such in the Divine presence, namely, affirmation coupled with sincerity, as affirmation by itself is not belief in reality. Hence, outwardly, it would have sufficed for Him to just say *Believe*. However, since affirmation by itself is belief outwardly—so that whoever professes the two testimonies of faith makes his life and property inviolable—it is possible to imagine it as subsumed under required belief through its being coupled with sincerity. Hence, outwardly, [*as human beings believe*] is a qualifier for the absolute [command] except that, in reality, it is an emphasis (*taʾkīd*) for required belief because the latter is coupled with sincerity sine qua non." (Z 1:143)

[665] "I.e. allegorically (*majāzan*), mentioning the result [interrogation arising from not knowing something] but intending the cause [denial]." (Q)

[666] Of fools. (Z)

[667] "I.e. those meant by *al-nās* according to the logic [implied by the definite article] of previous knowledge." (Q) "And they used to disclose this assertion among themselves, whereupon Allah revealed it.... or in themselves, and Allah exposed their innermost secrets." (Z)

(ب) أَوْ لِتَحْقِيرِ شَأْنِهِمْ ـ فَإِنَّ أَكْثَرَ الْمُؤْمِنِينَ كَانُوا فُقَرَاءَ، وَمِنْهُمْ مَوَالِي، كَصُهَيْبٍ وَبِلَالٍ ـ (ج) أَوْ لِلتَّجَلُّدِ وَعَدَمِ الْمُبَالَاةِ بِمَنْ آمَنَ مِنْهُمْ، إِنْ فُسِّرَ ﴿ٱلنَّاسُ﴾ بِعَبْدِ اللهِ بْنِ سَلَامٍ وَأَشْيَاعِهِ.

وَ(السَّفَهُ): خِفَّةٌ وَسَخَافَةُ رَأْيٍ يَقْتَضِيهِمَا نُقْصَانُ الْعَقْلِ؛ وَالْحِلْمُ يُقَابِلُهُ.

﴿أَلَآ إِنَّهُمْ هُمُ ٱلسُّفَهَآءُ وَلَٰكِن لَّا يَعْلَمُونَ﴾ رَدٌّ وَمُبَالَغَةٌ فِي تَجْهِيلِهِمْ؛ فَإِنَّ الْجَاهِلَ بِجَهْلِهِ الْجَازِمَ عَلَى خِلَافِ مَا هُوَ الْوَاقِعُ: أَعْظَمُ ضَلَالَةً وَأَتَمُّ جَهَالَةً مِنَ الْمُتَوَقِّفِ الْمُعْتَرِفِ بِجَهْلِهِ: فَإِنَّهُ رُبَّمَا يُعْذَرُ، وَتَنْفَعُهُ الْآيَاتُ وَالنُّذُرُ.

وَإِنَّمَا فُصِلَتِ الْآيَةُ بِـ﴿لَا يَعْلَمُونَ﴾ ....

(ii) or to belittle them, since most of the believers were poor and there were freedmen among them, such as Ṣuhayb and Bilāl;

(iii) or to feign courage and show indifference to those among them who believed, if *al-nās* is explained to refer to ʿAbd Allāh b. Salām and his faction.

Safah ⁽folly⁾ is levity and imbecility dictated by a deficient intellect. Its counterpart is *ḥilm* ⁽prudence⁾.

alā innahum humu-s-sufahāʾu wa-lākin lā yaʿlamūn ⁽*Behold! Truly it is they who are the fools; but they do not know*⁾: a rebuttal and intensive exposure of their ignorance. For the ignorant, with his ignorance positively asserting what is in direct opposition to facts, is in worse misguidance and greater nescience than the one who is undecided while acknowledging his ignorance. For the latter may be excused, and the wonders and warning signs may benefit him.

[The difference between "knowing" and "realizing"]

The reason the verse was sectioned off with *lā yaʿlamūn* ......

وَالَّتِي قَبْلَهَا بِـ﴿لَا يَشْعُرُونَ﴾، لِأَنَّهُ أَكْثَرُ طِبَاقاً لِذِكْرِ السَّفَهِ، وَلِأَنَّ الْوُقُوفَ عَلَى أَمْرِ الدِّينِ، وَالتَّمْيِيزَ بَيْنَ الْحَقِّ وَالْبَاطِلِ: مِمَّا يَفْتَقِرُ إِلَى نَظَرٍ وَفِكْرٍ؛ وَأَمَّا النِّفَاقُ، وَمَا فِيهِ مِنَ الْفِتَنِ وَالْفَسَادِ، فَإِنَّمَا يُدْرَكُ بِأَدْنَى تَفَطُّنٍ وَتَأَمُّلٍ فِيمَا يُشَاهَدُ مِنْ أَقْوَالِهِمْ وَأَفْعَالِهِمْ.

﴿وَإِذَا لَقُوا۟ ٱلَّذِينَ ءَامَنُوا۟ قَالُوٓا۟ ءَامَنَّا﴾ بَيَانٌ لِمُعَامَلَتِهِمِ الْمُؤْمِنِينَ وَالْكُفَّارَ. وَمَا صُدِّرَتْ بِهِ الْقِصَّةُ فَمَسَاقُهُ لِبَيَانِ مَذْهَبِهِمْ وَتَمْهِيدِ نِفَاقِهِمْ، فَلَيْسَ بِتَكْرِيرٍ.

رُوِيَ أَنَّ ابْنَ أُبَيٍّ وَأَصْحَابَهُ اسْتَقْبَلَهُمْ نَفَرٌ مِنَ الصَّحَابَةِ، فَقَالَ لِقَوْمِهِ: انْظُرُوا ....

‹they do not know› and the previous one with *lā yashʿurūn* ‹they do not realize› is because it is more congruent with the mention of folly, and because to grasp the matter of religion fully and distinguish truth from falsehood requires investigation and reflection. As for hypocrisy and its train of strifes and corruption, it can be detected with a modicum of awareness and consideration of what they let show of speech and acts.

[2:14] **wa-idhā laqū-l-ladhīna āmanū qālū āmannā** ‹*and when they light upon those who believe they say: We believe*› is an exposition of their interaction with [both] believers and unbelievers.

As for the opening of the account,[668] its narrative context is the show their posture and introduce their hypocrisy, so there is no repetition. It is narrated that

> Ibn Ubay and his friends[669] were met by a number of Companions, whereupon he said to his people: "Watch

[668] Namely, *and of people there are those who say we believe in Allah* to the end of the verse.... which is recounted to show their hypocrisy. (Z)
[669] See note 607.

كَيْفَ أَرُدُّ هٰؤُلَاءِ السُّفَهَاءَ عَنْكُمْ. فَأَخَذَ بِيَدِ أَبِي بَكْرٍ ـ رَضِيَ اللهُ عَنْهُ ـ فَقَالَ: مَرْحَباً بِالصِّدِّيقِ سَيِّدِ بَنِي تَيْمٍ، وَشَيْخِ الْإِسْلَامِ، وَثَانِي رَسُولِ اللهِ فِي الْغَارِ، الْبَاذِلِ نَفْسَهُ وَمَالَهُ لِرَسُولِ اللهِ ﷺ! ثُمَّ أَخَذَ بِيَدِ عُمَرَ ـ رَضِيَ اللهُ عَنْهُ ـ فَقَالَ: مَرْحَباً بِسَيِّدِ بَنِي عَدِيٍّ، الْفَارُوقِ الْقَوِيِّ فِي دِينِهِ، الْبَاذِلِ نَفْسَهُ وَمَالَهُ لِرَسُولِ اللهِ ﷺ! ثُمَّ أَخَذَ بِيَدِ عَلِيٍّ ـ رَضِيَ اللهُ عَنْهُ ـ فَقَالَ: مَرْحَباً بِابْنِ عَمِّ رَسُولِ اللهِ ﷺ وَخَتَنِهِ، سَيِّدَ بَنِي هَاشِمٍ، مَا خَلَا رَسُولَ اللهِ ﷺ! فَنَزَلَتْ.

how I will repel these fools from you." Then he took Abū Bakr's—Allah be well-pleased with him—hand and said: "Welcome to the all-trustful one (*ṣiddīq*), the liegelord of Banū Taym, elder of Islam and peer of the Messenger of Allah in the cave, who spent his life and property for the Messenger of Allah—upon him blessings and peace!" Then he took the hand of ʿUmar—Allah be well-pleased with him—and said: "Welcome to the liegelord of Banū ʿAdiy, the discerning one who is staunch in his religion, who spent his life and property for the Messenger of Allah—upon him blessings and peace!" Then he took the hand of ʿAlī—Allah be well-pleased with him—and said: "Welcome to the paternal cousin of the Messenger of Allah—upon him blessings and peace—and his son-in-law, the liegelord of the Banū Hāshim besides the Messenger of Allah—upon him blessings and peace!" Then this [verse] was revealed.[670]

[670] Narrated by al-Thaʿlabī in *al-Kashf wal-Bayān* (1:155) and al-Wāḥidī in *Asbāb al-Nuzūl* (Cairo: Maṭbaʿa Hindiyya, 1316/1898, rept. Beirut: ʿĀlam al-Kutub, n.d.) pp. 13-14 through Muḥammad b. Marwān al-Suddī al-Ṣaghīr (accused of forgery), from al-Kalbī (accused of lying), from Abū Ṣāliḥ (weak by agreement), from Ibn ʿAbbās—"the chain of mendacity (*silsilat al-kadhib*)" and "its text is the height of oddity" according to Ibn Ḥajar, respectively in *al-ʿUjāb fī Bayān al-Asbāb*, ed. ʿAbd al-Ḥakīm

وَ(اللِّقَاءُ): الْمُصَادَفَةُ؛ يُقَالُ: (لَقِيتُهُ) وَ(لَاقَيْتُهُ)، إِذَا صَادَفْتَهُ وَاسْتَقْبَلْتَهُ؛ وَمِنْهُ: (أَلْقَيْتُهُ) إِذَا طَرَحْتَهُ، فَإِنَّكَ بِطَرْحِهِ جَعَلْتَهُ بِحَيْثُ يُلْقَى.

﴿وَإِذَا خَلَوْا إِلَىٰ شَيَاطِينِهِمْ﴾ مِنْ (خَلَوْتُ بِفُلَانٍ وَإِلَيْهِ) إِذَا انْفَرَدْتَ مَعَهُ؛ أَوْ مِنْ (خَلَاكَ ذَمٌّ) أَيْ عَدَاكَ وَمَضَى عَنْكَ؛ وَمِنْهُ: (الْقُرُونُ الْخَالِيَةُ)؛ أَوْ مِنْ (خَلَوْتُ بِهِ) إِذَا سَخِرْتَ مِنْهُ.

وَعُدِّيَ بِـ(إِلَى) لِتَضَمُّنِ مَعْنَى الْإِنْهَاءِ.

Al-liqāʾ ‹coming across› is happenstance. One says, *laqītuhu* ‹you came across him› and *lāqaytuhu* ‹you encountered him› when you chanced upon him and faced him, whence *alqaytuhu* ‹you threw it› when you cast it off, since by casting it off you put it where it can be chanced upon.

wa-idhā khalaw ilā shayāṭīnihim ‹*and when they retire unto their devils*›:

(i) from *khalawtu bi-fulān* ‹I find yourself alone with X› and *[khalawtu] ilayh* ‹I retire to be with X› when you alone are with him;

(ii) or from *khallāka dhamm* ‹all blame has left you›, that is, it went past you and is now behind you; whence *al-qurūn al-khāliya* ‹bygone centuries›;

(iii) or from *khalawtu bihi* when you deride him.

It was transitivized with ***ilā*** ‹unto› because it entails the sense of termination.[671]

Muḥammad al-Anīs, 2 vols. (Dammām: Dār Ibn al-Jawzī, 1418/1997) 1:236 and *al-Kāfī al-Shāf* (p. 12 §22). "The marks of forgery are evident all over it: Sūrat al-Baqara was revealed very early in the Hijra, whereas ʿAlī only married Fāṭima in Year 2." (S)

671 I.e. they deride the believers, conveying that derision to their own kind. (Q, Z)

وَالْمُرَادُ بِـ﴿شَيَٰطِينِهِمْ﴾: الَّذِينَ مَاثَلُوا الشَّيْطَانَ فِي تَمَرُّدِهِمْ، وَهُمْ: (أ) الْمُظْهِرُونَ كُفْرَهُمْ ـ وَإِضَافَتُهُمْ إِلَيْهِم لِلْمُشَارَكَةِ فِي الْكُفْرِ ـ؛ (ب) أَوْ كِبَارُ الْمُنَافِقِينَ. وَالْقَائِلُونَ: صِغَارُهُمْ.

وَجَعَلَ سِيبَوَيْهِ نُونَهُ تَارَةً أَصْلِيَّةً عَلَى أَنَّهُ مِنْ (شَطَنَ) إِذَا بَعُدَ ـ فَإِنَّهُ بَعِيدٌ عَنِ الصَّلَاحِ ـ وَيَشْهَدُ لَهُ قَوْلُهُمْ: (تَشَيْطَنَ)، وَأُخْرَى زَائِدَةً، عَلَى أَنَّهُ مِنْ (شَاطَ) إِذَا بَطَلَ ـ وَمِنْ أَسْمَائِهِ: (الْبَاطِلُ).

﴿قَالُوٓاْ إِنَّا مَعَكُمْ﴾ أَيْ فِي الدِّينِ وَالِاعْتِقَادِ.

[The human devils]

What is meant by ***shayāṭīnihim*** ⟨their devils⟩ is those who typified Satan in their rebelliousness, namely,

(i) those who proclaimed their unbelief: their [possessive] annexation to [devils] stands for their mutual partnership in unbelief;

(ii) or the major hypocrites, the speakers being the minor ones.

Sībawayh in one place made its *nūn* an original [letter] whereby the root is *sh-ṭ-n*, "to be far"—since he is far from righteousness—and this is corroborated by their saying *tashayṭana* ⟨he acted like the devil⟩; and in another deemed it an augmentative affix, whereby the original is *shāṭa*, which is *baṭala* ⟨to be false⟩; and among his names is *al-Bāṭil* ⟨the false one⟩.[672]

qālū innā maʿakum ⟨*they say: Truly we are with you*⟩, that is, in religion and creed.

[672] As in the commentaries for the verse *Falsehood cannot come at it from before it or behind it* (Fuṣṣilat 41:42) and the hadith "Learn al-Baqara for taking it is a blessing and leaving it is woe, and the *baṭala* are powerless against it" narrated from Burayda by Aḥmad, al-Dārimī and others cf. Muḥammad b. Rizq b. Ṭarhūnī, *Mawsūʿat Faḍāʾil Suwar wa-Āyāt al-Qurʾān*, 2 vols. (Dammam: Dār Ibn al-Qayyim, 1409/1989) 1:113.

خَاطَبُوا الْمُؤْمِنِينَ بِالْجُمْلَةِ الْفِعْلِيَّةِ، وَالشَّيَاطِينَ بِالْجُمْلَةِ الْإِسْمِيَّةِ الْمُؤَكَّدَةِ بِـ(إِنَّ): (أ) لِأَنَّهُمْ قَصَدُوا بِالْأُولَى دَعْوَى إِحْدَاثِ الْإِيمَانِ، وَبِالثَّانِيَةِ تَحْقِيقَ ثَبَاتِهِمْ عَلَى مَا كَانُوا عَلَيْهِ؛ (ب) وَلِأَنَّهُ لَمْ يَكُنْ لَهُمْ بَاعِثٌ مِنْ عَقِيدَةٍ وَصِدْقِ رَغْبَةٍ فِيمَا خَاطَبُوا بِهِ الْمُؤْمِنِينَ، (ج) وَلَا تَوَقُّعُ رَوَاجِ ادِّعَاءِ الْكَمَالِ فِي الْإِيمَانِ عَلَى الْمُؤْمِنِينَ مِنَ الْمُهَاجِرِينَ وَالْأَنْصَارِ، بِخِلَافِ مَا قَالُوهُ مَعَ الْكُفَّارِ.

﴿إِنَّمَا نَحْنُ مُسْتَهْزِءُونَ﴾ (أ) تَأْكِيدٌ لِمَا قَبْلَهُ؛ لِأَنَّ الْمُسْتَهْزِئَ بِالشَّيْءِ .....

[Rhetorical difference between verbal and nominal clauses]

They addressed the believers with a verbal sentence and the devils with a nominal sentence emphasized by *inna* ‹truly›,

(i) because, by the first, they intended an aspersion at belief as something newfangled and by the second, the full affirmation of their standing firm on their original stance;[673]

(ii) also, because they were not being motivated by conviction and earnest desire regarding their words to the believers;

(iii) and they had no expectation for any claim of perfect belief to gain currency among believers such as the Emigrants and Helpers, contrary to what they said to the unbelievers.[674]

[The scoffing of the hypocrites]

innamā naḥnu mustahzi'ūna ‹*we only make scoff*› is (i) an emphasis for what precedes, for the one who mocks something and

[673] In order to pre-empt any misgivings on the part of their devils after they had told the believers *We believe.* (K) Also see notes 298, 557, 681 on nominal/verbal clauses.

[674] "If they had said *innā mu'minūn* ‹we are believers› to suggest pure belief, it would have never gained currency among the sincere believers due to their complete insight and sharp intelligence, so they avoided emphasis; as for the unbelievers, the claim of standing firm on Judaism can gain currency among them so they used emphasis." (Q)

الْمُسْتَخِفَّ بِهِ مُصِرٌّ عَلَى خِلَافِهِ؛ (ب) أَوْ بَدَلٌ مِنْهُ، لِأَنَّ مَنْ حَقَّرَ الْإِسْلَامَ فَقَدْ عَظَّمَ الْكُفْرَ؛ (ج) أَوِ اسْتِئْنَافٌ، فَكَأَنَّ الشَّيَاطِينَ قَالُوا لَهُمْ، لَمَّا ﴿قَالُوٓاْ إِنَّا مَعَكُمْ﴾: (إِنْ صَحَّ ذَٰلِكَ، فَمَا بَالُكُمْ تُوَافِقُونَ الْمُؤْمِنِينَ وَتَدَّعُونَ الْإِيمَانَ؟) فَأَجَابُوا بِذَلِكَ.

بالتشديد

وَ(الْاِسْتِهْزَاءُ): السُّخْرِيَةُ وَالْاِسْتِخْفَافُ؛ يُقَالُ: (هَزَأْتُ) وَ(اسْتَهْزَأْتُ) بِمَعْنًى، كَـ(أَجَبْتُ) وَ(اسْتَجَبْتُ). وَأَصْلُهُ الْخِفَّةُ، مِنَ (الْهَزْءِ)، وَهُوَ الْقَتْلُ السَّرِيعُ؛ يُقَالُ: (هَزَأَ فُلَانٌ) إِذَا مَاتَ عَلَى مَكَانِهِ، وَ(نَاقَتُهُ تَهْزَأُ بِهِ)، أَيْ تُسْرِعُ وَتَخِفُّ.

﴿ٱللَّهُ يَسْتَهْزِئُ بِهِمْ﴾: ....

makes light of it is obstinately following its opposite; (ii) or a substitute for it, because whoever belittles Islam has magnified unbelief; (iii) or a resumption, as if the devils had told them, in reply to their words *truly we are with you*, "If this is the case, then why do you concur with the believers and profess to have faith?" so they replied with that.

Istihzāʾ ‹scoffing, mockery› is derision and slighting. One says *hazaʾtu* and *istahzaʾtu* ‹I scoff/mock› in one and the same sense, like *ajabtu* and *istajabtu* ‹I answer›. Its basis is levity, from *al-hazʾ*,[675] which is speedy killing.[676] One says, *hazaʾa fulān* when X dies on the spot,[677] and *nāqatuhu tahzaʾu bih*, that is, his camel speeds up nimbly.

[2:15] **al-Lāhu yastahziʾu bihim** ‹*The One God scoffs at them*›:

[675] α, B, F: الهَزْء R: الهُزْء Ak, β, I, T: الهزء ε: الهزا In *Tāj al-ʿArūs*: هَزَأَ إِبِلَهُ هَزْءًا: قَتَلَها بِالبَرْدِ

[676] "Which is light in comparison to slow killing, so the congruence between the derivative and its root is complete." (Q)

[677] Cf. J and *Tāj al-ʿArūs*, under *h-z-ʾ*.

يُجَازِيهِمْ عَلَى اسْتِهْزَائِهِمْ. سُمِّيَ جَزَاءُ الْاِسْتِهْزَاءِ بِاسْمِهِ، كَمَا سُمِّيَ جَزَاءُ السَّيِّئَةِ سَيِّئَةً: (١) إِمَّا لِمُقَابَلَةِ اللَّفْظِ بِاللَّفْظِ؛ (٢) أَوْ لِكَوْنِهِ مُمَاثِلاً لَهُ فِي الْقَدْرِ؛ (٣) أَوْ يَرْجِعُ وَبَالُ الْاِسْتِهْزَاءِ عَلَيْهِمْ، فَيَكُونُ كَالْمُسْتَهْزِئِ بِهِمْ؛ (٤) أَوْ يُنْزِلُ بِهِمُ الْحَقَارَةَ وَالْهَوَانَ، الَّذِي هُوَ لَازِمُ الْاِسْتِهْزَاءِ أَوِ الْغَرَضُ مِنْهُ؛ (٥) أَوْ يُعَامِلُهُمْ مُعَامَلَةَ الْمُسْتَهْزِئِ: أَمَّا فِي الدُّنْيَا فَبِإِجْرَاءِ أَحْكَامِ الْمُسْلِمِينَ عَلَيْهِمْ،

He requites them for their scoffing.

[The divine scoffing]

The requital of scoffing was named by the same name as it, just as the requital of evil was named an evil,[678] (i) for homonymic correspondence; (ii) or because it is proportional to it; (iii) or [because] the bad consequences of mockery fall back on them, so that He is like one mocking them; (iv) or He visits upon them diminution and disgrace, which are the inseparable accompaniments of mockery or its objectives; (v) or he treats them the way a scoffer treats [the object of his scoffing]. In this world this takes place through their subjection to the same laws that apply to Muslims ....

[678] In the verse *The requital of an evil deed is an evil the like thereof* (al-Shūrā 42:40). "That is, a *majāz mursal* ‹synechdoche or hypallage› for *mushākala lafẓiyya* ‹homonymy› as he proceeded to say." (Q) However, the Shiʿi al-Sharīf al-Raḍī (359-406/970-1015) calls it a metaphor (*istiʿāra*) in his *Talkhīṣ al-Bayān fī Majāzāt al-Qur'ān*, ed. ʿAlī Maḥmūd Muqallid (Beirut: Dār Maktabat al-Ḥayāt, 1984?) pp. 29-30. On *majāz mursal* see Magdi Wahba, *A Dictionary of Literary Terms: English-French-Arabic* (Beirut: Librairie du Liban, 1974, rept. 1983) p. 229 §819, p. 557 §1742 and especially Abdul-Raof Hussein, *Arabic Rhetoric: A Pragmatic Analysis* (New York: Routledge, 2006) pp. 225-232. Cf. Geneva Bible, Hosea iv. 9: *I wil visit their wayes vpon them, and rewarde them their dedes.*

وَاسْتِدْرَاجِهِمْ بِالْإِمْهَالِ وَالزِّيَادَةِ فِي النِّعْمَةِ عَلَى التَّمَادِي فِي الطُّغْيَانِ؛ وَأَمَّا فِي الْآخِرَةِ: فَبِأَنْ يَفْتَحَ لَهُمْ ـ وَهُمْ فِي النَّارِ ـ بَاباً إِلَى الْجَنَّةِ، فَيُسْرِعُونَ نَحْوَهُ، فَإِذَا صَارُوا إِلَيْهِ، سَدَّ عَلَيْهِمُ الْبَابَ؛ وَذٰلِكَ قَوْلُهُ تَعَالَى: ﴿ فَٱلْيَوْمَ ٱلَّذِينَ ءَامَنُوا۟ مِنَ ٱلْكُفَّارِ يَضْحَكُونَ ﴿٣٤﴾ ﴾ [المطففين].

وَإِنَّمَا اسْتُؤْنِفَ بِهِ وَلَمْ يُعْطَفْ، لِيَدُلَّ عَلَى أَنَّ اللهَ تَعَالَى تَوَلَّى مُجَازَاتَهُمْ، وَلَمْ يُحْوِجِ الْمُؤْمِنِينَ إِلَى أَنْ يُعَارِضُوهُمْ، وَأَنَّ اسْتِهْزَاءَهُمْ لَا يُؤْبَهُ بِهِ فِي مُقَابَلَةِ مَا يَفْعَلُ اللهُ تَعَالَى بِهِمْ. وَلَعَلَّهُ لَمْ يَقُلْ: (اللهُ مُسْتَهْزِئٌ بِهِمْ) لِيُطَابِقَ قَوْلَهُمْ، إِيمَاءً بِأَنَّ الْاِسْتِهْزَاءَ يَحْدُثُ حَالاً فَحَالاً، وَيَتَجَدَّدُ حِيناً بَعْدَ حِينٍ، ....

and their beguilement by means of a respite and an increase in favors for them, while they themselves persist in their oppression. In the next life it is by His opening for them—while they are in hellfire—a doorway to Paradise, whereby they rush toward it, but when they reach it it is shut in their faces. That is the saying of Allah, *Today, then, those who believed shall laugh at the unbelievers* (al-Muṭaffifīn 83:34).

It was made a resumptive instead of being adjoined[679] to show that Allah Most High had taken it upon Himself to requite them and did not impose upon the believers the necessity to confront them and, furthermore, that their mockery is trifling in comparison to what Allah will do with them.

It may be that the reason He did not say "Allah is a scoffer of them"[680] to echo their own statement, is to allude to the fact that scoffing befalls in successive moments and recurs anew time af-

679 I.e., either with *They say: truly we are with you* or with *truly we are with you.* (Q)
680 I.e. *mustahzi'un bihim* as a nominal clause.

وَهٰكَذَا كَانَتْ نِكَايَاتُ اللهِ فِيهِمْ كَمَا قَالَ تَعَالَى ﴿أَوَلَا يَرَوْنَ أَنَّهُمْ يُفْتَنُونَ فِي كُلِّ عَامٍ مَّرَّةً أَوْ مَرَّتَيْنِ﴾ [التوبة ١٢٦].

﴿وَيَمُدُّهُمْ فِي طُغْيَانِهِمْ يَعْمَهُونَ﴾ مِنْ (مَدَّ الْجَيْشَ وَأَمَدَّهُ) إِذَا زَادَهُ وَقَوَّاهُ؛ وَمِنْهُ (مَدَدْتُ السِّرَاجَ وَالْأَرْضَ) إِذَا اسْتَصْلَحْتَهُمَا بِالزَّيْتِ وَالسَّمَادِ - لَا مِنَ الْمَدِّ فِي الْعُمُرِ، فَإِنَّهُ يُعَدَّى بِاللَّامِ، كَـ(أَمْلَى لَهُ). وَيَدُلُّ عَلَيْهِ قِرَاءَةُ ابْنِ كَثِيرٍ (وَيُمِدُّهُمْ).

وَالْمُعْتَزِلَةُ - لَمَّا تَعَذَّرَ عَلَيْهِمْ إِجْرَاءُ الْكَلَامِ عَلَى ظَاهِرِهِ - قَالُوا:

ter time;[681] thus indeed were Allah Most High's afflictions befalling them, as He said: *Lo! Do they not see that they are tested once or twice in every year?* (al-Tawba 9:126).

wa-yamudduhum fī ṭughyānihim yaʿmahūna ⟨*and keeps reinforcing them in their rebellion, all bewildered*⟩: from *madda/amadda al-jaysh*, "to increase and reinforce the army;" whence *madadtu al-sirāj wal-arḍ* ⟨I reinforce the candle and the land⟩ when you improve them with oil and manure respectively. It is not [meant in the sense] of an increase in life-span—for that is transitivized with *lām*, as in *amlā lahu* ⟨he gave him rein⟩. This is also indicated in the reading of Ibn Kathīr, *wa-yumidduhum*.[682]

[Non-Sunni figurations of the divine reinforcing of *ṭughyān*]

When the Muʿtazila found it unfeasible to let this discourse run according to its manifest locution,[683] they said:

681 See notes 298, 557 and 673 on the rhetorics of nominal and verbal clauses.

682 Ibn Kathīr, Ibn Muḥayṣin and Shibl. (*MQ*) It is *shādhdh* from Ibn Kathīr. (Naṣṣ)

683 "I.e. in their claim that Allah does not create something ugly." (A) "From the perspective that it contradicts what they claimed, namely, that whatever is optimal (*al-aṣlaḥ*) for the slave, it is incumbent on Allah Most High to take it into account; but giving reinforcement towards rebellion is among the ugly deeds, so it cannot be as-

(١) لمَّا مَنَعَهُمُ اللهُ تَعَالَى أَلْطَافَهُ الَّتِي يَمْنَحُهَا الْمُؤْمِنِينَ، وَخَذَلَهُمْ بِسَبَبِ كُفْرِهِمْ، وَإِصْرَارِهِمْ، وَسَدِّهِمْ طُرُقَ التَّوْفِيقِ عَلَى أَنْفُسِهِمْ - فَتَزَايَدَتْ بِسَبَبِهِ قُلُوبُهُمْ رَيْناً وَظُلْمَةً تَزَايُدَ قُلُوبِ الْمُؤْمِنِينَ انْشِرَاحاً وَنُوراً.

(٢) أَوْ مَكَّنَ الشَّيْطَانَ مِنْ إِغْوَائِهِمْ، ....

1. 'After Allah Most High deprived them of His graces which He grants believers,[684] and disappointed them because of their unbelief, obstinacy and self-induced blocking of their own access to the paths of success—and their hearts became further polluted and darkened as a consequence,[685] just as the hearts of the believers became more spacious and enlightened—

2. "or He enabled[686] Satan to seduce them, whereupon the latter

cribed to Him since He attributed that reinforcement to their brothers when He said, *and their brethren reinforce them in seduction* (al-Aʿrāf 7:202); how then can it be attributed to Him? And in light of the fact that He blamed them for that rebellion, if reinforcement toward it were really His then it would not be right to blame them for it. Consequently they were forced to interpret the verse figuratively, which they did in several ways." (Z) See also al-Qārī, *Minaḥ al-Rawḍ al-Azhar* (pp. 363 *lā yajib ʿalā Allāh shay'un min riʿāyat al-aṣlaḥ, khilāfan lil-Muʿtazila*). "The manifest (*ẓāhir*) is a word which has a clear meaning and yet is open to *ta'wīl* [interpretation], primarily because the meaning it conveys is not in harmony with the context in which it occurs. It is a word which has a literal/original meaning of its own but which leaves open the possibility of an alternative explanation." Mohammad Hashim Kamali, *Principles of Islamic Jurisprudence*, rev. ed. (Cambridge: Islamic Texts Society, 1991) p. 91. Hence Gimaret's translation of *ẓāhir* as "non parfaitement univoque" (*Doctrine* pp. 519-522).

684 "*Luṭf* is what the legally-responsible person chooses upon doing an act of obedience or avoiding a sin. Whatever is conducive to acts of obedience is called *tawfīq* and whatever is conducive to avoiding sins is called *'iṣma*. So each of these two is subsumed under *luṭf* as specific subsets of a general whole." (Z 1:149)

685 "The increase of pollution in their heart was named a reinforcement of rebellion and its supply was ascribed to Allah Most High. So in the predicate (*al-musnad*) there is a linguistic transference (*majāz lughawī*) and in the predication/ascription itself (*al-isnād*) a cognitive transference (*majāz 'aqlī*), because it is an ascription of the act to its causator, whereas [in their doctrine] the doer in reality is the unbelievers." (Z)

686 α, Ak, β, B, D, ε, F, Kh, P, R, Q, U, Ul, Z: أَوْ مَكَّنَ L, Sk: ومكن T: او من AQ, H, K,

فَزَادَهُمْ طُغْيَاناً: أُسْنِدَ ذٰلِكَ إِلَى اللهِ تَعَالَى إِسْنَادَ الْفِعْلِ إِلَى الْمُسَبِّبِ مَجَازاً؛ وَأَضَافَ الطُّغْيَانَ إِلَيْهِمْ، لِئَلَّا يُتَوَهَّمَ أَنَّ إِسْنَادَ الْفِعْلِ إِلَيْهِ عَلَى الْحَقِيقَةِ. وَمِصْدَاقُ ذٰلِكَ: أَنَّهُ، لَمَّا أَسْنَدَ الْمَدَّ إِلَى الشَّيَاطِينِ: أَطْلَقَ الْغَيَّ، وَقَالَ: ﴿وَإِخْوَٰنُهُمْ يَمُدُّونَهُمْ فِى ٱلْغَىِّ﴾ [الأعراف ٢٠٢].

(٣) أَوْ كَانَ أَصْلُهُ: (يَمُدُّ لَهُمْ)، بِمَعْنَى يُمْلِي لَهُمْ وَيَمُدُّ فِي أَعْمَارِهِمْ، كَيْ يَتَنَبَّهُوا وَيُطِيعُوا، فَمَا زَادُوا إِلَّا طُغْيَاناً وَعَمَهاً؛ فَحُذِفَتِ اللَّامُ وَعُدِّيَ الْفِعْلُ بِنَفْسِهِ، كَمَا فِي قَوْلِهِ تَعَالَى: ﴿وَٱخْتَارَ مُوسَىٰ قَوْمَهُۥ﴾ [الأعراف ١٥٥].

(٤) أَوِ التَّقْدِيرُ: يَمُدُّهُمْ اِسْتِصْلَاحاً، وَهُمْ مَعَ ذٰلِكَ يَعْمَهُونَ فِي طُغْيَانِهِمْ.

increased them in rebellion: that was ascribed to Allah Most High the way an act is ascribed to the causator allegorically; and He annexed rebellion to them lest one imagine the ascription of the act to Him is literal. In confirmation of the preceding, when He ascribed reinforcement to the devils He mentioned *al-ghayy* ⟨seduction⟩ in unqualified terms, saying *and their brethren reinforce them in seduction* (al-Aʿrāf 7:202).

3. "Or it is originally[687] *yamuddu lahum* in the sense of *yumlī lahum* ⟨He gives them rein/respite⟩ and He increases their lifespans so that they will heed and obey—but they increased only in rebellion and bewilderment, so the *lām* was suppressed and the verb was direct-transitivized as in the saying of the Most High, *and Mūsā chose his people* (al-Aʿrāf 7:155).[688]

4. "Or the subaudition is that He reinforces their reconciliation, but despite this they are bewildered in their rebellion."

MM: وأمكن inversion.
[687] B: أو كان α, Kh, R, Sk, U: أو كأنّ Ak, β, D, L, P, Q, T, Ul, Z: وقيل ε: و AQ, F, H, K, MM: أو
[688] "I.e. *wa-khtāra Mūsā min qawmihi* ⟨and Mūsā chose of his people⟩." (Z)

وَ(الطُّغْيَانُ) ـ بِالضَّمِّ وَالْكَسْرِ، كَـ(لُقْيَان) وَ(لِقْيَان) ـ: تَجَاوُزُ الْحَدِّ فِي الْعُتُوِّ، وَالْغُلُوُّ فِي الْكُفْرِ. وَأَصْلُهُ: تَجَاوُزُ الشَّيْءِ عَنْ مَكَانِهِ؛ قَالَ تَعَالَى: ﴿إِنَّا لَمَّا طَغَا ٱلْمَآءُ حَمَلْنَٰكُمْ﴾ [الحاقّة ١١].

وَ(الْعَمَهُ) فِي الْبَصِيرَةِ كَـ(الْعَمَى) فِي الْبَصَرِ، وَهُوَ التَّحَيُّرُ فِي الْأَمْرِ؛ يُقَالُ: (رَجُلٌ عَامِهٌ وَعَمِهٌ)، وَ(أَرْضٌ عَمْهَاءُ) لَا مَنَارَ بِهَا. قَالَ: [رجز]

أَعْمَى الْهُدَى بِالْجَاهِلِينَ الْعُمَّهْ * ....

﴿أُوْلَٰٓئِكَ ٱلَّذِينَ ٱشْتَرَوُاْ ٱلضَّلَٰلَةَ بِٱلْهُدَىٰ﴾: اِخْتَارُوهَا عَلَيْهِ، وَاسْتَبْدَلُوهَا بِهِ.

Ṭughyān ʿrebellionʾ is with *ḍamm* and also *kasr* [*ṭighyān*],[689] like *luqyān* and *liqyān* ʿchancing uponʾ. *Ṭughyān* is insolence that exceeds all bounds and exorbitant unbelief. Originally it is for something that goes beyond its own boundaries; Allah Most High said, *Truly, when the waters overflowed (ṭaghā), We carried you all* (al-Ḥāqqa 69:11).

ʿAmah ʿbewildermentʾ is in discernment—just as *ʿamā* ʿblindnessʾ is in eyesight—and consists in perplexity over something. One says a man is *ʿāmih* or *ʿamih* ʿperplexedʾ and a land is *ʿamhāʾ*: it has no lighthouse. [The poet] said: ["The trembling"]

it blinds (aʿmā) guidance to the perplexed (ʿummah) ignorant.[690]

[The purchase of ruin at the price of guidance]

[2:16] **ulāʾika-l-ladhīna shtarawu-ḍ-ḍalālata bil-hudā** ʿ*those are they who purchased error at the price of guidance*ʾ: they chose the former over the latter and exchanged one for the other.

[689] Two dialects. *Kasra* is the reading of Zayd b. ʿAlī. (*MQ*)

[690] Spoken by Ruʾba describing people who got lost in a forlorn place. See *Dīwān Ruʾbat b. al-ʿAjjāj* in *Majmūʿ Ashʿār al-ʿArab*, ed. Wilhelm Ahlwardt, 3 vols. (Berlin, Reuther & Reichard, 1903) 3:166.

وَأَصْلُهُ: بَذْلُ الثَّمَنِ لِتَحْصِيلِ مَا يُطْلَبُ مِنَ الْأَعْيَانِ، فَإِنْ كَانَ أَحَدُ الْعِوَضَيْنِ نَاضّاً، تَعَيَّنَ - مِنْ حَيْثُ إِنَّهُ لَا يُطْلَبُ لِعَيْنِهِ - أَنْ يَكُونَ ثَمَناً وَبَذْلُهُ اشْتِرَاءً؛ وَإِلَّا، فَأَيُّ الْعِوَضَيْنِ تَصَوَّرْتَهُ بِصُورَةِ الثَّمَنِ، فَبَاذِلُهُ مُشْتَرٍ، وَآخِذُهُ بَائِعٌ: وَلِذٰلِكَ عُدَّتِ الْكَلِمَتَانِ مِنَ الْأَضْدَادِ. ثُمَّ اسْتُعِيرَ لِلْإِعْرَاضِ عَمَّا فِي يَدِهِ مُحَصِّلاً بِهِ غَيْرَهُ، سَوَاءٌ كَانَ مِنَ الْمَعَانِي أَوِ الْأَعْيَانِ. وَمِنْهُ قَوْلُ الشَّاعِرِ:

[رَجَز]

Originally[691] [*shirā'* ⁽buying⁾] is the expenditure of cost to obtain the tangible properties one seeks. When one of the two instruments of exchange is current coin, it is ostensibly designated —since it is not sought for its own sake—as the cost, and its expenditure is the purchase. Otherwise,[692] whichever of the two instruments of exchange you construe to be the cost, the one who spends it is the *mushtarin* ⁽buyer⁾ and its taker the *bā'iʿ* ⁽seller⁾: hence both words[693] were deemed auto-antonyms.[694] Then it became a metaphor for the forsaking of what is in one's hand in order to obtain something else with it, whether abstractions or tangible properties. Hence the poet's words: ["The Trembling"]

691 "I.e. here 'literally' (*bi-maʿnā al-ḥaqīqa*), which is one of the conventional meanings for *aṣl*." (Q)

692 "I.e. when one of the two instruments of exchange is not current coin; for example, they are both current coin or both ready merchandise, or plots of land, or animals, or of disparate nature."" (Q)

693 "*Bayʿ* ⁽sale⁾ and *sharā'* ⁽purchase⁾. Auto-antonyms are words found in the language of the Arabs and used homophonically for two [semantic] opposites, such as *al-qur'* ⁽period⁾, which is used both for menses and for purity." (Q)

694 *Aḍdād*, translatable as antagonyms, autantonyms, contranyms or contronyms, self-antonyms and enantiodromes. See also Anṭūniūs Buṭrus, *al-Muʿjam al-Mufaṣṣal fil-Aḍdād* (Beirut: Dār al-Kutub al-ʿIlmiyya, 1424/2003) and Salim Soliman Khamash, *Aḍdād, a study of homo-polysemous opposites in Arabic*, unpublished Ph.D. diss. (Indianapolis: Indiana University, 1991).

بالضمّتين

أَخَذْتُ بِالجُمَّـةِ رَأْسـاً أَزْعَـرَا * وَبِالثَّنَايَا الْوَاضِحَاتِ الدُّرْدُرَا
وَبِالطَّوِيلِ الْعُمُرِ عُمْراً جَيْدَرَا * كَمَا اشْتَرَى الْمُسْلِمُ إِذْ تَنَصَّرَا

ثُمَّ اتُّسِعَ فِيهِ، فَاسْتُعْمِلَ لِلرَّغْبَةِ عَنِ الشَّيْءِ طَمَعاً فِي غَيْرِهِ. وَالْمَعْنَى: أَنَّهُمْ أَخَلُّوا بِالْهُدَى الَّذِي جَعَلَهُ اللهُ لَهُمْ بِالْفِطْرَةِ ﴿ٱلَّتِي فَطَرَ ٱلنَّاسَ عَلَيْهَا﴾ [الروم ٣٠]، مُحَصِّلِينَ الضَّلَالَةَ الَّتِي ذَهَبُوا إِلَيْهَا؛ أَوِ اخْتَارُوا الضَّلَالَةَ وَاسْتَحَبُّوهَا عَلَى الْهُدَى.

﴿فَمَا رَبِحَت تِّجَٰرَتُهُمْ﴾ تَرْشِيحٌ لِلْمَجَازِ: لَمَّا اسْتَعْمَلَ الْاِشْتِرَاءَ ....

I traded in the mane for a bald-head,
the sheer incisors for toothless gums,
and one long-lived for an abortive span—
as a Muslim purchased (ishtarā) when he turned Christian.[695]

Then its usage was extended to refer to something one grows uniterested in because of interest in something else.

The meaning is, they fell short of the guidance which Allah had made available them with the pristine nature *wherewith He originated all people* (al-Rūm 30:30) procuring, instead, the misguidance which they adopted; or they chose misguidance and loved it more than guidance.

fa-mā rabiḥat tijāratuhum ⟨*so their trading profited nothing*⟩ is an extended metaphor.[696] After He used "buying" ....

[695] Meaning: I exchanged a beautiful young woman for a toothless, hairless old hag. Spoken by al-Faḍl b. Qudāma al-ʿIjlī known as Abū al-Najm al-Rājiz, one of the major early poets known for their *rajaz*. (S) On him see Ibn Qutayba, *al-Shiʿr wal-Shuʿarāʾ*, ed. Aḥmad Muḥammad Shākir, 2 vols. (Cairo: Dār al-Maʿārif, 1982) 2:603-609. By "the Muslim" is meant Jabala b. al-Ayham, a Christian who came to Mecca in his best garb, became Muslim and circumambulated the Kaʿba, but someone trod on his pilgrim's cloth whereupon Jabala slapped him. The man complained to ʿUmar who ruled for requital. Jabala asked for respite until the next day but fled by night and returned to his prior beliefs, only to regret his pride in the end. (Afandi, Q)

[696] "*Tarshīḥ* is a vocable mentioned together with a transferred meaning and suited to

فِي مُعَامَلَتِهِمْ، أَتْبَعَهُ مَا يُشَاكِلُهُ تَمْثِيلاً لِخَسَارَتِهِمْ؛ وَنَحْوُهُ: [الطويل]

وَلَمَّا رَأَيْتُ النَّسْرَ عَزَّ ابْنَ دَأْيَةٍ * وَعَشَّشَ فِي وَكْرَيْهِ جَاشَ لَهُ صَدْرِي

وَ(**التِّجَارَةُ**): طَلَبُ الرِّبْحِ بِالْبَيْعِ وَالشِّرَاءِ.

وَ(**الرِّبْحُ**): الْفَضْلُ عَلَى رَأْسِ الْمَالِ؛ وَلِذٰلِكَ سُمِّيَ (شَفًا). وَإِسْنَادُهُ إِلَى التِّجَارَةِ - وَهُوَ لِأَرْبَابِهَا -: عَلَى الْاِتِّسَاعِ، ....

to represent their behavior, He followed it up with something conformant as a simile for their loss. Likewise: ["The Long"]

and when I saw the vulture beat the crow,
and nest in its two lairs—my bosom heaved.[697]

Al-tijāra ⁽trade⁾ is the pursuit of profit through buying and selling. *Al-ribḥ* ⁽profit⁾ is the surplus over the [outlay of] capital, hence it name of *shafā* ⁽edge⁾. It was ascribed to trade—when it [properly] belongs to its practicioners—metonymically, ...

its meaning, which is manifestly intended in the allegorical sense, whether already cited or about to be. The author here has decided that *tarshīḥ* is a proverbial metaphor (*istiʿāra tamthīliyya*)." (Q) "It is used mostly with metaphors." (S) "Carrying out a metaphor" in Margoliouth, *Chrestomathia* (pp. 72, 182 n. 409). "Catalysis—the use of a word or words without which an intended trope would not be realized. It is not peculiar to any one trope but may be the accompaniment of assimilation, parallelism, double entendre and many others" in Cachia, *Arch Rhetorician* (p. 62-63 §95) cf. verse 10 of al-Suyūṭī, *Naẓm al-Badīʿ fī Madḥi Khayri Shafīʿ*, ed. ʿAlī Muʿawwaḍ and ʿĀdil ʿAbd al-Mawjūd (Aleppo: Dār al-Qalam al-ʿArabī, 1416/ 1995) pp. 62-63; Ṭabāna, *Muʿjam al-Balāgha* (p. 252-253 §324); Aḥmad Maṭlūb, *Muʿjam al-Muṣṭalaḥāt al-Balāghiyya wa-Taṭawwuruhā*, 3 vols. (Baghdad, al-Majmaʿ al-ʿIlmī al-ʿIrāqī, 1983-1987) 2:132-134; and Inʿām ʿAkkāwī, *al-Muʿjam al-Mufaṣṣal fī ʿUlūm al-Balāgha*, 2nd ed. (Beirut: Dār al-Kutub al-ʿIlmiyya, 1417/1996) pp. 305-306.

697 Spoken by al-Kumayt b. Zayd, cf. *Shiʿr al-Kumayt b. Zayd al-Asadī*, ed. Dāwūd Sallūm, 3 vols. (Baghdad: Maktabat al-Andalus, 1969) 1:241. I.e. "when I saw the white hair of old age beat the black hair of youth, and take over both the hair and beard—like the crow's summer and winter nests—I sobbed." The nesting is a *tarshīḥ* for irreversible whitening and the two nests another *tarshīḥ*, standing for the hair and beard. (S)

لِتَلَبُّسِهَا بِالْفَاعِلِ، أَوْ لِمُشَابَهَتِهَا إِيَّاهُ مِنْ حَيْثُ إِنَّهَا سَبَبُ الرِّبْحِ وَالْخُسْرَانِ.

﴿وَمَا كَانُوا۟ مُهْتَدِينَ﴾ لِطُرُقِ التِّجَارَةِ؛ فَإِنَّ الْمَقْصُودَ مِنْهَا: سَلَامَةُ
رَأْسِ الْمَالِ وَالرِّبْحُ؛ وَهٰؤُلَاءِ قَدْ أَضَاعُوا الطَّلِبَتَيْنِ، لِأَنَّ رَأْسَ مَالِهِمْ كَانَ
الْفِطْرَةَ السَّلِيمَةَ وَالْعَقْلَ الصِّرْفَ؛ فَلَمَّا اعْتَقَدُوا هٰذِهِ الضَّلَالَاتِ، بَطَلَ
اسْتِعْدَادُهُمْ، وَاخْتَلَّ عَقْلُهُمْ، وَلَمْ يَبْقَ لَهُمْ رَأْسُ مَالٍ يَتَوَسَّلُونَ بِهِ إِلَى دَرْكِ مَعًا
الْحَقِّ، وَنَيْلِ الْكَمَالِ. فَبَقُوا خَاسِرِينَ، آيِسِينَ مِنَ الرِّبْحِ، فَاقِدِينَ لِلْأَصْلِ.

﴿مَثَلُهُمْ كَمَثَلِ ٱلَّذِى ٱسْتَوْقَدَ نَارًا﴾: لَمَّا جَاءَ بِحَقِيقَةِ حَالِهِمْ، عَقَّبَهَا
بِضَرْبِ الْمَثَلِ، زِيَادَةً فِي التَّوْضِيحِ وَالتَّقْرِيرِ. ....

because it possesses the characteristics of its agent, or because it resembles an agent from the perspective of being the cause for profit and loss.

wa-mā kānū muhtadīn ⟨*and they were not guided at all*⟩ to the ways of trade. For its objective is to safeguard capital and to profit, but those have completely failed to achieve either goal, because their capital was their sound pristine natures and pure minds; and when they embraced those fallacies their aptitude fell apart and their minds became muddled. No capital remained for them to use as a means to apprehend truth and acquire perfection. Thus they lingered in loss and despaired of reaping profit, having lost their principal.

[2:17] **mathaluhum ka-mathali-l-ladhī stawqada nāran** ⟨*their likeness is as the likeness of the one that kindled a fire*⟩: after describing the reality of their state, He followed up by setting forth a parable[698] as further elucidation and resolution. ....

698 "Parable: A comparison, a similitude; any saying or narration in which something

فَإِنَّهُ أَوْقَعُ فِي الْقَلْبِ وَأَقْمَعُ لِلْخَصْمِ الأَلَدِّ، لِأَنَّهُ يُرِيكَ الْمُتَخَيَّلَ مُحَقَّقاً وَالْمَعْقُولَ مَحْسُوساً. وَلِأَمْرٍ مَا، أَكْثَرَ اللهُ فِي كُتُبِهِ الأَمْثَالَ، وَفَشَتْ فِي كَلَامِ الأَنْبِيَاءِ وَالْحُكَمَاءِ.

وَ(الْمَثَلُ) فِي الأَصْلِ: بِمَعْنَى النَّظِيرِ؛ يُقَالُ: (مِثْلٌ)، وَ(مَثَلٌ)، وَ(مَثِيلٌ)، كَـ(شِبْهٍ)، وَ(شَبَهٍ)، وَ(شَبِيهٍ)؛ ثُمَّ قِيلَ لِلْقَوْلِ السَّائِرِ، الْمُمَثَّلِ مَضْرِبُهُ .....

[Parables, similes and proverbs]

For, truly, parables are more effective in the heart and more forceful against the bitterest enemy, because they visualize for you, realistically and sensibly, what is imagined and conceived in the mind. For some great purpose, Allah has multiplied parables in His Books and they are widespread in the discourses of the Prophets and sages.[699]

Al-mathal ˹likeness˺ originally means *al-naẓīr* ˹match˺. One says *mathal*, *mithl* ˹like˺, *mathīl* ˹equal˺, like *shabah* ˹similarity˺, *shibh* ˹similar˺, *shabīh* ˹resembling˺. Then it became applied to proverbs,[700] whereby the locus of coining is exemplified ....

is expressed in terms of something else.... *spec.* A fictitious narrative or allegory (usually something that might naturally occur), by which moral or spiritual relations are typically figured or set forth." *Oxford English Dictionary*. "Parabola: The explicit drawing of a parallel between two essentially dissimilar things, especially with a moral or didactic purpose" Burton, *Silva Rhetoricae, s.v.* 'A proverb is a short, generally known sentence of the folk which contains wisdom, truth, morals, and traditional views in a metaphorical, fixed and memorizable form and which is handed down from generation to generation" Wolfgang Mieder in his introduction to the re-edition of Archer Taylor, *The Proverb* (Cambridge, Mass., Harvard University Press, 1931), ed. Wolfgang Mieder (New York: Peter Lang, 1985) p. 119.

699 See Ibn al-Qayyim, *al-Amthāl fil-Qur'ān al-Karīm*, ed. Sa'īd al-Khaṭīb (Beirut: Dār al-Ma'rifa, 1981) and 'Abd Allāh al-Jarbū', *al-Amthāl al-Qur'āniyya al-Qiyāsiyya al-Maḍrūba lil-Īmān billāh*, 3 vols. (Medina: al-Jāmi'a al-Islāmiyya, 1424 /2003).

700 "Proverb: A short pithy saying in common and recognized use; a concise sentence,

بِمَوْرِدِهِ؛ وَلَا يُضْرَبُ إِلَّا مَا فِيهِ غَرَابَةٌ، وَلِذٰلِكَ حُوفِظَ عَلَيْهِ مِنَ التَّغْيِيرِ. ثُمَّ اسْتُعِيرَ لِكُلِّ حَالٍ، أَوْ قِصَّةٍ، أَوْ صِفَةٍ لَهَا شَأْنٌ وَفِيهَا غَرَابَةٌ، مِثْلَ قَوْلِهِ تَعَالَى: ﴿مَّثَلُ ٱلْجَنَّةِ ٱلَّتِى وُعِدَ ٱلْمُتَّقُونَ﴾ [الرعد ٣٥] وَقَوْلِهِ تَعَالَى: ﴿وَلِلَّهِ ٱلْمَثَلُ ٱلْأَعْلَىٰ﴾ [النحل ٦٠].

وَالْمَعْنَى: حَالُهُمُ الْعَجِيبَةُ الشَّأْنِ كَحَالِ مَنِ اسْتَوْقَدَ نَاراً. وَ﴿ٱلَّذِى﴾: (أ) بِمَعْنَى (الَّذِينَ) كَمَا فِي قَوْلِهِ تَعَالَى ﴿وَخُضْتُمْ كَٱلَّذِى خَاضُوٓا۟﴾ [التوبة ٦٩]،

by an original occurrence;[701] but only what is somewhat singular is coined as one, hence it is resistant to change.[702] Then it was borrowed to refer to every situation or account or description of importance that is singular, as in the saying of Allah Most High, *the likeness of the Garden that is promised to the God-fearing* (al-Raʿd 13:35) and His saying, *and Allah owns the most sublime likeness* (al-Naḥl 16:60).

[*The one* stands for a collective category: analysis of *al-ladhī*]

The meaning is that their very strange state is as that of those who kindled a fire, [etc.], while ***al-ladhī*** ⁽the one⁾ means

I. *al-ladhīna* ⁽those⁾—as in the saying of Allah Most High, *and you plunged like the one (kal-ladhī) they plunged* [=*like those (kal-*

often metaphorical or alliterative in form, which is held to express some truth ascertained by experience or observation and familiar to all; an adage, a wise saw" *OED*.

701 "For example, the proverb's original occurrence (*mawrid al-mathal*) for the saying 'In the summer you lost the milk' is the story of Dakhtanūs the daughter of Luqayt b. Zurāra, who was married to ʿAmr b. ʿAmr but disliked him because he was old. He divorced her and and a young man married her. She did not produce milk, so she sent word to ʿAmr asking for a milk-nurse, whereupon he said that phrase. The proverbial locus of coining (*maḍrib al-mathal*) here is the situation of someone who requests something which he previously wasted of his own doing." (S 1:416)

702 Taftāzānī and Jurjānī viewed its being a formal metaphor as a stronger reason. (S)

إِنْ جُعِلَ مَرْجِعُ الضَّمِيرِ فِي ﴿بِنُورِهِمْ﴾. وَإِنَّمَا جَازَ ذَلِكَ ـ وَلَمْ يَجُزْ وَضْعُ الْقَائِمِ مَوْضِعَ الْقَائِمِينَ ـ لِأَنَّهُ غَيْرُ مَقْصُودٍ بِالْوَصْفِ، بَلِ الْجُمْلَةُ الَّتِي هِيَ صِلَتُهُ. وَهُوَ: وُصْلَةٌ إِلَى وَصْفِ الْمَعْرِفَةِ بِهَا؛ لِأَنَّهُ لَيْسَ بِاسْمٍ تَامٍّ، بَلْ هُوَ كَالْجُزْءِ مِنْهُ؛ فَحَقُّهُ أَنْ لَا يُجْمَعَ ـ كَمَا لَا تُجْمَعُ أَخَوَاتُهَا ـ وَيَسْتَوِيَ فِيهِ الْوَاحِدُ وَالْجَمْعُ. وَلَيْسَ (الَّذِينَ) جَمْعُهُ الْمُصَحَّحُ، بَلْ ذُو زِيَادَةٍ زِيدَتْ لِزِيَادَةِ الْمَعْنَى؛ وَلِذَلِكَ جَاءَ بِالْيَاءِ أَبَدًا، ....

ladhīna) that plunged] (al-Tawba 9:69)[703]—if we make the pronoun in **bi-nūrihim** refer to it. This can be done—although we cannot give a word a double duty as both singular and plural[704]—only because [*al-ladhī*] is not meant to be described, but rather the sentence that is its definite relative clause. It itself serves as a [mere] connective to the description that it makes definite. Another reason is that it is not a full-fledged noun[705] but more like a portion of one; thus it deserves not to be pluralized—just as its siblings[706] are not pluralized—and to stand indifferently for the singular and the plural. Nor is *al-ladhīna* its sound plural form but rather a case of accretion added to reflect an added meaning. That is why it has forever come with a *yā'* [only], ...

---

[703] This is readable both as *wa-khuḍtum kal-ladhī[na] khāḍū* 'and you plunged like those that plunged' and as *wa-khuḍtum kal-[khawḍ al-]ladhī khāḍū* 'and you plunged into the same [corruption] they plunged in' cf. S (1:419) citing Ibn ʿAṭiyya; Aḥmad al-Kharrāṭ, *al-Mujtabā min Mushkil Iʿrāb al-Qurʾān al-Karīm*, 4 vols. (Medina: Mujammaʿ al-Malik Fahd li-Ṭibāʿat al-Muṣḥaf al-Sharīf, 1426/2005) 2:403; and Wahba al-Zuḥaylī, *al-Tafsīr al-Munīr fīl ʿAqīda wal-Sharīʿa wal-Manhaj*, 10th ed., 17 vols. (Damascus: Dār al-Fikr, 1430/2009) 5:653.

[704] "According to the majority; and they interpreted such cases figuratively." (Q)

[705] "Since it is not a full-fledged noun in conveying meaning as long as its *ṣila* does not accompany it, it is never constructed as a subject or object etc. except together with its *ṣila*." (Z)

[706] "Such as the connectives *man* and *mā*." (Q) All the mss.: أخواتها Q, Z: أخواته

عَلَى اللُّغَةِ الْفَصِيحَةِ الَّتِي عَلَيْهَا التَّنْزِيلُ. وَلِكَوْنِهِ مُسْتَطَالاً بِصِلَتِهِ، اِسْتَحَقَّ التَّخْفِيفَ: وَلِذَلِكَ بُولِغَ فِيهِ فَحُذِفَ يَاؤُهُ، ثُمَّ كَسْرَتُهُ، ثُمَّ اقْتُصِرَ عَلَى اللَّامِ فِي أَسْمَاءِ الْفَاعِلِينَ وَالْمَفْعُولِينَ. (ب) أَوْ قُصِدَ بِهِ جِنْسُ الْمُسْتَوْقِدِينَ، (ج) أَوِ الْفَوْجُ الَّذِي اسْتَوْقَدَ.

وَ(الْإِسْتِيقَادُ): طَلَبُ الْوُقُودِ وَالسَّعْيُ فِي تَحْصِيلِهِ؛ وَهُوَ سُطُوعُ النَّارِ وَارْتِفَاعُ لَهَبِهَا.

in conformity with the chaste idiom in which revelation came down. Now, because it was drawn out by its relative clause, it deserved alleviation,[707] which it got to extremes: its *yā'* was suppressed, then its *kasra*; and finally the *lām* was enough in the names of subjects and objects.[708]

II. Alternately, the species of those that kindle fires is intended;[709]

III. or the throng that kindled a fire.[710]

Al-istīqād ⟨kindling⟩ is the process of igniting something and doing all that is necessary to achieve it, namely, fire catching on and the rising of its flames.

707 "Through suppression of the *nūn*." (Z)

708 "When we say *al-ḍāribu abāh Zayd* ⟨the striker of his father is Zayd⟩, its meaning is *al-ladhī ḍaraba abāhu Zayd* ⟨the one that struck his father is Zayd⟩ as proved by the saying of Allah Most High *inna al-muṣṣaddiqīna wal-muṣṣaddiqāti wa-aqraḍū Allāha qarḍan ḥasanan* ⟨*Verily the givers of charity male and female and loan Allah an excellent loan*⟩ (al-Ḥadīd 57:18). The meaning here is *inna al-ladhīna iṣṣaddaqū wa-aqraḍū* ⟨*Verily those who give charity and loan...*⟩ except that the verb was produced in the form of the nominal agent or direct object according to contextual need... after the abbreviation of *al-ladhī* and its change to the *al-* form, but with the verbal sense unchanged. Hence the conjunctive sentence following *al-* was also a verbal clause." (Z)

709 "I.e. the assembly of those that kindle fires; for even if it is in the singular, what is meant is the multitude." (S)

710 "I.e. the object of description is subauded as a singular vocable carrying a plural sense, such as *al-jam'* ⟨the group⟩, *al-fawj* ⟨the throng⟩ and the like." (S)

بالفتح

وَاشْتِقَاقُ (النَّارِ) مِنْ (نَارَ يَنُورُ نَوْراً) إِذَا نَفَرَ لِأَنَّ فِيهَا حَرَكَةً وَاضْطِرَاباً.

﴿فَلَمَّآ أَضَآءَتْ مَا حَوْلَهُۥ﴾ أَيْ: النَّارُ مَا حَوْلَ الْمُسْتَوْقِدِ - إِنْ جَعَلْتَهَا مُتَعَدِّيَةً - وَإِلَّا: أَمْكَنَ أَنْ تَكُونَ مُسْنَدَةً إِلَى ﴿مَا﴾ - وَالتَّأْنِيثُ لِأَنَّ مَا حَوْلَهُ أَشْيَاءُ وَأَمَاكِنُ - أَوْ إِلَى ضَمِيرِ النَّارِ.

وَ﴿مَا﴾ مَوْصُولَةٌ فِي مَعْنَى الْأَمْكِنَةِ - نُصِبَ عَلَى الظَّرْفِ - أَوْ مَزِيدَةٌ. وَ ﴿حَوْلَهُۥ﴾ ظَرْفٌ. وَتَأْلِيفُ الْحَوْلِ لِلدَّوَرَانِ: وَقِيلَ لِلْعَامِ (حَوْلٌ) لِأَنَّهُ يَدُورُ.

﴿ذَهَبَ ٱللَّهُ بِنُورِهِمْ﴾: (أ) جَوَابُ ﴿لَمَّآ﴾؛ وَالضَّمِيرُ ....

Al-nār ⁽fire⁾ stems from *nāra* ⁽to become clear⁾ *yanūru nawran* when something is agitated, because it entails movement and shaking.

fa-lammā aḍā'at mā ḥawlahu ⁽*as soon as it illuminated his surroundings*⁾, that is, the fire [shining] on the surroundings of the kindler if you treat it as a transitive; otherwise it may be predicated to *mā* [= *but as soon as his surroundings shone*], in which case the feminine case [of the verb's subject pronoun] is because his surroundings are things and places, or [in the first case] as a pronoun for the fire.

Mā ⁽what, all⁾ is a definite conjunctive[711] in the sense of localities, in the accusative case as a local vessel; or an additive; and ***ḥawlahu*** ⁽around him⁾ is a local preposition. [The word] *ḥawl* is constituted to denote circularity.[712] The year is called *ḥawl* because it goes around.

dhahaba-l-Lāhu bi-nūrihim ⁽*the One God took away their light*⁾ is (i) the apodosis of *lammā* ⁽as soon as⁾ and the personal pro-

[711] Cf. the gloss for *man* in al-Baqara 2:8 above.

[712] "I.e. the composition of the letters of the vocable *ḥawl* in that particular order is to indicate circularity." (Z)

لـ﴿ٱلَّذِى﴾، وَجَمْعُهُ لِلْحَمْلِ عَلَى الْمَعْنَى. وَعَلَى هٰذَا إِنَّمَا قَالَ: ﴿بِنُورِهِمْ﴾، وَلَمْ يَقُلْ: (بِنَارِهِمْ)؛ لِأَنَّهُ الْمُرَادُ مِنْ إِيقَادِهَا.

(ب) أَوْ اِسْتِئْنَافٌ، أُجِيبَ بِهِ اعْتِرَاضُ سَائِلٍ يَقُولُ: مَا بَالُهُمْ شُبِّهَتْ حَالُهُمْ بِحَالِ مُسْتَوْقِدٍ اِنْطَفَأَتْ نَارُهُ؟

(ج) أَوْ بَدَلٌ مِنْ جُمْلَةِ التَّمْثِيلِ، عَلَى سَبِيلِ الْبَيَانِ.

وَالضَّمِيرُ عَلَى الْوَجْهَيْنِ: لِلْمُنَافِقِينَ؛ وَالْجَوَابُ مَحْذُوفٌ ـ كَمَا فِي قَوْلِهِ تَعَالَى: ﴿فَلَمَّا ذَهَبُوا۟ بِهِۦ﴾ [يوسف ١٥] ـ لِلْإِيجَازِ وَأَمْنِ الْإِلْتِبَاسِ.

noun refers back to *al-ladhī* ‹the one›. It was put in the plural because it is understood according to meaning, which is why He said *bi-nūrihim* ‹*their light*› and not *bi-nārihim* ‹*their fire*› as the former is the purpose of kindling the latter.

(ii) Or it is a resumption rebutting the objection of a questioner who asks, "Why was their state compared to that of a kindler whose fire went out?"

(iii) or a substitute for the parabolical clause for further elucidation.[713] The pronoun in both latter instances refers to the hypocrites[714] and the apodosis is suppressed—as in the saying of Allah Most High, *So when they took him away* (Yūsuf 12:15)[715]—for concision and unambiguity.[716]

713 "I.e. a substitute standing for an expository adjunction (*ʿaṭf al-bayān*) to clarify the antecedent(*al-matbūʿ*)." (Z)

714 "I.e. in *nūrihim* ‹their light› regardless whether *dhahaba Allāhu* is resumptive or a substitute." (Z)

715 *So when they took him away with them and resolved to put him into the bottom of the well—but We revealed to him: You will verily inform them [one day] about this act of theirs, they being unaware.* (Yūsuf 12:15)

716 "The subaudition then is: 'When it lit his surroundings, his fire died down and went out,' with the understanding that the subsequent state of the kindler is not de-

وَإِسْنَادُ الذَّهَابِ إِلَى اللهِ تَعَالَى: (أ) إِمَّـا لِأَنَّ الْكُـلَّ بِفِعْلِـهِ؛ (ب) أَوْ لِأَنَّ الْإِطْفَاءَ حَصَـلَ بِسَبَبٍ خَفِـيٍّ، أَوْ أَمْـرٍ سَـمَاوِيٍّ كَـرِيحٍ أَوْ مَطَـرٍ؛ (ج) أَوْ لِلْمُبَالَغَةِ؛ وَلِذٰلِكَ عُدِّيَ الْفِعْـلُ بِالْبَـاءِ دُونَ الْهَمْـزَةِ، لِـمَا فِيهَـا مِـنْ مَعْنَـى الْإِسْتِصْحَابِ وَالْإِسْتِمْسَاكِ. يُقَالُ: (ذَهَبَ السُّلْطَانُ بِمَالِهِ) إِذَا أَخَذَهُ. وَمَـا أَخَذَهُ اللهُ وَأَمْسَكَهُ، فَلَا مُرْسِلَ لَهُ! وَلِذٰلِكَ عَدَلَ عَـنِ الضَّـوْءِ ـ الَّـذِي هُـوَ مُقْتَضَى اللَّفْظِ ـ إِلَى النُّورِ؛ فَإِنَّهُ لَوْ قِيلَ: (ذَهَبَ اللهُ بِضَوْئِهِمْ)، احْتَمَلَ ذَهَابُهُ بِمَا فِي الضَّوْءِ مِنَ الزِّيَادَةِ، وَبَقَاءُ مَا يُسَمَّى نُوراً؛ وَالْغَرَضُ إِزَالَةُ النُّورِ عَنْهُمْ

[How Allah takes away light]

The predication of "taking away" to Allah Most High is

(i) either because everything is through His act;

(ii) or because the extinction took place through some hidden cause or heavenly event such as wind or or rain;

(iii) or for intensiveness, hence the verb was transitized with the *bā'* instead of the *hamza*,[717] due to the former's connotations of appropriation and seizure. One says *dhahaba al-sulṭān bi-mālih* ⁽the ruler took away his property⁾ when he seizes it; and whatever Allah seizes and withholds, none can release! That is why He shifted from *ḍaw'* ⁽illumination⁾—which is what the wording dictated—to *nūr* ⁽light⁾. Were it said "Allah took away their illumination" it might suggest that He took away the intensity of illumination while there remained what is called light, whereas the point is to do away with their light …...........................

scribed, just as in Sūrat Yūsuf—upon him peace—*so when they took him away with him*, in which the subaudition is: 'They did to him whatever they did of harm.'" (Z)

[717] I.e. *dhahaba bi-* ⁽to take away⁾ instead of *adhhaba* ⁽to do away with⁾.

رَأساً. أَلَا تَرَى كَيْفَ قَرَّرَ ذٰلِكَ وَأَكَّدَهُ بِقَوْلِهِ:

﴿وَتَرَكَهُمْ فِي ظُلُمَٰتٍ لَّا يُبْصِرُونَ﴾، فَذَكَرَ الظُّلْمَةَ الَّتِي هِيَ عَدَمُ النُّورِ وَانْطِمَاسُهُ بِالْكُلِّيَّةِ، وَجَمَعَهَا، وَنَكَّرَهَا، وَوَصَفَهَا بِأَنَّهَا ظُلْمَةٌ خَالِصَةٌ، لَا يَتَرَاءَى فِيهَا شَبَحَانِ؟ وَ(تَرَكَ) فِي الْأَصْلِ: بِمَعْنَى طَرَحَ وَخَلَّى؛ وَلَهُ مَفْعُولٌ وَاحِدٌ، فَضُمِّنَ مَعْنَى (صَيَّرَ)، فَجَرَى مَجْرَى أَفْعَالِ الْقُلُوبِ، كَقَوْلِهِ تَعَالَى

at once.[718] Do you not see how He resolved that and emphasized it by saying,

wa-tarakahum fī ẓulumātin lā yubṣirūna ⁽*and He left them in darknesses, sightless*⁾, mentioning darkness—the absence of light and its complete obliteration—which He made plural, left indefinite and described as pitch darkness in which no two forms can be distinguished one from another?

Taraka ⁽he left⁾ originally means *ṭaraḥa* ⁽cast off⁾ and *khallā* ⁽left alone⁾. It has a single direct object and so includes the sense of *ṣayyara* ⁽he turned [s.th.] into⁾ and is treated like verbs that signify mental operations,[719] as in the saying of Allah Most High

[718] "His allusion to *ḍaw'* ⁽illumination⁾ being more powerful than *nūr* ⁽light⁾ was mentioned by several. The author of *al-Falak al-Dā'ir [ʿalā al-Mathal al-Sā'ir* by the Muʿtazili ʿAbd al-Ḥamīd b. Hibat Allāh al-Madā'inī, known as Ibn Abī al-Ḥadīd (d. 655/1257), written in refutation of the Shāfiʿī philologist Ḍiyā' al-Dīn Ibn al-Athīr al-Jazarī's (d. 637/1240) *al-Mathal al-Sā'ir fī Adab al-Kātib wal-Shāʿir*] said, 'this is not true: we perused the books of language and did not find it as a corroborant for what they claimed, nor does current usage (*al-iṣṭilāḥ al-ʿurfī*) support it. Ibn al-Sikkīt in *Iṣlāḥ al-Manṭiq* said *al-nūr* is *al-ḍiyā'*, so he made them one and the same thing. Nor is there in the saying of Allah Most High *He is the one Who made the sun a ḍiyā' and the moon a nūr* (Yūnus 10:5) any indication of a difference.' Ṭībī replied that Ibn al-Sikkīt had expounded the literal meaning according to coinage (*al-waḍʿ*), not usage (*al-istiʿmāl*); but the perspective cited when differentiating is according to usage." (S)

[719] Such as *ẓanna, qaddara, ḥasiba, jaʿala, ʿalima*, e.g. "They consider him the leader." Also translated as "verbs of affectivity," cf. Antoine el-Dahdah, *A Dictionary of Uni-*

﴿وَتَرَكَهُمْ فِي ظُلُمَٰتٍ﴾، وَقَوْلِ الشَّاعِرِ: [الكامل]

فَتَرَكْتُهُ جَزَرَ السِّبَاعِ يَنُشْنَهُ * [يَقْضَمْنَ حُسْنَ بَنَانِهِ وَالْمِعْصَمِ]

وَ(الظُّلْمَةُ) مَأْخُوذَةٌ مِنْ قَوْلِهِمْ: (مَا ظَلَمَكَ أَنْ تَفْعَلَ كَذَا؟)، أَيْ مَا مَنَعَكَ؟، لِأَنَّهَا تَسُدُّ الْبَصَرَ وَتَمْنَعُ الرُّؤْيَةَ. وَظُلُمَاتُهُمْ:

(أ) ظُلْمَةُ الْكُفْرِ، وَظُلْمَةُ النِّفَاقِ، وَظُلْمَةُ يَوْمِ الْقِيَامَةِ - ﴿يَوْمَ تَرَى الْمُؤْمِنِينَ وَالْمُؤْمِنَٰتِ يَسْعَىٰ نُورُهُم بَيْنَ أَيْدِيهِمْ وَبِأَيْمَٰنِهِم﴾ [الحديد ١٢] - ....

and He left them in pitch darkness, and the poet's verse: ["The Perfect"]

So I left him a slaughter stock of beasts; they have at him.[720]

Al-ẓulma ⟨darkness⟩ is taken from the idiom *mā ẓalamaka an tafʿala kadhā* ⟨what darkened you from doing such?⟩, that is, what prevented you? because it obstructs sight and hinders vision. Their ***ẓulumāt*** ⟨darknesses⟩ are

(i) the darkness of unbelief, the darkness of hypocrisy and the darkness of the Day of Resurrection—*the day you will see the believers, men and women, with their light shining forth before them and on their right hands* (al-Ḥadīd 57:12);

versal Arabic Grammar: Arabic-English (Beirut: Librairie du Liban, 1992) p. 153.

720 Spoken by Abū al-Mughallas ʿAntara b. Shaddād b. Muʿāwiya al-Makhzūmī (d. 14BH?/608?) from his major poem that became one of the seven to be hung on the Kaʿba, cf. Ibn al-Anbārī, *Sharḥ al-Qaṣāʾid al-Sabʿ al-Ṭiwāl al-Jāhiliyyāt*, ed. ʿAbd al-Salām Hārūn, 5th ed. (Cairo: Dār al-Maʿārif, 1382/1963) pp. 374-375, verse 52; *Dīwān ʿAntara*, ed. Muḥammad Saʿīd Mawlawī (Beirut: al-Maktab al-Islāmī, 1390/1970) pp. 210-211 verse 57; and al-Khaṭīb al-Tabrīzī, *Sharḥ Dīwān ʿAntara*, ed. Majīd Ṭrād (Beirut: Dār al-Kitāb al-ʿArabī, 1412/.1992) pp.174-175 verse 57. Only the first hemistich is mentioned in α, Ak, β, B, D, ε, I, J, Kh, L, P, Q, R, T, U, Ul, Z. Second hemistich: in AQ, F, H, K, MM, Sk يَقْضَمْنَ حُسنَ بَنَانِهِ وَالْمِعْصَمِ *champing his graceful fingers and arms*; in A, S, Tabrīzī and Mawlawī مَا بَيْنَ قُلَّةِ رَأْسِهِ وَالمِعْصَمِ *from the crown of his head down to his feet.* Ibn al-Anbārī cites both versions. *Miʿṣam* is "the place for bracelets/armlets" but can also mean ankles by transference.

(ب) أَوْ ظُلْمَةُ الضَّلَالِ، وَظُلْمَةُ سَخَطِ الله، وَظُلْمَةُ الْعِقَابِ السَّرْمَدِيِّ،

(ج) أَوْ ظُلْمَةٌ شَدِيدَةٌ كَأَنَّهَا ظُلْمَةٌ مُتَرَاكِمَةٌ.

وَمَفْعُولُ ﴿لَا يُبْصِرُونَ﴾ مِنْ قَبِيلِ الْمَطْرُوحِ الْمَتْرُوكِ، فَكَأَنَّ الْفِعْلَ غَيْرُ مُتَعَدٍّ. وَالْآيَةُ:

(١) مَثَلٌ ضَرَبَهُ اللهُ لِمَنْ آتَاهُ ضَرْباً مِنَ الْهُدَى فَأَضَاعَهُ، وَلَمْ يَتَوَصَّلْ بِهِ إِلَى نَعِيمِ الْأَبَدِ، فَبَقِيَ مُتَحَيِّراً مُتَحَسِّراً، تَقْرِيراً وَتَوْضِيحاً لِمَا تَضَمَّنَتْهُ الْآيَةُ الْأُولَى. وَيَدْخُلُ تَحْتَ عُمُومِهِ:

(أ) هٰؤُلَاءِ الْمُنَافِقُونَ، فَإِنَّهُمْ أَضَاعُوا مَا نَطَقَتْ بِهِ أَلْسِنَتُهُمْ مِنَ الْحَقِّ ...

(ii) or the darkness of misguidance, the darkness of divine wrath and the darkness of everlasting retribution;

(iii) or a pitch darkness, as it were multi-layered.

The object of *lā yubṣirūn* ‹they do not see› is discarded and irrelevant, so the verb is tantamount to an intransitive.[721]

[Parables of error: hypocrites, atheists and false Sufis]

The verse

I. is a parable[722] Allah coined for one whom He gave some form of guidance and who then wastes it instead of using it to reach everlasting bliss, after which he remains confused and regretful, as a resolution and elucidation of everything the previous verse entails.[723] Its general meaning covers

(i) those hypocrites, for they neglected what their tongues ....

721 "I.e. there is no intended subaudition." (Z)

722 "That is, the citing of an equivalent." (Z)

723 "Namely, *those are they who purchased error at the price of guidance so their trading profited nothing and they were not guided at all* (al-Baqara 2:16)." (Z)

بِاسْتِبْطَانِ الْكُفْرِ وَإِظْهَارِهِ حِينَ خَلَوْا إِلَى شَيَاطِينِهِمْ؛

(ب) وَمَنْ آثَرَ الضَّلَالَةَ عَلَى الْهُدَى الْمَجْعُولِ لَهُ بِالْفِطْرَةِ، أَوِ ارْتَدَّ عَنْ دِينِهِ بَعْدَ مَا آمَنَ؛

(ج) وَمَنْ صَحَّ لَهُ أَحْوَالُ الْإِرَادَةِ، فَادَّعَى أَحْوَالَ الْمَحَبَّةِ، فَأَذْهَبَ اللهُ عَنْهُ مَا أَشْرَق عَلَيْهِ مِنْ أَنْوَارِ الْإِرَادَةِ؛ ....

had uttered of the truth by harboring unbelief and displaying it whenever they retired unto their devils;

(ii) whoever preferred misguidance to the right guidance that was granted him through his pristine nature or recanted his religion after first believing;

(iii) and whoever rightly possessed the states of an aspirant[724] but claimed the states of a lover,[725] whereupon Allah removed from him what He had shone upon him of the lights of aspiration.

[724] "What is meant by aspiration here is the first of the states of the wayfarer (*al-sālik*) for whom the light of aspiration has taken place in general terms as inferred from his saying Allah Most High removed from him etc.' Aspiration in the terminology of the Sufis—as gathered from the discourse of the authoritative commentators—is an ember from the fire of love in the heart that dictates compliance with the summons of truth. Love is the appurtenance (*ta'alluq*) of hearts to the beloved alone without regard for anything or anyone else. Its states are whatever happens to the seeker at that time. Its beginning is to delight in acts of worship and its end is love of the [Divine] Essence for the sake of the Essence in the presence of absolute Oneness." (Q 2:265)

[725] "I.e. the states typical of the great figures of spiritual connection, whereupon Allah removed from him etc., because he claimed arrival at a station higher than his, which is a lie similar to hypocrisy… likewise the student of knowledge who claims a station higher than his and scorns the masters of high stations because he thinks he is higher than them…. He remains in the darkness of compound ignorance (*jahl murakkab*), sightless of the way out; and that is the state of most students in our time… It also refers to those who desire spiritual realities for which they are not ready; for the wayfarer, when something higher than his station becomes disclosed to him, might not be able to carry it, and it will not firmly settle for him, so he will become gravely misguided because of it." (Q 2:265-266)

(٢) أَوْ مَثَلٌ (أ) لِإِيمَانِهِمْ -مِنْ حَيْثُ إِنَّهُ يَعُودُ عَلَيْهِمْ بِحَقْنِ الدِّمَاءِ، وَسَلَامَةِ الْأَمْوَالِ وَالْأَوْلَادِ، وَمُشَارَكَةِ الْمُسْلِمِينَ فِي الْمَغَانِمِ وَالْأَحْكَامِ- بِالنَّارِ الْمُوقَدَةِ لِلْاسْتِضَاءَةِ؛ (ب) وَلِذَهَابِ أَثَرِهِ، وَانْطِمَاسِ نُورِهِ بِإِهْلَاكِهِمْ وَإِفْشَاءِ حَالِهِمْ: بِإِطْفَاءِ اللهِ تَعَالَى إِيَّاهَا وَإِذْهَابِ نُورِهَا.

﴿صُمٌّ بُكْمٌ عُمْيٌ﴾: لَمَّا سَدُّوا مَسَامِعَهُمْ عَنِ الْإِصَاخَةِ إِلَى الْحَقِّ، وَأَبَوْا أَنْ يُنْطِقُوا بِهِ أَلْسِنَتَهُمْ وَيَتَبَصَّرُوا الْآيَاتِ بِأَبْصَارِهِمْ: جُعِلُوا كَأَنَّمَا أَيِفَتْ مَشَاعِرُهُمْ وَانْتَفَتْ قُوَاهُمْ، كَقَوْلِهِ: [بسيط]

II. Or it is a parable (i) for their belief—since it results in the safeguarding of their lives, the safety of their properties and children and their participation with the Muslims in the spoils of war and legal statutes—as a fire being kindled for the purpose of illumination; (ii) and for the disappearance of all trace of that [belief] and the obliteration of its light—through their destruction and the divulgence of their state[726]—as Allah Most High's extinguishment of that [fire] and the removal of its light.[727]

[The loss of hearing, speech and sight as a simile of unbelief]

[2:18] **ṣummun bukmun ʿumyun** ⁽*deaf, dumb, blind*⁾: since they turned a deaf ear so as to never pay heed to truth, refusing to let their tongues utter it or their sights to look into the great signs, they were made to seem bereft of their senses and disabled, as in the saying [of the poet]: ["The Outspread"]

726 I.e. His destroying them in the next life and His divulging their state in this. (Z)

727 "This interpretive variant was narrated by Ibn Jarīr [al-Ṭabarī] from Ibn ʿAbbās—Allah be well-pleased with him and his father—and it is the received exegesis and the preponderant one from both aspects of comprehension and transmission." (Kh)

صُمٌّ إِذَا سَمِعُوا خَيْراً ذُكِرْتُ بِهِ * وَإِنْ ذُكِرْتُ بِسُوءٍ عِنْدَهُمْ أَذِنُوا

وَكَقَوْلِهِ: [طويل]

أَصَمُّ عَنِ الشَّيْءِ الَّذِي لَا أُرِيدُهُ * وَأَسْمَعُ خَلْقِ اللهِ حِينَ أُرِيدُ

وَإِطْلَاقُهَا عَلَيْهِمْ: عَلَى طَرِيقَةِ التَّمْثِيلِ - لَا الِاسْتِعَارَةِ، إِذْ مِنْ شَرْطِهَا أَنْ يُطْوَى ذِكْرُ الْمُسْتَعَارِ لَهُ، بِحَيْثُ يُمْكِنُ حَمْلُ الْكَلَامِ عَلَى الْمُسْتَعَارِ مِنْهُ لَوْلَا الْقَرِينَةِ، كَقَوْلِ زُهَيْرٍ: [طويل]

Stone-deaf when they hear of good things touching me,
but if bad news about me reach them they give ear;[728]

and his saying: ["The Long"]

Utterly deaf to anything I do not want—
and the most hearing of God's creatures when I please;[729]

The application of these [attributes] to them is in the style of an assimilation,[730] not a metaphor; for the latter requires that the tenor[731] be left unmentioned, so that the discourse might be taken to refer to the vehicle[732] were it not for the context,[733] as in the saying of Zuhayr: ["The Long"]

[728] Spoken by the Umayyad poet Qaʿnab b. Umm Ṣāḥib al-Ghaṭafānī al-Fazārī (d. 295 /908) (S), and cited in *Dīwān al-Ḥamāsa* (Afandī).
[729] Spoken by an unknown poet.
[730] "That is, they are *ka-ṣumm* ʿas if deafʾ etc., so it is an assimilation and comparison as he said.... He did not call it an assimilation outright because the assimilative particle [the prefix *ka-*] was suppressed." (Q)
[731] Tenor: The underlying idea or subject to which a metaphor refers, as distinct from the literal meaning of the words used. *OED.*
[732] Vehicle: The literal meaning of the word or words used metaphorically, as distinct from the subject of the metaphor; the image or idea whose association with the subject constitutes the metaphor. *OED.*
[733] "He followed al-Zamakhsharī in this after the major authorities... as did al-Sakkākī (555-626/1160-1229) who said that a precondition of the metaphor is the possibility

لَدَى أَسَدٍ شَاكِي السِّلَاحِ مُقَذَّفٍ ❋ لَهُ لِبَدٌ أَظْفَارُهُ لَمْ تُقَلَّمِ

وَمِنْ ثَمَّ تَرَى الْمُفْلِقِينَ السَّحَرَةَ يَضْرِبُونَ عَنْ تَوَهُّمِ التَّشْبِيهِ صَفْحاً، كَمَا قَالَ أَبُو تَمَّامٍ الطَّائِيُّ: [مُتقارِب]

وَيَصْعَدُ حَتَّى يَظُنَّ الْجَهُولُ ❋ بِأَنَّ لَهُ حَاجَةً فِي السَّمَاءِ

وَهٰهُنَا، وَإِنْ طُوِيَ ذِكْرُهُ ....

With a lion full-weaponed, mammoth,
big-maned, with unpared claws.[734]

That is why you see the wonder-workers and magicians[735] steer clear of any semblance of comparison[736]—as Abū Tammām al-Ṭā'ī said: ["The Tripping"]

And he rises until the ignorant suspects
he might be fetching something in the sky.[737]

In the latter case, even if [the tenor] is left unsaid ....

of understanding the words literally on the surface and disregard the comparison, but 'Zayd is a lion' cannot be understood literally, so it cannot be a metaphor. The author of *al-Īḍāḥ* [by the Shāfi'ī Qāḍī al-quḍāt Jalāl al-Dīn Muḥammad b. 'Abd al-Raḥmān al-Qazwīnī, known as Khaṭīb Dimashq (d. 739/1339)] also followed him." (S)

734 Spoken by Zuhayr b. Abī Salmā, cf. his *Dīwān*, ed. 'Alī Ḥasan Fā'ūr (Beirut: Dār al-Kutub al-'Ilmiyya, 1408/1988) p. 108. *Muqadhdhāf* was also glossed as "one who throws himself into the fray," from *qadhafa* ⁽propel⁾. The verse's tenor is the description of Ḥuṣayn b. Ḍamḍam as fierce, tough, daunting and unyielding in combat—an example of *tajrīd al-isti'āra* ⁽naked metaphor⁾ with its *tarshīḥ* ⁽maturation⁾. (S)

735 "He means the masters of wordmanship who reach the highest ranks of expressiveness which astonishes listeners and boggles the mind... allegor[ies] for the apex of style as in the hadith: 'Truly some discourses are pure magic.'" (Kh) Hadith narrated from 'Ammār b. Yāsir by Muslim, Aḥmad, al-Dārimī and others.

736 "Because comparison calls for [mention of] both sides, so when one is suppressed and the subject of the comparison is diluted into the object it is being compared with, it is as if there is no comparison with it at all." (S)

737 From the funeral ode of Armenia's governor Khālid b. Yazīd al-Shaybānī. (S) Cf. al-Khaṭīb al-Tabrīzī, *Sharḥ Dīwān Abī Tammām*, ed. Muḥammad 'Abduh 'Azzām, 4th ed., 4 vols. (Cairo: Dār al-Ma'ārif, 1951-1965) 4:34.

بِحَذْفِ الْمُبْتَدَأِ، لٰكِنَّهُ فِي حُكْمِ الْمَنْطُوقِ بِهِ؛ وَنَظِيرُهُ: [كامل]

أَسَدٌ عَلَيَّ وَفِي الْحُرُوبِ نَعَامَةٌ * فَتْخَاءُ تَنْفُرُ مِنْ صَفِيرِ الصَّافِرِ

هٰذَا، إِذَا جَعَلْتَ الضَّمِيرَ لِلْمُنَافِقِينَ، عَلَى أَنَّ الْآيَةَ فَذْلَكَةُ التَّمْثِيلِ وَنَتِيجَتُهُ؛ وَإِنْ جَعَلْتَهُ لِلْمُسْتَوْقِدِينَ، فَهِيَ عَلَى حَقِيقَتِهَا. وَالْمَعْنَى: أَنَّهُمْ، لَمَّا أَوْقَدُوا نَاراً فَذَهَبَ اللهُ بِنُورِهِمْ وَتَرَكَهُمْ فِي ظُلُمَاتٍ هَائِلَةٍ، أَدْهَشَتْهُمْ بِحَيْثُ اخْتَلَّتْ حَوَاسُّهُمْ وَانْتَقَضَتْ قُوَاهُمْ.

وَثَلَاثَتُهَا قُرِئَتْ بِالنَّصْبِ، عَلَى الْحَالِ مِنْ مَفْعُولِ ﴿تَرَكَهُمْ﴾.

through the suppression of the inchoative, nevertheless it is virtually spoken,[738] the same as in the following: ["The Perfect"]

Towards me a lion—but in wars an ostrich
limp-winged, fleeing the very whistling of the wind.[739]

All this[740] applies if you make the pronoun[741] refer back to the hypocrites in the sense that the verse epitomizes assimilation and its consequence; and if you make it refer back to the kindlers then it is literal. In the latter case the meaning is that after they kindled the fire whereupon Allah took away their light and left them in dreadful darknesses that made them so distraught that their senses shut down and their powers unravelled.[742]

All three [epithets] were also read in the accusative[743] in the sense of participial state as an object of *tarakahum* ‹He left them›.

[738] "So it cannot be a metaphor as its precondition is no longer met." (Q)
[739] Spoken by the Khārijī warlord ʿImrān b. Ḥaṭṭān deriding al-Ḥajjāj. (S) Cf. al-Asfahānī, *Aghānī* (18:84).
[740] "I.e. his explanation 'since they turned a deaf ear.'" (Q)
[741] "I.e. their pronoun in *bi-nūrihim* ‹their light›; or they are subauded here, meaning *hum ṣumm* ‹they are deaf›." (Q)
[742] α, Ak, B, F, R, T: انتقضت β, ε, I: انتقصت
[743] By Ibn Masʿūd and Ḥafṣa the Mother of the Believers. (*MQ*)

وَ(الصَّمَمُ): أَصْلُهُ صَلَابَةٌ مِنِ اكْتِنَازِ الْأَجْزَاءِ؛ وَمِنْهُ قِيلَ (حَجَرٌ أَصَمُّ) وَ(قَنَاةٌ صَمَّاءُ)، وَ(صِمَامُ الْقَارُورَةِ). سُمِّيَ بِهِ فُقْدَانُ حَاسَّةِ السَّمْعِ لِأَنَّ سَبَبَهُ أَنْ يَكُونَ بَاطِنُ الصِّمَاخِ مُكْتَنِزاً، لَا تَجْوِيفَ فِيهِ فَيَشْتَمِلَ عَلَى هَوَاءٍ يُسْمَعُ الصَّوْتُ بِتَمَوُّجِهِ. وَ(الْبَكَمُ): الْخَرَسُ. وَ(الْعَمَى): عَدَمُ الْبَصَرِ عَمَّا مِنْ شَأْنِهِ أَنْ يُبْصَرَ؛ وَقَدْ يُقَالُ لِعَدَمِ الْبَصِيرَةِ.

﴿فَهُمْ لَا يَرْجِعُونَ﴾: (I) لَا يَعُودُونَ إِلَى الْهُدَى الَّذِي بَاعُوهُ وَضَيَّعُوهُ، أَوْ عَنِ الضَّلَالَةِ الَّتِي اشْتَرَوْهَا، ....

Al-ṣamam ⟨surdity⟩ is originally solidity stemming from compactness of parts, whence *ḥajar aṣamm* ⟨hard rock⟩, *qanāt ṣammā'* ⟨forceful spear⟩ and *ṣimām al-qārūra* ⟨plug of the flask⟩. It denotes loss of the sense of hearing since the latter is caused by the contraction of the internal auditory meatus and its missing a cavity for the passage of air by which sound can be heard as it vibrates.

Al-bakam ⟨dumbness⟩ is *al-kharas* ⟨muteness⟩.

Al-ʿamā ⟨cecity⟩ is the lack of sight of what should normally be seen. It is sometimes applied to lack of insight.[744]

fa-hum lā yarjiʿūn ⟨*so they will not return*⟩:

I. They do not go back (i) to the guidance which they sold away and wasted, (ii) or from the misguidance which they purchased.

744 "Allegorically, and the manifest locution in the discourse of certain scholars is that it is also used literally." (Kh) "Allegorically. For it to be literal is a weak view." (Q) Contra: "the heart is normally able to see, for truly its sight is true sight and its blindness is true blindness, as Allah Most High said: *for truly sights are not blind but rather hearts within bosoms are blind* (al-Ḥajj 22:46)." Ibn Taymiyya, *Majmūʿat al-Fatāwā*, ed. ʿĀmir al-Jazzār and Anwar al-Bāz, 3rd ed. 37 vols. (al-Manṣūra [Egypt]: Dār al-Wafā' lil-Ṭibāʿa wal-Nashr wal-Tawzīʿ, 1426/2005) 11:347.

(II) أَوْ فَهُمْ مُتَحَيِّرُونَ، لَا يَدْرُونَ أَيَتَقَدَّمُونَ أَمْ يَتَأَخَّرُونَ، وَإِلَى حَيْثُ ابْتَدَؤُوا مِنْهُ كَيْفَ يَرْجِعُونَ. وَالْفَاءُ: لِلدِّلَالَةِ عَلَى أَنَّ اتِّصَافَهُمْ بِالْأَحْكَامِ السَّابِقَةِ سَبَبٌ لِتَحَيُّرِهِمْ وَاحْتِبَاسِهِمْ.

﴿أَوْ كَصَيِّبٍ مِّنَ ٱلسَّمَآءِ﴾: عَطْفٌ عَلَى ﴿ٱلَّذِى ٱسْتَوْقَدَ﴾، أَيْ: كَمَثَلِ ذَوِي صَيِّبٍ، لِقَوْلِهِ: ﴿يَجْعَلُونَ أَصَٰبِعَهُمْ فِىٓ ءَاذَانِهِم﴾.

وَ(أَوْ) فِي الْأَصْلِ لِلتَّسَاوِي فِي الشَّكِّ؛ ثُمَّ اتُّسِعَ فِيهَا فَأُطْلِقَتْ لِلتَّسَاوِي مِنْ غَيْرِ شَكٍّ مِثْلَ (جَالِسِ الْحَسَنَ أَوِ ابْنَ سِيرِينَ) وَقَوْلِهِ تَعَالَى: ﴿وَلَا تُطِعْ مِنْهُمْ ءَاثِمًا أَوْ كَفُورًا﴾. ....

II. Or, "so they are utterly confused, they have no idea whether they are going forward or going backwards, and how they can possibly return to whence they started."

The *fā'* ⟨so⟩ serves to indicate that their description by the above-mentioned characteristics are the reason for their confusion and detention.

[The cloubdburst filled with darkness, thunder and lightning]

[2:19] **aw ka-ṣayyibin mina-s-samā'i** ⟨*or as a cloudburst from the sky*⟩: an adjunction with *the one that kindled a fire*. That is, as the likeness of those [caught under] a cloudburst since He says, *they put their fingers into their ears*.

Aw ⟨or⟩ originally is for parity in doubt,[745] then it was extended to apply to parity without doubt, for example: "Sit with al-Ḥasan or Ibn Sīrīn"[746] and the saying of Allah Most High, *and do not obey any felon or unbeliever among them* (al-Insān 76:24),

[745] "I.e. each of the two [sides] is equally doubtful." (Z)

[746] "'Or' here standing for parity in excellence." (Z) So the gist is, "Sit with the like of al-Ḥasan or Ibn Sīrīn."

فَإِنَّهَا تُفِيدُ التَّسَاوِي فِي حُسْنِ الْمُجَالَسَةِ وَوُجُوبِ الْعِصْيَانِ؛ وَمِنْ ذٰلِكَ قَوْلُهُ: ﴿أَوْ كَصَيِّبٍ﴾. وَمَعْنَاهُ: أَنَّ قِصَّةَ الْمُنَافِقِينَ مُشَبَّهَةٌ بِهَاتَيْنِ الْقِصَّتَيْنِ، وَأَنَّهُمَا سَوَاءٌ فِي صِحَّةِ التَّشْبِيهِ بِهِمَا، وَأَنْتَ مُخَيَّرٌ فِي التَّمْثِيلِ بِهِمَا أَوْ بِأَيِّهِمَا شِئْتَ.

وَ(الصَّيِّبُ): (فَيْعِلٌ) مِنَ الصَّوْبِ، وَهُوَ النُّزُولُ؛ يُقَالُ لِلْمَطَرِ وَلِلسَّحَابِ. قَالَ الشَّمَّاخُ: [طويل]

.... ❋ وَأَسْحَمُ دَانٍ صَادِقُ الرَّعْدِ صَيِّبُ

وَفِي الْآيَةِ: يَحْتَمِلُهُمَا. وَتَنْكِيرُهُ لِأَنَّهُ أُرِيدَ بِهِ نَوْعٌ مِنَ الْمَطَرِ شَدِيدٌ، ......

which [respectively] convey parity in the excellence of frequentation and the requirement of disobedience. His saying *or as a cloud-burst* is of the same type. It means that the account of the hypocrites is being compared to these two accounts and that they are both equal in being rightly comparable. You are free to choose to assimilate it to both of them or to either one you wish.

Ṣayyib (cloudburst)[747] is a *fay'al* form of *ṣawb* which means descent. It applies to rain and also to clouds; al-Shammākh said: ["The Long"]

and a low-lying black cloud true to its thunder, pouring (sayyib).[748]

In the verse both meanings are possible. It was left indefinite because what is meant by it is a kind of heavy rain.[749]

747 "Cloudburst [Ger. Wolkenbruch] (orig. U.S.), a violent storm of rain." *OED*

748 In *Dīwān al-Shammākh b. Ḍirār al-Dhabiyānī*, ed. Ṣalāḥ al-Dīn al-Hādī (Cairo: Dār al-Ma'ārif, [1388/1968]) p. 432. Also attributed to the major poet al-Nābigha (S) cf. *Dīwān al-Nābigha al-Dhabyānī*, ed. Ḥamdū Ṭammās, 2nd ed. (Beirut: Dār al-Ma'rifa, 1426/2005) p. 22.

749 "The fact that he says 'because what is meant by it is a kind of heavy rain' indicates the unlikeliness of its meaning the cloud." (Q) "What is firmly established in exegesis is that what is meant by it in the verse is the rain. Ibn Jarīr [al-Ṭabarī] narrated it from

وَتَعْرِيفُ ﴿ٱلسَّمَآءِ﴾: لِلدِّلَالَةِ عَلَى أَنَّ الْغَمَامَ مُطْبِقٌ، آخِذٌ بِآفَاقِ السَّمَاءِ كُلِّهَا، فَإِنَّ كُلَّ أُفُقٍ مِنْهَا يُسَمَّى سَمَاءً، كَمَا أَنَّ كُلَّ طَبَقَةٍ مِنْهَا سَمَاءٌ، وَقَالَ:

[طويل] وَمِنْ بُعْدِ أَرْضٍ بَيْنَنَا وَسَمَاءِ * ....

أَمَدَّ بِهِ مَا فِي الصَّيِّبِ مِنَ الْمُبَالَغَةِ مِنْ جِهَةِ الْأَصْلِ، وَالْبِنَاءِ، وَالتَّنْكِيرِ. وَقِيلَ: الْمُرَادُ بِـ﴿ٱلسَّمَآءِ﴾: السَّحَابُ؛ فَاللَّامُ لِتَعْرِيفِ الْمَاهِيَّةِ.

﴿فِيهِ ظُلُمَٰتٌ وَرَعْدٌ وَبَرْقٌ﴾: إِنْ أُرِيدَ بِالصَّيِّبِ الْمَطَرُ، فَظُلُمَاتُهُ ....

Al-samā' ⁽the sky⁾ was made definite to show that the clouds are covering everything from one skyline to another—as every skyline is called a sky, just as every layer of the latter is also a sky, and [the poet] said ["The Long"],

and across the distance of an earth between us and a sky.[750]

He reinforced with it what was already in *ṣayyib* ⁽cloudburst⁾ of intensiveness from the aspects of root,[751] morphology[752] and indefiniteness.[753] It was also said that what is meant by *samā'* is the cloud, so the definite article is for the definition of quiddity.

fīhi ẓulumātun wa-raʿdun wa-barqun ⁽*filled with darknesses, thunder and lightning*⁾: if, by *ṣayyib*, rain is meant, then its dark-

Ibn ʿAbbās, Ibn Masʿūd, Mujāhid, ʿAṭā', Qatāda, al-Rabīʿ, Ibn Zayd and Sufyān without contest." (S)

750 Spoken by an unknown. Its first hemistich is *O remembering her when I remember her!* cf. Jawharī, *Ṣiḥāḥ* (6:2225 *'-w-h*) and Ibn Jinnī, *Khaṣā'iṣ* (3:40).

751 "Al-Taftāzānī said: 'I.e. from its raw material (*al-māddat al-ūlā*) consisting of the *ṣād* which one of the self-elevated (*mustaʿliya*) phonemes, the doubled (*mushaddada*) *yā'* and the *bā'* which is one of the hard phonemes (*al-shadīda*); and from its secondary material because *al-ṣawb* is intense downpour and fall.'" (S)

752 "Because it was made in the *faywʿal* form, namely a quasi-participial adjective (*ṣifa mushabbaha*) that denotes something firmly established." (S)

753 "Which is used for magnification (*taʿẓīm*) and to inspire dread (*tahwīl*)." (S)

ظُلْمَةُ تَكَاثُفِهِ بِتَتَابُعِ الْقَطْرِ، وَظُلْمَةُ غَمَامِهِ مَعَ ظُلْمَةِ اللَّيْـلِ، وَجَعْلُـهُ مَكَانـاً لِلرَّعْدِ وَالْبَرْقِ، لِأَنَّهُـمَا فِي أَعْـلَاهُ وَمُنْحَـدَرِهِ، مُلْتَبِسَـيْنِ بِـهِ؛ وَإِنْ أُرِيـدَ بِـهِ السَّحَابُ، فَظُلُمَاتُهُ سُحْمَتُهُ وَتَطْبِيقُهُ مَعَ ظُلْمَةِ اللَّيْلِ.

وَارْتِفَاعُهَا بِالظَّرْفِ وِفَاقاً، لِأَنَّهُ مُعْتَمِدٌ عَلَى مَوْصُوفٍ.

وَ(الرَّعْدُ): صَوْتٌ يُسْمَعُ مِنَ السَّحَابِ. وَالْمَشْهُورُ أَنَّ سَبَبَهُ اضْطِرَابُ أَجْرَامِ السَّحَابِ وَاصْطِكَاكُهَا إِذَا حَدَتْهَا الرِّيحُ ....

nesses are the darkness of its opacity through uninterrupted rainfall and the darkness of its clouds together with the darkness of night. It was made the locus of thunder and lightning because they are in its top and bottom parts, coalescing with it.[754]

If the cloud is meant by it, then its darknesses are its blackness and the fact that it overlays the darkness of night.[755]

The nominative case [of *ẓulumātun*] is effected by the local vessel [*fīhi*] by agreement[756] because the latter rests on a qualified substantive.[757]

[The meteorological cause of thunder]

Al-raʿd ⁽thunder⁾ is a sound heard from the cloud—the current view is that it is caused by the disturbance of cloud formations and their mutual collision when driven by the wind[758]—

[754] "A type of naming one object by the name of something near it [metonymy] acc. to al-Ṭībī, which entails a metaphorical use of *fī* ⁽in⁾ acc. to al-Taftāzānī." (S)
[755] "Al-Taftāzānī: Through the establishing of three types of darkness in the *ṣayyib*, which is the minimum for the plural. The darkness of the night is inferred from the saying of Allah Most High, *Every time it sheds light on them* (al-Baqara 2:20)." (S)
[756] "Al-Taftāzānī: I.e. agreement over its [grammatical] permissibility." (S)
[757] "It is also possible that *fīhi* be a pre-positioned enunciative (*khabar muqaddam*) with *ẓulumātun* as the inchoative (*mubtadaʾ*); and this is the author's meaning." (Q)
[758] "He followed in this the *Kashshāf* and it carries no weight, because the hadiths and

مِنَ الْإِرْتِعَادِ، وَ(الْبَرْقُ) مَا يَلْمَعُ مِنَ السَّحَابِ، مِنْ (بَرِقَ الشَّيْءُ بَرِيقاً)؛ وَكِلَاهُمَا مَصْدَرٌ فِي الْأَصْلِ، وَلِذٰلِكَ لَمْ يُجْمَعَا.

﴿يَجْعَلُونَ أَصَٰبِعَهُمْ فِيٓ ءَاذَانِهِم﴾: الضَّمِيرُ لِأَصْحَابِ الصَّيِّبِ؛ وَهُوَ، وَإِنْ حُذِفَ لَفْظُهُ وَأُقِيمَ الصَّيِّبُ مُقَامَهُ، لٰكِنْ مَعْنَاهُ بَاقٍ، فَيَجُوزُ أَنْ يُعَوَّلَ عَلَيْهِ كَمَا عَوَّلَ حَسَّانُ فِي قَوْلِهِ: [طويل]

يَسْقُونَ مَنْ وَرَدَ الْبَرِيصَ عَلَيْهِمُ * بَرَدَى يُصَفَّقُ بِالرَّحِيقِ السَّلْسَلِ

from *irtiʿād* ⁽quivering⁾. ***Al-barq*** ⁽lightning⁾ is whatever gleams out of the cloud, from *bariqa al-shay'u barīqan* ⁽the thing flashed with a flashing⁾. Both [*raʿd* and *barq*] are infinitive nouns originally, and that is why neither was put in the plural.

yajʿalūna aṣābiʿahum fī ādhānihim ⁽*they put their fingers into their ears*⁾: the personal pronouns refer to those under the cloudburst. Although there is no [prior] verbal mention of them and the cloudburst was set up [as subject] instead, nevertheless their meaning remains,[759] just as Ḥassān depended [on other than the explicit antecedent] when he said: ["The Long"]

They give to drink whoever alights at al-Barīṣ to stay with them
a Baradā siphon-filtered[760] *with mellifluous fine wine.*[761]

reports say otherwise. Al-Ṭībī said: 'the sound view that is relied upon is what the hadiths say' [i.e., thunder is the sound of the crack of the whip of the angel in charge of herding the clouds wherever Allah commands them, as narrated from Ibn 'Abbās by Aḥmad and in the *Sunan*]." (S 1:440) On these reports see the latter as well as his *Ḥabā'ik fī Akhbār al-Malā'ik* and Ibn Abī al-Dunyā' monograph *al-Maṭar wal-Ra'd*. Of note (i) al-Bayḍāwī added the words "the current view is that" which are not found in J and (ii) the two explanations (angels and physics) are not necessarily incompatible.

759 "Since it was already mentioned that the subauded discourse is 'as the likeness of those [caught under] a cloud-burst' (*ka-mathali dhawī ṣayyib*)… so the gist relies on the fact that their meaning remains in referencing the plural pronouns back to it." (Z)

760 "Water was purified by transferring it from one vessel to another." (Q, Z) The Se-

حَيْثُ ذُكِّرَ الضَّمِيرُ لِأَنَّ الْمَعْنَى مَاءُ بَرَدَى.

وَالْجُمْلَةُ اسْتِئْنَافٌ؛ فَكَأَنَّهُ ـ لَمَّا ذُكِرَ مَا يُؤْذِنُ بِالشِّدَّةِ وَالْهَوْلِ ـ قِيلَ: فَكَيْفَ حَالُهُمْ مَعَ مِثْلِ ذٰلِكَ؟ فَأُجِيبَ بِهَا. وَإِنَّمَا أَطْلَقَ الْأَصَابِعَ مَوْضِعَ الْأَنَامِلِ لِلْمُبَالَغَةِ.

Here, the pronoun [in *yuṣaffaqu*] is in the masculine because the meaning is *mā'u Baradā* ⟨water from [the river] Baradā⟩.

The sentence is resumptive. It is as if—when He mentioned what intimates hardship and dread—someone asked, how are they faring in such conditions? and this answer came.

The term ***aṣābiʿ*** ⟨fingers⟩ was used instead of *anāmil* ⟨fingertips⟩ for intensiveness.

villian astronomer, inventor and mathematician Jābir b. Aflaḥ al-Ishbīlī (d. 540/1145) described various stills for purifying water that used wick siphons—a method that required a fibrous cord that would siphon water from one vessel to another, cf. http://www.freedrinkingwater.com/resource-history-of-clean-drinking-water.htm.

761 From a famed poem by the arch-poet of the Companions, cf. ʿAbd al-Raḥmān al-Barqūqī, *Sharḥ Dīwān Ḥassān b.Thābit al-Anṣārī* (Cairo: al-Maṭbaʿat al-Raḥmāniyya, 1347/1929) pp. 307-309. "The verb *yuṣaffaq* is in the masculine although its subject is *Baradā* which is traditionally feminine, because it refers back to the suppressed construct which is *mā'u Baradā* ⟨Baradā water⟩." (S) "The Baradā is Damascus's largest river. It originates from the county of al-Zabadānī near Baʿlabakk five parasangs from Damascus and pours into the town of al-Fīja two parasangs from Damascus, then another town called Dummar until Damascus where it pours into the lake of al-Marj. It is without doubt the purest river in the world." Yāqūt al-Ḥamawī, *Muʿjam al-Buldān*, 5 vols. (Beirut: Dār Ṣādir, 1397/ 1977) 1:378. "Its name comes from *baradī* < *faradīs* < *Gr. paradisos* > *Ar. firdaws*. Perhaps the reason it was named a river of Paradise is due to the oasis (*ghūṭa*) of Damascus, famed for its purity, beauty, rivers and trees. Thus did the Greeks name it. They also called it Chrysorrhoas—the river of gold." Aḥmad al-Ībish and Qutayba al-Shihābī, *Maʿālim Dimashq al-Tārikhiyya* (Damascus: Wizārat al-Thaqāfa, 1996) pp. 515-516. The Barīṣ is a tributary of the Baradā. (Q, S) "Its usage in poetry suggests that [Barīṣ] is the name of the entire oasis [of Damascus] (*ism al-ghūṭa bi-ajmaʿihā*)." Yāqūt, *Muʿjam al-Buldān* (1: 407). Mixing water (and herbs) into wine or vice-versa was a universal practice in the ancient world and the Middle Ages.

﴿مِنَ الصَّوَاعِقِ﴾ مُتَعَلِّقٌ بِـ﴿يَجْعَلُونَ﴾، أَيْ: مِنْ أَجْلِهَا يَجْعَلُونَ؛ كَقَوْلِهِمْ: سَقَاهُ مِنَ الْعَيْمَةِ. وَ(الصَّاعِقَةُ) قَصْفَةُ رَعْدٍ هَائِلٍ مَعَهَا نَارٌ، لَا تَمُرُّ بِشَيْءٍ إِلَّا أَتَتْ عَلَيْهِ؛ مِنَ (الصَّعْقِ)، وَهُوَ شِدَّةُ الصَّوْتِ. وَقَدْ تُطْلَقُ عَلَى كُلِّ هَائِلٍ مَسْمُوعٍ أَوْ مُشَاهَدٍ؛ يُقَالُ: (صَعَقَتْهُ الصَّاعِقَةُ) إِذَا أَهْلَكَتْهُ بِالْإِحْرَاقِ أَوْ شِدَّةِ الصَّوْتِ.

وَقُرِئَ (مِنَ الصَّوَاقِعِ)؛ وَهُوَ لَيْسَ بِقَلْبٍ مِنَ (الصَّوَاعِقِ)، لِاسْتِوَاءِ كِلَا الْبِنَاءَيْنِ فِي التَّصَرُّفِ. يُقَالُ: (صَقَعَ الدِّيكُ)، وَ(خَطِيبٌ مِصْقَعٌ)، وَ(صَقَعَتْهُ الصَّاقِعَةُ). ....

mina-s-sawāʿiq ⁽*from the thunderstrokes*⁾ pertains to *yajʿalūn* ⁽they put⁾, that is, "because of them, they put" the way they say, "he gave him to drink *min al-ʿayma* ⁽from his craving for milk⁾."

Al-ṣāʿiqa ⁽thunderstroke⁾ is a terrific clap of thunder together with fire that leaves nothing it touches unscathed, from *al-ṣaʿq* which is a very loud noise. It can apply to any frightful phenomenon heard or seen. One says *ṣaʿaqathu al-ṣāʿiqa* ⁽the thunderstroke struck him⁾ when it kills him by burning him or through its loud clap.

It was also read *min al-ṣawāqiʿ* ⁽from the thunderstrokes⁾,[762] which is not a transposition of *ṣawāʿiq*, as both forms are on a par in their employability.[763] One says *ṣaqaʿa al-dīk* ⁽the cock crowed⁾, *khaṭīb miṣqaʿ* ⁽a thunderous orator⁾ and *ṣaqaʿathu al-ṣāqiʿa* ⁽the thunderstroke killed him⁾.

[762] By al-Ḥasan al-Baṣrī; a dialect of Tamīm and some of Rabīʿa. (*MQ*)

[763] And mean the same thing. "And since they are on a par in conjugability and etymology then each stands on its own, because deeming one to be a transposition of the other is not more likely than not." (Sk)

وَهِيَ فِي الْأَصْلِ: إِمَّا صِفَةٌ لِقَصْفَةِ الرَّعْدِ، أَوْ لِلرَّعْدِ. وَالتَّاءُ لِلْمُبَالَغَةِ، كَمَا فِي (الرَّاوِيَةِ)، أَوْ مَصْدَرٌ، كَـ(الْعَافِيَةِ) وَ(الْكَاذِبَةِ).

﴿حَذَرَ ٱلْمَوْتِ﴾: نُصِبَ عَلَى الْعِلَّةِ، كَقَوْلِهِ: [طويل]

وَأَغْفِرُ عَوْرَاءَ الْكَرِيمِ ادِّخَارَهُ * وَأَصْفَحُ عَنْ شَتْمِ اللَّئِيمِ تَكَرُّمَا

وَ(الْمَوْتُ): زَوَالُ الْحَيَاةِ؛ وَقِيلَ: عَرَضٌ يُضَادُّهَا، لِقَوْلِهِ: ﴿خَلَقَ ٱلْمَوْتَ وَٱلْحَيَوٰةَ﴾ [الملك ٢]. وَرُدَّ بِأَنَّ (الْخَلْقَ): بِمَعْنَى التَّقْدِيرِ، وَالْأَعْدَامَ مُقَدَّرَةٌ.

Originally the word is a descriptive either for the thunderclap or for thunder. The [final] *tā'* is for intensiveness as in *al-rāwiya* ‹arch-narrator› or an infinitive noun as in *al-ʿāfiya* ‹haleness› and *al-kādhiba* ‹untruth›.

ḥadhara-l-mawt ‹*for fear of death*› is in the accusative in the causal sense, as in the [poet's] saying: ["The Long"]

and I forgive the honorable man's slur to preserve his affection;[764]
and I disregard the villain's curse out of sheer generosity.[765]

Al-mawt is the cessation of life. It was also said to be an accident that counters it, since Allah Most High said, *He created death and life* (al-Mulk 67:2); it was replied that "creating" [here] means appointing, and that non-entities are [only] appointed.[766]

764 Rather than "for future use of him" (*li-ddikhārih li-yawmin aḥtāj ilayh*) as it is usually glossed, which does not characterize noble character or patience in adversity. (Q)

765 Spoken by Ḥātim al-Ṭā'ī. (S) Cf. *Dīwān Shiʿr Ḥātim b. ʿAbd Allāh al-Ṭā'ī wa-Akhbāruh*, ed. ʿĀdil Sulaymān Jamāl, 2nd ed. (Cairo: Maktabat al-Khānjī, 1411/1990) p. 224 line 29. Second hemistich in α, AQ, F, H, I, K, Kh, MM, Sk, U but missing from Ak, β, L, D, ε, J, P, Q, R, S, T, Ul, Z.

766 "And a third group—from the experts of Hadith—consider that death is an actual body since several hadiths have said so explicitly... Be warned that the author has followed the writer of the *Kashshāf* on this issue, to the point of going along with his *madhhab*! Al-Māzarī said in *Sharḥ Muslim*: 'Death according to *Ahl al-Sunna* is an

﴿وَٱللَّهُ مُحِيطٌۢ بِٱلْكَٰفِرِينَ﴾: لَا يَفُوتُونَهُ، كَمَا لَا يَفُوتُ الْمُحَاطُ بِهِ الْمُحِيطَ: لَا يُخَلِّصُهُمُ الْخِدَاعُ وَالْحِيَلُ. وَالْجُمْلَةُ اِعْتِرَاضِيَّةٌ، لَا مَحَلَّ لَهَا.

﴿يَكَادُ ٱلْبَرْقُ يَخْطَفُ أَبْصَٰرَهُمْ﴾: اِسْتِئْنَافٌ ثَانٍ، كَأَنَّهُ جَوَابٌ لِمَنْ يَقُولُ: مَا حَالُهُمْ مَعَ تِلْكَ الصَّوَاعِقِ؟

وَ(كَادَ) مِنْ أَفْعَالِ الْمُقَارَبَةِ؛ وُضِعَتْ لِمُقَارَبَةِ الْخَبَرِ مِنَ الْوُجُودِ لِعُرُوضِ سَبَبِهِ، لٰكِنَّهُ لَمْ يُوجَدْ - إِمَّا لِفَقْدِ شَرْطٍ أَوْ لِوُجُودِ مَانِعٍ - وَ(عَسَى) مَوْضُوعَةٌ لِرَجَائِهِ؛ ....

wa-l-Lāhu muḥīṭun bil-kāfirīn ‹*and all the while the One God surrounds the unbelievers*›: They cannot elude Him, any more than the thing encompassed can elude the encompasser; neither ruse nor stratagem can rescue them. This clause is parenthetical and has no [desinential] place.

[2:20] **yakādu-l-barqu yakhṭafu abṣārahum** ‹*lightning almost snatches away their sights*› is a second resumption as if answering the question: how are they affected by those thunderstrokes?

[Analysis of *kāda* ‹it was almost fact›]

Kāda ‹it was almost fact› is of the verbs of propinquity. They were coined to suggest the near-actuality of something being reported due to the manifestation of its cause, but it never came to be—either for lack of a precondition or because of an obstacle—while [on the other hand] *ʿasā* ‹it may be that› was coined to denote its expectation. ....

accident (*ʿaraḍ*) and according to the Muʿtazila pure inexistence (*ʿadam maḥḍ*).' So you can see how the author began with the position that belongs to the Muʿtazila, letting it prevail, then mentioned the position of *Ahl al-Sunna* in second place and in dubitative terms (*bi-ṣīghat al-tamrīḍ*). Nor was this enough: he had to cite the latter's proof and reject it! But all that is only a summary of the words of the *Kashshāf*." (S 1:450) See note 140 also.

فَهِيَ خَبَرٌ مَحْضٌ ـ وَلِذٰلِكَ: جَاءَتْ مُتَصَرِّفَةً بِخِلَافِ (عَسَى). وَخَبَرُهَا مَشْرُوطٌ فِيهِ أَنْ يَكُونَ فِعْلاً مُضَارِعاً، تَنْبِيهاً عَلَى أَنَّهُ الْمَقْصُودُ بِالْقُرْبِ، مِنْ غَيْرِ (أَنْ)، لِتَوْكِيدِ الْقُرْبِ بِالدَّلَالَةِ عَلَى الْحَالِ. وَقَدْ تَدْخُلُ عَلَيْهِ، حَمْلاً لَهَا عَلَى (عَسَى)؛ كَمَا تُحْمَلُ عَلَيْهَا بِالْحَذْفِ مِنْ خَبَرِهَا لِمُشَارَكَتِهِمَا فِي أَصْلِ مَعْنَى الْمُقَارَبَةِ.

وَ(الْخَطْفُ): الْأَخْذُ بِسُرْعَةٍ. وَقُرِئَ: (أ) (يَخْطِفُ) بِكَسْرِ الطَّاءِ؛ .....

Thus, [*kāda*] is pure enunciation,[767] and that is why it is declinable,[768] as opposed to *ʿasā*. Furthermore it is a precondition for its enunciative to be a verb in the aorist tense, so as to serve notice that [the enunciative] is the purport of imminence, [and for that verb to be] devoid of *an* ⟨that⟩, so as to emphasize imminence by pointing instantly;[769] but it may also be prefixed with it when taken in the sense of *ʿasā*, just as [vice versa] the latter is taken in the sense of the former with the suppression [of *ʿan*] from its enunciative, as they both share the basic sense of imminence.[770]

Al-khaṭf ⟨snatching⟩ is to seize swiftly. It was also read

(i) *yakhṭifu* with a *kasra* under the *ṭāʾ*;[771]

767 "As opposed to being originative (*inshāʾī*)." (Q, Z)

768 "I.e. it has a past tense, a future tense, a passive voice, a jussive and a prohibitive just like any other of the verbs coined to express reports/enunciations (*akhbār*)." (Q)

769 "I.e. to indicate that the report is the purport of imminence among all the parts of speech in the clause to which *kāda* was prefixed. E.g., when we say *kāda Zaydun yajīʾu wa-rākiban* ⟨it was almost fact that Zayd came, and that he came riding⟩ it means that his coming was imminent. The reason the aorist (*al-muḍāriʿ*) serves notice of that is because it indicates recency (*al-ḥudūth*) together with the absence of actuality in the past (*al-taḥaqquq fīl-māḍī*)." (Sk)

770 "This suggests that the author considers that there is a sense of imminence in *ʿasā*" (Q) "as evinced in the poetic verse عسى الهم الذي امسيت فيه * يكون وراءه فرج قريب." (Z)

771 By Anas b. Mālik, Mujāhid, ʿAlī b. a-Ḥusayn, Yaḥyā b. Waththāb, al-Ḥasan al-Baṣrī,

(ب) وَ(يَخَطِّفُ) عَلَى أَنَّهُ يَخْتَطِفُ، فَنُقِلَتْ فَتْحَةُ التَّاءِ إِلَى الْخَاءِ ثُمَّ أُدْغِمَتْ فِي الطَّاءِ؛ (ج) وَ(يَخِطِّفُ) بِكَسْرِ الْخَاءِ لِالْتِقَاءِ السَّاكِنَيْنِ؛ (د) وَإِتْبَاعِ الْيَاءِ لَهَا؛ (ه) وَ(يَتَخَطَّفُ).

﴿كُلَّمَآ أَضَآءَ لَهُم مَّشَوْاْ فِيهِ وَإِذَآ أَظْلَمَ عَلَيْهِمْ قَامُواْ﴾: اِسْتِئْنَافٌ ثَالِثٌ، كَأَنَّهُ قِيلَ: مَا يَفْعَلُونَ فِي تَارَتَيْ خُفُوقِ الْبَرْقِ، وَخُفْيَتِهِ؟ فَأُجِيبَ بِذٰلِكَ.

(ii) *yakhaṭṭifu* to stand for *yakhtaṭifu*,[772] where the *fatḥa* of the *tā*ʾ was transferred to the *khā*ʾ and contracted into the *ṭā*ʾ;[773]

(iii) *yakhiṭṭifu* with a *kasra* under the *khā*ʾ due to the meeting of two quiescent consonants[774]

(iv) and the alliterative sequencing of the *yā*ʾ with it [*yikhiṭṭifu*];[775]

(v) and *yatakhaṭṭafu*.[776]

kullamā aḍāʾa lahum mashaw fīhi wa-idhā aẓlama ʿalayhim qāmū ⁽*every time it shines for them they walk in that, and when it darkens over them they stand*⁾ is a third resumption, as if it had been said, "What do they do in the two instances of the flashing of lightning and its obscuration?" and this answer came.

Abū Rajāʾ, Yūnus b. Ḥabīb al-Baṣrī, Abān b. Taghlib and Abān b. Yazīd, the latter two from ʿĀṣim. (*MQ*)

772 *Yakhtaṭifu* is the reading of ʿAlī and Ibn Masʿūd. (*MQ*)

773 By al-Ḥasan, al-Jaḥdarī and Ibn Abī Isḥāq. (*MQ*)

774 "I.e. when the *tā*ʾ is suppressed without transferring its vowel to the *khā*ʾ, a meeting of two quiescent consonants necessarily ensues, so it is vowelized with a *kasra*." (Q) It is the reading of al-Ḥasan, Abū Rajāʾ, ʿĀṣim al-Jaḥdarī, Qatāda, Yūnus b. Ḥabīb al-Baṣrī and al-Juʿfī, from Abū Bakr, from ʿĀṣim. Nevertheless some did read *yakhṭṭafu* and *yakhṭṭifu*. (*MQ*)

775 By al-Ḥasan and al-Aʿmash. (*MQ*)

776 By Ubay as consigned in his *muṣḥaf*. There is also the reading *yakhiṭifu*. (*MQ*) F, K and the Arab prints AQ, H, MM add *yukhaṭṭifu*, the reading of Zayd b. ʿAlī. (*MQ*)

وَ(أَضَاءَ) إِمَّا مُتَعَدٍّ، وَالْمَفْعُولُ مَحْذُوفٌ، بِمَعْنَى: كُلَّمَا نَوَّرَ لَهُمْ مَمْشَىً أَخَذُوهُ؛ أَوْ لَازِمٌ، بِمَعْنَى: كُلَّمَا لَمَعَ لَهُمْ مَشَوْا فِي مَطْرَحِ نُورِهِ.

وَكَذٰلِكَ (أَظْلَمَ)، فَإِنَّهُ جَاءَ مُتَعَدِّياً، مَنْقُولاً مِنْ (ظَلِمَ اللَّيْلُ)؛ وَيَشْهَدُ لَهُ قِرَاءَةُ (أُظْلِمَ) عَلَى الْبِنَاءِ لِلْمَفْعُولِ، وَقَوْلُ أَبِي تَمَّامٍ: [طويل]

هُمَا أَظْلَمَا حَالَيَّ ثُمَّتَ أَجْلَيَا * ظَلَامَيْهِمَا عَنْ وَجْهِ أَمْرَدَ أَشْيَبِ

مَعًا

Aḍāʾa ⟨to shine⟩ is either transitive with a suppressed direct object, in the sense "every time it lights a way for them they take it;" or intransitive, in the sense "every time it gleams for them they walk in the spot where its light falls." Likewise ***aẓlama*** ⟨to darken⟩,[777] which came as a transitive and was transferred from *ẓalima*[778] *al-layl* ⟨the night is dark⟩.

[Linguistic precedents and the diachronic status of poets]

Attesting to the latter are the reading *uẓlima* ⟨it was made dark⟩ in the passive voice[779] and Abū Tammām's saying, [“The Long”]

Both darkened (aẓlamā) my two states then lifted
their two palls from the face of a grizzled youth;[780]

777 "I.e. it is either transitive, in which case its subject is the pronoun [that stands] for lightning and the object is suppressed, in the sense 'whenever lightning darkens due to its being overlaid and its [absent] light covers up every avenue, they freeze'—the suppressed part here is considered absolute while it is considered partial and indeterminate there; he did not address [*aẓlama*] in its intransitive use as it is obvious." (Q)

778 B, F, P: ظَلِمَ H, R: ظَلَمَ A, Iṣ, Kh, S, Sk, Q, Z: بكسر اللام cf. Jawharī, *Ṣiḥāḥ* 5:1978a and *Lisān* after al-Farrāʾ, *Maʿānī al-Qurʾān* (1:18). For *fatḥ* see Saraquṣṭī's *Kitāb al-Afʿāl*, ed. Ḥusayn Sharaf and Muḥammad ʿAllām, 5 vols. (Cairo: al-Hayʾat al-ʿĀmma lil-Maṭābiʿ al-Amīriyya, 1395/1975; rept. Majmaʿ al-Lughat al-ʿArabiyya, 1413/1992) 3:579.

779 By Yazīd b. Quṭayb and al-Ḍaḥḥāk cf. Zamakhsharī, Ibn ʿAṭiyya and Abū Ḥayyān.

780 al-Khaṭīb al-Tabrīzī, *Sharḥ Dīwān Abī Tammām* (1:150). The two darkeners are his mind and era as indicated in the previous verse: *Are you (f.sing.) trying to guide me? My mind is my guide; / or do you strive to tutor me? My times are my tutor.* (Q, S) "Al-Quṭb, al-Taftāzānī and al-Sharīf said that the attribution of darkening to the mind is

فَإِنَّهُ، وَإِنْ كَانَ مِنَ الْمُحْدَثِينَ، لٰكِنَّهُ مِنْ عُلَمَاءِ الْعَرَبِيَّةِ، فَلَا يَبْعُدُ أَنْ يُجْعَلَ مَا يَقُولُهُ بِمَنْزِلَةِ مَا يَرْوِيهِ.

وَإِنَّمَا قَالَ مَعَ الْإِضَاءَةِ: ﴿كُلَّمَآ﴾، ....

for even though he is one of the moderns,[781] nevertheless he is one of the experts in Arabic, so it is not far-fetched to treat what he says as something he is actually narrating.[782]

The reason He said ***kullamā*** ⁽every time⁾ with the shining .....

because a rational person does not consider worldly life fulfilling." (S) His "two states" are days and nights; good and evil; poverty and wealth; sickness and health; hardship and ease. (Q, Z) The lifting of their palls stands for their imparting him with the two fruits of right direction and discipline. (Q) "A 'naked metaphor' for himself as a beardless youth in years but a grizzled man in life experience and wise counsel. That is, they lifted themselves from my face and left me a young man in years and a greying old man in the perfection of my mind and abundance of my knowledge." (Z)

781 "They are those who came after the early generations of Islam; they discourse cannot serve as a witness-text after language has generally become corrupt. The first among them is Bashshār b. Burd. (d. 167/784)." (S)

782 Meaning something of greater antiquity than his own time and thus more authoritative than the linguistic usage of his own generation-layer. "I.e. because he is trustworthy in narration; so if he did not first hear it from the Arabs he would not speak it. I say: this is patently problematic because if we were to open that door then everything in the poetry of the moderns could be used as a proof in the same way; yet, how much did grammarians and philologists rebut Abū Tammām, al-Mutanabbī and their ilk in many places and they denounced their solecisms!" (S) "Poets are in [six] categories: (1) those of Jāhiliyya such as Umru' al-Qays, Zuhayr b. Abī Salmā, Ṭarfa and al-Nābigha; (2) the "straddlers" (*mukhaḍram*): Jāhiliyya-born poets who died in Islam such as Ḥassān [b. Thābit] and Labīd; (3) early Muslims, namely poets of the first generations such as Jarīr and Farazdaq (see notes 527, 1042): all of these are authoritative linguistic references in their poetry; (4) the post-classical poets (*al-muwalladūn*) i.e. those after them such as Bashshār; (5) the moderns (*al-muḥdathūn*), namely those in later times such as Abū Tammām, al-Baḥtarī and al-Mutanabbī; and (6) latter-day poets (*al-muta'akhkhirūn*) such as those who come later among the poets of Ḥijāz and Iraq. These types cannot serve as linguistic or dialectical witness references in their poetry by agreement unless one treats the speech of the moderns as something they are actually narrating, as the author did." (Q 2:313, S 1:456)

وَمَعَ الْإِظْلَامِ: ﴿إِذَآ﴾، لِأَنَّهُمْ حُرَّاصٌ عَلَى الْمَشْيِ، فَكُلَّمَا صَادَفُوا مِنْهُ فُرْصَةً انْتَهَزُوهَا، وَلَا كَذٰلِكَ التَّوَقُّفُ. وَمَعْنَى ﴿قَامُوا﴾: وَقَفُوا؛ وَمِنْهُ: (قَامَتِ السُّوقُ) إِذَا رَكَدَتْ، وَ(قَامَ الْمَاءُ) إِذَا جَمَدَ.

﴿وَلَوْ شَآءَ ٱللَّهُ لَذَهَبَ بِسَمْعِهِمْ وَأَبْصَٰرِهِمْ﴾: أَيْ وَلَوْ شَاءَ اللهُ أَنْ يَذْهَبَ بِسَمْعِهِمْ بِقَصِيفِ الرَّعْدِ، وَأَبْصَارِهِمْ بِوَمِيضِ الْبَرْقِ: لَذَهَبَ بِهِمَا؛ فَحَذَفَ الْمَفْعُولَ لِدَلَالَةِ الْجَوَابِ عَلَيْهِ. وَلَقَدْ تَكَاثَرَ حَذْفُهُ فِي (شَاءَ) وَ(أَرَادَ)، حَتَّى لَا يَكَادُ يُذْكَرُ إِلَّا فِي الشَّيْءِ الْمُسْتَغْرَبِ، كَقَوْلِهِ: [طويل]

and ***idhā*** ⟨when⟩ with the darkening is that they are eager to walk, so whenever they chance upon an opportunity to do so they seize it—which is not the case for halting.

The meaning of ***qāmū*** ⟨they stand⟩ is *waqafū* ⟨they halt⟩, hence *qāmat al-sūq* ⟨the market stood⟩ when it stagnates[783] and *qāma al-māʾ* ⟨the water stood⟩ when it freezes.

[Effects are tied to causes yet befall only through divine will]

wa-law shāʾa-l-Lāhu la-dhahaba bi-samʿihim wa-abṣārihim ⟨*and if the One God willed He would take away their hearing and sights*⟩, that is, and if the One God willed to take away their hearing through the loud clap of thunder and their sights through the blinding flash of lightning, he would have taken them away." He suppressed the object as it was made clear in the apodosis. Its suppression is very frequent whenever *shāʾa* ⟨to will, wish⟩ and *arāda* ⟨to want, seek⟩ are used, to the point it is hardly ever mentioned except for something considered strange, as in his saying:

783 Since it was already mentioned (under verse 2:3 for *wa-yuqīmūn al-ṣalāt*) that *qāmat al-sūq* means "the market is up/brisk" it follows that this expression is one of the *aḍdād* ⟨auto-antonyms⟩ (Q, S, Z), cf. note 694.

Text and Translation

$$\text{فَلَوْ شِئْتُ أَنْ أَبْكِي دَمًا لَبَكَيْتُهُ} \quad * \quad ....$$

وَ﴿لَوْ﴾ مِنْ حُرُوفِ الشَّرْطِ؛ وَظَاهِرُهَا الدَّلَالَةُ عَلَى انْتِفَاءِ الْأَوَّلِ لِانْتِفَاءِ الثَّانِي، ضَرُورَةَ انْتِفَاءِ الْمَلْزُومِ عِنْدَ انْتِفَاءِ لَازِمِهِ.

وَقُرِئَ: ﴿لَأَذْهَبَ بِأَسْمَاعِهِمْ﴾، بِزِيَادَةِ الْبَاءِ، كَقَوْلِهِ ـ تَعَالَى ـ: ﴿وَلَا تُلْقُوا بِأَيْدِيكُمْ إِلَى التَّهْلُكَةِ﴾ [البقرة ١٩٥].

["The Long"]

If I wished to weep blood, I would weep it.[784]

Law ʿifʾ is of the conditional particles. Its manifest locution indicates the negation of the former due to the negation of the latter, the way that the premise[785] is automatically negated when its inseparable concomitant[786] is negated.

It was also read *laʾadhhaba bi-asmāʿihim*[787] ʿhe would have done away their hearing abilitiesʾ with the added *bāʾ* ʿwithʾ, as in the saying of Allah Most High, *wa-lā tulqū bi-aydīkum ilā-t-tahluka* ʿand do not throw up your hands unto destructionʾ[788] (al-Baqara 2:195).

---

[784] Spoken by al-Baḥtarī in his son's funeral eulogy (Z) or by Abū Yaʿqūb Isḥāq b. Ḥassān al-Sughdī al-Khuraymī (d. 214/829) in the funeral eulogy of the chief of Syro-Palestine's bedouins Abū al-Haydhām ʿUthmān b. ʿĀmir. (S) Cf. *Dīwān al-Khuraymī*, ed. ʿAlī Jawād al-Ṭāhir and Muḥammad Jabbār al-Muʿaybid (Beirut: Dār al-Kitāb al-Jadīd, 1971) p. 43; al-Mubarrid, *Kāmil* (3:1362) and al-Jurjānī, *Dalāʾil al-Iʿjāz* (p. 164).
[785] Or necessitating cause or hypothesis.
[786] Or conclusion, cf. Calverley-Pollock, *Nature, Man and God* (2:1146 *lāzim/malzūm*).
[787] By Ibn Abī ʿAbla. (*MQ*)
[788] The primary meaning here is that the hands are the direct object of the casting away with an additive *bāʾ* that does not affect direct transitiveness—as in *wa-huzzī ilayki bi-jidhʿi al-nakhlati* (Maryam 19:25)—with the specific meaning of "handing over control of your affairs to destruction" (by claiming penury to avoid *nafaqa* or by despairing of Divine mercy). This is stated by al-Ṭabarī, J and Ibn ʿĀshūr, *Taḥrīr*, contrary to the glosses (and translations) that make the *bāʾ* integral to meaning as an instrumental preposition and supply "yourselves" as the synecdochic direct object in-

وَفَائِدَةُ هٰذِهِ الشَّرْطِيَّةِ: (أ) إِبْدَاءُ الْمَانِعِ لِذَهَابِ سَمْعِهِمْ وَأَبْصَارِهِمْ مَعَ قِيَامِ مَا يَقْتَضِيهِ؛ (ب) وَالتَّنْبِيهُ عَلَى أَنَّ تَأْثِيرَ الْأَسْبَابِ فِي مُسَبَّبَاتِهَا مَشْرُوطٌ بِمَشِيئَةِ اللهِ تَعَالَى، وَأَنَّ وُجُودَهَا مُرْتَبِطٌ بِأَسْبَابِهَا، وَاقِعٌ بِقُدْرَتِهِ. وَقَوْلُهُ:

﴿إِنَّ ٱللَّهَ عَلَىٰ كُلِّ شَيْءٍ قَدِيرٌ﴾: كَالتَّصْرِيحِ بِهِ وَالتَّقْرِيرِ لَهُ.

وَ(الشَّيْءُ) يَخْتَصُّ بِالْمَوْجُودِ؛ لِأَنَّهُ فِي الْأَصْلِ مَصْدَرُ (شَاءَ)، أُطْلِقَ: (أ) بِمَعْنَى (شَاءٍ) تَارَةً ـ وَحِينَئِذٍ يَتَنَاوَلُ ....

The benefit of this conditionality is

I. to highlight the prevention of the loss of their hearing and sights—with the prevalence of [conditions] that would normally dictate it—and

II. to serve notice that (i) the efficacy of causes in their effects is conditional on the will of Allah Most High and (ii) the existence [of effects] is tied to their causes but befalls through His power.

Moreover, His saying

inna-l-Lāha ʿalā kulli shayʾin qadīr ⁽*truly the One God is over all things almighty*⁾ is like an explicit declaration to that effect and a resolution of it.

[For Ashʿarīs the term *shayʾ* applies only to existing entities]

[The term] ***shayʾ*** ⁽thing⁾ is exclusive to existents[789] because it is originally an infinitive noun for *shāʾa* ⁽to will⁾ used (i) in the sense of *shāʾin*[790] ⁽willer⁾ at times—whereupon it refers ....

stead of "your hands" cf. *Jalālayn*. In the latter scenario the meaning becomes generic self-destruction instead of self-imposed passivity that leads to destruction.

[789] This is the Ashʿarī position contrary to the Muʿtazila and Qadariyya, who apply the term *shay'* to non-existents as well, then proceed to restrict it to possibilities. See Kh (1:412-413), Ibn al-Munayyir's critique cited in the margins of J (1:209 n.1) and Ibn al-Tamjīd's *Ḥāshiya* in the margins of Q (1:322).

[790] α, Ak, B, I, P, R: شآءٍ A, AQ, β, D, Ɨ, H, K, Kh, L, MM, S, Sk, T, U: شاء ε: شا Iṣ, Q,

الْبَارِئَ تَعَالَى، كَمَا قَالَ: ﴿قُلْ أَيُّ شَيْءٍ أَكْبَرُ شَهَٰدَةً قُلِ ٱللَّهُ شَهِيدٌ﴾ [الأنعام ١٩] ـ؛ (ب) وَبِمَعْنَى (مَشِيءٍ) أُخْرَى؛ أَيْ مَشِيءٍ وُجُودُهُ.

وَمَا شَاءَ اللهُ وُجُودَهُ: فَهُوَ مَوْجُودٌ فِي الْجُمْلَةِ؛ وَعَلَيْهِ قَوْلُهُ تَعَالَى: ﴿إِنَّ ٱللَّهَ عَلَىٰ كُلِّ شَيْءٍ قَدِيرٌ﴾، ﴿ٱللَّهُ خَٰلِقُ كُلِّ شَيْءٍ﴾ [الزمر ٦٢]، فَهُمَا عَلَى عُمُومِهِمَا بِلَا مَثْنَوِيَّةٍ. وَالْمُعْتَزِلَةُ ـ لَمَّا قَالُوا: (الشَّيْءُ): مَا يَصِحُّ أَنْ يُوجَدَ ـ وَهُوَ يَعُمُّ الْوَاجِبَ وَالْمُمْكِنَ ـ؛ أَوْ مَا يَصِحُّ أَنْ يُعْلَمَ وَيُخْبَرَ عَنْهُ ـ فَيَعُمُّ الْمُمْتَنِعَ أَيْضاً ـ: لَزِمَهُمْ ……………………………

to the Exalted Creator, as He said, *Say: what thing (ayyu shay'in) is greatest in witnessing? Say: Allah is all-witnessing* (al-Anʿām 6:19); and (ii) in the sense of *mashī'in* ⁽willed⁾ other times, that is, something willed into existence.[791]

Whatever Allah Most High wills to exist exists in unqualified terms as understood from His saying *truly Allah is over all things almighty* (al-Baqara 2:20) and *Allah is the creator of all things* (al-Zumar 39:62). These [verses] are both [understood] in comprehensive terms without exception; but the Muʿtazila—who defined *al-shay'* as (i) what properly exists, which includes the necessary and the possible, or (ii) what can properly be known and accounted so that it also includes impossibles[792]—were forced to

Ul, Z: شائى A, S: أي مريد Q: فاعل... وهو مَن قامت به المشيئة كعدل بمعنى عادل

[791] "[He singled it out] on the basis that existence is nobler than inexistence, as [Divine] will appertains to inexistence when it is supervenient to existence (*al-ʿadam al-ṭāri' ʿalā al-wujūd*), thus inexistence is also willed since it is *majʿūl* ⁽disposed/made⁾ as he explicitly states toward the beginning of Sūrat al-Anʿām. What [Divine] will does not appertain to is primeval and beginningless non-existence." (Q)

[792] Ashʿarīs and the rest of *Ahl al-Sunna* applied the name *shay'* to existents exclusively of inexistents and impossibles whereas Muʿtazilis applied it to "anything that

التَّخْصِيصُ بِالْمُمْكِنِ فِي الْمَوْضِعَيْنِ بِدَلِيلِ الْعَقْلِ.

وَ(الْقُدْرَةُ): هُوَ التَّمَكُّنُ مِنْ إِيجَادِ الشَّيْءِ؛ وَقِيلَ: صِفَةٌ تَقْتَضِي التَّمَكُّنَ؛ وَقِيلَ: قُدْرَةُ الْإِنْسَانِ هَيْئَةٌ بِهَا يَتَمَكَّنُ مِنَ الْفِعْلِ؛ وَقُدْرَةُ اللهِ تَعَالَى: عِبَارَةٌ عَنْ نَفْيِ الْعَجْزِ عَنْهُ. وَ(الْقَادِرُ): هُوَ الَّذِي إِنْ شَاءَ فَعَلَ، وَإِنْ لَمْ يَشَأْ لَمْ يَفْعَلْ. وَ(الْقَدِيرُ): الْفَعَّالُ ....

restrict the meaning to possibles in both places through rational proofs.

[Human enablement and divine omnipotence]

Al-qudra ⟨power⟩ is the capacity to bring something into existence. It was also defined as an attribute that necessitates capacity. It was also said that a human being's *qudra* is a disposition by which he is capable of acting, while the *qudra* of Allah Most High is an expression for the negation of any incapacity in Him.

Al-qādir ⟨the potent⟩ is he who, if he wishes, acts, and if he does not wish, does not act. *Al-qadīr* ⟨the almighty⟩ is the effec-

could be reported or described" including impossibles. See al-Shahrastānī's seventh foundation in his *Nihāyat al-Iqdām fī ʿIlm al-Kalām*, ed. Alfred Guillaume (Cairo: Maktabat al-Mutanabbī, 1964) p. 151f.; al-Bāqillānī, *Tamhīd al-Awā'il wa-Talkhīṣ al-Dalā'il*, ed. Richard J. McCarthy (Beirut: Librairie Orientale, 1957) pp. 15-16 and his *Inṣāf* (p. 15); Calverley-Pollock, *Nature, Man and God* (1:213-221); Jurjānī, *Kitāb al-Taʿrīfāt*, ed. Gustavus Flügel (Leipzig: F.C.G. Vogelii, 1845; rept. Beirut: Librairie du Liban, 1985) pp. 135-136 *s.v.. shay'*; Ibn Ḥazm, *al-Fiṣal fil-Milal wal-Ahwā' wal-Niḥal*, 4 vols. (Cairo: al-Maṭbaʿa al-Adabiyya, 1317/1899) 5:43; Qadi ʿAbd al-Jabbār, *al-Mughnī fī Abwāb al-Tawḥīd wal-ʿAdl*, 20 vols., ed. Maḥmūd al-Khuḍayrī et al. (Cairo: al-Dār al-Miṣriyya lil-Ta'līf wal-Tarjama and others, 1374-1394/1955-1974) 5:249-252 and his *Mutashābih al-Qur'ān*, ed. ʿAdnān Muḥammad Zarzūr, 2 vols. (Cairo: Dār al-Turāth, 1969) 2:557; Naṣīr al-Dīn al-Ṭūsī, *Talkhīṣ al-Muḥaṣṣal*, ed. ʿAlī Ṣirāṭ al-Ḥaqq, 2nd ed. (Beirut: Dār al-Aḍwā', 1405/1985) p. 90; and Gimaret, *Doctrine* (pp. 29-32).

لِمَا يَشَاءُ عَلَى مَا يَشَاءُ؛ وَلِذَلِكَ قَلَّمَا يُوصَفُ بِهِ غَيْرُ الْبَارِي تَعَالَى.

وَاشْتِقَاقُ (الْقُدْرَةِ) مِنَ (الْقَدْرِ)، لِأَنَّ الْقَادِرَ يُوقِعُ الْفِعْلَ عَلَى مِقْدَارِ قُوَّتِهِ، أَوْ عَلَى مِقْدَارِ مَا تَقْتَضِيهِ مَشِيئَتُهُ. وَفِيهِ دَلِيلٌ عَلَى أَنَّ الْحَادِثَ حَالَ حُدُوثِهِ، وَالْمُمْكِنَ حَالَ بَقَائِهِ: مَقْدُورَانِ؛ وَأَنَّ مَقْدُورَ الْعَبْدِ: مَقْدُورٌ لِلهِ تَعَالَى، لِأَنَّهُ شَيْءٌ، وَكُلُّ شَيْءٍ مَقْدُورٌ لِلهِ تَعَالَى.

وَالظَّاهِرُ أَنَّ التَّمْثِيلَيْنِ مِنْ جُمْلَةِ التَّمْثِيلَاتِ الْمُؤَلَّفَةِ، وَهُوَ أَنْ تُشَبَّهَ كَيْفِيَّةٌ

tor for what He wills however He wills; hence one is seldom described by it other than the Exalted Producer of all.

Al-qudra is derived from *al-qadr* ⟨measure⟩, since the *qādir* causes the act to befall to the extent of his strength[793] or to the extent of what his will dictates.

There is in it[794] an indication that the originated, at its moment of origination, *and* the possible once it abides, are both apportioned;[795] and that the slave's apportionment is apportioned by Allah Most High, because it is a thing, and everything is apportioned by Allah.

[Multi-tiered allegories in the Qur'ān and Arabic poetry]

It appears that both allegories[796] are types of complex allegories, which consist in comparing some modality ....

793 α, β, B, ε, F, I, R, T: قوّته Ak: قدرته

794 "I.e. in his saying *truly Allah is over all things almighty*." (Q, Z)

795 He means to rebut those who contest the apportionment of abiding possibles. It was also said that he is rebutting—by saying 'at the moment of origination'—those who claim that capacity (*istiṭāʿa*) precedes acts. (Q) Hence, any time the originated phenomenon or the abiding possible stops obtaining the outpouring of the actual Effector's existentiation, it ceases to exist. (Z)

796 *Istawqada* and *ka-ṣayyibin*.

مُنْتَزَعَةً مِنْ مَجْمُوعٍ تَضَامَّتْ أَجْزَاؤُهُ وَتَلَاصَقَتْ حَتَّى صَارَتْ شَيْئاً وَاحِداً بِأُخْرَى مِثْلِهَا، كَقَوْلِهِ تَعَالَى: ﴿مَثَلُ ٱلَّذِينَ حُمِّلُواْ ٱلتَّوْرَىٰةَ ثُمَّ لَمْ يَحْمِلُوهَا﴾ [الجمعة ٥] الْآيَةَ؛ فَإِنَّهُ تَشْبِيهُ حَالِ الْيَهُودِ فِي جَهْلِهِمْ بِمَا مَعَهُمْ مِنَ التَّوْرَاةِ، بِحَالِ الْحِمَارِ فِي جَهْلِهِ بِمَا يَحْمِلُ مِنْ أَسْفَارِ الْحِكْمَةِ. وَالْغَرَضُ مِنْهُمَا: تَمْثِيلُ حَالِ الْمُنَافِقِينَ مِنَ الْحَيْرَةِ وَالشِّدَّةِ، بِمَا يُكَابِدُ مَنِ انْطَفَأَتْ نَارُهُ بَعْدَ إِيقَادِهَا فِي ظُلْمَةٍ، أَوْ بِحَالِ مَنْ أَخَذَتْهُ السَّمَاءُ فِي لَيْلَةٍ مُظْلِمَةٍ مَعَ رَعْدٍ قَاصِفٍ وَبَرْقٍ خَاطِفٍ وَخَوْفٍ مِنَ الصَّوَاعِقِ. وَيُمْكِنُ جَعْلُهُمَا مِنْ قَبِيلِ التَّمْثِيلِ الْمُفْرَدِ، وَهُوَ أَنْ تَأْخُذَ أَشْيَاءَ فُرَادَى فَتُشَبِّهَهَا بِأَمْثَالِهَا، كَقَوْلِهِ تَعَالَى:

extracted from a whole of which the parts came together and coalesced into a single body, to another identical [modality].

For example, the saying of Allah, *The likeness of those who were charged with the Torah then discharged themselves from it* (al-Jumuʿa 62:5)—[to the end of] the verse—is a comparison between the state of the Jews in their ignorance of what is with them of the Torah with the state of an ass in its ignorance of what it carries of the books of wisdom. The goal in both is to allegorize the state of the hypocrites—as caused by confusion and hardship—as something one endures when his fire goes out after he kindled it in pitch darkness, or as the state of one whom the sky caught on a dark night with shattering thunder and raptor lightning and fear from thunderstrikes.

It is also possible to treat them both as a type of single allegory (namely that which takes individual items and compares them to their like, as in the saying of Allah Most High, ...

﴿ وَمَا يَسْتَوِي ٱلْأَعْمَىٰ وَٱلْبَصِيرُ ۝١٩ وَلَا ٱلظُّلُمَٰتُ وَلَا ٱلنُّورُ ۝٢٠ وَلَا ٱلظِّلُّ وَلَا ٱلْحَرُورُ ۝٢١ ﴾ [فاطر]، وَقَوْلِ امْرِئِ الْقَيْسِ: [طويل]

كَأَنَّ قُلُوبَ الطَّيْرِ رَطْباً وَيَابِساً * لَدَى وَكْرِهَا الْعُنَّابُ وَالْحَشَفُ الْبَالِي

بِأَنْ يُشَبَّهَ (١) فِي الْأَوَّلِ: (أ) ذَوَاتُ الْمُنَافِقِينَ بِالْمُسْتَوْقِدِينَ؛ (ب) وَإِظْهَارُهُمُ الْإِيمَانَ بِاسْتِيقَادِ النَّارِ؛ (ج) وَمَا انْتَفَعُوا بِهِ ـ مِنْ حَقْنِ الدِّمَاءِ وَسَلَامَةِ الْأَمْوَالِ وَالْأَوْلَادِ وَغَيْرِ ذٰلِكَ ـ بِإِضَاءَةِ النَّارِ مَا حَوْلَ الْمُسْتَوْقِدِينَ؛ (د) وَزَوَالُ ذٰلِكَ عَنْهُم عَلَى الْقُرْبِ بِإِهْلَاكِهِمْ، ....

Not equal are the blind and the seeing, nor the darkness and the light, nor the shade and the torrid heat (Fāṭir 35:19-21) and the saying of Umru' al-Qays: ["The Long"]

As if the hearts of birds—some moist, some dry—
in its eyrie were drupes and spoiled keys),[797]

whereby there is a comparing,

I. in the first [allegory],

(i) of the persons of the hypocrites with the fire-kindlers;

(ii) of their exhibition of faith with the kindling of the fire;

(iii) of the benefits they reaped such as guaranteeing their lives and safeguarding their wealth and offspring among other things, with the fire shedding light on the surroundings of its kindlers;

[797] *Dīwān Umru' al-Qays* (p. 114). "He is describing the hawk (*al-ʿuqāb*), which does not eat the hearts of birds." (S) Cf. Kamāl al-Dīn Ilyās b. ʿAbd Allāh al-Damīrī, *Ḥayāt al-Ḥayawān al-Kubrā*, with Zakariyyā al-Qazwīnī's *Kitāb ʿAjā'ib al-Makhlūqāt wal-Ḥayawānāt wa-Gharā'ib al-Mawjūdāt*, 2nd ed., 2 vols. (Būlāq: Dār al-Ṭibāʿat al-ʿĀmira, 1284/1867) 2:152. "Al-Mubarrid said in *al-Kāmil* (2:922): 'This verse is, by consensus of the narrators, the best ever to compare an object in two different states to two different things.'" (S)

أَوْ بِإِفْشَاءِ حَالِهِمْ، وَإِبْقَائِهِمْ فِي الْخَسَارِ الدَّائِمِ وَالْعَذَابِ السَّرْمَدِ بِإِطْفَاءِ نَارِهِمْ وَالذَّهَابِ بِنُورِهِمْ.

(٢) وَفِي الثَّانِي: (أ) أَنْفُسُهُمْ بِأَصْحَابِ الصَّيِّبِ؛ (ب) وَإِيمَانُهُمُ الْمُخَالِطُ بِالْكُفْرِ وَالْخِدَاعِ بِصَيِّبٍ فِيهِ ظُلُمَاتٌ وَرَعْدٌ وَبَرْقٌ، مِنْ حَيْثُ إِنَّهُ، وَإِنْ كَانَ نَافِعاً فِي نَفْسِهِ، لٰكِنَّهُ لَمَّا وُجِدَ فِي هٰذِهِ الصُّورَةِ عَادَ نَفْعُهُ ضَرّاً؛ (ج) وَنِفَاقُهُمْ - حَذَراً عَنْ نِكَايَاتِ الْمُؤْمِنِينَ، وَمَا يَطْرُقُونَ بِهِ مَنْ سِوَاهُمْ مِنَ الْكَفَرَةِ - بِجَعْلِ الْأَصَابِعِ فِي الْآذَانِ مِنَ الصَّوَاعِقِ حَذَرَ الْمَوْتِ، مِنْ حَيْثُ إِنَّهُ لَا يَرُدُّ

(iv) of the imminent disappearance of all that with their destruction[798] or the exposure of their state, and their being made to abide[799] in everlasting loss and sempiternal punishment, with the extinction of their fire and the elimination of its light;

II. and in the second [allegory],

(i) of themselves with the characters of the cloudburst;

(ii) of their mixture of faith, unbelief and deceit with a cloudburst filled with darknesses, thunder and lightning, which, although beneficial in itself, nevertheless, because it exists in such a form, its benefit has turned into harm;

(iii) of their hypocrisy—in their wariness of the believers' blows and of what the latter inflict of such [blows] on the other unbelievers—with their placing their fingers into their ears from the thunderstrokes for fear of death, since it repels nothing of the

[798] "I.e. through the destruction of some of them with death, not killing, as there is no report of their being killed or combated." (Q)

[799] α, Ak, AQ, B, D, F, H, L, MM, P, Q, Sk, T, U: وابقائهم Kh, Ul, Z: وابقاؤهم β, I, R: وابقاءهم ε: والقاوهم

مِنْ قَدَرِ اللهِ تَعَالَى شَيْئاً، وَلَا يُخَلِّصُ مِمَّا يُرِيدُ بِهِمْ مِنَ الْمَضَارِّ؛ (د) وَتَحَيُّرُهُمْ لِشِدَّةِ الْأَمْرِ وَجَهْلُهُمْ بِمَا يَأْتُونَ وَيَذَرُونَ، بِأَنَّهُمْ كُلَّمَا صَادَفُوا مِنَ الْبَرْقِ خَفْقَةً اِنْتَهَزُوهَا فُرْصَةً ـ مَعَ خَوْفٍ أَنْ تَخْطَفَ أَبْصَارَهُمْ ـ فَخَطَوا خُطًى يَسِيرَةً؛ ثُمَّ إِذَا خَفِيَ وَفَتَرَ لَمَعَانُهُ، بَقُوا مُتَقَيِّدِينَ، لَا حَرَاكَ بِهِمْ.

وَقِيلَ: (أ) شَبَّهَ الْإِيمَانَ وَالْقُرْآنَ وَسَائِرَ مَا أُوتِيَ الْإِنْسَانُ مِنَ الْمَعَارِفِ الَّتِي هِيَ سَبَبُ الْحَيَاةِ الْأَبَدِيَّةِ: بِالصَّيِّبِ الَّذِي بِهِ حَيَاةُ الْأَرْضِ؛ (ب) وَمَا ارْتَبَكَتْ بِهَا مِنَ الشُّبَهِ الْمُبْطِلَةِ وَاعْتَرَضَتْ دُونَهَا مِنَ الْاِعْتِرَاضَاتِ الْمُشَكِّكَةِ: بِالظُّلُمَاتِ؛ ....

decree of Allah Most High, nor does it save them from the harms He intends for them;

(iv) and of their confusion in the midst of great peril and their ignorance of what they should do and what they should avoid with the fact that every time they experience a flash of lightning they jump at the opportunity—despite their fear that it might snatch away their sight—and take a few steps forward; then, when it disappears and its gleam lingers [before it is seen again], they stand fettered and unable to make the slightest movement.

[Allegorical interpretation of the storm and its elements]

It was also said that

(i) faith, the Qurʾān and all the types of knowledge a person is granted that are avenues for eternal life are being compared with the cloudburst through which there is life on earth;

(ii) their being mixed[800] with mortal misgivings and confronted with doubt-provoking objections is compared to the darknesses;

[800] All mss. and eds.: ارتبكت α, AQ, H, MM, P: ارتكبت inversion.

(ج) وَشَبَّهَ مَا فِيهَا مِنَ الْوَعْدِ وَالْوَعِيدِ بِالرَّعْدِ؛ (د) وَمَا فِيهَا مِنَ الْآيَاتِ الْبَاهِرَةِ بِالْبَرْقِ؛ (ه) وَتَصَامَّهُمْ عَمَّا يَسْمَعُونَ مِنَ الْوَعِيدِ بِحَالِ مَنْ يَهُولُهُ مخفف ومشدد
الرَّعْدُ، فَيَخَافُ صَوَاعِقَهُ، فَيَسُدُّ أُذُنَيْهِ عَنْهَا، مَعَ أَنَّهُ لَا خَلَاصَ لَهُمْ مِنْهَا؛ وَهُوَ مَعْنَى قَوْلِهِ تَعَالَى: ﴿وَاللَّهُ مُحِيطٌ بِالْكَافِرِينَ﴾؛ (و) وَاهْتِزَازُهُمْ لِمَا يَلْمَعُ لَهُمْ - مِنْ رُشْدٍ يُدْرِكُونَهُ، أَوْ رِفْدٍ تَطْمَحُ إِلَيْهِ أَبْصَارُهُمْ - بِمَشْيِهِمْ فِي مَطْرَحِ ضَوْءِ الْبَرْقِ ﴿كُلَّمَا أَضَاءَ لَهُم﴾؛ (ز) وَتَحَيُّرُهُمْ وَتَوَقُّفُهُمْ فِي الْأَمْرِ - حِينَ تَعْرِضُ لَهُمْ شُبْهَةٌ أَوْ تَعِنُّ لَهُمْ مُصِيبَةٌ - بِتَوَقُّفِهِمْ إِذَا أَظْلَمَ عَلَيْهِمْ.

(iii) the promises and threats contained in them are being compared with thunder;

(iv) their wondrous signs are being compared with lightning;

(v) their turning a deaf ear to whatever threats they hear is being compared to the state of one whom thunder terrifies,[801] so he dreads its thunderstrikes and stops his ears [to protect himself] from them, but they cannot escape—and that is the meaning of the saying of Allah Most High, *and all the while Allah surrounds the unbelievers* (al-Baqara 2:19);

(vi) their jumping at whatever shines before them—such as a right course that they take or a gift their sights are set upon—is being compared with their walking in the spots lit by lightning *every time it shines for them*;

(vii) and their perplexity and utter inaction, whenever some uncertainty pops up or a misfortune shows before them, are being compared with their halting whenever it is too dark for them.

801 Q: يهوله بالتخفيف والتشديد

وَنَبَّهَ ـ سُبْحَانَهُ ـ بِقَوْلِهِ: ﴿وَلَوْ شَآءَ ٱللَّهُ لَذَهَبَ بِسَمْعِهِمْ وَأَبْصَـٰرِهِمْ﴾ عَلَى أَنَّهُ تَعَالَى جَعَلَ لَهُمُ السَّمْعَ وَالأَبْصَارَ لِيَتَوَسَّلُوا بِهَا إِلَى الْهُدَى وَالْفَلَاحِ، ثُمَّ إِنَّهُمْ صَرَفُوهَا إِلَى الْحُظُوظِ الْعَاجِلَةِ، وَسَدُّوهَا عَنِ الْفَوَائِدِ الآجِلَةِ، وَلَوْ شَاءَ اللهُ لَجَعَلَهُمْ بِالْحَالَةِ الَّتِي يَجْعَلُونَهَا لِأَنْفُسِهِمْ، فَإِنَّهُ عَلَى مَا يَشَاءُ قَدِيرٌ.

﴿يَـٰٓأَيُّهَا ٱلنَّاسُ ٱعْبُدُوا۟ رَبَّكُمُ﴾: لَمَّا عَدَّدَ فِرَقَ الْمُكَلَّفِينَ وَذَكَرَ خَوَاصَّهُمْ وَمَصَارِفَ أُمُورِهِمْ، أَقْبَلَ عَلَيْهِمْ بِالْخِطَابِ عَلَى سَبِيلِ الْاِلْتِفَاتِ، هَزّاً لِلسَّامِعِ وَتَنْشِيطاً لَهُ وَاهْتِمَاماً بِأَمْرِ الْعِبَادَةِ، ....

Allah Most High drew attention, when He said *and if Allah willed He would take away their hearing and their sights*, to the fact that He had given them hearing and sights for them to use as means to guidance and success; but they applied them to ephemeral trappings and blocked them from next-worldly benefits. If Allah willed, He would have made them in the very state which they make for themselves,[802] for truly He is over all things almighty.

[Stylistic alarm through *iltifāt* ⁽apostrophic redirection⁾]

[2:21] **yā ayyuhā-n-nāsu ʿbudū rabbakumu** ⁽*O you people! worship your Nurturer*⁾: after enumerating the categories of those who are legally liable and mentioning their characteristics and main activities, He apostrophized them through redirection[803] in order to jolt the listener, stimulate him, apply attention to the matter of worship, ...

[802] I.e. He would have created them in the very state they acquired for themselves. (Q)
[803] *Iltifāt* was previously defined by the Qadi (*sub* Fātiḥa 1:5) as "switching from one style to another in order to refresh speech and stimulate the listener. For example, one will switch from the second person to the third and from the third person to the first

وَتَفْخِيماً لِشَأْنِهَا، وَجَبْراً لِكُلْفَةِ العِبَادَةِ بِلَذَّةِ المُخَاطَبَةِ.

و(يَا): حَرْفٌ وُضِعَ لِنِدَاءِ الْبَعِيدِ؛ وَقَدْ يُنَادَى بِهِ الْقَرِيبُ، تَنْزِيلاً لَهُ مَنْزِلَةَ الْبَعِيدِ، (أ) إِمَّا لِعَظَمَتِهِ، كَقَوْلِ الدَّاعِي: (يَا رَبِّ)، وَ(يَا الله) ـ وَهُوَ ﴿أَقْرَبُ إِلَيْهِ مِنْ حَبْلِ ٱلْوَرِيدِ﴾ [ق ١٦]؛ (ب) أَوْ لِغَفْلَتِهِ وَسُوءِ فَهْمِهِ؛ (ج) أَوْ لِلاِعْتِنَاءِ بِالمَدْعُوِّ لَهُ وَزِيَادَةِ الحَثِّ عَلَيْهِ.

وَهُوَ ـ مَعَ المُنَادَى ـ جُمْلَةٌ مُفِيدَةٌ، لِأَنَّهُ نَائِبٌ مَنَابَ فِعْلٍ.

amplify its importance and compensate for the trouble of worship with the pleasure of direct address.

Yā ⁽O⁾ was coined as a vocative particle for someone far. It is also used for someone near who is being treated as far,

(i) either due to his great rank, as in the supplicant's words, *yā Rabb* ⁽O Nurturer!⁾ and *yā Allāh* ⁽O Allah!⁾ when He is actually *nearer to him than his jugular vein* (Qāf 50:16);

(ii) or due to his inattention and denseness;[804]

(iii) or to hone in on the summons and add to its urgency.[805]

It—together with the callee—forms an informative proposition[806] because it stands for a verb.[807]

and back again." It is thus translated by our teacher Pierre Cachia in *The Arch Rhetorician* (p. 106 §143) where al-Nābulusī defines it as "an unexpected change from first, second or third person to one of the others, intended to reawaken interest and revive attention." Its translation as "enallage" (Howell as cited in Cachia, *Monitor* p. 89) falls short while "apostrophizing" (Margoliouth, *Chrestomathia* p. 127) is partial.

[804] "As in, 'O heedless one, listen for your own good!' where the callee's inattention and denseness are tantamount to his being distant, so they are given the status of physical distance, whence the use of the vocable *yā* metaphorically." (Q)

[805] See Shaykh Zādah's (1:176-177) luminous 26 lines on the meanings and uses of *yā* and his caution against anthropomorphism within the context of "distance."

[806] A more precise translation than "independent/simple sentence" since the latter

وَ(أَيٌّ): جُعِلَ وُصْلَةً إِلَى نِدَاءِ الْمُعَرَّفِ بِاللَّامِ؛ فَإِنَّ إِدْخَالَ (يَا) عَلَيْهِ مُتَعَذِّرٌ - لِتَعَذُّرِ الْجَمْعِ بَيْنَ حَرْفَيِ التَّعْرِيفِ، فَإِنَّهُمَا كَمِثْلَيْنِ - وَأُعْطِيَ حُكْمَ الْمُنَادَى، وَأُجْرِيَ عَلَيْهِ الْمَقْصُودُ بِالنِّدَاءِ وَصْفاً مُوَضِّحاً لَهُ، وَالْتُزِمَ رَفْعُهُ، إِشْعَاراً بِأَنَّهُ الْمَقْصُودُ. وَأُقْحِمَتْ بَيْنَهُمَا هَاءُ التَّنْبِيهِ تَأْكِيداً، وَتَعْوِيضاً عَمَّا يَسْتَحِقُّهُ - أَيْ مِنَ الْمُضَافِ إِلَيْهِ.

وَإِنَّمَا كَثُرَ النِّدَاءُ عَلَى هٰذِهِ الطَّرِيقَةِ فِي الْقُرْآنِ لِاسْتِقْلَالِهِ بِأَوْجُهٍ مِنَ التَّأْكِيدِ. ....

Ayyu serves as a connective to the calling of the definite article carrier, since prefixing the latter with *yā* is unfeasible for the same reason that joining together two definite articles is unfeasible, as they are quasi-identical. It was given callee status[808] and the actual purport of the summons[809] received the same desinential place as a descriptive of vividness for it. It invariably has to be put in the nominative case, to announce that it itself is the purport. The admonitory ***hāʾ*** was intercalated between the two[810] for emphasis, and in replacement of what *ayyu* deserves as a governed annex.

[The frequent Quranic summons *yā ayyuhā*]

This style of summoning[811] abounds in the Qurʾān because it uniquely possesses various emphatic senses. ....

includes questions and commands.

807 In the sense, "I call you all (*adʿūkum*)." (Z)

808 "What is meant by status here is consequential effect, that is, indeclinable *ḍamm* case-ending and being suffixed by the particle of indeclinability (*ḥarf al-bināʾ*)." (Q)

809 I.e. *al-nāsu*.

810 I.e. between *ayyu* and *al-nās*.

811 "Namely, using the vocative *yā* that was coined for the distant callee, anonymizing the latter and describing him with a generic name that serves to identify and explain

وَكُلُّ مَا نَادَى اللهُ لَهُ عِبَادَهُ ـ مِنْ حَيْثُ إِنَّهَا أُمُورٌ عِظَامٌ، مِنْ حَقِّهَا أَنْ يَتَفَطَّنُوا إِلَيْهَا، وَيُقْبِلُوا بِقُلُوبِهِمْ عَلَيْهَا، وَأَكْثَرُهُمْ عَنْهَا غَافِلُونَ ـ حَقِيقٌ بِأَنْ يُنَادَى لَهُ بِالْآكَدِ الْأَبْلَغِ.

وَالْجُمُوعُ وَأَسْمَاؤُهَا الْمُحَلَّاةُ بِاللَّامِ: لِلْعُمُومِ، حَيْثُ لَا عَهْدَ؛ وَيَدُلُّ عَلَيْهِ صِحَّةُ الِاسْتِثْنَاءِ مِنْهَا، أَوِ التَّأْكِيدُ بِمَا يُفِيدُ الْعُمُومَ، كَقَوْلِهِ تَعَالَى: ﴿فَسَجَدَ ٱلْمَلَٰٓئِكَةُ كُلُّهُمْ أَجْمَعُونَ﴾ [الحجر ٣٠؛ ص ٧٣] وَاسْتِدْلَالُ الصَّحَابَةِ بِعُمُومِهَا شَائِعاً وَذَائِعاً.

Indeed, everything to which Allah calls His slaves—from the perspective that they are grave matters that merit their full awareness[812] and their hearts' devotion, yet most of them are heedless of them—deserves to be summoned to through the most emphatic and powerful means possible.

[Belief and worship are universal duties, as Allah created all]

Plurals and their nouns that are fitted with the [definite article] *lām* denote universality as there is no previous knowledge. This is shown by

(i) the validity of their exceptive subsets;

(ii) emphases that convey universality, as in the saying of Allah Most High, *so the angels prostrated one and all, the whole lot of them* (al-Ḥijr 15:30; Ṣād 38:73);

(iii) and the fact that the Companions extensively and famously adduced it as evidence in its universal meaning.[813]

him, with the intercalation of the admonitory *hā* to further reawaken interest." (Z)

812 α, Ak, β, B, D, ε, F, I, P, Q, R, T, U, Ul, Z: يتفطنوا لها AQ, H, K, L, MM: يتفطنوا اليها

813 "An affirmation that what is being said is established by *ijmāʿ* ʿconsensusʾ." (Q)

فَـ﴿ٱلنَّاسُ﴾ يَعُمُّ (أ) المَوْجُودِينَ وَقْتَ النُّزُولِ لَفْظاً (ب) وَمَنْ سَيُوجَدُ، لِمَا تَوَاتَرَ مِنْ دِينِهِ ـ عَلَيْهِ الصَّلَاةُ وَالسَّلَامُ ـ أَنَّ مُقْتَضَى خِطَابِهِ وَأَحْكَامِهِ شَامِلٌ لِلْقَبِيلَيْنِ، ثَابِتٌ إِلَى قِيَامِ السَّاعَةِ، إِلَّا مَا خَصَّهُ الدَّلِيلُ.

وَمَا رُوِيَ عَنْ عَلْقَمَةَ وَالْحَسَنِ ـ أَنَّ كُلَّ شَيْءٍ نَزَلَ فِيهِ ﴿يَٰٓأَيُّهَا ٱلنَّاسُ﴾ فَمَكِّيٌّ، وَ﴿يَٰٓأَيُّهَا ٱلَّذِينَ ءَامَنُوٓاْ﴾: فَمَدَنِيٌّ ـ ....

Thus, ***al-nās*** ⟨people⟩ comprises

(i) those in existence at the time of revelation—lexically;

(ii) and those who will come later—in light of what is mass-transmitted as part of his religion (upon him blessings and peace) that the exigencies of his discourse and laws cover both parties[814] and endure to the rising of the Hour,[815] except for what the evidence specifies.[816]

As for what is narrated from ʿAlqama and al-Ḥasan stating that everything in the revelation that has *O you people* is Meccan while [everything that has] *O you who believe* is Medinan[817]—sup-

814 AQ, β, B, ε, F, I, K, Kh, L, MM, Q, R, Sk, T, U, Ul, Z: للقبيلين α, Ak, D, P: للقبيلتين

815 Such as the saying of Allah Most High, *that I may warn therewith you and whomever it may reach* (al-Anʿām 6:19), ... *to recite unto them His revelations and to make them grow, and to teach them... along with others of them who have not yet joined them* (al-Jumuʿa 62:2-3), and the Prophetic hadith, "I was sent to all people without exception" (*buʿithtu ilā al-nāsi kāffatan*) among other proofs to that effect, cf. al-Rāzī, *Mafātīḥ* (2:84) and *al-Maḥṣūl fī ʿIlm Uṣūl al-Fiqh*, ed. Ṭaha Jābir al-ʿAlwānī, 2nd ed. 6 vols. (Beirut: Mu'assasat al-Risāla, 1992) 2:388-389 and Badr al-Dīn al-Zarkashī, *al-Baḥr al-Muḥīṭ fī Uṣūl al-Fiqh*, ed. ʿAbd al-Qādir al-ʿĀnī, 2nd ed., 6 vols. (Kuwait: Wizārat al-Awqāf, 1413/1992) 3:184-185.

816 "I.e. the standing evidence that the general becomes specific when some types are excepted such as the minor and the demented." (Kh)

817 Narrated (i) from ʿAlqama by Ibn al-Ḍurays in *Faḍā'il al-Qur'ān wa-Mā Unzila min al-Qur'ān bi-Makkata wa-Mā Unzila bil-Madīna*, ed. ʿUrwa Budayr (Damascus:

إِنْ صَحَّ رَفْعُهُ، فَلَا يُوجِبُ تَخْصِيصَهُ بِالْكُفَّارِ، وَلَا أَمْرَهُمْ بِالْعِبَادَةِ؛ فَإِنَّ الْمَأْمُورَ بِهِ: هُوَ الْمُشْتَرَكُ بَيْنَ بَدْءِ الْعِبَادَةِ، وَالزِّيَادَةِ فِيهَا، وَالْمُوَاظَبَةِ عَلَيْهَا؛ فَالْمَطْلُوبُ (أ) مِنَ الْكُفَّارِ: هُوَ الشُّرُوعُ فِيهَا بَعْدَ الْإِتْيَانِ بِمَا يَجِبُ تَقْدِيمُهُ مِنَ الْمَعْرِفَةِ وَالْإِقْرَارِ بِالصَّانِعِ - فَإِنَّ مِنْ لَوَازِمِ وُجُوبِ الشَّيْءِ: ....

posing that its attribution up [to the Prophet] is correct—it does not require that it be specific to the unbelievers, nor that they are being ordered to worship.[818] In actuality what is being ordered is the common denominator[819] between the inception of worship, increase in it and perseverance with it. Thus what is demanded of the unbelievers is to commence it—after producing what must come first, such as cognizance and affirmation of the Maker. For among the inseparable accompaniments of an obligatory matter

Dār al-Fikr, 1408/1987) p. 38 §26; Abū ʿUbayd al-Qāsim b. Sallām in *Kitāb Faḍāʾil al-Qurʾān*, ed. Marwān al-ʿAṭiyya et al. (Damascus and Beirut: Dār Ibn Kathīr, 1416/1995) p. 367; and Ibn Abī Shayba, *Muṣannaf* (15:514 §30768); (ii) from al-Ḍaḥḥāk, *Tafsīr al-Ḍaḥḥāk*, ed. Muḥammad al-Zāwīti, 2 vols. (Cairo: Dār al-Salām, 1419/1999) p. 148 §26; (iii) from Maymūn b. Mahrān by Abū ʿUbayd cf. Ibn Kathīr *Kitāb Faḍāʾil al-Qurʾān*, ed. Abū Isḥāq al-Ḥuwaynī (Cairo: Maktabat Ibn Taymiyya, 1416/1995) p. 37-38 and (iv) from Ibn Masʿūd by al-Bazzār, *al-Baḥr al-Zakhkhār al-Maʿrūf bi-Musnad al-Bazzār*, ed. Maḥfūẓ al-Raḥmān Zayn Allāh et al., 18 vols. (Beirut: Muʾassasat ʿUlūm al-Qurʾān; Medina: Maktabat al-ʿUlūm wal-Ḥikam, 1409-1430/1988-2009) 4:336 §1531; al-Ḥākim, *Mustadrak* (3:18); and al-Bayhaqī, *Dalāʾil al-Nubuwwa wa-Maʿrifat Aḥwāl Ṣāḥib al-Sharīʿa*, ed. ʿAbd al-Muʿṭī Qalʿajī, 7 vols. (Beirut: Dār al-Kutub al-ʿIlmiyya and Dār al-Rayyān lil-Turāth, 1408/ 1988) 7:144. Al-Dāraquṭnī, *al-ʿIlal al-Wārida fil-Aḥādīth al-Nabawiyya*, ed. Maḥfūẓ al-Raḥmān Zayn Allah al-Salafi, 16 vols. (Riyadh: Dār Ṭayba, 1409/1989) 5:168-169 §800 averred that the correct version was the (weak) chain that stops at ʿAlqama rather than all the way to Ibn Masʿūd. No such report is narrated from al-Ḥasan. (S) See also Q (2:353) and especially S (2:76) and *Itqān*, end of Type 1 (*Ḍawābiṭ*) for a number of Makkī verses with *ayyuhā al-ladhīna āmanū* and Madanī with *ayyuhā al-nās*.

[818] Because the precondition of worship is belief; a rebuttal of the *Kashshāf* where J had said that *O you people* addresses the idolaters of Mecca. (Q, Sk, Z)

[819] Ak, B, ε, I, L, R, T: المشترك α: مشترك β: المشرك missp. AQ, F, H, K, MM: القدر المشترك

وُجُوبَ مَا لَا يَتِمُّ إِلَّا بِهِ - وَكَمَا أَنَّ الْحَدَثَ لَا يَمْنَعُ وُجُوبَ الصَّلَاةِ، فَالْكُفْرُ لَا يَمْنَعُ وُجُوبَ الْعِبَادَةِ: بَلْ يَجِبُ رَفْعُهُ، وَالْاِشْتِغَالُ بِهَا عَقِيبَهُ؛

(ب) وَمِنَ الْمُؤْمِنِينَ: ازْدِيَادُهُمْ وَثَبَاتُهُمْ عَلَيْهَا.

صح
وَإِنَّمَا قَالَ: ﴿رَبَّكُمُ﴾ تَنْبِيهاً عَلَى أَنَّ الْمُوجِبَ لِلْعِبَادَةِ: هِيَ الرَّبِّيَّةُ.

﴿ٱلَّذِى خَلَقَكُمْ﴾: صِفَةٌ جَرَتْ عَلَيْهِ تَعَالَى لِلتَّعْظِيمِ وَالتَّعْلِيلِ؛ وَيَحْتَمِلُ

is the obligatoriness of that without which it cannot be accomplished; and—just as ritual impurity does not preclude the obligatoriness of prayer—unbelief does not preclude the obligatoriness of worship: rather, it is obligatory to remove the former and involve oneself in the latter forthwith. [As for what is demanded] of the believers, it is to increase and remain firm in it.

The reason He said ***rabbakum*** ⁽your Nurturer⁾ is but to highlight the fact that what makes worship obligatory is nurturership.[820]

al-ladhī khalaqakum ⁽*Who created you*⁾ is a descriptive often applied to Him—exalted is He—for magnification and justification. It is also possible ....

[820] α, A, F, L, Q, R, Ul, Z: الربية B, ε, Iş, Kh, P, U: التربية Ak, AQ, β, D, H, I, MM, Sk, T: الربية بتشديد الاحرف الثلاثة بمعنى التربية كما في نسخة وفي اخرى الربوبية A: الربوبية "What he mentioned is because making status subsequent to description suggests causality." (Kh) "That is, to draw attention to the fact that the reason Allah made worship obligatory is that He made the worshipper reach his perfection gradually. That causality is twofold: first, nurture (*tarbiya*) prior to worship renders worship obligatory out of gratitude; second, worship itself is nurture for him, so obligatoriness stems from the will to nurture. When worship appertains to Him Who is unrelated to the slave except through nurture—while He is utterly exempt of deriving any benefit [therefrom], it becomes known that such worship was made obligatory for him out of nurture. Also among the benefits of His saying *rabbakum* is to serve notice to the addressee that the one commanding this is the Nurturer." (Iş)

التَّقْيِيدُ وَالتَّوْضِيحُ إِنْ خُصَّ الْخِطَابُ بِالْمُشْرِكِينَ، وَأُرِيدَ بِـ(الرَّبِّ) أَعَمُّ مِنَ الرَّبِّ الْحَقِيقِيِّ وَالْآلِهَةِ الَّتِي يُسَمُّونَهَا أَرْبَاباً.

وَ(الْخَلْقُ): إِيجَادُ الشَّيْءِ عَلَى تَقْدِيرٍ وَاسْتِوَاءٍ؛ وَأَصْلُهُ: التَّقْدِيرُ. يُقَالُ: (خَلَقَ النَّعْلَ) إِذَا قَدَّرَهَا وَسَوَّاهَا بِالْمِقْيَاسِ.

﴿وَالَّذِينَ مِن قَبْلِكُمْ﴾ مُتَنَاوِلٌ كُلَّ مَا يَتَقَدَّمُ الْإِنْسَانَ بِالذَّاتِ أَوْ بِالزَّمَانِ، مَنْصُوبٌ، مَعْطُوفٌ عَلَى الضَّمِيرِ الْمَنْصُوبِ فِي ﴿خَلَقَكُمْ﴾. ....

that it is a restrictive qualifier and one of vividness if the address is specifically directed to idolaters—in which case by *rabb* here is meant something more general than the true Nurturer and the deities which they call lords.

Al-khalq ⁽creating⁾ is to originate something according to a certain measure and proportion.[821] Its original meaning is *taqdīr* ⁽measuring⁾; one says *khalaqa al-naʿl* for measuring out the sandal [pattern] and making it symmetrical with a ruler.[822]

wal-ladhīna min qablikum ⁽*and those before you*⁾ covers all that precedes a human being in essence or in time.[823] It is accusative and adjoined to the accusative pronoun in *khalaqakum* ⁽created

821 "Fashioning (*al-takwīn*), invention (*al-ikhtirāʿ*), origination (*al-ījād*) and creation (*al-khalq*) are vocables that share a common meaning and differ in several meanings. The shared meaning is that something is existentiated *ex nihilo* which did not exist before, and it is more specific in its appurtenances (*taʿalluqan*) than *qudra* ⁽power⁾." Khwāja Naṣīr al-Dīn al-Ṭūsī, *Talkhīṣ al-Muḥaṣṣal lil-Rāzī*, ed. ʿAbd Allāh Nūrānī (Teheran: Intishārāt-i Muʾassasat-i Muṭālaʿāt-i Islāmī, 1980; rept. Beirut: Dār al-Aḍwāʾ, 1985) p. 312, *Masʾala: al-takwīn azalī wal-mukawwan muḥdath.*

822 I.e. its leather, before one proceeds to cut it. Cf. al-Jawharī, *Ṣiḥāḥ* (4:1470); al-Fayrūzābādī, *Qāmūs* (*s.v. kh-l-q*); al-Fārābī, *Dīwān al-Adab* (2:123); al-Khalīl al-Farāhīdī, *Kitāb al-ʿAyn*, ed. Mahdī al-Makhzūmī and Ibrāhīm al-Sāmarrāʾī, 8 vols. ([Baghdad]: Dār al-Rashīd, 1980-1985) 4:151; etc.

823 "The author of the *Irshād* [Abū al-Suʿūd] did right to leave out essential prece-

وَالْجُمْلَةُ أُخْرِجَتْ مُخْرَجَ الْمُقَرَّرِ عِنْدَهُمْ، إِمَّا لِاعْتِرَافِهِمْ بِهِ ـ كَمَا قَالَ اللهُ تَعَالَى: ﴿وَلَئِن سَأَلْتَهُم مَّنْ خَلَقَهُمْ لَيَقُولُنَّ ٱللَّهُ﴾ [الزخرف ٨٧] ـ أَوْ لِتَمَكُّنِهِمْ مِنَ الْعِلْمِ بِهِ بِأَدْنَى نَظَرٍ.

وَقُرِئَ (مَنْ قَبْلَكُمْ)، عَلَى إِقْحَامِ الْمَوْصُولِ الثَّانِي بَيْنَ الْأَوَّلِ وَصِلَتِهِ تَأْكِيداً، كَمَا أَقْحَمَ جَرِيرٌ فِي قَوْلِهِ: [بسيط]

يَا تَيْمُ تَيْمَ عَدِيٍّ لَا أَبَا لَكُمُ ❊ ....

you'. The sentence itself[824] was made to stand for something already resolved to them, either because they confessed it—as Allah Most High said, *and if you asked them who created them, they would assuredly say: Allah* (al-Zukhruf 43:87)—or because they were capable of knowing it with a modicum of investigation.[825]

It was also read *man qablakum* 'whoever [came] before you'[826] with the intercalation of the second relative between the first and its relative clause for emphasis, in the same way Jarīr intercalated, when he said, ["The Outspread"]

O Taym, Taym of 'Adīy! You fatherless sons![827]

dence and sufficed himself with temporal precedence, saying that *min* is inceptive (*ibtidā'iyya*) and appertains to an elliptic, that is: 'they were from a time before your time,' and it was also said 'whom He created before He created you.'" (Q)

824 I.e. *al-ladhī khalaqakum.*

825 "The sentence was made to stand for something already resolved following the exigency of what is obvious. For just as the learned is treated as an ignoramus when he does not act according to the exigency of knowledge, whereby he is addressed in the same fashion as the ignorant, likewise, the unlearned is treated as someone learned when the standing evidence is crystal-clear, and is addressed in the same fashion as the learned." (Z, Kh)

826 By Ibn al-Sumayfi' (*wa-khalaqa man qablakum*) and Zayd b. 'Alī (*wal-ladhīna man qablakum*). (*MQ*)

827 *Dīwān Jarīr* (1:212). "The meaning is 'O Taym of 'Adīy! O Taym of 'Adīy!'" (S)

تيماً الثَّاني، بَيْنَ الْأَوَّلِ وَمَا أُضِيفَ إِلَيْهِ.

﴿لَعَلَّكُمْ تَتَّقُونَ﴾: (١) حَالٌ (أ) مِنَ الضَّمِيرِ فِي ﴿اعْبُدُوا﴾، كَأَنَّهُ قَالَ: اعْبُدُوا رَبَّكُمْ رَاجِينَ أَنْ تَنْخَرِطُوا فِي سِلْكِ الْمُتَّقِينَ، الْفَائِزِينَ بِالْهُدَى وَالْفَلَاحِ، الْمُسْتَوْجِبِينَ لِجِوَارِ اللهِ تَعَالَى. نَبَّهَ بِهِ عَلَى أَنَّ التَّقْوَى مُنْتَهَى دَرَجَاتِ السَّالِكِينَ، وَهُوَ: التَّبَرِّي مِنْ كُلِّ شَيْءٍ سِوَى اللهِ تَعَالَى إِلَى اللهِ، وَأَنَّ الْعَابِدَ يَنْبَغِي أَنْ لَا يَغْتَرَّ بِعِبَادَتِهِ، وَيَكُونَ ذَا خَوْفٍ وَرَجَاءٍ. قَالَ تَعَالَى: ﴿يَدْعُونَ رَبَّهُمْ خَوْفًا وَطَمَعًا﴾ [السجدة ١٦] ﴿وَيَرْجُونَ رَحْمَتَهُ وَيَخَافُونَ عَذَابَهُ﴾ [الإسراء ٥٧].

the second "Taym" in between the first and its governed annex.

[The worshipper's *taqwā* is wariness between fear and hope]

laʿallakum tattaqūna ⁽*perhaps you will beware*⁾

I. is a participial state of the pronoun in ***uʿbudū*** ⁽worship!⁾ as if He were saying "Worship your Nurturer ardently hoping to enter into the line of the wary who triumph with guidance and success and ensure for themselves to deserve residing near Allah Most High" Thus He drew attention to the fact that wariness is the final level of the wayfarers and consists in ridding oneself[828] of everything but Allah Most High [on the way] to Allah.[829] Moreover, the worshipper must not be deluded by his own worship but must have fear and hope. Allah Most High said, *they call unto their Nurturer in fear and longing* (al-Sajda 32:16), *and they hope for His mercy and fear His punishment* (al-Isrā' 17:57).

[828] Ak, K, Kh, L, Ul, Z: التبري F, U: التبرّي β, T: التبرء α, B, I, R: التبراء ε: التبرا Sk: التبرأ

[829] This is the definition of *ḥaqīqat al-ikhlāṣ* (real sincerity) in al-Fayrūzābādī's *Baṣā'ir Dhawī al-Tamyīz fī Laṭā'if al-Kitāb al-ʿAzīz* as cited by al-Zabīdī in *Tāj al-ʿArūs* (entry *kh-l-ṣ*). "The expression *rājīn* ⁽ardently hoping⁾ hints that it is a tremendous level, because the seeker of truth never ceases to rise from one state to another.

(ب) أَوْ مِنْ مَفْعُولِ ﴿خَلَقَكُمْ﴾؛ وَالْمَعْطُوفُ عَلَيْهِ عَلَى مَعْنَى: أَنَّهُ خَلَقَكُمْ وَمَنْ قَبْلَكُمْ فِي صُورَةِ مَنْ يُرْجَى مِنْهُ التَّقْوَى، لِتَرَجُّحِ أَمْرِهِ بِاجْتِمَاعِ أَسْبَابِهِ، وَكَثْرَةِ الدَّوَاعِي إِلَيْهِ. وَغَلَّبَ الْمُخَاطَبِينَ عَلَى الْغَائِبِينَ فِي اللَّفْظِ؛ وَالْمَعْنَى عَلَى إِرَادَتِهِمْ جَمِيعاً. (٢) وَقِيلَ: تَعْلِيلٌ لِلْخَلْقِ؛ أَيْ: خَلَقَكُمْ لِكَيْ تَتَّقُوا، كَمَا قَالَ: ﴿وَمَا خَلَقْتُ ٱلْجِنَّ وَٱلْإِنسَ إِلَّا لِيَعْبُدُونِ ۝٥٦﴾ [الذاريات]. وَهُوَ ضَعِيفٌ، إِذْ لَمْ يَثْبُتْ فِي اللُّغَةِ مِثْلُهُ.

II. Or [it is a participial state] of the object of *khalaqakum* ⁽created you⁾, with the antecedent denoting that "He created you and those before you in the image of those from whom wariness is expected, as it was made all the likelier[830] by its many gathered causes and motives."

[In both scenarios] He gave preponderance to addressees over absentees verbally, but meaning-wise all are meant.

III. It was also said[831] it is the raison d'être of creation, that is, "He created you in order for you to beware," just as He said, *and I did not create the jinn and human beings for other than to worship Me* (al-Dhāriyāt 51:56). This is a weak view, since its like has no firm precedent in the language.[832]

This is called *sayr* ⁽journeying⁾ while *sulūk* ⁽wayfaring⁾ lexically means *dukhūl* ⁽entering⁾, then Sufis made it specific to entering a path that leads to truth, and the *sālik* ⁽wayfarer⁾ to them is one who journeys to Allah, mid-point between the *murīd* ⁽seeker⁾ and the *muntahī* ⁽accomplished⁾ for as long as he is journeying." (Kh 2:12).

830 Ak, β, B, ε, F, I, L, R, T: لترجّح α: ليترجح

831 By some of the philologists who view *la'alla* in the sense of *kay* ⁽in order that⁾. (Z)

832 "Because if it were not a weak view then it would have certainly been transmitted from the imams of language; however, their massive majority sufficed themselves in defining its literal meaning as high hope (*al-tarajjī*) and solicitude (*al-ishfāq*). If they meant it in the allegorical sense then the latter should not be resorted to unless the

وَالْآيَةُ تَدُلُّ عَلَى (أ) أَنَّ الطَّرِيقَ إِلَى مَعْرِفَةِ اللهِ تَعَالَى، وَالْعِلْمِ بِوَحْدَانِيَّتِهِ وَاسْتِحْقَاقِهِ لِلْعِبَادَةِ: النَّظَرُ فِي صُنْعِهِ، وَالِاسْتِدْلَالُ بِأَفْعَالِهِ، (ب) وَأَنَّ الْعَبْدَ لَا يَسْتَحِقُّ بِعِبَادَتِهِ عَلَيْهِ ثَوَاباً: فَإِنَّهَا، لَمَّا وَجَبَتْ عَلَيْهِ شُكْراً لِمَا عَدَّدَهُ عَلَيْهِ مِنَ النِّعَمِ السَّابِقَةِ، فَهُوَ كَأَجِيرٍ أَخَذَ الْأَجْرَ قَبْلَ الْعَمَلِ.

﴿ٱلَّذِى جَعَلَ لَكُمُ ٱلْأَرْضَ فِرَٰشًا﴾: صِفَةٌ ثَانِيَةٌ؛ أَوْ مَدْحٌ مَنْصُوبٌ، أَوْ مَرْفُوعٌ؛ أَوْ مُبْتَدَأٌ، خَبَرُهُ ﴿فَلَا تَجْعَلُوا۟﴾.

[Knowledge of Allah and of His rights over His creatures]

The verse indicates that

1. the way to greater knowledge of Allah Most High and cognizance of His absolute oneness and of the fact He indeed deserves to be worshipped is through investigation of His handiwork and inference from His acts;

2. and the slave does not become entitled, by worshipping Him, to any reward from Him; for since such [worship] became incumbent on him out of gratitude for all the past favors He enumerated for him, he is like a hired hand who took his wages before doing his job.[833]

[2:22] **al-ladhī jaʿala lakumu-l-arḍa firāshan** ⁽*Who has made for you the earth a bed*⁾ is (i) a second descriptive; (ii) or a complimentary expression in the accusative or the nominative;[834] (iii) or an inchoative of which the enunciative is *fa-lā tajʿalū* ⁽therefore do not make⁾.

literal sense is impractical (*mutaʿadhdhir*), which is not the case." (Z 1:185)

833 A rebuttal of the Muʿtazila, cf. the Qadi's explanation of the Sunni understanding of the believers' "deserving" in *lahum jannāt* ⁽for them are gardens⁾ (al-Baqara 2:25), see note 926.

834 See under verse 2:3 above, the gloss beginning "Or in the sense of a compliment in the accusative or the nominative..."

وَ(جَعَلَ): مِنَ الْأَفْعَالِ الْعَامَّةِ؛ يَجِيءُ عَلَى ثَلَاثَةِ أَوْجُهٍ: (أ) بِمَعْنَى (صَارَ وَطَفِقَ)، فَلَا يَتَعَدَّى؛ كَقَوْلِهِ: [وافر]

فَقَدْ جَعَلَتْ قَلُوصُ ابْنَيْ سُهَيْلٍ * مِنَ الْأَكْوَارِ مَرْتَعُهَا قَرِيبُ

(ب) وَبِمَعْنَى (أَوْجَدَ)، فَيَتَعَدَّى إِلَى مَفْعُولٍ وَاحِدٍ، كَقَوْلِهِ تَعَالَى: ﴿وَجَعَلَ ٱلظُّلُمَٰتِ وَٱلنُّورَ﴾ [الأنعام ١]؛ (ج) وَبِمَعْنَى (صَيَّرَ)، وَيَتَعَدَّى إِلَى مَفْعُولَيْنِ، كَقَوْلِهِ تَعَالَى: ﴿جَعَلَ لَكُمُ ٱلْأَرْضَ فِرَٰشًا﴾. وَالتَّصْيِيرُ يَكُونُ بِالْفِعْلِ تَارَةً،

Jaʿala ⟨to make⟩ is of the universal verbs[835] and comes in three different senses:

1. It can mean *ṣāra* ⟨start, become⟩, *ṭafiqa* ⟨set about⟩, in which case it is intransitive, as in the [poet's] saying: ["The Exuberant"]

The camel heifers of Suhayl's two sons set about (jaʿalat),
unburdened,[836] *their pasture near.*[837]

2. It can mean *awjada* ⟨bring into being⟩, in which case it is transitive and takes a single object, as in the saying of Allah Most High, *and He brought into being (jaʿala) darknesses and light* (al-Anʿām 6:1);

3. and it can mean *ṣayyara* ⟨turn s.th. to⟩, in which case it is transitive and takes two objects, as in the saying of Allah Most High, *He made for you the earth a bed. Al-taṣyīr* ⟨making [it/one] to be thus⟩ can be alternately by action, ...

[835] "Al-Rāghib said: '*Jaʿala* is an expression that is universal to all verbs, because it is more general than *faʿala* ⟨to do⟩, *ṣanaʿa* ⟨to make⟩ and all their siblings.'" (Kh)

[836] "*Al-akwār* is the plural of *kūr*—the saddle and its implements, just as al-Marzūqī and others said (cf. Iṣ). Whoever said *kawr* in the sense of a large pack of camels (cf. Z) is off the mark." (Kh) Cf. Abū ʿAlī al-Marzūqī, *Sharḥ Dīwān al-Ḥamāsa*, ed. Aḥmad Amīn and ʿAbd al-Salām Hārūn, 4 vols. in 2 (Beirut: Dār al-Jīl, 1411/1991) 1:310-311.

[837] Spoken by an anonymous poet, where the meaning is they are too exhausted to graze far so they stay near their saddles cf. al-Tabrīzī, *Sharḥ al-Ḥamāsa* (1:226).

وَبِالْقَوْلِ أَوِ الْعَقْدِ أُخْرَى.

وَمَعْنَى (**جَعَلَهَا فِرَاشاً**): أَنْ جَعَلَ بَعْضَ جَوَانِبِهَا بَارِزاً ظَاهِراً عَنِ الْمَاءِ، مَعَ مَا فِي طَبْعِهِ مِنَ الْإِحَاطَةِ بِهَا، وَصَيَّرَهَا مُتَوَسِّطَةً بَيْنَ الصَّلَابَةِ وَاللَّطَافَةِ، حَتَّى صَارَتْ مُهَيَّأَةً لِأَنْ يَقْعُدُوا وَيَنَامُوا عَلَيْهَا كَالْفِرَاشِ الْمَبْسُوطِ؛ وَذٰلِكَ لَا يَسْتَدْعِي كَوْنَهَا مُسَطَّحَةً، لِأَنَّ كُرِيَّةَ شَكْلِهَا ـ مَعَ عِظَمِ حَجْمِهَا وَاتِّسَاعِ جِرْمِهَا ـ لَا تَأْبَى الْافْتِرَاشَ عَلَيْهَا.

or it can be by speech or conviction.[838]

[Earth's levelness and rotundity at one and the same time]

The meaning of His making it a bed is that he made some of its parts rise high above water—although the latter naturally tends to encompass it[839]—and made it midway between something rock-hard and something subtle.[840] As a result it became suited for them to sit and sleep on top of it like a couch spread out. This does not require it to be level-planed, because its rotundity[841]—given its huge size and vast mass—does not preclude that one can lie down on top of it.[842]

838 "'By speech' such as naming the angels females… and 'by conviction' here means [to believe] something that contradicts fact." (Q, Z)

839 "Because earth is heavier than water." (Q)

840 "Such as water or air." (Kh)

841 The vowelization of كرية was defined by Aḥmad al-Fayyūmī in *al-Miṣbāḥ al-Munīr* (2:91) as كرية على لفظها meaning "conforming to the pronunciation of *kura*;" i.e. *kuriyya* as in the definitive edition of ʿAbd al-ʿAẓīm al-Shinnāwī (Cairo: Dār al-Maʿārif, 1397/1977) p. 531 and the Beirut: Maktabat Lubnān, 1987 ed. (p. 203), and not *kurayya* as given by H and the Beirut: al-Maktaba al-ʿIlmiyya ed. (2:532) of the *Miṣbāḥ*.

842 "Rotundity is the philosophers' position and seems to be the author's choice, following al-Rāzī…. but to follow the Predecessors is safer." (Q) Yet Ibn Ḥazm (384-456/994-1064) demonstrates that rotundity is implied in the Qur'ān and Sunna cf. *al-Fiṣal fil-Milal wal-Ahwā' wal-Niḥal*, 4 vols. (Cairo: al-Maṭbaʿa al-Adabiyya, 1317/1899) 2:97-

﴿وَٱلسَّمَآءَ بِنَآءً﴾: قُبَّةٌ مَضْرُوبَةٌ عَلَيْكُمْ. وَ(السَّماءُ): اِسْمُ جِنْسٍ، يَقَعُ عَلَى الْوَاحِدِ وَالْمُتَعَدِّدِ، كَـ(الدِّينَارِ) وَ(الدِّرْهَمِ)؛ وَقِيلَ: جَمْعُ (سَمَاءَةٍ).

وَ(الْبِنَاءُ): مَصْدَرٌ، سُمِّيَ بِهِ الْمَبْنِيُّ - بَيْتاً كَانَ أَوْ قُبَّةً أَوْ خِبَاءً - وَمِنْهُ: (بَنَى عَلَى امْرَأَتِهِ)، لِأَنَّهُمْ كَانُوا إِذَا تَزَوَّجُوا ضَرَبُوا عَلَيْهَا خِبَاءً جَدِيداً.

﴿وَأَنزَلَ مِنَ ٱلسَّمَآءِ مَآءً فَأَخْرَجَ بِهِۦ مِنَ ٱلثَّمَرَٰتِ رِزْقًا لَّكُمْ﴾ عَطْفٌ عَلَى ﴿جَعَلَ﴾.

wa-s-samāʾa bināʾan ⁽*and the sky a building*⁾: a dome pitched over them.

Al-samāʾ is a common noun denoting units and collectives, like "dinar" and "dirham." It is also said to be the plural of *samāʾa*.[843]

Al-bināʾ ⁽building⁾ is an infinitive noun by which the edifice is named, whether it is a house, a dome or a tent; whence *banā ʿalā imraʾatih* ⁽he built over his wife=consummated the marriage⁾, because whenever they married they would pitch a new tent over her.

wa-anzala mina-s-samāʾi māʾan fa-akhraja bihi mina-th-thamarāti rizqan lakum ⁽*and sent down, out of the sky, water whereby He produced some fruits as sustenance for you*⁾ is an adjunction to ***jaʿala*** ⁽*has made*⁾.

101, *Maṭlab bayān kurawiyyat al-arḍ*. The Muʿtazili Abū Rashīd Saʿīd b. Muḥammad al-Naysābūrī's (d. 440/1048) in *Masāʾil fil-Khilāf bayn al-Baṣriyyīn wal-Baghdādiyyīn*, ed. Maʿn Ziyāda and Riḍwān al-Sayyid (Beirut: Maʿhad al-Inmāʾ al-ʿArabī, 1979) pp. 71-74 §19: *Masʾala fī anna al-arḍa hal hiya kuriyyat al-shakl am lā?* correctly makes rotundity the Aristotelian and Ptolemaic view but, like Q, overlooks the fact that trigonometry and the planispheric astrolabe are specifically Muslim inventions whose models presuppose a spherical earth. See on this David A. King, *Astronomy in the Service of Islam* (Aldershot (UK): Variorum, 1993).

[843] I.e. the suppression of the feminine *tāʾ* indicates the plural, e.g. *baqara* → *baqar*. Cf. Q (3:94) but al-Zajjāj said "its singular is *samāt*, and some said *samāwa*." (S 2:179)

وَخُرُوجُ الثِّمَارِ بِقُدْرَةِ اللهِ تَعَالَى وَمَشِيئَتِهِ، وَلٰكِنْ (أ) جَعَلَ الْمَاءَ الْمَمْزُوجَ بِالتُّرَابِ سَبَباً فِي إِخْرَاجِهَا وَمَادَّةً لَهَا كَالنُّطْفَةِ لِلْحَيَوَانِ، بِأَنْ أَجْرَى عَادَتَهُ بِإِفَاضَةِ صُوَرِهَا وَكَيْفِيَّاتِهَا عَلَى الْمَادَّةِ الْمُمْتَزِجَةِ مِنْهُمَا؛ (ب) أَوْ أَبْدَعَ فِي الْمَاءِ قُوَّةً فَاعِلَةً وَفِي الْأَرْضِ قُوَّةً قَابِلَةً، يَتَوَلَّدُ مِنْ اجْتِمَاعِهِمَا أَنْوَاعُ الثِّمَارِ. وَهُوَ قَادِرٌ عَلَى أَنْ يُوجِدَ الْأَشْيَاءَ كُلَّهَا بِلَا أَسْبَابٍ وَمَوَادٍّ - كَمَا أَبْدَعَ نُفُوسَ الْأَسْبَابِ وَالْمَوَادِّ - وَلٰكِنْ لَهُ فِي إِنْشَائِهَا مُدَرَّجاً مِنْ حَالٍ إِلَى حَالٍ صَنَائِعُ

[The divine paradigms of fecundation and growth]

The budding of fruits is by the power of Allah Most High and His will; however,

(i) He made water that mixes with soil a means in their production and a material for them just like the sperm-drop for animals; that is, He made it His custom to pour out their forms and modalities over the material of their[844] admixture;

(ii) or He devised[845] in water an active force and in the earth a receptive force, out of the combination of which are generated the different kinds of fruit.[846]

He is able to bring all things into being without means and materials, just as He devised the means and materials themselves. However, in His originating them in gradual stages from state to state, He has designs ....

[844] "Namely water admixed with soil." (Q)

[845] α, Ak, β, B, D, I, Kh, L, P, R, Q, Sk, T, U, Ul, Z: ابدع F, H, K, MM, Iş: اودع "He stored/deposited." The first reading is Sunni, the second Mu'tazili! ε: ايداع error.

[846] "Meaning, the *bā'* ⟨whereby⟩ according to the first view is per the position of *Ahl al-Sunna wal-Jamā'a* and stands for customary causality (*al-sababiyya al-'ādiyya*) or, according to the second view, per that of the sages (*al-ḥukamā'*) [and the Mu'tazila] and stands for real causality (*al-sababiyya al-ḥaqīqiyya*)." (Kh) See also Q (2:385-386).

وَحِكَمٌ يُجَدِّدُ فِيهَا لِأُولِي الْأَبْصَارِ عِبَراً، وَسُكُوناً إِلَى عَظِيمِ قُدْرَتِهِ لَيْسَ فِي إِيجَادِهَا دَفْعَةً.

وَ﴿مِنَ﴾ الْأُولَى: لِلِابْتِدَاءِ، سَوَاءٌ أُرِيدَ بِالسَّمَاءِ السَّحَابُ ـ فَإِنَّ مَا عَلَاكَ سَمَاءٌ ـ أَوِ الْفَلَكُ. فَإِنَّ الْمَطَرَ يَبْتَدِئُ (أ) مِنَ السَّمَاءِ إِلَى السَّحَابِ وَمِنْهُ إِلَى الْأَرْضِ عَلَى مَا دَلَّتْ عَلَيْهِ الظَّوَاهِرُ؛ (ب) أَوْ مِنْ أَسْبَابٍ سَمَاوِيَّةٍ تُثِيرُ الْأَجْزَاءَ الرَّطْبَةَ مِنْ أَعْمَاقِ الْأَرْضِ إِلَى جَوِّ الْهَوَاءِ، فَتَنْعَقِدُ سَحَاباً مَاطِراً.

وَ﴿مِنَ﴾ الثَّانِيَةُ: (أ) لِلتَّبْعِيضِ، بِدَلِيلِ قَوْلِهِ تَعَالَى ﴿فَأَخْرَجْنَا بِهِۦ ثَمَرَٰتٍ﴾ [فاطر ٢٧]. وَاكْتِنَافُ الْمُنَكَّرَيْنِ لَهُ ـ أَعْنِي ﴿مَآءً﴾ وَ﴿رِزْقًا﴾ ـ كَأَنَّهُ قَالَ:

and wisdoms by which He renews [His] paradigms for those who can see, making them more confident of His irrepressible might, which would not be the case if they were created in one go.

[Rain formation]

The first ***min*** ⟨out of⟩ is inceptive—whether by *samā'* ⟨sky⟩ is meant *al-saḥāb* ⟨the cloud⟩—since whatever is above you is a *samā'*—or the hemisphere. For rain starts out (i) from the sky then to the cloud and from the latter to the earth according to external indicators;[847] (ii) or from celestial causes that drive up areas of moisture from the depths of the earth up into the atmosphere where they condense into rainclouds.

The second ***min*** is (i) partitive as shown in the saying of Allah Most High, *whereby We produce some fruits* (Fāṭir 35:27).[848] Its being sandwiched between two indefinites—I mean *mā'an* and *rizqan*—is as if He were saying: ....

[847] "I.e. the manifest locutions (*ẓawāhir*) of Quranic verses and reports." (S)

[848] "Shaykh Sa'd al-Dīn [al-Taftāzānī] said: The indefinite, especially in the plural of paucity (*jam' al-qilla*), intimates partitiveness (*ba'ḍiyya*)." (S)

(وَأَنْزَلْنَا مِنَ السَّمَاءِ بَعْضَ الْمَاءِ، فَأَخْرَجْنَا بِهِ بَعْضَ الثَّمَرَاتِ لِيَكُونَ بَعْضَ رِزْقِكُمْ). وَهٰكَذَا الْوَاقِعُ، إِذْ لَمْ يُنْزِلْ مِنَ السَّمَاءِ الْمَاءَ كُلَّهُ، وَلَا أَخرجَ بِالْمَطَرِ كُلَّ الثَّمَرَاتِ، وَلَا جعَلَ كُلَّ الْمَرْزُوقِ ثِمَاراً؛ (ب) أَوْ لِلتَّبْيِينِ، وَ﴿ رِزْقًا ﴾ مَفْعُولٌ بِمَعْنَى الْمَرْزُوقِ، كَقَوْلِكَ (أَنْفَقْتُ مِنَ الدَّرَاهِمِ أَلْفاً).

وَإِنَّمَا سَاغَ ﴿ٱلثَّمَرَٰتِ﴾ ـ وَالْمَوْضِعُ مَوْضِعُ الْكَثْرَةِ ـ (أ) لِأَنَّهُ أَرَادَ بِالثَّمَرَاتِ: جَمَاعَةَ الثَّمَرَةِ الَّتِي فِي قَولِكَ (أَدْرَكَتْ ثَمَرَةُ بُسْتَانِهِ)؛ وَيُؤَيِّدُهُ قِرَاءَةُ مَنْ قَرَأَ: (مِنَ الثَّمَرَةِ)، عَلَى التَّوْحِيدِ؛

"and We brought down from the sky some of the water, whereby We produced some of the fruits so that it would form some of your sustenance." That is the factual case, as not all the water came down from the sky, nor were all the fruits produced with rain, nor was all provision made to consist in fruit.

(ii) Or it is specificative, with ***rizqan*** as a direct object in the sense of the thing provided,[849] as when you say *anfaqtu min al-darāhim alfan* ‹I spent, of the dirhams, a thousand›.

[The plural of paucity standing for collectivity or abundance]

The reason why ***al-thamarāt*** ‹some fruits› is apt[850]—when the context is one of abundance—is (i) because He meant by *thamarāt* the collectivity of *al-thamara* which you use when you say, "The *thamara* ‹produce› of his orchard has matured." This is supported by the reading of those whoever reads it as *min al-thamarati* in the singular.[851]

[849] "I.e. He brought out a certain provision for you which consists in fruits" (*akhraja marzūqan lakum huwa al-thamarāt*). (Q, S)

[850] I.e. the plural of paucity instead of that of abundance i.e. *thamar* and *thimār* (Q), also *thumur* and *thumr* (Naṣṣ).

[851] Namely Ibn al-Sumayfiʿ—but in the sense of the plural like the mainstream. (*MQ*)

(ب) أَوْ لِأَنَّ الْجُمُوعَ يَتَعَاوَرُ بَعْضُهَا مَوْقِعَ بَعْضٍ، كَقَوْلِهِ تَعَالَى: ﴿كَمْ تَرَكُوا۟ مِن جَنَّٰتٍ وَعُيُونٍ ﴿٢٥﴾﴾ [الدخان] وَقَوْلِهِ: ﴿ثَلَٰثَةَ قُرُوٓءٍ﴾ [البقرة ٢٢٨]؛

(ج) أَوْ لِأَنَّهَا، لَمَّا كَانَتْ مُحَلَّاةً بِاللَّامِ، خَرَجَتْ عَنْ حَدِّ الْقِلَّةِ.

وَ﴿لَّكُمْ﴾: صِفَةُ ﴿رِزْقًا﴾ إِنْ أُرِيدَ بِهِ الْمَرْزُوقُ؛ وَمَفْعُولُهُ إِنْ أُرِيدَ بِهِ الْمَصْدَرُ، كَأَنَّهُ قَالَ: (رِزْقًا إِيَّاكُمْ).

﴿فَلَا تَجْعَلُوا۟ لِلَّهِ أَندَادًا﴾ مُتَعَلِّقٌ (١) بِـ﴿اعْبُدُوا۟﴾ عَلَى أَنَّهُ نَهْيٌ مَعْطُوفٌ

(ii) Or because plurals [of paucity and multitude] interchangeably stand for one another, as in the saying of Allah Most High, *How many were the gardens and the water springs that they left behind!* (al-Dukhān 44:25) and His saying *three periods* (al-Baqara 2:228).

(iii) Or because, once it was fitted with the [definite article] *lām*, it went beyond the parameter of paucity.[852]

Lakum ⁽for you⁾ is the descriptive of ***rizqan*** ⁽as sustenance⁾ if what is meant thereby is the thing provided;[853] or its object if by it is meant the infinitive noun, as if He were saying "sustainment of you."

fa-lā tajʿalū li-l-Lāhi andādan ⁽*therefore do not set up peers to the One God*⁾ appertains I. to ***uʿbudū*** ⁽Worship!⁾ in the sense of (i) a prohibition adjoined to it, ...

[852] "That is, there is no difference between the plurals of multitude and paucity when they are both affixed with the [definite article] *lām*." (Sk) "[The grammarian, exegete and jurist Bahā' al-Dīn 'Abd Allāh b. 'Abd al-Raḥmān] b. 'Aqīl [al-Ḥalabī] (d. 769/1368) said: '...the [definite article] *lām* intimates totality (*istighrāq*), at which time there is no difference anymore between a perfect plural (*jamʿ sālim*) and others.... furthermore, the two plurals [paucity and multitude] become equal through the totalizing of units on the part of the *lām*.'" (S 2:87)

[853] "I.e. sustenance that is yours." (S)

عَلَيْهِ؛ أَوْ نَفْيٌ مَنْصُوبٌ بِإِضْمَارِ (أَنْ)، جَوَابٌ لَهُ؛

(٢) أَوْ بِـ﴿لَعَلَّ﴾ عَلَى أَنَّ نَصْبَ ﴿تَجْعَلُواْ﴾ نَصْبُ ﴿فَأَطَّلِعَ﴾ فِي قَوْلِهِ تَعَالَى ﴿لَّعَلِّيٓ أَبْلُغُ ٱلْأَسْبَٰبَ ٣٦ أَسْبَٰبَ ٱلسَّمَٰوَٰتِ فَأَطَّلِعَ﴾ [غافر]، إِلْحَاقاً لَهَا بِالْأَشْيَاءِ السِّتَّةِ لِاشْتِرَاكِهَا فِي أَنَّهَا غَيْرُ مُوجِبَةٍ. وَالْمَعْنَى: (إِنْ تَتَّقُوا، لَا تَجْعَلُوا للهِ أَنْدَاداً)؛

(٣) أَوْ بِـ﴿ٱلَّذِى جَعَلَ﴾، إِنِ اسْتَأْنَفْتَ بِهِ، عَلَى أَنَّهُ نَهْيٌ وَقَعَ خَبَراً عَلَى تَأْوِيلِ مَقُولٍ فِيهِ: (لَا تَجْعَلُوا)؛ وَالْفَاءُ لِلسَّبَبِيَّةِ، أُدْخِلَتْ عَلَيْهِ ....

(ii) or a negation put in the accusative by an elliptic *an* ⁽that⁾, as its apodosis;[854]

II. or to ***laʿalla*** ⁽perhaps⁾ in the sense that the accusative of ***tajʿalū*** ⁽set up⁾ is the same accusative as *fa'aṭṭaliʿa* ⁽so that I will look upon⁾ in the saying of Allah Most High, *perhaps I will reach the means—the means of heavens—so that I will look in* (Ghāfir 40:36-37), if we sort it [*laʿalla*] as belonging with "the six things" with which it shares non-positiveness.[855] The meaning is: if you beware, do not set up rivals for Allah.

III. Or [it appertains] to ***al-ladhī jaʿala*** ⁽who has made⁾ if you resume [discourse] with the latter, in the sense that it [***fa-lā tajʿalū***] is a prohibition standing as an enunciative adjective if interpreted as a statement whose content is "Do not set up" The *fā'* ⁽therefore⁾ denotes illation[856] and was affixed to it because the

[854] "As an assimilation (*tashbīh*) to the apodosis of a command in light of its coming right after the command *Worship!*—not as its apodosis meaning-wise." (Q, Z)

[855] The six things are command (*amr*), prohibition (*nahy*), interrogation (*istifhām*), suggestion (*ʿarḍ*), wish (*tamannī*) and negation (*nafy*). Non-positiveness means nothing is being positively affirmed (*ʿadam al-ithbāt*). See ʿAbdul-Massih, *Khalīl* (p. 120, *al-ījāb*; p. 235 *al-sittat al-ashyā'*) and K (1:110).

[856] The illative *fā'* is a "particle [that] introduces a clause that expresses the result or

لِتَضَمُّنِ الْمُبْتَدَءِ مَعْنَى الشَّرْطِ. وَالْمَعْنَى: أَنَّ مَنْ خَصَّكُمْ بِهٰذِهِ النِّعَمِ الْجِسَامِ وَالْآيَاتِ الْعِظَامِ، يَنْبَغِي أَنْ لَا يُشْرَكَ بِهِ.

وَ(النِّدُّ): الْمِثْلُ الْمُنَاوِئُ؛ قَالَ جَرِيرٌ: [وافر]

أَتَيْماً تَجْعَلُونَ إِلَيَّ نِدّاً * وَمَا تَيْمٌ لِذِي حَسَبٍ نَدِيدُ

مِنْ (نَدَّ يَنِدُّ نُدُوداً) إِذَا نَفَرَ، وَ(نَادَدْتُ الرَّجُلَ): خَالَفْتُهُ؛ خُصَّ بِالْمُخَالِفِ الْمُمَاثِلِ فِي الذَّاتِ، كَمَا خُصَّ (الْمُسَاوِي) بِالْمُمَاثِلِ فِي الْقَدْرِ.

وَتَسْمِيَةُ مَا يَعْبُدُهُ الْمُشْرِكُونَ مِنْ دُونِ اللهِ ﴿أَندَادًا﴾ ـ وَمَا زَعَمُوا أَنَّهَا

inchoative implies the meaning of a conditional, in the sense that "He Who singled you out with these considerable favors and immense signs ought not to be associated with anything else [in worship]."

Al-nidd ⟨peer⟩ is the coequal rival—Jarīr said: ["The Exuberant"]

What! Taym you dare claim as my peer (ilayya niddan)?
—Taym, unfit to peer highborns![857]

It stems from *nadda,* [aorist] *yaniddu,* [inf. noun] *nudūdan* to denote fleeing. *Nādadtu al-rajulu* means "I opposed the man." It was made specific[858] to an opponent co-equal in essence[859] just as *al-musāwī* ⟨match⟩ was to the co-equal in proportion.

[Worship entails creed in the divine power of the worshipped]

The idolaters' objects of worship besides Allah were named *andādan*—although they did not claim that they ....

effect of a preceding clause." Wright 2:30 C.

857 *Dīwān Jarīr* (1:331) as part of a long lampoon of the Taym.

858 "I.e. in general convention or in sacred law, which is what is meant here." (Q)

859 Or "his co-sharer in substance" (*mushārikuh fil-jawhar*) per al-Rāghib, *Mufradāt* (p. 796, art. *n-d-d*). "Even if he differs from him in quantity and quality." al-Rāghib, *Tafsīr* (1:113).

تُسَاوِيهِ فِي ذَاتِهِ وَصِفَاتِهِ، وَلَا أَنَّهَا تُخَالِفُهُ فِي أَفْعَالِهِ ـ لِأَنَّهُمْ، لَمَّا تَرَكُوا عِبَادَتَهُ إِلَى عِبَادَتِهَا، وَسَمُّوهَا آلِهَةً، شَابَهَتْ حَالُهُمْ حَالَ مَنْ يَعْتَقِدُ أَنَّهَا ذَوَاتٌ وَاجِبَةٌ بِالذَّاتِ، قَادِرَةٌ عَلَى أَنْ تَدْفَعَ عَنْهُمْ بَأْسَ اللهِ، وَتَمْنَحَهُمْ مَا لَمْ يُرِدِ اللهُ بِهِمْ مِنْ خَيْرٍ؛ فَتَهَكَّمَ بِهِمْ، وَشَنَّعَ عَلَيْهِمْ بِأَنْ جَعَلُوا أَنْدَاداً لِمَنْ يَمْتَنِعُ أَنْ يَكُونَ لَهُ نِدٌّ. وَلِهٰذَا، قَالَ مُوَحِّدُ الجَاهِلِيَّةِ زَيْدُ بْنُ عَمْرِو بْنِ نُفَيْلٍ: [وافر]

أَرَبّاً وَاحِداً أَمْ أَلْفَ رَبٍّ ❁ أَدِينُ إِذَا تَقَسَّمَتِ الْأُمُورُ
تَرَكْتُ اللَّاتَ وَالْعُزَّى جَمِيعاً ❁ كَذٰلِكَ يَفْعَلُ الرَّجُلُ الْبَصِيرُ

﴿وَأَنتُمْ تَعْلَمُونَ﴾: حَالٌ مِنْ ضَمِيرِ ﴿فَلَا تَجْعَلُوا﴾.

matched Him in His Essence and Attributes, or that they opposed Him in His actions—because when they turned from worshipping Him to worshipping them and named them gods, their state became similar to that of those who believe such gods are self-necessary entities able to repel from them the wrath of Allah and bestow on them whatever goodness Allah did not wish for them. He therefore derided and reviled them for setting up peers for the One Who is absolutely precluded from having any peer. Hence the pure monotheist of Jāhiliyya, Zayd b. ʿAmr b. Nufayl, said: ["The Exuberant"]

Is it One Lord or a thousand lords
I should creed when matters fall apart?
I have given up al-Lāt and al-ʿUzzā both!—
and that is what a seeing man must do.[860]

wa-antum taʿlamūna ⁽*when you know full well!*⁾ is a participial state of the pronoun in *fa-lā tajʿalū* ⁽therefore do not set up⁾.

[860] Narrated from Asmā' bint Abī Bakr by Ibn ʿAsākir, *Tārīkh* (19:513-514).

وَمَفْعُولُ ﴿تَعْلَمُونَ﴾ (أ) مَطْرُوحٌ، أَيْ: وَحَالُكُمْ أَنَّكُمْ مِنْ أَهْلِ الْعِلْمِ وَالنَّظَرِ وَإِصَابَةِ الرَّأْيِ، فَلَوْ تَأَمَّلْتُمْ أَدْنَى تَأَمُّلٍ، اِضْطَرَّ عَقْلُكُمْ إِلَى إِثْبَاتِ مُوجِدٍ لِلْمُمْكِنَاتِ، مُنْفَرِدٍ بِوُجُوبِ الذَّاتِ، مُتَعَالٍ عَنْ مُشَابَهَةِ الْمَخْلُوقَاتِ؛ (ب) أَوْ مَنْوِيٌّ، وَهُوَ أَنَّهَا لَا تُمَاثِلُهُ، وَلَا تَقْدِرُ عَلَى مِثْلِ مَا يَفْعَلُهُ؛ كَقَوْلِهِ ـ سُبْحَانَهُ وَتَعَالَى ـ: ﴿هَلْ مِن شُرَكَآئِكُم مَّن يَفْعَلُ مِن ذَٰلِكُم مِّن شَيْءٍ﴾ [الروم ٤٠]. وَعَلَى هٰذَا، فَالْمَقْصُودُ مِنْهُ: التَّوْبِيخُ وَالتَّثْرِيبُ، لَا تَقْيِيدُ الْحُكْمِ وَقَصْرُهُ عَلَيْهِ؛ فَإِنَّ الْعَالِمَ وَالْجَاهِلَ الْمُتَمَكِّنَ مِنَ الْعِلْمِ سَوَاءٌ فِي التَّكْلِيفِ.

The object of *taʿlamūn* is

(i) discarded,[861] the sense being, "when you are supposed to be knowledgeable, judicious people and deciders, so that if you thought about it even a little, your own reason would be forced to affirm a Maker for all things in existence, Who alone is necessary in Himself, exalted beyond any resemblance to creatures;"

(ii) or intended, namely: [when you are perfectly aware] they do not resemble Him and are incapable to do what He does, as in the saying of Allah Most High, *Is there any of your associates who can do any of that?* (al-Rūm 30:40). Here the purport would be [unqualified] reprimand and censure, not subject to the status [of being knowledgeable] nor confined to it: for the learned and the ignorant who has access to knowledge are equally liable.

861 "I.e. completely disregarded so that it is neither implied nor intended, rather, the verb is treated as an intransitive and the objective for it to stand squarely in the agent and for the latter to be characterized by it (*ittiṣāfuh bih*) as a pretended hyperbole (*īhāman lil-mubālagha*) in that characterization. That is why he said, 'when you are supposed to be knowledgeable, etc.'" (Z)

وَاعْلَمْ أَنَّ مَضْمُونَ الْآيَتَيْنِ هُوَ الْأَمْرُ بِعِبَادَةِ اللهِ ـ سُبْحَانَهُ وَتَعَالَى ـ وَالنَّهْيُ عَنِ الْإِشْرَاكِ بِهِ تَعَالَى، وَالْإِشَارَةُ إِلَى مَا هُوَ الْعِلَّةُ وَالْمُقْتَضَى. وَبَيَانُهُ: أَنَّهُ رَتَّبَ الْأَمْرَ بِالْعِبَادَةِ عَلَى صِفَةِ الرُّبُوبِيَّةِ، إِشْعَاراً بِأَنَّهَا الْعِلَّةُ لِوُجُوبِهَا؛ ثُمَّ بَيَّنَ رُبُوبِيَّتَهُ بِأَنَّهُ ـ تَعَالَى ـ خَالِقُهُمْ وَخَالِقُ أُصُولِهِمْ وَمَا يَحْتَاجُونَ إِلَيْهِ فِي مَعَاشِهِمْ مِنَ الْمُقِلَّةِ وَالْمُظِلَّةِ وَالْمَطَاعِمِ وَالْمَلَابِسِ؛ فَإِنَّ الثَّمَرَةَ أَعَمُّ مِنَ الْمَطْعُومِ، وَالرِّزْقَ أَعَمُّ مِنَ الْمَأْكُولِ وَالْمَشْرُوبِ. ثُمَّ لَمَّا كَانَتْ هٰذِهِ الْأُمُورُ الَّتِي لَا يَقْدِرُ عَلَيْهَا غَيْرُهُ شَاهِدَةً عَلَى وَحْدَانِيَّتِهِ تَعَالَى، رَتَّبَ ـ تَعَالَى ـ عَلَيْهَا

[Why human beings are all under obligation to worship Allah]

Furthermore, you should know that the content of the two verses [21-22] is the command to worship Allah Most High and the prohibition from associating [anything] with Him, as well as an allusion to the cause[862] and exigency thereof.

To elaborate: He made the command to worship follow in sequence after the descriptive of nurtureship as an intimation that the latter was the cause for the obligatoriness of the former. Then He expounded His nurtureship in that He is their Creator and the Creator of their origins and all that they need for their livelihood: the earth that carries, the sky that shades, foodstuffs and garments—as "fruit" is more comprehensive than "foodstuff" and "sustenance" more comprehensive than "food and drink." Then, after these matters—which none but He is capable of controlling—witnessed to the Oneness of the most High, He

[862] "A cause alluded to in His saying, *your Nurturer Who created you* (2:21) which alludes to the reason behind the command to worship, as [His creation of you] is of the immense bounties which are causes for the obligatoriness of all types of worship." (Q)

النَّهْيَ عَنِ الْإِشْرَاكِ بِهِ. وَلَعَلَّهُ ـ سُبْحَانَهُ ـ أَرَادَ مِنَ الْآيَةِ الْأَخِيرَةِ ـ مَعَ مَا دَلَّ عَلَيْهِ الظَّاهِرُ وَسِيقَ فِيهِ الْكَلَامُ ـ الْإِشَارَةَ إِلَى تَفْصِيلِ خَلْقِ الْإِنْسَانِ وَمَا أَفَاضَ عَلَيْهِ مِنَ الْمَعَانِي وَالصِّفَاتِ عَلَى طَرِيقَةِ التَّمْثِيلِ؛ فَمَثَّلَ الْبَدَنَ بِالْأَرْضِ، وَالنَّفْسَ بِالسَّمَاءِ، وَالْعَقْلَ بِالْمَاءِ؛ وَمَا أَفَاضَ عَلَيْهِ مِنَ الْفَضَائِلِ الْعَمَلِيَّةِ وَالنَّظَرِيَّةِ، الْمُحَصَّلَةِ بِوَاسِطَةِ اسْتِعْمَالِ الْعَقْلِ لِلْحَوَاسِّ، وَازْدِوَاجِ الْقُوَى النَّفْسَانِيَّةِ وَالْبَدَنِيَّةِ: بِالثَّمَرَاتِ الْمُتَوَلِّدَةِ مِنْ اِزْدِوَاجِ الْقُوَى السَّمَاوِيَّةِ الْفَاعِلَةِ، وَالْأَرْضِيَّةِ الْمُنْفَعِلَةِ، بِقُدْرَةِ الْفَاعِلِ الْمُخْتَارِ. فَإِنَّ (**لِكُلِّ آيَةٍ ظَهْراً وَبَطْناً وَلِكُلِّ حَدٍّ مَطْلَعاً / مُطَّلَعاً**).

made the prohibition of associating anything with Him follow them in sequence.

[Quranic polysemy and the allegories of human creation]

It may be that Allah Most High also meant by the latter verse—beside what the manifest locution and the thread of discourse convey—to allude to the detailing of human creation, namely, what He lavished on human beings of inward qualities and attributes in an allegorical style. Thus, He represented the [human] body as the earth, the psyche as the sky and the mind as water, and [He represented] (i) what He lavished on them of practical and intellective gifts reaped through mind-informed use of the senses and (ii) the fusing of psychological and physical powers with the fruits generated by the fusing of active heavenly forces and passive earthly forces through the power of the All-Deciding Effecter. For truly "Each verse possesses a surface and a depth, and to each boundary there is a way up (or vantage-point)."[863]

[863] A Prophetic hadith narrated from Ibn Masʿūd by Abū Yaʿlā in his *Musnad*, ed. Ḥusayn Salīm Asad, 14 vols. (Damascus: Dār al-Maʾmūn lil-Turāth, 1407-1987) 9:80-

﴿وَإِن كُنتُمْ فِي رَيْبٍ مِّمَّا نَزَّلْنَا عَلَىٰ عَبْدِنَا فَأْتُوا۟ بِسُورَةٍ﴾: لَمَّا قَرَّرَ وَحْدَانِيَّتَهُ تَعَالَى، وَبَيَّنَ الطَّرِيقَ الْمُوَصِّلَ إِلَى الْعِلْمِ بِهَا، ذَكَرَ عَقِيبَهُ مَا هُوَ الْحُجَّةُ عَلَى نُبُوَّةِ مُحَمَّدٍ ﷺ: وَهُوَ الْقُرْآنُ، الْمُعْجِزُ (أ) بِفَصَاحَتِهِ الَّتِي بَذَّتْ فَصَاحَةَ كُلِّ مِنْطِيقٍ، (ب) وَإِفْحَامِهِ مَنْ طُولِبَ بِمُعَارَضَتِهِ مِنْ مَصَاقِعِ

[2:23] **wa-in kuntum fī raybin mimmā nazzalnā ʿalā ʿabdinā fa'tū bi-sūratin** ⁽*and if you are in doubt of what We brought down on Our slave, then produce a sura*⁾: after He resolved His absolute oneness and explained the way that leads to knowing it, He proceeded to mention what constitutes the overwhelming proof for the Prophethood of Muḥammad—upon him blessings and peace—namely the Qur'ān, most confounding both in its purity of style (which bested that of every great orator)[864] and its discomfiting of whosoever was summoned to challenge it of the cham-

84 §5149; al-Bazzār, *Musnad* (5:441-442 §2081); al-Ṭabarānī, *al-Muʿjam al-Kabīr* (10:105 §10107) and *al-Muʿjam al-Awsaṭ* (1:236 §773); al-Ṭaḥāwī, *Sharḥ Mushkil al-Āthār*, ed. Shuʿayb al-Arnā'ūṭ (Beirut: Mu'assasat al-Risāla, 1415/1994) 8:87 §3077 and 8:109 §3095; al-Ṭabarī, *Tafsīr, Muqaddima* (1:22); Ibn Ḥibbān, *Ṣaḥīḥ* (1:276 §75). See the complete wording in our introduction (see p. 25 on *aḥruf* and polysemy). "The 'way up' (or 'vantage-point') of the *ẓāhir* is to learn the Arabic disciplines from beginning to end and pursue all that outward knowledge depends on such as the circumstances of revelation, superseding verses and abrogated ones, absolute and particular understanding, what is vague, what is problematic, and other [issues] which are clarified in the principles of jurisprudence. And the 'way up' (or 'vantage-point') of the *bāṭin* is the purification of the self and spiritual training together with conformity to the sacred law through harsh physical efforts and curbing one's temperament, putting into practice the literal texts and proofs of the law as long as there is no strong context that dictates otherwise (through figurative interpretation of those pure outward meanings). At that time the veil will lift through the rising of the winds of subtle kindness from the All-Giving Outpourer (*al-Fayyāḍ al-Wahhāb*), and to him will be disclosed the wellsprings of wisdom and the minute points of greater knowledge. And he will see what others cannot see from the core of the Qur'ān and the realities of spiritual taste." (Q 2:411) See also Kh (2:29-30), S (2:91-92) and *Itqān* (6:2310-2315 type 78).

864 All mss. and eds.: منطيق AQ, H: منطق

الْخُطَبَاءِ مِنَ الْعَرَبِ الْعَرْبَاءِ ـ مَعَ كَثْرَتِهِمْ وَإِفْرَاطِهِمْ فِي الْمُضَادَّةِ وَالْمُضَارَّةِ، وَتَهَالُكِهِمْ عَلَى الْمُعَازَّةِ وَالْمُعَارَّةِ ـ وَعَرَّفَ مَا يُتَعَرَّفُ بِهِ إِعْجَازُهُ وَيُتَيَقَّنُ أَنَّهُ مِنْ عِنْدِ اللهِ كَمَا يَدَّعِيهِ.

وَإِنَّمَا قَالَ: ﴿مِّمَّا نَزَّلْنَا﴾ لِأَنَّ نُزُولَهُ نَجْماً فَنَجْماً بِحَسَبِ الْوَقَائِعِ ـ عَلَى مَا تَرَى عَلَيْهِ أَهْلَ الشِّعْرِ وَالْخَطَابَةِ ـ مِمَّا يُرِيبُهُمْ؛ كَمَا حَكَى اللهُ عَنْهُمْ، فَقَالَ: ﴿وَقَالَ ٱلَّذِينَ كَفَرُواْ لَوْلَا نُزِّلَ عَلَيْهِ ٱلْقُرْءَانُ جُمْلَةً وَٰحِدَةً﴾ [الفرقان ٣٢]. فَكَانَ الْوَاجِبُ تَحَدِّيَهُمْ عَلَى هٰذَا الْوَجْهِ، إِزَاحَةً لِلشُّبْهَةِ وَإِلْزَاماً لِلْحُجَّةِ.

وَأَضَافَ (الْعَبْدَ) إِلَى نَفْسِهِ تَعَالَى تَنْوِيهاً بِذِكْرِهِ، وَتَنْبِيهاً عَلَى أَنَّهُ مُخْتَصٌّ بِهِ، مُنْقَادٌ لِحُكْمِهِ تَعَالَى.

pions of eloquence among pure-blooded Arabs—despite their numbers, extreme antagonism, malignity and zeal for strife and defamation—and He defined that by which its inimitability is recognized and its Divine origin ascertained just as it claims.

The reason he said ***mimmā nazzalnā*** ⁽of what We brought down⁾ is because its descent piecemeal[865] and concurrently with events (just as you can see specialists of poetry and oratory do) was a cause of misgivings for them—as Allah Most High reported them saying, *and those who disbelieved said, if only the Qur'ān was sent down on him all at once* (al-Furqān 25:32)—so it was necessary to challenge them on that very aspect in order to silence objections and make the proof compelling.

He annexed *al-ʿabd* ⁽the slave⁾ to Himself to celebrate him and to serve notice that he exclusively belonged to Him and was bound by His authority.

[865] All mss. and eds.: نجما فنجما AQ, H, MM: نجما منجما

وَقُرِئَ (عِبَادِنَا)، يُرِيدُ مُحَمَّداً ﷺ وَأُمَّتَهُ.

وَ(السُّورَةُ): الطَّائِفَةُ مِنَ الْقُرْآنِ الْمُتَرْجَمَةُ الَّتِي أَقَلُّهَا ثَلَاثُ آيَاتٍ. وَهِيَ -إِنْ جُعِلَتْ وَاوُهَا أَصْلِيَّةً- مَنْقُولَةٌ (١) مِنْ (سُورِ الْمَدِينَةِ): (أ) لِأَنَّهَا مُحِيطَةٌ بِطَائِفَةٍ مِنَ الْقُرْآنِ، مُفْرَزَةٌ، مَحُوزَةٌ عَلَى حِيَالِهَا، (ب) أَوْ مُحْتَوِيَةٌ عَلَى أَنْوَاعٍ مِنَ الْعِلْمِ احْتِوَاءَ سُورِ الْمَدِينَةِ عَلَى مَا فِيهَا؛ (٢) أَوْ مِنَ (السُّورَةِ) الَّتِي هِيَ الرُّتْبَةُ. قَالَ النَّابِغَةُ: [كامل]

وَلِرَهْطِ حَرَّابٍ وَقَدٍّ سُورَةٌ ❊ فِي الْمَجْدِ لَيْسَ غُرَابُهَا بِمُطَارِ

It was also read *ʿibādinā* ⟨Our slaves⟩,[866] by which He meant Muḥammad and his nation.

Al-sūra ⟨sura⟩ is any section of the Qurʾān that has its own name and consists in at least three verses. The word itself,

I. if we consider the *wāw* to be there originally, is a transposition

(i) from the *sūr* ⟨wall⟩ of the city, as it encompasses a section of the Qurʾān that is sectioned off and comprehended within certain limits discretely, or it contains various categories of learning,[867] the way the city wall contains whatever is inside;

(ii) or from the *sūra* ⟨rank, station⟩ which denotes the level. Al-Nābigha said: ["The Perfect"]

And the band of Ḥarrāb and Qadd possess a rank
of glory, its flocks of ravens unruffled.[868]

[866] As in J—by unidentified readers. (*MQ*)

[867] "Respectively pertaining to creed, transactions, morals, stories and parables." (Q)

[868] Ḥarrāb b. Zuhayr and Qadd b. Mālik were two men of the Banū Asad. *Dīwān al-Nābigha* (p. 56). "An *istiʿāra tamthīliyya* ⟨proverbial metaphor⟩ meaning their glory is complete and firm, as it is said 'a land whose ravens cannot be made to fly away' meaning fertile and abundant in fruit." (Q, S)

لِأَنَّ السُّوَرَ كَالْمَنَازِلِ وَالْمَرَاتِبِ، يَتَرَقَّى فِيهَا الْقَارِئُ، أَوَّلُهَا مَرَاتِبُ فِي الطُّولِ وَالْقِصَرِ، وَالْفَضْلِ وَالشَّرَفِ، وَثَوَابِ الْقِرَاءَةِ؛ (٣) وَإِنْ جُعِلَتْ مُبْدَلَةً مِنَ الْهَمْزَةِ، فَمِنَ (السُّؤْرَةِ)، الَّتِي هِيَ الْبَقِيَّةُ وَالْقِطْعَةُ مِنَ الشَّيْءِ.

وَالْحِكْمَةُ فِي تَقْطِيعِ الْقُرْآنِ سُوَراً: إِفْرَادُ الْأَنْوَاعِ، وَتَلَاحُقُ الْأَشْكَالِ، وَتَجَاوُبُ النَّظْمِ، وَتَنْشِيطُ الْقَارِئِ، وَتَسْهِيلُ الْحِفْظِ، وَالتَّرْغِيبُ فِيهِ - فَإِنَّهُ إِذَا خَتَمَ سُورَةً نَفَّسَ ذٰلِكَ عَنْهُ، كَالْمُسَافِرِ إِذَا عَلِمَ ....

For the suras are like way-stops and levels by which the reciter progresses upwards, the first of which[869] being levels in length and brevity, merit and honor and the reward of recitation.

II. Or, if [the *wāw* of *sūra*] is deemed to be a substitute for the *hamza*, then [the word comes] from *al-su*ʾ*ra* ⟨leftover⟩, which is the remainder and portion of something.[870]

[Why the Qurʾān was sectioned into suras]

The wisdom behind the sectioning of the Qurʾān into suras includes

(i) the individualization of categories;

(ii) the close succession of forms;

(iii) the mutual harmony of structure;

(iv) the energizing of the reader;

(v) the facilitation of memorization;

(vi) and the motivation towards it. For when one concludes a sura he is relieved in the same way a traveller is when he knows

869 R: اوّلها with a *shadda*.

870 "Al-Jurjānī: 'There is weakness in this [derivation] lexically as it is unheard of, and from the viewpoint of meaning it suggests paucity and insignificance!" (S)

أَنَّهُ قَطَعَ مِيلاً أَوْ طَوَى بَرِيداً، وَالْحَافِظُ مَتَى حَذَقَهَا اعْتَقَدَ أَنَّهُ أَخَذَ مِنَ الْقُرْآنِ حَظّاً تَامّاً، وَفَازَ بِطَائِفَةٍ مَحْدُودَةٍ مُسْتَقِلَّةٍ بِنَفْسِهَا، فَعَظُمَ ذٰلِكَ عِنْدَهُ وَابْتَهَجَ بِهِ - إِلَى غَيْرِ ذٰلِكَ مِنَ الْفَوَائِدِ.

﴿مِّن مِّثْلِهِۦ﴾: (I) صِفَةُ (سُورَةٍ)؛ أَيْ: بِسُورَةٍ كَائِنَةٍ مِنْ مِثْلِهِ، وَالضَّمِيرُ:

(١) لِـ(مَا نَزَّلْنَا)؛ وَ(مِنْ) لِلتَّبْعِيضِ أَوْ لِلتَّبْيِينِ - وَزَائِدَةٌ عِنْدَ الْأَخْفَشِ - أَيْ بِسُورَةٍ مُمَاثِلَةٍ لِلْقُرْآنِ الْعَظِيمِ فِي الْبَلَاغَةِ وَحُسْنِ النَّظْمِ؛

(٢) أَوْ لِـ﴿عَبْدِنَا﴾، وَ(مِنْ) لِلِابْتِدَاءِ، أَيْ: بِسُورَةٍ كَائِنَةٍ مِمَّنْ هُوَ عَلَى حَالِهِ

he has crossed a milestone or put a travel-leg behind him. Also, when the memorizer has become proficient in it, he believes that he has taken a full share of the Qur'ān and carried off a distinct and independent portion in itself. This is of tremendous importance to him and he is elated by it.

There are other relevant benefits as well.

[Interpretations of the divine challenge]

min mithlihi ⟨*of its like/from his like*⟩ is

I. a descriptive for ***suratin*** ⟨a sura⟩, that is: "a sura that would be of its like," the pronoun referring

1. to ***mā nazzalnā*** ⟨what We brought down⟩, ***min*** ⟨of⟩ denoting division into parts or explication—it is redundant according to al-Akhfash[871]—that is, "a sura matching the magnificent Qur'ān in eloquence and beautiful structure;"

2. or to **'abdinā** ⟨Our slave⟩, *min* denoting [*ab quo*] commencement, that is: "a sura that would be from someone who has the same characteristics as him—upon him blessings and peace—

[871] According to J; but this is not found in the printed edition of al-Akhfash's *Ma'ānī al-Qur'ān*, ed. Hudā Maḥmūd Qarā'a, 2 vols. (Cairo: Maktabat al-Khānjī, 1411/1990).

ـ عَلَيْهِ الصَّلَاةُ وَالسَّلَامُ ـ مِنْ كَوْنِهِ بَشَراً أُمِّيّاً لَمْ يَقْرَأِ الْكُتُبَ وَلَمْ يَتَعَلَّمِ الْعُلُومَ.

(II) أَوْ صِلَةُ ﴿فَأْتُوا﴾، وَالضَّمِيرُ لِلْعَبْدِ ﷺ.

وَالرَّدُّ إِلَى الْمُنْزَلِ أَوْجَهُ، (أ) لِأَنَّهُ الْمُطَابِقُ لِقَوْلِهِ تَعَالَى: ﴿فَأْتُوا بِسُورَةٍ مِّن مِّثْلِهِۦ﴾ وَلِسَائِرِ آيَاتِ التَّحَدِّي؛ (ب) وَلِأَنَّ الْكَلَامَ فِيهِ، لَا فِي الْمُنْزَلِ عَلَيْهِ، فَحَقُّهُ أَنْ لَا يَنْفَكَّ عَنْهُ لِيَتَّسِقَ التَّرْتِيبُ وَالنَّظْمُ؛ (ج) وَلِأَنَّ مُخَاطَبَةَ الْجَمِّ الْغَفِيرِ بِأَنْ يَأْتُوا بِمِثْلِ مَا أَتَى بِهِ وَاحِدٌ مِنْ أَبْنَاءِ جِلْدَتِهِمْ أَبْلَغُ ....

such as being an unlettered human being who did not read books or learn the disciplines."

II. Or [*min mithlihi*] is a prepositional clause for *fa'tū* ⁽then produce⁾, the pronoun [his] referring to the slave—upon him blessings and peace.[872]

However, to refer [the pronoun in *mithlihi*] back to the revelation[873] is more apt,

(i) because it is in keeping with the saying of Allah Most High, *then produce a sura of its like* and with the rest of the verses of challenge;

(ii) because the thread is about it and not about the recipient of revelation, hence it deserves that [the thread] not dissociate itself from it so that sequence and structure can flow;

(iii) because to summon the vast multitudes to produce the like of what one of their own kith and kin has done is a more power-

[872] Thus in both scenarios I.2 and II the pronoun in *mithlih* refers back to the Prophet—upon him blessings and peace—with no difference in meaning other than *min mithlihi* being respectively descriptive or adverbial and Allah knows best.

[873] B: المُنْزَّل indicating *mukhaffaf* and *mushaddad* readings as both correct.

فِي التَّحَدِّي مِنْ أَنْ يُقَالَ لَهُمْ: (لِيَأْتِ بِنَحْوِ مَا أَتَى بِهِ هٰذَا آخَرُ مِثْلُهُ)؛ (د) وَلِأَنَّهُ مُعْجِزٌ فِي نَفْسِهِ، لَا بِالنِّسْبَةِ إِلَيْهِ، لِقَوْلِهِ تَعَالَى: ﴿قُل لَّئِنِ ٱجْتَمَعَتِ ٱلْإِنسُ وَٱلْجِنُّ عَلَىٰٓ أَن يَأْتُوا۟ بِمِثْلِ هَٰذَا ٱلْقُرْءَانِ لَا يَأْتُونَ بِمِثْلِهِۦ﴾ [الإسراء ٨٨]؛ (ه) وَلِأَنَّ رَدَّهُ إِلَى ﴿عَبْدِنَا﴾ يُوهِمُ إِمْكَانَ صُدُورِهِ مِمَّنْ لَمْ يَكُنْ عَلَى صِفَتِهِ: وَلَا يُلَائِمُهُ قَوْلُهُ تَعَالَى.

﴿وَٱدْعُوا۟ شُهَدَآءَكُم مِّن دُونِ ٱللَّهِ﴾، فَإِنَّهُ أَمَرَ بِأَنْ يَسْتَعِينُوا بِكُلِّ مَنْ يَنْصُرُهُمْ وَيُعِينُهُمْ.

وَ(الشُّهَدَاءُ) جَمْعُ شَهِيدٍ بِمَعْنَى ....

ful challenge than for them to be told, "Let something similar to what this one produced be produced by someone just like him;"

(iv) because it is inherently confounding, not just relatively to him,[874] since Allah Most High said, *Say: verily, if mankind and jinn united to produce the like of this Qur'ān they could not produce its like* (al-Isrā' 17:88);

(v) and because to refer it back to *Our slave* suggests the possibility of its production at the hands of someone who does not share his characteristics, which is inappropriate for the discourse of the Most High.

wa-dʿū shuhadā'akum min dūni-l-Lāhi ⁽*and call your witnesses as against the One God*⁾ for He has commanded that they avail themselves of any that would help and support them.

[Meanings of *shahīd* in Arabic usage]

Shuhadā' is the plural of *shahīd* ⁽witness⁾ in the sense of .....

[874] That is, as al-Rāzī pointed out (the list being based on him), the confounding challenge is not limited to a would-be lone and unschooled challenger but to all mankind.

(أ) الْحَاضِرِ، (ب) أَوِ الْقَائِمِ بِالشَّهَادَةِ، (ج) أَوِ النَّاصِرِ، (د) أَوِ الْإِمَامِ ـ وَكَأَنَّهُ سُمِّيَ بِهِ لِأَنَّهُ يَحْضُرُ النَّوَادِي وَتُبْرَمُ بِمَحْضَرِهِ الْأُمُورُ، إِذِ التَّرْكِيبُ لِلْحُضُورِ، إِمَّا بِالذَّاتِ أَوْ بِالتَّصَوُّرِ ـ (ه) وَمِنْهُ قِيلَ لِلْمَقْتُولِ فِي سَبِيلِ اللهِ: (شَهِيدٌ)، لِأَنَّهُ حَضَرَ مَا كَانَ يَرْجُوهُ، أَوِ الْمَلَائِكَةَ حَضَرُوهُ.

وَمَعْنَى ﴿دُونِ﴾: أَدْنَى مَكَانٍ مِنَ الشَّيْءِ؛ وَمِنْهُ: (تَدْوِينُ الْكُتُبِ)، لِأَنَّهُ إِدْنَاءُ الْبَعْضِ مِنَ الْبَعْضِ، وَ(دُونَكَ هٰذَا)، أَيْ: خُذْهُ مِنْ أَدْنَى مَكَانٍ مِنْكَ.

(i) an attendant, (ii) or a standing witness, (iii) or a helper, (iv) or the state leader. The latter seems to have been so named because he attends assemblies and official matters are ratified in his presence—as the construction [*sh-h-d*] is for "presence"[875]—either in essence or conceptually.[876] Hence (v) "the one killed in the path of Allah" is named *shahīd* because he attended what he was hoping to, or because the angels attended him.

[Meanings of *dūn* in Arabic usage]

The meaning of ***dūn*** ⁽beside⁾ is "the nearest point to something."[877] whence *tadwīn al-kutub* ⁽composing books⁾ because it consists in bringing them close to one another, and *dūnaka hādhā* ⁽this is right before you⁾, meaning: "Take it from the spot nearest to you" ....

875 "The fact that *shahīd* is in the sense of *imām* is but one of several instances of the meaning *ḥāḍir* ⁽present⁾, i.e. the letters of *shahīd* in whatever way they are combined and whatever meaning they are meant, always denote 'presence,' *imām* included." (Q)

876 "Presence 'in essence' and 'in person' is self-evident, as in *shahidtu kadhā* ⁽I witnessed such⁾ when I was right there, and 'conceptually' denotes knowledge because the latter is the occurrence of the mental concept of something (lit. its image in the mind), which is as in His saying *Why do you disbelieve in the signs of Allah when you are witnessing* (Āl 'Imrān 3:70), i.e. when you know." (Kh)

877 "But with slight physical lowness (*inḥiṭāṭ qalīl*)." (Q)

ثُمَّ اسْتُعِيرَ لِلرُّتَبِ، فَقِيلَ: (زَيْدٌ دُونَ عَمْرٍو)، أَيْ: فِي الشَّرَفِ؛ وَمِنْهُ: الشَّيْءُ الدُّونُ. ثُمَّ اتُّسِعَ فِيهِ، فَاسْتُعْمِلَ فِي كُلِّ تَجَاوُزِ حَدٍّ إِلَى حَدٍّ وَتَخَطِّي أَمْرٍ إِلَى آخَرَ. قَالَ تَعَالَى: ﴿لَا يَتَّخِذِ الْمُؤْمِنُونَ الْكَافِرِينَ أَوْلِيَاءَ مِن دُونِ الْمُؤْمِنِينَ﴾ [آل عمران ٢٨]، أَيْ: لَا يَتَجَاوَزُوا وَلَايَةَ الْمُؤْمِنِينَ إِلَى وَلَايَةِ الْكَافِرِينَ. قَالَ أُمَيَّةُ:

[بسيط] يَا نَفْسُ مَا لَكِ دُونَ اللهِ مِنْ وَاقٍ * ....

أَيْ: إِذَا تَجَاوَزْتِ وِقَايَةَ اللهِ فَلَا يَقِيكِ غَيْرُهُ.

وَ(مِنْ) مُتَعَلِّقَةٌ (I) بِـ﴿ادْعُوا﴾؛ وَالْمَعْنَى: (أ) وَادْعُوا لِلْمُعَارَضَةِ مَنْ حَضَرَكُمْ أَوْ ....

Then it was borrowed to denote rankings, as in *Zayd dūna ʿAmr* ⟨Zayd is below ʿAmr⟩, meaning in eminence; whence *al-shayʾ al-dūnu* ⟨trivial thing⟩. Finally the sense was extended to apply to any type of overpassing from one limit to another and crossing from one matter to another; Allah Most High said, *Let not the believers take the unbelievers as allies apart from the believers* (Āl ʿImrān 3:28), meaning: let them not overpass alliance with believers for alliance with unbelievers. Umayya said: ["The Outspread"]

O soul! you have not, besides (min dūn) Allah, any protector![878]

that is, "when you overpass the protection of Allah, no one else will protect you."

Min ⟨of, from⟩ pertains

I. to ***udʿū*** ⟨call⟩, where the meaning is,

(i) "and call in opposition whoever is present with you or whose

[878] The second hemistich states "and none perdures over the trials of time." *Dīwān Umayya b. Abī al-Ṣalt*, ed. Sajīʿ Jamīl al-Jubaylī (Beirut: Dār Ṣādir, 1998) p. 91 §83.

رَجَوْتُمْ مَعُونَتَهُ مِنْ إِنْسِكُمْ وَجِنِّكُمْ وَآلِهَتِكُمْ غَيْرَ اللهِ سُبْحَانَهُ وَتَعَالَى؛ فَإِنَّهُ لَا يَقْدِرُ عَلَى أَنْ يَأْتِيَ بِمِثْلِهِ إِلَّا اللهُ؛ (ب) أَوْ: وَادْعُوا مِنْ دُونِ اللهِ شُهَدَاءَ يَشْهَدُونَ لَكُمْ بِأَنَّ مَا أَتَيْتُمْ بِهِ مِثْلُهُ، وَلَا تَسْتَشْهِدُوا بِاللهِ: فَإِنَّهُ مِنْ دَيْدَنِ الْمَبْهُوتِ، الْعَاجِزِ عَنْ إِقَامَةِ الْحُجَّةِ.

(II) أَوْ بِـ﴿شُهَدَآءَكُم﴾، أَيْ: (أ) الَّذِينَ اتَّخَذْتُمُوهُمْ مِنْ دُونِ اللهِ أَوْلِيَاءَ وَآلِهَةً، وَزَعَمْتُمْ أَنَّهَا تَشْهَدُ لَكُمْ يَوْمَ الْقِيَامَةِ؛ (ب) أَوْ: الَّذِينَ يَشْهَدُونَ لَكُمْ بَيْنَ يَدَيِ اللهِ تَعَالَى عَلَى زَعْمِكُمْ - مِنْ قَوْلِ الْأَعْشَى: [طويل]

تُرِيكَ الْقَذَى مِنْ دُونِهَا وَهْيَ دُونَهُ * ....

لِيُعِينُوكُمْ.

support you expect among your humans, genies and gods other than Allah Most High; for truly none but He can bring its like;"

(ii) or, "and call apart from Allah witnesses that will witness on your behalf that what you produced is identical to it; and do not cite Allah as your witness—for that is typical of those who are utterly confounded and incapable of establishing any proof.

II. Or to ***shuhadāʾakum*** ⁽your witnesses⁾, that is:

(i) "those you have adopted *apart from* Allah as your allies and gods, claiming that they will witness on your behalf on the Day of Resurrection;"

(ii) or "those who will witness to your claim for you *in front of* Allah Most High—in the sense of al-Aʿshā's saying ["The Long"],

She shows the speck in front (dūnahā) but she's before it (dūnah)[879]

—in order to help you"

[879] Spoken of *al-ṣahbāʾ* ⁽the wine⁾ inside its glass bottle. The second hemistich says

وَفِي أَمْرِهِمْ أَنْ يَسْتَظْهِرُوا بِالْجَمَادِ فِي مُعَارَضَةِ الْقُرْآنِ الْعَزِيزِ: غَايَةُ التَّبْكِيتِ وَالتَّهَكُّمِ بِهِمْ. وَقِيلَ: ﴿مِّن دُونِ ٱللَّهِ﴾ أَيْ مِنْ دُونِ أَوْلِيَائِهِ ـ يَعْنِي فُصَحَاءَ الْعَرَبِ وَوُجُوهَ الْمَشَاهِدِ ـ لِيَشْهَدُوا لَكُمْ أَنَّ مَا أَتَيْتُمْ بِهِ مِثْلُهُ؛ فَإِنَّ الْعَاقِلَ لَا يَرْضَى لِنَفْسِهِ أَنْ يَشْهَدَ بِصِحَّةِ مَا اتَّضَحَ فَسَادُهُ وَبَانَ اخْتِلَالُهُ.

﴿إِن كُنتُمْ صَٰدِقِينَ﴾ أَنَّهُ مِنْ كَلَامِ الْبَشَرِ. وَجَوَابُهُ مَحْذُوفٌ، دَلَّ عَلَيْهِ مَا قَبْلَهُ.

In the command that they should take lifeless entities[880] as their friends and helpers in opposing the Mighty Qur'ān there is the most scathing rebuke and harshest sarcasm of them.

It was also said that ***min dūni-l-Lāh*** ⁽as against the One God⁾ is "as against His friends"—meaning the orators of the Arabs and those who preside over important gatherings—"witnessing on your behalf that what you produced is identical to it; for rational people do not stoop to bear witness to the veracity of something that is clearly corrupt and patently defective."

in kuntum ṣādiqīna ⁽*if you are truthful*⁾ in [your claim] that it is man-made speech. Its apodosis[881] is suppressed but what precedes points to it.

"Whoever tastes it smacks his tongue/licks his lips." *Dīwān al-A'shā* (p. 219 §33). "Al-Sharīf: he does not mean to say there is a speck but to vaunt the bottle's transparency hyperbolically, and there is in it *tajawwuz* ⁽tropology⁾ and a subtle *istikhdām* ⁽double usage⁾ [i.e. to refer grammatically to the wine—previously brought up in the poem—but semantically to the glass, of which there was no prior mention]." (Kh) "*Istikhdām* is to mention a term that has two meanings, whereby the first meaning is meant by the term itself, then the second meaning is meant through its pronoun, as in *And let any of you that witness the month fast it* (al-Baqara 2:185), where *the month* means the new moon, and *it* means the duration of time." al-Bustānī, *al-Bayān* (pp. 86-87).

880 I.e. their idols. (Iṣ) Or their gods: al-Farrā', *Ma'ānī al-Qur'ān* (1:19). Cf. below, "What is meant by 'the stones' is the idols they carved."

881 I.e. the apodosis of a conditional sentence introduced by *in* ⁽if⁾ of which the prota-

وَ(الصِّدْقُ): الْإِخْبَارُ الْمُطَابِقُ؛ وَقِيلَ: مَعَ اعْتِقَادِ الْمُخْبِرِ أَنَّهُ كَذٰلِكَ عَنْ دِلَالَةٍ أَوْ أَمَارَةٍ، لِأَنَّهُ تَعَالَى كَذَّبَ الْمُنَافِقِينَ فِي قَوْلِهِمْ: ﴿إِنَّكَ لَرَسُولُ ٱللَّهِ﴾ [المنافقون ١] ـ لَمَّا لَمْ يَعْتَقِدُوا مُطَابَقَتَهُ ـ وَرَدَّ بِصَرْفِ التَّكْذِيبِ إِلَى قَوْلِهِمْ: ﴿نَشْهَدُ﴾، لِأَنَّ الشَّهَادَةَ إِخْبَارٌ عَمَّا عَلِمَهُ، وَهُمْ مَا كَانُوا عَالِمِينَ بِهِ.

﴿فَإِن لَّمْ تَفْعَلُواْ وَلَن تَفْعَلُواْ فَٱتَّقُواْ ٱلنَّارَ ٱلَّتِي وَقُودُهَا ٱلنَّاسُ وَٱلْحِجَارَةُ﴾: لَمَّا بَيَّنَ لَهُمْ مَا يَتَعَرَّفُونَ بِهِ أَمْرَ الرَّسُولِ ﷺ وَمَا جَاءَ بِهِ، وَمَيَّزَ ....

[Truthfulness is to report accurately what one knows]

Al-ṣidq ⁽truthfulness⁾ is accurate reporting. Some add: with the reporter's conviction that it is so on the basis of a proof or some indication, because Allah Most High belied the hypocrites when they said, *verily you are indeed the Messenger of Allah* (al-Munāfiqūn 63:1) when in fact they did not consider it accurate, and He rebuffed with a peremptory denial their statement *we bear witness* (al-Munāfiqūn 63:1).[882] For bearing witness is to report what one knows, whereas they did not know it.

[2:24] **fa-in lam tafʿalū wa-lan tafʿalū fa-t-taqū-n-nāra-l-latī waqūduhā-n-nāsu wa-l-ḥijāratu** ⁽*but if you do not—and you will not—then beware the fire whose fuel is people and stones*⁾: after He exposed for them that by which they could recognize the mission of the Messenger and what he brought, and He discerned

sis is *if you are truthful,* and the unspoken apodosis is "Produce a sura of its like" or "Do all that" cf. Bahjat ʿAbd al-Wāḥid Ṣāliḥ, *al-Iʿrāb al-Mufaṣṣal li-Kitāb Allāh al-Murattal,* 12 vols. (Amman: Dār al-Fikr lil-Nashr wal-Tawzīʿ, 1413/1993) 1:31 and Muḥyī al-Dīn Darwīsh, *Iʿrāb al-Qurʾān al-Karīm wa-Bayānuh,* 7th ed., 4 vols. (Damascus and Beirut: al-Yamāma lil-Ṭibāʿa and Dār Ibn Kathīr, 1420/1999) 1:68.

[882] The verse states, *When the hypocrites come to you they say "We testify that verily you are indeed the Messenger of Allah;" and Allah knows that verily you are indeed His Messenger and Allah bears witness that the hypocrites are liars* (al-Munāfiqūn 63:1).

لَهُمُ الْحَقَّ عَنِ الْبَاطِلِ: رَتَّبَ عَلَيْهِ مَا هُوَ كَالْفَذْلَكَةِ لَهُ، وَهُوَ: (أَنَّكُمْ إِذَا اجْتَهَدْتُمْ فِي مُعَارَضَتِهِ وَعَجَزْتُمْ جَمِيعاً عَنِ الْإِتْيَانِ بِمَا يُسَاوِيهِ أَوْ يُدَانِيهِ: ظَهَرَ أَنَّهُ مُعْجِزٌ، وَالتَّصْدِيقُ بِهِ وَاجِبٌ، فَآمِنُوا بِهِ وَاتَّقُوا الْعَذَابَ الْمُعَدَّ لِمَنْ كَذَّبَ!) فَعَبَّرَ عَنِ الْإِتْيَانِ الْمُكَيَّفِ بِالْفِعْلِ الَّذِي يَعُمُّ الْإِتْيَانَ وَغَيْرَهُ إِيجَازاً، وَنَزَّلَ لَازِمَ الْجَزَاءِ مَنْزِلَتَهُ عَلَى سَبِيلِ الْكِنَايَةِ، تَقْرِيراً لِلْمُكَنَّى عَنْهُ، وَتَهْوِيلاً لِشَأْنِ الْعِنَادِ، وَتَصْرِيحاً بِالْوَعِيدِ مَعَ الْإِيجَازِ.

وَصَدَّرَ الشَّرْطِيَّةَ بِـ(إِنْ) الَّتِي لِلشَّكِّ ـ وَالْحَالُ يَقْتَضِي (إِذَا) الَّذِي .....

for them truth from falsehood, He followed up with something which is like the consequence of it all. Namely: "when you have striven hard to oppose it and found yourselves one and all incapable to produce its equal or something remotely like it, it will be obvious that it is inimitable and that confirming its truth is obligatory; therefore believe in it and beware the punishment that is prepared for those who belie."

Thus He rephrased the modalized "producing" into "doing"—a generic term that includes producing and other than that—for the sake of concision. He also treated the apodosis's inseparable concomitant as the apodosis itself[883] metonymically to resolve its tenor,[884] express the direness of obduracy and explicitly declare the threat of punishment with concision.

He initiated the conditional proposition with ***in*** ⁽if⁾, which is for doubt (whereas the situation called for *idhā* ⁽when⁾, which is

[883] The apodosis's inseparable concomitant (*lāzim al-jazā'*) is *fa-t-taqū-n-nār* ⁽then beware the fire⁾ while the apodosis itself is "it will be obvious that it is inimitable." (Q)

[884] "Which is 'Believe and cease obduracy!'" (Z)

لِلْوُجُوبِ، فَإِنَّ الْقَائِلَ سُبْحَانَهُ وَتَعَالَى لَمْ يَكُنْ شَاكّاً فِي عَجْزِهِمْ، وَلِذٰلِكَ نَفَى إِتْيَانَهُمْ مُعْتَرِضاً بَيْنَ الشَّرْطِ وَالْجَزَاءِ - تَهَكُّماً بِهِمْ وَخِطَاباً مَعَهُمْ عَلَى حَسَبِ ظَنِّهِمْ؛ فَإِنَّ الْعَجْزَ قَبْلَ التَّأَمُّلِ لَمْ يَكُنْ مُحَقَّقاً عِنْدَهُمْ.

وَ ﴿تَفْعَلُوا﴾ جُزِمَ بِـ﴿لَمْ﴾ لِأَنَّهَا وَاجِبَةُ الْإِعْمَالِ، مُخْتَصَّةٌ بِالْمُضَارِعِ، مُتَّصِلَةٌ بِالْمَعْمُولِ؛ وَلِأَنَّهَا لَمَّا صَيَّرَتْهُ مَاضِياً، صَارَتْ كَالْجُزْءِ مِنْهُ، وَحَرْفُ الشَّرْطِ كَالدَّاخِلِ عَلَى الْمَجْمُوعِ؛ فَكَأَنَّهُ قَالَ: (فَإِنْ تَرَكْتُمُ الْفِعْلَ)؛ وَلِذٰلِكَ سَاغَ اجْتِمَاعُهُمَا. ﴿وَلَن﴾: كَـ(لَا) فِي نَفْيِ الْمُسْتَقْبَلِ، ....

for inevitability, since the Speaker—may He be extolled and exalted!—did not doubt their incapability, hence He ruled out any producing [of anything] on their part parenthetically, between the protasis and the apodosis), to deride them and address them in terms of their own presumptions. For, prior to scrutiny, incapability had not yet become a certainty to them.

[The first] ***tafʿalū*** ⁽do⁾ is apocopated by *lam* ⁽not⁾[885] because the latter is categorically operative, specific to the aorist tense and connected to the governed [verb]; also, by turning it into the past, it became virtually part of it, with the conditional particle a virtual affix to the whole. Thus it is as if He were saying "but if you shun action"[886] and for that reason they work together well.

Lan ⁽will not⁾ is like *lā* ⁽do/will not⁾ as a future negative, how-

885 "As opposed to being apocopated by [the conditional] *in* ⁽if⁾ since two independent operatives cannot be governing a single regimen." (Z)

886 "This outwardly suggests that they shunned [action] while able to act, because *tark* is commonly understood as willful inaction, so it would make it clearer to say: 'if you are incapable of action—and you will be incapable.'... The purport in this context is the negation of the capability for action, not the negation of action." (Q)

غَيْرَ أَنَّهُ أَبْلَغُ؛ وَهُوَ حَرْفٌ مُقْتَضَبٌ عِنْدَ سِيبَوَيْهِ وَالْخَلِيلِ - فِي إِحْدَى الرِّوَايَتَيْنِ عَنْهُ، وَفِي الرِّوَايَةِ الْأُخْرَى: أَصْلُهُ (لَا أَنْ) - وَعِنْدَ الْفَرَّاءِ: (لَا)، فَأُبْدِلَتْ أَلِفُهَا نُوناً.

وَ(الْوَقُودُ) بِالْفَتْحِ: مَا تُوقَدُ بِهِ النَّارُ؛ وَبِالضَّمِّ: الْمَصْدَرُ. وَقَدْ جَاءَ الْمَصْدَرُ بِالْفَتْحِ؛ قَالَ سِيبَوَيْهِ: وَسَمِعْنَا مَنْ يَقُولُ (وَقَدْتُ النَّارَ وَقُوداً عَالِياً)، وَالْاِسْمُ بِالضَّمِّ. وَلَعَلَّهُ مَصْدَرٌ سُمِّيَ بِهِ، كَمَا قِيلَ: (فُلَانٌ فَخْرُ قَوْمِهِ وَزَيْنُ بَلَدِهِ)، وَقَدْ قُرِئَ بِهِ. ....

ever, it is more assertive.[887] Further, it is an improvised particle[888] according to Sībawayh and al-Khalīl in one of two narratives related from him;[889] the other says its origin is *lā an* ⟨not that⟩. Al-Farrā' said it is a *lā* whose *alif* was substituted by a *nūn*.

Al-waqūd ⟨fuel⟩ with a *fatḥa* is what is used to kindle a fire, and with *ḍamm* it is the infinitive noun. The latter also comes with *fatḥa*—Sībawayh said, "We have heard it said *waqadtu al-nāra waqūdan ʿāliyan* ⟨I kindled the fire into a fierce flaming⟩—and the name with *ḍamm*. The latter is probably an infinitive noun used as a noun, the way one says "X is *fakhru qawmih* ⟨the pride of his folk⟩ and *zaynu baladih* ⟨the adornment of his country⟩."[890] and there is a reading to that effect.[891]

887 See http://arabic.tripod.com/Negation5.htm "Future Tense Negative Sentences."

888 "I.e. cut off from others and not transferred from them. This is what was meant by those who call it *murtajal wuḍiʿa ibtidāʾan* ⟨extemporized, coined out of thin air⟩." (Q)

889 "It is also the preponderant position among latter-day authorities, Abū Ḥayyān and Ibn Hishām." (S)

890 "Linguistic transferences that mean *iftikhār* ⟨taking pride⟩ and *tazyīn* ⟨adorning⟩, then they were both used in the sense of what one takes pride in and what one adorns oneself with." (Z)

891 *Wuqūduhā* by ʿĪsā b. ʿUmar al-Hamdānī with the suppressed governing annex *dhū*,

وَالظَّاهِرُ أَنَّ الْمُرَادَ بِهِ الْإِسْمُ. وَإِنْ أُرِيدَ بِهِ الْمَصْدَرُ، فَعَلَى حَذْفِ مُضَافٍ، أَيْ: (وَقُودُهَا احْتِرَاقُ النَّاسِ وَالْحِجَارَةِ).

وَهِيَ جَمْعُ (حَجَرٍ)، كَـ(جِمَالَةٌ) جَمْعُ (جَمَلٍ)، وَهُوَ قَلِيلٌ غَيْرُ مُنْقَاسٍ. وَالْمُرَادُ بِهَا: (١) الْأَصْنَامُ الَّتِي نَحَتُوهَا، وَقَرَنُوا بِهَا أَنْفُسَهُمْ، وَعَبَدُوهَا طَمَعاً فِي شَفَاعَتِهَا وَالْإِنْتِفَاعِ بِهَا وَاسْتِدْفَاعِ الْمَضَارِّ بِمَكَانَتِهِمْ. وَيَدُلُّ عَلَيْهِ قَوْلُهُ تَعَالَى: ﴿إِنَّكُمْ وَمَا تَعْبُدُونَ مِن دُونِ ٱللَّهِ حَصَبُ جَهَنَّمَ﴾ [الأنبياء ٩٨]. عُذِّبُوا بِمَا هُوَ مَنْشَأُ جُرْمِهِمْ، كَمَا عُذِّبَ الْكَانِزُونَ ....

It appears the noun is meant; and if what is meant is the infinitive noun then it is so with a suppressed governing annex, that is: its fuelling is the combustion of *people and stones.*

The latter is the plural of *ḥajar*, as *jimāla* ⁽camels⁾ is the plural of *jamal*—a rare [form] underivable from any standard.[892]

[The meaning of *ḥijāra*]

What is meant by the stones is

I. the idols they carved, made their familiars and worshipped, expecting they would intercede for them, benefit them and repel harm from them through their standing.[893] This is indicated by the saying of Allah, *Truly you and what you worship apart from Allah are the firebrands of Gehenna* (al-Anbiyā' 21:98): they were punished with the resource of their crime—just as the hoarders[894]

in the sense of "the ingredient (*dhū*) of its kindling" according to Abū Ḥayyān. (*MQ*)

892 "The *Ṣiḥāḥ* says 'the plural of *ḥajar* is *aḥjār* for paucity, and for multitude *ḥijār* and *ḥijāra* as you would say *jamal* and *jimāla*, *dhakar* and *dhikāra* and it is rare.'" (Sk)

893 α, Ak, β, B, D, ε, F, I, Q, P, R, Sk: بمكانتهم L, Ul, Z: بمكانتها AQ, H, K, Kh, MM, U: لمكانتهم J: بمكانهم cf. al-Ṭībī, *Futūḥ* (1:414). "I.e. their [supposed] nearness and position in the divine presence." (Z)

894 α, Ak, β, B, D, ε, F, I, P, Q, R, Sk, U: الكانزون AQ, H, K, L, MM, Ul, Z: الكافرون typo

بِمَا كَنَزُوهُ؛ أَوْ بِنَقِيضِ مَا كَانُوا يَتَوَقَّعُونَ، زِيَادَةً فِي تَحَسُّرِهِمْ. (٢) وَقِيلَ: الذَّهَبُ وَالْفِضَّةُ الَّتِي كَانُوا يَكْنِزُونَهَا وَيَغْتَرُّونَ بِهَا؛ وَعَلَى هٰذَا، لَمْ يَكُنْ لِتَخْصِيصِ إِعْدَادِ هٰذَا النَّوْعِ مِنَ الْعَذَابِ بِالْكُفَّارِ وَجْهٌ. (٣) وَقِيلَ: حِجَارَةُ الْكِبْرِيتِ. وَهُوَ تَخْصِيصٌ بِغَيْرِ دَلِيلٍ وَإِبْطَالٌ لِلْمَقْصُودِ، إِذِ الْغَرَضُ: تَهْوِيلُ شَأْنِهَا وَتَفَاقُمُ لَهَبِهَا، بِحَيْثُ تَتَّقِدُ بِمَا لَا يَتَّقِدُ بِهِ غَيْرُهَا؛ ....

were punished with what they hoarded—or with the diametrical opposite of what they were expecting, to increase their sorrow.

II. It was also said [they mean] the gold and silver they used to hoard and delude themselves with; but in such a case the fact that such punishment is specifically prepared for the unbelievers makes no sense.[895]

III. It was also said [they are] brimstone—a pinpointing that has no proof[896] and nullifies the purport, as the point is to instil fear regarding it and the intense severity of its blaze, which is fueled as no other blaze is fueled. ....

[895] "*Used to hoard* i.e. they used not to remit its *zakāt* as the Qadi explicitly states under Sūrat al-Tawba [9:34].... Gold and silver are called *ḥajar* as in the *Qāmūs*. Punishment for the deniers of *zakāt* is not restricted to the unbelievers, hence the author did not accept this gloss... [but] the sense in which it is understood is that the Muslims' punishment, because it comes to an end, is like nothing in comparison." (Q)

[896] S condemns the Qadi's words here as mere opinion flying in the face of transmitted evidence—as he did before for the gloss of *ghayri al-maghḍūbi ʿalayhim* (see note 360, "This is truly bizarre..."): "Here he follows the *Kashshāf* among his other rejections of sound hadiths and established Prophetic exegeses with pure opinion. We belong to Allah! For the gloss of *ḥijāra* there as brimstone (*ḥijārat al-kibrīt*) is well-established as transmitted evidence and no other gloss is known of in Quranic commentaries." (S 2:116) Kh supports this criticism: "No other kind of stone is inflammable, moreover, it is firmly established in transmitted exegeses exclusively of any other gloss ... and such a gloss by the Companions regarding the hereafter has the status of a Prophetic report by consensus of hadith scholars and many commentators consider it

وَالْكِبْرِيتُ تَتَّقِدُ بِهِ كُلُّ نَارٍ وَإِنْ ضَعُفَتْ. فَإِنْ صَحَّ هٰذَا عَنِ ابْنِ عَبَّاسٍ - رَضِيَ اللهُ تَعَالَى عَنْهُمَا - ....

Sulphur, on the other hand, kindles every common fire, even small ones. Thus, if the report to that effect is sound from Ibn 'Abbās[897]—Allah be well-pleased with him and his father— ......

conclusive. They explain it as denoting more intensive heat, more flames and faster combustion together with its stench, abundant, thick smoke and tenacity to human bodies. So its pinpointing makes sense or rather many true senses both transmission-wise and explanation-wise." (Kh 2:53) But Q rejects S's characterization and Kh's reasoning as the Qadi's position is a strictly Quranic intertextual gloss which is not to be gainsaid by non-*mutawātir* reports: "This report's soundness is not known [i.e. as categorically established knowledge] and even if its soundness were conceded it must necessarily be interpreted figuratively as 'all stones (i.e. the stones they worship) stand in relation to that fire as brimstone stands etc.' and the motive for such interpretation is that the first two meanings are supported by Quranic verses as you know. As for saying that 'the Companions' statements regarding the hereafter have the status of Prophetic reports,' it is moot: lone-narrated reports cannot supplant Quranic verses. Likewise to say that 'many of the commentators consider it conclusive, etc. both transmission-wise and explanation-wise' is weak in light of what you already know, which is that such an objection does not stand up to the author's Qur'ān-supported arguments and his descriptive comparison of all stones in the hereafter to brimstone. I find it odd that some who, even after the author has ascertained his point in undeniable fashion, still relate these statements to suggest some problem." (Q 2:459-460)

897 Narrated *mawqūf* by al-Ṭabarī (1:404) from Mūsā b. Hārūn (*ṣadūq*), from 'Amr b. Ḥammād [al-Qannād] (*ṣadūq*), from Asbāṭ [b. Naṣr] (*ṣadūq kathīr al-khaṭa' yughrib*), from Ismā'īl al-Suddī (*ṣadūq*), from Ibn 'Abbās's students Abū Mālik Ghazwān al-Ghifārī (*thiqa*) and Abū Ṣāliḥ Bādhām Mawlā Umm Hāni' (*ḍa'īf*), from Ibn 'Abbās in the wording *fa-hiya ḥijāratun fil-nār min kibrītin aswad* but Ibn Abī Ḥātim narrates it in his *Tafsīr* (1:64 §245) with his chain through 'Amr as the *maqṭū'* saying of al-Suddī (d. 128/746) as confirmed in the printed edition of the latter's *Tafsīr*, ed. Muḥammad 'Aṭā Yūsuf (al-Manṣūra: Dār al-Wafā', 1414/1993) p. 457 under al-Taḥrīm 66:6. The same is also narrated as a saying of Ibn Mas'ūd, Ibn Jurayj, Mujāhid and Muḥammad b. 'Alī while several other glosses—contrary to al-Suyūṭī's claim—do not mention *kibrīt* cf. Anas, Abū Hurayra and 'Amr b. Dīnār: see al-Ṭabarī (1:403-404), Ibn Abī Ḥātim (1:64-65) and al-Suyūṭī, *Durr* (1:191-192). One gloss has "and these stones are under the second earth, like brimstone" (*mithla al-kibrīt*): *Tafsīr Muqātil* (1:94).

فَلَعَلَّهُ عَنَى بِهِ: أَنَّ الْأَحْجَارَ كُلَّهَا لِتِلْكَ النَّارِ كَحِجَارَةِ الْكِبْرِيتِ لِسَائِرِ النِّيرَانِ.

وَلَمَّا كَانَتِ الْآيَةُ مَدَنِيَّةً - نَزَلَتْ بَعْدَ مَا نَزَلَ بِمَكَّةَ قَوْلُهُ تَعَالَى فِي سُورَةِ التَّحْرِيمِ [٦] ﴿نَارًا وَقُودُهَا ٱلنَّاسُ وَٱلْحِجَارَةُ﴾ وَسَمِعُوهُ - صَحَّ تَعْرِيفُ النَّارِ وَوُقُوعُ الْجُمْلَةِ صِلَةً بِإِزَائِهَا؛ فَإِنَّهَا يَجِبُ أَنْ تَكُونَ قِصَّةً مَعْلُومَةً.

﴿أُعِدَّتْ لِلْكَٰفِرِينَ﴾: هُيِّئَتْ لَهُمْ وَجُعِلَتْ عُدَّةً لِعَذَابِهِمْ. وَقُرِئَ: (أُعْتِدَتْ) مِنَ الْعَتَادِ، بِمَعْنَى الْعُدَّةِ.

then he might have meant by it that all stones stand in relation to that fire as brimstone stands in relation to all other fires.[898]

Since the verse is Medinan—revealed subsequently to the Meccan revelation of the saying of Allah in Sūrat al-Taḥrīm, *a fire of which the fuel is people and stones* (66:6),[899] which they had heard—the fire could be put in the definite with a relative clause in its wake, for the latter needs to be a familiar story.

uʿiddat lil-kāfirīn ⁽*it was readied for the unbelievers*⁾: it was prepared for them and was made a provision for their punishment.

It was also read *uʿtidat* ⁽it was outfitted⁾[900] from *ʿatād* ⁽outfit⁾ in the sense of *ʿudda* ⁽gear⁾.

[898] "Ibn ʿAbbās's statement that they are brimstone is understood as an arch-effective simile (*maḥmūl ʿalā al-tashbīh al-balīgh*)." (Z)

[899] "This is a misapprehension on J's part by general agreement as exegetes all agree that Sūrat al-Taḥrīm is Medinan. It would have been enough for him to say that the latter was revealed before this verse, both of them in Medina." (S) "Except for 'a narration from Qatāda that its first ten verses are Medinan and the rest Meccan,' thus stated in the *Itqān*." (Sk)

[900] By Ibn Masʿūd cf. al-ʿUkbarī, *Iʿrāb al-Qirā'āt al-Shawādhdh*, ed. Muḥammad ʿAzzūz, 2 vols. (Beirut: ʿĀlam al-Kutub, 1417/1996) 1:137-138, "also *uʿtiddat* and *aʿtaddtu*."

وَالْجُمْلَةُ: اسْتِئْنَافٌ؛ أَوْ حَالٌ بِإِضْمَارِ (قَدْ) مِنَ النَّارِ لَا الضَّمِيرِ الَّذِي فِي ﴿وَقُودُهَا﴾ ـ وَإِنْ جَعَلْتَهُ مَصْدَراً ـ لِلْفَصْلِ بَيْنَهُمَا بِالْخَبَرِ.

وَفِي الْآيَتَيْنِ مَا يَدُلُّ عَلَى النُّبُوَّةِ مِنْ وُجُوهٍ: الْأَوَّلُ: مَا فِيهِمَا مِنَ التَّحَدِّي، وَالتَّحْرِيضِ عَلَى الْجِدِّ وَبَذْلِ الْوُسْعِ فِي الْمُعَارَضَةِ بِالتَّقْرِيعِ وَالتَّهْدِيدِ، وَتَعْلِيقِ الْوَعِيدِ عَلَى عَدَمِ الْإِتْيَانِ بِمَا يُعَارِضُ أَقْصَرَ سُورَةٍ مِنْ سُوَرِ الْقُرْآنِ. ثُمَّ إِنَّهُمْ ـ مَعَ كَثْرَتِهِمْ، وَاشْتِهَارِهِمْ بِالْفَصَاحَةِ، ....

The sentence is resumptive.[901] Alternately, it is a participial state with an implied *qad* (already) for *al-nār*—not for the pronoun in ***waqūduhā***,[902] even if you consider the latter an infinitive noun, because they are separated by the enunciative.[903]

[Proofs of Prophethood in the divine challenge]

In the two verses there are indicators of Prophethood from several perspectives. First, there is in them a defiant challenge and instigation for opponents to make every effort and do their utmost[904] by rebuking and threatening them as well as making next-worldly punishment hang on their incapacity to produce anything in opposition of even the shortest sura in all the Qur'ān.[905] Yet even after that, despite their numbers, famed elo-

[901] This shows the inadequacy of translating *uʿiddat* merely as an adjective (e.g. "prepared," "ready")—not to mention a relative clause ("which awaits," "which is prepared")—since resumption is "not adjoined to the preceding relative clause but rather underlines its own importance as the declarative purport in itself, not dependent on what precedes." (Q) This is also what al-Taftāzānī leans to. (S)

[902] "I.e. it is impermissible for the sentence to be a participial state of the annexed pronoun in *waqūduhā*." (Z)

[903] "Namely *al-nās* and its adjunct [*al-ḥijāra*]. The infinitive noun becomes inoperative (*lā yaʿmal*) when something extraneous crops up between it and its regimen because it is a weak-operant noun (*ism ḍaʿīf al-ʿamal*)." (Z)

[904] By saying *call your witnesses apart from Allah*. (Q)

[905] By saying *but if you do not—and you will not*. (Q)

وَتَهَالُكِهِمْ عَلَى الْمُضَادَّةِ ـ لَمْ يَتَصَدَّوا لِمُعَارَضَتِهِ، وَالْتَجَؤُوا إِلَى جَلَاءِ الْوَطَنِ وَبَذْلِ الْمُهَجِ. وَالثَّانِي: أَنَّهُمَا يَتَضَمَّنَانِ الْإِخْبَارَ عَنِ الْغَيْبِ عَلَى مَا هُوَ بِهِ؛ فَإِنَّهُمْ لَوْ عَارَضُوهُ بِشَيْءٍ، لَامْتَنَعَ خَفَاؤُهُ عَادَةً، سِيَّمَا وَالطَّاعِنُونَ فِيهِ أَكْثَرُ مِنَ الذَّابِّينَ عَنْهُ فِي كُلِّ عَصْرٍ. وَالثَّالِثُ: أَنَّهُ ﷺ لَوْ شَكَّ فِي أَمْرِهِ: لَمَا دَعَاهُمْ إِلَى الْمُعَارَضَةِ بِهٰذِهِ الْمُبَالَغَةِ، مَخَافَةَ أَنْ يُعَارَضَ، فَتُدْحَضَ حُجَّتُهُ.

وَقَوْلُهُ تَعَالَى: ﴿أُعِدَّتْ لِلْكَٰفِرِينَ﴾ دَلَّ عَلَى أَنَّ النَّارَ مَخْلُوقَةٌ، مُعَدَّةٌ الْآنَ لَهُمْ.

quence and fierce antagonistic zeal, they could not put up any resistance against it, resorting instead to ostracism and bloodshed. Second, they entail information about the unseen in precise terms.[906] Had they opposed it in any way, it would be typically unthinkable for such to remain hidden, especially when its would-be critics number more than its defenders in every era. Third, had the Prophet—upon him blessings and peace—been in any way uncertain about his own status, he would have never summoned them to oppose him with such intensity lest he be opposed and his proofs be dashed.[907]

The saying of Allah Most High *it is ready for the unbelievers* indicates that Hellfire has already been created and is ready for them as we speak.[908]

906 His saying *and you will not.* (Q)

907 "For no other reason than his trust in Allah Most High; and their inability to hurt him was through no other than His making him invulnerable to them. Such a situation constitutes a confirmation (*taṣdīq*) on the part of Allah; and that is the meaning of the confounding miracle. … He said this to clarify the Prophet's—upon him blessings and peace—boldness toward them." (Q)

908 Contrary to the Muʿtazila [who hold that it is not created yet]. (Q) This confirms the inadequacy of translating *uʿiddat* as merely adjectival as most have done. "As for the Muslim sinners in Hellfire, their punishment will not be everlasting and they will not be punished with the severest punishment nor with the most humiliating one.

﴿وَبَشِّرِ ٱلَّذِينَ ءَامَنُواْ وَعَمِلُواْ ٱلصَّٰلِحَٰتِ أَنَّ لَهُمْ جَنَّٰتٍ﴾ عطفٌ:

(أ) عَلَى الْجُمْلَةِ السَّابِقَةِ. وَالْمَقْصُودُ: عَطْفُ حَالِ مَنْ آمَنَ بِالْقُرْآنِ الْعَظِيمِ وَوَصْفِ ثَوَابِهِ عَلَى حَالِ مَنْ كَفَرَ بِهِ وَكَيْفِيَّةِ عِقَابِهِ، عَلَى مَا جَرَتْ بِهِ الْعَادَةُ الْإِلٰهِيَّةُ مِنْ أَنْ يَشْفَعَ التَّرْغِيبَ بِالتَّرْهِيبِ، تَنْشِيطاً لِاكْتِسَابِ مَا يُنْجِي وَتَثْبِيطاً عَنِ اقْتِرَافِ مَا يُرْدِي ـ لَا عَطْفُ الْفِعْلِ نَفْسِهِ حَتَّى يَجِبَ أَنْ يُطْلَبَ لَهُ مَا يُشَاكِلُهُ مِنْ أَمْرٍ أَوْ نَهْيٍ فَيُعْطَفَ عَلَيْهِ.

(ب) أَوْ عَلَى ﴿فَٱتَّقُواْ﴾، لِأَنَّهُمْ إِذَا لَمْ يَأْتُوا بِمَا يُعَارِضُهُ بَعْدَ التَّحَدِّي:

[2:25] **wa-bashshiri-l-ladhīna āmanū wa-ʿamilū-ṣ-ṣāliḥāti anna lahum jannātin** ⁽*and give glad tidings to those who believe and do righteous deeds, that for them are gardens*⁾ is an adjunction

I. to the previous sentence. The point is to adjoin the position of those who believe in the magnificent Qurʾān and the description of their reward to the position of those who disbelieved in it and in the modality of their retribution. This in accordance with the Divine habit of pairing encouragement with deterrence as a stimulus towards the acquisition of saving deeds and a preventive from the perpetration of ruinous ones. Thus, it is not an adjunction of the verb [*bashshir*] itself—in which case we would be required to look for its formal match such as [another] jussive or a prohibitive for it to be adjoined to.[909]

II. Or [it is adjoined] to ***fa-t-taqū*** ⁽then beware⁾; because once they could not produce anything to counter it after being chal-

Rather, they will be there for purification and preparation before entering the Abode of Safety." (Q)

909 "Al-Quṭb [al-Shīrāzī] said: 'This adjunction does not pertain to the vocable itself but to meaning.'" (S) On this type of semantic adjunction see note 601.

ظَهَرَ إِعْجَازُهُ؛ وَإِذَا ظَهَرَ ذٰلِكَ، فَمَنْ كَفَرَ بِهِ اسْتَوْجَبَ الْعِقَابَ، وَمَنْ آمَنَ بِهِ اسْتَحَقَّ الثَّوَابَ. وَذٰلِكَ يَسْتَدْعِي أَنْ يُخَوِّفَ هٰؤُلَاءِ وَيُبَشِّرَ هٰؤُلَاءِ.

وَإِنَّمَا أَمَرَ الرَّسُولَ ﷺ، أَوْ عَالِمَ كُلِّ عَصْرٍ، أَوْ كُلَّ أَحَدٍ يَقْدِرُ عَلَى الْبِشَارَةِ بِأَنْ يُبَشِّرَهُمْ ـ وَلَمْ يُخَاطِبْهُمْ بِالْبِشَارَةِ كَمَا خَاطَبَ الْكَفَرَةَ ـ تَفْخِيماً لِشَأْنِهِمْ وَإِيذَاناً بِأَنَّهُمْ أَحِقَّاءُ بِأَنْ يُبَشَّرُوا وَيُهَنَّؤُوا بِمَا أُعِدَّ لَهُمْ.

وَقُرِئَ (وَبُشِّرَ) عَلَى الْبِنَاءِ لِلْمَفْعُولِ عَطْفاً عَلَى ﴿أُعِدَّتْ﴾، فَيَكُونُ اسْتِئْنَافاً. وَ(الْبِشَارَةُ): الْخَبَرُ السَّارُّ، فَإِنَّهُ يُظْهِرُ أَثَرَ السُّرُورِ فِي الْبَشَرَةِ، وَلِذٰلِكَ قَالَ الْفُقَهَاءُ: الْبِشَارَةُ هِيَ الْخَبَرُ الْأَوَّلُ، ....

lenged, its inimitability became evident; and once that became evident, whoever rejects it must be penalized and whoever believes in it deserves reward; consequently, He had to intimidate the former and give glad tidings to the latter.

The order was given to the Messenger—upon him blessings and peace—or to the savant of every age, or to every individual capable of giving glad tidings, to do so. He did not direct the glad tidings to them directly—the way He addressed the unbelievers—in order to amplify their status and proclaim that they truly merit glad tidings and congratulations for what has been prepared for them.

It was also read *wa-bushshira* ⟨and were given glad tidings⟩[910] in the passive voice as an adjunct to *uʿiddat* ⟨it was readied⟩, in which case [the clause] is resumptive.

Al-bishāra ⟨glad tidings⟩ is "news that gladdens," since the latter causes the effect of gladness to show in the complexion. Hence the jurists said, "the *bishāra* is the first-heard news," so

[910] By Zayd b. ʿAlī (*MQ*).

حَتَّى لَوْ قَالَ الرَّجُلُ لِعَبِيدِهِ: (مَنْ بَشَّرَنِي) بِقُدُومِ وَلَدِي فَهُوَ حُرٌّ، فَأَخْبَرُوهُ فُرَادَى عَتَقَ أَوَّلُهُمْ؛ وَلَوْ قَالَ: (مَنْ أَخْبَرَنِي)، عَتَقُوا جَمِيعاً. وَأَمَّا قَوْلُهُ تَعَالَى: ﴿فَبَشِّرْهُم بِعَذَابٍ أَلِيمٍ﴾ [آل عمران ٢١]: فَعَلَى التَّهَكُّمِ أَوْ عَلَى طَرِيقَةِ قَوْلِهِ:

[الوافر] .... ❋ تَحِيَّةُ بَيْنِهِمْ ضَرْبٌ وَجِيعُ

وَ﴿الصَّالِحَاتِ﴾ جَمْعُ (صَالِحَةٍ)، وَهِيَ مِنَ الصِّفَاتِ الْغَالِبَةِ الَّتِي تَجْرِي مَجْرَى الْأَسْمَاءِ، كَـ(الْحَسَنَةِ). قَالَ الْحُطَيْئَةُ: [بسيط]

كَيْفَ الْهِجَاءُ وَمَا تَنْفَكُّ صَالِحَةٌ ❋ مِنْ آلِ لَأْمٍ بِظَهْرِ الْغَيْبِ تَأْتِينِي

that if one were to say to one's slaves, "Whoever *gives me the good news* of my son's coming is free," after which several of them inform him individually: [only] the first one of them is set free; but if he said, "Whoever *informs me*," then they would all be set free.

As for the saying of Allah Most High, *Give them the glad tidings of a painful punishment* (Āl ʿImrān 3:21), it is understood as sarcasm or as in the style of [the poet's] phrase: ["The Exuberant"]

Their mutual greetings are agonizing blows.[911]

Al-ṣāliḥāt is the plural of *ṣāliḥa* ʿrighteous deedʾ, one of the predominantly substantival epithets that are treated exactly as nouns such as *al-ḥasana* ʿexcellent deedʾ.[912] Al-Ḥuṭayʾa said: ["The Outspread"]

How to lampoon when righteous deeds constantly—from
the La'm folk, without my asking—keep coming to me?[913]

911 See note 641.

912 "In the sense that they are mentioned without a *mawṣūf* ʿthing described or qualifiedʾ." (Sk) "I.e. as *asmāʾ jāmida* ʿstationary nouns, nouns incapable of growthʾ" (Kh) "Like *al-naṭīḥa* ʿgored beastʾ." (Z)

913 Spoken in praise of the poet Ḥāritha b. La'm al-Ṭāʾī, known as Ibn Suʿdā, after

وَهِيَ مِنَ الْأَعْمَالِ مَا سَوَّغَهُ الشَّرْعُ وَحَسَّنَهُ؛ وَتَأْنِيثُهَا عَلَى تَأْوِيلِ الْخَصْلَةِ أَوِ الْخَلَّةِ. وَاللَّامُ فِيهَا: لِلْجِنْسِ. وَعَطْفُ الْعَمَلِ عَلَى الْإِيمَانِ ـ مُرَتِّباً لِلْحُكْمِ عَلَيْهِمَا ـ إِشْعَارٌ بِأَنَّ السَّبَبَ فِي اسْتِحْقَاقِ هٰذِهِ الْبِشَارَةِ مَجْمُوعُ الْأَمْرَيْنِ، وَالْجَمْعُ بَيْنَ الْوَصْفَيْنِ؛ فَإِنَّ الْإِيمَانَ الَّذِي هُوَ عِبَارَةٌ عَنِ التَّحْقِيقِ وَالتَّصْدِيقِ أُسٌّ، وَالْعَمَلُ الصَّالِحُ كَالْبِنَاءِ عَلَيْهِ. وَلَا غِنَاءَ بِأُسٍّ لَا بِنَاءَ عَلَيْهِ، ....

They are the types of acts which the sacred law has validated and approved.[914] The word is in the feminine in the sense of the *khaṣla* ⟨characteristic⟩ or *khalla* ⟨trait⟩,[915] while the [definite article] *lām* in it denotes species.[916]

He adjoined deeds to belief by making the stipulation[917] sequentially dependent upon the two of them, as a proclamation[918] that the reason for meriting such glad tidings is the sum of the two things and the combination of the two qualities. For belief—which is a term for verification and confirmation—is a foundation while righteous work is like an edifice on top of it. It is surely insufficient[919] to have a foundation with nothing built on it;

enviers had promised al-Ḥuṭay'a 100 camels if he lampooned him, whereupon he replied: "How can I lampoon a youth to whom I owe even the laces on my sandals?" cf. Afendi (p. 626) and *Dīwān al-Ḥuṭay'a bi-Riwāya wa-Sharḥ Ibn al-Sikkīt*, ed. Nuʿmān Ṭaha (Cairo: Maktabat al-Khānjī, 1407/1987) p. 295 §77.

914 "A warning that 'what is 'fine and good is what the Law deems fine and good' (*al-ḥasan ma ḥassanahu al-sharʿ*), which is the Ashʿarī position" (Q) as opposed to the Muʿtazila who made human reason—and not Allah—the arbiter of right and wrong.

915 "I.e. that is what the word described before it turned from an epithet to a noun." (Sk)

916 "As opposed to comprehensiveness (*istighrāq*), because no believer can do all the righteous deeds." (A, S)

917 "I.e. the stipulation of giving glad tidings." (Kh, Q)

918 Ak, B, Q, R, T: اشعارٌ α, AQ, β, D, ε, F, H,I, K, Kh, L, MM, P, Sk, U, Ul, Z: اشعارا which are both correct depending whether one reads وَعَطَفَ or وَعَطْفُ respectively.

919 "*Lā ghinā'a* with *kasr*, meaning *lā istighnā'a* ⟨one cannot dispense with⟩, whereas

وَلِذٰلِكَ قَلَّمَا ذُكِرَا مُنْفَرِدَيْنِ.

وَفِيهِ دَلِيلٌ عَلَى أَنَّهَا خَارِجَةٌ عَنْ مُسَمَّى الْإِيمَانِ، إِذِ الْأَصْلُ أَنَّ الشَّيْءَ لَا يُعْطَفُ عَلَى نَفْسِهِ، وَلَا عَلَى مَا هُوَ دَاخِلٌ فِيهِ.

﴿أَنَّ لَهُمْ﴾ مَنْصُوبٌ بِنَزْعِ الْخَافِضِ وَإِفْضَاءِ الْفِعْلِ إِلَيْهِ، أَوْ مَجْرُورٌ بِإِضْمَارِهِ مِثْلَ: (اللهِ لَأَفْعَلَنَّ).

وَ(الْجَنَّةُ): الْمَرَّةُ مِنَ (الْجَنِّ)، وَهُوَ مَصْدَرُ (جَنَّهُ) إِذَا سَتَرَهُ ـ وَمَدَارُ

hence they are seldom mentioned separately from one another.

In [the adjunction] there is also proof that [deeds] lie outside the designation of *īmān* ʿfaithʾ since, in principle, a thing is not adjoined to itself nor to something that is [already] part of it.[920]

Anna lahum ʿthat for themʾ is

1. in the accusative through (i) the removal of the genitival operative[921] and (ii) the reaching up of the verb to it;
2. or in the genitive through ellipsis [of the operative][922] as in *Allāhi la-afʿalanna* ʿ[I swear by] Allah I will certainly do it!ʾ.

[Meanings of the word *janna* and the names of paradise]

Al-janna ʿgardenʾ is a specimen of *jann* ʿover-coveringʾ which is the infinitive noun for *jannahu*, "it covered him" — the whole

to say *ghanāʾa* with *fatḥ* in the sense of 'benefit' suggests the negation of benefit altogether if one has faith and nothing else—which is the position of the Muʿtazila." (Sk)

920 "This statement of his is explicit in that the foundation by itself is sufficient, and he has said it explicitly in a previous passage [see note 486]. Thus there is an implied rebuttal of some of the Muʿtazila who said that all deeds are part of it." (Q) "When he says 'in principle' (*fīl-aṣl*) he alludes to the fact that such adjunction can happen contrary to principle as a subtle point, as in the adjunction of Jibrīl to the angels [in Sūrat al-Baqara 2:97], which is too well-known to need mention." (Kh)

921 "The accusative is the position of Sībawayh and al-Farrāʾ. In principle, it would be *bi-anna lahum*, so the annexing particle (*ḥarf al-jarr*) was suppressed." (Q, Z)

922 "This is the position of al-Khalīl and al-Kisāʾī." (Q, Z)

التَّرْكِيبِ عَلَى السَّتْرِ - سُمِّيَ بِهَا (أ) الشَّجَرُ الْمُظَلِّلُ لِالْتِفَافِ أَغْصَانِهِ، لِلْمُبَالَغَةِ، كَأَنَّهُ يَسْتُرُ مَا تَحْتَهُ سَتْرَةً وَاحِدَةً؛ قَالَ زُهَيْرٌ: [بسيط]

كَأَنَّ عَيْنَيَّ فِي غَرْبَيْ مُقَتَّلَةٍ * مِنَ النَّوَاضِحِ تَسْقِي جَنَّةً سُحُقَا

أَيْ نَخْلاً طِوَالاً؛ (ب) ثُمَّ الْبُسْتَانُ، لِمَا فِيهِ مِنَ الْأَشْجَارِ الْمُتَكَاثِفَةِ الْمُظَلِّلَةِ؛ (ج) ثُمَّ دَارُ الثَّوَابِ لِمَا فِيهَا مِنَ الْجِنَانِ. وَقِيلَ: سُمِّيَتْ بِذٰلِكَ لِأَنَّهُ سُتِرَ فِي الدُّنْيَا مَا أُعِدَّ فِيهَا لِلْبَشَرِ مِنْ أَفْنَانِ النِّعَمِ، كَمَا قَالَ سُبْحَانَهُ وَتَعَالَى: ﴿فَلَا تَعْلَمُ نَفْسٌ مَّآ أُخْفِيَ لَهُم مِّن قُرَّةِ أَعْيُنٍ﴾ [السجدة ١٧].

stem-form revolves around covering over[923] — and is a name for (i) shady trees because of their thick branchage for intensiveness, as if covering all that lies underneath with a single cover. Zuhayr said: ["The Outspread"]

As if my eyes were the two buckets a docile draught-camel used
among the beasts of burden to water a remote garden,[924]

that is, tall datepalms. Then [it came to denote]
(ii) an orchard because of the thick-branched, shady trees in it;
(iii) then the abode of rewards because of the gardens in it.

It was also said that the latter was thus named because all the varieties of divine bounties that were prepared for human beings in it were kept out of sight in this world, as Allah Most High said, *So no soul knows what was hidden for them of delight of the eyes* (al-Sajda 32:17).

[923] "I.e. the letters of *j-n-n* comprise the meaning of covering, whence a shield is called *junna*, the heart within is called *janān*; *junūn* ‹insanity› expresses the over-shadowing of reason; the *jinn* are thus called for being covered away from people's eyesights; and the *janīn* ‹fetus› is covered up inside his mother's belly." (Z)
[924] Zuhayr, *Dīwān* (p. 73).

وَجَمْعُهَا وَتَنْكِيرُهَا: لِأَنَّ الْجِنَانَ، عَلَى مَا ذَكَرَهُ ابْنُ عَبَّاسٍ - رَضِيَ اللهُ عَنْهُمَا - سَبْعٌ: جَنَّةُ الْفِرْدَوْسِ، وَجَنَّةُ عَدْنٍ، وَجَنَّةُ النَّعِيمِ، وَدَارُ الْخُلْدِ، وَجَنَّةُ الْمَأْوَى، وَدَارُ السَّلَامِ، وَعِلِّيُّونَ؛ وَفِي كُلِّ وَاحِدَةٍ مِنْهَا مَرَاتِبُ وَدَرَجَاتٌ مُتَفَاوِتَةٌ عَلَى حَسَبِ تَفَاوُتِ الْأَعْمَالِ وَالْعُمَّالِ.

وَاللَّامُ فِي ﴿لَهُمْ﴾ تَدُلُّ عَلَى اسْتِحْقَاقِهِمْ إِيَّاهَا لِأَجْلِ ....

They are in the plural and the indefinite because paradises, according to what Ibn ʿAbbās—Allah be well-pleased with him and his father—said, are seven:

1. the garden of Firdaws ⁽vineyard⁾,
2. the garden of ʿAdn ⁽permanence⁾,
3. the garden of Naʿīm ⁽bliss⁾,
4. the garden of Khuld ⁽eternity⁾,
5. the garden of Ma'wā ⁽settlement⁾,
6. the Abode of Peace,
7. and ʿIlliyyūn ⁽highmost⁾;[925]

and in each of them there are vastly differing ranks and levels corresponding with vastly differing deeds and their authors.

The *lām* in **lahum** ⁽for them⁾ indicates their deserving it[926] be-

925 The Qadi took this report from al-Rāghib's *Tafsīr* as did al-Qurṭubī in *al-Tadhkira* (with Dār al-Jalāl instead of ʿIlliyyūn), Ibn ʿĀdil, al-Shirbīnī, Abū al-Suʿūd and others in their *Tafsīr*s but it is undocumented as stated by S and al-Munāwī in the *Fatḥ*. All of the above are among the thirty-odd established names for paradise in the sources but they may all be synonymous collective names for paradise rather than referring to different places. For comprehensive references see Ibn Abī al-Dunyā's *Ṣifat al-Janna*, Abū Nuʿaym's *Ṣifat al-Janna*, Ibn al-Qayyim's *Ḥādī al-Arwāḥ ilā Bilād al-Afrāḥ* and in the last part of al-Mundhirī's *al-Targhīb wal-Tarhīb*.

926 A preamble to the author's rebuttal of the Muʿtazila who posited that belief and good deeds in themselves made it rationally incumbent upon Allah to bestow reward

مَا تَرَتَّبَ عَلَيْهِ مِنَ الْإِيمَانِ وَالْعَمَلِ الصَّالِحِ، لَا لِذَاتِهِ ـ فَإِنَّهُ لَا يُكَافِئُ النِّعَمَ السَّابِقَةَ، فَضْلاً عَنْ أَنْ يَقْتَضِيَ ثَوَاباً وَجَزَاءً فِيمَا يُسْتَقْبَلُ ـ بَلْ بِجَعْلِ الشَّارِعِ؛ وَمُقْتَضَى وَعْدِهِ تَعَالَى: لَا عَلَى الْإِطْلَاقِ، بَلْ بِشَرْطِ أَنْ يَسْتَمِرَّ عَلَيْهِ حَتَّى يَمُوتَ وَهُوَ مُؤْمِنٌ، لِقَوْلِهِ تَعَالَى: ﴿وَمَن يَرْتَدِدْ مِنكُمْ عَن دِينِهِۦ فَيَمُتْ وَهُوَ كَافِرٌ فَأُولَٰٓئِكَ حَبِطَتْ أَعْمَٰلُهُمْ﴾ [البقرة ٢١٧]، ....

cause of the immediately preceding sequence of belief and good deeds, not in themselves—for they hardly repay past [divine] bounties, let alone obligate reward and requital for the future—but by the Lawgiver's stipulation and the dictate of His promise;[927] and [even so] not in absolute terms, but on condition that one persevere with them until death as a believer, just as Allah Most High said, *and whoever among you recants his religion and dies an unbeliever: their deeds have come apart* (al-Baqara 2:217),

upon the believer, while the Sunni creed is that law, not reason, made belief and good deeds the avenues of reward through Divine generosity and not in themselves, as already shown in his *tafsīr* on *laʿallakum tattaqūn* [see note 833]. (Kh, Q, Z)

927 Such as the verses *Know you not that unto Allah belongs the Sovereignty of the heavens and the earth? He punishes whom He will, and forgives whom He will. Allāh is Able to do all things* (al-Māʾida 5:40); *Say : Who then can do anything against Allah, if He had willed to destroy the Messiah son of Mary, and his mother and everyone on earth? To Allāh belongs the Sovereignty of the heavens and the earth and all that is between them. He creates what He will. And Allah is Able to do all things* (al-Māʾida 5:17); *The sentence that comes from Me cannot be changed, and I am in no wise a tyrant unto the slaves* (Qāf 50:29). At the same time it is obligatorily known that Allah does not take back His promise to reward those who believe and do good and punish evil-doers: *But as for those who believe and do good works We shall bring them into gardens under which rivers flow, wherein they will abide for ever. It is a promise from Allah in truth; and who can be more truthful than Allah in utterance?* (al-Nisāʾ 4:122). The scholars have described the former evidence as a reason-based proof *(dalīl ʿaqlī)* and the latter as a law-based proof *(dalīl sharʿī)*, noting that it is the latter which takes precedence over the former, cf. Muḥammad Saʿīd al-Būṭī, *Kubrā al-Yaqīniyyāt al-Kawniyya*, 8th ed. (Damascus: Dār al-Fikr, 1982, rept. 1417/1997) p. 149.

وَقَوْلِهِ تَعَالَى لِنَبِيِّهِ ﷺ: ﴿لَئِنْ أَشْرَكْتَ لَيَحْبَطَنَّ عَمَلُكَ﴾ [الزمر ٦٥] وَأَشْبَاهِ ذَلِكَ. وَلَعَلَّهُ ـ سُبْحَانَهُ وَتَعَالَى ـ لَمْ يُقَيِّدْ هٰهُنَا اسْتِغْنَاءً بِهَا.

﴿تَجْرِي مِن تَحْتِهَا ٱلْأَنْهَٰرُ﴾: أَيْ مِنْ تَحْتِ أَشْجَارِهَا، كَمَا تَرَاهَا جَارِيَةً تَحْتَ الْأَشْجَارِ النَّابِتَةِ عَلَى شَوَاطِئِهَا. وَعَنْ مَسْرُوقٍ: أَنْهَارُ الْجَنَّةِ تَجْرِي فِي غَيْرِ أُخْدُودٍ.

وَاللَّامُ فِي ﴿ٱلْأَنْهَٰرُ﴾ لِلْجِنْسِ، كَمَا فِي قَوْلِكَ لِفُلَانٍ: (بُسْتَانٌ فِيهِ الْمَاءُ الْجَارِي)؛ أَوْ لِلْعَهْدِ، وَالْمَعْهُودُ: هِيَ الْأَنْهَارُ الْمَذْكُورَةُ فِي قَوْلِهِ تَعَالَى: ﴿فِيهَآ أَنْهَٰرٌ مِّن مَّآءٍ غَيْرِ ءَاسِنٍ﴾، الْآيَةَ [محمد ﷺ ١٥].

and He said to His Prophet—upon him blessings and peace—*if you associate [partners with Allah] your deeds will certainly fall apart* (al-Zumar 39:65) among similar verses. Perhaps Allah Most High did not qualify right here, because they sufficed.

[The rivers of paradise]

tajrī min taḥtihā-l-anhāru ⁽*underneath which run the rivers*⁾—that is underneath its trees, just as you see them flowing beneath the trees that shoot up on their banks. Masrūq said: "The rivers of Paradise run without river-beds."[928]

The [definite article] *lām* in ***al-anhār*** ⁽the rivers⁾ is for the species, as when you say to someone, "an orchard amidst flowing waters;" or for previous knowledge, namely the rivers previously mentioned in the saying of Allah Most High, *Therein are rivers of water unpolluted* (Muḥammad 47:15) and the rest of the verse.

[928] Narrated by Ibn Abī Shayba, *Muṣannaf* (18:407 §35091) and others. Also narrated as a saying of Anas by Ibn Abī al-Dunyā in *Ṣifat al-Janna wa-Mā Aʿadda Allāhu li-Ahlihā min al-Naʿīm*, ed. ʿAbd al-Raḥīm al-ʿAsāsila (Amman: Dār al-Bashīr; Beirut: Muʾassasat al-Risāla, 1417/1997) p. 90-91 §69.

وَ(النَّهْـرُ) بِالْفَتْحِ وَالسُّكُونِ: الْمَجْرَى الْوَاسِعُ، فَوْقَ الْجَدْوَلِ وَدُونَ
الْبَحْرِ، كَالنِّيلِ وَالْفُرَاتِ؛ وَالتَّرْكِيبُ لِلسَّعَةِ؛ وَالْمُرَادُ بِهَا مَاؤُهَا عَلَى الْإِضْمَارِ
أَوِ الْمَجَازِ، أَوِ الْمَجَارِي أَنْفُسُهَا. وَإِسْنَادُ الْجَرْيِ إِلَيْهَا مَجَازٌ، كَمَا فِي قَوْلِهِ
تَعَالَى: ﴿وَأَخْرَجَتِ الْأَرْضُ أَثْقَالَهَا ۝٢﴾، الْآيَةَ [الزلزلة].

﴿كُلَّمَا رُزِقُوا مِنْهَا مِن ثَمَرَةٍ رِّزْقًا قَالُوا هَٰذَا الَّذِي رُزِقْنَا﴾: (أ) صِفَةٌ
ثَانِيَةٌ لِـ﴿جَنَّٰتٍ﴾، (ب) أَوْ خَبَرُ مُبْتَدَإٍ مَحْذُوفٍ، (ج) أَوْ جُمْلَةٌ مُسْتَأْنَفَةٌ.

Al-nah(a)r—with *fatḥ* and *sukūn*—is the wide channel, bigger than a stream but smaller than the sea, such as the Nile and the Euphrates. The stem-formation [*n-h-r*] conveys vastness.[929] What is actually meant by them is their water—either elliptically or metonymically—or the channels themselves. As for the ascription of running to them it is figurative, as in the saying of Allah Most High *and the earth brought out its burdens* (al-Zalzala 99:2).

kullamā ruziqū minhā min thamaratin rizqan qālū hādhā-l-ladhī ruziqnā ‹*whenever they are provided thereof with fruit as a provision they say: This is what was provided to us*› is (i) a second descriptive for ***jannātin*** ‹gardens›;[930] (ii) or the enunciative of a suppressed inchoative;[931] (iii) or a resumptive clause.

929 "For *nahār* is the name for a vast light from the rising of the sun until its setting; it is said *anharta al-ṭaʿna* when you make a vast cut; *istanhara al-shay'* means something became large; and *anharta al-damm* means you shed a lot of blood." (Z) "*Manhara* is vacant space between people's courtyards where they trhrow their refuse." (S) "I.e. the forms of the root *n-h-r* all entail the meaning of vastness. As for *nahr* in the sense of censuring, what is meant by it is a harsh rebuke as al-Rāghib explained: so it entails moral vastness." (Q)

930 "I.e. a second complimentary epithet, the first being *tajrī*, so it is desinentially accusative." (Q)

931 "I.e. 'Those who (*al-ladhīna*), whenever they are provided,' or 'that which (*hiya*), whenever they are provided…'" (Q)

كَأَنَّهُ، لَمَّا قِيلَ: ﴿أَنَّ لَهُمْ جَنَّٰتٍ﴾، وَقَعَ فِي خَلَدِ السَّامِعِ: أَثْمَارُهَا مِثْلُ ثِمَارِ الدُّنْيَا أَوْ أَجْنَاسٌ أُخَرُ؟ فَأُزِيحَ بِذٰلِكَ. وَ﴿كُلَّمَا﴾ نُصِبَ عَلَى الظَّرْفِ، وَ﴿رِزْقًا﴾ مَفْعُولٌ بِهِ، وَ﴿مِن﴾ الْأُولَى وَالثَّانِيَةُ لِلِابْتِدَاءِ، وَاقِعَتَانِ مَوْقِعَ الْحَالِ. وَأَصْلُ الْكَلَامِ وَمَعْنَاهُ: (كُلَّ حِينٍ رُزِقُوا مَرْزُوقاً مُبْتَدَأً مِنَ الْجَنَّاتِ، مُبْتَدَأً مِنْ ثَمَرَةٍ). قَيَّدَ الرِّزْقَ بِكَوْنِهِ مُبْتَدِئاً مِنَ الْجَنَّاتِ، وَابْتِدَاؤُهُ مِنْهَا بِابْتِدَائِهِ مِنْ ثَمَرَةٍ، فَصَاحِبُ الْحَالِ الْأُولَى ﴿رِزْقًا﴾، وَصَاحِبُ الْحَالِ الثَّانِيَةِ ضَمِيرُهُ الْمُسْتَكِنُّ فِي الْحَالِ.

It is as if, when it was said *that for them are gardens*, the listener mused: "Are its fruits like the fruits of this world, or are they different species?" so it was put aside with that.

[The fruits of paradise]

Kullamā ⟨whenever⟩ is in the accusative as a temporal vessel. ***Rizqan*** ⟨as provision⟩ is a direct object. The first and second *min* are both for [*ab quo*] commencement and come as participial states.[932] Literally the meaning of the discourse is "every moment they are provided a certain provision starting from the gardens, starting from fruit:" He qualified provision as starting[933] from the gardens and its start from the latter is by starting from fruit. So the actor of the first participial state is *rizqan* while that of the second participial state is the covert personal pronoun [standing for *rizqan*] within the [first] participial state.

[932] "This is somewhat imprecise: for a particle to 'come as participial state' makes no sense. What is meant is that their appurtenances (*muta'alliqayhimā*) come as participial states, becoming two stable temporal-local vessels: respectively, *rizqan* and the covert pronoun within the participial state." (Q) See also Z (1:210) on this paragraph.

[933] B, F, Kh, U: مبتدئا x3 α: مُبْتَدِياً 3x R: مبتداء... مبتداءً... مبتداء Ak, T: مبتدًا... مبتدا... مبتدا I: مبتدِياً... مبتدءً... مبتدءً β: مبتدء... مبتداء... مبتديا ε: مبتدا... [missing]... مبتدا haplography H, K, L, MM, P, Sk, Ul, Z: مبتدأ 3x modern sp. for the same reading as Ak, R, T, ε.

وَيَحْتَمِلُ أَنْ يَكُونَ ﴿مِن ثَمَرَةٍ﴾ بَيَاناً تَقَدَّمَ، كَمَا فِي قَوْلِكَ: (رَأَيْتُ مِنْكَ أَسَداً)، وَهٰذَا إِشَارَةٌ إِلَى نَوْعِ مَا رُزِقُوا، كَقَوْلِكَ مُشِيراً إِلَى نَهْرٍ جَارٍ: (هٰذَا الْمَاءُ! لَا يَنْقَطِعُ)؛ فَإِنَّكَ لَا تَعْنِي بِهِ الْعَيْنَ الْمُشَاهَدَةَ مِنْهُ، بَلِ النَّوْعَ الْمَعْلُومَ الْمُسْتَمِرَّ بِتَعَاقُبِ جَرَيَانِهِ، وَإِنْ كَانَتِ الْإِشَارَةُ إِلَى عَيْنِهِ. فَالْمَعْنَى: (هٰذَا مِثْلُ الَّذِي)؛ وَلٰكِنْ لَمَّا اسْتَحْكَمَ الشَّبَهُ بَيْنَهُمَا، جُعِلَ ذَاتُهُ ذَاتَهُ، كَقَوْلِكَ: (أَبُو يُوسُفَ أَبُو حَنِيفَةَ).

It is also possible that ***min thamaratin*** ⟨with fruit⟩ is a preposed explicative as when you say, "I saw, out of you, a lion."[934] This would be an allusion to the species of what they are provided, as when you say, pointing to a running river, "This is water! It never ends," whereby you do not mean by that the individuated object you are observing but rather the identifiable species that keeps flowing without cease, even though the allusion you made was to its individuated object. So the meaning is, "This is identical to what was [provided]." However, since the resemblance between the two was so strong, they were made one and the same,[935] as when you say: "Abū Yūsuf is Abū Ḥanīfa."

[934] "Making it a *min tajrīdiyya* ⟨abstractive, highlighting a single quality⟩." (Q) "He put the explication ahead of the thing being explicated, namely *rizqan*, as when you say 'I saw of you a lion' when what you mean is 'you are a lion.' So the meaning of the verse would be, 'every time they are provided with some provision from the gardens being fruit or a specific kind of fruit." (Z) "Al-Raḍiy said: It is permissible to prepose the explicative *min* ahead of the unidentified object, similar to when you say 'I have of property what suffices' (*'indī min al-māl mā yakfi*), because the unidentified object being disclosed by the explicative *min* is virtually placed ahead, as if you had said, 'I have *something* of property that suffices,' and whatever follows is its explicative adjunction. In this sense it is correct that by *thamara* is meant the species (*al-naw'*) and by *jannāt* the specimen (*al-wāḥida*)." (Sk)

[935] "In that they share one and the same generic quiddity (*al-māhiyya al-naw'iyya*)." (Z)

﴿مِن قَبْلُ﴾: مِنْ قَبْلِ هٰذَا (I) فِي الدُّنْيَا؛ جَعَلَ ثَمَرَ الْجَنَّةِ مِنْ جِنْسِ ثَمَرِ الدُّنْيَا، (أ) لِتَمِيلَ النَّفْسُ إِلَيْهِ أَوَّلَ مَا يُرَى - فَإِنَّ الطِّبَاعَ مَائِلَةٌ إِلَى الْمَأْلُوفِ، مُتَنَفِّرَةٌ عَنْ غَيْرِهِ - (ب) وَيَتَبَيَّنَ لَهَا مَزِيَّتُهُ وَكُنْهُ النِّعْمَةِ فِيهِ؛ إِذْ لَوْ كَانَ جِنْساً لَمْ يُعْهَدْ، ظُنَّ أَنَّهُ لَا يَكُونُ إِلَّا كَذٰلِكَ.

(II) أَوْ فِي الْجَنَّةِ، لِأَنَّ طَعَامَهَا مُتَشَابِهٌ فِي الصُّورَةِ، كَمَا حُكِيَ عَنِ الْحَسَنِ: (أَنَّ أَحَدَهُمْ يُؤْتَى بِالصَّحْفَةِ فَيَأْكُلُ مِنْهَا، ثُمَّ يُؤْتَى بِأُخْرَى فَيَرَاهَا مِثْلَ الْأُولَى، فَيَقُولُ ذٰلِكَ، فَيَقُولُ الْمَلَكُ: ....

min qablu ⁽*in former times*⁾:[936] I. "before this in the world:" He made the fruit of paradise of the same species as the fruit of the world, (i) so that souls will be attracted to it from the first glimpse, since temperaments incline to the familiar and shun the rest; (ii) and so that its superiority and the extent of the divine favor therein become evident to them; for if it consisted in a previously unknown species it might be imagined that the latter is invariably like that.[937]

II. Or "[before this] in paradise," because its fare all looks similar,

(i) as attributed to al-Ḥasan—Allah Most High be well-pleased with him:[938] "One will be brought a large dish and eat from it; then another dish will be brought for him which he will view as identical to the first—and say so—whereupon the angel will say,

[936] α, B, R: من قبل هذا Ak, β, ε, F, I, Sk, T: اي من قبل هذا

[937] "If it were specimens of a previously unknown species, its superiority over all the other specimens of that species would not have come to light, rather, it would be imagined that all its specimens are just like that." (Z)

[938] α, Ak, β, B, D, ε, I, J, R, S, Sk, T: عن الحسن L, P, Q, U, Ul, Z: عن الحسن رضى الله تعالى عنه AQ, H, K, MM: ابن كثير عن الحسن رضى الله عنهما The latter is a corruption of the original text in al-Rāghib's *Tafsīr* (1:124) which reads: وإليه ذهب الحسن ويحيى بن أبي كثير

كُلْ، فَاللَّوْنُ وَاحِدٌ وَالطَّعْمُ مُخْتَلِفٌ)؛ أَوْ كَمَا رُوِيَ أَنَّهُ ـ عَلَيْهِ الصَّلَاةُ وَالسَّلَامُ ـ قَالَ: وَالَّذِي نَفْسُ مُحَمَّدٍ بِيَدِهِ، إِنَّ الرَّجُلَ مِنْ أَهْلِ الْجَنَّةِ لَيَتَنَاوَلُ الثَّمَرَةَ لِيَأْكُلَهَا، فَمَا هِيَ بِوَاصِلَةٍ إِلَى فِيهِ، حَتَّى يُبْدِلُ اللهُ تَعَالَى مَكَانَهَا مِثْلَهَا. فَلَعَلَّهُمْ، إِذَا رَأَوْهَا عَلَى الْهَيْئَةِ الْأُولَى، قَالُوا ذٰلِكَ. وَالْأَوَّلُ أَظْهَرُ، لِمُحَافَظَتِهِ عَلَى عُمُومِ ﴿كُلَّمَا﴾، فَإِنَّهُ يَدُلُّ عَلَى تَرْدِيدِهِمْ هٰذَا الْقَوْلَ كُلَّ مَرَّةٍ رُزِقُوا. وَالدَّاعِي لَهُمْ إِلَى ذٰلِكَ: فَرْطُ اسْتِغْرَابِهِمْ وَتَبَجُّحِهِمْ بِمَا وَجَدُوا ....

'Eat! the hue is one but the savors differ;"[939]

(ii) or as narrated from him—upon him blessings and peace:

> By Him in Whose Hand rests the soul of Muḥammad! Truly a man from the dwellers of paradise shall pluck a fruit to eat it and it will hardly reach his mouth before Allah Most High substitutes its like in its place.[940]

Hence, it may be that when they see it in the first form [a second time], they say that. However, the first explanation is more distinct because it preserves the comprehensiveness of ***kullamā*** ⟨whenever⟩, as it indicates that they repeat that statement every time they receive provision.[941] What impels them to do that is their great astonishment and exultation when they experience

[939] Narrated from Yaḥyā b. Abī Kathīr by al-Ṭabarī in his *Tafsīr* (1:410) and Ibn Abī Ḥātim in his (1:76 §261), as also narrated from Ibn 'Abbās, Ibn Mas'ūd, Abū al-'Āliya, Mujāhid, al-Rabī' b. Anas, al-Suddī and others cf. Ṭabarī (1:414-415) and Ibn Kathīr, *Tafsīr* (1:321-322). None of them mentions al-Ḥasan other than J and al-Rāghib.

[940] Narrated from Thawbān by al-Bazzār, *Musnad* (10:123 §4187); Ḥākim, *Mustadrak* (4:497 *ṣaḥīḥ 'alā sharṭ al-shaykhayn*); al-Ṭabarānī, *al-Mu'jam al-Kabīr* (2:102 §1449) through trustworthy narrators according to al-Haythamī, *Majma'al-Zawā'id* (10:414).

[941] "I consider the second explanation more conclusive because it is consistent with the meaning of the hadith of the mutual resemblance of the fruits of paradise and agrees with His saying afterwards, *and they are supplied with it, each resembling the other.*" (S)

مِنَ التَّفَاوُتِ الْعَظِيمِ فِي اللَّذَّةِ وَالتَّشَابُهِ الْبَلِيغِ فِي الصُّورَةِ.

﴿وَأُتُوا بِهِۦ مُتَشَٰبِهًا﴾ اِعْتِرَاضٌ يُقَرِّرُ ذٰلِكَ؛ وَالضَّمِيرُ (I) عَلَى الْأَوَّلِ: رَاجِعٌ إِلَى مَا رُزِقُوا فِي الدَّارَيْنِ، فَإِنَّهُ مَدْلُولٌ عَلَيْهِ بِقَوْلِهِ ـ عَزَّ مِنْ قَائِلٍ ـ: ﴿هَٰذَا الَّذِى رُزِقْنَا مِن قَبْلُ﴾. وَنَظِيرُهُ قَوْلُهُ ـ عَزَّ وَجَلَّ ـ: ﴿إِن يَكُنْ غَنِيًّا أَوْ فَقِيرًا فَاللَّهُ أَوْلَىٰ بِهِمَا﴾ [النساء ١٣٥]، أَيْ: بِجِنْسَيِ الْغَنِيِّ وَالْفَقِيرِ؛ (II) وَعَلَى الثَّانِي: إِلَى الرِّزْقِ.

such a vast difference in pleasure despite extreme resemblance in form.

wa-utū bihi mutashābihan ⁽*and they are supplied with it, all looking similar*⁾ is a parenthesis that resolves that.[942]

The personal pronoun [in *bihi*],

(i) according to the first explanation, refers to what they were provided in the two abodes.[943] For that is what is indicated in the saying of the Almighty *This is what was provided to us in former times.* Another example of it[944] is His saying *whether it is a rich man or a poor man yet Allah is more entitled to both* (al-Nisā' 4:135): that is, to the two categories of the rich and the poor.

(ii) According to the second [explanation], it refers to ***rizqan.***[945]

[942] "I.e. the resemblance of the provisions of the world and those of paradise." (Z)

[943] "I.e., the singular annexed pronoun in *bihi* refers to the first of the two glosses just mentioned, namely that *min qabl* ⁽in former times⁾ means 'in the world,' so that they were given it in the two abodes." (Kh) "I.e. they were given some provision in the two abodes, each looking like the other, some of it in the past and some in the future but using the past tense." (Sk)

[944] "I.e., of the reference to a singular when, in fact, the referent is multiple." (Z)

[945] "I.e. the singular annexed pronoun in *bihi* refers to *rizqan* per the second gloss in the sense that they were given provision in paradise that looks mutually similar." (Z)

فَإِنْ قِيلَ: التَّشَابُهُ هُوَ التَّمَاثُلُ فِي الصِّفَةِ، وَهُوَ مَفْقُودٌ بَيْنَ ثَمَرَاتِ الدُّنْيَا وَالْآخِرَةِ، كَمَا قَالَ ابْنُ عَبَّاسٍ - رَضِيَ اللهُ تَعَالَى عَنْهُمَا -: **لَيْسَ فِي الْجَنَّةِ مِنْ أَطْعِمَةِ الدُّنْيَا إِلَّا الْأَسْمَاءُ**؛ قُلْتُ: التَّشَابُهُ بَيْنَهُمَا حَاصِلٌ فِي الصُّورَةِ الَّتِي هِيَ مَنَاطُ الْإِسْمِ، دُونَ الْمِقْدَارِ وَالطَّعْمِ؛ وَهُوَ كَافٍ فِي إِطْلَاقِ التَّشَابُهِ.

هٰذَا؛ وَإِنَّ لِلْآيَةِ الْكَرِيمَةِ مَحْمَلاً آخَرَ: وَهُوَ أَنَّ مُسْتَلَذَّاتِ أَهْلِ الْجَنَّةِ فِي مُقَابَلَةِ مَا رُزِقُوا فِي الدُّنْيَا مِنَ الْمَعَارِفِ وَالطَّاعَاتِ مُتَفَاوِتَةٌ فِي اللَّذَّةِ بِحَسَبِ تَفَاوُتِهَا؛ فَيَحْتَمِلُ أَنْ يَكُونَ الْمُرَادُ مِنْ ﴿هَٰذَا ٱلَّذِى رُزِقْنَا﴾ أَنَّهُ ثَوَابُهُ، .....

If someone asks, "*Tashābuh* (similitude) is 'identity in character.' which is missing between the fruits of the world and those of paradise, as Ibn ʿAbbās said, 'There is nothing in paradise of the foods of the world[946] except the names,'"[947] I reply: 'Similitude' between them takes place in *form*, which is that on which the word hinges—as opposed to quantity and taste—which suffices to call [it] similitude.

[Allegorical interpretation of the "similar fruits" of paradise]

This said, the noble verse has a further meaning: namely, that the delights of the people of paradise, in comparison with what they were provided in the world of types of learning and acts of obedience, differ proportionately in pleasure.[948] So it is possible that what is meant by *This is what was provided to us* is its reward,[949] ....

[946] AQ, H : الدنيا missing—lacuna.
[947] Narrated by al-Ṭabarī, *Tafsīr* (1:416), Wakīʿ and Hannād's *zuhd* books and others.
[948] "I.e. the difference of the types of learning and acts of worship in their increase or decrease in quality and quantity." (Q)
[949] "I.e. that which is being provided in the hereafter is the reward of that which had been provided in the world." (Q)

وَمِنْ تَشَابُهِهِمَا تَمَاثُلُهُمَا فِي الشَّرَفِ وَالْمَزِيَّةِ وَعُلُوِّ الطَّبَقَةِ. فَيَكُونُ هٰذَا فِي الْوَعْدِ نَظِيرَ قَوْلِهِ: ﴿ذُوقُوا۟ مَا كُنتُمْ تَعْمَلُونَ﴾ [العنكبوت ٥٥] فِي الْوَعِيدِ.

﴿وَلَهُمْ فِيهَآ أَزْوَٰجٌ مُّطَهَّرَةٌ﴾ مِمَّا يُسْتَقْذَرُ مِنَ النِّسَاءِ وَيُذَمُّ مِنْ أَحْوَالِهِنَّ، كَالْحَيْضِ وَالدَّرَنِ وَدَنَسِ الطَّبْعِ وَسُوءِ الْخُلُقِ، فَإِنَّ (التَّطْهِيرَ) يُسْتَعْمَلُ فِي الْأَجْسَامِ وَالْأَخْلَاقِ وَالْأَفْعَالِ.

وَقُرِئَ: (١) (مُطَهَّرَاتٌ)، وَهُمَا لُغَتَانِ فَصِيحَتَانِ. يُقَالُ: (النِّسَاءُ فَعَلَتْ وَفَعَلْنَ)، وَ(هُنَّ فَاعِلَةٌ وَفَوَاعِلُ). قَالَ: [كامل]

وَإِذَا الْعَذَارَى بِالدُّخَانِ تَقَنَّعَتْ * وَاسْتَعْجَلَتْ نَصْبَ الْقُدُورِ فَمَلَّتِ

and, by their similitude, their being identical in honor, excellence and exalted status. Thus it is the promissory counterpart of the threat *Taste what you used to do* (al-ʿAnkabūt 29:55).

wa-lahum fīhā azwājun muṭahharatun ⁽*and they have therein spouses immaculate*⁾ from what is considered dirty in women and what is disapproved in their conditions, such as menses, filth, foul disposition and bad character; for "purification" can be applied to bodies, characters and deeds.

It was also read

(i) *muṭahharātun* ⁽fem. pl. form⁾.[950] Both [w. *muṭahharatun*] are chaste dialectical forms. One says "the womenfolk *faʿalat* ⁽did [sing.]⁾ and *faʿalna* ⁽did [pl.]⁾; they are *fāʿilatun* ⁽doer(s) [fem. sing.] and *fawāʿil* ⁽doers [fem. pl.]⁾." [The poet] said: ["The Perfect"]

And when the virgins wore masks (taqannaʿat) of smoke,
too impatient to set up pots, and grilled on cinders.[951]

[950] By Zayd b. ʿAlī. (*MQ*)
[951] Spoken by Sulmīy b. Rabīʿa of the Banū al-Sīd b. Ḍabba in reference to young

فَالْجَمْعُ عَلَى اللَّفْظِ، وَالْإِفْرَادُ عَلَى تَأْوِيلِ الْجَمَاعَةِ. (٢) وَ(مُطَّهِّرَةٌ) بِتَشْدِيدِ الطَّاءِ وَكَسْرِ الْهَاءِ، بِمَعْنَى (مُتَطَهِّرَةٌ).

وَ﴿ مُطَهَّرَةٌ ﴾ أَبْلَغُ مِنْ (طَاهِرَةٌ) وَ(مُتَطَهِّرَةٌ)، لِلْإِشْعَارِ بِأَنَّ مُطَهِّراً طَهَّرَهُنَّ: وَلَيْسَ هُوَ إِلَّا اللهَ عَزَّ وَجَلَّ.

وَ(الزَّوْجُ) يُقَالُ لِلذَّكَرِ وَالْأُنْثَى، وَهُوَ فِي الْأَصْلِ لِمَا لَهُ قَرِينٌ مِنْ جِنْسِهِ، كَـ(زَوْجِ الْخُفِّ). فَإِنْ قِيلَ: فَائِدَةُ الْمَطْعُومِ هُوَ التَّغَذِّي وَدَفْعُ ضَرَرِ الْجُوعِ، وَفَائِدَةُ الْمَنْكُوحِ التَّوَالُدُ وَحِفْظُ النَّوْعِ، وَهِيَ مُسْتَغْنًى عَنْهَا فِي الْجَنَّةِ؛ .....

So the plural reflects the letter of the text while the singular reflects its sense of a group.

(ii) and *muṭṭahhiratun*[952] with a double *ṭā'* and a *kasra* under the *hā'* in the sense of *mutaṭahhira* ‹self-purified›.

Muṭahhara is more expressive than *ṭāhira* ‹pure› and *mutaṭahhira*, to intimate that a purifier purified them—and that is none other than Allah Most High.

Zawj ‹spouse› can be used for both males and females. Originally it means the member of a matching pair as in *zawj al-khuff* ‹the other shoe›.

[The actual states of paradise are beyond comparison]

If one says, "The benefit derived by one who gets fed is nutrition and keeping the harm of hunger at bay; and the benefit derived by one who gets married is to reproduce and perpetuate

women who, goaded by famine to step out of their shy character, throw the meat on the cinders to cook it more quickly, not minding the smoke that filled their eyes and not leaving such work to others as they would usually do, cf. al-Tabrīzī, *Sharḥ Dīwān al-Ḥamāsa* (1:393). "The point was to show the use of *taqanna'at* ‹wore masks› in the singular [rather than *taqanna'na*] although it is understood that they are a group." (Q)

952 By 'Ubayd b. 'Umayr, based on the *idghām* of the original *mutaṭahhiratun*. (*MQ*)

قُلْتُ: مَطَاعِمُ الْجَنَّةِ، وَمَنَاكِحُهَا، وَسَائِرُ أَحْوَالِهَا: إِنَّمَا تُشَارِكُ نَظَائِرَهَا الدُّنْيَوِيَّةَ فِي بَعْضِ الصِّفَاتِ وَالْاِعْتِبَارَاتِ، وَتُسَمَّى بِأَسْمَائِهَا عَلَى سَبِيلِ الْاِسْتِعَارَةِ وَالتَّمْثِيلِ؛ وَلَا تُشَارِكُهَا فِي تَمَامِ حَقِيقَتِهَا حَتَّى تَسْتَلْزِمَ جَمِيعَ مَا يَلْزَمُهَا وَتُفِيدَ عَيْنَ فَائِدَتِهَا.

﴿وَهُمْ فِيهَا خَٰلِدُونَ﴾: دَائِمُونَ. وَ(الْخُلْدُ) وَ(الْخُلُودُ) فِي الْأَصْلِ: الثَّبَاتُ الْمَدِيدُ ـ دَامَ أَمْ لَمْ يَدُمْ ـ وَلِذَٰلِكَ قِيلَ لِلْأَثَافِيِّ وَالْأَحْجَارِ: (خَوَالِدُ)، وَلِلْجُزْءِ الَّذِي يَبْقَى مِنَ الْإِنْسَانِ عَلَى حَالِهِ مَا دَامَ حَيّاً: (خَلَدٌ). وَلَوْ كَانَ وَضْعُهُ لِلدَّوَامِ، كَانَ التَّقْيِيدُ ....

the species; but such is dispensed with in paradise," I say: the fare of paradise, its marriages and all of its states have some features and aspects in common with their worldly counterparts, and they share the same names *only metaphorically and by way of example*. They do not have one and the same nature in reality; thus they are not bound to have the same inseparable elements or denote the same precise meanings.

wa-hum fīhā khālidūna ⁽*and they will be therein, perduring*⁾: everlasting.

[The Sunni understanding of *khulūd* is literally "a long time"]

Khuld and *khulūd* ⁽perpetuity⁾ originally mean "long-standing fixity"—everlasting or not—whence hearthstones and rocks are referred to as *khawālid* ⁽durables⁾,[953] and the part of a person that remains unchanged for as long as he lives as the *khalad* ⁽heart⁾.[954] Had it been coined to signify everlastingness, qualify-

953 "Because the tripodal hearthstones (*athāfī*)—according to the *Ṣiḥāḥ*—endure even after houses have turned to ruins." (S)

954 Because it is described as "formed first and last to stop working" in *The Works of*

بِالتَّأْبِيدِ فِي قَوْلِهِ تَعَالَى ﴿خَٰلِدِينَ فِيهَآ أَبَدًا﴾ [النساء ٥٧ وغيرها] لَغْواً. وَاسْتِعْمَالُهُ حَيْثُ لَا دَوَامَ، كَقَوْلِهِمْ (وَقْفٌ مُخَلَّدٌ): يُوجِبُ اشْتِرَاكاً أَوْ مَجَازاً؛ وَالْأَصْلُ يَنْفِيهِمَا، بِخِلَافِ مَا لَوْ وُضِعَ لِلْأَعَمِّ مِنْهُ فَاسْتُعْمِلَ فِيهِ بِذَلِكَ الِاعْتِبَارِ - كَإِطْلَاقِ (الْجِسْمِ) عَلَى الْإِنْسَانِ - ....

ing it as eternal in the saying of Allah Most High, *perduring (khālidīna) therein eternally* (al-Nisā' 4:57, 122, 169; al-Mā'ida 5:119; al-Tawba 9:22, 100; al-Aḥzāb 33:65; al-Taghābun 64:9; al-Ṭalāq 65: 11; al-Jinn 72:23; al-Bayyina 98:8) would have been idle talk.[955] As for its usage when there is no everlastingness—for example in the term *waqfun mukhalladun* ⁽perpetual endowment⁾—such would require it to have more than one meaning or to be used figuratively; but the original term precludes[956] both of these scenarios. This is not the case when it has been coined to denote something more general [than everlastingness] and then is used to mean just that in light of its meaning [a very long time], as when *al-jism* ⁽body⁾ is used to refer to a human being;

Aristotle, vol. V: De Generatione Animalium (Oxford: Clarendon Press, 1912) Book II.5.741b, cf. Sk (p. 258) and Q (2:515). "This adducing of [linguistic] proofs serves to rebut the Mu'tazila, who consider the literal meaning of *khulūd* to be everlastingness and therefore claimed that whoever commits grave sins and dies without repentence is forever damned in light of the saying of Allah, *and whoever kills a believer wilfully, his requital is Gehenna, perpetually therein [khālidan fīhā]* (al-Nisā' 4:93), on the basis that *khulūd* literally means *dawām* ⁽everlastingness⁾, which is rejected in light of what the author mentioned; so *khulūd* in the latter verse [4:93] means a long period of time [for the Muslim]." (Q) Some of the Khawārij such as the Ibāḍiyya held the same views as the Mu'tazila on this issue but the former pronounced *takfīr* while the latter only pronounced *tafsīq*: see p. 260 above.

955 "In the sense that it offers no new information." (Z) *Ahl al-Sunna* consider *abadan* ⁽eternally⁾ in those verses to constitute *ta'sīs* ⁽fundamental speech⁾ and not mere emphasis as do their opponents. (Kh, Sk, Z)

956 "Because they impair mutual understanding: word structures aim to impart meaningful communication, so they are not structured without compelling reasons." (Sk)

مِثْلَ قَوْلِهِ تَعَالَى: ﴿وَمَا جَعَلْنَا لِبَشَرٍ مِّن قَبْلِكَ الْخُلْدَ﴾ [الأنبياء ٣٤]، لٰكِنِ الْمُرَادَ بِهِ هٰهُنَا: الدَّوَامُ عِنْدَ الْجُمْهُورِ، لِمَا يَشْهَدُ لَهُ مِنَ الْآيَاتِ وَالسُّنَنِ.

فَإِنْ قِيلَ: الْأَبْدَانُ مُرَكَّبَةٌ مِنْ أَجْزَاءٍ مُتَضَادَّةِ الْكَيْفِيَّةِ، مُعَرَّضَةٌ ....

for example, when Allah Most High says *and We did not appoint perpetuity for any human being before you* (al-Anbiyā' 21:34).[957]

However, what is meant by it right here is everlastingness according to the vast majority[958] as witnessed to by several verses [of the Qur'ān] and [hadiths from the] *Sunan.*

[The perfection of resurrected bodies: rebuttal of materialists]

If someone says: "Bodies are made up of components that are mutually exclusive in their respective qualities[959] and are prone

957 "This is an example demonstrating that the word *khuld* was coined to mean something more general than everlastingness but was used to denote it—not in light of its specificity but rather in light of its being one of the subsets of that whole, for [as the Qadi said] the term was coined 'originally to mean long-standing fixity—everlasting or not.'" (Z 1:214)

958 I.e. most of the Muslim sects at the exclusion of Jahm b. Ṣafwān and his followers who held that Paradise and Hellfire are finite because they are created (Kh, Q, Sk, Z). Among latter-day scholars Aḥmad b. Taymiyya also affirmed that the punishment of hellfire is finite, its people would be brought out of it and it would be extinguished, and he attributed this position to some Companions such as 'Umar b. al-Khaṭṭāb, Abū Hurayra, 'Abd Allāh b. Mas'ūd, Abū Sa'īd al-Khudrī and others. His student Shams al-Dīn Ibn Qayyim al-Jawziyya defended him strenuously in the discussion on Hell in his books *Ḥādī al-Arwāḥ, Shifā' al-'Alīl* and *al-Ṣawā'iq al-Mursala* but they were both dismissed as holding "a rejected, sickly position, which al-Subkī the father showed at length to be untenable [in the third epistle of his book *al-Durrat al-Muḍiyya fīl-Radd 'alā Ibn Taymiyya*, entitled *al-I'tibār bi-Baqā' al-Jannati wal-Nār*] and he did so excellently" by Ibn Ḥajar in *Fatḥ al-Bārī* (11:422). Another full-length refutation of Ibn Taymiyya and the Jahmiyya was penned by Muḥammad b. Ismā'īl al-Ṣan'ānī, entitled *Raf' al-Astār li-Ibṭāl Adillagt al-Qā'ilīn bi-Fanā' al-Nār.*

959 "He means the four humors of the ancient philosophers" (Q) namely water, earth, wind and fire.

لِلْاِسْتِحَالَاتِ الْمُؤَدِّيَةِ إِلَى الْاِنْفِكَاكِ وَالْاِنْحِلَالِ، فَكَيْفَ يُعْقَلُ خُلُودُهَا فِي الْجِنَانِ؟ قُلْتُ: إِنَّهُ ـ تَعَالَى ـ يُعِيدُهَا بِحَيْثُ لَا يَعْتَوِرُهَا الْاِسْتِحَالَةُ، بِأَنْ يَجْعَلَ أَجْزَاءَهَا مَثَلاً، مُتَقَاوِمَةً فِي الْكَيْفِيَّةِ، مُتَسَاوِيَةً فِي الْقُوَّةِ، لَا يَقْوَى شَيْءٌ مِنْهَا عَلَى إِحَالَةِ الْآخَرِ، مُتَعَانِقَةً، مُتَلَازِمَةً، لَا يَنْفَكُّ بَعْضُهَا عَنْ بَعْضٍ كَمَا يُشَاهَدُ فِي بَعْضِ الْمَعَادِنِ. هٰذَا؛ وَإِنَّ قِيَاسَ ذٰلِكَ الْعَالَمِ وَأَحْوَالِهِ عَلَى مَا نَجِدُهُ وَنُشَاهِدُهُ: مِنْ نَقْصِ الْعَقْلِ وَضَعْفِ الْبَصِيرَةِ.

وَاعْلَمْ أَنَّهُ، لَمَّا كَانَ مُعْظَمُ اللَّذَّاتِ الْحِسِّيَّةِ مَقْصُوراً عَلَى الْمَسَاكِنِ، وَالْمَطَاعِمِ، وَالْمَنَاكِحِ ـ عَلَى مَا دَلَّ عَلَيْهِ الْاِسْتِقْرَاءُ ـ وَكَانَ مِلَاكُ ذٰلِكَ كُلِّهِ الدَّوَامَ ....

to major changes[960] leading to decomposition and dissolution; how can anyone reasonably say that they will perdure in the gardens of paradise?" I say: Allah Most High shall restore them so that they will no longer be subject to successive changes. For example, He might make their components' qualities perfectly equivalent to one another and mutually proportionate in power so that none is capable of altering the other; they will all be complementary and cooperating with each another in full cohesion, as can be observed in certain minerals. Even so, to make analogies between that world and its states on the one hand and, on the other, what we experience and see [in this] betokens deficient minds and weak insight.

Know, then, that since the majority of sensory pleasures are limited to dwelling-places, aliments and coupling—as can be generally induced—the backbone of it all being[961] everlastingness

960 All mss. and eds.: للاستحالات H: للاستحلالات typo.
961 All mss. and eds. وكان AQ, F, H, K, MM: كان lacuna.

وَالثَّبَاتَ ـ فَإِنَّ كُلَّ نِعْمَةٍ جَلِيلَةٍ، إِذَا قَارَنَهَا خَوْفُ الزَّوَالِ، كَانَتْ مُنَغَّصَةً، غَيْرَ صَافِيَةٍ مِنْ شَوَائِبِ الْأَلَمِ ـ: بَشَّرَ الْمُؤْمِنِينَ بِهَا، وَمَثَّلَ مَا أَعَدَّ لَهُمْ فِي الْآخِرَةِ بِأَبْهَى مَا يُسْتَلَذُّ بِهِ مِنْهَا، وَأَزَالَ عَنْهُمْ خَوْفَ الْفَوَاتِ بِوَعْدِ الْخُلُودِ، لِيَدُلَّ عَلَى كَمَالِهِمْ فِي التَّنَعُّمِ وَالسُّرُورِ.

﴿إِنَّ اللَّهَ لَا يَسْتَحْيِۦٓ أَن يَضْرِبَ مَثَلًا مَّا بَعُوضَةً﴾: لَمَّا كَانَتِ الْآيَاتُ السَّابِقَةُ مُتَضَمِّنَةً لِأَنْوَاعٍ مِنَ التَّمْثِيلِ، عَقَّبَ ذٰلِكَ بِبَيَانِ حُسْنِهِ، وَمَا هُوَ الْحَقُّ لَهُ وَالشَّرْطُ فِيهِ: وَهُوَ أَنْ يَكُونَ عَلَى وَفْقِ الْمُمَثَّلِ لَهُ مِنَ الْجِهَةِ الَّتِي تَعَلَّقَ بِهَا التَّمْثِيلُ فِي الْعِظَمِ وَالصِّغَرِ، وَالْخِسَّةِ ....

and fixity—for every tremendous favor, when fear of its disappearance accompanies it, becomes marred and tainted by the stigmas of pain—He gave believers the glad tidings of those [favors], represented what He prepared for them in the hereafter by the most dazzling aspects of the delights they offer, and repelled from them all fear of termination with the promise of perpetuity, to show the perfection of their bliss and happiness.

[Method and power of similes/proverbs even in divine speech]

[2:26] **inna-l-Lāha lā yastaḥyī an yaḍriba mathalan mā baʿūḍatan**⁽*verily the One God is not ashamed to strike some similitude—of a gnat*⁾: after the previous verses had various examples of simile,[962] He followed up with an exposition of its beauty [as a trope], its rightful object and its precondition, which is congruence with the subject of assimilation from the perspective that the simile pertains to—with respect to being big or small, trivial

962 "Al-Ṭībī said that [J] did not mean by *tamthīl* here proverbial assimilation (*al-tashbīh al-tamthīlī*) nor proverbial metaphor (*al-istiʿāra al-tamthīliyya*) but something more general, while Shaykh Saʿd al-Dīn [al-Taftāzānī] said he meant *tashbīh* ⁽similitude⁾ in absolute terms." (S)

وَالشَّرَفِ، دُونَ الْمُمَثِّلِ. فَإِنَّ التَّمْثِيلَ إِنَّمَا يُصَارُ إِلَيْهِ لِكَشْفِ الْمَعْنَى الْمُمَثَّلِ لَهُ، وَرَفْعِ الْحِجَابِ عَنْهُ، وَإِبْرَازِهِ فِي صُورَةِ الْمُشَاهَدِ الْمَحْسُوسِ، لِيُسَاعِدَ فِيهِ الْوَهْمُ الْعَقْلَ وَيُصَالِحُهُ عَلَيْهِ؛ فَإِنَّ الْمَعْنَى الصِّرْفَ إِنَّمَا يُدْرِكُهُ الْعَقْلُ مَعَ مُنَازَعَةٍ مِنَ الْوَهْمِ، لِأَنَّ مِنْ طَبْعِهِ: الْمَيْلَ إِلَى الْحِسِّ وَحُبَّ الْمُحَاكَاةِ. وَلِذٰلِكَ: شَاعَتِ الْأَمْثَالُ فِي الْكُتُبِ الْإِلٰهِيَّةِ وَفَشَتْ فِي عِبَارَاتِ الْبُلَغَاءِ، وَإِشَارَاتِ الْحُكَمَاءِ؛ فَيُمَثَّلُ الْحَقِيرُ بِالْحَقِيرِ كَمَا يُمَثَّلُ الْعَظِيمُ بِالْعَظِيمِ، وَإِنْ كَانَ الْمُمَثِّلُ أَعْظَمَ مِنْ كُلِّ عَظِيمٍ؛ كَمَا مَثَّلَ فِي الْإِنْجِيلِ غِلَّ الصُّدُورِ بِالنُّخَالَةِ، ....

or worthy, but without respect to the assimilator['s identity].[963]

One resorts to simile in order to disclose the meaning which it represents, bring it into light and display it in a palpable, visible form. The aim thereby is for visualization to help reason to [comprehend] it and conciliate its acceptance of it. For pure meaning can be attained by reason only after some contention on the part of visualization, due to its bias for sensation and its love of portrayal. That is the reason why proverbs abound in the heavenly books, just as they are widespread in the phrases of the declaimers and the allusions of the sages. So the trivial is assimilated to the trivial just as the great is assimilated with the great, even if the assimilator himself[964] might be the greatest of the great—the way, in the Gospel,

• rancor of breasts was assimilated to dregs;

[963] "For example, the assimilation of idol-worship to a cobweb in consideration of feebleness and weakness: the subject of assimilation [idolatry] here is extremely worthless, so it is imperative that the object that it is being assimilated to be so as well." (Q)
[964] All mss. and eds.: الممثل AQ, H, MM: المثل typo.

وَالْقُلوبَ الْقَاسِيَةَ بِالْحَصَاةِ، وَمُخَاطَبَةَ السُّفَهَاءِ بِإِثَارَةِ الزَّنَابِيرِ؛ وَجَاءَ فِي كَلَامِ الْعَرَبِ: (أَسْمَعُ مِنْ قُرَادٍ)، وَ(أَطْيَشُ مِنْ فَرَاشَةٍ)، وَ(أَعَزُّ مِنْ مُخِّ الْبَعُوضِ). لَا مَا قَالَتِ الْجَهَلَةُ مِنَ الْكُفَّارِ:

لِمَا مَثَّلَ اللهُ حَالَ الْمُنَافِقِينَ بِحَالِ الْمُسْتَوْقِدِينَ؟ وَأَصْحَابَ الصَّيِّبِ وَعِبَادَةَ الْأَصْنَامِ فِي الْوَهْنِ وَالضَّعْفِ بِبَيْتِ الْعَنْكَبُوتِ؟ وَجَعَلَهَا أَقَلَّ مِنَ الذُّبَابِ، وَأَخَسَّ قَدْراً مِنْهُ؟ اللهُ سُبْحَانَهُ وَتَعَالَى أَعْلَى وَأَجَلُّ مِنْ أَنْ يَضْرِبَ الْأَمْثَالَ وَيَذْكُرَ الذُّبَابَ وَالْعَنْكَبُوتَ!

- hard hearts, to stones;
- and addressing fools, to stirring up hornets.

The Arabs, likewise, say in their aphorisms:

- "More perceptive than camel-ticks,"[965]
- "More heedless than a moth,"[966] and
- "Dearer than a gnat's head."[967]

Thus it is not as the ignorant among the unbelievers said:

> Why did Allah assimilate the state of the hypocrites to the state of the fire-kindlers and the people under the cloud-burst? and idol-worship, in frailty and weakness, to the cobweb? and make it less than a fly, and paltrier? Allah Most High is far above that! and too majestic to draw such similes, and mention flies and spiders![968]

[965] "Because they hear the sound of camel hooves from a day's distance and are set into motion by it." al-Maydānī, *Majmaʿ al-Amthāl*, ed. Muḥammad Muḥyī al-Dīn ʿAbd al-Ḥamīd, 2 vols. (Cairo: Maktabat al-Sunna al-Muḥammadiyya, 1374/1955) 1:349 §1878. "So when robbers see it move they know the caravan is near." (Q) See on some of their species: http://www.nhc.ed.ac.uk/index.php?page=25.119#Hyalomma

[966] "Because it throws itself into the fire." Al-Maydānī, *Majmaʿ* (1:438 §2327).

[967] An expression that conveys "rarity" (Q) or "the extreme difficulty of a task." (S)

[968] References to Surat al-Baqara 2:17-20; al-ʿAnkabūt 29:41; al-Ḥajj 22:73 respectively.

وَأَيْضاً، لَمَّا أَرْشَدَهُمْ إِلَى مَا يَدُلُّ عَلَى أَنَّ الْمُتَحَدَّى بِهِ وَحْيٌ مُنْزَلٌ، وَرَتَّبَ عَلَيْهِ وَعِيدَ مَنْ كَفَرَ بِهِ، وَوَعَدَ مَنْ آمَنَ بِهِ بَعْدَ ظُهُورِ أَمْرِهِ: شَرَعَ فِي جَوَابِ مَا طَعَنُوا بِهِ فِيهِ، فَقَالَ تَعَالَى: ﴿إِنَّ اللَّهَ لَا يَسْتَحْيِۦٓ﴾، أَيْ: لَا يَتْرُكُ ضَرْبَ الْمَثَلِ بِالْبَعُوضَةِ تَرْكَ مَنْ يَسْتَحْيِي أَنْ يُمَثِّلَ بِهَا لِحَقَارَتِهَا.

وَ(الْحَيَاءُ): اِنْقِبَاضُ النَّفْسِ عَنِ الْقَبِيحِ مَخَافَةَ الذَّمِّ؛ وَهُوَ الْوَسَطُ بَيْنَ الْوَقَاحَةِ - الَّتِي هِيَ الْجُرْأَةُ عَلَى الْقَبَائِحِ وَعَدَمُ الْمُبَالَاةِ بِهَا - وَالْخَجَلِ، الَّذِي هُوَ انْحِصَارُ النَّفْسِ عَنِ الْفِعْلِ مُطْلَقاً. وَاشْتِقَاقُهُ مِنَ (الْحَيَاةِ)، فَإِنَّهُ انْكِسَارٌ

Likewise, after apprising them of the divinely-revealed nature of the object of the challenge and making dire punishment the consequence of disbelief in it, with the promise of reward for whoever believed in it after its proclamation, He now set about answering the content of their criticism of it and said, *verily Allah is not ashamed.* That is, He does not shun coining the simile of a gnat the way that someone who is ashamed to use it as a simile—because of its insignificance—would.

[Definition of shame and meaning of its attribution to Allah]

Ḥayā' ⁽shame⁾ is the psyche's aversion to reprehensible matters out of fear of blame. It is an intermediate between *waqāḥa* ⁽impudence⁾, which is the audacity to do reprehensible matters with utter disregard for consequences, and *khajal* ⁽timidity⁾, the cowing of the psyche into complete inaction. It stems from *ḥayāt* ⁽life⁾, for it is a dejection ....

The Jews derided those verses as violating the canons of the divine style of address, whereupon the divine rebuttal came in Surat al-Baqara with the present verse, cf. *Tafsīrs* of ʿAbd al-Razzāq, al-Ṭabarī, Ibn Abī Ḥātim and al-Wāḥidī for 2:26 as well as the books of *Asbāb al-Nuzūl*, e.g. Salīm al-Hilālī and Muḥammad Āl Naṣr, *al-Istīʿāb fī Bayān al-Asbāb*, 3 vols. (Dammam: Dār Ibn al-Jawzī, 1425/2004) 1:21-23.

يَعْتَرِي الْقُوَّةَ الْحَيَوَانِيَّةَ فَيَرُدُّهَا عَنْ أَفْعَالِهَا؛ فَقِيلَ: (حَيِيَ الرَّجُلُ)، كَمَا يُقَالُ (نَسِيَ) وَ(حَشِيَ) إِذَا اعْتَلَّتْ نَسَاهُ وَحَشَاهُ. وَإِذَا وُصِفَ بِهِ الْبَارِي تَعَالَى - كَمَا جَاءَ فِي الْحَدِيثِ: إِنَّ اللهَ يَسْتَحْيِي مِنْ ذِي الشَّيْبَةِ الْمُسْلِمِ أَنْ يُعَذِّبَهُ؛ إِنَّ اللهَ حَيِيٌّ كَرِيمٌ، يَسْتَحْيِي، إِذَا رَفَعَ الْعَبْدُ يَدَيْهِ، أَنْ يَرُدَّهُمَا صِفْراً حَتَّى يَضَعَ فِيهِمَا خَيْراً - ....

that takes over the vital impulse and deters it from doing this or that. Hence it is said *ḥayiya al-rajulu* ⁽the man felt shame⁾ just as they say *nasiya* and *ḥashiya* when one's *nasā* ⁽sciatic nerves⁾ and *ḥashā* ⁽bowels⁾ are ailing.

When the Absolute Originator (exalted is He!) is described by it—as in the hadiths,

(i) "Verily Allah is too ashamed before the white-haired Muslim to punish him"[969] and

(ii) "Verily Allah is shy and generous: He is ashamed, when His slave raises his hands, to send them back empty; rather He will put something good in them"[970]—

[969] Narrated from Anas as a *ḥadīth qudsī* stating, "Truly I am ashamed before my slave and maidservant whose hair turns white in Islam, to punish them ever after that" by Ibn Abī al-Dunyā in *al-ʿUmr wal-Shayb*, ed. Najm Khalaf (Riyadh: Maktabat al-Rushd, 1412/1992) pp. 47-48 §2 and, through him, Abū Bakr al-Shāfiʿi in *al-Ghaylāniyyāt*, ed. Ḥilmī ʿAbd al-Hādī, 2 vols. (Riyadh: Dār Ibn al-Jawzī, 1997) 1:373-374 §395; al-Khaṭīb al-Baghdādī in *Muwaḍḍiḥ Awhām al-Jamʿ wal-Tafrīq*, 2 vols. (Hyderabad: Dā'irat al-Maʿārif al-ʿUthmāniyya, 1379/1960) 2:211 and the Shiʿi Yaḥyā al-Shajarī in §35 of his 40-topic hadith collection *al-Amālī al-Ḥadīthiyya*, 2 vols. (Cairo: Maṭbaʿat al-Fajjāla, 1376/1957; rept. 3rd ed. Beirut: ʿĀlam al-Kutub, 1403/1983) 2:240, all of them with a very weak chain of three discarded narrators, one of them a forger: Ibn Ḥibbān, *al-Majrūḥīn*, ed. Maḥmūd Ibrāhīm Zāyid, 3 vols. (Aleppo: Dār al-Waʿy, n.d.)1:167; Ibn al-Jawzī, *Mawḍūʿāt* (1:177-178). Suyūṭī adduces many variant chains and wordings in support of its authenticity: *al-La'ālī' al-Maṣnūʿa fil-Aḥādīth al-Mawḍūʿa*, 2 vols. (Cairo: al-Maṭbaʿat al-Adabiyya, 1317/1899; rept. Beirut: Dār al-Maʿrifa, n.d.) 1:133-137.

[970] A fair hadith narrated from Salmān by Aḥmad and in the *Sunan* as well as al-Ḥākim

فَالْمُرَادُ بِهِ: التَّرْكُ اللَّازِمُ لِلِانْقِبَاضِ؛ كَمَا أَنَّ الْمُرَادَ مِنْ رَحْمَتِهِ وَغَضَبِهِ: إِصَابَةُ الْمَعْرُوفِ وَالْمَكْرُوهِ اللَّازِمَيْنِ لِمَعْنَيَيْهِمَا.

وَنَظِيرُهُ قَوْلُ مَنْ يَصِفُ إِبِلاً: [طويل]

إِذَا مَا اسْتَحَيْنَ الْمَاءَ يَعْرِضُ نَفْسَهُ * كَرَعْنَ بِسِبْتٍ فِي إِنَاءٍ مِنَ الْوَرْدِ

what is meant by it is the refraining that is inseparable from aversion, just as what is meant by His mercy and His anger is, respectively, the befalling of beneficence and adversity that are inseparable from their respective meanings.[971]

The above [understanding] is illustrated by the following description of camels: [“The Long”]

When shamed (istaḥayna) by the water that offers itself, they gulp it down with a tanned hide[972] *from a flowery bowl.*[973]

and Ibn Ḥibbān in their *Ṣaḥīḥ*s among others, all of them without the second sentence except ʿAbd al-Razzāq al-Ṣanʿānī, *Muṣannaf*, ed. Ḥabīb al-Raḥmān al-Aʿẓamī, 2nd ed., 11 vols. (Gujerat, India: al-Majlis al-ʿIlmī, 1304/1983) 2:251 §3250 *Bāb rafʿ al-yadayn fīl-duʿāʾ*; al-Maḥāmilī (d. 330/942), *Amālī*, ed. Ibrāhīm al-Qaysī (Amman: al-Maktaba al-Islāmiyya and Dār Ibn al-Qayyim, 1412/1992); al-Kalābādhī (d. 380/990), *Baḥr al-Fawā'id al-Mashhūr bi-Maʿānī al-Akhbār*, ed. Wajīh Kamāl al-Dīn Zakī, 2 vols. (Cairo: Dār al-Salām, 1429/2008) 2:456 and al-Baghawī, *Sharḥ al-Sunna* (5:185 §1385).

971 As already discussed under the glosses of mercy and anger in *al-raḥmān al-raḥīm* and *al-maghḍūb ʿalayhim* (see pp. 168 and 205 above).

972 Var. *kariʿna bi-shībin*, “they gulp it down with slurps.”

973 Declaimed in 354/965 in a panegyric for the erudite Buwayhī vizier Abū al-Faḍl Muḥammad b. al-Ḥusayn b. al-ʿAmīd by al-Mutanabbī cf. ʿAbd al-Raḥmān al-Barqūqī, *Sharḥ Dīwān al-Mutanabbī*, 2nd ed., 4 vols. (Beirut: Dār al-Kitāb al-ʿArabī, 1357/1938) 1:165. The meaning is that there is so much water available due to the abundance ot rains that it is as if offering itself so that the camels drink it not out of thirst but just because it is there, their chops looking like tanned leather because they are clean and moist since they keep taking to water, and the flower-rich lands are compared to a drinking-bowl. “Its illustrative usage of *ḥayā'* is because its literal meaning is not imagined here but rather its concomitant, which is not to reject the water that offers itself, so it illustrates what is in the Hadith and the Qur'ān without difference.” (Q 3:17)

وَإِنَّمَا عَدَلَ بِهِ عَنِ التَّرْكِ لِمَا فِيهِ مِنَ التَّمْثِيلِ وَالْمُبَالَغَةِ. وَتَحْتَمِلُ الْآيَةُ خَاصَّةً أَنْ يَكُونَ مَجِيئُهُ عَلَى الْمُقَابَلَةِ لِمَا وَقَعَ فِي كَلَامِ الْكَفَرَةِ.

وَ(ضَرْبُ الْمَثَلِ): اِعْتِمَالُهُ، مِنْ (ضَرْبِ الْخَاتَمِ)؛ وَأَصْلُهُ: وَقْعُ شَيْءٍ عَلَى آخَرَ.

وَ﴿أَن﴾ بِصِلَتِهَا: مَخْفُوضُ الْمَحَلِّ عِنْدَ الْخَلِيلِ بِإِضْمَارِ (مِنْ)، مَنْصُوبٌ بِإِفْضَاءِ الْفِعْلِ إِلَيْهِ بَعْدَ حَذْفِهَا عِنْدَ سِيبَوَيْهِ. وَ﴿مَا﴾: (أ) إِبْهَامِيَّةٌ، تَزِيدُ النَّكِرَةَ إِبْهَاماً وَشِيَاعاً وَتَسُدُّ عَنْهَا طُرُقَ التَّقْيِيدِ، كَقَوْلِكَ (أَعْطِنِي كِتَاباً مَا)،

The reason why it was used—rather than *tark* ⁽refrain⁾—is because of its proverbial force and intensiveness. It is also possible that the verse itself used it as a retort to the words used in the unbelievers' discourse.[974]

Ḍarb al-mathal ⁽to strike a similitude⁾ means to construct it, from *ḍarb al-khātam* ⁽to engrave a seal⁾. Originally it means the striking down of something on something else.

An ⁽to⁾—with its conjunctive sentence—is (i) in the virtual genitive according to Khalīl with *min* implied;[975] (ii) or in the accusative when we make the verb govern it after suppressing [*min*] according to Sībawayh.

Mā ⁽some⁾ is (i) an anonymizer that adds to the vagueness and generalness of the indefinite, precluding it from being qualified in any way, as when you say *aʿṭinī kitāban mā* ⁽give me some ....

[974] J attributes to the unbelievers the words "Is not the lord of Muḥammad ashamed (*alā yastaḥyī rabbu Muḥammad*) to use flies and spiders in parables?" so the retort would be verbatim if such a report were authentic, but it is unverified in the books of *Asbāb al-Nuzūl*. Hence it retorts to the meanings meant by the unbelievers (see note 968) rather than their exact words.

[975] I.e. *lā yastaḥyī min an...*

أَيْ: أَيَّ كِتَابٍ كَانَ؛ (ب) أَوْ مَزِيدَةٌ لِلتَّأْكِيدِ، كَالَّتِي فِي قَوْلِهِ تَعَالَى: ﴿فَبِمَا رَحْمَةٍ مِّنَ ٱللَّهِ﴾ [آل عمران ١٥٩].

وَلَا نَعْنِي بِالْمَزِيدِ اللَّغْوَ الضَّائِعَ! فَإِنَّ الْقُرْآنَ كُلَّهُ هُدًى وَبَيَانٌ؛ بَلْ مَا لَمْ يُوضَعْ لِمَعْنًى يُرَادُ مِنْهُ؛ وَإِنَّمَا وُضِعَتْ لِأَنْ تُذْكَرَ مَعَ غَيْرِهِ، فَتُفِيدُ لَهُ وَثَاقَةً وَقُوَّةً؛ وَهُوَ زِيَادَةٌ فِي الْهُدَى، غَيْرُ قَادِحٍ فِيهِ.

وَ﴿بَعُوضَةً﴾: عَطْفُ بَيَانٍ لِـ﴿مَثَلًا﴾؛ أَوْ مَفْعُولٌ لِـ﴿يَضْرِبَ﴾؛ وَ﴿مَثَلًا﴾ حَالٌ تَقَدَّمَتْ عَلَيْهِ لِأَنَّهُ نَكِرَةٌ؛ أَوْ هُمَا مَفْعُولَاهُ لِتَضَمُّنِهِ مَعْنَى الْجَعْلِ.

book⁾, that is, any book whatsoever; (ii) or an emphatic additive like the one in the saying of Allah Most High, *And it was through some mercy of Allah!* (Āl ʿImrān 3:159).

[“Additive” particles in the Qurʾān play a stylistic role]

Nor do we mean by “additive” gratuitous idle talk[976]—for verily the entire Qurʾān is guidance and exposition!—but rather that *mā* was not coined for a sense that is meant [in particular]. It was coined only to be mentioned in tandem with another [sense] so as to impart to it solidity and strength. This is addition in guidance and does not detract from [the Qurʾān].

Baʿūḍatan ⁽gnat⁾ is (i) an explicative apposition for ***mathalan*** ⁽similitude⁾; (ii) or the object of ***yaḍriba*** ⁽to strike⁾ with ***mathalan*** as a participial state positioned ahead of it because it is indefinite; (iii) or they [***mathalan*** and ***baʿūḍatan***] are both its objects, as it also implies the meaning of “making.”

[976] Cf. S 2:152-153 and see note 357 above on the additive *lā* in *wa-lā-ḍ-ḍāllīn*.

وَقُرِئَتْ بِالرَّفْعِ، عَلَى أَنَّهُ خَبَرُ مُبْتَدَإٍ مَحْذُوفٍ. وَعَلَى هٰذَا: يَحْتَمِلُ ﴿مَّا﴾ وُجُوهاً أُخَرَ: (أ) أَنْ تَكُونَ مَوْصُولَةً حُذِفَ صَدْرُ صِلَتِهَا، كَمَا حُذِفَ فِي قَوْلِهِ: تَمَاماً عَلَى الَّذِي أَحْسَنُ [شاذّة للأنعام ١٥٤]؛ (ب) وَمَوْصُوفَةً بِصِفَةٍ كَذٰلِكَ - وَمَحَلُّهَا النَّصْبُ بِالْبَدَلِيَّةِ عَلَى الْوَجْهَيْنِ -؛ (ج) وَاسْتِفْهَامِيَّةً هِيَ الْمُبْتَدَأُ، ....

It was also read [*baʿūḍatun*] in the nominative,[977] in the sense that it is the enunciative of a suppressed inchoative. According to the latter scenario, ***mā*** ⁽some⁾ can have other senses as well:

(i) it could be a definite conjunctive of which the forefront was suppressed[978] the way it was suppressed in *tamāman ʿalā al-ladhī aḥsanu* ⁽*as a completion for that which is best*⁾.[979]

(ii) It could be an indefinite conjunctive likewise;[980] its virtual case-ending is accusative as a substitute[981] in both cases.

(iii) It could be an interrogative which is itself the inchoative, as

[977] By al-Ḍaḥḥāk, Ibrāhīm b. Abī ʿAbla, Abū Ḥātim, from Abū ʿUbayda, from Ru'ba b. al-ʿAjjāj, Quṭrub, Mālik b. Dīnār, al-Aṣmaʿī, from Nāfiʿ, and Ibn al-Sammāk. (*MQ*) Cf. ʿAbd al-ʿAlī al-Mas'ūl, *al-Qirā'āt al-Shādhdha: Ḍawābiṭuhā wal-Iḥtijāj bihā fīl-Fiqh wal-ʿArabiyya* (Cairo: Dār Ibn ʿAffān; Riyadh: Dār Ibn al-Qayyim, 1429/2008) p. 370.

[978] "Abū Ḥayyān said the suppressed part is *al-ladhī huwā* ⁽which is⁾, following the Kufans' position as they do not posit the precondition of a long conjunctive clause for the suppression of the pronoun as opposed to the Basrians" (S 2:155) so that "the subaudition is *an yaḍriba mathalan al-ladhī huwā baʿūḍatun* ⁽to strike a similitude which is a gnat⁾." (Z 1:219)

[979] I.e. in the non-canonical reading of Yaḥyā b. Yaʿmur, Ibn Abī Isḥāq, al-Ḥasan, al-Aʿmash, al-Sulamī and Abū Razīn (*MQ* 2:587-588) for al-Anʿām 6:154 "with *aḥsanu* in the nominative as a comparative of superiority in the sense of a suppressed inchoative" (Q 3:26) to mean "as a completion for that religion which is best" (Q 8:306).

[980] "Its subaudition being *an yaḍriba mathalan shay'an huwa baʿūḍatun* ⁽to strike a similitude—something which is a gnat⁾." (Z)

[981] "For *mathalan*." (Z)

كَأَنَّهُ، لَمَّا رَدَّ اسْتِبْعَادَهُمْ ضَرْبَ اللهِ الأَمْثَالَ، قَالَ بَعْدَهُ: (مَا الْبَعُوضَةُ فَمَا فَوْقَهَا حَتَّى لَا يُضْرَبَ بِهِ الْمَثَلُ؟ بَلْ لَهُ أَنْ يُمَثِّلَ بِمَا هُوَ أَحْقَرُ مِنْ ذٰلِكَ!) وَنَظِيرُهُ: (فُلَانٌ لَا يُبَالِي مِمَّا يَهَبُ: مَا دِينَارٌ وَدِينَارَانِ؟).

وَ(الْبَعُوضُ): فَعُولٌ مِنَ الْبَعْضِ؛ وَهُوَ الْقَطْعُ، كَالْبَضْعِ وَالْعَضْبِ؛ غَلَبَ عَلَى هٰذَا النَّوْعِ كَـ(الْخَمُوشِ).

﴿فَمَا فَوْقَهَا﴾: عَطْفٌ ....

if, when He rebutted their skepticism of the fact that Allah uses similes, He added: "What is a gnat or whatever is bigger that it should not be the subject of a similitude?" Rather, He may use as a simile something even more insignificant than that. It is further illustrated by [their saying], "X does not care how much he gives: what is one or two dinars?"[982]

Baʿūḍ ⁽gnat⁾ is the *faʿūl* form of *al-buʿḍ*, which is *al-qaṭʿ* ⁽cutting off⁾—likewise *al-baḍʿ* and *al-ʿaḍb*: that [meaning] became prevalent for those stem-letters—like *khamūsh* ⁽scratchy⁾.[983]

fa-mā fawqahā ⁽*or what is more than that*⁾ is an adjunction[984] to

[982] "That is, 'what is a gnat and whatever is bigger than it in size?' for all are equally proverbializable. It is as if someone said *ribā* ⁽usury⁾ is categorically prohibited in every foodstuff, whereupon someone else asked, 'what about quince? apples? almonds?' and you reply to him: it is categorically prohibited in every foodstuff, so what is the sense of your asking about apples and the rest?" (S)

[983] "Because the root letters *b-ʿ-ḍ* in any order they are put always denote cutting; then they were used mostly for that type of fly because it cuts—with its dart—the human face and the rest of the limbs; just as *khamūsh* is originally an epithet stemming from *al-khamsh*, which is *al-ḥadsh* and is not used for other than the face, then it became used mostly for the gnat." (Z) "*Khamūsh* is a Hudhayl name for the gnat." (Q)

[984] "Through the operation of the *fāʾ*, considered a *ʿāṭifa lil-tarākhī al-rutbī* ⁽adjunctive operator denoting decreasing order of importance⁾ whether what is intended by 'whatever is bigger than the gnat' something lowlier than it and even more insignificant, or something loftier than it and greater in mass." (Z)

عَلَى ﴿بَعُوضَةً﴾، أَوْ ﴿مَّا﴾ إِنْ جُعِلَ اِسماً. وَمَعْنَاهُ: مَا زَادَ عَلَيْهَا: (أ) فِي الْجُثَّةِ، كَالذُّبَابِ وَالْعَنْكَبُوتِ؛ كَأَنَّهُ قَصَدَ بِهِ رَدَّ مَا اسْتَنْكَرُوهُ. وَالْمَعْنَى: أَنَّهُ لَا يَسْتَحْيِي ضَرْبَ الْمَثَلِ بِالْبَعُوضِ فَضْلاً عَمَّا هُوَ أَكْبَرُ مِنْهُ؛ (ب) أَوْ فِي الْمَعْنَى الَّذِي جُعِلَتْ فِيهِ مَثَلاً: وَهُوَ الصِّغَرُ وَالْحَقَارَةُ، كَجَنَاحِهَا، فَإِنَّهُ - عَلَيْهِ الصَّلَاةُ وَالسَّلَامُ - ضَرَبَهُ مَثَلاً لِلدُّنْيَا. وَنَظِيرُهُ فِي الْاِحْتِمَالَيْنِ: مَا رُوِيَ أَنَّ رَجُلاً بِمِنىً خَرَّ عَلَى طُنُبِ فُسْطَاطٍ، فَقَالَتْ عَائِشَةُ - رَضِيَ اللهُ عَنْهَا -:

baʿūḍatan or to ***mā*** if we consider the latter a noun.[985]

[Sizes great and small are all relative in the divine sight]

It means whatever is more than it

(i) in mass, such as the fly and the spider, as if He aimed to rebut what they had objected to—meaning that He is not ashamed to strike a simile for a gnat, let alone what is bigger than that;

(ii) or in the meaning for which it was paradigmatized, namely minuteness and insignificance, like its wing—which the Prophet (upon him blessings and peace) made an allegory for the world.[986]

An illustration for it in both scenarios is the narration of the man in Minā who fell on the rope of a skin-tent,[987] whereupon ʿĀʾisha—Allah be well-pleased with her—said,

[985] "I.e. an adjunction to the first *mā*" (Q) "as a noun either as a *mawṣūla* ⁽definite conjunctive) or a *mawṣūfa* ⁽indefinite conjunctive⁾ or an *istifhāmiyya* ⁽interrogative⁾." (Z)

[986] "If the world was worth [*taʿdilu/tazinu*] a gnat's wing in the sight of Allah He would have never let an unbeliever drink a single sip of water [from it]." Narrated from Sahl b. Saʿd in the *Sunan* of Tirmidhī (*Zuhd, bāb mā jāʾa fī hawān al-dunyā ʿalā Allāh*; *ṣaḥīḥ*) and Ibn Mājah (*Zuhd, bāb mathal al-dunyā*); also from other Companions such as Ibn ʿUmar, Abū al-Dardāʾ, Ibn ʿAbbās, Abū Hurayra, ʿAmr b. Murra and unnamed men by Hannād b. Sary, Ibn al-Mubārak, al-Ṭabarānī, al-Bazzār, al-Ḥākim and others.

[987] "And he almost broke his neck or lost his eye" in some narrations.

سَمِعْتُ رَسُولَ اللهِ ﷺ قَالَ: مَا مِنْ مُسْلِمٍ يُشَاكُ شَوْكَةً فَمَا فَوْقَهَا، إِلَّا كُتِبَتْ لَهُ [بِهَا] دَرَجَةٌ، وَمُحِيَتْ عَنْهُ بِهَا خَطِيئَةٌ؛ فَإِنَّهُ يَحْتَمِلُ مَا تَجَاوَزَ الشَّوْكَةَ فِي الْأَلَمِ كَالْخُرُورِ، وَمَا زَادَ عَلَيْهَا فِي الْقِلَّةِ كَنَخْبَةِ النَّمْلَةِ، لِقَوْلِهِ عَلَيْهِ الصَّلَاةُ وَالسَّلَامُ مَا أَصَابَ الْمُؤْمِنَ مِنْ مَكْرُوهٍ فَهُوَ كَفَّارَةٌ لِخَطَايَاهُ حَتَّى نَخْبَةُ النَّمْلَةِ.

﴿فَأَمَّا ٱلَّذِينَ ءَامَنُوا۟ فَيَعْلَمُونَ أَنَّهُ ٱلْحَقُّ مِن رَّبِّهِمْ﴾: ....

> I heard the Messenger of Allah—upon him blessings and peace—say, "No Muslim is pricked by some thorn or what is more than that, but a higher level will be recorded for him because of it[988] and a sin will be erased from him because of it;"[989]

for it covers both what entails more pain than a thorn, such as a bad fall, and what is pettier than it, such as an ant-bite, since he —upon him blessings and peace—said,

> Whatever trouble affects the believer, such will surely be an expiation for his sins—even an ant-bite.[990]

fa-ammā al-ladhīna āmanū fa-yaʿlamūna annahu-l-ḥaqqu min rabbihim (*as for those who believe, they know it is the truth from their Nurturer*):

[988] Missing only from B: بها but present in all mss. and in compilations of this hadith.

[989] Narrated by Muslim, *Ṣaḥīḥ* (*al-Birr wal-ṣila wal-ādāb, bāb thawāb al-mu'min fī-mā yuṣībuh*) and in Bukhārī, *Ṣaḥīḥ* (*al-Marḍā, bāb mā jā'a fī kaffārat al-maraḍ*) and al-Tirmidhī, *Sunan* (*Tafsīr, sūrat al-Nisā'*), the latter two from Abū Hurayra.

[990] Narrated through many routes without the words "even an ant-bite" according to Ibn Ḥajar, *al-Kāfī al-Shāf* (p. 14 §29), which makes the hadith *gharīb jiddan* according to al-Zaylaʿī, *Takhrīj* (1:58 §37) and "nowhere to be found in such a wording" according to al-Ṭībī and Walī al-Dīn al-ʿIrāqī. (S) It is one of the forgeries which J alone adduces both in the *Kashshāf* and in *al-Fā'iq fī Gharīb al-Ḥadīth*, ed. ʿAlī al-Bijāwī and Muḥammad Ibrāhīm, 2nd ed., 4 vols. (Cairo: ʿĪsā al-Bābī al-Ḥalabī, 1390/1970, rept. Beirut: Dār al-Fikr, 1414/1993) 3:415 but its meaning is confirmed by the preceding.

(أَمَّا) حَرْفُ تَفْصِيلٍ، يُفَصِّلُ مَا أُجْمِلَ وَيُؤَكِّدُ مَا بِهِ صُدِّرَ، وَيَتَضَمَّنُ مَعْنَى الشَّرْطِ، وَلِذٰلِكَ يُجَابُ بِالْفَاءِ. قَالَ سِيبَوَيْهِ: أَمَّا زَيْدٌ فَذَاهِبٌ مَعْنَاهُ: مَهْمَا يَكُنْ مِنْ شَيْءٍ فَزَيْدٌ ذَاهِبٌ؛ أَيْ هُوَ ذَاهِبٌ لَا مَحَالَةَ وَأَنَّهُ مِنْهُ عَزِيمَةٌ. وَكَانَ الْأَصْلُ دُخُولَ الْفَاءِ عَلَى الْجُمْلَةِ لِأَنَّهَا الْجَزَاءُ، لٰكِنْ كَرِهُوا إِيلَاءَهَا حَرْفَ الشَّرْطِ، فَأَدْخَلُوهَا عَلَى الْخَبَرِ، وَعَوَّضُوا الْمُبْتَدَأَ عَنِ الشَّرْطِ لَفْظاً.

Ammā ʿas forʾ is an elaborative particle that details what was mentioned in vague terms, emphasizes whatever statement it initiates and implies the meaning of conditionality; hence its response is with a *fāʾ*.[991] Sībawayh said the meaning of *ammā Zaydun fa-dhāhibun* ʿas for Zayd he is goingʾ is that whatever happens, Zayd is leaving; that is, he is going no matter what and it is his unshakeable resolve.

In principle the *fāʾ* should have been affixed to the sentence since the latter is the apodosis of the conditional;[992] but they disliked to make it directly follow the conditional particle, so they affixed it to the enunciative and supplied the inchoative as compensation for the conditional verbally.[993]

[991] See Muḥammad Munīr al-Ḥāyik, *al-Fāʾ bayn al-Istijāba wal-Duʿāʾ* (Homs: Maṭbaʿat al-Yamāma, 1425/2004).

[992] "The original wording is *mahmā yakun min shayʾ* ʿno matter what happensʾ, where *mahmā* in an inchoative—and inchoatives are nominal by definition —and *yakun* the conditional verb, from which a follow-up *fāʾ* is usually invariable; but when *ammā* came up to play the role of both the inchoative and the conditional, it necessitated the *fāʾ*." (Kh 2:92-93)

[993] "I.e. the nominal sentence occurring after *ammā* because it is the apodosis of the suppressed conditional protasis… and the apodosis of a conditional protasis is a sentence sine qua non. However they disliked for the two particles of condition and apodosis to follow one another directly. So they affixed the latter to the enunciative and placed the inchoative ahead of it to serve as a separator between the two particles and

وَفِي تَصْدِيرِ الْجُمْلَتَيْنِ بِهِ: إِحْمَادٌ لِأَمْرِ الْمُؤْمِنِينَ، وَاعْتِدَادٌ بِعِلْمِهِمْ، وَذَمٌّ بَلِيغٌ لِلْكَافِرِينَ عَلَى قَوْلِهِمْ.

وَالضَّمِيرُ فِي ﴿أَنَّهُ﴾ لِلْمَثَلِ، أَوْ لِـ﴿أَن يَضْرِبَ﴾.

وَ(الْحَقُّ): الثَّابِتُ الَّذِي لَا يَسُوغُ إِنْكَارُهُ؛ يَعُمُّ الْأَعْيَانَ الثَّابِتَةَ، وَالْأَفْعَالَ الصَّائِبَةَ، وَالْأَقْوَالَ الصَّادِقَةَ؛ مِنْ قَوْلِهِمْ: (حَقَّ الْأَمْرُ) إِذَا ثَبَتَ. وَمِنْهُ: (ثَوْبٌ مُحَقَّقٌ): مُحْكَمُ النَّسْجِ.

﴿وَأَمَّا ٱلَّذِينَ كَفَرُواْ فَيَقُولُونَ﴾: كَانَ مِنْ حَقِّهِ: (وَأَمَّا الَّذِينَ

In the fact that He initiated the two sentences with [*ammā*] there is a commendation of the position of the believers and an appreciation of their knowledge together with a harsh censure of the unbelievers for what they said.

The personal pronoun in ***annahu*** ‹that it is› stands for the ***mathal*** ‹simile› or for ***an yaḍriba*** ‹to strike›.

[Definition of *ḥaqq*]

Al-ḥaqq ‹truth› is what is firmly established and unquestionable. It extends to individuated concrete objects, valid deeds and truthful statements, as when they say *ḥaqqa al-amr* ‹the matter has taken effect› when it becomes established, and *thawbun muḥaqqaq* ‹an accomplished garment›, perfectly woven.

wa-ammā-l-ladhīna kafarū fa-yaqūlūna ‹*but as for those who disbelieve, they say*›: normally it should be *wa-ammā-l-ladhīna*

serve as replacement for the suppressed conditional—I mean *mahmā yakun min shay'* ‹no matter what happens›." (Z 1:221) A direct object can be placed ahead of its governing verb to serve as a separator in the same way, for example in the verse *fa-ammā al-yatima fa-lā taqhar* ‹as for the orphan, do not crush him› (al-Sharḥ 93:9). (Kh)

كَفَرُوا فَلَا يَعْلَمُونَ)، لِيُطَابِقَ قَرِينَهُ وَيُقَابِلَ قَسِيمَهُ؛ لٰكِنْ لَمَّا كَانَ قَوْلُهُمْ هٰذَا دَلِيلاً وَاضِحاً عَلَى كَمَالِ جَهْلِهِمْ، عَدَلَ إِلَيْهِ عَلَى سَبِيلِ الْكِنَايَةِ، لِيَكُونَ كَالْبُرْهَانِ عَلَيْهِ.

﴿مَاذَآ أَرَادَ ٱللَّهُ بِهَٰذَا مَثَلًا﴾ يَحْتَمِلُ وَجْهَيْنِ: (أ) أَنْ يَكُونَ (مَا) اِسْتِفْهَامِيَّةً وَ(ذَا) بِمَعْنَى (الَّذِي)، وَمَا بَعْدَهُ صِلَتُهُ، وَالْمَجْمُوعُ خَبَرُ (مَا)؛ (ب) وَأَنْ يَكُونَ (مَا) مَعَ (ذَا) اِسْماً وَاحِداً بِمَعْنَى (أَيِّ شَيْءٍ)، مَنْصُوبَ الْمَحَلِّ عَلَى الْمَفْعُولِيَّةِ مِثْلَ (مَا أَرَادَ اللهُ). وَالْأَحْسَنُ فِي جَوَابِهِ: الرَّفْعُ عَلَى الْأَوَّلِ، وَالنَّصْبُ عَلَى الثَّانِي، لِيُطَابِقَ الْجَوَابُ السُّؤَالَ.

kafarū fa-lā yaʿlamūna (*but as for those who disbelieve: they do not know*) to match its fellow and complement its other half; but since that statement of theirs was such a patent proof of their utter ignorance, He shifted to [*they say*] in the style of a metonymy to serve as a demonstration of it.

mādhā arāda-l-Lāhu bi-hādhā mathalan (*what did the One God mean by [using] this as a simile?*) can be interpreted two ways:

(i) ***mā*** (what) is interrogative, ***dhā*** (this) is in the sense of *al-ladhī* (the one), what follows is its relative clause and the whole is the enunciative of ***mā***;

(ii) ***mā*** together with ***dhā*** forms a single noun in the sense of *ayyu shay'in* (what thing). It is a virtual accusative as an object, as in *mā arāda Allāh* (whatever Allah wants).

The best [parsing] concerning its reply is [to make it] nominative according to the first scenario and accusative according to the second, so that the reply will match the question.[994]

[994] "I.e. in its being a nominal sentence or a verbal one respectively." (S) "I.e. hypothetically; as for the noble verse there is no reply since, as you know, what was intended

وَ(الْإِرَادَةُ): نُزُوعُ النَّفْسِ وَمَيْلُهَا إِلَى الْفِعْلِ بِحَيْثُ يَحْمِلُهَا عَلَيْهِ؛ وَيُقَالُ لِلْقُوَّةِ الَّتِي هِيَ مَبْدَأُ النُّزُوعِ. وَالْأَوَّلُ مَعَ الْفِعْلِ، وَالثَّانِي قَبْلَهُ. وَكِلَا الْمَعْنَيَيْنِ غَيْرُ مُتَصَوَّرٍ اِتِّصَافُ الْبَارِي تَعَالَى بِهِ؛ وَلِذٰلِكَ اخْتُلِفَ فِي مَعْنَى إِرَادَتِهِ، فَقِيلَ: (١) إِرَادَتُهُ لِأَفْعَالِهِ: أَنَّهُ غَيْرُ سَاهٍ وَلَا مُكْرَهٍ؛ وَلِأَفْعَالِ غَيْرِهِ: أَمْرُهُ بِهَا. فَعَلَى هٰذَا، لَمْ تَكُنِ الْمَعَاصِي بِإِرَادَتِهِ. ....

Al-irāda ⟨will⟩ is the psyche's pining and propensity[995] for action which drive it to do it. It also designates the power that is the starting-point of pining. The first [definition] is together with action while the second is before it. Neither meaning can be conceived to describe Allah, whence the disagreement as to the precise meaning of His will.

[Definitions of the divine will]

I. Some said His willing of His acts is that He is neither inadvertent nor coerced,[996] and [His willing] of the acts of others is His command to do them.[997] According to this [definition], sins do not take place by His will.[998]

was objection, not enquiry." (Q) "Accordingly it is incorrect to make *yaḍillu bihi kathīran* the reply." (Iṣ)

995 "Propensity is like the explanation of pining and the benefit of adjoining them is to suggest that will is an involuntary propensity (*mayl ghayr ikhtiyārī*)" (Sk p. 268) and Muḥammad ʿAlī al-Tahānawī, *Mawsūʿat Kashshāf Iṣṭilāḥāt al-Funūn wal-ʿUlūm*, ed. Rafīq al-ʿAjam et al., 2 vols. (Beirut: Maktabat Lubnān, 1996) p. 132, art. *irāda*. The phrase became corrupted to "the benefit of adjoining them is to suggest that will is a voluntary propensity (*mayl ikhtiyārī*)" in the marginalia of P (p. 224)!

996 "This is the position of al-Najjār—one of the Muʿtazilis—as he considers will one of the eliminative attributes as opposed to affirmative." (S)

997 "I.e. His liability-imposing command, not His creational command (*al-amr al-taklīfī lā al-amr al-takwīnī*), as the latter is inseparable from the actualization of what is commanded." (Q)

998 The belief that sins do not take place by the divine will is the position of Muʿtazilis,

(٢) وَقِيلَ: عِلْمُهُ بِاشْتِمَالِ الْأَمْرِ عَلَى النِّظَامِ الْأَكْمَلِ، وَالْوَجْهِ الْأَصْلَحِ؛ فَإِنَّهُ يَدْعُو الْقَادِرَ إِلَى تَحْصِيلِهِ. (٣) وَالْحَقُّ: أَنَّهُ تَرْجِيحُ أَحَدِ مَقْدُورَيْهِ عَلَى الْآخَرِ وَتَخْصِيصُهُ بِوَجْهٍ دُونَ وَجْهٍ؛ أَوْ مَعْنًى يُوجِبُ هٰذَا التَّرْجِيحَ.

وَهِيَ أَعَمُّ مِنَ الِاخْتِيَارِ، فَإِنَّهُ مَيْلٌ مَعَ تَفْضِيلٍ.

وَفِي ﴿هٰذَا﴾: اسْتِحْقَارٌ وَاسْتِرْذَالٌ.

II. Others said it is His knowledge of the fact that the matter at hand entails the most perfect design and most beneficial pattern, for He summons every able person to implement it.[999]

III. The truth is that it is (i) to make one of its two potentials preponderant over the other and specify it through certain aspects at the exclusion of others;[1000] (ii) or a meaning that compels this giving of preponderance.[1001]

It is more general than choice, which is propensity together with preference.

Hādhā ⁽this⁾ connotes disparagement and contempt.[1002]

Qadaris, Manicheists and Christians cf. Imām al-Ḥaramayn, *al-Irshād* (p. 256, *dhamm al-qadariyya*).

999 "This is the position of al-Jāḥiẓ, al-Kaʿbī [Abū al-Qāsim al-Balkhī] and Abū al-Ḥasan al-Baṣrī, who belonged to the Muʿtazili sect." (S)

1000 "'One of its two potentials' means [preponderance of] one of the two sides of the possible over the other in actualization." (S) "The aspects meant are action and avoidance, beauty or ugliness, benefit or harm, and temporal and local contexts." (Q)

1001 "This is the position of the Ashʿaris, as it is a pre-eternal essential attribute that is differentiated from knowledge." (S) See on all the above positions the Qadi's own summations in *Ṭawāliʿ al-Anwār*, cf. Calverley and Pollock, *Nature, Man and God* (pp. 868-870 *God's will*) and Abū Manṣūr al-Baghdādī, *Uṣūl al-Dīn* (p. 102).

1002 "Because the demonstrative noun can be used for detraction [cf. Lat. *iste*] just as it can be used for magnification [cf. Lat. *ille*] according to context. The way it points to detraction is that when something is near it is easy to grasp—a quality which breeds contempt in most cases." (Q)

وَ﴿مَثَلًا﴾: نَصْبٌ عَلَى التَّمْيِيزِ، أَوِ الْحَالِ، كَقَوْلِهِ تَعَالَى: ﴿هَٰذِهِۦ نَاقَةُ ٱللَّهِ لَكُمْ ءَايَةً﴾ [الأعراف ٧٣].

﴿يُضِلُّ بِهِۦ كَثِيرًا وَيَهْدِى بِهِۦ كَثِيرًا﴾ (أ) جَوابُ ﴿مَاذَآ﴾، أَيْ: إِضْلَالُ كَثِيرٍ وَإِهْدَاءُ كَثِيرٍ. وَضَعَ الْفِعْلَ مَوْضِعَ الْمَصْدَرِ لِلْإِشْعَارِ بِالْحُدُوثِ وَالتَّجَدُّدِ. (ب) أَوْ بَيَانٌ لِلْجُمْلَتَيْنِ الْمُصَدَّرَتَيْنِ بِـ(أَمَّا) وَتَسْجِيلٌ بِأَنَّ الْعِلْمَ بِكَوْنِهِ حَقًّا: هُدًى وَبَيَانٌ، وَأَنَّ الْجَهْلَ بِوَجْهِ إِيرَادِهِ وَالْإِنْكَارَ لِحُسْنِ مَوْرِدِهِ: ضَلَالٌ وَفُسُوقٌ.

وَكَثْرَةُ كُلٍّ وَاحِدٍ مِنَ الْقَبِيلَيْنِ: بِالنَّظَرِ إِلَى أَنْفُسِهِمْ، ....

Mathalan ⁽as a similitude⁾ is an accusative of specification or of participial state, as in the saying of Allah Most High, *This is the she-camel of Allah as your sign* (al-Aʿrāf 7:73).

yuḍillu bihi kathīran wa-yahdī bihi kathīran ⁽*He misleads many thereby and He guides many thereby*⁾ is

(i) the answer to ***mādhā*** ⁽what⁾; that is, "the misguiding of many and the guiding of many."[1003] He placed a verb where the infinitive noun should have been, to intimate novelty and renewal;[1004]

(ii) or a clarification for the two clauses that begin with ***ammā*** and a ruling that knowledge of the fact that it is true is guidance and lucidity, while ignorance of the significance of its mention and denial of the excellence of its source[1005] are misguidance and deviance. The numerousness of each of the two clans is inherent

[1003] Ak, β, ε, F, I, R, T: اضلال كثير واهداء كثير :α اضلال كثير وهدّي كثير :B إضلال واهدآء

[1004] See note 298.

[1005] "Ignorance… and denial: this is an allusion to the fact that the question might actually be literal or it might be for denial." (Sk)

لَا بِالْقِيَاسِ إِلَى مُقَابِلِيهِمْ: فَإِنَّ الْمَهْدِيِّينَ قَلِيلُونَ بِالْإِضَافَةِ إِلَى أَهْلِ الضَّلَالِ، كَمَا قَالَ تَعَالَى: ﴿وَقَلِيلٌ مَّا هُمْ﴾ [ص ٢٤]، ﴿وَقَلِيلٌ مِّنْ عِبَادِيَ الشَّكُورُ﴾ [سبأ ١٣]. وَيَحْتَمِلُ أَنْ يَكُونَ كَثْرَةُ الضَّالِّينَ مِنْ حَيْثُ الْعَدَدِ، وَكَثْرَةُ الْمَهْدِيِّينَ بِاعْتِبَارِ الْفَضْلِ وَالشَّرَفِ، كَمَا قَالَ: [طويل]

.... * قَلِيلٌ إِذَا عُدُّوا كَثِيرٌ إِذَا شَدُّوا

وَقَالَ: [بسيط]

إِنَّ الْكِرَامَ كَثِيرٌ فِي الْبِلَادِ وَإِنْ * قَلُّوا كَمَا غَيْرُهُمْ قُلٌّ وَإِنْ كَثُرُوا

﴿وَمَا يُضِلُّ بِهِۦٓ إِلَّا ٱلْفَٰسِقِينَ﴾، أَيِ الْخَارِجِينَ عَنْ حَدِّ الْإِيمَانِ، كَقَوْلِهِ

to itself, not in comparison to its counterpart; for those who are well-guided are few in relation to the brood of misguidance—as Allah Most High said, *and truly few are they* (Ṣād 38:24), *and few of My slaves are the truly grateful* (Saba' 34:13). It is also possible that the numerousness of the misguided is in terms of numbers, while that of the well-guided is with regard to merit and honor, as [the poet] said: ["The Long"]

Few when counted, many when they fight,[1006]

and he said: ["The Outspread"]

Truly the noble are many in the lands, even if
they are few; just as the rest are scant, even if they abound.[1007]

wa-mā yuḍillu bihi illā-l-fāsiqīna ⁽*but He misleads none thereby other than the depraved*⁾, meaning those who pass the bounds of faith, as in the saying of Allah Most High, ...

[1006] Spoken by al-Mutanabbī in his panegyric of Muḥammad b. Sayyār b. Mukarram al-Tamīmī, cf. al-Barqūqī, *Sharḥ Dīwān al-Mutanabbī* (2:92).
[1007] Spoken by Abū Tammām al-Ṭā'ī in his panegyric of 'Umar b. 'Abd al-'Azīz al-Ṭā'ī al-Ḥimṣī, cf. al-Tabrīzī, *Sharḥ Dīwān Abī Tammām* (2:186).

تَعَالَى: ﴿إِنَّ ٱلْمُنَٰفِقِينَ هُمُ ٱلْفَٰسِقُونَ﴾ [التوبة ٦٧]؛ مِنْ قَوْلِهِمْ: (فَسَقَتِ الرُّطَبَةُ عَنْ قِشْرِهَا) إِذَا خَرَجَتْ. وَأَصْلُ الْفِسْقِ: الْخُرُوجُ عَنِ الْقَصْدِ. قَالَ رُؤْبَةُ: [رَجَز]

.... ❋ فَوَاسِقاً عَنْ قَصْدِهَا جَوَائِرَا

وَالْفَاسِقُ فِي الشَّرْعِ: الْخَارِجُ عَنْ أَمْرِ اللهِ بِارْتِكَابِ الْكَبِيرَةِ؛ وَلَهُ دَرَجَاتٌ ثَلَاثٌ: الْأُولَى: التَّغَابِي؛ وَهُوَ أَنْ يَرْتَكِبَهَا أَحْيَاناً، مُسْتَقْبِحاً إِيَّاهَا. الثَّانِيَةُ: الِانْهِمَاكُ؛ وَهُوَ أَنْ يَعْتَادَ ارْتِكَابَهَا، غَيْرَ مُبَالٍ بِهَا. الثَّالِثَةُ: الْجُحُودُ، وَهُوَ أَنْ يَرْتَكِبَهَا مُسْتَصْوِباً إِيَّاهَا. فَإِذَا شَارَفَ هٰذَا ....

verily the hypocrites—they are the depraved (al-Tawba 9:67), from their idiom *fasaqat al-ruṭaba ʿan qishrihā* ⁽the ripe moist date breaks away from its husk⁾ when it comes out.

Fisq originally means leaving the straight path. Ruʾba said: ["The Trembling"]

[Camels] deviating (fawāsiq) from their straight path, errant.[1008]

[The three types of *fāsiq*]

The ***fāsiq*** ⁽reprobate⁾ in the law is one who violates the divine command by committing a grave sin. There are three levels:

- The first level is mindlessness, which is for him to commit them at times, while considering them repugnant.
- The second level is immersion, which is for him to commit them habitually without second thought.
- The third level is disavowal, which is for him to commit them while considering them legitimate. Once he surveys the latter …

[1008] *Dīwān Ruʾba* in *Majmūʿ Ashʿār al-ʿArab* (3:192).

الْمَقَامَ وَتَخَطَّى خِطَطَهُ، خَلَعَ رِبْقَةَ الْإِيمَانِ مِنْ عُنُقِهِ، وَلَابَسَ الْكُفْرَ. وَمَا دَامَ هُوَ فِي دَرَجَةِ التَّغَابِي أَوِ الْانْهِمَاكِ، فَلَا يُسْلَبُ عَنْهُ اسْمُ الْمُؤْمِنِ، لِاتِّصَافِهِ بِالتَّصْدِيقِ الَّذِي هُوَ مُسَمَّى الْإِيمَانِ، وَلِقَوْلِهِ تَعَالَى: ﴿وَإِن طَآئِفَتَانِ مِنَ ٱلْمُؤْمِنِينَ ٱقْتَتَلُوا۟﴾ [الحجرات ٩].

وَالْمُعْتَزِلَةُ، لَمَّا قَالُوا: (الْإِيمَانُ عِبَارَةٌ عَنْ مَجْمُوعِ التَّصْدِيقِ وَالْإِقْرَارِ وَالْعَمَلِ، وَالْكُفْرُ تَكْذِيبُ الْحَقِّ وَجُحُودُهُ): جَعَلُوهُ قِسْماً ثَالِثاً نَازِلاً بَيْنَ مَنْزِلَتَي الْمُؤْمِنِ وَالْكَافِرِ، لِمُشَارَكَتِهِ كُلَّ وَاحِدٍ مِنْهُمَا فِي بَعْضِ الْأَحْكَامِ.

وَتَخْصِيصُ الْإِضْلَالِ بِهِمْ ....

position and maps out its grounds, he has doffed the noose of belief from his neck and donned the garment of unbelief. However, as long as he remains at the level of mindlessness or that of immersion, he retains the appellation of believer because he is still dressed with confirmation—which is the referent of belief—and because Allah Most High said, *And if two factions of the believers fall to fighting* (al-Ḥujurāt 49:9).

[The Muʿtazilis' intermediary damnation for sinful Muslims]

The Muʿtazila—since they said that belief stands for confirmation, affirmation and actions put together, while unbelief is the denial of truth and its disavowal—put him in a third category as "being positioned in-between the two positions of the believer and the unbeliever" because he shares with each of them some of the rulings that apply to them respectively.[1009]

The fact that their being subjects of misguidance is specified

[1009] See p. 259f. on the definition of belief and, on the "middle position," the entry on the Muʿtazila in our biographical glossary.

مُرَتَّباً عَلَى صِفَةِ الْفِسْقِ يَدُلُّ عَلَى أَنَّهُ الَّذِي أَعَدَّهُمْ لِلْإِضْلَالِ، وَأَدَّى بِهِمْ إِلَى الضَّلَالِ. وَذٰلِكَ لِأَنَّ كُفْرَهُمْ، وَعُدُولَهُمْ عَنِ الْحَقِّ، وَإِصْرَارَهُمْ بِالْبَاطِلِ صَرَفَتْ وُجُوهَ أَفْكَارِهِمْ عَنْ حِكْمَةِ الْمَثَلِ إِلَى حَقَارَةِ الْمُمَثَّلِ بِهِ، حَتَّى رَسَخَتْ بِهِ جَهَالَتُهُمْ وَازْدَادَتْ ضَلَالَتُهُمْ، فَأَنْكَرُوهُ وَاسْتَهْزَؤُوا بِهِ.

وَقُرِئَ (يُضَلُّ) عَلَى الْبِنَاءِ الْمَفْعُولِ، وَ(الْفَاسِقُونَ) بِالرَّفْعِ.

﴿ٱلَّذِينَ يَنقُضُونَ عَهْدَ ٱللَّهِ﴾ صِفَةٌ لِلْفَاسِقِينَ لِلذَّمِّ وَتَقْرِيرِ الْفِسْقِ. وَ(النَّقْضُ): فَسْخُ التَّرْكِيبِ. وَأَصْلُهُ ....

in direct sequence after the attribute of depravity shows that the latter is what made them apt to be misguided and led to their misguidance. That is because their unbelief, shunning of truth and persistence in falsehood turned their thoughts away[1010] from the wisdom of the simile and onto the insignificance of its vehicle. Then, through that [diverting away], their ignorance became deep-rooted and their misguidance increased, whereupon they denied it and mocked it.

It was also read *yuḍallu* ⟨are misled⟩ in the passive voice and *al-fāsiqūn* ⟨the depraved⟩ in the nominative.[1011]

[2:27] **al-ladhīna yanquḍūna ʿahda-l-Lāhi** ⟨*those who breach the covenant of the One God*⟩ is a descriptive for ***al-fāsiqīn*** ⟨the depraved⟩ for condemnation and the determination of depravity.[1012]

Al-naqḍ ⟨breach⟩ is the dissolution of an aggregate. Its orig-

[1010] Lit. "turned away the faces of their thoughts," "an implicit and conceptual/associative metaphor" (*istiʿāra mukanniya wa-takhyīliyya*). (Q)

[1011] By Zayd b. ʿAlī for all three verbs. (*MQ*)

[1012] "It is also considered possible that it is disjoined from what precedes and that it is an inchoative of which the enunciative is the clause of *ulā'ika*." (Kh)

فِي طَاقَاتِ الْحَبْلِ؛ وَاسْتِعْمَالُهُ فِي إِبْطَالِ الْعَهْدِ مِنْ حَيْثُ إِنَّ الْعَهْدَ يُسْتَعَارُ لَهُ الْحَبْلُ لِمَا فِيهِ مِنْ رَبْطِ أَحَدِ الْمُتَعَاهِدَيْنِ بِالْآخَرِ. فَإِنْ أُطْلِقَ مَعَ لَفْظِ الْحَبْلِ كَانَ تَرْشِيحاً لِلْمَجَازِ؛ وَإِنْ ذُكِرَ مَعَ الْعَهْدِ كَانَ رَمْزاً إِلَى مَا هُوَ مِنْ رَوَادِفِهِ، وَهُوَ أَنَّ الْعَهْدَ حَبْلٌ فِي ثَبَاتِ الْوُصْلَةِ بَيْنَ الْمُتَعَاهِدَيْنِ؛ كَقَوْلِكَ: (شُجَاعٌ، يَفْتَرِسُ أَقْرَانَهُ)، وَ(عَالِمٌ، يَغْتَرِفُ مِنْهُ النَّاسُ)؛ فَإِنَّ فِيهِ تَنْبِيهاً عَلَى أَنَّهُ أَسَدٌ فِي شَجَاعَتِهِ، بَحْرٌ بِالنَّظَرِ إِلَى إِفَادَتِهِ.

وَ(**الْعَهْدُ**): الْمَوْثِقُ. وَوَضْعُهُ لِمَا مِنْ شَأْنِهِ أَنْ يُرَاعَى وَيُتَعَهَّدَ، كَالْوَصِيَّةِ وَالْيَمِينِ، وَيُقَالُ لِلدَّارِ، مِنْ حَيْثُ إِنَّهَا تُرَاعَى بِالرُّجُوعِ إِلَيْهَا، وَالتَّارِيخِ لِأَنَّهُ يَحْفَظُ. ....

inal sense refers to the yarns of rope. Its use for the dissolution of a covenant comes from the metaphorization of the latter as a rope, since it ties the two covenantees to each other. If used with *ḥabl* ⁽rope⁾ it is an extended metaphor;[1013] and if it is mentioned together with **ʿahd** ⁽covenant⁾ it symbolizes one of its aftereffects, namely that the covenant is a rope in the solidity of the connection between the two convenantees—just as you say "he is fearless and devours his contemporaries" or "he is learned, people tap into his knowledge." There is, respectively, a notice that one is a lion in bravery and an ocean in the knowledge one contributes.

Al-ʿahd is *al-mawthiq* ⁽pact⁾ and was coined for something meant to be observed repetitively such as a testament or an oath. It also denotes (i) a house in the sense that it is tended by returning to it, and (ii) historical dating because it preserves. ....

[1013] See note 696 above, commentary on 2:16 *fa-mā rabiḥat tijāratuhum*.

وَهٰذَا الْعَهْدُ: (أ) إِمَّا الْعَهْدُ الْمَأْخُوذُ بِالْعَقْلِ - وَهُوَ الْحُجَّةُ الْقَائِمَةُ عَلَى عِبَادِهِ، الدَّالَّةُ عَلَى تَوْحِيدِهِ، وَوُجُوبِ وُجُودِهِ، وَصِدْقِ رَسُولِهِ - وَعَلَيْهِ أُوِّلَ قَوْلُهُ تَعَالَى: ﴿وَأَشْهَدَهُمْ عَلَىٰٓ أَنفُسِهِمْ﴾ [الأعراف ١٧٢]؛ (ب) أَوْ: الْمَأْخُوذُ بِالرُّسُلِ عَلَى الْأُمَمِ بِأَنَّهُمْ، إِذَا بُعِثَ إِلَيْهِمْ رَسُولٌ مُصَدَّقٌ بِالْمُعْجِزَاتِ: صَدَّقُوهُ وَاتَّبَعُوهُ، وَلَمْ يَكْتُمُوا أَمْرَهُ، وَلَمْ يُخَالِفُوا حُكْمَهُ. وَإِلَيْهِ أَشَارَ بِقَوْلِهِ: ﴿وَإِذْ أَخَذَ ٱللَّهُ مِيثَٰقَ ٱلَّذِينَ أُوتُوا۟ ٱلْكِتَٰبَ﴾ [آل عمران ١٨٧]، وَنَظَائِرُهُ.

وَقِيلَ: عُهُودُ اللهِ تَعَالَى ثَلَاثَةٌ: (١) عَهْدٌ أَخَذَهُ عَلَى جَمِيعِ ذُرِّيَّةِ آدَمَ بِأَنْ

[Types of divine covenants]

This [particular] ***ʿahd*** is either

(i) the covenant taken because of [the gift of] reason, which is the glaring proof [of Allah] over His slaves indicating His oneness, the necessity of His existence and the veracity of His Messenger. It is in this sense that the saying of Allah Most High *and He made them testify over themselves* (al-Aʿrāf 7:172) is interpreted.

(ii) Or it is the one taken through the Messengers from the nations, that when a certain messenger is sent to them who will be confirmed with stunning miracles, they must confirm him as true and follow him, without covering up his mission nor contravene his decisions, as pointed out by His saying, *And when Allah took a covenant from those who had received the Scripture* (Āl ʿImrān 3:187) and related verses.

It was also said that the covenants of Allah are three:

1. a covenant He took from all of the offspring of Adam whereby

يُقِرُّوا بِرُبُوبِيَّتِهِ؛ (٢) وَعَهْدٌ أَخَذَهُ عَلَى النَّبِيِّينَ بِأَنْ يُقِيمُوا الدِّينَ وَلَا يَتَفَرَّقُوا فِيهِ؛ (٣) وَعَهْدٌ أَخَذَهُ عَلَى الْعُلَمَاءِ بِأَنْ يُبَيِّنُوا الْحَقَّ وَلَا يَكْتُمُوهُ.

﴿مِنْ بَعْدِ مِيثَٰقِهِۦ﴾: الضَّمِيرُ لِلْعَهْدِ. وَ(الْمِيثَاقُ): اِسْمٌ لِمَا يَقَعُ بِهِ الْوَثَاقَةُ - وَهِيَ الْإِسْتِحْكَامُ - وَالْمُرَادُ بِهِ: مَا وَثَّقَ اللهُ بِهِ عَهْدَهُ مِنَ الْآيَاتِ وَالْكُتُبِ، أَوْ مَا وَثَّقُوهُ بِهِ مِنَ الْإِلْتِزَامِ وَالْقَبُولِ. وَيَحْتَمِلُ أَنْ يَكُونَ بِمَعْنَى الْمَصْدَرِ.

وَ(مِنْ) لِلْإِبْتِدَاءِ، فَإِنَّ ابْتِدَاءَ النَّقْضِ: بَعْدَ الْمِيثَاقِ.

their affirm His nurturership;

2. a covenant He took from the Prophets that they should establish religion and not diverge over it;

3. a covenant He took from the people of learning that they must show the truth and not conceal it.[1014]

min baʿdi mīthāqihi ⟨*after its thorough fastening*⟩: the personal pronoun stands for the covenant.

Al-mīthāq ⟨fastener⟩ is a name for that by which stability ensues, namely what makes something perfectly compact.[1015] What is meant by it is that whereby Allah has fastenened His covenant of verses and scriptures, or that whereby they themselves fastened it by way of observance and acceptance. It is also possible that it is meant as an infinitive noun.

Min ⟨from⟩ is inceptive, for the starting-point of the breach is after the fastening.

[1014] Respectively in al-Aʿrāf 7:172; Āl ʿImrān 3:81 and 3:187. Also in Hadith.

[1015] "Since it makes sense to object that, in light of *ʿahd*, *mīthāq* and *mawthiq* all meaning the same thing as he explicitly said before—'*al-ʿahd* is *al-mawthiq*'—making the personal pronoun stand for the covenant necessitates that an object refer to itself, he alluded to its rebuttal by saying that *mīthāq* here is not in the sense of covenant but a noun for that whereby *wathāqa* ensues, that is, *iḥkām* ⟨compactness⟩—so it is the name of a instrument, like *miftāḥ* ⟨key⟩." (Q)

﴿وَيَقْطَعُونَ مَآ أَمَرَ ٱللَّهُ بِهِۦٓ أَن يُوصَلَ﴾ يَحْتَمِلُ كُلَّ قَطِيعَةٍ لَا يَرْضَاهَا اللهُ تَعَالَى: كَقَطْعِ الرَّحِمِ، وَالْإِعْرَاضِ عَنْ مُوَالَاةِ الْمُؤْمِنِينَ، وَالتَّفْرِقَةِ بَيْنَ الْأَنْبِيَاءِ -عَلَيْهِمُ السَّلَامُ- وَالْكُتُبِ فِي التَّصْدِيقِ، وَتَرْكِ الْجَمَاعَاتِ الْمَفْرُوضَةِ وَسَائِرِ مَا فِيهِ رَفْضُ خَيْرٍ أَوْ تَعَاطِي شَرٍّ، فَإِنَّهُ يَقْطَعُ الْوُصْلَةَ بَيْنَ اللهِ وَبَيْنَ الْعَبْدِ الْمَقْصُودَةَ بِالذَّاتِ مِنْ كُلِّ وَصْلٍ وَفَصْلٍ.

وَ(الْأَمْرُ): هُوَ الْقَوْلُ الطَّالِبُ لِلْفِعْلِ؛ وَقِيلَ: مَعَ الْعُلُوِّ؛ وَقِيلَ: مَعَ الْاِسْتِعْلَاءِ. وَبِهِ سُمِّيَ ....

[Types of breaches condemned by Allah]

wa-yaqṭaʿūna mā amara-l-Lāhu bihi an yūṣala ⁽*and cut what the One God has commanded to be joined*⁾ can mean every type of severing that is not accepted by Allah such as (i) severing the ties of kinship; (ii) shunning allegiance to the believers; (iii) discriminating between prophets—upon them peace—and scriptures in what they confirm as true; (iv) shunning obligatory collective agreements;[1016] and the rest of what entails rejection of something good or taking something evil. For it [all] severs the relationship between Allah and the slave that is the essential purpose of every connection and every separation.

Al-amr ⁽command⁾[1017] denotes a verbal injunction to act—it was also said, together with [the commander's actual] superiority; or together with assumed aboveness. Then it came to also de-

[1016] "As in the saying of Allah *but do help one another unto righteousness and pious duty* (al-Mā'ida 5:2); *and exhort one another to truth and exhort one another to endurance* (al-ʿAṣr 103:3); and his saying—upon him blessings and peace: 'and be all slaves of Allah and brothers' and 'you must be with the largest mass.'" (Z)
[1017] Plural *awāmir.*

الْأَمْرُ الَّذِي هُوَ وَاحِدُ الْأُمُورِ، تَسْمِيَةً لِلْمَفْعُولِ بِهِ بِالْمَصْدَرِ؛ فَإِنَّهُ مِمَّا يُؤْمَرُ بِهِ، كَمَا قِيلَ لَهُ: (شَأْنٌ)، وَهُوَ الطَّلَبُ وَالْقَصْدُ؛ يُقَالُ: (شَأَنْتُ شَأْنَهُ)، إِذَا قَصَدْتَ قَصْدَهُ. وَ﴿أَن يُوصَلَ﴾ يَحْتَمِلُ النَّصْبَ وَالْخَفْضَ عَلَى أَنَّهُ بَدَلٌ مِنْ ﴿مَآ﴾، أَوْ ضَمِيرِهِ. وَالثَّانِي أَحْسَنُ لَفْظاً وَمَعْنًى.

﴿وَيُفْسِدُونَ فِى ٱلْأَرْضِ﴾ بِالْمَنْعِ عَنِ الْإِيمَانِ وَالْاسْتِهْزَاءِ بِالْحَقِّ، وَقَطْعِ الْوُصَلِ الَّتِي بِهَا نِظَامُ الْعَالَمِ وَصَلَاحُهُ.

﴿أُوْلَٰٓئِكَ هُمُ ٱلْخَٰسِرُونَ﴾ الَّذِينَ خَسِرُوا: (١) بِإِهْمَالِ الْعَقْلِ عَنِ النَّظَرِ

note *amr* as the singular of *umūr* ⁽matters⁾—the way the infinitive noun is used to name the direct object—since the latter is what one is commanded to do, just as it is also called *sha'n* ⁽affair⁾, which means "pursuit" and "purpose." It is said *sha'antu sha'nah* when I pursue a certain purpose.

It is possible for ***an yūṣala*** ⁽to be joined⁾ to be either in the accusative or in the genitive, in the sense of a substitute for ***mā*** or its personal pronoun respectively. The latter scenario is finer verbally and semantically.[1018]

wa-yufsidūna fīl-arḍi ⁽*and spread corruption on earth*⁾ by stopping [others] from believing, scoffing at truth and cutting the ties by which the order of the world and its haleness are kept.[1019]

ulā'ika humu-l-khāsirūna ⁽*those—they are the losers!*⁾ who have lost: 1. by neglecting [to use] theirs minds to investigate ....

1018 "Because it is a more powerful blame, since *the severing of what Allah has commanded to be joined* is more powerful than *the severing of the joining of what Allah has commanded*." (Kh, Q)

1019 This shows that the translation of *fasād* as "disorder" and "chaos" is interpretive, since it is clear they are not the same as corruption but rather its consequences.

وَاقْتِنَاصِ مَا يُفِيدُهُمُ الْحَيَاةَ الْأَبَدِيَّةَ؛ (٢) وَاسْتِبْدَالِ الْإِنْكَارِ وَالطَّعْنِ فِي الْآيَاتِ بِالْإِيمَانِ بِهَا، وَالنَّظَرِ فِي حَقَائِقِهَا، وَالْاِقْتِبَاسِ مِنْ أَنْوَارِهَا؛ (٣) وَاشْتِرَاءِ النَّقْضِ بِالْوَفَاءِ، وَالْفَسَادِ بِالصَّلَاحِ، وَالْعِقَابِ بِالثَّوَابِ.

﴿كَيْفَ تَكْفُرُونَ بِاللَّهِ﴾ اِسْتِخْبَارٌ فِيهِ إِنْكَارٌ وَتَعْجِيبٌ لِكُفْرِهِمْ بِإِنْكَارِ الْحَالِ الَّتِي يَقَعُ عَلَيْهَا عَلَى الطَّرِيقِ الْبُرْهَانِيِّ؛ لِأَنَّ صُدُورَهُ لَا يَنْفَكُّ عَنْ حَالٍ وَصِفَةٍ، فَإِذَا أُنْكِرَ أَنْ يَكُونَ لِكُفْرِهِمْ حَالٌ يُوجَدُ عَلَيْهَا: اِسْتَلْزَمَ ذٰلِكَ إِنْكَارُ وُجُودِهِ؛ فَهُوَ أَبْلَغُ وَأَقْوَى فِي إِنْكَارِ الْكُفْرِ مِنْ (أَتَكْفُرُونَ؟)، وَأَوْفَقُ لِمَا بَعْدَهُ مِنَ الْحَالِ.

and acquire what will profit them eternal life;

2. by substituting denial and criticism of the Quranic verses into the place of (i) belief in them, (ii) investigation of their realities (iii) and drawing from their lights;

3. and by purchasing (i) breach at the cost of observance, (ii) corruption at the cost of haleness (iii) and retribution at the cost of reward.

[2:28] **kayfa takfurūna bi-l-Lāhi** ⁽*how do you disbelieve in the One God*⁾ is a rhetorical query implying incredulity and stupefaction at their unbelief, through non-recognition of the state in which it takes place, in the manner of a demonstration. For its emergence [means it] has to possess some state and some attribute; when one cannot recognize any state in which their unbelief can exist, that inevitably means its existence is unrecognized. Thus it is more expressive and stronger in the non-recognition of unbelief than *atakfurūn* ⁽do you disbelieve?⁾ and more congruent with the participial-state constructions that follow it.

وَالْخِطَابُ: (I) مَعَ الَّذِينَ كَفَرُوا. لَمَّا وَصَفَهُمْ بِالْكُفْرِ وَسُوءِ الْمَقَالِ وَخُبْثِ الْفِعَالِ، خَاطَبَهُمْ عَلَى طَرِيقَةِ الْإِلْتِفَاتِ، وَوَبَّخَهُمْ عَلَى كُفْرِهِمْ مَعَ عِلْمِهِمْ بِحَالِهِمُ الْمُقْتَضِيَةِ خِلَافَ ذٰلِكَ. وَالْمَعْنَى: أَخْبِرُونِي عَلَى أَيِّ حَالٍ تَكْفُرُونَ!

﴿وَكُنتُمْ أَمْوَٰتًا﴾: أَيْ أَجْسَاماً لَا حَيَاةَ لَهَا: عَنَاصِرَ، وَأَغْذِيَةً، وَأَخْلَاطاً، وَنُطَفاً، وَمُضَغاً مُخَلَّقَةً وَغَيْرَ مُخَلَّقَةٍ.

﴿فَأَحْيَٰكُمْ﴾ بِخَلْقِ الْأَرْوَاحِ وَنَفْخِهَا فِيكُمْ. وَإِنَّمَا عَطَفَهُ بِالْفَاءِ لِأَنَّهُ مُتَّصِلٌ بِمَا عَطَفَ عَلَيْهِ، غَيْرُ مُتَرَاخٍ عَنْهُ، بِخِلَافِ الْبَوَاقِي.

[The three different possible addressees in *kayfa takfurūn?*]

The discourse addresses

I. those who disbelieved: when He attributed unbelief to them as well as evil speech and insidious acts, He addressed them by way of redirected apostrophe and scolded them for disbelieving when they know full well that their state dictates the opposite of that. The meaning is, "Tell me, in what possible way are you disbelieving?"

wa-kuntum amwātan ⟨*when you had been dead*⟩, that is, lifeless bodies—elements and nutrients and humors and zygotes and morsels of flesh, formed and unformed.

fa-aḥyākum ⟨*then He gave you life*⟩ by the creation of souls and their insufflation into you. The reason He adjoined it alone with the *fā'* ⟨then⟩ is because it is directly connected with its adjunct, without delay, contrary to the rest [of the adjunctive clauses].

﴿ثُمَّ يُمِيتُكُمْ﴾ عِنْدَ تَقَضِّي آجَالِكُمْ.

﴿ثُمَّ يُحْيِيكُمْ﴾ بِالنُّشُورِ ﴿يَوْمَ يُنفَخُ فِي ٱلصُّورِ﴾ [النبأ ١٨]، أَوْ لِلسُّؤَالِ فِي الْقُبُورِ.

﴿ثُمَّ إِلَيْهِ تُرْجَعُونَ﴾ بَعْدَ الْحَشْرِ، فَيُجَازِيكُمْ بِأَعْمَالِكُمْ؛ أَوْ تُنْشَرُونَ إِلَيْهِ مِنْ قُبُورِكُمْ لِلْحِسَابِ. فَمَا أَعْجَبَ كُفْرَكُمْ مَعَ عِلْمِكُمْ بِحَالِكُمْ هٰذِهِ!

فَإِنْ قِيلَ: إِنْ عَلِمُوا أَنَّهُمْ كَانُوا أَمْوَاتاً فَأَحْيَاهُمْ ثُمَّ يُمِيتُهُمْ، لَمْ يَعْلَمُوا أَنَّهُ يُحْيِيهِمْ ثُمَّ إِلَيْهِ يُرْجَعُونَ. قُلْتُ: تَمَكُّنُهُمْ مِنَ الْعِلْمِ بِهِمَا - لِمَا نَصَبَ لَهُمْ مِنَ الدَّلَائِلِ - مُنَزَّلٌ مَنْزِلَةَ عِلْمِهِمْ فِي إِزَاحَةِ ....

thumma yumītukum ⁽*then He will make you die*⁾ when their life terms are concluded.

thumma yuḥyīkum ⁽*then He will give you life*⁾ with resurrection *on the day the horn is blown* (al-Anʿām 6:73 etc.) or for the questioning in the grave.

thumma ilayhi turjaʿūna ⁽*then unto Him you shall be returned?*⁾ after the final gathering so that He will requite you for your works; or you will be gathered unto Him from your graves for the reckoning. How strange it is, then, that you should disbelieve when you are fully aware of your situation!

If someone asks: "They may have known that they had been dead then He gave them live and then He will cause them to die; but they had no knowledge that He would give them life and then unto Him they should be returned," I say: their capability of knowing the latter two[1020]—in light of the proofs He set up for them—is virtual knowledge on their part, so that it eliminates

[1020] "I.e. their soundness, not their actuality." (Q)

الْعُذْرِ، سِيَّما وَفِي الْآيَةِ تَنْبِيهٌ عَلَى مَا يَدُلُّ عَلَى صِحَّتِهِمَا، وَهُوَ أَنَّهُ تَعَالَى، لَمَّا قَدَرَ أَنْ أَحْيَاهُمْ أَوَّلاً: قَدَرَ عَلَى أَنْ يُحْيِيَهُمْ ثانياً؛ فَإِنَّ بَدْءَ الْخَلْقِ لَيْسَ بِأَهْوَنَ عَلَيْهِ مِنْ إِعَادَتِهِ. (II) أَوِ الْخِطَابُ مَعَ الْقَبِيلَيْنِ؛ فَإِنَّهُ - سُبْحَانَهُ وَتَعَالَى - لَمَّا بَيَّنَ دَلَائِلَ التَّوْحِيدِ وَالنُّبُوَّةِ، وَوَعَدَهُمْ عَلَى الْإِيمَانِ، وَأَوْعَدَهُمْ عَلَى الْكُفْرِ: أَكَّدَ ذٰلِكَ بِأَنْ عَدَّدَ عَلَيْهِمُ النِّعَمَ الْعَامَّةَ وَالْخَاصَّةَ، وَاسْتَقْبَحَ صُدُورَ الْكُفْرِ مِنْهُمْ، وَاسْتَبْعَدَهُ عَنْهُمْ مَعَ تِلْكَ النِّعَمِ الْجَلِيلَةِ؛ فَإِنَّ عِظَمَ النِّعَمِ يُوجِبُ عِظَمَ مَعْصِيَةِ الْمُنْعِمِ.

any excuse. This is even more the case when the verse draws attention to what shows the soundness of both[1021]—namely, that since Allah Most High had power to and gave them life[1022] in the first place, He has power to give them life a second time; for the producing of creation is not easier for Him than restoring it.[1023]

II. Alternately, the discourse addresses both parties.[1024] After Allah Most High clarified the evidentiary proofs of divine oneness and prophethood, promised them [Paradise] for belief and threatened them [with hellfire] for unbelief, He ascertained all that, by enumerating for them [His] general and specific favors. He then decried any show of unbelief from them and declared it improbable in light of those considerable favors; for the immensity of the favors spells the enormity of offending the Favorer.[1025]

1021 "I.e. the soundness of revival after death and being brought back to the Most High; for reason dictates the eventuality of resurrection and the return to the reckoning in many ways." (Z)

1022 α, B, β, ε, F, I, P, R, Sk, T: أن أحياهم Ak: على أن أحياهم U: على أحيائهم K, Kh, Q, Ul, Z: على احيائهم H, L, MM: على إحيائهم corruption making the sense subjunctive.

1023 As the Qadi explicitly states in his commentary on the verse *He it is who produces creation, then restores it—and it is easier for Him* (al-Rūm 30:27).

1024 "I.e. the believers and the unbelievers." (Z)

1025 All mss. and eds. المنعم AQ, H: النعم typo.

فَإِنْ قِيلَ: كَيْفَ تُعَدُّ الْإِمَاتَةُ مِنَ النِّعَمِ الْمُقْتَضِيَةِ لِلشُّكْرِ؟ قُلْتُ: لَمَّا كَانَتْ وُصْلَةً إِلَى الْحَيَاةِ الثَّانِيَةِ ـ الَّتِي هِيَ الْحَيَاةُ الْحَقِيقِيَّةُ، كَمَا قَالَ اللهُ تَعَالَى: ﴿وَإِنَّ ٱلدَّارَ ٱلْآخِرَةَ لَهِىَ ٱلْحَيَوَانُ﴾ [العنكبوت ٦٤] ـ كَانَتْ مِنَ النِّعَمِ الْعَظِيمَةِ؛ مَعَ أَنَّ الْمَعْدُودَ عَلَيْهِمْ نِعْمَةً: هُوَ الْمَعْنَى الْمُنْتَزَعُ مِنَ الْقِصَّةِ بِأَسْرِهَا ـ كَمَا أَنَّ الْوَاقِعَ حَالاً: هُوَ الْعِلْمُ بِهَا ـ لَا كُلُّ وَاحِدَةٍ مِنَ الْجُمَلِ؛ فَإِنَّ بَعْضَهَا مَاضٍ، وَبَعْضَهَا مُسْتَقْبَلٌ، وَكِلَاهُمَا لَا يَصِحُّ أَنْ يَقَعَ حَالاً.

(III) أَوْ: مَعَ الْمُؤْمِنِينَ خَاصَّةً، لِتَقْرِيرِ الْمِنَّةِ عَلَيْهِمْ وَتَبْعِيدِ الْكُفْرِ عَنْهُمْ، عَلَى مَعْنَى: (كَيْفَ يُتَصَوَّرُ ....

If someone asks, "How can the giving of death be counted among the favors that compel gratitude?" I say: since it is a junction to the second life, which is the real life—as Allah Most High said, *and verily the last abode—indeed that is the life* (al-'Ankabūt 29:64)—it is one of the immense favors. Yet what is being counted as the favor to them is the thrust of the account as a whole[1026]—just as what is presently taking place is knowledge of it—and not of each and every one of the sentences, since part of them is in the past and part in the future; so they cannot possibly be both taking place presently.

III. Alternately, [it addresses] the believers in particular, as a resolution of the bounty lavished on them and a distantiation of unbelief far from them. The sense would be: "How can anyone imagine ....

[1026] "Not every discrete item that was mentioned therein, lest it be objected, 'how can the giving of death be counted among the favors?' The thrust of the account is the extraction of antecedents for human beings out of two meanings: the context of inanimateness (*qarīnat al-jamādiyya*) and his gradual elevation to the apex of bliss, which is to connect with the divine." (Z)

مِنْكُمُ الْكُفْرُ وَكُنْتُمْ أَمْوَاتاً جُهَّالاً، فَأَحْيَاكُمْ بِمَا أَفَادَكُمْ مِنَ الْعِلْمِ وَالْإِيمَانِ، ثُمَّ يُمِيتُكُمُ الْمَوْتَ الْمَعْرُوفَ، ثُمَّ يُحْيِيكُمُ الْحَيَاةَ الْحَقِيقِيَّةَ، ثُمَّ إِلَيْهِ تُرْجَعُونَ، فَيُثِيبُكُمْ بِمَا لَا عَيْنٌ رَأَتْ، وَلَا أُذُنٌ سَمِعَتْ، وَلَا خَطَرَ عَلَى قَلْبِ بَشَرٍ؟)

وَ(الْحَيَاةُ): (I) حَقِيقَةٌ فِي الْقُوَّةِ الْحَسَّاسَةِ أَوْ مَا يَقْتَضِيهَا، وَبِهَا سُمِّيَ الْحَيَوَانُ حَيَوَاناً؛ (II) مَجَازٌ (أ) فِي الْقُوَّةِ النَّامِيَةِ ـ لِأَنَّهَا مِنْ طَلَائِعِهَا وَمُقَدِّمَاتِهَا

that you might disbelieve[1027] when you were dead and utterly unknowing, then He gave you life with what He imparted to you of knowledge and faith, then He will cause you to die the death known to all, then He will give you the true life and you will be returned unto Him, so that He will reward you with what no eye has ever seen or ear ever heard or heart of man ever conceived?"

[The definition of life in creatures]

Al-ḥayāt ⁽life⁾ is

I. a literal term in reference to the sensitive virtue or what presupposes it—whereby *ḥayawān* ⁽living animate nature⁾ receives its name—and

II. a metonymy[1028] in reference

(i) to the vegetative virtue[1029]—as the latter is one of its foresigns and preliminaries[1030]—

[1027] This is the gist of the translations that chose *How can/could you disbelieve…?* and it is the weakest of the three scenarios.

[1028] α, B, β, C, ε, F, K, Kh, Q, R, T, Ul, Z: حقيقة... مجاز Ak: حقيقة... ومجاز AQ, L, D, I, MM, P, Sk, U: حقيقة.... مجازاً H: حقيقية... مجازاً typo.

[1029] On these Aristotelian classes see, for example, Ibn Sīna on the *nafs* in his *Kitāb al-Najāt fīl-Ḥikmat al-Manṭiqiyya wal-Ṭabīʿiyya wal-Ilāhiyya*, ed. Mājid Fakhrī (Beirut: Dār al-Āfāq al-Jadīda, 1982) II.6.196 (*al-quwwat al-munmiya*) and the section on *al-ḥayawān* in the second part of his *Kitāb al-Shifā'* II.7 (*al-nafs al-ḥassasa=sensualitas*).

[1030] "In the fetus for example" (Z)

ـ (ب) وَفِيمَا يَخُصُّ الْإِنْسَانَ مِنَ الْفَضَائِلِ: كَالْعَقْلِ، وَالْعِلْمِ، وَالْإِيمَانِ، مِنْ حَيْثُ إِنَّهُ كَمَالُهَا وَغَايَتُهَا. وَ(الْمَوْتُ) بِإِزَائِهَا، يُقَالُ عَلَى مَا يُقَابِلُهَا فِي كُلِّ مَرْتَبَةٍ. قَالَ تَعَالَى: ﴿قُلِ ٱللَّهُ يُحْيِيكُمْ ثُمَّ يُمِيتُكُمْ﴾ [الجاثية ٢٦]؛ وَقَالَ: ﴿ٱعْلَمُوٓا۟ أَنَّ ٱللَّهَ يُحْيِ ٱلْأَرْضَ بَعْدَ مَوْتِهَا﴾ [الحديد ١٧]. وَقَالَ: ﴿أَوَمَن كَانَ مَيْتًا فَأَحْيَيْنَٰهُ وَجَعَلْنَا لَهُۥ نُورًا يَمْشِي بِهِۦ فِي ٱلنَّاسِ﴾ [الأنعام ١٢٢].

وَإِذَا وُصِفَ بِهِ الْبَارِي تَعَالَى: أُرِيدَ بِهَا صِحَّةُ اتِّصَافِهِ بِالْعِلْمِ وَالْقُدْرَةِ اللَّازِمَةِ لِهَٰذِهِ الْقُوَّةِ فِينَا، ....

(ii) and to whatever is specific to human beings of worthy qualities such as reason, knowledge and faith, as they are its completion and objective.

Al-mawt ⁽death⁾, on the other hand, is an appellation for the opposite at every level. Allah Most High said, *Say: "Allah—He gives you life then causes you to die"* (al-Jāthiya 45:26); *Know that Allah revives the earth after its death* (al-Ḥadīd 57:17); and *What about the one who was dead and We gave him life, and set for him a light whereby he walks among people?* (al-Anʿām 6:122).

[The description of Allah as possessing *ḥayāt* ⁽life⁾]

When the Absolute Originator—exalted is He—is described by it, what is meant is His sound characterization as [having] knowledge and power, [a characterization] concomitant with this virtue in ourselves,[1031] or a meaning inherent in His essence

[1031] The induction "origination<=>(power+knowledge)<=>life" is the three-tiered argument of Imām al-Ḥaramayn in *al-Shāmil fī Uṣūl al-Dīn*, ed. ʿAlī Sāmī al-Nashshār et al. (Alexandria: al-Maʿārif, 1389/1969) pp. 621-622. Others also add will such as al-Qushayrī in *al-Fuṣūl* (§28); and *idrāk*: "All that is soundly [described] as possessing life is soundly [described] as possessing knowledge, power, will and per-

أَوْ مَعْنًى قَائِمٌ بِذَاتِهِ يَقْتَضِي ذٰلِكَ، عَلَى الِاسْتِعَارَةِ.

وَقَرَأَ يَعْقُوبُ ﴿تَرْجِعُونَ﴾ بِفَتْحِ التَّاءِ فِي جَمِيعِ الْقُرْآنِ.

﴿هُوَ ٱلَّذِى خَلَقَ لَكُم مَّا فِى ٱلْأَرْضِ جَمِيعًا﴾: بَيَانُ نِعْمَةٍ أُخْرَى مُرَتَّبَةٍ عَلَى الْأُولَى ـ فَإِنَّهَا خَلْقُهُمْ أَحْيَاءً، قَادِرِينَ، مَرَّةً بَعْدَ أُخْرَى ـ وَهٰذِهِ: خَلْقُ مَا يَتَوَقَّفُ عَلَيْهِ بَقَاؤُهُمْ وَتَمَّ بِهِ مَعَاشُهُمْ. وَمَعْنَى ﴿لَكُم﴾: لِأَجْلِكُمْ وَانْتِفَاعِكُمْ (١) فِي دُنْيَاكُمْ، بِاسْتِنْفَاعِكُمْ بِهَا فِي مَصَالِحِ أَبْدَانِكُمْ ـ بِوَسَطٍ أَوْ

that presupposes that—metaphorically [either way].

Yaʿqūb read it ***tarjiʿūn*** ⁽you shall return⁾[1032] in all of the Qurʾān.

[2:29] **huwa-l-ladhī khalaqa lakum mā fī-l-arḍi jamīʿan** ⁽*He it is Who created for you what is in the earth—all of it*⁾ is an exposition of another favor, second in sequence to the first which consists in their being created living and able time and again, while this one is the creation of all that their survival hinges on and all by which their livelihood becomes complete.

The meaning of ***lakum*** ⁽for you⁾ is "for your sake and your benefit" in (i) your worldly affairs by your obtainment of benefit, through them, toward the interests of your bodies—with or

ceptions. ... If it is sound for us [to say] that the Maker is Knowing, Able and Willing —life being a precondition for these attributes in our school—then it is sound for us to deem that to be a proof that He is living." Al-Baghdādī, *Uṣūl al-Dīn* (pp. 29, 79, 105). Muʿtazilis, however, although they acknowledged Allah as knowing and powerful, nevertheless refused to admit knowledge and power as distinct divine attributes: al-Ashʿarī, *Maqālāt al-Islāmiyyīn wa-Ikhtilāf al-Muṣallīn*, ed. Helmut Ritter (Istanbul: 1929-1930, rept. Wiesbaden: Franz Steiner, 1980) pp. 164-167.

[1032] As did Mujāhid, Yaḥyā b. Yaʿmur, Ibn Abī Isḥāq, Ibn Muḥayṣin, Salām al-Ṭawīl, al-Fayyāḍ b. Ghazwān and al-Muṭawwaʿī. (*MQ*)

بِغَيْرِ وَسَطٍ ـ (٢) وَدِينِكُمْ، بِالْاِسْتِدْلَالِ وَالْاِعْتِبَارِ وَالتَّعَرُّفِ لِمَا يُلَائِمُهَا مِنْ لَذَّاتِ الْآخِرَةِ وَآلَامِهَا؛ لَا عَلَى وَجْهِ الْغَرَضِ، فَإِنَّ الْفَاعِلَ لِغَرَضٍ مُسْتَكْمِلٍ بِهِ؛ عَلَى أَنَّهُ كَالْغَرَضِ، مِنْ حَيْثُ إِنَّهُ عَاقِبَةُ الْفِعْلِ وَمُؤَدَّاهُ. وَهُوَ يَقْتَضِي إِبَاحَةَ الْأَشْيَاءِ النَّافِعَةِ، وَلَا يَمْنَعُ اخْتِصَاصَ بَعْضِهَا بِبَعْضٍ لِأَسْبَابٍ عَارِضَةٍ: فَإِنَّهُ يَدُلُّ عَلَى أَنَّ الْكُلَّ لِلْكُلِّ، لَا أَنْ كُلَّ وَاحِدٍ لِكُلِّ وَاحِدٍ.

without intermediary[1033]—and (ii) your spiritual affairs by proof-inference, due consideration and realization, and whatever is congruent with those [interests] among the delights of the hereafter and its torments.

[Its being created for their sake and benefit is] not in the sense of an ulterior purpose[1034]—for an agent [motivated] by an ulterior purpose is seeking completion through it—although it is like an ulterior purpose in that it is the aftermath of the act and what it leads to. Furthermore, it dictates the permissibility of beneficial things[1035] without precluding that some of them be exclusively restricted to some for non-essential reasons: for it indicates that all is for all, not each for each.[1036]

1033 "An allusion to venomous animals such as scorpions and snakes which are food for antelopes and hens which, in turn, are food for human beings, and their poisons can benefit also for defense against enemies. So the world, after careful consideration, is all created for the sake of human beings." (Q)

1034 "I.e. the 'for' of causality (*'illiyya*) is metaphorical and stands for wisdom and welfare in such verses as this or *I did not create jinns and human beings for any other reason than for them to worship Me* (al-Dhāriyāt 51:56)." (Z) This is an Ash'arī rule.

1035 "Meaning that the default (*al-aṣl*) in all things is licitness (*al-ḥill*).... as is the position of Hanafis and Shafi'is, and the preference of Imam al-Rāzī in *al-Maḥṣūl* where he made it an invariable rule." (Q)

1036 "Non-essential reasons validated by the Lawgiver such as marriage, purchase and

مَعًا
وَ﴿مَّا﴾ يَعُمُّ كُلَّ مَا فِي الْأَرْضِ، لَا الْأَرْضَ، إِلَّا إِذَا أُرِيدَ بِهَا جِهَةُ السُّفْلِ
كَمَا يُرَادُ بِالسَّمَاءِ جِهَةُ الْعُلُوِّ. وَ﴿جَمِيعًا﴾: حَالٌ عَنِ الْمَوْصُولِ الثَّانِي.

Mā ⁽*what*⁾ includes all that is on earth, excluding the earth[1037] —except when [we say that] what is meant by the latter is the nether direction [figuratively], just as by *samā'* ⁽sky⁾ is meant the upper direction.[1038]

Jamīʿan ⁽all of it⁾ is a participial state for[1039] the second conjunctive.[1040]

sale, gifts, leases and loans, all of which indicate that 'all,' meaning all that is on earth, 'is for all,' meaning all human beings, the discourse addressing everyone generally; not that every single thing created on earth is for every single individual among human beings lest everyone's property should also belong to others and every man's spouse be licit for others as claimed by the libertines—*Allah confound them! How they are perverted!* (al-Munāfiqūn 63:4)." (Q)

[1037] AQ, H, K, MM: missing [لا الأرض] lacuna.

[1038] "Or else it requires that something contain itself, which is impossible.... The author rejected the exegesis that it includes the earth as that requires a figurative interpretation [*arḍ*=belowness] in contradiction to the manifest locution without reason." (Z) "I say, rather, that it includes it as well, following another sense of Arabic eloquence which is to dispense with the governed annex (*muḍāf ilayh*) by only citing the governing annex (*muḍāf*) but meaning both in actuality, as in *rākib al-nāqa ṭalīḥān* ⁽the rider of the camel—both exhausted⁾... likewise in the verse His saying *mā fīl-arḍ* stands for the earth and what is in it," (S) cf. Ibn Jinnī, *Khaṣā'iṣ* (1:289-293) and below, note 1272. A locus classicus of this famous figure is verse 882 of Ibn Mālik's *Alfiyya*, where the words *bayna al-khayr* ⁽between goodness⁾ elliptically stand for "between goodness and me." The figure is also known as *rākib al-baʿīr ṭalīḥān* cf. Ibn Mālik, *Shawāhid al-Tawḍīḥ wal-Taṣḥīḥ li-Mushkilāt al-Jāmiʿ al-Ṣaḥīḥ*, ed. Ṭaha Muḥsin, 2nd ed. (Cairo: Maktabat Ibn Taymiyya, 1413/1993) p. 152. The figure sheds light on many concise and elliptical passages of Qur'ān and Hadith.

[1039] α, Ak, β, B, F, R, S: حال عن ε: حال على A, I, Kh, Q, Sk, T, Z: حال من

[1040] "I.e. *mā* in the sense of *kull* ⁽everything⁾... as opposed to *lakum* ⁽for you⁾ or *al-arḍ* ⁽the earth⁾, which do not entail intensiveness." (Kh) "because the conjunctive is an explicit second direct object" (Q) and "because the lavishing of favor (*imtinān*) can show only by exposing the abundance of favors, not the multitude of those favored." (S, Z)

﴿ثُمَّ ٱسْتَوَىٰ إِلَى ٱلسَّمَآءِ﴾: (١) قَصَدَ إِلَيْهَا بِإِرَادَتِهِ؛ مِنْ قَوْلِهِمْ (اِسْتَوَى إِلَيْهِ كَالسَّهْمِ الْمُرْسَلِ) إِذَا قَصَدَهُ قَصْداً مُسْتَوِياً، مِنْ غَيْرِ أَنْ يَلْوِيَ عَلَى شَيْءٍ. (٢) وَأَصْلُ (الْاِسْتِوَاءِ): طَلَبُ السَّوَاءِ. وَإِطْلَاقُهُ عَلَى الْاِعْتِدَالِ لِمَا فِيهِ مِنْ تَسْوِيَةِ وَضْعِ الْأَجْزَاءِ؛ وَلَا يُمْكِنُ حَمْلُهُ عَلَيْهِ، لِأَنَّهُ مِنْ خَوَاصِّ الْأَجْسَامِ. (٣) وَقِيلَ: (اِسْتَوَى) أَيْ: اِسْتَوْلَى وَمَلَكَ. قَالَ: [رَجَزٌ]

قَدِ اسْتَوَى بِشْرٌ عَلَى الْعِرَاقِ * مِنْ غَيْرِ سَيْفٍ وَدَمٍ مُهْرَاقِ

Thumma-stawā ilā-s-samāʾi ⟨*further, He proceeded to the sky*⟩: (1) He directed Himself to it with His will, from their saying *istawā ilayhi kas-sahm al-mursal* ⟨he proceeded to him like an arrow-shot⟩, meaning he directed himself straight to him without turning to anything else.

[*Istiwāʾ* literally means symmetry]

(2) The root meaning of ***istiwāʾ*** is the quest for symmetry.[1041] Its use to denote erectness is because of what the latter entails of making the arrangement of the parts equal. However, it cannot be said to mean that because such pertains exclusively to bodies.

(3) It was also said ***istawā*** means *istawlā* ⟨capture⟩ and *malaka* ⟨take possession⟩; [the poet] said: ["The Trembling"]

> *Bishr has taken over (istawā ʿalā) Iraq*
> *without any sword or bloodshed.*[1042]

[1041] "In al-Ṭībī's *Ḥāshiya*: *Istiwāʾ* literally means erectness, straightness and fullness of development and faculties." (S)

[1042] Spoken about the Umayyad prince Bishr b. Marwān b. al-Ḥakam b. Abī al-ʿĀṣ al-Marwānī by Abū Mālik Ghiyāth b. Ghawth b. al-Ṣalt al-Taghlubī al-Fadawkasī known as al-Akhṭal (19-92/640-711), a Damascene Umayyad Christian who excelled in finely-crafted panegyrics and lampoons and ranks with Jarīr and Farazdaq among the three strongest poets of their time. Maslama b. ʿAbd al-Malik said, "As for Akhṭal he comes

وَالْأَوَّلُ أَوْفَقُ (أ) لِلْأَصْلِ، (ب) وَالصِّلَةِ الْمُعَدَّى بِهَا، (ج) وَالتَّسْوِيَةِ الْمُتَرَتِّبَةِ عَلَيْهِ بِالْفَاءِ.

وَالْمُرَادُ بِـ﴿ٱلسَّمَآءِ﴾: هٰذِهِ الْأَجْرَامُ الْعُلْوِيَّةُ، أَوْ جِهَاتُ الْعُلُوِّ.

وَ﴿ثُمَّ﴾: لَعَلَّهُ لِتَفَاوُتِ مَا بَيْنَ الْخَلْقَيْنِ، وَفَضْلِ خَلْقِ السَّمَاءِ عَلَى خَلْقِ الْأَرْضِ، كَقَوْلِهِ تَعَالَى: ﴿ثُمَّ كَانَ مِنَ ٱلَّذِينَ ءَامَنُوا۟﴾ [البلد ١٧]؛ لَا لِلتَّرَاخِي فِي الْوَقْتِ، فَإِنَّهُ يُخَالِفُ ظَاهِرَ قَوْلِهِ تَعَالَى: ﴿وَٱلْأَرْضَ بَعْدَ ذَٰلِكَ دَحَىٰهَآ ﴿٣٠﴾﴾ [النازعات]: ....

The first[1043] is more congruent with (i) the root meaning, (ii) the conjunctive clause by which it was transitivized and (iii) the levelization that is made to follow it sequentially with ***fa*** ⁽then⁾.

What is meant by ***al-samā'*** ⁽the sky⁾ is these supernal bodies or the upward directions.

[Timing of the respective creations of heaven and earth]

Thumma ⁽further⁾ is probably due to the disparity between the two creations[1044] and the superiority of the creation of the sky over the creation of the earth—as in the saying of Allah Most High, *moreover (thumma), to be of those who believe* (al-Balad 90:17)—rather than temporal subsequence, which would contradict the manifest locution of the statement of Allah Most High *and the earth, after that—He spread it out* (al-Nāzi'āt 79:30).[1045]

in first place forever; as for al-Farazdaq he comes sometimes first and sometimes second; and as for Jarīr he comes sometimes first, sometimes second and sometimes last." Ibn Qutayba, *al-Shi'r wal-Shu'arā'*, ed. Aḥmad Muḥammad Shākir, 2nd ed. 2 vols. (Cairo: Dār al-Ma'ārif, 1386/1967) 1:483-496. Cf. *Shi'r al-Akhṭal*, ed. Fakhr al-Dīn Qibāwa, 4th ed. (Damascus and Beirut: Dār al-Fikr, 1416/1996) p. 557 §267.

1043 "I.e. *istiwā'* in the noble verse being in the sense of self-direction (*al-qaṣd*)." (Q)

1044 "Abū Ḥayyān said: in their extent and magnitude." (S)

1045 The Qadi goes on, in his commentary on *Who created the earth in two Days...*

فَإِنَّهُ يَدُلُّ عَلَى تَأَخُّرِ دَحْوِ الْأَرْضِ، الْمُتَقَدِّمِ عَلَى خَلْقِ مَا فِيهَا عَنْ خَلْقِ السَّمَاءِ وَتَسْوِيَتِهَا، إِلَّا أَنْ تَسْتَأْنِفَ بِـ﴿دَحَىٰهَآ﴾ مُقَدِّراً لِنَصْبِ ﴿الْأَرْضَ﴾ فِعْلاً آخَرَ دَلَّ عَلَيْهِ ﴿ءَأَنتُمْ أَشَدُّ خَلْقًا﴾ [النازعات ٢٧]، مِثْلَ: (تَعَرَّفَ الْأَرْضَ وَتَدَبَّرَ أَمْرَهَا بَعْدَ ذٰلِكَ)؛ لٰكِنَّهُ خِلَافُ الظَّاهِرِ.

﴿فَسَوَّىٰهُنَّ﴾: عَدَلَهُنَّ وَخَلَقَهُنَّ مَصُونَةً مِنَ الْعِوَجِ وَالْفُطُورِ. وَ(هُنَّ) ضَمِيرُ ﴿ٱلسَّمَآءِ﴾ إِنْ فُسِّرَتْ بِالْأَجْرَامِ، لِأَنَّهُ جَمْعٌ؛ أَوْ هُوَ فِي مَعْنَى الْجَمْعِ؛

The latter [verse] indicates the posteriority of the spreading out of the earth—which is itself prior to the creation of what is in it—to the creation and levelization of the sky. That is, unless you consider *daḥāhā* ⁽He spread it out⁾ a resumptive, subauding another verb—indicated by *Are you the harder to create?* (al-Nāziʿāt 79:27)—to make *al-arḍa* ⁽the earth⁾ accusative, like "he learned the lay of the land and administered its affairs after that;" but it contravenes the manifest locution.

fa-sawwāhunna ⁽*and He levelled them*⁾: He proportioned and fashioned them exempt of crookedness or gaps.[1046]

Hunna ⁽them⁾ is the personal pronoun for ***al-samāʾ*** ⁽the sky⁾ if the latter is glossed as the [celestial] bodies since it is a plural, or it is meant in the plural.[1047] ....

Then turned He to the sky... Then He ordained them seven skies (Fuṣṣilat 41:9-12) to discuss the priority of the creation of the earth from a different perspective. See also, on the reconciliation of these perspectives with additional consideration of the relevant hadiths: al-Qurṭubī's *Tafsīr* on al-Baqara 2:29 and S (2:176-178).

[1046] "Without disparity between parts, some being nearer to the center than others; rather, they are all equidistant from the center—an allusion to sphericality." (Q 3:93)

[1047] See above, under 2:22 and footnote: "*Al-samāʾ* is a common noun denoting units and collectives, like 'dinar' and 'dirham.' It is also said to be the plural of *samāʾa*."

وَإِلَّا: فَمُبْهَمٌ، يُفَسِّرُهُ مَا بَعْدَهُ، كَقَوْلِهِمْ: (رُبَّهُ رَجُلاً).

﴿سَبْعَ سَمَٰوَٰتٍ﴾: بَدَلٌ أَوْ تَفْسِيرٌ. فَإِنْ قِيلَ: أَلَيْسَ أَنَّ أَصْحَابَ الْأَرْصَادِ أَثْبَتُوا تِسْعَةَ أَفْلَاكٍ؟ قُلْتُ: فِيمَا ذَكَرُوهُ شُكُوكٌ؛ وَإِنْ صَحَّ، فَلَيْسَ فِي الْآيَةِ نَفْيُ الزَّائِدِ؛ مَعَ أَنَّهُ، إِنْ ضُمَّ إِلَيْهَا الْعَرْشُ وَالْكُرْسِيُّ، لَمْ يَبْقَ خِلَافٌ.

﴿وَهُوَ بِكُلِّ شَيْءٍ عَلِيمٌ﴾: فِيهِ: (١) تَعْلِيلٌ، كَأَنَّهُ قَالَ: (وَلِكَوْنِهِ ....

Otherwise it is an unidentified [pronoun] explained by what follows, as in their saying *rubbahu rajulan* ⟨many a one—a man⟩.[1048]

sabʿa samāwātin ⟨*as seven skies*⟩ is a substitute or an explication.

[The number of the heavenly spheres]

If someone says: "Is it not the case that those in charge of observatories affirm that there are nine heavenly spheres?"[1049] I reply: what they said is fraught with doubts; but if sound, there is nothing in the verse that negates additions—although if one adds to them the *ʿarsh* ⟨Throne⟩ and the *kursī* ⟨Footstool⟩ no disagreement remains.

[Divine creatorship, wisdom and resuscitatorship]

wa-huwa bi-kulli shayʾin ʿalīmun ⟨*and He is most knowing of all things*⟩ expresses (i) causation, as if He had said, "Because He is

[1048] This makes the clause "seven heavens" a *tamyīz* ⟨specificative⟩ for "them."

[1049] Rāzī in his *Tafsīr* (2:170-171) on this verse and again (4:199) for al-Baqara 2:164 adduces the post-Aristotelian model of the nine spheres of Arab cosmogony in ascending order of remoteness from the earth as the moon (*al-qamar*), Mercury (*ʿUṭārid*), Venus (*al-Zuhra*), the sun (*al-shams*), Mars (*al-Marrīkh*), Jupiter (*al-Mushtarī*), Saturn (*Zuḥal*), the sphere of the fixed stars (*al-kawākib al-thābita*) and the Greatest Sphere (*al-falak al-aʿẓam*) which S (2:180) rejects as the unprophetic speculations of Greek philosophy and excludes from his book on astronomy, *al-Hayʾat al-Sunniyya fīl-Hayʾat al-Saniyya*. See also on the Greek model al-Barjandī's *Sharḥ Risālat Naṣīr al-Dīn al-Ṭūsī fīl-Hayʾa* and http://starsandstones.wordpress.com/2010/07/16/on-the-nine-spheres-of-heaven/

عَالِماً بِكُنْهِ الْأَشْيَاءِ كُلِّهَا، خَلَقَ مَا خَلَقَ عَلَى هٰذَا النَّمَطِ الْأَكْمَلِ وَالْوَجْهِ الْأَنْفَعِ)؛ (٢) وَاسْتِدْلَالٌ بِأَنْ مَنْ كَانَ فِعْلُهُ عَلَى هٰذَا النَّسَقِ الْعَجِيبِ، وَالتَّرْتِيبِ الْأَنِيقِ: كَانَ عَلِيماً؛ فَإِنَّ إِتْقَانَ الْأَفْعَالِ، وَإِحْكَامَهَا، وَتَخْصِيصَهَا بِالْوَجْهِ الْأَحْسَنِ الْأَنْفَعِ، لَا يُتَصَوَّرُ إِلَّا مِنْ عَالِمٍ حَكِيمٍ رَحِيمٍ؛ (٣) وَإِزَاحَةٌ لِمَا يَخْتَلِجُ فِي صُدُورِهِمْ مِنْ أَنَّ الْأَبْدَانَ، بَعْدَمَا تَفَتَّتَتْ وَتَبَدَّدَتْ أَجْزَاؤُهَا، وَاتَّصَلَتْ بِمَا يُشَاكِلُهَا، كَيْفَ تُجْمَعُ أَجْزَاءُ كُلِّ بَدَنٍ مَرَّةً ثَانِيَةً بِحَيْثُ لَا يَشُذُّ شَيْءٌ مِنْهَا، وَلَا يَنْضَمُّ إِلَيْهَا مَا لَمْ يَكُنْ مَعَهَا فَيُعَادُ مِنْهَا كَمَا كَانَ؟ وَنَظِيرُهُ قَوْلُهُ تَعَالَى: ﴿وَهُوَ بِكُلِّ خَلْقٍ عَلِيمٌ﴾ [يس ٧٩].

knowing of the ultimate reality of all things, He created what He created in this most perfect pattern and most useful aspect;"

(ii) the inference that one whose acts follow such extraordinary order and refined arrangement must be most knowing: to perfect, thoroughly accomplish and signalize acts with their most beautiful and beneficial aspect is inconceivable other than on the part of one knowing, wise and most merciful;

(iii) and the quelling of the suspicion that might creep into their hearts, that "after body parts fall apart and disintegrate,[1050] joining whatever [elements] share their qualities,[1051] how can the parts of every body be collected a second time, so that none of them is mislaid in any way, and nothing is annexed that did not belong, so that they are returned exactly as they were?" Its equivalent is the saying of Allah Most High, *and He is most knowing of all things created* (Yāsīn 36:79).

1050 Ak, α, B, β, ε, F, I, P, Q, R, Sk, T: تفتتت وتبددت AQ, H, Kh, L, MM, U, Ul, Z: تبددت وتفتتت inversion.
1051 "Of liquid and dust." (Q)

وَاعْلَمْ أَنَّ صِحَّةَ الْحَشْرِ مَبْنِيَّةٌ عَلَى ثَلَاثِ مُقَدِّمَاتٍ، وَقَدْ بَرْهَنَ عَلَيْهَا فِي هَاتَيْنِ الْآيَتَيْنِ. أَمَّا الْأُولَى، فَهِيَ: (I) أَنَّ مَوَادَّ الْأَبْدَانِ قَابِلَةٌ لِلْجَمْعِ وَالْحَيَاةِ؛ وَأَشَارَ إِلَى الْبُرْهَانِ عَلَيْهَا بِقَوْلِهِ: ﴿وَكُنتُمْ أَمْوَٰتًا فَأَحْيَٰكُمْ ثُمَّ يُمِيتُكُمْ﴾، فَإِنَّ تَعَاقُبَ الِافْتِرَاقِ وَالِاجْتِمَاعِ وَالْمَوْتِ وَالْحَيَاةِ عَلَيْهَا يَدُلُّ عَلَى أَنَّهَا قَابِلَةٌ لَهَا بِذَاتِهَا؛ وَمَا بِالذَّاتِ: يَأْبَى أَنْ يَزُولَ وَيَتَغَيَّرَ. (II-III) وَأَمَّا الثَّانِيَةُ وَالثَّالِثَةُ: فَإِنَّهُ - عَزَّ وَجَلَّ - عَالِمٌ بِهَا وَبِمَوَاقِعِهَا، قَادِرٌ عَلَى جَمْعِهَا وَإِحْيَائِهَا؛ وَأَشَارَ إِلَى وَجْهِ إِثْبَاتِهِمَا (أ) بِأَنَّهُ تَعَالَى قَادِرٌ عَلَى إِبْدَائِهَا وَإِبْدَاءِ مَا هُوَ أَعْظَمُ خَلْقًا وَأَعْجَبُ صُنْعًا: فَكَانَ أَقْدَرَ عَلَى إِعَادَتِهِمْ وَإِحْيَائِهِمْ،

Know that the validity of the [Final] Gathering is based on three premises which He demonstrated in these two verses:

I. The first one is that the constituent parts of bodies are apt to be gathered up and given life; He alluded to its demonstration when He said, *when you had been dead then He gave you life, then He will make you die* (al-Baqara 2:28); for their successive [states] of disjointure, assemblage, death and life show that they are inherently fit for that; and what is inherent will not pass or change.

II-III. As for the second and third [premises]: truly the Almighty and Exalted is cognizant of them and their exact situations, able to collect them and give them life. He alluded to the sense in which He affirmed these two points with the facts that

(i) He is able to cause them to appear and even cause what is far more massive and extraordinary in its frame to appear [out of nothing]; so He is all the more able to return them back to life;

(ب) وَأَنَّهُ تَعَالَى خَلَقَ مَا خَلَقَ خَلْقاً مُسْتَوِياً مُحْكَماً، مِنْ غَيْرِ تَفَاوُتٍ وَاخْتِلَالٍ، مُرَاعىً فِيهِ مَصَالِحُهُمْ وَسَدُّ حَاجَاتِهِمْ. وَذٰلِكَ دَلِيلٌ عَلَى تَنَاهِي عِلْمِهِ وَكَمَالِ حِكْمَتِهِ - جَلَّتْ قُدْرَتُهُ وَدَقَّتْ حِكْمَتُهُ!

وَقَدْ سَكَّنَ نَافِعٌ وَأَبُو عَمْرٍو وَالْكِسَائِيُّ الْهَاءَ مِنْ نَحْوِ (فَهْوَ): ﴿وَهْوَ﴾، تَشْبِيهاً لَهُ بِـ(عَضْدٍ).

﴿وَإِذْ قَالَ رَبُّكَ لِلْمَلَٰٓئِكَةِ إِنِّي جَاعِلٌ فِي ٱلْأَرْضِ خَلِيفَةً﴾: تَعْدَادٌ لِنِعْمَةٍ ثَالِثَةٍ تَعُمُّ النَّاسَ كُلَّهُمْ، فَإِنَّ خَلْقَ آدَمَ ....

(ii) and He created whatever He created in a levelled and compact frame without any flaw or imperfection, thereby safeguarding their interests and meeting all their needs.

All the above is evidence of the infiniteness of His knowledge and perfection of His wisdom—how magnificent is His power and how fine His wisdom!

Nāfiʿ, Abū ʿAmr and al-Kisāʾī put a *sukūn* on the *hāʾ* in the like of *fa-hwa* and *wa-hwa*, in emulation of *ʿaḍdin*.[1052]

[The superiority of human beings to angels]

[2:30] **wa-idh qāla rabbuka li-l-malāʾikati innī jāʿilun fī-l-arḍi khalīfatan** ⁽*and behold! Your Nurturer said to the angels: Verily I am setting on earth a successor*⁾ is the enumeration of a third favor that includes all people.[1053] For the creation of Adam and his

[1052] Also Qālūn, Abū Jaʿfar, al-Ḥasan and al-Yazīdī. It is the dialect of Najd as opposed to that of the Ḥijāz. (*MQ*) "It is possible to put a *sukūn* on the *hāʾ* in *huwa* and *hiya* when they are prefixed with *wāw*, *fāʾ*, the inceptive *lām* and *thumma* such as in *fah-ya kal-ḥijāra, wah-wa bi-kulli shayʾin ʿalīm, lah-wal-ghaniyyul-ḥamīd, lah-yal-ḥayawān* and *thumma h-wa yawmal-qiyāmati min al-maqbūḥīn*, as in *ʿaḍud* [*ʿaḍd*] for *huwa* and *katif* [*katf*] for *hiya*." (Z) "And *rusul* [*rusl*]." (Q)

[1053] See below under verse 2:34 for the mention of a fourth favor.

وَإِكْرَامَهُ وَتَفْضِيلَهُ عَلَى مَلَائِكَتِهِ بِأَنْ أَمَرَهُمْ بِالسُّجُودِ لَهُ: إِنْعَامٌ يَعُمُّ ذُرِّيَّتَهُ.
وَ﴿إِذْ﴾: ظَرْفٌ وُضِعَ لِزَمَانِ نِسْبَةٍ مَاضِيَةٍ وَقَعَ فِيهِ أُخْرَى، كَمَا وُضِعَ (إِذَا)
لِزَمَانِ نِسْبَةٍ مُسْتَقْبَلَةٍ يَقَعُ فِيهِ أُخْرَى. وَلِذٰلِكَ (أ) يَجِبُ إِضَافَتُهُمَا إِلَى الْجُمَلِ
كَـ(حَيْثُ) فِي الْمَكَانِ؛ (ب) وَبُنِيَتَا تَشْبِيهاً لَهُمَا بِالْمَوْصُولَاتِ، (ج)
وَاسْتُعْمِلَتَا لِلتَّعْلِيلِ وَالْمُجَازَاةِ. ....

being given honor and preference over His angels—as He commanded them to prostrate before him—are a mark of favor that includes his progeny.

[Grammar and usage of *idh* and *idhā*]

Idh ⁽whereupon⁾ is a [temporal] vessel coined to denote a past temporal link inside which another link occurs, just as *idhā* ⁽when⁾ was coined for a futural temporal link inside which another link occurs. This is why

(i) it is required for both of them to be annexed to sentences like *ḥaythu* ⁽wherein⁾ with regard to place. Furthermore:

(ii) they are both indeclinable, to make them resemble relatives and conjunctives;[1054]

(iii) they are used causally and consequentially [respectively];[1055]

[1054] "Due to the fact that they both need a sentence to follow them and clarify how they are connected" (Z) "like *al-ladhī* ⁽that, who, which⁾." (Kh)

[1055] "There is here *laff wa-nashr mujmal* ⁽indeterminate [verbal] involution and evolution⁾, for it is *idh* that is used causally and *idhā* that is used consequentially, never the reverse." (S 2:181) Even so, "Abū Ḥayyān did not recognize any instance of *idh* used causally while Ibn Hishām said in *al-Mughnī* that the majority do not affirm it and that *idhā* does not effect apocopation (*jazm*) except in extreme cases of need." (S) Nevertheless the usages of *idh* and *idhā* are listed respectively as "*ẓarfiyya, fujā'iyya, taʿlīliyya*" and "*tafsīriyya, wa-ẓarfiyya, wa-fujā'iyya… wa-lā taʿmal idhā al-jazma illā fil-shiʿri lil-ḍarūra*" in al-Daqr, *Muʿjam al-Qawāʿid* (pp. 22-24). Cachia translates *laff wa-nashr* as "multiple attribution (rolling and unrolling):" *Arch Rhetori-*

(د) وَمَحَلُّهُمَا النَّصْبُ أَبَداً بِالظَّرْفِيَّةِ، فَإِنَّهُمَا مِنَ الظُّرُوفِ الْغَيْرِ الْمُتَصَرِّفَةِ لِمَا ذَكَرْنَاهُ. وَأَمَّا قَوْلُهُ تَعَالَى: ﴿وَٱذۡكُرۡ أَخَا عَادٍ إِذۡ أَنذَرَ قَوۡمَهُۥ بِٱلۡأَحۡقَافِ﴾ [الأحقاف ٢١] وَنَحْوُهُ، فَعَلَى تَأْوِيلِ: (أُذْكُرِ الْحَادِثَ إِذْ كَانَ كَذَا)، فَحُذِفَ الْحَادِثُ وَأُقِيمَ الظَّرْفُ مَقَامَهُ.

وَعَامِلُهُ فِي الْآيَةِ: (أ) ﴿قَالُوٓاْ﴾، (ب) أَوِ (اذْكُرْ) عَلَى التَّأْوِيلِ الْمَذْكُورِ، لِأَنَّهُ جَاءَ مَعْمُولاً لَهُ صَرِيحاً فِي الْقُرْآنِ كَثِيراً؛ (ج) أَوْ مُضْمَرٌ دَلَّ عَلَيْهِ مَضْمُونُ الْآيَةِ الْمُتَقَدِّمَةِ، مِثْلُ (وَبَدَأَ خَلْقَكُمْ إِذْ قَالَ). وَعَلَى هٰذَا، فَالْجُمْلَةُ مَعْطُوفَةٌ عَلَى ﴿خَلَقَ لَكُم﴾، دَاخِلَةٌ فِي حُكْمِ الصِّلَةِ. ....

(iv) and they are always construed as accusatives because of their adverbiality, since they are among the undeclinable temporal-local vessels for the reasons we mentioned.

As for the saying of Allah Most High *and recall ʿĀd's brother —whereupon (idh) he warned his people of the winding sands* (al-Aḥqāf 46:21) and its like, it is interpreted as "recall the incident whereupon such took place," where the incident was suppressed and the local vessel was set up in its place.

Its regent in the verse is (i) *qālū* ⸢they said⸣;[1056] (ii) or *udhkur* ⸢recall!⸣—following the aforementioned interpretation—as the latter explicitly came up as its governed element many times in the Qur'ān; (iii) or [another] implied [verb] indicated by the previous verse, such as *wa-bada'a khalqakum idh qāla* ⸢and He began creating you, whereupon He said⸣. Accordingly, the sentence is adjoined to ***khalaqa lakum*** ⸢created for you⸣ and is tantamount to a relative clause. ....

cian (p. 60 §92).

1056 In reference to the angels.

وَعَنْ مَعْمَرٍ أَنَّهُ مَزِيدٌ.

وَ(الْمَلَائِكَةُ) جَمْعُ (مَلْأَكٍ) عَلَى الْأَصْلِ، كَـ(الشَّمَائِلِ)؛ وَالتَّاءُ لِتَأْنِيثِ الْجَمْعِ. وَهُوَ مَقْلُوبُ (مَأْلَكٍ) مِنَ الْأَلُوكَةِ ـ وَهِيَ الرِّسَالَةُ ـ لِأَنَّهُمْ وَسَائِطُ

Maʿmar considered it an additive.[1057]

[The angels: name, nature and functions]

Al-malāʾika ʿthe angelsʾ is the plural of *malʾak*—originally—the way *shamāʾil* is the plural of *shamʾal* ʿnorth windʾ,[1058] and the [final] *tāʾ* is to feminize the plural.[1059] It is the inverted form of *maʾlak*[1060] from *alūka*, which means "message" as they are inter-

---

[1057] "Al-Zajjāj decried this interpretation and said that when a particle imparts a valid meaning it is impermissible to deem it an additive." (Z) Shah Waliyyullah summarily dismisses the need for a regent in all Quranic instances of *wa-idh* as superfluous, instead proposing a third view, which is to consider *idh* neither a temporal-local vessel (*ẓarf*) governed by an implied regent (*ʿāmil*) nor additive but a transference or metaphorization (*naql*) to a meaning of threat and intimidation (*takhwīf wa-tahwīl*), as it were a stand-alone ecphonesis or "exclamatory phrase" used for pathos when remembering and listing tremendous events: *al-Fawz al-Kabīr fī Uṣūl al-Tafsīr*, trans. from Persian by Saʿīd Aḥmad al-Bālanfūrī (Damascus: Dār al-Ghawthānī lil-Dirāsāt al-Qurʾāniyya, 1329/2008) p. 81 (section entitled *lā ḥājata ilā taftīsh al-ʿāmil fī kalimat idh*), translated by Ṭāhir Maḥmood Kiānī as *The Great Victory on Qurʾānic Hermeneutics* (London: Ta-Ha Publishers, 2014) pp. 104-105 (section entitled "There is no need to investigate the word that governs the word *idh*"). Also see note 357.

[1058] B, ε, R: كالشمايل Ak, β, F, I, T: كالشمائل جمع شمال a: كالشمائل في جمع شَمْأَل

[1059] "Otherwise the plural *malāʾik* would be aberrant, since the plural of *faʿal* is *fiʿāl* and *afʿul*, as in *jabal* → *jibāl*, *ajbul*; or *fiʿāla*, *afʿāl*, as in *ḥajar* → *ḥijāra*, *aḥjār*." (Z)

[1060] Namely, the *mafʿal* form of the root verb ʾ-l-k ʿto chewʾ, aorist *yalūku*, infinitive nouns *alk* and *ulūk*, the nouns *alūk(a)* and *maʾlūk(a)* signifying message, indicating the aural nature of messengership, cf. al-Farāhīdī, *ʿAyn* (5:380) and *Lisān s.v.* ʾ-l-k. "Their being named *malāʾika* is due to their extremely great strength, all of the cognates of *m-l-k* revolving around the senses of strength and toughness such as *malik* ʿkingʾ, *mālik* ʿownerʾ, *malaktu al-ʿajīn* 'I churned the dough'… It is enough for you that Allah Most High said of them *they laud night and day, they never wane* (al-Anbiyāʾ 21:20)—and what strength is greater than that!" (Z 1:240).

بَيْنَ اللهِ تَعَالَى وَبَيْنَ النَّاسِ، فَهُمْ رُسُلُ اللهِ ـ أَوْ كَالرُّسُلِ ـ إِلَيْهِمْ.

وَاخْتَلَفَ الْعُقَلَاءُ فِي حَقِيقَتِهِمْ، بَعْدَ اتِّفَاقِهِمْ عَلَى أَنَّهَا ذَوَاتٌ مَوْجُودَةٌ، قَائِمَةٌ بِأَنْفُسِهَا. فَذَهَبَ أَكْثَرُ الْمُسْلِمِينَ إِلَى أَنَّهَا أَجْسَامٌ لَطِيفَةٌ قَادِرَةٌ عَلَى التَّشَكُّلِ بِأَشْكَالٍ مُخْتَلِفَةٍ، مُسْتَدِلِّينَ بِأَنَّ الرُّسُلَ كَانُوا يَرَوْنَهُمْ كَذَٰلِكَ. وَقَالَتْ طَائِفَةٌ مِنَ النَّصَارَى: هِيَ النُّفُوسُ الْفَاضِلَةُ الْبَشَرِيَّةُ، الْمُفَارِقَةُ لِلْأَبْدَانِ. وَزَعَمَ الْحُكَمَاءُ ....

mediaries between Allah Most High and human beings, so they are the messengers of Allah—or like messengers—sent to them.

The thinkers differed as to their exact nature but agreed that they are created, autonomous entities.[1061] Most of the Muslims view them as subtle bodies able to take on various forms[1062]—as attested, they said, by the fact that the Messengers would see them thus—(a Christian sect said they were excellent human souls separated from their bodies[1063] while the sages claimed they

[1061] "Angels are spirits subsisting in subtle bodies of light, able to take on various forms by Divine permission, and not to be described as male or female." ʿAbd Allah b. Najīb Sirāj al-Dīn al-Ḥusaynī (1343-1422/1924-2002), *al-Īmān bil-Malāʾika* (Aleppo: Pub. by author, 1391/1972) p. 19.

[1062] Elsewhere the Qadi attributes the very same definition to "the majority of theologians" for "angels, jinns and devils:" Bayḍāwī, *Ṭawāliʿ al-Anwār min Maṭāliʿ al-Anẓār*, ed. ʿAbbās Sulaymān (Beirut: Dār al-Jīl: Cairo: al-Maktabat al-Azhariyya lil-Turāth, 1411/1991) p. 147. "In *Sharḥ al-Maqāṣid*: They are absolutely good, luminous bodies, while the jinn are subtle airy bodies divided into good and evil and the devils are evil fierybodies. It was said that the constitution of the three times is from the mixture of the elements, except that the dominant one in each is the one highlighted. Because fire and air are extremely subtle, angels, jinns and devils can enter windows and narrow places—even human cavities—unseen by the eyes, unless they put on other alloys dominated by earthiness and liquidity as vestments and coverings, at which time they can be seen in bodily forms such as human and other animal bodies." (Sk p. 287)

[1063] He attributes the very same position to "the sages" (*al-ḥukamāʾ*) in the *Ṭawāliʿ* (p.

أَنَّهُمْ جَوَاهِرُ مُجَرَّدَةٌ، مُخَالِفَةٌ لِلنُّفُوسِ النَّاطِقَةِ فِي الْحَقِيقَةِ، مُنْقَسِمَةٌ إِلَى قِسْمَيْنِ: (١) قِسْمٌ شَأْنُهُمُ الِاسْتِغْرَاقُ فِي مَعْرِفَةِ الْحَقِّ - جَلَّ جَلَالُهُ - وَالتَّنَزُّهُ عَنِ الِاشْتِغَالِ بِغَيْرِهِ - كَمَا وَصَفَهُمْ فِي مُحْكَمِ تَنْزِيلِهِ، فَقَالَ تَعَالَى: ﴿يُسَبِّحُونَ ٱلَّيْلَ وَٱلنَّهَارَ لَا يَفْتُرُونَ ۝٢٠﴾ [الأنبياء] - وَهُمُ الْعِلِّيُّونَ وَالْمَلَائِكَةُ الْمُقَرَّبُونَ؛ (٢) وَقِسْمٌ ﴿يُدَبِّرُ ٱلْأَمْرَ مِنَ ٱلسَّمَآءِ إِلَى ٱلْأَرْضِ﴾ [السجدة ٥] عَلَى مَا سَبَقَ بِهِ الْقَضَاءُ وَجَرَى بِهِ الْقَلَمُ الْإِلٰهِيُّ، ﴿لَّا يَعْصُونَ ٱللَّهَ مَآ أَمَرَهُمْ وَيَفْعَلُونَ مَا يُؤْمَرُونَ﴾ [التحريم ٦]، وَهُمُ الْمُدَبِّرَاتُ أَمْراً. فَمِنْهُمْ سَمَاوِيَّةٌ، وَمِنْهُم أَرْضِيَّةٌ، عَلَى تَفْصِيلٍ أَثْبَتُّهُ فِي كِتَابِ الطَّوَالِعِ.

were incorporeal substances that differ from articulate-speaking souls in their exact nature) and falling into two groups:

I. A group whose sole occupation is self-immersion in greater knowledge of the True and Real One—glorified is He!—and self-exemption from concern with anything else—as He described them in the decisive [verses] of His revelation, saying, *they laud night and day, they never wane* (al-Anbiyā' 21:20); these are the "highmost" and the "angels brought near."

II. A group that *administer the command from heaven to earth* (a-Sajda 32:5) according to the prior Decree and as penned in the Divine writ, *they do not disobey Allah in what He commanded them but they do what they are commanded* (al-Taḥrīm 66:6); these are the "executors of commands."

Thus some are heavenly and some earthly, per the scheme I finalized in *Kitāb al-Ṭawāliʿ* ('Book of the Rising Stars').[1064]

147), cf. Calverley and Pollock, *Nature, Man and God* (Ib:645).

[1064] *Ibid.* (Ib:644-723).

وَالْمَقُولُ لَهُمْ: الْمَلَائِكَةُ كُلُّهُمْ لِعُمُومِ اللَّفْظِ وَعَدَمِ الْمُخَصِّصِ؛ وَقِيلَ مَلَائِكَةُ الْأَرْضِ، وَقِيلَ إِبْلِيسُ وَمَنْ كَانَ مَعَهُ فِي مُحَارَبَةِ الْجِنِّ - فَإِنَّهُ تَعَالَى أَسْكَنَهُمْ فِي الْأَرْضِ أَوَّلاً فَأَفْسَدُوا فِيهَا، فَبَعَثَ إِلَيْهِمْ إِبْلِيسَ فِي جُنْدٍ مِنَ الْمَلَائِكَةِ فَدَمَّرَهُمْ وَفَرَّقَهُمْ فِي الْجَزَائِرِ وَالْجِبَالِ.

وَ﴿جَاعِلٌ﴾: مِنْ (جَعَلَ)، الَّذِي لَهُ مَفْعُولَانِ، وَهُمَا: ﴿فِي ٱلْأَرْضِ خَلِيفَةً﴾؛ أُعْمِلَ فِيهِمَا، ....

The audience referred to are the angels in their entirety due to the terms being general and the absence of a specifier; some said the earthly angels while others said Iblīs and those that were with him, fighting the jinns. For Allah Most High had made the latter dwell the earth first, after which they spread corruption in it, so He sent them Iblīs as part of an army of angels, destroying and dispersing them across islands and mountains.[1065]

Jāʿilun is from *jaʿala* ⁽to set⁾ which has two objects—namely ***fil-arḍi khalīfatan*** ⁽on earth a successor⁾—which it was made to

[1065] Al-Ṭabarī narrated in his *Tafsīr* (under al-Baqara 2:34) and his *Tārīkh al-Rusul wal-Mulūk*, ed. Muḥammad Abū al-Faḍl Ibrāhīm, 11 vols. 2nd ed. (Cairo: Dār al-Maʿārif; Beirut: Maktabat Suwaydān, 1960-1977) 1:81-82 from Ibn ʿAbbās that Allah Most High created the jinns and ordered them to inhabit the earth. They worshipped Allah until time seemed too long for them, so they disobeyed Allah and shed blood. They had a king or prophet called Yūsuf whom they killed. Allah sent against them an army of angels that were in the nearest sky. That army was called the jinn, and among them was Iblīs, commanding 4,000. They went down and banished the jinns' offspring from the earth and sent them into exile to the islands of the sea. Iblīs and the soldiers that were with him dwelt in the earth and found its life easy. It is said they lived there for 40 years before the creation of Adam and that the jinn had lived there before them for 2,000 years. Others said 40 years." Cf. Badr al-Dīn al-Shiblī, *Ākām al-Marjān fī Aḥkām al-Jānn* (Cairo: Maṭbaʿat al-Saʿāda, 1326/1908) pp. 155-156; al-Suyūṭī, *Laqaṭāt al-Marjān fī Aḥkām al-Jānn*, ed. Muṣṭafā ʿĀshūr (Cairo: Maktabat al-Qurʾān, 1408/1987) p. 189-190 and Q (3:109). Also see notes 1103 and 1127.

لِأَنَّهُ بِمَعْنَى الْمُسْتَقْبَلِ، وَمُعْتَمِدٌ عَلَى مُسْنَدٍ إِلَيْهِ. وَيَجُوزُ أَنْ يَكُونَ بِمَعْنَى (خَالِقٍ).

وَ(الْخَلِيفَةُ) مَنْ يَخْلُفُ غَيْرَهُ وَيَنُوبُ مَنَابَهُ؛ وَالْهَاءُ فِيهِ لِلْمُبَالَغَةِ. وَالْمُرَادُ بِهِ: (I) آدَمُ ـ عَلَيْهِ الصَّلَاةُ وَالسَّلَامُ ـ لِأَنَّهُ كَانَ (أ) خَلِيفَةَ اللهِ فِي أَرْضِهِ، وَكَذٰلِكَ كُلُّ نَبِيٍّ اِسْتَخْلَفَهُمُ اللهُ فِي عِمَارَةِ الْأَرْضِ، وَسِيَاسَةِ النَّاسِ، وَتَكْمِيلِ نُفُوسِهِمْ، وَتَنْفِيذِ أَمْرِهِ فِيهِمْ ـ لَا لِحَاجَةٍ بِهِ تَعَالَى إِلَى مَنْ يَنُوبُهُ، بَلْ لِقُصُورِ الْمُسْتَخْلَفِ عَلَيْهِ عَنْ قَبُولِ فَيْضِهِ وَتَلَقِّي ....

govern, because it has a meaning of future and depends on a correlative of attribute. It is also possible that it means *khāliqun* ⟨creating⟩.

[Hierarchical intermediacy of prophets and angels between Allah and creation]

Al-khalīfa ⟨successor⟩ is one who succeeds someone else and acts as his deputy. The [final] *hāʾ* in it is for intensiveness.

What is meant is

I. Adam—upon him blessings and peace—because he was

(i) the successor of Allah on His earth, as was every prophet whom Allah made successor in populating the earth, administering people, perfecting their souls and implementing His orders among them.

This was not because of some need Allah Most High had for someone to be His deputy,[1066] but rather due to the unreadiness of the recipients of succession to accept His outpouring and re-

[1066] "Contrary to all other successorships, which are born of the absence, weakness or deficiency of the one being succeeded." (Kh)

أَمْرِهِ بِغَيْرِ وَسَطٍ، وَلِذٰلِكَ لَمْ يَسْتَنْبِئْ مَلَكاً، كَمَا قَالَ اللهُ تَعَالَى: ﴿وَلَوْ جَعَلْنَٰهُ مَلَكًا لَّجَعَلْنَٰهُ رَجُلًا﴾ [الأنعام ٩]. أَلَا تَرَى أَنَّ الْأَنْبِيَاءَ، لَمَّا فَاقَتْ قُوَّتُهُمْ، وَاشْتَعَلَتْ قَرِيحَتُهُمْ بِحَيْثُ ﴿يَكَادُ زَيْتُهَا يُضِيٓءُ وَلَوْ لَمْ تَمْسَسْهُ نَارٌ﴾ [النور ٣٥]، أَرْسَلَ إِلَيْهِمُ الْمَلَائِكَةَ؟ وَمَنْ كَانَ مِنْهُمْ أَعْلَى رُتْبَةً كَلَّمَهُ بِلَا وَاسِطَةٍ، كَمَا كَلَّمَ مُوسَى ـ عَلَيْهِ السَّلَامُ ـ فِي الْمِيقَاتِ، وَمُحَمَّداً ﷺ لَيْلَةَ الْمِعْرَاجِ.

وَنَظِيرُ ذٰلِكَ فِي الطَّبِيعَةِ: أَنَّ الْعَظْمَ، لَمَّا عَجَزَ عَنْ قَبُولِ الْغِذَاءِ مِنَ اللَّحْمِ لِمَا بَيْنَهُمَا مِنَ التَّبَاعُدِ، جَعَلَ الْبَارِي تَعَالَى بِحِكْمَتِهِ بَيْنَهُمَا الْغُضْرُوفَ الْمُنَاسِبَ لَهُمَا، لِيَأْخُذَ مِنْ هٰذَا وَيُعْطِيَ ذَاكَ.

ceive His command without intermediary. Hence He did not make any angel a prophet, as Allah Most High said, *and had We made him an angel We would have still made him a man* (al-Anʿām 6:9). Do you not see how prophets, once their strength peaked and their innermost was set alight whereby *its oil almost radiates light even if no fire touches it yet* (al-Nūr 24:35)[1067]—He sent the angels to them? and how, to those who held a higher rank, He spoke without intermediary—such as speaking with Mūsā (upon him peace) at the appointed tryst and Muḥammad (upon him blessings and peace) on the Night of Ascent?

Its equivalent in nature is that in light of the bones' inability to accept nutrition from flesh because of their disparity, the exalted Producer of all, in His wisdom, placed between them cartilage which is well-adapted to both of them, so that it takes from one and gives to the other.

[1067] On this verse and intermediacy see our *Muhammadan Light in the Qur'ān, Sunna, and Companion-Reports* (London: Institute for Cultural and Spiritual Development, 2012) pp. 111-118 and 180-182, cf. Qāḍī ʿIyāḍ, *al-Shifā* III, introduction ("Prophets and Messengers are intermediaries (*wasāʾiṭ*) between Allah and His creation").

(ب) أَوْ خَلِيفَةَ مَنْ سَكَنَ الْأَرْضَ قَبْلَهُ؛ (II) أَوْ هُوَ وَذُرِّيَّتُهُ، لِأَنَّهُمْ يَخْلُفُونَ مَنْ قَبْلَهُمْ، أَوْ يَخْلُفُ بَعْضُهُمْ بَعْضاً؛ وَإِفْرَادُ اللَّفْظِ: إِمَّا لِلاِسْتِغْنَاءِ بِذِكْرِهِ عَنْ ذِكْرِ بَنِيهِ - كَمَا اسْتُغْنِيَ بِذِكْرِ أَبِي الْقَبِيلَةِ فِي قَوْلِهِمْ: (مُضَرُ) وَ(هَاشِمٌ) - أَوْ عَلَى تَأْوِيلِ (مَنْ يَخْلُفُ) أَوْ (خَلَفاً يَخْلُفُ).

وَفَائِدَةُ قَوْلِهِ تَعَالَى هٰذَا لِلْمَلَائِكَةِ: (١) تَعْلِيمُ الْمُشَاوَرَةِ؛ (٢) وَتَعْظِيمُ شَأْنِ الْمَجْعُولِ بِأَنْ بَشَّرَ - عَزَّ وَجَلَّ - بِوُجُودِهِ سُكَّانَ مَلَكُوتِهِ وَلَقَّبَهُ بِالْخَلِيفَةِ

(ii) Or [because Adam was] the successor of whoever dwelt the earth before him.

II. Or both he and his offspring, because they succeed those before them or they succeed one another, in which case the word [*khalīfa*] was put in the singular (i) either because it is sufficient to mention him without having to mention his sons—just as it is sufficient to mention the tribe's primogenitor when they say "Muḍar" and "Hāshim;" (ii) or in the sense of "someone/those who will succeed" or of "successors succeeding."[1068]

[The divine disclosure and the angels' verbal engagement]

The benefit of Allah's saying this to the angels is

1. the teaching of consultation;[1069]

2. the magnification of the appointee's status through Allah's glad tidings of his existence[1070] to the dwellers of His dominion and His titling him "successor" ....

[1068] α, B, R: خلفاً يخلف D, P, Sk: خلقا يخلف Ak, F, I, K, Kh, L, Q, U, Ul, Z: خلقا يخلفكم AQ, β, H, MM: خلفاً يخلفكم ε: او خلف مخلف

[1069] This shows the angels' questioning was neither extemporaneous nor inopportune (as those who anthropomorphize them suggest, to justify their own inclination to object) but in compliance with the divine invitation; even so they were silenced—thrice!—as the Qadi goes on to show, all the more to intensify the status of human *khilāfa*.

[1070] All mss. and eds.: بوجوده AQ, H, MM: بوجود

قَبْلَ خَلْقِهِ؛ (٣) وَإِظْهَارُ فَضْلِهِ الرَّاجِحِ عَلَى مَا فِيهِ مِنَ الْمَفَاسِدِ بِسُؤَالِهِمْ وَجَوَابِهِ؛ (٤) وَبَيَانٌ أَنَّ الْحِكْمَةَ تَقْتَضِي إِيجَادَ مَا يَغْلِبُ خَيْرُهُ، فَإِنَّ تَرْكَ الْخَيْرِ الْكَثِيرِ لِأَجْلِ الشَّرِّ الْقَلِيلِ شَرٌّ كَثِيرٌ؛ إِلَى غَيْرِ ذٰلِكَ.

﴿قَالُوٓا۟ أَتَجْعَلُ فِيهَا مَن يُفْسِدُ فِيهَا وَيَسْفِكُ ٱلدِّمَآءَ﴾: (I) تَعَجُّبٌ مِنْ (أ) أَنْ يُسْتَخْلَفَ لِعِمَارَةِ الْأَرْضِ وَإِصْلَاحِهَا مَنْ يُفْسِدُ فِيهَا؛ (ب) أَوْ يُسْتَخْلَفَ مَكَانَ أَهْلِ الطَّاعَةِ أَهْلُ الْمَعْصِيَةِ؛ (II) وَاسْتِكْشَافٌ عَمَّا خَفِيَ عَلَيْهِمْ مِنَ الْحِكْمَةِ الَّتِي بَهَرَتْ تِلْكَ الْمَفَاسِدَ وَأَلْغَتْهَا؛ ....

even before he was created;

3. the disclosure of his merit which prevails over whatever failings are in him, through their question and His answer;

4. and the exposition of the fact that wisdom dictates the creation of what is preponderantly good—for the abandonment of a great good because of a little evil is a great evil—among other [benefits].

[Angels wonder at how divine wisdom eradicates human sins]

qālū ataj'alu fīhā man yufsidu fīhā wa-yasfiku-d-dimā'a ⟨*they said: Will you set in it those who will spread corruption in it and shed blood?*⟩: [This question expresses]

I. astonishment (i) that the appointees for successorship in populating and civilizing the earth should be those who will spread corruption in it; (ii) or that, instead of the obedient, the disobedient should be appointed for successorship;

II. an exploration of what escaped their notice with regard to the wisdom that overcame those failings and eradicated them;

(III) وَاسْتِخْبَارٌ عَمَّا يُرْشِدُهُمْ وَيُزِيحُ شُبْهَتَهُمْ، كَسُؤَالِ الْمُتَعَلِّمِ مُعَلِّمَهُ عَمَّا يَخْتَلِجُ فِي صَدْرِهِ.

وَلَيْسَ بِاعْتِرَاضٍ عَلَى اللهِ تَعَالَى - جَلَّتْ قُدْرَتُهُ! - وَلَا طَعْنٍ فِي بَنِي آدَمَ عَلَى وَجْهِ الْغِيبَةِ: فَإِنَّهُمْ أَعْلَى مِنْ أَنْ يُظَنَّ بِهِمْ ذٰلِكَ، لِقَوْلِهِ تَعَالَى: ﴿... بَلْ عِبَادٌ مُّكْرَمُونَ ﴿٢٦﴾ لَا يَسْبِقُونَهُ بِالْقَوْلِ وَهُم بِأَمْرِهِ يَعْمَلُونَ ﴿٢٧﴾﴾ [الأنبياء].

وَإِنَّمَا عَرَفُوا ذٰلِكَ (أ) بِإِخْبَارٍ مِنَ اللهِ تَعَالَى، (ب) أَوْ تَلَقٍّ مِنَ اللَّوْحِ، (ج) أَوِ اسْتِنْبَاطٍ عَمَّا رَكَزَ فِي عُقُولِهِمْ أَنَّ الْعِصْمَةَ مِنْ خَوَاصِّهِمْ، (د) أَوْ قِيَاسٍ لِأَحَدِ الثَّقَلَيْنِ عَلَى الْآخَرِ.

III. and a quest for answers that might guide them and allay their misgiving, the way the learner asks his teacher about what creeps into his heart.

It is not an objection to Allah—may His might be exalted!—nor is it an aspersion cast on Adam's offspring in the way of slander, for they are above any such suspicion regarding them, since Allah Most High said, *nay, but they are honored slaves; they do not speak ahead of Him, but they act by His command alone* (al-Anbiyā' 21:26-27).

They became aware of that [*those who will spread corruption in it and shed blood*] only (i) because Allah Most High informed them; (ii) or by receiving it from the Tablet; (iii) or by inference from what was implanted in their minds to the effect that infallibility is one of their exclusive attributes; (iv) or by analogy of one of the Two Weighty Ones[1071] to the other.

[1071] See note 304.

وَ(السَّفْكُ) وَ(السَّبْكُ) وَ(السَّفْحُ) وَ(الشَّنُّ) أَنْوَاعٌ مِنَ الصَّبِّ. فَالسَّفْكُ يُقَالُ فِي الدَّمِ وَالدَّمْعِ؛ وَالسَّبْكُ: فِي الْجَوَاهِرِ الْمُذَابَةِ؛ وَالسَّفْحُ: فِي الصَّبِّ مِنْ أَعْلَى؛ وَالشَّنُّ: فِي الصَّبِّ مِنْ فَمِ الْقِرْبَةِ وَنَحْوِهَا، وَكَذٰلِكَ (السَّنُّ).

وَقُرِئَ (يُسْفَكُ) عَلَى الْبِنَاءِ لِلْمَفْعُولِ: فَيَكُونُ الرَّاجِعُ إِلَى ﴿مَن﴾، سَوَاءٌ جُعِلَ مَوْصُولاً أَوْ مَوْصُوفًا مَحْذُوفاً؛ أَيْ: يُسْفَكُ الدِّمَاءُ فِيهِمْ.

﴿وَنَحْنُ نُسَبِّحُ بِحَمْدِكَ وَنُقَدِّسُ لَكَ﴾: حَالٌ مُقَرِّرَةٌ لِجِهَةِ الْإِشْكَالِ، كَقَوْلِكَ: أَتُحْسِنُ إِلَى أَعْدَائِكَ وَأَنَا الصَّدِيقُ الْمُحْتَاجُ؟

Safk ‹shedding›, *sabk* ‹founding›, *safḥ* ‹pouring› and *shann* ‹splashing› are all types of *ṣabb* ‹pouring›; *safk* is said of blood and tears, *sabk* of molten precious metals, *safḥ* of pouring from above and *shann* of pouring from the mouth of a water-skin and the like, as also *sann* ‹streaming›. It was also read *yusfaku* ‹will be shed›[1072] in the passive, in which case the referent is ***man*** ‹those›, whether construed as a definite conjunctive or a suppressed indefinite conjunctive—that is, *yusfaku al-dimā'u fīhim* ‹among whom blood will be shed›.

[The angels inquired without objecting nor boasting]

wa-naḥnu nusabbiḥu bi-ḥamdika wa-nuqaddisu laka ‹*while we extol with Your praise and we hallow for You*› is a participial state and reaffirmation of the problematic perspective, as if you were to say, "Are you going to be gracious to your enemies when I am your friend in need?"[1073]

[1072] Thus in all the mss. and eds. as well as al-ʿUkbarī, *I'rāb* (1:144) and, after him, *MQ* (1:74), while Abū Naṣr al-Kirmānī cites it as *tusfaku al-dimā'u* in his *Shawādhdh al-Qirā'āt*, ed. Shimrān al-ʿAjlī (Beirut: Mu'assasat al-Balāgh, 2001) p. 57 although the latter could be a *taṣḥīf*. This is an unidentified reading according to al-ʿUkbarī.

[1073] Ak, β, B, ε, F, Kh, R, Sk, T, Ul, Z: الصديق المحتاج :I: الصِّدّيق المحتاج :α: الصديق القديم المحتاج

وَالمَعْنَى: أَتَسْتَخْلِفُ عُصَاةً وَنَحْنُ مَعْصُومُونَ، أَحِقَّاءُ بِذٰلِكَ؟ وَالمَقْصُودُ مِنْهُ: الْاِسْتِفْسَارُ عَمَّا رَجَّحَهُمْ ـ مَعَ مَا هُوَ مُتَوَقَّعٌ مِنْهُمْ ـ عَلَى الْمَلَائِكَةِ الْمَعْصُومِينَ فِي الْاِسْتِخْلَافِ، لَا الْعُجْبُ وَالتَّفَاخُرُ. وَكَأَنَّهُمْ عَلِمُوا أَنَّ الْمَجْعُولَ خَلِيفَةً ذُو ثَلَاثِ قُوًى، عَلَيْهَا مَدَارُ أَمْرِهِ: (أ) شَهْوِيَّةٌ (ب) وَغَضَبِيَّةٌ، تُؤَدِّيَانِ بِهِ إِلَى الْفَسَادِ وَسَفْكِ الدِّمَاءِ؛ (ج) وَعَقْلِيَّةٌ، تَدْعُوهُ إِلَى الْمَعْرِفَةِ وَالطَّاعَةِ؛ وَنَظَرُوا إِلَيْهَا مُفْرَدَةً، وَقَالُوا: «مَا الْحِكْمَةُ فِي اسْتِخْلَافِهِ، وَهُوَ ـ بِاعْتِبَارِ تَيْنِكَ الْقُوَّتَيْنِ ـ لَا تَقْتَضِي الْحِكْمَةُ إِيجَادَهُ، فَضْلًا عَنِ اسْتِخْلَافِهِ؟ وَأَمَّا بِاعْتِبَارِ الْقُوَّةِ الْعَقْلِيَّةِ، فَنَحْنُ نُقِيمُ مَا يُتَوَقَّعُ مِنْهَا سَلِيمًا عَنْ مُعَارَضَةِ تِلْكَ الْمَفَاسِدِ!» وَغَفَلُوا عَنْ فَضِيلَةِ كُلِّ وَاحِدَةٍ ....

The meaning is, "Are You going to appoint as Your successors sinners, when we are infallible and deserving of that?" but its intent is an inquiry about what gave them[1074] preponderance—despite what is expected of them—over the infallible angels in successorship; not vanity and self-pride.

[Complex humans and simple angels: mission of vicegerency]

It is as if they knew that the appointee to successorship possessed three faculties that defined him: (i) appetitive, (ii) wrathful—both leading him to corruption and bloodshed—and (iii) rational, drawing him to learning and obedience. Looking at each in isolation, they said: "What is the wisdom in making him successor when, with regard to those two faculties, wisdom does not dictate that he should even be created, not to mention made successor? As for the rational faculty, we ourselves can accomplish what is expected of it free and clear of the impediments of those failings." But they overlooked the merit of each of those two

[1074] B interlinear gloss: اي آدم واولاده "that is, Adam and his children."

مِنَ الْقُوَّتَيْنِ إِذَا صَارَتْ مُهَذَّبَةً مِطْوَاعَةً لِلْعَقْلِ، مُتَمَرِّنَةً عَلَى الْخَيْرِ: كَالْعِفَّةِ، وَالشَّجَاعَةِ، وَمُجَاهَدَةِ الْهَوَى، وَالْإِنْصَافِ. وَلَمْ يَعْلَمُوا أَنَّ التَّرْكِيبَ يُفِيدُ مَا يَقْصُرُ عَنْهُ الْآحَادُ كَالْإِحَاطَةِ بِالْجُزْئِيَّاتِ، وَاسْتِنْبَاطِ الصِّنَاعَاتِ، وَاسْتِخْرَاجِ مَنَافِعِ الْكَائِنَاتِ مِنَ الْقُوَّةِ إِلَى الْفِعْلِ، الَّذِي هُوَ الْمَقْصُودُ مِنَ الْاِسْتِخْلَافِ. وَإِلَيْهِ أَشَارَ تَعَالَى إِجْمَالاً بِقَوْلِهِ: ﴿قَالَ إِنِّيٓ أَعْلَمُ مَا لَا تَعْلَمُونَ﴾.

faculties when it becomes disciplined, docile to reason, trained for the goodness of continence, courage, the struggle against lust, and justice. They did not realize that combination affords what isolated elements do not—such as encompassment of particulars, the devising of industries and the extraction of the resources of created matter from potentiality to actuality, which is the very purpose of the appointment to successorship.[1075] Allah Most High alluded to that in indefinite terms, saying

qāla innī aʿlamu mā lā taʿlamūna ⁽*He said: Verily I know what you do not know*⁾.

[1075] "It appears that angels—upon them peace—because of their simplicity, do not have bodily faculties and external senses that are respectively apt to perceive any of the various objects of perception such as colors, sounds, savors and odors, or palpable modalities such as softness, coarseness, heat and cold. So their cognition does not encompass particular savors that are tasted because of the absence of a gustative faculty in them; nor particular observable colors because of the absence of optic power in them, nor particular audible sounds because of the absence of auditory power in them; likewise with regard to particular olfactory and palpatory objects. They also lack internal senses, so their cognition does not encompass particular forms imaginatively, nor particular meanings conceptually and so forth, on the basis of the fact that the divine custom has made it the rule that particulars cannot be grasped by using the intellective faculty except through the intermediary of corporeal faculties that are respectively apt for that.... So the complex (*al-murakkab*)—which is Adam (upon him peace) and his offspring—when they demarked themselves from the supernal angels through these merits, prevailed over them with the appointment to successorship, from the perspective that the reality of human beings that emerges from that reality is nobler. And Allah knows best concerning the truth of the matter." (Z 1:245)

وَ(التَّسْبِيحُ): تَبْعِيدُ الله تَعَالَى عَنِ السُّوءِ ـ وَكَذٰلِكَ التَّقْدِيسُ ـ مِنْ (سَبَحَ فِي الْأَرْضِ وَالْمَاءِ)، وَ(قَدَسَ فِي الْأَرْضِ) إِذَا ذَهَبَ فِيهَا وَأَبْعَدَ، وَيُقَالُ (قَدَّسَ) إِذَا طَهَّرَ، لِأَنَّ مُطَهِّرَ الشَّيْءِ مُبَعِّدُهُ عَنِ الْأَقْذَارِ.

وَ﴿بِحَمْدِكَ﴾ فِي مَوْضِعِ الْحَالِ، أَيْ: مُتَلَبِّسِينَ بِحَمْدِكَ عَلَى مَا أَلْهَمْتَنَا مَعْرِفَتَكَ وَوَفَّقْتَنَا لِتَسْبِيحِكَ! تَدَارَكُوا بِهِ مَا أَوْهَمَ إِسْنَادُ التَّسْبِيحِ إِلَى أَنْفُسِهِمْ.

﴿وَنُقَدِّسُ لَكَ﴾: نُطَهِّرُ نُفُوسَنَا ....

[The affirmation of divine transcendence]

Tasbīḥ ⟨extolling⟩ is the distantiation of Allah Most High far from evil, as is *taqdīs* ⟨hallowing⟩, from *sabaḥa fīl-arḍi wal-māʾ* ⟨he ran/swam on the ground and in the water⟩[1076] and *qadasa fīl-arḍ*, that is, he went far over the earth.[1077] One says *qaddasa*, "he made pure," because the one who purifies something is putting it far from impurities.

Bi-ḥamdika ⟨by Your praise⟩ is a virtual participial state, meaning: "Vested with praise of You for Your having inspired us knowledge of You and granted us success in extolling You!" They rectified thereby what the self-ascription of extolling had suggested. ***Wa-nuqaddisu laka*** ⟨and we hallow for You⟩: "we purify ourselves ....

[1076] The lexicons gloss *sabaḥa* as moving fast without a solid under-support as in water or in the air without mention of the ground—as pointed out by the supercommentaries—with the exception of the expression *sabbāḥ* for a wide-paced horse.

[1077] This rare meaning is cited by al-Rāzī and later exegetes after al-Zamakhsharī (as a rule spelled *qaddasa* cf. R: قدّس but see F, Z) and is undocumented in the lexicons other than al-Ṣāḥib b. ʿAbbād al-Ṭāliqānī's *al-Muḥīṭ fīl-Lugha*, ed. Muḥammad Ḥasan Āl Yāsīn, 11 vols. (Beirut: ʿĀlam al-Kutub, 1994) entry *q-d-s*. *Subḥān Allāh* can also mean "running fast to Him and lightness in obeying Him." *Ibid.* (entry *s-b-ḥ*).

عَنِ الذُّنُوبِ لِأَجْلِكَ، كَأَنَّهُمْ قَابَلُوا (أ) الْفَسَادَ ـ الْمُفَسَّرَ بِالشِّرْكِ عِنْدَ قَوْمٍ ـ بِالتَّسْبِيحِ، (ب) وَسَفْكَ الدِّمَاءِ ـ الَّذِي هُوَ أَعْظَمُ الْأَفْعَالِ الذَّمِيمَةِ ـ بِتَطْهِيرِ النُّفُوسِ عَنِ الْآثَامِ. وَقِيلَ: نُقَدِّسُكَ، وَاللَّامُ مَزِيدَةٌ.

﴿وَعَلَّمَ ءَادَمَ ٱلْأَسْمَآءَ كُلَّهَا﴾ إِمَّا بِخَلْقِ عِلْمٍ ضَرُورِيٍّ بِهَا فِيهِ، أَوْ إِلْقَاءٍ فِي رُوعِهِ. وَلَا يَفْتَقِرُ إِلَى سَابِقَةِ اصْطِلَاحٍ لِيَتَسَلْسَلَ.

وَ(التَّعْلِيمُ) فِعْلٌ يَتَرَتَّبُ عَلَيْهِ الْعِلْمُ غَالِباً، وَلِذٰلِكَ يُقَالُ: عَلَّمْتُهُ فَلَمْ يَتَعَلَّمْ.

from sins for Your sake," as if they had countered

(i) *fasād* ⁽corruption⁾—which is glossed by some[1078] as *shirk* ⁽polytheism⁾—with *tasbīḥ* ⁽extolment⁾,

(ii) and bloodshed—which is the gravest of abominable acts—with the purification of souls from offenses.

It was also said [that it means] *nuqaddisuka* ⁽we hallow You⁾, with the *lām* as an additive.

[The modality of the divine teaching of Adam]

[2:31] **wa-ʿallama Ādama-l-asmāʾa kullahā** ⁽*and He taught Adam the names—all of them*⁾ either by creating innate knowledge of them in him or by casting [it] into his innermost; nor is there need of a precedent of terminology [for such knowledge] to follow in succession.[1079]

Taʿlīm ⁽teaching⁾ is an act usually followed in sequence by knowledge, whence the expression *ʿallamtuhu fa-lam yataʿallam* ⁽I taught him but he learnt nothing!⁾.

[1078] E.g. Qatāda and al-Suddī cf. *Tafsīrs* of Makkī al-Qaysī, al-Samʿānī and al-Qurṭubī.
[1079] A rebuttal of the Muʿtazila, (Q) as that would necessitate circularity. (Z)

و(آدَمُ) اِسْمٌ أَعْجَمِيٌّ كَـ(آزَرَ) وَ(شَالَخ). وَاشْتِقَاقُهُ (أ) مِنَ (الْأُدْمَةِ)، (ب) أَوِ (الْأَدَمَةِ) بِالْفَتْحِ بِمَعْنَى الْأُسْوَةِ؛ (ج) أَوْ مِنْ (أَدِيمِ الْأَرْضِ) لِمَا رُوِيَ عَنْهُ ـ عَلَيْهِ الصَّلَاةُ وَالسَّلَامُ ـ ....

[The meaning of *Ādam*]

Ādam is a non-Arabic name like Āzar[1080] and Shālakh ⁽Shiloh⁾. Its derivation is

(i) from *al-udma* ⁽swarthiness⁾;

(ii) or from *al-adama* ⁽paragon⁾ in the sense of an examplar;[1081]

(iii) or from *adīm al-arḍ* ⁽the face of the earth⁾,[1082] in light of what is related from him—upon him blessings and peace—that

[1080] Āzar is considered to be the father of Ibrāhīm—upon him peace—"named Tāraḥ ⁽Terah⁾ in the histories, the two being different proper names for him, like Isrā'īl and Ya'qūb; or Āzar could mean 'the old man' or 'the cripple'... or it was the name of an idol he was named after for worshipping it assiduously" acc. to the Qadi *sub* al-An'ām 6:74. Āzar could also be Ibrāhīm's paternal uncle, one of the many brothers of Terah left unnamed in Genesis 11:25: 'And Nahor lived after he begat Terah 119 years, and begat sons and daughters," as the Qur'ān makes the father and the uncle synonyms and explicitly names both Ismā'īl and Isḥāq among Ya'qūb's fathers in al-Baqara 2:133, cf. the Prophetic hadith, "One's paternal uncle is the twin trunk (*ṣinw*) of one's father" (al-Tirmidhī from Abū Hurayra, *ṣaḥīḥ*) and 'Ā'isha's teknonym "Umm 'Abd Allāh" after her sister Asmā''s eldest son.

[1081] *Adama* is also "the inside of the skin (*bāṭin al-jild*, hypodermis) which is next to the flesh while the epidermis (*bashara*) is its exterior." *Ṣiḥāḥ, s.v. '-d-m.*

[1082] "It is authentically established that Ibn 'Abbās—Allah be well-pleased with him and his father—said Adam was thus named because he was created from *adīm al-arḍ* ⁽the surface of the earth⁾; narrated by al-Firyābī, Ibn Jarīr, Ibn Abī Ḥātim, al-Ḥākim—he declared it *ṣaḥīḥ*—and al-Bayhaqī in *al-Asmā' wal-Ṣifāt*. Something identical is related from 'Alī b. Abī Ṭālib and Ibn Mas'ūd—Allah be well-pleased with them—by Ibn Jarīr, and this strengthens the fact that it is an Arabic word, which is what [the linguist Abū Manṣūr Mawhūb b. Aḥmad] al-Jawālīqī (465-540/1073-1145) explicitly said in *al-Mu'arrab* [*min al-Kalām al-A'jamī*, ed. Aḥmad Muḥammad Shākir, 2nd ed., (Cairo: Maṭba'at Dār al-Kutub, 1389/1969) p. 61]: the names of the prophets—upon

أَنَّهُ تَعَالَى قَبَضَ قَبْضَةً مِنْ جَمِيعِ الْأَرْضِ - سَهْلِهَا وَحَزْنِهَا - فَخَلَقَ مِنْهَا آدَمَ، فَلِذٰلِكَ يَأْتِي بَنُوهُ أَخْيَافاً؛ (د) أَوْ مِنَ (الْأُدْمِ) أَوِ (الْأُدْمَةِ) بِمَعْنَى الْأُلْفَةِ: تَعَسُّفٌ - كَاشْتِقَاقِ (إِدْرِيسَ) مِنَ الدَّرْسِ وَ(يَعْقُوبَ) مِنَ الْعَقِبِ وَ(إِبْلِيسَ) مِنَ الْإِبْلَاسِ.

وَ(الْإِسْمُ) (١) بِاعْتِبَارِ الْاِشْتِقَاقِ: مَا يَكُونُ عَلَامَةً ....

Allah Most High grasped a handful from every corner of the earth—its valleys and cliffs—and created Adam from it all, whence his progeny come in different hues;[1083]

(iv) or from *udm* or *udma* in the sense of *ulfa* ‹congeniality›—[but that is] strained, as is deriving "Idrīs" from *dars* ‹study›, "Ya'qūb" from *'aqb* ‹posterity› and "Iblīs" from *iblās* ‹despair›.[1084]

Al-ism ‹the name› is, 1. etymologically,[1085] what serves as a sign

all of them the blessings of Allah—are all non-Arabic except four: Ādam, Ṣāliḥ, Shu'ayb and Muḥammad." (S 2:189-190)

1083 "Narrated by Aḥmad, Abū Dāwūd, al-Tirmidhī—he declared it *ṣaḥīḥ*—, Ibn Jarīr, Ibn al-Mundhīr, Ibn Mardūyah, al-Ḥākim—ditto—and al-Bayhaqī in *al-Asmā' wal-Ṣifāt*, from Abū Mūsā al-Ash'arī." (S) The actual wording states: "Verily Allah Almighty created Adam from a handful He grasped from every corner of the earth, thus human beings come just like the earth: among them are the red, the white, the black and in-between; the difficult, the easy and in-between; the foul, the clean and in-between." *Akhyāf* also means sons and daughters of the same mother from different fathers.

1084 "*Udm* and *udma* are *muwāfaqa* ‹congruity› and *ulfa* ‹congeniality›, as taken from the *idām* ‹condiment› of food. It is strained in light of what was already mentioned. *Idrīs* is from *dars* because of his abundant study of the sciences; *Ya'qūb* from *'aqb* because he comes after Isḥāq; and *Iblīs* from *iblās* because it despairs of the mercy of Allah, according to which scenario it is an Arabic name." (Kh) "In the *Ṣiḥāḥ*: *al-adm* is *ulfa* and *ittifāq* ‹agreement›. One says *adama Allāhu baynahumā* ‹may Allah harmonize their hearts›, that is, concile and accord; likewise *ādama Allāhu*. A hadith states, 'You might look at her, for it is more conducive to harmonize (*an yu'dama*) between the two of you' in the sense of there being between you love and agreement. So Adam was named after it because Allah made him congenialize with Eve." (Z 1:247)

1085 See the qadi's previous discussion on *ism* ‹name› deriving either from *sumūw*

لِلشَّيْءِ وَدَلِيلاً يَرْفَعُهُ إِلَى الذِّهْنِ، مِنَ الْأَلْفَاظِ وَالصِّفَاتِ وَالْأَفْعَالِ؛ (٢) وَاسْتِعْمَالُهُ عُرْفاً: فِي اللَّفْظِ الْمَوْضُوعِ لِمَعْنًى، سَوَاءٌ كَانَ مُرَكَّباً أَوْ مُفْرَداً، مُخْبَراً عَنْهُ أَوْ خَبَراً، أَوْ رَابِطَةً بَيْنَهُمَا. (٣) وَاصْطِلَاحاً: فِي الْمُفْرَدِ الدَّالِّ عَلَى مَعْنًى فِي نَفْسِهِ غَيْرِ مُقْتَرِنٍ بِأَحَدِ الْأَزْمِنَةِ الثَّلَاثَةِ.

وَالْمُرَادُ فِي الْآيَةِ: إِمَّا الْأَوَّلُ، أَوِ الثَّانِي - وَهُوَ يَسْتَلْزِمُ الْأَوَّلَ، لِأَنَّ الْعِلْمَ بِالْأَلْفَاظِ، مِنْ حَيْثُ الدَّلَالَةِ، مُتَوَقِّفٌ عَلَى الْعِلْمِ بِالْمَعَانِي.

وَالْمَعْنَى: أَنَّهُ تَعَالَى خَلَقَهُ مِنْ أَجْزَاءٍ ....

for something and its indicator, raising it up to the intellect: namely[1086] vocables, descriptives and operations.[1087]

2. In common parlance it is a vocable coined for a meaning—whether composite or simple, inchoative or enunciative, or the copulative between the two.

3. In conventional usage it denotes a simple that points to a meaning intrinsically, without connection to any of the three tenses.

[The meaning of the teaching of the names]

What is meant in the verse is either the first or the second [usage], which necessarily implies the first, since knowledge of vocables as being indicative of something hinges on knowledge of meanings.

The sense is that Allah Most High created him out of various

ʿheightʾ or from *sima* ʿbrandʾ, respectively the Basrian and Kufan views.

[1086] All eds. and mss.: من AQ, H, MM: مع typo.

[1087] "I.e. *ism* is a vocable coined opposite a thing, a descriptive or state qualifying it as to its benefit or harm, sweetness, whiteness and all its sensory, intelligible, imaginal and estimative modalities, or one of its operations such as 'reading it,' 'writing it,' 'sewing it'... All that constitutes marks pointing to that thing and its essence." (Z)

مُخْتَلِفَةٍ وَقِوىً مُتَبَايِنَةٍ، مُسْتَعِدّاً لِإِدْرَاكِ أَنْوَاعِ الْمُدْرَكَاتِ مِنَ الْمَعْقُولَاتِ، وَالْمَحْسُوسَاتِ، وَالْمُتَخَيَّلَاتِ، وَالْمَوْهُومَاتِ، وَأَلْهَمَهُ مَعْرِفَةَ ذَوَاتِ الْأَشْيَاءِ وَخَوَاصِّهَا وَأَسْمَائِهَا، وَأُصُولَ الْعُلُومِ، وَقَوَانِينَ الصِّنَاعَاتِ، وَكَيْفِيَّةَ آلَاتِهَا.

﴿ثُمَّ عَرَضَهُمْ عَلَى الْمَلَٰٓئِكَةِ﴾: الضَّمِيرُ فِيهِ لِلْمُسَمَّيَاتِ، الْمَدْلُولِ عَلَيْهَا ضِمْناً ـ إِذِ التَّقْدِيرُ: أَسْمَاءُ الْمُسَمَّيَاتِ، فَحُذِفَ الْمُضَافُ إِلَيْهِ لِدَلَالَةِ الْمُضَافِ عَلَيْهِ، وَعُوِّضَ عَنْهُ اللَّامُ، كَقَوْلِهِ تَعَالَى ﴿وَٱشْتَعَلَ ٱلرَّأْسُ شَيْبًا﴾ [مريم ٤] ـ

parts with distinct faculties, ready to perceive all kinds of perceptibles: the intelligible, sensory, imaginal and estimative; and He inspired to him knowledge of the essence of things, their properties and names, the foundations of the branches of knowledge, the canons of human crafts and the modalities of their implements.[1088]

thumma ʿaraḍahum ʿalā-l-malāʾikati ⁽*then He displayed them before the angels*⁾: the personal pronoun here stands for the referent-objects that are implicitly pointed to—as the subaudition is *asmāʾ al-musammayāt* ⁽[He taught him] the names of the referent-objects⁾, but the governed annex was suppressed because the governing annex was pointing to it and was compensated by the [definite] *lām* ⁽the⁾ as in the saying of Allah Most High *and the head is ablaze with white hair* (Maryam 19:4)[1089]—

[1088] "In the *Ḥāshiya* [of al-Ṭībī]: 'the scholars have three different views of what Adam was taught. (1) He was taught the vocables coined for physical objects and meanings; (2) He was taught their purposes and benefits; (3) both of the above, and this is J's position.' I say: The first position is the one narrated from Ibn 'Abbās [in al-Ṭabarī]." (S)

[1089] "Since his statement *Verily the bones of me wax feeble* (Maryam 19:4) precedes, the first person pronoun indicates that what is meant is '*my* head' so the speaker's pronoun was suppressed because it was understood and the definite article *lām* was

لِأَنَّ الْعَرْضَ لِلسُّؤَالِ عَنْ أَسْمَاءِ الْمَعْرُوضَاتِ، فَلَا يَكُونُ الْمَعْرُوضُ نَفْسَ الْأَسْمَاءِ، سِيَّمَا إِنْ أُرِيدَ بِهِ الْأَلْفَاظُ؛ وَالْمُرَادُ بِهِ ذَوَاتُ الْأَشْيَاءِ أَوْ مَدْلُولَاتُ الْأَلْفَاظِ. وَتَذْكِيرُهُ لِتَغْلِيبِ مَا اشْتَمَلَ عَلَيْهِ مِنَ الْعُقَلَاءِ. وَقُرِئَ (عَرَضَهُنَّ) وَ(عَرَضَهَا) ....

since the display is for the purpose of asking about the names of the things displayed. Hence what is being displayed cannot be the selfsame names[1090]—especially if by the latter the vocables are meant[1091]—and what is actually meant is the things themselves, or the significations of the vocables.[1092]

It was put in the masculine because, among its subsets, those endowed with reason were given predominance. It was also recited *ʿaraḍahunna* and *araḍahā* ʿHe displayed them [fem.]ʾ,[1093]

supplied instead, alluding to something known previously." (Z)

1090 All eds. and mss.: الأسماء AQ, H, MM: الأشياء typo.

1091 "Else the meaning is: tell me the names of the names, which makes no sense." (Z)

1092 "Know that I have a question here, which is that referent-objects can be physical objects and they can be abstract meanings; the display of the former is clear enough, but how were the abstract meanings displayed—such as pain and pleasure, joy and sadness, knowledge and ignorance, hunger and thirst and the infinitive nouns in their entirety? There is no answering that other than by what I resolved [in my works] more than once, namely that meanings are invisible only in this world; but as for the world of *malakūt* ʿpreternal dominionʾ they have various specific forms by which they can be seen and speak. This is similar to *ʿālam al-mithāl* ʿthe imaginal worldʾ which a group [of Sufis] have affirmed—pay no attention to those who denied it—and, as for us, we have enough standing proofs by which we can affirm it. Furthermore it is indicated by the hadiths transmitted on the enforming of belief, prayer, recitation, knowledge, days and nights, wombs, and the *dhikr* ʿinvocationsʾ of all the above-mentioned and their dialoguing. I have authored on this issue a treatise entitled *al-Maʿānī al-Daqīqa fī Idrāk al-Ḥaqīqa* ʿThe fine meanings regarding the perception of realityʾ. Likewise Shaykh ʿAbd al-Ghaffār al-Qawṣī said in his book *al-Tawḥīd wal-Maʿānī* ʿPure monotheism and abstract meaningsʾ: 'They take form and this is not precluded for Allah Most High.'" (S 2:194-195) See also Sirāj al-Dīn, *al-Īmān bil-Malāʾika* (pp. 32-48).

1093 By Ubay b. Kaʿb and ʿAbd Allāh b. Masʿūd respectively. (*MQ*)

عَلَى مَعْنَى عَرَضَ مُسَمَّيَاتِهِنَّ أَوْ مُسَمَّيَاتِهَا.

﴿فَقَالَ أَنۢبِـُٔونِي بِأَسۡمَآءِ هَٰٓؤُلَآءِ﴾ تَبْكِيتٌ لَهُمْ وَتَنْبِيهٌ عَلَى عَجْزِهِمْ عَنْ أَمْرِ الْخِلَافَةِ؛ فَإِنَّ التَّصَرُّفَ، وَالتَّدْبِيرَ، وَإِقَامَةَ الْمَعْدَلَةِ قَبْلَ تَحَقُّقِ الْمَعْرِفَةِ وَالْوُقُوفِ عَلَى مَرَاتِبِ الِاسْتِعْدَادَاتِ وَقَدْرِ الْحُقُوقِ: مُحَالٌ. وَلَيْسَ بِتَكْلِيفٍ لِيَكُونَ مِنْ بَابِ التَّكْلِيفِ بِالْمُحَالِ.

وَ(الْإِنْبَاءُ): إِخْبَارٌ فِيهِ إِعْلَامٌ، وَلِذٰلِكَ يُجْرَى مُجْرَى كُلٍّ وَاحِدٍ مِنْهُمَا.

﴿إِن كُنتُمۡ صَٰدِقِينَ﴾ فِي زَعْمِكُمْ أَنَّكُمْ أَحِقَّاءُ بِالْخِلَافَةِ لِعِصْمَتِكُمْ، ...

in the sense that He displayed their referents [as rational and impersonal feminine plurals respectively].

[The divine silencing of the angels' misassumption]

fa-qāla anbiʾūnī bi-asmāʾi hāʾulāʾi ʿ*and He said: inform Me of the names of these*ʾ: a silencing of them and notice of their impotence in the matter of succession. For managing and administering [creation] and establishing[1094] equity before complete cognition and ascertainment of the respective degrees of capacity and extents of due rights is impossible. It is not a tasking, so it cannot be claimed to be a form of "tasking with an impossibility."[1095]

Al-inbāʾ ʿinformingʾ is a reporting that contains a notification, whence it can mean either one of the two meanings.

in kuntum ṣādiqīna ʿ*if you are truthful*ʾ in your claim (i) that you are more deserving of successorship because of your infallibility

[1094] All mss. and eds.: وإقامة AQ, H, MM: إقامة lacuna.

[1095] Because it is a *taʿjīz* ʿincapacitationʾ rather than a *taklīf* ʿtaskingʾ. (Sk) On the issue of tasking beyond capacity see above, discussion on *Verily those who rejected belief, it is the same for them whether you warn them or you do not warn them* (al-Baqara 2:6).

أَوْ أَنَّ خَلْقَهُمْ وَاسْتِخْلَافَهُمْ ـ وَهٰذِهِ صِفَتُهُمْ ـ لَا يَلِيقُ بِالْحَكِيمِ: وَهُوَ ـ وَإِنْ لَمْ يُصَرِّحُوا بِهِ ـ لٰكِنَّهُ لَازِمُ مَقَالِهِمْ.

وَ(التَّصْدِيقُ) كَمَا يَتَطَرَّقُ إِلَى الْكَلَامِ بِاعْتِبَارِ مَنْطُوقِهِ، قَدْ يَتَطَرَّقُ إِلَيْهِ بِفَرْضِ مَا يَلْزَمُ مَدْلُولَهُ مِنَ الْأَخْبَارِ؛ وَبِهٰذَا الْإِعْتِبَارِ: يَعْتَرِي الْإِنْشَاءَاتِ.

﴿قَالُوا۟ سُبْحَٰنَكَ لَا عِلْمَ لَنَآ إِلَّا مَا عَلَّمْتَنَآ﴾: (١) اِعْتِرَافٌ بِالْعَجْزِ وَالْقُصُورِ؛ ....

or (ii) that "creating them and appointing them successors—when such is their ilk—is unbefitting the Most Wise" which, although they did not actually say it, is nevertheless the inescapable conclusion from their statement.[1096]

Taṣdīq ⁽averment⁾, just as it is applicable to discourse in the sense of its verbatim content, may also apply to it as the assumed factual reports that are the inescapable conclusion of its signification; in view of this it therefore covers originative sentences.[1097]

[2:32] **qālū subḥanaka lā ʿilma lanā illā mā ʿallamtanā** ⁽*they said, Extolled are You! We know nothing except what You taught us*⁾ is

1. an admission of helplessness and inadequacy;

[1096] I.e. their assumption that human beings are merely defined by corruption and bloodshed and are devoid of factors that would justify their successorship. (Kh) "It would be more appropriate to understand it differently: Ibn Jarīr narrated from Ibn ʿAbbās, al-Ḥasan al-Baṣrī, Qatāda and al-Rabīʿ b. Anas that the angels said: 'Our Lord did not create any creature He prizes more, nor more knowledgeable' and al-Wāḥidī endorsed it" (S)

[1097] I.e. sentences that express interrogation, command or wish as opposed to fact. "An implied response to the possible objection that the angels' statement was only an interrogative proposition qualified by a participial-state clause—namely, *Will you set in it those who will spread corruption in it and shed blood, while we extol with Your praise and we hallow for You?* whereas averment and infirmation do not apply to originative sentences, so what is the sense of asking them, *if you are truthful*?" (Kh)

(٢) وَإِشْعَارٌ (أ) بِأَنَّ سُؤَالَهُمْ كَانَ اسْتِفْسَاراً وَلَمْ يَكُنِ اعْتِرَاضاً، (ب) وَأَنَّهُ قَدْ بَانَ لَهُمْ مَا خَفِيَ عَلَيْهِمْ مِنْ فَضْلِ الْإِنْسَانِ وَالْحِكْمَةِ فِي خَلْقِهِ؛ (٣) وَإِظْهَارٌ لِشُكْرِ نِعْمَتِهِ بِمَا عَرَّفَهُمْ وَكَشَفَ لَهُمْ مَا اعْتَقَلَ عَلَيْهِمْ؛ (٤) وَمُرَاعَاةٌ لِلْأَدَبِ بِتَفْوِيضِ الْعِلْمِ كُلِّهِ إِلَيْهِ.

وَ(سُبْحَانَ) مَصْدَرٌ، كَـ(غُفْرَانَ)؛ وَلَا يَكَادُ يُسْتَعْمَلُ إِلَّا مُضَافاً منصوباً بِإِضْمَارِ فِعْلِهِ، كَـ(مَعَاذَ الله). وَقَدْ أُجْرِيَ عَلَماً لِلتَّسْبِيحِ بِمَعْنَى التَّنْزِيهِ - عَلَى الشُّذُوذِ - فِي قَوْلِهِ: [سريع]

.... * سُبْحَانَ مِنْ عَلْقَمَةَ الْفَاخِرِ.

2. a proclamation that (i) their question was an inquiry and not an objection, (ii) and that what was previously hidden to them of the merit of human beings and the wisdom in creating them was now abundantly clear to them;

3. a manifestation of gratitude for His favor in acquainting them of, and disclosing to them what had been incomprehensible before;

4. and keeping decorum in resigning all knowledge to Him.

Subḥān ⸢extolment⸣ is an infinitive noun like *ghufrān* ⸢pardon⸣. It is hardly used other than as a governing annex, made accusative by its implied verb as in *maʿādha-l-Lāh* ⸢God's refuge⸣.[1098]

It was used eponymically for *tasbīḥ* in the sense of disavowal —although this is highly irregular—in the saying: ["The Swift"]

Quittance from (subḥāna min) ʿAlqama the boastful![1099]

[1098] "I.e. *usabbiḥu-l-Lāha tasbīḥan* ⸢I extol Allah with true extolment⸣, like *aʿūdhu bi-l-Lāhi maʿādhan* ⸢I seek refuge in Allah as my [sole true] refuge⸣, where the verb was suppressed and the object was annexed to the infinitive noun." (Q) On *Subḥān Allāh* see note 1077.

[1099] Spoken by al-Aʿshā lampooning ʿAlqama b. ʿUlātha and praising his cousin ʿĀmir

وَتَصْدِيرُ الْكَلَامِ بِهِ: اِعْتِذَارٌ عَنِ الْاسْتِفْسَارِ وَالْجَهْلِ بِحَقِيقَةِ الْحَالِ؛ وَلِذٰلِكَ جُعِلَ مِفْتَاحَ التَّوْبَةِ، فَقَالَ مُوسَى ـ عَلَيْهِ السَّلَامُ ـ ﴿سُبْحَٰنَكَ تُبْتُ إِلَيْكَ﴾ [الأعراف ١٤٣]، وَقَالَ يُونُسُ: ﴿سُبْحَٰنَكَ إِنِّي كُنتُ مِنَ ٱلظَّٰلِمِينَ﴾ [الأنبياء ٨٧].

﴿إِنَّكَ أَنتَ ٱلْعَلِيمُ﴾: الَّذِي لَا يَخْفَى عَلَيْهِ خَافِيَةٌ.

﴿ٱلْحَكِيمُ﴾: الْمُحْكِمُ لِمُبْدَعَاتِهِ، الَّذِي لَا يَفْعَلُ إِلَّا مَا فِيهِ حِكْمَةٌ بَالِغَةٌ.

وَ﴿أَنتَ﴾ فَصْلٌ؛ وَقِيلَ: تَأْكِيدٌ لِلْكَافِ كَمَا فِي قَوْلِكَ: (مَرَرْتُ بِكَ أَنْتَ)،

The opening of discourse with it forms an apology for the inquiry and for the display of ignorance regarding the truth of the matter; hence it was made the key to repentence. Mūsā ‹Moses› —upon him peace—said *extolled are You! I repent to You* (al-Aʿrāf 7:143) and Yūnus ‹Jonah›—upon him peace, *extolled are You! Truly I was an oppressor* (al-Anbiyā' 21:87).

innaka anta al-ʿalīmu ‹*truly You—and You alone—are the most Knowing*› Whose notice no hidden thing escapes, **al-ḥakīmū** ‹*the most Wise*› Who perfects all His *ex nihilo* designs and Who does nothing but what entails utter wisdom.

Anta ‹You› is (i) a distinctive pronoun.[1100] (ii) It was also said it is an intensive for the [personal pronoun] *kāf* [in *innaka*], as when you say *marartu bika anta* ‹I passed by you yourself›, ……

b. al-Ṭufayl at the time they fell out and no Arab took sides with either, cf. *Dīwān al-Aʿshā* (p. 143). ʿAlqama was a Companion and the Prophet—upon him blessings and peace—actually forbade the recitation of this poem, cf. ʿAbd al-Qādir b. ʿUmar al-Baghdādī, *Khizānat al-Adab wa-Lubb Lubāb Lisān al-ʿArab*, ed. ʿAbd al-Salām Hārūn, 4th ed., 13 vols. (Cairo: Maktabat al-Khānjī, 1418/1997) 3:397-403.

[1100] See *hum* in the *tafsīr* for *wa-ulā'ika humu-l-mufliḥūn* (al-Baqara 2:5) above.

وَإِنْ لَمْ يَجُزْ: (مَرَرْتُ بِأَنْتَ)، إِذِ التَّابِعُ يَسُوغُ فِيهِ مَا لَا يَسُوغُ فِي الْمَتْبُوعِ؛ وَلِذٰلِكَ جَازَ: (يَا هٰذَا الرَّجُلُ)، وَلَمْ يَجُزْ: (يَا الرَّجُلُ). وَقِيلَ: مُبْتَدَأٌ، خَبَرُهُ مَا بَعْدَهُ، وَالْجُمْلَةُ خَبَرُ (إِنَّ).

﴿قَالَ يَٰٓـَٔادَمُ أَنۢبِئۡهُم بِأَسۡمَآئِهِمۡ﴾، أَيْ: أَعْلِمْهُمْ. وَقُرِئَ بِقَلْبِ الْهَمْزَةِ يَاءً، وَحَذْفِهَا بِكَسْرِ الْهَاءِ فِيهِمَا.

﴿فَلَمَّآ أَنۢبَأَهُم بِأَسۡمَآئِهِمۡ قَالَ أَلَمۡ أَقُل لَّكُمۡ إِنِّيٓ أَعۡلَمُ غَيۡبَ ٱلسَّمَٰوَٰتِ وَٱلۡأَرۡضِ وَأَعۡلَمُ مَا تُبۡدُونَ وَمَا كُنتُمۡ تَكۡتُمُونَ﴾: ....

although you cannot say *marartu bi-anta*, as what is permissible for the appositive is not permissible for the antecedent. Hence it can be said *yā hādhā al-rajul* ⟨O you fellow⟩ but it cannot be said *yā al-rajul*. (iii) It was also said it is an inchoative; the enunciative is what follows it and the whole clause is the enunciative of *inna*.

[2:33] **qāla yā Ādamu anbiʾhum bi-asmāʾihim** ⟨*He said, O Adam, inform them of their names*⟩, that is: notify them.

It was also read

(i) with a transposition of the *hamza* into a *yā'* [=*anbīhum*]; and

(ii) with suppression of the *hamza* and *kasra* inflection of the *hā'* [=*anbihim*]

(iii) in both instances [*anbīhim*].[1101]

fa-lammā anbaʾahum bi-asmāʾihim qāla alam aqul lakum innī aʿlamu ghayba-s-samāwāti wa-l-arḍi wa-aʿlamu mā tubdūna wa-mā kuntum taktumūna ⟨*when he informed them of their*

[1101] *Anbīhum*: al-Ḥasan and Hamza; *anbihim*: al-Ḥasan, al-Aʿraj, al-Zuhrī and Ibn Kathīr through al-Qawwās; *anbīhim*: al-Ḥasan, al-Aʿraj, Ibn Abī ʿAbla, Ibn ʿĀmir and al-Aʿmash. There is also *anbi'him*: Ibn ʿAbbās, Ibn Kathīr, al-Akhfash, Ibn Dhakwān, al-Bazzī, al-Walīd b. Muslim, Hishām and Ibn ʿĀmir. (*MQ*)

اِسْتِحْضَارٌ لِقَوْلِهِ تَعَالَى: ﴿إِنِّيٓ أَعْلَمُ مَا لَا تَعْلَمُونَ﴾ [البقرة ٣٠] لٰكِنَّهُ جَاءَ بِهِ عَلَى وَجْهٍ أَبْسَطَ يَكُونُ كَالْحُجَّةِ عَلَيْهِ؛ فَإِنَّهُ ـ تَعَالَى ـ لَمَّا عَلِمَ مَا خَفِيَ عَلَيْهِمْ مِنْ أُمُورِ السَّمَاوَاتِ وَالْأَرْضِ وَمَا ظَهَرَ لَهُمْ مِنْ أَحْوَالِهِمِ الظَّاهِرَةِ وَالْبَاطِنَةِ: عَلِمَ مَا لَا يَعْلَمُونَ. وَفِيهِ تَعْرِيضٌ بِمُعَاتَبَتِهِمْ عَلَى تَرْكِ الْأَوْلَى، وَهُوَ أَنْ يَتَوَقَّفُوا مُتَرَصِّدِينَ لِأَنْ يُبَيَّنَ لَهُمْ.

وَقِيلَ: ﴿مَا تُبْدُونَ﴾: قَوْلُهُمْ ﴿أَتَجْعَلُ فِيهَا مَن يُفْسِدُ فِيهَا﴾. وَمَا يَكْتُمُونَ: اسْتِبْطَانُهُمْ أَنَّهُمْ أَحِقَّاءُ بِالْخِلَافَةِ، وَأَنَّهُ تَعَالَى لَا يَخْلُقُ خَلْقاً أَفْضَلَ مِنْهُمْ. وَقِيلَ: ....

names He said: Did I not tell you? Verily I know what is invisible in the heavens and the earth, and I know what you disclose and what you try to keep hidden!⁾: a recalling of the saying of Allah Most High, *verily I know what you do not know* (al-Baqara 2:30) but in a more expansive manner that serves[1102] as a conclusive proof to that effect. Since Allah Most High knows what is hidden from them of heavenly and earthly matters, and knows what they comprehend of their own outward and inward states: He likewise knows what they do not know.

There is also in it an oblique rebuke of them for leaving the best course; the latter was for them to halt and wait for the clarification to come to them.

[The divine foreknowledge of Iblīs's planned disobedience]

It was said that ***mā tubdūna*** ⁽what you disclose⁾ is their saying, *Will you set in it those who will spread corruption in it* (al-Baqara 2:30) while ***taktumūna*** ⁽you keep hidden⁾ is their private musing that they are deserving of successorship and that He would not create a creature preferable to them; alternately: what-

[1102] α, B, ε, T: يكون Ak, β, F, I, R: ليكون

مَا أَظْهَرُوا مِنَ الطَّاعَةِ، وَأَسَرَّ إِبْلِيسُ مِنْهُمْ مِنَ الْمَعْصِيَةِ.

وَالْهَمْزَةُ لِلْإِنْكَارِ، دَخَلَتْ حَرْفَ الْجَحْدِ، فَأَفَادَتِ الْإِثْبَاتَ وَالتَّقْرِيرَ.

وَاعْلَمْ أَنَّ هٰذِهِ الْآيَاتِ تَدُلُّ (١) عَلَى شَرَفِ الْإِنْسَانِ؛ ....

ever obedience they displayed and whatever Iblīs concealed from them of his [planned] disobedience.[1103]

The *hamza* [in **alam**] is for disavowal: it was affixed to[1104] the negatory particle and therefore came to denote affirmation and resolution.

[Nine fundamental lessons in the *khilāfa* and *asmā'* verses]

Know that these verses show 1. the nobility of human beings;

[1103] In the sense that Iblīs was an angel among them as narrated from Ibn ʿAbbās and Ibn Masʿūd among other Companions, Mujāhid, Qatāda, Ibn al-Musayyib, Ibn Isḥāq and al-Ḍaḥḥāk by al-Ṭabarī (1:486-488; 1:507-511; 1:535-539), Ibn Abī Ḥātim, *Tafsīr* (1:79 §333-334; 1:84 §361-362) and al-Qushayrī, *al-Taysīr fī ʿIlm al-Tafsīr*, ed. ʿAbd Allāh al-Muṭayrī, unpublished Ph.D. diss. (Mecca: Jāmiʿat Umm al-Qurā, 1427/2006) pp. 514-517, cf. below on verse 2:34. "It is narrated Allah Most High commanded the angel of death—after the latter grasped a handful from each of the corners of the earth—that he ferment it and turn it into *ṭīnin lāzib* ⁽packed mud⁾ (al-Ṣāffāt 37:11) then *ḥama'in masnūn* ⁽moulded loam⁾ (al-Ḥijr 15:26, 28, 33); then *ṣalṣāl* ⁽clay⁾ (ditto and al-Raḥmān 55:40) and that he fashion from it Adam and place him on the road to Mecca for the angels who ascend from earth to heaven to see. He did so and placed Adam's body there for 40 years. Iblīs was an angel in charge of the nearest heaven, with a throng of angels called *Jinnī* because they were the custodians of *Janna*, and he was called *al-Jannān* as a man is called *Makkī, Madanī, Kūfī, Baṣrī*. Every time he passed by Adam he would say: 'For some reason you were created,' and he would strike it with his hand to make it resound. He then entered him through his nostrils and exited through his rear. He said to the angels that were with him: 'This hollow creature who is neither firm nor holding together—what do you think you will do if he is preferred over you?' They said, 'We will obey our Lord.' Iblis said in itself, 'By Allah, I will not obey him if he is preferred over me; and if I am preferred over him I will destroy him.'" (Z) Cf. Abū al-Shaykh, *al-ʿAẓama*, ed. Riḍā' Allāh Mubārakfūrī, 5 vols. (Riyadh: Dār al-ʿĀṣima, 1418/1998) 5:1679-1680 §1125-1128 and Ṭabarī, *Tafsīr* (1:486-488) from Ibn ʿAbbās, Ibn Masʿūd etc. Also see notes 1065, 1127.

[1104] All mss. and eds.: دخلت حرف Ak, Q: دخلت على حرف

(٢) وَمَزِيَّةِ الْعِلْمِ وَفَضْلِهِ عَلَى الْعِبَادَةِ؛ (٣) وَأَنَّهُ شَرْطٌ فِي الْخِلَافَةِ بَلِ الْعُمْدَةُ فِيهَا؛ (٤) وَأَنَّ التَّعْلِيمَ يَصِحُّ إِسْنَادُهُ إِلَى اللهِ تَعَالَى، وَإِنْ لَمْ يَصِحَّ إِطْلَاقُ (الْمُعَلِّمِ) عَلَيْهِ، لِاخْتِصَاصِهِ بِمَنْ يَحْتَرِفُ بِهِ؛ (٥) وَأَنَّ اللُّغَاتِ تَوْقِيفِيَّةٌ، فَإِنَّ الْأَسْمَاءَ تَدُلُّ عَلَى الْأَلْفَاظِ بِخُصُوصٍ أَوْ عُمُومٍ، وَتَعْلِيمُهَا ظَاهِرٌ فِي إِلْقَائِهَا عَلَى الْمُتَعَلِّمِ، مُبَيِّناً لَهُ مَعَانِيهَا، وَذٰلِكَ يَسْتَدْعِي سَابِقَةَ وَضْعٍ، وَالْأَصْلُ يَنْفِي أَنْ يَكُونَ ذٰلِكَ الْوَضْعُ مِمَّنْ كَانَ قَبْلَ آدَمَ، فَيَكُونُ مِنَ اللهِ سُبْحَانَهُ وَتَعَالَى؛ (٦) وَأَنَّ مَفْهُومَ الْحِكْمَةِ زَائِدٌ عَلَى ……………

2. the distinction of knowledge and its superiority to worship;

3. that [knowledge] is a precondition of successorship or rather its chief pillar;

4. that it is valid to ascribe teaching to Allah Most High—although it is invalid to call Him *al-muʿallim* ⟨teacher⟩, since that is specific to those who take up that occupation;

5. that languages are divinely ordained:[1105] for names point to vocables specifically or generally,[1106] and their teaching evidently consists in communicating them to the one learning them together with the clarification of their meanings, all this requiring prior coinage; but origin precludes that such coinage come from Adam's precursors, so it must come from Allah Most High;

6. that what is understood by wisdom is additional to what is

[1105] "The author takes the contrary view in his *Minhāj*." (Kh)

[1106] "I.e. in the customary specific sense, namely that of vocables specifically coined for a certain sense; and if explained in the lexical sense on the basis of etymological considerations from *sima* or *sumūw*, it includes all that serves as a sign and indicator for something as long as it evokes it to the mind, whether a vocable coined opposite that meaning or one of its inherent states or one of the acts that issue from it… so *al-asmāʾ*, no matter how it is explained, points to *al-alfaẓ* ⟨vocables⟩." (Z)

مَفْهُومِ الْعِلْمِ، وَإِلَّا لَتَكَرَّرَ قَوْلُهُ: ﴿إِنَّكَ أَنتَ ٱلْعَلِيمُ ٱلْحَكِيمُ﴾ [البقرة ٣٢]؛ (٧) وَأَنَّ عُلُومَ الْمَلَائِكَةِ وَكَمَالَاتِهِمْ تَقْبَلُ الزِّيَادَةَ؛ وَالْحُكَمَاءُ مَنَعُوا ذٰلِكَ فِي الطَّبَقَةِ الْعُلْيَا مِنْهُمْ، وَحَمَلُوا عَلَيْهِ قَوْلَهُ تَعَالَى: ﴿وَمَا مِنَّآ إِلَّا لَهُۥ مَقَامٌ مَّعْلُومٌ ﴿١٦٤﴾﴾ [الصافّات]؛ (٨) وَأَنَّ آدَمَ أَفْضَلُ مِنْ هٰؤُلَاءِ الْمَلَائِكَةِ لِأَنَّهُ أَعْلَمُ مِنْهُمْ، وَالْأَعْلَمُ أَفْضَلُ، لِقَوْلِهِ تَعَالَى: ﴿هَلْ يَسْتَوِى ٱلَّذِينَ يَعْلَمُونَ وَٱلَّذِينَ لَا يَعْلَمُونَ﴾ [الزمر ٩]؛ (٩) وَأَنَّهُ ـ تَعَالَى ـ يَعْلَمُ الْأَشْيَاءَ قَبْلَ حُدُوثِهَا.

understood by knowledge, otherwise there would be redundancy in His saying, *truly You—and You alone—are the most Knowing, the most Wise* (al-Baqara 2:32);

7. that the sciences and perfections of the angels are susceptible of increase—but not, the sages said, in their upper echelons, adducing to that effect the saying of Allah Most High, *And there is none of us but has a known station* (al-Ṣāffāt 37:164);

8. that Adam is better than those angels[1107] because he is more knowledgeable than them—and the more knowledgeable is superior, since Allah Most High said, *say: Are they equal, those who know and those who do not know?* (al-Zumar 39:9);

9. and that Allah Most High knows of things before they come into being.[1108]

[1107] Al-Rāzī in *al-Arbaʿīn fī Uṣūl al-Dīn*, ed. Aḥmad Ḥijāzī al-Saqqā, 2 vols. (Cairo: Maktabat al-Kulliyyāt al-Azhariyya, 1986) 2:177 *Masʾala* 33 attributes to Sunnis and Shiʿis the position that prophets are superior to angels, while "the philosophers and Muʿtazila said the heavenly angels are superior to human beings and it was the preference of al-Bāqillānī and al-Ḥalīmī among our [Ashʿarī] colleagues," all excepting the Prophet Muḥammad—upon him blessings and peace—who is superior to all creation without exception by consensus, cf. our article "The Prophetic Title *Best of Creation*" at http://www.livingislam.org/n/bc_e.html. Also see notes 1118, 1121 and 1126.

[1108] "As proved by His saying, *I am setting on earth a successor… Verily I know what you do not know* whereby He told of the creation and successorship of Adam before

﴿ وَإِذْ قُلْنَا لِلْمَلَٰٓئِكَةِ ٱسْجُدُواْ لِأٓدَمَ ﴾: لمَّا أَنْبَأَهُمْ بِأَسْمَائِهِمْ وَعَلَّمَهُمْ مَا لَمْ يَعْلَمُوا، أَمَرَهُمْ بِالسُّجُودِ لَهُ، اِعْتِرَافاً بِفَضْلِهِ، وَأَدَاءً لِحَقِّهِ، وَاعْتِذَاراً عَمَّا قَالُوا فِيهِ. وَقِيلَ: أَمَرَهُمْ بِهِ قَبْلَ أَنْ يُسَوِّيَ خَلْقَهُ، لِقَوْلِهِ تَعَالَى: ﴿ فَإِذَا سَوَّيْتُهُۥ وَنَفَخْتُ فِيهِ مِن رُّوحِى فَقَعُواْ لَهُۥ سَٰجِدِينَ ﴿٧٢﴾ ﴾ [ص]، اِمْتِحَاناً لَهُمْ وَإِظْهَاراً لِفَضْلِهِ.

[The angels' prostration to Adam]

[2:34] **wa-idh qulnā lil-malāʾikati sjudū li-Ādama** ⁽*and behold! We said to the angels: Prostrate to Adam*⁾: After he informed them of their names and taught them what they did not know, He ordered them to prostrate themselves to him in acknowledgment of his merit, in fulfillment of his right and in apology for what they had said about him. It is also said He ordered them to do so before He finished fashioning him—in light of His saying *and once I have fashioned him and breathed into him of My spirit, fall before him prostrate* (Ṣād 38:72)—as a test for them and to reveal his merit.

those events; then He told of the encompassment of His knowledge to everything which they did not know, including Adam's states and preferability over them due to his knowledge of the names together with their incapacity to know them [first], which necessarily means that He knew of Adam and his states before they came into being. Moreover His pre-existent knowledge does not update itself, nor is it changed by the updating of informations and their change; rather, the changes are in the appurtenances and the attributions (*al-taʿalluqāt wal-iḍāfāt*). Hishām b. al-Ḥakam claimed that Allah Most High did not know the particulars of events before their actual occurrence, whereupon He finds out about them only then, and that what He knows from pre-existence is only universal modalities and realities." (Z 1:255) Angels do not know the future (cf. al-Naml 27:65; al-Jinn 72:26-27), however, according to the majority of scholars they are aware of the innermost thoughts of human beings on the basis of the *ḥadīth qudsī* "When My slave wants to do an evil deed, do not record it against him until he does it, etc." (al-Bukhārī, *Ṣaḥīḥ, Tawḥīd, qawl Allāh yurīdūna an yubaddilū kalām Allāh*; Muslim, *Ṣaḥīḥ, Īmān, idhā hamma al-ʿabdu bi-ḥasana* cf. Sirāj al-Dīn, *al-Īmān bil-Malāʾika* p. 146-152).

وَالْعَاطِفُ عَطَفَ (أ) الظَّرْفَ عَلَى الظَّرْفِ السَّابِقِ إِنْ نَصَبْتَهُ بِمُضْمَرٍ؛ وَإِلَّا، عَطَفَهُ بِمَا يُقَدَّرُ عَامِلاً فِيهِ عَلَى الْجُمْلَةِ الْمُتَقَدِّمَةِ، (ب) بَلِ الْقِصَّةَ بِأَسْرِهَا عَلَى الْقِصَّةِ الْأُخْرَى؛ وَهِيَ نِعْمَةٌ رَابِعَةٌ عَدَّهَا عَلَيْهِمْ.

وَ(السُّجُودُ) فِي الْأَصْلِ: تَذَلُّلٌ مَعَ تَطَامُنٍ ـ قَالَ الشَّاعِرُ: [الطويل]

.... * تَرَى الْأُكْمَ فِيهَا سُجَّداً لِلْحَوَافِرِ

The copulative conjunction adjoins

I. the temporal vessel [*idh*] (i) to the previous vessel if you put it in the accusative by virtue of an implied [verb]—(ii) otherwise it adjoins it to its subauded regent per the previous sentence[1109]—

II. or rather, the entire account[1110] to the other account,[1111]

Furthermore, it is a fourth favor which He enumerated for them.[1112]

Al-sujūd ⁽prostration⁾, originally, is self-abasement together with stillness. The poet said: ["The Long"]

You could see bluffs there bowing (sujjadan) to the hooves;[1113]

1109 "Namely *wa-idh qāla rabbuka* (al-Baqara 2:30); but because there is full disparity between the two sentences in their respective assertory and originative parts he disregarded it by saying 'rather, the story in its entirety...'" (Q)

1110 α, β, B, ε, F, R, T: القصة Ak: الجملة المقصة

1111 "That is, the adjunction of the account indicated by the saying of Allah Most High, *wa-idh qulnā lil-malā'ikati sjudū li-Ādama* (al-Baqara 2:34) until His saying *wa-kāna min al-kāfirīn* (2:34) or even until *ulā'ika aṣḥāb al-nār hum fīhā khālidūn* (2:39) to the account indicated by His saying *wa-idh qāla Rabbuka lil-malā'ikati* (2:30) until His saying *wa-mā kuntum taktumūn* (2:33) regardless of the congruity or lack thereof in assertory and originative parts." (Z)

1112 After (1) granting life, (2) all creation and (3) caliphate (al-Baqara 2:28-31).

1113 Spoken by the Companion Zayd al-Khayl ⁽Zayd of the horse⁾—whom the Prophet renamed Zayd al-Khayr ⁽Zayd of goodness⁾—b. Muhalhal b. Zayd al-Ṭā'ī in reference to mounted riders who had no difficulty climbing even the steepest rocky slopes, as if they were trampling them underfoot, cf. Ibn Qutayba, *Ta'wīl Mushkil al-Qur'ān*, ed.

وَقَالَ: [طويل]

.... ✻ وَقُلْنَ لَهُ أَسْجِدْ لِلَيلَى فَأَسْجَدَا

يَعْنِي الْبَعِيرَ إِذَا طَأْطَأَ رَأْسَهُ - وَفِي الشَّرْعِ: وَضْعُ الْجَبْهَةِ عَلَى قَصْدِ الْعِبَادَةِ.

وَالْمَأْمُورُ بِهِ: (I) إِمَّا المَعْنَى الشَّرْعِيُّ: فَالْمَسْجُودُ لَهُ بِالْحَقِيقَةِ هُوَ اللهُ تَعَالَى، وَجُعِلَ آدَمُ قِبْلَةً لِسُجُودِهِمْ تَفْخِيماً لِشَأْنِهِ، أَوْ سَبَباً لِوُجُوبِهِ؛ فَكَأَنَّهُ - تَعَالَى - لَمَّا خَلَقَهُ بِحَيْثُ يَكُونُ ....

and he said,[1114] ["The Long"]

And they told it: "Bow (asjid) for Laylā!" so it bowed,[1115]

meaning the camel when it stoops its head.

In the sacred law it is the lowering of the forehead to the intent of worship.

What was commanded is

I. either the legal sense, in which case the one being bowed to in reality is Allah Most High, but he made Adam the direction to be faced in their prostration to amplify his status, or as the conditioning factor for [the onset of] its obligatoriness.[1116]

[Adam as archetype of everything in existence]

It is as if, once Allah Most High created him to become ......

Sayyid Aḥmad Ṣaqr, 2nd ed. (Cairo: Maktabat Dār al-Turāth, 1393/1973) p. 417 and Ṭabarī, *Tafsīr* (al-Baqara 2:58).

1114 All mss. and eds.: وقال AQ, H, K, MM: وقال آخر interpolation (gloss).

1115 Spoken by a Bedouin from Banū Asad in reference to maidservants telling Laylā's camel to kneel down so she could mount it, cf. al-Jawharī, *Ṣiḥāḥ* and al-Azharī, *Tahdhīb al-Lugha* (both under *s-j-d*).

1116 "The way the onset of the time for prayer was made the conditioning factor for the obligatoriness of prayer and the way the House was made the conditioning factor for the obligatoriness of pilgrimage." (Kh)

(أ) أُنْمُوذَجاً لِلْمُبْدَعَاتِ كُلِّهَا بَلِ الْمَوْجُودَاتِ بِأَسْرِهَا، (ب) وَنُسْخَةً لِمَا فِي الْعَالَمِ الرُّوحَانِي وَالْجُسْمَانِي، (ج) وَذَرِيعَةً لِلْمَلَائِكَةِ إِلَى اسْتِيفَاءِ مَا قُدِّرَ لَهُمْ مِنَ الْكَمَالَاتِ، (د) وَوُصْلَةً إِلَى ظُهُورِ مَا تَبَايَنُوا فِيهِ مِنَ الْمَرَاتِبِ وَالدَّرَجَاتِ: أَمَرَهُمْ بِالسُّجُودِ تَذَلُّلاً لِمَا رَأَوْا فِيهِ مِنْ عَظِيمِ قُدْرَتِهِ وَبَاهِرِ آيَاتِهِ، وَشُكْراً لِمَا أَنْعَمَ عَلَيْهِمْ بِوَاسِطَتِهِ. فَاللَّامُ فِيهِ ....

(i) an archetype[1117] for all *ex nihilo* designs—or even for existents in their entirety;[1118] (ii) an original pattern for all that is in the spiritual and corporeal worlds; (iii) an avenue for angels to obtain their allotted perfections;[1119] (iv) and a link to the manifestation of the disparity between all their [respective] ranks and levels:

He ordered them to prostrate out of humbleness before what they saw in him of the immensity of His power and the magnificence of His signs, and out of gratitude for the favors He lavished on them by means of him. So the *lām* ⁽to⁾ in it is ....

[1117] All mss. and eds.: انموذجا AQ, C, H, K, L, MM: نموذجا (both are lexically correct).

[1118] "The sense of upward gradation is that he is also an archetype for the Attributes of Allah Most High such as His life, knowledge and power, although an incomplete one. وجه الترقي هو نموذج أيضاً لصفاته تعالى كحياته وعلمه وقدرته مع كونه ناقصاً It does not harm that His attributes are in reality different from ours. Still, in truth it would have been more appropriate to leave out that gradation—hence he did not evoke it again under Sūrat al-Dhāriyāt." (Q 3:165) See note 305 above. "We say: when He *taught him the names—all of them* in the sense we have shown previously [f°100], to the point he could see only the exalted Lord and could no longer see himself, and he became in his entirety the exalted Lord (*wa-ṣāra bi-kulliyyatihi al-rabba taʿālā*!!), the angels were ordered to prostrate to him as a prostration to Allah." (Iṣ f°102a)

[1119] "On the basis of what was already mentioned, that the sciences and perfections of the angels are susceptible of increase—even if they belong to the upper echelons, contrary to the position of the Muslim philosophers." (Q)

كَاللَّامِ فِي قَوْلِ حَسَّانَ رَضِيَ اللهُ تَعَالَى عَنْهُ: [البسيط]

أَلَيْسَ أَوَّلَ مَنْ صَلَّى لِقِبْلَتِكُمْ ❋ وَأَعْرَفَ النَّاسِ بِالْقُرْآنِ وَالسُّنَنِ

أَوْ فِي قَوْلِهِ تَعَالَى: ﴿أَقِمِ ٱلصَّلَوٰةَ لِدُلُوكِ ٱلشَّمْسِ﴾ [الإسراء ٧٨].

(II) وَإِمَّا الْمَعْنَى اللُّغَوِيُّ، وَهُوَ التَّوَاضُعُ لِآدَمَ تَحِيَّةً وَتَعْظِيماً لَهُ، كَسُجُودِ إِخْوَةِ يُوسُفَ لَهُ، أَوِ التَّذَلُّلُ وَالْإِنْقِيَادُ بِالسَّعْيِ فِي تَحْصِيلِ مَا يَنُوطُ بِهِ .....

like the one in Ḥassān's saying—Allah Most High be well-pleased with him: ["The Outspread"]

Is he not the first who prayed ***toward*** *your qibla (li-qiblatikum),*
and best versed of people in the Qur'an and Prophetic ways?[1120]

or in the saying of Allah Most High, *Establish prayer* ***at*** *the going down (li-dulūk) of the sun* (al-Isrā' 17:78).

II. Or [what was commanded in the verse] was the lexical sense, namely

(i) to humble themselves to Adam as a greeting and magnification for him the way Yūsuf's brothers prostrated to him;

(ii) or self-abasement and compliance in doing everything necessary to obtain that on which their livelihood ....

[1120] Narrated "from one of the scions of Abū Lahab b. 'Abd al-Muṭṭalib" by al-Zubayr b. Bakkār in *al-Akhbār al-Muwaffaqiyyāt*, ed. Sāmī Makkī al-'Ānī, 2nd ed. (Beirut: 'Ālam al-Kutub, 1416/1996) p. 465 §380, namely al-Faḍl b. 'Abbās b. 'Utba b. Abī Lahab, cf. al-Burrī, *al-Jawhara fī Nasab al-Nabī wa-Aṣḥābihi al-'Ashara*, ed. Muḥammad al-Tūnjī (Riyadh: Dār al-Rifā'ī, 1403/1983) 2:276 while others attribute it to Khuzayma b. Thābit Dhūl-shahādatayn cf. Mughulṭāy, *Ikmāl Tahdhīb al-Kamāl*, ed. Usāma Ibrāhīm and 'Ādil Muḥammad, 12 vols. (Cairo: al-Fārūq al-Ḥadītha lil-Ṭibā'a wal-Nashr, 1422 /2001) 9:339-340; or the Mu'tazili Abū 'Ubayd Allāh al-Marzubānī cf. al-Sakhāwī, *Fatḥ al-Mughīth bi-Sharḥ Alfiyyat al-Ḥadīth*, ed. 'Alī Ḥusayn 'Alī, 4 vols. (Cairo: Maktabat al-Sunna, 1424/2003) 4:124 *tafḍīl al-ṣaḥābati ba'ḍahum 'alā ba'ḍ*. Al-Rāzī in his *Tafsīr* said it was spoken about 'Alī b. Abī Ṭālib in reaction to the election of Abū Bakr al-Ṣiddīq to the caliphate, a probable anachronism.

مَعَاشُهُمْ وَيَتِمُّ بِهِ كَمَالُهُمْ.

وَالْكَلَامُ فِي أَنَّ الْمَأْمُورِينَ بِالسُّجُودِ الْمَلَائِكَةُ كُلُّهُمْ، أَوْ طَائِفَةٌ مِنْهُمْ: مَا سَبَقَ.

﴿فَسَجَدُوٓاْ إِلَّآ إِبۡلِيسَ أَبَىٰ وَٱسۡتَكۡبَرَ﴾: اِمْتَنَعَ عَمَّا أُمِرَ بِهِ، اِسْتِكْبَاراً مِنْ أَنْ يَتَّخِذَهُ وُصْلَةً فِي عِبَادَةِ رَبِّهِ، أَوْ يُعَظِّمَهُ وَيَتَلَقَّاهُ بِالتَّحِيَّةِ، أَوْ يَخْدُمَهُ وَيَسْعَى

depends and by which their perfection becomes complete.

Whether those that were commanded to prostrate are the angels in their entirety or some of them is as [discussed] before.[1121]

[Iblīs's refusal to use Adam as a means to Allah]

fa-sajadū illā Iblīsa abā wa-stakbara ⁽*so they prostrated, except Iblīs: he refused and was arrogant*⁾: he declined doing what he had been ordered, too arrogant

(i) to take him as a link in the worship of his Nurturer;[1122]

(ii) to magnify him and welcome him with greetings;[1123]

(iii) or to serve him and do everything necessary wherein lie his

[1121] "Namely, his words 'Those that are referred to are the angels in their entirety due to the terms being general and the absence of a specifier; but some said the earthly angels, and some said Iblīs and those that were with him, fighting the jinns.' So the definite article in *lil-malā'ikati* here is for those made previously known there. It is as if He said, 'And when We said to those same angels to whom it had already been said *Verily I am setting on earth a successor*: Prostrate to Adam.' Therefore, those that were meant over there—whether generally or specifically—are those also meant right here. Most of the exegetes consider that all of the angels were ordered to prostrate to Adam, including the angels brought near, especially since He emphasized it, saying *kulluhum ajma'ūn* ⁽one and all, the whole lot⁾ (al-Ḥijr 15:30; Ṣād 38:73)." (Z 1:258)

[1122] "If the basis is that the sense of the command is the legal explanation of prostration i.e. Adam is either the *qibla* or the conditioning factor for worship of Allah." (Z)

[1123] "If the basis is that the sense of the command is the lexical explanations of prostration whether the first possibility—humbleness before Adam, greeting and magnification—or the second." (Z)

فِيمَا فِيهِ خَيْرُهُ وَصَلَاحُهُ. وَ(الْإِبَاءُ): اِمْتِنَاعٌ بِاخْتِيَارٍ. وَ(التَّكَبُّرُ): أَنْ يَرَى الرَّجُلُ نَفْسَهُ أَكْبَرَ مِنْ غَيْرِهِ. وَ(الْاِسْتِكْبَارُ): طَلَبُ ذٰلِكَ بِالتَّشَبُّعِ.

﴿وَكَانَ مِنَ ٱلْكَـٰفِرِينَ﴾ أَيْ فِي عِلْمِ اللهِ تَعَالَى؛ أَوْ صَارَ مِنْهُمْ بِاسْتِقْبَاحِهِ أَمْرَ اللهِ تَعَالَى إِيَّاهُ بِالسُّجُودِ لِآدَمَ اعْتِقَاداً بِأَنَّهُ أَفْضَلُ مِنْهُ - وَالْأَفْضَلُ لَا يَحْسُنُ أَنْ يُؤْمَرَ بِالتَّخَضُّعِ لِلْمَفْضُولِ وَالتَّوَسُّلِ بِهِ - كَمَا أَشْعَرَ بِهِ قَوْلُهُ ﴿أَنَا۠ خَيْرٌ مِّنْهُ﴾ [الأعراف ١٢] جَوَاباً لِقَوْلِهِ: ﴿مَا مَنَعَكَ أَن تَسْجُدَ لِمَا خَلَقْتُ بِيَدَيَّ أَسْتَكْبَرْتَ أَمْ كُنتَ مِنَ ٱلْعَالِينَ﴾ [ص ٧٥]، ....

benefit and welfare.

Ibāʾ (refusal) is wilful non-compliance. *Takabbur* (pride) is to consider oneself greater than others while ***istikbār*** (arrogance) is to pursue the same through *tashabbu*ʿ (presumption).[1124]

wa-kāna mina-l-kāfirīna (*and he was of the unbelievers*), that is, in the knowledge of Allah Most High; or he became one of them by despising the command of Allah Most High for him to prostrate to Adam (in his firm belief that he was better than him — and the better is unfit to be ordered to submit to an inferior and seek him as an intermediary—as intimated by his saying *I am better than him* (al-Aʿrāf 7:12) in answer to His saying *what prevented you from prostrating to what I created with My own hands? Are you self-puffed with pride or are you of the lofty ones?*

[1124] *Tashabbu*ʿ is literally feigned satiety. The *Ṣiḥāḥ* defines it as "adorning oneself with more than one actually has, whereby one pretends plentifulness and adorns oneself falsely." "*Pride* is unreasonable or inordinate self-esteem. *Arrogance* implies taking much upon ourselves and is pride attended with insolence and contempt.... By *presumption* is understood a blind and adventurous confidence.... *Pride* makes us value ourselves; *arrogance*, despise others... *Presumption* flatters us with having a vain power" John Trusler, *The difference, between words, esteemed synonymous: in the English language*, 2 vols. (London: printed, for J. Dodsley, 1766) 1:186 §177.

لَا بِتَرْكِ الْوَاجِبِ وَحْدَهُ.

وَالْآيَةُ تَدُلُّ عَلَى (١) أَنَّ آدَمَ عَلَيْهِ السَّلَامُ أَفْضَلُ مِنَ الْمَلَائِكَةِ الْمَأْمُورِينَ بِالسُّجُودِ لَهُ وَلَوْ مِنْ وَجْهٍ؛ (٢) وَأَنَّ إِبْلِيسَ كَانَ مِنَ الْمَلَائِكَةِ وَإِلَّا لَمْ يَتَنَاوَلْهُ أَمْرُهُمْ وَلَمْ يَصِحَّ اسْتِثْنَاؤُهُ مِنْهُمْ. وَلَا يَرِدُ عَلَى ذٰلِكَ قَوْلُهُ ـ سُبْحَانَهُ وَتَعَالَى ـ

(Ṣād 38:75)) and not only by not complying with a categorical command.[1125]

[Iblīs was originally an angel per the vast majority]

The verse indicates that

1. Adam (upon him peace) is superior to the angels that were ordered to prostrate to him—albeit in a particular sense[1126]—

2. and Iblīs was one of the angels,[1127] otherwise he would not have been included in the order given to them, nor would it have been valid to except him from them.[1128] This is not contradicted by the saying of Allah Most High, ...

[1125] "For the latter does not spell unbelief for *Ahl al-Sunna*, as mere lack of performance of a categorical obligation—without denial or legitimation—does not jeopardize belief in their view." (Q)

[1126] "As it does not automatically mean superiority in every sense, nor do we claim that; for they might be superior in the fact that they have no corporeal attachments and in their moral nearness to Allah Most High. It in this sense we understand the author's statement under Sūrat al-Naba' [concerning angels]: 'For these are those that are the most preferable of creatures and the nearest to Allah Most High.'" (Q) "For Adam is better than them in his knowledge of the names and his aptitude through the qualities and special perfections embedded in his complex form of which angels fall short; and they are superior to him in what we understand of their complete immersion in the worship of Allah, infallibility, subtle form and immateriality." Ibn al-Tamjīd's *Ḥāshiya* in the margins of Q (3:170).

[1127] Ibn ʿAbbās said, "His name was ʿAzāzīl [or ʿAzzāzīl] and he was among the nobility of the angels; he possessed four wings. After that he despaired (*ablasa*)... There was a sub-group or tribe of the angels called *al-jinn*.... they were created from the fire of samum among the angels, Iblīs being one of them, and his name was al-Ḥārith." Ibn Abī Ḥātim, *Tafsīr* (1:84 §361); al-Ṭabarī, *Tafsīr* (1:486-488, also from Ibn Masʿūd

﴿إِلَّآ إِبۡلِيسَ كَانَ مِنَ ٱلۡجِنِّ﴾ [الكهف ٥٠]، لِجَوَازِ أَنْ يُقَالَ: إِنَّهُ كَانَ مِنَ الْجِنِّ فِعْلاً وَمِنَ الْمَلَائِكَةِ نَوْعاً، وَلِأَنَّ ابْنَ عَبَّاسٍ - رَضِيَ اللهُ تَعَالَى عَنْهُمَا - رَوَى أَنَّ مِنَ الْمَلَائِكَةِ ....

except Iblīs—he was of the jinn (al-Kahf 18:50), because it is possible to say he was of the jinn behaviorally and of the angels generically;[1129] and because Ibn 'Abbās—Allah Most High be well-pleased with him and his father—related that "Among the angels

and others; 1:535-539); Abū al-Shaykh, *al-'Aẓama* (5:1676-1677 §1118-1119); al-Qushayrī, *Taysīr* (pp. 532-534); Ibn al-Anbārī, *Kitāb al-Aḍdād*, ed. Muḥammad Abū al-Faḍl Ibrāhīm (Sidon: al-Maktabat al-'Aṣriyya, 1407/1987) p. 336. "Iblīs was one of the angels according to the vast majority including Ibn 'Abbās, Ibn Mas'ūd, Ibn Jurayj, Ibn al-Musayyib, Qatāda and others; and it is the preferred position of Shaykh Abū al-Ḥasan [al-Ash'arī]. Al-Ṭabarī considered it the prevalent one and it is the apparent meaning of the verse. Ibn 'Abbās said: 'His name was 'Azāzīl, etc.'" al-Qurṭubī, *al-Jāmi' li-Aḥkām al-Qur'ān wal-Mubayyin li-mā Taḍammanahu min al-Sunna wa-Āy al-Furqān*, ed. 'Abd Allāh al-Turkī et al., 24 vols. (Beirut: Mu'assasat al-Risāla, 1427/ 2006) 1:440 (al-Baqara 2:34). According to this explanation the verse that states that *he was of the jinn* (al-Kahf 18:50) means that he was not "one of" but "among" the jinn, whom he was teaching at the time, or that he was an angel whose nature Allah changed into that of a jinn as narrated from Ibn 'Abbās and al-Suddī by Abū al-Shaykh in *al-'Aẓama* (5:1676-1677 §1119-1120; 5:1682 §1132 cf. J: al-Kahf 18:50). Taking the opposite position, Ibn Kathīr in his *Tafsīr* adduced Ṭabarī's report from al-Ḥasan al-Baṣrī that "Iblīs was not in the least an angel" since the latter himself says he was created from fire (al-A'rāf 7:12, Ṣād 38:76), while 'Abd al-Qāhir al-Baghdādī in *Uṣūl al-Dīn* (pp. 296-297) considered the exceptive particle *illā* in the verse to denote what the grammarians call a "disconnected exception" (*istithnā' munqaṭi'*), i.e. that Iblīs was merely with the angels at the time they were commanded to prostrate and thus was included in the command despite his not being one of their species.

1128 "Because the ground rule (*al-aṣl*) in exceptives is connectiveness—as that is its what it means literally—[i.e. the excepted is a subset, such as 'all the bakers stood, save one baker'] whereas disconnectedness [i.e. the excepted is extraneous, such as 'all the bakers stood, save one blacksmith'] is the allegorical sense." (Q) "Disconnected exceptions, however widespread and famous in Arabic discourse, nevertheless contravene the ground rule and so they do not take place in chaste speech." (Z)

1129 Cf. Ibn al-Anbārī, *Aḍdād* (pp. 337-338).

ضَرْباً يَتَوَالَدُونَ، يُقَالُ لَهُمُ الْجِنُّ؛ وَمِنْهُمْ إِبْلِيسُ؛ وَلِمَنْ زَعَمَ أَنَّهُ لَمْ يَكُنْ مِنَ الْمَلَائِكَةِ أَنْ يَقُولَ: إِنَّهُ كَانَ جِنِّيّاً نَشَأَ بَيْنَ أَظْهُرِ الْمَلَائِكَةِ، وَكَانَ مَغْمُوراً بِالْأُلُوفِ مِنْهُمْ، فَغُلِّبُوا عَلَيْهِ؛ أَوِ الْجِنُّ كَانُوا أَيْضاً مَأْمُورِينَ مَعَ الْمَلَائِكَةِ، لٰكِنَّهُ اسْتُغْنِيَ بِذِكْرِ الْمَلَائِكَةِ عَنْ ذِكْرِهِمْ: فَإِنَّهُ إِذَا عُلِمَ أَنَّ الْأَكَابِرَ مَأْمُورُونَ بِالتَّذَلُّلِ لِأَحَدٍ وَالتَّوَسُّلِ بِهِ، عُلِمَ أَنَّ الْأَصَاغِرَ أَيْضاً مَأْمُورُونَ بِهِ. ....

are a kind that procreate: they are called *al-jinn*, and among them is Iblīs."[1130]

Those who claimed that he was not an angel[1131] might say

(i) that he was a jinni who grew up among angels, one in a sea of thousands of them, so they were made to prevail over him [in being the only species cited];[1132]

(ii) or that the jinn were also commanded, together with the angels, however, He contented Himself with their mention and dispensed with theirs. For, once it is understood that seniors are commanded to humiliate themselves before someone and use him as an intermediary, it is understood that juniors, likewise, are commanded the same;

[1130] This report is nowhere to be found (S) in such a form, but the report ""Among the angels are a kind that are called *al-jinn*, and among them is Iblīs" is established: see notes 1065, 1103 and 1127.

[1131] "This is the position of most theologians (*mutakallimīn*), especially the Muʿtazilis among them, and is narrated from Ibn ʿAbbās, Ibn Zayd, al-Ḥasan, Qatāda and Abu Bakr al-Aṣamm. They said he is the primogenitor of the jinn as Adam is the primogenitor of human beings." (Z) Cf. Abū al-Shaykh, *al-ʿAẓama* (5:1645 §1088)

[1132] "It is narrated [from Ibn Masʿūd and Shahr b. Ḥawshab] that Iblīs was among the jinn who dwelt the earth before Adam and whom the angels fought, at which time they took him prisoner in his childhood, after which he was worshipping with them for eons; so he became of the angels virtually (*ḥukman*) per the hadith 'The client is part of the tribe' (*inna mawlā al-qawmi minhum*) even though he was a jinn by lineage." (Z 1:260, cf. al-Qushayrī, *Taysīr* p. 519; al-Qurṭubī, al-Baqara 2:34)

وَالضَّمِيرُ فِي ﴿فَسَجَدُوٓاْ﴾ رَاجِعٌ إِلَى الْقَبِيلَيْنِ، كَأَنَّهُ قَالَ: فَسَجَدَ الْمَأْمُورُونَ بِالسُّجُودِ إِلَّا إِبْلِيسَ. (٣) وَأَنَّ مِنَ الْمَلَائِكَةِ مَنْ لَيْسَ بِمَعْصُومٍ، وَإِنْ كَانَ الْغَالِبُ فِيهِمُ الْعِصْمَةُ؛ كَمَا أَنَّ مِنَ الْإِنْسِ مَعْصُومِينَ، وَالْغَالِبُ فِيهِمْ عَدَمُ الْعِصْمَةِ. وَلَعَلَّ ضَرْباً مِنَ الْمَلَائِكَةِ لَا يُخَالِفُ الشَّيَاطِينَ بِالذَّاتِ، وَإِنَّمَا يُخَالِفُهُمْ بِالْعَوَارِضِ وَالصِّفَاتِ، ....

The personal pronoun in ***fa-sajadū*** ⟨so they prostrated⟩ refers back to the two parties, as if He had said, "so those who were ordered to prostrate did so, except Iblīs."

[Certain angels are not infallible; *jinn* meaning "invisible"]

3. [The verse also shows that] certain angels are not infallible[1133] even if infallibility is prevalent among them—just as certain human beings are infallible but fallibility is prevalent among them. There might be a type of angels that are no different from devils in their essence but differ from them only in accidents and attrib-

[1133] "Hence the saying of Allah Most High about the angels, *honored slaves* (al-Anbiyā' 21:26) *who do not disobey Allah in what He ordered them and they do what they were ordered* (al-Taḥrīm 66:6) is an exposition of the state of their majority as the author goes on to expound." (Z) "Abū al-Mu'īn al-Nasafī was quoted as saying in his *'Aqīda*: 'As for the angels, anyone found to commit unbelief becomes a dweller of hellfire such as Iblīs; and anyone found to commit a sin but not unbelief incurs retribution, as proved by the story of Hārūt and Mārūt.' As you know their story originates with the Jews." (Q 3:174) The cited text is not found in al-Nasafī's *Tabṣirat al-Adilla*. As for *the two angels Hārūt and Mārūt* (al-Baqara 2:102), the account of their being fallen angels suggests mass transmission (*tawātur*) according to Ibn Ḥajar, *al-Qawl al-Musaddad fīl-Dhabb 'an Musnad al-Imām Aḥmad*, ed. 'Abd Allāh Darwīsh (Damascus and Beirut: al-Yamāma lil-Ṭibā'a wal-Nashr wal-Tawzī', 1405/1985) pp. 89-90 and al-Suyūṭī in *al-Zahr al-Mutanāthir*, *al-Durr al-Manthūr*, the *Ḥabā'ik* and *Manāhil al-Ṣafā* among others and is adopted by many commentaries. Nevertheless al-Qurṭubī and Ibn Kathīr consider them jinns while Ṭabarī avers that *the two angels* mentioned in the story were "Jibrīl and Mīkā'īl or some other two angels," Hārūt and Mārūt being two men from Babel who were called angels because of their righteousness.

كَالْبَرَرَةِ وَالْفَسَقَةِ مِنَ الْإِنْسِ؛ وَالْجِنُّ يَشْمُلُهُمَا؛ وَكَانَ إِبْلِيسُ مِنْ هٰذَا

الصِّنْفِ، كَمَا قَالَهُ ابْنُ عَبَّاسٍ. ....

utes[1134]—like the virtuous and wicked among humans—and the jinn comprise both [aspects],[1135] Iblīs being of this type, as stated by Ibn ʿAbbās ....

[1134] "He is reconciling between his words that Iblīs was an angel who disobeyed and committed unbelief and thus that not all angels are invariably infallible but only their majority, and the words of the Imam [al-Rāzī] who had said [in *Mafātīḥ al-Ghayb* 1:260 under al-Baqara 2:30], 'the massive majority of the religious scholars concur on the infallibility of all the angels from all sins, but some of the *Ḥashwiyya* ⟨vulgar anthropomorphists⟩ dissent' with the possibility that there are among angels a type that is in essence and in reality one with the devils but differ with their nature in accidents and external traits." (Z 1:260) "In *al-Taysīr* [*fī 'Ilm al-Tafsīr* by Najm al-Dīn ʿUmar b. Aḥmad al-Nasafī]: 'The description of the angels as *not disobeying* (al-Taḥrīm 66:6) and *not acting arrogant* (al-Anbiyā' 21:18) indicates that sin is conceivable for them. Were it not, they would not have been complimented with it. However, their obedience is their nature while their disobedience is a burden, while human beings' obedience is a burden and their hankering after lust is their nature. Nor is the commission of sins by angels completely disclaimable in light of the story of Hārūt and Mārūt.'" (Kh 2:134) "It would have behooved the author to steer clear from such discourse and relinquish it once and for all; but such is the fruit of wading into the philosophical sciences instead of imbuing oneself with hadiths and transmitted reports! What the latter indicate is that Iblīs is the primogenitor of the jinn just as Adam is that of human beings; that he was never for a moment an angel; and that the sound explanation of the exceptive is predominance since he was among them, or disconnection." (S 2:199) It can be seen that the assertion that "hadiths and transmitted reports indicate that Iblīs was never for a moment an angel" is patently incorrect. Also see note 1137.

[1135] "*Al-jinn* in the sense of the subtle body that is invisible to the eyes shares a common denominator with the two species of angels and devils." (Z) "Among what is explained, in the Book of Allah Most Glorious, with two mutually opposed explanations, is His saying, *except Iblīs—he was of the jinn* (al-Kahf 18:50). One says the jinn are the angels, they were named *jinn* because they hide themselves from people.... Ibn Isḥāq said *al-jinn* is whatever is invisible to people... Also showing that the angels are called *jinn* is al-Aʿshā's saying in mention of Sulaymān b. Dāwūd—upon both of them peace: *and He subjected from the jinns among angels (min jinni al-malā'iki) nine // who stood at his beck and call working without pay.*" Al-Anbārī, *Aḍdād* (pp. 334-335).

فَلِذٰلِكَ صَحَّ عَلَيْهِ التَّغَيُّرُ عَنْ حَالِهِ وَالْهُبُوطُ مِنْ مَحَلِّهِ، كَمَا أَشَارَ إِلَيْهِ بِقَوْلِهِ عَزَّ وَجَلَّ ﴿إِلَّآ إِبْلِيسَ كَانَ مِنَ ٱلْجِنِّ فَفَسَقَ عَنْ أَمْرِ رَبِّهِۦٓ﴾ [الكهف ٥٠].

لَا يُقَالُ: كَيْفَ يَصِحُّ ذٰلِكَ وَالْمَلَائِكَةُ خُلِقَتْ مِنْ نُورٍ وَالْجِنُّ مِنْ نَارٍ، لِمَا رَوَتْ عَائِشَةُ رَضِيَ اللهُ عَنْهَا أَنَّهُ ـ عَلَيْهِ الصَّلَاةُ وَالسَّلَامُ ـ قَالَ: خُلِقَتِ الْمَلَائِكَةُ مِنَ النُّورِ وَخُلِقَ الْجِنُّ مِنْ مَّارِجٍ مِنْ نَارٍ؟ لِأَنَّهُ كَالتَّمْثِيلِ لِمَا ذَكَرْتُ.

Hence it would be valid, in his case, [to speak of] a change in his state and a plummeting from his spot, as Allah Most High alluded when He said *except Iblīs—he was of the jinn, so he breached his Nurturer's command* (al-Kahf 18:50).

Let it not be said: "How could that be valid when the angels were created from light and the jinn from fire, since 'Ā'isha—Allah be well-pleased with her—related that the Prophet—upon him blessings and peace—said,

> The angels were created from light and the jinn were created from a blaze of fire?"[1136]

as that is precisely like a representation of what I discussed.[1137]

"The upshot is that jinn and angel are respectively general or specific for the same aspect. A jinn is [generically] what has aptitude for good and evil; if he does only good he is an angel and if he does only evil he is a devil; an angel is the one who does good regardless whether he is essentially good—without aptitude for evil whatsoever such as the *Karūbiyyūn* ('cherubim')—or accidentally good with essential aptitude for evil. Thus it is valid to count Iblīs among the angels, the jinn, and the devils without contrivance (*takalluf*) nor figurative interpretation (*ta'wīl*)." (Sk p. 307)

[1136] Narrated by Muslim, *Ṣaḥīḥ* (*al-Zuhd wal-Raqā'iq, bāb fī aḥādīth mutafarriqa*) and others, all with the continuation, "and Adam was created from what was described to you."

[1137] "If the author and his kind could construe every single hadith as 'a representation' they would, and this is inappropriate! Would that I knew, after he construed what was mentioned about the creation of angels and jinn as 'a representation,' what he would do with the rest of the hadith? Would he also construe what was mentioned of Adam's

فَإِنَّ الْمُرَادَ بِالنُّورِ: الْجَوْهَرُ الْمُضِيءُ؛ وَالنَّارُ كَذٰلِكَ، غَيْرَ أَنَّ ضَوْءَهَا مُكَدَّرٌ، مَغْمُورٌ بِالدُّخَانِ، مَحْذُورٌ عَنْهُ بِسَبَبِ مَا يَصْحَبُهُ مِنْ فَرْطِ الْحَرَارَةِ وَالْإِحْرَاقِ. فَإِذَا صَارَتْ مُهَذَّبَةً مُصَفَّاةً، كَانَتْ مَحْضَ نُورٍ، وَمَتَى نَكَصَتْ عَادَتِ الْحَالَةُ الْأُولَى جَذَعَةً، وَلَا تَزَالُ تَتَزَايَدُ حَتَّى يَنْطَفِئَ نُورُهَا وَيَبْقَى الدُّخَانُ الصِّرْفُ. ....

For what is meant by light is the substance that illuminates; and fire does likewise—except that its luminescence is tainted, obscured by smoke, and fearsome due to the extreme heat and combustion that accompany it. So, when it is under control and purified it becomes sheer light; and when it reverts, the former condition is rejuvenated and keeps intensifying until its light goes out and only absolute smoke remains.

creation as a representation? and that he was not really created from soil as per the verse's manifest locution? This is a diversion of the texts from their manifest locutions so let us beware of that path. For the Muʿtazila chiefly depend on it and are the first [sect] that did so in abundance, to the point they denied the questioning of Munkar and Nakīr, the punishment of the grave, the Balance, the Bridge, the Basin, intercession and the beast of the earth, construing all the hadiths to that effect as representations. Then they went and applied that to hadiths whose figurative interpretation does not impugn doctrine, such as the hadith of the fire's complaint and its breathing twice every year, the complaint of the wombs and others, and they were followed in that by all those who drank deep from the philosophical and rational disciplines without becoming accomplished in hadith, after which they applied this figurative interpretation to every verse and hadith without regard to externalities, and this is inadequate.... Those who do that and remove those hadiths from their exernal meanings, deem that such betokens verification and discernment and that taking external wordings goes against verification and discernment." (S 2:199-201) It can be replied that (i) "representation" is not mutually exclusive with the literal sense (cf. Q 3:176); (ii) although the Qadi is not a hadith expert, yet his sense of the evidence is more thorough than S admits; and (iii) to relegate his integrative approach to the Muʿtazilis' partial and *taʿṭīlī* ⟨divestive⟩ approach is rash. This is one of several unfair over-generalizations and misinterpretations found in *Nawāhid al-Abkār*. And Allah knows best.

فَهٰذَا أَشْبَهُ بِالصَّوَابِ وَأَوْفَقُ لِلْجَمْعِ بَيْنَ النُّصُوصِ. وَالْعِلْمُ عِنْدَ اللهِ سُبْحَانَهُ وَتَعَالَى.

وَمِنْ فَوَائِدِ الْآيَةِ: (أ) اِسْتِقْبَاحُ الْاِسْتِكْبَارِ؛ (ب) وَأَنَّهُ قَدْ يُفْضِي بِصَاحِبِهِ إِلَى الْكُفْرِ؛ (ج) وَالْحَثُّ عَلَى الْاِئْتِمَارِ لِأَمْرِهِ (د) وَتَرْكِ الْخَوْضِ فِي سِرِّهِ؛ (ه) وَأَنَّ الْأَمْرَ لِلْوُجُوبِ؛ (و) وَأَنَّ الَّذِي عَلِمَ اللهُ تَعَالَى مِنْ حَالِهِ أَنَّهُ يُتَوَفَّى عَلَى الْكُفْرِ: هُوَ الْكَافِرُ عَلَى الْحَقِيقَةِ، إِذِ الْعِبْرَةُ بِالْخَوَاتِيمِ، وَإِنْ كَانَ - بِحُكْمِ الْحَالِ - مُؤْمِناً. وَهُوَ (الْمُوَافَاةُ) الْمَنْسُوبَةُ إِلَى شَيْخِنَا أَبِي الْحَسَنِ الْأَشْعَرِيِّ، رَحِمَهُ اللهُ تَعَالَى.

Thus the latter seems like the most correct view and the best suited to make the texts consistent with each other; and knowledge is with Allah—may He be extolled and exalted![1138]

[Ashʿarīs define "the believer" as one who dies as a Muslim]

Among the benefits of this verse are (i) the condemnation of arrogance; (ii) the fact that the latter might lead one to unbelief; (iii) the exhortation to obey His order (iv) and refrain from probing its hidden aspects; (v) the fact that command constitutes obligatoriness; (vi) and that someone whom Allah Most High knows—right then—will eventually expire as an unbeliever: *that* is the true unbeliever; for what matters is the final moments,[1139] even if his status at that time is that of a believer. This is the "Ultimate Arrival" attributed to our teacher Abū al-Ḥasan al-

[1138] On the rigorous consistency of this view see the recapitulation in Z (1:261).

[1139] α, Ak, β, B, D, L, P, Q, S, Sk, T, U, Ul, Z: بالخواتيم AQ, C, F, H, I, K, Kh, MM, R: بالخواتم They are synonymous and equally correct but the hadith came in the former spelling: *innamā al-aʿmālu bil-khawātīm* ʿdeeds count only according to the last momentsʾ. Narrated from Sahl b. Saʿd by al-Bukhārī, *Ṣaḥīḥ* (*Qadar, bāb al-ʿamal bil-khawātīm*), also from Muʿāwiya, ʿĀʾisha and Ibn ʿUmar—Allah be well-pleased with them. (S)

﴿ وَقُلْنَا يَـٰٓـَٔادَمُ ٱسْكُنْ أَنتَ وَزَوْجُكَ ٱلْجَنَّةَ ﴾: (السُّكْنَى) مِنَ السُّكُونِ
لِأَنَّهَا اسْتِقْرَارٌ وَلَبْثٌ.

وَ﴿أَنتَ﴾ تَأْكِيدٌ؛ أَكَّدَ بِهِ الْمُسْتَكِنَّ لِيَصِحَّ الْعَطْفُ عَلَيْهِ. وَإِنَّمَا لَمْ يُخَاطِبْهُمَا
أَوَّلاً، تَنْبِيهاً عَلَى أَنَّهُ الْمَقْصُودُ بِالْحُكْمِ، وَالْمَعْطُوفُ عَلَيْهِ تَبَعٌ لَهُ.

وَ﴿ٱلْجَنَّةَ﴾ دَارُ الثَّوَابِ، لِأَنَّ اللَّامَ لِلْعَهْدِ، وَلَا مَعْهُودَ غَيْرُهَا.

Ashʿarī—may Allah Most High have mercy on him.[1140]

[2:35] **wa-qulnā yā Ādamu skun anta wa-zawjuka-l-jannata** ⸢*and We said: O Adam! inhabit the Garden—you and your wife—*⸣: ***al-suknā*** ⸢residence⸣ is from *sukūn* ⸢stillness⸣ because it consists in settlement and abidance.

[Husbands are liable primarily, ahead of wives]

anta ⸢you⸣ is an emphatic by which He emphasized the covert pronoun [in *uskun*] so that adjunction to it can be valid. The reason He did not address them as a pair at first is to draw attention to the fact that he is the intended party in the ruling, while his adjunct follows behind him.[1141]

[Paradise already exists and is beyond this world]

al-janna ⸢the Garden⸣ is the abode of reward,[1142] as the[definite article] *lām* is for previous knowledge—and there is no previously known garden other than it.

[1140] This is the Ashʿarī rationale for adding the dubitative "if Allah wills" to the affirmation "I am a believer" (*anā muʾminun in shāʾa Allāh*)—i.e. at the time of death, God willing—and the doctrinal differentiation between *islām* and *īmān*. See Kh (2:135); Z (1:262); "Ibn Ḥajar's Commentary on the Hadith of *Islām, Īmān, Iḥsān*" as translated in full in our *Sunna Notes III*; and Gimaret, *Doctrine* (pp. 479-483).

[1141] On this issue see further down, commentary on *fa-tāba ʿalayh* (al-Baqara 2:37).

[1142] "The author's statement 'abode of reward' dictates that there is legal tasking in the Garden, and the prominent position is the opposite, as detailed by Ibn Fūrak who

وَمَنْ زَعَمَ أَنَّهَا لَمْ تُخْلَقْ بَعْدُ قَالَ: إِنَّهُ بُسْتَانٌ كَانَ بِأَرْضِ فَلَسْطِينَ، أَوْ بَيْنَ فَارِسَ وَكِرْمَانَ، خَلَقَهُ اللهُ تَعَالَى امْتِحَاناً لِآدَمَ؛ وَحَمَلَ الْإِهْبَاطَ عَلَى الْاِنْتِقَالِ مِنْهُ إِلَى أَرْضِ الْهِنْدِ، كَمَا فِي قَوْلِهِ تَعَالَى: ﴿ٱهْبِطُواْ مِصْرًا﴾ [البقرة ٦١].

﴿وَكُلَا مِنْهَا رَغَدًا﴾: وَاسِعاً رَافِهاً، صِفَةُ مَصْدَرٍ مَحْذُوفٍ.

﴿حَيْثُ شِئْتُمَا﴾: أَيَّ مَكَانٍ مِنَ الْجَنَّةِ ....

Those who claimed that it had not been created yet[1143] said it was an orchard in the land of Palestine or somewhere between Fars and Kirman, which Allah Most High created as a test for Adam, and they construed *al-ihbāṭ* ⁽the casting down⁾ as a move thence to the land of India,[1144] as in the saying of Allah Most High, *alight (ihbiṭū) in a city* (al-Baqara 2:61).

wa-kulā minhā raghadan ⁽*and eat from it in plenty*⁾: in abundance, at leisure; an epithet for a suppressed infinitive noun.[1145]

ḥaythu shiʾtumā ⁽*wherever you both wish*⁾: wherever in the Gar-

said: 'Views differ regarding it, on group saying that there is no legal tasking in it at all, and whatever suggests the opposite is interpreted; as for what was mentioned about Adam, it is bliss lavished by Allah. Others said there is no legal tasking in it after the Final Gathering, but before it there is.... in which meaning is understood the covering of Adam's private parts, which was obligatory for him." (Kh 2:136)

[1143] "Namely the Muʿtazila and Abū Muslim al-Aṣfahānī; they claimed that (i) if Adam had been in the abode of eternity, Iblīs's deceit would never have affected him; (ii) he would have never been driven out of it; (iii) causing him to dwell in the abode of eternity without prior legal tasking goes against wisdom; and (iv) it had not been created yet—misgivings they adduced here." (Sk)

[1144] The story of the alighting on the mountain of Sarandīb (the Arabic name for present-day Sri Lanka) after the expulsion from Paradise is related from al-Ḥasan al-Baṣrī and Wahb b. Munabbih by Ibn Abī al-Dunyā in *al-Riqqa wal-Bukāʾ* and *al-ʿUqūbāt* and cited from Qatāda by Abū Ḥayyān in *al-Baḥr al-Muḥīṭ* as well as being adduced in the *Tafsīr*s (al-Baqara 2:36) of al-Baghawī, Abū al-Layth al-Samarqandī, al-Naysābūrī, al-Thaʿālibī, Ibn al-Jawzī, al-Qurṭubī and others.

[1145] "I.e. *kulā aklan raghadan* ⁽eat food in abundance⁾." (Q) Cf. below, verse 2:58.

شِئْتُمَا. وَسَّعَ الْأَمْرَ عَلَيْهِمَا إِزَاحَةً لِلْعِلَّةِ وَالْعُذْرِ فِي التَّنَاوُلِ مِنَ الشَّجَرَةِ الْمَنْهِيِّ عَنْهَا مِنْ بَيْنِ أَشْجَارِهَا الْفَائِتَةِ لِلْحَصْرِ.

﴿ وَلَا تَقْرَبَا هَٰذِهِ ٱلشَّجَرَةَ فَتَكُونَا مِنَ ٱلظَّٰلِمِينَ ﴾ فِيهِ مُبَالَغَاتٌ:

(١) تَعْلِيقُ النَّهْيِ بِالْقُرْبِ ـ الَّذِي هُوَ مِنْ مُقَدِّمَاتِ التَّنَاوُلِ ـ (أ) مُبَالَغَةً فِي تَحْرِيمِهِ وَوُجُوبِ الِاجْتِنَابِ عَنْهُ، (ب) وَتَنْبِيهاً عَلَى أَنَّ الْقُرْبَ مِنَ الشَّيْءِ يُورِثُ دَاعِيَةً وَمَيْلاً يَأْخُذُ بِمَجَامِعِ الْقَلْبِ وَيُلْهِيهِ عَمَّا هُوَ مُقْتَضَى الْعَقْلِ وَالشَّرْعِ؛ كَمَا رُوِيَ: حُبُّكَ الشَّيْءَ يُعْمِي وَيُصِمُّ.

den you both wish. He gave them both leeway in the matter to eliminate any cause or pretext for them to pick from the tree forbidden to them among all its trees that defy count.

[Wisdom of pre-emptive prohibition for the heart's haleness]

wa-lā taqrabā hādhihi-sh-shajarata fa-takūnā mina-ẓ-ẓālimīna *(but do not approach this Tree lest you be of the wrongdoers!)* contains hyperboles:

I. It makes the forbidding hinge upon proximity—which is one of the preliminaries of seizing—

(i) to emphasize the categorical prohibition of the latter and the imperativeness of steering clear from it,

(ii) and to serve notice that proximity to the object bequeaths motivation and inclination that tug at one's heartstrings, luring the heart away from the dictates of reason and sacred law, as narrated:

Your love of something will make [you] blind and deaf.[1146]

[1146] A Prophetic hadith narrated from **(1)** Abū al-Dardā' by Abū Dāwūd in his *Sunan* (*Adab, bāb fīl-hawā*) and others such as Aḥmad, al-Ṭabarānī in *al-Mu'jam al-Awsaṭ*,

فَيَنْبَغِي أَنْ لَا يَحُومَا حَوْلَ مَا حَرَّمَ اللهُ عَلَيْهِمَا مَخَافَةً أَنْ يَقَعَا فِيهِ.

(٢) وَجَعْلَهُ سَبَباً لِأَنْ يَكُونَا مِنَ الظَّالِمِينَ: الَّذِينَ ظَلَمُوا أَنْفُسَهُمْ بِارْتِكَابِ الْمَعَاصِي، أَوْ بِنَقْصِ حَظِّهِمَا بِالْإِتْيَانِ بِمَا يُخِلُّ بِالْكَرَامَةِ وَالنَّعِيمِ؛ فَإِنَّ الْفَاءَ تُفِيدُ السَّبَبِيَّةَ سَوَاءٌ جُعِلَتْ لِلْعَطْفِ عَلَى النَّهْيِ أَوِ الْجَوَابِ لَهُ.

وَ(الشَّجَرَةُ) هِيَ الْحِنْطَةُ؛ أَوِ الْكَرْمَةُ؛ أَوِ التِّينَةُ؛ أَوْ ....

Therefore they must not hover about what Allah has made categorically prohibited for them both, lest they fall in it.

II. It made proximity an avenue for them to be of the wrongdoers—those who wronged themselves (i) by committing sins,[1147] (ii) or by diminishing their share through doing what compromises honor and bliss.[1148] For the *fā'* ⁽lest⁾ communicates causality whether it is used as an adjunct to a prohibition or its apodosis.

[The Forbidden Tree]

Al-shajara ⁽the tree⁾ is wheat, or the vine, or the fig-tree[1149] or

al-Bayhaqī in the *Sunan al-Kubrā* and *al-Ādāb* and al-Quḍā'ī in *Musnad al-Shihab*; also—in the wording *ḥubbuka lil-shay'*—al-Bukhārī in *al-Tārīkh*, Ibn 'Adī in *al-Kāmil fīl-Ḍu'afā'*, Ibn al-A'rābī in his *Mu'jam* and al-Kharā'ṭī; **(2)** Abū Barza by al-Kharā'iṭī in *I'tilāl al-Qulūb*; **(3)** 'Abd Allāh b. Unays by Abū Ḥanīfa in his *Musnad* and Ibn 'Asākir in *Tārīkh Dimashq*; **(4)** Abū al-Dardā' as his own saying by Abū Dāwūd in *al-Zuhd*. Al-'Iraqī deemed the hadith fair per al-Sakhāwī in *al-Maqāṣid al-Ḥasana*.

1147 "If His saying *and do not approach this tree* is construed as a forbidding of categorical prohibition (*nahy taḥrīm*), because proximity to it would be categorically prohibited and the commission of the categorically prohibited is a sin." (Z)

1148 "If the forbidding is construed as one of preference (*nahy tanzīh*), in which case prozimity to it, even if it is not categorically prohibited or a sin, nevertheless , because it leads to their expulsion from the Garden, it compromises the honorific gifts they obtained in paradise. Picking from it in the first scenario has to be before prophethood while in the second it can be either before it or after it, for there is no proof of the necessity of infallibility before prophethood." (Z 1:263)

1149 For an anthology of the reports describing the wheat-tree's mind-boggling beauty

شَجَرَةٌ، مَنْ أَكَلَ مِنْهَا أَحْدَثَ. وَالْأَوْلَى أَنْ لَا تُعَيَّنَ مِنْ غَيْرِ قَاطِعٍ - كَمَا لَمْ تُعَيَّنْ فِي الْآيَةِ - لِعَدَمِ تَوَقُّفِ مَا هُوَ الْمَقْصُودُ عَلَيْهِ.

وَقُرِئَ بِكَسْرِ الشِّينِ؛ وَ(تِقْرَبَا) بِكَسْرِ التَّاءِ؛ وَ(هٰذِي) بِالْيَاءِ.

﴿فَأَزَلَّهُمَا ٱلشَّيْطَٰنُ عَنْهَا﴾: أَصْدَرَ زَلَّتَهُمَا عَنِ الشَّجَرَةِ وَحَمَلَهُمَا عَلَى الزَّلَّةِ بِسَبَبِهَا. وَنَظِيرُ (عَنْ) هٰذِهِ فِي قَوْلِهِ تَعَالَى ﴿وَمَا فَعَلْتُهُۥ عَنْ أَمْرِى﴾ [الكهف ٨٢]؛

a tree that caused whoever ate from it to lose their ritual purity.[1150] It is best left unnamed in the absence of decisive evidence, just as it was not named in the verse, as the purport of the latter does not depend on it.

It was also read [*shijara*] with a *kasra* under the *shīn*, *tiqrabā* with one under the *tāʾ*, and *hādhī* with a *yāʾ*.[1151]

[How Satan duped Adam and Eve]

[2:36] **fa-azallahumā-sh-shayṭānu ʿanhā** ⁽*then Satan caused them to slip from it*⁾: (i) he produced their slip out of the very tree and drove them to slip because of it. An example of this particular *ʿān* is in the saying of Allah Most High *wa-mā faʿaltuhu ʿan amrī* ⁽I did not do it of my own command⁾ (al-Kahf 17:82);

see al-Diyārbakrī, *Tārīkh al-Khamīs fī Akhbār Anfas Nafīs*, 2 vols. (Cairo: al-Maṭbaʿa al-Wahbiyya, 1283/1866) p. 48. Other candidates include camphor/cinnamon: Badr al-Dīn Ibn Jamāʿa, *Ghurar al-Tibyān fī-man lam Yusamma fil-Qurʾān*, ed. ʿAbd al-Jawād Khalaf (Damascus: Dār Qutayba, 1410/1990); spikenard, olive or colocynth: al-Balansī, *Tafsīr Mubhamāt al-Qurʾān al-Mawsūm bi-Ṣilat al-Jamʿ wa-ʿĀʾid al-Tadhyīl li-Mawṣūl Kitābay al-Iʿlām wal-Takmīl*, ed. Ḥanīf al-Qāsimī, 2 vols. (Beirut: Dār al-Gharb al-Islāmī, 1411/1991); and vine, wheat, almond, citron, or date: al-Suyūṭī, *Mufḥimāt al-Aqrān fī Mubhamāt al-Qurʾān*, ed. Iyād Khālid al-Ṭabbāʿ (Beirut: Muʾassasat al-Risāla, 1406/1986), all under this verse.

1150 "I.e. to defecate, and there is no loss of purity nor defecation in paradise. The verbal oppositeness (*muqābala*) suggests that eating from wheat, the vine or the fig-tree did not cause one to lose one's purity or defecate; and this requires reflection." (Q)

1151 Respectively: (i) by Hārūn al-Aʿwar, a dialect of the Banū Sulaym; (ii) Yaḥyā b. Waththāb as done by some of the Ḥijāzīs and (iii) Ibn Muḥayṣin and Ibn Kathīr. (*MQ*)

أَوْ أَزَلَّهُمَا عَنِ الْجَنَّةِ بِمَعْنَى (أَذْهَبَهُمَا). وَيَعْضُدُهُ قِرَاءَةُ حَمْزَةَ (فَأَزَالَهُمَا)؛ وَهُمَا مُتَقَارِبَانِ فِي الْمَعْنَى، غَيْرَ أَنْ (أَزَلَّ) يَقْتَضِي عَثْرَةً مَعَ الزَّوَالِ.

وَإِزْلَالُهُ: قَوْلُهُ ﴿هَلْ أَدُلُّكَ عَلَىٰ شَجَرَةِ ٱلْخُلْدِ وَمُلْكٍ لَّا يَبْلَىٰ﴾ [طه ١٢٠] وَقَوْلُهُ ﴿مَا نَهَىٰكُمَا رَبُّكُمَا عَنْ هَٰذِهِ ٱلشَّجَرَةِ إِلَّآ أَن تَكُونَا مَلَكَيْنِ أَوْ تَكُونَا مِنَ ٱلْخَٰلِدِينَ﴾ [الأعراف ٢٠] وَمُقَاسَمَتُهُ إِيَّاهُمَا بِقَوْلِهِ ﴿إِنِّي لَكُمَا لَمِنَ ٱلنَّٰصِحِينَ﴾ [الأعراف ٢١]. وَاخْتُلِفَ فِي (١) أَنَّهُ تَمَثَّلَ لَهُمَا فَقَاوَلَهُمَا بِذَٰلِكَ، أَوْ أَلْقَاهُ إِلَيْهِمَا عَلَىٰ طَرِيقِ الْوَسْوَسَةِ.

(ii) or he caused them to slip from the Garden[1152] in the sense that he made them go away, which is supported by Ḥamza's reading *fa-azālahumā*.[1153] They are closely similar in meaning except that *azalla* presupposes a stumbling down as well as removal.

His tripping [of them] is his saying *shall I point you to the tree of immortality and a kingdom that never fades?* (Ṭaha 20:120) his saying, *the only reason Your Nurturer prohibited you both from this tree is lest you become angels or become of the immortals* (al-Aʿrāf 7:20) and his solemn oath to both of them[1154] when he said, *verily I am to both of you of the most faithful counselors* (al-Aʿrāf 7:21). Views differed

I. whether he came to them disguised and argued with them to that effect, or cast it to them by way of whisperings;[1155]

[1152] "As witnessed by the verse *just as he brought out your two foreparents from the Garden* (al-Aʿrāf 7:27)." (S)

[1153] By al-Ḥasan, Abū Rajā', Ḥamza, ʿĀṣim and al-Aʿmash. (*MQ*)

[1154] All mss. and eds.: اياها AQ, H, MM: إياها typo.

[1155] "The argument here is that they both knew him and would not have accepted his discourse face to face, which is weak since he could take another form by which they did not recognize him, so what prevails is face to face talk, hence he put it first." (Q)

(٢) وَأَنَّهُ كَيْفَ تَوَصَّلَ إِلَى إِزْلَالِهِمَا بَعْدَ مَا قِيلَ لَهُ ﴿فَٱخْرُجْ مِنْهَا فَإِنَّكَ رَجِيمٌ﴾
[ص ٧٧]؟ فَقِيلَ: إِنَّهُ مُنِعَ مِنَ الدُّخُولِ عَلَى جِهَةِ التَّكْرِمَةِ كَمَا كَانَ يَدْخُلُ مَعَ
الْمَلَائِكَةِ؛ وَلَمْ يُمْنَعْ أَنْ يَدْخُلَ لِلْوَسْوَسَةِ، إِبْتِلَاءً لِآدَمَ وَحَوَّاءَ. وَقِيلَ: قَامَ
عِنْدَ الْبَابِ فَنَادَاهُمَا. وَقِيلَ: تَمَثَّلَ بِصُورَةِ دَابَّةٍ، فَدَخَلَ وَلَمْ تَعْرِفْهُ الْخَزَنَةُ.
وَقِيلَ دَخَلَ فِي فَمِ الْحَيَّةِ حَتَّى دَخَلَتْ بِهِ. وَقِيلَ أَرْسَلَ بَعْضَ أَتْبَاعِهِ فَأَزَلَّهُمَا.
وَالْعِلْمُ عِنْدَ اللهِ سُبْحَانَهُ وَتَعَالَى.

﴿فَأَخْرَجَهُمَا مِمَّا كَانَا فِيهِ﴾، أَيْ مِنَ الْكَرَامَةِ وَالنَّعِيمِ.

﴿وَقُلْنَا ٱهْبِطُوا﴾: خِطَابٌ ....

II. and how could he arrive at tripping them after being told, *So get out from it, for you are repudiated* (Ṣād 38:77)?

(i) Some said he was barred from entering in a priviledged way—as when he used to enter with the angels—but he was not barred from entering for whispering, as a test for Adam and Ḥawwā' ⁽Eve⁾; (ii) others said he stood at the gate and called out to them; (iii) others said he disguised himself as an animal, entering unbeknown to the custodians; (iv) others said he lodged himself in the snake's muzzle until it entered with him inside;[1156] (v) others said he sent one of his followers and the latter tripped them both; and knowledge is with Allah—may He be extolled and exalted!

[The fall from paradise to earth]

fa-akhrajahumā mimmā kānā fīhi ⁽*and he drove them out of what they were both in*⁾, that is, of honor and bliss.

wa-qulnā hbiṭū ⁽*and We said: All go down*⁾ is addressed ....

[1156] Narrated from Ibn ʿAbbās and Ibn Masʿūd among other Companions as well as Wahb b. Munabbih, Abū al-ʿĀliya and Muḥammad b. Qays (1:561-563, 566-567 al-Baqara 2:36) but al-Rāzī rejects its authenticity on rational bases. (Z)

(١) لِآدَمَ وَحَوَّاءَ - عَلَيْهِمَا السَّلَامُ - لِقَوْلِهِ: ﴿قَالَ ٱهْبِطَا مِنْهَا جَمِيعًا﴾ [طه ١٢٣]. وَجَمْعُ الضَّمِيرِ: لِأَنَّهُمَا أَصْلَا الْإِنْسِ، وَكَأَنَّهُمَا الْجِنْسُ كُلُّهُمْ؛ (٢) أَوْ هُمَا وَإِبْلِيسَ، أُخْرِجَ (أ) مِنْهَا ثَانِياً بَعْدَ مَا كَانَ يَدْخُلُهَا لِلْوَسْوَسَةِ، أَوْ دَخَلَهَا مُسَارَقَةً؛ (ب) أَوْ مِنَ السَّمَاءِ.

﴿بَعْضُكُمْ لِبَعْضٍ عَدُوٌّ﴾: حَالٌ أُسْتُغْنِيَ فِيهَا عَنِ الْوَاوِ بِالضَّمِيرِ. وَالْمَعْنَى: مُتَعَادِينَ، يَبْغِي بَعْضُكُمْ عَلَى بَعْضٍ بِتَضْلِيلِهِ.

I. to Adam—upon him blessings and peace—and Ḥawwā' ⁽Eve⁾ per the saying of Allah Most High *He said: Both get down (ihbiṭā) hence—all of you!* (Ṭaha 20:123). The personal pronoun [in ***ihbiṭū***] was put in the plural because they both are the two origins of human beings, and it is as if the two of them[1157] make up the species in its entirety.[1158]

II. Alternately [the address is to] both of them and Iblīs.[1159]

The latter was driven out (i) from it a second time after he used to enter it for whispering; (ii) or [after] he entered it surreptitiously;[1160] (iii) or from the sky.

baʿḍukum li-baʿḍin ʿaduwwun ⁽*one another's enemy*⁾ is a participial state where the *wāw* was dispensed with through the personal pronoun. The meaning is *mutaʿādīn* ⁽in a state of mutual enmity⁾, each oppressing the other with his misguiding.

1157 α, β, R: لانهما اصلا الانس وكانهما الجنس كلهم Ak, ε, Sk, T: فكانهما I: لانهما اصلا الناس فكانهما الجنس كلهم B: لأنهما اصلا الإنسِ وكانهم الجنسُ كلّه F, K: لأنّهما أصْلا الجنسِ فكأنّهما الانس كلّهم inversion? Kh, L, Q, U, Ul, Z: لانهما اصلا الانس فكانهما الانس كلهم dittography? G: فالذرية داخلون في الخطاب، يدل عليه قوله (**بعضكم لبعض عدو**) لأن التعادي إنما يكون بين ذرية آدم

1158 "This is indicated by the saying of Allah Most High, *therefore whoever follows My guidance, there will be no fear for them and they will not grieve* (al-Baqara 2:38)." (Sk)

1159 "This is the relied-upon position, as narrated from Ibn ʿAbbās and others." (S)

1160 "As it was said, namely in the form of an animal, unrecognized, or in the snake's muzzle." (Z)

﴿وَلَكُمْ فِى ٱلْأَرْضِ مُسْتَقَرٌّ﴾: مَوضِعُ اسْتِقْرَارٍ؛ أَوِ اسْتِقْرَارٌ.

﴿وَمَتَٰعٌ﴾: تَمَتُّعٌ. ﴿إِلَىٰ حِينٍ﴾: يُرِيدُ بِهِ وَقْتَ المَوْتِ؛ أَوِ القِيَامَةِ.

﴿فَتَلَقَّىٰٓ ءَادَمُ مِن رَّبِّهِۦ كَلِمَٰتٍ﴾: اِسْتَقْبَلَهَا بِالْأَخْذِ وَالْقَبُولِ وَالْعَمَلِ بِهَا حِينَ عَلِمَهَا.

وَقَرَأَ ابْنُ كَثِيرٍ بِنَصْبِ ﴿آدَمَ﴾ وَرَفْعِ (الْكَلِمَاتِ) عَلَى أَنَّهَا اسْتَقْبَلَتْهُ وَبَلَغَتْهُ. وَهِيَ قَوْلُهُ تَعَالَى: ﴿رَبَّنَا ظَلَمْنَآ أَنفُسَنَا﴾ [الأعراف ٢٣] ـ الآيَةَ.

wa-lakum fīl-arḍi mustaqarrun ⁽*and you can have in the earth a settlement*⁾: a place to settle or [the act of] settling.

wa-matāʿun ⁽*and some benefit*⁾:[1161] enjoyment.

ilā ḥīnin ⁽*until a certain time*⁾: He means by it the moment of death or resurrection.[1162]

[The divine gift of human repentance]

[2:37] **fa-talaqqā Ādamu min rabbihi kalimātin** ⁽*then Adam welcomed from his Nurturer certain words*⁾: he met them with adoption, acceptance and practice as soon as he was taught them.

Ibn Kathīr read it *Ādama* in the accusative and *kalimātun* in the nominative[1163] [*then Adam was welcomed by certain words from His Nurturer*] in the sense that they met him and reached him; namely, (i) the saying of Allah Most High, *Our Nurturer, we have wronged ourselves* (al-Aʿrāf 7:23) to the end of the verse.[1164]

1161 قال الطيبي: فالمتاع بمعنى التحقير في الاستمتاع والتقليل في المكث. حاشية السيوطي

1162 Narrated respectively from Ibn ʿAbbās and Mujāhid by al-Ṭabarī. (S)

1163 Also Ibn Muḥayṣin. (*MQ*)

1164 *Our Nurturer, we have wronged ourselves, and if You do not forgive us and grant us mercy we will most surely be of the losers.* This is narrated from al-Ḥasan, Abū al-ʿĀliya, Mujāhid, Qatāda and Ibn Zayd by al-Ṭabarī (1:581-586) and also from Ibn ʿAbbās, Saʿīd ibn Jubayr, Abū al-ʿĀliya, Muḥammmad b. Kaʿb, al-Rabīʿ b. Anas,

وَقِيلَ: سُبْحَانَكَ اللّٰهُمَّ وَبِحَمْدِكَ، وَتَبَارَكَ اسْمُكَ، وَتَعَالَى جَدُّكَ لَا إِلٰهَ إِلَّا أَنْتَ ظَلَمْتُ نَفْسِي فَاغْفِرْ لِي، إِنَّهُ لَا يَغْفِرُ الذُّنُوبَ إِلَّا أَنْتَ. وَعَنِ ابْنِ عَبَّاسٍ - رَضِيَ اللهُ تَعَالَى عَنْهُمَا - قَالَ: يَا رَبِّ أَلَمْ تَخْلُقْنِي بِيَدِكَ؟ قَالَ: بَلَى؛ قَالَ: يَا رَبِّ أَلَمْ تَنْفُخْ فِيَّ الرُّوحَ مِنْ رُوحِكَ؟ قَالَ: بَلَى؛ قَالَ: أَلَمْ تُسْكِنِّي جَنَّتَكَ؟ قَالَ: بَلَى؛ قَالَ: يَا رَبِّ إِنْ تُبْتُ وَأَصْلَحْتُ أَرَاجِعِيَّ أَنْتَ إِلَى الْجَنَّةِ؟

(ii) It was also said they are:

> Extolled are You, Allah, and most praised! Hallowed be Your name, exalted be Your honor, there is no god but You! I have wronged myself, therefore forgive me! Truly none forgives sins but You.[1165]

(iii) [It is also narrated] from Ibn ʿAbbās—Allah be well-pleased with him and his father that

> [Adam] said: "My Nurturer, did You not create me with Your hand?" He said yes. He said: "My Nurturer, did You not breathe into me the spirit from Your spirit?" He said yes. He said: "Did you not make me dwell in Your paradise?"[1166] He said yes. He said: "My Nurturer, if I repent and do good, will You be returning me to paradise?" ....

Khālid b. Maʿdān and ʿAṭāʾ al-Khurāsānī (S). Al-Ṭabarī considers it the most probative but allows that "we may also attribute additional expressions to Adam."

[1165] A hadith narrated from (i) Anas by al-Bayhaqī, *al-Zuhd* (S); (ii) Abū Barza by al-Ṭabarānī in *al-Kabīr* per al-Haythamī in *Majmaʿ al-Zawāʾid* (8:198) (iii) Mujāhid and (iv) ʿAbd al-Raḥmān b. Yazīd b. Muʿāwiya by al-Ṭabarī in his *Tafsīr* (1:584-585); (v) Muḥammad al-Bāqir by Ibn al-Mundhir per al-Suyūṭī in *al-Durr al-Manthūr* (al-Baqara 2:37); and (vi) Wahb b. Munabbih by Ibn Qudāma in *al-Riqqa wal-Bukāʾ* and *al-Tawwābīn*. It is narrated without mention of Adam from several Companions including Burayda and ʿAlī, from the Prophet—upon him blessings and peace.

[1166] α, B, ε, I, T: يا رب ألم تنفخ في الروح من روحك، قال: بلى، قال: ألم تسكني جنتك β: يا رب ألم تسبق رحمتك غضبك، قال: بلى، قال: يا رب ألم تنفخ في الروح من روحك، قال: بلى، قال: يا رب ألم تسكني جنتك

قَالَ: نَعَمْ. وَأَصْلُ (الْكَلِمَةِ): (الْكَلْمُ)؛ وَهُوَ التَّأْثِيرُ الْمُدْرَكُ بِإِحْدَى الْحَاسَّتَيْنِ - السَّمْعِ وَالْبَصَرِ - كَالْكَلَامِ وَالْجِرَاحَةِ.

﴿فَتَابَ عَلَيْهِ﴾: رَجَعَ عَلَيْهِ بِالرَّحْمَةِ وَقَبُولِ التَّوْبَةِ. وَإِنَّمَا رَتَّبَهُ بِالْفَاءِ عَلَى تَلَقِّي الْكَلِمَاتِ لِتَضَمُّنِهِ مَعْنَى التَّوْبَةِ: وَهُوَ الِاعْتِرَافُ بِالذَّنْبِ، وَالنَّدَمُ عَلَيْهِ، وَالْعَزْمُ عَلَى أَنْ لَا يَعُودَ إِلَيْهِ.

He said yes.[1167]

The root of ***kalima*** ‹word› is *al-kalmu* ‹slashing›, namely, an impact perceptible through one of the two senses of hearing and sight such as speech and wounding [respectively].[◊]

fa-tāba ʿalayhi ‹*whereupon He relented towards him*›: He turned back to him with mercy and the acceptance of repentance.[1168] The reason He put it—by using the *fāʾ*—in sequence after the welcoming of the words is because the latter implies the meaning of repentance, namely, the acknowledgment of one's fault, remorse over it and the resolution never to relapse.

F: يا رب ألم تنفخ في الروح من روحك، قال: بلى، قال: يا رب ألم تسبق رحمتك غضبك، قال: بلى، قال: يا رب ألم تسكني جنتك

Ak: يا رب ألم تنفخ في الروح من روحك، قال: بلى، قال: يا رب ألم تسكني جنتك، قال: بلى، قال: يا رب ألم تسبق رحمتك غضبك

1167 Narrated with a fair chain by al-Ḥākim, *Mustadrak* (2:454); al-Ājurrī, *Kitāb al-Sharīʿa*, ed. ʿAbd Allāh al-Dumayjī, 6 vols. (Riyadh: Dār al-Waṭan, 1418/1997) 3:1345 §910 and others including al-Ṭabarī, *Tafsīr* (1:580-582), Ibn Abī al-Dunyā in *al-Tawba* and Ibn Abī Ḥātim, *Tafsīr* (1:90-91 §407).

◊ Cf. *wa-rubba kalāmin yaʿūdu kalman* ‹some speech turns into slashing›: Sharaf al-Dīn ʿAbd al-Muʾmin b. Hibat Allāh al-Maghribī al-Aṣfahānī, *Aṭbāq al-Dhahab*, ed. Shaykh Yūsuf al-Nabhānī (Beirut: al-Maṭbaʿa al-Adabiyya, 1309/1892) §74 (p. 84 l.1).

1168 "It is narrated from Shahr b. Ḥawshab that Adam's gaze for 300 years remained downcast out of shame. Ibn ʿAbbās said Adam and Ḥawwāʾ wept for that long over what they had lost of the bliss of paradise, and they did not eat or drink for forty days, and Adam did not approach Ḥawwāʾ for a year. It is also narrated that the Prophet—upon him blessings and peace—said, "If the weeping of the people of the world, that of Dāwūd and that of Nūḥ were put together, that of Adam would exceed it." (Z)

وَاكْتَفَي بِذِكْرِ آدَمَ لِأَنَّ حَوَّاءَ كَانَتْ تَبَعاً لَهُ فِي الْحُكْمِ؛ وَلِذٰلِكَ طُوِيَ ذِكْرُ النِّسَاءِ فِي أَكْثَرِ الْقُرْآنِ وَالسُّنَنِ.

﴿إِنَّهُۥ هُوَ ٱلتَّوَّابُ﴾: الرَّجَّاعُ عَلَى عِبَادِهِ بِالْمَغْفِرَةِ، أَوِ الَّذِي يُكْثِرُ إِعَانَتَهُمْ عَلَى التَّوْبَةِ. وَأَصْلُ (التَّوْبَةِ): الرُّجُوعُ. فَإِذَا وُصِفَ بِهَا الْعَبْدُ، كَانَ رُجُوعاً عَنِ الْمَعْصِيَةِ؛ وَإِذَا وُصِفَ بِهَا الْبَارِي تَعَالَى، أُرِيدَ بِهَا الرُّجُوعُ مِنَ الْعُقُوبَةِ إِلَى الْمَغْفِرَةِ. ﴿ٱلرَّحِيمُ﴾: الْمُبَالِغُ فِي الرَّحْمَةِ.

[Women follow behind men with regard to legal status]

He contented Himself with the mention of Adam because Ḥawwā' follows behind him with regard to legal status; and that is why the mention of women is tucked away in most of the Qur'ān and Sunna reports.[1169]

innahu huwa-t-tawwābu ⁽*truly He—and He alone—is the Oft-Relenting*⁾: the Oft-Returning to His slaves with forgiveness, or the one Who assists them much to repent.

The root [meaning] of ***tawba*** ⁽repentance⁾ is *al-rujū'* ⁽returning⁾. When the slave is described by it, it denotes renouncing sin; and when the Creator is described by it, what is meant is renouncing retribution in favor of forgiveness.

ar-raḥīmu ⁽*the Most Merciful*⁾: one who is extremely merciful.

[1169] "I.e. left unexplicit." (Kh 2:140) "I.e. Allah Most High contented Himself with the mention of Adam's repentance when He said *then Adam welcomed* etc. without mentioning Ḥawwā''s repentance, and He did not say *fa-tāba 'alayhimā* ⁽whereupon He relented towards both of them⁾ as an allusion that she follows after him and is not meant in herself; and since women follow behind men, their mention was tucked away in the Qur'ān and Hadith except in rare cases." (Z 1:270) "I.e. he is the one being faced with command and prohibition… In the *Kashshāf* legal status is not mentioned and that is better, since Ḥawwā' does not follow behind him in obeying commandments and avoiding prohibitions; nor in repentance." (Q 3:197)

وَفِي الْجَمْعِ بَيْنَ الْوَصْفَيْنِ: وَعْدٌ لِلتَّائِبِ بِالْإِحْسَانِ مَعَ الْعَفْوِ.

﴿قُلْنَا ٱهْبِطُوا۟ مِنْهَا جَمِيعًا﴾: كُرِّرَ (I) لِلتَّأْكِيدِ، (II) أَوْ (١) لِاخْتِلَافِ الْمَقْصُودِ ـ فَإِنَّ الْأَوَّلَ دَلَّ عَلَى أَنَّ هُبُوطَهُمْ إِلَى دَارِ بَلِيَّةٍ يَتَعَادَوْنَ فِيهَا وَلَا يَخْلُدُونَ؛ وَالثَّانِي أَشْعَرَ بِأَنَّهُمْ أُهْبِطُوا لِلتَّكْلِيفِ، فَمَنِ اهْتَدَى الْهُدَى نَجَا، وَمَنْ ضَلَّهُ هَلَكَ ـ (٢) وَالتَّنْبِيهِ عَلَى (أ) أَنَّ مَخَافَةَ الْإِهْبَاطِ الْمُقْتَرِنِ بِأَحَدِ هٰذَيْنِ الْأَمْرَيْنِ وَحْدَهَا كَافِيَةٌ لِلْحَازِمِ أَنْ تَعُوقَهُ عَنْ مُخَالَفَةِ حُكْمِ اللهِ تَعَالَى، فَكَيْفَ بِالْمُقْتَرِنِ بِهِمَا؟ وَلٰكِنَّهُ نَسِيَ ﴿وَلَمْ نَجِدْ لَهُۥ عَزْمًا﴾ [طه ١١٥]؛ (ب) وَأَنَّ كُلَّ وَاحِدٍ مِنْهُمَا ....

[Adam represents all repentants and followers of guidance]

In putting together the two descriptives there is glad tidings of lavish treatment for the repentant together with pardon.

[2:38] **qulnā hbiṭū minhā jamīʿan** ⟨*We said: Go down from it, all of you!*⟩: it was reiterated: I. for emphasis;

II. or (1) because the intent differs—the first instance points to the fact that they are going down to an abode of trial in which they will be enemies to one another and they will not be immortal, while the second announces that they are made to go down for task-work; then, whoever heeds guidance is safe and whoever strays from it perishes—

(2) and to serve notice that (i) fear of being cast down, together with either one of those two matters,[1170] is enough by itself to deter the judicious from contravening the edict of Allah Most High, let alone both of them at once; still, *he forgot and We found no firm resolve in him* (Ṭaha 20:115); (ii) and that each of

[1170] "First, mutual enmity and lack of immortality; second, task-work leading to requital (*jazāʾ*)." (Z)

كَفَى بِهِ نَكَالاً ﴿لِّمَنْ أَرَادَ أَن يَذَّكَّرَ﴾ [الفرقان ٦٢]. (III) وَقِيلَ: الْأَوَّلُ مِنَ الْجَنَّةِ إِلَى السَّمَاءِ الدُّنْيَا، وَالثَّانِي مِنْهَا إِلَى الْأَرْضِ؛ وَهُوَ كَمَا تَرَى.

وَ﴿جَمِيعًا﴾ حَالٌ فِي اللَّفْظِ، تَأْكِيدٌ فِي الْمَعْنَى؛ كَأَنَّهُ قِيلَ: اِهْبِطُوا أَنْتُمْ أَجْمَعُونَ. وَلِذَٰلِكَ لَا يَسْتَدْعِي اجْتِمَاعَهُمْ عَلَى الْهُبُوطِ فِي زَمَانٍ وَاحِدٍ، كَقَوْلِكَ: (جَاءُوا جَمِيعاً).

﴿فَإِمَّا يَأْتِيَنَّكُم مِّنِّي هُدًى فَمَن تَبِعَ هُدَايَ فَلَا خَوْفٌ عَلَيْهِمْ وَلَا هُمْ يَحْزَنُونَ﴾: الشَّرْطُ الثَّانِي مَعَ جَوَابِهِ: جَوَابُ الشَّرْطِ الْأَوَّلِ. ....

the two suffices as exemplary punishment *for him who wishes to be mindful* (al-Furqān 25:62).

III. It was also said that the first instance is from the Garden to the nearest sky, and the second from the latter to the earth—and this needs no comment.[1171]

Jamīʿan ⁽all⁾ is a participial state in verbal form and an emphasizer in meaning, as if it had been said: "Go down, the whole lot of you!" Hence it is not required for them to be going down together at the same time, as when you say, "they all came."

fa-im-mā yaʾtiyannakum minnī hudan fa-man tabiʿa hudāya fa-lā khawfun ʿalayhim wa-lā hum yaḥzanūna ⁽*and if ever comes to you—as it will—a guidance from Me: then whoever follows My guidance, there shall be no fear for them, nor shall they grieve*⁾: the second condition together with its apodosis form the apodosis of the first condition.

[1171] "I.e. it is weak, because it would then treat the settlement and benefit in the earth as a participial state of the first instance—although that was implied—and because the personal pronoun in *minhā* ⁽from it⁾ manifestly refers to the Garden that was mentioned prior in the verse, not to the sky." (Sk)

وَ(مَا) مَزِيدَةٌ، أُكِّدَتْ بِهِ (إِنْ)؛ وَلِذٰلِكَ حَسُنَ تَأْكِيدُ الْفِعْلِ بِالنُّونِ، وَإِنْ لَمْ يَكُنْ فِيهِ مَعْنَى الطَّلَبِ. وَالْمَعْنَى: إِنْ يَأْتِيَنَّكُمْ مِنِّي هُدىً بِإِنْزَالٍ أَوْ إِرْسَالٍ، فَمَنْ تَبِعَهُ مِنْكُمْ نَجَا وَفَازَ. وَإِنَّمَا جِيءَ بِحَرْفِ الشَّكِّ ـ وَإِتْيَانُ الْهُدَى كَائِنٌ ـ لِأَنَّهُ مُحْتَمَلٌ فِي نَفْسِهِ، غَيْرُ وَاجِبٍ عَقْلاً.

وَكَرَّرَ لَفْظَ الْهُدَى وَلَمْ يُضمِرْ، لِأَنَّهُ أَرَادَ بِالثَّانِي أَعَمَّ مِنَ الْأَوَّلِ: وَهُوَ مَا أَتَى بِهِ الرُّسُلُ وَاقْتَضَاهُ الْعَقْلُ؛ أَيْ: فَمَنْ تَبِعَ مَا أَتَاهُ مُرَاعِياً فِيهِ مَا يَشْهَدُ بِهِ

Mā [in ***immā***] is additive and serves to emphasize ***in*** ⟨if⟩; thus it is most excellent to emphasize the verb with a *nūn*, even when it entails no sense of demand. The meaning is, "If there assuredly comes to you a guidance from Me through revelation or a message, then whoever among you follows that, will find salvation and victory." The reason the particle of doubt was adduced—although the coming of guidance will take place[1172]—is because the latter is inherently supposible and not rationally necessary.[1173]

He repeated the vocable for ***hudā*** ⟨guidance⟩ instead of pronomination because the second one is meant in a more inclusive sense than the first, namely: whatever messengers bring and the mind dictates.[1174] In other words whoever follows what He brings him, faithfully observing, in the process, what is attested by the

[1172] All mss., Sk, T: كائن K, Kh, L, Q, U, Ul, Z: كائن لا محالة see next note.

[1173] In rebuttal of J who had said "the bringing of guidance will take place and is inevitably necessary" (*ityān al-hudā kā'in, lā maḥālata li-wujūbih*): *Kashshāf* (1:257). This is the Mu'tazili belief in the law-making capacity of the mind through *taḥsīn* and *taqbīḥ* (declaring this and that excellent or ugly) while the doctrine of *Ahl al-Sunna* is that nothing is necessary nor compulsory upon Allah Most High, cf. Ibn al-Munayyir, *Intiṣāf* as quoted in al-Ghāmidī, *al-Masā'il al-I'tizāliyya* (p. 213).

[1174] "This [rational stipulation] and its like in this work are all Zamakhsharian copyisms (*mashyat qalam mimmā fīl-Kashshāf*), as that is definitely not our *madhhab*!" (S)

الْعَقْلُ، فَلَا خَوْفٌ عَلَيْهِمْ، فَضْلاً عَنْ أَنْ يَحُلَّ بِهِمْ مَكْرُوهٌ، وَلَا هُمْ يَفُوتُ
عَنْهُمْ مَحْبُوبٌ فَيَحْزَنُوا عَلَيْهِ ـ فَالْخَوْفُ عَلَى الْمُتَوَقَّعِ وَالْحُزْنُ عَلَى الْوَاقِعِ ـ:
نَفَى عَنْهُمُ الْعِقَابَ وَأَثْبَتَ لَهُمُ الثَّوَابَ عَلَى آكَدِ وَجْهٍ وَأَبْلَغِهِ.

وَقُرِئَ (هُدَيَّ) عَلَى لُغَةِ هُذَيْلٍ، وَ(لَا خَوْفَ) بِالْفَتْحِ.

﴿وَالَّذِينَ كَفَرُوا وَكَذَّبُوا بِآيَاتِنَا أُولَٰئِكَ أَصْحَابُ النَّارِ هُمْ فِيهَا خَالِدُونَ ﴿٣٩﴾﴾:
عَطْفٌ عَلَى ﴿فَمَن تَبِعَ﴾ إِلَى آخِرِهِ، قَسِيمٌ لَهُ، كَأَنَّهُ قَالَ: (أ) وَمَنْ لَمْ يَتْبَعْ بَلْ
كَفَرُوا بِاللهِ، وَكَذَّبُوا بِآيَاتِهِ؛ (ب) أَوْ كَفَرُوا بِالْآيَاتِ جَنَاناً وَكَذَّبُوا بِهَا
لِسَاناً، فَيَكُونَ الْفِعْلَانِ مُتَوَجِّهَيْنِ إِلَى الْجَارِّ وَالْمَجْرُورِ.

mind: there will be no fear for them, even less any hateful thing affecting them, and they will not be frustrated of anything beloved over which they would be sad. For fear is over something expected while sadness is over something factual. He precluded any punishment for them while affirming their reward in the most emphatic and intensive way possible.

It was also read *hudayya*[1175] after the Hudhayl dialect and *lā khawfa* with a *fatḥa*.[1176]

[2:39] **wa-l-ladhīna kafarū wa-kadhdhabū bi-āyātinā ulāʾika aṣḥābu-n-nāri hum fīhā khālidūna** ⁽*as for those who disbelieve and belie Our signs: those are the dwellers of the fire; they will abide therein forever*⁾ is adjoined to **fa-man tabiʿā** ⁽*then whoever follows*⁾ to the end of that [clause] and on a par with it, as if He had said: (i) "And those who do not follow but rather disbelieve in Allah and belie His signs," or (ii) "disbelieve in the signs at heart and belie them *viva voce*," in which case both verbs are directed to the same genitival object [*bi-āyātinā*].

1175 By ʿĀṣim al-Jaḥdarī and Ibn Abī Isḥāq, cf. Ibn ʿAṭiyya, *Muḥarrar* (1:247).
1176 By al-Zuhrī, ʿĪsā al-Thaqafī and Yaʿqūb, cf. Abū Ḥayyān, *Baḥr*. (*MQ*)

وَ(الْآيَةُ) فِي الْأَصْلِ: الْعَلَامَةُ الظَّاهِرَةُ؛ وَيُقَالُ (أ) لِلْمَصْنُوعَاتِ مِنْ حَيْثُ إِنَّهَا تَدُلُّ عَلَى وُجُودِ الصَّانِعِ وَعِلْمِهِ وَقُدْرَتِهِ؛ (ب) وَلِكُلِّ طَائِفَةٍ مِنْ كَلِمَاتِ الْقُرْآنِ الْمُتَمَيِّزَةِ عَنْ غَيْرِهَا بِفَصْلٍ.

وَاشْتِقَاقُهَا مِنْ (أَيٍّ)، لِأَنَّهَا تُبَيِّنُ أَيّاً مِنْ أَيٍّ؛ أَوْ مِنْ (أَوَى إِلَيْهِ). وَأَصْلُهَا (أَيَّةٌ) أَوْ (أَوْيَةٌ) كَـ(تَمْرَةٍ) ـ فَأُبْدِلَتْ عَيْنُهَا أَلِفاً عَلَى غَيْرِ قِيَاسٍ؛ أَوْ (أَيَيَةٌ) كَـ(رَمَكَةٍ)، فَأُعِلَّتْ؛ أَوْ (آئِيَةٌ) كَـ(قَائِلَةٍ)، فَحُذِفَتِ الْهَمْزَةُ تَخْفِيفاً.

[Meaning, etymology and interpretation of *āya*]

Al-āya ⁽the sign⁾, originally, is the visible mark. It applies to (i) created entities, in which sense they point to the existence of the Maker, His knowledge and His power;[1177] and (ii) to every grouplet of the words of the Qur'ān that are set apart from the rest with a divider.

Its derivation is from *ayy* ⁽what/which⁾ because it distinguishes which from which; or from *awā ilayh* ⁽he sought shelter besides him⁾, its origin being [respectively]

1. *ayya*[1178]

2. or *awya*—as in *tamra* ⁽date⁾—then its middle letter was changed into an *alif* irregularly;[1179]

3. or *ayaya*—as in *ramaka* ⁽draft horse⁾—where it was impaired;

4. or *ā'iya*—as in *qā'ila* ⁽speaker [f.]⁾—then the *hamza* was suppressed to make it lighter.

[1177] "As in the saying of Allah Most High, *And how many a sign in the heavens and the earth they pass by and ignore* (Yūsuf 12:105)." (Z)

[1178] α, Ak, B, D, ε, F, MM, P, Q, R, S, Sk, U, Ul, Z: أيّة I, L: ايية AQ, C, H: أأية β: أئية او اية

[1179] "Because when two weak letters are joined, normally the second one is changed, as in *jawan* and *hawan*." (Kh)

وَالْمُرَادُ ﴿بِـَٔايَـٰتِنَآ﴾: (أ) الْآيَاتُ الْمُنْزَلَةُ؛ (ب) أَوْ مَا يَعُمُّهَا وَالْمَعْقُولَةَ.

وَقَدْ تَمَسَّكَتِ الْحَشْوِيَّةُ بِهٰذِهِ الْقِصَّةِ عَلَى عَدَمِ عِصْمَةِ الْأَنْبِيَاءِ - عَلَيْهِمُ السَّلَامُ - مِنْ وُجُوهٍ:

* الْأَوَّلُ: أَنَّ آدَمَ - صَلَوَاتُ اللهِ عَلَيْهِ - كَانَ نَبِيًّا، وَارْتَكَبَ الْمَنْهِيَّ عَنْهُ، وَالْمُرْتَكِبُ لَهُ: عَاصٍ.

* وَالثَّانِي: أَنَّهُ جُعِلَ بِارْتِكَابِهِ مِنَ الظَّالِمِينَ - وَالظَّالِمُ مَلْعُونٌ، لِقَوْلِهِ تَعَالَى: ﴿أَلَا لَعْنَةُ ٱللَّهِ عَلَى ٱلظَّـٰلِمِينَ﴾ [هود ١٨].

What is meant by ***āyātinā*** ⁽Our signs⁾ is (i) the revealed signs; (ii) or what includes both them and those that reason detects.

[Adam's mistake in light of the infallibility of prophets][1180]

Note:[1181] the Ḥashwiyya latched onto this account to assert the lack of infallibility of prophets—upon them blessings and peace—from various perspectives:

• First, Adam—upon him the blessings of Allah—was a prophet, yet he committed what was forbidden; and whoever does that is a rebel.[1182]

• Second, he was put, because of what he perpetrated, among the wrongdoers—and the wrongdoer is cursed since Allah Most High said, *Behold! The curse of Allah is on the wrongdoers* (Hūd 11:18).

[1180] Objections and rebuttals are abridged from Rāzī's *Tafsīr* and *'Iṣmat al-Anbiyā'*.

[1181] α, β, B, D, I, Kh, L, P, Q, R, Sk, U, Z: تنبيه; missing from Ak, C, ε, F, H, MM, Ul

[1182] "The *'iṣyān* ⁽disobedience⁾ of prophets is a cause of nearness to Allah for them and of benefits for their nations. They are not called *'uṣāt* ⁽rebels⁾. We say: 'Adam disobeyed' *('aṣā)*, but not 'he is a rebel' *('āṣin)*." Ibn Khafīf, *al-'Aqīda al-Ṣaḥīḥa*, in 'Alī b. Muḥammad al-Daylamī, *Sīrat al-Shaykh al-Kabīr Ibn Khafīf al-Shīrāzī*, ed. Ibrāhīm al-Dasūqī Shattā (Cairo: Majma' al-Buḥūth al-Islāmiyya, 1977) p. 340-365 §112.

* وَالثَّالِثُ: أَنَّهُ تَعَالَى أَسْنَدَ إِلَيْهِ الْعِصْيَانَ، فَقَالَ ﴿وَعَصَىٰٓ ءَادَمُ رَبَّهُۥ فَغَوَىٰ﴾ [طه ١٢١].

* وَالرَّابِعُ: أَنَّهُ تَعَالَى لَقَّنَهُ التَّوْبَةَ، وَهِيَ الرُّجُوعُ عَنِ الذَّنْبِ وَالنَّدَمُ عَلَيْهِ.

* وَالْخَامِسُ: اِعْتِرَافُهُ بِأَنَّهُ خَاسِرٌ لَوْلَا مَغْفِرَةُ اللهِ تَعَالَى إِيَّاهُ بِقَوْلِهِ: ﴿وَإِن لَّمْ تَغْفِرْ لَنَا وَتَرْحَمْنَا لَنَكُونَنَّ مِنَ ٱلْخَٰسِرِينَ﴾ [الأعراف ٢٣]، وَالْخَاسِرُ: مَنْ يَكُونُ ذَا كَبِيرَةٍ.

* وَالسَّادِسُ: أَنَّهُ لَوْ لَمْ يُذْنِبْ، لَمْ يَجْرِ عَلَيْهِ مَا جَرَى.

وَالْجَوَابُ مِنْ وُجُوهٍ:

* الْأَوَّلُ: أَنَّهُ لَمْ يَكُنْ نَبِيّاً حِينَئِذٍ؛ وَالْمُدَّعِي ....

• Third, Allah Most High ascribed rebellion and errancy to him, saying *and Adam disobeyed his Nurturer and erred* (Ṭaha 20:121).

• Fourth, Allah Most High instructed him with repentance, which is to renounce sin and to feel remorse over it.

• Fifth, he confessed that he would be a loser were it not that Allah Most High forgave him when he said, *and if You do not forgive us and grant us mercy we will certainly be of the losers* (al-A'rāf 7:23)—and the loser is the one who committed an enormous sin.

• Sixth, if he had not committed a sin, all that happened to him would not have happened.

The answer is from several perspectives:

• First, he was not yet a prophet at that time;[1183] whoever claims

[1183] "Because he had no community and had not yet been commanded to convey anything. Even if it were granted [that he already was a prophet], the prohibition was preferential (*tanzīhī*) and the loss and wrongdoing are in their lexical sense." (Kh)

مُطَالَبٌ بِالْبَيَانِ.

* وَالثَّانِي: أَنَّ النَّهْيَ لِلتَّنْزِيهِ؛ وَإِنَّمَا سُمِّيَ (ظَالِمًا) وَ(خَاسِرًا) لِأَنَّهُ ظَلَمَ نَفْسَهُ وَخَسِرَ حَظَّهُ بِتَرْكِ الْأَوْلَى لَهُ. وَأَمَّا إِسْنَادُ الْغَيِّ وَالْعِصْيَانِ إِلَيْهِ، فَسَيَأْتِي الْجَوَابُ عَنْهُ فِي مَوْضِعِهِ إِنْ شَاءَ اللهُ تَعَالَى. وَإِنَّمَا أُمِرَ بِالتَّوْبَةِ تَلَافِيًا لِمَا فَاتَ عَنْهُ؛ وَجَرَى عَلَيْهِ مَا جَرَى مُعَاتَبَةً لَهُ عَلَى تَرْكِ الْأَوْلَى، وَوَفَاءً بِمَا قَالَهُ لِلْمَلَائِكَةِ قَبْلَ خَلْقِهِ.

otherwise has to prove it.

• Second, the prohibition was one of preference. He was called "wrongdoer" and "loser" only because he wronged himself and lost his share by giving up what was best for him. As for the ascription of errancy and rebellion to him the reply will be given in the proper place, if Allah wills.[1184]

He was commanded to repent only as a consolation for what had eluded his grasp,[1185] and what happened to him happened as a reproach to him for giving up what was best and in fulfillment of what He had said to the angels before creating him.[1186]

1184 Namely, under the verse *and Adam disobeyed his Nurturer and erred* (Ṭaha 20:121) where he says, "*Ghawā* ⟨he erred⟩, that is, he strayed from his objective and reaped disappointment when he sought immortality by eating from the tree; or he strayed from the right direction when he became deluded by the enemy's words. To make him notorious for rebellion and errancy—despite the minor nature of his slip—magnifies the slip or forms a momentous dissuasion against it for his offspring." "It is as if they were being told: "Look and heed how it was recorded against the infallible prophet—the beloved of Allah for whom it is impossible to commit a small sin deemed abhorrent—a slip through this mistake. In this hideous word there is an indication of the ugliness of your own excessive evils and small sins, not to mention your reckless involvement in enormous sins." (Z 1:277)

1185 "And as a discipline for him in the most perfect way." (Kh)

1186 "And not as a humiliation but rather as a realization of the successorship (*khilāfa*)

* وَالثَّالِثُ: أَنَّهُ فَعَلَهُ نَاسِياً لِقَوْلِهِ ـ سُبْحَانَهُ وَتَعَالَى ـ ﴿فَنَسِيَ وَلَمْ نَجِدْ لَهُۥ عَزْمًا﴾ [طه ١١٥]. وَلٰكِنَّهُ (أ) عُوتِبَ بِتَرْكِ التَّحَفُّظِ عَنْ أَسْبَابِ النِّسْيَانِ، وَلَعَلَّهُ ـ وَإِنْ حُطَّ عَنِ الْأُمَّةِ ـ لَمْ يُحَطَّ عَنِ الْأَنْبِيَاءِ لِعِظَمِ قَدْرِهِمْ، كَمَا قَالَ ـ عَلَيْهِ الصَّلَاةُ وَالسَّلَامُ ـ: **أَشَدُّ النَّاسِ بَلَاءً الْأَنْبِيَاءُ، ثُمَّ الْأَوْلِيَاءُ، ثُمَّ الْأَمْثَلُ فَالْأَمْثَلُ**.

• Third, he did it forgetfully, since Allah Most High and Exalted said, *but he forgot and We found no firm resolve in him* (Ṭaha 20:115); but

(i) he was rebuked for letting down his guard against the causes of forgetfulness: it may be that, even if the Community was excused from the onus of that, nevertheless, prophets were not,[1187] due to the magnificence of their rank, as the Prophet—upon him blessings and peace—said,

> The people tested with the severest hardships are the prophets, then the friends [of Allah], then those with most merit, then those with most merit.[1188]

that had been promised. Even if it were granted that it was an enormity and that the prohibition was categorical (*taḥrīmī*), nevertheless what he did was out of forgetfulness so it does not count as a sin or it counts as a minor one for him, because even if forgetfulness is forgiven for all communities, it is not forgiven for prophets—upon them blessings and peace—due to their majestic rank; hence a president is reproached in a way others are not, and al-Junayd said, 'The good deeds of the virtuous are the evil deeds of those brought near.' It is also said that forgetfulness was not forgiven for the previous communities in absolute terms and that such is exclusively the prerogative of this particular community, as mentioned in the sound hadiths." (Kh 2:144)

1187 "Nor were the previous communities in their entirety, for the lack of liability for forgetfulness is among the exclusive characteristics of this Community." (S)

1188 This is the wording cited in the *Tafsīrs* of al-Qushayrī and al-Rāzī as well as the works of al-Ghazālī whereas the established wordings are: **(I)** "The people tested with the severest hardships are the prophets, then those with most merit, then those with

(ب) أَوْ أَدَّى فِعْلُهُ إِلَى مَا جَرَى عَلَيْهِ عَلَى طَرِيقِ السَّبَبِيَّةِ الْمُقَدَّرَةِ دُونَ الْمُؤَاخَذَةِ عَلَى تَنَاوُلِهِ، كَتَنَاوُلِ السُّمِّ عَلَى الْجَاهِلِ بِشَأْنِهِ. لَا يُقَالُ إِنَّهُ بَاطِلٌ لِقَوْلِهِ تَعَالَى ﴿مَا نَهَىٰكُمَا رَبُّكُمَا﴾، ﴿وَقَاسَمَهُمَآ﴾ الْآيَتَيْنِ [الأعراف ٢٠-٢١]، لِأَنَّهُ لَيْسَ فِيهِمَا مَا يَدُلُّ عَلَى أَنَّهُ تَنَاوَلَهُ حِينَ مَا قَالَ لَهُ إِبْلِيسُ. فَلَعَلَّ مَقَالَهُ أَوْرَثَ فِيهِ مَيْلاً طَبِيعِيّاً، ثُمَّ إِنَّهُ كَفَّ نَفْسَهُ عَنْهُ مُرَاعَاةً لِحُكْمِ اللهِ تَعَالَى، إِلَى أَنْ نَسِيَ ذٰلِكَ، ....

(ii) Or his act led to what happened to him, in the fashion of preset causality without reproach for partaking of it, like the partaking of poison by one unaware of its nature. Let it not be said that this is false on the basis of the saying of Allah Most High, *and he said, The only reason Your Nurturer prohibited you both* etc. *and he swore to them* etc. (al-Aʿrāf 7:20-21), as there is nothing in these two verses to show that he actually partook of it at the time Iblīs said this to him. So it may be that the latter's statement awoke in him a natural inclination which he resisted in observance of the Divine ruling until he forgot that; ....

most merit," narrated from Saʿd b. Abī Waqqāṣ by al-Tirmidhī, *Sunan* (*Zuhd, al-ṣabr ʿala al-balāʾ, ḥasan ṣaḥīḥ*); al-Dārimī, *Sunan* (*Riqāq, ashadd al-nās balāʾan*); Aḥmad, *Musnad* (3:87, 128, 159 §1494, 1555, 1607); Ibn Mājah, *Sunan* (*Fitan, al-ṣabr ʿalā al-balāʾ*); al-Nasāʾī, *al-Sunan al-Kubrā* (*Ṭibb, ayyu al-nās ashaddu balāʾan*); al-Ṭaḥāwī, *Sharḥ Mushkil al-Āthār* (5:456 §2207) and others; **(II)** "the prophets then the righteous (*al-ṣāliḥūn*) then those with most merit, then those with most merit," narrated from (i) Saʿd by Aḥmad (3:78 §1481 *isnād ḥasan*); (ii) Fāṭima bint al-Yamān al-ʿAbsiyya by al-Ṭabarānī, *al-Muʿjam al-Kabīr* (24:245 §629) with a sound chain according to al-ʿIrāqī in his documentation of *Iḥyāʾ ʿUlūm al-Dīn*; and (iii) Abū Hurayra according to al-Tirmidhī; **(III)** ditto, without the phrases "then those..." from Abū Saʿīd al-Khudrī by al-Bukhārī, *al-Adab al-Mufrad* (p. 134 §510 *hal yakūn qawl al-marīd innī wajiʿ shikāya?*); Ibn Mājah, *Sunan* (*Fitan, al-ṣabr ʿalā al-balāʾ*) with a fair chain; al-Ṭabarānī, *al-Muʿjam al-Awsaṭ* (9:31 §9047); al-Ḥākim, *Mustadrak* (4:307) and others; and **(IV)** "the prophets, then the knowledgeable (*al-ʿulamāʾ*), then those with most merit, then those with most merit," narrated from Saʿd by al-Ḥākim, *Mustadrak* (1:99).

وَزَالَ الْمَـانِعُ، فَحَمَلَهُ الطَّبْعُ عَلَيْهِ.

* وَالرَّابِعُ: أَنَّهُ ـ عَلَيْهِ السَّلَامُ ـ أَقْدَمَ عَلَيْهِ بِسَبَبِ اجْتِهَادٍ أَخْطَأَ فِيهِ؛ فَإِنَّهُ ظَنَّ (أ) أَنَّ النَّهْيَ لِلتَّنْزِيهِ، (ب) أَوِ الْإِشَارَةِ إِلَى عَيْنِ تِلْكَ الشَّجَرَةِ، فَتَنَاوَلَ مِنْ غَيْرِهَا مِنْ نَوْعِهَا ـ وَكَانَ الْمُرَادُ بِهَا الْإِشَارَةَ إِلَى النَّوعِ ـ كَمَا رُوِيَ أَنَّهُ ـ عَلَيْهِ الصَّلَاةُ وَالسَّلَامُ ـ **أَخَذَ حَرِيراً وَذَهَباً بِيَدِهِ وَقَالَ: هٰذَانِ حَرَامٌ عَلَى ذُكُورِ أُمَّتِي، حِلٌّ لِإِنَاثِهَا.**

وَإِنَّمَا جَرَى عَلَيْهِ مَا جَرَى تَعْظِيماً لِشَأْنِ الْخَطِيئَةِ، لِيَجْتَنِبَهَا أَوْلَادُهُ.

then the impediment disappeared and his inclination drove him to do it.

• Fourth, he—upon him peace—ventured it due to judicious exertion in which he reached the wrong conclusion. For he thought that the prohibition

(i) was merely preferential,

(ii) or that it was referring to that specific tree, so he partook of another tree of the same kind, whereas the reference was to the [whole] kind, as in the narration in which the Prophet—upon him blessings and peace—held up silk and gold, saying:

> These two are categorically prohibited for males in my Community, licit for females;[1189]

and what happened to him happened only as an emphasis of the gravity of sin so that his children would avoid it.[1190]

[1189] Narrated from ʿAlī in the four *Sunan.* (S) "Spoken about gold and silk which he held in the right and left hand respectively, without meaning to refer to the specific objects, as in the hadith of his ablutions after which he says, 'This is a *wuḍū'* without which Allah accepts no prayer.'" (Z)

[1190] "Even though error in juridical exertion is forgivable; but as a horrification of the

وَفِيهَا دِلَالَةٌ عَلَى أَنَّ الْجَنَّةَ مَخْلُوقَةٌ، وَأَنَّهَا فِي جِهَةٍ عَالِيَةٍ، وَأَنَّ التَّوْبَةَ مَقْبُولَةٌ، وَأَنَّ مُتَّبِعَ الْهُدَى مَأْمُونُ الْعَاقِبَةِ، وَأَنَّ عَذَابَ النَّارِ دَائِمٌ، وَأَنَّ الْكَافِرَ فِيهِ مُخَلَّدٌ، وَأَنَّ غَيْرَهُ لَا يُخَلَّدُ فِيهِ، بِمَفْهُومِ قَوْلِهِ تَعَالَى: ﴿هُمْ فِيهَا خَالِدُونَ﴾.

[Other paradigms and teachings in Adam's story]

There is also in [the account] an indication that

1. the Garden is already created;

2. it is somewhere high;

3. repentance is accepted;

4. the follower of guidance will have a safe outcome;

5. the punishment of hellfire is everlasting;

6. the unbeliever abides therein eternally

7. while others will not,[1191] as inferred from the saying of Allah Most High, *they will abide therein forever* (al-Baqara 2:39).

gravity of sin, as it draws attention to the fact that if he is rebuked for it in the context of juridical exertion, what about when there is no juridical exertion to begin with?... Do you not see that the verse was revealed to the Prophet—upon him blessings and peace—*were it not for a writ of Allah foreordained you would have all incurred an awful punishment* (al-Anfāl 8:68) although the taking of ransom from the prisoners was through judicial exertion? The author's preference is that prophets practice that and that they may be mistaken in it: both issues are disagreed upon among scholars but his is the correct position. However, prophets are not maintained for long in a mistake but are quickly notified of it, and the notification here consists in being brought down from the Garden.... The upshot of his words is that his preferred position is that Adam—upon him peace—was a prophet before coming out of the Garden and that the prohibition can be either categorical or preferential, but the former is the prevalent and chosen position as he himself explicitly said in his commentary on *but do not approach this tree* etc. (al-Baqara 2:35) As Allah is my witness, what a marvelous examination of the pros and cons, in which he first rejected, then conceded what he had rejected as is the right way in sound dispositions and rightful scrutiny." (Q 3:213)

[1191] Contrary to the doctrines of the Muʿtazila and Khawārij in this respect.

وَاعْلَمْ أَنَّهُ ـ سُبْحَانَهُ وَتَعَالَى ـ لَمَّا ذَكَرَ دَلَائِلَ التَّوْحِيدِ وَالنُّبُوَّةِ وَالْمَعَادِ، وَعَقَّبَهَا تَعْدَادَ النِّعَمِ الْعَامَّةِ تَقْرِيراً لَهَا وَتَأْكِيداً ـ فَإِنَّهَا، مِنْ حَيْثُ إِنَّهَا حَوَادِثُ مُحْكَمَةٌ تَدُلُّ عَلَى مُحْدِثٍ حَكِيمٍ لَهُ الْخَلْقُ وَالْأَمْرُ وَحْدَهُ لَا شَرِيكَ لَهُ؛ وَمِنْ حَيْثُ إِنَّ الْإِخْبَارَ بِهَا عَلَى مَا هُوَ مُثْبَتٌ فِي الْكُتُبِ السَّابِقَةِ مِمَّنْ لَمْ يَتَعَلَّمْهَا، وَلَمْ يُمَارِسْ شَيْئاً مِنْهَا: إِخْبَارٌ بِالْغَيْبِ مُعْجِزٌ يَدُلُّ عَلَى نُبُوَّةِ الْمُخْبِرِ عَنْهَا؛ وَمِنْ حَيْثُ اشْتِمَالِهَا عَلَى خَلْقِ الْإِنْسَانِ وَأُصُولِهِ وَمَا هُوَ أَعْظَمُ مِنْ ذٰلِكَ، تَدُلُّ عَلَى أَنَّهُ قَادِرٌ عَلَى الْإِعَادَةِ كَمَا كَانَ قَادِراً عَلَى الْإِبْدَاءِ ـ: خَاطَبَ أَهْلَ

Know that Allah Most High first mentioned the proofs of pure monotheism, prophethood and the Return and followed them up with the enumeration of universal bounties in affirmation and emphasis of them. For

I. by virtue of being accomplished originated entities, they point to a wise Originator Who owns creation and command alone, without partner;

II. by the fact that their retelling exactly as they were recorded in the previous books—which he had not learned and with which he was not familiar in any way whatsoever—constitutes a stunning miraculous disclosure of something hidden, they point to the prophethood of their describer;

III. and by virtue of encompassing the creation of human beings, their origins and what is greater yet, they point to Him as being able to return them back to life just as He was able to originate them in the first place.

[The divine address to all learned people and to the Israelites]

After that, He addressed the people ....

الْعِلْمِ وَالْكِتَابِ مِنْهُمْ، وَأَمَرَهُمْ أَنْ يَذْكُرُوا نِعَمَ اللهِ تَعَالَى عَلَيْهِمْ، وَيُوفُوا بِعَهْدِهِ فِي اتِّبَاعِ الْحَقِّ وَاقْتِفَاءِ الْحُجَجِ، لِيَكُونُوا أَوَّلَ مَنْ آمَنَ بِمُحَمَّدٍ ﷺ وَمَا أُنْزِلَ عَلَيْهِ؛ فَقَالَ:

﴿يَٰبَنِيٓ إِسۡرَٰٓءِيلَ﴾ أَيْ أَوْلَادُ يَعْقُوبَ.

وَ(الِابْنُ) مِنَ (الْبِنَاءِ) لِأَنَّهُ مَبْنَى أَبِيهِ. وَلِذٰلِكَ يُنْسَبُ الْمَصْنُوعُ إِلَى صَانِعِهِ، فَيُقَالُ: (أَبُو الْحَرْبِ) وَ(بِنْتُ فِكْرٍ).

وَ﴿إِسْرَائِيلُ﴾ لَقَبُ يَعْقُوبَ - عَلَيْهِ السَّلَامُ - وَمَعْنَاهُ بِالْعِبْرِيَّةِ: صَفْوَةُ اللهِ؛ وَقِيلَ: عَبْدُ اللهِ.

of learning and of Scripture among them,[1192] commanding them to remember the favors Allah Most High lavished on them and to fulfill His covenant in pursuing truth and treading the path of overwhelming proofs so that they would be the first of those who believe in Muḥammad —upon him blessings and peace— and what He sent down upon him. So He said:

[2:40] **yā banī Isrā'īla** ⁽*O sons of Israel*⁾: that is, the children of Ya'qūb ⁽Jacob⁾.

Al-ibn ⁽son⁾ is from *al-binā'* ⁽building⁾ because the son is his father's edifice. Hence one attributes the handiwork to its worker with expressions such as *abū al-ḥarb* ⁽father of war⁾ and *bintu fikrin* ⁽daughter of thought⁾.[1193]

Isrā'īl ⁽Israel⁾ is the surname of Ya'qūb ⁽Jacob⁾—upon him peace—and its meaning in Hebrew is *ṣafwat Allāh* ⁽elite of Allah⁾. It was also said it means "slave of Allah"

1192 "Them" meaning all human beings. "He adjoined Scripture to learning to make clear that those that are meant are not the learned of the Israelites but the Israelites in absolute terms." (Q)

1193 α, Ak, β, B, ε, F, I, R, T: بنت فكر All eds.: بنت الفكر *alif-lām* diplology, modernism.

وَقُرِئَ (إِسْرَائِلَ) بِحَذْفِ الْيَاءِ وَ(إِسْرَالَ) بِحَذْفِهِمَا وَ(إِسْرَايِيلَ) بِقَلْبِ الْهَمْزَةِ يَاءً.

﴿اذْكُرُوا نِعْمَتِيَ الَّتِي أَنْعَمْتُ عَلَيْكُمْ﴾ أَيْ بِالتَّفَكُّرِ فِيهَا وَالْقِيَامِ بِشُكْرِهَا.

وَتَقْيِيدُ النِّعْمَةِ بِهِمْ: لِأَنَّ الْإِنْسَانَ غَيُورٌ، حَسُودٌ بِالطَّبْعِ، فَإِذَا نَظَرَ إِلَى مَا أَنْعَمَ اللهُ عَلَى غَيْرِهِ، حَمَلَهُ الْغَيْرَةُ وَالْحَسَدُ عَلَى الْكُفْرَانِ وَالسَّخَطِ؛ وَإِنْ نَظَرَ إِلَى مَا أَنْعَمَ اللهُ بِهِ عَلَيْهِ، حَمَلَهُ حُبُّ النِّعْمَةِ عَلَى الرِّضَاءِ وَالشُّكْرِ.

It was also read

(i) *Isrā'il* with the *yā'* suppressed;[1194]

(ii) *Isrāl* with both [the *yā'* and the *hamza*] suppressed;[1195]

(iii) and *Isrāyīl* with a transposition of the *hamza* into a *yā'*.[1196]

ᵘ**dhkurū niʿmatiya-l-latī anʿamtu ʿalaykum** ⁽*remember My favor which I lavished on you*⁾, that is, by reflecting on it and showing deep gratitude for it.

The restriction of favor to them[1197] is because human beings are naturally jealous and envious: when they look at what Allah has lavished of favors on others, jealousy and envy drive them to denial and angry dismissal; but when they look at what Allah has lavished on them, their love of gifts drives them to satisfaction[1198] and gratitude.

1194 By Warsh from Nāfiʿ. (*MQ*)

1195 By Khārija from Nāfiʿ and it is al-Ḥasan's reading. (*MQ*)

1196 By Abū Jaʿfar, al-Aʿmash, ʿĪsā b. ʿUmar, al-Ḥasan, al-Zuhrī, Ibn Abī Isḥāq, ʿĪsā, Nāfiʿ, al-Azraqī and al-Muṭawwaʿī. There are many other readings such as *Isra'il*, *Isrā'al*, *Isrā'ill*, *Isra'al*, *Isrél* with *imāla*, *Isrā'īn*, *Isrāyil*, *Srāl* etc. (*MQ*)

1197 "An allusion to the fact that what is meant by the said favor right here is what was lavished on all human beings." (Z) "That is, the ascription of *niʿma* ⁽favor⁾ to the [personal pronoun] *yā'* ⁽=my⁾ imparts totality (*istighrāq*)." (Q)

1198 α, B, D, I, P, Q, R Sk: الرضاء β, F, Kh, U: الرضا Ak, AQ, C, ε, H, L, MM, Ul, Z: الرضى

وَقِيلَ: أَرَادَ بِهَا مَا أَنْعَمَ اللهُ بِهِ (أ) عَلَى آبَائِهِمْ مِنَ الْإِنْجَاءِ مِنْ فِرْعَوْنَ وَالْغَرَقِ، وَمِنَ الْعَفْوِ عَنِ اتِّخَاذِ الْعِجْلِ؛ (ب) وَعَلَيْهِمْ مِنْ إِدْرَاكِ زَمَنِ مُحَمَّدٍ ﷺ.

وَقُرِئَ (اِذَّكِرُوا)؛ وَالْأَصْلُ: (اِفْتَعِلُوا). وَ(نِعْمَتِي) بِإِسْكَانِ الْيَاءِ وَقْفاً، وَإِسْقَاطِهَا دَرْجاً: وَهُوَ مَذْهَبُ مَنْ لَا يُحَرِّكُ الْيَاءَ الْمَكْسُورَ مَا قَبْلَهَا.

﴿وَأَوْفُوا۟ بِعَهْدِىٓ﴾ بِالْإِيمَانِ وَالطَّاعَةِ.

﴿أُوفِ بِعَهْدِكُمْ﴾ بِحُسْنِ الْإِثَابَةِ.

It was also said that He meant by it whatever favor Allah had lavished (i) on their forefathers by saving them from Pharaoh and from drowning, and by pardoning them for resorting to the Calf;[1199] (ii) and on them for making them live in the time of Muḥammad —upon him blessings and peace.

It was also read *ⁱdhdhakirū*[1200] which is originally [the form] *ⁱftaʿilū*;[1201] as for *niʿmatī* ⁽my favor⁾ with a *sukūn* over the *yāʾ*[1202] —when followed by a pause—and its suppression mid-phrase, it is the school of those who do not vowelize a *yāʾ* preceded by a *kasra*.[1203]

[Levels of the respective divine and human covenants]

wa-awfū bi-ʿahdī ⁽*and fulfill My covenant*⁾ of belief and obedience.

ūfi bi-ʿahdikum ⁽*I shall fulfill the covenant made to you*⁾ of an excellent retribution.

1199 Cf. further down on al-Baqara 2:50.

1200 By Ibn Masʿūd and Yaḥyā b. Waththāb. (*MQ*)

1201 All mss. and eds.: افتعلوا AQ, F, H, MM: اذتكروا gloss ε: افتكروا error.

1202 By Ibn Muḥayṣin, al-Ḥasan and al-Mufaḍḍal from ʿĀṣim. (*MQ*)

1203 "That is, their dialect." (Q) "As it invariably leads to two *kasras* side by side." (Sk)

وَ(الْعَهْدُ) يُضَافُ إِلَى الْمُعَاهِدِ وَالْمُعَاهَدِ؛ وَلَعَلَّ الْأَوَّلَ مُضَافٌ إِلَى الْفَاعِلِ وَالثَّانِي إِلَى الْمَفْعُولِ: فَإِنَّهُ ـ تَعَالَى ـ عَهِدَ إِلَيْهِمْ بِالْإِيمَانِ وَالْعَمَلِ الصَّالِحِ بِنَصْبِ الدَّلَائِلِ وَإِنْزَالِ الْكُتُبِ، وَوَعَدَ لَهُمْ بِالثَّوَابِ عَلَى حَسَنَاتِهِمْ.

وَلِلْوَفَاءِ بِهِمَا عَرْضٌ عَرِيضٌ، فَأَوَّلُ مَرَاتِبِ الْوَفَاءِ مِنَّا: هُوَ الْإِتْيَانُ بِكَلِمَتَيِ الشَّهَادَةِ، وَمِنَ اللهِ تَعَالَى: حَقْنُ الدَّمِ وَالْمَالِ؛ وَآخِرُهَا مِنَّا: الْاِسْتِغْرَاقُ فِي بَحْرِ التَّوْحِيدِ بِحَيْثُ يَغْفُلُ عَنْ نَفْسِهِ فَضْلاً عَنْ غَيْرِهِ، وَمِنَ اللهِ تَعَالَى: الْفَوْزُ بِاللِّقَاءِ الدَّائِمِ.

Al-ʿahd ⟨the covenant⟩ can be annexed to the covenanter as well as the covenantee. [Here] it may be that the first one is annexed to the subject while the second one is annexed to the object. For Allah Most High has enjoined upon them to have faith and do good works by setting up the proofs and sending down the Books; and He promised them reward in exchange of their excellent deeds.

[Self-extinction in Allah is the last level of *tawḥīd*]

The respective fulfillments of the two [covenants] cover a very vast range.[1204] The first of the levels of fulfillment consists, on our part, in professing the two testimonies of faith; and, on the part of Allah, in the shedding of [our] blood and seizure of [our] property becoming forbidden. The last level on our part consists in full immersion in the ocean of pure monotheism whereby one loses notice of oneself—let alone others; and, on the part of Allah, in [our] being awarded the everlasting meeting.

1204 "That is, many levels characterized by disparity on top of one another." (Q)

وَمَا رُوِيَ عَنِ ابْنِ عَبَّاسٍ - رَضِيَ اللهُ تَعَالَى عَنْهُمَا -: ﴿أَوْفُوا بِعَهْدِيٓ﴾
فِي اتِّبَاعِ مُحَمَّدٍ ﷺ، ﴿أُوفِ بِعَهْدِكُمْ﴾ فِي رَفْعِ الْآصَارِ وَالْأَغْلَالِ؛ وَعَنْ
غَيْرِهِ ﴿أَوْفُوا﴾ بِأَدَاءِ الْفَرَائِضِ وَتَرْكِ الْكَبَائِرِ ﴿أُوفِ﴾ بِالْمَغْفِرَةِ وَالثَّوَابِ؛
أَوْ ﴿أَوْفُوا﴾ بِالِاسْتِقَامَةِ عَلَى الطَّرِيقِ الْمُسْتَقِيمِ، ﴿أُوفِ﴾ بِالْكَرَامَةِ
وَالنَّعِيمِ الْمُقِيمِ: فَبِالنَّظَرِ إِلَى الْوَسَائِطِ.

I. As for what is narrated from Ibn ʿAbbās—may Allah be well-pleased with him and his father:

> *Keep the promise made to Me* with regard to following Muḥammad—upon him blessings and peace—*I shall keep the promise made to you* in removing [your] burdens and yokes;[1205]

II. and from someone else,

> *Keep the promise* of accomplishing the categorical obligations and avoiding the major sins, *I shall keep the promise* of forgiving and rewarding [you];[1206]

III. or,

> *Keep your promise* by strictly following the straight path,
> *I shall keep mine* by [granting] honor and unending bliss:

it is all with respect to ways and means.

1205 As stated by al-Rāghib and al-Rāzī in their *Tafsīrs* and as narrated in theirs—all with *al-iṣr* in the singular—by al-Ṭabarī (1:597) and Ibn Abī Ḥātim (1:95-96 §439, 441) who said its gist is also related from Abū al-ʿĀliya, al-Ḍaḥḥāk, al-Suddī and al-Rabīʿ b. Anas. It is also narrated as Ibn Isḥāq's commentary in his *Sīra*, cf. *Tafsīr Muḥammad b. Isḥāq*, ed. Muḥammad Abū Ṣuʿaylīk (Beirut: Mu'assasat al-Risāla, 1417/1996) p. 21-22. Al-Ṭabarī's chain was graded sound (S) and the report is considered authentic by Yāsīn, *Tafsīr Ṣaḥīḥ* (1:146).

1206 "That is also from Ibn ʿAbbās and narrated by Ibn Jarīr [al-Ṭabarī] from him, but with a weak chain" (S) and different wording, cf. *Tafsīrs* of al-Ṭabarī (1:598) and Ibn Abī Ḥātim (1:95-96 §437, 440).

وَقِيلَ: كِلَاهُمَا مُضَافٌ إِلَى الْمَفْعُولِ، وَالْمَعْنَى: أَوْفُوا بِمَا عَاهَدْتُمُونِي مِنَ الْإِيمَانِ وَالْتِزَامِ الطَّاعَةِ، أُوفِ بِمَا عَاهَدْتُكُمْ مِنْ حُسْنِ الْإِثَابَةِ.

وَتَفْصِيلُ الْعَهْدَيْنِ فِي سُورَةِ الْمَائِدَةِ، فِي قَوْلِهِ تَعَالَى: ﴿وَلَقَدْ أَخَذَ ٱللَّهُ مِيثَٰقَ بَنِىٓ إِسْرَٰٓءِيلَ﴾ إِلَى قَوْلِهِ: ﴿وَلَأُدْخِلَنَّكُمْ جَنَّٰتٍ تَجْرِى مِن تَحْتِهَا ٱلْأَنْهَٰرُ﴾ [المائدة ١٢].

وَقُرِئَ (أُوَفِّ) بِالتَّشْدِيدِ، لِلْمُبَالَغَةِ.

﴿وَإِيَّٰىَ فَٱرْهَبُونِ﴾ فِيمَا تَأْتُونَ وَتَذَرُونَ، وَخُصُوصاً فِي نَقْضِ الْعَهْدِ.

It was also said that both [covenants] are annexed to the direct object, in which case the sense would be "*Keep your promise in what you covenanted with Me* of faith and strict obedience, *I shall keep My promise in what I covenanted with you* of a beautiful retribution." The two covenants are detailed in Sūrat al-Mā'ida where Allah Most High said: *Allah made a covenant of old with the Israelites; and We raised among them twelve chiefs, and Allah said: Truly I am with you. If you but establish prayer, pay the poor-due, believe in My messengers and support them, and lend unto Allah a kindly loan, I shall certainly remit your evils and I shall certainly bring you into Gardens underneath which rivers flow* (al-Mā'ida 5:12).

It was also read *uwaffi*[1207]—with a double consonant—for intensiveness.

[The divine reminder to the people of the Covenant]

wa-iyyāya fa-rhabūni ⟨*and Me alone do dread*⟩ in all that you execute or leave out, particularly in the breach of the covenant; and

[1207] By al-Zuhrī. (*MQ*)

وَهُوَ آكَدُ فِي إِفَادَةِ التَّخْصِيصِ مِنْ ﴿إِيَّاكَ نَعْبُدُ﴾ [الفاتحة ٥] لِمَا فِيهِ - مَعَ التَّقْدِيمِ - مِنْ تَكْرِيرِ الْمَفْعُولِ وَالْفَاءِ الْجَزَائِيَّةِ، الدَّالَّةِ عَلَى تَضَمُّنِ الْكَلَامِ مَعْنَى الشَّرْطِ، كَأَنَّهُ قِيلَ: إِنْ كُنْتُمْ رَاهِبِينَ شَيْئاً، فَارْهَبُونِي!

وَ(الرَّهْبَةُ): خَوْفٌ مَعَ تَحَرُّزٍ.

وَالْآيَةُ مُتَضَمِّنَةٌ لِلْوَعْدِ وَالْوَعِيدِ، دَالَّةٌ عَلَى وُجُوبِ الشُّكْرِ وَالْوَفَاءِ بِالْعَهْدِ، وَأَنَّ الْمُؤْمِنَ يَنْبَغِي أَنْ لَا يَخَافَ أَحَداً إِلَّا اللهَ.

﴿وَءَامِنُوا۟ بِمَآ أَنزَلْتُ مُصَدِّقًا لِّمَا مَعَكُمْ﴾ إِفْرَادٌ لِلْإِيمَانِ بِالْأَمْرِ بِهِ وَالْحَثِّ عَلَيْهِ، لِأَنَّهُ الْمَقْصُودُ وَالْعُمْدَةُ لِلْوَفَاءِ بِالْعُهُودِ.

it is even more emphatic in its particularization than *iyyāka naʿbud* ⁽You do we worship⁾ because—together with being put first—it contains a repetition of the object, and because of the *fāʾ* of apodosis, which indicates that the discourse implies conditionality, as if the statement were: "If you are to dread something then dread Me!"

Al-rahba ⁽dread⁾ is fear together with guardedness.

The verse entails the divine ultimate promise and threat and points to the obligatoriness of gratitude and of fulfilling the covenant as well as the fact that a believer must fear no one but Allah Most High.

[2:41] **wa-āminū bi-mā anzaltu muṣaddiqan li-mā maʿakum** ⁽*and believe in what I have sent down in confirmation of what is with you*⁾ singles out belief by commanding it and exhorting to it, because it is the goal and the pillar of reliance toward the fulfillment of covenants.

وَتَقْيِيدُ الْمُنْزَلِ بِأَنَّهُ مُصَدِّقٌ لِمَا مَعَهُمْ مِنَ الْكُتُبِ الإِلٰهِيَّةِ، مِنْ حَيْثُ إِنَّهُ: (١) نَازِلٌ حَسْبَمَا نُعِتَ فِيهَا، (٢) أَوْ مُطَابِقٌ لَهَا (أ) فِي الْقِصَصِ وَالْمَوَاعِيدِ، وَالدُّعَاءِ إِلَى التَّوْحِيدِ، وَالأَمْرِ بِالْعِبَادَةِ وَالْعَدْلِ بَيْنَ النَّاسِ، وَالنَّهْيِ عَنِ الْمَعَاصِي وَالْفَوَاحِشِ؛ (ب) وَفِيمَا يُخَالِفُهَا مِنْ جُزْئِيَّاتِ الأَحْكَامِ بِسَبَبِ تَفَاوُتِ الأَعْصَارِ فِي الْمَصَالِحِ، مِنْ حَيْثُ إِنَّ كُلَّ وَاحِدَةٍ مِنْهَا حَقٌّ بِالإِضَافَةِ إِلَى زَمَانِهَا، مُرَاعًى فِيهِ صَلَاحُ مَنْ خُوطِبَ بِهَا، حَتَّى لَوْ نَزَلَ الْمُتَقَدِّمُ فِي أَيَّامِ الْمُتَأَخِّرِ لَنَزَلَ عَلَى وَفْقِهِ، وَلِذٰلِكَ قَالَ ـ عَلَيْهِ الصَّلَاةُ وَالسَّلَامُ: لَوْ كَانَ مُوسَى حَيّاً لَمَا وَسِعَهُ إِلَّا اتِّبَاعِي: ....

[The time-contextual suitability of variant heavenly rulings]

The restriction of revelation to that which confirms whatever they have of heavenly books is in the sense that it is

1. descending according to[1208] what was described in them;

2. or conforming with them (i) in respect of narrative accounts, divine promises, summons to pure monotheism, the command to worship and treat people with justice and the prohibition of sins and depravities;[1209]

(ii) as well as in whatever peculiar rulings differ with them due to time-specific considerations of public interest (in the sense that each respective ruling is right in its historical context and duly protects the welfare of those concerned by it, to the point that if the earlier [ruling] had come down in the time of the later one, it would have come down in complete agreement with it, hence the Prophet, upon him blessings and peace, said: "If Mūsā were alive, he would have no other choice but to follow

[1208] B: حَسْبَمَا whereas in the preamble it was vowelized حَسَبَمَا

[1209] I.e. in whatever agrees with them of unabrogated accounts etc. (Kh)

تَنْبِيهٌ عَلَى أَنَّ اتِّبَاعَهَا لَا يُنَافِي الْإِيمَانَ بِهِ، بَلْ يُوجِبُهُ؛ وَلِذٰلِكَ عَرَّضَ بِقَوْلِهِ:
﴿وَلَا تَكُونُوٓاْ أَوَّلَ كَافِرِۭ بِهِۦ﴾ بِأَنَّ الْوَاجِبَ: أَنْ يَكُونُوا أَوَّلَ مَنْ آمَنَ بِهِ،

me.")[1210]

[Jews and Christians are most expected to become Muslims]

[The restriction] serves notice that following [the books] does not annul belief in [this revelation] but dictates it.[1211] Hence He hinted—by saying

wa-lā takūnū awwala kāfirin bihi ⁽*and do not be the first disbeliever therein*⁾—to the fact that it behooves them to be the first of those who believe therein,[1212] ....

[1210] Part of a longer hadith narrated from **(i)** Jābir through Mujālid b. Saʿīd al-Hamdānī by Aḥmad, *Musnad* (22:468 §14631, 23:349 §15156); al-Dārimī, *Sunan* (*Muqaddima, mā yuttaqā min tafsīr ḥadīth al-Nabī*); Ibn Abī Shayba, *Muṣannaf* (13:458-459 §26949); al-Bazzār, *Musnad*: see al-Haythamī, *Kashf al-Astār ʿan Zawāʾid al-Bazzār ʿalā al-Kutub al-Sitta*, ed. Ḥabīb al-Raḥmān al-Aʿẓamī, 4 vols. (Beirut: Muʾassasat al-Risāla, 1399/1979) 1:78-79 §124; Abū Yaʿlā, *Musnad* (4:102 §2135); Ibn Abī ʿĀṣim, *al-Sunna*, ed. Bāsim al-Jawābira (Riyadh: Dār al-Ṣumayʿī, 1419/1998) 1:67 §50 *ḥasan li-ghayrih*; al-Bayhaqī, *Sunan* (2:10-11) and *Shuʿab al-Īmān* (1:199-200 §176-179); Ibn ʿAbd al-Barr, *Jāmiʿ Bayān al-ʿIlm* (2:805-806 §1497); al-Baghawī, *Sharḥ al-Sunna* (1:270 §126 *ḥadīth ḥasan*); **(ii)** ʿAbd Allāh b. al-Ḥārith through Jābir al-Juʿfī by ʿAbd al-Razzāq, *Muṣannaf* (6:113 §10164, 10:313-314 §19213); al-Bayhaqī, *Shuʿab* (4:307 §5201); Ibn ʿAbd al-Barr, *Jāmiʿ* (2:804 §1495); and Ibn al-Ḍurays, *Faḍāʾil al-Qurʾān* (p. 54-55 §90); **(iii)** and *mursal* from al-Ḥasan by Ibn al-Ḍurays, *Faḍāʾil* (p. 54 §89) and al-Khaṭīb, *al-Jāmiʿ li-Akhlāq al-Rāwī* (1991 ed. 2:228 §1531). Another *mursal* chain from Abū Qilāba for the same incident omits this particular segment while a broken-chained Prophetic variant from Ḥafṣa by ʿAbd al-Razzāq, *Muṣannaf* (6:113-114 §10165) and al-Bayhaqī, *Shuʿab* (4:308-309 §5205) mentions Yūsuf instead of Mūsā. Mujālid is slightly weak, cf. al-Haythamī, *Majmaʿ al-Zawāʾid* (1:173-174) while Jābir al-Juʿfī is very weak but their respective chains and the *mursal* ones strengthen one another, especially in light of the fact that Mujālid was used by Muslim in his *Ṣaḥīḥ* for corroborants and witness-chains, cf. al-Ghamrī, *Fatḥ al-Mannān* (3:191 §458 *ṣaḥīḥ li-ghayrih*).

[1211] On Islam's supercession and final abrogation of prior dispensations see further down, the Qadi's commentary on al-Baqara 2:62 and note.

[1212] "A metonymic oblique hinting (*taʿrīḍ kināʾī*)." (Kh)

وَلِأَنَّهُمْ كَانُوا أَهْلَ النَّظَرِ فِي مُعْجِزَاتِهِ، وَالْعِلْمِ بِشَأْنِهِ، وَالْمُسْتَفْتِحِينَ بِهِ، وَالْمُبَشِّرِينَ بِزَمَانِهِ.

other reasons being that they possessed insight into his[1213] staggering miracles, were cognizant of his affair, used to pray for victory through him[1214] and had been announcing the glad tidings of his coming time.[1215]

[1213] "Its manifest locution is that the author has chosen to reference the personal pronoun of *bihi* to the Prophet—upon him peace—who is not mentioned explicitly but implicitly, although it is incompatible with what he says further down, 'For whoever disbelieves in the Qur'ān,' which is quasi-explicit in making the personal pronoun refer back to the Qur'ān. The way to reconcile this is that he made the pronoun refer back to the Prophet—upon him peace—but it is knowledge of his affair and staggering miracles that is conducive to belief in him for most, and that in turn dictates belief in the Qur'ān. So what he mentions later exposes the logical conclusion of the meaning. What is more apparent is the pronoun refers back to the Qur'ān since it is mentioned verbatim and because it is compatible with his saying 'that is why He alluded obliquely.'" (Q 3:234) "Referencing the personal pronoun to Muḥammad—upon him blessings and peace—is the position of Abū al-ʿĀliya. It was also said to refer to *what is with you*, namely the Torah, for it contains the complete description of Muḥammad—upon him blessings and peace—and that is the position of al-Zajjāj." (Kh) The Qadi brings up the latter interpretation a few lines down. Al-Ṭabarī, *Tafsīr* (1:602-603) considers both interpretations "far-fetched but not linguistically impossible."

[1214] Before Islam the Jews would fight the Aws and Khazraj of Yathrib praying for victory "by the worth of Muḥammad" *(bi-ḥaqqi Muḥammad)* as narrated from Ibn ʿAbbās by al-Ājurrī, *al-Sharīʿa* (3:1452 §978); al-Ḥākim, *Mustadrak* (2:263) and al-Bayhaqī, *Dalā'il* (2:76)—all through a very weak chain because of ʿAbd al-Malik b. Hārūn b. ʿAntara—among other wordings related from many Companions and Successors cf. *Tafsīrs* of al-Ṭabarī (2:236-241) and Ibn Abī Ḥātim (1:171-172 §903-906); the books of *Asbāb al-Nuzūl* cf. al-Wāḥidī (p. 18), Ibn Ḥajar, *al-ʿUjāb* (1:280-285) and others, and as stated by Ibn al-Qayyim in *Hidāyat al-Ḥayārā fī Ajwibat al-Yahūd wal-Naṣārā*, ed. ʿUthmān Ḍumayriyya (Mecca: Dār ʿĀlam al-Fawā'id, 1429/2008) p. 45, 185-186 (also his *Badā'iʿ al-Fawā'id* and *Madārij al-Sālikīn*) in explanation of the verse *And when there came to them a Book from Allah verifying that which they had, and aforetime they used to pray for victory against those who disbelieve, but when there came to them that which they knew, they disbelieved in him; so let the curse of Allah be on the unbelievers* (al-Baqara 2:89).

[1215] "In the Torah and the Gospel" (Kh) cf. further down on al-Baqara 2:62 and note.

وَ﴿أَوَّلَ كَافِرٍ بِهِۦ﴾ وَقَعَ خَبَراً عَنْ ضَمِيرِ الْجَمْعِ، بِتَقْدِيرِ (أَوَّلَ فَرِيقٍ أَوْ فَوْجٍ)؛ أَوْ بِتَأْوِيلِ (لَا يَكُنْ كُلُّ وَاحِدٍ مِنْكُمْ أَوَّلَ كَافِرٍ بِهِ)، كَقَوْلِكَ (كَسَانَا حُلَّةً). فَإِنْ قِيلَ: كَيْفَ نُهُوا عَنِ التَّقَدُّمِ فِي الْكُفْرِ وَقَدْ سَبَقَهُمْ مُشْرِكُو الْعَرَبِ؟ قُلْتُ: الْمُرَادُ بِهِ (١) التَّعْرِيضُ، لَا الدِّلَالَةُ عَلَى مَا نَطَقَ بِهِ الظَّاهِرُ، كَقَوْلِكَ: (أَمَّا أَنَا فَلَسْتُ بِجَاهِلٍ)؛ (٢) أَوْ: لَا تَكُونُوا أَوَّلَ كَافِرٍ بِهِ مِنْ أَهْلِ الْكِتَابِ؛ (٣) أَوْ مِمَّنْ كَفَرَ بِمَا ....

Awwala kāfirin bih ʿthe first disbeliever thereinʾ stands in as the enunciative of the plural personal pronoun [in ***takūnū***] with the subaudition "first party or throng" or figuratively interpreted as "let not each and every one of you be the first disbeliever therein" in the same way as you would say "he gave us a tunic to wear."[1216]

If someone asks: how could they be forbidden to be first in unbelief when evidently Arab idolaters preceded them? I say: what is meant by it is

1. oblique hinting,[1217] as opposed to indicativeness according to what the manifest locution expresses in absolute terms[1218]—as when you would say, "for my part I am not an idiot;"

2. or "and do not be the first disbeliever therein among the People of Scripture;"

3. or "among those who disbelieve in ....

[1216] "I.e. he gave each of us a tunic, not one tunic for all of us." (Q)

[1217] Cf. Cachia, *Arch Rhetorician* (p. 66-67 §101 *taʿrīḍ*): "Obliqueness—(Laterality), Hinting: An indirect indication of the speaker's intention, the sense being understood neither from the use of words in their literal meaning nor through *transference* [*kināya*], but from the general tenor of the discourse." *Innuendo* is the same but in a depreciatory sense, cf. *OED*.

[1218] α, Ak, β, ε, F, I, Kh, R, Sk, T, Z: نَطَقَ B: يُطلق

مَعَهُ؛ فَإِنَّ مَنْ كَفَرَ بِالْقُرْآنِ فَقَدْ كَفَرَ بِمَا يُصَدِّقُهُ؛ (٤) أَوْ مِثْلَ مَنْ كَفَرَ مِنْ مُشْرِكِي مَكَّةَ.

وَ(أَوَّلُ): (أَفْعَلُ) لَا فِعْلَ لَهُ؛ وَقِيلَ: أَصْلُهُ (أَوْأَلُ) مِنْ (وَأَلَ)، فَأُبْدِلَتْ هَمْزَتُهُ وَاواً تَخْفِيفاً غَيْرَ قِيَاسِيٍّ؛ أَوْ (أَأْوَلُ) مِنْ (آلَ)، فَقُلِبَتْ هَمْزَتُهُ وَأُدْغِمَتْ.

﴿وَلَا تَشْتَرُوا۟ بِـَٔايَٰتِى ثَمَنًا قَلِيلًا﴾: وَلَا تَسْتَبْدِلُوا بِالْإِيمَانِ بِهَا وَالْاتِّبَاعِ لَهَا حُظُوظَ الدُّنْيَا، فَإِنَّهَا ـ وَإِنْ جَلَّتْ ـ قَلِيلَةٌ، مُسْتَرْذَلَةٌ بِالْإِضَافَةِ إِلَى مَا يَفُوتُ عَنْكُمْ مِنْ حُظُوظِ الْآخِرَةِ بِتَرْكِ الْإِيمَانِ.

قِيلَ: كَانَ لَهُمْ رِئَاسَةٌ فِي قَوْمِهِمْ ……………………

what they have,"[1219] for whoever disbelieves in the Qur'ān has certainly disbelieved in what confirms its truth;

IV. or "like those who disbelieved among the idolaters of Mecca."

Awwal ⟨first⟩ is an *af'al* form that has no basic verb. It is also said its root is *aw'al* ⟨push to refuge⟩, stemming from *wa'ala* ⟨take refuge⟩, whereby the *hamza* was substituted into a *wāw* irregularly; or *a'wal* ⟨drive⟩ from *āla* ⟨end up⟩, where the *hamza* was transposed into a *wāw* and then contracted.[1220]

wa-lā tashtarū bi-āyātī thamanan qalīlan ⟨*and do not trade off My signs for a small price*⟩: "and do not exchange belief in them and following them for the goods of this world." For truly, however weighty the latter may seem, they are scant and despised next to what will be forever lost to you of the goods of the hereafter if you abandon faith.

[The rabbinate and clergy feared losing their worldly status]

It was said that they held leadership among their people and

[1219] "Meaning that the personal pronoun in *bihi* refers back to *what is with you.*" (Sk)
[1220] α, β, B, ε, F: فقلبت همزته وادغمت Ak, I, R, T: فقلبت همزته واوا وادغمت diplology.

وَرُسُومٌ وَهَدَايَا مِنْهُمْ، فَخَافُوا عَلَيْهَا لَوِ اتَّبَعُوا رَسُولَ اللهِ ﷺ فَاخْتَارُوهَا عَلَيْهِ.

وَقِيلَ: كَانُوا يَأْخُذُونَ الرُّشَى فَيُحَرِّفُونَ الْحَقَّ وَيَكْتُمُونَهُ.

﴿وَإِيَّىٰ فَاتَّقُونِ﴾ بِالْإِيمَانِ وَاتِّبَاعِ الْحَقِّ وَالْإِعْرَاضِ عَنِ الدُّنْيَا. وَلَمَّا كَانَتِ الْآيَةُ السَّابِقَةُ مُشْتَمِلَةً عَلَى مَا هُوَ كَالْمَبَادِي لِمَا فِي الْآيَةِ الثَّانِيَةِ، فُصِلَتْ بِالرَّهْبَةِ الَّتِي هِيَ مُقَدِّمَةُ التَّقْوَى؛ وَلِأَنَّ الْخِطَابَ بِهَا عَمَّ الْعَالِمَ وَالْمُقَلِّدَ: أَمَرَهُمْ بِالرَّهْبَةِ الَّتِي هِيَ مَبْدَأُ السُّلُوكِ؛ وَالْخِطَابُ بِالثَّانِيَةِ - لَمَّا خَصَّ أَهْلَ الْعِلْمِ - أَمَرَهُمْ بِالتَّقْوَى الَّتِي هِيَ مُنْتَهَاهُ.

received remuneration and gifts from them, which they were afraid to lose if they were to follow the Messenger of Allah—upon him blessings and peace—so they chose them over him.

It was also said they would accept bribes, after which they would tamper with the truth and conceal it.[1221]

wa-iyyāya fa-ttaqūna ⁽*and of Me do beware!*⁾ through faith, following truth and turning away from the world.

[The first step of wariness (*taqwā*) is dread (*rahba*)]

After the previous verse comprised, as it were, the first principles of what is [mentioned] in the second verse, it was concluded with dread which is the premise of wariness. Since it addresses the learned and the imitator inclusively, it orders them [all] to have dread, which is the first step of wayfaring, while the address of the second [verse]—since it specifies the people of knowledge—orders them to have wariness, which is its culmination.

[1221] Cf. al-Mā'ida 5:63 and al-Tawba 9:34.

﴿وَلَا تَلْبِسُوا۟ ٱلْحَقَّ بِٱلْبَٰطِلِ﴾: عَطفٌ عَلَى مَا قَبْلَهُ.

وَ(اللَّبْسُ): الْخَلْطُ؛ وَقَدْ يَلْزَمُهُ جَعْلُ الشَّيْءِ مُشْتَبِهاً بِغَيْرِهِ. وَالْمَعْنَى: لَا تَخْلِطُوا الْحَقَّ الْمُنْزَلَ بِالْبَاطِلِ الَّذِي تَخْتَرِعُونَهُ وَتَكْتُبُونَهُ حَتَّى لَا يُمَيَّزَ بَيْنَهُمَا؛ أَوْ: وَلَا تَجْعَلُوا الْحَقَّ مُلْتَبِساً بِسَبَبِ خَلْطِ الْبَاطِلِ الَّذِي تَكْتُبُونَهُ فِي خِلَالِهِ، أَوْ تَذْكُرُونَهُ فِي تَأْوِيلِهِ.

﴿وَتَكْتُمُوا۟ ٱلْحَقَّ﴾: (I) جَزْمٌ دَاخِلٌ تَحْتَ حُكْمِ النَّهْيِ، كَأَنَّهُمْ أُمِرُوا بِالْإِيمَانِ وَتَرْكِ الضَّلَالِ، وَنُهُوا عَنِ الْإِضْلَالِ بِالتَّلْبِيسِ عَلَى مَنْ سَمِعَ الْحَقَّ

[2:42] **wa-lā talbisū-l-ḥaqqa bi-l-bāṭili** ⟨*and do not confound the truth with falsehood*⟩ is adjoined to what comes before it.[1222]

[The Jews and Christians' deliberate muddling of the truth]

Al-labs ⟨confusion⟩ is *al-khalṭ* ⟨muddling⟩, which may at times be concomitant with making something seem like something else. The meaning is, "Do not mix up the God-sent truth[1223] with the falsehood that you invent and write[1224] so that they cannot be told apart," or "Do not muddle up the truth with an intermixing of falsehood which you write between its lines or bring up in its interpretation."

wa-taktumū-l-ḥaqqa ⟨*and conceal the truth*⟩ is

I. an apocopate subsumed under virtual prohibition, as if they had been ordered to believe and renounce misguidance, and were forbidden to misguide others through deception of those who heard the truth ....

[1222] "It is possible to adjoin it to either one of the two preceding prohibitions." (Kh)
[1223] All mss. and eds.: الحق المنزل AQ, H, K, L, MM: الحق المنزل عليكم gloss.
[1224] α, Ak, B, F, R, T: وتكتبونه β, ε, I: وتكتمونه

وَالْإِخْفَاءِ عَلَى مَنْ لَمْ يَسْمَعْهُ.

(II) أَوْ نَصْبٌ بِإِضْمَارِ (أَنْ) عَلَى أَنَّ الْوَاوَ لِلْجَمْعِ، أَيْ لَا تَجْمَعُوا لَبْسَ الْحَقِّ بِالْبَاطِلِ وَكِتْمَانِهِ؛ وَيَعْضُدُهُ أَنَّهُ فِي مُصْحَفِ ابْنِ مَسْعُودٍ: (وَتَكْتُمُونَ)، أَيْ: وَأَنْتُمْ تَكْتُمُونَ بِمَعْنَى (كَاتِمِينَ). وَفِيهِ إِشْعَارٌ بِأَنَّ اسْتِقْبَاحَ اللَّبْسِ لِمَا يَصْحَبُهُ مِنْ كِتْمَانِ الْحَقِّ.

﴿وَأَنتُمْ تَعْلَمُونَ﴾، عَالِمِينَ بِأَنَّكُمْ لَابِسُونَ كَاتِمُونَ، فَإِنَّهُ أَقْبَحُ؛ إِذِ الْجَاهِلُ قَدْ يُعْذَرُ.

﴿وَأَقِيمُوا۟ ٱلصَّلَوٰةَ وَءَاتُوا۟ ٱلزَّكَوٰةَ﴾: ....

and through concealment from those who did not hear it.

II. Or it is an accusative through the ellipsis of *an* ⟨that⟩ in the sense that *wāw* ⟨and⟩ stands for combination;[1225] meaning, "do not add confounding truth through falsehood to [your already] concealing it." This [sense] is strengthened by the fact that Ibn Mas'ūd's codex has *wa-taktumūna*,[1226] that is, "while you conceal" in the [participial] sense of *kātimīna* ⟨concealing⟩.

The clause conveys that the condemnation of wilful confusion is due to what accompanies it of the concealment of truth.

wa-antum taʿlamūna ⟨*when you know full well!*⟩ "aware that you are confounding and concealing" which is even uglier, for the ignoramus might be excused.

[Non-Muslim worship is as zero prayer and zero charity]

[2:43] **wa-aqīmū-ṣ-ṣalāta wa-ātū-z-zakāta** ⟨*and establish the pray-*

[1225] All mss. and eds.: الواو للجمع AQ, H, K, MM: الواو للجمع بمعنى مع gloss interpolation.

[1226] Cf. J (1:260) and Abū Ḥayyān, *Tafsīr al-Baḥr al-Muḥīṭ*, ed. ʿĀdil Aḥmad ʿAbd al-Mawjūd et al., 8 vols. (Beirut: Dār al-Kutub al-ʿIlmiyya, 1413/1993) 1:335 but "such is not found in the printed edition of Ibn Masʿūd's *Muṣḥaf*." (*MQ*)

يَعْنِي صَلَاةَ الْمُسْلِمِينَ وَزَكَاتَهُمْ، فَإِنَّ غَيْرَهُمَا كَلَا صَلَاةٍ وَلَا زَكَاةٍ. أَمَرَهُمْ بِفُرُوعِ الْإِسْلَامِ بَعْدَ مَا أَمَرَهُمْ بِأُصُولِهِ. وَفِيهِ دَلِيلٌ عَلَى أَنَّ الْكُفَّارَ مُخَاطَبُونَ بِهَا.

وَ(**الزَّكَاةُ**) مِنْ (زَكَا الزَّرْعُ) إِذَا نَمَا؛ فَإِنَّ إِخْرَاجَهَا يَسْتَجْلِبُ بَرَكَةً فِي الْمَالِ وَيُثْمِرُ لِلنَّفْسِ فَضِيلَةَ الْكَرَمِ؛ أَوْ مِنَ (الزَّكَاءِ) بِمَعْنَى الطَّهَارَةِ؛ فَإِنَّهَا تُطَهِّرُ الْمَالَ مِنَ الْخَبَثِ وَالنَّفْسَ مِنَ الْبُخْلِ.

﴿وَارْكَعُوا مَعَ الرَّاكِعِينَ﴾ أَيْ فِي جَمَاعَتِهِمْ؛ فَإِنَّ ....

er and remit the charity tax⸣, meaning the prayer prayed by Muslims and charity tax remitted by them; for any other kinds are as zero prayer and zero charity.

[The pillars of Islam are universally binding]

He ordered them [to implement] the branches of Islam after ordering them [to implement] its foundations: this constitutes a proof that the unbelievers are [also] charged in that respect.[1227]

Zakāt ⸢charity tax⸣ is (i) from *zakā al-zarʿ* ⸢the crop increases⸣ when it grows; for its disbursement attracts blessing for one's property and bears the fruit of meritorious generosity for one's soul; (ii) or from *al-zakāʾ*[1228] ⸢cleansing⸣ in the sense of purity, for it purifies property from dross and the soul from avarice.

wa-rkaʿū maʿa-r-rākiʿīna ⸢*and bow with those who bow*⸣, that is, in their congregation; for ....

[1227] "As is the position of al-Shāfiʿī and the Iraqis among the Hanafis. What is meant is that they are charged with the obligation of implementation in the world, and this is what is not agreed upon; as for their legal liability for it in the next, they are charged by general agreement. There is also no disagreement as to (i) the impermissibility of implementation while in the state of unbelief and (ii) the non-obligatoriness of make-up after becoming Muslim." (Q 3:248, cf. Kh 2:153)

[1228] α, F, I, R, T: الزكاء ε: الزكا β, B: الزكاة synonyms.

صَلَاةُ الْجَمَاعَةِ تَفْضُلُ صَلَاةَ الْفَذِّ بِسَبْعٍ وَعِشْرِينَ دَرَجَةً لِمَا فِيهَا مِنْ تَظَاهُرِ النُّفُوسِ.

وَعَبَّرَ عَنِ الصَّلَاةِ بِـ(الرُّكُوعِ) احْتِرَازاً عَنْ صَلَاةِ الْيَهُودِ. وَقِيلَ: الرُّكُوعُ: الْخُضُوعُ وَالِانْقِيَادُ لِمَا يُلْزِمُهُمُ الشَّارِعُ. قَالَ الْأَضْبَطُ السَّعْدِيُّ: [الْمُنْسَرِح]

لَا تُذِلَّ الضَّعِيفَ عَلَّكَ أَنْ تَرْ * كَعَ يَوْماً وَالدَّهْرُ قَدْ رَفَعَهْ

﴿أَتَأْمُرُونَ ٱلنَّاسَ بِٱلْبِرِّ﴾: تَقْرِيرٌ مَعَ تَوْبِيخٍ وَتَعْجِيبٍ.

Congregational prayer is superior to individual prayer twenty-seven times[1229]

because of the souls' mutual assistance in it.

He referred to prayer as bowing to guard it from being confused with the prayer of the Jews.[1230] It was also said that bowing is submission and compliance for what the Lawgiver made incumbent upon them. Al-Aḍbaṭ al-Saʿdī said: [The Flowing"]

Do not humiliate the weak; you may stoop (tarkaʿ)
one day while times will have exalted him.[1231]

[They enjoined virtue and even Islam but practiced neither]

[2:44] **ataʾmurūna al-nāsa bi-l-birri** ⁽*do you order people to practice virtue*⁾ is a resolution in addition to reproach and stupefaction.

[1229] A Prophetic hadith narrated from Ibn ʿUmar and—with the number 25 instead of 27—from Abū Hurayra in the Nine Books.

[1230] Which is devoid of bowing. (Kh, Q, Sk, Z) I.e. as an integral *sine qua non* as indicated by its disappearance and reappearance in Jewish prayer rituals through various historical periods and cultural localities. Likewise prostration was practised then disappeared. Also see note 1371 on "shokeling."

[1231] Cf. Abū al-Faraj al-Aṣfahānī, *Aghānī* (16:154-155); Ibn Qutayba, *al-Shiʿr wal-Shuʿarāʾ* (1:382-383) and al-Baghdādī, *Khizāna* (11:452-456).

وَالْبِرُّ: التَّوَسُّعُ فِي الْخَيْرِ ـ مِنَ (الْبَرِّ) وَهُوَ الْفَضَاءُ الْوَاسِعُ ـ يَتَنَاوَلُ كُلَّ خَيْرٍ؛ وَلِذٰلِكَ قِيلَ: الْبِرُّ ثَلَاثَةٌ: بِرٌّ فِي عِبَادَةِ اللهِ تَعَالَى، وَبِرٌّ فِي مُرَاعَاةِ الْأَقَارِبِ، وَبِرٌّ فِي مُعَامَلَةِ الْأَجَانِبِ.

﴿وَتَنسَوْنَ أَنفُسَكُمْ﴾: وَتَتْرُكُونَهَا مِنَ الْبِرِّ كَالْمَنْسِيَّاتِ. وَعَنِ ابْنِ عَبَّاسٍ ـ رَضِيَ اللهُ عَنْهُمَا ـ أَنَّهَا نَزَلَتْ فِي أَحْبَارِ الْمَدِينَةِ، كَانُوا يَأْمُرُونَ سِرّاً مَنْ نَصَحُوهُ بِاتِّبَاعِ مُحَمَّدٍ ﷺ، وَلَا يَتَّبِعُونَهُ. وَقِيلَ: كَانُوا يَأْمُرُونَ بِالصَّدَقَةِ وَلَا يَتَصَدَّقُونَ.

Al-birr ⁽virtue⁾ is the extensive practice of goodness—from *al-barr* ⁽land⁾, which is vast space—and it pertains to every kind of goodness. Hence it is said that virtue is of three types: virtue in worshipping Allah Most High, virtue in mindfulness of relatives and virtue in interacting with strangers.

wa-tansawna anfusakum ⁽*and forget yourselves?*⁾: leaving your own selves, when it comes to virtue, as forgotten objects.

It is narrated from Ibn ʿAbbās—Allah be well-pleased with him and his father—that [this verse] was revealed in reference to the rabbis of Medina: they used to secretly command whoever they advised to follow Muḥammad—upon him blessings and peace—but they themselves did not follow him.[1232] It is also said that they would command others to give charity but they themselves did not give it.

[1232] The Jews would thus advise their Muslim in-laws. Narrated by al-Wāḥidī, *Asbāb* (p. 15) with a very weak chain containing Muḥammad b. al-Sā'ib al-Kalbī who is discarded, but its content is confirmed through other chains from (i) Ibn ʿAbbās himself by al-Ṭabarī, *Tafsīr* (1:614); (ii) Qatāda by ʿAbd al-Razzāq, *Tafsīr*, ed. Muṣṭafā Muslim Muḥammad, 3 vols. (Riyadh: Maktabat al-Rushd, 1410/1989) 1:44; (iii) Ibn Jurayj in ʿAlī Ḥasan ʿAbd al-Ghanī, *Tafsīr Ibn Jurayj* (Cairo: Maktabat al-Turāth al-Islāmī, 1413 /1992) pp. 32-33 as culled from al-Ṭabarī, al-Qurṭubī and Abū Ḥayyān; (iv-v) al-

﴿وَأَنتُمْ تَتْلُونَ ٱلْكِتَٰبَ﴾ تَبْكِيتٌ، كَقَوْلِهِ: ﴿وَأَنتُمْ تَعْلَمُونَ﴾ [البقرة ٢٢، ٤٢]، أَيْ تَتْلُونَ التَّوْرَاةَ، وَفِيهَا الْوَعِيدُ عَلَى الْعِنَادِ وَتَرْكِ الْبِرِّ وَمُخَالَفَةِ الْقَوْلِ الْعَمَلَ.

﴿أَفَلَا تَعْقِلُونَ﴾ قُبْحَ صَنِيعِكُمْ فَيَصُدَّكُمْ عَنْهُ؟ أَوْ: أَفَلَا عَقْلَ لَكُمْ يَمْنَعُكُمْ عَمَّا تَعْلَمُونَ وَخَامَةَ عَاقِبَتِهِ؟

وَ(الْعَقْلُ) فِي الْأَصْلِ: الْحَبْسُ؛ سُمِّيَ بِهِ (أ) الْإِدْرَاكُ الْإِنْسَانِيُّ، لِأَنَّهُ يَحْبِسُهُ عَمَّا يَقْبُحُ، وَيَعْقِلُهُ عَلَى مَا يَحْسُنُ، (ب) ثُمَّ الْقُوَّةُ الَّتِي بِهَا النَّفْسُ تُدْرِكُ هٰذَا الْإِدْرَاكَ.

wa-antum tatlūna-l-kitāba ⁽*yet you rehearse the Book!*⁾ is a harsh rebuke, like His saying *wa-antum taʿlamūna* ⁽when you know full well!⁾ (al-Baqara 2:22, 2:42); that is, "you rehearse the Torah wherein is a divine threat against obduracy, against the disregard of virtue and against disparity of speaking and doing."

a-fa-lā taʿqilūna ⁽*have you no understanding*⁾ of the ugliness of your handiwork so that you will be deterred from it? or, "Have you no mind that might restrain you from that which you know will lead to a baleful end?"

Al-ʿaql ⁽mind⁾ originally is *al-ḥabs* ⁽confinement⁾. It became a name for human cognition because it bars [the human being] from all that is ugly and fastens one to what is beautiful.[1233] Later it became a name for the faculty by which the psyche perceives that cognition.

Suddī and ʿAbd al-Raḥmān b. Zayd b. Aslam by al-Ṭabarī, *Tafsīr* (1:614-615). Cf. Ibn Ḥajar, *al-ʿUjāb* (1:252-253).

1233 "Mostly and in the majority of cases; or rather, it is susceptible of doing so. Clearly it did not bar evil rabbis from committing ugly acts!" (Q)

وَالْآيَةُ نَاعِيَةٌ عَلَى مَنْ يَعِظُ غَيْرَهُ وَلَا تَتَّعِظُ نَفْسُهُ سُوءَ صَنِيعِهِ وَخُبْثَ
نَفْسِهِ، وَأَنَّ فِعْلَهُ فِعْلُ الْجَاهِلِ بِالشَّرْعِ أَوِ الْأَحْمَقِ الْخَالِي عَنِ الْعَقْلِ؛ فَإِنَّ
الْجَامِعَ بَيْنَهُمَا تَأْبَى عَنْهُ شَكِيمَتُهُ. وَالْمُرَادُ بِهَا حَثُّ الْوَاعِظِ عَلَى تَزْكِيَةِ النَّفْسِ
وَالْإِقْبَالِ عَلَيْهَا بِالتَّكْمِيلِ لِيَقُومَ، فَيُقِيمَ؛ لَا مَنْعُ الْفَاسِقِ عَنِ الْوَعْظِ: فَإِنَّ
الْإِخْلَالَ بِأَحَدِ الْأَمْرَيْنِ الْمَأْمُورِ بِهِمَا لَا يُوجِبُ الْإِخْلَالَ بِالْآخَرِ.

﴿وَٱسۡتَعِينُواْ بِٱلصَّبۡرِ وَٱلصَّلَوٰةِۚ﴾ ....

The verse unmasks those who admonish others without rebuking themselves,[1234] exposing their evil handiwork and the wickedness of their own souls as well as showing that theirs is the act of those who have no knowledge of sacred law or, worse, mindless imbeciles. For whoever joins together between [knowledge and mind][1235] will never allows himself such [behavior].

What is meant by it is the exhortation of every admonisher to cleanse his own soul and devote himself to perfecting it so that he can meet his duties in order to help others to meet theirs. It is not meant to prevent the corrupt from exhorting [others]; for the failure to meet one of two compulsory requirements does not automatically mean the failure of the other.

[2:45] **wa-staʿīnū bi-ṣ-ṣabri wa-ṣ-ṣalāti** ⁽*and seek help in endurance*

[1234] B, Sk: تَتَعظُ نفسُه α, β, F, I, Kh, P, R, T, U: يتعظ نفسَه Ak, ε, L, Q, Ul, Z: يتعظ بنفسه

[1235] "In the *ḥawāshī saʿdiyya* ⁽commentaries on J by Saʿd al-Dīn al-Taftāzānī⁾: 'If someone says: This is the strongest proof that the ugliness of these matters is a rational criterion [as opposed to revealed]! we reply: rather, it is a sacred legal one in that such rebuke was made the consequence of what they perpetrated *after* rehearsing the Book. Allah Most High followed up their blame with two rulings that ascertain their guilt: the first one is His saying, *yet you rehearse the Book!* [i.e.] you ponder the Torah; the second one is His saying, *do you not understand?* to draw attention to the fact that whoever puts together mind and continuous book-study ought not to be ordering others to do what they themselves do not.'" (Z 1:292)

مُتَّصِلٌ بِمَا قَبْلَهُ، كَأَنَّهُمْ لَمَّا أُمِرُوا بِمَا يَشُقُّ عَلَيْهِمْ لِمَا فِيهِ مِنَ الْكُلْفَةِ، وَتَرْكِ الرِّيَاسَةِ، وَالْإِعْرَاضِ عَنِ الْمَالِ: عُولِجُوا بِذٰلِكَ. وَالْمَعْنَى: «اِسْتَعِينُوا عَلَى حَوَائِجِكُمْ (١) بِانْتِظَارِ النُّجْحِ وَالْفَرَجِ تَوَكُّلاً عَلَى اللهِ؛ (٢) أَوْ بِالصَّوْمِ، الَّذِي هُوَ صَبْرٌ عَنِ الْمُفَطِّرَاتِ لِمَا فِيهِ مِنْ كَسْرِ الشَّهْوَةِ وَتَصْفِيَةِ النَّفْسِ؛ (٣) وَالتَّوَسُّلِ بِالصَّلَاةِ وَالْاِلْتِجَاءِ إِلَيْهَا، فَإِنَّهَا جَامِعَةٌ لِأَنْوَاعِ الْعِبَادَاتِ النَّفْسَانِيَّةِ وَالْبَدَنِيَّةِ - مِنَ الطَّهَارَةِ، وَسَتْرِ الْعَوْرَةِ، وَصَرْفِ الْمَالِ فِيهِمَا، وَالتَّوَجُّهِ إِلَى الْكَعْبَةِ، ....

and prayer⁾ is connected to what precedes[1236] as if, after they were ordered something difficult for them due to its heavy burden and the fact that they would have to give up leadership and income, they were assuaged with that.

The meaning is: "Seek help, for all your needs,

1. in the awaiting of success and deliverance with reliance on Allah;

2. or in fasting, which is endurance away from the things that vitiate the fast, as it curbs lust and purifies the soul;

[The benefits of prayer]

3. and in seeking the means of prayer and taking refuge in it; for it gathers up all kinds of moral and physical acts of worship:

- purity,
- the covering of nakedness,
- the expenditure of wealth towards such acts,
- turning one's face to the Kaʿba,

[1236] "Whereby he suggests the address is [still] to the Israelites not to all Muslims." (Q)

وَالْعُكُوفِ لِلْعِبَادَةِ، وَإِظْهَارِ الْخُشُوعِ بِالْجَوَارِحِ، وَإِخْلَاصِ النِّيَّةِ بِالْقَلْبِ، وَمُجَاهَدَةِ الشَّيْطَانِ، وَمُنَاجَاةِ الْحَقِّ، وَقِرَاءَةِ الْقُرْآنِ، وَالتَّكَلُّمِ بِالشَّهَادَتَيْنِ وَكَفِّ النَّفْسِ عَنِ الْأَطْيَبَيْنِ - حَتَّى تُجَابُوا إِلَى تَحْصِيلِ الْمَآرِبِ وَجَبْرِ الْمَصَائِبِ.»

رُوِيَ أَنَّهُ - عَلَيْهِ الصَّلَاةُ وَالسَّلَامُ - كَانَ إِذَا حَزَبَهُ أَمْرٌ فَزِعَ إِلَى الصَّلَاةِ.

- keeping to worship,
- manifesting humbleness in the limbs,
- the refinement of intention with the heart,
- struggling against the devil,
- conversing with the Real,
- reading the Qur'ān,
- uttering the two testimonies of faith
- and depriving the self from the two sweetest pleasures,[1237]

until your plea is fulfilled so that you will obtain all your ardent wishes and remedy your troubles."

It is narrated that

> the Prophet—upon him blessings and peace—whenever any matter worried[1238] him, would quickly resort to prayer.[1239]

[1237] Food and sex. (Q, Sk, Z)

[1238] A, B, β, F, I, S, Sk: حَزَبَهُ α, Ak, ε, R: جزبه T: خوفه

[1239] Narrated from Ḥudhayfa b. al-Yamān by Aḥmad, *Musnad* (38:330-331 §23299); Abū Dāwūd, *Sunan* (*Ṣalāt, Bāb waqt qiyām al-Nabī fil-layl*); al-Ṭabarī, *Tafsīr* (1:619); al-Bayhaqī, *Shuʿab* (3:154 §3181-3182) and others, all with the simpler wording "he would pray" (*ṣallā*) but for Ibn Qāniʿ, *Muʿjam al-Ṣaḥāba*, ed. Ṣalāḥ al-Miṣrātī, 3 vols. (Medina: Maktabat al-Ghurabā' al-Athariyya, 1998) 2:189 §684 who alone narrates it

وَيَجُوزُ أَنْ يُرَادَ بِهَا الدُّعَاءُ.

﴿وَإِنَّهَا﴾: أَيْ وَإِنَّ الْإِسْتِعَانَةَ بِهِمَا أَوِ الصَّلَاةَ - وَتَخْصِيصُهَا بِرَدِّ الضَّمِيرِ إِلَيْهَا: لِعِظَمِ شَأْنِهَا وَاسْتِجْمَاعِهَا ضُرُوباً مِنَ الصَّبْرِ - أَوْ جُمْلَةَ مَا أُمِرُوا بِهَا وَنُهُوا عَنْهَا.

﴿لَكَبِيرَةٌ﴾: لَثَقِيلَةٌ شَاقَّةٌ كَقَوْلِهِ تَعَالَى ﴿كَبُرَ عَلَى ٱلْمُشْرِكِينَ مَا تَدْعُوهُمْ إِلَيْهِ﴾ [الشورى ١٣].

It is also possible that what is meant by [*ṣalāt*] is supplication.

wa-innahā ⁽*and truly that*⁾, meaning, (i) "truly, seeking help in both of them;" (ii) or "[in] prayer"—in which case it was singled out by referring the personal pronoun back to it, because of its tremendous importance and the fact that it collects together so many avenues of endurance; (iii) or the entirety of what they were commanded and forbidden.[1240]

la-kabīratun ⁽*is too much*⁾, "too heavy, grueling" as in His saying, *Grievous (kabura) for the idolaters is that unto which you call them* (al-Shūrā 42:13).

in the wording the Qadi cites. It is further confirmed by (i) the Prophetic narration from Ṣuhayb, "Whenever they were alarmed, the prophets would quickly resort to prayer," Aḥmad, *Musnad* (31:267-268 §18937); (ii) another one from ʿAbd Allāh b. Salām, "Whenever the Prophet's wives faced hardship he would order them to pray and recite *And command your wives to pray and remain steadfast with it* (Ṭaha 20:132); (iii) a *mursal* narration from Thābit that the Prophet would say, whenever he faced a financial hardship: "My family, pray! Pray!"; and (iv) by Thābit's own saying: "Whenever the Prophets faced hardship they would quickly resort to prayer," the latter three reports in al-Bayhaqī, *Shuʿab* (3:153 §3180, 3:155 §3185). Hence al-Mundhirī and al-Ḍiyā' al-Maqdisī deemed it authentic and included it in *al-Targhīb wal-Tarhīb* and *al-Aḥādīth al-Mukhtāra* respectively.

[1240] Ak, β, B, ε, F, I, K, Kh, L, R, Sk, U: أمروا بها ونهوا عنها α: امروا به ونهوا عنها Ul, Q, Z: الأمورالتي أمر بها بنو إسرائيل ونهوا عنها J: امروا ونهوا عنه T: أمروا به ونهوا عنه

﴿إِلَّا عَلَى ٱلْخَٰشِعِينَ﴾ أَيِ الْمُخْبِتِينَ. وَ(الْخُشُوعُ): الإِخْبَاتُ؛ وَمِنْهُ:
(الْخُشْعَةُ) لِلرَّمْلَةِ الْمُتَطَامِنَةِ. وَ(الْخُضُوعُ): اللِّينُ وَالِانْقِيَادُ؛ وَلِذٰلِكَ يُقَالُ:
الْخُشُوعُ بِالْجَوَارِحِ، وَالْخُضُوعُ بِالْقَلْبِ.

﴿ٱلَّذِينَ يَظُنُّونَ أَنَّهُم مُّلَٰقُواْ رَبِّهِمْ وَأَنَّهُمْ إِلَيْهِ رَٰجِعُونَ ٤٦﴾، أَيْ يَتَوَقَّعُونَ
لِقَاءَ اللهِ تَعَالَى وَنَيْلَ مَا عِنْدَهُ؛ أَوْ يَتَيَقَّنُونَ أَنَّهُمْ يُحْشَرُونَ إِلَى اللهِ فَيُجَازِيهِمْ.
وَيُؤَيِّدُهُ أَنَّ فِي مُصْحَفِ ابْنِ مَسْعُودٍ: (يَعْلَمُونَ). ....

illā ʿalā-l-khāshiʿīna ⸢*except for those who are humble*⸣, that is, the lowly.[1241] *Khushūʿ* ⸢humility⸣ is lowliness—whence *khushʿa* ⸢low hillock⸣, said of a low-lying track of earth—while *khuḍūʿ* ⸢submissiveness⸣ is compliancy and docility. That is why it is said that humility is with the limbs while submissiveness is with the heart.[1242]

[2:46] **al-ladhīna yaẓunnūna annahum mulāqū rabbihim wa-annahum ilayhi rājiʿūna** ⸢*those who presume that they are going to meet their Nurturer and are returning back to Him*⸣: that is,

(i) they expect to meet Allah Most High and secure what He has in store [for them];

or (ii) they are certain that they will be gathered unto Allah, after which He will repay them in full. The latter is supported by the variant *yaʿlamūna* ⸢who know⸣ in Ibn Masʿūd's Codex.[1243] As

1241 *Mukhbit* can also be translated as "tranquil surrenderer" cf. Maḥmūd al-Ṭanāḥī, *Min Asrār al-Lugha fīl-Kitāb wal-Sunna*, 2 vols. (Mecca: al-Maktaba al-Makkiyya; Amman: Dār al-Fatḥ, 1428/2008) 2:481-482.

1242 But the contrary is also said cf. Abū Hilāl al-ʿAskarī, *al-Furūq al-Lughawiyya*, ed. Muḥammad Ibrāhīm Salīm (Cairo: Dār al-ʿIlm wal-Thaqāfa, 1418/1997) p. 243 and al-Ṭanāḥī, *Asrār* (2:509).

1243 Cf. J (1:262) and Abū Ḥayyān, *Baḥr* (1:342).

وَكَأَنَّ الظَّنَّ، لَمَّا شَابَهَ الْعِلْمَ فِي الرُّجْحَانِ، أُطْلِقَ عَلَيْهِ، لِتَضْمِينِ مَعْنَى التَّوَقُّعِ. قَالَ أَوْسُ بْنُ حَجَرٍ: [الطويل]

فَأَرْسَلْتُهُ مُسْتَيْقِنَ الظَّنِّ أَنَّهُ * مُخَالِطُ مَا بَيْنَ الشَّرَاسِيفِ جَائِفُ

وَإِنَّمَا لَمْ يَثْقُلْ عَلَيْهِمْ ثِقَلَهَا عَلَى غَيْرِهِمْ - فَإِنَّ نُفُوسَهُمْ مُرْتَاضَةٌ بِأَمْثَالِهَا، مُتَوَقِّعَةٌ فِي مُقَابَلَتِهَا مَا يُسْتَحْقَرُ لِأَجْلِهِ مَشَاقُّهَا وَيُسْتَلَذُّ بِسَبَبِهِ مَتَاعِبُهَا - وَمِنْ ثَمَّةَ قَالَ - عَلَيْهِ الصَّلَاةُ وَالسَّلَامُ -: **وَجُعِلَتْ قُرَّةُ عَيْنِي فِي الصَّلَاةِ.**

﴿يَٰبَنِيٓ إِسۡرَٰٓءِيلَ ٱذۡكُرُواْ نِعۡمَتِيَ ٱلَّتِيٓ أَنۡعَمۡتُ عَلَيۡكُمۡ﴾: ....

it were, since presumption resembles knowledge in preponderance, the former was used to express the latter because the meaning of expectation is implied. Aws b. Ḥajar said: ["The Long"]

So I loosed it, positively presuming[1244] *it went*
smack in between the rib-ends and into the gut.[1245]

It did not weigh heavily upon them as opposed to others. For their souls were disciplined through its like and expected, in return, that for which they did not care how much hardship they incurred and in return for which all difficulties felt sweet. This is why the Prophet—upon him blessings and peace—said,

and the coolness of my eye was made to be in prayer.[1246]

[The divine preferentiation of the Israelites at one time]

[2:47] **yā banī Isrā'īla dhkurū niʿmatiya-l-latī anʿamtu ʿalaykum** (*O sons of Isrā'īl! Remember My favor which I lavished on you*): He

[1244] All mss. and eds.: مستيقن الظن AQ, H: مستيقن الظل typo.

[1245] Spoken in reference to the onager. *Dīwān Aws b. Ḥajar*, ed. Muḥammad Yūsuf Najm (Beirut: Dār Bayrūt, 1400/1980) p. 72 with *arsalahu* instead of *arsaltuhu*.

[1246] Narrated from Anas by Aḥmad (19:305-306 §12293), al-Nasā'ī, *Sunan* (*'Ushrat al-nisā', bāb ḥubb al-nisā'*) and al-Ḥākim, *Mustadrak* (2:160) among others with a fair chain according to al-Ḍiyā' al-Maqdisī, al-'Irāqī, Ibn Ḥajar, al-Suyūṭī and others.

كَرَّرَهُ لِلتَّأْكِيدِ، وَتَذْكِيرِ التَّفْضِيلِ الَّذِي هُوَ أَجَلُّ النِّعَمِ خُصُوصــاً؛ وَرَبَطَهُ بِالْوَعِيدِ الشَّدِيدِ، تَخْوِيفاً لِمَنْ غَفَلَ عَنْهَا وَأَخَلَّ بِحُقُوقِهَا.

﴿ وَأَنِّي فَضَّلْتُكُمْ ﴾: عَطْفٌ عَلَى ﴿ نِعْمَتِيَ ﴾.

﴿ عَلَى ٱلْعَٰلَمِينَ ﴾، أَيْ عَالَمِي زَمَانِهِمْ. يُرِيدُ بِهِ تَفْضِيلَ آبَائِهِمْ ـ الَّذِينَ كَانُوا فِي عَصْرِ مُوسَى، عَلَيْهِ الصَّلَاةُ وَالسَّلَامُ، وَبَعْدَهُ، قَبْلَ أَنْ يُغَيِّرُوا ـ بِمَا مَنَحَهُمُ اللهُ تَعَالَى مِنَ الْعِلْـمِ وَالْإِيمَانِ وَالْعَمَـلِ الصَّالِـحِ، وَجَعَلَهُمْ أَنْبِيَاءَ وَمُلُوكـاً مُقْسِطِينَ. وَاسْتُدِلَّ بِهِ عَلَى تَفْضِيلِ الْبَشَرِ عَلَى الْمَلَكِ؛ وَهُوَ ضَعِيفٌ.

repeated it for emphasis and the reminder of preferentiation—which is the most tremendous of favors—in particular, and he tied it to the direst threat as a deterrent for those who are heedless of it and remiss in its [resulting] obligations.

wa-annī faḍḍaltukum ⁽*and that I have preferred you*⁾: adjunction to ***niʿmatī***.

ʿalā-l-ʿālamīna ⁽*over the worlds*⁾, that is the worlds of their time,[1247] by which He means the preference given to their forefathers (in the time of Mūsā—upon him blessings and peace—and thereafter, before they changed[1248]) in what Allah Most High had granted them of knowledge, faith and good deeds, making them prophets and kings who ruled justly. [The verse] was used as proof of the preferentiation of human beings over angels—a weak view.

1247 Narrated from (i) Mujāhid, (ii) Abū al-ʿĀliya, (iii) Qatāda, (iv) ʿAbd al-Raḥmān b. Zayd b. Aslam by al-Ṭabarī, *Tafsīr* (1:629-630); and in similar terms (v) al-Rabīʿ b. Anas and (vi) Ismāʿīl b. Abī Khālid cf. Ibn Abī Ḥātim, *Tafsīr* (1:104 §497). "Shaykh Saʿd al-Dīn [al-Taftāzānī] said: "*Ālamīn* does not refer to all other than Allah (to necessarily deduce they were preferred over the angels); nor to all people (to necessarily deduce they were preferred over our Prophet and his Community). Hence it was explained as the worlds of their time."" (S 2:229)

1248 All eds. and mss: يغيّروا AQ, F, H, MM: يُضِرّوا blunder.

﴿ وَٱتَّقُواْ يَوۡمًا ﴾، أَيْ مَا فِيهِ مِنَ الْحِسَابِ وَالْعَذَابِ.

﴿ لَّا تَجۡزِي نَفۡسٌ عَن نَّفۡسٖ شَيۡـٔٗا ﴾: لَا تَقْضِي عَنْهَا شَيْئاً مِنَ الْحُقُوقِ؛ أَوْ شَيْئاً مِنَ الْجَزَاءِ، فَيَكُونُ نَصْبُهُ عَلَى الْمَصْدَرِ.

وَقُرِئَ (لَا تُجْزِئُ) مِنْ (أَجْزَأَ عَنْهُ) إِذَا أَغْنَى؛ وَعَلَى هٰذَا، تَعَيَّنَ أَنْ يَكُونَ مَصْدَراً.

وَإِيرَادُهُ مُنَكَّراً - مَعَ تَنْكِيرِ النَّفْسَيْنِ - لِلتَّعْمِيمِ وَالْإِقْنَاطِ الْكُلِّيِّ.

وَالْجُمْلَةُ صِفَةٌ لِـ﴿ يَوۡمًا ﴾؛ وَالْعَائِدُ فِيهَا مَحْذُوفٌ، تَقْدِيرُهُ: لَا تَجْزِي فِيهِ. وَمَنْ لَمْ يُجَوِّزْ ....

[2:48] **wa-t-taqū yawman** ⁽*and beware a day*⁾, that is, what is in that day of accounting and punishment.

lā tajzī nafsun ʿan nafsin shayʾan ⁽*a soul cannot pay anything on behalf of another soul*⁾: no soul can repay on behalf of another (i) any of the rights it owes; or (ii) any compensation,[1249] in which case the accusative denotes an infinitive noun.

It was also read *lā tujziʾu*[1250]—from *ajzaʾa ʿanhu* ⁽make satisfaction on his behalf⁾ when someone suffices his need—in which case it is definitely an infinitive noun.

[***Shayʾan*** ⁽a thing⁾] is adduced as an indefinite—as are the two instances of ***nafs*** ⁽soul⁾—for universalization and total hopelessness.

The [entire] sentence is a qualificative for ***yawman*** ⁽a day⁾. Its connector-pronoun is suppressed and the subaudition is *lā tajzī fīhi* ⁽whereupon it cannot pay⁾. Those who deem it incorrect to

[1249] In absolute terms. (Q)
[1250] By Abū al-Sammāl al-ʿAdawī and Abū al-Sawwār al-Ghanawī. (*MQ*)

حَذفَ الْعَائِدِ الْمَجْرُورِ قَالَ: اِتُّسِعَ فِيهِ، فَحُذِفَ عَنْهُ الْجَارُّ وَأُجْرِيَ مُجْرَى الْمَفْعُولِ بِهِ، ثُمَّ حُذِفَ كَمَا حُذِفَ مِنْ قَوْلِهِ: [الوافر]

.... * .... أَمْ مَالٌ أَصَابُوا

﴿وَلَا يُقْبَلُ مِنْهَا شَفَٰعَةٌ وَلَا يُؤْخَذُ مِنْهَا عَدْلٌ﴾، أَيْ مِنَ النَّفْسِ الثَّانِيَةِ الْعَاصِيَةِ؛ أَوْ مِنَ الْأُولَى. وَكَأَنَّهُ أُرِيدَ بِالْآيَةِ نَفْيُ أَنْ يَدْفَعَ الْعَذَابَ أَحَدٌ عَنْ أَحَدٍ مِنْ كُلِّ وَجْهٍ مُحْتَمَلٍ. ....

suppress the annexed connector-pronoun said that by rhetorical license the preposition was suppressed from it and it was treated as a direct object; then it was suppressed [entirely] just as it was suppressed in the [poet's] saying:[1251] ["The Exuberant"]

or some fortune they made (mālun aṣābū)?[1252]

wa-lā yuqbalu minhā shafāʿatun wa-lā yuʾkhadhu minhā ʿadlun ⁽*and no intercession will be accepted from it and no redemption taken*⁾, that is, from the second, sinful soul;[1253] or from the first, as if the verse were meant as a denial that anyone can save anyone else from punishment in any possible way whatsoever.

1251 "Namely, when the *ẓarf* ⁽temporal-local vessel⁾ is treated as a *mafʿūl bihi* ⁽direct object⁾ governed by the verb transitively without its appropriate word, as in his saying *wa-yawmin shahidnāhu Sulayman wa-ʿĀmiran* ⁽and a day we witnessed Sulaym and ʿĀmir⁾ when it is normally *shahidnā fīhi* ⁽in which we witnessed⁾... so when it became possible to suppress its word with the vessel, the annexed connector-pronoun was suppressed by rhetorical license in that the preposition was suppressed—since that is its vessel—and the pronominal object of the preposition was attached to the verb, becoming accusative; then it was wholly suppressed from the qualifying clause." (Z 1:297)

1252 "I.e. *aṣābūh* ⁽that they made⁾." (Q) The full verse says "I do not know—has some ill report changed them, // and long absence, or some fortune they made?" Spoken by the Jāhiliyya-born Companion and physician al-Ḥārith b. Kalada addressing his cousins for their protracted silence and lack of response to his many letters in "one of the gentlest rebukes ever composed." Ibn al-Shajarī, *al-Amālī*, ed. Maḥmūd al-Ṭanāḥi, 3 vols. (Cairo: Maktabat al-Khānjī, 1413/1992) 1:10, 2:71, 3:107.

1253 "He suggests it as the preferred position, also in the following clause and as echoed

فَإِنَّهُ إِمَّا أَنْ يَكُونَ قَهراً أَوْ غَيْرَهُ. وَالْأَوَّلُ: النُّصرَةُ؛ وَالثَّانِي: إِمَّا أَنْ يَكُونَ مَجَّاناً أَوْ غَيْرَهُ. وَالْأَوَّلُ: أَنْ يَشْفَعَ لَهُ؛ وَالثَّانِي: إِمَّا بِأَدَاءِ مَا كَانَ عَلَيْهِ ـ وَهُوَ أَنْ يُجْزَى عَنْهُ ـ أَوْ بِغَيْرِهِ، وَهُوَ أَنْ يُعْطِيَ عَنْهُ عَدْلاً.

وَ(**الشَّفَاعَةُ**) مِنَ (الشَّفْعِ)؛ كَأَنَّ الْمَشْفُوعَ لَهُ كَانَ فَرْداً، فَجَعَلَهُ الشَّفِيعُ شَفْعاً بِضَمِّ نَفْسِهِ إِلَيْهِ. وَ(**الْعَدْلُ**): الْفِدْيَةُ؛ وَقِيلَ: الْبَدَلُ؛ وَأَصْلُهُ التَّسْوِيَةُ، سُمِّيَ بِهِ الْفِدْيَةُ لِأَنَّهَا سُوِّيَتْ بِالْمَفْدِيِّ.

وَقَرَأَ ابْنُ كَثِيرٍ وَأَبُو عَمْرٍو: ﴿**وَلَا تُقْبَلُ**﴾ بِالتَّاءِ.

For such is either by violent means—which is succor—or otherwise; the latter is either gratuitous—which is for one to intercede for another—or otherwise. The latter is either by fulfilling someone's obligation—namely that it be paid on his behalf—or otherwise, namely, to give some redemption on his behalf.

Shafāʿa ⁽intercession⁾ is from *shafʿ* ⁽pairing⁾, as if the beneficiary of intercession was alone at first, then the intercessor turned him into a pair by joining up with him.

ʿAdl ⁽redemption⁾ is *fidya* ⁽ransom⁾. It was also said it means a substitute. Literally it means sameness, and the ransom was thus named because it was made identical[1254] with the thing ransomed.

Ibn Kathīr and Abū ʿAmr read it *wa-lā tuqbalu* with a *tāʾ*.[1255]

in al-Baqara 2:123.... however, it is more apparent that the first soul is meant since the verse was revealed in rebuttal of the Jews who were claiming that their forefathers would intercede from them" (Kh), which the Qadi himself states further down.

[1254] All mss. and eds.: سويت AQ, H: سميت typo.

[1255] As did Yaʿqūb, Ibn Muḥayṣin and al-Yazīdī. It is the preferred reading of the Meccans and Basrians. (*MQ*)

﴿وَلَا هُمْ يُنصَرُونَ﴾: يُمْنَعُونَ مِنْ عَذَابِ الله. وَالضَّمِيرُ: لِمَا دَلَّتْ عَلَيْهِ النَّفْسُ الثَّانِيَــــةُ ـ الْمُنَكَّرَةُ الْوَاقِعَةُ فِي سِيَاقِ النَّفْيِ ـ مِنَ النُّفُوسِ الْكَثِيرَةِ؛ وَتَذْكِيرُهُ بِمَعْنَى الْعِبَادِ، أَوِ الْأَنَاسِيِّ.

وَ(النَّصْرُ) أَخَصُّ مِنَ الْمَعُونَةِ، لِاخْتِصَاصِهِ بِدَفْعِ الضُّرِّ.

وَقَدْ تَمَسَّكَتِ الْمُعْتَزِلَةُ بِهَذِهِ الْآيَةِ عَلَى نَفْيِ الشَّفَاعَةِ لِأَهْلِ الْكَبَائِرِ؛ وَأُجِيبَ بِأَنَّهَا مَخْصُوصَةٌ بِالْكُفَّارِ لِلْآيَاتِ وَالْأَحَادِيثِ الْوَارِدَةِ …………

wa-lā hum yunṣarūna ʿ*nor will they get any succor*ʾ, [i.e.] have any defense against the divine punishment.

The personal pronoun stands for what the second soul signified—as an indefinite within a negative statement[1256]—of a multitude of souls; it is a masculine in the sense of "worshippers" or "human beings."[1257]

Al-naṣr ʿsuccorʾ is more specific than *al-maʿūna* ʿassistanceʾ because it is specific to the repelling of harm.

[The non-Sunni claim that once in hellfire always in hellfire]

The Muʿtazila clang to this verse to disprove intercession for grave sinners.[1258] The reply is that such is specific[1259] to the unbelievers in light of the verses and hadiths that came up regard-

[1256] All mss. and eds.: في سياق النفى AQ, H, MM: في سياق النفس typo.
[1257] "Al-Ḥalabī said: 'True, but the grammarians have stipulated that such [syntax] is only in case of absolute necessity (*ḍarūra*). So it is more appropriate that it refer back to the unbelievers who are presupposed by the verse, as Ibn 'Aṭiyya said." (S) Cf. al-Samīn al-Ḥalabī, *al-Durr al-Maṣūn fī 'Ulūm al-Kitāb al-Maknūn*, ed. Aḥmad al-Kharrāṭ, 11 vols. (Damascus: Dār al-Qalam, 1406/1986) 1:339-340 and Ibn 'Aṭiyya, *al-Muḥarrar al-Wajīz* (1:139).
[1258] Cf. our glossary of persons and sects.
[1259] All mss. and eds.: مخصوصة H: خصوصة typo.

فِي الشَّفَاعَةِ. وَيُؤَيِّدُهُ أَنَّ الْخِطَابَ مَعَهُمْ، وَالْآيَةُ نَزَلَتْ رَدّاً لِمَا كَانَتِ الْيَهُودُ تَزْعُمُ أَنَّ آبَاءَهُمْ تَشْفَعُ لَهُمْ.

﴿وَإِذْ نَجَّيْنَٰكُم مِّنْ ءَالِ فِرْعَوْنَ﴾ تَفْصِيلٌ لِمَا أَجْمَلَهُ فِي قَوْلِهِ ﴿ٱذْكُرُوا۟ نِعْمَتِىَ ٱلَّتِىٓ أَنْعَمْتُ عَلَيْكُمْ﴾ [البقرة ٤٠]، وَعَطْفٌ عَلَى ﴿نِعْمَتِىَ﴾ عَطْفَ ﴿جِبْرِيلَ﴾ وَ﴿مِيكَائِيلَ﴾ على المَلَائِكَةِ. وَقُرِئَ (نَجَّيْتُكُمْ).

وَأَصْلُ (آلٍ): (أَهْلٌ)، لِأَنَّ تَصْغِيرَهُ: (أُهَيْلٌ). وَخُصَّ بِالْإِضَافَةِ إِلَى أُولِي الْخَطَرِ، كَالْأَنْبِيَاءِ وَالْمُلُوكِ.

ing intercession. This is further supported by the fact that it is addressed to them, and the verse came down in rebuttal of the claim of the Jews that their forefathers would intercede for them.

[2:49] **wa-idh najjaynākum min āli Firʿawna** ⟨*and when We saved you from the house of Pharaoh*⟩ is an exposition for what was left unexplained when He said *Remember My favor which I lavished on you* (al-Baqara 2:40) and is adjoined to ***niʿmatī*** ⟨My favor⟩ the way *Jibraʾīl*[1260] and *Mīkāʾīl* were adjoined to *al-malāʾika* [in *Whoever is an enemy to Allah, His angels, His messengers, Jibraʾīl and Mīkāʾīl* (al-Baqara 2:98)]. It was also read *najjaytukum.*[1261]

The origin of ***āl*** ⟨house⟩ is *ahl* ⟨family⟩ because its diminutive is *uhayl.*[1262] Its use in construct was made specific to those of momentous rank such as prophets and kings.[1263]

[1260] α, B, D, ε, I, P, T: جبرئيل Ak, β, F, H, K, Kh, L, MM, U, Ul, Z: جبريل R, Q, Sk: جبرائيل

[1261] B, J: نَجَّيْتُكُمْ : thus read by Ibrāhīm al-Nakhaʿī and cited by J. (*MQ*) α, Ak, β, ε, F, I, K, R, Sk, T: أَنْجَيْتُكُمْ : an unidentified, anomalous reading but its existence was confirmed by al-Samīn al-Ḥalabī in *al-Durr al-Maṣūn*. Kh, L, Q, U, Ul, Z: أنجيتكم ونجيتكم

[1262] Cf. al-ʿAskarī, *al-Talkhīṣ fī Maʿrifat Asmāʾ al-Ashyāʾ*, ed. ʿIzzat Hasan, 2nd ed. (Damascus: Dāt Ṭlās, 1996) p. 132 and Ibn Sīdah, *Mukhaṣṣaṣ* (3:128).

[1263] See art. *āl* in ʿAbd al-Nabī b. ʿAbd al-Rasūl Aḥmadnagarī, *Mawsūʿat Muṣṭalaḥāt Jāmiʿ al-ʿUlum al-Mulaqqab bi-Dustūr al-ʿUlamāʾ*, ed. ʿAlī Dahrūj et al. (Beirut:

وَ(فِرْعَوْنُ) لَقَبٌ لِمَنْ مَلَكَ الْعَمَالِقَةَ، كَـ(كِسْرَى) وَ(قَيْصَرَ) لِمَلِكَي الْفُرْسِ وَالرُّومِ. وَلِعُتُوِّهِمُ اشْتُقَّ مِنْهُ (تَفَرْعَنَ الرَّجُلُ) إِذَا عَتَا وَتَجَبَّرَ. وَكَانَ فِرْعَوْنُ مُوسَى ـ مُصْعَبُ بْنُ رَيَّانَ، وَقِيلَ: ابْنُهُ وَلِيدُ ـ مِنْ بَقَايَا عَادٍ. وَفِرْعَوْنُ يُوسُفَ ـ عَلَيْهِ السَّلَامُ ـ رَيَّانُ، وَكَانَ بَيْنَهُمَا أَكْثَرُ مِنْ أَرْبَعِمِائَةِ سَنَةٍ.

﴿يَسُومُونَكُمْ﴾: يَبْغُونَكُمْ؛ مِنْ (سَامَهُ خَسْفاً) إِذَا أَوْلَاهُ ظُلْماً. وَأَصْلُ (السَّوْمِ): الذَّهَابُ فِي طَلَبِ الشَّيْءِ.

Firʿawn ‹*Pharaoh*› is a title for whoever holds sway over the Amalekites,[1264] like "Kisrā" ‹Chosroes› and "Qayṣar" ‹Caesar› for the two kings of Persia and Rome respectively. Because of their rebellious pride the expression *tafarʿana al-rajul* ‹the man acts pharaonic› was derived from it to describe someone who rebels and becomes a tyrant.

Mūsā's Pharaoh was Muṣʿab b. Rayyān—some say his son[1265] Walīd[1266]—and he was from the remnant of [the people of] ʿĀd. The Pharaoh of Yūsuf ‹Joseph›—upon him peace—was Rayyān, with more than four hundred years between the two.

yasūmūnakum ‹*as they persecuted you*›: "targeted you" from *sāmahu khasfan* ‹he brought harm upon him› when one works injustice upon another. *Sawm*, literally, is to go in pursuit of something.

Maktabat Lubnān, 1997).

1264 "The Amalekites are the children of ʿImlīq ‹Amalek› b. Lāwudh ‹Lud? Eliphaz?› b. Iram ‹Aram? Edom?› b. Sām ‹Shem› b. Nūḥ ‹Noah› according to al-Taftāzānī." (S)

1265 α, Ak, AQ, B, D, F, H, I, K, Kh, L, MM, P, U, Ul, Z: ابنه T: ابنه with interlinear superscript اسمه ε, Q, S, Sk: اسمه error β: واسمه ابنه interpolation.

1266 I.e. Walīd b. Muṣʿab b. Rayyān. "And the latter is the most famous view, held by Ibn Isḥāq and most of the exegetes." (S) Cf. also *Ṣiḥāḥ* and *Tāj al-ʿArūs*.

﴿سُوٓءَ ٱلۡعَذَابِ﴾: أَفْظَعَهُ؛ فَإِنَّهُ قَبِيحٌ بِالْإِضَافَةِ إِلَى سَائِرِهِ.

وَ(السُّوءُ) مَصْدَرُ (سَاءَ يَسُوءُ)، وَنَصْبُهُ عَلَى الْمَفْعُولِ لِـ﴿يَسُومُونَكُمۡ﴾.

وَالْجُمْلَةُ حَالٌ مِنَ الضَّمِيرِ فِي ﴿نَجَّيۡنَٰكُم﴾؛ أَوْ مِنْ ﴿ءَالِ فِرۡعَوۡنَ﴾؛ أَوْ مِنْهُمَا جَمِيعاً، لِأَنَّ فِيهَا ضَمِيرَ كُلٍّ وَاحِدٍ مِنْهُمَا.

﴿يُذَبِّحُونَ أَبۡنَآءَكُمۡ وَيَسۡتَحۡيُونَ نِسَآءَكُمۡ﴾: بَيَانٌ لِـ﴿يَسُومُونَكُمۡ﴾، وَلِذٰلِكَ لَمْ يُعْطَفْ. وَقُرِئَ (يَذْبَحُونَ) بِالتَّخْفِيفِ.

وَإِنَّمَا فَعَلُوا بِهِمْ ذٰلِكَ لِأَنَّ فِرْعَوْنَ رَأَى فِي الْمَنَامِ، أَوْ قَالَ لَهُ الْكَهَنَةُ: ...

sūʾa-l-ʿadhābi ⁽*with evil torment*⁾: with the most heinous torment—for it was truly foul in comparison to all other types.

Sūʾ ⁽evil⁾ is the infinitive noun for *sāʾa*, [aorist] *yasūʾu* ⁽to be evil⁾. It is in the accusative as the direct object of *yasūmūnakum* ⁽they persecuted you⁾. The whole clause is a participial state for the [object] personal pronoun in ***najjaynākum*** ⁽We saved you⁾, or for ***āli Firʿawna*** ⁽the house of Pharaoh⁾ or for both of them together, since it contains the personal pronoun of each respectively.

yudhabbiḥuna abnāʾakum wa-yastaḥyūna nisāʾakum ⁽*massacring your sons and sparing your females*⁾ is an exposition of ***yasūmūnakum*** ⁽they persecuted you⁾, hence it was not adjoined [with a conjunction].

It was also read *yadhbaḥūna* in a lighter form.[1267]

The reason they were doing this to them was that Pharaoh had seen in a dream or had been told by the oracles there would

[1267] By al-Zuhrī and Ibn Muḥayṣin. Another lighter reading was *yudhbiḥūna*, while the reading *yuqattilūna* ⁽killing indiscriminately⁾ is related from Ibn Masʿūd. (*MQ*)

سَيُولَدُ مِنْهُمْ مَنْ يَذْهَبُ بِمُلْكِهِ. فَلَمْ يَرُدَّ اجْتِهَادُهُمْ مِنْ قَدَرِ اللهِ شَيْئاً.

﴿وَفِي ذَٰلِكُم بَلَآءٌ﴾: (أ) مِحْنَةٌ - إِنْ أُشِيرَ بِـ﴿ذَٰلِكُم﴾ إِلَى صَنِيعِهِمْ - (ب) وَنِعْمَةٌ - إِنْ أُشِيرَ بِهِ إِلَى الْإِنْجَاءِ. وَأَصْلُهُ: الِاخْتِبَارُ؛ لٰكِنْ لَمَّا كَانَ اخْتِبَارُ اللهِ تَعَالَى عِبَادَهُ تَارَةً بِالْمِحْنَةِ وَتَارَةً بِالْمِنْحَةِ، أُطْلِقَ عَلَيْهِمَا. وَيَجُوزُ أَنْ يُشَارَ بِـ﴿ذَٰلِكُم﴾ إِلَى الْجُمْلَةِ؛ وَيُرَادَ بِهِ الِامْتِحَانُ الشَّائِعُ بَيْنَهُمَا.

﴿مِّن رَّبِّكُمْ﴾ بِتَسْلِيطِهِمْ عَلَيْكُمْ؛ أَوْ بِبَعْثِ مُوسَى - عَلَيْهِ السَّلَامُ - وَتَوْفِيقِهِ لِتَخْلِيصِكُمْ؛ أَوْ بِهِمَا. ﴿عَظِيمٌ﴾: صِفَةُ ﴿بَلَآءٌ﴾.

be born one in their midst who would wrest dominion from him; but all their striving availed them nothing against the appointed decree of Allah.

[Ordeals and blessings are both divine tests]

wa-fī dhālikum balā'un ‹*and in that you faced a trial*›:

(i) an ordeal, if ***dhālikum*** ‹that› refers to what they perpetrated;

(ii) and a blessing if it refers to their deliverance.

Literally, [***balā'***] is *ikhtibār* ‹testing›, but because Allah Most High tests His servants alternately through banes (*miḥna*) and boons (*minḥa*),[1268] it applies to both; and it is also possible that ***dhālikum*** refers to the sentence, whereby what is meant is the testing both of them[1269] have in common.

min Rabbikum ‹*on the part of your Nurturer*› consisting in His unleashing them on you, or in sending forth Mūsā—upon him peace—and granting him success for their deliverance, or both.

'aẓīmun ‹*tremendous!*› is a descriptive for ***balā'*** ‹trial›.

[1268] An alliterative wordplay of the type *jinās maqlūb* ‹anagrammatic paronomasia›, cf. Cachia, *Arch Rhetorician* (p. 27 §40) typically used to mnemonic and didactic ends.

[1269] "I.e. favor and trouble." (Q)

وَفِي الْآيَةِ تَنْبِيهٌ عَلَى أَنَّ مَا يُصِيبُ الْعَبْدَ مِنْ خَيْرٍ أَوْ شَرٍّ: إِخْتِبَارٌ مِنَ اللهِ تَعَالَى؛ فَعَلَيْهِ أَنْ يَشْكُرَ عَلَى مَسَارِّهِ وَيَصْبِرَ عَلَى مَضَارِّهِ، لِيَكُونَ مِنْ خَيْرِ الْمُخْتَبَرِينَ.

﴿وَإِذْ فَرَقْنَا بِكُمُ الْبَحْرَ﴾: فَلَقْنَاهُ وَفَصَلْنَا بَيْنَ بَعْضِهِ وَبَعْضٍ، حَتَّى حَصَلَتْ فِيهِ مَسَالِكُ (أ) بِسُلُوكِكُمْ فِيهِ؛ (ب) أَوْ بِسَبَبِ إِنْجَائِكُمْ؛ (ج) أَوْ مُلْتَبِساً بِكُمْ، كَقَوْلِهِ: [الوافر]

.... * تَدُوسُ بِنَا الْجَمَاجِمَ وَالتَّرِيبَا

وَقُرِئَ (فَرَّقْنَا) عَلَى بِنَاءِ التَّكْثِيرِ، لِأَنَّ الْمَسَالِكَ كَانَتِ اثْنَي عَشَرَ، بِعَدَدِ الْأَسْبَاطِ.

In the verse there is a notification that whatever good or evil affects a servant is a test from Allah Most High. Let one, therefore, give thanks for one's happy states and be steadfast in adversities, so that one will be among the best testees.

[2:50] **wa-idh faraqnā bikumu-l-baḥra** ⁽*and when We parted the sea with you*⁾: "We cleaved it and sectioned off its various parts so that there were pathways in it (i) "by means of your passing through it;" (ii) or "for the sake of saving you;" (iii) or "mixing with you," as in [the poet's] saying: ["The Exuberant"]

[our mounts] trampling with us (binā) skulls and breastbones.[1270]

It was also read *farraqnā* ⁽We split into parts⁾ as a stem-form of multitude, because the pathways were twelve, to the number of the Tribes.

1270 Second hemistich of a verse spoken by al-Mutanabbī of riders so valiant that their horses became accustomed to riding over the dead without fear, in his panegyric of ʿAlī b. Muḥammad b. Sayyār al-Tamīmī, cf. al-Barqūqī, *Sharḥ Dīwān al-Mutanabbī* (1:265). The first hemistich says *So they passed unfazed over them.*

﴿فَأَنجَيۡنَٰكُمۡ وَأَغۡرَقۡنَآ ءَالَ فِرۡعَوۡنَ﴾: أَرَادَ بِهِ فِرْعَوْنَ وَقَوْمَهُ؛ وَاقْتَصَرَ عَلَى ذِكْرِهِمْ لِلْعِلْمِ بِأَنَّهُ كَانَ أَوْلَى بِهِ؛ وَقِيلَ: شَخْصَهُ - كَمَا رُوِيَ أَنَّ الْحَسَنَ كَانَ يَقُولُ: (اللّٰهُمَّ صَلِّ عَلَى آلِ مُحَمَّدٍ) أَيْ شَخْصِهِ - وَاسْتَغْنَى بِذِكْرِهِ عَنْ ذِكْرِ أَتْبَاعِهِ.

[The word *āl* means *ahl* ⁽family, people⁾ including their head]

fa-anjaynākum wa-aghraqnā āla Firʿawna ⁽*whereupon We saved you and drowned the house of Pharaoh*⁾: He meant by it [both] Pharaoh and his nation.[1271] It was enough to mention the latter alone because it is understood he is even more deserving of it.[1272] It is also said [***āl***] means his actual person[1273]—as in the report that al-Ḥasan would say, *Allāhumma ṣalli ʿalā Āli Muḥammad!* ⁽O Allah, bless the house of Muḥammad⁾,[1274] meaning his person—so that mentioning him alone was enough, without need to mention his followers.

[1271] Just as it is said "Banū Hāshim" to mean both Hāshim and his sons, and "Banū Ādam" to mean both Adam and human beings. (Z)

[1272] "He should have said '*Or*' to introduce this as an alternate meaning: if they were punished by drowning, the wellspring of obduracy and head of misguidance was more deserving of that." (Z) "It is best to consider it a case of the figure *rākib al-nāqa ṭalīḥān* ⁽the rider of the camel—both exhausted⁾ (see note 1038) in view of the annex construct, rather than one of suppression of one or the other of a pair of adjuncts as the author said." (S)

[1273] Cf. Abū Hilāl al-ʿAskarī (d. 395/1005), *al-Wujūh wal-Naẓā'ir*, ed. Muḥammad ʿUthmān (Cairo: Maktabat al-Thaqafa al-Dīniyya, 1428/2007) p. 84; al-Qaysī (567?/1172?), *Īḍāḥ Shawāhid al-Īḍāḥ*, ed. Muḥammad al-Daʿjānī, 2 vols. (Beirut: Dār al-Gharb al-Islāmī, 1408/1987) 1:270; and al-Rāghib, *Mufradāt*, *s.v.* "The use of *āl* to mean the very person is lexically established, however, it is faulty (*rakīk*) as there is no need for it." (Z)

[1274] Neither al-Suyūṭī nor al-Munāwī documents it but it is adduced in elucidation of the second half of the well-established hadith "Say: *Allāhumma ṣalli ʿalā Muḥammadin wa-ʿalā Āli Muḥammadin, wa-ṣalli ʿalā Āli Ibrāhīma*" in the *Ṣiḥāḥ* and *Sunan*, cf. Ibn al-Munayyir (620-683/1223-1284), *al-Mutawārī ʿalā Tarājim Abwāb al-Bukhārī*, ed.

﴿وَأَنتُمْ تَنظُرُونَ﴾ ذٰلِكَ: أَيْ (أ) غَرَقَهُمْ وَإِطْبَاقَ الْبَحْرِ عَلَيْهِمْ؛ (ب) أَوِ انْفِلَاقَ الْبَحْرِ عَنْ طُرُقٍ يَابِسَةٍ مُذَلَّلَةٍ؛ (ج) أَوْ جُثَثَهُمُ الَّتِي قَذَفَهَا الْبَحْرُ إِلَى السَّاحِلِ؛ (د) أَوْ يَنْظُرُ بَعْضُكُمْ بَعْضاً. رُوِيَ أَنَّهُ تَعَالَى أَمَرَ مُوسَى ـ عَلَيْهِ السَّلَامُ ـ أَنْ يَسْرِيَ بِبَنِي إِسْرَائِيلَ، فَخَرَجَ بِهِمْ، فَصَبَّحَهُمْ فِرْعَوْنُ وَجُنُودُهُ وَصَادَفُوهُمْ عَلَى شَاطِئِ الْبَحْرِ، فَأَوْحَى اللهُ تَعَالَى إِلَيْهِ ﴿أَنِ ٱضْرِب بِّعَصَاكَ ٱلْبَحْرَ﴾ [الشعراء ٦٣]، فَضَرَبَهُ، فَظَهَرَ فِيهِ اثْنَا عَشَرَ طَرِيقاً يَابِساً، فَسَلَكُوهَا، فَقَالُوا: يَا مُوسَى نَخَافُ أَنْ يَغْرَقَ بَعْضُنَا وَلَا نَعْلَمُ! فَفَتَحَ اللهُ فِيهَا كُوىً، فَتَرَاءَوْا وَتَسَامَعُوا حَتَّى عَبَرُوا الْبَحْرَ، ثُمَّ لَمَّا وَصَلَ إِلَيْهِ فِرْعَوْنُ وَرَآهُ .....

[Meaning of the Israelites' "looking on" at the Red Sea]

wa-antum tanẓurūna ‹*as you looked on*› that, namely (i) their drowning as they were submerged in the sea; (ii) or the cleaving of the sea, revealing dry, practicable pathways; (iii) or their dead bodies after the sea cast them onto the shore; (iv) or "as you were looking at one another." It is narrated that

> Allah Most High ordered Mūsā—upon him peace—to travel by night with the Israelites. He led them out but Pharaoh and his armies caught up with them at dawn and came upon them at the seashore. Allah Most High inspired him to *strike the sea with your staff* (al-Shuʿarāʾ 26:63). He struck it and there appeared in it twelve dry paths which they proceeded to take. They said: "Mūsā! We fear some of us might drown unbeknownst to us.[1275] Then Allah opened up garret windows in them through which they could see and hear one another until they crossed the sea. When Pharaoh reached it and saw

Ṣalāḥ al-Dīn Maqbūl Aḥmad (Kuwait: Maktabat al-Muʿallā, 1407/1987) p. 324.

[1275] Ak, B, β, ε, F, T: ولا نعلم α, I, R: فلا نعلم

مُنْفَلِقاً، اِقْتَحَمَ فِيهِ هُوَ وَجُنُودُهُ، فَالْتَطَمَ عَلَيْهِمْ وَأَغْرَقَهُمْ أَجْمَعِينَ.

وَاعْلَمْ أَنَّ هٰذِهِ الْوَاقِعَةَ مِنْ أَعْظَمِ مَا أَنْعَمَ اللهُ بِهِ عَلَى بَنِي إِسْرَائِيلَ، وَمِنَ الْآيَاتِ الْمُلْجِئَةِ إِلَى الْعِلْمِ بِوُجُودِ الصَّانِعِ الْحَكِيمِ وَتَصْدِيقِ مُوسَى ـ عَلَيْهِ الصَّلَاةُ وَالسَّلَامُ ـ ثُمَّ إِنَّهُمْ بَعْدَ ذٰلِكَ ﴿ٱتَّخَذُواْ ٱلْعِجْلَ﴾ [النساء ١٥٣] وَقَالُوا: ﴿لَن نُّؤْمِنَ لَكَ حَتَّىٰ نَرَى ٱللَّهَ جَهْرَةً﴾ [البقرة ٥٥] وَنَحْوَ ذٰلِكَ؛ فَهُمْ بِمَعْزِلٍ ـ فِي الْفِطْنَةِ وَالذَّكَاءِ وَسَلَامَةِ النَّفْسِ وَحُسْنِ الِاتِّبَاعِ ـ عَنْ أُمَّةِ مُحَمَّدٍ ﷺ، مَعَ أَنَّ مَا تَوَاتَرَ مِنْ مُعْجِزَاتِهِ: أُمُورٌ نَظَرِيَّةٌ [نسخة: مِثْلُ: الْقُرْآنِ، وَالتَّحَدِّي بِهِ،

it was parted open, he went in together with his armies; then it came crashing down on them and drowned them all.[1276]

[The qualitative differences between Israelites and Muslims: the former disbelieved in full sight of sensory miracles; the latter believed although their chief miracle required thought]

Know that this event was among the greatest of the favors Allah ever lavished on the Israelites and of the signs that leave one no choice other than to know that the all-wise Maker exists and to confirm the truthfulness of Mūsā—upon him blessings and peace. Yet, after that, *they resorted to the Calf* (al-Nisā' 4:153) and said *we will not believe merely for your sake but only when we see the One God openly* (al-Baqara 2:55) and other such things. Thus they are far removed in understanding, intelligence, haleness of souls and excellent followership from the community of Muḥammad—upon him blessings and peace—even though what is mass-transmitted of the latter's stunning miracles consists in matters that require reasoning[1277] <such as the Qur'ān, the chal-

[1276] Narrated from Ibn 'Abbās, al-Suddī and 'Abd al-Raḥmān b. Zayd b. Aslam by al-Ṭabarī, *Tafsīr* (1:658-662).

[1277] "As opposed to self-evident knowledge (see note 519)—except that his stunning

وَالْفَضَائِلِ الْمُجْتَمِعَةِ فِيهِ، الشَّاهِدَةِ عَلَى نُبُوَّةِ مُحَمَّدٍ ﷺ] دَقِيقَةٌ، يُدْرِكُهَا الْأَذْكِيَاءُ؛ وَإِخْبَارُه ـ عَلَيْهِ الصَّلَاةُ وَالسَّلَامُ ـ عَنْهَا: مِنْ جُمْلَةِ مُعْجِزَاتِهِ، عَلَى مَا مَرَّ تَقْرِيرُهُ.

﴿وَإِذْ وَعَدْنَا مُوسَىٰٓ أَرْبَعِينَ لَيْلَةً﴾: لَمَّا عَادُوا إِلَى مِصْرَ بَعْدَ هَلَاكِ فِرْعَوْنَ، وَعَدَ اللهُ مُوسَى أَنْ يُعْطِيَهُ ....

lenge thereby and the virtues gathered therein that witness to Muḥammad's prophethood (upon him blessings and peace)>[1278] and sagacity, which [only] the intelligent can grasp. His reporting it is itself one of his stunning miracles, as resolved before.[1279]

[2:51] **wa-idh waᶜadnā**[1280] **Mūsā arbaᶜīna laylatan** ⁽*and when We promised Mūsā forty nights*⁾ when they returned to Egypt after Pharaoh perished,[1281] Allah promised Mūsā that He would give

miracles were not exclusively speculative. Rather, among them are many sensory ones such as the gushing of water [from his fingers], the multiplication of food, the splitting of the moon and other than that. It may be that the author does not concede their mass-transmitted status." (Kh, Z)

1278 Thus in α, Ak, AQ, ε, H, K, Kh, MM, Sk, U but the clause "such as the Qur'ān… Muḥammad" is missing from B, β, D, F, I, L, P, Q, R, T, Ul, Z and seems to be a gloss.

1279 "Because it is from the unseen, since he did not read books for him to look them up. And in his saying *as you looked on* there is *tajawwuz* ⁽tropology⁾ in the sense: 'as your forefathers looked on,' so he made their forefathers' sighting like something visually sensory because of its absolute certainty." (Kh, Z)

1280 Ak, β, ε, F, I (*alif* crossed out), K, Kh, R (blank space after the *wāw* suggesting the *alif* was inscribed then scratched out), Z: **وعدنا** per the minority reading of Abū ʿAmr (one of the Seven), Abū Jaʿfar (one of the Ten), Yaʿqūb (one of the Ten), Shayba, al-Yazīdī, Ibn Muḥayṣin, al-Ḥasan, Abū Rajā', ʿĪsā b. ʿUmar, Qatāda and Ibn Abī Isḥāq, also preferred by Abū ʿUbayda, Abū Ḥātim, Makkī and many of the philologists (*MQ*), a spelling missed by all the modern editions from the Teheran 1272/1856 ed. onwards except K but including J, who all have the majority reading **واعدنا** as do α and B. Yet the context of J (which the Qadi follows, cf. his words "Ibn Kathīr, Nāfiʿ, Āṣim etc.") indicates he took the reading of Abū ʿAmr which, as one of the Main Seven canonical readers, is also mass-transmitted as pointed out by Abū Ḥayyān, *Baḥr* (1:356-357).

1281 "He followed J in this and it is not recognized nor has it been transmitted in any

التَّوْرَاةَ، وَضَرَبَ لَهُ مِيقَاتاً ذَا الْقَعْدَةِ وَعَشْرَ ذِي الْحِجَّةِ. وَعَبَّرَ عَنْهَا بِاللَّيَالِي لِأَنَّهَا غُرَرُ الشُّهُورِ.

وَقَرَأَ ابْنُ كَثِيرٍ وَنَافِعٌ وَعَاصِمٌ وَابْنُ عَامِرٍ وَحَمْزَةُ وَالْكِسَائِيُّ: ﴿وَٰعَدْنَا﴾، لِأَنَّهُ تَعَالَى وَعَدَهُ الْوَحْيَ، وَوَعَدَهُ مُوسَى - عَلَيْهِ السَّلَامُ - الْمَجِيءَ لِلْمِيقَاتِ إِلَى الطُّورِ.

﴿ثُمَّ ٱتَّخَذْتُمُ ٱلْعِجْلَ﴾ إِلٰهاً أَوْ مَعْبُوداً.

﴿مِنۢ بَعْدِهِۦ﴾: مِنْ بَعْدِ مُوسَى - عَلَيْهِ السَّلَامُ - أَوْ ....

him the Torah and He set a dedicated time for him in Dhū-l-Qaʿda and [the first] ten of Dhū-l-Ḥijja. He referred to them as nights because the latter inaugurate the months.

Ibn Kathīr, Nāfiʿ, ʿĀṣim, Ibn ʿĀmir, Ḥamza and al-Kisāʾī[1282] all read ***wāʿadnā*** ⟨*We gave a mutual appointment*⟩ because the Most High promised him the revelation while Mūsā—upon him peace—promised Him to come to the Mount for the Tryst.

thumma-t-takhadhtumu-l-ʿijla ⟨*then you resorted to the Calf*⟩ as a god or an object of worship.

min baʿdihi ⟨*after him*⟩: "after Mūsā"—upon him peace—or .....

report that they ever went back to Egypt after exiting it. Rather, the Qurʾān spoke to the contrary in a number of places, namely that they were in Syro-Palestine, such as the saying of Allah Most High, *and We caused the folk who were devised to inherit the eastern parts of the land and the western parts thereof which We had blessed* (al-Aʿrāf 7:137), meaning Syro-Palestine, as narrated from the authorities in *tafsīr* among the *Tābiʿīn* [i.e. al-Ḥasan and Qatāda, by ʿAbd al-Razzāq, ʿAbd b. Ḥumayd in his *Musnad*, al-Ṭabarī, Ibn al-Mundhir and Ibn Abī Ḥātim in their *Tafsīrs*, Abū al-Shaykh and Ibn ʿAsākir as mentioned in al-Suyūṭī's *Durr*; and Ibn ʿAbd al-Salām in *Targhīb Ahl al-Islām fī Suknā al-Shām*]. Nor did Mūsā attend the tryst other than on Mount Sinai, which is in Syro-Palestine, not Egypt." (S 2:240, A f°162, Kh 2:160, Z 1:301)

1282 "He confined himself to readers from the Seven; otherwise, from the Ten, there is also Khalaf." (A) And from others: Mujāhid, Ḥafṣ, al-Aʿraj and al-Aʿmash. (*MQ*)

مُضِيِّهِ.

﴿وَأَنتُمْ ظَٰلِمُونَ﴾ بِإِشْرَاكِكُمْ.

﴿ثُمَّ عَفَوْنَا عَنكُم﴾ حِينَ تُبْتُمْ. وَالْعَفْوُ مَحْوُ الْجَرِيمَةِ مِنْ (عَفَا) إِذَا دَرَسَ.

﴿مِّنۢ بَعْدِ ذَٰلِكَ﴾، أَيِ الِاتِّخَاذِ.

﴿لَعَلَّكُمْ تَشْكُرُونَ﴾: لِكَيْ تَشْكُرُوا عَفْوَهُ.

﴿وَإِذْ ءَاتَيْنَا مُوسَى ٱلْكِتَٰبَ وَٱلْفُرْقَانَ﴾، يَعْنِي التَّوْرَاةَ، الْجَامِعَ بَيْنَ كَوْنِهِ كِتَاباً وَحُجَّةً يَفْرُقُ بَيْنَ الْحَقِّ وَالْبَاطِلِ.

his departure.[1283]

wa-antum ẓālimūna ⟨*transgressing*⟩ with your polytheism.[1284]

[2:52] **thumma ʿafawnā ʿankum** ⟨*then We pardoned you*⟩ when you repented.

Al-ʿafw ⟨pardon⟩ is *maḥw al-jarīma* ⟨the deletion of crime⟩, from *ʿafā* when something becomes obliterated.

min baʿdi dhālika ⟨*after that act*⟩, that is, "that resorting."

laʿallakum tashkurūna ⟨*perhaps you will give thanks*⟩, that is, "in order that you give thanks for His pardon."

[The Book and the *Furqān* given to Mūsā]

[2:53] **wa-idh ātaynā Mūsā-l-kitāba wa-l-furqāna** ⟨*and when We gave Mūsā the Book and discernment*⟩, meaning the Torah, which is at one and the same time a book[1285] and conclusive proof that separates between truth and falsehood.

[1283] "I.e. for the Mount." (A) "One ms. has *ay muḍiyyih* ⟨meaning his departure⟩." (Kh)

[1284] "His saying 'with your polytheism' made *wa-antum ẓālimūn* a participial state; if it were made a resumptive (*mustaʾnaf*) or parenthetical (*muʿtariḍ*) the meaning would be 'and you are inveterate wrongdoers.'" (Q)

[1285] All mss. and F, S, Sk: كَونه كتابا All remaining eds.: كونه كتابا منزلا

وَقِيلَ: أَرَادَ بِالْفُرْقَانِ: (١) مُعْجِزَاتِهِ الْفَارِقَةَ (أ) بَيْنَ الْمُحِقِّ وَالْمُبْطِلِ فِي الدَّعْوَى، (ب) أَوْ بَيْنَ الْكُفْرِ وَالْإِيمَانِ؛ وَقِيلَ: (٢) الشَّرْعَ الْفَارِقَ بَيْنَ الْحَلَالِ وَالْحَرَامِ؛ (٣) أَوِ النَّصْرَ الَّذِي فَرَقَ بَيْنَهُ وَبَيْنَ عَدُوِّهِ، كَقَوْلِهِ تَعَالَى: ﴿يَوْمَ ٱلْفُرْقَانِ﴾ [الأنفال ٤١]، يُرِيدُ بِهِ يَوْمَ بَدْرٍ.

It was also said that by *furqān* He meant

1. his staggering miracles that separate (i) truthful claimants from frauds, or (ii) between unbelief and faith;

2. the sacred law which separates the licit from the unlawful;

3. or the victory that separated between him and his enemy, as in the saying of Allah Most High *the day of the Discerning* (al-Anfāl 8:41), by which He meant the day of [the battle of] Badr.[1286]

[1286] The Quranic appellation of *furqan* for the battle of Badr prophetically sums up its historical, strategic and geopolitical ramifications as the first step in the domino-like demise and assimilation of all the non-Muslim powers in the Arabian peninsula and its fringes one by one—Arabs, Jews, Romans and Persians—followed by outward expansion. The early Muslims viewed Badr as one of the major signs of end times; the Basrian *Jāhiliyya*-born *Tābiʿī* exegete Abū al-ʿĀliya Rufayʿ b. Mahrān al-Riyāḥī al-Tamīmī (d. 90/709) said: "We considered that *the day when We shall seize them with the greater seizure (then), in truth We shall punish* (al-Dukhān 44:16) was the Day of Badr" (in Ibn Abī Shayba, *Kitāb al-Maghāzī*, ed. ʿAbd al-ʿAzīz b. Ibrāhīm al-ʿUmarī, 2nd ed. (Riyadh: Dār Ishbīliā, 1422/2001) pp. 216-217 §204)—and it was indeed Ibn Masʿūd's (d. 32/ca.653) famous exegesis of " the greater seizure" (*al-baṭshat al-kubrā*) in that verse and his view that it had already taken place (al-Bukhārī, *Ṣaḥīḥ*, *Tafsīr*, *yaghshā al-nās, hādhā ʿadhābun alīm*; Muslim, *Ṣaḥīḥ*, *ṣifat al-qiyāma, al-dukhān*). Badr as *furqān* also encapsulates the Muslims' sense of self as *the* people of Belief, who can never be one again with the people of Unbelief regardless of parentage, tribe or national affiliation. The more analytical works of *sīra* have elaborated these and other global consequences of Badr at great length, cf. Muḥammad Ṣādiq ʿArjūn, *Muḥammad Rasūl Allāh*, 2nd ed., 4 vols. (Damascus: Dār al-Qalam, 1415/1995) 3:284-538; Muḥammad Abū Shahba, *al-Sīra al-Nabawiyya fī Ḍawʾ al-Qurʾān wal-Sunna*, 2nd ed., 2 vols. (Damascus, Dār al-Qalam, 1412/1992) 2:123-178; Muḥammad Saʿīd al-Būṭī, *Fiqh al-Sīra al-Nabawiyya*, 10th ed. (Damascus: Dār al-Fikr; Beirut: Dār al-Fikr al-

﴿لَعَلَّكُمْ تَهْتَدُونَ﴾: لِكَيْ تَهْتَدُوا بِتَدَبُّرِ الْكِتَابِ وَالتَّفَكُّرِ فِي الْآيَاتِ.

﴿وَإِذْ قَالَ مُوسَىٰ لِقَوْمِهِۦ يَٰقَوْمِ إِنَّكُمْ ظَلَمْتُمْ أَنفُسَكُم بِٱتِّخَاذِكُمُ ٱلْعِجْلَ فَتُوبُوٓاْ إِلَىٰ بَارِئِكُمْ﴾:

(I) فَاعْزِمُوا عَلَى التَّوْبَةِ وَالرُّجُوعِ إِلَى مَنْ خَلَقَكُمْ بَرِيئاً مِنَ التَّفَاوُتِ، وَمُمَيِّزاً بَعْضَكُمْ عَنْ بَعْضٍ بِصُوَرٍ وَهَيْئَاتٍ مُخْتَلِفَةٍ.

وَأَصْلُ التَّرْكِيبِ: لِخُلُوصِ الشَّيْءِ عَنْ غَيْرِهِ، إِمَّا عَلَى سَبِيلِ التَّقَصِّي، كَقَوْلِهِمْ: بَرِئَ الْمَرِيضُ مِنْ مَرَضِهِ وَالْمَدْيُونُ مِنْ دَيْنِهِ؛ أَوِ الْإِنْشَاءِ، كَقَوْلِهِمْ: بَرَأَ اللهُ آدَمَ مِنَ الطِّينِ.

la'allakum tahtadūna ⁽*perhaps you will be guided*⁾: "in order that you will follow guidance" by pondering the Book and reflecting on the signs.

[2:54] **wa-idh qāla Mūsā li-qawmihi yā qawmi innakum ẓalamtum anfusakum bi-ttikhādhikumu-l-ʿijla fa-tūbū ilā bāriʾikum** ⁽*and when Mūsā said to his nation: My nation! truly you have wronged yourselves by resorting to the Calf, therefore repent to your Producer*⁾: I. "firmly resolve to repent and return to the One Who created you exempt of inconsistency and distinguished you all from one another with various looks and forms."

The stem-form [***b-r-ʾ***] is originally for something being free and clear of something else, either exhaustively—as in *bariʾa al-mariḍu min maradih* ⁽the patient is clear of all trace of illness⁾ and *al-madyūnu min daynih* ⁽the debtor is free of his debt⁾—or in the sense of origination as in *baraʾa-l-Lāhu Ādama min al-ṭīn* ⁽Allah produced Adam out of mud⁾.

Muʿāṣir, 1419/1998) pp. 229-247.

(II) أَوْ: فَتُوبُوا، ﴿فَٱقْتُلُوٓاْ أَنفُسَكُمْ﴾ إِتْمَاماً لِتَوْبَتِكُـــــــمْ (أ) بِالْبَخْعِ، (ب) أَوْ قَطْعِ الشَّهَوَاتِ، كَمَا قِيلَ: مَنْ لَمْ يُعَذِّبْ نَفْسَهُ لَمْ يُنَعِّمْهَا، وَمَنْ لَمْ يَقْتُلْهَا لَمْ يُحْيِهَا؛ (ج) وَقِيلَ: أُمِرُوا أَنْ يَقْتُلَ بَعْضُهُمْ بَعْضاً؛ ....

[Autogenocide atoned for the enormity of the golden calf]

II. Or [it means] "repent

fa-qtulū anfusakum ⁽*and kill yourselves*⁾" as completion for your repentence: (i) through suicide; (ii) or through quitting lusts[1287] as in the adage, "Whoever does not punish his soul will never bless it and whoever does not kill it will never give it life."[1288] (iii) It was also said they were ordered to kill one another.[1289] ....

[1287] An exegesis popularized by al-Sulamī in his *Ḥaqā'iq al-Tafsīr*, ed. Sayyid ʿImrān, 2 vols. (Beirut: Dār al-Kutub al-ʿIlmiyya, 1421/2001) 1:59-60. "According to *Asās al-Balāgha*, using *bakhʿ* ⁽suicide⁾ to signify hardship rather than killing is an allegorical transference (*majāz*). As for saying it means the quitting of lusts, this was mentioned by some of the adepts of ruminations (*arbāb al-khawāṭir*); [but] a group [of scholars] said it is impermissible to explain it that way due to the consensus of the exegetes that what is meant here is literal killing." (S 2:244)

[1288] "As if they had been ordered to kill themselves as an allusion (*ishāra*) to the fact that whoever does not kill his enemy—which is the ego—it will kill him, so that others might see it as an example." (Iṣ) "Whoever does not punish his soul with spiritual hardships (*riyāḍāt*) will never bless it with spiritual inspirations and whoever does not kill it with the quitting of lusts will never give it life with spiritual witnessings" (Sk) "Strenuous obligations were imposed on the Israelites such as cutting off the spot of ritual impurity [e.g. on a cloth], fifty prayers in a day and night, the remittance of a quarter of one's wealth as almsgiving etc." (Q)

[1289] Which they did with knives and swords as related in al-Ṭabarī, *Tafsīr* (1:679-685), some narrations stating "in facing rows," some "including fathers and sons" and some "excluding," Mūsā all the while standing, hands raised in supplication and weeping, surrounded by the distraught women and children until he became exhausted, then some went over and held up his arms for him, until Allah accepted their repentence and they stopped utterly sad and dejected. Ibn ʿAbbās said the number of the dead reached 70,000. Allah said to Mūsā: "What makes you sad? Those of you that were killed are *alive with Me, fully provided*, and as for those who remain, I have certainly accepted their repentence." This consoled them. Qatada, Ibn Jurayj, Ibn Zayd and

وَقِيلَ: أُمِرَ مَنْ لَمْ يَعْبُدِ الْعِجْلَ أَنْ يَقْتُلَ الْعَبَدَةَ. رُوِيَ أَنَّ الرَّجُلَ كَانَ يَرَى بَعْضَهُ وَقَرِيبَهُ، فَلَمْ يَقْدِرِ الْمُضِيَّ لِأَمْرِ اللهِ، فَأَرْسَلَ اللهُ ضَبَابَةً وَسَحَابَةً سَوْدَاءَ لَا يَتَبَاصَرُونَ، فَأَخَذُوا يَقْتُلُونَ مِنَ الْغَدَاةِ إِلَى الْعَشِيِّ، حَتَّى دَعَا مُوسَى وَهَارُونُ، فَكُشِفَتِ السَّحَابَةُ وَنَزَلَتِ التَّوْبَةُ، وَكَانَتِ الْقَتْلَى سَبْعِينَ أَلْفاً. وَ(الْفَاءُ) الْأُولَى لِلتَّسْبِيبِ، وَالثَّانِيَةُ لِلتَّعْقِيبِ.

(iv) It was also said that those who had not worshipped the Calf were ordered to kill those who had.[1290] It is narrated that

> one would see one of his own [flesh and blood], or his friend,[1291] and be unable to carry out[1292] the divine command, whereupon Allah sent a fog and a black cloud so that they could not see one another. They set to killing[1293] from dawn to dusk. Then Mūsā and Hārūn supplicated so that the cloud was lifted and repentence came down. Those who were killed numbered seventy thousand.[1294]

The first ***fā'*** [i.e. in ***fa-tūbū***] is for illation[1295] while the second one [i.e. in ***fa-qtulū***] is for nextness.

others said: "It was *shahāda* for the dead and *tawba* for the survivors."

1290 Those doing the killing were armed with knives and circulating while those being killed were sitting, one report identifying the executioners as a group of 70 men who had gone away at the time of the Calf-worship, including Hārūn as narrated from Ibn ʿAbbās by al-Ṭabarī, *Tafsīr* (1:680 and 1:685-685). Another report has "12,000." (Sk)

1291 I, R, Sk: وقرينه All others have وقريبه but Kh, Z acknowledge the variant. The latter is both more logical and more in line with the reports.

1292 α, B, β, I, R, T: يقدر المضى Ak, ε, F: يقدر على المضى

1293 All mss. and eds.: يقتلون AQ, H, K, MM: يقتتلون lectio facilior grammatically but contextually incoherent.

1294 Or roughly 12% of a total of 600,000 who had fled Pharaoh and his million-strong horse (one report states 620,000 versus 1,700,000) cf. al-Ṭabarī, *Tafsīr* (1:657-660).

1295 α, β, B, ε, G, J, Kh, L, Q, Sk, T, U, Ul, Z: للتسبيب AQ, D, F, H, I, K, MM, P, R: للتسبب A, Ak, S: للسببية. Or "resultative," commonly identified as *taʿlīliyya* (Q) or *sababiyya.*

﴿ذَٰلِكُمْ خَيْرٌ لَّكُمْ عِندَ بَارِئِكُمْ﴾ مِنْ حَيْثُ إِنَّهُ طُهْرَةٌ مِنَ الشِّرْكِ، وَوُصْلَةٌ إِلَى الْحَيَاةِ الْأَبَدِيَّةِ وَالْبَهْجَةِ السَّرْمَدِيَّةِ.

﴿فَتَابَ عَلَيْكُمْ﴾: (I) مُتَعَلِّقٌ بِمَحْذُوفٍ إِنْ جَعَلْتَهُ مِنْ كَلَامِ مُوسَى ـ عَلَيْهِ السَّلَامُ ـ لَهُمْ، تَقْدِيرُهُ: إِنْ فَعَلْتُمْ مَا أُمِرْتُمْ بِهِ فَقَدْ تَابَ عَلَيْكُمْ؛ (II) وَعَطْفٌ عَلَى مَحْذُوفٍ إِنْ جَعَلْتَهُ خِطَابًا مِنَ اللهِ تَعَالَى لَهُمْ عَلَى طَرِيقَةِ الْإِلْتِفَاتِ، كَأَنَّهُ ....

dhālikum khayrun lakum ʿinda bāriʾikum⁽*such indeed*[1296] *is best for you in the sight of your Producer*⁾ from the perspective that it is a cleansing from idolatry and a link to eternal life and everlasting happiness.

fa-tāba ʿalaykum ⁽*then He relented towards you*⁾ I. pertains to a suppressed [clause] if you make it part of Mūsā's —upon him peace—discourse to them, whose subaudition is, "If you do what you are ordered then be sure He has forgiven you;"[1297]

II. and/or is adjoined[1298] to a suppressed [clause] if you make it a divine address to them by way of apostrophic redirection, as if

[1296] The *bayānī* ⁽stylistic⁾ difference between *dhālika* and *dhālikum*—other than pronominal number—is that the latter may connote (i) *taṭwīl* ⁽contextual lengthiness⁾ as opposed to concision (e.g. *dhālikum* in a long listing of divine favors in al-Anʿām 6:99 versus *dhālika* in the concise listing in al-Naḥl 16:12) or (ii) *tawkīd* ⁽emphasis⁾ as opposed to mere preference, in addition to contextual lengthiness (e.g. *dhālikum* in al-Baqara 2:232 in reference to several unabrogable and everlasting divorce rulings versus *dhālika* in al-Mujādila 58:12 for the abrogated, isolated and preferential ruling of preceding one's petition with almsgiving. See Fāḍil al-Sāmarrāʾī, *Maʿānī al-Naḥw*, 2nd ed., 4 vols. (Cairo: Sharikat al-ʿĀtik li-Ṣināʿat al-Kitāb, 1423/2003) 1:93-97. Here it points to a horrific consequence through *tafkhīm* ⁽amplification⁾ and Allah knows best.

[1297] "Which means the *fāʾ* here is a *fāʾ faṣīḥa* ⁽revelatory/correct *fāʾ*⁾, thus named because it reveals what is suppressed and because its speaker speaks pure Arabic." (Kh)

[1298] α, Ak, β, D, ε, F, I, Kh, Q, R, Sk, T, U, Z: وعطف AQ, B, H, K, L, MM, P, Ul: او عطف "or is adjoined."

قَالَ: فَفَعَلْتُمْ مَا أُمِرْتُمْ بِهِ، فَتَابَ عَلَيْكُمْ بَارِئُكُمْ.

وَذِكْرُ الْبَارِئِ وَتَرْتِيبُ الْأَمْرِ عَلَيْهِ: إِشْعَارٌ (أ) بِأَنَّهُمْ بَلَغُوا غَايَةَ الْجَهَالَةِ وَالْغَبَاوَةِ، حَتَّى تَرَكُوا عِبَادَةَ خَالِقِهِمِ الْحَكِيمِ إِلَى عِبَادَةِ الْبَقَرِ الَّتِي هِيَ مَثَلٌ فِي الْغَبَاوَةِ؛ (ب) وَأَنَّ مَنْ لَمْ يَعْرِفْ حَقَّ مُنْعِمِهِ حَقِيقٌ بِأَنْ يُسْتَرَدَّ مِنْهُ. وَلِذَٰلِكَ أُمِرُوا بِالْقَتْلِ وَفَكِّ التَّرْكِيبِ.

﴿إِنَّهُۥ هُوَ ٱلتَّوَّابُ ٱلرَّحِيمُ﴾ الَّذِي يُكْثِرُ تَوْفِيقَ التَّوْبَةِ أَوْ قَبُولَهَا مِنَ الْمُذْنِبِينَ، وَيُبَالِغُ فِي الْإِنْعَامِ عَلَيْهِمْ.

He were saying, "then you did what you were ordered, so your Producer relented towards you."

[Significance of the divine name *al-Bāriʾ* ⟨Producer of all⟩]

The mention of "the Producer" and making the matter consequent upon Him is to proclaim (i) that they have reached the far end of willful ignorance and stupidity, to the point they quit worshipping their all-wise Creator only to worship bovines, which are proverbially stupid;[1299] (ii) and that whoever fails to recognize the right of his benefactor amply deserves to have his benefits repossessed.[1300] Hence they were sentenced to execution and disintegration.[1301]

innahu huwa-t-tawwābu-r-raḥīmu ⟨*truly He—and He alone—is the Oft-Relenting, the Most Merciful!*⟩: the one[1302] who multiplies the prosperity of divine relentment or its acceptance on the part of sinners and abundantly favors them.

[1299] "The Arabs say, 'Denser than a bull.'" (J, Q)

[1300] All mss. and eds.: بأن يسترد منه AQ, H, MM: بأن لا يسترد منه !! blunder.

[1301] "We say: they were sentenced to execution because they annulled the existence of the One God by affirming divinity for the Calf (*al-ʿijl*), so they were requited in this life (*ʿājilan*) with the very same, namely the annullment of their existence." (Iṣ)

[1302] All mss. and eds.: الذي AQ, H, MM: للذي typo.

﴿وَإِذْ قُلْتُمْ يَٰمُوسَىٰ لَن نُّؤْمِنَ لَكَ﴾، أَيْ لِأَجْلِ قَوْلِكَ؛ أَوْ: لَنْ نُقِرَّ لَكَ.

﴿حَتَّىٰ نَرَى ٱللَّهَ جَهْرَةً﴾: عِيَاناً؛ وَهِيَ - فِي الْأَصْلِ - مَصْدَرُ قَوْلِكَ: (جَهَرْتُ بِالْقِرَاءَةِ)، اُسْتُعِيرَتْ لِلْمُعَايَنَةِ؛ وَنَصْبُهَا عَلَى الْمَصْدَرِ، لِأَنَّهَا نَوْعٌ مِنَ الرُّؤْيَةِ؛ أَوِ الْحَالِ مِنَ الْفَاعِلِ؛ أَوِ الْمَفْعُولِ.

وَقُرِئَ (جَهَرَةً) بِالْفَتْحِ عَلَى أَنَّهَا مَصْدَرٌ كَـ(الْغَلَبَةِ)، أَوْ جَمْعٌ كَـ(الْكَتَبَةِ)،

[2:55] **wa-idh qultum yā Mūsā lan nuʾmina laka** ⁽*and when you said, O Mūsā, we will not believe just for you*⁾, that is, "on the mere basis of what you say;" or "we will not recognize your authority."

ḥattā narā-l-Lāha jahratan ⁽*but only when we see Allah openly*⁾: with their own eyes.[1303]

The latter [sc. ***jahr*** ⁽speaking out⁾] is originally the infinitive noun of the expression *jahartu bil-qirāʾa* ⁽I made my recitation audible⁾, metaphorically used for "viewing before one's eyes." It is in the accusative (i) as an objective complement[1304] because it is a type of sighting; (ii) or as a participial state describing the doer or the act.

It was also read *jaharatan* with a mid-*fatḥa*[1305] in the sense (i) of an infinitive noun as in *ghalaba* ⁽ascendency⁾; (ii) or a plural [of *jāhir* ⁽proclaimer⁾] as in *kataba* ⁽pl. of *kātib*= scribe⁾, ...

1303 This exact same gloss is narrated from ʿAbd al-Raḥmān b. Zayd b. Aslam by al-Ṭabarī in his *Tafsīr* (1:696 under verse 2:56, and 2:46 under 2:63): "He said: 'These tablets contain the Book of Allah, His commands that He commands you and His prohibitions that He prohibits you.' They said: '*wa-man yaʾkhudhuhu bi-qawlika ant?* And who is going to take it just because you say so? No, by Allah! Not until we see Allah openly and until He comes up and faces us and says: This is My Book, so take it!'"

1304 Also known as an absolute object, cf. Wright, *Grammar* (2:54 §26).

1305 By Ibn ʿAbbās, Sahl b. Shuʿayb, Ḥumayd b. Qays and Ṭalḥa, a dialect often heard among the Basrians when the mid-letter is an unvowelized laryngeal phoneme preceded by a *fatḥa*. (*MQ*)

فَيَكُونُ حَالاً مِنَ الْفَاعِلِ قَطْعاً. وَالْقَائِلُونَ: هُمُ السَّبْعُونَ الَّذِينَ اخْتَارَهُمْ مُوسَى ـ عَلَيْهِ السَّلَامُ ـ لِلْمِيقَاتِ. وَقِيلَ: عَشَرَةُ آلَافٍ مِنْ قَوْمِهِ. وَالْمُؤْمَنُ بِهِ: أَنَّ اللهَ الَّذِي أَعْطَاكَ التَّوْرَاةَ وَكَلَّمَكَ؛ أَوْ أَنَّكَ نَبِيٌّ.

﴿فَأَخَذَتْكُمُ ٱلصَّٰعِقَةُ﴾ لِفَرْطِ الْعِنَادِ وَالتَّعَنُّتِ وَطَلَبِ الْمُسْتَحِيلِ؛ فَإِنَّهُم ظَنُّوا أَنَّهُ ـ تَعَالَى ـ يُشْبِهُ الْأَجْسَامَ، فَطَلَبُوا رُؤْيَتَهُ رُؤْيَةَ الْأَجْسَامِ فِي الْجِهَاتِ وَالْأَحْيَازِ الْمُقَابِلَةِ لِلرَّائِي، وَهِيَ مُحَالٌ؛ بَلِ الْمُمْكِنُ: أَنْ يُرَى رُؤْيَةً مُنَزَّهَةً عَنِ الْكَيْفِيَّةِ: وَذٰلِكَ لِلْمُؤْمِنِينَ فِي الْآخِرَةِ وَلِأَفْرَادٍ مِنَ الْأَنْبِيَاءِ فِي بَعْضِ الْأَحْوَالِ فِي الدُّنْيَا.

in which case it is definitely a participial state of the doer.

The speakers are the seventy whom Mūsā selected for the Tryst—by another account ten thousand—from his nation.[1306] The object of belief [in their statement *we will not believe*] was "that it is indeed Allah Who gave you the Torah and spoke to you" or "that you are indeed a prophet."

[Prophet's vision of Allah in *dunyā*; believers' vision in *ākhira*]

fa-akhadhatkumu-ṣ-ṣāʿiqatu⁽*whereupon the thunderstroke seized you*⁾ because of excessive obduracy, carping and demanding impossibilities. For they presumed that Allah Most High resembled bodies and demanded to see Him the way one sees bodies —within the directions and zones facing the onlooker—which is impossible. Rather, what is possible is for Him to be seen with a vision devoid of all modality. That vision befalls the believers in the hereafter and the very rarest of all prophets on some occasions in this world.[1307]

[1306] See note 1290.

[1307] "Namely the Prophet Muḥammad—upon him blessings and peace—during the

Night of Ascension" (Q) "as is the position of many of the early Muslims" (Kh) such as Ibn ʿAbbās and all his students, Abū Dharr, Anas, ʿAbd al-Raḥmān b. ʿĀʾish, the totality of Banū Hāshim, Abū Hurayra (in one narration), Ibn Masʿūd (ditto), ʿUrwa b. al-Zubayr, al-Ḥasan al-Baṣrī, al-Zuhrī; Kaʿb al-Aḥbār, Aḥmad b. Ḥanbal, al-Ṭabarī and al-Ashʿarī, cf. Ibn Khuzayma, *Kitāb al-Tawḥīd wa-Ithbāt Ṣifāt al-Rabb ʿazza wa-jall*, ed. ʿAbd al-ʿAzīz al-Shahawān, 5th ed., 2 vols. (Riyadh: Maktabat al-Rushd, 1414/1994) 2:477-563; al-Dāraquṭnī, *al-Ruʾya*, ed. Aḥmad al-Rifāʿī and Ibrāhīm al-ʿAlī (al-Zarqāʾ: Maktabat al-Manār, 1411/1990) pp. 73-74 and Khalīl Ibrāhīm Mullā Khāṭir, *Makānat al-Ṣaḥīḥayn* (Cairo: al-Maṭbaʿat al-ʿArabiyya al-Ḥadītha, 1402/1982) pp. 448-465. Ibn ʿAbbās said everything the Prophet saw on the night of *Isrāʾ* and *Miʿrāj* was with his very eyes (*ruʾyā ʿayn*) as narrated by al-Bukhārī, *Ṣaḥīḥ* (*Faḍāʾil al-Ṣaḥāba, bāb al-Miʿrāj*). "The *Isrāʾ* (Night Journey) with the Prophet—upon him blessings and peace—took place twice [cf. Abū Shāma, ʿIyāḍ, al-Suhaylī, Ibn Sayyid al-Nās, Ibn al-ʿArabī, al-Muhallab, Ibn Kathīr, al-Ṭībī, Ibn Ḥajar and others]: once during sleep [viz. Anas from Mālik b. Ṣaʿṣaʿa from the Prophet in the two *Ṣaḥīḥ*s] and once awake [viz. all other reports]; and he saw his Lord Most High on the Night Journey with the two eyes of his head. That is the sound position, stated by Ibn ʿAbbās and most of the Companions and scholars—may Allah be well-pleased with all of them." Al-Nawawī, *Fatāwā al-Imām al-Nawawī al-Musammāt bil-Masāʾil al-Maʾthūra*, ed. Muḥammad al-Ḥajjār, 6th ed. (Beirut: Dār al-Bashāʾir al-Islāmiyya, 1417/1996) p. 37 and *Sharḥ Ṣaḥīḥ Muslim* (*Īmān, bāb maʿnā qawlihi ʿazza wa-jall: wa-laqad raʾāhu nazlatan ukhrā*), cf. Anwar Shāh Kashmīrī, *Fayḍ al-Bārī*, ed. Muḥammad Badr al-Mīrtahī, 6 vols. (Lahore: al-Maṭbaʿa al-Islāmiyya al-Saʿūdiyya, 1978; rept. Beirut: Dār al-Kutub al-ʿIlmiyya, 2055/1426) 6:600. There is no agreement on its exact timing and up to eleven different positions among the scholars are reported by Ibn Ḥajar, *Fatḥ al-Bārī* (7:213). Anas's long narration of the Ascension through Sharīk in al-Bukhārī's *Ṣaḥīḥ* (*Tawḥīd, bāb wa-kallama Allāhu Mūsā taklīman*) has (i) "until he reached the Lote-Tree of the Farthest Boundary and *the All-Powerful, the Lord of Might approached (wa-danā al-Jabbāru Rabbu al-ʿIzza) then came down until He was two bow-lengths, or closer yet* to him" and (ii) "He was brought back up to the Almighty Most High and said *in the same place*: 'Lord, lighten our burden.'" The narration ends with the words "then he woke up in the mosque" and was rejected by Ibn Ḥazm and others as a non-Prophetic report by Anas narrated only from Sharīk "and contradicting other reports" such as in the above expressions; but this was itself refuted as inaccurate: ʿIyāḍ said the final mention of the waking up is a postposition and does not preclude that the actual *Isrāʾ* followed rather than preceded, and the ascription of *approached then came down* to Allah Most High is confirmed by other authentic Prophetic narrations from Ibn ʿAbbās, Anas and Abū Saʿīd al-Khudrī cf. al-Ṭabarī, *Tafsīr* (22:14-15); Ibn Ḥajar, *Fatḥ* (13:480-484); and Khāṭir, *Makānat al-Ṣaḥīḥayn* (pp. 421-456).

قِيلَ: جَاءَتْ نَارٌ مِنَ السَّمَاءِ فَأَحْرَقَتْهُمْ. وَقِيلَ: صَيْحَةٌ. وَقِيلَ: جُنُودٌ، سَمِعُوا بِحَسِيسِهَا فَخَرُّوا صَعِقِينَ مَيِّتِينَ يَوْماً وَلَيْلَةً.

﴿وَأَنتُمْ تَنظُرُونَ﴾ مَا أَصَابَكُمْ ـ بِنَفْسِهِ أَوْ أَثَرِهِ.

﴿ثُمَّ بَعَثْنَاكُم مِّنْ بَعْدِ مَوْتِكُمْ﴾ بِسَبَبِ الصَّاعِقَةِ. وَقَيَّدَ الْبَعْثَ لِأَنَّهُ قَدْ يَكُونُ عَنْ إِغْمَاءٍ أَوْ نَوْمٍ، كَقَوْلِهِ تَعَالَى: ﴿ثُمَّ بَعَثْنَاهُمْ﴾ [الكهف ١٢].

﴿لَعَلَّكُمْ تَشْكُرُونَ﴾ نِعْمَةَ الْبَعْثِ، أَوْ مَا كَفَرْتُمُوهُ لَمَّا رَأَيْتُمْ بَأْسَ اللهِ بِالصَّاعِقَةِ.

It is said that a fire came from the sky and blasted them; another view states that it was din-and-destruction.[1308] A third one mentions "angelic soldiers" whose invisible presence they heard, upon which they fell thunderstruck, dead, for a day and a night.

wa-antum tanẓurūna ˹*as you looked on*˺ at the very thing that befell you or at its sequels.

[Allah's successive gifts and the Israelites' successive treasons]

[2:56] **thumma baʿathnākum min baʿdi mawtikum** ˹*then We raised you up after your death*˺ because of the thunderstroke.

The rising[1309] was restrictively qualified because it can also take place after fainting or after sleep, as in the saying of Allah Most High, *then We awoke them (baʿathnāhum)* (al-Kahf 18:12).

laʿallakum tashkurūna ˹*perhaps you will be thankful*˺ for the blessing of arising, or for what you had previously disbelieved, in light of what you saw of the wrath of Allah through the thunderstroke.

1308 Both in al-Ṭabarī, *Tafsīr* (1:690).

1309 All mss. and eds.: البعث AQ, H, MM: للبعث typo.

﴿وَظَلَّلْنَا عَلَيْكُمُ ٱلْغَمَامَ﴾: سَخَّرَ اللهُ لَهُمُ السَّحَابَ يُظِلُّهُم مِنَ الشَّمْسِ حِينَ كَانُوا فِي التِّيهِ.

﴿وَأَنزَلْنَا عَلَيْكُمُ ٱلْمَنَّ وَٱلسَّلْوَىٰ﴾: التَّرَنْجُبِينَ وَالسُّمَانَى. قِيلَ: كَانَ يَنزِلُ عَلَيْهِمُ الْمَنُّ مِثْلَ الثَّلْجِ مِنَ الْفَجْرِ إِلَى الطُّلُوعِ، وَتَبْعَثُ الْجَنُوبُ عَلَيْهِمُ السُّمَانَى، وَيَنزِلُ بِاللَّيْلِ عَمُودُ نَارٍ يَسِيرُونَ فِي ضَوْئِهِ، وَكَانَتْ ثِيَابُهُمْ لَا تَتَّسِخُ وَلَا تَبْلَى.

﴿كُلُوا۟ مِن طَيِّبَٰتِ مَا رَزَقْنَٰكُمْ﴾ عَلَى إِرَادَةِ الْقَوْلِ. ﴿وَمَا ظَلَمُونَا﴾: فِيهِ اخْتِصَارٌ، وَأَصْلُهُ: (فَظَلَمُوا بِأَنْ كَفَرُوا هٰذِهِ النِّعَمَ، وَمَا ظَلَمُونَا).

[2:57] **wa-ẓallalnā ʿalaykumu-l-ghamāma** ⁽*and We overshadowed you with clouds*⁾: Allah subjected the clouds to them as it was shading them from the sun while they were wandering in the desert.

wa-anzalnā ʿalaykumu-l-manna wa-s-salwā ⁽*and We brought down upon you manna and game*⁾: camelthorn sap and quails. It is said manna would come down on them like snow from dawn to sunrise; the southerly propelled quails over them; at night, a pillar of fire would descend so that they could walk in its light; and their clothes would neither soil nor wear out.

kulū min ṭayyibāti mā razaqnākum ⁽*eat of the agreeable things We provided you*⁾ is meant as direct speech.

[The harm of ingratitude to Allah is only reflexive]

wa-mā ẓalamūnā ⁽*and they did not wrong Us*⁾: there is a type of abridgment[1310] for what is originally "they did wrong in denying these favors; and they did not wrong Us."

[1310] Of a type named *ījāz ḥadhf* ⁽elliptic brevity⁾ by al-Nābulusī, cf. Cachia, *Arch Rhetorician* (p. 52-53 §81c).

﴿وَلَٰكِن كَانُوٓاْ أَنفُسَهُمۡ يَظۡلِمُونَ﴾ بِالْكُفْرَانِ، لِأَنَّهُ لَا يَتَخَطَّاهُمْ ضَرَرُهُ.

﴿وَإِذۡ قُلۡنَا ٱدۡخُلُواْ هَٰذِهِ ٱلۡقَرۡيَةَ﴾ يَعْنِي بَيْتَ الْمَقْدِسِ؛ وَقِيلَ: أَرِيحَا. أُمِرُوا بِهِ بَعْدَ التِّيهِ.

﴿فَكُلُواْ مِنۡهَا حَيۡثُ شِئۡتُمۡ رَغَدٗا﴾: وَاسِعاً؛ وَنَصْبُهُ عَلَى الْمَصْدَرِ، أَوِ الْحَالِ مِنَ الْوَاوِ.

﴿وَٱدۡخُلُواْ ٱلۡبَابَ﴾ أَيْ بَابَ الْقَرْيَةِ أَوِ الْقُبَّةِ الَّتِي كَانُوا يُصَلُّونَ إِلَيْهَا: فَإِنَّهُمْ لَمْ يَدْخُلُوا بَيْتَ الْمَقْدِسِ فِي حَيَاةِ مُوسَى ـ عَلَيْهِ الصَّلَاةُ وَالسَّلَامُ.

wa-lākin kānū anfusahum yaẓlimūna ⁽*but rather they were wronging themselves*⁾ with ingratitude, because its harm does not reach beyond themselves.

[2:58] **wa-idh qulnā-dkhulū hādhihi-l-qaryata** ⁽*and when We said, Enter this town*⁾,[1311] meaning the House of the Hallowed [Jerusalem]. It was also said it means Jericho.[1312] They were ordered to enter it after the wandering in the desert.

fa-kulū minhā ḥaythu shiʾtum raghadan ⁽*and eat from it wherever you wish in plenty*⁾: in abundance; it was put in the accusative as an objective complement[1313] or as a participial state for the [subject] *wāw* [in *kulū*].[1314]

[The effortless avenue of divine forgiveness]

wa-dkhulū-l-bāba ⁽*and enter the gate*⁾, meaning the gate of the town or that of the round tent toward which they used to pray.[1315] For they did not enter Jerusalem in the life of Mūsā—upon him

[1311] Namely, the eighth favor, which entails within itself many other favors. (Z)

[1312] The latter is related from Ibn ʿAbbās, the former from Qatāda, al-Suddī and al-Rabīʿ. (Z)

[1313] Cf. above, verse 2:35. See note 1304 also.

[1314] "I.e. *rāghidīna*" (Q) in the sense of *mukthirīna* ⁽without stint⁾.

[1315] "As their prayer was not valid unless performed inside a synagogue of theirs." (Q)

﴿سُجَّدًا﴾: مُتَطَامِنِينَ مُخْبِتِينَ؛ أَوْ سَاجِدِينَ لله شُكْراً عَلَى إِخْرَاجِهِمْ مِنَ التِّيهِ.

﴿وَقُولُوا حِطَّةٌ﴾، أَيْ: مَسْأَلَتُنَا ـ أَوْ أَمْرُكَ ـ حِطَّةٌ؛ وَهِيَ فِعْلَةٌ مِنَ الْحَطِّ، كَـ(الْجِلْسَةِ). وَقُرِئَ بِالنَّصْبِ عَلَى الْأَصْلِ، بِمَعْنَى: حُطَّ عَنَّا ذُنُوبَنَا حِطَّةً، أَوْ عَلَى أَنَّهُ مَفْعُولُ ﴿وَقُولُوا﴾، أَيْ: قُولُوا هٰذِهِ الْكَلِمَةَ.

وَقِيلَ: مَعْنَاهُ (أَمْرُنَا حِطَّةٌ)؛ أَيْ: أَنْ نَحُطَّ فِي هٰذِهِ الْقَرْيَةِ وَنُقِيمَ بِهَا.

blessings and peace.

sujjadan *(submissively)* stooping and lowly, or prostrating to Allah out of gratitude for bringing them out of the wandering in the desert.

wa-qūlū ḥiṭṭatun *(and say: a reprieve!)*, that is, "our request—or Your command—is a reprieve."[1316] [The word] is a single-instance deverbal form[1317] from *al-ḥaṭṭ* *(lowering down)* as in *al-jilsa* *(a single sitting)*.[1318]

It was also read in the default accusative,[1319] as an objective complement in the sense *ḥuṭṭa ʿannā dhunūbanā ḥiṭṭatan* *(unburden us of our sins, a thorough unburdening)*, or in the sense that it is the direct object of *qūlū* *(say)*, that is, "Say this word."

It was also said its meaning is *amrunā ḥiṭṭatun* *(our decision is to unload)*, that is, to unsaddle in this town and stay there.[1320]

[1316] "[It is narrated] from Ibn ʿAbbās and ʿIkrima that they said, '*Ḥiṭṭa* is *lā ilāha illā-l-Lāh* (there is no god but Allah). It was named thus because it lays down sins." Makkī al-Qaysī, *al-Hidāya ilā Bulūgh al-Nihāya*, ed. al-Shāhid al-Būshaykhī et al., 13 vols. (Sharjah: Kulliyyat al-Dirāsāt al-ʿUlyā, Jāmiʿat al-Shāriqa, 1429/2008) 1:280. Al-Ṭabarī, *Tafsīr* (1:717) narrates it only from ʿIkrima.
[1317] Nomen vicis, cf. Wright, *Grammar* (1:109 §193, 1:122-123 §219, 2:53-56 §26).
[1318] This entire sentence is missing from R but found in α, Ak, β, ε, I, T and in the eds.
[1319] By Ibrāhīm b. Abī ʿAbla, al-Akhfash, Ibn al-Sumayfiʿ and Ṭāwūs al-Yamanī. (MQ)
[1320] "This is the position of Abū Muslim al-Aṣfahānī and was deemed weak because

﴿نَغْفِرْ لَكُمْ خَطَايَاكُمْ﴾ بِسُجُودِكُمْ وَدُعَائِكُمْ. وَقَرَأَ نَافِعٌ بِالْيَاءِ، وَابْنُ عَامِرٍ بِالتَّاءِ عَلَى الْبِنَاءِ لِلْمَفْعُولِ. وَ(خَطَايَا) أَصْلُهُ: (خَطَائِيَ) كَـ(خَطَايِعَ)؛ فَعِنْدَ سِيبَوَيْهِ أَنَّهُ أُبْدِلَتِ الْيَاءُ الزَّائِدَةُ هَمْزَةً لِوُقُوعِهَا بَعْدَ الْأَلِفِ، وَاجْتَمَعَتْ هَمْزَتَانِ فَأُبْدِلَتِ الثَّانِيَةُ يَاءً ثُمَّ قُلِبَتْ أَلِفاً، وَكَانَتِ الْهَمْزَةُ بَيْنَ الْأَلِفَيْنِ فَأُبْدِلَتْ يَاءً. وَعِنْدَ الْخَلِيلِ: قُدِّمَتِ الْهَمْزَةُ عَلَى الْيَاءِ ثُمَّ فُعِلَ بِهِمَا مَا ذُكِرَ.

naghfir lakum khaṭāyākum ⁽*whereby We shall forgive you your errors*⁾ by means of your prostration and supplication. Nāfiʿ read it with *yāʾ* and Ibn ʿĀmir with *tāʾ*[1321] in the passive.[1322]

The root of ***khaṭāyā*** ⁽errors⁾ is *khaṭāʾiya* as in *khaṭāyiʿa.*[1323] According to Sībawayh, the extra *yāʾ* [in *khaṭāyiʾ*, pl. of *khaṭīʾa*] was replaced with a *hamza* because it fell after an *alif*, whereupon two *hamza*s were contiguous so the second one was replaced with a *yāʾ* which was then turned into an *alif*; but there was now a *hamza* between two *alif*s, so it was replaced with a *yāʾ*. For al-Khalīl, the *hamza* came before the *yāʾ*, then they both underwent what we said.[1324]

it fails to highlight how it pertains to forgiveness and to the next verse; although it is possible to say that it means 'to unsaddle in it in obedience to Your order… and reside in it in fulfillment of the promise' as the reason for forgiveness." (Q)

1321 Ak, β, I, Sk, T: عامر بالتاء على البناء α, ε, F, R: عامر بها على البناء B: عامر على البناء with two marginal inserts: بها صح and بالتاء صـ which may mean, respectively: "thus in original ms. (صحّ نقلاً)" and "correct in meaning (الصواب معنىً)."

1322 *Naghfir*: Ibn Kathīr, Abū ʿAmr, ʿĀṣim, Ḥamza and al-Kisāʾī; *yaghfir*: Abū Bakr, al-Juʿfī, ʿĀṣim, al-Aʿmash, al-Ḥasan, Nāfiʿ and Abān; *yughfar*: Nāfiʿ, Abū Jaʿfar, Qatāda, al-Ḥasan and Abū Ḥaywa; *tughfar*: Ibn ʿĀmir, Mujāhid, al-Jaḥdarī, Qatāda, Abū Ḥaywa and Jabala from al-Mufaḍḍal; *taghfir*: a group. (*MQ*)

1323 α, Ak, B, G, R, T: خطائي كخطايع D: خطائي كخطائع L, Ul, Q: خطائي كخضائع Sk: خطائى كخضايع I: خطايئ كخضايع Kh, P, U, Z: خطايئ كخضائع AQ, F, H, K, MM: خطايئ كخطآيع ε: خطايي كخطآيع

1324 I.e. خطيئة → خطايئ → خطائئ → خطائي → خطاءا → خطايا cf. Sībawayh, *Kitāb* (3:551 and 4:377-378); and خطائئ → خطائي → خطاءا → خطايا cf. al-Khalīl, *al-ʿAyn* (4:292).

﴿ وَسَنَزِيدُ ٱلْمُحْسِنِينَ ﴾ ثَوابـاً. جَعَلَ الِامْتِثَالَ تَوْبَةً لِلْمُسِيءِ وَسَبَبَ زِيَادَةِ الثَّوَابِ لِلْمُحْسِنِ، وَأَخْرَجَهُ عَنْ صُورَةِ الْجَوَابِ إِلَى الْوَعْدِ، إِيهَامـاً بِأَنَّ الْمُحْسِنَ بِصَدَدِ ذٰلِكَ وَإِنْ لَمْ يَفْعَلْهُ ـ فَكَيْفَ إِذَا فَعَلَـهُ! ـ وَأَنَّهُ ـ تَعَالَى ـ يَفْعَلُ لَا مَحَالَةَ.

﴿ فَبَدَّلَ ٱلَّذِينَ ظَلَمُوا۟ قَوْلًا غَيْرَ ٱلَّذِى قِيلَ لَهُمْ ﴾: بَدَّلُوا بِمَا أُمِرُوا بِهِ مِنَ التَّوْبَةِ وَالِاسْتِغْفَارِ بِطَلَبِ مَا يَشْتَهُونَ مِنْ أَعْرَاضِ الدُّنْيَا.

﴿ فَأَنزَلْنَا عَلَى ٱلَّذِينَ ظَلَمُوا۟ ﴾ كَرَّرَهُ ....

[The divine honoring of well-doers no matter what]

wa-sa-nazīdu-l-muḥsinīna ⁽*and We will increase the well-doers*⁾ in reward: faithful obedience was made to form repentence for the transgressor and cause for increase for the well-doer. Furthermore He brought it out of the pattern of apodosis and into that of a promise to suggest that the well-doer is facing that even if he does not do it—how then if he does!—and that He shall do it no matter what.[1325]

[2:59] **fa-baddala-l-ladhīna ẓalamū qawlan ghayra-l-ladhī qīla lahum** ⁽*then those who did wrong replaced what they had been told with some other words*⁾: they replaced what they had been ordered of repentence and asking forgiveness with the pursuit of what they craved of the perishables of this world.

[The parody of *Ḥiṭṭa* and the mockery of forgiveness]

fa-anzalnā ʿala-l-ladhīna ẓalamū ⁽*so We sent down on the wrong-doers*⁾: He repeated the latter ....

[1325] "I.e. the apocopation was removed and replaced by a promise for the verb of increase for the well-doers to show that they will be positively increased in any case, whether they obey or not." (Z) "It is not far-fetched to also read the phrase 'he shall do it not matter what' as referring to the well-doer, who will obey no matter what." (Q)

مُبَالَغَةً فِي تَقْبِيحِ أَمْرِهِــمْ وَإِشْعَاراً بِأَنَّ الإِنْزَالَ عَلَيْهِمْ لِظُلْمِهِمْ بِوَضْعِ غَيْرِ الْمَـأْمُورِ بِهِ مَوْضِعَهُ، أَوْ عَلَى أَنْفُسِهِـمْ بِأَنْ تَرَكُــوا مَا يُوجِبُ نَجَاتَهَا إِلَى مَا يُوجِبُ هَلَاكَهَا.

﴿رِجْزًا مِّنَ ٱلسَّمَآءِ بِمَا كَانُوا۟ يَفْسُقُونَ﴾: عَذَاباً مُقَدَّراً مِنَ السَّمَاءِ بِسَبَبِ فِسْقِهِمْ. وَ(الرِّجْزُ) فِي الأَصْلِ: مَا يُعَافُ عَنْهُ، وَكَذٰلِكَ (الرِّجْسُ). وَقُرِئَ بِالضَّمِّ، وَهُوَ لُغَةٌ فِيهِ.

to intensively stigmatize[1326] their affair and as a proclamation that the sending down was caused by their wrong-doing (i) in putting other than what they had been commanded in its place[1327] or (ii) against their own souls in leaving what would guarantee their salvation in favor of what would guarantee their ruin.

rijzan mina-s-samā'i bi-mā kānū yafsuqūna ⁽*a bane from the sky because of their transgressions*⁾: a punishment apportioned out of the sky because of their transgressing. ***Rijz*** ⁽bane⁾ originally is that from which one keeps safely away; likewise *rijs* ⁽filth⁾. It was also read [*rujzan*] with *ḍamm*—a dialectical form.[1328]

1326 As in the rhetorical figure of pathos known as *conduplicatio*, "repetition of a word or words in adjacent phrases or clauses, either to amplify the thought or to express emotion." Burton, *Silva Rhetoricae, s.v.*

1327 I.e. instead of saying *ḥiṭṭatun* ⁽reprieve⁾ they made up derisive parodic phrases such as *ḥabbatun fī sha'ra* ⁽a seed on a hair⁾ which they blurted out as they entered the gate shifting on their backsides: narrated from Abū Hurayra by Bukhārī, *Ṣaḥīḥ* (*Anbiyā'* and *Tafsīr*) and Muslim, *Ṣaḥīḥ* (*Tafsīr*) or, in another version from Ibn Mas'ūd in al-Ḥākim, *Mustadrak* (2:352), "a strong red ear of wheat containing a black hair!" In one report they said, "Mūsā wants nothing other than to toy with us, *ḥiṭṭatun ḥiṭṭatun*! What thing is that—*ḥiṭṭatun*?" and they said to each other: *ḥinṭa* ⁽wheat⁾. Narrated by al-Ṭabarī, *Tafsīr* (1:723-729).

1328 By Ibn Muḥayṣin, a dialect of the Banū al-Ṣu'udāt according to Abū Ḥayyān and others (*MQ*). I found no trace or mention of that tribal group in any of the sources.

وَالْمُـرَادُ بِهِ: الطَّاعُونُ. رُوِيَ أَنَّهُ مَاتَ فِي سَاعَةٍ أَرْبَعَةٌ وَعِشْرُونَ أَلْفاً.

﴿ وَإِذِ ٱسْتَسْقَىٰ مُوسَىٰ لِقَوْمِهِۦ ﴾ لَمَّا عَطِشُوا فِي التِّيهِ.

﴿ فَقُلْنَا ٱضْرِب بِّعَصَاكَ ٱلْحَجَرَ ﴾: اللَّامُ فِيهِ: (I) لِلْعَهْدِ عَلَى مَا رُوِيَ أَنَّـــــهُ: (أ) كَانَ حَجَراً طُورِيّاً مُكَعَّباً حَمَلَهُ مَعَهُ، وَكَانَتْ تَنْبُعُ مِنْ كُلِّ وَجْهٍ ثَلَاثُ أَعْيُنٍ، تَسِيلُ كُلُّ عَيْنٍ فِي جَدْوَلٍ إِلَى سِبْطٍ؛ وَكَانُوا سِتَّمِائَةِ أَلْفٍ؛ ....

What is meant thereby is the plague.[1329] It was reported that 124,000 died all at once.

[The miracle of Mūsā's water-rock in the desert]

[2:60] **wa-idhi-stasqā Mūsā li-qawmihi** ⁽*and when Mūsā sought water for his nation*⁾ when they became thirsty during the wandering in the desert.[1330]

fa-qulnā-ḍrib-bi-ʿaṣāka-l-ḥajara⁽*so We said, strike with your staff the rock*⁾: the [definite article] *lām* in the latter denotes

I. previous knowledge, in accordance with the reports that it was (i) a mountain rock which he had carried with him and which gushed out from each side three springs, each flowing in a separate stream to one of the tribes[1331]—they were 600,000[1332] ....

[1329] As in the Prophetic report narrated from Usāma b. Zayd, Saʿd b. Mālik and Khuzayma b. Thābit by al-Ṭabarī, *Tafsīr* (1:729-730) and Ibn Abī Ḥātim, *Tafsīr* (1:120 §591) and per al-Shaʿbī's exegesis ("pestilence or hail") in the latter (§594). On the other hand the categorical glossing of *rijz* as "punishment" is one of the "invariables without exception" (*kulliyyāt muṭṭarida*) in the Qur'ān according to Ibn ʿAbbās as narrated by al-Ṭabarī, *Tafsīr* (1:730) and Ibn Abī Ḥātim, *Tafsīr* (1:120 §592), cf. al-Qarnī, *Kulliyyāt* (1:312-325); the latter misquotes the hadith from Usāma in al-Ṭabarī.

[1330] Entire clause and *āya* missing from main body in B but added in margin.

[1331] Narrated from Ibn ʿAbbās etc. by al-Ṭabarī, *Tafsīr* (2:6-8) and Ibn Abī Ḥātim, *Tafsīr* (1:121 §598-603), "light, like a human head, or that of a cat or of a bull." (Z)

[1332] Ibn Khaldūn at the very beginning of his *Muqaddima* cited this figure as a case of unrealistic exaggeration that "fails to take into consideration the dimensions of Egypt

وَسَعَةُ الْمُعَسْكَرِ اثْنَا عَشَرَ مِيلاً؛ (ب) أَوْ حَجَراً أَهْبَطَهُ آدَمُ مِنَ الْجَنَّةِ، وَوَقَعَ إِلَى شُعَيْبٍ، فَأَعْطَاهُ مَعَ الْعَصَا؛ (ج) أَوِ الْحَجَرَ الَّذِي فَرَّ بِثَوْبِهِ لَمَّا وَضَعَهُ عَلَيْهِ لِيَغْتَسِلَ، وَبَرَّأَهُ اللهُ بِهِ عَمَّا رَمَوْهُ بِهِ مِنَ الْأُدْرَةِ، فَأَشَارَ إِلَيْهِ جِبْرَئِيلُ ـ عَلَيْهِ السَّلَامُ ـ بِحَمْلِهِ؛ ....

and the width of the campsite was 12 miles;[1333] (ii) or a rock Adam had brought down from the Garden and which befell Shuʿayb ⁽Jethro, Reuel⁾ who then gave it,[1334] along with the staff; (iii) or the rock which had fled with his clothes after he had placed them on it before washing, at the time Allah justified him against their charge that he had dropsy of the scrotum,[1335] after which Jibraʾīl ⁽Gabriel⁾—upon him peace—instructed him to carry it away.

and Syro-Palestine" as well as the probably much smaller number of Jews having been born in the intervening generations between Mūsā and Yaʿqūb—only four forefathers and 120 years—and the comparatively much more ancient, vaster and more powerful Persian dominion whose armies nevertheless counted, at best, only 120,000 at the battle of Qādisiyya. Furthermore, he says, other Israelite reports fix at 12,000 the army of Sulaymān while his private guard numbered 1,000 and his horse 400 "at the height of their power and kingdom, and that is the correct one of their reports, so pay no heed to the elucubrations of their rabble." Cf. Muḥammad Abū Shahba, *al-Isrāʾīliyyāt wal-Mawḍūʿāt fī Kutub al-Tafsīr*, 4th ed.(Cairo: Maktabat al-Sunna, 1408/1988) p. 178-180.

1333 12 miles =12x1.5m=18km per Nasība al-Ḥarīrī, *al-Maqāyīs wal-Maqādīr ʿinda al-ʿArab*, ed. Muḥammad Fatḥi al-Ḥarīrī (Cairo: Dār al-Faḍīla, 2002) pp. 66-68, cf. Ibn al-Rifʿa, *al-Īḍāḥ wal-Tibyān fī Maʿrifat al-Mikyāl wal-Mīzān*, ed. Muḥammad Aḥmad al-Khārūf (Mecca: Jāmiʿat al-Malik ʿAbd al-ʿAzīz, 1400/1980) p. 89. As of July 27, 2014 the Zaatari Syrian refugee camp in Jordan was estimated at 81,000 refugees and covered an area of 3.3km^2. By the ratio of 18km^2:600,000 a surface of 3.3km^2 yields a population of 110,000 which lends credence to the proportionality of the numbers adduced by the Qadi, who took them from J.

1334 All mss. and Sk: فاعطاه Kh, Z: فاعطاه اياه gloss. All others incl. F: فأعطاه لموسى gloss.

1335 Narrated from Abū Hurayra by al-Bukhārī, *Ṣaḥīḥ* (*Ghusl, man ightasala ʿuryānan*) and Muslim, *Ṣaḥīḥ* (*Faḍāʾil, faḍāʾil Mūsā ʿalayhi al-salām*).

(II) أَوْ لِلْجِنْسِ، وَهٰذَا أَظْهَرُ فِي الْحُجَّةِ؛ قِيلَ: لَمْ يَأْمُرْهُ بِأَنْ يَضْرِبَ حَجَراً بِعَيْنِهِ، وَلٰكِنْ لَمَّا قَالُوا: كَيْفَ بِنَا لَوْ أَفْضَيْنَا إِلَى أَرْضٍ لَا حِجَارَةَ بِهَا؟ حَمَلَ حَجَراً فِي مِخْلَاتِهِ، وَكَانَ يَضْرِبُهُ بِعَصَاهُ إِذَا نَزَلَ فَيَنْفَجِرُ، وَيَضْرِبُهُ بِهِ إِذَا ارْتَحَلَ فَيَيْبَسُ؛ فَقَالُوا: إِنْ فَقَدَ مُوسَى عَصَاهُ مُتْنَا عَطَشاً! فَأَوْحَى اللهُ إِلَيْهِ: لَا تَقْرَعِ الْحِجَارَةَ، وَكَلِّمْهَا، تُطِعْكَ؛ لَعَلَّهُمْ يَعْتَبِرُونَ!

وَقِيلَ: كَانَ الْحَجَرُ مِنْ رُخَامٍ، وَكَانَ ذِرَاعاً فِي ذِرَاعٍ، وَالْعَصَا عَشَرَةُ أَذْرُعٍ، عَلَى طُولِ مُوسَى ـ عَلَيْهِ السَّلَامُ ـ مِنْ آسِ الْجَنَّةِ، وَلَهَا شُعْبَتَانِ تَتَّقِدَانِ فِي الظُّلْمَةِ.

II. Or it denotes the species, which is a more conclusive proof:[1336] it was said that He did not order him to strike any rock in particular, but when they said, "What will happen to us if we end up in a land devoid of rocks?" he carried a rock in his pack and would strike it with his staff whenever he alighted so it would burst out; then, before departure, he would strike it with it[1337] and it would dry up. After that they said, "If Mūsā were to lose his staff we would all die of thirst!" At that time Allah revealed to him, "Do not beat on the rock anymore, just speak to it and it will obey you; perhaps they will learn!"

It was also said the rock was made of marble and measured a cubit square, while the staff measured ten cubits—the height of Mūsā himself[1338]—and was from the myrtle of the Garden with two forks that would light up in the dark.

[1336] A position attributed to al-Ḥasan al-Baṣrī in the commentaries.

[1337] Ak, B, ε, F, R, T: ويضربه به α, β: ويضربه I, eds.: ويضربه بها

[1338] The length of the staff and of Mūsā were thus narrated from al-Suddī and Nawf by al-Ṭabarī, *Tafsīr* (8:309, 8:315).

﴿فَٱنفَجَرَتۡ مِنۡهُ ٱثۡنَتَا عَشۡرَةَ عَيۡنٗاۖ﴾: مُتَعَلِّقٌ بِمَحْذُوفٍ، تَقْدِيرُهُ: (فَإِنْ ضَرَبْتَ فَقَدِ انْفَجَرَتْ مِنْهُ)؛ أَوْ (فَضَرَبَ فَانْفَجَرَتْ)، كَمَا مَرَّ فِي قَوْلِهِ تَعَالَى: ﴿فَتَابَ عَلَيۡكُمۡۚ﴾. وَقُرِئَ (عَشِرَةَ) بِكَسْرِ الشِّينِ وَفَتْحِهَا، وَهُمَا لُغَتَانِ فِيهِ.

﴿قَدۡ عَلِمَ كُلُّ أُنَاسٖ﴾: كُلُّ سِبْطٍ. ﴿مَّشۡرَبَهُمۡۖ﴾: عَيْنَهُمُ الَّتِي يَشْرَبُونَ مِنْهَا. ﴿كُلُواْ وَٱشۡرَبُواْ﴾ عَلَى تَقْدِيرِ الْقَوْلِ.

﴿مِن رِّزۡقِ ٱللَّهِ﴾: يُرِيدُ بِهِ مَا رَزَقَهُمْ مِنَ الْمَنِّ وَالسَّلْوَى وَمَاءِ الْعُيُونِ؛

fa-nfajarat minhu-thnatā ʿashrata ʿaynan ⁽*whereupon there burst forth from it twelve springs*⁾ pertains to a suppressed [clause], the subaudition being, "whenever it is struck there burst forth," or "whereupon he struck, so it burst forth" as previously in the saying of Allah Most High *fa-tāba ʿalaykum* ⁽*then He relented towards you*⁾ (al-Baqara 2:54).

It was also read *ʿashirata* and *ʿasharata* with *kasr* and *fatḥ* of the *shīn* respectively, which are two dialectical forms.[1339]

qad ʿalima kullu unāsin ⁽*each people knew well*⁾: each tribe.[1340]

mashrabahum ⁽*their drinking-place*⁾: their spring from which they may drink.

kulū wa-shrabū ⁽*eat and drink*⁾ is subauded as direct speech.

min rizqi-l-Lāhi ⁽*of the provision of the One God*⁾: He means by that what He provided them of manna, game and spring water.

[1339] *ʿAshrata* is the reading of the majority and the dialect of the Ḥijāz and of Asad; *ʿashirata* is the reading of Abū ʿAmr, Mujāhid, Ṭalḥa, ʿĪsā, Yaḥyā b. Waththāb, Ibn Abī Laylā, Yazīd, al-Muṭawwaʿī, al-Aʿmash, Nuʿaym al-Saʿdī and Abū Jaʿfar and it is the dialect of Tamīm and Rabīʿa; *ʿasharata* is the reading of Ibn al-Faḍl al-Anṣārī and al-Aʿmash and is a weak dialect according to some, anomalous according to others. (*MQ*)

[1340] "An allusion to the fact that *kull* ⁽every⁾ here is for the encompassment of kind not that of individual persons… and that what is meant by *unās* is not 'all the people' but the people present with Mūsā—upon him peace—namely the tribes. Also, the twelve springs indicate that what is meant is *sibṭ* as 'tribe' not as single grandchild." (Q 3:330)

وَقِيلَ: الْمَاءَ وَحْدَهُ، لِأَنَّهُ يُشْرَبُ وَيُؤْكَلُ مِمَّا يَنْبُتُ بِهِ.

﴿وَلَا تَعْثَوْا فِي ٱلْأَرْضِ مُفْسِدِينَ﴾: لَا تَعْتَدُوا حَالَ إِفْسَادِكُمْ. وَإِنَّمَا قَيَّدَهُ لِأَنَّهُ - وَإِنْ غَلَبَ فِي الْفَسَادِ - قَدْ يَكُونُ مِنْهُ مَا لَيْسَ بِفَسَادٍ، كَمُقَابَلَةِ الظَّالِمِ الْمُعْتَدِي بِفِعْلِهِ؛ وَمِنْهُ مَا يَتَضَمَّنُ صَلَاحاً رَاجِحاً، كَقَتْلِ الْخَضِرِ الْغُلَامَ وَخَرْقِهِ السَّفِينَةَ. وَيَقْرُبُ مِنْهُ الْعَيْثُ، غَيْرَ أَنَّهُ يَغْلُبُ فِيمَا يُدْرَكُ حِسّاً.

It was also said it means water alone, since one drinks it and eats of what grows because of it.[1341]

wa-lā taʿthaw fī-l-arḍi mufsidīna ⟨*and do not wreak havoc in the land by spreading corruption!*⟩: "Do not exceed limits when you are spreading corruption." He put it within the latter limitation[1342] because even though [havoc] is almost always used to mean corruption there might be a kind that is not, such as facing a transgressing tyrant with [the same kind of act as] his act. There is also a kind that involves a preponderant advantage, such as al-Khaḍir's killing of the boy and his scuttling of the ship.

Close to it is *al-ʿayth* ⟨mischief⟩,[1343] except the latter is almost always used for something perceptible by the senses.[1344]

[1341] "Shaykh Saʿd al-Dīn [al-Taftāzānī] said: the author [i.e. J] did not accept the latter view because, first, their food during the wandering in the desert was not from produce or fruit grown out of that water; second, because it would be a conflation of the literal and the figurative, whereas the meaning is 'eat of the provision of Allah and drink of the provision of Allah' without conflation." (S 2:255)

[1342] There is disagreement among the linguist-exegetes whether *mufsidīn* here is a *ḥāl muʾakkida* ⟨emphatic participial state⟩ or rather, as the Qadi indicated, a *ḥāl muqayyida* ⟨restrictive participial state⟩. (S) Al-Ṭībī was of the former opinion while al-Bābirtī, al-Taftāzānī and al-Rāghib followed the latter.

[1343] "I.e. close to [the infinitive noun] *al-ʿathā* ⟨havoc⟩ which is is indicated by the saying of Allah *wa-lā taʿthaw* ⟨and do not wreak havoc⟩." (Q)

[1344] Cf. al-Rāghib, *Tafsīr* (1:206) and *Mufradāt* (p. 546, art. *ʿ-th-y*).

وَمَنْ أَنْكَرَ أَمْثَالَ هٰذِهِ الْمُعْجِزَاتِ، فَلِغَايَــــةِ جَهْلِهِ بِاللهِ وَقِلَّةِ تَدَبُّرِهِ فِي عَجَائِبِ صُنْعِهِ؛ فَإِنَّهُ لَمَّا أَمْكَنَ أَنْ يَكُونَ مِنَ الْأَحْجَارِ مَا يَحْلِقُ الشَّعْرَ وَيَنْفِرُ الْخَلَّ وَيَجْذِبُ الْحَدِيدَ: لَمْ يَمْتَنِعْ أَنْ يَخْلُقَ اللهُ حَجَراً يُسَخِّرُهُ لِجَذْبِ الْمَاءِ مِنْ تَحْتِ الْأَرْضِ، أَوْ لِجَذْبِ الْهَوَاءِ مِنَ الْجَوَانِبِ، وَيُصَيِّرُهُ مَاءً بِقُوَّةِ التَّبْرِيــــدِ وَنَحْوِ ذٰلِكَ.

﴿وَإِذْ قُلْتُمْ يَـٰمُوسَىٰ لَن نَّصْبِرَ عَلَىٰ طَعَامٍ وَٰحِدٍ﴾: يُرِيدُونَ بِهِ مَا رُزِقُوا فِي التِّيهِ مِنَ الْمَنِّ وَالسَّلْوَى؛ وَبِوَحْدَتِهِ أَنَّهُ (أ) لَا يَخْتَلِفُ وَلَا يَتَبَدَّلُ، كَقَوْلِهِمْ: (طَعَامُ مَائِدَةِ الْأَمِيرِ ....

[Deniers of the miracles wrought for Mūsā and the Israelites]

Whoever denies the like of these stunning miracles, it is because of his utmost ignorance of Allah and his lack of pondering the wonders of His handiwork. For when it is conceivable that there might be stones that shave hair, shrink away from vinegar or attract metal,[1345] it is not inconceivable that Allah may create a rock and make it disposed to attract subterranean water, or attract winds from the [four] corners and turn that into water through a process of cooling and the like.

[2:61] **wa-idh qultum yā Mūsā lan naṣbira ʿalā ṭaʿāmin wāḥidin** ⁽*and when you all said: O Mūsā, we will no longer put up with the same food*⁾: they meant by it what they were being provided of manna and game during the wandering in the desert and, by its sameness, (i) the fact that it never differed nor changed, as in the expression *ṭaʿāmu māʾidati al-amīr wāḥid* ⁽the prince's menu

[1345] "He means the *ḥajarat al-nūra* ⁽pumice-stone or limestone⁾, *al-ḥajar al-bāghiḍ lil-khall* ⁽vinegarophobic stone⁾ and *mighnaṭīs* ⁽magnetite, lodestone⁾ respectively." (Kh) Al-Bīrūnī in *bāb al-khumāhān wal-kark* ⁽chapter on malachite and opal⁾ of his *Jamāhir fī Maʿrifat al-Jawāhir* said he was not able to observe any vinegarophobic stone.

وَاحِدٌ): يُرِيدُونَ أَنَّهُ لَا تَتَغَيَّرُ أَلْوَانُهُ؛ وَبِذٰلِكَ أَجِمُوا؛ (ب) أَوْ ضَرْبٌ وَاحِدٌ، لِأَنَّهُمَا طَعَامُ أَهْلِ التَّلَذُّذِ ـ وَهُمْ كَانُوا فَلَّاحَةً ـ فَنَزَعُوا إِلَى عِكْرِهِمْ وَاشْتَهَوا مَا أَلِفُوهُ. ﴿فَٱدْعُ لَنَا رَبَّكَ﴾: سَلْهُ لَنَا بِدُعَائِكَ إِيَّاهُ.

﴿يُخْرِجْ لَنَا﴾: يُظْهِرْ وَيُوجِدْ. وَجَزْمُهُ بِأَنَّهُ جَوَابُ ﴿فَٱدْعُ﴾، فَإِنَّ دَعْوَتَهُ سَبَبُ الْإِجَابَةِ. ﴿مِمَّا تُنۢبِتُ ٱلْأَرْضُ﴾: مِنَ الْإِسْنَادِ الْمَجَازِيِّ وَإِقَامَةِ الْقَابِلِ مَقَامَ الْفَاعِلِ. وَ(مِنْ) لِلتَّبْعِيضِ.

﴿مِنۢ بَقْلِهَا وَقِثَّآئِهَا وَفُومِهَا وَعَدَسِهَا وَبَصَلِهَا﴾: تَفْسِيرٌ وَبَيَانٌ وَقَعَ

is monotonous⁾ to mean there is no variety in its dishes: hence they became disgusted with it;[1346] (ii) or the fact that it is a single type of food, as they are both the food of gourmets whereas they were peasants; so they yearned for their original state and missed what they were used to.

fa-dʿu lanā rabbaka ⁽*therefore call upon your Nurturer for us*⁾: "Ask Him for us through your supplication to Him."

yukhrij lanā ⁽*and He will bring out for us*⁾: "He will make appear and bring into existence." Its apocopation is because it is the apodosis of **fa-dʿu** ⁽*therefore call upon*⁾, for truly his supplication is the reason for the answer.

mimmā tunbitu-l-arḍu ⁽*of what the earth grows*⁾ is an example of allegorical predication and the setting up of the recipient to represent the agent. ***Min*** ⁽of⁾ is partitive.

[They longed for the rustic food they were used to]

min baqlihā wa-qiththāʾihā wa-fūmihā wa-ʿadasihā wa-baṣalihā ⁽*—of its herbs and its cucumbers and its grains and its lentils and its onions*⁾ is an explanation and exposition that comes ………..

[1346] All mss. and eds.: ولذلك اجموا AQ, H, MM: وبذلك أجمعوا typos.

مَوْقِعَ الْحَالِ؛ وَقِيلَ: بَدَلٌ، بِإِعَادَةِ الْجَارِّ. وَ(الْبَقْلُ): مَا أَنْبَتَتْهُ الْأَرْضُ مِنَ الْخُضَرِ؛ وَالْمُرَادُ بِهِ: أَطَايِبُهُ الَّتِي تُؤْكَلُ؛ وَ(الْفُومُ): الْحِنْطَةُ؛ وَيُقَالُ لِلْخُبْزِ، وَمِنْهُ: (فَوِّمُوا لَنَا)؛ وَقِيلَ: الثُّومُ.

وَقُرِئَ (قُثَّائِهَا) بِالضَّمِّ، وَهُوَ لُغَةٌ فِيهِ.

as a participial state. It was also said that it is a substitute, with a reiterated preposition.

Al-baql ⁽herbs⁾ is whatever the earth grows of greens. What is meant is its sweet leaf-vegetables that are edible.

Al-fūm ⁽grains⁾ is wheat and is a term for bread,[1347] whence *fawwimū lanā* ⁽bake us some bread⁾; it is also said it is *al-thūm* ⁽garlic⁾.[1348]

It was also read *quththā'ihā* with *ḍamm*[1349]—a dialectical form.

[1347] Cf. J, Abū ʿUbayda, *Majāz* (1:41), al-Ṭabarī, *Tafsīr* (2:15-18) al-Rāghib and others in that order together with *al-ḥabb* ⁽grains⁾ as per the reports from Ibn ʿAbbās, ʿAṭā', al-Suddī, Mujāhid, Qatāda, al-Ḥasan, Abū Mālik and Ibn Zayd. Similarly Abū Ḥayyān in his *Tuḥfat al-Arīb bimā fīl-Qur'ān min al-Gharīb*, ed. Aḥmad Maṭlūb and Khadīja al-Ḥudaythī (Beirut: Maktabat Lubnān, 2001) p. 125 defines *wa-fūmihā* as *al-ḥinṭa, wa-qīl al-thūm* ⁽wheat, and it was also said garlic⁾ cf. Z. Sufyān glossed *fūm* simply as "bread" cf. *Tafsīr Sufyān al-Thawrī*, ed. Imtiyāz ʿAlī ʿArshī (Rampur: Reza Library, 1965; rept. Beirut: Dār al-Kutub al-ʿIlmiyya, 1403/1983) p. 45-46 §19. Others put the meaning of *thūm* ⁽garlic⁾ first followed by bread, wheat and grains (cf. next note).

[1348] As per the reading of Ibn Masʿūd, Ibn ʿAbbās and Ubay b. Kaʿb. (*MQ*) Cf. also Abū Jaʿfar Aḥmad b. ʿAbd al-Ṣamad al-Khazrajī (d. 582/1186), *Tafsīr al-Khazrajī al-musammā Nafas al-Ṣabāḥ fī Gharīb al-Qur'ān wa-Nāsikhih wa-Mansūkhih*, ed. Aḥmad Farīd al-Mazyadī (Beirut: Dār al-Kutub al-ʿIlmiyya, 1429/2008) p. 21 and Tāj al-Qurrā' Maḥmūd b. Ḥamza al-Kirmānī (d. 505?/1112) in his *Gharā'ib al-Tafsīr wa-ʿAjā'ib al-Ta'wīl*, ed. Shamrān al-ʿIjlī, 2 vols. (Jeddah: Dār al-Qibla; Damascus: Mu'assasat ʿUlūm al-Qur'ān, 1408/1988) 1:144 and it is the order preferred by al-Rāzī and Q on the grounds that "(i) garlic is more congruent with the mention of onions and (ii) if it meant wheat it would be impermissible to call it inferior as wheat is the noblest food."

[1349] By Yaḥyā b. Waththāb, Ṭalḥa b. Muṣarrif, Ibn Masʿūd, al-Ashhab, al-Aʿmash, Abū Rajā' and Qatāda; it is the dialect of Tamīm and some of Banū Asad. (*MQ*)

﴿قَالَ﴾ أَيِ اللهُ، أَوْ مُوسَى.

﴿أَتَسْتَبْدِلُونَ ٱلَّذِى هُوَ أَدْنَىٰ﴾: أَقْرَبُ مَنْزِلَةً وَأَدْوَنُ قَدْراً. وَأَصْلُ (الدُّنُوِّ): الْقُرْبُ فِي الْمَكَانِ؛ فَاسْتُعِيرَ لِلْخِسَّةِ، كَمَا اسْتُعِيرَ الْبُعْدُ لِلشَّرَفِ وَالرِّفْعَةِ، فَقِيلَ: (بَعِيدُ الْمَحَلِّ)، (بَعِيدُ الهِمَّةِ). وَقُرِئَ (أَدْنَأُ)، مِنَ الدَّنَاءَةِ.

﴿بِٱلَّذِى هُوَ خَيْرٌ﴾: يُرِيدُ بِهِ الْمَنَّ وَالسَّلْوَى، فَإِنَّهُ خَيْرٌ فِي اللَّذَّةِ وَالنَّفْعِ وَعَدَمِ الْحَاجَةِ إِلَى السَّعْيِ.

﴿ٱهْبِطُواْ مِصْرًا﴾: انْحَدِرُوا إِلَيْهِ مِنَ التِّيهِ. يُقَالُ: (هَبَطَ الْوَادِي) إِذَا نَزَلَ بِهِ، وَ(هَبَطَ مِنْهُ) إِذَا خَرَجَ مِنْهُ. ....

qāla ⁽*He said*⁾, that is, Allah; or Mūsā—upon him peace.

a-tastabdilūna-l-ladhī huwa adnā ⁽*will you take what is inferior in exchange*⁾: nearer in position and of lesser value. The literal meaning of *dunūw* ⁽nearness⁾ is local proximity, then it was borrowed for what is contemptible the same way *buʿd* ⁽remoteness⁾ was borrowed for honor and eminence, whence the expressions *baʿīd al-maḥall* ⁽far-reaching⁾ and *baʿīd al-himma* ⁽far-aspiring⁾.

It was also read *adna'u* ⁽viler⁾,[1350] from *danā'a* ⁽vileness⁾.

bi-l-ladhī huwa khayrun ⁽*for what is best?*⁾ by which He means manna and game, as they are more delicious and beneficial and they require no effort.

ʾhbiṭū miṣran ⁽*go down into some city*⁾: "descend there and out of the wandering in the desert."

One says *habaṭa al-wādī* ⁽he went down into the valley⁾ if he alights there and *habaṭa minh* ⁽he dropped out from it⁾ when he exits it.

[1350] By Zuhayr al-Furqubī [a contemporary of ʿĀṣim] a.k.a. Zuhayr al-Kisā'ī. (*MQ*)

وَقُرِئَ بِالضَّمِّ.

وَ(الْمِصْرُ): الْبَلَدُ الْعَظِيمُ؛ وَأَصْلُهُ: الْحَدُّ بَيْنَ الشَّيْئَيْنِ. وَقِيلَ: أَرَادَ بِهِ الْعَلَمَ، وَإِنَّمَا صَرَفَهُ لِسُكُونِ وَسَطِهِ، أَوْ عَلَى تَأْوِيلِ (الْبَلَدِ)؛ وَيُؤَيِّدُهُ أَنَّهُ غَيْرُ مُنَوَّنٍ فِي مُصْحَفِ ابْنِ مَسْعُودٍ. وَقِيلَ: أَصْلُهُ (مِصْرَائِيمُ)، فَعُرِّبَ.

﴿فَإِنَّ لَكُم مَّا سَأَلْتُمْ وَضُرِبَتْ عَلَيْهِمُ ٱلذِّلَّةُ وَٱلْمَسْكَنَةُ﴾: أُحِيطَتْ بِهِمْ إِحَاطَةَ الْقُبَّةِ بِمَنْ ضُرِبَتْ عَلَيْهِ؛ أَوْ أُلْصِقَتْ بِهِمْ، مِنْ (ضَرَبَ ....

It was also read [^{u}hbuṭū] with *ḍamm.*[1351]

Al-miṣr ⁽city⁾ is the vast territory and, originally, the boundary between two things. It was also said He meant by it the proper noun [Egypt],[1352] which He inflected only because its middle letter is quiescent, or for it to be interpreted as meaning "the City." The latter is supported by the fact that it is not nunated in Ibn Mas'ūd's Codex.[1353] It was also said its original form is *Miṣrā'īm* ⁽Mizraim⁾ then it was Arabized.

[The stamping of odious states on the Israelites]

fa-inna lakum mā sa'altum wa-ḍuribat ʿalayhimu-dh-dhillatu wa-l-maskanatu ⁽*then you shall have what you ask. And humiliation and misery were pitched upon them*⁾: they were made to encompass them the way a tent encompasses those over whom it was pitched; or they were made to cling to them, from *ḍaraba*

[1351] By Abū Ḥaywa, al-Ḥasan al-Baṣrī and Ayyūb al-Sikhtiyānī. (*MQ*)

[1352] As narrated from Abū al-ʿĀliya and al-Rabīʿ by al-Ṭabarī, *Tafsīr* (2:23), also from Mālik b. Anas, cf. Ḥamīd Laḥmar, *al-Imām Mālik Mufassiran* (Beirut: Dār al-Fikr, 1415/1995) p. 73 §17.

[1353] *Miṣra* without *tanwīn* is the reading of al-Ḥasan, Ṭalḥa, al-Aʿmash, Abān b. Taghlub, Ibn ʿAbbās, Ubay b. Kaʿb and Ibn Masʿūd. (*MQ*) Al-Ṭabarī (2:25) disallowed it as well as the suppression of the final *alif* in *miṣran* in light of the unanimity of the established script in the Quranic volumes. However, he considered it equally possible that *miṣran* in the verse may mean Egypt or any town of Syro-Palestine indifferently.

الطِّينَ عَلَى الْحَائِطِ)، مُجَازَاةً لَهُمْ عَلَى كُفْرَانِ النِّعْمَةِ.

وَالْيَهُودُ فِي غَالِبِ الْأَمْرِ أَذِلَّاءُ مَسَاكِينُ، إِمَّا عَلَى الْحَقِيقَةِ، أَوْ عَلَى التَّكَلُّفِ مَخَافَةَ أَنْ تُضَاعَفَ جِزْيَتُهُمْ.

﴿وَبَآءُو بِغَضَبٍ مِّنَ ٱللَّهِ﴾: رَجَعُوا بِهِ؛ أَوْ صَارُوا أَحِقَّاءَ بِغَضَبِهِ، مِنْ (بَاءَ فُلَانٌ بِفُلَانٍ) إِذَا كَانَ حَقِيقاً بِأَنْ يُقْتَلَ بِهِ. وَأَصْلُ (الْبَوْءِ): الْمُسَاوَاةُ.

﴿ذَٰلِكَ﴾ إِشَارَةٌ إِلَى مَا سَبَقَ مِنْ ضَرْبِ الذِّلَّةِ وَالْمَسْكَنَةِ وَالْبَوْءِ بِالْغَضَبِ.

﴿بِأَنَّهُمْ كَانُوا يَكْفُرُونَ بِـَٔايَٰتِ ٱللَّهِ وَيَقْتُلُونَ ٱلنَّبِيِّـۧنَ بِغَيْرِ ٱلْحَقِّ﴾ (I) بِسَبَبِ كُفْرِهِمْ (أ) بِالْمُعْجِزَاتِ، الَّتِي مِنْ جُمْلَتِهَا مَا عَدَّ عَلَيْهِمْ مِنْ فَلْقِ الْبَحْرِ

al-ṭīna ʿalā al-ḥāʾiṭ ⁽he cemented the mortar on the wall⁾, in requital for their denial of the favors [lavished on them].

Indeed, Jews for the most part are lowly and destitute, in reality or in pretense, out of fear that their tribute be increased.

wa-bāʾū bi-ghaḍabin mina-l-Lāhi ⁽*and they finally bore the anger of the One God*⁾: they brought it on themselves; or they became deserving of His anger, from *bāʾa fulānun bi-fulān* ⁽X tallied Y⁾, in the sense that X became fit to be executed in retaliation for Y: the literal meaning of *al-bawʾ/al-būʾ* is *al-musāwāt* ⁽equivalence⁾.

dhālika ⁽*that is*⁾: an allusion to what preceded of the pitching of humiliation, misery and the final deserving of anger.

bi-annahum kānū yakfurūna bi-āyāti-l-Lāhi wa-yaqtulūna-n-nabiyyīna bi-ghayri-l-ḥaqqi ⁽*on account of their constant disbelief in the signs of the One God and their killing the prophets unrightly*⁾ due to I. their disbelief (i) in stunning miracles, among which those that were enumerated [as evidence] against them: the cleaving of the sea, ...

وَإِظْلَالِ الْغَمَامِ، وَإِنْزَالِ الْمَنِّ وَالسَّلْوَى، وَانْفِجَارِ الْعُيُونِ مِنَ الْحَجَرِ؛ (ب) أَوْ بِالْكُتُبِ الْمُنْزَلَةِ كَالْإِنْجِيلِ وَالْفُرْقَانِ، وَآيَةِ الرَّجْمِ، وَالَّتِي فِيهَا نَعْتُ مُحَمَّدٍ ﷺ مِنَ التَّوْرَاةِ؛ (II) وَقَتْلِهِمُ الْأَنْبِيَاءَ: فَإِنَّهُمْ قَتَلُوا شَعْيَاءَ وَزَكَرِيَّا وَيَحْيَى وَغَيْرَهُمْ بِغَيْرِ الْحَقِّ عِنْدَهُمْ، إِذْ لَمْ يَرَوْا مِنْهُمْ مَا يَعْتَقِدُونَ بِهِ جَوَازَ قَتْلِهِمْ. وَإِنَّمَا حَمَلَهُمْ ....

the shading of the clouds, the sending down of manna and game, and the bursting of springs from the rock; (ii) or in the revealed books—such as the Gospel and the Discernment[1354]—as well as the Verse of Lapidation and those/the one in which there is a description of Muḥammad—upon him blessings and peace—in the Torah;[1355]

II. and their killing of prophets: for they killed Shaʿyāʾ ⁽Isaiah⁾, Zakariyyā ⁽Zechariah⁾, Yaḥyā ⁽John⁾ and others[1356] without right by their own admission, as they never saw them do anything for which their own creed permits them to kill them. What drove

[1354] Namely, the two books that they continue to deny whereas the above-mentioned miracles were denied by their forefathers. (Q)

[1355] For the verses of lapidation in the Torah see Deuteronomy (chapters 13 and 22) and Leviticus (20 and 24). The flagrant covering up of one such verse in Prophetic times is related in the *Muwaṭṭaʾ*, *Ṣaḥīḥayn*, *Sunan* and the *Musnad* of Aḥmad. The Torah's description of the Prophet is in Deuteronomy 33:2-3; in the Muslim sources it is related from the former rabbi Kaʿb al-Aḥbār by Dārimī, *Sunan* (*Muqaddima, Ṣifat al-Nabī fīl-Kutub qabla Mabʿathih*) thus: "We find him named Muḥammad b. ʿAbd Allāh. His birthplace is Mecca, his place of migration Ṭāba and his kingdom Syro-Palestine. He is not coarse of speech or boisterous in the market-places. He does not return wrong with wrong but forgives and pardons," among other Biblical passages e.g. Gn 49:10, Dt 18:18-20, Is 42:1-4, 10-13, Hb 3:3, Sg 5:16, Jn 14:16, 15:26, 16:7 etc.

[1356] As described in Talmudic literature cf. killing of Isaiah in *Tractate Yebamoth* 49b; killing of Zechariah ben Jehoiada [not the father of John the Baptist but a much earlier figure] in *Tractate Gittin* 57b, *Tractate Sanhedrin* 96b and *Lamentations Rabbah* iv.13. Other Jewish prophets killed by the Jews were Jeremiah, Ezekiel, Micah and Amos.

عَلَى ذٰلِكَ اتِّبَاعُ الْهَوَى وَحُبُّ الدُّنْيَا كَمَا أَشَارَ إِلَيْهِ بِقَوْلِهِ:

﴿ذَٰلِكَ بِمَا عَصَوا وَّكَانُوا يَعْتَدُونَ﴾، أَيْ: جَرَّهُمُ الْعِصْيَانُ وَالتَّمَادِي وَالِاعْتِدَاءُ فِيهِ إِلَى الْكُفْرِ بِالْآيَاتِ وَقَتْلِ النَّبِيِّينَ: فَإِنَّ صِغَارَ الذُّنُوبِ سَبَبٌ يُؤَدِّي إِلَى ارْتِكَابِ كِبَارِهَا، كَمَا أَنَّ صِغَارَ الطَّاعَاتِ أَسْبَابٌ مُؤَدِّيَةٌ إِلَى تَحَرِّي كِبَارِهَا.

وَقِيلَ: كَرَّرَ الْإِشَارَةَ لِلدِّلَالَةِ عَلَى أَنَّ مَا لَحِقَهُمْ، كَمَا هُوَ بِسَبَبِ الْكُفْرِ وَالْقَتْلِ، فَهُوَ بِسَبَبِ ارْتِكَابِهِمُ الْمَعَاصِي وَاعْتِدَائِهِمْ حُدُودَ اللهِ تَعَالَى.

وَقِيلَ: الْإِشَارَةُ إِلَى الْكُفْرِ وَالْقَتْلِ، وَالْبَاءُ بِمَعْنَى (مَعَ). ....

them to do all that was but he fact that they followed their evil inclinations and loved this world, to which He alluded when He said,

dhālika bi-mā ʿaṣaw wa-kānū yaʿtadūna ⁽*that is on account of their disobedience and constant transgressions*⁾: that is, their disobedience, obduracy in it and transgressing all limits in it gradually drove them to disbelief in the signs and killing the prophets. For small sins are a cause for committing major ones just as minor acts of piety are avenues of endeavor after major ones.

It was said that He reiterated the demonstrative as an indication that what befell them, just as it had been caused by unbelief and murder, was also caused by their commission of sins and their trespassing of the boundaries set by Allah Most High.

It was also said that the demonstrative points to "unbelief" and "killing" while the *bā'* is in the sense of *maʿa* ⁽together with⁾.

John was beheaded by the Jewish Roman-client tetrarch of Judea, Herod Antipas cf. Luke 3:19–20 and *Encyclopaedia Judaica*, ed. Fred Skolnik et al., 2nd ed., 22 vols. (Detroit etc.: Thomson Gale, 2007) 11:380-381.

وَإِنَّمَا جُوِّزَتِ الْإِشَارَةُ بِالْمُفْرَدِ إِلَى شَيْئَيْنِ فَصَاعِداً عَلَى تَأْوِيلِ (مَا ذُكِرَ، أَوْ تَقَدَّمَ) لِلْإِخْتِصَارِ. وَنَظِيرُهُ فِي الضَّمِيرِ: قَوْلُ رُؤْبَةَ يَصِفُ بَقَرَةً: [الرَّجَز]

فِيهَا خُطُوطٌ مِنْ سَوادٍ وَبَلَقْ ❊ كَأَنَّهُ فِي الْجِلْدِ تَوْلِيعُ الْبَهَقْ

وَالَّذِي حَسَّنَ ذٰلِكَ أَنَّ تَثْنِيَةَ الْمُضْمَرَاتِ وَالْمُبْهَمَاتِ وَجَمْعَهَا وَتَأْنِيثَهَا لَيْسَتْ عَلَى الْحَقِيقَةِ؛ وَلِذٰلِكَ جَاءَ (الَّذِي) بِمَعْنَى الْجَمْعِ.

﴿إِنَّ ٱلَّذِينَ ءَامَنُوا۟﴾ بِأَلْسِنَتِهِمْ؛ يُرِيدُ بِهِ الْمُتَدَيِّنِينَ بِدِينِ مُحَمَّدٍ ﷺ الْمُخْلِصِينَ

Note that it is allowed to use a singular demonstrative [pronoun] to refer to two or more objects when the latter are paraphrased as "what was mentioned or preceded" for brevity. An example of such usage with the personal pronoun is the saying of Ru'ba as he describes a cow: ["The Trembling"]

In it there are threads of blackness and piebald
as if it [sing.] *were, in its coat, a shimmer of white spots.*[1357]

What makes that beautiful is that the dual number of implied and anonymous items, their plural and their feminine are not literal. This is why *al-ladhī* ⟨who, which⟩ can be in the sense of the plural.[1358]

[2:62] **inna-l-ladhīna āmanū** ⟨*verily those who believed*⟩ with their tongues, by which is meant those that professed the religion of Muḥammad (upon him blessings and peace)—both the sincere

[1357] Cf. al-ʿAskarī, *Dīwān al-Maʿānī*, ed. Aḥmad Ḥasan Basaj, 2 vols. (Beirut: Dār al-Kutub al-ʿIlmiyya, 1414/1994) 2:481 and al-Baghdādī, *Khizāna* (1:88). Other editions have *ka'annahā*, which defeats the purpose as the latter fits the plural of *khuṭūṭ*, cf. Wilhelm Ahlwardt's edition of *Dīwān Ru'ba* in *Majmūʿ Ashʿār al-ʿArab* (3:104) and likewise al-Jurjānī in *Asrār al-Balāgha*, ed. Maḥmūd Shākir (Cairo: Maṭbaʿat al-Madanī; Jeddah: Dār al-Madanī, n.d.) p. 194.

[1358] "As already shown in the exegesis of the verse *as the likeness of the one that (al-ladhī) kindled a fire* (al-Baqara 2:17)." (Z)

مِنْهُمْ وَالْمُنَافِقِينَ؛ وَقِيلَ: المُنَافِقِينَ، لِانْخِرَاطِهِمْ فِي سَلْكِ الْكَفَرَةِ.

﴿وَٱلَّذِينَ هَادُواْ﴾: تَهَوَّدُوا، يُقَالُ (هَادَ وَتَهَوَّدَ) إِذَا دَخَلَ فِي الْيَهُودِيَّةِ.

وَ(يَهُودُ): إِمَّا عَرَبِيٌّ، مِنْ (هَادَ) إِذَا تَابَ - سُمُّوا بِذٰلِكَ لَمَّا تَابُوا مِنْ عِبَادَةِ الْعِجْلِ - وَإِمَّا مُعَرَّبُ (يَهُوذَا)، وَكَأَنَّهُمْ سُمُّوا بِاسْمِ أَكْبَرِ أَوْلَادِ يَعْقُوبَ، عَلَيْهِ السَّلَامُ.

﴿وَٱلنَّصَـٰرَىٰ﴾: جَمْعُ (نَصْرَانٍ)، كَـ(النَّدَامَى)؛ وَالْيَاءُ فِي (نَصْرَانِيٍّ) لِلْمُبَالَغَةِ، كَمَا فِي (أَحْمَرِيٍّ). سُمُّوا بِذٰلِكَ لِأَنَّهُمْ نَصَرُوا المَسِيحَ عَلَيْهِ السَّلَامُ،

and the hypocrites among them. It was also said it [just] means the hypocrites[1359] because they file up in the strand of the unbelievers:

wa-l-ladhīna hādū ⁽*and those who Judaized*⁾: became Jewish. One says *hāda* and *tahawwada* for someone who embraces Judaism.

Yahūdun ⁽Jews, Yehudim⁾[1360] is either Arabic [derived] from [the verb] *hāda*, "he repented"—they were called thus when they repented of the worship of the Calf[1361]—or the Arabized form of Yahūdhā ⁽Judah⁾, whereby it would seem they were named after the eldest of the sons of Yaʿqūb ⁽Jacob⁾—upon him peace.[1362]

wa-n-naṣārā ⁽*and the Nazarenes/Christians*⁾, plural of *naṣrānin* as in *nadāmā* and *nadmānun* ⁽regretful⁾. The *yā'* in *naṣrānī* is for intensiveness the same way as in *aḥmarī* ⁽ruby red⁾. They were called thus because of their support for the Christ—upon him…

1359 As narrated from Sufyān al-Thawrī and as held as the primary exegesis here by al-Taymī al-Asbahānī, Makkī al-Qaysī, Ibn ʿAṭiyya and al-Nasafī in their *Tafsīrs*.

1360 α, Ak, β, F, I, R, Sk: ويهود B: وتهوّد diplology ε: وىهود undotted

1361 As in Sūrat al-Aʿrāf 7:156 and per the explanation of Ibn Jurayj. (S)

1362 Al-Jawālīqī gives the latter derivation first and the former one second in his *al-Muʿarrab min al-Kalām al-Aʿjamī ʿalā Ḥurūf al-Muʿjam*, ed. Aḥmad Muḥammad Shākir, 2nd ed. (Cairo: Maṭbaʿat Dār al-Kutub, 1389/1969) p. 405.

أَوْ لِأَنَّهُمْ كَانُوا مَعَهُ فِي قَرْيَةٍ يُقَالُ لَهَا (نَصْرَانَ) أَوْ (نَاصِرَةَ) فَسُمُّوا بِاسْمِهَا، أَوْ مِنْ اسْمِهَا.

﴿وَالصَّابِئِينَ﴾: قَوْمٌ بَيْنَ النَّصَارَى وَالمَجُوسِ. وَقِيلَ أَصْلُ دِينِهِمْ دِينُ نُوحٍ - عَلَيْهِ السَّلَامُ؛ وَقِيلَ: هُمْ عَبَدَةُ المَلَائِكَةِ؛ وَقِيلَ: عَبَدَةُ الكَوَاكِبِ. وَهُوَ، إِنْ كَانَ عَرَبِيًّا فَمِنْ (صَبَأَ) إِذَا خَرَجَ.

peace—or because they were with him in a town called Naṣrān or Nāṣira ⁽Nazareth⁾, so they were named by its very name or after its name.

wa-ṣ-ṣābi'īna ⁽*and the Sabians*⁾: a people between Christians and Jews.[1363] It is also said the origin of their religion is the religion of Nūḥ ⁽Noah⁾—upon him peace. It is also said they are angelolaters. It is also said they are astrolaters. The term itself, if it is Arabic, comes from *ṣaba'a*, "he exits."

[1363] Ibn Abī Ḥātim cites eight different definitions of the Sabians, *Tafsīr* (1:127-128 §637-645) and they were considered People of the Book by al-Suddī and Isḥāq b. Rāhawayh as mentioned by al-Ṭabarī and al-Qurṭubī under this verse. They are also known as "MANDAEANS. A small religious sect in Iran and S Iraq, who maintain an ancient belief resembling that of gnosticism and that of the Parsis. They are also known as Christians of St. John, Nasoreans, Sabians, and Subbi. A few Mandaeans survive, some near the Tigris and Euphrates rivers, others in the area of Shushtar, Iran, and in cities of Asia Minor. Their customs and writings indicate early Christian, perhaps pre-Christian, origins. Their system of astrology resembles those of ancient Babylonia and the cults of the Magi in the last centuries BC. Their emanation system and dualism suggest a Gnostic origin, but unlike the Gnostics they abhor asceticism and emphasize fertility. Although some of their practices were influenced by Christianity, Judaism and Islam, they reject all three. They respect St. John the Baptist because of his baptizing, since their principal concern is ritual cleanliness and their chief rite is frequent baptism.... [R]ecent scholarship places their origin in Palestine or Syria. Their chief holy book, the *Ginza Rba*, like their other books, is a compendium of cosmology, cosmogony, prayers, legends, and rituals, written at various times and often contradictory" *New Columbia Encyclopedia*, ed. William H. Harris and Judith S. Levey (New York and London: Columbia University Press, 1975).

وَقَرَأَ نَافِعٌ وَحْدَهُ بِالْيَاءِ، إِمَّا لِأَنَّهُ خَفَّفَ الْهَمْزَةَ وَأَبْدَلَهَا يَاءً، أَوْ لِأَنَّهُ مِنْ (صَبَا) إِذَا مَالَ، لِأَنَّهُمْ مَالُوا عَنْ سَائِرِ الْأَدْيَانِ إِلَى دِينِهِمْ، أَوْ مِنَ الْحَقِّ إِلَى الْبَاطِلِ.

﴿مَنْ ءَامَنَ بِٱللَّهِ وَٱلْيَوْمِ ٱلْءَاخِرِ وَعَمِلَ صَٰلِحًا﴾: مَنْ كَانَ مِنْهُمْ فِي دِينِهِ قَبْلَ أَنْ يُنْسَخَ، مُصَدِّقاً بِقَلْبِهِ بِالْمَبْدَإِ وَالْمَعَادِ، عَامِلاً بِمُقْتَضَى شَرْعِهِ. وَقِيلَ: مَنْ آمَنَ مِنْ هٰؤُلَاءِ الْكَفَرَةِ إِيمَاناً خَالِصاً وَدَخَلَ فِي الْإِسْلَامِ دُخُولاً صَادِقاً.

﴿فَلَهُمْ أَجْرُهُمْ عِندَ رَبِّهِمْ﴾ الَّذِي وَعَدَ لَهُمْ ....

Nāfiʿ alone read it with *yā*ʾ [*ṣābīna*],[1364] either because he lightened the *hamza* and substituted it with a *yā*ʾ, or because it comes from *ṣabā*,[1365] "he inclines," as they inclined away from all the religions to their own, or from truth to falsehood.

[Islam abrogates previous faiths]

man āmana bi-l-Lāhi wa-l-yawmi-l-ākhiri wa-ʿamila ṣāliḥan ⁽*whoever believed in the One God and in the Last Day and did good*⁾: "whoever among them had followed his religion before it was abrogated,[1366] confirming with all his heart original creation and the final return and acting upon the dictates of his religious law;" it was also said, "whoever believes, out of those unbelievers, with unalloyed belief and enters Islam truthfully."[1367]

fa-lahum ajruhum ʿinda rabbihim ⁽*undoubtedly for them is their reward with their Nurturer Himself*⁾ which He promised them…

[1364] Also Abū Jaʿfar, al-Zuhrī and, in case of pause, Ḥamza. (*MQ*) "'Nāfiʿ alone' among the Seven; otherwise, among the Ten, so did Abū Jaʿfar." (A) "'Nāfiʿ alone with *yā*ʾ' meaning 'with *yā*ʾ only,' without *hamza*." (Q)

[1365] All mss. and eds.: صبا اذا مال AQ, H, MM: صبأ اذا مال dittography

[1366] See our introduction, section entitled "*Naskh*: The pre-Islamic viability and post-Islamic inviability of Judaism, Christianity and other superseded faiths."

[1367] I.e. believing in Muḥammad—upon him blessings and peace—cf. *Tafsīrs* of al-Ṭabarī (2:32, 2:38), al-Zajjāj, al-Taymī, al-Qurṭubī and others.

عَلَى إِيمَانِهِمْ وَعَمَلِهِمْ.

﴿وَلَا خَوْفٌ عَلَيْهِمْ وَلَا هُمْ يَحْزَنُونَ﴾ حِينَ يَخَافُ الْكُفَّارُ مِنَ الْعِقَابِ، وَيَحْزَنُ الْمُقَصِّرُونَ عَلَى تَضْيِيعِ الْعُمْرِ وَتَفْوِيتِ الثَّوَابِ.

وَ﴿مَنْ﴾ مُبْتَدَأٌ، خَبَرُهُ ﴿فَلَهُمْ أَجْرُهُمْ﴾؛ وَالْجُمْلَةُ: خَبَرُ ﴿إِنَّ﴾، أَوْ بَدَلٌ مِنْ اسْمِ ﴿إِنَّ﴾، وَخَبَرُهَا ﴿فَلَهُمْ أَجْرُهُمْ﴾. وَالْفَاءُ: لِتَضَمُّنِ الْمُسْنَدِ إِلَيْهِ مَعْنَى الشَّرْطِ. وَقَدْ مَنَعَ سِيبَوَيْهِ دُخُولَهَا فِي خَبَرِ (إِنَّ) مِنْ حَيْثُ إِنَّهَا لَا تَدْخُلُ الشَّرْطِيَّةَ، ....

for their belief and their deeds.

wa-lā khawfun ʿalayhim wa-lā hum yaḥzanūna ⁽*and they have nothing to fear, nor shall they grieve*⁾ at a time the unbelievers will fear divine retribution and the negligent will grieve over wasting their lives and missing their rewards.

Man ⁽whoever⁾ is an inchoative whose enunciative is ***fa-lahum ajruhum*** ⁽assured for them is their reward⁾. The whole clause is the enunciative of ***inna*** ⁽verily⁾, or a substitute for the noun of ***inna*** so that the enunciative of the latter is ***fa-lahum ajruhum***.

[Refutation of Sībawayh regarding the *fāʾ* of apodosis]

The ***fāʾ*** reflects the fact that the correlative of attribute[1368] implies the meaning of a condition. Sībawayh, on the other hand, disallowed its affixing to the enunciative of *inna* from the perspective that it is never affixed[1369] to conditional statements—

[1368] "Namely *man*, whether *man amana* is made out to be a *badal* ⁽substitute⁾ or a *mubtadaʾ* ⁽inchoative⁾—but this is not what he means in light of his words 'Sībawayh, on the other hand,' etc. which explicitly show that what is meant by the *mustanad ilayh* ⁽correlative of attribute⁾ is the first *mawṣūl* ⁽conjunctive⁾, namely, *al-ladhīna hādū* ⁽those who Judaized⁾.... nor is Sībawayh's position here of any weight. Bayḍāwī only brought up the issue to refute him." (Q)

[1369] H: تتدخّل dittography.

وَرُدَّ بِقَوْلِهِ تَعَالَى: ﴿إِنَّ ٱلَّذِينَ فَتَنُوا۟ ٱلْمُؤْمِنِينَ وَٱلْمُؤْمِنَٰتِ ثُمَّ لَمْ يَتُوبُوا۟ فَلَهُمْ عَذَابُ جَهَنَّمَ﴾ [البروج ١٠].

﴿وَإِذْ أَخَذْنَا مِيثَٰقَكُمْ﴾ بِاتِّبَاعِ مُوسَى وَالْعَمَلِ بِالتَّوْرَاةِ.

﴿وَرَفَعْنَا فَوْقَكُمُ ٱلطُّورَ﴾ حَتَّى أَعْطَيْتُمُ الْمِيثَاقَ. رُوِيَ أَنَّ مُوسَى لَمَّا جَاءَهُمْ بِالتَّوْرَاةِ فَرَأَوْا مَا فِيهَا مِنَ التَّكَالِيفِ الشَّاقَّةِ، كَبُرَتْ عَلَيْهِمْ وَأَبَوْا قَبُولَهَا، فَأَمَرَ جِبْرَئِيلَ فَقَلَعَ الطُّورَ فَظَلَّلَهُ فَوْقَهُمْ حَتَّى قَبِلُوا.

a position invalidated by the saying of Allah Most High, *truly those (inna-l-ladhīna) who persecute the believing men and women then do not repent: assured for them (fa-lahum) is the torment of Gehenna* (al-Burūj 85:10).

[The Damoclean mountain used to extract Israelite obedience]

[2:63] **wa-idh akhadhnā mīthāqakum** ⁽*and when We took your binding promise*⁾[1370] to follow Mūsā and act upon the Torah.

wa-rafaʿnā fawqakumu-ṭ-ṭūra ⁽*and We made the mountain hang over you*⁾ until you gave the binding promise. It is narrated that

> when Mūsā—upon him blessings and peace—brought them the Torah and they saw what it comprised of tasking duties they considered it overwhelming and refused to accept it; whereupon Jibra'īl ⁽Gabriel⁾ was ordered to uproot the mountain from the earth and overshadow them with it until they accepted.[1371]

[1370] "And this is the tenth divine favor lavished on them." (Q)

[1371] Narrated from Ibn Zayd (see note 1303), Qatāda, Mujāhid, Abū al-ʿĀliya, ʿIkrima, ʿAṭā' and al-Suddī by al-Ṭabarī (2:48-50) and Ibn Abī Ḥātim (1:129-130 §653-654) in their *Tafsīrs*. Al-Suddī's version adds that they prostrated on one flank and turned up the other to see if the mount was still falling on them. This writer has heard a Turkish storyteller cite the above account as the origin of "shokeling," the swaying or rocking of the body back and forth during Jewish prayer—which has also been scripturally justified (Numbers 8:13, Psalms 35:10, Proverbs 20:27) among other etiologies such as

﴿ خُذُواْ ﴾: عَلَى إِرَادَةِ الْقَوْلِ. ﴿ مَآ ءَاتَيْنَٰكُم ﴾ مِنَ الْكِتَابِ ﴿ بِقُوَّةٍ ﴾: جِدٍّ وَعَزِيمَةٍ. ﴿ وَٱذْكُرُواْ مَا فِيهِ ﴾: ادْرُسُوهُ وَلَا تَنْسَوْهُ؛ أَوْ تَفَكَّرُوا فِيهِ، فَإِنَّهُ ذِكْرٌ بِالْقَلْبِ؛ أَوِ اعْمَلُوا بِهِ. ﴿ لَعَلَّكُمْ تَتَّقُونَ ﴾: لِكَيْ تَتَّقُوا الْمَعَاصِيَ؛ أَوْ رَجَاءً مِنْكُمْ أَنْ تَكُونُوا مُتَّقِينَ. وَيَجُوزُ عِنْدَ الْمُعْتَزِلَةِ أَنْ يَتَعَلَّقَ بِالْقَوْلِ الْمَحْذُوفِ، أَيْ: (قُلْنَا خُذُوا وَاذْكُرُوا إِرَادَةً أَنْ تَتَّقُوا).

﴿ ثُمَّ تَوَلَّيْتُم مِّنۢ بَعْدِ ذَٰلِكَ ﴾: أَعْرَضْتُمْ عَنِ الْوَفَاءِ بِالْمِيثَاقِ بَعْدَ أَخْذِهِ.

khudhū ⁽*Take*⁾ is meant as direct speech.

mā ātaynākum ⁽*what We gave you*⁾ of the Book.

bi-quwwatin ⁽*with strength*⁾: with earnest resolve.

wa-dhkurū mā fīhi ⁽*and remember what is in it*⁾: "study it and do not forget it;" or "ponder it, for the latter act is remembrance with the heart;" or "put it into practice."

laʿallakum tattaqūna ⁽*perhaps you will beware*⁾: "so that you will beware of sins," or "because what is expectated of you is that you will become wary."

It is also possible, in the view of the Muʿtazila, that the latter [clause] pertains to a suppressed statement, meaning, "We said: take and remember, to the intention that you would beware."

[2:64] **thumma tawallaytum min baʿdi dhālika** ⁽*yet you turned away even after that*⁾: "you failed to fulfill your binding promise after pledging it."

mnemonics, gymnastics or emotionalism, cf. *Encyclopaedia Judaica* (16:460). The term *tahawwada* ⁽to become a Jew⁾ itself has been glossed by Abū ʿAmr b. al-ʿAlāʾ as "meaning 'they sway during the reading of the Torah, and they say that heavens and earth swayed when Allah gave Mūsā the Torah.'" Al-Baghawī, *Maʿālim al-Tanzīl*, ed. ʿAbd al-Razzāq al-Mahdī, 5 vols. (Beirut: Dār Iḥyāʾ al-Turāth al-ʿArabī, 1420/1999) 1:124.

﴿فَلَوْلَا فَضْلُ ٱللَّهِ عَلَيْكُمْ وَرَحْمَتُهُۥ﴾ بِتَوْفِيقِكُمْ لِلتَّوْبَةِ، أَوْ بِمُحَمَّدٍ ﷺ يَدْعُوكُمْ إِلَى الْحَقِّ وَيَهْدِيكُمْ إِلَيْهِ.

﴿لَكُنتُم مِّنَ ٱلْخَٰسِرِينَ﴾: الْمَغْبُونِينَ بِالْانْهِمَاكِ فِي الْمَعَاصِي، أَوْ بِالْخَبْطِ وَالضَّلَالِ فِي فَتْرَةٍ مِنَ الرُّسُلِ.

وَ(لَوْ) فِي الْأَصْلِ: لِامْتِنَاعِ الشَّيْءِ لِامْتِنَاعِ غَيْرِهِ؛ فَإِذَا دَخَلَ عَلَى (لَا): أَفَادَ إِثْبَاتاً؛ وَهُوَ امْتِنَاعُ الشَّيْءِ لِثُبُوتِ غَيْرِهِ؛ وَالْاسْمُ الْوَاقِعُ بَعْدَهُ ـ عِنْدَ سِيبَوَيْهِ ـ مُبْتَدَأٌ، خَبَرُهُ وَاجِبُ الْحَذْفِ لِدَلَالَةِ الْكَلَامِ عَلَيْهِ وَسَدِّ الْجَوَابِ مَسَدَّهُ؛ وَعِنْدَ الْكُوفِيِّينَ: فَاعِلُ فِعْلٍ مَحْذُوفٍ.

fa-law-lā faḍlu-l-Lāhi ʿalaykum wa-raḥmatuhu ⟨*indeed, were it not for the favor of the One God over you and His mercy*⟩ "by facilitating for you the prosperity of repentence;" or "in the person of Muḥammad—upon him blessings and peace—summoning you to the truth and guiding you towards it."

la-kuntum mina-l-khāsirīna ⟨*you would have been of the losers*⟩, those who are defrauded through immersion in sins; or by stumbling along in error during the slow period devoid of prophets.

[The expression *law* ⟨if it were⟩]

Law ⟨if it were⟩, originally, is for the preclusion of something because of the preclusion of something else; when affixed[1372] to ***lā*** ⟨not⟩ it conveys assertion, namely the preclusion of something because of the firm establishment of something else. The name that comes after it is, (i) according to Sībawayh, an inchoative whose enunciative must be suppressed because the tenor already points it out and the apodosis takes its place; (ii) and, according to the Kufans, the subject of a suppressed verb.

[1372] All mss. and eds.: دخل B: دخلت

﴿ وَلَقَدْ عَلِمْتُمُ ٱلَّذِينَ ٱعْتَدَوْا۟ مِنكُمْ فِى ٱلسَّبْتِ ﴾: اللَّامُ مُوَطِّئَةٌ لِلْقَسَمِ. وَ(السَّبْتُ): مَصْدَرُ (سَبَتَتِ الْيَهُودُ) إِذَا عَظَّمَتْ يَوْمَ السَّبْتِ؛ وَأَصْلُهُ: الْقَطْعُ. أُمِرُوا بِأَنْ يُجَرِّدُوهُ لِلْعِبَادَةِ، فَاعْتَدَى فِيهِ نَاسٌ مِنْهُمْ فِي زَمَنِ دَاوُدَ - عَلَيْهِ السَّلَامُ - وَاشْتَغَلُوا بِالصَّيْدِ، وَذٰلِكَ أَنَّهُمْ كَانُوا يَسْكُنُونَ قَرْيَةً عَلَى سَاحِلٍ يُقَالُ لَهَا: أَيْلَةُ، وَإِذَا كَانَ يَوْمُ السَّبْتِ ....

[2:65] **wa-la-qad ʿalimtumu-l-ladhīna-ʿtadaw minkum fi-s-sabti** ⁽*and you know very well of those among you who transgressed in the Sabbath*⁾: the *lām* [in **wa-la-qad**] paves the way for the oath.[1373]

Al-sabt ⁽sabbath⁾ is the infinitive noun of *sabatat al-Yahūdu* ⁽the Jews sabbathized⁾[1374] to mean they observed the Sabbath-day reverently. Its literal sense is *qaṭʿ* ⁽severing⁾.

[The simianization of the Sabbath-breakers]

They were commanded to devote it exclusively to worship but some of them transgressed against it in the time of Dāwūd ⁽David⁾—upon him peace—and took to fishing. The story goes, they dwelt a shore town named Ayla ⁽Eilat⁾.[1375] Every Sabbath-

[1373] "Rather, it is the *lām jawāb al-qasam* ⁽*lām* that corresponds to, or is the complement of an oath⁾." (K) "It goes against the terminology of the grammarians… When you say *la-in akramtanī la-ukrimannak* ⁽indeed if you honor me I will most certainly honor you⁾ with a subauded initial oath, the *lām* affixed to the conditional particle [*in*] is the *lām muwatti'a* ⁽the *lām* that paves the way⁾ while the *lām* that comes after the condition is the *lām jawāb al-qasam*." (Z) "It might be a slip of the copyist; the correct description is *lām taqdīr al-qasam* ⁽*lām* of subaudition of the oath⁾, that is, 'By Allah! You certainly do know.'" (Iṣ, Kh) "Abū Ḥayyān said it is a *lām* of inception as in *la-Zaydun qā'imun* ⁽Zayd, behold, is standing⁾, and it is possible for it to be the complement of a suppressed oath whereby He swore that they knew those who transgressed." (S, Kh) "What the author said is in the lexical sense, therefore it makes no sense to take his words as a slip. The subaudition is, 'And, by Allah! You know full well of the Sabbath transgressors and the examplary punishment they incurred, so be cautious not to do what they did in light of the consequences of their deed.'" (Q, Kh)

[1374] All mss. and Kh, S, Sk: مصدر سبتت K, Z and modern eds.: مصدر قولك سبتت gloss.

[1375] A city on the Syro-Palestinian shore of the Red Sea according to Yāqūt al-Ḥamawī,

لَمْ يَبْـقَ حُوتٌ فِي الْبَحْرِ إِلَّا حَضَرَ هُنَـاكَ وَأَخْرَجَ خُرْطُومَـهُ، فَـإِذَا مَضَى، تَفَرَّقَتْ؛ فَحَفَرُوا حِيَاضـاً وَشَرَّعُوا إِلَيْهَا الْجَدَاوِلَ، وَكَانَتِ الْحِيتَانُ تَدْخُلُهَا يَوْمَ السَّبْتِ فَيَصْطَادُونَهَا يَوْمَ الْأَحَدِ.

﴿فَقُلْنَا لَهُمْ كُونُوا قِرَدَةً خَاسِئِينَ﴾: جَامِعِينَ بَيْنَ صُورَةِ الْقِرْدِ وَالْخُسُوءِ، وَهُوَ الصَّغَارُ وَالطَّرْدُ. وَقَالَ مُجَاهِدٌ: مَا مُسِخَتْ صُوَرُهُمْ وَلَكِنْ قُلُوبُهُـمْ، فَمُثِّلُوا بِالْقِرْدِ كَمَا مُثِّلُوا بِالْحِمَارِ فِي قَوْلِـهِ تَعَالَى: ﴿كَمَثَلِ الْحِمَارِ يَحْمِلُ أَسْفَارًا﴾ [الجمعة ٥].

> day there was no fish left in the sea but was present there, poking out its snout. When it passed they would disperse. So they dug out ponds and opened up channels leading thereto so that fish would enter them on the Sabbath-day and they would net them on the first day of the week.[1376]

fa-qulnā lahum kūnū qiradatan khāsiʾīna⁽*whereupon We said to them: Be apes, kept at bay!*⁾, joining together the outward form of apes[1377] and *khusūʾ*, which is abjectness and expulsion. Mujāhid, on the other hand, said,

> Their physical appearances were not metamorphosed but rather their hearts, whence they were proverbialized as apes just as they were proverbialized as an ass in the saying of Allah Most High *as the likeness of an ass loaded with tomes* (al-Jumuʿa 62:5).[1378]

present-day ʿAqaba in Jordan according to Muḥammad Shurrāb, *al-Maʿālim al-Athīra fīl-Sunnati wal-Sīra* (Damascus: Dār al-Qalam; Beirut: al-Dār al-Shāmiyya, 1411/1991) p. 40 and Muḥammad al-Marʿashlī et al., *Mawsūʿat al-Sīrat al-Nabawiyya al-Sharīfa* (Beirut: Dār al-Nafāʾis, 1429/2008) pp. 133-134.

1376 Narrated from al-Suddī by al-Ṭabarī in his *Tafsīr* (2:63-64).

1377 α, B, R: بالقرد... القرد Ak, β, ε, F, I, Sk, T: بالقردة... القردة ε: : بالقرد... [missing] lacuna.

1378 Cf. *Tafsīr al-Imām Mujāhid b. Jabr*, ed. Muḥammad ʿAbd al-Salām Abū al-Nīl (Madīnat Naṣr: Dār al-Fikr al-Islāmī al-Ḥadītha, 1410/1989) p. 205. Al-Ṭabarī in his *Tafsīr* (2:65-66) took issue with this gloss as contradicting the manifest locution of the

وَقَوْلُهُ: ﴿كُونُوا﴾ لَيْسَ بِأَمْرٍ، إِذْ لَا قُدْرَةَ لَهُمْ عَلَيْهِ؛ وَإِنَّمَا الْمُرَادُ بِهِ: سُرْعَةُ التَّكْوِينِ، وَأَنَّهُمْ صَارُوا كَذٰلِكَ كَمَا أَرَادَ بِهِمْ.

وَقُرِئَ (قَرِدَةً) بِفَتْحِ الْقَافِ وَكَسْرِ الرَّاءِ، وَ(خَاسِينَ) بِغَيْرِ هَمْزَةٍ.

﴿فَجَعَلْنَاهَا﴾: أَيِ الْمَسْخَةَ؛ أَوِ الْعُقُوبَةَ.

His saying *kūnū* ⁽be!⁾ is not a command—since they are incapable of it—but rather what is meant by it is the speed of instant formation[1379] and the fact that they became such just as He willed it for them.

It was also read *qaridatan* with a *fatḥa* on the *qāf* and a *kasra* on the *rā*ʾ, and *khāsīn* without *hamza*.[1380]

[2:66] **fa-jaʿalnāhā** ⁽*then We made it*⁾, that is, the metamorphosis; or the retribution.

Qurʾān and exegetical consensus. Likewise Makkī al-Qaysī, *Hidāya* (1:301) stated "The totality of exegetes said otherwise, as they were metamorphosed into apes literally" Abū Manṣūr al-Māturīdī in *Taʾwīlāt al-Qurʾān*, ed. Ertuğrul Boynukalin and Bekir Topaloğlu, 18 vols. (Istanbul: Dār al-Mīzān, 2006) 1:151 brings up a third scenario: "He turned their *jawhar* ⁽material constitution⁾ into that of apes while maintaining humanity in them with respect to understanding and reason." This is supported by Ibn ʿAbbās's remarkable account that the apes wept and signaled their former identities to their human relatives when the latter discovered them metamorphosed as narrated by al-Shāfiʿī in *Aḥkām al-Qurʾān*, al-Wāḥidī, al-Baghawī and Ibn ʿĀdil in their *Tafsīr*s under this verse, al-Ḥākim, *Mustadrak* (2:322-323) and al-Bayhaqī, *Sunan* and *Maʿrifat al-Sunan wal-Āthār*. It is strange that Dr. ʿAlī al-Ṣābūnī in *Ṣafwat al-Tafāsīr*, 4th ed., 3 vols. (Beirut: Dār al-Qurʾān al-Karīm, 1402/1981) 1:65 forwards Mujāhid's figurative gloss as the majority exegesis and cites the literal one as "the saying of one exegete," by which he means al-Jamal in his supercommentary on the *Jalālayn*—when al-Jamal's gloss only reiterates what is found everywhere else and is so very far from being isolated that al-Damīrī stated in *Ḥayāt al-Ḥayawān* (2:290) that Mujāhid alone had said it among the totality of the exegetes.

1379 "It is an *amr taḥwīl* ⁽metamorphizing command⁾." Al-Taymī al-Aṣfahānī (457-535 /1065-1141), *Kitāb al-Īḍāḥ fīl-Tafsīr*, offset rept. of complete Tehran Kitabkhanah ms. dated 531/1137 (Tehran: Markaz Nashr Danshagahī, 1384P/2006) p. 18.

1380 Respectively al-Khalīl, and al-Hudhalī from al-Nahrawānī from Ibn Wardān. (*MQ*)

﴿نَكَٰلًا﴾: عِبْرَةً تُنَكِّلُ المُعْتَبِرَ بِهَا، أَيْ تَمْنَعُهُ. وَمِنْهُ: (النِّكْلُ) لِلْقَيْدِ.

﴿لِّمَا بَيْنَ يَدَيْهَا وَمَا خَلْفَهَا﴾ لِمَا قَبْلَهَا وَمَا بَعْدَهَا مِنَ الأُمَمِ إِذْ ذُكِرَتْ حَالُهُمْ فِي زُبُرِ الْأَوَّلِينَ، وَاشْتَهَرَتْ قِصَّتُهُمْ فِي الآخِرِينَ؛ أَوْ لِمُعَاصِرِيهِمْ وَمَنْ بَعْدَهُمْ؛ أَوْ لِمَا بِحَضْرَتِهَا مِنَ الْقُرَى وَمَا تَبَاعَدَ عَنْهَا؛ أَوْ لِأَهْلِ تِلْكَ الْقَرْيَةِ وَمَا حَوَالِيهَا؛ أَوْ لِأَجْلِ مَا تَقَدَّمَ عَلَيْهَا مِنْ ذُنُوبِهِمْ وَمَا تَأَخَّرَ مِنْهَا.

﴿وَمَوْعِظَةً لِّلْمُتَّقِينَ﴾ مِنْ قَوْمِهِمْ؛ أَوْ لِكُلِّ مُتَّقٍ سَمِعَهَا.

﴿وَإِذْ قَالَ مُوسَىٰ لِقَوْمِهِۦٓ إِنَّ ٱللَّهَ يَأْمُرُكُمْ أَن تَذْبَحُوا۟ بَقَرَةً﴾: أَوَّلُ هَٰذِهِ

nakālan⸢*a deterrent punishment*⸣: a lesson that deters the one that takes heed of it in the sense that it inhibits him; wence *al-nikl*, "shackle."

li-mā bayna yadayhā wa-mā khalfahā ⸢*for all behind it and all ahead of it*⸣: (i) "for all before it and all after it" among the communities, since their situation was chronicled in the writs of the ancients and their story acquired fame among the moderns; (ii) or "for their contemporaries and those who succeed them;" (iii) or "for their neighboring towns and the outlying ones;" (iv) or "for the people of that town and whatever is around it;" (v) or "due to their sins prior to it and thereafter."[1381]

wa-mawʿiẓatan li-l-muttaqīna ⸢*and an admonishment for those who beware*⸣ among their nation; or for every wary one who hears of it.

[The story of the divinatory yellow cow]

[2:67] **wa-idh qāla Mūsā li-qawmihi inna-l-Lāha yaʾmurukum an tadhbaḥū baqaratan** ⸢*and when Mūsā said to his nation: Verily the One God commands you to slaughter a cow*⸣: the start of this

[1381] Al-Ṭabarī (*Tafsīr* 2:72) advocates yet a sixth meaning, namely a combination of the first part of (v) and the latter part of (ii).

الْقِصَّةِ قَوْلُهُ تَعَالَى ﴿ وَإِذْ قَتَلْتُمْ نَفْسًا فَادَّارَءْتُمْ فِيهَا ﴾ [البقرة ٧٢]، وَإِنَّمَا فُكَّتْ
عَنْهُ وَقُدِّمَتْ عَلَيْهِ لِاسْتِقْلَالِهَا بِنَوْعٍ آخَرَ مِنْ مَسَاوِيهِمْ: وَهُوَ الِاسْتِهْزَاءُ
بِالْأَمْرِ، وَالِاسْتِقْصَاءُ فِي السُّؤَالِ، وَتَرْكُ الْمُسَارَعَةِ إِلَى الِامْتِثَالِ. وَقِصَّتُهُ: أَنَّهُ
كَانَ فِيهِمْ شَيْخٌ مُوسِرٌ، فَقَتَلَ ابْنَهُ بَنُو أَخِيهِ طَمَعاً فِي مِيرَاثِهِ، وَطَرَحُوهُ عَلَى
بَابِ الْمَدِينَةِ، ثُمَّ جَاءُوا يُطَالِبُونَ بِدَمِهِ؛ فَأَمَرَهُمُ اللهُ أَنْ يَذْبَحُوا بَقَرَةً
وَيَضْرِبُوهُ بِبَعْضِهَا لِيَحْيَى، فَيُخْبِرَ بِقَاتِلِهِ.

﴿ قَالُوٓاْ أَتَتَّخِذُنَا هُزُوًا ﴾، أَيْ مَكَانَ هُزْءٍ؛ أَوْ أَهْلَهُ، ....

account is the saying of Allah Most High *and when you killed a soul and repelled one another concerning it* (al-Baqara 2:72). It was detached thence and put ahead because it independently [conveys] another instance of their evil deeds—namely, their mockery of commandments, their going to extremes in questioning and their nonchalance in obeying. The story goes,

> there was among them a rich man advanced in years. His son was killed by his brother's sons, who coveted his inheritance. They flung his body outside the city gate and then came to demand his blood-wite. Eventually, Allah ordered them to slaughter a cow and strike him over with part of it so that he would come back to life and reveal his killer.[1382]

qālū a-tattakhidhunā huzuʾan[1383] ⁽*they said: Are you making us your laughing-stock?*⁾: that is, (i) "the butt of ridicule," (ii) or "fit

[1382] Narrated alongside variants from Ibn ʿAbbās, ʿAbīdat al-Salmānī, Abū al-ʿĀliya, al-Suddī, Mujāhid, Wahb b. Munabbih, Muḥammad b. Kaʿb and Muḥammad b. Qays by al-Ṭabarī in his *Tafsīr* (2:76-81).

[1383] F, T: هُزُؤًا B: هُزُءًا K, Kh, U, Ul, Z: هزؤا I: هُزْؤًا R: هُزْوًا α: هُزُوًا Ak, β, ε, Sk: هزوا
What we established as the Qadi's text—*huzu'an*—is the reading of Nāfiʿ, Ibn Kathīr, Abū ʿAmr, Ibn ʿĀmir, ʿĀṣim, al-Kisāʾī, Shuʿba and Yaʿqūb in Ruways's narration (*MQ*) and the majority reading. The *rasm* in the old volumes is هزوا cf. Tayyar Altikulaç, *Al-Muṣḥaf Al-Sharif: Attributed To ʿUthmān Bin ʿAffān (The Copy At The Topkapi Palace*

وَمَهْزُوءاً بِنَا؛ أَوِ الْهُزْءَ نَفْسَهُ لِفَرْطِ الْاِسْتِهْزَاءِ، اِسْتِبْعَاداً لِمَا قَالَهُ وَاسْتِخْفَافاً بِهِ. وَقَرَأَ حَمْزَةُ وَإِسْمَاعِيلُ عَنْ نَافِعٍ بِالسُّكُونِ، وَحَفْصٌ عَنْ عَاصِمٍ بِالضَّمِّ وَقَلْبِ الْهَمْزَةِ وَاواً.

﴿قَالَ أَعُوذُ بِٱللَّهِ أَنْ أَكُونَ مِنَ ٱلْجَٰهِلِينَ﴾ لِأَنَّ الْهُزْءَ فِي مِثْلِ ذٰلِكَ: جَهْلٌ وَسَفَهٌ. نَفَى عَنْ نَفْسِهِ مَا رُمِيَ بِهِ عَلَى طَرِيقَةِ الْبُرْهَانِ، وَأَخْرَجَ ذٰلِكَ فِي صُورَةِ الْاِسْتِعَاذَةِ اسْتِفْظَاعاً لَهُ.

﴿قَالُوا۟ ٱدْعُ لَنَا رَبَّكَ يُبَيِّن لَّنَا مَا هِىَ﴾، ....

for it" and "something utterly mocked" (iii) or "the definition of a farce" to convey excessive mockery in incredulity at what he said and derision of it.[1384]

Ḥamza and Ismāʿīl—[narrating] from Nāfiʿ—read it [*huz'an*] with *sukūn* and Ḥafṣ from ʿĀṣim [*huzuwan*] with *ḍamm* and the transposition of *hamza* into *wāw*.[1385]

qāla aʿūdhu bi-l-Lāhi an akūna mina-l-jāhilīna ⁽*he said: I take refuge in the One God from ever being of the ignorant!*⁾ because mockery in such matters is ignorance and foolishness. He rejected the charge against him demonstratively and couched that in terms of seeking refuge, to show that it was abominable.

[2:68] **qalū-dʿu lanā rabbaka yubayyin lanā mā hiya** ⁽*they said: Call upon your Nurturer for us to make clear to us what she is*⁾,

Museum), 2 vols. (Istanbul: Organization of the Islamic Conference Research Centre for Islamic History, Art and Culture, 1428/2007) 2:12 line 3.

1384 From al-Suddī: When Mūsā told them of the command they said: "We are asking you about the murdered man and the identity of his killer, and you say 'Slaughter a cow'? Are you mocking us?" Ibn Abi Ḥātim, *Tafsīr* (1:136 §691).

1385 *huz'an*: Ḥamza, Ismāʿīl, Khalaf, Yaʿqūb, al-Muṭawwaʿī, al-Qazzāz from ʿAbd al-Wārith, al-Mufaḍḍal, and Nāfiʿ in Ismāʿīl's narration; *huzuwan*: ʿĀṣim from Ḥafṣ and al-Shanbūdhī; *huzzan*: Abū Jaʿfar and Shayba. (*MQ*)

أَيْ مَا حَالُهَا وَصِفَتُهَا. وَكَانَ حَقُّهُ أَنْ يَقُولُوا: أَيُّ بَقَرَةٍ هِيَ؟ أَوْ: كَيْفَ هِيَ؟ لِأَنَّ (مَا) يُسْأَلُ بِهِ عَنِ الْجِنْسِ غَالِباً؛ لٰكِنَّهُمْ لَمَّا رَأَوْا مَا أُمِرُوا بِهِ عَلَى حَالٍ لَمْ يُوجَدْ بِهَا شَيْءٌ مِنْ جِنْسِهِ، أَجْرَوْهُ مُجْرَى مَا لَمْ يَعْرِفُوا حَقِيقَتَهُ وَلَمْ يَرَوْا مِثْلَهُ.

﴿قَالَ إِنَّهُۥ يَقُولُ إِنَّهَا بَقَرَةٌ لَّا فَارِضٌ وَلَا بِكْرٌ﴾: لَا مُسِنَّةٌ وَلَا فَتِيَّةٌ؛ يُقَالُ: (فَرَضَتِ الْبَقَرَةُ فُرُوضاً)، مِنَ الْفَرْضِ ـ وَهُوَ الْقَطْعُ ـ كَأَنَّهَا فَرَضَتْ سِنَّهَا؛ وَتَرْكِيبُ (الْبِكْرِ) لِلْأَوَّلِيَّةِ، وَمِنْهُ: (الْبُكْرَةُ) وَ(الْبَاكُورَةُ).

﴿عَوَانٌ﴾: نَصَفٌ. قَالَ: [الوافر] .... ✻ نَوَاعِمُ بَيْنَ أَبْكَارٍ وَعُونِ

that is, what her state is and how she is described. It would have been right for them to say *ayyu baqaratin hiya* ‹which cow is she› or *kayfa hiya* ‹which kind is she›[1386] because *mā* ‹what› is asked[1387] mostly to define species;[1388] but when they saw that what they had been commanded was of a condition that no specimen of its species had, they treated it as something whose reality they did not know and the like of which they had never seen before.

qāla innahu yaqūlu innahā baqaratun lā fāriḍun wa-lā bikrun ‹*he said: verily He says it is a cow neither cull nor yearling*›: neither aged nor immature. One says *faraḍat al-baqaratu furūḍan* ‹the cow has become aged›, [inf. noun] *furūḍan*, from *farḍ* which is *qaṭ*ʿ ‹cutting›, as if it had cut away its teeth.

The stem-form ***bikr*** spells primacy, whence *bukra* ‹daybreak› and *bākūra* ‹first-fruits›.

ʿawānun‹*middling*›: middle-aged. [The poet] said: ["The Exuberant"]

Sensuous women, between virgins and middlings (ʿūn).[1389]

[1386] All mss. and eds.: اي بقرة هي او كيف هي B: ايٌّ بقرة هي lacuna.
[1387] B: يُسأَل R: يساءل α, I, Sk, T: يُسئل A, F: يُسْأل β: يسئال Ak: يسال ε: يسيل
[1388] "Including *māhiyya* ‹quiddity› and *ḥaqīqa* ‹literal sense›." (Q)
[1389] Spoken by al-Ṭirmāḥ b. Ḥakīm b. al-Ḥakam al-Ṭā'ī (d.ca. 125/743), one of the Syr-

﴿بَيْنَ ذَٰلِكَ﴾: أَيْ بَيْنَ مَا ذُكِرَ مِنَ الْفَارِضِ وَالْبِكْرِ. وَلِذٰلِكَ أُضِيفَ إِلَيْهِ (بَيْنَ)، فَإِنَّهُ لَا يُضَافُ إِلَّا إِلَى مُتَعَدِّدٍ.

وَعَوْدُ هٰذِهِ الْكِنَايَاتِ، وَإِجْرَاءُ تِلْكَ الصِّفَاتِ عَلَى بَقَرَةٍ: يَدُلُّ عَلَى أَنَّ الْمُرَادَ بِهَا مُعَيَّنَةٌ؛ وَيَلْزَمُهُ تَأْخِيرُ الْبَيَانِ عَنْ وَقْتِ الْخِطَابِ. وَمَنْ أَنْكَرَ ذٰلِكَ زَعَمَ أَنَّ الْمُرَادَ بِهَا بَقَرَةٌ مِنْ شِقِّ الْبَقَرِ غَيْرُ مَخْصُوصَةٍ، ثُمَّ انْقَلَبَتْ مَخْصُوصَةً بِسُؤَالِهِمْ؛ وَيَلْزَمُهُ النَّسْخُ قَبْلَ الْفِعْلِ، فَإِنَّ التَّخْصِيصَ إِبْطَالٌ لِلتَّخْيِيرِ الثَّابِتِ بِالنَّصِّ.

bayna dhālika ⁽*between that*⁾, that is, in-between what was mentioned of the cull and the yearling, hence ***bayna*** ⁽between⁾ was annexed to it, which is done only for something plural.

[Abrogation and other scenarios of the cow's particularization]

The referencing of these denotatives and assignation of these attributes back to a cow indicate that what is meant thereby is a particular cow. Concomitantly it means that the exposition [of precisely what cow is meant] has to be delayed until after the time of the initial address.[1390] Those who deny that [scenario][1391] claim that what was meant by it was any cow of the bovine species without specification, which was then switched into a specific one through their questioning. Concomitantly it means abrogation occurred before implementation, as specification[1392] is an invalidation of textually-established latitude.

ian *fuḥūl* ⁽"stallion satirists"⁾ of Islam. Its first hemistich has several variants, among them "Tall, like coverings on the necks of horses" (Kh, S) and "Decorous wives, donning high face-veils" cf. Afandī, *Tanzīl al-Āyāt* (p. 262).

1390 This is permissible for Shāfiʿīs (Q) or rather for *Ahl al-Sunna* in general (Z), and there is agreement that what is impermissible is to delay exposition from the time of need for action (*waqt al-ḥāja ilā al-ʿamal*). (Q, Z)

1391 I.e. the Muʿtazila. (Z)

1392 "That is, *taqyīd* ⁽restrictiveness⁾." (Q)

وَالْحَقُّ: جَوَازُهُمَا. وَيُؤَيِّدُ الرَّأْيَ الثَّانِي: (I) ظَاهِرُ اللَّفْظِ؛ (II) وَالْمَرْوِيُّ عَنْهُ ـ عَلَيْهِ الصَّلَاةُ وَالسَّلَامُ ـ: لَوْ ذَبَحُوا أَيَّ بَقَرَةٍ أَرَادُوا لَأَجْزَأَتْهُمْ، وَلَكِنْ شَدَّدُوا عَلَى أَنْفُسِهِمْ فَشَدَّدَ اللهُ عَلَيْهِمْ؛ (III) وَتَقْرِيعُهُمْ بِالتَّمَادِي وَزَجْرُهُمْ عَلَى الْمُرَاجَعَةِ بِقَوْلِهِ:

﴿فَٱفْعَلُواْ مَا تُؤْمَرُونَ﴾، أَيْ مَا تُؤْمَرُونَهُ، بِمَعْنَى تُؤْمَرُونَ بِهِ، مِنْ

The truth is both [scenarios] are possible.[1393] The second view is well-supported I. by the manifest locution; II. by what was narrated from the Prophet—upon him blessings and peace:

> Had they slaughtered any cow they wished it would have been sufficient for them; but they made it difficult for themselves so Allah made it difficult for them;[1394]

III. and by their being rebuked for their obduracy and chided for constantly arguing in His saying,

fa-fʿalū mā tuʾmarūna ⁽*so do what you are commanded!*⁾, that is, (i) *mā tuʾmarūnahu* ⁽that which you are commanded⁾ in the sense of *tuʾmarūna bih* ⁽you are commanded to do⁾ as in the saying:

[1393] "That is, it is both possible that the exposition was delayed until after the time of initial address—as imposed by the first sense—and that abrogation took place before implementation but after enablement to believe (*al-tamakkun bil-iʿtiqād*). This is supported by the abrogation of the obligation of fifty prayers in the hadith of the Ascent. What is precluded is only abrogation before enablement to believe, by agreement. Furthermore the meaning of abrogation here is not in the sense of the abrogation of the initial command and the cancellation of the ruling completely so that the restricted [ruling] now needs a fresh command; but rather in the sense that its ruling is cancelled with regard to all but the restricted aspect, while slaughtering remains specifically incumbent, which constitutes obedience to the initial order." (Q 3:390).

[1394] Narrated from Ibn ʿAbbās, Qatāda, ʿAbīdat al-Salmānī, ʿIkrima, Mujāhid, Abū al-ʿĀliya and Ibn Zayd as their own saying by al-Ṭabarī, *Tafsīr* (2:98-100); and through al-Ḥasan from Abū Hurayra by Ibn Mardūyah, Ibn Abī Ḥātim and al-Bazzār according to Ibn Ḥajar in *al-Kāfī al-Shāf* (p. 16 §39).

قَوْلِه: [بسيط] أَمَرْتُكَ الْخَيْرَ فَافْعَلْ مَا أُمِرْتَ بِهِ ✻ ....

أَوْ (أَمْرَكُمْ) بِمَعْنَى (مَأْمُورَكُمْ).

﴿قَالُوا۟ ٱدْعُ لَنَا رَبَّكَ يُبَيِّن لَّنَا مَا لَوْنُهَا ۚ قَالَ إِنَّهُۥ يَقُولُ إِنَّهَا بَقَرَةٌ صَفْرَآءُ فَاقِعٌ لَّوْنُهَا﴾: (الْفُقُوعُ) نُصُوعُ الصُّفْرَةِ، وَلِذَلِكَ يُؤَكَّدُ بِهِ، فَيُقَالُ: (أَصْفَرُ فَاقِعٌ)، كَمَا يُقَالُ (أَسْوَدُ حَالِكٌ). وَفِي إِسْنَادِهِ إِلَى اللَّوْنِ - وَهُوَ صِفَةُ ﴿صَفْرَآءُ﴾ - لِمُلَابَسَتِهِ بِهَا: فَضْلُ تَأْكِيدٍ، كَأَنَّهُ قِيلَ: صَفْرَاءُ شَدِيدَةُ الصُّفْرَةِ صُفْرَتُهَا؛ وَعَنِ الْحَسَنِ: سَوْدَاءُ شَدِيدَةُ السَّوَادِ؛ ....

["The Outspread"] "I commanded you goodness, so do what you were commanded to do;"[1395] (ii) or *amrakum* ⸢your command⸣ in the sense of *ma'mūrakum* ⸢what was commanded to you⸣.

[2:69] **qālū-dʿu lanā rabbaka yubayyin lanā mā lawnuhā qāla innahu yaqūlu innahā baqaratun ṣafrāʾu fāqiʿun lawnuhā** ⸢*they said: Call upon your Nurturer for us to make clear to us what her color is. He said: Verily He says it is a yellow cow of intensely bright color*⸣: ***Fuqūʿ*** ⸢intense yellowness⸣ is the pureness of the color yellow and hence serves to reinforce the latter in the expression *aṣfarun fāqiʿ* ⸢bright yellow⸣, just as one says *aswadun ḥālik* ⸢jet-black⸣. Its ascription to ***lawn*** ⸢color⸣, although it is the attribute of ***ṣafrāʾ*** ⸢yellow⸣—because of the intimate connection between the former and the latter[1396]—is a superadded emphasis, as if it had been said, "yellow, with an intensely yellow yellowness."

Al-Ḥasan relatedly glossed it as "of intensely black color."[1397]

[1395] Attributed to the Companion ʿAmr b. Maʿdīkarib by Sībawayh, *Kitāb* (1:37).
[1396] "I.e. the intimate connection of *al-lawn* with *al-ṣufra* the way the *muṭlaq* ⸢unqualified⸣ is connected with the *muqayyad* ⸢restricted⸣." (Q)
[1397] Narrated by al-Ṭabarī who goes on to cite al-Aʿshā's verse, *Tafsīr* (2:92-94), and

وَبِهِ فُسِّرَ قَوْلُهُ تَعَالَى: ﴿جِمَٰلَتٌ صُفْرٌ﴾ [المرسلات ٣٣]. قَالَ الْأَعْشَى: [الخفيف]

تِلْكَ خَيْلِي مِنْهُ وَتِلْكَ رِكَابِي ❋ هُنَّ صُفْرٌ أَوْلَادُهَا كَالزَّبِيبِ

وَلَعَلَّهُ عَبَّرَ بِالصُّفْرَةِ عَنِ السَّوَادِ لِأَنَّهَا مِنْ مُقَدِّمَاتِهِ، أَوْ لِأَنَّ سَوَادَ الْإِبِلِ تَعْلُوهُ صُفْرَةٌ؛ وَفِيهِ نَظَرٌ، لِأَنَّ الصُّفْرَةَ بِهَٰذَا الْمَعْنَى لَا تُؤَكَّدُ بِالْفُقُوعِ.

﴿تَسُرُّ ٱلنَّٰظِرِينَ﴾، أَيْ تُعْجِبُهُمْ. وَ(السُّرُورُ): أَصْلُهُ لَذَّةٌ فِي الْقَلْبِ عِنْدَ حُصُولِ نَفْعٍ، أَوْ تَوَقُّعِهِ، مِنَ (السِّرِّ).

This is how the saying of Allah Most High, *herds of* ṣufr *camels* (al-Mursalāt 77:33) was explained.[1398] Al-Aʿshā said: ["The Nimble"]

There are my horses—his gifts—and there my camel-mounts:
they are jet black (ṣufrun) and their colts like raisins.[1399]

It may be that He expressed blackness in terms of yellowness because the latter is among the hues that turn into the former,[1400] or because the black of camels is topped by yellow. Yet this [gloss] needs reconsideration because yellowness in this sense is never reinforced with *fuqūʿ*.

[*Surūr* among the types of mirth]

tasurru-n-nāẓirīna ⟨*that gladdens the beholders*⟩, that is, it excites their admiration. ***Surūr*** ⟨gladness⟩ is originally a pleasure in the heart at the occurrence of a benefit or in expectation of one, and stems from *sirr* ⟨secret⟩.[1401]

Ibn Abī Ḥātim, *Tafsīr* (1:140 §715).

1398 By al-Ḥasan and Qatāda according to al-Ṭabarī while al-Māwardī and Makkī al-Qaysī added Mujāhid and al-Wāḥidī added Ibn ʿAbbās, al-Kalbī and Muqātil.

1399 Spoken by al-Aʿshā in praise of Abū al-Ashʿath Qays b. Maʿdīkarb's generosity. Black camels topped with golden spots were extremely prized. Narrated by al-Ṭabarī, *Tafsīr* (2:94), cf. *Dīwān al-Aʿshā* (p. 335 §68 v.18).

1400 "As in most yellow plants and fruits." (Q)

1401 "The subtlety of restricting the pleasure as being 'in the heart' is evident as it pre-

﴿قَالُوا۟ ٱدْعُ لَنَا رَبَّكَ يُبَيِّن لَّنَا مَا هِىَ﴾: تَكْرِيرٌ لِلسُّؤَالِ الأَوَّلِ وَاسْتِكْشَافٌ زَائِدٌ. وَقَوْلُهُ:

﴿إِنَّ ٱلْبَقَرَ تَشَـٰبَهَ عَلَيْنَا﴾ اعْتِذَارٌ عَنْهُ؛ أَيْ: إِنَّ الْبَقَرَ الْمَوْصُوفَ بِالتَّعْوِينِ وَالصُّفْرَةِ كَثِيرٌ، فَاشْتَبَهَ عَلَيْنَا.

وَقُرِئَ (إِنَّ الْبَاقِرَ) - وَهُوَ اسْمٌ لِجَمَاعَةِ الْبَقَرِ - وَ(الأَبَاقِرَ)؛ وَ(الْبَوَاقِرَ)؛

[2:70] **qālū-dʿu lanā rabbaka yubayyin lanā mā hiya** ⁽*they said: Call upon your Nurturer for us to make clear to us what she is*⁾ is a reiteration of the first question and further investigation, while His saying

inna-l-baqara tashābaha ʿalaynā ⁽*verily cows all look the same to us*⁾ is an apology for that. That is, "verily the cows described as middle-aged and yellow are many, so it is confusing to us."

It was also read (i) *inna-l-bāqira* ⁽verily herds⁾[1402]—a name for a company of oxen; (ii) *al-abāqir*; (iii) and *al-bawāqir*;[1403]

empts other pleasures such as in the gustative, auditive, visual and other faculties.... The reason for not choosing the literal meaning [of *tasurru* as 'gladdens the heart'] here is that the literal meaning [of *surūr*] is pleasure—that is, a delighting (*iltidhādh*) —and a dilation that take place in the heart exclusively, without any outward trace. *Ḥubūr* ⁽joy⁾, on the other hand, is that of which the *ḥibr* or 'trace' is visible on the surface of the skin [in paradise as in al-Rūm 30:15 and al-Zukhruf 43:70]. Hence *surūr* and *ḥubūr* are both praiseworthy. As for *faraḥ* ⁽jollity⁾, it is out of *baṭar* ⁽exultation⁾ and *kibr* ⁽arrogance⁾, hence it is very often blamed [e.g. al-Qaṣaṣ 28:76, Hūd 11:10, al-Raʿd 13:26 etc.]... and all three terms might also be used interchangeably." (Q 3:396)

1402 By ʿIkrima, Yaḥyā b. Yaʿmur, Ibn Abī Laylā, Ibn Abī ʿAbla and Muḥammad Dhūl-Shāma. (*MQ*)

1403 The latter two readings were left unsourced in the commentaries. As for morphology it was said *bāqir* is a plural of three or more *baqara*s while *abāqir* and *bawāqir* are the plurals of *abqūr* and *bayqūr* respectively. (Q) "*Bāqir* is the noun of a company... its plural is *bāqūr*. *Bawāqir* seems to be the plural of *bāqira* and *abāqir*; the plurals differ according to the difference in the original term." (Kh)

وَ(تَتَشَابَهُ) بِالتَّاءِ وَالْيَاءِ؛ وَ(تَشَابَهُ) بِطَرْحِ التَّاءِ؛ وَإِدْغَامِهَــــا عَلَى التَّذْكِيرِ، وَالتَّأْنِيثِ؛ وَ(تَشَابَهَتْ) مُخَفَّفاً، وَمُشَدَّداً؛ وَ(تَشَّبَّهُ) بِمَعْنَى تَتَشَبَّهُ؛ وَ(تَشَبَّـهَ) بِالتَّذْكِيرِ؛ وَ(مُتَشَابِهٌ)؛ وَ(مُتَشَابِهَةٌ)؛ ....

and (i) *tatashābahu* with a *tā*ʾ;[1404]

(ii) [*yatashābahu*] with a *yā*ʾ;[1405]

(iii) *tashābahu* with the *tā*ʾ discarded[1406]

(iv) and [*yashshābahu*] with its contraction in the masculine[1407]

(v) and in the feminine [*viz. tashshābahu*];[1408]

(vi) *tashābahat*, both alleviated[1409]

(vii) and doubed [*tashshābahat*,[1410] *ttashābahat*[1411]];

(viii) *tashshabbahu* in the sense of *tatashabbahu*[1412]

(ix) and *tashabbaha*[1413] in the masculine;[1414]

(x) *mutashābihun*[1415]

(xi) and *mutashābihatun*;[1416]

1404 "Read by some." *(MQ)* Cited by Mujāhid, cf. Abū Naṣr al-Kirmānī, *Shawādhdh* (p. 65).

1405 By Zayd b. ʿAlī according to Abū Naṣr al-Kirmānī, *Shawādhdh* (p. 65).

1406 By al-Ḥasan and Yaḥyā b. Yaʿmur. (*MQ*)

1407 By Ibn Masʿūd, Muḥammad Dhūl-Shāma, Yaḥyā b. Yaʿmur, al-Muṭṭawwaʿī. (*MQ*)

1408 By al-Aʿraj, al-Ḥasan, Yaḥyā b. Yaʿmur, Ibn Masʿūd, ʿAbbās from Abū ʿAmr. (*MQ*)

1409 By Ubay b. Kaʿb. (*MQ*)

1410 By Ibn Abī Isḥāq and Ubay b. Kaʿb. (*MQ*)

1411 Narrated by Ibn Hishām from Ibn Mahrān's book *al-Shawādhdh*; this is produced by the supposed contraction of the two *tā*ʾ from either *al-baqara tatashābahat* or *al-baqarata tashābahat.* (*MQ*)

1412 By Mujāhid, cf. al-ʿUkbarī, *Iʿrāb al-Qirāʾāt al-Shawādhdh* (1:174).

1413 B: يُشْبِهُ but there is no such reading. Furthermore context confirms it is a masc. version of the same *rasm* as *tashshabbahu.*

1414 By Mujāhid. (*MQ*)

1415 "By Ibn Masʿūd" according to Abū Naṣr al-Kirmānī, *Shawādhdh* (p. 65).

1416 Both by al-Aʿmash, al-Ḥasan and Ibn Masʿūd. (*MQ*)

وَ (مُشْتَبِهٌ)؛ وَ (مُتَشَبِّهٌ).

﴿وَإِنَّآ إِن شَآءَ ٱللَّهُ لَمُهْتَدُونَ﴾ إِلَى الْمُرَادِ ذَبْحُهَا، أَوْ إِلَى الْقَاتِلِ.

وَفِي الْحَدِيثِ: لَوْ لَمْ يَسْتَثْنُوا، لَمَا بُيِّنَتْ لَهُمْ آخِرَ الْأَبَدِ.

وَاحْتَجَّ بِهِ أَصْحَابُنَا عَلَى أَنَّ الْحَوَادِثَ بِإِرَادَةِ اللهِ ـ سُبْحَانَهُ وَتَعَالَى ـ ....

(xii) *mushtabihun*;[1417]

(xiii) and *mutashabbihun*.[1418]

[All is by His will but His order may differ from His will]

wa-innā in shāʾa-l-Lāhu la-muhtadūna ⁽*then we will be, if the One God wills, assuredly well-guided*⁾ to the one meant to be slaughtered; or to the killer.

It is stated in a hadith,

> Had they not stated the exceptive condition, she would have never been made clear to them for all eternity.[1419]

Our colleagues adduced it as a decisive proof that all events are by the will of Allah[1420]—may He be exalted and glorified!—

[1417] B, α: مُشْتَبِهٌ I: مُشَبَّهَةٌ R: مُشْتَبِهَةٌ I could not find any of those readings.

[1418] Cited by al-Dānī. (*MQ*) "By Ibn Masʿūd" according to Abū Naṣr al-Kirmānī, *Shawādhdh* (p. 65). I, R: مُتَشَبِّهَةٌ

[1419] Narrated by Ibn Abī Ḥātim, *Tafsīr* (1:141 §722) from Abū Hurayra; Ṭabarī (2:99-100, 2:77-78) in *mursal* mode from Abū al-ʿĀliya, Qatāda and *muʿḍal* from Ibn Jurayj; and Saʿīd b. Manṣūr in his *Sunan* (2:565 §193) from ʿIkrima.

[1420] "As opposed to the Muʿtazila, who claimed that some of the contingencies befall by the servant's will despite the fact that His own will pertains to the opposite. The way this verse serves as proof is that the declaration of guidance as conditional on His will—even if it was uttered by Mūsā's nation, since the hadith cited resolves it—shows that being guided can only happen for them through Allah's will; yet being guided is among the contingencies (*ḥawādith*); if it is entirely dependent on His will, then so are all contingencies also dependent on His will, as there is no reason to make any hierarchy. This establishes that all contingencies happen by His will and that Mūsā's nation, despite their coarse understanding and mindlessness, were more knowledgeable

وَأَنَّ الْأَمْرَ قَدْ يَنْفَكُّ عَنِ الْإِرَادَةِ، وَإِلَّا لَمْ يَكُنْ لِلشَّرْطِ بَعْدَ الْأَمْرِ مَعْنًى.

وَالْمُعْتَزِلَةُ وَالْكَرَّامِيَّةُ عَلَى حُدُوثِ الْإِرَادَةِ؛ وَأُجِيبَ بِأَنَّ التَّعْلِيقَ بِاعْتِبَارِ التَّعَلُّقِ.

and that the divine command might be one thing while the divine will is another; otherwise the proviso [of the latter], once the command has been issued, would no longer make sense.[1421]

The Muʿtazila and Karrāmiyya, however, held that the divine will is temporally originated; this was rebutted with the doctrine that the hinging of temporal origination is [understood] with respect to appurtenance.[1422]

of Allah and more complete in their monotheism than the Muʿtazila because of that, while the Muʿtazila say: 'Allah surely wills that all legally-responsible servants believe, obey and be guided to what truth is in deeds and character except that most will otherwise, so their will supplants His wherever matters are as they willed and not as Allah wills.' We seek refuge in Allah from error in creed and action! So the verse is a final proof for us regarding divine will." (Z 1:325)

1421 "The upshot is that whatever Allah does not will will not be, and the reverse of its opposite is that whatever is and took place is nothing but His will, as they verified it regarding the saying of the Prophet—upon him blessings and peace—'Whatever Allah willed was and whatever He did not will was not' [Abū Dāwūd, *Sunan, Adab, mā yaqūl idhā aṣbaḥ*]. So it can be known from this exposition that just as that wording shows that all created events are by the will of Allah, it also shows that everything that Allah wills inevitably takes place. The Muʿtazila wrangle with us over these two issues and the verse constitutes a final proof against them." (Q 3:400)

1422 I.e when the pre-eternal divine will pertains to created events, such as, e.g., the revelation of the Qur'ān in time, the attribute of divine will does not become created but rather what is created is the appurtenance (*taʿalluq*) of the will to the event. A locus classicus of this doctrine was given by Imam Ahmad b. Ḥanbal in his exchange with the Muʿtazili prosecutor regarding the use of the epithet *muḥdath* ʿcontingent, createdʾ in relation to the revelation of Qur'ān: "Questioner: '*Never comes there unto them a novel reminder (dhikrun muḥdathun) from their Lord* (al-Anbiyā 21:2). Can something novel be anything but created?' Aḥmad: 'It is possible that it is the Qur'ān's revelation to us *(tanzīluhu ilaynā)* that is new; not the *dhikr* itself. Allah said: *Ṣād. By the Qur'ān that contains the Reminder* (Ṣād 38:1). *The* reminder is the Qur'ān; the

﴿قَالَ إِنَّهُۥ يَقُولُ إِنَّهَا بَقَرَةٌ لَّا ذَلُولٌ تُثِيرُ ٱلْأَرْضَ وَلَا تَسْقِى ٱلْحَرْثَ﴾ أَيْ لَمْ تُذَلَّلْ لِلْكِرَابِ وَسَقْيِ الْحَرْثِ. وَ﴿لَا ذَلُولٌ﴾ صِفَةٌ لِـ﴿بَقَرَةٌ﴾ بِمَعْنَى غَيْرُ ذَلُولٍ؛ وَ﴿لَا﴾ الثَّانِيَةُ مَزِيدَةٌ لِتَأْكِيدِ الْأُولَى؛ وَالْفِعْلَانِ صِفَتَا ﴿ذَلُولٌ﴾، كَأَنَّهُ قِيلَ: لَا ذَلُولٌ مُثِيرَةٌ وَسَاقِيَةٌ. وَقُرِئَ (لَا ذَلُولَ) بِالْفَتْحِ - أَيْ حَيْثُ هِيَ، كَقَوْلِكَ: مَرَرْتُ بِرَجُلٍ لَا بَخِيلَ وَلَا جَبَانَ، أَيْ حَيْثُ هُوَ - وَ(تُسْقِي)، مِنْ (أَسْقَى).

﴿مُسَلَّمَةٌ﴾: سَلَّمَهَا اللهُ تَعَالَى مِنَ الْعُيُوبِ؛ أَوْ أَهْلُهَا مِنَ الْعَمَلِ؛ أَوْ أُخْلِصَ لَوْنُهَا، ....

[2:71] **qāla innahu yaqūlu innahā baqaratun lā dhalūlun tuthīru-l-arḍa wa-lā tasqī-l-ḥartha** ⁽*he said: Verily He says it is a cow unbroken to plowing the earth or watering tillage*⁾: that is, it was never subjected to tilling[1423] and watering the fields.

Lā dhalūlun ⁽not a broken one⁾ is an epithet for ***baqaratun*** ⁽a cow⁾ in the sense of *ghayru dhalūlin* ⁽other than broken⁾. The second ***lā*** ⁽nor⁾ is additive to emphasize the first. The two verbs are epithets of ***dhalūlun*** as if it were said *lā dhalūlun muthīratun wa-sāqiyatun* ⁽not a broken one plowing and irrigating⁾.

It was also read *lā dhalūla* ⁽no broken one⁾ with a *fatḥa*[1424]—in the sense of "in itself," as when you say *marartu bi-rajulin lā bakhīla wa-lā jabāna* ⁽I passed by a man—no miser nor coward⁾, that is, in himself—and *tusqī*,[1425] from *asqā* ⁽irrigate⁾.

musallamatun ⁽*flawless*⁾: Allah Most High kept it free of defects; or her owners [kept it free] of work; or it was given a solid color,

other verse does not say *the*'" In Ibn Kathīr, *al-Bidāya wal-Nihāya* (14:385, 400) and Ibn al-Subkī, *Ṭabaqāt al-Shāfi'iyya al-Kubrā* (2:46-47), cf. Ṣaliḥ b. Aḥmad, *Sīrat al-Imām Aḥmad*, ed. Muḥammad Zughlī (Beirut: al-Maktab al-Islāmī, 1997) pp. 32-47.

1423 All mss. and Kh, S, Sk, T, Z: للكراب F, K and modern eds.: لكراب الأرض gloss.

1424 By Abū 'Abd al-Raḥmān al-Sulamī. (*MQ*)

1425 A common Arab dialect, cf. Abū Naṣr al-Kirmānī, *Shawādhdh al-Qirā'āt* (p. 65).

مِنْ (سَلِمَ لَهُ كَذَا) إِذَا خَلَصَ لَهُ.

﴿لَّا شِيَةَ فِيهَا﴾: لَا لَوْنَ فِيهَا يُخَالِفُ لَوْنَ جِلْدِهَا؛ وَهِيَ فِي الْأَصْلِ مَصْدَرُ (وَشَاهُ) ـ (وَشْياً) وَ(شِيَةً) ـ إِذَا خَلَطَ بِلَوْنِهِ لَوْناً آخَرَ.

﴿قَالُوا۟ ٱلْـَٔـٰنَ جِئْتَ بِٱلْحَقِّ﴾، أَيْ بِحَقِيقَةِ وَصْفِ الْبَقَرَةِ، وَحَقَّقْتَهَا لَنَا. وَقُرِئَ (آلْآنَ؟) بِالْمَدِّ، عَلَى الِاسْتِفْهَامِ، وَ﴿الَانَ﴾ بِحَذْفِ الْهَمْزَةِ وَإِلْقَاءِ حَرَكَتِهَا عَلَى اللَّامِ.

﴿فَذَبَحُوهَا﴾: فِيهِ اخْتِصَارٌ؛ وَالتَّقْدِيرُ: فَحَصَلُوا الْبَقَرَةَ الْمَنْعُوتَةَ فَذَبَحُوهَا.

from *salima lahu kadhā* ⟨it is his, participant-free⟩ when it becomes uniformly his.

lā shiyata fīhā ⟨*without one spot on her*⟩: "without any color on her different from the color of her hide." [***Shiyatun***] is originally the infinitive noun of *washāhu* ⟨he taints it⟩—[inf. nouns] *washy* and *shiya*—when one mixes into its [original] color another.

qālū-l-āna jiʾta bi-l-ḥaqqi ⟨*they said: Now you have given the precise terms!*⟩,[1426] that is, the literal description of the cow, and "you have made it real for us" It was also read (i) *ā-l-āna* ⟨what? now?⟩ with prolongation[1427] in the interrogative sense; (ii) and *a-lāna* with the *hamza* suppressed, its vowel dropped onto the *lām*.[1428]

fa-dhabaḥūhā ⟨*finally they slaughtered it*⟩: there is ellipsis here. The subaudition is, "then they obtained the cow that had been described, and finally they slaughtered it."

[1426] "And not 'the truth,' which would constitute unbelief on their part." (Q, Z, Kh) In this respect most of the 50+ English translations are off the mark except for the five or six that have "right description," "accurate description" or something similar.

[1427] By Ibn al-Sammāl, cf. Abū Naṣr al-Kirmānī, *Shawādhdh al-Qirāʾāt* (p. 65).

[1428] By Nāfiʿ (*qālu-lāna*); Warsh, Ibn Wardān and Abū Jaʿfar (*qālū alāna*). (*MQ*)

﴿وَمَا كَادُواْ يَفْعَلُونَ﴾، (١) لِتَطْوِيلِهِمْ وَكَثْرَةِ مُرَاجَعَاتِهِمْ، (٢) أَوْ لِخَوْفِ الْفَضِيحَةِ فِي ظُهُورِ الْقَاتِلِ، (٣) أَوْ لِغَلَاءِ ثَمَنِهَا؛ إِذْ رُوِيَ أَنَّ شَيْخاً صَالِحاً مِنْهُمْ كَانَ لَهُ عِجْلَةٌ، فَأَتَى بِهَا الْغَيْضَةَ وَقَالَ: اللَّهُمَّ إِنِّي اسْتَوْدَعْتُكَهَا لِابْنِي حَتَّى يَكْبُرَ؛ فَشَبَّتْ، وَكَانَتْ وَحِيدَةً بِتِلْكَ الصِّفَاتِ فَسَاوَمُوهَا الْيَتِيمَ وَأُمَّهُ حَتَّى اشْتَرَوْهَا بِمِلْءِ مَسْكِهَا ذَهَباً؛ وَكَانَتِ الْبَقَرَةُ إِذْ ذَاكَ بِثَلَاثَةِ دَنَانِيرَ.

وَ(كَادَ) مِنْ أَفْعَالِ الْمُقَارَبَةِ، وُضِعَ لِدُنُوِّ الْخَبَرِ حُصُولاً؛ فَإِذَا دَخَلَ عَلَيْهِ النَّفْيُ، قِيلَ: مَعْنَاهُ الْإِثْبَاتُ مُطْلَقاً؛ ....

wa-mā kādū yafʿalūna ⁽*after they almost did not*⁾

1. because of their procrastination and endless arguing;
2. or for fear of exposure in case the killer were discovered;
3. or due to its exorbitant price. It is narrated that

> a pious elder[1429] among them owned a heifer. He brought it to a grassy woodland and said: "O Allah, I entrust it to You on my son's behalf until he should come of age." She grew and was the only one with those characteristics. They bargained for her with the orphan[1430] and his mother until they bought her for the fill of her skin in gold, at a time when the price of cows was but three dinars.[1431]

Kāda ⁽he almost⁾ is of the verbs of propinquity coined for the near-befalling of an event;[1432] but when negation is affixed to it, some said, it acquires the meaning of absolute affirmation; oth-

[1429] All mss. and eds. incl. J: شيخا صالحا α, B: شخصا صالحا homomorphism.
[1430] All mss. and eds. incl. J: فساوموها اليتيم K and modern eds.: فساوموها من اليتيم
[1431] Narrated by al-Ṭabarī in his *Tafsīr* (2:114-116) in brief and by al-Baghawī in his.
[1432] "Its full study came up under *yakādu-l-barqu yakhṭafu abṣārahum* ⁽*lightning almost snatches away their sights*⁾ (al-Baqara 2:20) and the only reason he had to clarify it here is to introduce his statement 'but when negation is affixed to it...' as the latter needed clarification." (Q)

وَقِيلَ: مَاضِيـاً. وَالصَّحِيحُ: أَنَّهُ كَسَائِرِ الْأَفْعَالِ؛ وَلَا يُنَافِي قَوْلُـهُ: ﴿وَمَا كَادُواْ يَفْعَلُونَ﴾ قَوْلَـهُ: ﴿فَذَبَحُوهَا﴾ لِاخْتِلَافِ وَقْتَيْهِمَا؛ إِذِ الْمَعْنَى: أَنَّهُمْ مَا قَارَبُوا أَنْ يَفْعَلُوا حَتَّى انْتَهَتْ سُؤَالَاتُهُـمْ، وَانْقَطَعَتْ تَعَلُّلَاتُهُـمْ، فَفَعَلُوا كَالْمُضْطَرِّ الْمُلْجَأِ إِلَى الْفِعْلِ.

﴿وَإِذْ قَتَلْتُمْ نَفْسًا﴾: خِطَابُ الْجَمْعِ، لِوُجُودِ الْقَتْلِ فِيهِمْ.

﴿فَادَّارَءْتُمْ فِيهَا﴾: اِخْتَصَمْتُمْ فِي شَأْنِهَا، إِذِ الْمُتَخَاصِمَانِ يَدْفَعُ بَعْضُهُمَا بَعْضاً؛ أَوْ: تَدَافَعْتُمْ بِأَنْ طَرَحَ قَتْلَهَـا كُلٌّ عَنْ نَفْسِـهِ إِلَى صَاحِبِـهِ. وَأَصْلُـهُ: (تَدَارَأْتُمْ)، فَأُدْغِمَتِ التَّاءُ فِي الدَّالِ وَاجْتُلِبَتْ لَهَا هَمْزَةُ الْوَصْلِ.

﴿وَاللَّهُ مُخْرِجٌ مَّا كُنتُمْ تَكْتُمُونَ﴾: مُظْهِرُهُ ....

ers said past affirmation. The sound view is that it is like all other verbs. Nor does the saying of Allah **wa-mā kādū yafʿalūna** ⁽*after they almost did not*⁾ contradict His saying **fa-dhabaḥūhā** ⁽*finally they slaughtered it*⁾ since their respective timings differ, as the meaning is: they hardly acted upon it until their nagging questions first came to an end and they ran out of subterfuges; and so they did it as one coerced who has no other recourse left.

[2:72] **wa-idh qataltum nafsan** ⁽*and when you killed a soul*⁾ as a collective address, since the killing took place among them.

fa-d-dāraʾtum fīhā ⁽*then jostled one another over it*⁾: "you wrangled concerning it"—as the two contenders shove one another; or "you shoved one another" in that each disclaimed responsibility for its murder and imputed it to the other. It is originally *tadāraʾtum*, then the *tāʾ* was contracted into the *dāl* and a *hamza* of conjunctive compression was procured.

wa-l-Lāhu mukhrijun mā kuntum taktumūna ⁽*but the One God was to be the discloser of what you were concealing*⁾: its exposer...

لَا مَحَالَةَ. وَأُعْمِلَ ﴿مُخْرِجٌ﴾ لِأَنَّهُ حِكَايَةُ مُسْتَقْبَلٍ، كَمَا أُعْمِلَ ﴿بَاسِطٌ ذِرَاعَيْهِ﴾ [الكهف ١٨]، لِأَنَّهُ حِكَايَةُ حَالٍ مَاضِيَةٍ.

﴿فَقُلْنَا اضْرِبُوهُ﴾: عَطْفٌ عَلَى ﴿ادَّارَأْتُمْ﴾ وَمَا بَيْنَهُمَا اعْتِرَاضٌ؛ وَالضَّمِيرُ لِلنَّفْسِ؛ وَالتَّذْكِيرُ عَلَى تَأْوِيلِ الشَّخْصِ أَوِ الْقَتِيلِ.

﴿بِبَعْضِهَا﴾، أَيَّ بَعْضٍ كَانَ؛ وَقِيلَ: بِأَصْغَرَيْهَا؛ وَقِيلَ: بِلِسَانِهَا؛ وَقِيلَ: بِفَخِذِهَا الْيُمْنَى؛ وَقِيلَ: بِالْأُذُنِ؛ وَقِيلَ: بِالْعَجْبِ.

without fail. ***Mukhrijun*** ⟨discloser⟩ was given regental force because it is citing a [contextually] future event, just as *bāsiṭun dhirāʿayhi* ⟨stretching its two paws⟩ (al-Kahf 18:18) was given regental force because it is citing a [contextually] past event.

[2:73] **fa-qulnā-ḍribūhu** ⟨*so We said: Strike it*⟩ is adjoined to ***d-dāra'tum*** ⟨jostled one another⟩ and the intervening clause is parenthetical. The personal pronoun refers to the soul. Its masculine gender reflects the interpretation of the latter as *al-shakhṣ* ⟨the individual⟩ or *al-qatīl* ⟨the murdered man⟩.

bi-baʿḍihā ⟨*with part of her*⟩, any part.[1433]

(i) It was also said: with its two smallest organs.[1434]

(ii) It was also said: with its tongue.

(iii) It was also said: with its right thigh.

(iv) It was also said: with the ear.

(v) It was also said: with the coccyx.[1435]

1433 "He understood the construct [*baʿḍihā*] to refer to species as there is no contextual indicator of *ʿahdiyya* ⟨previous knowledge⟩. It also reveals divine power in more perfect fashion. It also draws attention to the fact that there is no cause for specifying a particular organ." (Q)

1434 "I.e. the heart and the tongue because they are the two noblest organs." (Q)

1435 "It is the first bone created [in the fetus] and the last to disintegrate." (S) "It was also said the most compelling position is to say nothing." (Z)

﴿كَذَٰلِكَ يُحۡيِ ٱللَّهُ ٱلۡمَوۡتَىٰ﴾: يَدُلُّ عَلَى مَا حُذِفَ، وَهُوَ (فَضَرَبُوهُ فَحَيِيَ). وَالْخِطَابُ مَعَ مَنْ حَضَرَ حَيَاةَ الْقَتِيلِ، أَوْ نُزُولَ الْآيَةِ.

﴿وَيُرِيكُمۡ ءَايَٰتِهِۦ﴾: دَلَائِلَهُ عَلَى كَمَالِ قُدْرَتِهِ.

﴿لَعَلَّكُمۡ تَعۡقِلُونَ﴾: (أ) لِكَيْ يَكْمُلَ عَقْلُكُمْ وَتَعْلَمُوا أَنَّ مَنْ قَدَرَ عَلَى إِحْيَاءِ نَفْسٍ قَدَرَ عَلَى إِحْيَاءِ الْأَنْفُسِ كُلِّهَا؛ (ب) أَوْ تَعْلَمُونَ عَلَى قَضِيَّتِهِ.

وَلَعَلَّهُ تَعَالَى إِنَّمَا لَمْ يُحْيِهِ ابْتِدَاءً، وَشَرَطَ فِيهِ مَا شَرَطَ، لِمَا فِيهِ ....

ka-dhālika yuḥyī-l-Lāhu-l-mawtā ⁽*thus does the One God revive the dead*⁾ points to what was suppressed, namely, "so they struck him and he came back to life." The discourse addresses those who were present at the time the murdered man came alive, or at the time the verse was revealed.

wa-yurīkum āyātihi ⁽*and show you His signs*⁾: His indicators of the perfection of His power.

laʿallakum taʿqilūna ⁽*perhaps you will understand*⁾:

(i) "so that your intelligence will become complete[1436] and so that you will know that He Who has power to bring a soul back to life has power to bring all souls back to life;"

(ii) or "you will know[1437] according to its dictates."[1438]

[Divine teachings in the story of the yellow cow]

It may be that Allah Most High did not revive him from the first moment and made all those stipulations because they entail

[1436] "He gave a figurative interpretation because it is ascertained that they do understand and it is not still in the form of something that is merely hoped. However, because of their failure to act according to the dictates of intelligence, they were made to appear to lack it." (Kh)

[1437] α, B, ε, L, R: تعلمون Ak, β, Kh, Q, Sk, T, U, Ul, Z: تعملون AQ, D, F, H, I, K, MM, P: تعملوا All three readings are possible but the first is the strongest and most logical.

[1438] "I.e. the dictates of their *ʿaql* ⁽intelligence⁾." (A)

مِنَ (أ) التَّقَرُّبِ، (ب) وَأَدَاءِ الْوَاجِبِ، (ج) وَنَفْعِ الْيَتِيمِ، (د) وَالتَّنْبِيهِ عَلَى بَرَكَةِ التَّوَكُّلِ، (ه) وَالشَّفَقَةِ عَلَى الْأَوْلَادِ، (و) وَأَنَّ مِنْ حَقِّ الطَّالِبِ أَنْ يُقَدِّمَ قُرْبَةً، (ز) وَالْمُتَقَرِّبِ أَنْ يَتَحَرَّى الْأَحْسَنَ وَيُغَالِيَ بِثَمَنِهِ - كَمَا رُوِيَ عَنْ عُمَرَ رَضِيَ اللهُ تَعَالَى عَنْهُ: أَنَّهُ ضَحَّى بِنَجِيبَةٍ اِشْتَرَاهَا بِثَلَاثِمِائَةِ دِينَارٍ - (ح) وَأَنَّ الْمُؤَثِّرَ فِي الْحَقِيقَةِ هُوَ اللهُ تَعَالَى، وَالْأَسْبَابُ أَمَارَاتٌ لَا أَثَرَ لَهَا،

(i) means of drawing near to Allah,

(ii) fulfillment of obligations,

(iii) and benevolence to orphans;

while drawing attention to

(iv) the blessing of God-reliance,

(v) compassion to children,

(vi) the fact that it behooves the petitioner to offer a sacrifice

(vii) and the sacrificer to do his utmost to find the very best [animal] and spend a considerable amount for it, as narrated from ʿUmar—may Allah be well-pleased with him—that he sacrificed a prize she-camel he had bought for three hundred dinars;[1439]

(viii) the fact that the effecter in reality is Allah Most High, while causes are but tokens without effect;[1440]

[1439] ʿUmar said: "Messenger of Allah, I was given a *bukhtiyya* ⁽she-Bactrian⁾ as a gift and got an offer of three hundred dinars for it. Shall I sell it and buy *budnan* ⁽sacrificial camels⁾ [i.e. older] for its price?" He replied: "No, sacrifice it itself." Narrated by Abū Dāwūd, *Sunan* (*Manāsik, Bāb tabdīl al-hady*); Aḥmad, *Musnad* (10"403-404 §6325); Ibn Khuzayma, *Ṣaḥīḥ*, ed. Muḥammad Muṣṭafā al-Aʿẓamī, 4 vols. (Beirut: al-Maktab al-Islāmī, 1400/1980) 4:292 §2911; and others.

[1440] "As the dead man was revived by striking it with dead remnants, which cannot be imagined to have any effect in any way whatsoever, for the generating of life through the touching of the dead by the dead is neither intelligible nor imaginable." (Z 1:329)

(ط) وَأَنَّ مَنْ أَرَادَ أَنْ يَعْرِفَ أَعْدَى عَدُوِّهِ ـ السَّاعِي في إِمَاتَتِهِ المَوْتَ الْحَقِيقِيَّ ـ فَطَرِيقُهُ أَنْ يَذْبَحَ بَقَرَةَ نَفْسِهِ الَّتِي هِيَ الْقُوَّةُ الشَّهْوِيَّةُ حِينَ زَالَ عَنْهَا شَرَهُ الصِّبَى، وَلَمْ يَلْحَقْهَا ضَعْفُ الْكِبَرِ، وَكَانَتْ مُعْجِبَةً، رَائِقَةَ الْمَنْظَرِ، غَيْرَ مُذَلَّلَةٍ فِي طَلَبِ الدُّنْيَا، مُسَلَّمَةً عَنْ دَنَسِهَا، لَا سِمَةَ بِهَا مِنْ مَقَابِحِهَا، بِحَيْثُ يَصِلُ أَثَرُهُ إِلَى نَفْسِهِ: فَتَحْيَى حَيَاةً طَيِّبَةً، وَيُعْرِبُ عَمَّا بِهِ يَنْكَشِفُ الْحَالُ، وَيَرْتَفِعُ مَا بَيْنَ الْعَقْلِ وَالْوَهْمِ مِنَ التَّدَارُءِ وَالنِّزَاعِ.

[Slaying one's ego to know one's enemy and revive one's soul]
(ix) and the fact that whoever wants to know his worst enemy —which strives in every way to inflict true death upon him— the way for him is to slaughter the cow in his own self, namely the appetitive faculty at the time the rapacity of adolescence is gone but the weakness of old age has not yet taken over, when it still excites [his] admiration and looks ravishing [to him], has not yet been brought low in the pursuit of this world and is still free of its stain, without any speck of its disgrace on it.[1441] Then the effect of that [slaying] will reach his soul: it will come alive with a good life and he will openly express that whereby the reality of things will show; and all trace of jostling and contention will be removed between understanding and envisioning.[1442]

[1441] "The stain of contravening the law and reason and running after pleasures, and the disgraces of corrupt belief, false doctrines and bad character. A knower said that *without one spot on her* draws attention to the fact that the most commendable of all states for the servant is to be ʿalā lawnin wāḥid (monochrome) in his interaction with Allah Most High—without the concerns of this world interfering with him and without the pursuit of lusts befalling him. Allah Most High put the resuscitation of the victim in the slaughtering of the cow to notify His servants that reviving one's heart cannot happen without the slaying of one's own self; so whoever slays it through different kinds of spiritual discipline, Allah will revive his heart with the lights of witnessing" (Z 1:330) "The assimilation of the appetitive faculty to the cow is because of its resemblance in eating much and indulging what is of no benefit but rather is harmful." (Q)
[1442] "It will come alive with a good life and gaze upon the reality of things through be-

﴿ثُمَّ قَسَتْ قُلُوبُكُم﴾: الْقَسَاوَةُ عِبَارَةٌ عَنِ الْغِلَظِ مَعَ الصَّلَابَةِ، كَمَا فِي الْحَجَرِ. وَقَسَاوَةُ الْقَلْبِ مَثَلٌ فِي نُبُوِّهِ عَنِ الْاِعْتِبَارِ؛ وَ﴿ثُمَّ﴾ لِاسْتِبْعَادِ الْقَسْوَةِ.

﴿مِّنْ بَعْدِ ذَٰلِكَ﴾: يَعْنِي إِحْيَاءَ الْقَتِيلِ، أَوْ جَمِيعَ مَا عَدَّدَ مِنَ الْآيَاتِ، فَإِنَّهَا مِمَّا يُوجِبُ لِينَ الْقَلْبِ.

﴿فَهِيَ كَالْحِجَارَةِ﴾ فِي قَسْوَتِهَا.

[2:74] **thumma qasat qulūbukum** ⁽*yet your hearts hardened*⁾: ***Qasāwa*** ⁽hardness⁾ stands for coarseness together with solidity, as in rocks. "Hardness of heart" is a proverb for its alienation from heedfulness. ***Thumma*** ⁽yet⁾ signifies the preposterousness of such hardness.

min baʿdi dhālika ⁽*even after that*⁾, meaning the reviving of the murdered man, or all the signs that had been enumerated—for such signs compel softness of heart.

[Hearts are harder than rocks as the latter feel and surrender]

fa-hiya ka-l-ḥijārati ⁽*indeed, they are like rocks*⁾ in hardness.[1443]

coming enlightened with the lights of *mushāhadāt* ⁽witnessings⁾ and *tajalliyāt* ⁽manifestations⁾ after it had been erring blindly in the valleys of misguidance, bound for spiritual destruction. At that time he can clearly distinguish what brings him eternal bliss from what brings him damnation and destruction. So he becomes mature, well-guided in himself as well as guiding and uplifting others, and he openly expresses to them that which was obscure to them of the reality of things. Thus his saying 'and openly express that whereby the reality of things will show' is inferred from the saying of Allah, *but Allah was to be the discloser of what you were concealing* (al-Baqara 2:72)." (Z 1:330) Al-Qūnawī added a tenth benefit: "As for the point of having a cow slaughtered as opposed to any other type of beast, it is that prior to that, they used to worship the Calf, then they repented and returned to the worship of Allah Most High, so He wanted to test them through the slaughter of what was made beloved to them, to make manifest the truth of repentence." (Q 3:416)

1443 All mss.: في قسوتها B: في القَسْوَةِ

﴿أَوْ أَشَدُّ قَسْوَةً﴾ مِنْهَا. وَالْمَعْنَى: (أ) أَنَّهَا فِي الْقَسَاوَةِ مِثْلُ الْحِجَارَةِ أَوْ أَزْيَدُ عَلَيْهَا؛ (ب) أَوْ أَنَّهَا مِثْلُهَا، أَوْ مِثْلُ مَا هُوَ أَشَدُّ مِنْهَا قَسْوَةً كَالْحَدِيدِ. فَحُذِفَ الْمُضَافُ وَأُقِيمَ الْمُضَافُ إِلَيْهِ مُقَامَهُ. وَيَعْضُدُهُ قِرَاءَةُ الْجَرِّ بِالْفَتْحِ عَطْفًا عَلَى ﴿الْحِجَارَةِ﴾. وَإِنَّمَا لَمْ يَقُلْ (أَقْسَى) لِمَا فِي ﴿أَشَدُّ﴾ مِنَ الْمُبَالَغَةِ، وَالدَّلَالَةِ عَلَى اشْتِدَادِ الْقَسْوَتَيْنِ وَاشْتِمَالِ الْمُفَضَّلِ عَلَى زِيَادَةٍ.

aw ashaddu qaswatan ⁽*or more intense yet in hardness*⁾ than them. The meaning is, (i) they are, in terms of hardness, like rocks or even superior to them; (ii) or they are like them, or like what is harder yet than them—such as metal—in which case the governing annex was suppressed and the governed annex was made to stand in its stead.[1444] The latter sense is reinforced by the reading of prepositional attraction with *fatḥa* [*aw ashadda*][1445] in adjunction to ***ḥijārati*** ⁽rocks⁾.

He did not say *aqsā* ⁽harder⁾ because of (i) the hyperbole *ashadd* ⁽more intense⁾ entails;[1446] (ii) its pointing to the intensity of both kinds of hardness; (iii) and the addition [in meanings] comprised in the superior comparate.[1447]

1444 "I.e *mithl* ⁽like⁾ was suppressed and *ashadd* ⁽harder⁾ was made to stand in its stead and given its declension, which is the nominative." (Q)

1445 Ak, B, D, ε, I, Iṣ, L, P, Sk, T: الجر بالفتح J, Kh, U, Ul, Z: الأعمش بالفتح β: الحسن بالفتح α: الحسن بالجر بالفتح AQ, F, H, K, MM, R: الحسن بالجر The reading *aw ashadda* is sourced to al-Aʿmash and Abū Ḥaywa. (*MQ*) None of the sources checked cite al-Ḥasan.

1446 "The intent of of his citing that it is indicative of hyperbole in the hardness of hearts is that the object of the comparative of superiority is the intensity of hardness, not hardness itself; so their common denominator is intensity of hardness and the meaning is to expose the fact that hearts are more intensely hard than them: the latter meaning, without doubt, is more powerful—when attributing hardness to hearts—than just saying they have more than rocks of hardness itself." (Z 1:331)

1447 "As *ashaddu qaswatan* ⁽more intense in hardness⁾ indicates addition in both materia and form" (Kh) "while *aqsā* ⁽harder⁾ indicates addition in form only." (Q)

وَ﴿أَوْ﴾ لِلتَّخْيِيرِ أَوْ لِلتَّرْدِيدِ، بِمَعْنَى أَنَّ مَنْ عَرَفَ حَالَهَا، شَبَّهَهَا بِالْحِجَارَةِ أَوْ بِمَا هُوَ أَقْسَى مِنْهَا.

﴿وَإِنَّ مِنَ ٱلْحِجَارَةِ لَمَا يَتَفَجَّرُ مِنْهُ ٱلْأَنْهَٰرُ ۚ وَإِنَّ مِنْهَا لَمَا يَشَّقَّقُ فَيَخْرُجُ مِنْهُ ٱلْمَآءُ ۚ وَإِنَّ مِنْهَا لَمَا يَهْبِطُ مِنْ خَشْيَةِ ٱللَّهِ ۗ﴾: تَعْلِيلٌ لِلتَّفْضِيلِ؛ وَالْمَعْنَى أَنَّ الْحِجَارَةَ تَتَأَثَّرُ وَتَنْفَعِلُ ـ فَإِنَّ مِنْهَا مَا يَتَشَقَّقُ فَيَنْبُعُ مِنْهُ الْمَاءُ وَتَنْفَجِرُ مِنْهُ الْأَنْهَارُ؛ وَمِنْهَا مَا يَتَرَدَّى مِنْ أَعْلَى الْجَبَلِ انْقِيَاداً لِمَا أَرَادَ اللهُ تَعَالَى بِهِ ـ وَقُلُوبُ هٰؤُلَاءِ لَا تَتَأَثَّرُ وَلَا تَنْفَعِلُ عَنْ أَمْرِهِ تَعَالَى.

وَ(التَّفَجُّرُ): التَّفَتُّحُ بِسَعَةٍ وَكَثْرَةٍ. ....

Aw ⟨or⟩ denotes (i) optionality, (ii) or reiteration in the sense that whoever is familiar with their state compares them to rocks or to whatever is harder than them.[1448]

wa-inna mina-l-ḥijārati la-mā yatafajjaru minhu-l-anhāru wa-inna minhā la-mā yashshaqqaqu fa-yakhruju minhu-l-māʾu wa-inna minhā la-mā yahbiṭu min khashyati-l-Lāhi ⟨*but truly there are certain rocks out of which rivers burst forth; and truly there are some that cleave asunder so that water issues from them; and truly there are some that crash down in fear of the One God!*⟩: this is a justification for preferentiation in the sense that rocks themselves feel and are affected—as there are some that cleave asunder so that water gushes out of them and rivers burst forth, and there are some that throw themselves from mountaintops in utter submission to what Allah wants of them—yet the hearts of those [creatures] feel nothing and remain unaffected by His commands.

Tafajjur ⟨bursting forth⟩ is a vast and abundant opening up

1448 "*Aw* here denotes 'either/or' or 'and' or 'but rather.'" Al-Ṭabarī, *Tafsīr* (2:132).

وَ(الْخَشْيَةُ) مَجَازٌ عَنِ الِانْقِيَادِ.

وَقُرِئَ (إِنْ) عَلَى أَنَّهَا الْمُخَفَّفَةُ مِنَ الثَّقِيلَةِ - وَتَلْزَمُهَا اللَّامُ الْفَارِقَةُ بَيْنَهَا وَبَيْنَ النَّافِيَةِ - وَ(يَهْبُطُ) بِالضَّمِّ.

﴿وَمَا ٱللَّهُ بِغَٰفِلٍ عَمَّا تَعۡمَلُونَ ﴿٧٤﴾﴾: وَعِيدٌ عَلَى ذَلِكَ. وَقَرَأَ ابْنُ كَثِيرٍ وَنَافِعٌ وَيَعْقُوبُ وَخَلَفٌ وَأَبُو بَكْرٍ بِالْيَاءِ ضَمًّا إِلَى مَا بَعْدَهُ، وَالْبَاقُونَ بِالتَّاءِ.

while ***khashya*** ⁽fear⁾ is a metonymy for docility.

It was also read *in* ⁽verily⁾ as the lightened form of the heavy *inna*[1449]—which is always accompanied by the "*lām* that distinguishes it from the negatory *in*"[1450]—and *yahbuṭu* ⁽crash down⁾ with a *ḍamma*.[1451]

wa-mā-l-Lāhu bi-ghāfilin ʿammā taʿmalūna ⁽*and the One God is not at all unaware of what you do!*⁾ is a threat over that.[1452]

Ibn Kathīr, Nāfiʿ, Yaʿqūb, Khalaf and Abū Bakr all read it with a *yā'*—putting it together with what follows—while the rest all read it with a *tā'*.[1453]

[END OF *ḤIZB* I]

[1449] By Qatāda. (*MQ*)

[1450] Cf. Daqr, *Muʿjam* (p. 97); Wright, *Grammar* (2:81 D).

[1451] By al-Aʿmash al-Muṭawwaʿī, a dialect. (*MQ*)

[1452] "I.e. intense hardness and indocility." (Q)

[1453] Only Ibn Kathīr read *yaʿmalūna* here. (*MQ*) Nāfiʿ, Yaʿqūb, Khalaf and Abū Bakr read *yaʿmalūna* with a *yā'* only in verses 2:85 and 2:144 but not here, so this passage is counted as a mistake. (S 2:273, Q 3:428, Z 1:332) "The *yā'* reading entails redirection from second to third-person as a putdown for them away from the pleasure of auditorship; as for [the *tā'* reading in] the form of direct address then the meaning would be rebuke—as the address of enemies consists in rebuke—and shifting from it is for distantiation from the arena of direct address. *Al-nukātu mutafāwitatun bi-ḥasabi al-maqāmāt* ⁽nuances vary according to rhetorical contexts⁾." (Q 3:429)

Arabic-English glossary of technical terms

of grammar, rhetoric, lexicography, phonetics, prosody, theology, philosophy and law, indexed in the form cited in the text

(Columns proceed from left to right)

permissibility إباحة

inchoative, inceptive إبتداء، مبتدأ

more expressive, intensive, powerful, significant أبلغ

augmentative forms أبنية المزيد

vagueness إبهام

anonymizer إبهاميّة

alliterative sequencing إتْباع

poetic license إتساع

judicious exertion اجتهاد

treating إجراءً مُجرى

received the same desinential place أُجْرِيَ عليه

it was deemed as such أُجرِيَ مُجْراه

mentioned in vague terms أُجمِل

factual reports أخبار

exclusivity إختصاص

made to stand for أُخرِج مَخْرَج

siblings (lingu.) أخوات

affixed أُدْخِلَ

insert أَدخَلَ

human cognition الإدراك الإنساني

contraction إدغام

fusing ازدواج

resumption استئناف

resumptive استإنافية

a posteriori استتباعاً

declare the exceptive condition استثنى

as an exceptive بالاستثناء

quest for answers استخبار

metaphor استعارة

metaphorically used استُعير

totality الاستغراق

inquiry استفسار

interrogative استفهام

virtue إستقامة

inductive survey استقراء

uniquely possesses استقلاله بـ

exploration استكشاف

inseparably means استلزم

inference استنباط

nomen speciei اسم الجنس

agential noun إسم الفاعل

إقرار affirmation

اِلتفات apostrophic redirection, redirected apostrophe

إلتقاء الساكنين meeting of two quiescent consonants

إلقاء casting

الأمر imperative

إمكان contingency

أمْن الالتباس unambiguity

إنشاءات originative sentences

انفعالات affects

أُنْمُوذَج archetype

الأنواع categories

أوجَه more apt

أوقعتَه موقِعَ treat it as

إيجاب بالذات ontic necessity

إيجاد origination

إيجاز concision

الأظهر predominant view

باعتبار الاشتقاق etymologically

باعتبار الغايات in consideration of outcomes

إعجاز incapacitation, inimitability

إعراب desinential syntax, parsing

إعلال vowel-weakness

أُعِلَّت impaired

أُعْمِلَ given regental force

أفاد communicates, conveys, imparts

إفتقار dependency

إفراد individualization

أفعال المقارَبة verbs of propinquity

أفعال acts

أقبل بالخطاب apostrophize

اقتضى dictates, see also *muqtaḍā*

إسم فاعل active participle

إسم، أسماء nouns

إسناد ascription, predication

أُسْنِد ascribed

إشتقاق derivation

الأشكال forms

إشمام *z*-sound

اصطلاح conventional usage

أصل etymon or root, literal meaning, origin or form, principle

أصله، في الأصل literally, originally

أضاف annexed

إضافة annexation

إضمار ellipsis, pronomination

بإضمار by implying

إطباق over-covering [of tongue and palate]

أُطلِقَ used as a syntactical absolute

الباري Absolute Originator, Producer of all

بدل substitute

بدل الكل substituting the whole

بسملة theonymic invocation

البسيط The Outspread

بصيرة discernment

البِناء morphology

بناء التكثير stem-form of multitude

بناء على السكون indeclinable mute case

بني للمبالغة intensive form

بُنِيَت properly used

بيان (هو التمييز) clarification, determination, elucidation, exposition

بيان تقدّم preposed explicative

تأكيد emphasis, emphasizer

تابع appositive

تَبِعَه depending

تبعيض division into parts

تبعيضية partitive

تبكيت scathing rebuke, silencing

تبيين explication

للتبيين specificative

تجاوُب mutual harmony

تَجَرُّد being unaugmented

تحريف textual corruption

تحقيق verification

تخصيص particularization

بالتخفيف with alleviation

ترتُّب الحكم على making the status subsequent, when a certain status follows in sequence

ترشيح المجاز extended metaphor

تركيب stem-formation

تَسَبُّب illation

تسجيل ruling

تسوية sameness

تصريح explicit declaration

تضمّن contains, entails, implies

تعذّر unfeasability

تعريض oblique hinting

تعريف definite article

تعريف الماهيا definition of quiddity

تعظيم magnification

تعقيب nextness

تَعَلُّق appurtenance

تعليل justification, rationale

للتعليل causally

تعيين determination

تفخيم amplify, glottal accentuation

تفسير explication

تقدير subaudition

جهة الإشكال problematic perspective

جواب apodosis

جوهر، جواهر substance(s)

حال complement of state, participial state

حالّ immanent

حدوث origination, see also *ḥawādith*

حُذِفَ elided

حَذْف elision, ellipsis

حرف، حروف particles

حرف الشك particle of doubt

حرف تفصيل elaborative particle

حرف مُقتَضَب improvised particle

حرف اللِّين soft phoneme

حروف البدل letters of permutation

حروف التنبيه admonitory interjections

التوحيد pure monotheism

توضيح elucidation, vividness

توكيد emphasis

ثبات stability

جارّ ومجرور preposition and its complement

جارٍ عليه apply

الجرّ prepositional attraction

الجزاء apodosis

جَزْم apocopate

جُزِمَ apocopated

جِزْيَة tribute

جزئيّات الأحكام peculiar rulings

جُسماني corporeal

الجمع المصحَّح sound plural form

الجملة المبتدأة introductive sentence

جملة مفيدة informative proposition

الجنس species, genus

تقرير determination, resolution

تقييد restriction, restrictive qualifier

تكليف legal responsibility

تكوين instant formation

تلاحُق close succession

تمثيل assimilation, representation

التمثيل المفرد single allegory

تمثيلاً as a simile

تمثيلات مؤلَّفة complex allegories

طريقة التمثيل allegorical style

جملة التمثيل parabolical clause

تمييز specification

تنبيهاً highlighting

للتنزيه preferential (*fiqh*)

تنصيص stipulation

تهكُّم sarcasm

روحاني spiritual
رُوع innermost
زائدة redundant, additive
زكاة obligatory almsgiving
الساكن، السكون quiescent
سُباعي septiliteral
سبب conditioning factor
سببية causality, illation
سدّ مسدّه fills in
سَنيّ refined
شاذّ aberrant
شُبْهَة misgiving, skepticism, suspicion
الشرط protasis
الشريعة sacred Law
شَمَل comprise, encompass
شِياع generalness
صحة soundness, validity

حكاية verbatim citation
حَمْلها على take it to refer
حوادث originated entities
حَيِّز annexure to
الخافض genitival operative
خالية عن الإعراب devoid of inflection
خبر enunciative, predicate
خِفّة nimbleness
داخلة في حكم tantamount to
دخول affixing
دل designate
دليل sign, proof, indication
بذاتها inherently
ذَلْق اللسان tongue-tip
رابِطة copulative
الرَجَز The Trembling
رذيلة، رذائل vices
رَمْز symbolism

الحروف الحَلْقيّة laryngeal phonemes
الحروف الذَّلْقِية tipped phonemes
الحروف الرِّخوة limp phonemes
الحروف الشديدة hard phonemes
حروف الشرط conditional particles
حروف القلقلة plosive phonemes
الحروف المجهورة outspoken phonemes
الحروف المستعلية self-elevated phonemes
الحروف المطبَقة over-covered phonemes
الحروف المنخفضة depressed phonemes
الحروف المنفتحة opened-up phonemes
الحروف المهموسة voiceless phonemes
حقيقة literal term, quiddity

صَرَّف inflect

صِلَة prepositional or relative clause

صوت، أصوات sound(s)

ضرورةً automatically

ضروري indispensable

ضمناً inclusively

الضمير المستكنّ covert pronoun

ضمير منفصل disconnected pronoun

الطويل The Long

ظاهر manifest locution

ظرف temporal-local preposition, vessel

الظرفية adverbiality

العاطف copulative conjunction

العالَم الكبير macrocosm

عامل، عوامل regents

عائد connector-pronoun

عِبَر paradigms

عُدول عن shunning of

عُدِّيَ transitivized

عُدِّي بنفسه direct-transitivized

عَرَض، أعراض accidents

عُرْف common parlance

عُرْف مجدَّد modern convention

عَطْف adjoining, adjunction

عِلم ضروري innate knowledge

على الاتساع in a wider sense

على الاستعارة metaphorically

على المصدر as an objective complement

على تأويل paraphrased as

على سبيل الكناية metonymically

على طريقة in the style of

على غير قياس irregularly

عمل regency

عموم universality

العَهْد previous knowledge

العَين individuated object

غاية outcome

غَرَض point, ulterior purpose

غلب عليه usage

غلب، تغليباً overwhelming or predominant usage

غير قارّة unfixed

غير مصروف indeclinable

الفاء الجزائيّة *fā'* of apodosis

الفاعل المختار Agent of free choice

فاعلية agency

فائدة function, import

فَرْعي subsidiary

فصاحة purity of style, chasteness; Sacy: élégance

فصلٌ distinctive pronoun, separative pronoun

فَعْلَةٌ single-instance deverbal form

الفقهاء jurists

في حَيِّز annexed to

في مَحَلّ construed as

في نفسه intrinsically

قابلة fit

قائم بذاته inherent in His essence

قدس الجبروت world of Holiness and Might

قرّر resolved

القرينة context

قَسَمِيّ juratory

بالقطع disjunctively

قَلْب Transposition

القوّة الحسّاسة sensitive virtue

القوّة الحيوانيّة vital impulse

القوّة النّامية vegetative virtue

قوّة فاعلة active force

قوّة قابلة receptive force

كسبي acquired

الكلم words

كمال integrity

كنايات denotatives

كون الشيء غير موجَب non-positiveness

كيفية modality

لا النافية للجنس ***lā*** that negates the whole genus

لا تقتضيه بَدِيْهَة العقل unintuited

لازم inescapable conclusion or concomitant

لوازم inseparable accompaniments

لَحْن solecism

لطيفة، لطائف subtleties

لغة dialectical form

لَفْظ vocable

لَقَب nickname, title

لم تَلِها العوامل ungoverned

ما تحتَه subaltern

ما حُذِف صدرُه initial elisions

ما وُضِعَ لَهُ semantic usage

ما يُتَلَقّى به القَسَم juratory term

مادَّة material

المبادئ inceptions

مبالَغة intensive(ness), hyperbole, going to every length

مُبْدَعات *ex nihilo* designs

مُبدَل منه alternant

مبنيّ الأصل indeclinable

مبنيّ على الفتح indeclinable *fatḥa* case ending

مُبهَم unidentified

مُبيِّن expository

متبوع antecedent

مضاف governing annex

مضاف إليه governed annex

مُضْمَر implied

مطروح discarded

مُطلَقاً in unqualified terms

المُظْهَر other than pronouns

المعاني meanings

مُعاهَد covenantee

مُعاهِد covenanter

مُعْجِز confounding

مَعرفة cognition

معطوف adjoined

المعطوف عليه adjunct, antecedent

معمول governed element

المعنى المنتزَع thrust

معهود one in particular

المفردات المعدودة word-lists

مُحَلًّى fitted

مُخبَرٌ عنه inchoative

مخفوض genitive

المدّ prolongation

مدلول signification

المرَّة specimen

مرفوع nominative

مُركَّب compound

مَزيدة additive

مستطال drawn out

المستعار له tenor

المستعار منه vehicle

مُسَمًّى referent

المُسَمَّيات referent-objects

مُسنَد إليه correlative of attribute

المصاحبة accompaniment

مَصالح considerations of public interest

مصدر infinitive noun

مضارع aorist

المتحدَّى به content of the challenge

المتحرِّك vowelized consonant

مترتِّبة عليه made to follow sequentially

متشابه ambiguous

متعلق بـ pertains to

المتقارب The Tripping

مُتَقَطِّعَة separate

متناوِل covering

متوقِّفٌ على hinges on

متوَلِّد generated

مَثَلٌ parable

مَجاز metonymy

للمُجازاة consequentially

مجرور genitive-case

مُجْمَل unexplained

محتَمَل في نفسه inherently supposible

محذوف ellipsis

مُحكَم accomplished, clinched

منصوب accusative

مُوازِن، موازِنة commensurable

المؤثِّر effecter, Mover

الموجودات existents

موحِّد pure monotheist

موصوف qualified substantive

موصوفة indefinite conjunctive

الموصول conjunctive noun, relative pronoun

الموصولات relatives and conjunctives

موطِّئة للقَسَم paves the way for the oath

الميقات the Tryst

نائب منابَ stands for

النِّسبة referent, relation

نَسْخ abrogation

نُسْخَة original pattern

نَصْب accusative

نظريّ requiring reasoning

ملتبِس به coalescing with it

ملزوم premise

المُلْك والملكوت Sovereignty and preternal Dominion

المُمَثِّل assimilator

المُمَثَّل له vehicle, subject of assimilation

الممكن possibles

من حيثُ إنَّ from the perspective that

من طريق المفهوم in substance

مِن للابتداء **min** for *ab quo* commencement

المنادَى callee

مَناط الاسم that on which the word hinges

مُنتَزَع extracted

منتهَى culmination

مُنَزَّل مَنْزِلَةَ كذا to be treated as

منصوب المَحَلّ virtual accusative

مفصول عنه distinct pronoun

المفضَّل superior comparate

مفعول object

المقارَبة من الوجود near-actuality

مقامَ to represent

مقتضى corollary, exigencies

مُقحَم intercalated

مُقَدَّر subauded

مقدِّراً subauding

مقدِّمات premises, preliminaries

مقدور potential

المُقَرَّر resolved

مقرِّرَة reaffirming

المقصود goal, intent, purport, pursuit

مقلوب inverted form

مقيِّد restrictive, restricting sense

مِلَّة religious denomination

وَقَعَ، واقعٌ موقِعَ comes as

وقف التمام pause of termination of meaning

وهبيّ gifted

يختصّ بـ exclusive to

يُدغَم contracted; Sacy: *tashdīd*-insertion

يستدعي requires

يستلزم necessarily implies or means

يشاكله conformant

يُشَمّ given a smack of (phon.)

يشهد له witnessing to it

يفسِّره glossed

يَقتضي follows from, dictates, presupposes

يَلحَق annexed

يوجِب compel, impose, require

واجب الإعمال categorically operative

واجب الوجود Necessary Being

واجب عقلاً rationally necessary

واجب لذاته self-necessary

الوافر The Exuberant

الوجوب inevitability

وحدانية absolute oneness

الوسائط ways and means

وصْف موَضِّح descriptive of vividness

وُصْلَة link, connective, nexus

وُضِعَت لـ ... coined for…

الوعد والوعيد divine ultimate promise and threat

وَقَعَ خبراً standing as an enunciative adjective

النظم structure

نظيره exactly like it

نعت descriptive epithet

نُعِتَ به used as a qualificative

النفس psyche

نفساني psychological

النقل transference, metaphorization

نقيض antithesis, contrary

نُكْتة، نُكَت allusions

نَكِرَة indefinite

نهي forbidding

النوع المعلوم identifiable species

الهَزَج The Trilling

همزة الوصل conjunctive compression

همزة glottal stop

هيئة disposition

هيئات عارضة accidental aspects

Glossary of persons and sects cited by al-Bayḍāwī

ʿAbd Allāh b. Mughaffal b. ʿAbd Ghanm or Nahm, Abū Saʿīd and Abū Ziyād al-Muzanī (d. 59 or 60/679 or 680): a Companion and father of two famous Companions (Saʿīd and Ziyād), he was known as "one of the oft-weepers." He took part in the Pledge at the Tree (*bayʿat al-riḍwān*, year 6/628) and the expedition of Tabūk then lived and died in Basra where ʿUmar had sent him among ten teachers in charge of Islamic education. He was the first Muslim to enter the gate of the city of Tustar. He stipulated for Abū Barza al-Aslamī to pray over him at his funeral, which Abū Barza did.[1454]

ʿAbd Allāh b. Salām b. al-Ḥārith al-Qaynuqāʿī al-Anṣārī, Abū Yūsuf the Israelite (d. 43/663), a Companion said to have been a descendant of the Prophet Yūsuf—upon him blessings and peace. Al-Ṭabarī, Ibn Saʿd and Yaʿqūb b. Sufyān narrated he was named al-Ḥuṣayn before he became Muslim in the first or the eighth year of the Hijra at the hands of the Prophet—upon him blessings and peace—who changed his name and revealed that he was one of the dwellers of Paradise. He was an ally of the Nawāfil among the Khazraj. From him narrated his two sons Yūsuf and Muḥammad and, among the Companions and those after them: Abū Hurayra, ʿAbd Allah b. Miʿqal, Unays, ʿAbd Allāh b. Ḥanẓala, Kharasha b. al-Ḥurr, Qays b. ʿAbbād, Abū Salama b. ʿAbd al-Raḥmān and others. He became Muslim as soon as the Prophet—upon him and his family blessings and peace—first came to Medina or, in a weaker version, in the year 8/629. Aḥmad and the *Sunan* compilers narrated from him the

1454 Ibn Ḥajar, *al-Iṣāba fī Tamyīz al-Ṣaḥaba*, 8 vols. in 4 (Cairo: al-Maṭbaʿa al-Sharafiyya, 1327/1909; rept. in 5 vols. with indices Beirut: Dār al-Kutub al-ʿIlmiyya, n.d.) 4:132 §4963.

report: "When the Prophet—upon him and his family blessings and peace—came to Medina I was among those who kept their distance; but when I finally beheld his face I knew for sure that such was never the face of a liar. Then I heard him say, 'Give salaam and feed others,'" etc. He came to the Prophet and said: "I want to ask you about three matters only a prophet would know," to the end of the hadith, which includes his story with the Jews and his calling them "a calumniating folk." In another version he said: "I bear witness that you are the Messenger of Allah in truth, and that you are bringing truth. You do know that I am their leader and the most learned of them, so ask them about me before they learn of my submission,'" etc.

Saʿd b. Abī Waqqāṣ said: "I never heard the Prophet—upon him and his family blessings and peace—ever say about someone walking on the face of the earth that he was one of the people of paradise except ʿAbd Allāh b. Salām." Yazīd b. ʿUmayr said: "Muʿādh was at the point of death when someone said to him, 'Advise us.' He replied: 'Seek knowledge with Abū al-Dardā', Salmān, Ibn Masʿūd and ʿAbd Allāh b. Salām who used to be a Jew then he submitted. I heard the Messenger of Allah—upon him and his family blessings and peace—say that he was the tenth of ten people who will be in paradise.'" ʿAbd Allāh b. Miʿqal said, "'ʿAbd Allāh b. Salām forbade ʿAlī from leaving for Iraq and said, 'Stay close to the pulpit of the Messenger of Allah—upon him and his family blessings and peace—for if you leave it you will never see it again.' ʿAlī said, 'Truly he is a righteous man, one of us.'" Abū Burda b. Abī Mūsā: "I came to the mosque in Medina and, behold, I saw ʿAbd Allāh b. Salām sitting in the back in a humble posture, bearing the mark of goodness." When they were trying to kill ʿUthmān ʿAbd Allāh b. Salām declared his support of him and said publicly: "My name in Jāhiliyya was So-and-so, after which the Messenger of Allah —upon him and his family blessings and peace—renamed me ʿAbd Allāh, and certain verses of the Book of Allah were revealed concerning me: *a witness from the Israelites witnesses over the same* (al-Aḥqāf 46:10) was revealed about me, and *say: Allah is enough of a witness between me and you and whoever has the knowledge of the Book* (al-Raʿd 13:43) was revealed about me.'" He died by unanimous agreement in Medina in 43/663.[1455]

ʿAbd Allāh b. Ubay b. Salūl: The leader of the Khazraj and Aws and chief of the *munāfiqūn* (hypocrites) of Medina. The Prophet—upon him blessings and peace—once passed by his house and waited for him to invite him in, but he sent word: "Look for those who invited you and stay with them." The Prophet mentioned this to a group of the *Anṣār* whereupon Saʿd b. ʿUbāda said in excuse of Ibn Salūl: "Allah bestowed you upon us, Messenger of Allah, at a time we were intending to crown him king over us." He is the one quoted as saying, during the return from the expedition against the Banū Muṣṭaliq, *Surely, after we go back to Medina the mightier will soon drive out the weaker* (al-Munāfiqūn 63:8) in reference to his driving out the Prophet, among many other verses revealed concerning him. The "Great Calumny" (*al-Ifk*) against ʿĀʾisha took place at that time, whereby the hypocrites of Medina, led by Ibn Salūl, spread a malicious scandal against her, enrolling some of the Muslims in their campaign which lasted more than a month, during which she stayed with her parents. The Prophet visited her in that situation and told her, "If you are innocent, Allah will acquit you; otherwise, you have to beg for His forgiveness and pardon." She said, "I have no recourse but the words Yūsuf's father, *Patience is most fitting. And it is Allah alone Whose Help is sought against that which you assert* (Yūsuf 12:18)" Then the ten verses acquitting

[1455] Ibn Ḥajar, *Iṣāba* (4:80-91 §4716), al-Khafājī, *ʿInāyat al-Qāḍī* (1:336).

her of all the accusations were revealed, beginning, *Verily those who brought forth the slander are a group among you* (al-Nūr 24:11). The culprits—Misṭaḥ b. Uthātha, Ḥassān b. Thābit and Ḥamna bint Jaḥsh (Zaynab's sister)—were flogged eighty stripes as was the principal instigator ʿAbd Allāh b. Ubay b. Salūl whom his own Muslim son ʿAbd Allāh b. ʿAbd Allāh was poised to kill, had not the Prophet prevented him. Another version states he was spared the flogging due to a lack of evidence of his involvement.

When the Prophet defeated the Banū Qaynuqāʿ after a siege of 15 days and took them prisoner ʿUbāda b. al-Ṣamit stood with the Prophet and dissolved his alliance with them but Ibn Salūl interceded in virulent terms on their behalf: "My allies! 400 of them unarmored and 300 of them in mail defended me, are you going to mow them down in one morning? I am, by Allah, a man who fears consequences!" whereupon the Prophet released them and the verses were revealed, *O believers, do not take the Jews and Christians as your allies* (al-Mā'ida 5:51-56). He also criticized the campaign of Tabūk (9/630) which he joined only to secede from it, returning to Medina with a party of followers, which earned him a dire rebuke and damnation (cf. al-Tawba 9:81-89).

He died the following year after a 20-day illness during which the Prophet would visit and say to him: "Did I not tell you not to love the Jews?" He replied: Asʿad b. Zurāra hated them: what good did it bring him?" Then he said: "Messenger of Allah, this is not the time for reproach; I am dying. Once I am dead, attend my washing, give me your shirt for a shroud, pray over me and ask forgiveness for me," all of which the Prophet—upon him blessings and peace—did. Al-Dhahabī rejected the authenticity of the latter report but then cited the report in al-Bukhārī and

Muslim that after Ibn Salūl was placed in his grave the Prophet came, ordered that he be brought back up, placed him on his lap, blew on his face and dressed him with his own shirt.[1456] Ibn Ḥajar mentioned that Abū Nuʿaym had compiled all the narrative routes of the above incident in a monograph, *Juzʾ jumiʿa fīh ṭuruq ḥadīth al-ṣalāt ʿalā ʿAbd Allāh ibn Ubay.*[1457] All of Ibn Salūl's many children were Muslims.

Abū ʿAlī: The brilliant near-centenarian grammarian Abū ʿAlī al-Ḥasan b. Aḥmad b. ʿAbd al-Ghaffār al-Fārisī al-Naḥwī (d. 377/987) was a student of al-Zajjāj, rival of al-Mubarrid and teacher of Ibn al-Jinnī. He lived in Syria and died in Baghdad.[1458]

Abū al-ʿĀliya: Rufayʿ b. Mihrān al-Riyāḥī—*mawlāhum*—al-Baṣrī (d. 93 or 106), born in *Jāhiliyya*, became Muslim two years after the death of the Prophet—upon him blessings and peace—and took Qurʾān from Ubay b. Kaʿb, Zayd b. Thābit and Ibn ʿAbbās. He was one of the imams of the exegetical schools of the senior Successors, a first-rate jurist whom Abū Isḥāq al-Shīrāzī included in his *Ṭabaqāt al-Fuqahāʾ*, and a hadith master whom al-Dhahabī included in his *Tadhkirat al-Ḥuffāẓ*. He met and/or narrated from ʿUmar, ʿAlī, Ibn Masʿūd, Abū Ayyūb, ʿĀʾisha, Abū Hurayra and others. Among his students were Qatāda, Abū ʿAmr b. al-ʿAlāʾ, Khālid al-Ḥadhdhāʾ, Dāwūd b. Abī Hind, ʿAwf al-Aʿrābī, Ḥafṣa bint Sīrīn, al-Rabīʿ b. Anas—who narrated his *Tafsīr*—and many others. Abū Bakr b. Abī Dāwūd said: "After the *Ṣaḥāba* there is none more knowledgeable of the Qurʾān than

[1456] Ibn Isḥāq and others as cited in Ibn Kathīr, *Bidāya* (4:492; 5:13-14, 320-322); al-Dhahabī, *Siyar Aʿlām al-Nubalāʾ*, ed. Shuʿayb al-Arnāʾūṭ et al., 3rd ed. 25 vols. (Beirut: Muʾassassat al-Risāla, 1405/1985) 2:258.

[1457] Ibn Ḥajar, *Fatḥ* (8:339).

[1458] Cf. al-Khaṭīb, [*Tārīkh Baghdād*] *Tārīkh Madīnat al-Salām*, 17 vols., ed. Bashshār Awwād Maʿrūf (Beirut: Dār al-Gharb al-Islāmī, 1422/2001) 8:217 §3716 and al-Suyūṭī, *Bughyat al-Wuʿāt* (1:496-497 §1030).

Abū al-ʿĀliya, followed by Saʿīd b. Jubayr." They ranked him with Ibrāhīm al-Nakhaʿī in learning.[1459]

Abū ʿAmr b. al-ʿAlāʾ: Abū ʿAmr Zabbān b. al-ʿAlāʾ b. ʿAmmār al-Tamīmī al-Māzinī al-Baṣrī (68-154/688-771) was one of the "Main Seven" canonical readers of Qurʾān. He studied in the Two Sanctuaries and Iraq with more teachers than any of the other canonical readers, among them Anas, al-Ḥasan, Ḥumayd al-Aʿraj, Abū al-ʿĀliya, Saʿīd b. Jubayr, Shayba, ʿĀṣim, the two ʿIkrimas, Ibn Kathīr, ʿĀṭāʾ b. Abī Rabāḥ, Mujāhid, and others. Among his students: Khatan al-Layth, Khārija, Ḥusayn al-Juʿfī, al-Yashkurī, Aḥmad b. Mūsā al-Luʾluʾī, Ibn al-Mubārak, al-Aṣmaʿī, Sībawayh and others. "He was the most knowledgeable of people in Qurʾān and the Arabic language in addition to his trustworthiness and asceticism" (Ibn al-Jazarī). Abū ʿUbayda said: "His notebooks reached to the ceilings of his house, hen he devoted himself to worship and had them all burnt, and he would make sure to recite the entire Qurʾān in three days." Al-Aṣmaʿī said: "I heard him say, 'I never saw anyone before me more learned than me;' and I myself never saw after Abū ʿAmr anyone more learned than him; and I also heard him say: 'I bear witness that Allah misguides and guides, and despite that He possesses the conclusive argument over His slaves.'" Shuʿba said that the Quranic reading followed in his time in Syro-Palestine, the Hijaz, Yemen and Egypt was that of Abū ʿAmr.[1460]

Abū Bakr al-Ṣiddīq: ʿAbd Allāh b. ʿUthmān b. ʿĀṣim al-Qurashī al-Taymī, nicknamed ʿAtīq b. Abī Quḥāfa (d. 13/634)) was the intimate friend of the Prophet (upon him blessings and peace),

[1459] Cf. al-Dawūdī, *Ṭabaqāt al-Mufassirīn*, ed. ʿAlī Muḥammad ʿUmar, 2nd ed., 2 vols. (Cairo: Maktabat Wahba, 1415/1994) 1:172-173 §170.

[1460] Ibn al-Jazarī, *Ghāyat al-Nihāya fī Ṭabaqāt al-Qurrāʾ*, 2 vols. (Beirut: Dār al-Kutub al-ʿIlmiyya, 1427/2006, based on the three-volume ed. by Gotthelf Bergsträsser and Otto Pretzl (Cairo: Maṭbaʿat al-Saʿāda, 1933-1935) 1:262-265 §1283.

exclusive companion at his Basin and in the Cave, greatest supporter and closest confidant, first of the men who believed in him and the only one who did so unhesitatingly, first of the four Rightly-Guided Caliphs, first of the Ten promised Paradise, first of the Community of Islam to enter Paradise, "the Venerable of the Community," "truthful, dutiful, well-guided, and following the right" and the best of creation after Prophets.

The Prophet described him as the foremost genealogist of the Quraysh and the best of them at interpreting dreams according to Ibn Sīrīn. He once said: "I saw in dream black sheep succeeded by dirt-white sheep. Abū Bakr! Interpret it." The latter said, "Messenger of Allah, these are the Arabs following you, then the non-Arabs succeed them until they completely engulf them in their number." The Prophet said: "Just so did the angel interpret it [to me] before the dawn."[1461]

Alone among the Companions, Abū Bakr's genealogical tree regroups four successive generations of Companions of the Prophet: his parents Abū Quḥāfa and Umm al-Khayr, himself, his daughter Asmā' and her son ʿAbd Allāh, in addition to Abū Bakr's son ʿAbd al-Raḥmān and his grandson Abū ʿAtīq.

When the Quraysh confronted the Prophet after the Night Journey, they went to Abū Bakr and said: "Do you believe what he said—that he went last night to the Hallowed House and came back before morning?" He replied: "If he said it then I believe him. And I believe him regarding what is farther: I believe the news of heaven he brings, whether in the space of a morning or in that of an evening journey!" Because of this, Abū Bakr was

[1461] Narrated from ʿAbd al-Raḥmān b. Abī Laylā, [1] from Abū Ayyūb al-Anṣārī by al-Ḥākim (4:395) and [2] from Abū Bakr himself but al-Dāraquṭnī in his *ʿIlal* (1:289) avers that this narration is more probably *mursal* from Ibn Abī Laylā cf. Ibn Abī Shayba (6:176 §30479). Also narrated *mursal* from the *Tābiʿī* Abū Maysara ʿAmr b. Shuraḥbīl al-Hamdānī and something similar *mursal* from Qatāda.

named *al-Ṣiddīq*.[1462] The Prophet confirmed that title for him in the hadiths of the shaking of the two mountains: Uḥud (together with 'Umar and 'Uthmān)—at which time he said: "Be firm, Uḥud! There is none on top of you but a Prophet, a *Ṣiddīq*, and two martyrs"[1463]—and Ḥirā' (together with 'Umar, 'Uthmān, 'Alī, Ṭalḥa and al-Zubayr)—at which time he said: "Be still! There is none on top of you but a Prophet, a *Ṣiddīq*, or a martyr."[1464]

Abū Bakr, also alone among the Companions, repeatedly led the Community in prayer in the lifetime of the Prophet—upon him blessings and peace.[1465] Imam Aḥmad said: "When the Prophet was taken ill he ordered Abū Bakr to lead the prayer although there others were present who were more Qur'ān-proficient, but he was pointing to the Caliphate."[1466] Imām al-Shāfi'ī preceded him in this view.

Abū Bakr's caliphate lasted two years and three months in which he brought Syro-Palestine and Iraq into Islam (the "one or two bucketfuls" in the dream of the Prophet) and suppressed apostasy among the Arab tribes in forty days. He fought Najd's false prophets—Ṭulayḥa al-Asadī,[1467] Musaylima the Arch-Liar and his wife Sajāḥ who were killed in the devastating battle of Yamāma and Fujā'at al-Sulāmī, as well as the false prophet of

[1462] Narrated from 'Ā'isha by al-Ḥākim, *Mustadrak* (3:62, 3:76 *isnāduhu ṣaḥīḥ*); Ibn Sa'd, Ibn Abī 'Āṣim, al-Ṭabarānī and others; also from Anas and 'Alī by Abū Nu'aym in *Ma'rifat al-Ṣaḥāba* cf. al-Suyūṭī, *Durr* (4:155).

[1463] Narrated from Anas by al-Bukhārī, Tirmidhī, Abū Dāwūd, al-Nasā'ī and Aḥmad.

[1464] Narrated from Abū Hurayra by Muslim, al-Tirmidhī and Aḥmad.

[1465] As narrated from Abū Mūsā al-Ash'arī by al-Bukhārī and Muslim. This is mass-transmitted, also from 'Ā'isha, Ibn Mas'ūd, Ibn 'Abbās, Ibn 'Umar, Abū Sa'īd al-Khudrī, 'Abd Allāh b. Zam'a, 'Alī and Ḥafṣa.

[1466] Narrated from Abū Bakr al-Marwazī by Ibn al-Jawzī in *Manāqib al-Imām Aḥmad*, ed. Muḥammad Amīn al-Khānjī al-Kutbī, 2nd ed. (Beirut: Khānjī wa-Ḥamdān, 1349/1930-1931) p. 160.

[1467] He repented before the death of Abū Bakr and died a martyr on the Muslim side in the battle of Nahāwand in the year 21/642).

Yemen al-Aswad al-ʿAnsī. The harshest and most devastating of all these campaigns by far was the battle of Yamāma in which the Muslims sustained the heaviest losses and after winning which Abū Bakr went into the thanksgiving prostration.[1468]

Al-Nawawī in *Tahdhīb al-Asmā' wal-Lughāt* states that only 142 Prophetic hadiths are narrated from Abū Bakr.[1469] He comments: "The reason for this scarcity, despite the seniority of his companionship to the Prophet, is that his death predated the dissemination of hadiths and the endeavor of the Successors to hear, gather, and preserve them." It is also related that Abū Bakr had the written record of all the hadiths in his possession burnt lest a mistake slip into them. It is related that ʿĀ'isha said: "My father gathered Hadith from the Messenger of Allah and it was 500 hadiths. One night he kept tossing and turning and it worried me. I said, 'Are you tossing and turning because of some ailment or have you heard bad news?' In the morning he said, 'Daughter, bring me the hadiths you have with you.' I brought them, then he called for fire and burnt them. He said, 'I fear lest I die while those are still in your possession and there might be among them hadiths from someone I trusted and believed, but it was not as he said to me, and I would have imitated him.'"[1470]

[1468] Ibn Abī Shayba, *Muṣannaf* (5:459 §8499 *Kitāb al-ṣalāt, Sajdat al-shukr*) and al-Bayhaqī, *Sunan* (2:519 §3940) through a nameless narrator but the rest of the narrators are trustworthy; Muḥammad b. al-Ḥasan cited it in *Kitāb al-Siyar* without chain and he cited the same act by ʿAlī after fighting the Khawārij at Nahrawān as narrated by al-Bazzār, *Musnad* (2:186) and Ibn Abī Shayba (5:460-463 §8502-8503, §8508) cf. al-Sarakhsī, *Sharḥ Kitāb al-Siyar al-Kabīr*, ed. Abū ʿAbd Allāh Muḥammad Ḥasan al-Shāfiʿī, 5 vols. (Beirut: Dār al-Kutub al-ʿIlmiyya, 1417/1997) 1:153-154. The thanksgiving prostration and the thanksgiving prayer are both mentioned in several authentic hadiths contrary to what certain jurists claimed.

[1469] I.e. without repetitions through various chains. Suyūṭī in *Tārīkh al-Khulafā'* documents over 100 of them which he follows up with over 100 of Abū Bakr's sayings.

[1470] Narrated by al-Ḥākim as stated by Ibn Kathīr in the *Musnad al-Ṣiddīq* inside his *Jāmiʿ al-Asānīd*.

Among Abū Bakr's sayings: "Whoever fights his ego *(nafs)* for the sake of Allah, He will protect him against what he hates."[1471] When Yemenis came in the time of his caliphate and heard the Qur'an they took to weeping, whereupon he said: 'Thus were we before, then the hearts hardened (*qasat al-qulūb*).'"[1472] Abū Nu'aym said: "*The hearts hardened* means they became strong and tranquil through knowledge of Allah."[1473]

Abū Bakr: Shu'ba b. 'Ayyāsh b. Sālim al-Asadī al-Nahshalī al-Kūfī (95-193/714-809) was a major imam of Quranic reading and Sunna who took the readings from 'Āṣim thrice, 'Aṭā' b. al-Sāyib and Aslam al-Minqarī. In his very old age he would say: "I am half of all knowledge." He is known to have "prayed *fajr* with the ablutions of *'ishā'* for forty years" and "not spread out a bed for fifty years" and was considered one of the *awliyā'*. Among his famous sayings: "The Sunna in Islam is more rare and precious than Islam itself is rare and precious among the rest of the faiths;"[1474] and "Abū Bakr [al-Ṣiddīq] did not best you because of praying or fasting more but because of something that has firmly settled in his heart." On his deathbed he showed his sister a corner and said: "Why do you weep? Look at that corner, this is where I have made 18,000 *khatma*s of the Qur'ān."[1475]

Abū Ḥanīfa: al-Nu'mān b. Thābit b. Kāwūs b. Hurmuz b. Marzubān al-Taymī—*mawlāhum*—al-Kūfī (80-150/699-767), called "the true *Faqīh*" by Mālik, "the Imām" by Abū Dāwūd,

[1471] Cited by Muḥammad b. Qudāma in *Minhāj al-Qāṣidīn*.

[1472] Narrated by al-Qāsim b. Sallām in *Faḍā'il al-Qur'ān* (p. 135) and Ibn Abī Shayba (19:452-453 §36673).

[1473] Abū Nu'aym al-Aṣfahānī, *Ḥilyat al-Awliyā' wa-Ṭabaqāt al-Aṣfiyā'*, 10 vols. (Cairo: Maṭba'at al-Sa'āda, 1399/1979, rept. Beirut: Dār al-Kutub al-'Ilmiyya, 1409/1988) 1:33-34.

[1474] Narrated by al-Khaṭīb in *al-Jāmi' li-Akhlāq al-Rāwī wal-Sāmi'* (2:172).

[1475] Ibn al-Jazarī, *Ghāyat al-Nihāya* (1:295-296 §1321). The figure of 18,000 is equivalent to a daily *khatma* for 49 years.

Faqīh al-Milla by al-Dhahabī, and "the Imām, one of those who have reached the sky" by Ibn Ḥajar, first of the four *mujtahid* Imams whose school survived to our time and acquired the greatest following among Sunnī schools, known in the Community as "The Greatest Imām" *(al-imām al-aʿẓam)* and teacher to Abū Yūsuf, Muḥammad b. al-Ḥasan al-Shaybānī, and Zufar among others.[1476]

Abū al-Ḥasan al-Ashʿarī: ʿAlī b. Ismāʿīl b. Abī Bishr Isḥāq b. Salīm b. Ismāʿīl b. ʿAbd Allāh b. Mūsā b. Bilāl b. Abī Burda b. Abī Mūsā al-Yamānī al-Baṣrī al-Baghdādī (260-324/874-936).[1477] A descendent of the Yemeni Companion Abū Mūsā al-Ashʿarī and eponymous founder of the Ashʿarī School, he was in the first half of his scholarly career a disciple of his father-in-law, the Muʿtazili teacher Abū ʿAlī al-Jubbāʾī, whose doctrines he abandoned in his 40th year after asking him a question al-Jubbāʾī failed to resolve over the issue of the supposed Divine obligation to "abandon the good for the sake of the better" *(al-ṣāliḥ wal-aṣlaḥ)*. At that time he adopted the doctrines of the *ṣifatiyya*, those of *Ahl al-Sunna* who assert that the Divine Attributes are obligatorily (i) characterized by perfection, (ii) unchanging and (iii) without beginning, but He is under no obligation whatsoever to abandon the good for the sake of the better.[1478] He left

1476 See more in our *Four Imams and Their Schools.*

1477 These dates were given by Ibn ʿAsākir in *Tabyīn Kadhib al-Muftarī*, Ibn al-Subkī in *Ṭabaqāt al-Shāfiʿiyya al-Kubrā* (3:347, 3:352), al-Dhahabī, *Siyar* (15:85) and *Tadhkirat al-Ḥuffāẓ*, Ibn Kathīr, *Bidāya* (15:101) and *Ṭabaqāt al-Fuqahāʾ al-Shāfiʿiyyīn* (1:208-214) and Ibn Qāḍī Shuhba in *Ṭabaqāt al-Shāfiʿiyya*, ed. ʿAbd al-ʿAlīm Khān, 5 vols. (Hyderabad Deccan: Dāʾirat al-Maʿārif al-ʿUthmāniyya, 1398/ 1978) 1:114 §60 while al-Khaṭīb in *Tārīkh Baghdād* (11:346) gives the obitus 330/942 as does Ibn al-Athīr according to Ibn Kathīr. Cf. also Ibn al-ʿImād, *Shadharāt al-Dhahab* (2:303) and Ibn Khallikān, *Wafayāt al-Aʿyān* (2:446).

1478 Cf. al-Shahrastānī, *al-Milal wal-Nil al* (Ṣifātiyya 1:126-127, Ashāʿira 1:139) and Ibn al-Subkī, *Ṭabaqāt al-Shāfiʿiyya al-Kubrā* (3:356). See also Nūr al-Dīn Aḥmad b. Mahmūd al-Ṣābūnī (d. 1184/1770), *al-Bidāya min al-Kifāya fī Uṣūl al-Dīn.*

Basra and went to Baghdad where he took *fiqh* from the Shāfiʿī jurist Abū Isḥāq al-Marwazī (d. 340).[1479] He devoted the next 24 years to the refutation of "the Muʿtazila, the Rāfiḍa, the Jahmiyya, the Khawārij, and the rest of the various kinds of innovators" in the words of al-Khaṭīb. His student Bundār related that his yearly expenditure was a meager 17 dirhams.

"Al-Ashʿarī became the sign-post of Sunni learning in his time and his word has since then become synonymous with the position of *Ahl al-Sunna wal-Jamāʿa*."[1480] On his deathbed he said: "Bear witness over me that I do not declare any of the people of the *Qibla* an unbeliever *(kāfir)*, as all of them point to One Object of worship; and all of this [disagreement] is just differences in terminology."[1481]

Abū Hurayra: ʿAbd al-Raḥmān b. Ṣakhr al-Yamanī al-Dawsī (19BH-57/603-677)—formerly named ʿAbd al-Shams then renamed ʿAbd al-Raḥmān by the Prophet and nicknamed by him Abū Hirr—is the most abundant Companion-narrator of hadith from the Prophet, having accompanied him day and night at home and abroad, in public and in private, on pilgrimage and military expeditions for three full years, during which time he was content to live from hand to mouth. The number of those who narrates from him reaches 800 including both Companions and Successors. At his burial Ibn ʿUmar said: "He preserved the Hadith of the Prophet for Muslims" and "O Abū Hurayra! You were the most assiduous among us in accompanying the Messenger of Allah and the most knowledgeable of us all in his hadith." Abū Ayyūb al-Anṣārī said: "Abū Hurayra heard what we

[1479] Abū Isḥāq al-Isfarāyīnī and Ibn Fūrak considered al-Ashʿarī a Shāfiʿī in *fiqh* cf. Ibn Qāḍī Shuhba, *Ṭabaqāt al-Shāfiʿiyya* (1:83).

[1480] Munīr ʿAbduh Aghā, *Namūdhaj min al-Aʿmāl al-Khayriyya fīl-Maṭbaʿat al-Munīriyya* (Riyadh: Maktabat al-Imām al-Shāfiʿī, 1988) p. 134.

[1481] In al-Dhahabī, *Siyar Aʿlām al-Nubalāʾ* (15:88).

did not hear, and I certainly prefer to narrate from him than to quote the Prophet [on my own]." Hence, al-Shāfi'ī named Abū Hurayra "the foremost in memorization among those who narrated hadith in his time"—meaning Companions and Successors.

Among Abū Hurayra's sayings: "I divided my nights into three parts: in one third I would pray, in another sleep, and in the last third I would recollect the hadith of the Prophet." And this is also how al-Shāfi'ī said he himself lived. He also said: "I preserved from the Messenger of Allah two large vessels of knowledge. I disseminated the first one among the people. Were I to disseminate the second, my gullet would be cut." That was in reference to his knowledge of the political strifes to come including the murder of al-Ḥusayn, the sack of the Ka'ba and the names of those involved.

Abū Hurayra used to fast in the daytime and pray in the dead of night with his wife and daughter. He was content with little, eating five dates for his pre-fast meal and breaking his fast with five, sometimes tying a stone to his stomach to contain his hunger. He had several prayer-spots in his house and within his doorstep, and prayed in each of them once every time he entered or exited. He was slightly swarthy, wide-shouldered, tooth-gapped, wore two braids (*ḍafīratayn*) and dyed his white hair and beard with red henna. He wore a black turban. He was of gentle and humble disposition, played with children, rode a donkey, and carried wood on his back from the marketplace even after he became governor of Medina. He possessed a thread with 2,000 knots and would not sleep until he had used six times in *dhikr*. He said: "I make glorification (*tasbīḥ*) of Allah Most High every day according to my ransom (*qadar diyatī*): 12,000 times."

His high rank is indicated by the hadith of the Prophet: "None hears a word, or two, or three, or four, or five words pertaining to what Allah has commanded, then learns them and teaches them to others, except he certainly enters Paradise."[1482]

Abū Jahl: ʿAmr b. Hishām b. al-Mughīra al-Makhzūmī (d. 2/624) was one of the rank enemies of Muslims among Meccan leaders. Previously known as Abū al-Ḥakam (Father of the Wise), he was renamed Abū Jahl (Father of Ignorance) by the Prophet—upon him blessings and peace—who forbade it for anyone to call him Abū al-Ḥakam; he also named him "the Pharaoh of this Community." Al-Akhnas al-Thaqafī asked him after they witnessed the Qur'ān being recited: "What do you think of what you heard?" He replied: "What have I heard? We and the Banū ʿAbd Manāf had always competed for eminence. They would feed people, so we would feed people. They would equip them, so we would equip them. They gave, so we gave. We were like two front runners; until they said: 'There is a prophet among us who receives revelation from heaven.' How are we going to match that? By Allah, we will never believe in him nor accept him as truthful—ever!" He was killed at the battle of Badr.[1483]

Abū Lahab: Literally "flamer," thus named because of his beauty, ʿAbd al-ʿUzzā b. ʿAbd al-Muṭṭalib was a paternal uncle of the Prophet—upon him blessings and peace—and the only one of his Meccan opponents to be mentioned in the Qur'ān by name. When the Prophet was commanded to warn his near relatives (al-Shuʿarā' 26:214), he ascended Mount Ṣafā and shouted out: "All of you be warned!" When the people gathered around him, he mentioned each tribe and family by name and said: "If I were to inform you that mounted troops are about to come out from

1482 See references at http://www.livingislam.org/k/ahpp_e.html.

1483 Ibn Hishām, *al-Sīra al-Nabawiyya*, ed. Muṣṭafā al-Saqqā et al., 2nd ed., 4 vols. in 2 (Beirut: Dār al-Wifāq, 1375/1955) 1:316.

behind this mountain, would you believe me?" They said yes. He continued: "I warn you of a great impending punishment!" and summoned them to believe in him. At this Abū Lahab said: "Perish your hands (*tabbat yadāk*)! Is this why you gathered us?" Then Sūrat al-Masad was revealed.[1484] He contracted *ʿadasa*, a contagious form of anthrax after which his family abandoned him and no one tended to his dead body for three days. When the stench became unbearable they had some slaves remove it and throw it down a hole.[1485]

Abū al-Shaʿthāʾ: Also known as Abū Ashʿath, the trustworthy *Tābiʿī* Salīm (or Sulaym) b. al-Aswad al-Muḥāribī al-Kūfī al-Kinānī (d. 125?/743?) is one of al-Bukhārī's narrators in his *Ṣaḥīḥ* and narrated from his father, Ibn Masʿūd, Ibn ʿUmar, and Ḥudhayfa. He died in Kūfa in the time of al-Ḥajjāj. Al-Bayḍāwī mentions him in the context of a variant *qirāʾa*, although he is not known as a Quranic reading specialist and Ibn al-Jazarī does not mention him in *Ṭabaqāt al-Qurrāʾ*.

Abū Tammām al-Ṭāʾī: Ḥabīb b. Aws b. al-Ḥārith (d. 231/846) was a Syrian poet who authored *Fuḥūl al-Shuʿarāʾ* and *Dīwān al-Ḥamāsa*. The latter received several commentaries, three of them available in print (by al-Tibrīzī, al-Marzūqī and Abū al-ʿAlāʾ al-Maʿarrī). Famed for his eloquence and forceful style, he went to Egypt then Baghdad and was lauded by the caliph al-Muʿtaṣim above the poets of his time.

al-Aḍbaṭ al-Saʿdī: Abū Jaʿfar Aḍbaṭ b. Quraynʿ b. ʿAwf b. Kaʿb al-Saʿdī al-Tamīmī, nicknamed Anf al-Nāqa (Camel Snout), was a pre-Islamic poet (not Umawī as claimed by S in *Nawāhid al-*

[1484] Bukhārī, *Ṣaḥīḥ* (*Tafsīr, Sūrat Tabbat*); Muslim, *Ṣaḥīḥ* (*Īmān, fī qawlihi taʿālā Wa andhir ʿashīratak al-aqrabīn*); al-Tirmidhī, *Sunan* (*Tafsīr, Sūrat Tabbat*); etc.

[1485] Ibn Saʿd, *Kitāb al-Ṭabaqāt al-Kabīr*, ed. ʿAlī Muḥammad ʿUmar, 11 vols. (Cairo: Maktabat al-Khānjī, 1421/2001) 4:67; Ibn Ḥajar, *Fatḥ al-Bārī* (*Tafsīr*, al-Masad 111).

Abkār and *Sharḥ Abyāt al-Mughnī*, but predating Islam by four or five centuries) who was harmed by his tribe—the Banū Saʿd—and left it to join another tribe who also mistreated him, then another until he returned to the first and bitterly remarked, *bi-kulli wādin Banū Saʿd*, "In every vale there are Banū Saʿd!"[1486]

ʿĀʾisha: ʿĀ'isha bt. Abī Bakr al-Ṣiddīq, *Umm al-Mu'minīn* (7 BH?-57/615?-677), the only virgin the Prophet ever married and most beloved of all women after Khadīja to him. He dubbed her Umm ʿAbd Allāh and nicknamed her Ḥumayrā' (fair young woman), ʿĀ'ish and ʿUwaysh. She was the teacher of the Community and a paragon of women, "the most eloquent of speakers after the Messenger of Allah" (Muʿāwiya, Mūsā b. Ṭalḥa and al-Aḥnaf b. Qays), "absolutely the most knowledgeable woman in the *Umma* or rather in humankind" (al-Dhahabī), "comprehensive in knowledge, unique in her intelligence, a *mujtahida*, the epitome of learning and teaching" (al-Suyūṭī). Her mother was Umm Rūmān the daughter of ʿĀṣim b. ʿUwaymir b. ʿAbd Shams b. ʿAttāb b. Udhayna al-Kināniyya.

ʿĀ'isha was nineteen to twenty years younger than her sister Asmā' (27 BH-74/596-693) and about five to eight years Fāṭima's junior. The Prophet married her after the death of his first wife Khadīja bint Khuwaylid, a year or two before his emigration to Medina, and he first cohabited with her in Shawwāl of the second year after the Hijra, following the battle of Badr. She was among those who bade farewell to the Badr combatants as they were leaving Medina, as narrated by Muslim in his *Ṣaḥīḥ*. On the day of Uḥud (year 3624), Anas—at the time only twelve or thirteen years old—reports seeing an eleven-year old ʿĀ'isha and his mother Umm Sulaym having pulled up their dresses and carrying water skins back and forth to the combatants, as

[1486] Ibn Qutayba, *al-Shiʿr wal-Shuʿarā'* (1:382-383); Baghdādī, *Khizāna* (11:452-456).

narrated by al-Bukhārī and Muslim.

When the Prophet gave her the news of her exoneration of the accusations against her in the incident of the Great Calumny (*al-Ifk*) instigated by ʿAbd Allāh b. Ubay (*q.v.*) she said: "Thanks and praise to Allah, not anyone else, and not to you!"[1487] Al-Sharnūbī in *Sharḥ al-Ḥikam* said that "this was because she was oblivious to causes and effects and immersed in the One Over-whelming Creator of causes, which is the 'station of oblivion' *(iṣṭilām)* while the higher station of 'abiding' *(baqā')*—that of Abū Bakr—acknowledges the working of causes" Muḥammad al-Ṭāhir al-Kattānī in *Maṭāliʿ al-Saʿāda* said it was a liberty born of *tadallul* ʿlovelorn endearmentʾ she did not mean literally.

ʿĀʾisha is with Abū Hurayra the foremost instructor of the *Umma* and a principal conveyer of the Sunna from the Prophet to the Companions and subsequent generations. She narrated abundantly from him—up to 2,210 hadiths directly, as well as through Abū Bakr, ʿUmar, Fāṭima, Saʿd, Ḥamza b. ʿAmr al-Aslamī and Judāma bt. Wahb according to Dhahabī. She taught over 30 Companions and her students among the Successors number in the hundreds. She was famed as a jurisprudent of the first rank. Seven famous Jurisprudents among the Companions were known as "the Masters of fatwa:" ʿUmar, ʿAlī, Ibn Masʿūd, Ubay b. Kaʿb, Abū Mūsā al-Ashʿarī, Zayd b. Thābit, and ʿĀʾisha. Masrūq was asked if she had knowledge of inheritance laws. He replied: "By the One in Whose Hand is my soul! I saw the senior Companions asking her about inheritance law."[1488] She is also famous for her judicious corrections (*istidrākāt*) of older Companions, which al-Zarkashī compiled.

The Prophet praised her in several reports: "Many men

[1487] Narrated by al-Bukhārī.

[1488] Narrated by al-Dārimī and al-Ḥākim (4:11).

reached perfection but, among women, only Āsya the wife of Pharaoh and Maryam bint ʿImrān; and the superexcellence of ʿĀʾisha over all women is like that of meat and gruel *(tharīd)* over all foods."[1489] Ibn Ḥajar cites other versions from Ṭabarānī and Abū Nuʿaym that add, after the mention of Maryam bint ʿImrān, "Khadīja bint Khuwaylid and Fāṭima bint Muḥammad." This is confirmed by the hadith in Aḥmad with a fair chain from Abū Saʿīd al-Khudrī: "Fāṭima is the best of the women of Paradise except for Maryam." When ʿĀʾisha asked him: "Which of your wives are in Paradise?" He replied: "You are surely one of them!"[1490]

The relationship between the Prophet and her was tender and playful. One time he raced with her and she beat him. Some time later, they raced again and he beat her. He then said: "One all!" *(hādhihi bi-tilk)*.[1491] He once said to her: "I know for sure when you are happy with me and when you are angry with me!" She said, "And how do you know, Messenger of Allah?" He said: "When you are happy with me, you say, 'No, by the Lord of Muḥammad!' And when you are angry with me, you say, 'No, by the Lord of Ibrāhīm!'" She said: "Yes, by Allah! I do not stay away from more than your name."[1492] Abū Bakr one day sought permission to enter the Prophet's apartment. As he entered he heard ʿĀʾisha shouting at the Prophet. He caught her and said: 'Am I seeing you shouting at the Prophet?" and he wanted to slap her but the Prophet held him back by the waist and saved ʿĀʾisha. Abū Bakr went out angry. When he had gone, the

[1489] Narrated from Abū Mūsā al-Ashʿarī by al-Bukhārī, Muslim, al-Tirmidhī, Ibn Mājah, and Aḥmad.

[1490] Narrated from ʿĀʾisha by Ibn Ḥibbān (16:8), al-Ṭabarānī in *al-Awsaṭ* (8:84 §8039), and al-Ḥākim (1990 ed. 4:14 *ṣaḥīḥ*).

[1491] Narrated from ʿĀʾisha by Abū Dāwūd, Aḥmad and Ibn Mājah.

[1492] Narrated from ʿĀʾisha by al-Bukhārī and Muslim.

Prophet said to her: "Well? Did I save you from the man?" After a few days, Abū Bakr again sought permission to enter and saw that the Prophet and ʿĀʾisha were at peace. He said: "Let me enter in your peace as I had entered in your dispute." The Prophet said: "We do, we do (*qad faʿalnā, qad faʿalnā*)."[1493]

She once asked the people: "Who gave you the fatwa to fast on ʿĀshūrā'?" They replied, ʿAlī. She said: "He is truly most knowledgeable of the Sunna!"[1494] ʿAmmār b. Yāsir said to the people of Kūfa when ʿAlī sent him there to mobilize against ʿĀʾisha before the Battle of the Camel: "We know for certain that she is the wife of the Messenger of Allah in the world and in the hereafter, but Allah is testing you through her."[1495]

In addition to her superlative knowledge and understanding of Hadith, she was a mine of information on Arabic medicine because, she said, of her retentive memory. She was also, like her father, imbued with the oral heritage of pre-Islamic Arabs and could quote at will from their poetry. Like Fāṭima, she had an intense sense of woman's privacy and modesty in dress. She defined woman's public dress thus: "When a woman reaches puberty she must cover whatever her mother and grandmother must cover,"[1496] their *khimār* being "nothing short of what covers both the hair and skin,"[1497] "without transparency."[1498] She said: "By Allah! I never saw any better women than the women of the *Anṣār* nor stronger in their confirmation of the book of Allah! When Sūrat al-Nūr was revealed *and to draw their khumūr over*

[1493] Narrated from Nuʿmān b. Bashīr by Abū Dāwūd and Aḥmad with good chains.

[1494] Narrated by Ibn ʿAbd al-Barr in *al-Istīʿāb*.

[1495] Narrated from Abū Wāʾil by al-Bukhārī and Aḥmad as well as Ibn Abī al-Jaʿd in his *Musnad*.

[1496] Narrated by al-Bayhaqī, *Sunan* (6:57) and Ibn Abī Shayba (2:229).

[1497] Narrated by ʿAbd al-Razzāq, *Muṣannaf* (3:133).

[1498] Narrated by Mālik in his *Muwaṭṭaʾ*, book of clothing.

their bosoms (24:31) – their men went back to them reciting to them what Allah had revealed to them in that [sura or verse], each man reciting it to his wife, daughter, sister, and relative. Not one woman among them remained except she got up on the spot, tore up her waist-wrap and covered herself from head to toe *(i'jtajarat)* with it. They prayed the very next dawn prayer covered from head to toe *(mu'tajirāt)*."[1499] She forbade women from going to mosques for congregational prayers, including the five prescribed prayers, let alone *Tarāwīḥ*. She gave her reason in the famous statement: "If the Messenger of Allah had seen what the women of our time do, he would have forbidden them to go to the mosques just as the Israelite women were forbidden!"[1500] She did pray *Tarāwīḥ* in congregation but at home, and she often led other women in prayer.

When 'Umar was mortally stabbed he sent his son 'Abd Allāh with a message to 'Ā'isha to "Ask her if I can be buried with my two companions," that is, in her room, next to the Prophet and Abū Bakr. 'Ā'isha replied: "Yes, by Allah!" Another narration states that she said: "I wanted the spot for myself, but I shall put him before me today." It had been her habit that if a man from among the Companions asked her that spot she would always refuse. She herself gave the following instructions before her death: "Bury me with my lady-friends (the wives of the Prophet in al-Baqī') and do not bury me with the Prophet in the house, for I dislike to be held in reverence *(innī akrahu an uzakkā)*." Ibn 'Umar came back with the news, whereupon

[1499] Narrated by Ibn Abī Ḥātim in his *Tafsīr* as mentioned by Ibn Kathīr in his *Tafsīr* (Dār al-Fikr 1981 ed. 3:285) and Ibn Ḥajar in *Fatḥ al-Bārī* (8:490) while al-Bukhārī narrates something similar. Ibn Ḥajar notes that 'Ā'isha said something similar about the women of the *Muhājirīn* (*i.e.* the women of Mecca) but that the two reports are reconciled by the fact that the women of Medina were the first to apply the verse.
[1500] Narrated by al-Bukhārī, Muslim, and in the books of *Sunan*.

'Umar said: "Nothing in the world was more important to me than that resting-place.[1501] 'Ā'isha said: "I used to enter my house—where the Messenger of Allah and my father (Abū Bakr) were buried —and undress thinking it is only my husband and my father. But when 'Umar b. al-Khaṭṭāb was later buried [there], I did not enter the room except that I wore my garment close to me, out of shyness before 'Umar."[1502]

As a rule she did not shorten prayers in travel and gave as her reason the fact she found no hardship in travel, whereas *qaṣr* was stipulated to alleviate hardship. She even fasted while travelling and deemed shortening to two a dispensation *(rukhṣa)*. This is the Shāfi'ī and Ḥanbalī position. Qāsim b. Muḥammad b. Abī Bakr al-Ṣiddīq related that his aunt 'Ā'isha practiced lifelong fasting *(kānat taṣūmu al-dahr)*.[1503]

al-Akhfash: Abū al-Ḥasan Sa'īd b. Mas'ada al-Balkhī *thumma* al-Baṣrī al-Mujāshi'ī *mawlāhum* (d. 210/825 or 221/836), known as al-Awsaṭ (the Middle) to differentiate him from two other famous Akhfash. He was a client of the Banū Mujāshi' b. Dārim in Balkh and lived in Basra and Baghdad. He studied grammar under Sībawayh although older than him, and took hadith from Ibrāhīm al-Nakha'ī, Hishām b. 'Urwa and al-Kalbī. A Mu'tazili in doctrine, he authored *al-Awsaṭ* and *al-Maqāyīs* in grammar, *Ma'ānī al-Qur'ān* on the desinential syntax of the Qur'ān (not to be confused with the same-titled *tafsīr* by Abū Zakariyyā Yaḥyā b. Ziyād al-Farrā', *q.v.*), *al-Ishtiqāq* on etymology, *al-'Arūḍ wal-Qawafī* on prosody among other works.[1504]

[1501] Compare this to the impious saying of some people that "there is nothing there."

[1502] Narrated by Aḥmad with a sound chain as stated by al-Haythamī, by al-Ḥākim (4:7 and 3:61) who said it is sound by the criteria of al-Bukhārī and Muslim.

[1503] Cf. al-Dhahabī, *Siyar* (2:187).

[1504] al-Suyūṭī, *Bughyat al-Wu'āt* (1:590-591 §1244).

ʿAlī: Abū al-Ḥasan ʿAlī b. Abī Ṭālib b. ʿAbd al-Muṭṭalib b. Hishām b. ʿAbd Manāf al-Qurashī al-Hāshimī (16BH-40/606-661) was the first of people to become Muslim according to many scholarly authorities. He was born 10 years before the Prophetic mission according to the sound version and was raised in the home of the Prophet—upon him and his family blessings and peace—and was always with him. He took part in all the battles with him except for the campaign of Tabūk, at which time the Prophet said to him, by way of explanation why he should stay in Medina: "Are you not pleased to have, in relation to me, the position of Hārūn in relation to Mūsā?" He gave him his daughter Fāṭima in marriage and the Prophet's standard was in his hand in most battles. When the Prophet—upon him and his family blessings and peace—paired the Companions in brotherhood he said to him: "You are my brother."

His merits are very many. Imam Aḥmad b. Ḥanbal said, "None of the Companions has as many merits reported about them as ʿAlī does." Another scholar said the reason for this was the Banū Umayya's hatred for him, which made anyone of the Companions that possessed any knowledge of his immense merits step forward and recount it; and the more they tried to quell it and threatened whoever talked about his merits, the more they were disseminated. Al-Nasāʾī compiled many reports with chains of transmission that are good for the most part. The Rāfiḍa, on the other hand, invented many fabricated merits of his.

He narrated much from the Prophet—upon him and his family blessings and peace—and from him narrated: (I) among the Companions: his two sons al-Ḥasan and al-Ḥusayn, Ibn Masʿūd, Abū Mūsā, Ibn ʿAbbās, Abū Rāfiʿ, Ibn ʿUmar, Abū Saʿīd, Ṣuhayb, Zayd b. Arqam, Jarīr, Abū Umāma, Abū Juḥayfa, al-Barāʾ b. ʿĀzib, Abū al-Ṭufayl and others; (II) among the Successors who are *mukhaḍram* [born in Jāhiliyya] or saw the Prophet as non-believers: ʿAbd Allāh b. Shaddād b. al-Hād, Ṭāriq b. Shihāb, ʿAbd al-Raḥmān b. al-Ḥārith b. Hishām, ʿAbd Allāh b. al-Ḥārith b. Nawfal, Masʿūd b. al-Ḥakam, Marwān b. al-Ḥakam and others; (III) among the rest of the Successors a great many, among the most distinguished of them his sons Muḥammad, ʿUmar and al-ʿAbbās—the latter became famous as a courageous and fearless knight [...].

He was one of the members of the *shūrā* whom ʿUmar had stipulated [for caliphate], so ʿAbd al-Raḥmān b. ʿAwf offered it to him and made conditions, part of which he refused; so ʿAbd al-Raḥmān went over to ʿUthmān, who accepted, whereupon he was made caliph. ʿAlī consented and pledged to ʿUthmān. [...] When ʿUthmān was killed people gave him their pledge, after which a group of the Companions demanded reparation for ʿUthmān's murder, among them Ṭalḥa, al-Zubayr and ʿĀʾisha, at which time the notorious battle of the Camel took place. Then Muʿāwiya rose among the people of Syro-Palestine—he had been its governor under ʿUthmān and under ʿUmar before that—similarly demanding reparation, and thus the battle of Ṣiffīn took place. [...] His opponents held that they should catch the killers and he should execute them; but he deemed that punishment without actual prosecution and establishment of a clear proof was indefensible. Each party applied juridical exertion while a group of the Companions did not take part in any of the conflict. Then the killing of ʿAmmār showed that the side of right was ʿAlī's, and *Ahl al-Sunna* agreed on this. [...]

Among ʿAlī's exclusive characteristics: the saying of the Prophet—upon him and his family blessings and peace—at the time of the battle of Khaybar, "Tomorrow I will hand over the flag to a man who loves Allah and His Prophet and whom Allah and His Prophet love, at whose hands Allah will grant victory." When the Messenger of Allah—upon him and his family blessings and peace—arose in the morning, he asked, "Where is ʿAlī b. Abī Ṭālib?" They replied, "He is suffering from ophthalmia." He was brought and the Prophet spat into his eyes, supplicated for him and he was cured. He gave him the flag [...] after which the last of the people had hardly gotten up before Allah gave them victory. He also sent him to recite Barāʾa to the Quraysh and said, "None is to go except a man who is part of me and I am part of him." He also said to ʿAlī: "You are my bondsman in this world and the next." He also placed his garment over ʿAlī, Fāṭima, al-Ḥasan and al-Ḥusayn, saying *Allah wishes but to remove uncleanness far from you, O Folk of the Household, and cleanse you with a thorough cleansing!* (al-Aḥzāb 33:33). ʿAlī wore his garment and slept in his place at the time the pagans had plotted to kill the Prophet—upon him and his family blessings and peace. [...] He said to him, "You are the patron of every believer after me." He blocked all the doors [to the mosque] except the door of ʿAlī, so he could enter the mosque in a state of major ritual impurity as that was his path and he had no other path. He also said, "Whoever I am patron to, now ʿAlī is his patron." [...]

Yaḥyā b. Saʿīd al-Anṣārī said, as related from Saʿīd b. al-Musayyib: 'Umar used to seek refuge in Allah from any problem that Abu Ḥasan could not solve. Saʿīd b. Jubayr said that Ibn ʿAbbās would say: "When a way up comes to us from ʿAlī, we look no other way." Wahb b. ʿAbd Allāh said, as narrated from Abal-Ṭufayl: "ʿAlī used to say, "Ask me, ask me about the Book of Allah Most High! For, by Allah, there is not one verse but I would know whether it was revealed by night or by day." [...]

Al-Tirmidhī narrated—and its basis is in Muslim—from ʿAlī: "The Messenger of Allah—upon him and his family blessings and peace—has guaranteed this for me: 'None loves you but a believer and none hates you but a hypocrite.'" [...] In Aḥmad's *Musnad* with a good chain from ʿAlī: It was asked, "Messenger of Allah, to whom should we give leadership after you?" He said, "If you give leadership to Abū Bakr you will find him trustworthy, living simply in this world and desiring the next world; if you give leadership to ʿUmar you will find him strong and trustworthy, fearing no blame for the sake of Allah; and if you give leadership to ʿAlī—and I do not think you will—you will find him guiding and well-guided, and he will take you on the right path."

The murder of ʿAlī took place on the night before 27 Ramadan 40/2 February 661and the duration of his caliphate was short of five years by three and a half months, since the pledge was made to him after the murder of ʿUthmān in Dhūl-Ḥijja 35/June 656. The Battle of the Camel was in Jumādā 36/656, that of Ṣiffīn the following year and that of Nahrawān with the Khawārij the year after that. Then he spent two years pressing for military action against rebels but this did not take place, then he died.[1505]

ʿAlqama: Abū Shibl ʿAlqama b. Qays b. ʿAbd Allāh b. Mālik al-Nakhaʿī al-Kūfī (d. 61/681, 65/685 or 72/691) the trustworthy, most humble and self-effaced arch-jurist of Kufa, *mujtahid* imam and memorizer of Qur'ān and Hadith, maternal uncle to al-Aswad b. Yazīd and paternal uncle to Ibrāhīm al-Nakhaʿī. He is a *mukhaḍram* born during the days of Prophecy who became Ibn Masʿūd's top student and took the Qur'ān from him until he became one of the senior scholars of Iraq in his time. He related

[1505] Ibn Ḥajar, *Iṣāba* (4:-269-271 §5682).

hadith from ʿUmar, ʿUthmān, ʿAlī, Salmān, Abū al-Dardā', Khālid b. al-Walīd, Ḥudhayfa, Khabbāb, ʿĀ'isha, Saʿd, ʿAmmār, Abū Masʿūd al-Badrī, Abū Mūsā, and others. From him narrated Abū Wā'il, al-Shaʿbī, Ibrāhīm, Salama b. Kuhayl, Yaḥyā b. Waththāb and others. He fought at Ṣiffīn on the side of ʿAli b. Abī Ṭālib. He would complete the Qur'ān every five days, disliked to visit princes and preferred to graze his sheep over teaching and becoming famous. When Ibn Masʿūd heard them say, "ʿAlqama is not the most learned of us" he replied: "Yes, by Allah, ʿAlqama is indeed the most learned of you!" Qābūs b. Abī Ẓabyān said he asked his father: "Why do you go and see ʿAlqama instead of going to see the Companions of the Prophet—upon him blessings and peace?" He replied: "I saw many of the Companions of the Prophet—upon him blessings and peace—asking ʿAlqama questions and fatwas." Abū Nuʿaym al-Nakhaʿī said he lived ninety years.[1506]

ʿAmr b. Qurra: More than one historian included him among the Companions on the sole evidence of the report which ʿAbd al-Razzāq al-Ṣanʿānī narrated with a very weak chain from Makḥūl that ʿAmr b. Qurra said to the Prophet—upon him blessings and peace: "Messenger of Allah, I do not see myself making a livelihood other than by banging my drum with my hand; therefore give me permission to sing without indecency." The Prophet did not give him permission and ordered him to seek a licit means of livelihood, saying: "That is jihad in the path of Allah."[1507]

Anas b. Mālik b. al-Naḍr b. Ḍamḍam al-Najjārī (10BH-90/613-709), Abū Ḥamza al-Anṣārī al-Khazrajī, was the servant of the Messenger of Allah—upon him and his house blessings and

[1506] Al-Dhahabī, *Siyar* (4:53-61 §14).
[1507] Ibn Ḥajar, *Iṣāba* (5:11-12 §5937).

peace—and one of those who narrated very abundantly from him. It is soundly established (i) that he said, "The Prophet—upon him and his house blessings and peace—came to Medina when I was 10;" (ii) that his mother Umm Sulaym brought him to the Prophet—upon him and his house blessings and peace—when he arrived and said to him, "This is Anas, a boy who will serve you," and he accepted him; (iii) and that he nicknamed him Abū Ḥamza ("Sourish") because he was holding a certain vegetable in his hand at the time. The Prophet would joke with him and call him "O Big-Eared!" (*ya dhāl-udhunayn*).

Muḥammad b. ʿAbd Allāh al-Anṣārī said: "Anas went out with the Messenger of Allāh—upon him and his house blessings and peace—to Badr as a boy, serving him. My father informed me, from a freedman that had belonged to Anas, that the latter asked Anas whether he had taken part in Badr, whereupon Anas replied: 'And how would I not be present at Badr, you motherless son!'" Ibn Ḥajar said the only reason they did not mention him among the veterans of Badr was that he was not of combatant age. He took part in eight campaigns with the Prophet—upon him and his house blessings and peace.

He lived on in Medina after the Prophet's time and took part in the conquests, after which he lived in Basra where he died. ʿAlī b. al-Madīnī said he was the last Companion to die in Basra, where he had an orchard that produced twice-yearly harvests and it grew fragrant plants that gave off a scent of musk. He once said, "None remains who prayed in both directions other than I." Thābit al-Bunānī said, "Anas b. Mālik told me, 'This is a hair from the hair of the Messenger of Allah—upon him and his house blessings and peace—and I want you to place it under my tongue.' So I placed it under his tongue and he was buried with it under his tongue."

Umm Sulaym said, "Messenger of Allah, supplicate Allah for Anas," whereupon he said, "O Allah, Make his property and offspring abundant and put blessing in it for him, and enter him into Paradise." Anas said: "I have seen the first two and I hope for the third. In my life I have outlived 125 of my own loins not counting my grandchildren, and behold, my land gives harvests twice a year!" Thābit al-Bunānī said: "I was with Anas when his right-hand man (*qahramān*) came and said, "Abū Ḥamza, our land is parched!" Anas got up, made ablutions, went out into the wilderness and prayed two rakʿats then supplicated. I saw the clouds gather up then it rained until everything was filled. When the rain abated Anas sent out one of his household and said, "Check to where the rain reached." They checked and saw it had not gone outside his own land except a little, and that was in the summer.

ʿAlī b. al-Jaʿd said, from Shuʿba, from Thābit, that Abū Hurayra said: "I never saw anyone resemble the Prophet—upon him and his house blessings and peace—in his prayer more than Ibn Umm Sulaym," meaning Anas. Al-Ṭabarānī narrated in *al-Awsaṭ* [...] from Abū Hurayra: "Anas b. Mālik informed me that the Prophet—upon him and his house blessings and peace—would gesture inside prayer." He said Abū Hurayra is not known to narrate any other hadith from Anas besides this one. Muḥammad b. ʿAbd Allāh al-Anṣārī said [...] from Mūsā b. Anas, that when Abū Bakr was made caliph, he summoned Anas to send him to Baḥrayn for *zakāt* collection, whereupon ʿUmar went in and he consulted with him. The latter said, "Send him, for he is conscientious and can write." So he sent him. Anas's immense merits are very many indeed.[1508]

Anṣār: See Emigrants and Helpers.

[1508] Ibn Ḥajar, *Iṣāba* (1:71-73 §275).

al-Aʿshā: Abū Baṣīr Maymūn b. Qays b. Jandal, known as al-Aʿshā (d. 7/629) was one of the major poets of Jāhiliyya ranking with Umru' al-Qays, al-Nābigha and al-Akhṭal.

ʿĀṣim: The ultra-meticulous Abū Bakr ʿĀṣim b. Abī al-Nujūd al-Asadī (d. 127/745) was the teacher of Shuʿba and Ḥafṣ b. Sulaymān al-Asadī and one of the main seven canonical readers.

Aws b. Ḥajar b. ʿAttāb al-Tamīmī (1-96BH/530-620): The foremost poet of Muḍar and Tamīm in the Time of Ignorance until al-Nābigha and Zuhayr surpassed him. He used proverbs, spoke wisdom in his poetry and excelled in the description of onagers and arms, especially bows, as in his saying

Muted, filling the hand, peerless,
its grip could not better fit the hand.
Whenever they use it you will hear its sound
when they let loose, a hum and a purr.

Al-Aṣmaʿī said: "I never heard a better opening for a funeral eulogy than his line: *O soul! make graceful your lament: Truly what you feared has now come to pass*."[1509]

al-Awzāʿī: Abū ʿAmr ʿAbd al-Raḥmān b. ʿAmr b. Yuḥmad al-Awzāʿī (88-158/707-775), *Shaykh al-Islām*, the saintly, wise scholar of Greater Syria, one of the *mujtahid* Imams of the *Salaf* whose school did not survive along with Sufyān al-Thawrī, al-Ṭabarī, and Dāwūd, the first—with Ibn Jurayj and Abū Ḥanīfa—to compile the Sunna of the Prophet and the Companions under *fiqh* subheadings. Born orphaned and poor in Baʿlabak, Lebanon and raised in al-Kark in the Biqāʿ valley, he came to live in the area known as—and populated by—the *Awzāʿ* or "variegated tribes" in Damascus then moved to Beirut where he re-

[1509] Ibn Qutayba, *al-Shiʿr wal-Shuʿarā'* (1:202-209).

mained garrisoned until his death, his fame having spread worldwide.

Bilāl: Bilāl b. Rabāḥ al-Ḥabashī (d. 20/641) the muezzin. His mother was named Ḥamāma. Abū Bakr al-Ṣiddīq bought him from the pagans who used to torture him because of his monotheism, and he freed him. After that Bilāl kept close to the Prophet—upon him and his family blessings and peace—raising the call to prayer for him, and he took part in all his battles. The Prophet made him and Abū ʿUbayda b. al-Jarrāḥ brothers. After the time of the Prophet Bilāl would go out on jihad and he died in Syro-Palestine. Abū Nuʿaym said: "He was the friend of Abū Bakr and the store-keeper of the Prophet." Abū Isḥāq al-Jūzajānī narrated in his *Tārīkh* through Manṣūr, from Mujāhid, that ʿAmmār said: "Everyone concurred that they—meaning the pagans—wanted to harm no one more than Bilāl." His merits are many and famous. […] Umayya b. Khalaf would bring him out when the noonday was very hot and cast him down on his back in the Meccan plain, then order for a huge boulder to be placed on top of his chest, saying: "Let him stay like that until he dies or until he disbelieves in Muḥammad!" Bilāl would say all the while: *Aḥad! Aḥad!* (One!). Abū Bakr passed by him and bought him from Umayya in exchange for a tough black slave he owned. Al-Bukhārī said he died in Syro-Palestine in the time of ʿUmar. Ibn Bukayr said he died in the time of the plague of ʿAmwās. ʿAmr b. ʿAlī said he died in the year 20/641. Ibn Zubar said, "He died in our house." Ibn Mandah's *Maʿrifat al-Ṣaḥāba* states he was buried in Aleppo.[1510]

Ibn ʿAsākir narrates that Bilāl saw the Prophet in dream telling him: "What separation is this, Bilāl? When will you come and visit me?" whereupon he woke up in a fright and travelled

[1510] Ibn Ḥajar, *Iṣāba* (1:170-171 §732).

from Damascus to Medina with the expressed intention of visiting the Prophet—upon him and his family blessings and peace. Upon arrival he rubbed his face against the Prophetic grave and proceeded to raise the *adhān* upon the request of the two grandsons of the Prophet, hearing which all the Medinans came out weeping.[1511]

Companions and Successors: A Companion (*ṣahābī*, pl. *ṣaḥāba*) is whoever encountered the Prophet—upon him blessings and peace—believing in him and died as a Muslim while a Successor (*tābiʿī*, pl. *tābiʿūn*) is someone who met one of the Companions according to the same terms.[1512]

Emigrants and Helpers: An Emigrant (*muhājir*, pl. *muhājirūn*) is a Muslim who emigrated to Medina (from Mecca or elsewhere) before the conquest of Mecca in the year 10/631 and a Helper (pl. only, *Anṣār*) is a Medinan Muslim contemporary of the Prophet—upon him blessings and peace.

al-Farrāʾ: Yaḥyā b. Ziyād b. ʿAbd Allāh al-Daylamī al-Farrāʾ (144-207/761-822) was the leading grammarian and philologist of the Kufans as well as a jurist and theologian who leaned to Muʿtazilism like his Basran contemporary al-Akhfash, and like him he authored a *tafsīr* entitled *Maʿānī al-Qurʾān*.

Ḥamza: The trustworthy imam, *ḥujja*, hadith master, canonist and specialist of inheritance law Abū ʿUmāra Ḥamza b. Ḥabīb b. ʿUmāra al-Zayyāt al-Kūfī al-Taymī *mawlāhum* (80-156/699-773), the client of ʿIkrima b. Rabīʿ al-Taymī, was a specialist of Arabic and one of the "Main Seven" canonical readers. He took Qurʾān from al-Aʿmash, who called him "the arch-scholar (*ḥabr*) of the

[1511] Narrated by Ibn ʿAsākir, *Tārīkh Dimashq* (7:137) with a good chain *(sanad jayyid)* per al-Shawkānī in *Nayl al-Awṭār* (5:180) at the end of *Kitāb al-Manāsik*.
[1512] Ibn Ḥajar, *Nukhbat al-Fikar fī Muṣṭalaḥ Ahl al-Athar*, ed. Maḥmūd Muḥammad Ḥamūda (Cairo: Maktabat al-Ādāb, 1422/2011) p. 27.

Qur'ān." Ḥumrān b. A'yan, Abū Isḥāq al-Sabī'ī, Ibn Abī Laylā, Layth b. Abī Sulaym, Ja'far al-Ṣādiq, and others. Among his students were Ibrāhīm b. Ad-ham and dozens of others, the most famous one being al-Kisā'ī and the most precise one Sulaym b. 'Īsā. Sufyān al-Thawrī said: "Ḥamza did not read a single letter of the Book of Allah except on the basis of a proof from hadith."[1513]

al-Ḥasan: al-Ḥasan b. Abī al-Ḥasan Yasār Abū Sa'īd al-Baṣrī (d. 110/728) was one of the major Imams of jurisprudence, Hadith (he transmits over 1,400 narrations in the top nine canonical books) and Qur'ānic exegesis, considered by the Basrians to be the greatest of the *Tābi'īn* and by the *Salaf* (such as Qatāda) to be one of the "Substitute-Saints" *(Abdāl)*. He was the son of a freedwoman of Umm Salama the Mother of the Believers (who nursed him) and a freedman of Zayd b. Thābit, the stepson of the Prophet—upon him and them blessings and peace. His mother took him as a child to 'Umar who supplicated for him with the words: "O Allah! Make him wise in the Religion and beloved to people." He became famous for strict embodiment of the Sunna of the Prophet, knowledge, piety and simple living *(zuhd)*, fearless remonstrance of the authorities and power of attraction both in discourse and appearance. One of the early formal Sufis in both the general and the literal sense, he wore all his life a cloak of wool *(ṣūf)*. He used to swear by Allah that the true believer could not feel other than sadness in this world[1514] and was the reason Ḥabīb al-'Ajamī abandoned trading and entered the path of asceticism and perpetual worship.[1515] He defined the *faqīh* as "he who has renounced the world, longs for the hereafter, pos-

[1513] Ibn al-Jazarī, *Ghāyat al-Nihāya* (1:236-238 §1190).

[1514] Narrated from Shumayṭ, 'Abbād b. Hishām, Ḥazm b. Abī Ḥazm and others by Abū Nu'aym al-Aṣfahānī in *Ḥilyat al-Awliyā'* (2:133).

[1515] Cf. chapter on Ḥabīb al-'Ajamī in Ibn al-Mulaqqin, *Ṭabaqāt al-Awliyā'*.

sesses insight in his Religion, and worships his Nurturer without cease" and he described the vigil prayer (*tahajjud*) as "the hardest thing I have ever seen; it is the act of the wary (*muttaqīn*) and it is obligatory (*farḍ*) upon the Muslims, if only the time it takes to milk an ewe."[1516] About the memorizers of Qur'ān in his time al-Ḥasan said:

> The reciters of Qur'ān are three types. The first take the Qur'ān as a merchandise by which to earn their bread; the second uphold its letters and lose its laws, aggrandizing themselves over the people of their country and seeking gain through it from the rulers. Many *qurrā'* belong to that type. May Allah not increase them! Finally, the third type have sought the healing of the Qur'ān and applied it over their sick hearts, fleeing with it to their places of prayer, wrapping themselves in it. Those have felt fear and put on the garment of sadness. Those are the ones for whose sake Allah sends rain and victory over the enemies. By Allah! That kind of *qāri'* is rarer than red sulphur.[1517]

Ḥashwiyya or **Ḥashawiyya**: Lit. "visceralists," the term refers to a sect that attributed corporal attributes to Allah and, like the Jews and Christians, declared prophets capable of intentionally committing enormous sins as well as contemptible minor ones in violation of the consensus of the early Muslims over the impossibility of either. They are also known as *Mujassima* (those who attribute a body to Allah) and *Mushabbiha* (those who liken Allah to creation).

Ḥassān: Ḥassān b. Thābit b. Mundhir b. Ḥarām al-Anṣārī al-Khazrajī of the Banū Najjār was the poet of the Messenger of Allāh—upon him and his family blessings and peace. His

[1516] Ibn al-Jawzī, *Ādāb al-Ḥasan al-Baṣrī* (ed. Sulaymān al-Ḥarsh, Damascus: Dār al-Ṣiddīq, 1426/2005) p. 29-31.

[1517] In al-Qāsim b. Sallām, *Faḍā'il al-Qur'ān* (ed. Wahbī Sulaymān Ghāwjī, Beirut: Dār al-Kutub al-'Ilmiyya, 1411/1991) p. 60 §4.

mother was al-Furayʿa bt. Khālid b. Ḥubaysh, also a Khazrajī and a Muslim who gave her *bayʿa.* His most famous teknonym was Abū al-Walīd. He narrated several hadiths from the Prophet —upon him blessings and peace. From him narrated Saʿīd b. al-Musayyib, Abū Salama b. ʿAbd al-Raḥmān, ʿUrwa b. al-Zubayr and others. Abū ʿUbayda said Ḥassān excelled all poets in three things: he was the poet of the *Anṣār* in the Jāhiliyya, the poet of the Prophet in the days of Prophecy, and the poet of all Yemen in Islam. Ibn Ḥajar said he lacked bravery.

In the two *Ṣaḥīḥ*s through Saʿīd b. al-Musayyib: ʿUmar passed by and saw Ḥassān reciting poetry in the mosque whereupon he scolded him. Ḥassān said: "I used to recite when there was in it someone better than you." Then he turned to Abū Hurayra and said: "I ask you to tell me by Allah! Did you not hear the Prophet—upon him and his family blessings and peace —say [to me]: 'Answer for me. O Allah! Support him with the Spirit of Holiness'?" [...] Another narration states: "Lampoon them, and Jibrīl is with you." Abū Dāwūd narrated [...] from ʿĀ'isha that the Prophet—upon him and his family blessings and peace—would set up a pulpit for Ḥassān in the mosque for him to stand and lampoon those who lampooned the Prophet, whereupon the latter said, "Truly the Spirit of Holiness is with Ḥassān for as long as he speaks back in defense of the Messenger of Allah."

Ibn Isḥāq narrated in the *Maghāzī* [...] that Ṣafiyya bt. ʿAbd al-Muṭṭalib was [sheltered] in one of the quarters of Ḥassān's fort. She said, "Ḥassān was right there with us, with the women and children, at which time one of the Jews came by us and started to roam around the fort." She told Ḥassān: "I fear this Jew will reveal our vulnerability, so go down and kill him." He replied: "May Allah forgive you, daughter of ʿAbd al-Muṭṭalib!

You know very well I am not suitable for this." Upon this, Ṣafiyya took up a pole and went down from the fort until she killed the Jew. Then she said, "Ḥassān! Come down and take his spoils," but he replied, "I have no need of his spoils."

According to Khalīfa, Ḥassān died before the year 40/660. Others said he died that year, or in 50/670, or in 54/674 which is the position of Ibn Hishām as related from him by Ibn al-Barqī who added, "at the age of 120 years or thereabout." Ibn Isḥāq mentioned that at the time the Prophet—upon him and his family blessings and peace—came to Medina Ḥassan was 60. I say: This is probably the position of those who say that he died in the year 40 at the age of 100 or less; or in 50 at the age of 110; or in 54 at the age of 114. The vast majority hold that he lived 120 years. It was also said he lived 104 years and this was categorically affirmed by Ibn Abī Khaythama, from al-Madā'inī. Ibn Sa'd said he lived 60 years in Jāhiliyya and 60 years in Islam, and died at 120.[1518]

Helpers: See Emigrants and Helpers.

Hishām: Abū al-Walīd Hishām b. 'Ammār b. Naṣīr b. Maysara al-Sulamī (153-245/770-859) was the imam, Qur'ān teacher, mufti and *muḥaddith* of the people of Damascus. He took the readings from Ayyūb b. Tamīm, 'Arāk b. Khālid, Suwayd b. 'Abd al-'Azīz, al-Walīd b. Muslim, Ṣadaqa b. Khālid and Mudrik b. Abī Sa'd among others. Among his students were Abū 'Ubayd al-Qāsim b. Sallām, Ibrāhīm b. Duḥaym, al-Akhfash and many others. He was heard saying in his *khuṭba*: "Say the truth and al-Ḥaqq will show you the abodes of the people of truth on the Day the sole criteria of judgment will be truth." He said:

> I asked Allah for seven needs and he gave me six, as for the seventh I am not sure yet. I asked him to forgive me and my

[1518] Ibn Ḥajar, *Iṣāba* (2:8-9 §1699).

> parents and that is the one I am not sure about; I asked Him to grant me to perform pilgrimage and He did; I asked Him to grant me to reach 100 years of age and He did; I asked Him to make me one who confirms/blesses the Messenger of Allah—upon him blessings and peace—and He did; I asked Him to make people travel to me for study and He did; I asked Him to make me pronounce the sermon on the pulpit of Damascus and He did; and I asked Him to bestow 1,000 dinars on me and He did.[1519]

Ḥudhayfa b. al-Yamān: Ḥudhayfa b. Ḥisl or Ḥusayl b. Jābir b. Rabīʿa al-ʿAbsī. One of the major Companions. His father Ḥisl was wanted for a crime and sought asylum in Medina, where he entered into an alliance with the Banū ʿAbd al-Ahshal and thereafter became known as al-Yamān because he was allied with the Yemenis. Ḥudhayfa was born there and they both became Muslim. Al-Yamān died a martyr in the battle of Uḥud and it is also authentically related that he was mistakenly killed by the Muslims there. Ḥudhayfa said to his killers at the time: "May Allah forgive you, and He is the most merciful of the merciful." When news of this reached the Prophet—upon him and his family blessings and peace—he praised Ḥudhayfa and took it on himself to repay him the blood-wite. He narrated much from the Prophet —upon him and his family blessings and peace—and also from ʿUmar. From him narrated Jābir, Jundub, ʿAbd Allāh b. Yazīd and Abū al-Ṭufayl among others; also, among the Successors, his son Bilāl, Rabʿī b. Ḥirāsh, Zayd b. Wahb, Zirr b. Ḥubaysh, Abū Wāʾil and others. He took part in the conquest of Iraq where many of his vestiges are famous. ʿUmar appointed him governor of al-Madāʾin where he died in 36/657, forty days after the murder of ʿUthman and ʿAlī's *bayʿa*. Among his sayings: "The Prophet—upon him and his family blessings and peace—offered me to choose between [the status

[1519] Ibn al-Jazarī, *Ghāya* (2:308-310 §3787).

of] emigration and [that of] helpship and I chose helpship." "The Prophet—upon him and his family blessings and peace—informed me of what was and what was to be until the Hour rose." Abū al-Dardā' called him "the keeper of the secrets of the Messenger of Allah, which no one else knows."[1520]

al-Hudhalī: The Companion Abū Khirāsh Khuwaylid b. Murra al-Hudhalī was one of the renowned poets of his tribe and died of a snake-bite in the time of 'Umar b. al-Khaṭṭāb—Allah be well-pleased with them.

al-Ḥuṭay'a: Abū Mulayka Jarwal b. Aws b. Mālik al-'Absī was born in Jāhiliyya, became Muslim in the time of the Prophet—upon him blessings and peace—but never saw him, recanted, then died a Muslim in the time of Mu'āwiya (20BH-60/602-680) or Ibn 'Abbās (2 or 3BH-68/619-688). One of the major poets, he excelled in panegyrics, lampoons and genealogies. He inherited ill repute as the fruit of his father's adultery with his mother's slave. He lampooned his parents, uncles on both sides, brother, wife, stepfather, half-brothers, tribe and any tribe that displeased him, switching his affiliation from one to another. Al-Zubayr b. Bakkār said that whenever Ḥuṭay'a came to Mecca the Quraysh lavished gifts on him, fearing his venomous tongue. On a slow day he even lampooned himself in a poem that begins "My lips will not refrain today from ill speech, but I know not whom to smear." He admired the poetry of Ka'b b. Zuhayr who reciprocated ambiguously on his deathbed. The moniker Ḥuṭay'a means either "Runt" in reference to his diminutive size, "Flatfoot" or "Farter." The author of the *Aghānī* unsurprisingly attributes to him blasphemous, Rabelaisian deathbed banter.[1521]

1520 Ibn Ḥajar, *Iṣāba* (1:332-333 §1642 *s.v.* "Ḥudhayfa b. al-Yamān," 2:13-14 §1715 *s.v.* "Ḥusayl b. Jābir").
1521 al-Baghdādī, *Khizānat al-Adab* (2:406-413); Ibn Ḥajar, *Iṣāba* (*s.v.* "al-Ḥuṭay'a").

Ibn ʿAbbās: ʿAbd Allāh b. al-ʿAbbās b. ʿAbd al-Muṭṭalib b. Hāshim b. ʿAbd Manāf al-Qurashī al-Hāshimī, Abū al-ʿAbbās (3BH-68/619-688), the paternal cousin of the Messenger of Allāh—upon him and his house blessings and peace. His mother was Umm al-Faḍl Lubāba bt. al-Ḥārith al-Hilāliyya. He was born when the Banū Hāshim were in the Shiʿb before the Hijra by three years. He is narrated to say that the time of the Prophet's demise he was ten, but al-Wāqidī said he was 13. He declared seeing the angel Jibrīl twice. In the *Ṣaḥīḥ*, also from him: "The Prophet—upon him and his house blessings and peace—hugged me and said: 'O Allah! Teach him wisdom.'"

Abū Bakra said: "Ibn ʿAbbas came to us in Basra and there was no one like him among the Arabs in dignity, knowledge, garb, handsomeness, and perfection." Ibn Mandah said: "He was white, tall, yellowish, big, handsome, of cheerful countenance, with long hair which he daubed with henna." Muḥammad b. ʿUthman b. Abī Shayba said in his *Tārīkh* that Abū Isḥāq said: "I saw Ibn ʿAbbās, he was a big man with a receding front hairline and hair down to his shoulders." Abū ʿAwāna said that Abū Ḥamza said whenever Ibn ʿAbbās sat he would take the place of two men.

In al-Baghawī's *Muʿjam*: Ibn ʿUmar would tell Ibn ʿAbbās to come near and he would say: "Truly I saw the Messenger of Allah—upon him and his house blessings and peace—call you, pat you on the head, insufflate (*tafala*) into your mouth and say: 'O Allah! Give him deep understanding of the religion and teach him interpretation.'" In Ibn Saʿd's *Ṭabaqāt*: "The Messenger of Allah—upon him and his house blessings and peace—supplicated for me and patted me on my forehead saying, 'O Allah, teach him wisdom and the interpretation of the Book.'" al-Zubayr b. Bakkār also narrated from Ibn ʿUmar that the

Prophet—upon him and his house blessings and peace—supplicated for Ibn ʿAbbās saying: "O Allah! put blessings in him and propagate [blessings] from him." Al-Dārimī and al-Ḥārith said in their respective *Musnad*s that Ibn ʿAbbās said: "I would hear of a certain hadith a man [among them] had heard and I would go and knock on his door as he was asleep so I would roll up my mantle into a cushion and wait at his door as the wind blew sand on me. Then he would come out, see me and say, 'Cousin of the Messenger of Allah! Whatever brought you? Why did you not send for me to come to you?' But I would reply: 'No, you are more deserving that I come to you,' and I would ask him about that hadith." Muḥammad b. Hārūn al-Rūyānī narrated in his *Musnad* from Abū Rāfiʿ that Ibn ʿAbbās would come to the latter and ask him: "What did the Prophet—upon him and his house blessings and peace—do on such and such a day?" and he had someone with him writing down his answer.

ʿAbd al-Razzāq said: Maʿmar informed us from al-Zuhrī: "The Emigrants said to ʿUmar: 'Why do you not call on us the way you call on Ibn ʿAbbās?' He said: 'That boy of yours is the champion of shaykhs! He has an inquisitive tongue and an intellectual heart." In *al-Mujālasa* through al-Madāyinī, ʿAlī said of Ibn ʿAbbās: "Truly we are looking at the rain of mercy through a thin veil" in reference to his mind and perspicuity. [It was narrated] through Ibn al-Mubārak, from Dāwūd—namely Ibn Abī Hind—from al-Shaʿbī that he said: "Zayd b. Thābit was about to mount his horse, whereupon Ibn ʿAbbās took hold of the stirrup. Zayd said: 'Do not, cousin of the Messenger of Allah!' but he replied, 'That is what we were commanded to do with our people of learning.' At this Zayd b. Thābit kissed his hand and said, 'And this is what we were commanded to do with the People of the House of our Prophet.'" Yaʿqūb b. Sufyān and al-Bayhaqī narrated that ʿAbd Allāh b. Masʿūd said: "Behold!

Had ʿAbd Allāh b. ʿAbbās been our age none of us could have been his equal." He would also say: "What a wonderful translator of the Qur'ān Ibn ʿAbbās is!" In the *Tārīkhs* of Muḥammad b. ʿUthmān b. Abī Shayba and Abū Zurʿa al-Dimashqī: Ibn ʿUmar was asked about something and he replied, "Ask Ibn ʿAbbās for he is the most knowledgeable of those who are still alive in what Allah has revealed to Muḥammad." Abū Nuʿaym narrated that a man asked Ibn ʿAbbās about His saying, *they [heavens and earth] were both 'ratqan' then we cleaved them* (al-Anbiyā' 21:30) whereupon he said: "The heavens were compact and rainless and the earth was compact and barren, so He cleaved this one with rain and that one with vegetation."

In Baghawī's *Muʿjam*: ʿAṭā' said, "I never saw more generous a gathering than that of Ibn ʿAbbās, nor any more abundant in learned jurists or greater in fear of Allah. Truly the experts in law were there with him, and the experts in Qur'ān were there with him, and the experts in poetry were there with him—and he presided over all of them by miles!" Mujāhid said: "Ibn ʿAbbās is called the Sea because of the abundance of his knowledge." Masrūq said: "Whenever you saw Ibn ʿAbbās you would say he is the most handsome of people; whenever he spoke you would say he is the most chaste and correct in speech; and whenever he narrated hadith you would say he is the most learned of people." Abū Wā'il said, "Ibn ʿAbbās recited Sūrat al-Nūr then took to explaining it, whereupon a man said, 'If Daylam [in Persia] were to hear this they would all become Muslims.'" Al-Aʿmash: "Ibn ʿAbbās predicated—as he was in charge of the pilgrimage season—and took to reciting and commenting [Qur'ān], so I said to myself: if Persia and Byzantium heard him they would all become Muslims." Saʿīd b. Jubayr: "I would hear hadith from Ibn ʿAbbās and, if he had given me permission, I would have kissed his head."

Ibn Saʿd also narrated with a sound chain from ʿAbd Allāh b. Abī Yazīd: "Whenever Ibn ʿAbbās was asked he would reply if the answer was in the Qur'ān or if it was in what the Messenger of Allah—upon him and his house blessings and peace—had said or in what Abū Bakr and ʿUmar had said. Otherwise he would give his well-considered opinion (*ijtahada ra'yah*)."

Ibn ʿAbbās died in al-Ṭā'if and Ibn al-Ḥanafiyya prayed over him, at which time a white bird came and entered his shroud. It was not seen coming out. They deemed it to be his knowledge. There are differing positions on his obitus: year 65/685, some saying 67/687, some 68/688 and the latter is the correct one according to the vast majority. They differed as to his age when he died, some saying 71, some 72, some 74; the strong view is the first one.[1522]

Ibn ʿĀmir: ʿAbd Allāh b. ʿĀmir b. Yazīd b. Tamīm al-Yaḥṣubī 8-118/629-736) the trustworthy Successor, leader of the canonical readers in Syro-Palestine—where his reading was taught until the sixth Hijri century—and one of the "Main Seven" canonical readers. Al-Dānī said Ibn ʿĀmir studied the Qur'ān under Abū al-Dardā' and al-Mughīra b. Abī Shihāb the companion of ʿUthmān. He took hadith from Muʿāwiya, al-Nuʿmān b. Bashīr, Wāthila b. al-Asqaʿ and Fuḍāla b. ʿUbayd. Among his students were his successor in Quranic teaching Yaḥyā b. al-Ḥārith al-Dhammārī, his brother ʿAbd al-Raḥmān b. ʿĀmir, Rabīʿa b. Yazīd and others. Ṭabarī's critique of him is counted among al-Ṭabarī's lapses; similarly other criticism of the fact that Ibn ʿAmir was appointed qadi of Damascus was rejected by the majority of the scholars.[1523]

Ibn Jinnī: Abū al-Fatḥ ʿUthmān b. Jinnī al-Mawṣilī (bef. 330-

[1522] Ibn Ḥajar, *Iṣāba* (4:90-94 §4772).
[1523] Ibn al-Jazarī, *Ṭabaqāt al-Qurrā'* (1:380-381 §1790).

392/bef. 942-1001) the greatest student of Abū ʿAlī al-Fārisī and author of many books in grammar and morphology as well as poetry and philology.

Ibn Kathīr: The Successor ʿAbd Allāh b. Kathīr al-Dārī al-Makkī (d. 120/738), one of the "Main Seven" canonical readers and teacher to Qunbul among others.

Ibn Masʿūd: Abū ʿAbd al-Raḥmān ʿAbd Allāh b. Masʿūd b. Ghāfil b. Ḥabīb b. Samiḥ b. Fār b. Makhzūm b. Ṣāhila b. al-Ḥārith b. Taym b. Saʿd b. Hudhayl al-Hudhalī, (d. bef. 34/655) was an ally of the Banū Zuhra as his father had been. His mother was Umm ʿAbd Allāh bt. ʿAbd Wudd b. Sawāʾa; she became Muslim and accompanied the Prophet—upon him blessings and peace. One of *the Foremost and First* who became Muslim early, he took part in the Two Emigrations, Badr and the great battles after it, and kept close to the Prophet—upon him and his house blessings and peace—whose sandals he carried. He narrated much from him as well as from ʿUmar and Saʿd b. Muʿādh. From him narrated his two sons ʿAbd al-Raḥmān and Abū ʿUbayda, his nephew ʿAbd Allāh b. ʿUtba, his wife Zaynab al-Thaqafiyya and, among the Companions: the ʿAbd Allāhs Abū Mūsā, Abū Rāfiʿ, Abū Shurayḥ and Abū Saʿīd, Jābir, Anas, Abū Juḥayfa, Abū Umāma and Abū al-Ṭufayl; among the Successors: ʿAlqama, Abū al-Aswad, Masrūq, al-Rabīʿ b. Khuthaym, Shurayḥ al-Qāḍī, Abū Wāʾil, Zayd b. Wahb, Zarr b. Ḥubaysh, Abū ʿAmr al-Sufyānī, ʿAbīda b. ʿAmr al-Salmānī, ʿAmr b. Maymūn, ʿAbd al-Raḥmān b. Abī Laylā, Abū ʿUthmān al-Nahdī, al-Ḥārith b. Suwayd, Rabʿī b. Ḥirāsh and others.

The Prophet—upon him and his house blessings and peace—made him the brother of al-Zubayr and, after Emigration, that of Saʿd b. Muʿādh. He said to him early in Islam: "Truly you are a learned young man!" Al-Baghawī narrated that he said: "I can still see myself when I was the sixth of six Muslims at a time there were no other Muslims than us on the face of the earth" and, with a sound chain from Ibn ʿAbbās: "The Prophet—upon him and his house blessings and peace—made Anas and Ibn Masʿūd brothers." Abū Nuʿaym said he was the sixth to become Muslim and that he used to say, "I took from the mouth of the Messenger of Allah—upon him and his house blessings and peace—seventy suras." Al-Bukhārī narrated it. He is the first to have recited the Qurʾān out loud in Mecca as mentioned by Ibn Isḥāq. The Prophet—upon him and his house blessings and peace—said: "Whoever is glad to recite the Qurʾān as fresh as when it was first revealed, let him recite it acording to the reading of Ibn Umm ʿAbd."

ʿAlqama said, "Is there not among you the carrier of the two sandals, the toothstick, and the cushion?" meaning ʿAbd Allāh. The Messenger of Allah—upon him and his house blessings and peace—told Ibn Masʿūd: "I give you permission to raise the veil and hear from my intimates until I say otherwise." The *Ṣaḥīḥ* compilers narrated the latter two. Ibn Masʿūd said the Messenger of Allah—upon him and his house blessings and peace—said: "Hold fast to the covenant of Ibn Umm ʿAbd!" Tirmidhī narrated it as part of a longer report as he also narrated that Abū Mūsā said, "We would not doubt that he was a member of the house of the Prophet—upon him and his house blessings and peace—because we saw him and his mother go in to see him so often."

Ḥudhaydfa said, "The closest of all people in well-guidedness and evidence and probity to the Messenger of Allah—upon him and his house blessings and peace—was Ibn Masʿūd. The protected ones (*al-maḥfūẓūn*) among Muḥammad's Companions—upon him and his house blessings and peace—knew that Ibn

Umm 'Abd was one of the nearest of them to Allah" Al-Tirmidhī narrated it with a sound chain. After the time of the Prophet—upon him and his house blessings and peace—he took part in the conquests of Syro-Palestine and 'Umar made him travel to Kufa to teach them the essentials of their religion. He also sent 'Ammār to be its governor and said, "They are among the elite (*al-nujabā'*) of the Companions of Muḥammad, so follow them closely!" Then 'Uthmān put him in charge of Kufa and after a while he removed him and ordered him to return to Medina. 'Alī said that the Messenger of Allah—upon him and his house blessings and peace—said to someone: "'Abd Allāh is heavier in the Scale than anyone." Aḥmad narrated it with a fair chain.

When news of the demise of 'Abd Allāh b. Mas'ūd reached Abū al-Dardā' he said, 'He has left no-one like him to succeed him.'" Al-Bukhārī said he died before the murder of 'Umar; others said earlier, but the former is better established.[1524]

Ibn al-Mubārak: Abū 'Abd al-Raḥmān 'Abd Allāh b. al-Mubārak b. Wāḍiḥ al-Ḥanẓalī—*mawlāhum*—al-Turkī (118-181/736-797), Shaykh al-Islām, *Amīr al-Mu'minīn fil-Ḥadīth*, was one of the foremost, major pious Imāms and ḥadīth masters of the Predecessors. Al-Bukhārī began his career by memorizing his compilations.

Ibn Salām: See 'Abd Allāh b. Salām.

Ibn Sīrīn: Abū Bakr Muḥammad b. Sīrīn al-Anasī a-Baṣrī (33-110/654-729 the freedman of Anas b. Mālik, Shaykh al-Islām, older brother to Anas b. Sīrīn—among seven siblings from four different mothers—and considered by the Basrians to be the senior authority of the Successors after al-Ḥasan. "He was a

[1524] Ibn Ḥajar, *Iṣāba* (4:129-130 §4945).

jurist, a learned scholar, Godfearing, a man of letters, he narrated hadith much, he was truthful and a proof in the religion" (al-Ṭabarī). "He was divinely supported in his interpretation of dreams" (al-Dhahabī).

He met 30 Companions according to Hishām b. Ḥassān and narrated from Abū Hurayra, ʿImrān b. Ḥuṣayn, Ibn ʿAbbās, ʿAdiy b. Ḥātim, Ibn ʿUmar, ʿAbīdat al-Salmānī, Shurayḥ the qadi, Anas b. Mālik and many others. From him narrated Saʿīd b. Abī ʿArūba, Qatāda, Yūnus b. ʿUbayd, Khālid al-Ḥadhdhā', Ayyūb, Ibn ʿAwn and others. He would fast one day and break one or two days. He was short and paunchy with long parted hair, wore a white turban and a signet-ring marked "Abū Bakr" on the left hand, loved merriment—except when it came to hadith narration or the lawful and the unlawful—and used to dye his hair with henna or indigo without shaving his moustache. He narrated hadith strictly word by word, like al-Qāsim b. Muḥammad and Rajā' b. Ḥaywa, as opposed to al-Ḥasan who narrated the gist, as did Ibrāhīm b. al-Ḥasan and al-Shaʿbī.

ʿUthmān al-Battī said Ibn Sīrīn was the most expert judge in Basra. ʿAwf al-Aʿrabī cited his knowledge of inheritance law and arithmetics as well. Ibn Yūnus said he was more judicious than al-Ḥasan in certain things. Abū Qilāba considered him the sharpest and most scrupulous of his contemporaries. Abū ʿAwāna said: "I saw Muḥammad b. Sīrīn in the marketplace. No one would set eyes on him except they would make *dhikr* of Allah." Zuhayr al-Aqṭaʿ said: "Whenever Muḥammad b. Sīrīn mentioned death he would die limb by limb." Sufyān al-Thawrī said: "No Kufan or Basrian matched the Godfearingness of Muḥammad b. Sīrīn." Thābit al-Bunānī said: "al-Ḥasan was in hiding from al-Ḥajjāj when one of his daughters died. I went to see him, hoping he would ask me to pray over her. He wept until his moaning became audible then he said to me, 'Go and get Muḥammad b. Sīrīn and tell him to pray over her.' At that time it became clear that he put no one on the same level as Ibn Sīrīn." Among his sayings: "Truly this knowledge is religion; so look well from whom you take your religion;" "Knowledge has gone and nothing remains of it but specks gathered up in many different vessels." Ḥudhayfa said: "Only three types of people may give fatwa: one who knows whatever of the Qur'ān was abrogated"—they asked: who knows that? He replied: 'Umar—"or a leader who is forced to do so, or an affected imbecile." Ibn Sīrīn said: "I am neither of the first two and hate to be the third."

Ibn Sīrīn bought olive oil on credit for 40,000 dirhams but when he saw a dead mouse in one of the containers he spilled it or gave it all away. Unable to repay his debt he was taken to prison and said: I am being punished for saying to a man many years ago: "You bankrupt one!" Abū Sulaymān al-Dārānī commented: "The sins of the folk were so few that they knew exactly what was wrong; our sins are so many that we have no idea anymore." The jailer would tell him: "Go home at night, then come back in the morning" but Ibn Sīrīn would say, "No, by Allah, I will not be your accomplice in betraying the sultan!"[1525]

Ibn Ubay: See 'Abd Allāh b. Ubay b. Salūl.

Ismā'īl: Abū Isḥāq Ismā'īl b. Ja'far b. Abī Kathīr al-Anṣārī, *mawlāhum*, also known as Abū Ibrāhīm al-Madanī (130-180/748-796) took the Quranic readings from Shayba b. Naṣṣāḥ, Nāfi', Sulaymān b. Muslim b. Jammāz and 'Īsā b. Wardān. He taught al-Kisā'i, Qutayba, al-Qāsim b. Sallām, al-Dūrī, Khalaf b. Hishām and others of the major masters of that discipline.[1526]

[1525] Al-Dhahabī, *Siyar* (4:606- §246).

[1526] Ibn al-Jazarī, *Ghāyat al-Nihāya* (1:148 §758). The 2000 ed. of the *Anwār* (1:109 n.1) misidentifies him as Abū 'Alī Ismā'īl b. al-Qāsim b. 'Aydhūn b. Hārūn al-Baghdādī,

Jarīr: Abū Ḥazra Jarīr b. ʿAṭiyya b. Ḥudhayfa al-Khaṭafī al-Kulaybī al-Tamīmī (d. 110 or 114/728 or 732) is one of the three giants among Muslim poets, the other two being al-Farazdaq and al-Akhṭal.[1527]

Jibraʾīl: Gabriel, the chief angel, named in al-Baqara 2:97-98 and al-Taḥrīm 66:4 and known as *al-Rūḥ* (the Spirit), *Rūḥ al-qudus* (the Spirit of Holiness) and *al-rūḥ al-amīn* (the Trusted Spirit) in charge of all revealed Scripture.[1528] His name has over a dozen lexical forms and canonical readings: Jibrīl (the Ḥijāzīs' reading), Jabrīl, Ja/ibraʾīl, Jabrāʾil, Jabraʾil, Jabraʾill, Ja/ibrāʾīl, Ja/ibrāyīl; Jabrayl, etc. (the Banū Asad substituted *n* for the final *l* yielding the impermissible readings Ja/ibrīn and Ja/ibrāʾīn),[1529] glossed as "slave of Allah" by the lexicographers. The Jews deemed him their enemy and Mikāʾīl their ally according to the glosses on al-Baqara 2:97 and the disclosure of the Companion and former rabbi ʿAbd Allah b. Salām—Allah be well-pleased with him—to that effect.[1530]

Karrāmiyya: The followers of the Khurasanian Muḥammad b. Karrām—who was expelled or jailed wherever he went for most of his lifetime—they are considered anthropomorphists who believed that Allah actually comes in contact with the upper

known as al-Qālī (288-356/901-967) which could not possibly be correct since the Qadi says that he narrated from Nāfiʿ, not to mention that al-Qālī was a grammarian-philologist and not a specialist of *qirāʾāt*.

1527 See Ibn Qutayba, *al-Shiʿr wal-Shuʿarāʾ* (1:464); Abū al-Faraj al-Aṣfahānī, *Aghānī* (8:3); and Ibn Khallikān, *Wafayāt al-Aʿyān wa-Anbāʾ Abnāʾ al-Zamān*, ed. Iḥsān ʿAbbās, 8 vols. (Beirut: Dār al-Thaqāfa, rept. Dār Ṣādir, 1972) 1:321.

1528 See al-Baqara 2:87, 253, al-Māʾida 5:110, al-Shuʿarāʾ 26:192-195, al-Muʾmin 40:15, al-Maʿārij 70:4, al-Nabaʾ 78:38, al-Qadr 97:4 and Muḥammad al-Amīn al-Shinqīṭī's *Aḍwāʾ al-Bayān fī Īḍāḥ al-Qurʾān bil-Qurʾān*, 9 vols. (Mecca: Dār ʿIlm al-Fawāʾid, 1426/2005) on those verses.

1529 *MQ* (1:157-159).

1530 al-Bukhārī, *Ṣaḥīḥ* (*Badʾ al-Khalq, dhikr al-malāʾika*)

surface of the Throne which is located in a high place, goes up and down and moves about.[1531] They shared with the Mu'tazila the view that Allah creates His will in time and with the Murji'a the position that belief is oral affirmation without conviction in the heart, so that the hypocrites in the time of the Prophet—upon him blessings and peace—in their opinion, were true believers.[1532] Their school in Naysābūr was razed at the end of the fifth/11th century yet they endured to al-Rāzī's time since they are suspected of poisoning him after he defeated them in debate after debate. Shahrastānī described their doctrines at length.[1533]

al-Khaḍir (alt. sp. **al-Khiḍr**): Lit. "the Verdant" because, the Prophet—upon him blessings and peace—said, "he once sat on withered grass and it became verdant again."[1534] The anonymous mention of *one of Our slaves, unto whom We had given mercy from Us, and whom We taught knowledge from Our presence* in Sūrat al-Kahf (18:65) is identified in al-Bukhārī and Muslim and by the massive majority of the scholars as "al-Khaḍir—upon him peace—and his full name is Balyā b. Malkān. It was also said his name was al-Yasa', and others yet said Ilyās."[1535] He is considered a prophet "by general agreement" according to Ibn al-Ṣalāḥ in his *Fatāwā* and al-Nawawī; al-Tha'labī, al-Rāzī, al-Qurṭubī, Abū Ḥayyān and al-Ālūsī in their *Tafsīrs*; Zayn al-Dīn al-'Irāqī in *al-Bā'ith 'alā al-Khalāṣ*, Ibn Ḥajar in *al-Zahr al-Naḍir fī Ḥāl al-Khaḍir*, al-Suyūṭī in *al-Wajh al-Naḍir fī Tarjīḥ Nubuwwat al-Khaḍir* and others, while Baghawī and al-Maḥallī

1531 al-Qūnawī, *Ḥāshiya* (2:109).

1532 On the first doctrine see *Anwār al-Tanzīl* (under al-Baqara 2:70); on the second, al-Ash'arī, *Maqālāt al-Islāmiyyīn* (p. 141).

1533 al-Shahrastānī, *al-Milal wal-Niḥal*, ed. Aḥmad Fahmī Muḥammad, 3 vols. (Beirut: Dār al-Surūr, 1368/1948) 1:159-170.

1534 Al-Bukhārī, *Ṣaḥīḥ* (*Anbiyā', ḥadith al-Khaḍir ma'a Mūsā 'alayhimā al-salām*) and Muslim, *Ṣaḥīḥ* (*Faḍā'il, faḍā'il al-Khaḍir*).

1535 The Qadi under Sūrat al-Kahf 18:65.

in their *Tafsīrs* and Ibn Taymiyya in his *Fatāwā* forward the claim that "the majority of the Ulema do not consider him a Prophet," which is also the view of "Abū Ya'lā and Ibn Abī Mūsā among the Ḥanbalīs and Ibn al-Anbārī" as related by Ibn Ḥajar in his *Zahr*. They differed similarly about his being alive and ageless across the centuries. A weak but many-chained report states that 'Alī b. Abī Ṭālib identified an invisible but audible supplicant at the Prophet's funeral as being al-Khaḍir. Ya'qūb b. Sufyān al-Fasawī in *al-Ma'rifa wal-Tārīkh* narrated from 'Umar b. 'Abd al-'Azīz that a man the latter was seen walking with was actually al-Khaḍir. Ibn Ḥajar declared it sound and said it was the most authentic report he had seen on the topic.[1536]

Khalaf: Abū Muḥammad Khalaf b. Hishām b. Tha'lab (or b. Ṭālib) al-Asadī al-Bazzār al-Baghdādī (150-229/767-844) was a trustworthy and ascetic erudite scholar, the tenth of the "Main Ten" canonical readers and a student of Sulaym and others. He memorized the Qur'ān at age 10 and began his studies at 13. He did not read Qur'ān from al-Kisā'ī but only the dialectical variants (*al-ḥurūf*). He died in hiding, pursued by the Jahmiyya. Among his students: Ibrāhīm al-Qaṣṣār, Idrīs al-Ḥaddād, al-Faḍl b. Aḥmad al-Zabīdī and many others.[1537]

al-Khalīl: al-Khalīl b. Aḥmad b. 'Amr al-Farāhīdī al-Baṣrī (100-178/719-794) the grammarian and prosodist, Sībawayh's teacher and the author of *al-'Ayn*, the first dictionary of Arabic.

Khawārij: pl. of Khārijī. "Seceders." Originally a group of puritan followers of 'Alī b. Abī Ṭālib who rebelled violently against his leadership. They began as a group of 20,000 pious worshippers and memorizers of the Qur'ān—without a single Companion among them—who were part of his army but walked out on him

[1536] Ibn Ḥajar, *Fatḥ al-Bārī* (6:435).
[1537] Ibn al-Jazarī, *Ghāyat al-Nihāya* (1:246-247 §1235).

after he accepted arbitration in the crises with Muʿāwiya b. Abī Sufyān and ʿĀ'isha. Their ostensibly strict position was on the basis of the verses *The decision rests with Allah only* (6:57, 12:40, 12:67) and *Whoso judges not by that which Allah has revealed: such are disbelievers* (5:44). ʿAlī summarized their stance in his famous statement: "A word of truth spoken in the way of falsehood!" They deemed themselves "emigrants from unbelief to belief" (cf. al-Nisā' 4:101) and "sellers of their own lives for Paradise" (cf. al-Baqara 2:103 and al-Tawba 9:12). The title came to describe dozens of mutually anathemizing sects that all waged armed rebellion (*al-khurūj ʿalā al-amīr*), damning (*ikfār/ takfīr*) of Muslims and conspicuous religiosity such as praying and fasting above the norm. Abū Manṣūr al-Baghdādī said:

> The *Khawārij* are considered legally to belong to the Umma in certain rulings such as burial in Muslim cemeteries, share in the spoils of war and praying in the masjids; and they are outside the *Umma* in other rulings, such as not being prayed upon after death, nor does one pray behind them in life,[1538] their *dhabīḥa* is *ḥarām* not *ḥalāl*, their marriage with a Sunni woman is invalid and a Sunni man is forbidden from marrying one of their women if she adheres to their doctrines. ʿAlī b. Abī Ṭālib said to the *Khawārij*: "Our responsibility toward you is threefold: we shall not initiate fighting with you; we will not prevent you from praying in the mosques of Allah in which His name is remembered; we do not prevent you from your share in the spoils as long as you fight along with us."[1539]

Al-Bayḍāwī said in his commentary on al-Fātiḥa: "Whoever comes short of deeds is a *fāsiq* ⁽transgressor⁾ by agreement; the Khawārij deem the latter an unbeliever and the Muʿtazila (*q.v.*)

[1538] Or one must repeat the prayer after praying behind them, neither ruling being unanimously agreed upon since Ibn ʿUmar prayed behind them.

[1539] ʿAbd al-Qādir Abū Manṣūr al-Baghdādī, *al-Farq bayn al-Firaq*, ed. Muḥammad Mḥyī al-Dīn ʿAbd al-Ḥamīd (Sidon and Beirut: al-Maktabat al-ʿAṣriyya, 1416/1995) p. 14; see also pp. 20, 24, 72-113.

consider him outside belief and unbelief both." Hence Khawārij are also known as *Wa'īdiyya* (<*wa'īd*, threat of punishment) or "Punishists" because they considered the perpetrators of major sins apostates eternally condemned to hellfire even if they were Muslims, and they also considered small sins to be major ones if committed deliberately.[1540]

They are the extreme opposite of the Murji'a who overemphasized *wa'd* (promise of bliss) by saying that a believer who sins incurs no punishment at all,[1541] while the Mu'tazila put unrepentant grave sinners in an "intermediary status between the respective statuses" (of believers and unbelievers) but stopped short of declaring them apostates. Both they and the Khawārij agreed, however, on denying all intercession—Prophetic or otherwise—to all but the dwellers of Paradise. Their sects and beliefs are described at length in heresiology books such as al-Ash'arī's *Maqālāt al-Islāmiyyīn*, Baghdādī's *al-Farq bayn al-Firaq* and *al-Milal wal-Niḥal*, Ibn Ḥazm's *al-Fiṣal fil-Milal wal-Ahwā' wal-Niḥal* and Shahrastānī's *Milal wal-Niḥal.*

al-Kisā'ī: The grammarian 'Alī b. Ḥamza al-Kisā'i (d. 189/805) was one of the "Main Seven" canonical readers.

Ma'mar: Abū 'Ubayda Ma'mar b. al-Muthannā al-Baṣrī Mawlā Banī Taym (110-209/728-824) was the encyclopedic student of Yūnus b. Ḥabīb al-Baṣrī and Abū 'Amr b. al-'Alā' in the Quranic readings and al-Akhfash in grammar. Al-Dhahabī said he was born the night al-Ḥasan al-Baṣrī died and that he was not one of the hadith masters, yet several of them were his students such as

[1540] "The Wa'īdiyya fall under the Khawārij:" al-Shahrastānī, *al-Milal wal-Niḥal* (1:64 [Wāṣiliyya], 1:69-170 [Karrāmiyya (end)-Khawārij (beg.)]) and Ibn al-Wazīr, *Īthār al-Ḥaqq 'alā al-Khalq*, 2nd ed. (Beirut: Dār al-Kutub al-'Ilmiyya, 1407/1987) p. 362. Margoliouth calls them 'Wa'īdites' and identifies them purely as Mu'tazilis: *Chrestomathia Baidawiana* (p. 149 n. 50) cf. Z 1:106.

[1541] Cf. al-Ghazālī, *Mankhūl* (*Kitāb al-'umūm wal-khuṣūṣ*).

ʿAlī b. al-Madīnī, al-Qāsim b. Sallām, Abū ʿUthmān al-Māzinī, ʿUmar b. Shubba, al-Athram and others (but not al-Bukhārī and Muslim as erroneously claimed by al-Qūnawī).[1542] He was an exceptional philologist and reputedly the first to author a *gharīb* compendium of obscure and difficult words in hadith among 200 works. Hārūn al-Rashīd invited him to Baghdad and studied some of them under him. It is said he surpassed al-Aṣmaʿī and Abū Zayd [Saʿīd b. Aws al-Anṣārī] in knowledge of Arab history, genealogy and arguably grammar although, al-Dhahabī insisted, he was no expert in Qur'ān, Sunna, *fiqh* or *khilāf*. The son of a Persian Jew, he was an Ibāḍī Khārijī and Arabophobe (*shuʿūbī*) who authored *Mathālib* ("demerit" literature) and other works against them. His contemporaries apparently loathed him for it and he died alone.[1543]

Mālik: Abū ʿAbd Allāh Mālik b. Anas b. Mālik b. ʿAmr al-Ḥimyarī al-Aṣbaḥī al-Madanī (93-179/712-795) was the Imam of the Abode of Emigration and "Knowledgeable Scholar of Medina" predicted by the Prophet—upon him blessings and peace. The second of the four major *mujtahid* Imāms, his school filled North Africa, al-Andalus, much of Egypt, and some of al-Shām, Yemen, Sudan, Iraq, and Khurāsān. He authored the *Muwaṭṭa'* and taught al-Shāfiʿī among others.

Masrūq: Abū ʿĀ'isha Masrūq b. al-Ajdāʿ b. Mālik b. Umayya al-Hamdānī al-Kūfī (d. 63/683) was a pious arch-erudite *tābiʿī* scholar who narrated from the Rightly-Guided Caliphs and other major Companions. ʿAlī b. al-Madīnī considered him the most knowledgeable of Ibn Masʿūd's students. His narrations are found in the Six Books.[1544]

[1542] Q (3:105).

[1543] al-Dhahabī, *Siyar Aʿlām al-Nubalā'* (9:445-447 §168); al-Suyūṭī, *Bughyat al-Wuʿāt* (2:294-296 §2010).

[1544] Ibn Ḥajar, *Tahdhīb al-Tahdhīb*, 14 vols. (Hyderabad Deccan: Dā'irat al-Maʿārif al-

al-Mubarrid: Muḥammad b. Yazīd al-Azdī (210-286/825-899), known as al-Mubarrid or "The Cooler" in reference to his wisdom, was the Basra-born imam of philologists in Baghdad in his time and famed author of two major linguistic reference-works, *al-Kāmil* and *al-Muqtaḍab*, among other works. He is also known as al-Mubarrad.

Muḥammad b. al-Ḥasan: Abū ʿAbd Allāh Muḥammad b. al-Ḥasan b. Farqad al-Ḥarastānī *thumma* al-Wāsiṭī al-Shaybānī—*mawlāhum*—al-Kūfī (132-189/ca.749-805), the godly Syrian-born *mujtahid* imam, *faqīh*, and mufti of the Irāqis who became, with Abū Yūsuf (113-182/731-798)—his second teacher, whom he succeeded as head judge for Hārūn al-Rashīd—the spokesman of the School of their teacher Abū Ḥanīfa so that they are known as "the Two Colleagues" *(al-ṣāḥibān)*.

Mujāhid: Abū al-Ḥajjāj Mujāhid b. Jabr al-Makkī al-Qurashī al-Makhzūmī *mawlāhum* (21-102/642-721) was a major commentator of the Qur'ān, jurist and hadith master of the *Tābiʿīn*. Ibn Saʿd relates in his *Ṭabaqāt* and elsewhere that he went over the explanation of the Qur'ān together with Ibn ʿAbbās thirty times. Al-Aʿmash said: "Mujāhid was like someone who carried a treasure: whenever he spoke, pearls came out of his mouth." After praising him in similar terms al-Dhahabī said in his *Mīzān al-Iʿtidāl* and *Siyar Aʿlām al-Nubalā'*:

> He has certain strange sayings pertaining to knowledge and exegesis which are disclaimed and condemned. A report has reached us whereby he went to Babel and asked its governor to show him [the angels] Hārūt and Mārūt. Mujāhid said: "The governor sent a Jew to go with me until we arrived at a grotto under the earth and he showed them to me. They were suspended upside down. I said: 'I believe in the One Who created the two of you.' At that time they shuddered,

Niẓāmiyya, 1327/1909; rept. Beirut: Dār al-Fikr, 1984) 10:109-111 §205.

and both I and the Jew fainted. We came to after a while, and the Jew said to me: You nearly caused our death!"

Al-Dhahabī also quotes al-A'mash's judgment of Mujāhid's *Tafsīr* whereby Mujāhid was among those who narrate from the books of *Ahl al-Kitāb*. Al-Dhahabī then proceeds to mention Mujāhid's established commentary on the verse of the Exalted Station as one of the most objectionable statements he made: "The saying of Allah: *It may be that your Nurturer will raise you to an Exalted Station* (al-Isrā' 17:79) means He will seat the Prophet with Him on His Throne *(yujlisuhu ma'ahu 'alā 'arshih)*." Far from deeming this report objectionable, however, al-Ṭabarī defends it at length in his own *Tafsīr* of the same verse. Among Mujāhid's famous sayings: "There is no creature of Allah but you may take or leave what they said except the Prophet."[1545]

Muʿtazila: pl. of Muʿtazili. "Isolationists." A sect that made human reason the ultimate criterion of truth, forged a political alliance with the Shīʿa and, like them, held the Qur'an to be created and the Divine Attributes to be null in themselves and to mean none other than the Essence. They held that once in hellfire always in hellfire and therefore denied Prophetic intercession *(shafā'a)* as well as the miraculous gifts (*karāmāt*) of the *awliyā'*. "All Muʿtazilīs are Qadarīs but not vice-versa" (al-Maghnīsāwī). They devised five principles integral to their creed:

(i) In the chapter of *tawḥīd* the Muʿtazila—and the Shīʿa in their wake—held that Allah cannot be seen at all whether in the world or on the Day of Resurrection, as that would necessitate corporeality and direction for Him. In contrast, *Ahl al-Sunna* held that Allah will be seen by the believers on the

[1545] Narrated from Mujāhid and also from al-Ḥakam ibn 'Utayba by Ibn Ḥazm in *al-Iḥkām fī Uṣūl al-Aḥkām*, ed. Aḥmad Muḥammad Shākir, 8 vols. in 2 (Cairo: Maṭba'at al-'Āṣima, 1388/1968; rept. Beirut: Dār al-Āfāq al-Jadīda, 1980) 6:29-293 and Ibn 'Abd al-Barr in *al-Jāmi' fī Bayān al-'Ilm* (2:925-926 §1761-1765). See also Abū Nu'aym, *Ḥilyat al-Awliyā'* (3:280).

Day of Resurrection without our specifying how. Furthermore, they—and the Shīʿa in their wake—held that the Attributes are none other than the Essence—"otherwise," they claimed, "there would be a multiplicity of pre-eternal entities" *(taʿaddud al-qudamā')*; whereas for *Ahl al-Sunna* "what is impossible is that the beginningless essence(s) be multiple —not the Attributes of a single essence" (al-Būṭī).[1546]

(ii) In the chapter of Divine justice *(al-ʿadl)*, the Muʿtazila— and the Qadariyya, Shīʿa and Christians likewise—held that Allah cannot possibly create the evil deeds of His slaves, therefore they are in charge of their own destinies and create the latter themselves through a power which He deposited in them. This belief is the core of Qadarism and was refuted by al-Bukhārī in his *Khalq Afʿāl al-ʿIbād*, al-Ashʿarī in *Khalq al-Aʿmal* and his student Ibn Khafīf in *al-ʿAqīda al-Ṣaḥīḥa*.

(iii) In the chapter of reward and punishment the Muʿtazila held that Allah *of necessity* must reward those who do good and punish those who do evil; that Muslims who commit grave sins and die without repentence will remain in Hellfire eternally; that Prophetic intercession cannot bring out anyone from hellfire; *Ahl al-Sunna* held that Allah rewards and punishes without being obliged to do so; that no Muslim whatsoever remains in hellfire eternally and that the Prophet's intercession is firmly established by mass transmission.

(iv) In the chapter of *īmān* the Muʿtazila held that grave sinners were considered neither believers nor disbelievers and so construed for them a "half-way status" *(al-manzila bayn al-manzilatayn)*. They claimed that grave sinners belonged eternally in hellfire—as mentioned in the previous heading —but in a less harsh situation than pure unbelievers.

(v) In the chapter of commanding goodness and forbidding evil the Muʿtazila held, as do *Ahl al-Sunna* and the Shīʿa, that such is obligatory upon believers. However, in deriving this and the previous four headings, the Muʿtazila and Shīʿa gave precedence to reason and reason-based methods over the

1546 Muḥammad Saʿīd al-Būṭī, *Kubrā al-Yaqīniyyāt* (p. 119 n. 1).

Sunna, the Sunna-based principles of the imams of the *Salaf* and the Consensus of the Companions and *Salaf*. They picked and chose whatever verses and narrations suited their views and rejected the rest either through manipulation of meaning or through flat denial of transmissive authenticity, as did the rest of the sects with limited or no knowledge of the Sunna and its methodology and probativeness.[1547]

al-Nābigha: Abū Umāma Ziyād b. Muʿāwiya b. Ḍabāb al-Muḍarī al-Ghaṭafānī (d. 18BH/604) was a major Jāhilī poets from the Hijaz, nicknamed al-Nābigha (Prodigy) for his brilliant style.[1548]

Nāfiʿ: Abū Ruwaym Nāfiʿ b. ʿAbd al-Raḥmān b. Abī Nuʿaym al-Madanī (d. 169/786) transmitted the Qurʾān from Abū Jaʿfar Ibn al-Qaʿqāʿ (the ninth of the "Main Ten" canonical readers) and seventy of the *Tābiʿīn* among the students of Ibn ʿAbbās, Abū Hurayra and Ubay b. Kaʿb, then went on to become one of the "Main Seven" canonical readers. The most famous narrations from him are those of Warsh and Qālūn.

People of the *Qibla*: The Muslims, as all pray toward the same direction or *qibla*.

Qunbul: Ibn Kathīr's student Abū ʿUmar Muḥammad b. ʿAbd al-Raḥmān b. Khālid al-Makhzūmī al-Makkī (d. 291/904), one of the canonical readers.

Quṭrub: Abū ʿAlī Muḥammad b. al-Mustanīr al-Baṣrī, known as Quṭrub (d. 206/821) took grammar from Sībawayh and *kalām* from the Muʿtazili al-Naẓẓām. He died in Baghdad. Among his many works: *Maʿānī al-Qurʾān*, *Gharīb al-Āthār*, and *al-Ishtiqāq*. Finding him at his door early every morning Sībawayh would say to him: "You are a real *quṭrub* (night-owl)!"[1549]

[1547] See for example note 914 above.

[1548] Kaḥḥāla, *Muʿjam al-Muʾallifīn* (4:188-189).

[1549] Al-Qūnawī, *Ḥāshiyat al-Qūnawī ʿalā Tafsīr al-Imām al-Bayḍāwī*, ed. ʿAbd Allāh Maḥmūd ʿUmar (Beirut: Dār al-Kutub al-ʿIlmiyya, 1422/2001) 1:354.

Ru'ba: b. 'Abd Allāh al-'Ajjāj b. Ru'ba al-Tamīmī al-Sa'dī (d. 145/762) was a Basrian *rajaz* poet of the first rank—as was his father 'Abd Allāh al-Ṭawīl—and imam of language whose life spanned both the Umayyad and Abbasid rules. He died in the desert, at which time al-Khalīl said: "We have buried poetry, language and purity of style."[1550]

Ruways: Abū 'Abd Allāh Muḥammad b. al-Mutawakkil al-Lu'lu'ī al-Baṣrī (d. 238/ca.852), among the foremost students of Ya'qūb the great canonical reader.

Salmān: Salmān al-Fārisī, Abū 'Abd Allāh the Persian (d. 32?/ 653?), was also called Salmān b. al-Islām and Salmān al-Khayr. He hailed from Rām Hurmuz or, it is also said, from Ispahan. He had heard that the Prophet—upon him and his house blessings and peace—would be sent forth so he went out in search of him. He was captured and sold in Medina and thus he worked as a slave until his first great battle, which was The Trench. He also took part in the rest of the battles and the conquests of Iraq. Ibn 'Abd al-Barr said it is said he also took part in Badr.

He was learned and ascetic. From him narrated Anas, Ka'b b. 'Ujra, Ibn 'Abbās, Abū Sa'īd and others of the Companions and, among the Successors, Abū 'Uthmān al-Nahdī, Ṭāriq b. Shihāb, Sa'īd b. Wahb, and others who came after them. It was also said his name was Mābih b. Būd. Ibn Mājah narrated it with his chain and even adduced a lineage for him. It was said he met 'Īsā b. Maryam or rather—as was also said—the latter's legatee. His story to that effect is narrated through many routes, among its most authentic is what Aḥmad narrated of his own recounting. In the thread of his account of how he became Muslim there are divergences that are difficult to reconcile. Al-Bukhārī narrated from him that he passed through two to three dozen

[1550] al-Baghdādī, *Khizānat al-Adab* (1:90-91).

masters. Al-Dhahabī said, "I found different statements regarding his age all indicating that he had passed 250 years of age; they only differ as to how much older than that he was. Then I revised that finding and it became apparent to me that he did not live beyond the age of 80." Ibn Ḥajar commented, "If what they mentioned is true it would be one of those breaches of custom with respect to him; who can object? Indeed, Abū al-Shaykh narrated in *Ṭabaqāt al-Aṣbahāniyyīn* through al-ʿAbbās b. Yazīd that the latter said: 'The people of learning hold that Salmān lived 350 years. As for 250, they consider it beyond doubt.'"

Abū Rabīʿa al-Iyādī said, from Abū Burayda, from his father, that the Prophet—upon him and his house blessings and peace—said, "Truly Allah loves, among my Companions, four" and he mentioned him among them. Sulaymān b. al-Mughīra said, from Ḥumayd b. Hilāl, that the Prophet—upon him and his house blessings and peace—made Abū al-Dardā' and Salmān brothers. The same is found in Bukhārī in the hadith of Abū Juḥayfa on his story, which contains this passage: "The Prophet—upon him and his house blessings and peace—said to Abū al-Dardā': 'Salmān has more understanding (*afqah*) than you.'"

After the conquest of Iraq he was made governor of Madā'in and is buried there. When the state donation went out to him he would give it all away in charity. He used to weave palm leaves and eat from the earnings of his hand. He died in the year 36/657 per Abū 'Ubayd or 37 per Khalīfa; but 'Abd al-Razzāq narrated from Anas that "Ibn Masʿūd went in to see Salmān on his deathbed," which shows he died before Ibn Masʿūd, who died before 34. So it would seem Salmān died in 33 or 32.[1551]

[1551] Ibn Ḥajar, *Iṣāba* (3:113-114 §3350). al-Dhahabī's *Juz' fīhi Ahl al-Mi'ā*, ed. Abū Yaḥyā al-Kandarī and Abū 'Abd Allāh Būqurayṣ (Beirut: Dār Ibn Ḥazm, 1417/1997), p. 31 §1 has: "It became apparent to me that he did not reach 90 years of age."

al-Shāfiʿī: Abū ʿAbd Allāh Muḥammad b. Idrīs b. al-ʿAbbās b. ʿUthmān b. Shāfiʿ b. al-Sā'ib b. ʿUbayd b. ʿAbd Yazīd b. Hāshim b. al-Muṭṭalib b. ʿAbd Manāf b. Quṣay, al-Imām al-Shāfiʿī al-Ḥijāzī al-Makkī al-Azdī al-Qurashī al-Hāshimī al-Muṭṭalibī (150-204/767-819), the offspring of the House of the Prophet—upon him blessings and peace, peerless one of the great *mujtahid* Imāms and jurisprudent *par excellence*, the scrupulously pious ascetic and Friend of Allah, praised by Aḥmad b. Ḥanbal as "like the sun over the world and good health for people—do these two have replacements or successors?"[1552] He laid down the foundations of *fiqh* in his *Risāla*, which he said he revised and re-read eighty times, then said: "Only the Book of Allah Most High is perfect and free from error."[1553]

al-Shammākh: Al-Shammākh b. Ḍirār b. Ḥarmala al-Māzinī al-Dhabyānī al-Ghaṭafānī (d. 22/643)—also called Maʿqil b. Ḍirār, whereby Shammākh (Lofty) is his nickname—was a *mukhaḍram* (*Jāhiliyya*-born Muslim) poet famed as an extemporizer in the *rajaz* ("Trembling") meter and for his unrivaled descriptions of shooting bows and wild asses, a contemporary of Labīd and al-Nābigha. He fought at al-Qādisiyya and died in the Mawqān campaign. His brother Muzarrid was also a famed poet.[1554]

Shuʿayb: Shuʿayb b. Mīkā'īl b. Yasjur b. Madyan b. Ibrāhīm, the prophet sent to the people of Madyan (Midian) who, like him, descended from the same-named son of the prophet Ibrāhīm—upon them peace. He was nicknamed *khaṭīb al-anbiyā'* (orator of prophets) because of the excellent way he preached to his nation.[1555]

[1552] Cited by Ibn ʿAbd al-Barr, *al-Intiqā' fī Faḍā'il al-A'immat al-Thalāthat al-Fuqahā'*, ed. ʿAbd al-Fattāḥ Abū Ghudda (Beirut: Dār al-Bashā'ir al-Islāmiyya, 1997) p. 125.

[1553] See more in our *Four Imams and Their Schools*.

[1554] Cf. Ibn Qutayba, *al-Shiʿr wal-Shuʿarā'* (1:315-319).

[1555] Bayḍāwī, *Anwār al-Tanzīl* under al-Aʿrāf 7:85.

Sībawayh: Abū Bishr ʿAmr b. ʿUthmān b. Qanbar al-Shīrāzī *thumma* al-Baṣrī, known as Sībawayh (148-180/765-796), is famous as the great grammarian of the Arabic language who surpassed his master al-Khalīl al-Farāhīdī and taught al-Akhfash although younger than him. He authored *al-Kitāb*, the first systematic grammar of the Arabic language.

Successors: See Companions and Successors.

Ṣuhayb b. Sinān b. Mālik b. Saʿd b. Judaym al-Namirī, Abū Yaḥyā (32BH-38/591-659). His mother was from the Banū Mālik b. ʿAmr b. Tamīm. He is known as al-Rūmī because the Byzantines took him prisoner in his childhood, then a man from Kalb bought him and sold him to ʿAbd Allāh b. Jadʿān al-Tamīmī who set him free. It is also narrated that he ran away from the Byzantines and came to Mecca where he became an ally of Ibn Jadʿān. Ibn Saʿd related that he became Muslim with ʿAmmār when the Prophet—upon him and his family blessings and peace—was in Dār al-Arqam. The vizier Abū al-Qāsim al-Maghribī related that his name was ʿUmayra while al-Baghawī related that "Ṣuhayb" (Reddish) referred to his complexion, and that he had a large head of hair which he dyed with henna. He was one of the defenseless ones (*al-mustaḍʿafīn*) who would be tortured for submitting to Allah. He emigrated to Medina with ʿAlī b. Abī Ṭālib with the last batch of emigrants that year. They arrived there in mid-Rabīʿ al-Awwal. He took part in Badr and all the battles after that. Ibn ʿAdī narrated from Ṣuhayb: "I kept company with the Messenger of Allah—upon him and his family blessings and peace—before he received his mission."

It is said that when he left Mecca for Medina a group of the pagans followed in his tracks aiming to capture him. He said: "O Quraysh! Truly I am one of your best archers and you will not reach me before I first target you with every arrow in my quiver, after which I will strike you with my sword; but if you want my property I will tell you where it is." They relented and he kept his word and told them where it was. They returned and seized his property. When he arrived the Prophet—upon him and his family blessings and peace—told him: "Your trade was gainful." At that time the verse was revealed, *And among people there is the one who buys himself out in pursuit of the good pleasure of Allah* (al-Baqara 2:207). The preceding was narrated by Ibn Saʿd and Ibn Abī Khaythama through Ḥammād from ʿAlī b. Zayd, from Saʿīd b. al-Musayyib and also through another chain; al-Kalbī in his *Tafsīr* from Abū Ṣāliḥ, from Ibn ʿAbbās; Ibn ʿAdī from Anas; and al-Ṭabarānī from Umm Hāniʾ, all in relation to the circumstances of the revelation of that verse.

The latter also has Abū Umāma's narration that the Prophet—upon him and his family blessings and peace—said: "The forerunners are four: I am the forerunner of the Arabs, Ṣuhayb the forerunner of the Byzantines, Bilāl the forerunner of the Abyssinians and Salmān the forerunner of the Persians." Ibn ʿUyayna in his *Tafsīr* and Ibn Saʿd narrated through Manṣūr, from Mujāhid: "The first of those who publicized their *islām* are seven people," and he mentioned him among them. Ibn Saʿd also narrated through ʿUmar b. al-Ḥakam: "ʿAmmār b. Yāsir was among those who were tortured until he did not know what he was saying; likewise Ṣuhayb, Abū Qāʾid, ʿĀmir b. Fuhayra and others. It was in reference to them that the verse was revealed, *Then verily, your Lord is, for those who emigrated after being persecuted then fought and were steadfast, verily, your Lord afterwards is for them indeed Forgiving, Merciful* (al-Naḥl 16:110).

Al-Baghawī narrated through Zayd b. Aslam, from his father:[1556] "I went out with ʿUmar until we reached Ṣuhayb in al-

[1556] This chain is as cited in the printed edition of the *Iṣāba*; however, the printed edi-

'Aliyya. When the latter saw him, he cried out: "People! People! (*ya nās ya nās*)." 'Umar said, "What is the matter with him? Why is he calling out to the people?" I said, "He is only calling his boy Nukhays." He then said: "Ṣuhayb, I find no fault in you except three traits: you claim Arab ancestry yet the way you speak is foreign; your teknonym contains the name of a Prophet, and you are a spendthrift." He replied: "As for my being a spendthrift, I spend only on what is right; as for my teknonym it was given to me by the Prophet—upon him and his family blessings and peace—and as for my affiliation to the Arabs, the Byzantines took me prisoner when I was little, so I acquired their language." Before 'Umar died he stipulated that Ṣuhayb should pray over his remains and that he should people in prayer until they decided on a leader. Al-Bukhārī narrated it in his *Tārīkh*.

Al-Ḥumaydī and al-Ṭabarānī narrated from Ṣuhayb: "The Messenger of Allah—upon him and his family blessings and peace—never fought a battle except I took part in it, to his right or to his left; and he never received a pledge except I was present, and he never sent out an expedition except I was present, and he never went on a raid except I was with him, to his right or his left, and they never feared to be in front except I was in front, nor in the back except I was in the back, and I never placed the Messenger of Allah between myself and the enemy until he died."

Ṣuhayb died in 38/659; it was also said he died in 39/660. From him narrated his sons Ḥabīb, Ḥamza, Sa'd, Ṣāliḥ, Ṣayfī, 'Abbād, 'Uthmān and Muḥammad, and his grandson Ziyād b. Ṣayfī. The Companion Jābir also narrated from him, as did Sa'īd

tion of al-Baghawī's *Mu'jam al-Ṣaḥāba*, ed. Muḥammad al-Amīn al-Jankī, 5 vols. (Kuwait: Maktabat Dār al-Bayān, 1421/2000) 3:345 has "Yaḥyā b. 'Abd al-Raḥmān b. Ḥāṭib, from his father" but the wording of the hadith differs.

b. al-Musayyib, ʿAbd al-Raḥmān b. Abī Laylā and others. Al-Wāqidī said: Abū Ḥudhayfa one of the descendants of Ṣuhayb narrated to me, from his father, from his grandfather, that Ṣuhayb died in Shawwāl 38/March 659 aged 70.[1557]

Tābiʿī(n): See Companions and Successors.

Ubay: Ubay b. Kaʿb b. Qays b. ʿUbayd b. Zayd b. Muʿāwiya b. ʿAmr b. Mālik b. al-Najjār al-Anṣārī al-Najjārī (d. 22/643), Abū al-Mundhir and Abū al-Ṭufayl, was the Leader of Qurʾān Reciters (*sayyid al-qurrāʾ*) among the Companions. He was one of the participants of the Second ʿAqaba [Pledge] and he took part in Badr and all the battles. The Prophet—upon him and his Family blessings and Peace—said to him: "Let knowledge congratulate you (*lyahnaʾka/liyahnika al-ʿilm*), Abū al-Mundhir!" [*Saḥīḥ Muslim*] He also said to him: "Verily Allah has ordered me to recite to you." ʿUmar would call him the master of Muslims (*sayyid al-Muslimīn*) and say: "Recite, Ubay!" This is also related from the Prophet himself.

The Imams all documented his hadiths in their *Ṣaḥīḥ*s. Masrūq counted him among the six who specialized in giving fatwa. Al-Wāqidī said, "He is the first who took dictation from the Prophet—upon him and his Family blessings and Peace—and the first who wrote, at the end of whatever he wrote, 'Signed, X son of Y' (*wa-kataba Fulān b. Fulān*)." He was of medium build and had a white beard—he would not change it to a different color. ʿUmar was among those of the Companions who narrated from him and he would ask Ubay when tribulations took place and yield to his decision in problems. Others who narrated from him: Abū Ayyūb, ʿUbāda b. al-Ṣāmit, Sahl b. Saʿd, Abū Mūsā, Ibn ʿAbbās, Abū Hurayra, Sulaymān b. Ṣurad and others.

[1557] Ibn Ḥajar, *Iṣāba* (3:254-255 §4099).

Someone asked, "Messenger of Allah, you see these illnesses that target us? What do we gain out of them?" He replied, "Expiations." Ubay b. Kaʿb said, "Messenger of Allah, even small ones?" He replied, "Even a thorn and what is smaller yet (*wa-in shawkatun fa-mā fawqahā*)." Hearing this, Ubay supplicated that fever (*al-waʿak*) never leave him until he died and that it not distract him from pilgrimage or ʿUmra or jihad or obligatory prayer in congregation. After that, no one would ever touch his body except they found it hot, and so until he died. It was narrated by Aḥmad, Abū Yaʿlā and Ibn Abī al-Dunyā, and Ibn Ḥibbān declared it sound. Al-Ṭabarānī related its gist from Ubay b. Kaʿb and its chain is fair.[1558]

ʿUmar: ʿUmar b. al-Khaṭṭāb b. Nufayl b. ʿAbd al-ʿUzza, *Amīr al-Muʾminīn*, Abū Ḥafs al-Qurashī al-ʿAdawī al-Fārūq (d. 23/644), was the second Caliph of the Prophet after Abū Bakr. He embraced Islam in the year 6 of the Prophethood at age 27 after having fought it, the divine answer to the Prophet's supplication, "O Allah! Strengthen Islam with ʿUmar b. al-Khaṭṭāb." He was famous for his sagacity and fierce stand for the truth and took up the task of caliphate with utmost diligence, to an unprecedented extent with regard to strength of character and perfect justice. He spent all in the way of Allah as the Prophet predicted and was an exceptional statesman and ruler. He was fair-skinned with some reddishness, tall with a large build, fast-paced, a skilled fighter and horseman of immense courage, and a scrupulously Godfearing leader who wept much and was martyred as the Prophet had predicted.

The Prophet said: "I have two ministers from the dwellers of heaven and two ministers from the dwellers of the earth. The former are Jibrīl and Mīkāʾīl, and the latter are Abū Bakr and

[1558] Ibn Ḥajar, *Iṣāba* (1:16-17 §32).

'Umar."[1559] He said of the latter: "These two are [my] hearing and eyesight"[1560] and instructed the Companions: "Follow those that come after me: Abū Bakr and 'Umar."[1561] "In the nations before you were *muḥaddathūn* (people who received communications) although they were not prophets. If there is any of them in my Community, truly it is 'Umar b. al-Khaṭṭāb."[1562] This narration is further elucidated by the narrations "Allah has engraved truth on the tongue of 'Umar and his heart"[1563] and "Had there been a Prophet after me, truly, it would have been 'Umar."[1564]

He was intransigent and severe in separating truth from falsehood and the Prophet conferred on him the title of *al-Fārūq*, saying: "Indeed, the devil parts ways with 'Umar."[1565] He also said: "This is a man who does not like vanity *(al-bāṭil)*. This is 'Umar b. al-Khaṭṭāb."[1566] He also had the distinction of having

1559 Narrated from Abū Sa'īd al-Khudrī by al-Tirmidhī who said it is *ḥasan*, and from Ibn 'Abbās by al-Ḥākim with a chain al-Dhahabī graded *ḥasan* in the *Siyar* (1/2:511).

1560 Narrated *mursal* from the *Tābi'ī* 'Abd Allāh b. Ḥanṭab by al-Tirmidhī, al-Ḥākim (3:69), and others cf. al-Qārī, *al-Mirqāt* (1994 ed. 10:424 §6064).

1561 Narrated from Ḥudhayfa by Aḥmad, al-Tirmidhī and Ibn Mājah with chains al-Dhahabī said were fair.

1562 Narrated from Abū Hurayra and 'Ā'isha by al-Bukhārī and Muslim, the latter without the words "although they were not Prophets."

1563 Narrated from Ibn 'Umar by al-Tirmidhī *(ḥasan ṣaḥīḥ gharīb)*, Aḥmad and Ibn Ḥibbān (15:318 §6895); from Abū Dharr by Aḥmad, Abū Dāwūd and al-Ḥākim; from Abū Hurayra by Aḥmad, Ibn Ḥibbān (15:312-313 §6889), Abū Ya'lā, al-Ḥākim, Ibn Abī Shayba (12:21), Ibn Abī 'Āṣim in *al-Sunna* (§1250), and al-Bazzār (§2501) with a sound chain as indicated by al-Haythamī (9:66); and from Bilāl and Mu'āwiya by al-Ṭabarānī in *al-Kabīr*. See al-Baghawī, *Sharḥ al-Sunna* (14:85) and Ibn Abī 'Āṣim, *al-Sunna* (p.567 §1247-1250).

1564 Narrated from 'Uqba b. 'Āmir by Aḥmad and al-Tirmidhī who graded it *ḥasan*, and by al-Ḥākim (3:85) who graded it *ṣaḥīḥ*. Also narrated from 'Iṣma b. Mālik by al-Ṭabarānī in *al-Kabīr* (17:298)with a weak chain as stated by al-Haythamī (9:68).

1565 Narrated from Burayda by Aḥmad with a strong chain, al-Tirmidhī as part of a longer hadith with the wording "the devil certainly fears 'Umar," and Ibn Ḥibbān. Al-Tirmidhī said it is *ḥasan ṣaḥīḥ gharīb*.

1566 Narrated from al-Aswad b. Sarī' by Aḥmad through two slightly weak chains several of his suggestions to the Prophet confirmed by the Revelation in the Holy Qur'ān, such as praying behind Ibrāhīm's Station (al-Baqara 2:125), covering up the wives of the Prophet (al-Aḥzab 33:53) and other rulings. He excelled at the interpretation of dreams.

The conquest of the territories of Syro-Palestine was completed in his time as well as those of Egypt and most of Persia. He routed Chosroes and "scissored Caesar to size" *(qaṣṣara Qayṣara)*. He spent their spoils in the way of Allah just as the Messenger of Allah had predicted and promised. The Prophet called him "my little brother" *(ukhayya)* and asked him to pray for him.[1567] Among the Companions who narrated from him: ʿAlī, Ibn Masʿūd, Ibn ʿAbbās, Abū Hurayra, and especially his son Ibn ʿUmar upon whose reports Mālik relied in the *Muwaṭṭa*ʾ.

His caliphate lasted ten years and a half during which Islam covered all Egypt, Syria, Sijistān, most of Persia and other regions. He died while at prayer, stabbed in the back by a disgruntled Sabean or Zoroastrian slave at sixty-six years of age. The Prophet said: "I dreamt I was presented a vessel of milk, so I drank from it, then I gave the rest of it to ʿUmar b. al-Khaṭṭāb." They asked: "What do you say its meaning is, Messenger of Allah?" He replied: "Knowledge."[1568] Ibn Masʿūd said: "When ʿUmar died we considered that nine tenths of all learning had disappeared."

because of ʿAlī b. Zayd. This narration describes ʿUmar as "swarthy and tall, bald, and left-handed."

1567 Hadith: "My little brother, join us in your supplication and do not forget us." *(Ay ukhayya ashriknā fī duʿāʾik wa-lā tansanā)*. Narrated from ʿUmar by al-Tirmidhī (*ḥasan ṣaḥīḥ*), Ibn Mājah and al-Nasāʾī. Al-Nawawī in *al-Adhkār* and others cited it as an example of (i) the permissibility of asking for supplication and (ii) asking from one less meritorious than the one who asks.

1568 Narrated from Ibn ʿUmar by Bukhārī, Muslim, Tirmidhī, al-Dārimī and Aḥmad.

He was the first Muslim ruler to levy *ʿushr*, the 10% Customs or Import Duty levied on the goods of the traders of other countries who chose to trade in the Muslim dominions on merchandise meant for sale if valued at more than two hundred dirhams. Instructions were issued to the officials that no personal luggage was to be searched, and *ʿushr* was applied only to goods that were declared as being for the purpose of trade. Muslims paid a lower rate of 2½% while *Dhimmī*s paid 5%. Other firsts mentioned in Abū Hilāl al-ʿAskarī's *Kitāb al-Awāʾil* ("Book of Firsts") and al-Ṭabarī's *Tārīkh* included: the establishment of the public treasury, courts of justice and appointment of judges; the Hijri calendar which continues to this day; assumption of the title of *Amīr al-Muʾminīn*; organization of the war department; putting army reserves on the payroll; establishment of land revenue; survey and assessment of lands; census building of canals; founding of the cities of Kūfa, Baṣra, al-Jazīra, Fusṭāṭ, and Mawṣil; division of conquered countries into provinces; imposition of customs duties; and many others. He was also the first ruler in history to separate the judiciary from the executive.

One of his famous excellent innovations during his caliphate was his gathering the multifarious groups praying *tarāwīḥ* into a single congregation. Ubay b. Kaʿb said: "This was never done before!" ʿUmar replied: "I am fully aware but it is good!"[1569] He also said: "And a fine innovation this is!" *(niʿmati al-bidʿatu hādhih).*"[1570] He was also the first caliph to prohibit the Jahiliyya practice of *mutʿa* or temporary marriage, according to the Prophet's earlier prohibition.[1571] This was confirmed by ʿAlī himself: "The Messenger of Allah forbade temporary marriage during

[1569] Cited in Ibn Rajab, *Jāmiʿ al-ʿUlūm wal-Ḥikam* (al-Arnāʾūṭ ed. 2:128).

[1570] Narrated from ʿAbd al-Raḥmān b. ʿAbd by Mālik, *Muwaṭṭaʾ (niʿmati al-bidʿatu hādhih)* and al-Bukhārī in his *Ṣaḥīḥ (niʿma al-bidʿatu hādhih).*

[1571] On the abrogated character of *mutʿa* see, for example, *Iʿlāʾ al-Sunan* (11:58-59).

Khaybar and the consumption of the meat of the domestic asses."[1572] On *rajm* (stoning as a criminal penalty) 'Umar said:

> Allah sent Muḥammad with the truth. He revealed the Book to him. Among what He revealed to him was the verse of *rajm*. We recited it, learnt it, and the Prophet did *rajm* and so did we after him. I reckon that in due time someone will come up and say: "We do not find the verse of *rajm* in the Book of Allah." whereupon they will follow misguidance by leaving a categorical obligation Allah revealed. *Rajm* is incumbent against any man or woman that commits adultery if one is married, if the proof is absolutely established, or if there is pregnancy, or confession. I swear by Allah that were it not that people might claim that 'Umar added something to the Book of Allah, I would write it down![1573]

Yet he always sought a way out from capital punishment and always tried to find a legal excuse for perpetrators so as to let them escape with their lives. This took place many times in his caliphate. He took pains to provide effective and speedy justice. He set up an effective system of judicial administration under which justice was administered according to the principles of Islam. Qadis were appointed at all administrative levels for the administration of justice and were chosen for their integrity and learning. High salaries were paid to them and they were appointed from the among the wealthy and those of high social standing so as not to be influenced by the social position of any litigants. They were not allowed to engage in trade.

He would go to the villages every seventh day of the week and, if he found a slave doing work that was too much for him, lightened it for him. He also used to go out at night searching for people he might help.[1574] It is related he once said to 'Amr b.

[1572] Narrated in the Nine Books except Abū Dāwūd.

[1573] Narrated in the Nine Books.

[1574] In *al-Muwaṭṭa'* ('Abd al-Bāqī ed. 2:980 toward the end of book 54, *Isti'dhān*), Ibn

al-ʿĀṣ the governor of Egypt: "ʿAmr, when did you start turning people into slaves when their mothers gave birth to them as free men?"[1575] ʿUmar would pray *ʿishā* with the people then enter his house and not cease praying until dawn, and he did not die before acquiring the habit of fasting permanently.[1576] He wrote to all his deputies around the Muslim world: "Your most important urgent matter, in my view, is prayer. Whoever guards it well and persistently has guarded his Religion and whoever is careless with it is even more careless *(aḍyaʿ)* with everything else."[1577]

ʿAbd Allāh b. ʿĪsā b. Abī Laylā related: "There were always tracks in ʿUmar's face caused by tears." Al-Ḥasan al-Baṣrī and Hishām b. al-Ḥasan narrated that he sometimes lost consciousness after reciting a verse from the Qur'ān, whereupon he would be taken ill and visited for days.[1578]

Although ʿUmar loved his wives tenderly and they treated him with affection and care, particularly Umm ʿĀṣim Jamīla bint Thābit al-Awsiyya – who never let him out to the Mosque without walking him to the door and kissing him goodbye[1579] –

al-Jawzī, *Manāqib ʿUmar* (p. 71); al-Samhūdī, *Tārīkh al-Madīna* (2:759); Ibn Qudāma, *al-Mughnī* (7:301).

1575 Narrated by Ibn ʿAbd al-Ḥakam in *Futūḥ Miṣr wa-Akhbāruhā* (p. 114) and Ibn al-Jawzī in *Manāqib ʿUmar* (p. 120) cf. *Kanz al-ʿUmmāl* (12:660), all with a broken chain through Abū ʿAbda Yūsuf b. ʿAbdah al-Azdī whose narrations from Thābit (such as this one) are disclaimed *(munkar)*. In addition the content itself is disclaimed, namely the claim that ʿUmar ordered both ʿAbd Allāh b. ʿAmr and his father to be lashed and insulted them. Modern writers such as Sayyid Quṭb in *Fī Ẓilāl al-Qur'ān* (3:1364, 6:3969), Maḥmūd ʿAqqād in *ʿAbqariyyat ʿUmar* and al-Kāndihlawī in *Ḥayāt al-Ṣaḥāba* nevertheless gave currency to these stories.

1576 Ibn Kathīr, *Bidāya* (7:135).

1577 Narrated by Mālik in his *Muwaṭṭa'*.

1578 Narrated by Ibn Abī Shayba (13:269); Abū Nuʿaym, *Ḥilya* (1:88 §133) through Abū Bakr b. Abī Shayba; Ibn al-Jawzī, *Manāqib ʿUmar* (p. 168); Ibn Qudāma, *al-Riqqa wa al-Bukā'* (p. 166); al-Dhahabī in the *Siyar*.

1579 According to Ibn al-Jawzī in *Manāqib ʿUmar* (p. 206).

yet his reputation is that of a severe critic of women. "What! He is too rough to live with and harsh on women!" relatedly exclaimed Umm Kulthūm the daughter of ʿAlī b. Abī Ṭālib when ʿĀ'isha asked her why she would turn down his proposal for marriage.[1580] In reality, he was intensely scrupulous with everyone and not with any group in particular, and he was even stricter with his own household—men and women. He birched one of his sons whom he had seen wearing new clothes and letting his hair down. When his wife asked him why, he said: "I saw him puffed up with self-approval and wished to teach his ego a lesson."[1581] He took away his other son's profit from the sale of a camel and poured it into the public treasury with the words: "Tend the camel of the son of the Commander of the believers! Feed the camel of the son of the Commander of the believers! Clean the camel of the son of the Commander of the believers!" He took his wife ʿĀtika's prayer rug and struck her on the head with it when she told him it was a gift from Abū Mūsā al-Ashʿarī then called the latter and struck him with it too, with the words: "Do not gift anything to my wives, we have no need of your gifts!" He distributed woolen garments to the women of Madīna to the last piece, which he then gave to an old woman in preference to his own wife Umm Kulthūm the daughter of ʿAlī, with the words: "Umm Sulayṭ deserves it more, she sewed for the people at the battle of Uḥud."[1582] He himself gave the reason for this stricter standard at home, when he gathered his entire household and told them:

> I have forbidden the people to do such-and-such. People look to you the way birds look at a piece of meat. When you fall, they fall. When you fear, they fear. By Allah! Let me not

[1580] Narrated through al-Wāqidī by al-Ṭabarī in his *Tārīkh* (2:564) and others.

[1581] Narrated by ʿAbd al-Razzāq (10:416).

[1582] Narrated from Thaʿlaba b. Abī Mālik by al-Bukhārī in two places.

> see one of you brought to me for falling into what I have forbidden the people people to do, or I will double the punishment for him due to his relationship to me![1583]

During his caliphate ʿUmar forbade certain actions out of precautionary pre-emption *(sadd al-dharāʾiʿ)*. For example, he forbade Anas from praying towards a grave after seeing him do so;[1584] he hit a man for praying while facing another and hit the latter for facing the former through his *ṣalāt*;[1585] he forbade Muslims in non-Muslim countries (Azerbaijan at the time) from dressing in the manner of non-Muslims;[1586] he forbade the fasting of Rajab lest it be confused with Jāhiliyya-time over-veneration of that month. He also forbade praying in churches whether or not they contained statues while Ibn ʿAbbās prayed in them as long as they did not contain them.[1587] When a man from Iraq named Ṣabīgh b. ʿIsl came to Madīna and began to ask about the meaning of the ambiguous verses *(mutashābihāt)* of Qurʾān ʿUmar summoned him and asked him: "Who are you?" He replied: "I am the servant of Allah, Ṣabīgh." ʿUmar said: "And I am the servant of Allah, ʿUmar." Then he struck him on the head with a birch. This went on until his head bled. Ṣabīgh said: "Commander of the believers, stop! No trace remains of what was in my head."[1588] In another version, ʿUmar

1583 Narrated by Ibn Saʿd (3:289) with a chain meeting the criteria of al-Bukhārī and Muslim.

1584 Narrated by Ibn Abī Shayba (1:106) and ʿAbd al-Razzāq (1:404).

1585 Narrated by ʿAbd al-Razzāq (2:38) and others.

1586 Narrated by Aḥmad in his *Musnad* with a sound chain according to al-Arnaʾūṭ (1:252-253 §92). Ibn Taymiyya in his *Iqtiḍāʾ al-Ṣirāṭ al-Mustaqīm* (1907 ed. p. 60) said: "This is a prohibition on the part of ʿUmar directed at Muslims against all that belongs to the manner of dress of non-Muslims *(mushrikūn)*." For some reason, this particular passage was left out of the English translation of the *Iqtiḍāʾ* entitled *Ibn Taymiyya's Struggle Against Popular Religion* (1976).

1587 Narrated by al-Bukhārī in *taʿlīqan* mode.

1588 Narrated from Sulaymān b. Yasār with a sound chain by al-Dārimī and cited by

said to him: "Uncover your head." He did, revealing two braids. 'Umar said: "By Allah! Had I found you tonsured, I would have cut off your head."[1589] Meaning, if you had been a recidivist, because they used to shave the heads of convicts (as took place with 'Umar's own son, 'Abd al-Raḥmān, for drunkenness).[1590]

'Umar disliked the compilation of ḥadīth in books, however, he commanded people to learn ḥadīth by heart exactly as they had to learn the Qur'an. He did so during his caliphate in writing: "Learn the inheritance laws, the *Sunna*, and grammar the same way you learn the Qur'ān!"[1591]

Ṭāriq b. Shihāb narrated: "When 'Umar came to Syro-Palestine the army came to him as he was wearing a waist-wrap, two *khuff*s, and a turban *('imāma)*; he took his camel by the reins and waded into the water, whereupon they said to him: 'Commander of the Believers! The army and patriarchs of Shām are meeting you and you are in this state?' 'Umar said: 'We are a nation Allah ennobled and made mighty with Islam. We shall not seek nobility and might with other than it.'"[1592]

Al-Qurṭubī in his *Tafsīr* on the verse *Allah knows that which*

al-Qurṭubī in his commentary on *Āl 'Imrān* 3:7. Imām Mālik narrated in *al-Muwaṭṭa'* that al-Qāsim b. Muḥammad said: "I heard a man asking 'Abd Allāh b. 'Abbās about the spoils of war. The latter answered: 'Horses are part of the spoils of war, and the battle-gear and property carried by the enemy killed in battle *(al-salab)*.' Then the mean asked the same question again and Ibn 'Abbās gave the same answer. Then the man said: 'The spoils Allah mentioned in His Book, what are they?' and he did not stop asking him until he almost created a nuisance for him. Then Ibn 'Abbās said: 'Do you know what this man is like? He is like Ṣabīgh whom 'Umar beat up.'"

1589 Narrated from al-Ḥasan by al-Firyābī cf. al-Suyūṭī, *al-Durr al-Manthūr* (7:614).

1590 Narrated by 'Abd al-Razzāq (9:232-233).

1591 Narrated through trustworthy narrators by Ibn Abī Shayba (10:459, 11:236), al-Dārimī, Sa'īd b. Manṣūr at the very beginning of his *Sunan*, al-Bayhaqī in his (6:209), and Ibn 'Abd al-Barr in *Jāmi' Bayān al-'Ilm* (2:1008-1009 §1920-1921).

1592 Narrated by Ibn Abī Shayba (7:10, 7:93) and others.

every female bears and that which the wombs absorb and that which they grow. And everything with Him is measured (al-Raʿd 13:8) mentioned that a man came to ʿUmar stating that he found his wife pregnant after two years of absence. ʿUmar held a consultation regarding her lapidation or adultery. Muʿādh b. Jabal said to him: "You may have jurisdiction over her, but not over the foetus. Leave her until she gives birth." She then gave birth to a boy whose front teeth were coming out. The husband recognized a resemblance in him and exclaimed: "This is my son, by the Lord of the Kaʿba!" ʿUmar said: "Women can no longer give birth to the like of Muʿādh; were it not for Muʿādh, ʿUmar would have perished!" *(lawlā Muʿādhun la-halaka ʿUmar.)*[1593]

Al-Bukhārī narrated in his *Ṣaḥīḥ* that in a time of drought ʿUmar accomplished the prayer for rain through the intercession of al-ʿAbbās b. ʿAbd al-Muṭṭalib, the uncle of the Prophet, saying: "O Allah! We would use our Prophet as a means to You and You then sent us rain; now we use our Prophet's uncle as a means to You, therefore send us rain!"[1594] Among his sayings: "Learn before you become leaders!"[1595] "Take account of your-

[1593] Narrated by Ibn Abī Shayba, Ibn Saʿd, Ibn ʿAsākir, al-Bayhaqī in *al-Sunan al-Kubrā* (7:443 §15335), al-Dāraquṭnī and Saʿīd b. Manṣūr in their *Sunan* and others cf. al-Dhahabī, *Siyar* (1:452) and Ibn Ḥajar, *Iṣāba* (6:137). This report is the basis of the *majnūna* narration in Abū Dāwūd and Aḥmad but the latter two do not have the words "Were it not...". It was corrupted to read "ʿAlī" instead of "Muʿādh" in the Shiʿi sources beginning with the *Musnad* attributed to Zayd b. ʿAlī (p. 335) and some Sunni sources without chain cf. Ibn Qutayba, *Ta'wīl Mukhtalif al-Ḥadīth* (Dār al-Jīl ed. p. 162), Ibn ʿAbd al-Barr in *al-Istīʿāb* (3:1103)—although he himself cites the true version in *Jamiʿ Bayān al-ʿIlm* (2:919 §1742)—and certain *tafsīrs*. Aḥmad al-Ghumārī's claim in *al-Burhān al-Jalīy* (p. 71) that Ibn Abī Khaythama relates it in his *Tārīkh* is incorrect.

[1594] Narrated from Anas by al-Bukhārī in the book of *Istisqā'* of his *Ṣaḥīḥ* as quoted in the 1959 edition of *Fatḥ al-Bārī* (2:494), al-Baghawī in *Sharḥ al-Sunna* (3:409), Ibn Khuzayma in his *Ṣaḥīḥ* (2:337-338 §1421), Ibn Ḥibbān in his (7:110-111 §2861).

[1595] Narrated by al-Khaṭīb in *Naṣīḥat Ahl al-Ḥadīth* (p. 24).

selves before you are brought to account;"[1596] "Would that I were resurrected with a clear account, with nothing for me and nothing against me;"[1597] "If a stray camel or a sheep died on the shore of the Euphrates I would fear that Allah would ask me to account for it;"[1598] "O Allah, I am rough, so make me gentle! I am stingy, so make me generous! I am weak, so make me strong!"[1599] "Whoever displays humility to the people beyond what is in his heart only displays hypocrisy on top of hypocrisy;"[1600] Anas said: "I heard 'Umar say as he was alone behind a wall: 'By Allah! You shall certainly fear Allah, O son of Khaṭṭāb, or He will punish you!"[1601] "People resemble their times more than they resemble their own parents."[1602] "We found that the goodness of our lives was patience."[1603] "Know that greed is poverty and despair sufficiency. When a man despairs of something, he does without it." "By Allah! My heart has softened for the sake of Allah until it became softer than butter, and it has hardened for the sake of Allah until it became harder than stone." "If it were announced from the heaven: 'O people! You are all entering Paradise except one,' I would fear to be he; and if it were announced: 'O people! You are all entering the Fire except one,' I would hope to be he."

'Umar remarked to Ḥudhayfa that he sometimes refrained

[1596] Abū Nu'aym, *Ḥilya* (1:88 §135); Ibn al-Jawzī, *Ṣifat al-Ṣafwa*, chapter on 'Umar.

[1597] Cited by Ibn al-Jawzī in *Ṣayd al-Khāṭir* (p. 241).

[1598] Narrated by Ibn Sa'd (3:105).

[1599] Narrated by Abū Nu'aym in *Ḥilyat al-Awliyā'* (1985 ed. 1:53) and Ibn Sa'd in *al-Ṭabaqāt al-Kubrā* (3:275) cf. al-Zamakhsharī, *al-Fā'iq* (4:113).

[1600] Narrated by al-Dīnawarī as cited in *Kanz al-'Ummāl* (§22527).

[1601] Ibn Qudāma, *Mukhtaṣar Minhāj al-Qāṣidīn li-Ibn al-Jawzī* (p. 426) and al-Dhahabī.

[1602] Narrated by Ibn Qutayba in *'Uyūn al-Akhbār* (2:1) as a saying of 'Umar; and by Abū Nu'aym in the *Ḥilya* (2:177) as a saying of 'Urwa.

[1603] This and the next nine reports in Abū Nu'aym's *Ḥilya* (1:86-91).

from praying the funeral prayer over one of the deceased so the latter told him that the Prophet had revealed to him the names of twelve of the hypocrites, whereupon 'Umar asked Ḥudhayfa, "I adjure you by Allah! Tell me, am I one of them?" Ḥudhayfa replied, "No, and I will not tell anyone anything further after this."[1604] 'Umar was see carrying a slaughtered animal on his back. He was asked why, and he replied: "I was infatuated with myself and wanted to humble myself."[1605] He gave a sermon when he was caliph wearing a waist-wrap patched in twelve places.[1606] He memorized Sūrat al-Baqara in twelve years and when he had learned it completely he slaughtered a camel.[1607]

As 'Umar's head lay in his son Ibn 'Umar's lap after his stabbing he said to him: "Lay my cheek on the ground." Then he said: "Woe to me, my mother's woe to me if my Lord does not grant me mercy!"[1608] The next morning al-Miswar woke him for the dawn prayer. 'Umar rose saying: "Yes, and there is no part in Islam for whoever leaves prayer." He prayed bleeding from his wounds.[1609] To the visitors who told him *Jazāka Allāhu khayran* he would reply: "I am hopeful and fearful" *(rāghib wa rāhib)*.[1610]

Ibn 'Abbas narrated: When 'Umar was placed on his death-bed, the people gathered around him, invoked Allah, and prayed for him before the body was taken away, and I was among them. Suddenly I felt somebody taking hold of my

[1604] Narrated by al-Ṭabarī in his *Tafsīr*, al-Bazzār through trustworthy narrators according to al-Haythamī (3:42), al-Bayhaqī in his *Sunan al-Kubrā* (8:200), Ibn Abī Shayba and others.

[1605] Al-Suyūṭī in *Tārīkh al-Khulafā'* and al-Dhahabī.

[1606] Abū Nu'aym, *Ḥilya* (1:89 §140).

[1607] Narrated from Ibn 'Umar by al-Dhahabī.

[1608] Ibn Sa'd (3:344), Abū Nu'aym, *Ḥilya* (1:89 §137), and al-Dhahabī.

[1609] Narrated from al-Miswar b. Makhrama by Mālik in his *Muwaṭṭa'*, Ibn Sa'd (3:350-351), and Ibn al-Jawzī in *Manāqib 'Umar* (p. 222).

[1610] Narrated from Ibn 'Umar by al-Bukhārī and Muslim.

shoulder and saw that it was 'Alī b. Abī Ṭālib. He invoked Allah's Mercy for 'Umar and said: "O 'Umar! You have not left behind you a person whose deeds I like to imitate more than yours, nor would I more prefer to meet Allah with other than your deeds. By Allah! I always thought that Allah would keep you with your two companions, for very often I used to hear the Prophet saying: I, Abū Bakr and 'Umar went somewhere; I, Abū Bakr and 'Umar entered someplace; and I, Abū Bakr and 'Umar went out." Muslim and Mālik narrated it.

'Umar had nine sons and four daughters: the great Imām 'Abd Allāh Abū 'Abd al-Raḥmān (from Zaynab bint Maẓ'ūn); 'Abd al-Raḥmān the Elder (from Zaynab also); Zayd the Elder (from Umm Kulthūm bint 'Alī b. Abī Ṭālib min Fāṭimat al-Zahrā'); 'Āṣim (from Umm Kulthūm Jamīla bint 'Āṣim b. Thābit; Zayd the Younger (from Mulayka bint Jarwal al-Khuzā'iyya); 'Ubayd Allah (from Mulayka also); 'Abd al-Raḥmān the Middle, known as Abū Shaḥmat al-Majlūd (from Lahiyya, a slavewoman); 'Abd al-Raḥmān the Younger, known as Abū al-Mujabbar (from a slavewoman); 'Iyāḍ (from 'Ātika bint Zayd); Ḥafṣa (from Zaynab also); Ruqayya (from Umm Kulthūm bint 'Alī also); Fāṭima (from Umm Ḥakīm bint al-Ḥārith); and Zaynab (from Fukayha, a slavewoman).

Among his descendants in the Middle East are the following families: Abū Bakr, Abū al-Hudā, al-Baysār, al-Tājī al-Fārūqī, al-Ḥāmidī, al-Khaṭṭābiyya, al-Khayrī (family of the famous Ḥanafī authority Khayr al-Dīn al-Ramlī d. 1081), al-Rāfi'ī, al-Zuwaytīnī, 'Abd al-Hādī, al-'Absī, 'Uthmān, al-'Arāqīb, al-'Aqqād, al-'Uqaylī, al-'Alabī, al-'Umarī, al-'Anānī, Fūflayya (tree of 'Abd al-Ghanī al-Nābulusī and the Banū Qudāma and Jammā'ilī Ḥanbalīs), al-Lādiqī, al-Masādīn, al-Nābulusī (cf. above), al-Nuṣūlī, and al-Nu'mān.

'Umar was the barrier between the Prophet's Community and the onset of dissension. His death is one of the earliest signs of the Final Hour. One day he asked Ḥudhayfa about the "dissension that shall surge like the waves of the sea" mentioned by the Prophet. Ḥudhayfa answered: "You need not worry about it, Commander of the Believers, for between you and it there is a gate closed shut!" 'Umar said: "Will the gate be opened or broken?" Ḥudhayfa said: "Broken!" 'Umar replied: "That is more appropriate than that it be let open." The narrator [Abū Wā'il] said: "We feared to ask Ḥudhayfa who was that gate, so we sent Masrūq to ask him and he said: 'That gate was 'Umar.'" They asked him, "Did 'Umar know that?" He replied, "Yes, as surely as night precedes tomorrow, and I was speaking to him unambiguously!"[1611]

Umayya: Abū al-Ḥakam 'Abd Allāh b. Abī Rabī'a b. 'Awf al-Thaqafī, known as Umayya b. Abī al-Ṣalt (d. 5/626) was one of the well-travelled leaders of Thaqīf and a jinn-familiar poet of Jāhiliyya who read the Scriptures, frequented the Christians and Jews of Syro-Palestine, shunned idolatry and polytheism and taught the Quraysh the expression *bi-smik Allāhumma* ⁽in Your Name, O Allah⁾. He disbelieved in the Prophet—upon him blessings and peace—either out of envy or out of loyalty for his maternal cousins killed at Badr, whence the Prophet compared him to the archetypal learned apostate in the verse *Recite to them the news of him to whom We sent Our signs, but he sloughed them off* (al-A'rāf 7:175) which, alternately, may have been revealed in actual reference to him.[1612] He once said: "Little sister! I am a man for whom Allah desired great goodness, but I refused it." The Prophet enjoyed listening to his poetry, endorsing some as true and critiquing some. He said of him: "He almost became

[1611] Narrated from Abū Wā'il Shaqīq b. Salama by al-Bukhārī and Muslim.
[1612] *Tafsīrs* of 'Abd al-Razzāq, al-Ṭabarī, al-Baghawī and others.

Muslim in his poetry," "His tongue believed but his heart disbelieved" and "Allah knows of Umayya b. Abī al-Ṣalt."[1613]

Umm Salama: Umm Salama bt. Abī Umayya b. al-Mughīra b. Abd Allāh b. ʿAmr b. Makhzūm al-Qurashiyya al-Makhzūmiyya (d. ca. 63/683), the Mother of the Believers, was named Hind. A weaker report says her name was Ramla. Her father's name was Ḥudhayfa—it is also said, Suhayl—and his nickname Zād al-Rākib (Rider's Provision) because he was one of those famed for generosity: whenever he travelled he would let no one come with their own provision but he would take care of all their needs himself. Her mother was ʿĀtika bt. ʿĀmir b. Rabīʿa b. Mālik al-Kināniyya of the Banū Firās. Umm Salama was the wife of her paternal cousin Abū Salama b. ʿAbd al-Asad b. al-Mughīra. He died before her, after which the Prophet—upon him and his house blessings and peace—married her in Jumādā II of the year 4/625, some said the year 3.

She and her husband were among the first to become Muslim. They both emigrated to Abyssinia and she gave birth to his son, Salama. Then they came back to Mecca and emigrated again to Medina, where she gave birth to his other children ʿUmar, Durra and Zaynab per Ibn Isḥāq. She related:

> When Abū Salama resolved to leave to Medina, he equipped one of his camels and carried, together with me, my son Salama. Then he went out, leading his camel, but when the men of Banū al-Mughīra saw him they confronted him and said: 'As for yourself you have the better of us but what about her, our kin? On what account are we to just let you roam the lands with her?' Then they snatched the bridle from his hand and took me. At this the Banū ʿAbd al-Asad became

[1613] Cf. Ibn ʿAsākir, *Tārīkh* (9:255-287); Ibn Qutayba, *al-Shiʿr wal-Shuʿarā'* (1:459-462); Ibn Sallām al-Jumaḥī, *Ṭabaqāt Fuḥūl al-Shuʿarā'*, ed. Maḥmūd Muḥammad Shākir, 2 vols. (Jeddah: Dār al-Madanī, 1974) 1:260-267. "There is no contest among the authorities in history that Umayya ibn Abī al-Ṣalt died an unbeliever." Ibn Ḥajar, *Iṣāba* (1:133 §549).

> angry and rushed to Abū Salama's side, saying: 'We swear by Allah that we will not leave our son with her if you snatch her away from our kin.' And they started dragging my son Salama back and forth until they dislocated his shoulder. The Banū 'Abd al-Asad and group of Abū Salama went off with the boy while the Banū al-Mughīra detained me. My husband Abū Salama made for Medina. I had been separated from my husband and my son. Every morning I would go out to al-Abṭaḥ and sit there, crying without cease until the evening. Seven days or so passed. A man came by, one of my paternal cousins, and saw how my face had changed. He told the Banū al-Mughīra: 'Will you not let this poor woman leave? You separated her from her husband and her son!' So they said: 'Join your husband if you wish.' At this the Banū 'Abd al-Asad gave me back my son. I saddled my camel, put my son in my lap and went out heading for my husband in Medina with no creature accompanying me. I would inform whoever I met of my plan until I reached al-Tanʿīm where I met 'Uthmān b. Ṭalḥa the brother of the Banū 'Abd al-Dār. He asked where I was going and I told him. He said, 'Do you have anyone with you?' I said, 'No, by Allah, except Allah and my son here.' He said, 'By Allah! You will not be left on your own.' He took the bridle of the camel and left with me, leading me. By Allah! I never accompanied a nobler Arab man. Whenever he made a pit stop he would kneel down my mount then move away to some tree and lie down under it. When it was time to leave again he would go up to my camel, bring it forward and saddle it, then step back and tell me to mount, after which he would come back, take the bridle and lead me on until the next stop. He kept doing that until we reached Medina. When he saw the town of the Banū 'Amr b. 'Awf in Qubā' he said, 'Your husband is in this town'—Abū Salama had alighted there.

It is said she was the first woman to emigrate to Abyssinia and the first woman to have entered Madina as a lone female rider. It is also said that Laylā the wife of 'Āmir b. Rabīʿa shared that distinction with her. Nasā'ī narrated with a sound chain that after her waiting period [after widowhood of Abū Salama] was over, Abū Bakr proposed to her but she did not accept his proposal. Then the Prophet—upon him and his house blessings and peace—sent his proposal to her after she gave birth to her daughter Zaynab and she said, "Tell the Messenger of Allah that I am a jealous woman, that I have several boys, and that I have none of my relatives to act as guardian for me." He said: "Tell her, 'I will supplicate Allah and your jealousy will leave you; your boys will be provided for; and none of your relatives will dislike that proposal.'" When she heard this she said to her son 'Umar, "Rise and betrothe me to the Messenger of Allah."

After they married he would visit her and ask, "Where is Zunāb? [Little Zaynab]" [= who will look after the baby?] until 'Ammār b. Yāsir came and took care of her needs—as she would nurse her and he said, "This infant is hindering the Messenger of Allah—upon him and his house blessings and peace—from his need." Then the Prophet came one day and said, "Where is Zunāb?" whereupon Qarība bt. Abī Umayya—who happened to be there —said, "'Ammār b. Yāsir took her." He said, "I will come to you tonight," and she prepared food for him and joined him in bed.

Ibn Sa'd related from 'Ā'isha that she said, "When the Messenger of Allah married Umm Salama I became despondent because we had been told she was very beautiful, so I sneaked in to see her and I saw that she was even more beautiful than what they had said." Ibn Hajar commented: "Umm Salama was indeed described as very beautiful, very intelligent and very wise. Her suggestion to the Prophet—upon him and his house blessings and peace—on the Day of Ḥudaybiya is proof enough of the latter."

She narrated [Hadith] from the Prophet as well as from Abū Salama and Fāṭima al-Zahrā'. From her narrated her two children 'Umar and Zaynab, her brother 'Āmir, her nephew Muṣ'ab b. 'Abd Allāh, her posthumous freedman Nabhān, her freedmen 'Abd Allāh b. Rāfi', Nāfi', Safīna, his son, Abū Kathīr,

Khayra the mother of al-Ḥasan, and also—from those who are counted among the Companions—Ṣafiyya bt. Shayba, Hind bt. al-Ḥārith al-Firāsiyya, Qubayṣa bt. Dhu'ayb and 'Abd al-Raḥmān b. al-Ḥārith b. Hishām; and from the senior Successors: Abū 'Uthmān al-Nahdī, Abū Wā'il, Sa'īd b. al-Musayyib, Abū Salama and Ḥumayd the two sons of 'Abd al-Raḥmān b. 'Awf, 'Urwa, Abū Bakr b. 'Abd al-Raḥmān, Sulaymān b. Yasār and others.

Ibn Abī Khaythama said she died in the caliphate of Yazīd b. Mu'āwiya, which was toward the end of the year 60/678. Abū Nu'aym said she died in 62/682 and that she was among the last of the Mothers of the Believers to die. Ibn Ḥajar said: "Rather, she is the very last one of them to die, since it is firmly established in Muslim's *Ṣaḥīḥ* that al-Ḥārith b. 'Abd Allāh b. Abī Rabī'a and 'Abd Allāh b. Ṣafwān went in to see Umm Salama during the caliphate of Yazīd b. Mu'āwiya and they asked about the army that would be engulfed by the earth. This was when Yazīd b. Mu'āwiya was preparing to send Muslim b. 'Uqba with the army of Syro-Palestine to Medina, then the event of al-Ḥarra took place in 63/683, and Allah knows best."[1614]

Umru' al-Qays: Umru' al-Qays b. Ḥujr b. 'Amr al-Kindī (d. 80? before Hijra/540?) of the Banū Kinda, author of the first of the ten pre-Islamic odes, beginning with the famous hendiadys, "*Stop! Let us weep at the reminder of a friend and a resting-place at the dune's fall between Dakhūl then Ḥawmal.*"[1615]

Wa'īdiyya: See "Khawārij" and "Mu'tazila."

al-Walīd b. al-Mughīra b. 'Abd Allāh b. 'Umar b. Makhzūm al-Qurashī al-Makhzūmī (d. 1/623): One of the Meccan arch-enemies of the Prophet—upon him blessings and peace—and the father of the great military commander Khālid b. al-Walīd.

[1614] Ibn Ḥajar, *Iṣāba* (8:240-242 §1302).
[1615] Cf. Ibn Qutayba, *al-Shi'r wal-Shu'arā'* (1:105-136).

Al-Walīd b. al-Mughīra was the first to be bold enough to apply the pickaxe to the Kaʿba at the time of its planned rebuilding by the Quraysh, which he did with the words, "O Allah, no fear for you! O Allah, we intend only goodness." He once came to see the Prophet who recited Qur'ān for him, and al-Walīd seemed to soften up upon hearing it. News of this reached his nephew Abū Jahl who came to see him and said: "You need to say you disapprove of it or that you abhor it." Al-Walīd said: "What can I say? By Allah, none of you who knows poetry better than I, and by Allah, nothing of what he says resembles any of that. By Allah, that discourse of his which he recites is sweet and fluid, its top bears fruit and its bottom is well-watered. It rises high and nothing rises above it. Nay, it shatters everything below it." Abū Jahl said, "Your people will never accept other than that you attack it." He said, "Let me think about it." After a while he came out and said of the Qur'ān: "This is only magic passed on, he took it from someone who passed it on to him." Then the verse was revealed *Leave me with the one I created destitute* etc. (al-Muddaththir 74:11). He or Saʿīd b. al-ʿĀṣ was the elder who, when everyone prostrated upon hearing the entirety of Sūrat al-Najm in Mecca —five years or less before the Emigration—took a handful of earth and pressed it upon his forehead. When al-Walīd said: "Does Allah send down revelations to Muḥammad and ignore me, the greatest chief of Quraysh, to say nothing of Abū Masʿūd ʿAmr b. ʿUmayr al-Thaqafī, the chief of Thaqīf, we being the great ones of Ṭā'if and Mecca?" Then the verse was revealed: *They said, "If but this Qur'ān had been revealed to a great man of the two towns!"* (al-Zukhruf 43: 30). Another verse, *Verily We have taken care of the scoffers for you* (al-Ḥijr 15:95), was explained by Ibn ʿAbbās as referring to al-Walīd b. al-Mughīra, al-Aswad b. ʿAbd Yaghūth al-Zuhrī, al-Muṭṭalib b. Banī Asad b. ʿAbd al-ʿUzzā, al-Ḥārith b. ʿAyṭal al-Sahmī and al-

ʿĀṣ b. Wā'il, to each of whom Jibrīl pointed in a vision, saying: "He has been taken care of for you." After he pointed to a vein in al-Walid's ankle the latter passed by a man of Khuzāʿa who was feathering his arrow and one arrow nicked his ankle-vein, after which he bled to death.[1616]

Yaʿqūb: Abū Isḥāq Yaʿqūb b. Isḥāq al-Ḥaḍramī (d. 205/ca.820) is the tenth of the "Main Ten" canonical readers and was teacher to Rawḥ and Ruways.

Zayd b. ʿAmr b. Nufayl b. ʿAbd al-ʿUzzā al-Qurashī al-ʿAdawī: Called "the monotheist of Jāhiliyya" by the Qadi, he was reputed to detest idols and shun the food dedicated to them. Having gone to Syria in search of true religion he leaned neither to Judaism nor Christianity but instead returned to Mecca and announced he was following the religion of Ibrāhīm and denouncing idol worship. He was then expelled by the Quraysh and took up residence in Ḥirā', entering Mecca only by night, and so until his death when the Prophet—who saw him—was 35.

Zuhayr: Zuhayr b. Abī Salmā Rabīʿa b. Rabāḥ al-Muzanī (d. 13/634): Nicknamed the sage of *Jāhiliyya* poets, he was also the son, nephew, brother and father of famed poets. His verse was collectively known as *al-Ḥawliyyāt* and he authored one of the seven *Muʿallaqāt* (poems hanged on the Kaʿba).[1617]

[1616] Al-Dhahabī, *Tārīkh al-Islām wa-Wafayāt al-Mashāhīr wal-Aʿlām*, ed. ʿUmar ʿAbd al-Salām Tadmurī, 52 vols.. 2nd ed. (Beirut: Dār al-Kitāb al-ʿArabī, 1409/1989) *al-Sīra al-Nabawiyya*:67, 155, 187, 224.

[1617] Cf. Ibn Qutayba, *al-Shiʿr wal-Shuʿarā'* (1:137-153).

Bibliography

'Abd al-Razzāq al-Ṣan'ānī. *Muṣannaf*. Ed. Ḥabīb al-Raḥmān al-A'ẓamī. 2nd ed. 11 vols. Gujerat, India: al-Majlis al-'Ilmī, 1304/ 1983.

Abdul-Massih, George and Hani Tabri. *al-Khalīl: A Dictionary of Arabic Grammar Terminology*. Beirut: Librairie du Liban, 1410/ 1990.

Abū Dāwūd Sulaymān b. al-Ash'ath al-Azdī al-Sijistānī. *Sunan*. 5 vols. Ed. Muḥammad 'Awwāma. 2nd ed. Jeddah: Dār al-Qibla lil-Thaqāfat al-Islāmiyya; Beirut: Mu'assasat al-Rayyān, 1425/2004.

Abū Ḥayyān al-Andalusī. *Tafsīr al-Baḥr al-Muḥīṭ*. Ed. 'Ādil Aḥmad 'Abd al-Mawjūd et al. 8 vols. Beirut: Dār al-Kutub al-'Ilmiyya, 1413/1993.

Abū Nu'aym. *Ḥilyat al-Awliyā' wa-Ṭabaqāt al-Aṣfiyā'*. 10 vols. Cairo: Maktabat al-Khānjī and Maktabat al-Sa'āda, 1932-1938. Rept. Beirut: Dār al-Kitāb al-'Arabī, 1967-1968.

Abū al-Shaykh. *Kitāb al-'Aẓama*. Ed. Riḍā' Allāh Mubārakfūrī. 5 vols. Riyadh: Dār al-'Āṣima, 1418/1998.

Abū 'Ubayda Ma'mar b. al-Muthannā al-Taymī. *Majāz al-Qur'ān*. Ed. Muḥammad Fu'ād Sezgin. 2nd ed. 2 vols. Beirut: Mu'assasat al-Risāla, 1401/1981.

al-Adnahwī, Aḥmad b. Muḥammad. *Ṭabaqāt al-Mufassirīn*. Ed. Sulaymān b. Ṣāliḥ al-Khizzī. Medina: Maktabat al-'Ulūm wal-Ḥikam, 1417/1997.

Afandī, Muḥibb al-Dīn. [*Sharḥ Shawāhid al-Kashshāf*] *Tanzīl al-Āyāt 'alā al-Shawāhid min al-Abyāt*. With Ibn Ḥajar, *al-Kāfī al-Shāf fī Takhrīj Aḥādīth al-Kashshāf*. Beirut: Dār Iḥyā' al-Turāth al-'Arabī, 1418/1997.

Aḥmad b. Muḥammad b. Ḥanbal. *al-Musnad*. Ed. Shu'ayb al-Arnā'ūṭ et al. 50 vols. Beirut: Mu'assasat al-Risāla, 1999-2001.

al-Ājurrī. *Kitāb al-Sharī'a*. Ed. 'Abd Allāh al-Dumayjī. 6 vols. Riyadh: Dār al-Waṭan, 1418/1997.

'Alī, Yūsuf Aḥmad. *al-Bayḍāwī wa-Manhajuh fīl-Tafsīr*. Unpub. doctoral thesis. Mecca: Jāmi'at Umm al-Qurā, n.d.

al-'Āmilī, Bahā' al-Dīn Muḥammad b. Ḥusayn. *Ta'līqāt Anwār al-Tanzīl*. Teheran: s.n., 1272/1856.

al-Anṣārī. See Zakariyyā al-Anṣārī.

al-Aṣfahānī, Abū al-Faraj. *Kitāb al-Aghānī*. Ed. Iḥsān ʿAbbās et al. 3rd ed. 25 vols. Beirut: Dār Ṣādir, 1429/2008.

al-Aʿshā. *Dīwān al-Aʿshā al-Kabīr*. Ed. Muḥammad Ḥusayn. Cairo: Maktabat al-Ādāb, [1950].

al-ʿAskarī, Abū Hilāl al-Ḥasan b. ʿAbd Allāh b. Sahl. *Kitāb Jamharat al-Amthāl*. Ed. Aḥmad ʿAbd al-Salām and Muḥammad basyūnī Zaghlūl. 2 vols. Beirut: Dār al-Kutub al-ʿIlmiyya, 1408/1988.

al-Azharī, Abū Manṣūr Muḥammad ibn Aḥmad. *Tahdhīb al-Lugha*. Ed. ʿAbd al-Salām Muḥammad Hārūn et al. 15 vols. Cairo: al-Dār al-Miṣriyya lil-Taʾlīf wal-Tarjama, 1966.

al-Baghawī, Abū Muḥammad al-Ḥusayn b. Masʿūd al-Farrāʾ. *Tafsīr al-Baghawī al-Musammā Maʿālim al-Tanzīl*. Ed. ʿAbd al-Razzāq al-Mahdī. 5 vols. Beirut: Dār Iḥyāʾ al-Turāth al-ʿArabī, 1420/2000.

_______. *Sharḥ al-Sunna*. Ed. Shuʿayb al-Arnāʾūṭ. 2nd ed. 15 vols. Beirut: al-Maktab al-Islāmī, 1403/1983.

al-Baghdādī, ʿAbd al-Qādir b. ʿUmar. *Khizānat al-Adab wa-Lubb Lubāb Lisān al-ʿArab*. Ed. ʿAbd al-Salām Hārūn. 4th ed. 13 vols. Cairo: Maktabat al-Khānjī, 1418/1997.

al-Bayḍāwī, Nāṣir al-Dīn Abū Saʿīd ʿAbd Allah b. ʿUmar. *Anwār al-Tanzīl wa-Asrār al-Taʾwīl, al-Maʿrūf bi-Tafsīr al-Bayḍāwī*. Ed. Muḥammad ʿAbd al-Raḥmān al-Marʿashlī. Beirut: Dār Iḥyāʾ al-Turāth al-ʿArabī and Muʾassasat al-Tārīkh al-ʿArabī, 1418/ 1998.

_______. *al-Ghāyat al-Quṣwā fī Dirāyat al-Fatwā*. Ed. ʿAlī Muḥyī al-Dīn ʿAlī Qarah Dāghī. 2 vols. Shubrā Miṣr: Dār al-Naṣr lil-Ṭibāʿat al-Islāmiyya, 1402/1982.

_______. *Tafsīr al-Bayḍāwī al-Musammā Anwār al-Tanzīl wa-Asrār al-Taʾwīl*. Ed. Muḥammad Ṣubḥī Ḥallāq and Maḥmūd al-Aṭrash. 3 vols. Damascus: Dār al-Rashīd; Beirut: Muʾassasat al-Īmān, 1421/ 2000.

_______. *Tuḥfat al-Abrār Sharḥ Maṣābīḥ al-Sunna*. Ed. Muḥammad Isḥāq Ibrāhīm. 3 vols. Riyadh: Pub. by editor, 1432/2011.

al-Bayhaqī, Abū Bakr Aḥmad b. al-Ḥusayn. *Maʿrifat al-Sunan wal-Āthār*. Ed. ʿAbd al-Muʿṭī Amīn Qalʿajī, 15 vols. Aleppo and Cairo: Dār al-Waʿī, 1411/1991.

_______. *Shuʿab al-Īmān*. Ed. Muḥammad Saʿīd Basyūnī Zaghlūl. 7 vols. Beirut: Dār al-Kutub al-ʿIlmiyya, 1410/ 1980.

_______. *al-Sunan al-Kubrā*. With Ibn al-Turkmānī's *al-Jawhar al-Naqī* in the margins. 10 vols. Hyderabad Deccan: Maṭbaʿat Majlis Dā'irat al-Maʿārif al-ʿUthmāniyya, 1355/1937.

al-Bazzār. [*Musnad.*] *al-Baḥr al-Zakhkhār al-Maʿrūf bi-Musnad al-Bazzār*. Ed. Maḥfūẓ al-Raḥmān Zayn Allāh et al. 18 vols. Beirut: Mu'assasat ʿUlūm al-Qur'ān; Medina: Maktabat al-ʿUlūm wal-Ḥikam, 1409-1430/1988-2009.

al-Bukhārī, Muḥammad b. Ismāʿīl al-Juʿfī. *al-Jāmiʿ al-Ṣaḥīḥ: wa-Huwa al-Jāmiʿ al-Musnad al-Ṣaḥīḥ al-Mukhtaṣar min Umūr Rasūl Allāh Ṣallā Allāhu ʿalayhi wa-Sallam wa-Sunanih wa-Ayyāmih*. 2nd ed. 8 vols. in 3. Ed. Muḥammad Zuhrī al-Ghamrāwī. Bulāq: al-Maṭbaʿat al-Kubrā al-Amīriyya, 1314/1896. Repr. Cairo: al-Maṭbaʿat al-Maymūniyya [Muṣṭafā Bābā al-Ḥalabī et al.], 1323/1905.

Burton, Gideon O. *Silva Rhetoricae: The Forest of Rhetoric*. http://rhetoric.byu.edu

al-Bustānī, Karam. *al-Bayān*. Beirut: Maktabat Ṣādir, n.d.

al-Būṭī, Muḥammad Saʿīd. *Kubrā al-Yaqīniyyāt al-Kawniyya*. 8th ed. Damascus: Dār al-Fikr, 1982. Rept. 1417/1997.

Cachia, Pierre Jacques Élie. *The Arch Rhetorician or The Schemer's Skimmer: A Handbook of Late Arabic* badīʿ *drawn from ʿAbd al-Ghanī an-Nābulusī's* Nafaḥāt al-azhār ʿalā nasamāt al-asḥār. Wiesbaden: Harrasowitz Verlag, 1998.

_______. "Bayḍāwī on the *Fawātiḥ*: A Translation of His Commentary on *alif-lām-mīm* in Sūrah 2, v. 1." *Journal of Semitic Studies* 13 (1968) 218-231.

_______. *The Monitor: A Dictionary of Arabic Grammatical Terms*. Beirut: Librairie du Liban and London: Longman, 1973.

Çelebi, Saʿdī Çelebi and Shaykh Zādah. *Ḥāshiyatā Saʿdī Shalabī wa-Shaykh Zādah ʿalā Anwār al-Tanzīl*. Riyadh: King Saʿūd University ms. 6750.

al-Daqr, ʿAbd al-Ghanī. *Muʿjam al-Qawāʿid al-ʿArabiyya fīl-Naḥw wal-Taṣrīf*. Damascus: Dār al-Qalam, 1406/1986.

al-Dāraquṭnī, Abū al-Ḥasan ʿAlī b. ʿUmar b. Aḥmad b. Mahdī. *al-ʿIlal al-Wārida fīl Aḥādīth al-Nabawiyya*. Ed. Maḥfūẓ al-Raḥmān Zayn Allāh al-Salafī. 16 vols. Riyadh: Dār Ṭayba, 1405/1985.

______. *al-Sunan*. With *al-Taʿlīq al-Mughnī ʿalā al-Dāraquṭnī* by Muḥammad Shams al-Ḥaqq al-ʿAẓīm Ābādī. Ed. al-Sayyid ʿAbd Allāh Hāshim Yamānī al-Madanī. 4 vols. in 2. Beirut: Dār al-Maʿrifa, 1966. Rept. Beirut: Dār Iḥyāʾ al-Turāth al-ʿArabī, 1993.

______. *al-Sunan*. With *al-Taʿlīq al-Mughnī ʿalā al-Dāraquṭnī* by Muḥammad Shams al-Ḥaqq al-ʿAẓīm Ābādī. Ed. Shuʿayb al-Arnaʾūṭ et al. 6 vols. Beirut: Muʾassasat al-Risāla, 1424/2004.

al-Dārimī. *Sunan*. See al-Ghamrī.

al-Dāwūdī. *Ṭabaqāt al-Mufassirīn*. Ed. ʿAlī Muḥammad ʿUmar. 2nd ed. 2 vols. Cairo: Maktabat Wahba, 1415/1994.

al-Dhahabī, Muḥammad b. Aḥmad b. ʿUthmān. *Siyar Aʿlām al-Nubalāʾ*. Ed. Shuʿayb al-Arnāʾūṭ et al. 3rd ed. 25 vols. Beirut: Muʾassassat al-Risāla, 1405/1985.

al-Dhahabī, Muḥammad Ḥusayn. *al-Tafsīr wal-Mufassirūn*. 7th ed. 3 vols. Cairo: Maktabat Wahba, 2000.

De Sacy. See Sacy.

Encyclopædia Iranica. Ed. Ehsan Yarshater. 16 vols. Boston: Routledge & Kegan Paul, 1982.

Fakhrulḥasan, Sayyid. *al-Taqrīr al-Ḥāwī fī Ḥall al-Bayḍāwī*. 4 vols. Deoband: Kutubkhānah-i Fakhriyyah, 1970. Rept. 4 vols. in 1. Karachi: Islāmī Kutubkhānah, 2004.

al-Farāhīdī, al-Khalīl. *Kitāb al-ʿAyn*. Ed. Mahdī al-Makhzūmī and Ibrāhīm al-Sāmarrāʾī. 8 vols. [Baghdad]: Dār al-Rashīd, 1980-1985.

al-Farrāʾ. *Maʿānī al-Qurʾān*. Ed. Muḥammad ʿAlī al-Najjār & Aḥmad Yūsuf Najātī. 3rd ed. 3 vols. Beirut: ʿĀlam al-Kutub, 1403/1983.

al-Fayrūzābādī, Muḥammad b. Yaʿqūb. *al-Qāmūs al-Muḥīṭ*. Ed. Yūsuf al-Shaykh Muḥammad al-Biqāʿī. Beirut: Dār al-Fikr, 1995/1410.

al-Ghāmidī, Ṣāliḥ. *al-Masāʾil al-Iʿtizāliyya fī Tafsīr al-Kashshāf lil-Zamakhsharī fī Ḍawʾi mā Warada fī Kitāb al-Intiṣāf li-Ibni al-Munayyir: ʿArḍ wa-Naqd*. 2 vols. Ḥāʾil (Saudi Arabia): Dār al-Andalus, 1418/1998.

al-Ghamrī, Abū ʿĀṣim Nabīl. *Fatḥ al-Mannān Sharḥ wa-Taḥqīq Kitāb al-Dārimī Abī Muḥammad ʿAbd Allāh b. ʿAbd al-Raḥmān.* 10 vols. Mecca and Beirut: al-Maktaba al-Makkiyya and Dār al-Bashā'ir al-Islāmiyya, 1419/ 1999.

Gimaret, Daniel. *La doctrine dal-Ashʿarī.* Paris: Cerf, 1990.

Haddad, Gibril Fouad. *The Four Imams and Their Schools: Abū Ḥanīfa, Mālik, al-Shāfiʿī, Aḥmad b. Ḥanbal.* London: Muslim Academic Trust, 2007.

_______. *Sunna Notes III: The Binding Proof of the Sunna.* Birmingham: al-Qur'an wal-Sunna Association, 2010.

Ḥājjī Khalīfa. *Kashf al-Ẓunūn ʿan Asāmī al-Kutub wal-Funūn.* Ed. Muḥammad Sharaf al-Dīn Yāltaqāyā and Rifʿat Bīlkah al-Kilīsī. 2 vols. Istanbul: Maṭābiʿ Wikālat al-Maʿārif al-Jalīla, 1941-1943. Rept. Beirut: Dār Iḥyā' al-Turāth al-ʿArabī, n.d.

al-Ḥākim al-Naysābūrī. *al-Mustadrak ʿalā al-Ṣaḥīḥayn.* With al-Dhahabī's *Talkhīṣ al-Mustadrak.* 5 vols. Hyderabad Deccan: Dā'irat al-Maʿārif al-Niẓāmiyya, 1334-1342/1916-1923. Rept. Beirut: Dār al-Maʿrifa, 1986 with indices by Yūsuf al-Marʿashlī.

al-Ḥakīm al-Tirmidhī, Abū ʿAbd Allāh Muḥammad b. ʿAlī b. al-Ḥasan. *Nawādir al-Uṣūl fī Maʿrifat Aḥādīth al-Rasūl.* Ed. Tawfīq Takla. 2nd ed. 7 vols. Damascus: Dār al-Nawādir, 1432/2011.

al-Haythamī. *Majmaʿ al-Baḥrayn fī Zawā'id al-Muʿjamayn.* Ed. ʿAbd al-Quddūs b. Muḥammad Nadhīr. 9 vols. Riyadh: Maktabat al-Rushd, 1413/1992.

_______. *Majmaʿ al-Zawā'id wa-Manbaʿ al-Fawā'id.* 10 vols. Beirut: Dār al-Fikr, 1412/1992.

al-Ḥuṣarī, Maḥmūd Khalīl. *Aḥkām Qirā'at al-Qur'ān al-Karīm.* Ed. Muḥammad Ṭalḥa Bilāl Minyār. 4th ed. Cairo: al-Maktabat al-Makkiyya; Beirut: Dār al-Bashā'ir al-Islāmiyya, 1999.

Ibn ʿAbd al-Barr. *Jāmiʿ Bayān al-ʿIlm wa-Faḍlih.* Ed. Abū al-Ashbāl al-Zuhayrī. 2 vols. Dammam: Dār Ibn al-Jawzī, 1414/1994.

Ibn Abī ʿĀṣim. *al-Sunna.* Ed. Bāsim al-Jawābira. Riyadh: Dār al-Ṣumayʿī, 1419/1998.

Ibn Abī Ḥātim al-Rāzī. *Tafsīr al-Qur'ān al-ʿAẓīm Musnadan ʿan Rasūl Allāh ṣallā Allāhu ʿalayhi wa-sallama wal-Ṣaḥābati wal-Tābiʿīn.* Ed.

As'ad Muḥammad al-Ṭayyib. 14 vols. Mecca and Riyadh: Maktabat Nizār Muṣṭafā al-Bāz, 1417/1997.

Ibn Abī Shayba. *al-Muṣannaf*. Ed. Muḥammad 'Awwāma. 26 vols. Beirut: Dār Qurṭuba, 1428/2006.

Ibn 'Adī. *al-Kāmil fil-Ḍu'afā'*. Ed. 'Ādil Aḥmad 'Abd al-Mawjūd et al. 9 vols. Beirut: Dār al-Kutub al-'Ilmiyya, 1997.

[Ibn] al-Anbārī. *Kitāb al-Aḍdād*. Ed. Muḥammad Abū al-Faḍl Ibrāhīm. Sidon: al-Maktabat al-'Aṣriyya, 1407/1987.

Ibn 'Asākir. *Tārīkh Madīnat Dimashq*. Ed. Muḥibb al-Dīn 'Amrawī. 80 vols. Beirut: Dār al-Fikr, 1421/2001.

Ibn 'Āshūr, Muḥammad al-Fāḍil b. Muḥammad al-Ṭāhir. *al-Tafsīr wa-Rijāluh*. Silsilat al-Buḥūth al-Islāmiyya no. 2, year 28. Cairo: Majma' al-Buḥūth al-Islāmiyya fīl-Azhar, 1970; rept. 1417/1997.

Ibn 'Āshūr, Muḥammad al-Ṭāhir. *Tafsīr al-Taḥrīr wal-Tanwīr*. 30 vols. Tunis: al-Dār al-Tūnisiyya lil-Nashr, 1984.

Ibn 'Aṭiyya al-Andalusī, Abū Muḥammad 'Abd al-Ḥaqq b. Ghālib. *al-Muḥarrar al-Wajīz fī Tafsīr al-Kitāb al-'Azīz*. Ed. 'Abd al-Salām 'Abd al-Shāfī Muḥammad. 6 vols. Beirut: Dār al-Kutub al-'Ilmiyya, 1422/2001.

Ibn Durayd, Abū Bakr Muḥammad b. al-Ḥasan. *al-Ishtiqāq*. Ed. 'Abd al-Salām Muḥammad Hārūn. Beirut: Dār al-Jīl, 1411/1991.

Ibn al-Ḍurays. *Faḍā'il al-Qur'ān wa-Mā Unzila min al-Qur'ān bi-Makkata wa-Mā Unzila bil-Madīna*. Ed. 'Urwa Budayr. Damascus: Dār al-Fikr, 1408/1987.

Ibn Ḥajar al-'Asqalānī, Shihāb al-Dīn Abū al-Faḍl Aḥmad b. 'Alī. *al-Durar al-Kāmina fī A'yān al-Mi'at al-Thāmina*. 4 vols. Hyderabad Deccan: Maṭba'at Dā'irat al-Ma'ārif al-'Uthmāniyya, 1350/1931.

_______. *Fatḥ al-Bārī bi-Sharḥ Ṣaḥīḥ al-Bukhārī*. Ed. Muḥammad Fu'ād 'Abd al-Bāqī et al. 13 vols. Beirut, Dār al-Ma'rifa, 1379/1959.

_______. *al-Iṣāba fī Tamyīz al-Ṣaḥāba*. Ed. 8 vols. in 4. Cairo: al-Maṭba'at al-Sharafiyya, 1327/1909. Rept. in 5 vols. with indices Beirut: Dār al-Kutub al-'Ilmiyya, n.d.

_______. *al-Kāfī al-Shāf fī Takhrīj Aḥādīth al-Kashshāf*. See Afandī, *Sharḥ Shawāhid al-Kashshāf*.

_______. *al-ʿUjāb fī Bayān al-Asbāb*. Ed. ʿAbd al-Ḥakīm Muḥammad al-Anīs. 2 vols. Dammām: Dār Ibn al-Jawzī, 1418/1997.

Ibn Ḥibbān. *Ṣaḥīḥ Ibn Ḥibbān bi-Tartīb Ibn Balbān*. Ed Shuʿayb al-Arnāʾūṭ. 2nd ed. 18 vols. Beirut: Muʾassasat al-Risāla, 1414/1993.

Ibn Hishām al-Maʿāfirī, Abū Muḥammad ʿAbd al-Malik. *al-Sīrat al-Nabawiyya*. Ed. Muṣṭafā al-Saqqā et al. 2nd ed. 4 vols. in 2. Beirut: Dār al-Wifāq, 1375/1955.

Ibn al-Jawzī, Abū al-Faraj ʿAbd al-Raḥmān b. ʿAlī b. Muḥammad. *Manāqib Amīr al-Muʾminīn ʿUmar b. al-Khaṭṭāb*. Ed. Zaynab Ibrāhīm al-Qārūt. Beirut: Dār al-Kutub al-ʿIlmiyya, 1980.

_______. *Kitāb al-Mawḍūʿāt*. Ed. ʿAbd al-Raḥmān ʿUthmān. 3 vols. Medina: al-Maktabat al-Salafiyya, 1386/1966.

_______. *Kitāb al-Mawḍūʿāt min al-Aḥādīth al-Marfūʿāt*. Ed. Nūr al-Dīn b. Shukrī Būyājīlār. 4 vols. Riyadh: Aḍwāʾ al-Salaf, 1418/1997.

Ibn Jinnī. *al-Khaṣāʾiṣ*. Ed. Muḥammad al-Najjār. 3 vols. Cairo: Dār al-Kutub al-Miṣriyya, 1371/1952.

Ibn Kamāl Bāshā (Kemalpaşazade). *Ḥāshiya ʿalā Tafsīr al-Bayḍāwī* [Surat al-Baqara 2:21 to 2:95, with a fragment of Surat al-Fātiḥa]. Baltimore: Walters Art Museum ms. W.584.

Ibn Kathīr. *al-Bidāya wal-Nihāya*. Ed. ʿAbd Allāh al-Turkī. 21 vols. Cairo: Dār Hajar, 1417/1997.

_______. *Ṭabaqāt al-Fuqahāʾ al-Shāfiʿiyyīn*. Followed by Ibn al-Maṭarī al-ʿUbādī's *Dhayl Ṭabaqāt al-Shāfiʿiyyīn*. Ed. Muḥammad Zaynuhum ʿAzb and Aḥmad Hāshim. 3 vols. Cairo: Maktabat al-Thaqāfat al-Dīniyya, 1413/ 1993.

_______. *Tafsīr al-Qurʾān al-ʿAẓīm*. Ed. Muṣṭafā al-Sayyid Muḥammad et al. 15 vols. Jīza: Muʾassasat Qurṭuba, 1421/2000.

Ibn Mājah. *Sunan*. Ed. Bashshār ʿAwwād Maʿrūf. 6 vols. Beirut: Dār al-Jīl, 1418/1998.

Ibn Manẓūr, Abū al-Faḍl Jamāl al-Dīn Muḥammad b. Mukarram. *Lisān al-ʿArab*. 15 vols. Beirut: Dār Ṣādir, [1968].

Ibn al-Maṭarī. See Ibn Kathīr, *Ṭabaqāt al-Fuqahāʾ al-Shāfiʿiyyīn*.

Ibn Qutayba. *al-Shiʿr wal-Shuʿarāʾ*. Ed. Aḥmad Muḥammad Shākir. 2nd ed. 2 vols. Cairo: Dār al-Maʿārif, 1386/1967.

Ibn Sa'd. *Kitāb al-Ṭabaqāt al-Kabīr*. Ed. 'Alī Muḥammad 'Umar. 11 vols. Cairo: Maktabat al-Khānjī, 1421/2001.

Ibn Sīdah. *al-Mukhaṣṣaṣ*. Ed. Muḥammad Maḥmūd al-Tarkazī al-Shinqīṭī et al. 17 vols. Cairo: al-Maṭba'at al-Amīriyya, 1321/1903.

Ibn al-Subkī, Tāj al-Dīn Abū Naṣr 'Abd al-Wahhāb b. Taqī al-Dīn 'Alī b. 'Abd al-Kāfī. *Ṭabaqāt al-Shāfi'iyya al-Kubrā*. Ed. Maḥmūd al-Ṭannāḥī and 'Abd al-Fattāḥ al-Ḥilw. 2nd. ed. 10 vols. Jīza: Dār Hijr, 1992.

Ibrahim, Lutpi. *The Theological Questions at Issue between az-Zamakhsharī and al-Bayḍāwī with special reference to al-Kashshāf and Anwār at-Tanzīl*. Unpub. Ph.D. thesis. Edinburgh: University of Edinburgh, 1977.

Imām al-Ḥaramayn, Abū al-Ma'ālī 'Abd al-Malik al-Juwaynī. *al-Irshād ilā Qawāṭi' al-Adilla fī Uṣūl al-I'tiqād*. Ed. Muḥammad Mūsā and 'Alī 'Abd al-Ḥamīd. Cairo: Maktabat al-Khānjī, 1369/1950.

'Iṣam, see al-Isfarāyīnī.

al-Isfarāyīnī, 'Iṣām al-Dīn Ibrāhīm b. Muḥammad b. 'Arab Shāh. *Ḥāshiya 'alā Tafsīr al-Bayḍāwī*. Riyadh: King Sa'ūd University ms. 6096.

al-Isnawī, Jamāl al-Dīn. *Ṭabaqāt al-Shāfi'iyya*. Ed. Kamāl Yūsuf al-Ḥūt, 2 vols. Beirut: Dār al-Kutub al-'Ilmiyya, 1407/1987.

'Itr, Nūr al-Dīn. *'Ulūm al-Qur'ān al-Karīm*. 6th ed. Damascus: Pub. by author, 1416/1996.

'Iyāḍ b. Mūsā al-Yaḥṣubī, Qāḍī. *al-Shifā bi-Ta'rīfi Ḥuqūq al-Muṣṭafā*. Ed. 'Abduh 'Alī Kawshak. Damascus: Maktabat al-Ghazālī; Beirut: Dār al-Fayḥā', 1420/2000.

Jarīr. *Dīwān Jarīr*. Ed. Nu'mān Amīn Ṭaha. 3rd ed. 2 vols. Cairo: Dār al-Ma'ārif, 1969-1971.

al-Jawharī. *al-Ṣiḥāḥ: Tāj al-Lugha wa-Ṣiḥāḥ al-'Arabiyya*. Ed. Aḥmad 'Abd al-Ghafūr 'Aṭṭār. 4th ed. 6 vols. Beirut: Dār al-'Ilm lil-Malāyīn, 1410/1990.

al-Juwaynī, Abū al-Ma'ālī 'Abd al-Malik, see Imām al-Ḥaramayn.

al-Kāzarūnī, 'Abd Allāh b. Ḥasan al-Ṣiddīqī. *Ḥāshiyat al-Kāzarūnī 'alā Tafsīr al-Bayḍāwī*. Ed. Muḥammad al-Zuhrī al-Ghamrāwī, 4 vols. Cairo: Dār al-Kutub al-'Arabiyya al-Kubrā, 1330/1912.

_______. *Ḥāshiya*. Ed. ʿAbd al-Qādir ʿIrfān al-ʿAshshā Ḥassūna. 5 vols. Beirut: Dār al-Fikr, 1996, rept. 2005 and 2009.

al-Khafājī, Shihāb al-Dīn Aḥmad b. Muḥammad b. Aḥmad. *Ḥāshiyat al-Shihāb al-Musammāt ʿInāyat al-Qāḍī wa-Kifāyat al-Rāḍī*. Ed. Muḥammad al-Ṣabbāgh. 8 vols. Bulāq: Dār al-Ṭibāʿa al-ʿĀmira, 1283/1867. Rept. Beirut: Dār Ṣādir, 1974-1975.

al-Khaṭīb, ʿAbd al-Laṭīf. *Muʿjam al-Qirāʾāt*. 11 vols. Damascus, Dār Saʿd al-Dīn, 1422/2002.

al-Khaṭīb al-Baghdādī. *al-Jāmiʿ li-Akhlāq al-Rāwī wa-Ādāb al-Sāmiʿ*. Ed. Muḥammad ʿAjāj al-Khaṭīb. 2 vols. Beirut: Muʾassasat al-Risāla, 1412/1991.

Khiḍr, Sihām. *al-Iʿjāz al-Lughawī fī Fawātiḥ al-Suwar*. Beirut: Dār al-Kutub al-ʿIlmiyya, 2008.

al-Kirmānī, Abū Naṣr. *Shawādhdh al-Qirāʾāt*. Ed. Shimrān al-ʿAjlī. Beirut: Muʾassasat al-Balāgh, 2001.

Lane, Edward William. *Arabic-English Lexicon*. 8 vols. London and Edinburgh: Williams and Norgate, 1863-1893. Rept. 2 vols. Cambridge: Islamic Texts Society, 1984.

_______. *Selections from the Ḳur-án, commonly called, in England, The Koran*. London: James Madden and Co., 1843.

Lisān al-ʿArab. See Ibn Manẓūr.

Mardīnī, Fāṭima Muḥammad. *al-Tafsīr wal-Mufassirūn*. Damascus: Dār Ghār Ḥirāʾ and Bayt al-Ḥikma, 1430/2009.

Margoliouth. David S. *Chrestomathia Baidawiana: The Commentary of El-Baiḍāwī on Sura III, translated and explained for the students of Arabic*. London: Luzac & Co., 1894.

al-Maydānī al-Naysābūrī, Abū al-Faḍl Aḥmad b. Muḥammad. *Majmaʿ al-Amthāl*. Ed. Muḥammad Muḥyī al-Dīn ʿAbd al-Ḥamīd. 2 vols. Cairo: Maṭbaʿat al-Sunnat al-Muḥammadiyya, 1374/1955.

al-Mubarrid. *al-Kāmil*. Ed. Muḥammad Aḥmad al-Dālī. 2nd ed. 4 vols. Beirut: Muʾassasat al-Risāla, 1412/1992.

al-Munāwī, Zayn al-Dīn Muḥammad ʿAbd al-Raʾūf b. Tāj al-Dīn. *al-Fatḥ al-Samāwī bi-Takhrīj Aḥādīth al-Qāḍī al-Bayḍāwī*. Ed. Aḥmad Mujtabā al-Salafī. 3 vols. Riyadh: Dār al-ʿĀṣima, 1409/1989.

Muqātil b. Sulaymān al-Balkhī. *Tafsīr Muqātil*. Ed. ʿAbd Allāh Maḥmūd Shaḥḥāta. 5 vols. Beirut: Muʾassasat al-Tārīkh al-ʿArabī lil-Ṭibāʿa wal-Nashr wal-Tawzīʿ, 1423/2002.

Muslim b. al-Ḥajjāj b. Muslim al-Qushayrī al-Naysābūrī. [*Ṣaḥīḥ*.] *al-Jāmiʿ al-Ṣaḥīḥ*. 8 vols. [Istanbul]: al-Maṭbaʿat al-ʿĀmira, 1334/1916.

al-Nābigha. *Dīwān al-Nābigha al-Dhabyānī*. Ed. Ḥamdū Ṭammās. 2nd ed. Beirut: Dār al-Maʿrifa, 1426/2005.

al-Nābulusī, ʿAbd al-Ghanī b. Ismāʿīl. *al-Ajwiba ʿalā Miʾatin wa-Wāḥidin wa-Sittīna Suʾālan*. Ed. Imtithāl al-Ṣaghīr. Damascus: Dār al-Fārābī lil-Maʿārif, 1422/2001.

al-Nasāʾī, Abū ʿAbd al-Raḥmān Aḥmad b. Shuʿayb b. ʿAlī. *Sunan al-Nasāʾī bi-Sharḥ al-Ḥāfiẓ Jalāl al-Dīn al-Suyūṭī wa-Ḥāshiyat al-Imām al-Sindī*. 8 vols. [Cairo]: al-Maṭbaʿat al-Miṣriyya, 1348/1930. Rept. 8 vols. in 4. Beirut: Dār Iḥyāʾ al-Turāth al-ʿArabī, n.d.

_______. *al-Sunan al-Kubrā*. Ed. Ḥasan ʿAbd al-Munʿim Shalabī et al. 12 vols. Beirut: Muʾassasat al-Risāla, 1421/2001.

Nuwayhiḍ, ʿĀdil. *Muʿjam al-Mufassirīn min Ṣadr al-Islām ḥattā al-ʿAṣr al-Ḥāḍir*. 3rd ed. 2 vols. Beirut: Muʾassasat Nuwayhiḍ al-Thaqāfiyya, 1409/1988.

Qarah Dāghī. See al-Bayḍāwī, *al-Ghāyat al-Quṣwā fī Dirāyat al-Fatwā*.

al-Qārī, Mullā ʿAlī b. Muḥammad Sulṭān. *al-Asrār al-Marfūʿa fīl-Akhbār al-Mawḍūʿa*. Ed. Muḥammad Luṭfī al-Ṣabbāgh. 2nd ed. Beirut: al-Maktab al-Islāmī, 1406/1986.

_______. Encyclopedia of Hadith Forgeries: *al-Asrār al-Marfūʿa fīl-Akhbār al-Mawḍūʿa*. Sayings Misattributed to the Prophet Muḥammad, صلى الله عليه وآله وصحبه وسلّم. Introduction, translation and notes by Gibril Fouad Haddad. London: Beacon Books, 2013.

al-Qarnī, Burayk b. Saʿīd. *Kulliyyāt al-Alfāẓ fīl-Tafsīr*. 2 vols. Ryadh: Pub. by author, 1426/2006.

Quiring-Zoche, Rosemarie. "An early manuscript of al-Bayḍāwī's *Anwār al-tanzīl* and the model it has been copied from." *From Codicology to Technology: Islamic Manuscripts and Their Place in Scholarship*. Ed. Stephanie Brinkmann and Beate Wiesmüller. Berlin: Frank & Timme, 2009. Pp. 33-45.

al-Qūnawī, ʿIṣām al-Dīn Ismāʿīl b. Muḥammad. *Ḥāshiyat al-Qūnawī ʿalā Tafsīr al-Bayḍāwī.* With Ibn al-Tamjīd, *Ḥāshiya.* Ed. ʿAbd Allāh ʿUmar. 20 vols. Beirut: Dār al-Kutub al-ʿIlmiyya, 1422/2001.

al-Qurṭubī. *al-Tadhkira fī Aḥwāl al-Mawtā wa-Umūr al-Ākhira.* 3 vols. Ed. Yūsuf ʿAlī Budaywī. Damascus and Beirut: Dār Ibn Kathīr, 1419/1999.

_______. [*Tafsīr.*] *al-Jāmiʿ li-Aḥkām al-Qurʾān wal-Mubayyin li-mā Taḍammanahu min al-Sunna wa-Āy al-Furqān.* Ed. ʿAbd Allāh b. ʿAbd al-Muḥsin al-Turkī and Muḥammad Riḍwān ʿAraqsūsī. 24 vols. Beirut: Muʾassasat al-Risāla, 1427/2006.

al-Qushayrī. *al-Taysīr fī ʿIlm al-Tafsīr.* Ed. ʿAbd Allāh al-Muṭayrī. Unpublished Ph.D. diss. Mecca: Jāmiʿat Umm al-Qurā, 1427/2006.

al-Rāghib al-Aṣfahānī. *Mufradāt Alfāẓ al-Qurʾān.* Ed. Ṣafwān Dāwūdī. 4th ed. Damascus: Dār al-Qalam, 1430/2009.

_______. *Tafsīr al-Rāghib al-Aṣfahānī: min awwal sūrat Āl ʿImrān wa-ḥattā nihāyat al-āya 113 min sūrat al-Nisāʾ.* Ed. ʿĀdil ʿAlī al-Shidī. 2 vols. Riyadh: Madār al-Waṭan lil-Nashr, 1424/2003.

al-Rāzī, Fakhr al-Dīn Muḥammad b. ʿUmar. *Tafsīr al-Fakhr al-Rāzī al-Mushtahar bil-Tafsīr al-Kabīr wa-Mafātīḥ al-Ghayb.* 32 vols. Beirut: Dār al-Fikr, 1401/1981.

De Sacy, Antoine-Isaac Silvestre. "Extrait du Commentaire de Béïdhawi sur l'Alcoran." In *Anthologie Grammaticale Arabe.* Paris: Imprimerie Royale, 1829.

Saʿīd b. Manṣūr. *Sunan Saʿīd b. Manṣūr.* Ed. Saʿd b. ʿAbd Allāh Āl Ḥumayyid. 5 vols. Riyadh: Dār al-Ṣumayʿī, 1414/1993.

al-Sayālkūtī, ʿAbd al-Ḥakīm [b. Shams al-Dīn]. *Ḥāshiyat al-ʿAllāma ʿAbd al-Ḥakīm al-Sayālkūtī ʿalā al-Tafsīr lil-Qāḍī al-Bayḍāwī.* Bulāq: Dār al-Ṭibāʿat al-ʿĀmira, 1270/1854. Rept. Kootah (Jammu and Kashmir): Maktaba-e-islamia, 1977.

Shaykh Zādah al-Qawjawī, Muḥyī al-Dīn Muḥammad b. Muṣṭafā. *Ḥāshiyat Muḥyī al-Dīn Shaykh Zādah ʿalā Tafsīr al-Bayḍāwī.* 3 vols. Istanbul: al-Maktabat al-ʿUthmāniyya, 1306/1889. Rept. Istanbul: Hakikat Kitabevi, 1990.

_______. Ed. Muḥammad ʿAbd al-Qādir Shāhīn. 8 vols. Beirut: Dār al-Kutub al-ʿIlmiyya, 1419/1999.

_______. See also Çelebi, Saʿdī.

al-Shihrī, ʿAbd al-Raḥmān. Nine audio lessons on al-Bayḍāwī's *Anwār al-Tanzīl* (Fātiḥa). http://ar.islamway.net/lesson/132243 (Arabic)

al-Subkī, see Ibn al-Subkī.

al-Suyūṭī, Jalāl al-Dīn Abū al-Faḍl ʿAbd al-Raḥmān b. Kamāl al-Dīn Abī Bakr. *al-Ashbāh wal-Naẓā'ir fīl Naḥw*. 4 vols. Hyderabad Deccan: Dā'irat al-Maʿārif al-ʿUthmāniyya, 1359-1361/1940-1942.

_______. *Bughyat al-Wuʿāt fī Ṭabaqāt al-Lughawiyyīn wal-Nuḥāt*. Ed. Muḥammad Abū al-Faḍl Ibrāhīm. 2nd ed. 2 vols. Beirut: Dār al-Fikr, 1399/1979.

_______. *al-Durr al-Manthūr fīl-Tafsīr bil-Ma'thūr*. Ed. ʿAbd Allāh b. ʿAbd al-Muḥsin al-Turkī. 17 vols. Cairo: Markaz Hajar lil-Buḥūth, 1424/2003.

_______. *al-Itqān fī ʿUlūm al-Qur'ān*. Ed. Markaz al-Dirāsāt al-Qur'āniyya. 7 vols. Medina: Mujammaʿ al-Malik Fahd li-Ṭibāʿat al-Muṣḥaf al-Sharīf, 1426/2005.

_______. *Nawāhid al-Abkār wa-Shawārid al-Afkār* [*Ḥāshiyat Tafsīr al-Bayḍāwī*]. Ed. Muḥammad Kamāl ʿAlī. Unpublished Ph.D. diss. 3 vols. Mecca: Jāmiʿat Umm al-Qurā, 1423-24/ 2002-2003.

al-Ṭabarānī, Abū al-Qāsim Sulaymān b. Aḥmad b. Ayyūb. *al-Duʿā'*. Ed. Muḥammad Saʿīd al-Bukhārī. 3 vols. Beirut: Dār al-Bashā'ir al-Islāmiyya, 1407/1987.

_______. *al-Muʿjam al-Awsaṭ*. Ed. Ṭāriq b. ʿAwaḍ Allāh b. Muḥammad and ʿAbd al-Muḥsin al-Ḥusaynī. 10 vols. Cairo: Dār al-Ḥaramayn, 1415/1995.

_______. *al-Muʿjam al-Kabīr*. Ed. Ḥamdī ʿAbd al-Majīd al-Salafī. 2nd ed. 25 vols. Baghdad: Wizārat al-Awqāf, 1984-1990. Rept. Cairo: Maktabat Ibn Taymiyya, n.d.

_______. *al-Muʿjam al-Ṣaghīr*. Ed. ʿAbd al-Raḥmān Muḥammad ʿUthmān. 2 vols. Medina: al-Maktaba al-Salafiyya, 1388/1968. Rept. 2 vols. Beirut: Dār al-Kutub al-ʿIlmiyya, 1403/1983.

al-Ṭabarī, Abū Jaʿfar Muḥammad b. Jarīr. *Tārīkh al-Rusul wal-Mulūk*. Ed. Muḥammad Abū al-Faḍl Ibrāhīm. 11 vols. 2nd ed. Cairo: Dār al-Maʿārif; Beirut: Maktabat Suwaydān, 1960-1977.

_______. *Tafsīr al-Ṭabarī: Jāmiʿ al-Bayān ʿan Taʾwīl Āy al-Qurʾān.* Ed. ʿAbd Allāh b. ʿAbd al-Muḥsin al-Turkī et al. 26 vols. Cairo: Dār Hajar, 1422/2001.

al-Tabrīzī. *Sharḥ Dīwān Abī Tammām.* Ed. Muḥammad ʿAbduh ʿAzzām. 4th ed. 4 vols. Cairo: Dār al-Maʿārif, 1951-1965.

_______. *Sharḥ Dīwān al-Ḥamāsa li-Abī Tammām.* Ed. Ghurayd al-Shaykh. 2 vols. Beirut: Dār al-Kutub al-ʿIlmiyya, 1421/2000.

_______. *Tahdhīb al-Āthār wa-Tafṣīl al-Thābit ʿan Rasūl Allāh min al-Akhbār.* Ed. Maḥmūd Muḥammad Shākir. 6 vols. Cairo: Maṭbaʿat al-Madanī, 1402/1982.

Tahdhīb al-Lugha. See al-Azharī.

al-Taymī al-Aṣfahānī. *al-Targhīb wal-Tarhīb.* Ed. Ayman Shaʿbān. 3 vols. Cairo: Dār al-Ḥadīth, 1993.

al-Thaʿlabī al-Naysābūrī, Abū Isḥāq Aḥmad b. Muḥammad b. Ibrāhīm. *al-Kashf wal-Bayān al-Maʿrūf bi-Tafsīr al-Thaʿlabī.* Ed. Ibn ʿĀshūr and Naẓīr al-Sāʿidī. 10 vols. Beirut: Dār Iḥyāʾ al-Turāth al-ʿArabī, 1422/2002.

al-Ṭībī. *Futūḥ al-Ghayb fīl-Kashf ʿan Qināʿ al-Rayb.* Ed. Ḥikmat Yāsīn. Unpub. Ph.D. diss. 7 vols. Medina: al-Jāmiʿa al-Islāmiyya, 1413-1416/1992-1996.

al-Ṭihrānī, Muḥammad Muḥsin Aghā Buzurg. *al-Dharīʿa ilā Taṣānīf al-Shīʿa.* Ed. Sayyid Aḥmad al-Ḥusaynī. 26 vols. Beirut: Dār al-Aḍwāʾ, 1983.

al-Tirmidhī. [*Sunan.*] *al-Jāmiʿ al-Ṣaḥīḥ.* Ed. Aḥmad Shākir et al. 5 vols. 2nd ed. Cairo: Muṣṭafā Bābī al-Ḥalabī, 1398/1978.

al-ʿUkbarī. *Iʿrāb al-Qirāʾāt al-Shawādhdh.* Ed. Muḥammad ʿAzzūz. 2 vols. Beirut: ʿĀlam al-Kutub, 1417/1996.

Van Ess, Josef. "Biobibliographische Notizen zur islamischen Theologie," *Die Welt des Orients,* Bd. 9, H. 2 (1978) 255-283.

al-Wāḥidī. *Asbāb al-Nuzūl.* Cairo: al-Maṭbaʿa al-Hindiyya, 1316/1898. Rept. Beirut: ʿĀlam al-Kutub, n.d.

Wright, William. *A Grammar of the Arabic Language: Translated from the German of [Carl P.] Caspari.* 3rd ed. Revised by W. Robertson Smith and M.J. de Goeje. Ed. Pierre Cachia. 2 vols. Beirut: Librairie du Liban, 1996.

Yāsīn, Ḥikmat Bashīr. *al-Tafsīr al-Ṣaḥīḥ: Mawsūʿat al-Ṣaḥīḥ al-Masbūr min al-Tafsīr bil-Maʾthūr*. 4 vols. Medina: Dār al-Maʾāthir, 1420/1999.

al-Zabīdī, al-Sayyid Muḥammad Murtaḍā al-Ḥusaynī. *Tāj al-ʿArūs min Jawāhir al-Qāmūs*. Ed. ʿAbd al-Sattār Farāj. 40 vols. Kuwait: Wizārat al-Irshād wal-Anbāʾ, 1385/1965.

Zādah. See Shaykh Zādah.

Zakariyyā al-Anṣārī. *Fatḥ al-Jalīl bi-Bayān Khafī Anwār al-Tanzīl*. Damascus: Ẓāhiriyya ms. *ʿUlūm al-Qurʾān* 266.

al-Zamakhsharī, Abū al-Qāsim Jār Allāh Maḥmūd b. ʿUmar. *al-Kashshāf ʿan Ḥaqāʾiq Ghawāmiḍ al-Tanzīl wa-ʿUyūn al-Aqāwīl fī Wujūh al-Taʾwīl*. Eds. ʿĀdil Aḥmad ʿAbd al-Mawjūd et al. 6 vols. Riyadh: Maktabat al-ʿUbaykān, 1418/1998.

_______. *al-Mustaqṣā min Amthāl al-ʿArab*. 2 vols. Hyderabad: Dāʾirat al-Maʿārif al-ʿUthmāniyya, 1381/1962.

al-Zarkashī, Badr al-Dīn Muḥammad b. ʿAbd Allāh. *al-Burhān fī ʿUlūm al-Qurʾān*. Ed. Muḥammad Abū al-Faḍl Ibrāhīm. 3rd ed. 4 vols. Cairo: Dār al-Turāth, 1404/1984.

Index of Sura References

al-ʿĀdiyāt, 92
al-Aḥqāf, 277, 506, 693
al-Aḥzāb, 39, 53, 144, 458, 714
Āl ʿImrān, 22-23, 29, 38, 41, 56-57, 77, 143, 200, 206, 247, 250, 265, 278, 291, 314, 425-426, 441, 468, 484-485, 762, 785
al-Aʿlā, 159
al-Anʿām, 28, 52, 82, 166, 197, 261, 263, 385, 397, 405, 469, 490, 494, 512, 521, 620
al-Anbiyā', 23
al-Anfāl, 573, 616
al-ʿAnkabūt, 197, 257, 455, 463, 492
al-Aʿrāf, 28, 37, 39, 183, 195, 249, 283, 288, 296, 314, 346-347, 478, 484-485, 529, 541, 543, 555, 558, 568, 571, 614, 646, 749, 767
al-ʿAṣr, 486
al-Balad, 196, 499
Banū Isrā'īl, see al-Isrā'
al-Baqara, 22-23, 33, 35, 37-39, 43-47, 51-54, 61-62, 76, 80-85, 90, 103, 108, *124-139*, 179, 206, 213, *214-679*, 737-739, 751, 756, 765, 781
Barā'a, see al-Tawba
al-Bayyina, 302, 458
al-Burūj, 23, 650
al-Dahr, see al-Insān
al-Dhāriyāt, 179, 403, 496, 538
al-Dukhān, 411, 616
al-Fatḥ, 249, 318
al-Fātiḥa, 22, 33, 46, 51, 60-61, 83-84, 97, 101, *123*, *147-213*, 295, 740, 781
Fāṭir, 188, 269, 330, 389, 409
al-Furqān, 143, 419, 563
al-Ḥadīd, 356, 361, 494
al-Ḥajj, 59, 368, 463
al-Ḥāqqa, 348
al-Ḥijr, 22, 39, 56, 92, 150, 238, 332, 396, 532, 540, 772
Hūd, 154, 270, 567, 664
al-Ḥujurāt, 261, 481
Ibrāhīm, 196, 202
al-Infiṭār, 180, 286
al-Insān, 369
al-Inshiqāq, 144
al-Isrā', 56, 197, 248, 303, 402, 424, 539, 744
al-Jāthiya, 304, 494
al-Jinn, 458, 535
al-Jumuʿa, 388, 397, 654
al-Kāfirūn, 56
al-Kahf, 22, 64, 82, 288, 299, 543, 546-547, 554, 625, 672, 738
al-Layl, 23

Luqmān, 22, 238
al-Mā'ida, 28
al-Ma'ārij, 737
al-Mā'ida, 39, 52, 62, 175, 207, 261, 292, 299, 446, 458, 486, 580, 587, 694, 737
Maryam, 239, 383, 524
al-Masad, 36, 705
al-Mā'ūn, 267
al-Muddaththir, 772
Muḥammad, 447
al-Mujādila, 24, 261, 620
al-Mulk, 55, 376
al-Mu'min, 737
al-Mu'minūn, 23
al-Munāfiqūn, 300, 429, 497, 693
al-Mursalāt, 663
al-Muṭaffifīn, 344
al-Muzzammil, 244
al-Naba', 206, 542, 737
al-Naḥl, 22, 27, 143, 176, 261, 299, 354, 620, 751
al-Najm, 59, 772
al-Naml, 28, 238, 535
al-Nāzi'āt, 23, 499, 500
al-Nisā', 28, 57, 267
al-Nūr, 512, 694, 709, 730
al-Qadr, 737
Qāf, 23, 144, 216, 305, 394, 446
al-Qaṣaṣ, 28, 92, 238, 279
al-Qiyāma, 52, 331
al-Ra'd, 41, 238, 354, 664, 693
al-Raḥmān, 159, 532
al-Rūm, 350, 415, 491, 664
Saba', 22, 23
Ṣād, 56, 143, 216, 241, 396, 479, 535, 540-543, 556, 667
al-Ṣāffāt, 195, 251, 532, 534
al-Sajda, 402, 444
al-Sharḥ, 474
al-Sharī'a, see al-Jāthiya
al-Shu'arā', 193, 229, 238, 611, 704, 737
al-Shūrā, 239, 343, 597
al-Taghābun, 458
Ṭaha, 555, 557, 562, 568-570, 597
al-Taḥrīm, 56, 435, 436, 509, 545-546, 737
al-Ṭalāq, 458
al-Tawba, 23, 76, 91, 193, 314, 325, 345, 355, 434, 458, 480, 560, 587, 694, 714, 740
al-'Uqūd, see al-Mā'ida
al-Wāqi'a, 23, 89, 268
Yāsīn, 502
Yūnus, 23
Yūsuf, 22
al-Zalzala, 448
al-Zukhruf, 401, 664, 772
al-Zumar, 385, 447, 534

Index of Hadiths & Early Reports

ʿAbd Allāh b. Masʿūd is heavier in the Scale than anyone, 734

ʿAbd Allāh b. Salām became Muslim as soon as the Prophet came to Medina, 691

ʿAbd Allāh b. Salām declared his support of ʿUthmān, 692

ʿAbd Allāh b. Salām is the tenth of ten people who will be in paradise, 692

Abrogation of the obligation of fifty prayers in the hadith of the Ascent, 662

Abū Bakr did not best you because of praying or fasting more, 700

Abū Bakr went into the thanksgiving prostration, 699

Abū Hurayra heard what we did not hear, 703

Abū Hurayra preserved the Prophet's Hadith, 702

Abū Hurayra! You were the most assiduous among us in accompanying the Messenger of Allah, 702

Adam and Eve wept for 300 years over what they had lost of the bliss of paradise, 561

Adam was taught the vocables coined for physical objects and meanings, 525

Adam was thus named because he was created from *adīm al-arḍ*, 522

Adam's gaze for 300 years was downcast out of shame, 561

ʿĀ'isha did lifelong fasting, 711

ʿĀ'isha did not shorten prayers in travel, 711

ʿĀ'isha fasted while travelling, 711

ʿĀ'isha forbade women from going to mosques for congregational prayers, 710

ʿĀ'isha was of those who bade farewell to Badr combatants, 706

ʿAlī identified an invisible audible supplicant at the Prophet's funeral as Khiḍr, 739

ʿAlī is most knowledgeable of the Sunna, 709

ʿAlī said to the *Khawārij*: "Our responsibility toward you is threefold…, 740

ʿAlī took part in all the battles with him except for the campaign of Tabūk, 712

ʿAlī was born 10 years before the Prophetic mission, 712
ʿAlī was one of the members of the *shūrā* whom ʿUmar had stipulated for caliphate, 713
ʿAlī was raised in the home of the Prophet, 712
ʿAlī went into the thanksgiving prostration after fighting the Khawārij, 699
ʿAlī wore the Prophet's garment and slept in his place, 714
Alif is of Allah, *lām* of Jibraʾīl, *mīm* of Muḥammad, 231
Alif lām rāʾ, *ḥā mīm*, and *nūn* all form *al-Raḥmān*, 231
Alif stands for bounties of Allah, *lām* is His kindness, 230
Allah commanded the angel of death to grasp earth from its four corners and ferment it into packed mud, 533
Allah grasped a handful from every corner of the earth and created Adam, 523
Allah has engraved truth on ʿUmar's tongue and heart, 755
Allah has ordered me to recite to you [Ubay], 753
Allah is ashamed, when His slave raises his hands, to send them back empty, 466
Allah is shy and generous, 466
Allah is testing you through her [ʿĀʾisha], 709
Allah is too ashamed before the white-haired Muslim to punish him, 466
Allah knows of Umayya b. Abī al-Ṣalt, 768
Allah most certainly granted you pure sustenance! But you chose what He forbade, 270
Allah opened garret windows through which the Israelites saw and heard one another until they crossed the Sea, 612
Allah ordered Mūsā to travel by night with the Israelites, 612
Allah shall send to this Nation, every 100 years, one/those who will renew religion, 42
ʿAlqama is indeed the most learned of you, 716
ʿAlqama would complete the Qurʾān every five days, 716
Am I seeing you shouting at the Prophet? and he wanted to slap her, 708
Āmīn is the seal of the Nurturer of the worlds, 211
ʿAmmār b. Yāsir was among those who were tortured, 751
Among the angels are a kind that procreate, they are called *al-jinn*, 544
ʿAmr, when did you start turning people into slaves when their mothers gave birth to them as free men?, 759

Anas made ablutions, went out and prayed for rain, 718
Anas saw ʻĀ'isha and his mother Umm Sulaym at Uḥud, 706
Anas was the last Companion to die in Basra, 717
Anas went out with the Messenger of Allāh to Badr as a boy, 717
And He left them in darknesses is a parable for the disappearance of belief, 365
And of people there are those who say refers to ʻAbd Allāh b. Ubay and 470 hypocrites of Medina, 312
And We said: All go down was addressed to both of them and Iblīs, 558
Angel came to him and said, "Receive the glad tidings of two lights, An, 213
Angels were created from light and the jinn were created from a blaze of fire, 548
Answer for me. O Allah! Support him with the Spirit of Holiness, 724
Apes wept and signaled their former identities to their human relatives, The, 656
Are you not pleased to stand, in relation to me, like Hārūn in relation to Mūsā, 712
As for my teknonym it was given to me by Prophet, 752
As you judge, so shall you be judged, 182
Ask her if I can be buried with my two companions, the Prophet and Abū Bakr, 710
Ask Ibn ʻAbbās for he is the most knowledgeable of those who are still alive, 730
Be firm, Uḥud! There is none on top of you but a Prophet, a *Ṣiddīq*, and two martyrs, 698
Be still [Ḥīrā']! There is none on top of you but a Prophet, a *Ṣiddīq*, or a martyr., 698
Belief, prayer, recitation, knowledge, days and nights, wombs, and *dhikr* will all be given form and speech, 526
Bilāl rubbed his face against the Prophetic grave and proceeded to raise the *adhān*, 721
Bilāl was the friend of Abū Bakr and the store-keeper of the Prophet, 720
Bilāl would say all the while: *Aḥad! Aḥad!*, 720
Bury me with my lady-friends the wives of the Prophet, 710
By the Name of Allah, with Whose Name nothing can harm, 155
By the status of Muḥammad!, 585

Certain words Adam received were: *Our Nurturer, we have wronged ourselves*, 559
Charity tax is the archway of Islam, 257
Client is part of the tribe, A, 545
Closest of all in well-guidedness and evidence and probity was Ibn Masʿūd, The, 733
Congregational prayer bests individual prayer 27 times, 592
Construe Qur'ān according to its most beautiful aspects, 25
Coolness of my eye was made to be in prayer, The, 600
Covering up of a verse of lapidation in the Torah, 644
Deeds count only according to the last moments, 550
Devil parts ways with ʿUmar, The, 755
Did I not tell you not to love the Jews?, 694
Do not gift my wives anything, we have no need of gifts!, 760
Doubt is misgivings, truthfulness peace of mind, 246
Dwellers of paradise shall pluck fruit and Allah substitutes its like, The, 453
Each verse has a surface and a depth and each boundary has a way up, 418
Eat! the hue is one but savors differ, 453
Establish prayer means they make integrals equal and protect it from corruption, 265
Even a thorn and smaller yet, 754
Every verse in each of them has a surface and an inward, 25
Every wording has a surface and an inward, each wording a boundary and each boundary a way up, 25
Everything that has *O you people* is Meccan while everything that has *O you who believe* is Medinan, 398
Everything the Prophet saw on the night of *Isrā'* and *Miʿrāj* was with his very eyes, 625
Faḍḍaltukum ʿalā-l-ʿālamīna refers neither to all other than Allah nor to all people, 601
Faḍḍaltukum ʿalā-l-ʿālamīna refers to the worlds of their time, 601
Faqīh is he who has renounced the world and longs for the hereafter, The, 722
Fatiha is a panacea, The, 149
Fatiha is like the seal over the book, The, 210
Fatiha is soundly established as Meccan, The, 150
Fāṭima is the best of the women of Paradise but for Maryam, 708
Fine innovation this is!, A, 757

First of those who publicized their *islām* are seven people, The, 751
Follow those that come after me: Abū Bakr and ʿUmar, 755
Forerunners are four: I am the forerunner of the Arabs, 751
Fruits of paradise resemble each other, The, 453
Give salaam, feed others, 692
Greed is poverty and despair sufficiency, 764
Had ʿAbd Allāh b. ʿAbbās been our age none of us could have been his equal, 730
Had I found you tonsured, I would have cut off your head, 762
Had there been a Prophet after me, truly, it would have been ʿUmar, 755
Had they not said *in shāʾ Allah*, she would have never ever been made clear to them, 667
Had they slaughtered any cow they wished it would have been sufficient for them, 662
Hadith of Jibrīl on submission, belief and excellence (*Islām, Īmān, Iḥsān*), 200, 551
Ḥijāra are brimstone, 435
Ḥiṭṭa is *lā ilāha illā-l-Lāh*, thus named because it lays down sins, 629
Hold fast to the covenant of Ibn Umm ʿAbd, 733
Horses are part of the spoils of war, and the battle-gear and property carried by the enemy killed in battle, 762
Ḥudhayfa was the keeper of the Prophet's secrets, 727
I am half of all knowledge, 700
I am hopeful and fearful, 765
I am the master of the children of Adam on the Day of Resurrection, 184
I asked Allah for seven needs and he gave me six, 725
I bear witness you are truly the Messenger of Allah, and that you are bringing truth, 692
I divided my nights into three parts, 703
I do not see myself making a livelihood other than banging my drum, 716
I do not stay away from more than your name, 708
I dreamt I drank from a vessel of milk then gave the rest of it to ʿUmar—knowledge, 756
I give you permission to raise the veil and hear from my intimates, 733
I have made 18,000 *khatma*s of the Qurʾān, 700

I have two ministers from the dwellers of heaven and two from the dwellers of earth, 754
I have wronged myself, forgive me! None forgives sins but You, 560
I kept company with the Messenger of Allah before he received his mission, 750
I know for sure when you are happy with me and when you are angry with me, 708
I never saw any better women than the women of the *Anṣār* nor stronger, 709
I said to myself: if Persia and Byzantium heard him they would all be Muslims, 730
I saw even senior Companions asking her about inheritance law, 707
I saw him puffed up with self-approval and wished to teach his ego a lesson, 760
I dreamt of black sheep succeeded by dirt-white sheep. Abū Bakr! Interpret it, 697
I saw many of the Companions asking ʿAlqama questions and fatwas, 716
I saw the Messenger of Allah call you, pat you, and insufflate into your mouth, 728
I took from the mouth of the Messenger of Allah 70 suras, 733
I used to hear the Prophet say: I, Abū Bakr and ʿUmar went somewhere, 766
I want to ask you matters only a prophet would know, 692
I wanted the spot for myself, but I shall put him before me today, 710
I was infatuated with myself and wanted to humble myself, 765
I was sent to all people without exception, 398
I was the sixth of six Muslims on the face of the earth, 733
I went out with ʿUmar until we reached Ṣuhayb, 751
I will supplicate Allah and your jealousy will leave you, 770
Iblīs is the primogenitor of the jinn as Adam is that of human beings, 545
Iblīs lodged himself in the snake's muzzle until it entered with him into paradise, 557
Iblīs was an angel in charge of the nearest heaven, 533
Iblīs was an angel whose nature Allah changed into that of a jinn, 544
Iblīs was not "one of" but "among" the jinn, 544

Iblīs was not in the least an angel, 544
Iblīs was of the jinn who dwelt the earth before Adam, 545
Iblīs's name was 'Azāzīl and he was among the nobility of the angels, 543
Ibn 'Abbās declared seeing the angel Jibrīl twice, 728
Ibn 'Abbās is called the Sea because of the abundance of his knowledge, 730
Ibn Mas'ūd has left no-one like him to succeed him, 734
Ibn Mas'ūd is the first to have recited the Qur'ān out loud in Mecca, 733
Ibn Mas'ūd was the carrier of the sandals, the toothstick, and the cushion, 733
Ibn Mas'ūd went in to see Salmān on his deathbed, 748
Ibn Ubay and his friends were met by Companions, 338, 339
Ibn Umm 'Abd [=Ibn Mas'ūd] was one of the nearest of them to Allah, 734
Ibrāhīm lied on three occasions, 327, 328
If a stray camel or a sheep died on the shore of the Euphrates I would fear that Allah would ask me to account, 764
If Daylam heard this they would all become Muslims, 730
If he had permitted it I would have kissed his head, 730
If he said it then I believe him. And I believe him regarding more yet, 697
If the Messenger of Allah had seen what our women do, he would have forbidden them to go to the mosques, 710
If Mūsā were alive, he would have no other choice but to follow me, 583, 584
If one's *āmīn* coincides with the angels', one's sins are all forgiven, 212
If the weeping of all people, that of Dāwūd and that of Nūḥ were put together, that of Adam exceeds it, 561
If the world fetched a gnat's wing to Allah He would have never let an unbeliever drink a sip of water from it, 472
If you are innocent, Allah will acquit you; otherwise, beg for His forgiveness, 693
If you give leadership to Abū Bakr you will find him trustworthy, 715
If you give leadership to 'Alī you will find him guiding, 715
If you give leadership to 'Umar you will find him strong, 715
Ihbiṭū miṣran was said to mean the proper noun [Egypt], 642

In the nations before you were people who received communications, non-prophets, 755
In their hearts is a sickness denotes moral vices, 45
Infāq means a man's expenditure on his family, 271
Infāq (spending) means *zakāt* (charity tax), 271
Inna-l-ladhīna āmanū [in al-Baqara 2:62] was said to mean the hypocrites, 647
Israelites accused Mūsā of having dropsy of the scrotum, The, 634
Israelites deemed Jibrīl their enemy and Mikā'īl their ally, The 737
Israelites dug ponds and opened channels so that fish entered on the Sabbath, The, 655
Israelites in the desert were 600,000, The, 633
Israelites made it difficult for themselves so Allah made it difficult for them, The, 662
Israelites made up derisive phrases as they entered the gate shifting on their backsides, The, 632
Israelites' physical appearances were not metamorphosed but rather their hearts, The, 655
Israelites prostrated on one flank and turned up the other to see if the mount was still falling on them, The, 651
Israelites set to killing from dawn to dusk. Mūsā and Hārūn supplicated and repentence came down, The, 620
Israelites used to pray for victory through the Prophet, 585
Israelites were metamorphosed into apes literally, The, 656
Israelites who had not worshipped the Calf were ordered to kill those who had, The, 620
Iyyāka naʿbudu means, "We worship You, and none other than You", 192
Jibra'īl taught me *āmīn* whenever I finish reciting the Fatiha, 210
Jibra'īl was ordered to uproot the mountain and overshadow them with it, 651
Jibrīl made me read according to one *ḥarf* so I kept asking him for more, 23
Just so did the angel interpret it before the dawn, 697
Keep the promise of the obligations and avoiding sins, *I shall keep the promise* of forgiving and rewarding, 580
Keep the promise with regard to following Muḥammad *I shall keep the promise* in removing your burdens, 580

Khatama and *ghishāwa* are a literal sealing and a literal cover, 298
Khiḍr sat on withered grass and it became verdant again, 738
Killing of 'Ammār showed that the side of right was 'Alī's, The, 713
Knowledge has gone, nothing remains but specks gathered up in different vessels, 736
Lampoon them, and Jibrīl is with you, 724
Land and its western parts which We had blessed means Syro-Palestine, The 615
Learn al-Baqara, for taking it is a blessing and leaving it is woe, 341
Learn before you lead, 763
Learn the inheritance laws, the *Sunna*, and grammar the way you learn Qur'ān, 762
Learning left unspoken is like a treasure left unspent, 272
Leave what causes you misgivings for what does not cause you misgivings, 246
Let knowledge congratulate you, Abū al-Mundhir, 753
Let me enter in your peace as I had entered in your dispute, 709
Māliki yawmi-d-dīn is a Prophetic narration, 180
Maliki yawmi-d-dīn is also related from the Prophet, 180
Many men reached perfection but, among women, only Āsya the wife of Pharaoh and Maryam bint 'Imrān, 708
Meaning of *alif lām mīm* is, "I, Allah, know best," The, 231
Meaning of *Āmīn* is, "Do!", The, 209
Messenger of Allah forbade temporary marriage and eating the meat of the domestic asses, The, 758
Messenger of Allah never fought a battle except I [Ṣuhayb] took part in it, The, 752
Messenger of Allah recited the Fatiha and counted, The, 152
Messenger of Allah smiled, The, 232
Messenger of Allah, I was given a *bukhtiyya* as a gift! "Sacrifice it", 675
Mūsā had a rock which gushed out from each side three springs, 633
Mūsā struck the sea and there appeared twelve paths, 612
Mūsā wants nothing other than to toy with us: *ḥiṭṭatun ḥiṭṭatun*!, 632
Mūsā's staff measured ten cubits —the height of Mūsā, 635

Mūsā's staff was from the myrtle of Paradise with two forks that lit up in the dark, 635
Muttaqīn are *those who believe in the unseen*, The, 273
My family, pray! Pray!, 598
My father called for fire and burnt the hadiths he had in his possession, 699
My father gathered Hadith from the Messenger of Allah and it was 500 hadiths, 699
My heart softened like butter and hardened like stone for the sake of Allah, 764
My mother's woe if my Lord does not grant mercy!, 765
My Nurturer, did You not create me with Your hand?" 560
No Kufan or Basrian matched the Godfearingness of Ibn Sīrīn, 735
No Muslim is pricked by a thorn but a higher level will be recorded, 473
No newborn is born except the devil touches it at the time of its birth, 55
No one would set eyes on Ibn Sīrīn except they would make *dhikr* of Allah, 735
None has better belief than belief without seeing, 264
None hears a word, or two, or three, or four, or five words pertaining to what Allah has commanded..., 704
None is to go except a man who is part of me and I am part of him, 714
None loves you ['Alī] but a believer and none hates you but a hypocrite, 715
None of the Companions has as many merits reported about them as 'Alī does, 712
None remains who prayed in both directions other than I, 717
None resembled the Prophet at prayer more than Anas, 718
Not one woman among them remained except she covered herself from head to toe, 710
Nothing in the world was more important to me than that resting-place, 711
Nothing short of what covers both the hair and skin, without transparency, 709
O Allah! Give him deep understanding of the religion and teach him interpretation, 728
O Allah! I am rough, make me gentle! I am stingy, make me generous! I am weak, make me strong!, 764
O Allah! Make his property and offspring abundant and put blessing in it for him, 718

O Allah! Make him wise in the Religion and beloved to people, 722
O Allah! put blessings in him and propagate [blessings] from him, 729
O Allah! Strengthen Islam with ʿUmar b. al-Khaṭṭāb, 754
O Allah! teach him wisdom and the interpretation of the Book, 728
O Allah! We used our Prophet as a means to You, 763
O *kāf hā yā ʿayn ṣād*! O *ḥā mīm ʿayn sīn qāf*!, 238
O ʿUmar! You have not left behind you a person whose deeds I like to imitate more than yours, 766
One all!, 708
One would see one of his own [flesh and blood], or his friend, and be unable to carry out the divine command, 620
One's paternal uncle is the twin trunk of one's father, 522
Only 142 Prophetic hadiths are narrated from Abū Bakr, 699
Only three types of people may give fatwa, 736
Opening Letters allude to the lifespans of peoples, The, 232
Opening Letters are a secret known only to Allah, The, 239
Opening Letters are names for Allah Most High, The, 238
Opening Letters are names for the Qurʾān, The, 238
Opening Letters are names for the suras, The, 234
Opening of the Book and the closing verses of Surat al-Baqara, The, 213
Opening of the Book is seven verses, first of which, The, 152
Opening of the Book! Truly it is the Seven Oft-Repeated, The, 212
Our Lord did not create any creature He prizes more, nor more knowledgeable than human beings, 528
Pagans wanted to harm no one more than Bilāl, The, 720
People look to you the way birds look at a piece of meat, 760
People resemble their times more than they resemble their own parents, 764
People tested with the severest hardships are the prophets, then those with most merit, The, 571
Pious elder among them owned a heifer, A, 671
Prayer is the pillar of the Religion, 257

Prophet blocked all doors [to the mosque] except the door of 'Alī, The, 714
Prophet called 'Umar "my little brother", The, 756
Prophet came to Medina when I [Anas] was 10, The, 717
Prophet did *rajm* and so did we after him, The, 758
Prophet does not return wrong with wrong but forgives and pardons, The, 644
Prophet enjoyed listening to Umayya's poetry, endorsing some as true, 767
Prophet hugged Ibn 'Abbās, The, 728
Prophet is not coarse of speech or boisterous in the market-places, The, 644
Prophet made Anas and Ibn Mas'ūd brothers, The, 733
Prophet made Ibn Mas'ūd the brother of al-Zubayr and of Sa'd b. Mu'ādh, The, 732
Prophet offered me to choose between emigration and helpship, The, 727
Prophet passed by Ibn Ubay's house and waited for him to invite him in, 693
Prophet placed his garment over 'Alī, Fāṭima, al-Ḥasan and al-Ḥusayn, 714
Prophet praised Ḥudhayfa and took it on himself to repay him the blood-wite, 726
Prophet reached the Lote-Tree of the Farthest Boundary and *the All-Powerful, the Lord of Might approached*, The, 625
Prophet revealed 'Abd Allāh b. Salām was one of the dwellers of Paradise, The, 691
Prophet saw his Lord Most High on the Night Journey with the two eyes of his head, 625
Prophet spat into his eyes, supplicated for him and he was cured, 714
Prophet swore to avoid his concubine Māriya, 56
Prophet was brought back up to the Almighty Most High and said *in the same place*: 'Lord, lighten our burden,' 625
Prophet would gesture inside prayer, 718
Prophet would joke with Anas and call him "O Big-Eared!", 717
Prophet would say *āmīn* after reciting *wa-lā-ḍ-ḍāllīn* and raise his voice, The, 211
Prophet would set up a pulpit for Ḥassān in the mosque, The, 724
Prophet's standard was in 'Alī's hand in most battles, The, 712

Prophets, then the righteous then those with most merit, 572
Prophets, then the knowledgeable, then those with most merit, 572
Qalb (heart) is the seat of knowledge but can mean the mind, 305
Qur'ān is tractable, 25
Qur'ān was sent according to seven wordings, The, 24
Quraysh! Truly I am one of your best archers and you will not reach me, 750
Rabbis of Medina would secretly tell whoever they advised to follow Muḥammad, , 593
Reciters of Qur'ān are three types. The first take it as merchandise, The, 723
Rijzan mina-s-samā' means pestilence or hail, 633
Rivers of Paradise run without river-beds, The, 448
Rock fled with Mūsā's clothes after he had placed them on it before washing, A, 634
Ṣafrā'u fāqi'un lawnuhā means "of intensely black color", 663
Salmān did not reach 90 years of age, 748
Salmān had heard the Prophet would be sent forth so he went out in search of him, 747
Salmān has more understanding than Abū al-Dardā', 748
Salmān lived 350 years, 748
Salmān took part in the Trench, the rest of the battles and the conquests of Iraq, 747
Say the truth and al-Ḥaqq will show you the abodes of the people of truth, 725
Seek a licit means of livelihood. That is jihad in the path of Allah, 716
Seventy men were away at the time of the Calf-worship including Hārūn, 620
Shall I not tell you of a sura the like of which was never sent down?, 212
Shu'ayb was nicknamed *khaṭīb al-anbiyā'* because of the excellent way he preached, 749
Silent *āmīn* is related from 'Alī, Ibn Mas'ūd and 'Umar, The, 212
Sins of the folk were so few that they knew exactly what was wrong; ours are so many we have no idea, 736
Some discourses are pure magic, 367
Someone will come up and say: "We do not find the verse of *rajm* in the Book of Allah", 758

Spirit of Holiness is with Ḥassān for as long as he speaks back in defense of the Messenger of Allah, The, 724
Stay close to the pulpit of the Messenger of Allah for if you leave it you will never see it again, 692
Strike with your staff the rock denotes any rock, 635
Ṣuhayb became Muslim with ʿAmmār when the Prophet was in Dār al-Arqam, 750
Ṣuhayb, I find no fault in you except three traits, 752
Ṣuhayb took part in Badr and all the battles after that, 750
Sunna in Islam is more rare and precious than Islam itself is rare and precious among the rest of the faiths, The, 700
Superexcellence of ʿĀʾisha over women is like that of meat and gruel over foods, The, 708
Tafsīr has four different perspectives (*awjuh*): one is familiar to Arabs, 26
Take account of yourselves before you are brought to account, 764
Tell me, am I one of the hypocrites?, 765
Thanks and praise to Allah, not anyone else, and not to you!, 707
That boy of yours is the champion of shaykhs!, 729
That is what we were ordered to do with our learned people, 729
There is no creature of Allah but you may take or leave what they said except the Prophet, 744
There is no part in Islam for whoever leaves prayer, 765
There is not one verse but I would know whether it was revealed by night or by day, 714
There is nothing in paradise of the foods of the world except the names, 455
There was a sub-group of the angels called *al-jinn*, created from the fire of samum, 543
There were always tracks in ʿUmar's face caused by tears, 759
These are Arabs following you, then non-Arabs succeed them until they completely engulf them in their number, 697
These tablets contain the Book of Allah, His commands and His prohibitions, 623
These two [Abū Bakr and ʿUmar] are [my] hearing and eyesight, 755

These two [silk and gold] are categorically prohibited for males in my Community, licit for females, 573
They are among the elite of the Companions of Muḥammad, 734
This ['Umar] is a man who does not like vanity, 755
This is a *wuḍū'* without which Allah accepts no prayer, 573
This is from the hair of the Messenger of Allah and I want you to place it under my tongue, 717
This is what we were commanded to do with the People of the House of our Prophet, 729
Those that are meant by *and when it is said to them* have not yet appeared, 328
Those who incurred anger are the Jews while *those who are astray* are the Christians, 207
Thunder is the sound of the crack of the whip of the angel in charge of herding the clouds, 374
Thunderstroke seized you means a fire came from the sky and blasted them, or din-and-destruction, The, 626
Thus were we before, then our hearts hardened, 700
Tomorrow I will hand over the flag to someone who loves Allah and His Prophet and whom Allah and His Prophet love, 714
True believer could not feel other than sadness in this world, The, 722
Truly Allah loves, among my Companions, four, 748
Truly he is a righteous man, one of us, 692
Truly this knowledge is religion; so look well from whom you take your religion, 736
Truly we are looking at the rain of mercy through a thin veil, 729
Truly, Allah might visit on a people inevitable, destined punishment, but..., 213
Truthfulness/goodness is peace of mind and mendacity is misgivings, 246
Ubay is the first who took dictation from the Prophet, 753
Ubay took part in Badr and all the battles, 753
Ubay was the Leader of Qur'ān Reciters, 753
Ubay was a participant in the Second 'Aqaba Pledge, 753
'Umar accomplished the prayer for rain through intercession

of ʿAbbās b. ʿAbd al-Muṭṭalib, 763
ʿUmar b. ʿAbd al-ʿAzīz was seen walking with al-Khaḍir, 739
ʿUmar came to Syro-Palestine wearing a waist-wrap, two *khuffs*, and a turban, 762
ʿUmar commanded people to learn ḥadīth by heart exactly as they had to learn Qur'an, 762
ʿUmar disliked the compilation of ḥadīth in books, 762
ʿUmar excelled at interpreting dreams, 756
ʿUmar forbade certain actions out of precautionary pre-emption *(sadd al-dharāʾiʿ)*, 761
ʿUmar memorized Sūrat al-Baqara in twelve years, 765
ʿUmar passed by and saw Ḥassān reciting poetry in the mosque, 724
ʿUmar sacrificed a prize she-camel he had bought for three hundred dinars, 675
ʿUmar stipulated that Ṣuhayb should pray over his remains, 752
ʿUmar used to seek refuge in Allah from any problem ʿAlī could not solve, 714
ʿUmar was the barrier between the Community and the onset of dissension, 767
ʿUmar wore a waist-wrap patched in twelve places, 765
ʿUmar would call Ubay the master of Muslims, 753
Umayya almost became Muslim in his poetry, 767-768
Umayya disbelieved in the Prophet either out of envy or out of loyalty for his cousins killed at Badr, 767
Umayya's tongue believed but his heart disbelieved, 768
Umm Salama and her husband were among the first, 768
Umm Salama was the first woman to migrate to Abyssinia 769
Umm Sulayṭ deserves it more, she sewed for the people at the battle of Uḥud, 760
Vigil prayer (*tahajjud*) is the hardest thing I have ever seen, 723
We are a nation Allah ennobled and made mighty with Islam, 762
We find him named Muḥ. b. ʿAbd Allāh. His birthplace is Mecca, his place of migration Ṭāba, 644
We found that the goodness of our lives was patience, 764

We would not doubt that Ibn Masʿūd was a member of the house of the Prophet, 733

Well? Did I save you from the man?, 709

Were it not for Muʿādh, ʿUmar would have perished, 763

Were it not people might claim that ʿUmar added something to the Book of Allah, I would write it down, 758

What a wonderful translator of the Qurʾān Ibn ʿAbbās is!, 730

What did the Prophet do on such and such a day?, 729

What do we gain out of all our illnesses? "Expiations", 754

What separation is this, Bilāl? When will you come and visit me?, 720

What thing is that—*ḥiṭṭatun*?, 632

Whatever trouble affects the believer, such will surely be an expiation, 473

When I finally beheld his face I knew for sure that such was never the face of a liar, 692

When the imam says *wa-lā-ḍ-ḍāllīn*, let all of you say *āmīn*, 212

When the Jews came to him he recited to them, *Alif, lām, mīm*, 232

When Mūsā brought them the Torah and they saw what it comprised..., 651

When the Prophet first came to Medina I was among those who kept their distance, 692

When the Prophet was taken ill he ordered Abū Bakr to lead the prayer, 698

When ʿUmar died we considered nine tenths of learning had disappeared, 756

When ʿUmar was mortally stabbed he sent his son ʿAbd Allāh with a message, 710

When a way up comes to us from ʿAlī, we look no other way, 714

When a woman reaches puberty she must cover whatever her mother and grandmother must cover, 709

When you are happy with me, you say, 'No, by the Lord of Muḥammad!', 708

Whenever any matter worried him, the Prophet would quickly resort to prayer, 597

Whenever Ibn ʿAbbās sat he would take the place of two men, 728

Whenever Ibn Sīrīn mentioned death he would die limb by limb, 735

Whenever the Prophet's wives faced hardship he would order them to pray, 598
Whenever they were alarmed, the prophets would quickly resort to prayer, 598
Where is Zunāb?, 770
Which of your wives are in Paradise? "You are surely one of them!", 708
Who is going to take it just because you say so? No, by Allah! Not until we see Allah!, 623
Whoever displays humility to the people beyond what is in his heart only displays hypocrisy, 764
Whoever fights his ego *(nafs)* for the sake of Allah, He will protect him, 700
Whoever helps to kill a Muslim even by half a word, 230
Whoever I am patron to, now 'Alī is his patron, 714
Whoever reads one letter of the Book of Allah has one good deed, 215
Whoever speaks about the Qur'ān based on his mere opinion and is correct, is incorrect, 43
Whoever wants to recite Qur'ān as it was first revealed, let him recite it according to Ibn Mas'ūd's reading, 733
Why do you not call on us the way you call on Ibn 'Abbās?, 729
Width of the Israelites' campsite was 12 miles, The, 634
Would that I were resurrected with a clear account, 764
Yahūd stems from *hāda*, "he repented," when they repented of the Calf-worship, 647
You ['Alī] are my brother, 712
You are my bondsman in this world and the next, 714
You are a learned young man, 732
You are more deserving that I come to you, 729
You are the patron of every believer after me, 714
You might look at her, for it is more conducive to harmony, 523
You shall certainly fear Allah, O son of Khaṭṭāb!, 764
You will never understand until you see the Qur'ān's different aspects/perspectives, 26
Your Lord will raise you to an Exalted Station means He will seat the Prophet with Him on His Throne, 744

Index of Poetic Verses

Alas and woe to Zayyāba because of al-Ḥārith, 274
Amīn! then Allah increased our mutual estrangement, 210
And a low-lying black cloud true to its thunder, pouring, 370
And across the distance of an earth between us and a sky, 371
And Allah named you with a name blessed, 158
And the band of Ḥarrāb and Qadd possess a rank, 420
And cavalry-men approaching one another, 325
And he rises until the ignorant suspects, 366
And I disregard the villain's curse out of sheer generosity, 376
And I forgive the honorable man's slur to preserve his affection, 376
And I may pass by the scoundrel hurling insults at me,, 204
And may Allah have mercy on a slave who says āmīn, 210
And none perdures over the trials of time, 426
And nothing's left but enmity, 183
And they told it "Bow for Laylā!" so it bowed, 537
And when I saw the vulture beat the crow, 351
And when the virgins wore masks of smoke, 455
Are you trying to guide me? My mind is my guide, 380
As if the hearts of birds—some moist, some dry—, 389
As if my eyes were the two buckets a docile draught-camel used, 444
Baradā siphon-filtered with mellifluous fine wine, A, 373
Bishr has taken over Iraq, 498
Both darkened my two states then lifted, 380
Camel heifers of Suhayl's two sons set about, The, 405
Countries where we lived and which we loved, 333
Death surely keeps bursting upon unsuspecting folk, 311
Decorous wives, donning high face-veils, 660
Deviating from their straight path, errant, 480
Do not humiliate the weak; you may stoop, 591
Few when counted, many when they fight, 479
Futḥul went far from me for my asking him, 210

Ghazāla pulled up the market of sword fights, 265
Graciousness earned you three things from me, 174
Have you all not seen Iram and ʿĀd?, 164
How to lampoon when righteous deeds constantly..., 441
I commanded you goodness so do what you were commanded to do, 662
I do not know—has some ill report changed them?, 602
I have given up al-Lāt and al-ʿUzzā both!, 414
I told her, "Stop!" so she said, "Qāf!", 230
I traded in the mane for a bald-head, 350
If I wished to weep blood, I would weep it, 383
In it there are threads of blackness and piebald, 645
In the name of Him Whose Name is in every sura, 159
Is he not the first who prayed toward your qibla..., 539
Is it One Lord or a thousand lords, 414
It blinds guidance to the perplexed ignorant, 348
Like a solemn oath of Abū Rabāḥ, 164
Lo! I swear by the sire of the carrion-birds squatting mid-morning, 282
Lo! May Allah never bless Suhayl, 167
Long is your night with antimonied eyes, 188
Lovely to me were made the two fire-workers, 279
Muted, filling the hand, peerless, 719
My two daughters wished for their father to live on, 160
O my Lord! do not deprive me of her love—ever!, 210
O remembering her when I remember her!, 371
O soul! make graceful your lament, 719
O soul! you have not, besides Allah, any protector!, 426
O Taym, Taym of ʿAdīy! You fatherless sons!, 401
Or some fortune they made, 602
Quittance from ʿAlqama the boastful!, 528
Sensuous women, between virgins and middlings, 659
She shows the speck in front but she's before it, 427
So I left him a slaughter stock of beasts, 361
So I loosed it, positively presuming it went, 599
Stone-deaf when they hear of good things touching me, 365
Stop! Let us weep at the reminder of a friend and a resting-place, 771

Tall, like coverings on the necks of horses, 660
Their mutual greetings are agonizing blows, 325, 441
There are my horses—his gifts—and there my camel-mounts, 663
They give to drink whoever alights at al-Barīṣ to stay with them, 373
To the bull camel, king of magnificent designs, 274
Towards me a lion—but in wars an ostrich, 367
Trampling with us skulls and breastbones, 609
Truly the noble are many in the lands, 479
Up to one year—then the Name of Peace on you both, 160
Utterly deaf to anything I do not want, 365
What! Taym you dare claim as my peer?, 413
When people were people and times were times, 333
When shamed by the water that offers itself, 466
Whoever tastes it smacks his tongue, 428
With a lion full-weaponed, mammoth, 366
You could see bluffs there bowing to the hooves, 536

General Index

'Abbād b. Hishām, 722
al-'Abbādī, 17
'Abbās b. 'Abd al-Muṭṭalib, 728, 763
'Abbās b. Yazīd, 748
'Abbās, Faḍl Ḥasan, 65
Abbasid, 747
'Abd al-'Azīz b. Ziyād, 170
'Abd al-Bāqī, Miṣbāḥ Allāh, 72
'Abd Allāh b. 'Abbās, 732
'Abd Allāh b. 'Abd Allāh b. Ubay, 694
'Abd Allāh b. Abī Yazīd, 731
'Abd Allāh b. 'Amr b. al-'Āṣ, 732
Abd Allāh b. Ḥanṭab, 755
'Abd Allāh b. Ḥanẓala, 691
'Abd Allāh b. al-Ḥārith b. Nawfal, 713
'Abd Allāh b. Jābir, 149
'Abd Allah b. Mi'qal, 691-692
'Abd Allāh b. Mughaffal, 211, 691
'Abd Allāh b. Ṣafwān, 771
'Abd Allāh b. Salām, 273, 336, 597, 691-692, 734, 737
'Abd Allāh b. Shaddād, 713
'Abd Allāh al-Ṭawīl, 747
'Abd Allāh b. Ubay b. Salūl, 312-313, 337, 693, 736
'Abd Allāh b. 'Umar, 732
'Abd Allāh b. 'Utba, 732
'Abd Allāh b. Yazīd, 726
'Abd Allāh b. Zam'a, 698
'Abd al-Malik b. Marwān, 266
'Abd al-Malik b. 'Umayr, 149
'Abd al-Qāhir al-Jurjānī, 48
'Abd al-Raḥmān b. 'Abd Allāh b. Mas'ūd, 732
'Abd al-Raḥmān b. 'Āmir, 731
'Abd al-Raḥmān b. Aslam, 234
'Abd al-Raḥmān b. 'Awf, 180, 713, 771
'Abd al-Raḥmān b. Ḥārith, 713, 771
'Abd al-Raḥmān b. Ḥāṭib, 752
'Abd al-Raḥmān b. Sābiṭ, 170
'Abd al-Raḥmān b. 'Umar b. al-Khaṭṭāb, 762
'Abd al-Raḥmān, Jalāl al-Dīn, 13
'Abd al-Razzāq al-Ṣan'ānī, 174, 182, 238, 464, 466, 583, 592, 614, 651, 709, 716, 729, 748, 760-762, 767
'Abd al-Tawwāb, Ramaḍān, 230
abdāl, 722
'Abduh, Muḥammad, 65, 69, 74, 206, 366, 702
'Abduh Aghā, Munīr, 702
Abdul-Massih, George M., 156, 158, 183, 329, 332
'Abīda b. 'Amr al-Salmānī, 657, 661, 732, 735
'Abqariyyat 'Umar, 759
Abrahamov, Binyamin, 276
abrogation, 24, 33, 37-43, 201, 418, 582-583, 620, 648, 660-661, 689, 736, 757
Abū 'Abd al-Malik al-Shāmī, 182
Abū 'Alī al-Fārisī, 50, 214, 695, 732
Abū 'Alī al-Jubbā'ī, 701
Abū al-'Āliya, 46, 179, 231-232, 239, 312, 452, 556, 558, 579, 584, 600, 616, 641, 650, 657, 661, 666, 695-696
Abū 'Amr b. al-'Alā', 146, 180-181, 189, 199, 294, 305, 307, 320, 326, 504, 603, 613, 629, 635, 651, 657, 665, 695-696, 732, 741
Abū 'Amr al-Sufyānī, 732
Abū al-Aswad, 189, 732
Abū 'Awāna, 728, 735
Abū Ayyūb, 695, 697, 702, 753

Abū Bakr al-Ṣiddīq, 272, 338, 539, 696-700 707, 710, 715, 720, 754, 755, 769
Abū Bakr b. ʿAbd al-Raḥmān, 771
Abū Bakra, 728
Abū Barza al-Aslamī, 691
Abū Burayda, 748
Abū Burda b. Abī Mūsā, 692
Abū al-Dardāʾ, 26, 180, 182, 257, 471, 552, 692, 716, 727, 731, 734, 748
Abū Dāwūd, 26, 42, 210, 522, 552, 596, 667, 674, 698, 700, 708-709, 724, 755, 758, 763
Abū Dharr, 207, 624, 755
Abū al-Faraj al-Aṣfahānī. See *al-Aghānī*
Abū Firākh, Muḥammad Aḥmad, 230
Abū Ḥamdūn, 199
Abū Ḥamza, 717, 728
Abū Ḥanīfa, 151, 181, 211, 262, 450, 553, 700, 719, 743
Abu al-Ḥasan, Muḥammad, 63
Abū Ḥātim al-Sijistānī, 180, 182, 239, 311
Abū Ḥaywa, 181, 307, 319-320, 629, 641, 677
Abū Ḥayyān al-Andalusī, 19, 57-58, 91, 145, 231, 239, 294, 306, 380, 397, 432-433, 469, 499, 505, 551, 565, 589, 592, 598, 613, 631, 639, 653, 738
Abū Hurayra, 42, 151-152, 180-181, 211-212, 272, 328, 435, 459, 471, 472, 521, 571, 591, 624, 631, 633, 661, 666, 691, 695, 698, 702-703, 707, 718, 724, 735, 746, 753, 755-756
Abū Hurayra Ibn al-Dhahabī, 8, 120
Abū ʿIkrima al-Ḍabbī, 159
Abū Isḥāq al-Ḥaḍramī, 773
Abū Isḥāq al-Isfarāyīnī, 702
Abū Isḥāq al-Jūzajānī, 720,
Abū Isḥāq al-Marwazī, 702,
Abū Isḥāq al-Sabīʿī 722, 728
Abū Isḥāq al-Shīrāzī, 15, 49, 260, 695
Abū Jaʿfar Ibn al-Qaʿqāʿ, 146, 180, 199, 294, 320, 326, 330, 504, 576, 613, 629, 635, 648, 658, 669, 705, 746
Abū Jahl, 35-36, 288, 295, 704, 772
Abū Juḥayfa, 712, 732, 748
Abū Lahab, 35-36, 288, 295, 539, 704
Abū al-Layth al-Samarqandī, 209, 237, 551
Abū Manṣūr al-Azharī, 51
Abū Masʿūd al-Badrī, 716
Abū Maysara, 210, 697
Abū Mūsā al-Ashʿarī, 522, 698, 701, 707-708, 753, 760
Abū Muslim al-Aṣfahānī, 58, 551, 628
Abū al-Najm al-Rājiz, 350
Abū Nawfal, 182
Abū Nuʿaym al-Aṣbahānī, 445, 695, 698, 700, 708, 716, 720, 722, 730, 733, 744, 759, 765, 771
Abū Qāʾid, 751
Abū al-Qāsim al-Maghribī, 750
Abū Qilāba, 182, 583, 735
Abū Rabīʿa al-Iyādī, 748
Abū Rāfiʿ, 712, 729, 732
Abū Rajāʾ, 180, 307, 379, 555, 613, 639
Abū Saʿīd al-Khudrī, 1, 149, 175, 459, 571, 624, 691, 698, 708, 712, 732, 747, 755,
Abū Salama b. ʿAbd al-Asad al-Makhzūmī, 691, 724, 768-770
Abū Salama b. ʿAbd al-Raḥmān, 691, 724
Abū Ṣāliḥ, 182, 209, 338, 435, 751
Abū al-Sawwār al-Ghanawī, 190, 601
Abū Shahba, Muḥammad, 59
Abū al-Shaʿthāʾ, 251, 705
Abū al-Shaykh, 532, 543-544, 614, 748

Abū Shurayḥ, 732
Abū Sulaymān al-Dārānī, 736
Abū al-Su'ūd, 19, 64, 90, 237, 400, 445
Abū Ṭāhir, 180
Abū Ṭālūt, 321
Abū Tammām, 183, 274, 366, 380-381, 479, 705
Abū al-Ṭufayl, 713, 726, 732, 753
Abū 'Ubayd. *See* al-Qāsim b. Sallām
Abū 'Ubayda b. 'Abd Allāh b. Mas'ūd, 732
Abū 'Ubayda b. al-Jarrāḥ, 720
Abū 'Ubayda Ma'mar b. al-Muthannā, 21, 160, 189, 230, 469, 613, 639, 696, 720, 724, 741
Abū Umāma, 712, 732, 751
Abū 'Uthmān al-Māzinī, 741
Abū 'Uthmān al-Nahdī, 182, 732, 747, 771
Abū Wā'il Shaqīq b. Salama, 709, 716, 726, 730, 732, 767, 771
Abū Ya'lā, 417, 583, 739, 754-755
Abū al-Yusr 'Ābidīn, 119
Abū Yūsuf, 450, 691, 701, 743
Abū Zahra, Muḥammad, 66, 239
Abu Zayd al-Anṣārī, 66, 159, 179, 259, 742
Abū Zuhayr al-Numayrī, 210
Abū Zur'a al-'Irāqī, 213
Abyssinia, Abyssinians, 751, 768, 769
accidents, 202, 689
accompaniment, 155, 265, 351, 687
'Ād, 143
Adab al-Kātib, 176, 233
al-Adab al-Mufrad, 305, 571
al-'Adadī, Aḥmad b. Muḥ., 161
Adam, 40, 79, 130-131, 184, 232, 484, 504, 510-524, 530-547, 550-551, 554-562, 567-569, 573, 610, 617, 633
Aḍbaṭ al-Sa'dī, 591, 705
aḍdād, 80, 349, 382, 543, 546
al-Aḍdād, a study of homopolysemous opposites in Arabic, 349
additives, 206, 332, 357, 383, 468, 507, 520, 564, 668, 685, 687
al-Adhkār, 155, 756
'Adī b. Ḥātim, 207, 735
Adil, Muhammad Nazim, xliii
adjunction, 283, 306, 358, 369, 407, 439, 443, 450, 470-471, 536, 550, 600, 677, 685
al-Adnahwī, 2, 11
'Adnān, 143
'Aḍudiyya, 85
Aḍwā' al-Bayān fī Īḍāḥ al-Qur'ān bil-Qur'ān, 20, 28, 737
Afandī, Muḥibb al-Dīn, 159, 265, 365, 660
affirmation, 207, 249, 259-262, 283, 293-294, 316, 331, 334-335, 341, 396, 398, 481, 519, 532, 550, 574, 670-671, 682, 738
Afifi al-Akiti, Muhammad, xliii
al-Afrād, 257
al-Aghānī, 266, 333, 367, 591, 727, 737
al-Aḥādīth al-Mukhtāra, 170, 597
al-Aḥādīth al-Mushkila al-Wārida fī Tafsīr al-Qur'ān al-Karīm, 58
'ahd. See previous knowledge
Aḥkām Qirā'at al-Qur'ān al-Karīm, 12-13, 218-224, 543, 655
Ahl al-Ḥadīth, 260-261
Ahl al-Kitāb, 744; *See also* Christians; Jews
Ahl al-Sunna, 269, 298, 316, 376, 385, 408, 458, 542, 564, 660, 701-702, 713, 744-745
Aḥmad Āghā b. Hūlāgū, 6
Aḥmad b. Ḥanbal, 149, 182, 207, 214, 246, 328, 340, 366, 373, 465, 522, 545, 552, 571, 583, 596-599, 624, 643, 667-668, 674, 691, 698, 708-712, 715, 734, 747, 749, 754-756, 761
Aḥmad b. Mūsā al-Lu'lu'ī, 696
Aḥmadnagrī, 'Abd al-Nabī b. 'Abd al-Rasūl, 166

Aḥnaf b. Qays, 706
aḥruf, 22-24, 418
al-Aḥruf al-Sabʿa wa-Manzilat al-Qirā'āt minhā, 24
ʿĀ'isha, 170, 182, 471, 521, 547, 549, 693, 698-699, 706-713, 716, 724, 755, 760, 770
al-Ajwiba ʿalā Mi'atin wa-Wāḥidin wa-Sittīna Su'ālan, 146
al-Ajwibat al-Marḍiyya, 155
al-Ajwibat al-Muḥarrara ʿan al-As'ilat al-ʿAshara, 290
Ākām al-Marjān fī Aḥkām al-Jānn, 510
al-Akhfash, 233, 306, 422, 530, 628, 711, 721, 725, 741, 750
al-Akhnas, 704
al-Akhṭal, 498, 719, 737
ʿAkkāwī, Inʿām, 351
al-Aʿlām, 1, 3, 695, 702, 742-743, 773
L'Alcoran de Mahomet, 67, 69
Alcoran of Mahomet, 68
Alcorani textus universus, 69
L'Alcorano di Macometto, 68
ʿAlī b. Abī Ṭalḥa, 20
ʿAlī b. Abī Ṭālib, 52, 150, 170, 181, 190, 205, 207, 212, 238, 257, 266, 305, 339, 521, 539, 692, 695, 698, 709, 712-716, 726, 739, 740, 750, 756-757, 760, 766
ʿAlī b. al-Madīnī, 717, 741-742
ʿAlī b. Zayd, 751
ʿAlī, Yūsuf Aḥmad, 8, 10, 14, 16, 30, 49, 50-56, 60, 164
ʿĀlim, Aḥmad, 153
ʿĀlim, ʿUmar Luṭfī, 85
al-ʿAliyya, 752
allegory, 61, 335, 347, 353, 388-390, 471, 683
alliteration. See *jinās*
ʿAlqama, 180, 201, 207, 397, 528, 715, 732-733
al-Ālūsī, 19, 58, 64, 230, 239, 738
al-Aʿmash, 180, 182, 194, 205, 293-294, 307, 326, 379, 469, 530, 555, 576, 614, 629, 635, 639, 641, 665, 677, 679, 721, 730, 743-744
ambiguous verses. See *mutashābihāt*
al-ʿĀmilī, Bahā' al-Dīn, 64, 86, 114
ʿĀmir b. Fuhayra, 751
ʿĀmir b. Rabīʿa, 769
ʿĀmir b. al-Ṭufayl, 528-529
ʿĀmir b. ʿUwaymir, 706
ʿAmmār b. Yāsir, 366, 709, 713, 716, 720, 734, 750-751, 770
Amol, 31
Amos, 643
ʿAmr b. ʿAlī, 720
ʿAmr b. al-ʿĀṣ, 759
ʿAmr b. Maʿdīkarb, 325
ʿAmr b. Maymūn, 732
ʿAmr b. Qurra, 270, 716
ʿAmr b. Shuraḥbīl, 697
ʿAmr b. ʿUmayr al-Thaqafī, 772
ʿAmrāwī, Muḥammad, 290
al-Amthāl al-Qur'āniyya al-Maḍrūba lil-Īmān billāh, 353
al-Amthāl fil-Qur'ān al-Karīm, 353
al-Amwāl, 272
ʿAmwās, 720
anapodoton, 330
Anas b. Mālik, 170, 181-182, 211, 238, 378, 435, 447, 465, 559, 599, 624, 641, 696, 698, 706, 716-718, 732-735, 747-751, 761, 764
al-Andalus, 351, 742
angels, 44, 53, 79, 129-130, 178, 192, 203, 212, 275, 303, 325, 373, 396, 406, 425, 443, 504-518, 524-527, 532-547, 555-569, 600, 605, 743
anger, 44, 123, 136, 203, 204, 205, 206, 207, 209, 466, 642
Anmāṭī, ʿUthmān b. Saʿīd, 6
anonymizer, 21, 467, 681
Anṣār, 63, 341, 693, 709, 718, 721, 724-725, 743
Anthologie Grammaticale Arabe. See Sacy, Silvestre de
anthropomorphism, 54, 290, 314, 394, 723, 737; *see also* Ḥashwiyya

antithesis, 689
aorist, 164, 177, 194, 378, 413, 431, 507, 607, 687
apodosis, 236, 330, 357-358, 382, 412, 428-431, 473, 553, 563, 581, 630, 638, 649, 652, 684, 686
Approaches to the History of the Interpretation of the Qur'ān, 78
appurtenance (*ta'alluq*), 290, 363, 667, 683
al-'Aqaba, 654, 753
al-'Aqīda al-Niẓāmiyya, 261
al-'Aqīda al-Ṣaḥīḥa, 567, 745
'Aqīl, 330
'aql, 275, 593, 673
al-'Aqqād, Maḥmūd, 759
Arabic Rhetoric: A Pragmatic Analysis, 79, 343
Arabic-English Lexicon. See Lane
Die Arabischen Studien in Europa, 85
Arabs, 10, 26, 32, 74, 86, 143, 157, 179, 183, 188, 222, 225, 230, 233, 244, 259, 263, 349, 381, 419, 428, 463, 616, 621, 697, 709, 728, 751-752; Arabophobe, 742
'Arā'is al-Bayān fī Ḥaqā'iq al-Qur'ān, 240
A'raj, 180, 530, 614, 665
'Arāk b. Khālid, 725
Arba'īn al-Ruhāwī, 155
al-Arba'īn fī Uṣūl al-Dīn, 534
Arberry, Arthur John, 75
Arch Rhetorician or The Schemer's Skimmer: A Handbook of Late Arabic badī' *drawn from 'Abd al-Ghanī an-Nābulusī's* Nafaḥāt al-azhār 'alā nasamāt al-asḥār, 168, 332, 351, 394, 506, 585, 608, 626
Arghun, 4
Aristotle, 232, 458
Arrivabene, Andrea, 68
'Āṣ b. Wā'il, 773
Asad, 194
As'ad b. Zurāra, 694
al-Aṣamm, 58, 544
Asās al-Taqdīs, 57
asbāb al-nuzūl, 43
Asbāb al-Nuzūl, 338, 464, 467, 584
al-Aṣfahānī al-Taymī. *See* al-Taymī al-Aṣfahānī
al-A'shā, 164, 427, 428, 528, 546, 662, 663, 719
al-Ash'arī Abū al-Ḥasan, 36, 160, 260-261, 495, 543, 549-550, 624, 701-702, 738, 740, 745
Ash'arīs and Ash'arism, 1, 32-33, 36, 54-58, 73, 160, 196, 200, 260-262, 269, 384-385, 442, 495-496, 534, 550, 701-702, 740
al-Ashbāh wal-Naẓā'ir fīl Naḥw, 34, 165
Ashqar, Muḥammad Sulaymān, 66
'Āṣim, 146, 152, 180-182, 199, 293, 306, 320, 326, 379, 555, 565, 577, 583, 614, 629, 640, 657-658, 696, 698, 700, 719, 766
al-'Askarī, Abū Hilāl, 182, 598, 605, 610, 645, 757
aṣl, 80, 301, 349, 443, 496, 543
Aslam al-Minqarī, 700
al-aṣlayn, 43
al-Asmā' wal-Ṣifāt, 169, 182, 238, 521, 522
al-Aṣma'ī, 189, 469, 696, 719, 742
Asrār al-Balāgha, 21, 48, 645
Asrār al-Ḥurūf wa-Ḥisāb al-Jummal, 232
al-Asrār al-Marfū'a fīl-Akhbār al-Mawḍū'a, 257
astronomy, 10, 16, 501
al-Aswad, 180, 201, 207, 699, 705, 715, 755, 772
al-Aswad al-'Ansī, 699
Aswad b. 'Abd Yaghūth, 772
Āsya, 708
'Aṭā' al-Khurāsānī, 170, 559
'Aṭā' b. Abī Rabāḥ, 6, 696
'Aṭā' b. al-Sāyib, 700
Atābak, 1
Aṭbāq al-Dhahab, 560

ʿaṭf, 29, 310, 358
atheism, 334
al-Athram, 741
ʿĀtika bint ʿĀmir, 768
ʿĀtika bint ʿUmays, 760
al-Aṭrash, Maḥmūd Aḥmad, 14, 90
augmentative, 224, 340, 681
auto-antonym. See *aḍdād*
autogenocide, 618-619
al-Awāʾil, 757
ʿAwf al-Aʿrabī, 695, 735
ʿAwn al-ʿUqaylī, 182
ʿAwn b. Abī Shaddād, 182
Aws, 584, 599, 693
Aws b. Ḥajar, 719
Awsaṭ, 257
ʿAwwāma, Muḥammad, 210
al-Awzāʿī, 151, 155, 719
Ayman b. Khuraym, 265
al-ʿAyn, 400, 507, 629, 739
ʿAyn al-Maʿānī fī Tafsīr al-Kitāb al-ʿAzīz wal-Sabʿ al-Mathānī, 239
Aysar al-Tafāsīr, 66
Ayyūb, 735
Ayyūb b. Tamīm, 725
Azerbaijan, 1, 12, 31, 761
al-Azhar, 63, 72-73, 74, 88, 115, 117, 119-120
al-ʿAzīz Sharḥ al-Wajīz, 153
al-Azraq, 294
ʿAzzāwī, ʿAbbās, 15
al-Bāb al-Ḥādi ʿAshar, 12
Bābilī, Shams al-Dīn, 120
al-Bābirtī, Akmal al-Dīn, 48, 91, 636
Badāʾiʿ al-Ṣanāʾiʿ, 49
Badawī, Aḥmad, 48
badīʿ, 42, 168
Badr, 397, 554, 616, 624, 704, 706, 717, 732, 747, 750, 753, 767
al-Badr al-Ṭāliʿ bi-Maḥāsin man baʿd al-Qarn al-Sābiʿ, 11
al-Baghawī, 11, 15, 19, 31, 88, 153, 174, 231, 238, 264, 466, 551, 583, 651, 655, 670, 728, 730, 732, 738, 750-752, 755, 763, 767
Baghdad, 9, 12, 15, 31, 48, 351, 400, 695, 702, 705, 711, 742, 743, 746
al-Baghdādī, Abū Manṣūr, 260
Bahai sect, 232
Bāhir al-Burhān fī Maʿānī Mushkilāt al-Qurʾān, 57
Baḥr al-Madhhab, 153
al-Baḥr al-Muḥīṭ. See Abū Ḥayyān
Baḥrayn, 718
al-Bāʿith ʿalā al-Khalāṣ, 738
Bakar, Osman, xxv, xliii, 11, 12, 202, 795
Bakr b. Wāʾil, 181
Baʿlabakk, 236, 374, 719
Balāgha as an Instrument of Qurʾān Interpretation in al-Kashshāf, 48
al-Balbīsī, 21
Bālī, 12
Balkh, 30, 711
al-Bannāʾ, Ḥasan, 65
Banū ʿAbd al-Ahshal, 726
Banū ʿAbd al-Asad, 768
Banū ʿAbd al-Dār, 769
Banū ʿAbd Manāf, 704
Banū ʿAdiy, 338
Banū ʿĀmir, 602
Banū ʿAmr b. ʿAwf, 769
Banū Asad, 330, 420, 537, 639, 737
Banū Firās, 768
Banū Hāshim, 338, 610, 624, 728
Banū Kalb, 159, 199, 750
Banū Kinda, 771
Banū al-Mughīra, 768
Banū Muṣṭaliq, 693
Banū al-Qayn, 199
Banū Qaynuqāʿ, 694
Banū Salūl, 204
Banū Sulaym, 602
Banū Tamīm. *See* Tamīm
Banū Taym, 338
Banū Zuhra, 732
Baqīʿ, 710
al-Bāqillānī, 260, 327, 386, 534
al-Barāʾ b. ʿĀzib, 713
Barelwis, 91

Baṣra, 30, 151, 691, 702, 711, 717, 728, 735, 743, 757
al-Baṣrī, ʿAbd Allāh b. Sālim, 120
Basrians, Basrian school, 32, 157-158, 183, 206, 246, 265, 326, 469, 523, 603, 616, 622, 722, 734-735, 747
Basūs war, 183
Battle of the Camel, 709, 713-715
bayān, 42, 358, 407
al-Bayān, 157
al-Bayān fī ʿAdd Āy al-Qur'ān, 150
Bayān al-Ḥaqq al-Naysābūrī, 57
bayʿat al-riḍwān, 691
Bayḍā', 1
Bayḍāwī on the Fawātiḥ: A Translation of His Commentary on alif-lām-mīm, 76, 214, 222, 224, 225
al-Bayḍāwī wa-Ārā'uh al-Iʿtiqādiyya: ʿArḍ wa-Naqd, 54
al-Bayḍāwī wa-Manhajuh, 8, 10, 14, 16, 30, 49, 50-56, 60
al-Bayḍāwī wa-Manhajuh fil-Tafsīr, 164
Bayḍāwī's Commentary on Sūrah 12 of the Qur'ān, 77
al-Bayhaqī, 149, 152-153, 169-170, 174, 182, 211-212, 238, 257, 261, 272, 398, 521-522, 553, 559, 583-584, 596, 655, 699, 709, 729, 762-765
al-Bazzār, 146, 170, 398, 418, 452, 471, 583, 661, 699, 739, 755, 765
Beeston, Alfred Felix Landon, 77
beguilement, 344-347
Beidhawii Commentarius in Coranum: ex codd. Parisiensibus, Dresdensibus et Lipsiensibus, 85
Bellamy, James A., 237
Bible, 343, 644
  Biblical passages mentioning the Prophet, 643
  See also Gospel; Torah
Bibliander, Theodorus, 67, 68
al-Bidāya min al-Kifāya fī Uṣūl al-Dīn, 701
al-Bidāya wal-Nihāya, 2, 11, 668, 695, 701, 759
Bidāyat al-Sūl fī Tafḍīl al-Rasūl, 184
Bilāl, 336, 701, 720, 726, 751, 755
Bint al-Shāṭi', ʿĀ'isha b. ʿAbd al-Raḥmān, 208
al-Biqāʿ, 719
al-Bizzī, 199
blasphemy, 324
braids, 703, 762
Brockelmann, Carl, 3, 63
Browne, Edward G., 2, 16, 73, 82-84
Bruinessen, Martin van, 78
Bughyat al-Wuʿāt fī Ṭabaqāt al-Lughawiyyīn wal-Nuḥāt, 2, 11, 695, 711, 742
al-Bukhārī, 23, 27, 55-56, 182, 208, 212, 232, 246, 264, 305, 328, 472, 535, 549, 553, 571, 610, 616, 624, 631, 633, 694, 698, 705-711, 720, 733-734, 737-738, 741, 745-748, 752, 755-757, 760-767
al-Bukhārī, ʿAlā' al-Dīn, 40
al-Bulqīnī, 48, 161, 167, 208
al-Bunānī, 37
Bundār, 702
al-Būnī, Aḥmad b. ʿAlī, 232
Burayda, 340, 559, 755
al-Burda, 16, 60, 692, 701
al-Burhān al-Jalīy, 763
al-Burhān fī ʿUlūm al-Qur'ān, 24, 27
Burman, Thomas E., 67
Burton, Gideon O., 332, 353, 631
al-Būshakānī/Būshanjānī, 4, 7, 10, 48
al-Būṣīrī, 4, 16, 60, 264
Bustānī, Karam, 157, 428
al-Būṭī, 237, 446, 616, 745
Buṭrus, Anṭūniūs, 349
Byzantines, 750, 751, 752
Cachia, Pierre, 76-79, 156, 168, 214, 219, 220-225, 233-234, 243, 332, 351, 394, 505, 585, 608, 626
Caesar, 606, 756
Caldwell, Roswell Walker, 76

Calverley, Edwin E., 2, 12-13, 48, 78, 383, 386, 477, 509
canonical readings, canonicity, 7, 24, 31, 49, 83, 199, 737; see also *shādhdh*
Çelebi, Sa'dī, 30, 64, 84
Chaldeans, 232
China, 16
Chrestomathia Baidawiana: The Commentary of El-Baiḍāwī on Sura III, 16, 77, 210, 351, 394, 741
Christianity, Christians, 22, 37-38, 207, 273, 278, 477, 583-590, 646-648, 694, 723, 745, 767, 773
circularity, 357, 520
Classification of Knowledge in Islam, 11
classification of the sciences, 16
codicology, 199
cosmogony, cosmology, 501, 647
conformant, 351, 689
Conger, George Perrigo, 179
conjunctive, 32, 157-158, 288, 297, 312, 356-357, 467, 469, 471, 497, 499, 516, 649, 671, 688-689
Consensus, 745
Constantinople, 87, 90
contextualization, 36, 296
contingency, contingencies, 80, 178, 180, 290, 300, 303, 666, 682
covenant, 129, 132, 482-485, 575-581, 733
covenantee, 578, 688
creation of the Qur'an, 744
credal doctrine, 15, 80
Daf' Īhām al-Iḍṭirāb 'an Āyāt al-Kitāb, 58
Dahdah, Antoine, 360
al-Ḍaḥḥāk, 192, 210, 231, 380, 398, 469, 532, 579
Ḍaḥḥāk b. Ḥumra, 258
al-Dājūnī, 305
Dakhtanūs daughter of Luqayt b. Zurāra, 354
Dakhūl, 771
Dalā'il al-I'jāz, 48, 288
Dalā'il al-Nubuwwa, 170, 383, 386, 398, 584
Damascus, 10, 14, 26, 82-83, 90, 119, 374, 719, 721, 725-726, 731
al-Dāmighānī, 21
Ḍāmin, Ḥātim Ṣāliḥ, 48
al-Dānī, 150, 242, 666, 731
al-Daqr, 'Abd al-Ghanī, 156, 505, 679
Dār al-Arqam, 750
al-Dāraquṭnī, 25, 152, 398, 624, 697, 763
al-Dārimī, 149, 214-215, 272, 340, 366, 571, 583, 643, 707, 729, 756, 761-762
al-Dārimī, 'Uthmān b. Sa'īd, 238
Darrūza, Muḥammad 'Izzat, 229
Daryabadi, Abdul Majid, 75
al-Ḍaw' al-Lāmi' li-Ahl al-Qarn al-Tāsi', 86, 121
Dāwūd, 59, 653
Dāwūd b. Abī Hind, 695, 729
Dāwūd al-Ẓāhirī, 719
al-Dāwūdī, 2, 9, 198, 696
Ḍayf, Shawqī, 66
Daylam, 730
Deobandis, 63, 75, 89
descriptive of vividness, 395, 689
desinential syntax, 216, 711
Determinists. *See* Jabriyya
devil. *See* Iblīs
al-Dhahabī, 1, 8, 10, 42, 64, 153, 211, 694, 695, 701-702, 706-707, 711, 716, 735-736, 741-744, 748, 755, 759, 763-765, 773
al-Dhahabī, Abū Hurayra b., 8, 120
al-Dhahabī, Muḥammad Ḥusayn, 14, 19, 29, 54
al-Dhammārī, 731
al-Dharī'a ilā Taṣānīf al-Shī'a, 2, 86
Dhayl Ṭabaqāt al-Fuqahā' al-Shāfi'iyyīn, 3, 5
dhikr, 21, 525, 667, 703, 735, 737
Dhū Jadan al-Ḥimyarī, 311
Dhūl-Qarnayn, 288

diagnostication, 323
dialectical forms, 157, 175, 177, 181, 190, 194, 209, 631, 639, 686
A Dictionary and Glossary of the Kor-ân, 79
Dictionary of Arabic Grammar Terminology, 156
Dictionary of Literary Terms English-French-Arabic, 79, 343
Dictionary of Stylistics and Rhetoric, 79
Dictionary of Universal Arabic Grammar: Arabic-English, 361
Dictionnaire des orientalistes de langue française, 76
Dictionnaire détaillé des noms des vêtements chez les Arabes, 163
al-Dihlī, Najm al-Dīn 2
al-Dīnawarī, 149, 764
Dirāsāt fī Manāhij al-Mufassirīn, 29
Disjointed Letters, 26, 45, 214-242
Divine Attributes, 54, 701, 744
Dīwān al-Adab, 289, 400
Dīwān ʿAntara, 361
Dīwān al-Aʿshā, 164
Dīwān al-Ḥamāsa, 183, 274, 333, 365, 405, 456, 705, 825
Dīwān al-Hudhaliyyīn, 282
Dīwān Jarīr, 280, 401, 413
Dīwān Majnūn Laylā, 210
Dīwān al-Nābigha al-Dhabyānī, 370
Dīwān Ru'ba, 348, 480, 645
Dīwān al-Shammākh b. Ḍirār, 370
Dīwān Umru' al-Qays, 188-189, 389
La doctrine d'al-Ashʿarī. See Gimaret
Dozy, Reinhart, 163
Drāz, Muḥammad ʿAbd Allāh, 206
al-Duʿā', 170, 211, 473
al-Durar al-Kāmina fī Aʿyān al-Mi'at al-Thāmina, 8, 11
al-Dūrī, 305, 736
al-Durr al-Manthūr fīl-Tafsīr bil-Ma'thūr, 19-20, 149, 152, 175, 211, 231, 233, 435, 545, 559, 604-605, 614, 698, 762
al-Durr al-Maṣūn, 19
Durrat al-Aslāk fī Dawlat al-Atrāk, 2, 4, 118
Durrat al-Ta'wīl fī Mutashābih al-Tanzīl, 57
ego, 62, 618, 675, 700, 760
Egypt, 63, 66, 77, 289, 613-614, 632, 641, 696, 705, 742, 756, 759
embryological stages, 40
emphasis, 38, 156, 200, 286, 295, 315, 331, 335, 341, 395, 401, 458, 562, 572, 574, 600, 620, 662, 683-684
Encyclopædia Iranica, 4, 11
Encyclopaedia Judaica, 644, 651
Encyclopædia of Islam, 69
equilibrium, 45, 323, 329
equivocation, 328
Etymologies, 44
etymology, 32, 42, 44, 48, 50, 158, 161, 173, 284, 375, 566, 711
Eve. *See* Ḥawwā'
ex nihilo designs, 529, 538, 687
existents, 384, 385, 538, 688
Ezekiel, 643
faculties, 44, 202, 498, 517-518, 524, 664, 795
  appetitive faculty, 62, 675
  vegetative faculty/virtue, 493, 686
Faḍā'il al-Qur'ān, 723
al-Fāḍil al-Yamanī, 48
al-Fāḍil b. al-Ṭāhir b. ʿĀshūr, 18, 41, 70, 164
al-Faḍl al-Riqāshī, 190
al-Faḍl b. Aḥmad, 739
al-Faḍl b. Dukayn, 257
al-Faḍl b. Qudāma al-ʿIjlī, 350
Fahras al-Makhṭūṭāt al-ʿArabiyya al-Maḥfūẓa fī Maktabat al-Asad, 17
al-Fahras al-Shāmil lil-Turāth al-ʿArabī al-Islāmī al-Makhṭūṭ, 17, 63
al-Fā'iq fī Gharīb al-Ḥadīth, 21, 472, 764
Fakhrulḥasan, Sayyid, 63, 89
al-Falak al-Dā'ir ʿalā al-Mathal al-Sā'ir, 360

fanā', 61
Fann al-Jinās, 256
Fanṣūrī, 'Abd al-Ra'ūf (=Singkili), 78
Fārābī, 146, 289, 400
Faraghlī, Zakī Muḥammad, 65
Farazdaq, 381, 498, 737
Farq bayn al-Firaq, 740
Farrā', 177, 237, 380, 428, 432, 443, 711, 721
Farrūja Muḥammad b. Ṣāliḥ, 155
Fars, 1, 6, 551
Fāshānī, Muḥammad b. Aḥmad, 5
fāsiq, 51, 480, 740
fasting permanently, 759
Fatāwā Ibn al-Ṣalāḥ, 738
Fatāwā Ibn Taymiyya, 739
Fatḥ al-Bārī bi-Sharḥ Ṣaḥīḥ al-Bukhārī, 56, 59, 83, 102, 150, 155, 175-176, 209, 211-212, 233, 249, 318, 445, 459, 539, 583, 598, 624, 695, 705, 710, 739, 763
Fatḥ al-Mannān fī Tafsīr al-Qur'ān, 11
Fatḥ al-Mannān Sharḥ wa-Taḥqīq Kitāb al-Dārimī, 149
al-Fatḥ al-Mubīn bi-Sharḥ al-Arba'īn, 37
Fatḥ al-Mun'im Sharḥ Ṣaḥīḥ Muslim, 261
Fatḥ al-Qadīr, 66
al-Fatḥ al-Rabbānī min Fatāwā al-Imām al-Shawkānī, 40
Fatḥ al-Raḥmān, 72
al-Fatḥ al-Samāwī fī Takhrīj Aḥādīth al-Bayḍāwī, 89, 152, 192, 211, 231, 327, 328
Fatḥ al-Wahhāb bi-Takhrīj Aḥādīth al-Shihāb, 258
Fatiha
  names, 147
Fāṭima, 53, 339, 571, 706-709, 712, 714, 766, 770
al-Fawā'id al-Muntaqāt al-Ḥisān min al-Ṣiḥāḥ wal-Gharā'ib al-Ma'rūfa bil-Khila'iyyāt, 272
Fawā'id fī Mushkil al-Qur'ān, 58
fawāṣil of Qur'ān, 172
al-Fawz al-Kabīr fī Uṣūl al-Tafsīr, 75, 507
Fayḍ al-Bārī fī Takhrīj Aḥādīth Tafsīr al-Bayḍāwī, 89
al-Fayrūzābādī, 69, 88, 162, 177, 400, 402
al-Fayyūmī, Aḥmad b. Muḥammad, 162, 406
Fell, Winand, 85
Fī Ẓilāl al-Qur'ān, 65, 237, 759
fiqh, 5, 7, 8, 15, 18, 43, 49-50, 58, 702, 719, 742, 749
Fir'awn, 288, 606
al-Firdaws bi-Ma'thūr al-Khiṭāb, 257
Fleischer, Heinrich, 69-70, 85, 113
forgery, 4, 155, 170, 258, 270, 338
The Four Imams and Their Schools, 701, 749
Frank, Richard M., 261
From Codicology to Technology: Islamic Manuscripts and Their Place in Scholarship, 4
Fück, Johann, 85
Fūda, Sa'īd, 4, 290
Fuḍāla b. 'Ubayd, 731
Fuḥūl al-Shu'arā', 705, 768
Fujā'at al-Sulāmī, 698
Furay'a bt. Khālid, 724
Fusṭāṭ, 757
al-Fuṣūl fil-Uṣūl, 196
Futḥul, 210
Futūḥ al-Ghayb fil-Kashfi 'an Qinā' al-Rayb. See al-Ṭībī
Futūḥ Miṣr wa-Akhbāruhā, 759
Gallipoli, 87
Gätje, Helmut, 78
gematria, 232
genealogy, 183, 742
genus. *See* species
Geschichte des Qorâns, 69
al-Ghāmidī, Ṣāliḥ, 54, 564
al-Ghamrāwī, 63, 117, 170
Ghamrī, Abū 'Āṣim Nabīl, 149, 583

Gharā'ib al-Qur'ān, 19
Gharīb al-Āthār, 746
Gharīb al-Ḥadīth, 174, 472, 742
Ghāwjī, Wahbī Sulaymān, 261, 723
Ghāyat al-Nihāya fī Ṭabaqāt al-Qurrā', 5, 8-9, 13, 696, 700, 722, 726, 736, 739
al-Ghāyat al-Quṣwā fī Dirāyat al-Fatwā, 4, 8, 12, 15
al-Ghayṭī, Najm al-Dīn, 120
Ghazāla, 265-266
Ghazala, Hasan, 79
al-Ghazālī, 5, 31, 39, 49-50, 179, 212, 327, 570, 741
al-Ghaznawī, 31, 209, 239
al-Ghazzī, Najm al-Dīn, 86
Ghulām Tha'lab, 31
Ghumārī, Aḥmad, 149, 155, 258, 763
Ghurar al-Tibyān fī man lam Yusamma fīl-Qur'ān, 312
Gimaret, Daniel, 160, 261, 346, 386, 550
Glazemaker, 68
Goldziher, Ignaz, 69, 70
Gospel, 38, 39, 212, 277, 302, 462, 584, 643-644
grammar, 9, 13, 15, 18, 20, 31, 42, 48-50, 58, 65, 76-81, 91, 157, 164, 204, 681, 711, 732, 741, 746, 750, 762
Grammar of the Arabic Language. See Wright, William
A Grammar of the Classical Arabic Language, 79
Gunasti, Susan, 63
Gunny, Aḥmad, 68
Ḥabannaka, 'Abd al-Raḥmān, 66
Ḥabīb al-'Ajamī, 722
Ḥabīb al-Siyar, 4
Ḥabīb b. Aws. *See* Abū Tammām
Ḥadath al-Aḥdāth fīl-Islām: al-Iqdām 'alā Tarjamat al-Qur'ān, 74
Ḥādī al-Arwāḥ ilā Bilād al-Afrāḥ, 278
Hadiyyat al-'Ārifīn, 3, 8
Ḥaḍramawt, 236
Ḥafṣ b. Sulaymān, 719
Ḥafṣa bint Sīrīn, 695
Ḥafṣa bint 'Umar, 367, 583, 695, 698, 766
Ḥajdarī, 180, 181
al-Ḥajjāj, 266, 367, 705, 735
Ḥājjī Khalīfa, 14, 22, 30, 48, 58-59, 86, 725, 748
Ḥakam b. 'Abd Allāh al-Aylī, 170
Ḥakam b. 'Utayba, 744
al-Ḥākim, 42, 152, 170, 212, 264, 398, 452, 465, 471, 521-522, 560, 571, 584, 599, 631, 655, 697-699, 707-708, 711, 755
Ḥall Mutashābihāt al-Qur'ān, 57
Ḥallāq, Muḥammad Ṣubḥī, 14, 34, 40, 87, 90
Ḥalwānī, Aḥmad, 224
Ḥamāsa. See *Dīwān al-Ḥamāsa*
Ḥamīdullah, Muḥammad, 72, 74
Ḥammād b. Salama, 751
Ḥammūda, 'Abd al-Wahhāb, 229
Ḥamna bint Jaḥsh, 694
Ḥamza b. 'Amr al-Aslamī, 707
Ḥamza al-Kūfī, 17, 146, 180, 182, 199, 293, 320, 326, 555, 614, 629, 639, 648, 658, 707, 716, 718, 721-722, 752
Hand-List of the Muḥammadan Manuscripts in the Library of the University of Cambridge, 82-84
Hankī, 9
ḥaqīqī, 166
al-Harawī al-Anṣārī, 73
al-Ḥārith b. 'Abd Allāh b. Abī Rabī'a, 771
al-Ḥārith b. Abī Usāma, 729
Ḥārith b. 'Ayṭal, 772
Ḥārith b. Suwayd, 732
Hārūn, 619, 712
Hārūn, 'Abd al-Salām, 143, 204, 289, 361, 405, 529
Hārūn al-'Atakī, 175
Hārūn al-A'war, 554
Hārūn al-Rashīd, 742, 743

Hārūt and Mārūt, 59, 545, 546, 743
al-Ḥasan b. ʿAlī b. Abī Ṭālib, 83, 246, 712, 714
al-Ḥasan al-Baṣrī, 46, 175, 177, 180, 182, 234, 293, 307, 312, 326, 330, 369, 375, 378-379, 397-398, 451-452, 469, 504, 527, 530, 543-544, 551, 555, 558, 576-577, 583, 610, 613-614, 624, 629, 634, 639, 641, 661, 663, 665, 677, 696, 722-723, 734-735, 741, 759, 762, 771
al-Ḥusayn b. ʿAlī b. Abī Ṭālib, 466, 703, 712, 714
al-Ḥasanī, Badr al-Dīn, 119
Ḥāshiyat al-ʿAlawī ʿalā Tafsīr al-Bayḍāwī, 91-92
Ḥāshiyat al-Kāzarūnī ʿalā Tafsīr al-Bayḍāwī, 63, etc.
Ḥāshiya on al-Maḥallī, 37
Ḥāshiyat Muḥyī al-Dīn Shaykh Zādah, 86, 149, etc.
Ḥāshiyat al-Qūnawī. See Qūnawī
Ḥashwiyya, 52, 546, 567, 723
Ḥassān b. Abī Sinān, 246
Ḥassān b. Thābit, 694, 723
al-Ḥathth ʿalā al-Tijāra wal-Ṣināʿa wal-ʿAmal, 272
al-Ḥawliyyāt, 773
Ḥawmal, 771
Ḥawwāʾ, 522, 554-557, 560-561
Ḥayāt al-Ṣaḥāba, 759
al-Hayek, Muhammad Munir, xliii
al-Haytamī, Aḥmad b. Ḥajar, 37, 42-43, 62, 120
al-Haythamī, 175, 258, 452, 559, 583, 711, 755, 765
Ḥāzimī, Aḥmad, 176
Ḥazm b. Abī Ḥazm, 722
hellfire, 278, 285, 314-315, 344, 459, 491, 545, 573, 604, 741, 744-745
henna, 703, 728, 735, 750
hermeneutics, 29, 41, 43, 50
Herod Antipas, 644
Hijaz, Hijazis, 195, 294, 326, 554, 696, 737, 746
al-Ḥillī. *See* Ibn al-Muṭahhar
Ḥilyat al-Awliyāʾ wa-Ṭabaqāt al-Aṣfiyāʾ, 700, 722, 744, 759, 764, 765
Hind bt. al-Ḥārith al-Firāsiyya, 771
Ḥirāʾ, 698, 773
al-Ḥīrī, 21
Hishām b. ʿAbd al-Malik, 279
Hishām b. ʿAmmār al-Sulamī, 293-294, 329, 725
Hishām b. al-Ḥasan, 759
Hishām b. ʿUrwa, 711
History of the Qurʾān, 72
homonymy, 343
Howell, Mortimer, 79, 394
Ḥudaybiya, 770
al-Hudhalī, 24, 282, 655, 727, 732
Ḥudhayfa, 213, 596, 705, 716, 727, 736, 753, 755, 764, 767-768
Ḥudhayfa b. al-Yamān, 726
Hudhayl, 194
ḥudūth, 80, 176, 378
Ḥujja, 264
al-Ḥujja fī Bayān al-Maḥajja, 261
Ḥukm al-Basmala fil-Ṣalāt, 153
Ḥumayd al-Aʿraj, 696
Ḥumayd b. Hilāl, 748
Ḥumrān b. Aʿyan, 722
Hurgronje, Snouck, 69, 78
al-ḥurūf al-muqaṭṭaʿa. See disjointed letters
ḥurūfiyyūn, 232
al-Ḥusām al-Māḍī fī Sharḥ Gharīb al-Qāḍī, 62
al-Ḥuṣarī, Maḥmūd Khalīl. *See Aḥkām Qirāʾat al-Qurʾān*
Ḥusayn al-Juʿfī, 696
Ḥusayn b. al-Faḍl, 239
Hussein, Abdul-Raof, 79, 343
Ḥuṭayʾa, 441, 442, 727
Hyderabad, 16
hypallage, 326, 343
hyperbole, 281, 415, 677, 687
hypocrisy, hypocrites, 38, 264, 310-313, 334-337, 340-341, 358, 361-

363, 367, 370, 388-390, 429, 463, 480, 646, 693, 738, 764-765
Ibāḍī, 742
al-Ibāna 'an Uṣūl al-Diyāna, 36
al-'Ibar fī Akhbāri man 'Abar, 1
Iblīs, 55, 59, 130, 301, 340, 510, 522, 531-532, 540-547, 551, 557, 571, 596, 755
Ibn 'Abbās, 6, 20, 23, 26, 29, 37, 46, 149-150, 174, 180, 192, 200, 207, 209, 213, 230-231, 234-235, 238-239, 267, 271-273, 288, 293-294, 338, 364, 371, 373, 435-436, 445, 452, 454, 471, 510, 521, 524, 527, 530, 532, 542-546, 556-560, 579, 584, 592, 612, 618-619, 622, 624, 627-628, 632, 639, 641, 655, 657, 661, 663, 695, 698, 712, 714, 727, 728-735, 743, 746-747, 751, 753, 755-756, 761-762, 772
Ibn 'Abd al-Barr, 150, 272, 583, 709, 744, 747, 749, 762-763
Ibn 'Abd al-Ḥakam, 759
Ibn 'Abd al-Salām, 57, 168, 184, 614
Ibn Abī 'Āṣim, 755
Ibn Abī 'Abla, 177, 469, 628
Ibn Abī 'Adī, 182
Ibn Abī Dāwūd, 199, 201, 695
Ibn Abī al-Dunyā, 174, 272, 373, 445, 447, 465, 551, 560, 754
Ibn Abī al-Ḥadīd, 360
Ibn Abī Ḥātim, 19, 31, 46, 174, 192, 207, 231, 233, 239, 264, 267, 328, 435, 452, 464, 521, 532, 542, 560, 579, 584, 600, 614, 632, 647, 650, 661, 663, 666, 710
Ibn Abī Hind, 729
Ibn Abī Isḥāq, 293-294, 379, 469, 495, 565, 576, 613, 665
Ibn Abī al-Ja'd, 709
Ibn Abī Khaythama, 725, 751, 763, 771
Ibn Abī Laylā, 635, 664, 697, 722, 732, 753, 759
Ibn Abī Mūsā, 739
Ibn Abī al-Qāsim, 53
Ibn Abī Sabra, 321
Ibn Abī Shayba, 170, 210, 272, 398, 447, 583, 616, 697-700, 709, 755, 759-765
Ibn Abī Uṣaybi'a, 59
Ibn 'Ābidīn, 121
Ibn 'Adī, 182, 211, 258, 553, 750-751
Ibn 'Ādil, 168, 445, 655
Ibn 'Allāb al-Mālikī, 120
Ibn al-'Amīd Atqānī, 53
Ibn 'Āmir, 146, 180-181, 199, 238, 293, 320, 326, 330, 530, 614, 629, 657, 731
Ibn al-Anbārī, 159, 239, 274, 361, 543, 739
Ibn al-A'rābī, 26, 189, 553
Ibn 'Arabī, 11
Ibn 'Asākir, 54, 170, 272, 414, 553, 614, 701, 720, 721, 763, 768
Ibn 'Āshūr, 29, 71, 209, 383
Ibn 'Aṭā' Allāh, 296
Ibn 'Aṭā' Allāh et la naissance de la confrérie šāḏilite, 296
Ibn al-Athīr, Ḍiyā' al-Dīn, 360
Ibn al-Athīr, Majd al-Dīn, 11, 701
Ibn 'Aṭiyya, 14, 19-20, 29, 145, 190, 238-239, 355, 380, 565, 604, 646
Ibn 'Awn, 735
Ibn al-Bādhish, 146
Ibn Bannā' al-Marrākishī, 161
Ibn al-Barqī, 725
Ibn Bukayr, 720
Ibn Dhakwān, 293, 305, 530
Ibn Durayd, 143
Ibn Faraḥ al-Lakhmī, 211
Ibn Fāris, 289
Ibn Fūrak, 29, 31, 36, 57, 260, 327, 550, 702
Ibn al-Fuwaṭī, 1
Ibn Ghalbūn, 146
Ibn Ḥabīb al-Ḥalabī, 2, 4, 118
Ibn Ḥajar al-'Asqalānī, 8, 11, 42, 56, 59, 83, 89, 120, 150, 152, 155, 159,

163, 209, 211-212, 257-258, 264, 338, 459, 472, 545, 550, 584, 593, 599, 624, 661, 691, 693, 695, 701, 705, 708, 710, 715-721, 724-727, 731, 734, 738-739, 742, 748, 753-754, 768, 771
Ibn al-Ḥājib, 9, 11, 12, 15
Ibn Ḥamdūn, 222
Ibn Ḥasnūn, 27
Ibn Ḥazm, 149, 386, 406, 624, 740, 744, 748
Ibn Ḥibbān, 25, 207, 418, 465, 466, 708, 754, 755, 763
Ibn Himmāt, 89
Ibn Hishām, 432, 505, 665, 704, 725
Ibn al-ʿImād, 2, 701
Ibn Isḥāq, 233, 532, 546, 579, 606, 695, 724-725, 733, 768
Ibn Jadʿān, 750
Ibn Jamāʿa, 312
Ibn al-Jawzī, 20-21, 34, 170, 211, 231, 258, 272, 339, 464-465, 551, 698, 723, 759, 764-765
Ibn al-Jazarī, 146, 220-221, 696, 700, 705, 722, 726, 731, 736, 739
Ibn Jinnī, 50, 168, 218, 221, 230, 280, 371, 497, 695, 731
Ibn Jubayr, 180
Ibn Jundab, 180
Ibn Jurayj, 6, 180, 233, 238, 435, 543, 592, 618, 646, 666, 719
Ibn Juzay, 231
Ibn Kamāl Bāshā, 64, 83, 101
Ibn Karrām, 737
Ibn Kathīr al-Dārī, 146, 180, 199, 205, 294, 320, 326, 345, 530, 554, 558, 603, 613-614, 629, 657, 679, 696, 732, 746
Ibn Kathīr al-Dimashqī, 11, 16-20, 39, 65, 152, 170, 192, 210, 230, 237-238, 312, 398, 452, 543, 545, 624, 668, 695, 699, 701, 710, 759
Ibn Khafīf, 567, 745
Ibn Khallikān, 58, 701, 737
Ibn Khuzayma, 152, 624, 674, 763
Ibn Mājah, 238, 270, 328, 471, 571, 708, 747, 755-756
Ibn Mandah, 264, 720, 728
Ibn Manīʿ al-Marwarūdhī, 264
Ibn Manẓūr, 23
Ibn al-Marjānī, 120
Ibn Masʿūd, 10, 24, 46, 170, 180, 201, 205, 207, 212, 215, 238-239, 264, 271-272, 307, 319, 367, 371, 379, 398, 417, 435-436, 452, 459, 521, 525, 532, 542, 544, 556, 577, 589, 598, 607, 616, 624, 631, 639, 641, 665-666, 692, 695, 698, 705, 707, 712, 715, 729, 732-734, 742, 748, 756
Ibn al-Maṭarī, 3, 16
Ibn al-Mubārak, 151, 471, 696, 729, 734
Ibn Muḥayṣin, 180, 205, 294, 330, 345, 495, 554, 558, 577, 603, 607, 613, 631
Ibn al-Mulaqqin, 722
Ibn al-Munayyir, 53, 54, 56, 261, 269, 384, 564, 610
Ibn al-Mundhir, 231, 233, 238, 559, 614
Ibn al-Muṭahhar al-Hillī, 12-13
Ibn Nabhān, 306
Ibn Qāḍī Shuhba, 11, 701-702
Ibn Qaʿqāʿ. *See* Abū Jaʿfar b. al-Qaʿqāʿ
Ibn al-Qayyim, 28, 234, 278, 340, 353, 445, 466, 469, 584
Ibn Qudāma, 559, 759, 764
Ibn Qutayba, 57, 176, 178, 233-234, 350, 499, 536, 591, 706, 720, 737, 749, 763-764, 768, 771, 773
Ibn Rāfiʿ, 11
Ibn Saʿd, 691, 698, 705, 725, 728, 731, 743, 750-751, 761-765, 770
Ibn al-Ṣāʾigh, 4, 63, 322
Ibn al-Ṣalāḥ, 208, 257, 738
Ibn al-Sammāl, 669
Ibn al-Sikkīt, 360, 442
Ibn al-Subkī, 3, 9, 31, 37, 41, 48, 59, 62, 155, 668, 701

Ibn al-Sumayfiʿ, 175, 179, 182, 401, 410, 628
Ibn al-Tamjīd, 90, 145, 384, 542
Ibn al-Turkmānī, 212
Ibn al-Wazīr, 741
Ibn al-Zubayr, 201, 205, 207, 624
Ibn Sallām. *See* al-Qāsim b. Sallām
Ibn Salūl. *See* ʿAbd Allāh b. Ubay
Ibn Shaddād, 321, 361
Ibn Shāhīn, 257
Ibn Sīdah, 177, 265, 311, 605
Ibn Sīrīn, 180, 369, 697, 734-736
Ibn Taghrī Bardī, 11, 13
Ibn Taymiyya, 13, 57, 175, 237, 368, 398, 459, 497, 739, 761
Ibn Ubay. *See* ʿAbd Allāh b. Ubay
Ibn ʿUmar, 6, 180, 182, 257, 272, 471, 549, 591, 698, 702, 705, 710, 712, 728, 730, 735, 740, 755-756, 765
Ibn Umm ʿAbd, 733, 734
Ibn ʿUyayna, 175, 751
Ibn Wardān, 655, 669
Ibn Yaʿīsh, 311
Ibn Yūnus, 735
Ibn Zubar, 720
Ibrāhīm, 328, 708, 749
Ibrāhīm b. Ad-ham, 722
Ibrāhīm b. Duḥaym, 725
Ibrāhīm b. al-Ḥasan, 735
Ibrahim, Lutpi, 3, 16, 54
Ibrāhīm al-Nakhaʿī, 605, 696, 711, 715
Ibrāhīm al-Qaṣṣār, 739
al-Īḍāḥ, 15, 366
al-Īḍāḥ fil-Tafsīr, 655
Īḍāḥ al-Maknūn fil-Dhayl ʿalā Kashf al-Ẓunūn, 63
Īḍāḥ Shawāhid al-Īḍāḥ, 610
al-Īḍāḥ wal-Tibyān fī Maʿrifat al-Mikyāl wal-Mīzān, 633
Īḍāḥ al-Waqf wal-Ibtidā', 159
idolatry, 37, 249, 273, 296, 462, 620, 767
Idrīs al-Ḥaddād, 739
al-Iḥkām fī Uṣūl al-Aḥkām, 744
Iḥyā' ʿUlūm al-Dīn, 179, 571
iʿjāz. See inimitability
al-Iʿjāz al-Lughawī fī Fawātiḥ al-Suwar, 48, 88, 230-234, 237-241, 383
al-Ījī, 9
ijmāʿ, 150, 396
ijtihād, 13, 20, 41, 62, 75
ʿIkrima, 20, 46, 234, 257, 628, 650, 661, 664, 666, 696, 721
al-ʿIlal al-Mutanāhiya fil-Aḥādīth al-Wāhiya, 258
al-ʿIlal al-Wārida fil Aḥādīth al-Nabawiyya, 152
Iʿlām al-Ṭalabat al-Nājiḥīn, 8, 121
ʿilm ḍarūrī. *See* necessary knowledge
ʿIlm al-Tafsīr, 19, 532, 546
iltifāt. See redirection
al-ʿImādī, Ḥāmid b. ʿAlī, 29
imāla, 23, 190, 305, 307, 576
al-Imām al-Ḥakīm Fakhr al-Dīn al-Rāzī min Khilāl Tafsīrih, 59
Imām al-Ḥaramayn, 5, 53, 261, 327, 477, 494
al-Imām Waliyyullāh al-Dihlawī wa-Tarjamatuhu lil-Qur'ān, 72
al-Īmān, 264
ʿImrān b. Ḥuṣayn, 735
ʿInāyat al-Qāḍī wa-Kifāyat al-Rāḍī ʿalā Tafsīr al-Bayḍāwī, 3, 87, 149, 693
inceptive, 156, 242, 401, 409, 485, 504, 681
inchoative, 156, 175, 181, 250-253, 258, 280, 284, 292, 306, 367, 372, 404, 413, 448, 469, 473, 482, 523, 530, 649, 652, 681, 687
indeclinable, 32, 156-157, 172, 210, 242, 251, 286, 395, 505, 682, 686-687
India, 18, 63, 74, 466, 551
individualization, 421, 682
inductive survey, 225, 681
infallibility (*ʿiṣma*), 52-56, 59, 327, 346, 515, 517, 526, 542, 545, 546, 553, 567, 569

infāq, 271
infinitive noun, 164, 175, 177, 244-247, 255, 263, 291-292, 305, 307, 326, 332, 376, 384, 407, 411, 432-433, 437, 443, 478, 485, 487, 528, 551, 601, 607, 622, 636, 653, 669, 687
inimitability (*iʿjāz*), 13, 30, 50, 254, 419, 440, 682
innuendo, 331, 585
al-Inṣāf bil-Muḥākama bayna al-Tamyīz wal-Itḥāf, 54
al-Inṣāf fī Masāʾil al-Khilāf bayn al-Kūfiyyīn wal-Baṣriyyīn, 274
al-Inṣāf fī-mā Yajib Iʿtiqāduh wa-lā Yajūz al-Jahlu bih, 260
integrity, 45, 323, 329-330, 686, 758
intensives, 168-169, 177, 200, 227, 244, 255, 263, 307, 315, 319, 325-326, 330, 336, 359, 371, 374, 376, 435, 444, 467, 497, 511, 513, 529, 565, 580, 631, 646, 681, 683, 687
intercalated, 160, 395, 401, 688
intercession, 51, 548, 602-605, 741, 744-745, 763
al-Intiqāʾ fī Faḍāʾil al-Aʾimmat al-Thalāthat al-Fuqahāʾ, 749
al-Intiṣāf min al-Kashshāf, 53-54, 269, 564
al-Intiṣār li-mā fīl-Iḥyāʾ min al-Asrār, 179
invariables, 26-29, 49, 534, 632
al-ʿIqd al-Mufīd fī ʿIlm al-Tajwīd, 219
al-Iqnāʿ fīl-Qirāʾāt al-Sabʿ, 146
Iqtiḍāʾ al-Ṣirāṭ al-Mustaqīm, 761
iʿrāb, 15, 30, 216
Iʿrāb al-Qirāʾāt al-Shawādhdh, 60, 436, 665
Iʿrāb al-Qurʾān, 87
Iraq, 12, 84, 104, 230, 381, 498, 647, 692, 696, 698, 715, 726, 742, 747-748, 761
al-ʿIrāqī, Abū al-Faḍl Zayn al-Dīn, 208, 351, 472, 571, 599, 738
al-ʿIrāqī, Abū Zurʿa Walī al-Dīn, 212
irregular variants. See *shādhdh*
Irshād al-ʿAql al-Salīm, 19, 64, 237
al-Irshād ilā Qawāṭiʿ al-Adilla fī Uṣūl al-Iʿtiqād, 53, 261
Irshād al-Sārī ilā Durar Tafsīr al-Bayḍāwī, 65
Irshād al-Thiqāt ilā Ittifāq al-Sharāʾiʿ ʿalā al-Tawḥīd wal-Maʿād wal-Nubuwwāt, 40
ʿĪsā b. ʿAbd al-ʿAzīz al-Lakhmī, 576, 635
ʿĪsā b. Maryam, 55, 201, 232, 747
ʿĪsā b. ʿUmar al-Hamdānī, 179, 432, 576, 613
ʿĪsā b. Wardān, 736
Isaiah, 643
al-Iṣāba fī Tamyīz al-Ṣaḥāba, 163, 691, 693, 715-720, 725, 727, 731, 734, 748, 751-754, 763, 768, 771
al-Isfarāyīnī, ʿIṣām al-Dīn, 64, 84 etc.
al-Isfarāyīnī, Shāhfūr, 73
al-Ishāra ghayr al-Shafawiyya fīl-Aḥādīth al-Nabawiyya, 230
al-Ishāra ilā al-Ījāz fī Baʿḍ Anwāʿ al-Majāz, 169
al-Ishāra ilā Madhhab Ahl al-Ḥaqq, 260
ishmām, 199
ishtiqāq, 32, 42, 173, 270
al-Ishtiqāq, 143, 711, 746
Isidore of Seville, 44
Iṣlāḥ al-Manṭiq, 360
Islamic Civilisation and the Modern World, 12, 202, 795
ʿiṣma. See infallibility
ʿIṣma b. Mālik, 755
Ismāʿīl b. Jaʿfar b. Abī Kathīr, 294, 736
Ismāʿīl Bāshā, 3, 63
Ismāʿīlīs, 232
ʿIṣmat al-Anbiyāʾ, 328, 567
Ispahan, 31, 747
Israelite reports, 59, 633, 744
Israelites, 22, 37, 59, 207, 232-233, 273, 278, 288, 312-313, 388, 464,

545, 574-679, 691-694, 710, 723-724, 737, 742-743, 767
al-Isrāʾīliyyāt wal-Mawḍūʿāt fī Kutub al-Tafsīr, 59, 633
Iṣṭakhr, 1
Istanbul, 17
al-Istīʿāb fī Maʿrifat al-Aṣḥāb, 464, 709, 763
al-Istiʿādha wal-Ḥasbala mimman Ṣaḥḥaḥa Ḥadīth al-Basmala, 155
istiʿāra, 168, 319, 343, 351, 366, 420, 461, 482
al-Istidhkār al-Jāmiʿ li-Madhāhib Fuqahāʾ al-Anṣār, 150
istiqrāʾ, 23, 80, 225
istiṣḥāb, 13
istithnaʾ, 24
Itḥāf al-Khiyara bi-Zawāʾid al-Masānīd al-ʿAshara, 264
al-Itḥāf bi-Tamyīz mā Tabiʿa fīhi al-Bayḍāwī Ṣāḥib al-Kashshāf, 53
Īthār al-Ḥaqq ʿalā al-Khalq, 741
Ithbāt al-Imāma, 86
al-Itqān fī ʿUlūm al-Qurʾān, 21-24, 42, 47, 148, 172, 229, 238, 276, 398, 418, 436
ʿItr, Ḥasan, 24
ʿItr, Nūr al-Dīn, xliii, 20, 29, 43, 119, 208, 228, 236
Jabala b. al-Ayham, 350
Jābir, 374, 397, 583, 726, 727, 732, 752
Jabriyya, 36, 191
Jadd b. Qays, 312
Jaʿfar al-Ṣādiq, 722
Jāhiliyya, 381, 414, 602, 616, 692, 695, 713, 719, 724-727, 749, 757, 761, 767, 773
al-Jāḥiẓ, 48, 477
Jahmiyya, 459, 702, 739
Jalāʾ al-Afhām, 28
al-Jalālayn. See *Tafsīr al-Jalālayn*
Jamʿ al-Jawāmiʿ, 37, 42
Jamharat al-Amthāl, 182
al-Jāmiʿ li-Akhlāq al-Rāwī wa-Ādāb al-Sāmiʿ, 155, 700
Jāmiʿ al-Asānīd, 699
Jāmiʿ al-Bayān ʿan Taʾwīl Āy al-Qurʾān. See al-Ṭabarī
Jāmiʿ Bayān al-ʿIlm wa-Faḍlih, 272, 744, 762-763
al-Jāmiʿ al-Ṣaghīr, 149, 175
Jāmiʿ al-Uṣūl, 11
Jamīla bint ʿĀṣim, 766
Jamīla bint Thābit, 759
al-Janā al-Dānī min Ḥurūf al-Maʿānī, 288
Janbāz, Muḥammad Ghiyāth, 31
al-Jārabardī, 9, 48
al-Jarbūʿ, ʿAbd Allāh, 353
Jarīr, 279-280, 381, 401, 413, 498-499, 712, 737
al-Jawāhir al-Ḥisān fī Tafsīr al-Qurʾān, 19, 551
al-Jawhar al-Naqī, 212
al-Jawharī, 162, 198, 371, 380, 400, 537
al-Jazāʾirī, Abū Bakr, 66
al-Jazarī. *See* Ibn al-Jazarī
al-Jazariyya, 219
al-Jazīra, 757
Jeremiah, 643
Jews. *See* Israelites
Jibraʾīl, Jibrīl, 23, 200, 210, 231, 275-276, 443, 545, 605, 633, 650, 724, 728, 737, 754, 773
Jinān al-Jinās fī ʿIlm al-Badīʿ, 256
jinās, 256, 608
al-Jindī, ʿAlī, 256
jins. See species
John the Baptist, 643
Johns, A.H., 46
Jubayr b. Muṭʿim, 181
al-Jubbāʾī, 58, 701
Judaism, 37, 38, 77, 341, 646-648, 773; *see also* Israelites
Judāma bt. Wahb, 707
Judea, 644
al-Jūharī, Shihāb al-Dīn, 120

al-Jundī, Darwīsh, 48
Jundub, 726
juratory, 241, 331, 686, 687
Jurjān, 31
al-Jurjānī, Abū al-Ḥasan, 31
al-Jurjānī, ʿAbd al-Qāhir, 31, 48, 288, 383, 645
al-Jurjānī, Muḥammad b. Ibrāhīm b. Jaʿfar, 212
al-Jurjānī, al-Sharīf, 46, 48, 91, 178, 283, 310, 354, 386, 421
jussive, 156, 378, 439
al-Juwaybārī, 213
al-Juwaynī. *See* Imām al-Ḥaramayn
Juzʾ fīhi Ahl al-Miʾā, 748
al-Jūzajānī, 720
Kaʿb b. ʿUjra, 747
Kaʿba, 350, 361, 595, 703, 772, 773
Kabbani, Muhammad Hisham, xliii
kadhib, 27, 55, 170, 270, 326-328, 338, 370, 598
al-Kafawī, Ayyūb, 27
al-Kāfī al-Shāf fī Takhrīj Aḥādīth al-Kashshāf, 89, 159, 209, 211, 258, 339, 472, 661
al-Kāfiya, 9, 15
Kaḥḥāla, ʿUmar Riḍā, 3, 75, 746
kalām, 8, 12, 15, 58, 535, 746
kalām nafsī, 290
al-Kalbī, 209, 234, 238, 338, 592, 663, 711, 751
Kalima ḥawla Tarjamat al-Qurʾān al-Karīm, 74
Kallās, Adīb, 119
Kamali, Mohammad Hashim, 346
al-Kāmil, 158, 383, 389, 743
al-Kāmil fīl-Ḍuʿafāʾ, 182, 211, 258, 553
al-Kāmil fīl-Qirāʾāt al-ʿAshr, 24
Kanʿān, Muḥammad b. Aḥmad, 64
al-Kāndihlawī, Muḥ. Yūsuf, 759
Kanz al-ʿIrfān fī Fiqh al-Qurʾān, 12
Kanz al-ʿUmmāl, 764, 759
Karrāmiyya, 316, 334, 667, 737, 741
al-Kāsānī, 49
Kashf al-Aqwāl al-Mubtadhala fī Sabqi Qalam al-Bayḍāwī li-Madhhab al-Muʿtazila, 54
Kashf al-Asrār ʿan Uṣūl Fakhr al-Islām al-Pazdawī, 40, 262
al-Kashf wal-Bayān, 69, 209, 338
Kashf Mushkilāt al-Qurʾān, 57
Kashf al-Sarāʾir fī Maʿnā al-Wujūh wal-Ashbāh wal-Naẓāʾir, 21
Kashf al-Ẓunūn ʿan Asāmī al-Kutub wal-Funūn, 14, 22, 30, 48, 59, 63
al-Kashshāf ʿan Ḥaqāʾiq Ghawāmiḍ al-Tanzīl. See al-Zamakhsharī
Kashshāsh, Muḥammad, 230, 233
al-Kathitāʾī (or Kathitānī), 6
al-Kattānī, Muḥammad b. Jaʿfar, 155
al-Kattānī, Muḥammad Ṭāhir, 707
al-Kawākib al-Sāʾira bi-Aʿyān al-Miʾat al-ʿĀshira, 86
al-Kawrāʾī, ʿAbd al-Karīm, 63, 91
al-Kawtharī, Muḥammad Zāhid, 182, 260, 328
al-Kāzarūnī, ʿAfīf al-Dīn, 7, 10, 17, 63, 88-89, 115, 116, 170, etc.
al-Kāzarūnī, Muḥ. al-Khaṭīb, 88
Kemalism, 74
Khabbāb, 716
Khabīr b. al-Aḍbaṭ, 210
Khadīja bint Khuwaylid, 706, 708
al-Khaḍir, 636, 738, 741
al-Khafājī, Shihāb al-Dīn, 3, 55-59, 64, 87, 90, 149, 225, 233, 693, etc.
Khalaf b. Hishām, 146, 180, 182, 293, 320, 326, 465, 554, 614, 658, 679, 736, 739
Khālid al-Ḥadhdhāʾ, 695, 735
Khālid b. al-Walīd, 716, 771
Khalīfa, Ḥājjī. *See* Ḥājjī Khalīfa
Khalīfa, Ibrāhīm ʿAbd al-Raḥmān, 29
Khalīfa, Rashād, 232
al-Khalīl, 329, 332
Khalīl al-Farāhīdī, 3, 42, 51, 156, 183, 189, 214, 228, 234, 294, 312, 400, 412, 432, 443, 467, 624, 629, 655, 739, 747, 750

al-Khallāl, Abū Bakr, 272
Khallūf, Muṣṭafā Shāhir, 255
Khalq Af'āl al-'Ibād, 745
Khalq al-A'mal, 745
Khamash, Salim Soliman, 349
Khan, Muḥ. 'Abd al-Ḥakīm, 74
Kharasha b. al-Ḥurr, 691
Khārija, 576, 696
Khārijīs. *See* Khawārij
Kharrāṭ, Aḥmad, 355
al-Khaṣā'iṣ, 230, 280, 371, 497
al-khāṣṣ wal-'āmm, 24
Khatan al-Layth, 696
al-Khaṭīb al-Baghdādī, 155, 366, 380, 465, 583, 695, 700-702, 763
al-Khaṭīb, 'Abd al-Laṭīf, 175
al-Khaṭṭābī, 48, 174
Khawārij, 20, 38, 158, 160, 260, 266, 285, 367, 458, 573, 699, 702, 715, 739, 740-742, 771
Khaybar, 713, 758
al-Khāzin, 19, 78, 88, 153
Khazraj, 584, 691, 693
al-Khiḍr. *See* al-Khaḍir
Khiḍr, Sihām, 230-234, 237-241, 741
khilāfa, 318
Khilāfiyyāt, 153, 211
al-Khila'ī, 272
Khizānat al-Adab, 529, 591, 645, 706, 727, 747
Khomeini, Ruhollah, 65
Khulāṣat al-Athar fī A'yān al-Qarn al-Ḥādī 'Ashar, 121
Khurasan, 9, 31, 742
Khuraym, 266
Khuwaylid b. Nufayl, 35, 166
Khuwayy, 31, 59, 182, 229
Khuzā'a, 773
Khvānṣārī, 3-4, 6, 8, 11, 13, 48, 53
Khwāndamīr, 4
Khwarizm, 30, 31
kināya, 322, 585
al-Kindī, 288, 771
King Sa'ūd University, 50, 82, 84, 97
al-Kirmānī Abū Naṣr, 7, 171, 230, 516, 639, 665-669
al-Kisā'ī, 146, 179-180, 199, 293, 305, 307, 320, 326, 329, 443, 504, 614, 629, 640, 657, 722, 736, 739, 741
Kitāb al-Siyar, 699
Kitāb al-Zuhd, 26
Kitāb Sībawayh, 750
Kubrā al-Yaqīniyyāt al-Kawniyya, 446, 745
Kufa, Kufan school, 32, 151, 158, 206, 242, 265, 287, 306, 469, 652, 705, 709, 715, 721, 734, 757
kufr, 21, 289, 316
kulliyyāt. See invariables
al-Kulliyyāt, 10
Kulliyyāt al-Alfāẓ fīl-Tafsīr, 27, 632
al-Kulliyyāt: Mu'jam fīl-Muṣṭalaḥāt wal-Furūq al-Lughawiyya, 27
al-Kumayt b. Zayd al-Asadī, 351
kunh, 80
al-Kūrānī, 59
al-Kuzbarī, 121
Labīd b. Rabī'a al-'Āmirī, 160, 381, 749
Lagarde, Michel, 59
Lamentations Rabbah, 643
Lane, Edward William, 68, 79-80, 83, 156, 183, 308
Lange, Johan, 68
Laqaṭāt al-Marjān fī Aḥkām al-Jānn, 510
Larzul, Sylvette, 76
Lāshīn, Mūsā, 261
Last Day, 38, 125, 136, 263, 309, 313-316, 648
al-Laṭā'if al-Bahiyya Sharḥ al-Minḥat al-Saniyya, 224
Lawāmi' al-Bayyināt Sharḥ Asmā' Allāh Ta'ālā wal-Ṣifāt, 165
Laylā wife of 'Āmir b. Rabī'a, 769
Layth b. Abī Sulaym, 722
lāzim, 80, 290, 383, 430
Levy, Ruben, 4

Lex Mahumet pseudoprophete, 66-67
Lex Saracenorum, 68
Liber Alchorani, 67
lifelong fasting, 711
The Light of Inspiration and Secret of Interpretation, being a translation of the Chapter of Joseph, 77
Lisān al-ʿArab, 23, 163, 179, 210, 222, 380, 507, 529
literal, literalization, 29, 45-46, 51, 55, 72, 80, 168, 184, 222, 262, 267, 286-287, 298, 304, 317, 323, 346-347, 360, 365-368, 403-404, 418, 458, 466, 478, 493, 548, 585, 618, 636, 640, 642, 645, 653, 655, 659, 664, 669, 682, 684, 722
Literary History of Persia, 16, 73
logic, 16, 18, 58, 85, 335
López-Morillas, Consuelo, 72
Lubāb al-Ta'wīl fī Maʿānī al-Tanzīl, 19, 78, 88, 153
al-Lubāb fī ʿUlūm al-Kitāb, 168
Lubāba bt. al-Ḥārith. *See* Ibn ʿAbbas
Lubb al-Albāb fī ʿIlm al-Iʿrāb, 15, 30
Lucknow, 63
lugha, 42
al-Lughāt fil-Qur'ān, 27
al-Lumaʿ fil-Radd ʿalā Ahl al-Zaygh wal-Bidaʿ, 36, 260
al-Lumʿat al-Saniyya fī Taḥqīq al-Ilqā' fil-Umniyya, 59
lust, 281, 518, 546, 595, 618, 675
luṭf, 346
lying. See *kadhib*
mā al-kāffa (neutralizing *mā*), 332
Mā Tamassu ilayhi Ḥājatu al-Qārī li-Ṣaḥīḥ al-Imām al-Bukhārī, 208
Maʿadd, 143
Maʿālim al-Tanzīl, 19, 88, 231, 651
Maʿallamī, ʿAbd al-Raḥmān, 59, 328
maʿānī, 42
Maʿānī al-Aḥruf al-Sabʿa, 24
Maʿānī al-Qur'ān, 177, 230-231, 380, 422, 428, 711, 721, 746. *See also* al-Zajjāj
al-Maʿarrī, 705
al-Mabsūṭ, 72
Madā'in, 726, 748
al-Madā'inī, 725, 729
Madārik al-Tanzīl wa-Ḥaqā'iq al-Ta'wīl, 19, 62, 64, 88
Madīna, 397, 759-761
al-Madkhal ilā al-Sunan al-Kubrā, 272
al-Madrāsī, ʿAbd Allāh b. Ṣibghat Allāh, 89
Madyan, 749
Mafātīḥ al-Ghayb, 19, 27, 30, 33, 39, 41, 43, 58-59, 69, 164-165, 227, 317, 397, 546
Mafātīḥ al-Asrār wa-Maṣābīḥ al-Abrār, 41
Maghreb, 18, 161
al-Maḥallī, 37, 64, 69, 738
Maḥāsin al-Iṣṭilāḥ, 208
al-Mahdali, Sayyid Hamid, xliii
maḥfūẓūn, 733
Mahomet's Koran, 68
al-Maḥṣūl fil-Uṣūl, 15, 50, 397, 496
majāz, 168, 215, 298, 322, 333, 335, 343, 346, 618
Majāz al-Qur'ān, 21, 160, 230
Majdūb, ʿAbd al-ʿAzīz, 59
Majmaʿ al-Ādāb fī Muʿjam al-Alqāb, 1
Majmaʿ al-Amthāl, 182, 463
Majmaʿ al-Baḥrayn fī Zawā'id al-Muʿjamayn, 175, 258
Majmaʿ al-Zawā'id wa-Manbaʿ al-Fawā'id. See al-Haythamī
Majmūʿ Ashʿār al-ʿArab, 348, 480, 645
Majmūʿ al-Athbāt al-Ḥadīthiyya li-Āl Kuzbarī al-Dimashqiyyīn, 121
Majmūʿ al-Fatāwā, 175
Makhlūf, Muḥammad Ḥasanayn, 74
Makḥūl, 716
Mālik b. Anas, 6, 151, 239, 641, 700, 709, 742, 756-759, 762, 765-766
Mālik b. Dīnār, 182

al-Mālikī, Sharīfa Aḥmad, 54
Maʿmar b. al-Muthannā. *See* Abū ʿUbayda
Maʿmar b. Rāshid, 729
Maʾmūn b. Aḥmad al-Harawī, 213
Manāhij al-Mufassirīn min al-ʿAṣr al-Awwal ilā al-ʿAṣr al-Ḥadīth, 20
Manāhil al-ʿIrfān fī ʿUlūm al-Qurʾān, 24
Manāqib Aḥmad, 698
Manāqib ʿUmar, 759, 765
Mandæans. *See* Sabians
Manhaj al-Naqd fī ʿUlūm al-Ḥadīth, 208
manifest locution, 345, 368, 383, 417, 497-500, 548, 584-585, 654, 661, 685
al-Mankhūl, 741
mansūkh. See abrogation
al-Manṣūr, 751
manzila bayn al-manzilatayn, 745
Maqālāt al-Ashʿarī, 36, 260
al-Maqālat al-Fākhira fī Ittifāq al-Sharāʾiʿ ʿalā Ithbāt al-Dār al-Ākhira, 40
Maqālāt al-Islāmiyyīn, 495, 738, 740
Maragheh observatory, 12
al-Marāghī, 8, 65, 69, 75
al-Marāghī, Aḥmad b. Muṣṭafā, 65, 69, 74
Marāghī, Muḥ. b. Muṣṭafā, 74-75
al-Marāghī, ʿUmar b. Ilyās, 8, 121
al-Marʿashlī, Muḥammad ʿAbd al-Raḥmān, 17, 90, 242, 264, 654...
al-Marʿashlī, Yūsuf, 42
Mardīnī, Fāṭima Muḥammad, 29, 54
Margoliouth, David Samuel, 16, 76-77, 210, 351, 394, 741
al-Maʿrifa wal-Tārīkh, 739
Maʿrifat al-Ṣaḥāba, 698, 720
Maʿrifat al-Sunan wal-Āthār, 152, 655
Marracci, Ludovico, 67, 68, 69
Marwān b. al-Ḥakam, 180, 498, 713
Maryam bint ʿImrān, 708
al-Marzūqī, 405, 705
Maṣābīḥ al-Sunna, 15, 43, 200
al-Māṣāḥif. See Ibn Abī Dāwūd
al-Masāʾil al-Iʿtizāliyya fī Tafsīr al-Kashshāf lil-Zamakhsharī, 54
Masrūq, 447, 707, 730, 732, 742, 753, 767
mass-transmitted, 22, 31, 306, 397, 435, 612, 613, 698
Masʿūd b. al-Ḥakam, 713
Maṭāliʿ al-Anẓār, 2, 15, 508
Maṭāliʿ al-Saʿāda, 707
al-Maṭālib al-ʿĀliya bi-Zawāʾid al-Masānīd al-Thamāniya, 264
Matar, Nabil, 68
Materialien zur arabischen Literaturgeschichte, 3
materialists, 44, 459
mathal. *See* allegory; proverbs
al-Mathal al-Sāʾir fī Adab al-Kātib wal-Shāʿir, 360
Maṭlūb, Aḥmad, 351, 639
Māturīdīs, 33, 36, 200, 316, 655
Mawāhib al-Jalīl min Tafsīr al-Bayḍāwī, 64
al-Mawāqif, 85, 268
al-Māwardī, 19, 25, 663
al-Mawḍūʿāt, 16, 170, 465
Mawḍūʿāt al-ʿUlūm, 16
Mawdūdī, 65
Mawqān campaign, 749
Mawṣil, 757
al-Mawsūʿa al-Muyassara fī Tarājim Aʾimmat al-Tafsīr, 54
Mawsūʿat Muṣṭalaḥāt Jāmiʿ al-ʿUlūm: al-Mulaqqab bi-Dustūr al-ʿUlamāʾ, 166
al-Maydānī, Abū al-Faḍl, 182, 463
Meaning of the Glorious Koran, 74
Mecca, 8, 28, 32, 54, 59, 75, 84, 107, 149-151, 164, 170, 175-176, 232, 350, 398, 532, 584, 586, 598, 633, 643, 710, 721, 727, 733, 737, 750, 768, 772-773
Medina, 2, 19, 33, 47, 54, 150-151, 170, 257, 312, 353, 355, 398, 436,

592, 596, 691-694, 703, 706, 710, 712, 717, 721, 725, 726, 734, 742, 747, 750, 768, 771
Medinans, 326, 721
Merv, 31
metaphor, metaphorizing, 45-46, 51, 62, 168, 184, 205, 266, 298-299, 305, 319, 343, 349-354, 365-367, 372, 381, 394, 420, 457, 461, 483, 495-496, 507, 622, 681, 683, 686, 689
metonymy, 34, 166, 168, 351, 372, 430, 448, 475, 493, 679, 686-687
Micah, 643
microcosm, 179
Mieder, Wolfgang, 353
Mīkā'īl, 275, 754, 737
al-Milal wal-Nil al, 701, 738-741
al-Minaḥ al-Makkiyya fī Sharḥ al-Hamziyya, 37
Minaḥ al-Rawḍ al-Azhar fī Sharḥ al-Fiqh al-Akbar, 261, 269, 290, 346
Minhāj al-Qāṣidīn, 700, 764
Minhāj al-Sunna al-Nabawiyya, 13
Minhāj al-Wuṣūl ilā 'Ilm al-Uṣūl, 8-9, 15, 50, 56, 533, 700, 764
miracles, 44-45, 248, 297, 484, 584, 612-613, 616, 637, 642-643
Mir'āt al-Jinān wa-'Ibrat al-Yaqẓān, 3
Mirqāt al-Mafātīḥ Sharḥ Mishkāt al-Maṣābīḥ, 43, 755
Miṣbāḥ al-Arwāḥ, 4, 8, 15
al-Miṣbāḥ al-Munīr fī Gharīb al-Sharḥ al-Kabīr lil-Rāfi'ī, 162
Miṣbāḥ al-Mutahajjid, 12
missionary Arabists, 76-78
Misṭaḥ b. Uthātha, 694
Miswar b. Makhrama, 180, 765
Mīzān al-I'tidāl, 743
Mizzī, 237
modality, 169, 298, 387, 388, 439, 520, 623, 686
Monitor: Dictionary of Arabic Grammatical Terms, 79, 156, 224, 394
monotheism, 33, 40, 154, 165, 259, 525, 574, 578, 582, 667, 684, 720
morphology, 42, 48, 157, 161, 169, 371, 664, 682, 732
Mosul, 266
Mu'ādh b. Jabal, 170, 180, 763
Mu'allaqāt, 160, 773
Mu'ammal b. 'Abd al-Raḥmān b. al-'Abbās, 211
al-Mu'ammarīn min al-'Arab, 311
Mu'attab b. Qushayr, 312
Mu'āwiya, 549, 559, 706, 713, 727, 731, 755, 771
al-Mubarrid, 51, 158, 218, 224, 237, 288, 383, 389, 695, 742-743
mubham, 43
Muḍar, 160, 513, 719
al-Mudāwī li-'Ilal al-Jāmi' al-Ṣaghīr wa-Sharḥay al-Munāwī, 149
Mudrik b. Abī Sa'd, 725
al-Mufaḍḍal al-Ḍabbī, 306
al-Mufassirūn: Maḍarisuhum wa-Manāhijuhum, 65
Mufradāt Alfāẓ al-Qur'ān, 21, 57, 67, 162, 198, 297, 413, 610, 636
Mughīra b. Abī Shihāb, 731
al-Mughnī, 196, 386, 505, 759
al-Muhadhdhab, 49
Muhājirūn, 341, 710, 718, 721, 725, 729, 739, 743
Muḥ. b. 'Abd Allāh al-Anṣārī, 717-718
Muḥ. b. al-Ḥasan, 7, 151, 699, 701, 743
Muḥammad b. Ka'b al-Quraẓī, 152
Muḥammad b. Qudāma, 700
Muḥ. b. 'Uthman b. Abī Shayba, 728
Muḥammad, 'Abd al-Salām, 20
al-Muḥarrar al-Wajīz fī Tafsīr al-Kitāb al-'Azīz, 14, 19-20, 604
al-Muḥibbī, 121

al-Muḥkam wal-Muḥīṭ al-Aʿẓam fil-Lugha, 266
al-Muḥtasab fī Tabyīn wujūh Shawādhdh al-Qirā'āt, 168, 230
Mujāhid, 29, 46, 150, 180, 230, 238, 371, 378, 435, 452, 495, 532, 558-600, 614, 629, 635, 639, 650, 654, 657, 661, 663, 665, 696, 720, 730, 743, 744, 751
al-Mujālasa wa-Jawāhir al-ʿIlm, 149, 729
Muʿjam al-Balāghā al-ʿArabiyya, 332
al-Muʿjam fī Fawātiḥ al-Suwar, 230
al-Muʿjam al-Jāmiʿ fil-Muṣṭalaḥāt al-ʿUthmāniyya, 87
al-Muʿjam al-Kabīr, 170, 211, 418, 452, 571
Muʿjam Maqāyīs al-Lugha, 289
Muʿjam al-Maṭbūʿāt al-ʿArabiyya wal-Muʿarraba, 11
Muʿjam al-Mu'allifīn, 3, 75, 746
al-Muʿjamal-Mufaṣṣalfil-Aḍdād, 349
al-Muʿjam al-Mufaṣṣal fī ʿUlūm al-Balāgha, 351
Muʿjam al-Mufassirīn, 3, 31, 63, 86, 87
Muʿjam al-Muṣṭalaḥāt al-Balāghiyya wa-Taṭawwuruhā, 351
Muʿjam al-Qawāʿid al-ʿArabiyya fil-Naḥw wal-Taṣrīf, 156, 679
Muʿjam al-Qirā'āt, 175
al-Muʿjam al-Ṣaghīr, 170
Muʿjam al-Ṣaḥāba, 596, 728, 752
Muʿjam al-Uṣūliyyīn, 3, 11
al-mujmal wal-mufassar, 24, 43, 505
al-Mujtabā min Mushkil Iʿrāb al-Qur'ān al-Karīm, 355
mujtahid, 41, 701, 715, 719, 742, 743, 749
mukallaf, 36
al-Mukhaṣṣaṣ, 311, 605
Mukhtalaf al-Shīʿa fī Aḥkām al-Sharīʿa, 13
Mukhtaṣar Khilāfiyyāt al-Bayhaqī, 211
Mukhtaṣar Minhāj al-Qāṣidīn, 764
Mukhtaṣar Muntahā al-Sūl wal-Amal fil-Uṣūl wal-Jadal, 9, 11, 15
al-Muktafā fil-Waqf wal-Ibtidā, 242
al-Mulḥa fī Iʿtiqād Ahl al-Ḥaqq, 169
al-Mullawī, Shihāb al-Dīn, 120
multiplicity of pre-eternal entities, 745
al-Munājāt, 296
al-Munāwī, ʿAbd al-Ra'ūf, 89, 149, 152, 175, 192, 209, 211, 231, 233, 327-328, 445, 610
al-Mundhirī, 170, 258, 445, 597
Muntahā al-Munā Sharḥ Asmā' Allāh al-Ḥusnā, 15
al-Muntakhab, 15
muqaddar, 175, 255
Muqaddima fī Uṣūl al-Tafsīr, 57
Muqātil b. Sulaymān al-Balkhī, 20, 30, 150, 435, 663
muqtaḍā, 80
al-Muqtaḍab, 224, 743
al-Murabbī al-Kābulī fīman Rawā ʿan al-Babilī, 121
Murji'a, 738, 741
Mūsā, 23, 134, 195, 201, 277, 288, 347, 512, 529, 582-583, 600, 606, 608, 611-624, 627, 631-637, 640, 650, 651, 656, 658, 666, 712, 716, 718, 738
Mūsā b. Ṭalḥa, 706
Muṣʿab b. ʿAbd Allāh, 770
Muṣannaf, 174, 182, 210, 272, 398, 447, 466, 583, 699, 709
Musaylima, 171, 698
al-muṣḥāf al-imām, 199
mushāhadāt, 676
mushākala, 343
Mushkil al-Ḥadīth wa-Bayānuh, 57
Mushkil al-Wasīṭ, 257
Muslim b. Ḥajjāj, 213, 328, 694, 698, 705, 708, 710, 738, 741
Muslim b. Khālid, 6
Muslim b. ʿUqba, 771

Musnad Aḥmad. See Aḥmad b. Ḥanbal
Musnad Ibn Manīʿ, 264
Musnad al-Shihāb, 257, 272
al-Mustadrak ʿalā al-Ṣaḥīḥayn, 42, 152, 170, 264, 398, 452, 560, 571, 584, 599, 631, 655, 698
al-Mustaqṣā min Amthāl al-ʿArab, 21, 182
al-Mustaṣfā min ʿIlm al-Uṣūl, 39, 50
Mustawfī al-Qazwīnī, 2
al-Muʿtabar, 9
Mutahhari, Murtadha, 13
Muʿtarak al-Aqrān fī Mushtarak al-Qur'ān, 21
mutashābihāt, 23-26, 29, 41, 761
al-Muʿtaṣim, 40, 705
al-Mutawallī, 196
Mutawallī al-Shaʿrāwī, Muḥ., 66
mutawātir. See mass-transmitted
al-Muṭawwiʿī, 194
Muʿtazila, 12, 30, 38, 51-55, 58, 165, 186, 198, 200, 230, 260, 268, 271, 285, 290, 300, 303, 345-346, 360, 377, 384, 385, 404, 407-408, 438, 442-445, 458, 477, 481, 520, 534, 539, 548, 551, 564, 573, 604, 651, 660, 666-667, 701-702, 711, 721, 738, 740-741, five principles: 744-746, 771
al-muṭlaq wal-muqayyad, 24, 50
al-Muṭṭalib b. Banī Asad, 772
al-Muwāfaqāt, 28
al-Muwarriq al-ʿIjlī, 321
al-Muwaṭṭa', 643, 709, 742, 756-759, 765
al-Muzanī, 6, 691, 773
al-Muzarrid, 749
al-Naba' al-ʿAẓīm: Naẓarāt Jadīda fīl-Qur'ān al-Karīm, 206
Nabhān, 770
al-Nabhānī, Yūsuf, 64, 560
al-Nābigha, 370, 381, 420, 719, 746, 749
al-Nābulusī, ʿAbd al-Ghanī, 54, 146, 168, 394, 626, 766
al-Nābulusī, Badr al-Dīn, 8
Nāfiʿ, 6, 146, 180, 199, 279, 294, 320, 326, 330, 469, 504, 576, 613-614, 629, 648, 657-658, 669, 679, 736-737, 746, 770
Nahāwand, 698
Nahrawān, 699, 715
Nahshalī, Aḥmad b. ʿImrān, 155
naḥw, 15, 42
Nakhaʿī, 180, 194, 715
Nallino, Carlo A., 69
Name of Allah, 33-35, 161-167
name other than the named, 159
Namūdhaj min Aʿmāl al-Khayr fīl-Maṭbaʿat al-Munīriyya, 702
Naqḍ Bishr al-Marrīsī, 238
al-Nasafī, 4, 19, 36, 48, 62, 64, 88, 150, 237, 545-546, 646
al-Nasafiyya, 85
al-Nasā'ī, 212-213, 246, 571, 599, 698, 712, 756, 769
Nashr al-Ṣināʿa, 218
Naṣīḥat Ahl al-Ḥadīth, 763
al-nāsikh. See abrogation
Naṣīr al-Dīn al-Ṭūsī, 10-12, 386, 400, 501
al-naṣṣ wal-mu'awwal, 24
al-Naṣṣ, Muḥammad Sāmer, xliii, 119, 345, 410
Natural Medicine, 323
natural sciences, 58
Nature, Man and God in Medieval Islam, 2, 12-13, 48, 383, 386, 477, 509
al-Nawādir fīl-Lugha, 159, 259
Nawādir al-Uṣūl fī Maʿrifat Aḥādīth al-Rasūl, 174
Nawāhid al-Abkār wa-Shawārid al-Afkār, 14, 34, 46, 48, 51, 53, 56, 89, 91, 148, 155, 165, 179, 327, 548, 705, etc.
al-Nawawī, 155, 208, 257, 327, 624, 699, 738, 756

Nawfal, Ahmad, 66
Nawwās b. Sam'ān, 175
Nayl al-Awṭār, 34, 165, 721
Naẓariyyat 'Abd al-Qāhir fil-Naẓm, 48
Naẓariyyat al-Naẓm: Tārīkh wa-Taṭawwur, 48
Naẓm al-Badī' fī Madḥi Khayri Shafī', 351
al-Naẓẓām, 746
necessary knowledge, 259, 276, 279, 289, 425, 612
nifāq, 313
Nine Books, 591, 758
Nishapur, 31
Niẓām al-Dīn al-Naysābūrī, 19
Niẓām al-Tawārīkh, 15
Nöldeke, Theodor, 69-72
non-canonical readings. See *shādhdh*
non-Muslims, 289, 589, 616, 761
non-Sunni beliefs, 51, 58, 232, 285, 300, 345, 604
North Africa, 742
Nūbī, Aḥmad al-, 54
Nūḥ, 22, 560, 606, 647
nujabā', 734
al-Nujūm al-Zāhira fī Mulūk Miṣr wal-Qāhira, 11, 13
al-Nukat wal-'Uyūn, 19, 25
nukta, 146, 254, 303
Nu'mān b. Bashīr, 709, 731
numerology, 232, 233
Nuwayhiḍ, 'Ādil, 3, 11, 17, 31, 63, 86, 87
Nuzhat al-A'yun al-Nawāẓir fī 'Ilm al-Wujūh wal-Naẓā'ir, 21
oaths, 241, 242, 287, 331
oblique hinting, 583, 585, 683
ontic necessity, 186, 682
Opening Letters. *See* Disjointed Letters
Orientalism, 66, 69, 70
origination, 175, 180, 185, 387, 400, 494, 617, 667, 682, 684
originative, 378, 527, 536, 682
Ottomans, 63, 64, 72, 74, 86-87
parables, 352, 362, 364, 687
Paradise, 163, 278, 314-315, 344, 374, 447, 459, 491, 550-551, 691, 697, 704, 708, 718, 739, 741, 764
paronomasia. See *jinās*
parsing, 15, 29, 30, 47, 87, 475, 682
participial state (*ḥāl*), 181, 194, 205, 252, 264, 295, 367, 402-403, 414, 437, 449, 468, 478, 497, 516, 519, 557, 563, 607, 615, 622-623, 627, 636, 639, 684
passive anonymizers. See *tamrīḍ*
al-Pazdawī, 262
Penrice, John, 75, 79
permutation, 199, 221, 222, 684
Persia, Persians, 16, 232, 606, 616, 730, 751, 756
Persian Literature: A Biobibliographical Survey, 73
philosophy, 58, 501, 681
phonemes, phonetics, 49, 80, 199, 218-224, 371, 681, 684
Pickthall, Muḥammad Marmaduke, 74-75
poets, poetry, 12, 15-16, 20-21, 32, 172, 183, 235-236, 350, 374, 380-381, 387, 419, 498, 705, 709, 719, 724, 727, 730, 732, 737, 746, 767-768, 772-773
Pollock, James W., 2, 12-13, 48, 383, 386, 477, 509
polysemy, 19-22, 25-26, 29, 49, 417-418
polytheism, 273, 520, 615, 767
previous knowledge (*'ahd*), 284, 288, 312, 331, 333, 335, 396, 447, 483-485, 550, 578, 632, 672, 686
Principles of Islamic Jurisprudence, 346
privatives, 308
prohibitive, 378, 439
prophethood, 201, 259, 334, 491, 553, 574, 613
propinquity, 377, 670, 682

prosody, 42, 80, 157, 681, 711
protasis, 429, 431, 473, 685
proverbs, 182, 292, 353-354, 676
The Proverb, 353
Psalms, 39, 182, 650
psyche, 44-45, 205, 246, 298, 323, 417, 464, 476, 593, 689
psycholinguistics, psychology, 36, 44, 45, 323, 417, 689
Pythagoras, 232
Qābūs b. Abī Ẓabyān, 716
Qadarīs, Qadarism, 52-54, 191, 269, 384, 269, 744-745
Qāḍī ʿAbd al-Jabbār, 58
al-Qāḍī al-Bayḍāwī, 14, 16, 164
al-Qāḍī al-Bayḍāwī wa-Atharuhu fī Uṣūl al-Fiqh, 13
Qāḍī al-Hind, 182
Qadi ʿIyāḍ, 231
al-Qādisiyya, 633, 749
al-Qaffāl al-Kabīr, 31
al-Qaffāl al-Ṣaghīr, 5
Qaḥṭān, 143
al-Qaḥṭānī, Ṭāriq, 232
al-Qālī, 7, 737
al-Qalqashandī, 1
Qālūn, 294, 504, 746
al-Qamūlī, 59
al-Qāmūs al-Muḥīṭ, 162, 177, 297, 400, 434
al-Qanānī, Abū Khālid, 158
al-Qaranī, ʿĀʾiḍ, 66
al-Qārī, Mullā ʿAlī, 43, 214, 257, 261, 269, 290, 346, 755
Qarība bt. Abī Umayya, 770
al-Qarnī, Burayk b. Saʿīd, 27-29, 632
qaṣaṣ, 43
al-Qāsim b. Muḥammad, 170, 711, 735, 762
al-Qāsim b. Sallām, 180, 182, 152, 398, 539, 700, 723, 725, 736, 741, 748, 768
Qatāda, 46, 150, 174, 180, 199, 238, 312, 321, 371, 379, 436, 520, 527, 532, 543-544, 551, 558, 592, 600, 613-614, 627, 629, 639, 650, 661, 663, 666, 679, 695, 697, 722, 735
Qawāʿid al-Anām fī Maʿrifat al-Ḥalāl wal-Ḥarām, 13
al-Qawāʿid al-Rukniyya, 12
al-Qawl al-Faṣl fī Tarjamat al-Qurʾān al-Karīm ilā al-Lughāt al-Aʿjamiyya, 73
al-Qawl al-Sadīd fī Ḥukm al-Qurʾān al-Majīd, 75
al-Qawwās, 199, 530
Qays, 194, 330
Qays b. ʿAbbād, 691
al-Qazwīnī, 2-3, 48, 366, 389
qibla, 539, 540, 746
qirāʾāt, 43
al-Qirāʾāt al-Shādhdha Ḍawābiṭuhā wal-Iḥtijāj bihā fīl-Fiqh wal-ʿArabiyya, 469
al-Qirāʾāt al-Shādhdha wa-Tawjīhuhā fī Tafsīr al-Bayḍāwī, 31-32; see also *shādhdh*
Qubāʾ, 769
Qubayṣa bt. Dhuʾayb, 771
al-Quḍāʿī, 257, 272, 553
quiddity, 321, 371, 450, 659, 683, 684
Quiring-Zoche, Rosemarie, 4, 14, 82, 85
al-Qūnawī, 11, 34, 35-36, 62, 64, 90, 145, 158, 201, 676, 738, 741, 746...
Qunbul, 199, 732, 746
The Qurʾān: An Encyclopedia, 15, 79
al-Qurʾān al-Majīd maʿa Maʿānīh bil-Faransiyya, 72
Quraysh, 27, 143, 194, 199, 294, 697, 714, 727, 750, 767, 772-773
Qurrat al-ʿAyn min al-Bayḍāwī wal-Jalālayn, 64
al-Qurṭubī, Aḥmad, 29
al-Qurṭubī, Muḥ. 209, 231, 239, 445, 500, 520, 543, 544-545, 551, 592, 647-648, 738, 762
al-Quṣayyir, Aḥmad, 58

al-Qushayrī, 31, 60-61, 196, 261, 494, 532, 543-544, 570
Quṭb, Sayyid, 65, 759
Qutayba, 374, 554, 736
Quṭb al-Dīn Shīrāzī, 7-12, 48, 91
Quṭrub, 168, 229, 237, 469, 746
al-Rabīʿ b. Anas, 207, 231, 452, 527, 558, 579, 600, 695
al-Rabʿī b. Ḥirāsh, 726, 732
al-Rabīʿ b. Khuthaym, 239, 732
al-Rabīʿ b. Sulaymān, 6, 29
Rabīʿa, 160, 194, 307, 375, 455, 635, 726, 731, 748, 767-768, 773
Rabīʿa b. Yazīd, 731
al-Raḍī, al-Sharīf, 343
Rafʿ al-Ikhtilāf ʿan Kalāmay al-Qāḍī wal-Kashshāf, 54
Rāfiḍa. *See* Shiʿism
al-Rāfiʿī, 153, 162, 766
al-Rāghib al-Aṣfahānī, 30, 42, 57, 67, 70, 162, 164, 198, 259, 297, 333, 405, 413, 445, 448, 451-452, 579, 610, 636, 639
Rajāʾ b. Ḥaywa, 735
rajaz, 350, 747, 749
rajm, 643, 758, 763
Rām Hurmuz, 747
Rasāʾil fil-Iʿjāz in Iʿjāz al-Qurʾān al-Karīm ʿAbr al-Tārīkh, 48
Rashīd al-Dīn Faḍl Allāh, 4
rational proofs/arguments, 30, 44, 46, 178, 187, 245, 304, 381, 386, 428, 517, 526, 548, 556, 564, 594
Rawḍāt al-Jannāt fī Aḥwāl al-ʿUlamāʾ al-Sādāt, 3, 6, 8, 11, 13, 48, 53
Rawḥ, 182, 293, 773
Ray, 30-31
al-Rāzī, 15, 19, 23, 27, 30-34, 39, 46, 48, 50, 56-59, 69, 91, 164-165, 196, 215, 227, 229, 231, 233-234, 238-239, 260, 288-289, 317, 327-328, 334, 397, 400, 406, 424, 496, 501, 519, 534, 539, 546, 556, 567, 570, 579, 639, 738
al-Rāzī, Abū al-Faḍl, 24
al-Razzāz, Saʿīd b. Muḥammad, 5
Reading the Qurʾān in Latin Christendom, 1140-1560, 67
redirection (*iltifāt*), 60, 188, 393, 620, 679, 682
redundancy, 206, 534
referent/denominate, 29, 32, 158-160, 200, 215, 333-334, 453, 481, 516, 524-525, 687, 689
relative, 3, 204, 256, 275, 278, 280, 312, 355, 356, 401, 436-437, 471, 475, 506, 685, 688, 710
repentance, 134, 289, 334, 529, 558-561, 568-569, 573, 615-618, 646, 650, 676, 698
Report on Arab (Unani) Medicine & the State of Kuwait, 202
requital, 184, 259, 318, 343, 350, 446, 458, 562, 642
resumption, resumptive, 29, 235, 280, 319, 331, 342, 344, 358, 374, 377, 379, 437, 440, 448, 500, 615, 681
resurrection, 40, 259, 490-491, 558
rhetoric, 18, 42, 50, 57-58, 65, 80, 164, 332, 681
Richtungen der islamischen Koranauslegung, 69
Riḍā, Muḥammad Rashīd, 43, 59, 65, 69, 73, 75, 206, 229
Riddell, Peter, 15, 78
Rieu, Charles, 2, 3
Rightly-Guided Caliphs, 180, 697, 742
al-Riqqa wa al-Bukāʾ, 759
al-Risāla, 749
Risāla fī Anwāʿ al-Jinās, 256
Risāla fī Iʿjāz al-Qurʾān, 88
Risāla Sharīfa fīmā Yataʿallaq bil-Aʿdād wal-Ḥurūf, 232
Riyāḍ al-Ṣāliḥin min Kalām Sayyid al-Mursalīn, 327
Riyadh, 50
Rizāzādah Shafaq, 16
Robert of Ketton, 66, 67, 68

Robson, james, 3
rock, 45, 135, 368, 406, 632-634, 637, 643, 720
Ross, Alexander, 68
Ru'ba b. 'Ajjāj, 159, 175, 348, 469, 480, 645, 747
al-Rūḥ, 278
Rūḥ al-Maʿānī, 19, 58, 64
al-Ruhāwī, 155
al-Rummānī, 48
Ruways, 199, 294, 330, 657, 747, 773
al-Rūyānī, 153, 729
Rūzbahān, 8, 31, 60, 240
Ryer, André du, 67, 68, 69
Saʿd b. Abī Waqqāṣ, 707
Ṣabbāgh, 'Abbās, 87
Sabbath, 653-654
Sabean, 756
Sabians, Sabianism, 22, 37-38, 647
Ṣabīgh b. 'Isl, 761
Sabtī, Ḥimyar, 328
al-Ṣābūnī, Muḥammad 'Alī, 66, 237, 655, 701
Sacy, Silvestre de, 16, 69, 76, 87, 108-109, 216, 223-229, 234, 243, 248, 282, 686, 689
Saʿd b. Abī Waqqāṣ, 182, 571, 692, 716
Saʿd b. Bakr, 294
Saʿd b. Muʿādh, 732
Saʿd b. 'Ubāda, 693
Ṣadaqa b. Khālid, 725
sadd al-dharāʾiʿ, 761
Saʿdī, 'Abd al-Raḥmān, 65
Ṣafā, 545, 704
al-Ṣafadī, 2, 13, 256
Ṣafiyya bint 'Abd al-Muṭṭalib, 724
Ṣafiyya bint Shayba, 771
Ṣafwat al-Tafāsīr, 237, 655
Ṣaḥīḥ al-Bukhārī. See al-Bukhārī
Ṣaḥīḥ Ibn Ḥibbān bi-Tartīb Ibn Balbān. See Ibn Ḥibbān
Ṣaḥīḥ Muslim. See Muslim
Sahl b. Saʿd, 471, 549, 753
Saʿīd b. Abī 'Arūba, 735
Saʿīd b. al-'Āṣ, 772
Saʿīd b. Jubayr, 231, 238-239, 695-696, 714, 730
Saʿīd b. Manṣūr, 215, 264, 666, 763
Saʿīd b. al-Musayyib, 714, 724, 751, 753, 771
Saʿīd b. Wahb, 747
al-Sajāwandī, 308
al-Sakhāwī, 86, 121, 155, 539, 553
al-Sakhtiyānī, Ayyūb, 209
Salafis, 50, 54, 72-73. *See also* Wahhabis
Salama b. Dhuhl, 274
Salama b. Kuhayl, 716
Ṣalāt, 257
Sale, George, 68
Saleh, Walid A., 70-72
Ṣaliḥ b. Aḥmad b. Ḥanbal, 668
al-Ṣāliḥ, Ṣubḥī, 229
al-Ṣāliḥī, Muḥammad b. 'Alī, 54
Salmān al-Fārisī, 28, 72, 272, 328, 465, 692, 716, 747-751
al-Samʿānī, 31, 231, 520
al-Samīn al-Ḥalabī, 19, 27, 57, 604, 605
al-Ṣanʿānī, 176, 232, 459, 466, 716
Ṣanʿat Allāh fī Ṣīghat Ṣibghat Allāh, 214
al-Sanhūrī, Abū al-Najā, 120
Saqqā, Ibrāhīm, 119
al-Sarakhsī, 72, 699
Sardār al-Ḥalabī, 8, 121
Sarkīs, Yūsuf, 11
Sarra Man Raʾā, 234
Satan, 131, 340, 346, 554; *see* Iblīs
al-Sayālkūtī, 64, 76, 85, 86, 90
Ṣayd al-Khāṭir, 764
Sayf, Ṣalāḥ Ṣāliḥ, 219
Sayyid 'Alī, Maḥmūd al-Naqrāshī, 20
Sayyid Quṭb, 237
Schweiggern, Salomon, 68
Les secrets de l'invisible: Essai sur le Grand Commentaire de Faẖr al-Dîn al-Râzî, 59

sects, 38, 51, 80, 232, 459, 691, 740, 746
Selections from the Kuran, 68
self-evident knowledge. *See* necessary knowledge
self-exegesis, 49
self-extinction, 61, 192, 197
Sellheim, Rudolf, 3
seven *aḥrūf*. See *aḥruf*
al-Sha'bī, 182, 238-239, 632, 716, 729, 735
Shabīb b. Yazīd b. Nu'aym, 266
Shadd al-Izār fī Ḥaṭṭ al-Awzār 'an Zuwwār al-Mazār, 7-11
Shadharāt al-Dhahab fī Akhbār man Dhahab, 2, 701
shādhdh, 31, 49, 146, 205, 345
al-Shāfi'ī, 6, 10, 151, 260, 590, 655, 698-703, 742, 749
Shāfi'īs, 29, 58, 149, 151, 153, 327, 660
Shāh Jahān Ābād, 85
Shah, Muhammad Sultan, 67
Shahl b. Shaybān, 183
al-Shahrastānī, 31, 40-41, 386, 701, 738, 740-741
Shākir, Aḥmad Muḥammad, 231
Shākir, Maḥmūd Muḥ., 288, 768
Shākir, Muḥammad, 2, 73, 74, 231, 233, 350, 499, 521, 645-646, 744
Shalṭūt, Maḥmūd, 66
Shām. *See* Syro-Palestine
al-Shammākh, 370, 749
Shams al-Ma'ārif, 232
al-Shanbūdhī, 330, 658
Shaqīq b. Salama. *See* Abū Wā'il
Sharaf al-Dīn al-Maghribī, 560
al-Sha'rānī, Muḥ. Mutawallī, 239
Sharbajī, Muḥammad Yūsuf, 21
Sharḥ Abyāt al-Mughnī, 706
Sharḥ al-'Aqā'id al-Nasafiyya, 37
Sharḥ Dīwān al-Ḥamāsa, 183
Sharḥ Dīwān 'Antara, 361
Sharḥ al-Ḥikam, 707
Sharḥ Kitāb al-Siyar al-Kabīr, 699
Sharḥ Ma'ānī al-Āthār, 150, 152
Sharḥ al-Muntakhab, 15
Sharḥ al-Qaṣā'id al-Sab' al-Ṭiwāl al-Jāhiliyyāt, 361
Sharḥ Qawā'id al-I'rāb, 146
Sharḥ Shawāhid al-Kashshāf, 497, 610
Sharḥ al-Shifā, 59
Sharḥ al-Sunna, 11, 153, 174, 466, 583, 755, 763
Sharḥ Ṭayyibat al-Nashr fīl-Qirā'āt al-'Ashr, 146
Sharjah, 66, 628
al-Sharnūbī, 707
al-Shāṭibī, 28
Shāṭir, Muḥammad Muṣṭafā, 75
Shawādhdh al-Qirā'āt, 516, 668, 669
al-Shawkānī, 11, 34, 40, 66, 165, 239, 721
Shayba, 180, 199
Shayba b. Naṣṣāḥ, 736
Shaykh al-Islam, 58, 83, 86-87, 101, 114, 119-121, 719, 734
Shaykh Zādah, 62, 64, 84, 85, 86, 90, 149, 394
Shibl, 199, 345, 715
Shiblī, Badr al-Dīn, 510
al-Shifā, 231
Shifā' al-Ghalīl fī-mā fī Kalām al-'Arab min al-Dakhīl, 87, 233
al-Shihrī, 'Abd al-Raḥmān, 4, 22, 50, 195
Shi'is, Shi'ism, Rāfiḍa, 7, 12-13, 38, 52-53, 86, 114, 230, 232, 290, 343, 465, 534, 702, 712, 744-745
al-Shinqīṭī, Muḥammad al-Amīn, 20, 28-29, 58, 66, 737
al-Shi'r wal-Shu'arā', 350, 499, 591, 706, 720, 737, 749, 768, 771, 773
Shiraz, 1, 4, 10, 12, 31
Shīrāznāmah, 3, 12
al-Shirbīnī, 19, 64, 445
Shu'ab al-Īmān, 149, 152, 174, 257, 583
Shu'ayb, 522, 633, 749

Shuʿba b. ʿAyyāsh (Abū Bakr), 211, 657, 679, 696, 700, 718, 719
shubha, 80
al-Shukru lil-Lāh ʿazza wa-jall, 174
al-Shukūk, 9
Shumayṭ, 722
shūrā, 713
Shurayḥ al-Qāḍī, 732, 735
Shurayḥ b. Yazīd, 182
Sībawayh, 50, 204, 221, 228, 234, 236, 294, 306, 312, 340, 432, 443, 467, 473, 629, 649, 652, 662, 696, 711, 739, 746, 750
Ṣibghat Allāh b. Rawḥ Allāh, 214
al-ṣifāt al-salbiyya/al-thubūtiyya, 166
Ṣiffīn, 266, 713, 715, 716
al-Ṣiḥāḥ: Tāj al-Lugha wa-Ṣiḥāḥ al-ʿArabiyya, 162, 198, 371, 380, 400, 433, 457, 521-522, 537, 541, 606, 610
al-Sijāwandī, 239
Sijistān, 756
Silva Rhetoricae: The Forest of Rhetoric, 332, 353, 631
al-Sinbāwī, Muḥammad, 121
sincerity, 334, 335, 402
Singkili, ʿAbd al-Ra'uf, 78
al-Sīra al-Nabawiyya, 616, 704, 773
Sirāj al-Dīn, ʿAbd Allāh, 119
Sirāj al-Dīn, Najīb, 119
al-Sirāj al-Munīr fīl-Iʿānati ʿalā Maʿrifati Baʿḍi Maʿānī Kalām Rabbinā al-Khabīr, 19, 64
Sirr Ṣināʿat al-Iʿrāb, 168
Siyar Aʿlām al-Nubalāʾ, 1, 695, 699, 701-702, 711, 716, 736, 742, 743, 755, 759, 763
slavery, 441, 705, 720, 727, 747, 756-759, 766
species/genus, 171, 176, 227, 251, 254, 256, 284, 312-313, 331-332, 335-356, 442, 447-451, 457, 463, 543-546, 557, 634, 659-660, 672, 684, 686, 689
Spirit of Holiness, 724, 737
spiritual discipline, 675
Staatsbibliothek Preußischer Kulturbesitz, 82
station of abiding, 707
station of oblivion, 707
Storey, Charles, 73
Study Quran, The, 76
stylistics, 60
subaudition, subauded, 153, 240-241, 250, 252, 258, 264, 301, 347, 356, 358-359, 362, 367, 373, 469, 524, 536, 585, 601, 620, 635, 653, 669, 683, 688
Ṣubḥ al-Aʿshā fī Kitābat al-Inshā, 1
al-Subkī, 6, 11, 12, 16, 56, 459. *See also* Ibn al-Subkī
substitute, substituted, 41, 200, 203, 251, 295, 342, 358, 421, 432, 469, 487, 501, 586, 603, 639, 648-649, 682, 737
Successors, 89, 149, 210, 721, 731, 732
Sudan, 742
al-Suddī, 238, 435, 452, 520, 543, 579, 593, 612, 627, 634, 639, 647, 650, 654, 657-658
al-Suddī, Muḥammad b. Marwān, 338
Sufis, sufism, 16, 32, 60-62, 148, 232, 239, 362, 363, 403, 525, 675, 722
Sufyān al-Thawrī, 38, 190, 211, 239, 639, 646, 719, 722, 735
Ṣuhayb, 336, 597, 712, 750, 751, 752
al-Suhaylī, 233, 624
Suḥnūn, 49, 59
al-Suhrawardī, 7, 10
suicide, 618
al-Sulamī, Abū ʿAbd al-Raḥmān ʿAbd Allāh b. Ḥabīb, 180, 469, 668
al-Sulamī, Abū ʿAbd al-Raḥmān Muḥ. b. al-Ḥusayn, 31, 60-61, 618
Sulaym b. ʿĪsā, 722
Sulaymān, 59, 633
Sulaymān b. al-Mughīra, 748

Sulaymān b. Muslim b. Jammāz, 736
Sulaymān b. Ṣurad, 753
Sulaymān b. Yasār, 761, 771
Sulaymān, ʿAbbās, 16
Sulaymān, Muḥammad, 74
Sullam al-Samāwāt, 7
Sunan, 25, 42, 149, 152-153, 210-212-215, 264, 270, 272, 327, 459, 471-472, 553, 571-572, 583, 596, 599, 610, 643, 655, 666-667, 674, 691, 149, 211, 328, 373, 465, 552-553, 571, 699, 705, 709-710, 757, 762-765
superadded *mā*. See additive
Supplement to the Catalogue of the Arabic Manuscripts in the British Museum, 2
al-Sūsī, 3, 11
Suwayd b. ʿAbd al-ʿAzīz, 725
al-Suyūṭī, 2, 11, 14, 19-24, 34, 42-48, 51-56, 62, 64, 69, 76, 89-91, 148, 152, 155, 165, 170, 172, 175, 179, 208, 211, 229, 231, 233, 237-238, 257, 276, 323, 327, 351, 435, 465, 510, 545, 554, 559, 599, 610, 614, 695, 698-699, 706, 711, 738, 742, 762, 765; see also *al-Ashbāh wal-Naẓā'ir*; *al-Durr al-Manthūr*; *al-Itqān fī ʿUlūm al-Qur'ān*; *Nawāhid al-Abkār*; *Tafsīr al-Jalālayn*
synechdoche, 343
syntax, 30, 48-50, 250, 294, 604, 682, 711
Syria, 151, 289, 647, 695, 719, 756, 773
Syriac, 167
Syro-Palestine, 119, 383, 614, 633, 641, 643, 696, 698, 713, 720, 731, 734, 742, 756, 762, 767, 771
ta'wīl, 29
Ta'wīl Mukhtalif al-Ḥadīth, 763
Ta'wīl Mushkil al-Qur'ān, 57
Ṭabāna, Badawī, 332, 351
Ṭabaqāt al-Aṣbahāniyyīn, 748
Ṭabaqāt al-Awliyā', 722
Ṭabaqāt al-Fuqahā', 695
Ṭabaqāt al-Fuqahā' al-Shāfiʿiyyīn, 3, 16, 701
al-Ṭabaqāt al-Kubrā. *See* Ibn Saʿd
Ṭabaqāt al-Mufassirīn, 2, 9, 11, 696
Ṭabaqāt al-Qurrā', 696, 705
Ṭabaqāt al-Shāfiʿiyya, 3, 11-12, 16, 31, 48, 59, 701-702
Ṭabaqāt al-Shāfiʿiyya al-Kubrā, 3, 11-12, 31, 48, 59, 155, 668, 701
Ṭabaqāt al-Shāfiʿiyya al-Wusṭā, 3
al-Ṭabarānī, 152, 170, 175, 211-212, 257, 418, 452, 471, 552, 559, 571, 698, 708, 718, 751-752, 754-755
al-Ṭabarī, 19-20, 25-26, 31, 46, 59, 67, 73, 160, 174, 180, 192, 205, 212, 230-234, 238, 267, 271, 273, 288, 306, 328, 364, 370, 383, 418, 435, 452, 454, 464, 510, 524, 532, 537, 542, 545, 558-560, 579, 584, 592, 596, 600, 612, 614, 618-619, 622, 624, 625, 628, 631-634, 639, 641, 647, 648, 650, 654-657, 661-663, 666, 670, 678, 691, 719, 731, 735, 744, 757, 760, 765, 767
al-Ṭabbākh, Muḥammad Rāghib, 208
Tabri, Hani George, 156
Tabriz, 1, 4, 8-13
Tabṣirat al-Adilla fī Uṣūl al-Dīn, 37
Tabṣirat al-Mutaʿallimīn fī Aḥkām al-Dīn, 12
Tabūk, 691, 694, 712
Tabyīn Kadhib al-Muftarī, 54, 701
tadallul, 707
taḍammun, 80
al-Tadhkira fīl-Qirā'āt al-Thamān, 146
al-Tadhkirat al-Ḥamdūniyya, 222
Tadhkirat al-Ḥuffāẓ, 695, 701
Tadrīb al-Rāwī, 175
Tafhīm al-Qur'ān, 65
Tafrīj al-Shidda, 16

al-Tafṣīl fīl-Farq bayn al-Tafsīr wal-Ta'wīl, 29
al-tafsīr bil-athar, 19
al-tafsīr al-lughawī, 19
al-tafsīr bil-ra'y, 19, 58
al-tafsīr al-taḥlīlī, 19
Tafsīr al-Rāzī. See *Mafātīḥ al-Ghayb*
Tafsīr Gharīb al-Qur'ān, 178
Tafsīr Ibn al-Jawzī. See *Zād al-Masīr*
Tafsīr Ibn Kathīr, 152, 192
Tafsīr al-Jalālayn, 19, 64, 66-69, 78, 84, 111, 239, 384, 655
Tafsīr al-Jawharī, 65
Tafsīr al-Khazrajī: Nafas al-Ṣabāḥ fī Gharīb al-Qur'ān wa-Nāsikhih wa-Mansūkhih
al-Tafsīr al-Lughawī lil-Qur'ān, 19-20
Tafsīr al-Manār, 65, 206, 229, 239
al-Tafsīr al-Manhajī, 66
Tafsīr al-Marāghī, 65
Tafsīr al-Māwardī. See *al-Nukat wal-'Uyūn*
al-Tafsīr al-Mawḍū'ī, 66
al-Tafsīr wal-Mufassirūn, 14, 29, 54, 64
al-Tafsīr al-Munīr fīl 'Aqīda wal-Sharī'a wal-Manhaj, 355
al-Tafsīr al-Muyassar, 66
Tafsīr al-Qurṭubī. See al-Qurṭubī
Tafsīr al-Qushayrī. See al-Qushayrī
Tafsīr al-Rāghib al-Aṣfahānī, 57, 259
al-Tafsīr wa-Rijāluh, 18, 41, 164
Tafsīr Rūzbahān. See Rūzbahān
al-Tafsīr al-Ṣaḥīḥ: Mawsū'at al-Ṣaḥīḥ al-Masbūr min al-Tafsīr bil-Ma'thūr, 19
Tafsīr al-Shahrastānī, 41
Tafsīr al-Ṭabarī. *See* al-Ṭabarī
Tafsīr al-Tha'labī. See *al-Kashf wal-Bayān*
Tafsīr al-Tha'ālibī. See *al-Jawāhir al-Ḥisān*
Tafsīr al-Tustarī. See al-Tustarī
Tafsīr al-Zajjāj. See *Ma'ānī al-Qur'ān*
al-Taftāzānī, 34, 37, 48, 56, 91, 310, 319, 326, 354, 371-372, 380, 409, 437, 461, 594, 600, 606, 636
tahajjud, 723
al-Ṭaḥāwī, 150, 152, 418, 571
Tahdhīb al-Akhlāq, 16
Tahdhīb al-Asmā' wal-Lughāt, 699
Tahdhīb al-Āthār, 212
Tahdhīb al-Lugha, 179, 210, 537
Tahdhīb Sharḥ al-Sanūsiyya Umm al-Barāhīn, 290
Tafsīr al-Shinqīṭī. See *Aḍwā' al-Bayān fī Īḍāḥ al-Qur'ān bil-Qur'ān*
Tahdhīb al-Tahdhīb, 742
Tahdhīb Ṭuruq al-Wuṣūl ilā 'Ilm al-Uṣūl, 12
al-Ṭāhir b. 'Āshūr, 66, 237
al-Taḥrīr wal-Tanwīr, 29, 66, 151, 237, 383
Ṭā'if, 731, 772
Tāj al-'Arūs, 236, 342, 402, 606
tajaddud, 176
tajalliyāt, 676
Tajrīd al-Kashshāf, 53
Takhrīj al-Aḥādīth wal-Āthār al-Wārida fī Tafsīr al-Kashshāf, 89, 175, 257-258
al-takhyīl wa-taṣwīr, 55
taklīf, 35, 36, 37, 526
Ṭalḥa, 180, 713
Ta'līqāt Anwār al-Tanzīl, 86, 114
Talkhīṣ al-Bayān fī Majāzāt al-Qur'ān, 343
Talkhīṣ al-Ḥabīr, 152, 257
Talkhīṣ al-Mustadrak, 42
Talmud, 643
Tamīm, 194, 199, 222, 293-294, 375, 635, 639, 719, 750
tamrīḍ, 21-22, 208, 308, 327, 377
al-Tanbīh fīl-Fiqh, 15, 49
al-Tankīl bi-mā fī Ta'nīb al-Kawtharī min al-Abāṭīl, 328
Tanqīḥ al-Taḥqīq, 211, 257
Ṭanṭāwī b. Jawharī, 65

Ṭanṭāwī, Muḥammad al-Sayyid, 65, 66
Tanwīr al-Miqbās min Tafsīr Ibn ʿAbbās,69, 88
Tanzīh al-Anbiyāʾ ʿammā Nasaba ilayhim Ḥuthālat al-Aghbiyāʾ, 328
Tanzīl al-Āyāt ʿalā al-Shawāhid min al-Abyāt. See *Sharḥ Shawāhid al-Kashshāf*
Taqrīr al-Ḥāwī fī Ḥall al-Bayḍāwī, 63, 89
Taqyīd wal-Īḍāḥ li-mā Uṭliqa wa-Ughliqa min Muqaddimat Ibn al-Ṣalāḥ, 208
tarāwīḥ, 710
al-Targhīb wal-Tarhīb, 170, 257-258, 445, 597, 614
al-Taʿrīf bil-Muʾarrikhīn fī ʿAhd al-Maghūl wal-Turkmān, 15
Tārīkh al-Adab al-Fārisī, 16
Tārīkh Baghdād, 695, 701
Tārīkh al-Bukhārī, 752
Taʾrīkh-i Guzida, 2
Tārīkh Ḥarakat al-Istishrāq, 85
Tārīkh Ibn Abī Shayba, 728
Tārīkh al-Islām, 1, 773
Tārīkh al-Khulafāʾ, 699
Tārīkh Madīnat Dimashq, 272
Tārīkh ʿUlamāʾ Baghdād, 11
Ṭāriq b. Shihāb, 713, 747, 762
Tarjamat al-Qurʾān wamā fīhā min al-Mafāsid wa-Munāfāt al-Islām, 73
Tarjumān al-Mustafīd, 69, 78
tarshīḥ, 351, 366
al-Taṣārīf: Tafsīr al-Qurʾān mimmā Ishtabahat Asmāʾuhu wa-Taṣarrafat Maʿānīh, 21
Tasbīʿ al-Burda, 60
Ṭāshköprüzāde (Ṭāsh Kubrī Zādah), 87
tasking beyond capacity, 35, 295, 526
Taṣnīf al-ʿUlūm bayna al-Ṭūsī wal-Bayḍāwī, 16
taṣrīf, 42
Tawāliʿ al-Anwār, 2, 8, 15, 477, 508, 509
tawfīq, 346
taʾwīl, 346, 547
Taʾwīlāt al-Qurʾān, 316, 655
Tawjīh al-Naẓar ilā Uṣūl al-Athar, 208
Ṭāwūs, 307, 628
Taylor, Archer, 353
al-Taymī al-Aṣfahānī, Abū al-Qāsim, 31, 170, 257, 261, 264
Taysīr al-Bayḍāwī: Taʿlīqāt wa-Sharḥ ʿalā Anwār al-Tanzīl, 63
Taysīr al-Karīm al-Raḥmān fī Tafsīr Kalām al-Mannān, 65
Tazyīn al-Maqāmāt, 87
teknonym, 521, 724, 752
tenor, 21, 62, 168, 292, 293, 365, 366, 430, 585, 652, 687
Thaʿlaba b. Abī Mālik, 760
al-Thaʿālibī, ʿAbd al-Raḥmān, 19, 551
al-Thaʿālibī, ʿĪsā, 121
Thabat al-Amīr al-Kabīr, 121
Thabat Ibn ʿĀbidīn: ʿUqūd al-Laʾālī fil-Asānīd al-ʿAwālī, 121
Thabat Shams al-Dīn al-Bābilī, 121
Thabat Shaykh al-Islām al-Qāḍī Zakariyyā al-Anṣārī, 121
Thābit al-Bunānī, 717, 718, 735
Thābit b. ʿAjlān, 214
Thaʿlab, 51, 739
al-Thaʿlabī, 31, 68, 69, 174, 209, 213, 231, 338, 738
Thalāth Rasāʾil lil-Qushayrī, 196
Thamarāt al-Naẓar fī ʿIlm al-Athar, 176
Thamūd, 143, 196
thanksgiving prayer/prostration, 699
Thaqīf, 767, 772
tharīd, 708
Theological Questions at Issue between Zamakhsharī and Bayḍāwī, 3, 12, 16, 54

Theories of Macrocosms and Microcosms in the History of Philosophy, 179
Thomson, Robert, 323, 644
Thuʿaylib, 119
al-Ṭībī, 33, 46, 48, 56, 91, 156, 165-166, 183, 216, 245-246, 280, 284, 302, 326, 360, 372-373, 433, 461, 472, 498, 524, 624, 636, 759
al-Tibrīzī, 9, 63, 183, 361, 366, 380, 405, 456, 479, 705
al-Tibyān fī Aqsām al-Qurʾān, 234
al-Tibyān fī Iʿrāb al-Qurʾān, 60
al-Ṭihrānī, 2, 86
Time of Ignorance, 719
al-Tirmidhī, 174, 207-208, 212, 215, 246, 257, 327, 471-472, 521-522, 571, 698, 705, 708, 715, 733-734, 755-756
Toledo, Mark of, 67
Torah, 38-39, 182, 212, 277, 302, 313, 388, 584, 593-594, 614-615, 623, 643, 650-651
Tractate Gittin, Sanhedrin, etc., 643
transference, 51, 322, 346, 361, 507, 585, 618, 689
transitivized, 339, 345, 347, 499, 685
transmissive proofs / arguments, 19, 304, 746
Tryst, 614, 623, 689
Tuḥfat al-Abrār Sharḥ Maṣābīḥ al-Sunna, 5, 15, 200
Tuḥfat al-Rāwī fī Takhrīj Aḥādīth Tafsīr al-Bayḍāwī, 89
Ṭulayḥa al-Asadī, 698
Tunisia, 63
Turkish Encyclopedia, 4
Ṭuruq ḥadīth al-ṣalāt ʿalā ʿAbd Allāh ibn Ubay, 695
Ṭūs, 31
al-Ṭūsīʾ, 8
Tustar, 30, 691
al-Tustarī, 30, 60, 231
Two Sanctuaries, 16, 181, 696
ʿUbāda b. al-Ṣāmit, 753
ʿUbādī, 3, 5, 7, 16
Ubay b. Kaʿb, 150, 180, 205, 207, 525, 639, 641, 665, 695, 707, 746, 753-754, 757
ʿUbayd b. ʿAqīl, 199
ʿUbayd b. ʿUmayr, 181, 194, 307, 456
ʿUdhra, 199
Uḥud, 698, 706, 726, 760
al-ʿUjāb fī Bayān al-Asbāb, 338, 584, 593
ʿUkbarī, 60, 436, 516, 665
ʿUkl, 307
Uljaytu, 13
ʿUlūm al-Ḥadīth, 208
ʿulūm al-Qurʾān, 50
ʿUlūm al-Qurʾān, 20, 29, 43, 47, 228, 398, 639
ʿUmar b. ʿAbd al-ʿAzīz, 180-181, 479, 739
ʿUmar b. al-Ḥakam, 751
ʿUmar b. al-Khaṭṭāb, 201, 205, 207, 212, 338, 459, 674, 691, 695, 707, 711, 713, 718, 720, 722, 724, 726-727, 732, 734, 736, 753-769
ʿUmar b. Shubba, 741
Umayya b. Abī al-Ṣalt, 270, 426, 712, 720, 742, 767-768
Umayya b. Khalaf, 720
Umayyad, 365, 498, 747
ʿUmdat al-Ḥuffāẓ fī Tafsīr Ashraf al-Alfāẓ, 27, 57
Umm ʿAbd Allāh bint ʿAbd Wudd, 732
Umm al-Faḍl, 728
Umm Hāniʾ, 435, 751
Umm Ḥuṣayn, 180
Umm Kulthūm, 760, 766
Umm Rūmān, 706
Umm Salama, 152, 180, 722, 768, 770-771
Umm Sulaym, 706, 717-718
Umm Sulayṭ, 760
Umma, 17, 201, 706-707, 740

Umru' al-Qays, 188, 189, 381, 389, 719, 771
Unays, 553, 691
uncreatedness of Qur'ān, 667
Universiti Brunei Darussalam, 92
'Unwān al-Dalīl fī Marsūm Khaṭṭ al-Tanzīl, 161
'Uqba b. 'Āmir, 755
'Urwa b. al-Zubayr, 724, 764
usage, 22, 32, 34, 35, 79, 80, 162, 165, 178, 192, 198, 208, 222, 230, 235, 291, 322, 333, 350, 360, 374, 381, 424, 425, 428, 458, 466, 505, 523, 645, 682, 686, 687
'ushr, 757
Uslūb al-Ḥadhf fil-Qur'ān al-Karīm wa-Atharuh fil-Ma'ānī wal-I'jāz, 255
Usmani, Muhammad Taqi, 75
Uṣūl al-Dīn, 260, 477, 494, 534, 543
'Uthmān al-Battī, 735
'Uthmān b. Abī Sulaymān, 182
'Uthman b. Affan, 726
'Uthmān b. Affan, 230, 713, 715
'Uthmān b. 'Affān, 199, 692
'Uthmān b. Ṭalḥa, 769
'Uthmānic Codex, 151
Uyūn al-Akhbār, 764
'Uyūn al-Anbā' fī Ṭabaqāt al-Aṭibbā', 59
vagueness, 467, 681
van Ess, Josef, 2, 3, 4
verbal and nominal clauses, 154, 175-176, 341, 344-345, 356, 473, 475
verbatim et literatim vs. *ad sensum* translation, 75
verb-like particles, 332
vision of Allah, 60-61, 186-187, 197, 622-623
Vollstaendiges türckisches Gesetz-Buch oder Alkoran, 68
Wafayāt al-A'yān, 58, 701, 737
al-Wāfī bil-Wafayāt, 2, 13
Wahb b. 'Abd Allāh, 714
Wahba, Magdi, 79, 343
Wahhabis, Wahhabism, 50, 54, 91, 179. *See also* Salafis
al-Wāḥidī, 7, 31, 42, 58, 338, 464, 527, 584, 592, 655, 663
Wa'īdiyya, 285, 740-741, 771
Wā'il b. Ḥujr, 211
al-Wajh al-Naḍir fī Tarjīḥ Nubuwwat al-Khaḍir, 738
Wajīh al-Dīn al-'Alawī, 92
al-Wajīz fī Fiqh al-Imām al-Shāfi'ī, 49
al-Wajīz fī Tafsīr al-Qur'ān, 66
Walīd b. al-Mughīra, 288, 771
Walīd b. Muslim, 530, 725
Walīd b. 'Uqba b. Abī Mu'ayṭ, 230
Waliyyullāh, Shāh, 72, 75, 507
wandering in the desert, 626-628, 632, 636-637, 640
waqf jā'iz/lāzim, 29
al-Wāqidī, 728, 753, 760
Warsh, 279, 294, 576, 669, 746
al-Wasīṭ fil-Madhhab, 212
Wāthila b. al-Asqa', 731
women, 163, 189, 312, 350, 361, 455-456, 550, 561, 597, 618, 650, 659-660, 706-710, 722, 724, 740, 756-760, 766, 769, 890
World Bibliography of Translations of the Meanings of the Qur'ān, 72
Wright, William, 79, 156-158, 224, 236, 244, 413, 622, 628, 679
Wujūh al-Qur'ān, 21
wujūh al-tafsīr, 22
al-Wujūh wal-Naẓā'ir fil-Qur'ān, 20
al-Yāfi'ī, 3
Yaḥyā b. 'Abd al-Raḥmān b. Ḥāṭib, 752
Yaḥyā b. al-Ḥārith, 731
Yaḥyā b. Sallām, 21, 69
Yaḥyā b. Waththāb, 180, 194, 378, 554, 577, 635, 639, 716
Yaḥyā b. Ya'mur, 180-181, 469, 495, 664-665
Yamāma, 171, 429, 473, 545, 698

Yaʿqūb, 146, 180, 199, 294, 320, 326, 383, 495, 521-522, 565, 575, 603, 613, 633, 646, 657-658, 679, 691, 729, 739, 747
Yaʿqūb b. Sufyān, 691, 729, 739
al-Yashkurī, 696
Yāsīn, Ḥikmat Bashīr, 19
Yazīd b. Muʿāwiya, 771
Yazīd b. ʿUmayr, 692
Yazīdī, 294, 305, 504, 603, 613
Yemen, 696, 699, 724, 742
Yūnus b. Ḥabīb, 379, 741
Yūnus b. ʿUbayd, 735
Yūnus b. Yazīd al-Aylī, 170
Yūsuf Aḥmad ʿAlī. *See al-Bayḍāwī wa-Manhajuh*
al-Zabīdī, 54, 121, 236, 326, 402, 739
Zād al-Masīr, 20
Zadeh, Travis, 73
al-Zāhidī, 73
ẓāhir, 46, 276, 346, 418
Ẓāhirīs, 298
al-Zahr al-Naḍir fī Ḥāl al-Khaḍir, 738
Zahrat al-Tafāsīr, 66
Zain, Ibrahim, xliii
al-Zajjāj, 51, 205, 230, 306, 407, 507, 584, 648, 695
Zakariyyā al-Anṣārī, 63, 83, 102, 120-121, 256…
zakāt, 267, 271, 434, 718
al-Zamakhsharī, 3, 9, 11, 13, 19-21, 30-34, 42, 48-58, 67-71, 90, 164, 182, 316, 365, 380, 519, 764…
al-Zarkashī, 24, 27-29, 234, 397, 707
Zarkūb Shīrāzī, 3, 12
al-Zarqānī, 24
Zarr b. Ḥubaysh, 732
Zayd b. ʿAlī, 175, 179, 194, 201, 251, 307, 348, 379, 401, 440, 455, 482, 665, 763
Zayd b. ʿAmr, 414, 773
Zayd b. Arqam, 712
Zayd b. Aslam, 207, 234, 238, 593, 600, 612, 622, 751
Zayd b. Thābit, 695, 707, 722, 729
Zayd b. Wahb, 726, 732
Zaydiyya, 260
al-Zaylaʿī, 89, 175, 212, 257, 258, 472
Zaynab al-Thaqafiyya, 732
Zaynab bint Umm Salama, 770
Zaytūna, 63, 66
Zechariah ben Jehoiada, 643
Zendiks, 334
al-Ziriklī, 3
Zirr b. Ḥubaysh, 194, 726
Ziyād b. Ṣayfī, 752
Zoroastrian, 756
al-Zubayr b. Awwām, 180, 713, 732
Zubayr b. Bakkār, 539, 727, 728
Zubdat al-Tafsīr, 66
Zubir, Badri N., 48
Zufar, 701
al-Zuḥaylī, Muḥammad, 14, 164
al-Zuḥaylī, Wahba, 66, 355
Zuhayr, 365-366, 381, 420, 444, 640, 719, 727, 773
Zuhayr al-Aqṭaʿ, 735
Zuhayr al-Farqabī, 251
zuhd, 454, 722
al-Zuhd, 182, 214
al-Zuhd al-Kabīr, 182
al-Zuhrī, 63, 117, 170, 180, 294, 530, 565, 576, 580, 607, 624, 648, 729, 772

Other Works by Gibril Fouad Haddad

Advice to Our Brethren the Scholars of Najd. By Shaykh Yusuf Hashim al-Rifaʿi. Introduction by Dr. Muhammad Saʿid al-Buti. With the introduction of ʿAlawi b. Hasan al-Haddad's *Misbah al-Anam fi Radd Shubuhat al-Najdi al-Lati Adalla biha al-ʿAwamm* (1802).

Afdal al-Khalq Sayyiduna Muhammad. The Prophetic Attribute "Best of Creation."

Ahl al-Sunna Versus the "Salafi" Movement. By Shaykh Hisham Kabbani.

Albani and His Friends: A Concise Guide to the "Salafi" Movement.

Al-Arbaʿun fi Fadl al-Sham wa-Ahlih wal-Hijrati ila Allah wa-Rasulih Salla Allah wa-Sallama ʿalayhi wa-ʿala Alih. Foreword by Shaykh Mustafa al-Turkmani.

Correct Islamic Doctrine. By Ibn Khafif.

Defending the Transgressed by Censuring the Reckless Against the Killing of Civilians. By Shaykh Muhammad Afifi al-Akiti.

The Divine Names and Attributes. al-Asmaʾ wal-Sifat. By al-Bayhaqi.

Doctrine of the Muslims. By Ibn ʿArabi.

The Doctrine of the People of Truth. al-Mulha fi Iʿtiqad Ahl al-Haqq. By Ibn ʿAbd al-Salam.

Encyclopedia of Hadith Forgeries by Mulla ʿAli al-Qari: Sayings Misattributed to the Prophet Muhammad.

Encyclopedia of Islamic Doctrine. By Shaykh Hisham Kabbani.

The Excellence of Syro-Palestine—al-Shām—and Its People: Forty Hadiths. Forewords by Shaykh Mustafa al-Turkmani, Shaykh Adib Kallas, Shaykh Wahbi Sulayman Ghawji al-Albani and Shaykh Salah al-Din Fakhri.

Fayd al-Salam bi-Suhbat al-Shaykh Hisham wa-Minnat Mawlana al-Shaykh Nazim ʿala al-Khass wal-Amm.
The Four Imams and Their Schools: Abu Hanifa, Malik, al-Shafiʿi, Ahmad ibn Hanbal.
From the Two Holy Sanctuaries: A Hajj Journal. With historical illustrations.
The Integrated Encyclopedia of the Qur'ān. With Muzaffar Iqbal et al.
Jesus Christ the Son of Mary & His Most Blessed Mother, upon them peace. By Ḥabib Ali al-Jifri.
The Lights of Revelation & the Secrets of Interpretation: Hizb I of the Commentary on Qur'an by al-Baydawi.
Mawlana's Open Door in Johore and Singapore.
Mawlid: Celebrating the Birth of the Holy Prophet, upon him blessings and peace.
Moonrises and the Meeting of Hearts concerning the Harmony between Islamic Jurisprudence and Astronomy and the Correlation of Computation and Sighting. By Dr. Muhammad Afifi al-Akiti.
The Muhammadan Light in the Qur'an, Sunna, and Companion-Reports.
Musnad Ahl al-Bayt, al-Musamma Husn al-Ma'al wal-Ma'arib fi Fadl al-Al wal-Aqarib bi-Arbaʿina Hadithan Musnadan ʿan Arbaʿīna Sharifan min Arbaʿina Kitaban.
The Prophet's Night Journey and Heavenly Ascent. By Shaykh Muḥammad ibn Alawi al-Maliki.
Qubrus al-Tarab fi Suhbati Rajab—The Joy of Cyprus in the Association of Rajab: Discourses of Shaykh Nazim al-Haqqani.
Refutation of Ibn Taymiyya Who Attributes Direction to Allah. By Ibn Jahbal al-Kilābī.
The Remembrance of God. Sibahat al-Fikr fil-Jahri bil-Dhikr. By al-Suyuti.

Sayyiduna Abu Bakr al-Siddiq radya Allahu ʿanh.
The Staff in Islam.
Sunna Notes I: Hadith History and Principles. With Ibn Hajar's *Nukhbat al-Fikar.*
Sunna Notes II: The Excellent Innovation in the Qur'an and Ḥadith. Foreword by Shaykh Wahbi Sulayman Ghawji. With Ibn Rajab's *The Sunna of the Caliphs.*
Sunna Notes III: The Binding Proof of the Sunna. Foreword by Dr. Muhammad Saʿid Ramadan al-Buti. With Ibn Hajar's *The Hadith of Gibril.*
Tuhfat al-Labib bi-Nusrat al-Habib ʿAli al-Jifri wa-Munaqashat al-Mukhalifin fil-Masa'il al-Sufiyya. Foreword by Sayyid Yusuf al-Rifa'i.
The Turban in Islam.

Other Publications by Beacon Books

Haddad, Gibril Fouad. Qari's Encyclopedia of Hadith Forgeries: *al-Asrār al-Marfū'a fīl-Akhbār al-Mawḍū'a*. Sayings misattributed to the Prophet Muhammad صلى الله عليه وآله وصحبه وسلّم.

Kiani, T. M. *Usul ash-Shashi; The Principles of Hanafi Jurisprudence.*

Lawrence, Bruce. *Nizam Ad-Din Awliya: Morals for the Heart.*

O'Kane, John and Radtke, Bernd. *Pure Gold from the Words of Sayyidī 'Abd al-Azīz al-Dabbāgh.*

Shackle, Christopher. *The Life, Teaching and Poems of Khwaja Ghulam Fareed*

Sabuni, 'Ali and Rashad Jameer. *The Infallibility of the Prophets.*

Zahuri, Jamiluddin Morris. *The Divan of Hafiz of Shiraz: English rendition in rhymed couplets with Parsi text and transliteration.*

Other Publications by UBD Press

Bakar, Osman. *Islamic Civilisation and the Modern World.*

Bakar, Osman. *Qur'anic Pictures of the Universe: The Scriptural Foundation of Islamic Cosmology.*

Bakar, Osman and Mesut Idriz. *Islam in Southeast Europe: Past Reflections and Future Prospects.*

Muhammad, Norhazlin. *The Education System in Brunei Darussalam in Light of Al-Attas' Philosophy of Education.*

Kartanegara, Mulyadhi. *Essentials of Islamic Epistemology.*

CPSIA information can be obtained
at www.ICGtesting.com
Printed in the USA
BVOW03s0850260617
487831BV00003B/238/P